nual Report, 1965.

of the

Secretary of the Treasury

on the

State of the Finances

For the Fiscal Year Ended June 30, 1965

TREASURY DEPARTMENT

DOCUMENT NO. 3236

Secretary

UNITED STATES GOVERNMENT PRINTING OFFICE, WASHINGTON : 1966

For sale by the Superintendent òf Documents, U.S. Government Printing Office
Washington, D.C., 20402 - Price $2.50 (paper cover)

1 MONTH OF FREE READING

at

www.ForgottenBooks.com

By purchasing this book you are eligible for one month membership to ForgottenBooks.com, giving you unlimited access to our entire collection of over 1,000,000 titles via our web site and mobile apps.

To claim your free month visit:

www.forgottenbooks.com/free922823

ISBN 978-0-260-02168-7
PIBN 10922823

This book is a reproduction of an important historical work. Forgotten Books uses
state-of-the-art technology to digitally reconstruct the work, preserving the original format
whilst repairing imperfections present in the aged copy. In rare cases, an imperfection in
the original, such as a blemish or missing page, may be replicated in our edition. We do,
however, repair the vast majority of imperfections successfully; any imperfections that
remain are intentionally left to preserve the state of such historical works.

Regulations

Legislation

FINANCIAL POLICY

MONETARY DEVELOPMENTS

PUBLIC DEBT MANAGEMENT

TAXATION DEVELOPMENTS

INTERNATIONAL FINANCIAL AND MONETARY DEVELOPMENTS

SUMMARY OF FISCAL OPERATIONS

CONTENTS

SECRETARIES, UNDER SECRETARIES, GENERAL COUNSEL, ASSISTANT SECRETARIES, SPECIAL ASSISTANT TO THE SECRETARY (FOR ENFORCEMENT), AND DEPUTY UNDER SECRETARIES FOR MONETARY AFFAIRS, SERVING IN THE TREASURY DEPARTMENT FROM JANUARY 20, 1965, THROUGH DECEMBER 31, 1965 [1]

Term of service		Official
From	To	
		Secretaries of the Treasury
Jan. 21, 1961	Apr. 1, 1965	Douglas Dillon, New Jersey.
Apr. 1, 1965	--------------	Henry H. Fowler, Virginia.
		Under Secretary
Apr. 29, 1965	--------------	Joseph W. Barr, Indiana.
		Under Secretary of the Treasury for Monetary Affairs
Feb. 1, 1965	--------------	Frederick L. Deming, Minnesota.
		General Counsel
Nov. 16, 1962	Jan. 31, 1965	G. d'Andelot Belin, Massachusetts.
		Assistant Secretaries
Apr. 24, 1961	--------------	Stanley S. Surrey, Massachusetts.
Dec. 20, 1961	Sept. 1, 1965	James A. Reed, Massachusetts.
Sept. 18, 1963	--------------	Robert A. Wallace, Illinois.
Apr. 29, 1965	--------------	Merlyn N. Trued, New Jersey.
Sept. 14, 1965	--------------	W. True Davis, Jr., Missouri.
		Special Assistant to the Secretary (for Enforcement)
Sept. 16, 1965	--------------	David C. Acheson, District of Columbia.
		Deputy Under Secretaries of the Treasury for Monetary Affairs
Dec. 3, 1963	Nov. 23, 1965	Paul A. Volcker, New Jersey.
Nov. 24, 1965	--------------	Peter D. Sternlight, New York.
		Fiscal Assistant Secretary
June 15, 1962	--------------	John K. Carlock, Arizona.
		Assistant Secretary for Administration
Sept. 14, 1959	--------------	A. E. Weatherbee, Maine.

[1] For officials from Sept. 11, 1789, to Jan. 20, 1965, see exhibit 69.

PRINCIPAL ADMINISTRATIVE AND STAFF OFFICERS OF THE TREASURY DEPARTMENT AS OF DECEMBER 31, 1965

Secretary of the Treasury_____ Henry H. Fowler
   Special Assistant to the Secretary_____ Douglass Hunt
Under Secretary of the Treasury_____ Joseph W. Barr
Under Secretary for Monetary Affairs_____ Frederick L. Deming
   Deputy Under Secretary for Monetary Affairs___ Peter D. Sternlight
   Director, Office of Domestic Gold and Silver
      Operations_____ Leland Howard
   Director, Office of Financial Analysis_____ John H. Auten (Acting)
   Director, Office of Debt Analysis_____ R. Duane Saunders
   Assistant to the Secretary (Debt Management)__ Franklin R. Saul
General Counsel_____ Fred B. Smith (Acting)
   Deputy General Counsel_____ Fred B. Smith
   Assistant General Counsel_____ Roy T. Englert
   Assistant General Counsel_____ Charlotte Tuttle Lloyd
   Assistant General Counsel_____ Hugo A. Ranta
   Assistant General Counsel_____ Vacancy
   Chief Counsel, Foreign Assets Control_____ Stanley L. Sommerfield
   Director of Practice_____ Thomas J. Reilly
Assistant Secretary_____ Stanley S. Surrey
   Director, Office of Tax Analysis_____ Gerard M. Brannon
      (Acting)
   Tax Legislative Counsel_____ Lawrence M. Stone
   Special Assistant for International Tax Affairs___ Richard O. Loengard, Jr.
Assistant Secretary_____ Robert A. Wallace
   Special Assistant to Assistant Secretary_____ Thomas W. Wolfe
   Director, Employment Policy Program_____ Mrs. Mary F. Nolan
Assistant Secretary_____ Merlyn N. Trued
   Deputy Assistant Secretary_____ Winthrop Knowlton
   Deputy to Assistant Secretary for International
      Monetary Affairs_____ George H. Willis
   Deputy to Assistant Secretary for International
      Financial and Economic Affairs_____ Ralph Hirschtritt
Assistant Secretary_____ W. True Davis, Jr.
   Deputy Assistant Secretary_____ James P. Hendrick
   Aide to the Assistant Secretary_____ Commander G. H. Patrick
      Bursley, USCG
   Assistant to the Assistant Secretary_____ Matthew J. Marks
Special Assistant to the Secretary (for Enforcement)_ David C. Acheson
   Staff Assistant_____ Robert E. Jordan, III
   Staff Assistant_____ Anthony A. Lapham
   Director, Office of Law Enforcement Coordination_ Arnold Sagalyn
Fiscal Assistant Secretary_____ John K. Carlock
   Deputy Fiscal Assistant Secretary_____ George F. Stickney
   Assistant Fiscal Assistant Secretary_____ Hampton A. Rabon, Jr.
   Assistant to Fiscal Assistant Secretary_____ Boyd A. Evans
   Assistant to Fiscal Assistant Secretary_____ Sidney Cox
Assistant Secretary for Administration_____ A. E. Weatherbee
   Deputy Assistant Secretary for Administration
      and Director, Office of Budget and Finance___ Ernest C. Betts, Jr.
   Director, Office of Personnel_____ Amos N. Latham, Jr.
   Director, Office of Management and Organization_ James H. Stover
   Director, Office of Administrative Services_____ Paul McDonald
   Director, Office of Security_____ Thomas M. Hughes
   Director, Office of Planning and Program Evalu-
      ation_____ Vacancy
Assistant to the Secretary (Congressional Relations)__ Joseph M. Bowman, Jr.
   Deputy Assistant to the Secretary (Congressional
      Relations)_____ Joseph L. Spilman

Assistant to the Secretary (Public Affairs)_____ Dixon Donnelley
　　Deputy Assistant to the Secretary (Public
　　　Affairs)_____ Mark T. Sheehan
Assistant to the Secretary (National Security Affairs)_ Charles A. Sullivan
　　Financial Adviser_____ Robert W. Bean
　　National Security Affairs Adviser_____ Raymond J. Albright
　　Director, Office of Foreign Assets Control_____ Mrs. Margaret W.
　　　　　　　　　　　　　　　　　　　　　　　　　　　Schwartz
Senior Consultant_____ Seymour E. Harris
Special Assistant to the Secretary and Director,
　　Executive Secretariat_____ Robert J. Moody

BUREAU OF ACCOUNTS

Commissioner of Accounts_____ Sidney S. Sokol
Assistant Commissioner_____ L. D. Mosso
Comptroller_____ Ray T. Bath
Chief Disbursing Officer_____ Lester W. Plumley
Deputy Commissioner for Central Accounts and
　　Reports_____ Howard A. Turner
Deputy Comissioner for Deposits and Investments___ Sebastian Fama

BUREAU OF CUSTOMS

Commissioner of Customs_____ Lester D. Johnson
Assistant Commissioner of Customs_____ Edwin F. Rains
Deputy Commissioner, Office of Administration_____ N. G. Strub
Deputy Commissioner, Office of Investigations_____ Lawrence Fleishman
Deputy Commissioner, Office of Operations_____ David C. Ellis
　　Deputy Commissioner, Appraisement_____ Walter G. Roy
　　Deputy Commissioner, Technical_____ George Vlases, Jr.
　　Deputy Commissioner, Collectors Operations____ Thomas J. Gorman, Jr.
Deputy Commissioner, Office of Regulations and
　　Rulings_____ Robert V. McIntyre
Deputy Commissioner, Classification and Draw-
　　backs_____ William E. Higman
Deputy Commissioner, Entry, Value, and Pen-
　　alties_____ Vacancy
　　Acting Deputy Commissioner, Marine Admin-
　　　istration_____ John P. Tebeau
Chief Counsel_____ Donald L. Ritger

BUREAU OF ENGRAVING AND PRINTING

Director, Bureau of Engraving and Printing_____ Henry J. Holtzclaw
Assistant Director, Bureau of Engraving and Print-
　　ing_____ Frank G. Uhler

BUREAU OF THE MINT

Director of the Mint_____ Miss Eva Adams
Assistant Director of the Mint_____ Frederick W. Tate

BUREAU OF NARCOTICS

Commissioner of Narcotics_____ Henry L. Giordano
Deputy Commissioner of Narcotics_____ George H. Gaffney
Assistant to the Commissioner of Narcotics_____ John R. Enright

BUREAU OF THE PUBLIC DEBT

Commissioner of the Public Debt_____ Donald M. Merritt
Assistant Commissioner_____ Ross A. Heffelfinger, Jr.
Deputy Commissioner_____ Michael E. McGeoghegan
Deputy Commissioner in Charge, Chicago Office_____ Jack P. Thompson

INTERNAL REVENUE SERVICE

Commissioner of Internal Revenue	Sheldon S. Cohen
Deputy Commissioner	Bertrand M. Harding
Assistant Commissioner (Administration)	Edward F. Preston
Assistant Commissioner (Inspection)	Vernon D. Acree
Assistant Commissioner (Compliance)	Donald W. Bacon
Assistant Commissioner (Data Processing)	Robert L. Jack
Assistant Commissioner (Planning and Research)	William H. Smith
Assistant Commissioner (Technical)	Harold T. Swartz
Chief Counsel	Mitchell Rogovin

OFFICE OF THE COMPTROLLER OF THE CURRENCY

Comptroller of the Currency	James J. Saxon
First Deputy Comptroller	William D. Camp
Administrative Assistant to the Comptroller	Anthony G. Chase
Deputy Comptroller (Bank Supervision and Examination)	Justin T. Watson
Deputy Comptroller (Mergers and Branches)	R. J. Blanchard
Deputy Comptroller (New Charters)	Thomas G. DeShazo
Deputy Comptroller (Domestic Bank Operations)	R. C. Egertson
Deputy Comptroller (Trusts)	Dean E. Miller
Deputy Comptroller (International Banking and Finance)	E. R. Park
Director, Department of Banking and Economic Research	Victor Abramson
Chief Counsel	Robert Bloom
Chief National Bank Examiner	Vacant

OFFICE OF THE TREASURER OF THE UNITED STATES

Treasurer of the United States	Mrs. Kathryn O'Hay Granahan
Deputy Treasurer	William T. Howell
Assistant Deputy Treasurer	Willard E. Scott

UNITED STATES COAST GUARD

Commandant, U.S. Coast Guard	Admiral Edwin J. Roland
Assistant Commandant	Vice Admiral W. D Shields
Chief of Staff	Rear Admiral Paul E. Trimble

UNITED STATES SAVINGS BONDS DIVISION

National Director	William H. Neal
Assistant National Director	Bill McDonald

UNITED STATES SECRET SERVICE

Director	James J. Rowley
Assistant Director (Investigations)	Thomas J. Kelley
Assistant Director (Protective Forces)	Rufus Youngblood
Assistant Director (Protective Intelligence)	Walter Young

COMMITTEES AND BOARD

Chairman, Treasury Management Committee	A. E. Weatherbee
Chairman, Treasury Awards Committee	Amos N. Latham, Jr.
Chairman, Treasury Wage Board	Amos N. Latham, Jr.
Employment Policy Officer	Robert A. Wallace
Principal Compliance Officer	Robert A. Wallace

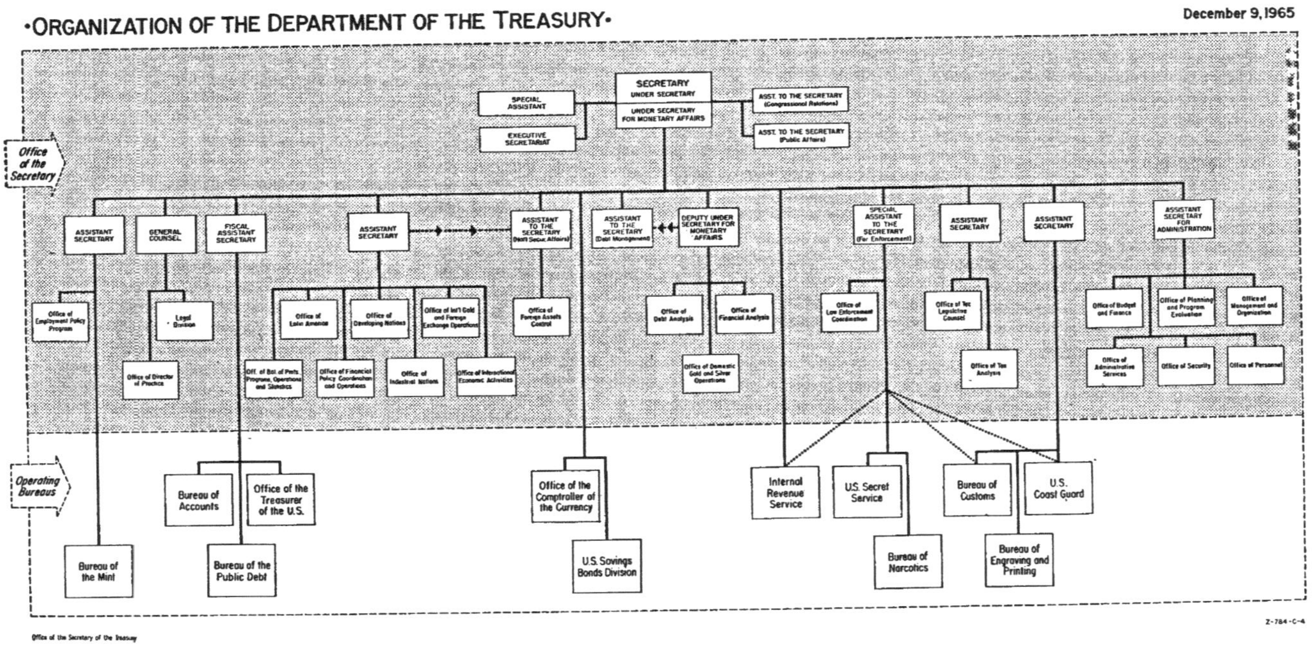
•ORGANIZATION OF THE DEPARTMENT OF THE TREASURY•
December 9, 1965
Office of the Secretary
Operating Bureaus
SECRETARY
UNDER SECRETARY
UNDER SECRETARY FOR MONETARY AFFAIRS
SPECIAL ASSISTANT
EXECUTIVE SECRETARIAT
ASST. TO THE SECRETARY (Congressional Relations)
ASST. TO THE SECRETARY (Public Affairs)
ASSISTANT SECRETARY
GENERAL COUNSEL
FISCAL ASSISTANT SECRETARY
ASSISTANT SECRETARY
ASSISTANT TO THE SECRETARY
ASSISTANT TO THE SECRETARY (Debt Management)
DEPUTY UNDER SECRETARY FOR MONETARY AFFAIRS
SPECIAL ASSISTANT TO THE SECRETARY (For Enforcement)
ASSISTANT SECRETARY
ASSISTANT SECRETARY
ASSISTANT SECRETARY FOR ADMINISTRATION
Office of Employment Policy Program
Legal Division
Office of Director of Practice
Office of Latin America
Office of Developing Nations
Office of Int'l Gold and Foreign Exchange Operations
Off. of Bal. of Pmts. Programs, Operations and Statistics
Office of Financial Policy Coordination and Operations
Office of Industrial Nations
Office of International Economic Activities
Office of Foreign Assets Control
Office of Debt Analysis
Office of Financial Analysis
Office of Domestic Gold and Silver Operations
Office of Law Enforcement Coordination
Office of Tax Legislative Counsel
Office of Tax Analysis
Office of Budget and Finance
Office of Planning and Program Evaluation
Office of Management and Organization
Office of Administrative Services
Office of Security
Office of Personnel
Bureau of the Mint
Bureau of Accounts
Office of the Treasurer of the U.S.
Bureau of the Public Debt
Office of the Comptroller of the Currency
U.S. Savings Bonds Division
Internal Revenue Service
U.S. Secret Service
Bureau of Narcotics
Bureau of Customs
U.S. Coast Guard
Bureau of Engraving and Printing
Z-784-C-4
Office of the Secretary of the Treasury

CHART 1

ANNUAL REPORT ON THE FINANCES

Treasury Department,
Washington, May 9, 1966.

Sirs: I have the honor to report to you on the finances of the Federal Government for the fiscal year 1965. Details on Treasury operations and administrative reports for the fiscal year 1965 will be found in the full text of this report. This introduction will be concerned with major fiscal and financial developments during the calendar year 1965 and the early part of 1966.

Overall Review

The period under review was one of challenge and accomplishment, both domestically and internationally. At home a continuing expansion in production and incomes, unparalleled in our peacetime history, carried us closer to the goals of a Great Society. Although margins of unutilized industrial capacity and unemployed labor remained by the end of 1965, they had been narrowed significantly by the pace of steady expansion, supported by an act of Congress in June eliminating most excise taxes and reducing others. But, as 1965 drew to a close, it was becoming apparent that our steadfast commitment to the cause of freedom in Viet Nam would entail a much larger claim upon the nation's resources, both material and human. The new economic challenge was to insure the balanced growth of a nearly fully employed economy, free from inflationary excesses, while providing all that our commitments in Southeast Asia and elsewhere might require.

There was every reason for confidence that the vast productive power of our economy, strengthened during recent years by tax reduction and high rates of investment, would be equal to the foreseeable demands that might be placed upon it. But, it was essential, if serious inflationary strains were to be avoided, that the Federal fiscal influence should shift from one of steady stimulus to aggregate demand to one of moderate restraint. Therefore, the President's January 1966 budgetary recommendations combined strict economy in non-defense expenditure programs with proposals for further tax action to augment the increases in social security and medicare taxes already going into effect at the beginning of 1966. Prompt congressional enactment of that further tax action, in almost the exact form requested, was an impressive demonstration of the flexibility of fiscal policy, and of the willingness of the Congress to act promptly to prevent overstraining the economy. Whether further fiscal action

xvii

would be required was uncertain, but the President had made it amply clear in his Budget Message that:

> "if . . . events in Southeast Asia so develop that additional funds are required, I will not hesitate to request the necessary sums. And should that contingency arise, or should unforeseen inflationary pressures develop, I will propose such fiscal actions as are appropriate to maintain economic stability."

In our international financial relations, the challenge at the beginning of 1965 was twofold. First, it was essential to reverse the worsening in our balance-of-payments position that had developed in late 1964 and to move promptly toward a secure equilibrium in our international accounts. Second, beyond that immediate necessity, there was the very great desirability of making timely progress toward agreement with other nations on the form that improved international monetary arrangements should take.

The President's comprehensive voluntary balance-of-payments program announced February 10, 1965, and further tightened in December 1965, was chiefly responsible for an approximate halving of our 1964 balance-of-payments deficit as measured on the liquidity basis. The goal of the Administration was to cover the remaining distance to payments equilibrium by the end of 1966, although it was recognized that the direct and indirect impact of Viet Nam might temporarily delay achievement of that goal.

Following a series of bilateral talks with the financial officials of a number of other countries, new negotiating machinery was established in September 1965, to achieve improvements in the international monetary situation. The major objective is to arrange for dependable new sources of liquidity as required in the future to finance growing international trade in the absence of dollar deficits. Negotiations have been pursued actively and progress is being made toward reaching a consensus on the essential features of an international system for creating reserves.

Treasury debt management faced new challenges in the past year even though the Treasury's net cash borrowings were relatively modest. The rise in longer-term interest rates after mid-1965 was the first significant upturn during the present extended period of prosperity and created a new environment for debt management. As described below and discussed more fully in the text of this report, financing operations were successfully adjusted to the changing market situation, and continued to serve the overall objectives of economic policy.

In addition to these major domestic and international financial developments, the past year was an active and important one for the Treasury in many other respects, a few of which are noted below.

At a conference in Manila in early December 1965, the United States and 21 other countries signed the charter of an Asian Develo ment Bank with an authorized capital of $1 billion, of which the U.S. subscription is $200 million. Nine other countries became charter members by signing and making a pledge by January 31, 1966. In his Message to the Congress recommending approval of U.S. participation, President Johnson pointed out that the new Bank "is the product of Asian initiative, and it offers the nucleus around which Asians can make a cooperative response to the most critical economic problems—national and regional." The Congress approved the enabling legislation and it was signed by President Johnson on March 16, 1966.

As an outgrowth of action initiated at the September 1964 meeting of the International Monetary Fund, the Congress authorized an increase of $1.035 billion in the U.S. quota in the International Monetary Fund in June 1965. The U.S. action was part of a general increase by all of the participating countries in their respective Fund quotas, to become effective upon ratification by members holding two-thirds of present quotas. This point was reached on February 23, 1966. The quota expansion had been strongly supported by President Johnson and by his National Advisory Council on International Monetary and Financial Problems.

The realities of the silver supply situation made it impossible to continue indefinitely the production of high-content silver coins. Therefore, a necessary change in our coinage system was made with the passage of the Coinage Act of 1965 which removed silver from the dime and quarter and reduced the silver content of the half dollar to 40 percent. New coinage alloys, reflecting the latest developments in modern technology, insured the consistent operation of the new dimes, quarters, and half dollars in all of our millions of coin-operated machines. Late in 1965, the new quarters began to go into circulation, followed by the dimes and half dollars in early 1966. Details of the new coinage system and a description of the successful efforts of the Bureau of the Mint in overcoming recent coin shortages will be found in the accompanying report (pages 131–4).

A comprehensive study, initiated in 1963, on the mission, organization, and management of the Bureau of Customs was released in March 1965. At the same time, President Johnson announced a major program, under the terms of Reorganization Plan No. 1 of 1965 which became effective May 25, to make maximum use of the skill and talent of the career employees of the Customs Service and to achieve annual savings estimated at $9 million. Major management improvements in other Treasury agencies and bureaus are described in the accompanying report.

Tax Policy

The economic expansion that began in early 1961 continued strongly through calendar year 1965 and into 1966. National output rose 5½ percent in real terms during 1965 and our record of cost-price stability remained superior to that of any other major industrial nation, despite growing pressures by the end of the year. Unemployment was reduced to just over 4 percent by the end of 1965 and declined further in early 1966.

Tax reduction and reform was again a central element in overall economic policy. Forward impetus was provided to the economy by the second-stage tax reductions of the Revenue Act of 1964, which has convincingly demonstrated its success, and by the first stage of the Excise Tax Reduction Act of 1965, signed into law by President Johnson on June 21, 1965.

Very general agreement had developed that many of our excise taxes had no place in a permanent tax system. Extensive hearings had been held on excise tax reduction before the House Ways and Means Committee in the summer of 1964 preparing the way for prompt action in 1965. The President stated in his Budget Message of January 25, 1965, that attention should now be given to the repeal of some excise taxes and the reduction of others. Such action would provide further aid to economic growth and minimize the burden on consumers and business resulting from taxes which were often costly and difficult to administer and which frequently distorted consumer choices as among different goods. On May 17 the President sent a message to the Congress with the details of an excise tax reduction program, modified in the light of the current and prospective economic situation, and totaling $3.9 billion at estimated fiscal 1966 levels of income. To insure the maximum contribution to continued price stability and balanced prosperity, the President requested that business promptly pass forward to consumers the full amount of excise tax reductions. This request was emphasized again when he signed the bill on June 21, and, by and large, was carried into effect in ensuing months.

The tax repeals or reductions under the final legislation amounted to $4.7 billion at fiscal 1966 levels of income, rather than the $3.9 billion recommended by the President. This resulted chiefly from eventual reduction of the tax on passenger automobiles to one percent, rather than five percent as recommended, and to a lesser extent from minor changes which are detailed later in this report (pages 37–40). Of the total $4.7 billion, about $1.75 billion became effective on June 22, 1965, and an approximately equal amount became effective on January 1, 1966, with additional reductions to be effective in three stages, on January 1, 1967, 1968, and 1969.

Another taxation development during 1965 that deserves mention here was the modification of the depreciation guideline procedures initiated in 1962. Those 1962 procedures were instituted as part of a thoroughgoing depreciation reform designed to encourage the use of more rapid equipment modernization in industry. At that time, taxpayers were allowed a three-year transitional period. Study of the depreciation practices of several hundred large firms conducted at the request of the Treasury in 1964 by the National Industrial Conference Board and independent studies by the Internal Revenue Service suggested that some liberalization of guideline procedures was necessary if businesses were to obtain full benefit from the 1962 depreciation reform. At the same time, the Treasury recognized the need to apply limitations in the use of certain accounting techniques found to be incompatible with the guideline procedure. The combination of the new liberalized rules and the new limitations was estimated to result in increasing depreciation tax benefits during 1965 by some $600 million–$800 million over what they would have been if the 1962 reform had not been modified.

The overall fiscal position in late 1965 and early 1966 was substantially influenced by the amendment of the Social Security Act in July 1965, in line with recommendations by the President. Old age benefits were liberalized retroactively to January 1, 1965, with disbursement of the retroactive portion made in September 1965. However, the increase of some $2 billion annually in transfer payments was to be more than offset by the increase in social security and medicare payroll taxes of $6 billion, annual rate, going into effect January 1, 1966. With medicare payments not beginning until the second half of 1966, the net effect would be some increase in fiscal restraint in the first half of 1966 because of the higher payroll taxes.

Late in 1965 it became apparent that the increased commitment in Viet Nam might be sufficiently large to require offsetting fiscal action, beyond that which would result from the higher payroll taxes and rigorous control of nondefense expenditures. In his Budget Message of January 24, 1966, President Johnson announced that apart from the special military and economic assistance costs in Viet Nam, expenditures for the regular programs of the Federal Government in fiscal 1967 were estimated at $102.3 billion, a rise of $0.6 billion from fiscal 1966, only six-tenths of one percent. But, because increased special costs associated with Viet Nam would add an estimated $4.7 billion in fiscal year 1966 expenditures and $10.5 billion in fiscal year 1967 expenditures over the amounts estimated in January 1965, it would be necessary to raise additional revenues.

As the President had expressed the matter on January 19, 1966: "Under these circumstances, I was faced with three choices:

  —A deficit in excess of $6.5 billion, which would require the Government to borrow the additional money.

  —An increase in corporate and personal income tax rates, or other new taxes.

  —Temporary restoration of certain excise taxes, and adoption of graduated withholding of individual income taxes and current payment of corporate income taxes—to put the American people on a pay-as-you-go basis without increasing the total tax bill due.

"Over the past several weeks I discussed these alternatives and countless variations of them with my advisers. I made two decisions.

"First, we could raise revenue or borrow it. I chose to raise the money.

"Second, I chose to raise that money without any increases in personal and corporate income tax liabilities, but through changes that affect only the timing of tax payments and the temporary restoration of certain excise taxes on telephones and automobiles."

Therefore, the President recommended tax legislation involving (a) temporary restoration of the rates of excise taxes on automobiles and telephones that were in effect at the end of 1965 and (b) the adoption of collection procedures which would put income and self-employment tax payments closer to a pay-as-you-go system, thereby increasing current revenues without changing income tax rates and without changing anyone's final tax liabilities. It took only about 60 days from the time the tax program was outlined in mid-January for it to be enacted, essentially in its original form as regards the impact on fiscal years 1966 and 1967, as the Tax Adjustment Act of 1966. That legislation was expected to generate approximately $6 billion extra revenue in the 15 months following its enactment—through fiscal year 1967. In terms of cash payments, the changes in the new law were estimated to take about $2.7 billion out of the individual and corporate spending stream in calendar 1966.

Whether the degree of fiscal restraint embodied in the Tax Adjustment Act of 1966 would prove sufficient, or whether further fiscal or other action would be required, could only be determined with the passage of time. Full effects of the Federal Reserve's monetary tightening signaled by the December 1965 increase in the discount rate were yet to be registered, and further evidence was needed on the strength of private spending plans. It was clear, however, that the flexible adaptation of fiscal policy to changing needs had already been convincingly demonstrated.

In the recent past, tax reduction actions had included the investment credit in the Revenue Act of 1962, the individual and corporate income tax reductions in the Revenue Act of 1964, the Excise Tax Reduction Act of 1965, and the administrative depreciation reforms of 1962 and 1965. Despite tax reductions that cut the burden of taxes by some $20 billion at current levels of income, revenues were estimated at $21 billion higher in fiscal year 1966 than in fiscal year 1961. This contrasts with a growth in receipts of only $10 billion in the 5 years preceding 1961, a period in which there was no significant tax reduction.

In commenting upon this remarkable growth in revenues in his January 24, 1966, Budget Message, President Johnson noted that we have had a clear illustration of the direct relationship between tax policies, economic growth, and Federal revenues. He went on to observe that: "Tax policy, however, must be used flexibly. We must be equally prepared to employ it in restraint of an overly rapid economic expansion as we were to use it as a stimulus to a lagging economy. The current situation calls for a modest measure of fiscal restraint."

Balance of Payments

The U.S. balance-of-payments deficit increased sharply during the last half of calendar 1964, reaching an annual rate of $5.5 billion in the fourth quarter (liquidity basis), primarily because of a substantial increase in net outflows of U.S. private capital. By leading to temporarily excessive increases in foreign dollar holdings the larger deficit was aggravating the gold outflow problem. Therefore, President Johnson announced a comprehensive balance-of-payments program on February 10, 1965. The program was the result of a careful review of the situation by the Cabinet Committee on the Balance of Payments, chaired by the Secretary of the Treasury. The essentially new element in the program was its reliance upon the voluntary cooperation of the commercial and financial community.

U.S. banks were asked to hold total claims outstanding on foreign residents to 105 percent of the level at the end of 1964. Guidelines developed by the Board of Governors of the Federal Reserve System for implementing this program were designed to assure that credits to finance U.S. exports, and loans to less-developed countries, could be adequately met. In addition, consideration for the special positions of Canada, Japan, and the United Kingdom was requested. Within these broad guidelines each bank was to decide the direction of its particular overseas activities. A similar approach was permitted nonbank financial institutions in their foreign lending and investing activities.

U.S. industrial corporations also were asked to improve their individual balance-of-payments accounts, combining all transactions such as exports, dividend income, royalties, fees, and capital outflows from the United States. The objective was to leave the corporations free to adjust these components of their individual payments accounts while achieving a significant net payments improvement.

To reduce the tourist deficit, Americans as well as foreigners were encouraged to travel more in this country. Legislation was recommended and subsequently enacted on June 30, 1965 (Public Law 89–62), reducing the duty exemption on purchases made abroad by returning U.S. residents.

The February 10 program also called for extension of the interest equalization tax for two years beyond December 31, 1965, broadening its coverage to include nonbank credit of one-to-three year maturity, and activation of the Presidential authority under the Gore Amendment to the act to apply the interest equalization tax to bank loans of one year or more. (The Interest Equalization Act was broadened in coverage and extended to July 31, 1967, by Public Law 89–243, October 9, 1965.) To stop any excessive flow of funds to Canada under its special exemption from the interest equalization tax, the President sought and received firm assurance that the policies of the Canadian Government would be directed toward limiting borrowing in the United States to the maintenance of a stable level of Canada's foreign exchange reserves. The program also called for an intensification of U.S. Government efforts to minimize the foreign exchange costs of our defense and aid programs; an increase in our efforts to promote U.S. exports; and, finally, encouragement of more investments from abroad, by increasing, through new tax legislation, the incentive of foreigners to invest in U.S. securities.

The program of voluntary cooperation that President Johnson called for in his Balance-of-Payments Message of February 10, 1965, proved to be highly effective. For the year 1965, there was a $1.5 billion net reduction in the payments deficit on a liquidity basis despite heavy outflows on private capital account during the early months and despite setbacks for the year as a whole in trade and other accounts. The $1.3 billion deficit in 1965 was the smallest since 1957 and less than half the size of our deficits of $2.8 billion in 1964 and $2.7 billion in 1963. On the other principal accounting basis, official reserve transactions, our deficit in 1965 was also $1.3 billion, about the same as the 1964 deficit on that basis.

Gold outflows rose sharply to $1.665 billion for the year as a whole. However, there was a pattern of steady improvement during the course of the year. From a high of $832 million in the first quarter, the outflow declined to $590 million in the second quarter (including a $259 million payment of the gold portion of the increased U.S. subscription to the IMF), and fell further to $124 million in the third quarter, and $119 million in the fourth quarter.

Late in 1965, at the request of the President, the Cabinet Committee on the Balance of Payments, under the chairmanship of the Secretary of the Treasury, conducted an intensive review of the U.S. balance-of-payments situation. The recommended measures for 1966 involve, essentially, a sharpening and reinforcing of the 1965 program with continued emphasis upon its voluntary, comprehensive, and balanced character.

Corporations are requested, through a strengthened Commerce Department Program, to meet overall balance-of-payment targets similar to those of 1965; and also to meet specific targets for direct investment which are expected to result in balance-of-payments savings of up to $1 billion in 1966. Ceilings on lending under the Federal Reserve voluntary program are to rise by the end of 1966 to

109 percent of the December 1964 base for banks and nonbank financial institutions and small banks will be permitted to increase their loans somewhat more than this. These changes recognize the outstanding contribution of banking institutions to the 1965 program, and will help to insure more fully the adequacy of credit for financing of U.S. exports and the achievement of other desired objectives. Other important features of the program include an intensified effort to hold down the balance-of-payments cost of Government programs, encouragement of both foreign and domestic tourism in the United States, stepped-up effort to expand U.S. export trade, and the recommendation that legislation to encourage foreign investment in the United States now before the Congress be enacted as soon as possible.

The main balance-of-payments imponderables in early 1966 were the exact extent to which there would be rising balance-of-payments costs in Southeast Asia in both the military and aid programs and the direct and indirect impact of Viet Nam on the domestic economy and the balance of trade.

International Financial Arrangements

A summary of a wide range of developments in international financial affairs will be found in the text of this report (pages 49–65). The discussion here will be limited to a brief review of the major steps taken during the calendar year 1965 to achieve further progress toward improved international monetary arrangements.

The need for improved arrangements arises from the fact that growth in international monetary reserves—primarily gold and dollars—has been largely dependent over the past decade upon increases in official foreign dollar holdings. New gold supplies moving into monetary use have been accounting for a relatively small proportion of total reserve growth. Therefore, as the U.S. payments deficit is removed, the major source of recent growth in international liquidity will also be removed. To assure ample world liquidity for the years ahead—when U.S. payments will not be in chronic deficit— the United States, in cooperation with other leading financial countries, is seeking workable ways of strengthening and improving international financial arrangements.

In a Ministerial Statement of August 1964, the Group of Ten countries—Belgium, Canada, France, Germany, Italy, Japan, the Netherlands, Sweden, the United Kingdom, and the United States— stated that while supplies of gold and reserve currencies are fully adequate for the present and are likely to be for the immediate future, the continuing growth of world trade and payments is likely to require larger international liquidity. It was recognized that world liquidity needs might be met by larger credit facilities or might call for some new form of reserve asset. Therefore, a Study Group was set up "to examine various proposals regarding the creation of reserve assets either through the IMF or otherwise." Their valuable study—the so-called Ossola Report—was submitted to the Group of Ten on June 1, 1965, and was published later.

By mid-1965 with this and other technical studies completed and with the U.S. balance-of-payments program demonstrating its effectiveness, it was appropriate to press forward toward a stage of more conclusive negotiations. Therefore, on July 10, 1965, the Secretary of the Treasury announced his intention of conducting a series of informal discussions with ranking financial officials of other Group of Ten countries to ascertain firsthand their views on the most practical and promising ways of furthering progress toward improved international monetary arrangements. In that statement, it was made clear that the United States was prepared to participate in an international monetary conference at some appropriate future time. It was also pointed out that before such a conference took place, there should be reasonable certainty of measurable progress through prior agreement on basic points.

It was announced at the same time that President Johnson had approved the recommendation of the Secretary of the Treasury and had created an Advisory Committee on International Monetary Arrangements, chaired by the former Secretary of the Treasury, Douglas Dillon. The Advisory Committee membership includes: Robert V. Roosa, former Under Secretary of the Treasury for Monetary Affairs; Kermit Gordon, former Director of the Bureau of the Budget; Edward Bernstein, economic consultant specializing in international monetary policy; Andre Meyer, of the investment banking firm of Lazard Freres; David Rockefeller, President of the Chase Manhattan Bank; Charles Kindleberger, Professor of Economics at Massachusetts Institute of Technology; Walter Heller, former Chairman of the Council of Economic Advisers; and Frazar Wilde, Chairman of the Board of Trustees, Committee for Economic Development.

In September, following a series of bilateral talks between the Secretary of the Treasury and foreign financial officials, new negotiating machinery was established at the time of the annual meeting of the International Monetary Fund. The Finance Ministers of the Group of Ten countries instructed their Deputies to seek a basis of agreement on the improvements needed in the international monetary system, including arrangements for the future creation of reserve assets. It was further provided that once a basis for agreement on essential points was reached, it would be necessary to proceed from this first phase to a second phase, involving a much larger group of countries.

At the same time, the Managing Director of the IMF, who participates in the ministerial meetings of the Group of Ten, indicated that the Fund would pursue its own investigation of the ways and means of creating international reserves. Since last fall, negotiations have been pursued actively. The Deputies are proceeding to draft their report to the Ministers, which it is hoped will show considerable progress toward a consensus on the essential features of an international system for creating reserves.

Debt Management

During the course of calendar 1965, record flows of funds moved through our domestic financial markets but at higher rates of interest. For short-term rates, this marked a continuation of the more or less steady advance dating from the beginning of the current expansion in early 1961, which has made our own short-term rates more competitive with key rates abroad. For longer term rates, the rise after mid-1965 was the first significant upturn since the present expansion began.

Yields moved upward in all maturity ranges of Treasury securities from mid-1965 until early December, and then rose sharply following the December 6 increase in the Federal Reserve discount rate (yields from 1960 to mid-1965 are shown in chart 3, page 18 of the accompanying report). The yield on 3-month bills advanced from about 3.80 percent at mid-1965 to 4⅛ percent in early December, rose sharply to about 4½ percent by the end of the year, and worked its way irregularly higher in early 1966. Treasury coupon issues in the 5-year range, which were a bit above 4⅛ percent at midyear, rose to about 4½ percent by early December, and 4⅞ by yearend. Longer term yields in the 20-year range moved from a little below 4¼ percent at mid-1965, to around 4½ percent by the end of 1965. This background of rising rates, which continued into early 1966, formed the environment for Treasury debt management operations after mid-1965. (A detailed review of public debt management and ownership developments during fiscal 1965 is provided on pages 17–34 of the accompanying report.)

Following an August 1965 refunding operation, the Treasury conducted the bulk of its financing for the rest of the year in the form of tax anticipation bills. A $4 billion tax anticipation bill package in September was followed by a November auction of another $2.5 billion in tax bills. On October 27 the Treasury announced the terms for refinancing $9.7 billion of notes maturing November 15. The refinancing took the form of a cash offering of a new 18-month, 4¼ percent note, priced to yield about 4.37 percent. At the end of 1965 the average length of the marketable interest-bearing public debt was 5 years, the same as a year earlier but 4 months shorter than the average maturity at the end of fiscal 1965 which had reflected the lengthening impact of an advance refunding in January 1965.

In early 1966, after a $1.5 billion cash offering and $1 billion in additional tax anticipation bills in January, the Treasury took advantage of favorable market conditions in February to achieve some moderate but useful debt lengthening, and also to lighten the task of refunding issues that would be maturing later in the year. The successful February operation was a combined refunding of February 15 and April 1 debt maturities into 18-month or 4¾ year notes, along with a prerefunding of issues maturing in May and August into the 4¾ year option. With its completion, Treasury financing operations for the fiscal year were virtually completed, except for routine rollovers.

The savings bond program received an important stimulus early in 1966 when President Johnson announced an increase in the rate to 4.15 percent from the previous 3.75 percent effective from December 1, 1965. The Presidential action also raised the earnings after December 1, 1965, of outstanding Series E and H savings bonds. The new, higher rate was clearly justified not only in view of the higher rates available on various private savings accounts, but also in the light of current needs to sustain vigorous noninflationary growth and manage the public debt soundly. Corporate and Federal campaigns to increase participation in the payroll savings plan were being pressed intensively and substantial results were expected.

HENRY H. FOWLER,
Secretary of the Treasury.

To THE PRESIDENT OF THE SENATE.
To THE SPEAKER OF THE HOUSE OF REPRESENTATIVES.

REVIEW OF FISCAL OPERATIONS

Summary of Financial Operations

The administrative budget deficit for the fiscal year 1965 was $3.4 billion, $4.8 billion less than the 1964 deficit and $2.8 billion less than estimated in the 1966 budget document. Net administrative budget receipts during the year totaled $93.1 billion and net expenditures amounted to $96.5 billion—receipts being $3.6 billion higher and expenditures $1.2 billion lower than the preceding year.

Net receipts of trust funds during fiscal 1965 exceeded net trust expenditures by $1.4 billion, with net receipts rising to $31.0 billion and net expenditures to $29.6 billion.

On the basis of a consolidated cash statement, total receipts from the public during the year amounted to $119.7 billion, and total payments to the public amounted to $122.4 billion, resulting in an excess of payments to the public of $2.7 billion.

The public debt outstanding June 30, 1965, totaled $317.3 billion, a net increase of $5.6 billion during the year. A summary of the Government's fiscal operations during the 1964–65 fiscal years and their effect on the public debt follows:

	In billions of dollars	
	1964	1965
Administrative budget receipts and expenditures:		
Net receipts (−)	−89.5	−93.1
Net expenditures	97.7	96.5
Administrative budget deficit	8.2	3.4
Trust receipts and expenditures:		
Net receipts (−)	−30.3	−31.0
Net expenditures	28.9	29.6
Excess of receipts (−), or expenditures	−1.4	−1.4
Net investments in public debt and agency securities	2.8	2.4
Net sales (−) of Government agency securities in the market	−1.9	−1.4
Increase (−), or decrease in checks outstanding, deposits in transit (net), etc.	−.9	.9
Increase (−), or decrease in public debt interest accrued	(*)	−.1
Change in cash balances, increase, or decrease (−):		
Treasurer's account	−1.1	1.6
Held outside Treasury	.2	.2
Net increase in cash balances	−.9	1.8
Increase in public debt	5.9	5.6

*Less than $50 million.

3

Administrative Budget Receipts and Expenditures

Chart 2

The Administrative Budget

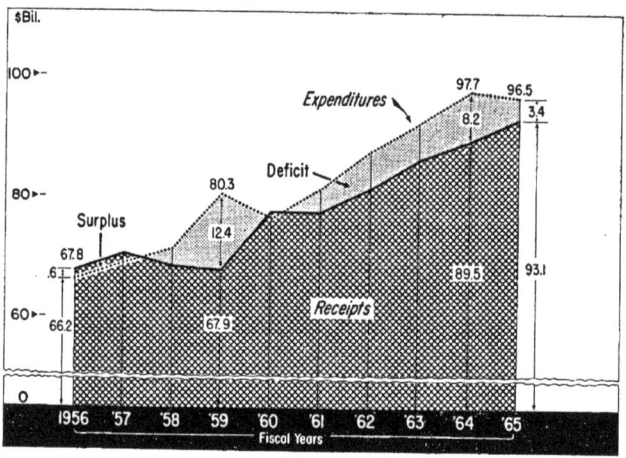

Receipts

The increase of $3.6 billion in net administrative budget receipts during fiscal 1965 brought the total to $93.1 billion, thus marking the fourth successive year in which new peaks have been established. This overall rise occurred despite the impact of reduced individual and corporate income tax rates under the Revenue Act of 1964. The bulk of the tax reduction went into effect early in the calendar year 1964 and the remainder on January 1, 1965.

Economic activity continued to expand throughout the fiscal year 1965 and tax receipts accompanied this general rise.

A comparison of net administrative budget receipts by major sources for fiscal years 1964 and 1965 is shown below. Additional data for 1965 on the gross basis are presented in table 18.

Source	1964	1965	Increase
	In millions of dollars		
Internal revenue:			
Individual income taxes	48, 697	48, 792	95
Corporation income taxes	23, 493	25, 461	1, 968
Excise taxes	10, 211	10, 911	700
Estate and gift taxes	2, 394	2, 716	323
Total internal revenue	84, 794	87, 880	3, 086
Customs duties	1, 252	1, 442	190
Miscellaneous receipts	3, 412	3, 749	337
Net administrative budget receipts	89, 459	93, 072	3, 613

Individual income taxes.—Receipts from individual income taxes amounted to $48.8 billion in fiscal 1965, accounting for over one-half of total budget revenues but, because of the rate reduction, for only 3 percent of the year's increase. The net gain of $95 million over fiscal 1964 occurred despite the effect of the tax reduction under the Revenue Act of 1964.

Corporation income taxes.—Corporation income tax receipts rose to $25.5 billion in the fiscal year 1965, $2.0 billion above the previous year's receipts, despite the reduced tax rates.

Receipts from corporation income taxes depend primarily on the amount of corporation profits earned during the calendar year which ends within the fiscal year. Corporation profits rose substantially from calendar year 1963 to 1964, up $6.2 billion on a national accounts basis. Tax receipts in fiscal 1965 were further bolstered by the speedup in estimated payments required under the Revenue Act of 1964. This speedup in payments adds to Government receipts in the fiscal years involved but does not affect the tax liabilities computed under the new lower rates.

Excise taxes.—Receipts from excise taxes are shown in the following table.

Source	1964	1965	Increase, or decrease (−)
	In millions of dollars		
Alcohol taxes	3,577	3,773	195
Tobacco taxes	2,053	2,149	96
Taxes on documents, other instruments, and playing cards	172	186	15
Manufacturers excise taxes	6,021	6,418	398
Retailers excise taxes	475	513	38
Miscellaneous excise taxes	1,547	1,786	239
Undistributed depositary receipts and unapplied collections	106	−32	−139
Gross excise taxes	13,950	14,793	843
Less:			
Refunds of receipts	220	223	3
Transfers to highway trust fund	3,519	3,659	139
Net excise taxes	10,211	10,911	700

Net excise tax receipts, after deduction of refunds and transfers to the highway trust fund, rose $700 million to $10.9 billion for the fiscal year 1965. Increases were pervasive among the many forms of excises reflecting the sustained expansion in economic activity. Miscellaneous excise taxes showed the largest relative increase, the bulk of it due to increased collections from telephone and other communications services.

Estate and gift taxes.—Estate and gift tax collections reached $2.7 billion in fiscal 1965, $323 million larger than in the previous fiscal year. Since estate taxes are not payable until 15 months after death and the valuation of the estate is the lesser of the value at time of death or one year later, the rise reflected the strong upsurge in stock prices which began late in the calendar year 1962.

Customs.—Customs duties increased 15 percent during the year reaching a net total of $1,442 million. This rise reflected a substantial increase in taxable imports accompanying the general rise in economic activity.

Miscellaneous receipts.—Miscellaneous receipts are the total of receipts by the Government of varied forms of income other than taxes. The total of $3.7 billion received in the fiscal year 1965 was $337 million or 10 percent larger than in 1964. The net overall rise is a composite of divergent movements in the various forms of nontax receipts. Sales of Government property and products, dividends and other earnings, and seigniorage showed advances, offset in part by smaller realizations on loans and investments.

Estimate of receipts

The Secretary of the Treasury is required each year to prepare and submit in his annual report to Congress estimates of public revenue for the current fiscal year and for the fiscal year next ensuing (act of February 26, 1907 (5 U.S.C. 265)).

The estimates of receipts from taxes and customs for the current and ensuing fiscal years are prepared by the Treasury Department. In general, the estimates of miscellaneous receipts are prepared by the agencies depositing these receipts in the Treasury.

The estimates of receipts and the legislative and economic assumptions upon which they are based are the same as those presented in the Budget message of the President of January 24, 1966. Briefly, the recommendations involve (a) rescheduling the 1966–69 reductions in the automobile and telephone excise taxes to the period 1968–71 and (b) the adoption of certain collection procedures which will put income tax payments closer to a pay-as-you-go system, thereby increasing current revenues without changing income tax rates and without changing final tax liabilities.

Excise tax rates on automobiles and general and long distance telephone and teletype services would be restored to the rates in effect before January 1, 1966, and the successive reductions scheduled until January 1, 1969, would be deferred. The estimate assumes that the telephone and teletype taxes would return to 10 percent on April 1, 1966, and the tax on automobiles would return to 7 percent from 6 percent on March 15, 1966.

The proposed graduated withholding schedule on wage and salary income tax liabilities affects the timing of tax payments during the year, but it does not change the tax liabilities. Under present legislation, a flat 14 percent is withheld on taxable salaries and wages; this corresponds to the tax on the lowest income bracket, and it is applied regardless of the amount of income. As a result, the taxes withheld on higher bracket wage earners are generally too small. The proposed new schedule would increase the amounts withheld as taxable salaries and wages increase, and thereby would reduce underwithholding to a small proportion of total income tax liability. The new withholding schedules are assumed to become effective on May 1, 1966.

Under present law quarterly corporation payments on estimated tax liabilities greater than $100,000 per year are being adjusted to a schedule that would run concurrently with the accrual of tax liabilities during each tax year. The size of payments on estimated tax is being adjusted gradually to reach an even quarterly pattern by calendar year 1970. The legislation proposed in this budget would require a more rapid adjustment and would complete the transition in the 1967 tax year. The accelerated schedule would first apply to payments due April 15, 1966.

Legislation authorizing additional user charges and extending others is recommended, in keeping with the policy that a greater share of the costs of certain programs which provide special benefits or privileges should be borne by identifiable primary beneficiaries. The user charges program also is being extended by administrative action throughout the executive branch where legislative authority exists, and present charges are reexamined regularly to assure that they adequately reflect the costs incurred.

The tax on air passenger traffic would be raised from 5 percent to 6 percent until January 1, 1969. A tax of 2 percent on air freight waybills would be instituted and an additional 2 percent added on January 1, 1969, raising this tax to 4 percent. The growth of air transportation should generate sufficient receipts from these taxes to meet commercial aviation's share of the cost of the Federal airways. Accordingly, the present 2 cents per gallon tax on gasoline used in commercial aviation would be repealed, leaving fuels used in commercial aviation untaxed. Gasoline and jet fuels used in general aviation would be taxed at 4 cents per gallon, and all of the receipts retained in the general fund.

A user charge of 2 cents per gallon is proposed on fuel used by vessels navigating the inland waterways.

User charges are also being recommended in several other programs. Some of these charges would become miscellaneous receipts of the general fund. In other instances, the charges would be used to offset the costs of operation, as in: (1) meat and poultry inspections; (2) commodity inspection and classification and warehouse inspecting and licensing; (3) administration of workmen's compensation and safety programs for longshoremen and harbor workers; and (4) overtime border inspections of private vessels and aircraft.

Legislation has been requested to create revolving funds for the Rural Electrification Administration (REA) and three power administrations—Bonneville, Southeastern, and Southwestern. With authority to operate as revolving funds, the agencies would be able to use collections on outstanding loans and revenues from power sales to help finance their current operations and necessary capital outlays, while remaining subject to control through the regular appropriations process. Enactment of this legislation will reduce, equally, miscellaneous receipts of the Treasury and expenditures by the agencies without effect upon the budgetary surplus or deficit.

The nation's output of goods and services for calendar year 1966 is expected to be within a $10 billion range centered on $722 billion, an increase of $46½ billion over 1965 at the midpoint of the range. Substantial gains in personal income and corporate profits will accompany the growth in output. Specifically, the fiscal year revenue estimates are based on the following economic assumptions:

	Calendar years		
	1964 actual	1965 preliminary	1966 estimate
	In billions of dollars		
Gross national product	628.7	675.6	722
Personal income	495.0	530.7	567
Corporate profits before taxes	64.8	74.6	80

Estimates of tax revenues cannot be derived directly and simply from the assumed levels of aggregate economic performance. The definitions of taxable income in the tax statutes, which determine tax liabilities, differ from the economic or statistical definitions of income which are used to measure economic performance. In addition, tax payments are received by the Treasury after the period in which tax liabilities are incurred. For example, corporation income tax collections lag six months behind the period when the taxable income was earned; there is also some lag between the time when individual income and social security taxes are deducted from earnings and the time employers transfer these sums to the Treasury.

The 1964 income tax legislation decreased tax liabilities by successively greater amounts in calendar years 1964 and 1965. Despite the losses from income tax reduction and, in fiscal 1966, from the excise tax cuts of 1965, total revenues rose in fiscal 1964 and 1965 and are expected to continue rising in the fiscal years 1966 and 1967. Receipts for fiscal 1966 are estimated to increase $7 billion over actual receipts in 1965 to $100 billion. A further increase of $11 billion to a total of $111 billion is estimated for 1967. Receipts will have risen for six consecutive years by the fiscal year 1967, reaching a level $33 billion above 1961. This revenue gain reflects an increase of $218 billion in gross national product from the calendar year 1960 to the calendar year 1966.

Actual administrative budget receipts for the fiscal year 1965 and estimated receipts for 1966 and 1967 are compared by major sources in the accompanying table. Amounts shown for each revenue source are the net amounts after deduction of refunds, transfers to trust funds, and interfund transactions.

	Fiscal years			
	1965 actual	1966 estimate	1967 estimate	Increase, or decrease (—), 1966 to 1967
	In millions of dollars			
Individual income taxes	48,792	51,400	56,240	4,840
Corporation income taxes	25,461	29,700	34,400	4,700
Excise taxes	10,911	9,169	8,879	—290
Estate and gift taxes	2,716	2,932	3,301	369
Customs	1,442	1,655	1,845	190
Miscellaneous receipts	3,749	5,144	6,335	1,191
Net administrative budget receipts	93,072	100,000	111,000	11,000

Individual income taxes.—Collections of individual income taxes amounted to $48.8 billion in fiscal year 1965. They are estimated to rise to $51.4 billion in fiscal 1966 and to $56.2 billion in fiscal 1967, an increase of $4.8 billion. The rise of $2.6 billion in fiscal 1966 reflects a substantial increase in the individual income tax base offset in part by the second stage reduction of tax rates which went into effect on January 1, 1965. The larger rise in 1967 is almost wholly due to higher incomes, bolstered by the proposed introduction of a graduated withholding system.

Corporation income taxes.—Corporate receipts which amounted to $25.5 billion in the fiscal year 1965, are expected to reach $29.7 billion in 1966, and $34.4 billion in 1967. Receipts in 1966 are depressed by the second stage of tax rate reduction but are increased by $1.0 billion because of the further speedup in the payment schedule. The 1967 revenue increase of $4.7 billion reflects both increased profits and a $3.2 billion effect of the proposed speedup.

Excise taxes.—Net excise tax revenues, excluding taxes collected and transferred to the highway trust fund, are estimated to fall to $9.2 billion in fiscal year 1966 from $10.9 billion in 1965. A further decrease to $8.9 billion is estimated for 1967. Losses in 1967 from the several excises repealed as of January 1, 1966, will be substantially offset if the proposals relating to the auto and telephone excises are accepted by the Congress.

Also, there would be some offset if the various user charge proposals are adopted. Collections are also increasing from the excises not affected by the excise reduction act, reflecting increased sales of the products and services involved.

Estate and gift taxes.—Estate and gift tax receipts are estimated to increase from $2.7 billion in 1965 to $2.9 billion in 1966. A rise to $3.3 billion is expected in 1967. Receipts from this source arise mostly from collections of estate taxes which are payable 15 months after death. The estimated increases in the fiscal years 1966 and 1967 therefore reflect rises in asset valuations occurring some time earlier.

Customs.—Customs receipts are estimated to increase from $1,442 million in fiscal year 1965, to $1,655 million in 1966, and to $1,845 million in 1967. Enlarged receipts from customs duties reflect increasing imports associated with a continued expansion of economic activity.

Miscellaneous receipts.—Miscellaneous receipts, which are all those received by the general fund of the Treasury except for taxes and customs duties, are shown in the above table net of interfund transactions. Such receipts are estimated to increase from $3.7 billion in fiscal 1965, to $5.1 billion in 1966, and to $6.3 billion in 1967. Over half of the increases of $1.4 billion in 1966 and $1.2 billion in 1967 are attributable to seigniorage profits arising from full-scale production of coins with the new composition authorized by the Coinage Act of 1965.[1] Also adding to the increases are accelerated sales of excess strategic and critical materials, increased receipts from the Outer Continental Shelf lands as new areas are opened for exploration, and higher payments of earnings by the Federal Reserve System.

Expenditures

Net administrative budget expenditures decreased more than $1 billion in fiscal 1965 from the preceding fiscal year, the first such year-to-year reduction in expenditures in five years. A two-year comparative summary by major functions is set forth below; more detailed information on administrative budget expenditures is contained in table 15.

---

[1] See exhibit 23.

Program	1964	1965	Increase, or decrease (−)
	In millions of dollars		
National defense	54,181	50,163	−4,018
Interest payments	10,765	11,435	670
Health, labor, and welfare	5,475	5,898	423
Veterans' benefits and services	5,492	5,495	3
Space research and technology	4,171	5,093	922
International affairs and finance	3,687	4,304	617
Agriculture and agricultural resources	r 5,475	4,898	−577
Commerce and transportation	3,002	3,499	497
Other 1	r 6,102	6,592	490
Less interfund transactions	664	870	206
Total	97,684	96,507	−1,177

r Revised.
1 Includes programs relating to natural resources, housing and community development, education, and general government.

Expenditures for national defense, though significantly below the preceding year, accounted for 52 percent of total administrative budget expenditures. Interest payments increased during the year to account for 12 percent of administrative budget expenditures; health, labor, and welfare programs accounted for over 6 percent; and veterans' benefits and services something less than 6 percent.

Estimates of expenditures

Administrative budget expenditures in the fiscal years 1966 and 1967 are expected to be $106.4 billion and $112.8 billion, respectively. The following summary shows the estimated expenditures for these two years by major programs. Table 18 shows estimated administrative budget expenditures for these years by agencies.

Program	1965 actual	1966 estimate	Increase, or decrease (−), 1966 from 1965	1967 estimate	Increase, or decrease (−), 1967 from 1966
	In millions of dollars				
National defense	50,163	56,560	6,397	60,541	3,981
Interest payments	11,435	12,104	669	12,854	750
Health, labor, and welfare	5,898	8,377	2,479	9,962	1,585
Veterans' benefits and services	5,495	5,122	−373	5,721	599
Space research and technology	5,093	5,600	507	5,300	−300
International affairs and finance	4,304	3,932	−372	4,177	245
Agriculture and agricultural resources	4,898	4,313	−585	3,372	−941
Commerce and transportation	3,499	3,202	−297	2,672	−530
Other 1	6,592	7,866	1,274	8,960	1,094
Less interfund transactions	870	647	−223	712	65
Total	96,507	106,428	9,921	112,847	6,419

1 Includes programs relating to natural resources, housing and community development, education, and general government.

Trust Receipts and Expenditures

Receipts

In fiscal 1965, net trust receipts rose to $31.0 billion, an increase of $.7 billion over 1964. Detailed information on net trust receipts is given in table 5; the following summary shows the two year comparison of net trust receipts, by source for fiscal years 1964 and 1965.

Source	1964	1965	Increase
	In millions of dollars		
Employment taxes	16,832	16,905	73
Unemployment tax deposits by States	3,042	3,052	10
Excise taxes	3,519	3,659	140
Interest on trust funds	1,613	1,770	157
Other trust receipts [1]	5,845	6,299	454
Less interfund transactions	521	638	117
Net trust receipts	30,331	31,047	716

[1] Includes Federal employee and agency payments to retirement funds, veterans' life insurance premiums, and other miscellaneous trust receipts.

Estimates of receipts

In the fiscal years 1966 and 1967 trust receipts are expected to rise to $33.5 billion and $41.6 billion, respectively. The rise will be due principally to employment tax receipts. In fiscal 1966, employment taxes are estimated to increase $1.9 billion over 1965, and in 1967 by $5.5 billion over 1966. These increases will develop primarily from the higher social security tax rates and larger wage base, effective January 1, 1966. On that date the combined employer-employee rate is raised from 7.25 percent to 8.4 percent and the covered annual wage base from $4,800 to $6,600. On January 1, 1967, existing law provides for the combined tax rate to be further increased to 8.8 percent.

Detailed estimates of trust fund receipts are contained in table 19; a summary by principal source follows:

Source	1965 actual	1966 estimate	Increase, or decrease (−), 1966 from 1965	1967 estimate	Increase, or decrease (−), 1967 from 1966
	In millions of dollars				
Employment taxes	16,905	18,819	1,914	24,339	5,520
Unemployment tax deposits by States	3,052	2,900	−152	2,900	
Excise taxes	3,659	3,859	200	4,378	519
Interest on trust funds	1,770	1,822	52	1,970	148
Other [1]	6,299	6,933	634	8,787	1,854
Less interfund transactions	638	795	157	767	−28
Net trust receipts	31,047	33,539	2,492	41,608	8,069

[1] Includes Federal employee and agency payments to retirement funds, veterans' life insurance premiums, and other miscellaneous trust receipts.

Expenditures

Net trust expenditures in fiscal 1965 amounted to $29.6 billion, an increase over the preceding year of $.7 billion. Programs of a health, labor, and welfare nature accounted for 78 percent of total trust expenditures, while commerce and transportation programs (mainly highway trust fund expenditures) made up 13 percent of the total. Details regarding trust expenditures are contained in table 5; a summary by major function follows comparing fiscal 1965 trust expenditures with those of 1964.

Program	1964	1965	Increase, or decrease (−)
	In millions of dollars		
Health, labor, and welfare	22,733	23,186	453
Commerce and transportation	3,482	3,864	382
Housing and community development	1,889	1,136	−753
Veterans' benefits and services	666	624	−42
Agriculture and agricultural resources	496	927	431
National defense	487	751	264
Other [1]	−348	−213	135
Less interfund transactions	521	638	117
Net trust expenditures	28,885	29,637	752

[1] Includes programs relating to natural resources, international affairs and finance, education, and general government; also includes net transactions in deposit fund accounts.

Estimates of expenditures

In the fiscal years 1966 and 1967 trust expenditures are expected to reach $33.8 billion and $37.9 billion, respectively. The following summary shows by major functions the estimated trust expenditures for 1966 and 1967, compared with the preceding year. Trust expenditures for these years are shown in more detail in table 19.

Program	1965 actual	1966 estimate	Increase, or decrease (−), 1966 from 1965	1967 estimate	Increase, or decrease (−), 1967 from 1966
	In millions of dollars				
Health, labor, and welfare	23,186	26,589	3,403	31,110	4,521
Commerce and transportation	3,864	3,780	−84	3,895	115
Housing and community development	1,136	1,988	852	1,194	−794
Veterans' benefits and services	624	554	−70	682	128
Agriculture and agricultural resources	927	600	−327	623	23
National defense	751	875	124	898	23
Other [1]	−213	194	407	248	54
Less interfund transactions	638	795	157	767	−28
Net trust expenditures	29,637	33,786	4,149	37,882	4,096

[1] Includes programs relating to natural resources, international affairs and finance, education, and general government; also includes net transactions in deposit funds.

Receipts From and Payments to the Public

A summary of Federal Government cash transactions with the public during fiscal year 1965 shows total receipts from the public to have amounted to $119.7 billion, while total payments to the public reached $122.4 billion, resulting in an excess of payments totaling $2.7 billion.

The consolidated cash statement is considered helpful in assessing the results of the Federal Government's financial operations, since it presents the flow of cash transactions between the Federal Government and the public. The totals of the administrative budget receipts and expenditures are added to the trust fund receipts and expenditures, with appropriate deductions for intragovernmental transactions, an adjustment to expenditures for debt issuances in lieu of checks, and certain other adjustments for transactions not involving cash exchanges with the public. The 1962 annual report, page 31, contains a detailed explanation of the procedure for compiling the consolidated cash statement.

Table 17 provides an 11-year comparative table showing details of cash transactions with the public. The following summary shows such transactions for fiscal years 1964–65 and estimates for 1966–67.

Receipts from and payments to the public	Actual		Estimated	
	1964	1965	1966	1967
	In millions of dollars			
Receipts from the public:				
Administrative budget (net)	89,459	93,072	100,000	111,000
Trust and other (net)	30,331	31,047	33,539	41,608
Intragovernmental and other noncash items (−)	−4,259	−4,420	−5,385	−7,069
Total receipts from the public	115,530	119,699	128,154	145,539
Payments to the public:				
Administrative budget (net)	97,684	96,507	106,428	112,847
Trust and other (net)	28,885	29,637	33,786	37,882
Intragovernmental and other noncash items (−)	−6,237	−3,749	−5,166	−5,681
Total payments to the public	120,332	122,395	135,048	145,048
Excess of cash receipts from, or payments to (−), the public	−4,802	−2,696	−6,894	491

Corporations and Other Business-Type Activities of the Federal Government

The business-type programs which Government corporations and agencies administer are financed by various means: appropriations, sales of capital stock, borrowings from either the U.S. Treasury or the public, or by revenues derived from their own operations.

Corporations or agencies having legislative authority to borrow from the Treasury issue their formal securities to the Secretary of the Treasury. Amounts borrowed are reported in the periodic financial statements of the Government corporations and agencies as part of the Government's net investment in the enterprise. In fiscal 1965, borrowings from the Treasury, exclusive of refinancing transactions, totaled $7,450 million, repayments were $8,352 million, and outstanding loans on June 30, 1965, totaled $28,354 million.

Those agencies having legislative authority to borrow from the public must either consult with the Secretary of the Treasury regarding the proposed offering, or have the terms of the securities to be offered approved by the Secretary.

During fiscal 1965 Congress granted new authority to borrow from the Treasury in the total amount of $1,050 million, and reduced existing authority by $924 million, resulting in a net increase of $126 million. The status of borrowing authority and the amount of corporation and agency securities outstanding as of June 30, 1965, are shown in table 109.

Unless otherwise specifically fixed by law, the Treasury each month determines interest rates on its loans to agencies by considering the Government's cost for its borrowings in the current market, as reflected by prevailing market yields on Government securities with comparable maturities. A description of the Federal agencies' securities held by the Treasury on June 30, 1965, is shown in table 110.

During fiscal 1965, $1.1 billion was received by the Treasury as interest on borrowings by agencies, dividends, and similar payments.

Quarterly statements of financial condition, income and expense, and source and application of funds are submitted to the Treasury by Government corporations and agencies. Semiannual statements of financial contingencies are also submitted. These statements serve as the basis for the combined financial statements compiled by the Treasury which, together with the individual statements, are published periodically in the *Treasury Bulletin*. Summary statements of the financial condition of Government corporations and other business-type activities, as of June 30, 1965, are shown in table 111.

Account of the Treasurer of the United States

Gold, silver, and the general account are the three major categories of the account of the Treasurer of the United States. On June 30, 1965, gold held was valued at $13,934 million, the principal amount being at the Fort Knox Depository with lesser amounts at mints and assay offices. Gold liabilities totaled $13,826 million and included gold certificates (series 1934), the reservation for the gold certificate fund of the Federal Reserve Board of Governors, and reserves against Federal Reserve notes and U.S. notes.

Assets of the silver account, consisting of silver bullion and silver dollars had a value of $1,270 million as of June 30, 1965. Liabilities against the silver account (currency issued against free silver, etc.) amounted to $889 million, leaving a silver balance totaling $382 million.

Transactions affecting the account of the Treasurer of the United States, fiscal year 1965

[In millions of dollars]

Balance June 30, 1964_____ 11,036

Excess of deposits, or withdrawals (−), budget, trust, and other accounts:

    Deposits_____ 125,464

    Withdrawals (−)_____ 126,395   −931

Excess of deposits, or withdrawals (−), public debt accounts:

    Increase in gross public debt_____ 5,561

    Deduct:

        Excess of Government agencies' investments in public debt issues_____ 2,422

        Accruals on savings and retirement plan bonds and Treasury bills (included in increase in gross public debt above)_____ 3,717

        Certain public debt redemptions (included above in withdrawals, budget, trust, and other accounts)_____ −3,467

        Net deductions_____ 2,672   2,889

Excess of sales of Government agencies' securities in the market_____ 201

Net transactions in clearing accounts (documents not received or classified by the Office of the Treasurer)_____ −584

Balance June 30, 1965_____ 12,610

The assets of the general account of the Treasurer at fiscal yearend included the gold and silver balances against which there were no reserves or specific liabilities, cash in the form of currency and coin, unclassified collections, and funds on deposit with Federal Reserve banks and other depositaries. During the year the balance in the general account increased by $1,575 million. The net change is accounted for in the preceding table.

Table 58 is a balance sheet presentation of the account of the Treasurer of the United States.

Public Debt Management and Ownership

In the fiscal year 1965 Treasury debt management operations were primarily designed to secure the funds needed for Government expenditures in excess of revenues and for the refinancing of maturing Treasury securities. In addition to meeting these basic housekeeping requirements, decisions were also shaped by major economic policy objectives—including the achievement of progress toward equilibrium in the U.S. balance of payments, and the achievement of growth and price stability of the domestic economy. In brief, these goals called for maintaining a level of short-term interest rates that would be sufficiently competitive with rates available in other financial centers, while avoiding an excessive buildup in short dated debt (with its implicit inflationary potential) or upward pressure on long-term interest rates, which would impede domestic investment. At the same time a continuing effort was made to retain and improve upon a debt maturity structure that would assure flexibility in future financing decisions. With the domestic economy expanding and total credit flows proceeding at record levels, these objectives presented no serious conflict with one another. Flows of funds proceeded through the market at record levels, helping to lift economic activity to new highs while longer term interest rates were essentially steady—despite sizable sales of long-term Treasury issues through the advance refunding of shorter debt. The price level in the economy rose slightly during the year. The balance of payments was in deficit for the period as a whole, but showed a marked improvement within the year and actually registered a surplus in the April–June 1965 quarter. This improvement largely reflected the initial impact of President Johnson's voluntary restraint program of February 10, 1965, but the higher level of short-term interest rates in this country was also helpful.

782–556—66——2

The form and scope of Treasury borrowing operations in fiscal 1965 depended to a great extent upon the investment environment at each particular financing juncture. Early in the fiscal year the investment climate was generally marked by investor confidence in the existing yield levels which, in turn, reflected the noticeable improvement in the U.S. balance-of-payments situation in the second half of the previous fiscal year and the continued steady growth of the domestic economy.

This favorable atmosphere was clouded during the fall months, however, as the extent of the British balance-of-payments problems became publicized and the increase in the Bank of England bank rate was closely followed in late November by a rise in the Federal Reserve discount rate. The credit market impact of the British payments crisis was almost entirely confined to the money market area where, for example, average issuing rates on three-month Treasury bills rose from 3½ percent early in the fiscal year to 3⅞ percent by calendar yearend. (See chart 3.) Prices of long-term securities faltered, but recovered quickly as a steady volume of investment demand continued to be the predominate factor in capital markets. The extent of this demand was highlighted by the very active investor participation in the Treasury's advance refunding offering in January and the aggressive bidding for corporate and municipal securities offered at that time.

CHART 3

Market Yields At Constant Maturities¹ 1960-'65

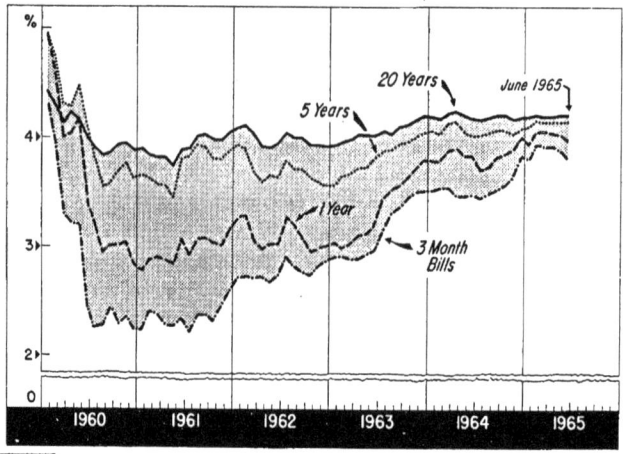

¹ Estimated yields of U.S. Government securities at 1, 5, and 20 years; bank discount rates on bills; monthly averages of end of week figures.

Short-term rates, after declining somewhat from December highs, turned up again in January and reached record levels in late February 1965 for the current business expansion. Growing concern over the deteriorating U.S. balance-of-payments position and the accompanying gold losses created uncertainties in the money market, which were in part abated by the President's February 10 message to Congress introducing the voluntary foreign credit restraint program. As the efficacy of this program became apparent, investor confidence re-emerged and short-term as well as long-term interest rates were generally steady to lower throughout the remainder of the fiscal year. By the end of the fiscal year the market rate on 3-month bills, after reaching 4.0 percent, declined to about 3.8 percent while the average yield on long-term Treasury bonds fell slightly to about 4⅛ percent.

The Treasury was also aided in debt management efforts by a continuation of the trend of recent years toward smaller year-to-year increases in the Federal debt (the public debt and guaranteed debt not owned by the Treasury). The total debt rose by $5.3 billion in fiscal 1965 compared with increases of $6.1 billion in fiscal 1964, $7.8 billion in fiscal 1963, and $9.4 billion in fiscal 1962. Marketable securities, which comprised almost two-thirds of the debt on June 30, 1965, totaled just $2.2 billion higher than a year earlier, marking the smallest fiscal year increase in this category of debt since fiscal year 1957. Moreover, the supply of marketable Treasury securities held by the public actually declined by $2.4 billion as Government investment accounts and the Federal Reserve System absorbed $4½ billion of marketable issues during the year. Official accounts also added $2 billion to their holdings of nonmarketable securities, for a total net acquisition that was $1.2 billion greater than the $5.3 billion increase in the Federal debt.

As illustrated by chart 4, commercial banks (particularly large reserve city banks) continued to liquidate holdings of Government securities during the past fiscal year. These holdings declined by $2 billion, following a $4 billion decline in fiscal 1964. Large nonfinancial corporations were also net sellers of governments in fiscal 1965 as the yields on alternative money market instruments attracted an increasingly larger share of the corporate short-term investment funds which remained after heavier capital spending outlays. As was true in fiscal 1964 net new investment in Federal securities in fiscal 1965, other than that represented by Government investment account and Federal Reserve purchases, was largely concentrated in the portfolios of State and local government general and pension funds, individuals, and corporate pension funds.

CHART 4

Changes in Public Debt Holdings by Investor Classes

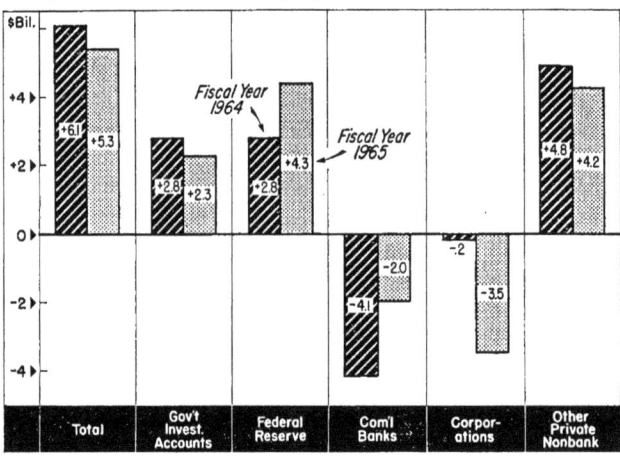

FINANCING OPERATIONS

As the new fiscal year began the financing outlook had improved from earlier projections due to the stronger than anticipated budget position during the last few months of fiscal 1964. The Treasurer's account balance reached a relatively high level of $11 billion on June 30, 1964, and earlier expectations of moderately heavy cash borrowing in the upcoming July–September period were revised downward. The budget deficit for fiscal 1965 was viewed as certain to be significantly less than the $8¼ billion fiscal 1964 total with expenditures held below the level of the previous year and revenues rising somewhat. Reflecting the seasonally light flow of receipts the budget deficit in the first six months of the new fiscal year was expected to approach $9 billion, followed by a substantial surplus in the subsequent six-month period. However, by drawing down the seasonally high cash balance at the start of the fiscal year and entering the market for about $2 billion of new money in July or August, it appeared that the Treasury could postpone the bulk of new cash borrowing until the October–December quarter.

This favorable cash outlook, together with outward signs of strength in the Government securities market, presented the Treasury with an opportunity to make a major debt restructuring effort. Consideration centered on the possibility of including an early refunding in advance of maturity of issues due in August and November 1964 into longer term securities in addition to the advance refunding of selected issues in the short to intermediate maturity range. With close to $30 billion of coupon issues maturing on the 4 quarterly refunding dates of fiscal year 1965 and $16½ billion of the total held by the public (that is, in the hands of individual, business, and institutional investors other than the Federal Reserve banks and Government investment accounts) it was hoped to refund a significant portion of these nearby maturities, along with some other short-term issues, in the existing receptive market. A reduction in the volume of short dated debt also would provide greater flexibility in the later fall cash operations by making it possible to borrow through regular bills and tax anticipation bills without adding so much to the economy's liquidity as to be an inflationary influence.

Accordingly, on July 8, the Treasury announced that the improvement of its cash position made unnecessary any immediate substantial cash borrowing. At the same time, an advance refunding offering was made to holders of $42 billion of 9 selected note and bond issues maturing from August 1964–February 1967. This first financing of the new fiscal year provided an opportunity for holders of these issues ($26½ billion in public hands) to exchange for reopened 4 percent bonds of October 1969, new 4⅛ percent bonds of 1973, and reopened 4¼ percent bonds of August 1987–92. The terms of the offering were well received by investors and public subscriptions reached a record high for advance refundings of $9.3 billion, 35 percent of eligible public holdings. As a result of the large conversion public holdings of issues maturing in fiscal year 1965 were reduced by some $4½ billion, $1¼ billion was added to the volume of long-term debt outstanding, and the average maturity of the marketable debt rose by almost 5 months to the highest level in 8 years. The successful offering was particularly helpful in tightening the August and November maturities, reducing public holdings of issues maturing in each of those months to a very manageable $2¼ billion.

The Treasury also announced at the time of the advance refunding in July that the immediate cash needs of the Treasury would be met through increases in the regular weekly bill offerings beginning with a $100 million addition to the weekly auction of bills dated July 16. The following two weekly auctions were increased by a like amount. The demand for bills expanded sharply during the refunding period, however, as some sellers of advance refunding "rights" entered the bill market and reinvestment demand also developed from holders of the $2 billion one year bills maturing July 15. Bill rates moved appreciably lower. Responding to the market demand, and mindful of near-term needs for additional cash, the Treasury announced, on July 20, a cash offering of a $1 billion strip of bills consisting of an additional $100 million each of 10 weekly series dated October 15—

December 17, 1964. Bill rates immediately steadied and then turned upward as supplies were enlarged and as market observers interpreted the move as a sign of official concern over the trend and level of short-term rates compared with those abroad.

The $4 billion remainder of the 5 percent notes and 3¾ percent notes maturing on August 15 were refinanced through a cash offering of new 3⅞ percent 18-month notes, at par. The cash refinancing offer was favorably received and subscriptions totaled $14.9 billion for the $4 billion, or thereabouts, to be issued. Subscriptions received from States and funds of other political subdivisions, Government investment accounts, Federal Reserve banks, international organizations and foreign official accounts totaled $2.0 billion and were allotted in full upon receipt of the required certification of ownership of the maturing securities. Subscriptions for less than $100,000 were allotted in full while larger subscriptions were subject to a 15-percent allotment but were assured of a minimum award of $100,000.

The second major step taken to meet the anticipated cash requirements of the fall period was announced on August 21, 1964. Subscriptions were invited for $1 billion of 201-day tax anticipation bills to be dated September 2, 1964, and to mature March 22, 1965. On August 31, the Treasury announced a $100 million increase in the following regular weekly bill auction, and similar additions were made for the next three weeks bringing the net new cash borrowed through the first three months of fiscal 1965 to $2½ billion.

Treasury financing decisions through the remainder of the calendar year 1964 were influenced by a combination of international and domestic developments. In the international area uncertainties arose over the British and U.S. balance-of-payments positions and were strengthened by the sterling crisis and resultant increases in the British bank rate and Federal Reserve discount rate in late November. Added to these concerns there were increased discussions in the market of the possibility that domestic price stability might be threatened by rising private credit demand associated with expanding business activity. The outcome of the labor negotiations in the automobile industry also generated a degree of market caution.

In mid-October Treasury again entered the Government securities market to borrow $1½ billion through the auction of additional March 22, 1965, tax anticipation bills. This step had been anticipated by market observers in view of expected Treasury cash requirements and commercial banks bid aggressively in the auction to obtain the Treasury tax and loan account credit which was permitted up to 50 percent of bank allotments.

On October 28, the Treasury announced plans to refinance the $8¾ billion of 4⅞ percent notes and 3¾ percent notes maturing November 15, 1964. The Treasury offered $9¼ billion, or thereabouts, of new 4 percent 18-month notes for cash in order to pay off the maturing securities and raise a moderate amount of new money. Subscriptions totaling $21.9 billion were received for the issue and those received from States, political subdivisions, Government investment accounts, Federal Reserve banks, international organizations and foreign official accounts were allotted in full if accompanied by the required certification of ownership of the maturing notes. All other subscriptions were allotted in full up to $100,000 and larger subscriptions were subject to a 16.5 percent allotment ratio with a minimum award of $100,000.

Additional new cash was raised in November with an offering of $1.5 billion of tax anticipation bills to mature in June 1965. As in October, the Treasury allowed commercial banks to pay for 50 percent of their purchases through direct crediting of tax and loan accounts, and this resulted again in vigorous bank bidding for the bills.

This offering marked the completion of the borrowing program (aside from regular bill rollovers) for the July–December half of the fiscal year with a total of $6½ billion of new cash raised, primarily through bills, and $22 billion of notes and bonds issued in exchange and cash refunding operations.

Throughout the closing months of the calendar year the Treasury considered possibilities for borrowing operations in the January–June 1965 period. While financial developments in late November, as mentioned earlier, provided an additional complication, plans continued to focus on advance refunding possibilities should conditions favor such an undertaking in the months ahead. Remaining cash borrowing needs for the fiscal year were expected to be relatively light with most of the total to be raised through additional June tax anticipation bills. The market for longer term governments improved in early December and prices climbed back to the levels existing before the discount rate increase in November. While bond prices declined moderately by yearend, there appeared to be sufficient demand for intermediate and longer term governments to warrant another advance refunding offering in early January. A good availability of funds for long-term investment was in evidence with some signs of easing in the demand for mortgage loans and no particular pressures noticeable in either the corporate or municipal sectors.

The flow of liquid savings continued at record high levels and it was felt that by moving ahead at the turn of the calendar year, the Treasury would remove some uncertainties surrounding new investment programs for the coming year, and provide investors with an opportunity to extend their holdings at then current yield levels. It would also be useful for the Treasury to gain the benefit of private investors' desires to achieve debt extention and thus increase the flexibility of future Treasury operations.

The announcement on December 30 of an advance refunding offering was well received by the market. Holders of $33 billion of 8 outstanding issues, including the nearby maturing February 1965 bonds, in addition to those maturing from November 1965—November 1967, were given an opportunity to extend their holdings into new 4 percent bonds of February 1970, new 4⅛ percent bonds of February 1974, and reopened 4¼ percent bonds of August 1987–92. A total of $9.1 billion or 41 percent of the $22.1 billion of eligible public holdings, were exchanged for the new issues. The Treasury was well satisfied with the results of the offering, which exceeded earlier expectations, and welcomed the expression of investor confidence in current interest rate levels. Secondary distribution proceeded smoothly assisted by a favorable market reaction to the President's Budget Message and news of improvement in the British balance-of-payments situation.

At the same time that the January advance refunding was announced, the Treasury indicated the intent to borrow shortly from $1½ billion to $2 billion by adding to the outstanding June tax anticipation bill. The formal offering of $1¾ billion of this issue was made on January 6, for cash subscription on January 12. Commercial banks were again allowed a 50 percent credit to their Treasury tax and loan accounts in payment for their allotments and as a result the auction attracted good commercial bank participation.

A technical shortage of short-term regular bills developed in the market during the advance refunding period as strong reinvestment demand originated from sellers of "rights." To help counteract this shortage and maintain international short-term interest rate relationships, as well as help cover some of the remaining fiscal year 1965 cash borrowing needs, the Treasury announced on January 13 that $100 million would be added to the regular weekly auctions in coming weeks. Each of the seven auctions for the bills issued from January 21—March 4, was increased by this amount as well as the auctions for the March 25, April 1, and April 15 issues. One auction, the issue of April 8, was increased by $200 million to even out the existing pattern, leaving a cycle of $2.2 billion regular weekly bills maturing and offered each week: $1.2 billion of the 13-week bill and $1.0 billion of the 26-week issue. This cycle was maintained through the balance of fiscal 1965, along with the regular cycle of one-year bills maturing on month-end dates, each in the amount of $1 billion.

The remainder of the 2⅝ percent bonds maturing February 15, 1965, were paid off in cash from the proceeds of a routine offering of an equivalent amount of 4 percent, 21-month notes priced at 99.85, to yield 4.09 percent.   The $2.2 billion of these 2⅝s to reach final maturity represented less than one-third of the amount originally issued in June 1958.   The issue had been made eligible in three advance refunding offerings and in the last of these, in January, $1.8 billion was exchanged for the longer term securities then being offered.

Subscriptions for the new 4 percent notes totaled $10.6 billion and those received from official institutions and public funds were allotted in full.   Subscriptions of $100,000 or less were also allotted in full while larger subscriptions were subject to a 15 percent allotment ratio but assured of a $100,000 minimum award.   The 21-month maturity of the notes offered in this refinancing represented a slight departure from the length of short-term securities in recent cash and exchange offerings and, in fact, was the only such maturity issued in more than 20 years.

The final financing operation of fiscal year 1965 consisted of the refinancing of $8½ billion securities maturing May 15, 1965.   The two maturing issues were a 4⅝ percent note and a 3⅞ percent note with some $4.1 billion of the maturing total in public hands.   This total represented the largest public holding of the four quarterly refundings during the year and the largest since the $4.2 billion public holding of May 1964, just a year earlier.   The market environment was also similar to that of the previous spring, with long-term yields down slightly and intermediate rates generally unchanged from a year earlier.   The only significant change in the yield structure had occurred in the short-term area where the three-month bill rate had climbed nearly one-half of one percent and one-year yields had increased a little over one-eighth of one percent.   The budget picture was also one of improvement from the latest January estimates, with projected revenue flows adequate to meet expenditures through the remainder of the fiscal year.

The securities offered in the May refunding, in exchange for the maturing notes were also similar to those offered a year earlier.   Investors were given the opportunity to exchange for 4 percent 15-month notes (priced to yield 4.12 percent) and 4¼ percent, 9-year bonds (priced to yield 4.22 percent).   The latter option was the same issue that had been offered in 1964, reopened at a slight premium.   Interest centered primarily on the 4¼ percent bonds and public subscriptions to this issue totaled $2.0 billion, compared to $1.7 billion for the shorter term notes.

The two accompanying tables summarize the Treasury's major financing operations during the fiscal year and table 45 provides data on allotments by investor classes. The exhibits on public debt operations provide further information on public offerings and allotments by issues in tables and representative circulars.

Public offerings of marketable Treasury securities excluding refinancing of regular bills (three-month, six-month, and one-year) fiscal year 1965

[In millions of dollars]

Date	Description	Issued for cash		Issued in exchange		Total
		For new money	For refunding	For maturing issue	In advance refunding	
1964	BONDS AND NOTES					
Apr. 1	1½% exchange note–Apr. 1, 1969 [1]	_____	_____	[2] 48	_____	48
July 22	4% bond–Oct. 1, 1969, additional_____	_____	_____	_____	3,726	3,726
July 22	4⅛% bond–Nov, 15, 1973_____	_____	_____	_____	4,357	4,357
July 22	4¼% bond–Aug. 15, 1987–92, additional_____	_____	_____	_____	1,198	1,198
Aug. 15	3⅞% note–Feb. 15, 1966 [3]	_____	_____	4,040	_____	4,040
Oct. 1	1½% exchange note–Oct. 1, 1969 [1]	_____	_____	159	_____	159
Nov. 15	4% note–May 15, 1966 [3]	811	8,708	_____	_____	9,519
1965						
Jan. 15	4% bond–Feb. 15, 1970_____	_____	_____	_____	4,381	4,381
Jan. 15	4⅛% bond–Feb. 15, 1974_____	_____	_____	_____	3,130	3,130
Jan. 15	4¼% bond–Aug. 15, 1987–92, additional_____	_____	_____	_____	2,254	2,254
Feb. 15	4% note–Nov. 15, 1966 [3]	86	2,168	_____	_____	2,254
Apr. 1	1½% exchange note–Apr. 1, 1970 [1]	_____	_____	31	_____	31
May 15	4% note–Aug. 15, 1966, additional at 99.85_____	_____	_____	5,904	_____	5,904
May 15	4¼% bond–May 15, 1974, additional at 100.25_____	_____	_____	2,062	_____	2,062
	Total bonds and notes_____	897	14,916	8,204	19,046	43,063
	BILLS [4] (MATURITY VALUE)					
	Increase in three-month and six-month bills:					
1964	July through September_____	608	_____	_____	_____	608
	October through December_____	100	_____	_____	_____	100
1965	January through March_____	802	_____	_____	_____	802
	April through June_____	399	_____	_____	_____	399
	Total increase_____	1,909	_____	_____	_____	1,909
1964	Other bill offerings:					
July 29	3.505% 109.6-day average for strip [5]	1,001	_____	_____	_____	1,001
Sept. 2	3.580% 201-day (tax anticipation) Mar. 22, 1965___	1,001	_____	_____	_____	1,001
Oct. 26	3.518% 147-day (tax anticipation) Mar. 22, 1965, additional_____	1,503	_____	_____	_____	1,503
Nov. 24	3.639% 210-day (tax anticipation) June 22, 1965___	1,505	_____	_____	_____	1,505
1965						
Jan. 18	3.711% 155-day (tax anticipation) June 22, 1965, additional_____	1,758	_____	_____	_____	1,758
	Total bills_____	8,677	_____	_____	_____	8,677
	Total public offerings_____	9,574	14,916	8,204	19,046	51,740

[1] Issued only on demand in exchange for 2¾% Treasury Bonds, Investment Series B–1975–80.
[2] Issued subsequent to June 30, 1964.
[3] A cash offering (all subscriptions subject to allotment) was made for the purpose of paying off the maturing securities in cash. Holders of the maturing securities were permitted to present them in payment in lieu of cash to the extent subscriptions were allotted. For further detail see exhibit 1.
[4] Treasury bills are sold on a discount basis with competitive bids for each issue. The average price for auctioned issues gives an approximate yield on a bank discount basis as indicated for each series.
[5] Consists of additional amounts of 10 series of outstanding regular weekly Treasury bills $100 million maturing each week from Oct. 15 through Dec. 17, 1964.

Disposition of marketable Treasury securities excluding regular bills (three-month, six-month, and one-year) fiscal year 1965

[In millions of dollars]

Date of refunding or retirement	Securities		Redeemed for cash or carried to matured debt	Exchanged for new issue		Total
	Description and maturity date	Issue date		At maturity	In advance refunding	
1964	BONDS AND NOTES					
July 22	5% note-Aug. 15, 1964	Oct. 15, 1959			845	845
July 22	3¾% note-Aug. 15, 1964	Aug. 1, 1961			1,175	1,175
July 22	4⅞% note-Nov. 15, 1964	Feb. 15, 1960			600	600
July 22	3¾% note-Nov. 15, 1964	Aug. 15, 1963			519	519
July 22	3⅞% note-May 15, 1965	Nov. 15, 1963			1,357	1,357
July 22	3⅝% note-Feb. 15, 1966	May 15, 1962			2,392	2,392
July 22	3¾% bond-May 15, 1966	Nov. 15, 1960			612	612
July 22	4% note-Aug. 15, 1966	Feb. 15, 1962			664	664
July 22	3⅝% note-Feb. 15, 1967	Mar. 15, 1963			1,117	1,117
Aug. 15	5% note-Aug. 15, 1964	Oct. 15, 1959	1,061	[1] 137		1,198
Aug. 15	3¾% note-Aug. 15, 1964	Aug. 1, 1961	1,094	[1] 1,817		2,910
Oct. 1	1½% exchange note-Oct. 1, 1964	Oct. 1, 1959	490			490
Nov. 15	4⅞% note-Nov. 15, 1964	Feb. 15, 1960	901	[1] 2,366		3,267
Nov. 15	3¾% note-Nov. 15, 1964	Aug. 15, 1963	1,182	[1] 4,260		5,441
1965						
Jan. 15	2⅝% bond-Feb. 15, 1965	June 15, 1958			1,808	1,808
Jan. 15	3½% note-Nov. 15, 1965	Nov. 15, 1962			1,337	1,337
Jan. 15	4% note-Nov. 15, 1965	May 15, 1964			461	461
Jan. 15	3⅝% note-Feb. 15, 1966	May 15, 1962			1,065	1,065
Jan. 15	3⅞% note-Feb. 15, 1966	Aug. 15, 1964			1,443	1,443
Jan. 15	3¾% bond-May 15, 1966	Nov. 15, 1960			563	563
Jan. 15	3¾% note-Aug. 15, 1967	Sept. 15, 1962			1,504	1,504
Jan. 15	3⅝% bond-Nov. 15, 1967	Mar. 15, 1961			1,584	1,584
Feb. 15	2⅝% bond-Feb. 15, 1965	June 15, 1958	1,649	[1] 518		2,168
Apr. 1	1½% exchange note-Apr. 1, 1965	Apr. 1, 1960	466			466
May 15	4⅝% note-May 15, 1965	May 15, 1960	281	1,535		1,816
May 15	3⅞% note-May 15, 1965	Nov. 15, 1963	189	6,431		6,620
	Total bonds and notes		7,313	17,064	19,046	43,423
1965	BILLS					
Mar. 22	3.580% (tax anticipation)	Sept. 22, 1964	[2] 1,001			1,001
Mar. 22	3.518% (tax anticipation)	Oct. 26, 1964	[2] 1,503			1,503
June 22	3.639% (tax anticipation)	Nov. 24, 1964	[2] 1,505			1,505
June 22	3.711% (tax anticipation)	Jan. 18, 1965	[2] 1,758			1,758
	Total bills		5,767			5,767
	Total securities		13,080	17,064	19,046	49,190

[1] Accepted in payment in lieu of cash.
[2] Including tax anticipation issues returned for taxes.

Public debt changes

The Treasury issued $51.7 billion of new marketable securities during fiscal 1965, exclusive of the refinancing of regular three-month, six-month, and one-year bills, or slightly more than the $51.6 billion volume of fiscal 1964. Over $9.6 billion of the 1965 total represented securities for new cash, of which $5.8 billion was seasonal borrowing through tax anticipation bills issued and redeemed within the fiscal year. Of the remaining $3.8 billion new cash raised, $2.2 billion represented an increase in the marketable debt. The remaining $1.6 billion was used to pay off maturing exchange notes in October 1964 and April 1965, to retire unexchanged maturing securities in the May refunding, and to redeem Treasury bonds during the year for the payment of estate taxes. In addition to new cash operations, $19 billion of longer term securities were placed with investors in the advance refundings of July 1964 and January 1965, and over $23 billion of notes and bonds were issued to replace securities maturing during the year. Over one-fourth of the $155¾ billion marketable notes and bonds outstanding on June 30, 1964, were extended during the subsequent 12 months, while the $50¾ billion outstanding bills were rolled over an average of almost two and one-half times.

Class of debt	June 30, 1964	June 30, 1965	Increase, or decrease (−)
	In billions of dollars		
Public debt:			
Marketable public issues, maturing:			
Within one year	81.4	87.6	6.2
One to five years	65.5	56.2	−9.3
Five to twenty years	43.3	47.6	4.3
Over twenty years	16.3	17.2	.9
Total marketable issues	206.5	208.7	2.2
Nonmarketable public issues:			
Savings bonds:			
Series E and H	47.7	48.8	1.1
Other series	1.6	1.2	−.3
Investment series bonds	3.5	3.3	−.3
Foreign series securities	.4	1.1	.7
Foreign currency series securities	.8	1.1	.3
Other nonmarketable debt	.2	.2	(*)
Total nonmarketable issues	54.2	55.8	1.5
Special issues to Government investment accounts	46.6	48.6	2.0
Noninterest-bearing debt	4.4	4.2	−.2
Total public debt	311.7	317.3	5.6
Guaranteed debt not owned by Treasury	.8	.6	−.2
Total gross public debt and guaranteed debt	312.5	317.9	5.3

*Less then $50 million.

Although the shortest term marketable debt—that maturing within the following year—increased by $6¼ billion in fiscal 1965 as the volume of regular Treasury bills rose and the terms of outstanding issues shortened, the debt maturing within the potentially troublesome one-to-five year area declined by $9¼ billion. The total of debt maturing beyond 5 years was increased by $5¼ billion, or by almost 9 percent. Further use of the advance refunding technique played a major role in achieving this rise in longer term debt. In the advance refundings of July 1964 and January 1965 holders of $19 billion of issues maturing within 3 years elected to exchange for bonds maturing in from 5 to 28 years. Of the exchanges, $3½ billion were for 27–28 year maturities, $7½ billion for the approximately 9-year issues, and the remaining $8 billion for the 5-year issues made available. The net effect of all Treasury financing operations during fiscal year 1965 was to increase the average maturity of the marketable debt by 4 months to 5 years 4 months, the highest June 30 level since 1956.

Public nonmarketable debt increased by $1.5 billion during the year, reaching $55.8 billion on June 30, 1965. The change during the year was largely the result of $1.1 billion increase in Series E and H savings bonds and $1.1 billion increase in securities issued directly to foreign official agencies, offset by declines in discontinued Series J and K savings bonds and investment Series A and B bonds. The increase in Series E and H savings bonds, which are purchased principally by individuals, brought the total for these two series to $48.8 billion, or 16 percent of the total interest-bearing debt on June 30, 1965. The $0.7 billion increase in foreign series securities and the $0.3 billion increase in securities denominated in foreign currencies are discussed on page 32.

Special securities issued directly to Government trust funds and accounts rose by $2.0 billion during fiscal 1965, mainly reflecting the surplus of receipts over expenditures in the civil service retirement, unemployment, and Federal old age and survivors insurance trust funds. The fiscal year 1965 income, expenditure and investment activities of the major trust funds and accounts are detailed in tables 66—83 and discussed on page 33.

Guaranteed debt not owned by Treasury consists of $20 million District of Columbia stadium bonds, due in 1979, and $569 million Federal Housing Administration debentures issued under the Housing Act of 1934. The $0.2 billion decline in this category during fiscal 1965 was entirely the result of FHA debentures called for redemption during the year.

OWNERSHIP OF FEDERAL SECURITIES

Of the $317.9 billion Federal securities outstanding at the end of the fiscal year 1965, Government investment accounts and Federal Reserve banks held $102.5 billion, or close to one-third of the total. Commercial banks held $58.3 billion, or just under one-fifth, and private nonbank investors held almost one-half, or $157.1 billion. The June 30, 1965, ownership distribution of the debt is graphically illustrated in chart 5 and a further classification of investor ownership on selected dates is presented in the following table.

Individuals, the investor group with the largest holdings of the public debt, increased their ownership of Federal securities by $2.0 billion during fiscal 1965. Although more than half of this increase was due to the continued rise in the value of their Series E and H savings bond holdings, individuals also added to their accumulation of marketable Government securities. The increase in holdings of marketable securities in fiscal 1965 was in all probability concentrated within the personal trust and partnership areas, however, certain long-term deep discount securities continue to be attractive to wealthy individuals as evidenced by the $0.3 billion unmatured Treasury bonds redeemed during fiscal 1965 in payment of estate taxes.

CHART 5

Ownership of the Federal Debt, June 30, 1965

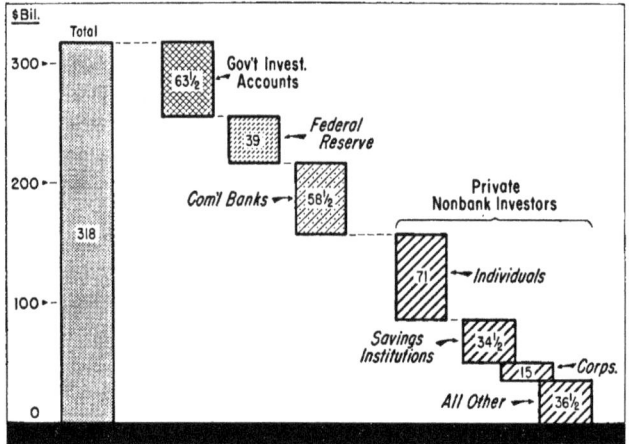

Ownership of Federal securities[1] by investor classes on selected dates, 1941–65

[Dollar amounts in billons]

	June 30, 1941	Feb. 28, 1946 [2]	June 30, 1964	June 30, 1965	Change during fiscal year 1965
Estimated ownership by:					
Private nonbank investors:					
Individuals: [3]					
Series E and H saving bonds	$0.2	$30.8	$47.3	$48.3	$1.0
Other securities	11.0	33.3	21.9	22.8	.9
Total individuals	11.2	64.1	r 69.2	71.1	2.0
Insurance companies	7.1	24.4	10.9	10.6	—.3
Mutual savings banks	3.4	11.1	6.0	5.8	—.2
Savings and loan associations	.1	2.5	6.7	7.2	.5
State and local governments	.6	6.7	22.5	24.1	1.6
Foreign and international [4]	.2	2.4	15.6	15.7	.1
Corporations [5]	2.0	19.9	r 18.5	15.1	—3.5
Miscellaneous investors [6]	.4	4.0	7.0	7.6	.5
Total private nonbank investors	25.0	135.1	156.4	157.1	.7
Commercial banks	19.7	93.8	60.2	58.3	—2.0
Federal Reserve banks	2.2	22.9	34.8	39.1	4.3
Federal Government investment accounts	8.5	28.0	61.1	63.4	2.3
Total gross debt outstanding	55.3	279.8	312.5	317.9	5.3
			Percent		
Percent owned by:					
Individuals	20	23	22	23	
Other private nonbank investors	25	25	28	27	
Commercial banks	36	34	19	18	
Federal Reserve banks	4	8	11	12	
Federal Government investment accounts	15	10	20	20	
Total gross debt outstanding	100	100	100	100	

r Revised.
[1] Gross public debt, and guaranteed debt of the Federal Government held outside the Treasury.
[2] Immediate postwar peak of debt.
[3] Includes partnerships and personal trust accounts. Nonprofit institutions and corporate pension trust funds are included under "Miscellaneous investors."
[4] Includes the investments of foreign balances and international accounts in the United States.
[5] Exclusive of banks and insurance companies.
[6] Includes nonprofit institutions, corporate pension trust funds, and nonbank Government security dealers.

The Government security holdings of insurance companies declined during fiscal 1965 as life companies liquidated $0.3 billion and fire, casualty and marine companies showed a small increase for the year. On June 30, 1965, life insurance companies held $5.2 billion governments while property and casualty insurance companies held $5.4 billion. Although the average maturity of marketable governments held by life insurance companies fell nine months during fiscal 1965, the end-of-year level was still high at 19 years 11 months, as these institutions continue to hold a large proportion of their portfolios in long-term securities. In contrast the fire, casualty and marine companies, with a less predictable claim experience, tend to hold short and intermediate-term securities as primary and secondary reserves. However, the average maturity of their marketable governments rose sharply during the fiscal 1965, from 5 years 9 months at the beginning of the year to 6 years 11 months on June 30, 1965, as these companies exchanged for higher-yielding issues in the July 1964 and January 1965 advance refundings.

Mutual savings banks reduced their holdings of governments by $0.2 billion in fiscal 1965 to a level of $5.8 billion at yearend. These institutions typically use short-term Treasury securities as a form of liquid reserve and as temporary investments for funds earmarked for future mortgage acquisitions, while maintaining an investment position in longer term issues. During the fiscal year 1965 their holdings of Treasury bills rose by $0.2 billion, other securities declined by $0.4 billion, and the average maturity of all marketables increased by three months to 10 years 10 months. The increase in the average maturity of marketable holdings was also primarily due to participation in the two advance refundings during the fiscal year.

Savings and loan associations have increased their holdings of Government securities during each of the past 11 fiscal years, rising from less than $2 billion on June 30, 1954, to $7.2 billion at the end of fiscal 1965. Held primarily as liquidity reserves, the Federal securities purchased by savings and loan associations are generally short to intermediate-term maturities. Close to 75 percent of their Government portfolio matures within 10 years with the heaviest concentration of holdings in bonds with from 5–10 years to maturity.

State and municipal governments held $24.1 billion of Federal securities on June 30, 1965, $1.6 billion more than at the end of the fiscal year 1964. Pension funds of State and municipal employees continued to add to holdings of governments, acquiring a net $0.5 billion during fiscal 1965. As would be expected by the nature of these funds the bulk of investment is in long-term Treasury issues, as evidenced by the 20 year 10 month average maturity of their June 30, 1965, holdings.   The general purpose funds of States and municipalities, on the other hand, are invested in governments for a relatively short period of time, generally as seasonally surplus tax revenues.   During the high revenue spring months these investments are increased, only to be drawn down during the fall months when expenditures exceed current revenues.   As a result the shortest term Treasury securities are purchased (to avoid the risk of price fluctuations) and Treasury bills are in particularly heavy demand for this purpose.   In addition to excess tax revenues the proceeds of capital market borrowings are also invested in Treasury securities until needed, as are the receipts to special purpose funds, such as sinking, endowment, and workmen's compensation funds.   During the fiscal year 1965 all of the nonretirement type funds showed an increase of $1.1 billion in holdings of Government securities.

Foreign and international investments in U.S. Government securities rose by $0.1 billion in fiscal 1965 as a $0.4 billion increase (from $9.9 billion to $10.3 billion) in foreign holdings was partially offset by a $0.3 billion reduction (from $5.7 billion to $5.4 billion) in securities held by international and regional institutions.   Within the foreign group, liquidation of official French and German holdings, totaling $1.0 billion, was more than balanced by Italian and United Kingdom acquisitions totaling $1.1 billion, also primarily for official accounts.   Special nonmarketable securities, issued directly to foreign monetary authorities, were increased by $1.1 billion during the fiscal year while holdings of marketable Treasury securities fell by $0.7 billion.

The decline in international and regional institutions' holdings consisted of a $0.2 billion drop in marketable securities held by the International Bank for Reconstruction and Development and a $0.1 billion reduction of special noninterest-bearing notes issued to the International Monetary Fund.   On June 30, 1965, the securities held for international and regional accounts consisted of $3.5 billion noninterest-bearing special notes and $1.9 billion marketable Treasury bills, notes, and bonds.

Nonfinancial corporations were heavy liquidators of Federal securities during the fiscal year as holdings fell to the lowest levels since the recession induced lows of 1958.   Almost all of the $3.5 billion fiscal year 1965 decline in corporate holdings of governments appear to be related to switching on the part of large industrial firms into higher yielding alternative short-term investments.   Federal securities have historically been used by corporations as convenient investments of funds earmarked for income tax, dividend, and other anticipated near-term payments.   During the past few years, however, commercial bank certificates of deposit and open market paper have assumed a major role in this area. The trend toward greater investment in non-Federal money market instruments began in the early 1960s and became pronounced in the fiscal years 1964 and 1965 following the July 1963 and November 1964 revisions in the maximum rates payable by Federal Reserve member banks on time and savings deposits. Prior to fiscal 1965 much of the flow into these instruments appeared to be net new investment and conversion of demand deposits to time, with holdings of governments remaining relatively stable from year to year. During the fiscal year 1965, however, corporate investment in governments declined by almost 20 percent as holdings of negotiable certificates of deposit and commercial paper combined increased by approximately 30 percent, or $41½ billion.

Activity of the remaining private nonbank investor groups (nonprofit institutions, nonbank dealers, corporate pension funds, and miscellaneous smaller institutions) resulted in a $0.5 billion increase during the fiscal year.

Commercial banks were net sellers of Federal securities in fiscal year 1965 for the third consecutive year. Although banks were active purchasers of governments during most of the first six months of the fiscal year, heavy liquidation in the last half of the year brought total holdings down by $2.0 billion for the full 12-month period. The larger reserve city commercial banks acquired $1.4 billion governments from June 30 to December 31, 1964, then sold a net $3.3 billion during the following six months in order to meet sharply rising loan demands. Smaller commercial banks (country and nonmember institutions) were also actively purchasing governments through December 1964, adding a total of $2.4 billion, and then liquidating a like amount in the following 6-month period.

The Federal Reserve System acquired a net $4.3 billion Government securities in fiscal year 1965, $1.5 billion more than in fiscal 1964. The increase in net purchases during fiscal 1965 was necessary in order to offset reserve drains caused by increased sales of gold and other technical factors as well as to provide for growth in member bank reserves. Acquisitions of Treasury bills accounted for $2.8 billion of the increase and the remaining $1.5 billion was in coupon securities. The average maturity of the $39.1 billion Federal securities held in the System Open Market Account on June 30, 1965, was 15½ months, two months lower than a year earlier.

The holdings of Government investment accounts rose by $2.3 billion in the fiscal year 1965, or by $0.5 billion less than in fiscal 1964. The largest increases during 1965 were registered by the Government employee retirement funds ($1.2 billion) and the unemployment trust fund ($1.0 billion). Of the $63.4 billion Federal securities held by these accounts on June 30, 1965, $48.6 billion, or over three-fourths of the total, was in the form of special issues held only by these accounts. The remaining one-fourth of the total consisted of $2.2 billion of non-marketable securities (primarily investment series bonds) and $12.4 billion of intermediate and longer term marketable issues.

A summary of the Treasury survey of ownership of the interest-bearing public debt and guaranteed debt for fiscal 1965 is shown in table 57.

Taxation Developments

Taxation developments in 1965 were highlighted by the passage of the Excise Tax Reduction Act of 1965. The measure was designed to simplify the tax system, lessen the burden of regressive taxes, and provide more purchasing power with the consequent creation of employment opportunities for the expanding labor force.

The legislation eliminated, as of June 22, 1965, the 10-percent retailers excise tax on such items as toilet articles, wallets and handbags, jewelry, and furs. In addition, manufacturers excise taxes on many other items were eliminated or reduced on the same date with later reductions scheduled for January 1, 1966, January 1, 1967, January 1, 1968, and January 1, 1969.

The total annual excise tax reduction, when the program is in full effect, will be about $4.7 billion. About $1.75 billion of the reduction became effective on June 22, 1965, and an approximately equal amount will become effective on January 1, 1966. The tax reduction for 1966 will thus total about $3.4 billion. The additional reductions will be effective in three stages, on January 1, 1967, 1968, and 1969.

Modifications of the application of the depreciation guideline procedure initiated in 1962 liberalized the manner in which depreciation deductions may be taken and increased depreciation benefits in 1965 by some $600 million to $800 million as compared to the results that would have occurred if the procedure had remained unchanged.

The Interest Equalization Tax Extension Act of 1965, designed to strengthen our international economic position, was pending before the Ways and Means Committee at the end of fiscal 1965 and was subsequently approved.

In response to requests by the Senate Committee on Finance and the House Committee on Ways and Means, the Treasury Department examined the activities of private foundations for possible tax abuses. The Department's report on this subject, which was printed by the Committee on Finance on February 2, 1965,[1] indicated that serious abuse·of the tax exemption privilege occurred among only a minority

---

[1] See exhibit 37.

of foundations. Recommendations were made for additional legislative measures to meet problems disclosed by the study.

Excise Tax Reduction Act of 1965

The Excise Tax Reduction Act of 1965, Public Law 89–44, was approved by President Johnson on June 21, 1965.

Since the revenue acts of 1962 and 1964 had been devoted to income tax adjustments and reductions, the President stated in his budget message of January 25, 1965, that attention should now be given to excise reductions as a means of providing further aid to economic growth and of minimizing the burden on consumers and business resulting from the taxes on sales of selected goods and services. Accordingly, the President stated that he planned to transmit to the Congress an excise reduction program, $1,750 million of which was to be effective before July 1, 1965. Other excise proposals in the budget message related to user charges for highways, airways, and waterways.

The highway user charge proposals of the President involved increasing the tax on diesel fuel from 4 cents to 7 cents a gallon, increasing the use tax on heavy trucks from $3 to $5 per 1,000 pounds, and increasing the tax on tread rubber from 5 cents to 10 cents a pound. Increased revenue from the proposals was estimated to be $206 million per year. The highway user charge proposals had two objectives: To provide increased revenues to meet the new cost estimates of completing the Interstate System and to obtain from heavier trucks the highway construction costs attributable to them. To finance the increased construction costs, the President recommended an extension of the taxes used to finance the highway trust fund beyond the present expiration date of September 30, 1972. The President subsequently recommended an extension to February 28, 1973.

The President recommended, as an airways user charge system, continuation of the 5-percent tax on amounts paid for transportation of persons by air, a tax of 2 percent on air freight waybills, a tax of 2 cents a gallon on jet fuel (which is not now taxed although aviation gasoline is taxed at 2 cents a gallon), and an additional tax of 2 cents a gallon on fuel used in general (noncommercial) aviation. He recommended that revenues from the tax on aviation gasoline be retained in the general fund of the Treasury rather than transferred to the highway trust fund. Revenue from the recommendations for these tax increases was estimated at $86 million.

As a waterways user charge, the President recommended a tax of 2 cents a gallon on all fuel used in boats with a draft of 15 feet or less using the domestic waterways and not engaged in foreign trade. Gasoline, but not diesel fuel or bunker fuel, used in boats is now taxable at a net rate of 2 cents a gallon. The present tax thus is largely limited to fuel used in pleasure boats. The new tax was estimated to raise $8 million.

On May 17 the President sent a message [1] to the Congress with the details of an excise reduction program totaling $3.9 billion at estimated fiscal 1966 levels of income. Highlights of the program had been made public by the President on May 15. Of the total, a reduction of $1,750 million was recommended for July 1, 1965, about the same amount for January 1, 1966, and further reductions totaling $464 million for January 1, 1967, 1968, and 1969. The increase from the amount recommended in January was made possible by the improved economic situation over that foreseen in January. The reductions suggested for January 1966 were deemed desirable to avoid the possibility that the tax system would be taking too much buying power out of the private economy.

To insure that the reductions made the maximum contribution to continued price stability and balanced prosperity, the President requested that business promptly pass forward to consumers the full amount of the reductions. The President reemphasized this when he signed the Excise Tax Reduction Act of 1965 on June 21. [2] The hearings published by the Senate Finance Committee, as a result of a request by a member of the committee, contain copies of telegrams to the Chairman of the Committee from the four largest domestic passenger car manufacturers expressing their intention to reflect any excise reduction in their suggested retail prices on passenger cars.

The President's recommendations in May contemplated eventual repeal of all excises except those on: (1) alcoholic beverages, (2) tobacco products, (3) passenger automobiles (to be reduced by one-half), (4) truck parts and accessories, (5) pistols and revolvers, and (6) a number of levies designed as control measures (e.g., the taxes on narcotics, white phosphorous matches, wagers, and machine guns). The taxes used to finance specific expenditure programs, or which were in the nature of user charges were also to be retained. These were the taxes on motor fuels, trucks, tires and tubes, tread rubber, truck use, fishing equipment, sporting firearms and ammunition, and transportation of persons by air. It was also recommended that the tax reductions scheduled for July 1, 1965, on alcoholic beverages, cigarettes, and truck parts, and the repeal of the tax on air transportation be removed from the law.

Refunds of tax already paid on items subject to manufacturers excises and held by wholesalers and retailers for sale on the date of tax reduction or repeal were recommended in all cases except: fountain

---

[1] See exhibit 30.
[2] See exhibit 33.

and ball-point pens and mechanical pencils, cigarette lighters, playing cards, passenger automobile parts and accessories, and sporting goods.

An innovation in Federal tax policy was the recommendation for a refund to consumers (through the medium of the manufacturers and their dealers) of the tax on purchases of passenger automobiles and air conditioners between May 15 and the effective date of the law. May 15 was recommended because the President's statement on that date specifically mentioned his intended recommendations with respect to reduction and repeal of these taxes. Such refunds were proposed in order to prevent disruption of sales as a result of consumer anticipation of price reductions. Air conditioners have a unique seasonal pattern with a high proportion of retail sales normally occurring in June. In the case of automobiles, the large dollar amount per unit of the proposed tax reduction was deemed a possible sales deterrent. The consumer refund recommendation was limited to these two items because other businesses affected by the tax reduction recommendations felt that the complexity and cost of the paperwork involved would outweigh the benefits.

Since the House Ways and Means Committee had held extensive hearings on excise tax reduction in the summer of 1964, the committee held no further hearings on the President's recommendations. Hearings before the Senate Finance Committee were limited to statements by Secretary Fowler and Assistant Secretary Surrey on June 8.[1]

The House and Senate agreed to the conference report on the President's recommendations on June 17, 1965. On June 21, the President signed the bill to become effective on June 22. The Congress had provided that the effective date should be the day after enactment of the law in order to minimize the postponement of purchases by consumers and distributors.

Tax repeals or reductions under the act ultimately will total $4.7 billion at fiscal 1966 levels of income. (See exhibit 33). Practically all of the difference from the $3.9 billion program recommended by the President [2] is accounted for by the fact that the act provides for eventual reduction of the tax on passenger automobiles to one percent of manufacturers sales prices, rather than to five percent recommended by the President. The additional four points reduction will result in a revenue loss of $760 million. Reductions taking effect in fiscal 1966, however, will be practically the same as the $3.5 billion recommended by the President.

The House Ways and Means Committee decided not to consider user charges as part of the excise tax legislation, except to make permanent the 5-percent tax on amounts paid for transportation of per-

[1] See exhibits 31 and 32.
[2] See exhibit 30.

sons by air. Consequently, the other recommendations of the President respecting user charges were not considered in the course of the legislation.

Another variation from the President's recommendations was the repeal of the 10 cents per pound tax on smoking and chewing tobacco and snuff effective January 1, 1966. The estimated revenue loss is $18 million. Conversely, the act retains the 6 cents per gallon tax on lubricating oil if used in a highway motor vehicle. Taxation was continued because the Congress felt that repeal would seriously affect operations of rerefiners of used oil and add to the water pollution problem if waste oil were disposed of in streams because it was not collected by rerefineries. In the case of the taxes on truck parts and accessories and lubricating oil, provision was made for the transfer of the revenues therefrom from the general fund to the highway trust fund beginning January 1, 1966. Revenues to be so transferred are estimated to be $50 million per year from lubricating oil and $20 million from truck parts.

The effective date for repeal of the tax on conveyances of realty was advanced from January 1, 1966, as originally recommended by the President, to January 1, 1968, in order to give the States time to enact a similar tax if they wished.

A number of new exemptions from taxes not otherwise repealed were added by the act. So called camper coaches and bodies for mobile homes were exempted from the taxes on manufacturers sales of trucks (10 percent) or truck parts (8 percent). Exempted from the tax on trucks were three wheel trucks if the gross weight of the chassis does not exceed 1,000 pounds and the motor is not over 18 brake horsepower. The tax on trucks also was removed from school buses sold to any person for use in transporting students and employees of public and private nonprofit schools. Also exempted from the truck tax and truck parts tax were bodies and parts and accessories primarily designed for use in processing, hauling, spreading, loading or unloading, feed, seed, or fertilizer for use on farms. Exemption from the tax on transportation of persons by air was provided within the concept of "uninterrupted international air transportation" for payments by servicemen traveling in uniform at their own expense if they purchase their tickets for the second portion of their trip within 6 hours after the end of the first portion and utilize the first accommodations available for such subsequent portion. An exemption from the wagering tax retroactive to March 10, 1964, was enacted for sweepstakes or lotteries conducted by a State. As of the end of fiscal 1965 New Hampshire was the only State operating sweepstakes.

In addition to the floor stocks refunds recommended by the President, provision was made for refunds on passenger automobile parts and accessories, sporting goods, playing cards, and cutting oil.

Under prior law, refunds (in whole or in part) of the excise tax on gasoline were made to the ultimate purchaser for gasoline used on a farm for farming purposes, for nonhighway purposes, and for certain local transit operations. Under the Excise Tax Reduction Act, such "refunds" will be made in the form of credits against income tax. In the case of a typical calendar year taxpayer, the credit will be taken first on the income tax return filed for the calendar year 1966 and will cover gasoline used from July 1, 1965, through December 31, 1966. However, the United States, a State, or political subdivision, and organizations exempt from income tax under section 501 of the Internal Revenue Code (other than those subject to income tax on certain income) will continue to apply directly for refunds. In the case of gasoline used for off-highway and local transit purposes, a direct claim for refund is permitted for any of the first three quarters of the user's taxable year for any quarter in which the claim is $1,000 or more. Prior law contained this quarterly refund provision, but for all four quarters of the year.

A similar system for credit against income tax, direct quarterly refunds, or direct refunds to the United States, etc., was enacted for the 6 cents a gallon tax on lubricating oil for oil used other than in a highway motor vehicle after December 31, 1965. Credits or refunds will not be available for oil previously used, since the sale of used or rerefined oil is not subject to tax. Cutting oil, which is to be exempted from tax as of January 1, 1966, will qualify for exemption under the normal procedure rather than through a credit or refund to the ultimate purchaser.

The act also contains a number of technical revisions of taxes continued in effect.

The definitions of a cigarette and cigar were revised in recognition of the development and use of homogenized tobacco for use as wrappers of tobacco products. Prior law defined a cigarette as a roll of tobacco wrapped in paper or any substance other than tobacco. A cigar was defined as a roll of tobacco wrapped in tobacco. The new law expands the definitions to make the classification of a product also dependent on its appearance, type of tobacco used in the filler, and its packing and labeling.

Gasoline was redefined as "all products commonly or commercially known or sold as gasoline which are suitable for use as a motor fuel." Prior law did not include the "suitability" test, and the law specifically included casinghead and natural gasoline. Thus, some products, such as casinghead and natural gasoline and certain petrochemicals, were taxed as gasoline although they could not be used in a modern automobile. The retail tax on special motor fuels was amended, however, to tax casinghead and natural gasoline if sold for use or used as a fuel for a motor vehicle, motorboat, or airplane.

The definitions of local telephone service (previously general telephone service), toll telephone service, and teletypewriter exchange service were revised to clarify the services taxable.

Other technical changes covered: Determination of tax on installment sales made before tax repeals or reductions; electric light bulbs incorporated in other articles between June 22 and December 31, 1965; the definition of truck parts or accessories; the definition of the taxable price of truck parts made with used components furnished by the customer; the use of new parts in rebuilding and reconditioning automobile and truck parts; bonding requirements for producers and importers of gasoline; registration by purchasers of tax-free supplies for vessels or aircraft; the method of payment of the tax on foreign insurance policies; credit or refund of tax for distilled spirits returned to bonded premises; exemption from rectification tax for certain mingling of distilled spirits; refund or credit of tax for distilled spirits returned to bonded premises and voluntarily destroyed; redistillation of articles containing denatured distilled spirits; relanding of exported distilled spirits; the amount of carbon dioxide permitted in still wines; wine inventory reserve requirements and certain restrictions relating to the use of sugar in wines; the tax-free shipment of distilled spirits to possessions of the United States; credit to the manufacturer or importer for tax on tobacco products or cigarette papers or tubes withdrawn from the market or destroyed by casualty; the definition of "manufacturer of tobacco products"; and the form in which a return has to be filled out to start the running of the statute of limitations.

Other excise tax legislation

Legislation approved August 31, 1964 (26 U.S.C. 5062(c)), provided for credit or refund of internal revenue taxes on imported alcoholic beverages which, after having been found to be unmerchantable or not to conform to sample or specifications, are returned to customs custody, and then exported or destroyed. Domestic alcoholic beverages already were accorded substantially similar treatment.

The Land and Water Conservation Fund Act of 1965, Public Law 88–578, approved September 3, 1964, provided that the estimated revenues from the taxes on gasoline and special motor fuels used in motorboats shall be transferred to the land and water conservation fund. Transfers are effective with respect to revenues received after January 1, 1965, and before July 1, 1989. Previously, such revenues accrued to the highway trust fund. For the fiscal year 1966, it is estimated that $28 million will be so transferred.

Rate reductions and revenue loss under the Excise Tax Reduction Act of 1965

[Dollar amounts in millions]

Tax	Rate prior to Excise Tax Reduction Act	Rate under Excise Tax Reduction Act	Full year revenue loss [1]
Changes effective June 22, 1965:			
Retail taxes:			
Jewelry	10%	0	$220
Furs	10%	0	30
Toilet preparations	10%	0	210
Luggage	10%	0	90
Subtotal			550
Manufacturers taxes:			
Automobiles [3]	10%	7%	570
Trucks and truck parts:			
"Camper coaches" [3]	10% and 8%	0	6
School buses	10%	0	4
Farm feed, seed, and fertilizer equipment.	10% and 8%	0	(*)
Small three-wheeled trucks	10%	0	(*)
Business machines	10%	0	75
Sporting goods (except fishing equipment).	10%	0	25
Phonograph records	10%	0	30
Musical instruments	10%	0	27
Television sets	10%	0	135
Radios and phonographs	10%	0	90
Photographic equipment	Cameras and film, 10%; projectors, 5%.	0	40
Refrigerators and freezers	5%	0	41
Room air conditioners [3]	10%	0	34
Electric, gas, and oil appliances	5%	0	85
Pens and mechanical pencils	10%	0	8
Lighters	10%, not to exceed 10¢ per unit.	0	3
Matches	Plain, 10%, not to exceed 2¢ per 1,000; fancy wooden, 5½¢ per 1,000.	0	4
Playing cards	13¢ per pack	0	11
Subtotal			1,188
Other taxes: [4]			
Coin-operated amusement devices.	$10 per device per year	0	6
Bowling alleys, billiard, and pool tables.	$20 per alley or table per year	0	⁴
Leases of safe deposit boxes	10% of amount paid	0	⁴
Wagering:			
State-conducted sweepstakes [5]	10% of amount wagered; $50 per year for each person receiving wagers.	0	(*)
Subtotal			20
Total effective June 22, 1965			1,758
Changes effective January 1, 1966:			
Tobacco taxes:			
Chewing and smoking tobacco and snuff.	10¢ per pound	0	18
Manufacturers taxes:			
Automobiles	10%	6%	190
Automobile parts and accessories, except truck parts.	8%	0	230
Lubricating oil:			
Cutting oil	3¢ per gallon	0	} 28
Other, used other than in a highway vehicle.	6¢ per gallon	0 ⁶	
Electric light bulbs	10%	0	45
Subtotal			511
Admissions and club dues:			
General admissions [7]	1¢ for each 10¢ in excess of $1; race tracks, 1¢ for each 5¢ of full price.	0	55
Cabarets [7]	10% of bill	0	47
Club dues and initiation fees [8]	20% of amount paid if annual dues are in excess of $10.	0	85
Subtotal			187

Footnotes at end of table.

Rate reductions and revenue loss under the Excise Tax Reduction Act of 1965—
Continued

[Dollar amounts in millions]

Tax	Rate prior to Excise Tax Reduction Act	Rate under Excise Tax Reduction Act	Full year revenue loss [1]
Changes effective January 1, 1966— Continued			
Communications taxes:			
Local and long distance telephone service and teletypewriter exchange service.	10% of amount paid	3% of amount paid	$639
Private telephonic communications service.	10% of amount paid	0	130
Telegraph service	10% of amount paid	0	17
Wire and equipment service	8% of amount paid	0	15
Subtotal			801
Documentary stamp taxes:			
Issuance of stocks and bonds:			
Stocks, except mutual funds	10¢ per $100 of actual value	0	
Mutual fund shares	4¢ per $100 of actual value	0	
Bonds	11¢ per $100 of face value	0	
Transfer of stocks and bonds:			
Stocks	4¢ per $100 of actual value, but not more than 8¢ per share or less than 4¢ per sale.	0	153
Bonds	5¢ per $100 of face value	0	
Total effective January 1, 1966			1,652
Total 1965 and 1966 changes			3,410
Changes effective January 1, 1967:			
Automobiles	10% of manufacturers price	4% of manufacturers price.	380
Local and long distance telephone service and teletypewriter exchange service.	10% of amount paid	2% of amount paid	91
Total effective January 1, 1967			471
Changes effective January 1, 1968:			
Automobiles	10% of manufacturers price	2% of manufacturers price.	380
Local and long distance telephone service and teletypewriter exchange service.	10% of amount paid	1% of amount paid	91
Deeds of conveyance	55¢ per $500 of the consideration if in excess of $100.	0	42
Total effective January 1, 1968			513
Changes effective January 1, 1969:			
Automobiles	10% of manufacturers price	1% of manufacturers price.	190
Local and long distance telephone service and teletypewriter exchange service.	10% of amount paid	0	92
Total effective January 1, 1969			282
Grand total			4,676

*Less than $1 million.
[1] At fiscal 1966 levels of income.
[2] Effective May 15, 1965.
[3] Includes bodies for self-propelled mobile homes.
[4] Effective July 1, 1965.
[5] Effective Mar. 10, 1964.
[6] Exemption achieved by refund to ultimate purchaser.
[7] Effective at noon, Dec. 31, 1965.
[8] Effective July 1, 1965, for initiation fees to a new club which first makes its facilities available to members on or after that date.

Public Law 88–653, approved October 13, 1964, made three amendments to the excise tax provisions. Rebuilt automobile parts were exempted from the 8-percent manufacturers tax on automobile parts and accessories. The value of a television picture tube taken in trade on a rebuilt tube was excluded from the taxable price for purposes of the 10 percent manufacturers tax on radio and television parts. Exclusion of the value of a "trade in" had previously been in effect for purposes of computing the tax on rebuilt automobile parts. The act also contained a provision making it possible to produce wine by removing the volatile fruit-flavor concentrate from the juice before fermentation and then to add it back to the wine after fermentation. The act made clear that such an operation would not result in the wine having to be classified as "imitation" wine.

Depreciation developments

On February 19, 1965, the Treasury Department announced [1] several measures modifying the application of the new depreciation guideline procedure initiated in 1962 (Revenue Procedure 62–21).

In general, the new measures liberalized the manner in which income tax deductions for depreciation of plant and equipment can be taken to insure that business may reap the full benefit of the 1962 depreciation reform. At the same time, the Treasury limited the ways in which guideline depreciation can be calculated to exclude certain accounting techniques that are incompatible with the guideline procedure.

The combination of the new liberalized rules and the new limitations was estimated to result in increasing depreciation tax benefits during 1965 by some $600 million to $800 million over what they would have been if the 1962 reform had not been modified.

The new liberalizing measures and limitations were subsequently set forth in Revenue Procedure 65–13 of May 7, 1965, supplementing Revenue Procedure 62–21, *Depreciation Guidelines and Rules*.

The new liberalizing measures are: (1) a method (called the "guideline form of the reserve ratio test") which allows each taxpayer to compute a reserve ratio upper limit more correctly tailored to his individual circumstances, as an alternative to determining such limit from the Reserve Ratio Table under the "tabular form" of the test; (2) a "transitional allowance rule" which eases and extends the transition from previous depreciation practices and gives taxpayers additional time to conform their replacement policy to the new guideline lives; it will do so by raising the effective reserve ratio upper limit, determined under either the tabular form or the guideline form of the test, over a new lengthened transition period equal to one guideline life beginning with the termination of the original three-year moratorium on the application of the reserve ratio test; and (3) a "minimal adjustment rule" which reduces the lengthening adjustments of depreciable life in cases where the reserve ratio test is not met from generally 25 percent under the original procedure to 5 percent or 10 percent, de-

---

[1] See exhibit 35.

pending on the extent by which the taxpayer fails to meet the reserve ratio test.

Also added are limitations on the use of depreciation calculation techniques, involving the use of multiple-asset open end accounts in conjunction with the straight line or sum-of-the-years-digits method, designed to prevent exaggerated depreciation deductions under the guideline procedure, particularly during the liberalized transition period. Accounts depreciated under the declining balance method are not affected.

Without the new liberalization, an estimated 60 percent of larger firms would not have qualified under the reserve ratio test in 1965. This would have reduced total tax benefits in 1965 resulting from the 1962 guideline revision, estimated at $1.8 billion, by some $700 million to $900 million. The three liberalizing measures will allow the great bulk of firms which would have failed the test in 1965 to meet it, continuing some $600 million to $800 million of the benefits which otherwise they would not have been eligible to receive.

Other legislation enacted

Legislation approved July 17, 1964 (26 U.S.C. 512(b)(14)), provides an exemption from the tax on unrelated business income in the case of labor unions and agricultural or horticultural organizations where three conditions are met. First, the income must be used to establish, maintain, or operate a retirement home, hospital, or similar facility operated for the exclusive use of aged and infirm members of such organizations. Second, the income must be derived from agricultural pursuits on ground contiguous to the home, hospital, etc. Third, this income may not represent more than 75 prcent of the cost of maintaining and operating the facilities.

Public Law 88–484, approved August 22, 1964, amends the "collapsible corporation" provisions of the tax laws so that they will not apply to the sale of stock in a corporation which consents to a special tax treatment on any later disposition by it of its noncapital assets as of the date of sale of the stock.

Public Law 88–554, approved August 31, 1964, extends for two more years certain temporary rules with respect to the deductibility of accrued vacation pay.

Public Law 88–570, approved September 2, 1964, provides that gain from installment obligations which were transmitted to a taxpayer at the time of death of a decedent in taxable years before 1954, but on which payments are still being made, may be reported by the recipient on a pro rata basis as he receives installment payments without the necessity, heretofore required, of maintaining a bond with the Internal Revenue Service to assure this reporting of income. This law also provided that where real property is sold and the seller receives a mortgage on such property, and subsequently is forced to repossess the property, any gain resulting from such repossession is to be limited to money (and value of other property) received by the seller before the repossession to the extent such amounts have not already been reported as income.

Public Law 88–571, approved September 2, 1964, makes five modifications in the tax treatment of life insurance companies and two other amendments. The life insurance modifications are as follows: First, it extends the 8-year loss carryover to new life insurance companies regardless of whether they are affiliated with other companies. Second, it corrects an imperfection in prior law which permitted a double inclusion in the "shareholders surplus account" with respect to the excess of net long-term capital gains over net short-term capital losses. This double inclusion, which was removed by the act, permitted the distribution to shareholders of an amount equal to twice this capital gain without the payment of tax at the time of distribution (with certain other adjustments) under what is called "phase 3." Third, the act corrects an imperfection in the additions which are required to be made to the "policyholders surplus account." The new law provides that if any amount added to the policyholders surplus account for any year increases or creates a loss from operations, and part or all of that loss cannot be used in any other year to reduce the company's taxable income, then the policyholders surplus account for the last year to which this loss may be carried is to be reduced by the amount of the unused loss or, if less, the amount in the policyholders account (before making any subtractions for that year). Fourth, the act adds a new exception to the phase 3 tax which makes that tax inapplicable in the case of spin-offs of the stock of an 80-percent controlled fire or casualty subsidiary to the shareholders of a life insurance company, subject to certain restrictions. Fifth, the new law permits the investment income of life insurance companies to remain free of tax to the extent attributable to reserves for retirement annuities of public school systems. In addition, the act provides that all ores of beryllium are to receive the same percentage depletion treatment when domestically produced as domestically produced beryl, and that foreign expropriation capital losses may be carried over 10 years rather than for the usual period of 5 years.

Public Law 88–650, approved October 13, 1964, contains provisions affecting the old-age, survivors, and disability insurance program in three ways: first, it permits a disabled worker to establish the beginning of his disability, for purposes of social security protection, as of the date he actually became disabled regardless of when he files his application; second, it extends through April 15, 1965, the time within which certain ministers can elect to be covered under social security;

and, third, it validates certain earnings reported under social security of engineering aides working for soil and water conservation districts in Oklahoma.

Legislation pending as of June 30, 1965

H.R. 6675, passed by the House on April 8, 1965, and reported with amendments by the Senate Finance Committee on June 30, 1965, includes provisions which establish a health insurance system, increase social security benefits, raise the wage base and the rates of contribution for employees, employers, and the self-employed, and make some changes in the income tax treatment of medical expenses. As passed by the House, the bill would terminate the special treatment of the medical expenses of taxpayers who are 65 or over. Thus, the provision of present law limiting medical expense deductions for a taxpayer, his spouse, or his dependents under age 65 to the amount of such expenses in excess of three percent of adjusted gross income, including expenses for medicine and drugs to the extent they exceed one percent of adjusted gross income, is extended to all taxpayers, spouses, and dependents regardless of age. In addition, the bill provides that all taxpayers itemizing their deductions are to be granted a deduction, without regard to the three-percent floor, for one-half the cost of medical care insurance but not to exceed $250. The other half of any premiums paid, plus any excess over the $250 limit for medical care insurance, will continue to be subject to the three-percent floor and only when they plus any other allowable medical expenses exceed three percent of adjusted gross income will they be deductible. The House bill would also cover tips under social security and the withholding of income tax.

Administration, interpretation, and clarification of tax laws

During the fiscal year the Treasury Department stepped up its program of issuing regulations under the Internal Revenue Code.

Seventy-seven final regulations, 13 Executive orders, and 58 notices of proposed rulemaking, relating to matters other than alcohol and tobacco taxes, were published in the *Federal Register*.

A special effort was made to publish those regulations interpreting the important provisions of the revenue acts of 1962 and 1964. Fifteen of the published Treasury decisions related to regulations under the Revenue Act of 1964, and nine notices of proposed rulemaking were published in connection with other regulations under that act. Fourteen of the published Treasury decisions related to regulations under the Revenue Act of 1962, and six notices of proposed rulemaking were published in connection with other regulations under that act.

At the end of fiscal 1965, final or proposed regulations had been published for every significant provision of the 1962 act and for all but eight of the significant provisions under the 1964 act. In addition, the Treasury decisions published in 1965 included significant regulations under other revenue acts and some significant amendments in earlier regulations.

Among the issues covered in the Treasury decisions published were the sick pay exclusion, the deduction of moving expenses, the limitation on the medicine and drug deduction, the acceleration of corporate estimated tax, lobbying expenses, the minimum standard deduction, the retirement income credit, the denial of a deduction for certain State and local taxes, the income of export trade corporations and foreign investment companies, professional service corporations, distributions by foreign corporations, foreign controlled corporations, and foreign investment companies.

Notices of proposed rulemaking published during the fiscal year and still pending at the end of the year included those relating to: group term insurance; foreign expropriation losses and other net operating loss deductions; employee stock options and purchase plans; interest on deferred payments; and investment credit recapture.

International tax matters

H.R. 4750, the Interest Equalization Tax Extension Act of 1965,[1] was pending before the House Ways and Means Committee on June 30, 1965. (It was enacted and approved by President Johnson on October 9, 1965 (Public Law 89–243).) It extends the termination date of the interest equalization tax on the acquisition by a U.S. person of stock of a foreign issuer, or a debt obligation of a foreign obligor with a period remaining to maturity of three years or more, from December 31, 1965, to July 31, 1967, and enlarges its scope to make taxable the acquisition after February 10, 1965 (the date of President Johnson's Special Message to Congress on the Balance of Payments) by a U.S. person of a debt obligation of a foreign obligor with a period remaining to maturity between one year and three years. Other technical amendments included in the act have the effect of granting exclusions for specific acquisitions whose deterrence is not required to further the balance-of-payments policies implemented by the tax.

H.R. 5916, a bill to encourage investment by foreign persons in the United States which was prompted by the 1964 Report of the Fowler Task Force, was also pending before the House Ways and Means Committee on June 30, 1965. A new bill embodying committee amendments (H.R. 11297) was introduced in September 1965 and circulated for public comment.

The new income tax convention with Luxembourg was ratified by the Senate in July 1964. Instruments of ratification were exchanged

---

[1] See exhibit 46.

in December 1964, and the treaty is effective for taxable years beginning on or after January 1, 1964.

Two supplementary protocols to the tax convention with Japan came into force during fiscal year 1965. The first, signed in May 1960, came into force in September 1964. The second, signed in August 1962, came into force in May 1965.

Discussions on a protocol to the income tax treaty with Belgium were concluded during the year, and a protocol was signed in May 1965, which revises the treaty largely to take account of the 1962 Belgian income tax law. Discussions were concluded during the year with Germany on a protocol to update the present German income tax treaty. Both protocols were signed and were the subject of hearings before the Subcommittee on Tax Treaties of the Senate Committee on Foreign Relations.

Negotiations were begun with France to revise the present French treaty signed in 1945. Although negotiations were still in progress at the close of fiscal 1965, it is expected that the new treaty will be patterned after the model income tax convention prepared by the Organization for Economic Cooperation and Development (OECD). Negotiations were also initiated with Portugal on an income tax convention.

Three income tax treaties were negotiated with less-developed countries during fiscal 1965: A treaty was signed with the Philippines on October 10, 1964; on March 1, 1965, a treaty was signed with Thailand; and on June 29, 1965, one was signed with Israel. The Israeli and Thai treaties contain provisions which have not appeared previously in U.S. tax treaties and which are designed specifically for income tax treaties with less-developed countries. The most important of these is a credit to be granted American investors against their U.S. tax liability on income from any source equal to seven percent of the capital invested in a qualified enterprise in the less-developed country and a similar credit for the reinvestment of amounts in excess of one-half the profits of such enterprise. Hearings were held by the Senate Subcommittee on the treaty with Thailand but action on it was deferred until 1966.

Income tax treaty negotiations were also held with India during the year, but were not concluded. Tentative agreement was reached to include the investment credit provision in the new Indian treaty.

Treasury representatives participated in the preparation of a report on "Fiscal Incentives for Private Investment in Developing Countries" which was adopted by the OECD Fiscal Committee and published during the year. The Fiscal Committee also made progress toward completion of a model estate tax convention.

International Financial Affairs

The U.S. balance of payments and gold and dollar movements

The U.S. balance of payments.—The payments situation deteriorated during the last half of the calendar year 1964, reaching an annual rate of $6.2 billion during the fourth quarter. The deficit resulted from a substantial increase in net outflows of private U.S. capital. On February 10, 1965, President Johnson transmitted a special Balance-of-Payments Message to the Congress calling for a wide range of new, primarily voluntary, measures to extend the balance-of-payments program to the bulk of our international transactions.

The American commercial and financial communities responded with their immediate support of the new payments program. Particularly significant was the reversal of the flow of short-term U.S. liquid funds, which swung from a heavy net outflow to a net inflow. In March the United States had a substantial payments surplus. The improvement continued throughout the second quarter of 1965 when the first quarterly surplus in several years was registered.

The net deficit registered during the first half of calendar 1965 resulted from the combination of large deficits in January and February, and surpluses in March through June. While the turnaround was in good part ascribable to the President's payments program, the improvement also reflected certain special, transient factors.

During the first half of 1965 the payments deficit on regular transactions ran at an annual rate of $1.3 billion, seasonally adjusted; this compared favorably with the more than $6 billion annual rate deficit registered in the fourth quarter of 1964, and the $3.1 billion deficit recorded for the calendar year 1964.

U.S. gold sales (excluding the increased gold subscription to the International Monetary Fund) amounted to $1.2 billion. These were the counterpart of a reduction in holdings of foreign official dollar balances of nearly $1.0 billion. The cashing-in of these holdings for gold reflected in part the unusually large foreign official acquisitions during the fourth quarter of 1964.

The U.S. payments deficit on regular transactions, which excludes special inter-Government transactions, amounted to $3.1 billion in 1964, a slight improvement over the 1963 deficit. The overall 1964 deficit—which includes as receipts, in addition to the regular transactions, any net inflows arising out of special intergovernmental transactions (sales of special nonmarketable, nonconvertible Treasury bonds to official foreign institutions, prepayments to the U.S. Government of official foreign debts, and prepayments for U.S. Government military exports)—came to $2.8 billion, compared with $2.7 billion in 1963.

However, the full measure of the deterioration in the U.S. payments position is masked by these year-to-year comparisons. In the fourth quarter of 1963 the overall deficit at an annual rate was $612 million, compared with $5.5 billion in the fourth quarter of 1964. This $4.9 billion deterioration mainly reflected the $4.3 billion increase in outflows of private U.S. capital. Over the same period the U.S. commercial current account surplus rose by $1.6 billion to an annual rate of $5.5 billion.

The President's program.—The President's message of February 10, 1965, recommended a new balance-of-payments program which was the result of a careful review of the situation by the Cabinet Committee on the Balance of Payments, chaired by the Secretary of the Treasury. It was designed to respect the criteria and decisions of the marketplace, as opposed to the use of compulsory controls. Therefore, a prime element in the program was its reliance on the voluntary cooperation of the U.S. commercial and financial community.

U.S. banks were asked to hold total claims outstanding on foreign residents to 105 percent of the level at the end of 1964. Guidelines developed by the Board of Governors of the Federal Reserve System for implementing this program were designed to assure that credits to finance U.S. exports, and loans to less-developed countries, could be adequately met. In addition, consideration for the special positions of Canada, Japan, and the United Kingdom was requested. Within these broad guidelines each bank decides the direction of its particular overseas activities. A similar approach was permitted nonbank financial institutions in their foreign lending and investing activities.

U.S. industrial corporations also were asked to improve their individual balance-of-payments accounts, combining all transactions such as exports, dividend income, royalties, fees, and capital outflows from the United States. The objective was to leave the corporations free to adjust these components of their individual payments accounts while achieving a significant net payments improvement.

To reduce the tourist deficit, Americans as well as foreigners were encouraged to travel more in this country. Legislation was recommended and subsequently enacted on June 30, 1965 (Public Law 89–62), reducing the duty exemption on purchases made abroad by returning U.S. residents.

The February 10 program also: Extended the interest equalization tax through July 1967; broadened the interest equalization tax to include lending of one to three years' maturity; and activated the President's authority to apply the interest equalization tax to bank loans of one year or more maturity. To stop any excessive flow of funds to Canada under its special exemption from the interest equalization tax, the President sought and received firm assurance that the policies of the Canadian Government would be directed toward limiting such outflows to the maintenance of a stable level of Canada's foreign exchange reserves. The program also called for an intensification of U.S. Government efforts to minimize the foreign exchange costs of our defense and aid programs; an increase in our efforts to promote U.S. exports; and finally, encouraging more investments from abroad, by increasing, through new tax legislation, the incentive of foreigners to invest in U.S. securities.

The effect of the payments program.—On the basis of seasonally adjusted data, an improvement of $950 million in the overall payments balance was achieved from the first to the second quarters of the calendar year 1965. The details of quarterly balance-of-payments statistics from January 1964—June 1965 are contained in table 99.

The reduction in the net outflow of private U.S. capital, from $1.5 billion in the first quarter of 1965 to $264 million in the second quarter accounted for a good part of the improvement. The largest quarter-to-quarter change occurred in U.S. net bank claims on foreigners: an outflow of $435 million in the first quarter was converted to an inflow of $369 million in the second quarter. This improvement reflected a reduction in net U.S. bank loans to developed countries, indicating bank compliance with the priorities suggested by the Federal Reserve guidelines. The total bank inflows from March through June were sufficient to place banks under the ceilings suggested in the Federal Reserve guidelines and to leave adequate room for expansion of bank credits to finance U.S. exports.

U.S. corporations repatriated large amounts of short-term liquid investments abroad in the March–June period. In the first two quarters of 1965 nonbank, short-term U.S. capital showed an inflow of $575 million seasonally adjusted, compared to an outflow of $588 million in the full year 1964.

U.S. direct investment outlays in the second quarter amounted to about $880 million. While this represented a decline from the first quarter rate, it was at an annual rate considerably above the total for 1964. This continued high level of direct investment outlays may have reflected in part the difficulty in tapering off already-developed capital expenditure plans.

Treasury foreign exchange reporting system.—A number of steps were taken in fiscal 1965 to improve the reporting of capital movements statistics which enter into the U.S. balance of payments, particularly by nonbanking concerns. Procedures for the monthly reports of liquid assets held abroad by large companies were changed to expand the reporting group and to ensure more accurate reporting of monthly changes in holdings. At the same time the exemption level for the quarterly reports was raised to exempt smaller firms from the reporting requirement, without significantly affecting the statistics. Special instructions were issued to reporting firms to ensure proper reporting of funds placed abroad. Following the initiation in February 1965 of the President's voluntary balance-of-payments program, various types of nonbanking financial firms were informed of the Treasury reporting requirements.

Early in the year, a survey was made to ascertain the types of short-term dollar liabilities to foreigners, aside from deposits and Government obligations, held for the account of foreigners. In connection with the publication of the capital movements statistics in the *Treasury Bulletin*, a number of changes were introduced, including the publication of liabilities to foreign official institutions by area (beginning with the September 1964 issue), and a breakdown by type of short-term liabilities and claims of nonbanking concerns (first published in May 1965).

Gold and dollar holdings.—The gold and dollar holdings of foreign countries (excluding gold holdings of the U.S.S.R., other Eastern European countries, and China Mainland) amounted to an estimated $51.4 billion as of June 30, 1965. Of this total, official gold holdings were $26.9 billion. Official and private short-term dollar assets held with banks in the United States were $22.9 billion, and estimated official and private holdings of marketable U.S. Government bonds and notes amounted to $1.6 billion. (See table 96.)

During fiscal 1965 gold and dollar holdings of foreign countries increased by $3.4 billion. Official gold holdings derived from all sources increased by $1.9 billion. The increase of $1.5 billion in the dollar holdings of foreign countries accrued entirely to private accounts, with official holdings declining by $13 million.

Western European countries increased their gold and dollar assets by $2.5 billion during fiscal 1965, substantially more than the gain of $1.1 billion during fiscal 1964. Italy gained $785 million; the United Kingdom $662 million; and France $643 million. The gold and dollar assets of most other Western European countries increased, except for the decreases of $698 million for the Federal Republic of Germany and $17 million for Austria.

Canadian gold and dollar holdings declined by $141 million and African holdings by $164 million. Latin American holdings rose by $251 million. The total gain of Asiatic countries was $807 million, of which $377 million was made by Japan. The rest of the world gained $115 million.

The gold and dollar holdings of international and regional organizations decreased by $874 million during fiscal 1965: Those of the International Monetary Fund declined by $649 million, while the holdings of other international and regional organizations declined by $225 million. The Fund gold holdings exclude payments made to it in anticipation of increases in quotas, including the $259 million in gold paid by the United States in June 1965 as part of its increase. These payments will not be taken into the Fund's regular accounts until the requisite number of countries (having two-thirds of the quotas in effect on February 26, 1965) consent to their quota increases.

The official gold holdings of the world (excluding the U.S.S.R., other Eastern European countries, and China Mainland) increased by an estimated $75 million during fiscal 1965, amounting on June 30, 1965, to $43.0 billion. Of the world total, the United States held $14.0 billion and international and regional institutions $1.8 billion. See tables 96 and 97.

Treasury exchange and stabilization agreements

During the fiscal year 1965 Treasury exchange agreements were in effect with Brazil, Chile, the Dominican Republic, and Mexico. A one year Treasury exchange agreement in the amount of $6,250,000 was concluded with the Dominican Republic [1] on August 10, 1964. A $16,120,000 Treasury exchange agreement with Chile [2] was signed on February 4, 1965, effective for one year. On February 23, 1965, a one year Treasury exchange agreement in the amount of $53,660,000 was signed with Brazil. [3]

Foreign exchange operations

The dollar, after generally weakening against most major currencies from July–December 1964, showed renewed strength in the exchange markets after the President's February 1965 message. Despite the large U.S. payments deficit incurred in the last quarter of 1964 and the severe pressure, at times, on sterling, the dollar was not under speculative attack. This was largely because speculation has been discouraged by the network of defenses which have been steadily erected over the past five years and because the President in his Balance-of-Payments Message of February 10 reaffirmed the determination of the United States to eliminate its deficit.

The dominant force on exchange markets during the year was selling pressure on sterling. Through November, short-term assistance to the Bank of England in financing market operations was provided by a number of foreign central banks as well as through utilization of the Federal Reserve swap arrangement. This assistance was repaid in early December when the United Kingdom drew $1 billion from the IMF. At the end of November, in further support of the United

---

[1] See exhibit 52 and table 100.
[2] See exhibit 58 and table 100.
[3] See exhibit 61 and table 100.

Kingdom's determination to defend sterling, the United States joined 10 other countries and the Bank for International Settlements in arrangements to provide the United Kingdom with the equivalent of $3 billion of additional assurance.   Through the next six months the United Kingdom utilized portions of this to help finance exchange operations.   On May 28, 1965, it drew $1.4 billion from the IMF, a large part of which was used to repay drawings from the $3 billion "package."

Cumulative deficits in the U.S. balance of payments over recent years, accentuated by a heavy capital outflow in the last three months of 1964 and in January 1965, led to an accumulation of dollar reserves by certain foreign central banks in excess of desired levels and to large purchases of gold in the latter part of the fiscal year.   One important objective of Treasury and Federal Reserve foreign exchange operations was to ease demands for gold by absorbing dollars held by the central banks and facilitating shifts from official to private holdings. To some extent, official dollar gains resulted from flows which appeared likely to be reversed in the future.   These could appropriately be offset by short-term operations such as the utilization of Federal Reserve swap facilities, forward market operations, and swaps with the Bank for International Settlements involving foreign currencies. In addition, the Treasury issued further amounts of special medium-term, nonmarketable securities to Austria, Germany, and Switzerland.

The operations undertaken by the Treasury and Federal Reserve are described in detail in articles published semiannually by the Federal Reserve Bank of New York which, as agent or manager, carries out the operations of both the Treasury and the Federal Reserve.   See exhibits 48 and 49.

The International Monetary Fund

During fiscal 1965, 27 member countries drew the equivalent of $3,180.7 million in convertible currencies from the Fund, an increase of 41.5 percent in the total assistance made available by the Fund since it began operations in 1947.   Total drawings as of June 30, 1965, were $10,841.2 million equivalent.

The exceptional activity of the Fund reflected the support operation for the pound sterling.   Assistance to the United Kingdom totaled $2,400 million equivalent, or more than three-fourths of total Fund lending during the fiscal year.   For the first time, the General Arrangements to Borrow (GAB) was activated.   The GAB is an agreement among 10 major industrial countries (the Group of Ten) to provide mutual financial assistance.   The Fund borrowed $405 million equivalent from 8 countries for relending to the United Kingdom in December 1964, and $525 million in May 1965.   In associated transactions Switzerland made available to the United Kingdom the equivalent of $80 million and $40 million, respectively. Switzerland is not a member of the Ten, but is associated with them by special agreement. In neither instance did the Fund borrow from the United States.

The United States was the second largest user of the Fund during fiscal 1965, with drawings amounting to $350 million.[1] All U.S. drawings of currencies were intended for sale for U.S. dollars at par by the United States to countries holding reserves in dollars and wishing to make repurchases of their own currencies from the Fund. Under Article V, Section 7(b), the Fund is precluded from accepting for repurchase any currency of which the Fund's holdings are 75 percent of the country's quota. During all of fiscal 1965 the Fund's holdings of dollars exceeded 75 percent of the U.S. quota and no repayments were accepted in dollars. The U.S. drawings, however, enabled countries holding dollars to make repayments to the Fund without inconvenience.

The Deutsche Mark was the currency most used in Fund transactions. The equivalent of $862.2 million in Deutsche Marks (27.1 percent of total drawings) was drawn from the Fund, compared with drawings of $485.5 million in dollars. Repurchases amounted to $492.1 million equivalent, of which $276.4 million (56.2 percent) were made in Deutsche Marks. The United States has made no repurchases from the Fund, but its net indebtedness had been reduced to $123.4 million as of June 30, 1965, as the result of drawings by other countries.

During fiscal 1965, 22 countries arranged standby credit facilities amounting to $2,127.8 million with the Fund. Of this amount, $1,643.1 million was actually drawn during the year.

Fund membership remained at 102 throughout the year. Preparations have been made to increase member quotas by 25 percent to about $21 billion, subject to ratification of members holding two-thirds of the total quota. In addition, several countries have consented to an increase in their quota by more than 25 percent. Legislation authorizing a 25 percent increase in the U.S. quota was approved in June 1965 (Public Law 89–21). One quarter of the $1,035 million increase or $258.75 million, was paid in gold on June 30, 1965; the remainder is represented by a letter of credit. The U.S. gold payment is exactly offset by an increase in the amount of credit automatically available to the United States from the Fund. The total potential credit available to the United States under normal Fund policy relating to the credit tranches will be increased by an amount equal to the quota increment.

---

[1] See exhibits 53, 54, 56, and 62.

Both in the IMF and in other forums there was continuing study of proposals to strengthen the international monetary system, including proposals for increasing international liquidity in the future through the creation of a new type of reserve asset. The "Study Group on the Creation of Reserve Assets" of the Group of Ten published a report (Ossola Report) on August 1, 1965, examining several of these proposals.

Programs for financing economic development

The International Bank.—During fiscal 1965 the International Bank for Reconstruction and Development (IBRD) authorized 38 loans in 27 countries amounting to $1,023 million. Loans to Asia and the Middle East amounted to $395.5 million; to Europe, $292.5 million; to the Western Hemisphere, $212.3 million; and to African countries, $123 million. India received the largest loan, $134 million. Distribution of IBRD loans by purpose was as follows: transportation, $411.7 million; electric power, $321.4 million; industry, $179 million; agriculture, $78.2 million; water supply, $27 million; and education, $6 million. Disbursements amounted to $606 million, compared with $559 million in fiscal 1964.

The Bank's funded debt increased by about $232 million to $2,724 million as a result of its active borrowing. New bonds amounted to $299.6 million, including an issue of $200 million in the United States (the first U.S. issue in three years). In addition, $298 million of maturing bonds and notes were refunded through placements outside the United States, including a maturing $100 million issue of U.S. dollar bonds. Two issues, both held outside the United States, totaling $18.4 million, were paid off. Borrowers repaid $300 million on outstanding Bank loans during fiscal 1965: $137 million to the Bank and $163 million to investors holding participations in Bank loans. Sales for the year of portions of Bank loans totaled $106 million, compared to $173 million the year before. Sales from portfolio accounted for $76 million and the remaining $30 million represented participations by investors who agreed to take up parts of Bank loans at the time loan agreements were signed. The reduction in sales was due in part to the policy of the Bank not to sell the obligations of countries subject to the U.S. interest equalization tax in the United States.

Through June 30, 1965, the Bank had extended a total of 424 loans in 77 countries and territories, with gross commitments amounting to $8,954.6 million, of which $6,590.1 million had been disbursed. A total of $1,884.8 million in outside participations had been sold by the Bank. This, along with exchange adjustments, cancellations, and repayments, reduced net IBRD commitments to $5,966.8 million. Total reserves were $956.5 million. Subscribed capital amounted to $21,669.4 million. Eight members increased their subscriptions to the Bank's capital stock as a concomitant to increases in their Fund quotas.

The Bank has adopted a policy of differentiating between the interest rates on loans to developing countries and those on loans to industrialized countries. Therefore, a loan to Japan carried an interest rate of 6½ percent and one to Italy at shorter maturity a rate of 6¼ percent, compared to 5½ percent for all other loans.

During the year the Executive Directors completed a draft of a Convention on the Settlement of Investment Disputes between States and Nationals of Other States. The convention provides for the establishment of an International Center for Settlement of Investment Disputes under the auspices of the Bank. It will provide facilities for conciliation and arbitration, on a voluntary basis, of disputes arising between any contracting nation and investors who are nationals of other countries. The convention will become effective after it has been signed and ratified by at least 20 governments. At the end of fiscal 1965 it was before the member governments for appropriate action.

The Bank continued its technical, advisory, and planning assistance, as well as its activities in helping to coordinate the aid projects of major capital-exporting countries to certain countries. The Bank is a member of consortia on India, Pakistan, Greece, and Turkey and participates in Consultative Groups for Colombia, Nigeria, the Sudan, Tunisia, and Ecuador. Most of these consortia and Consultative Groups have been formed at the initiative of the IBRD.

The International Development Association.—The International Development Association (IDA) an affiliate of the IBRD, during fiscal 1965 approved 20 credits totaling $309 million in 11 member countries—an increase of $26 million over authorizations in the preceding fiscal year. Aggregate credits approved by the IDA through June 30, 1965, were thereby increased to a cumulative net total of $1,085.5 million, covering 77 credits in 29 countries and territories. Disbursements during the 1965 fiscal year increased from $192.5 million on June 30, 1964, to $414.7 million as of June 30, 1965, or about 38 percent of net credits authorized.

With the addition of Belgium in July 1964, the membership of the IDA on June 30, 1965, increased to 94, consisting of 18 Part I (economically advanced) members, and 76 Part II members.

As indicated in the 1964 annual report, page 58, the proposed increase of $750 million in the freely usable resources of the IDA became effective on June 29, 1964, when 12 members (including the

United States) formally notified the Association that they would contribute new resources to the IDA in excess of the required $600 million. As of July 1965, all of the remaining Part I countries had agreed to contribute the amounts allotted to them.

The International Finance Corporation.—The International Finance Corporation (IFC) is an affiliate of the IBRD designed to encourage the growth of private enterprise in less-developed countries by investing in debt and equity issues of private firms without governmental guaranty of repayment. The Corporation acts for the IBRD and the IDA and on its own behalf in the technical and financial appraisal, preparation, and supervision of industrial, mining, and development finance company projects.

During fiscal 1965 the IFC invested $26 million in 11 countries in 15 enterprises, mostly basic industries, including cement, steel, textiles, paper, and food products. Eight of these investments, totaling $9.9 million, represented second or third commitments to firms in which IFC had outstanding investments. New commitments included approximately $15 million in loans and $11 million in equity.

As of June 30, 1965, the IFC had made total commitments of $137 million involving 103 transactions in 32 countries. About 56 percent ($77 million) of this represents investments in the Western Hemisphere. The IFC has been able to revolve more than one-third of its entire commitments through sales from its portfolio and principal repayments. Membership remained unchanged during the year at 78.

Amendments to the Articles of Agreement of the IFC and of the IBRD were proposed to the members by the Board of Governors in September 1964, to permit the Bank to lend to the IFC and to permit the IFC to borrow from the Bank in an amount up to four times the unimpaired subscribed capital and surplus of the IFC. Member governments, including the United States, approved the amendments,[1] which became effective after the close of the fiscal year. Approximately $400 million will be added to the potential resources of the IFC for relending to private enterprise.

The Inter-American Development Bank.—The Inter-American Development Bank (IDB) was established on December 30, 1959, began operations in the fall of 1960, and made its first loan on February 3, 1961. All of the countries of the Organization of American States are members of the IDB. Cuba is not a member and is no longer eligible to join.

The Bank has up to now carried on its financing operations through three "windows."

---

[1] The necessary legislation was passed by the U.S. Senate June 30, 1965.   The bill became law on Aug. 14, 1965 (79 Stat. 519).

The Ordinary Capital resources provide development funds on conventional terms in much the same manner as the World Bank. It commenced operations with governmental subscriptions but now obtains its funds largely from private financial markets in the same way as the World Bank.

The Fund for Special Operations offers financing on easy repayment terms entirely from resources provided by the United States and the Latin American members of the Bank.

The Social Progress Trust Fund has been administered by the Bank since mid-1961 on behalf of the United States, which provided all of its funds. Loans from the Fund are repayable on easy terms and are made in four areas of social development: water supply and sanitation, advanced education, housing, and land settlement and improved land use.

The authorized Ordinary Capital of the Bank is the equivalent of $2,150 million (of which the total U.S. share is $762 million), composed of $475 million in paid-in capital (U.S. portion, $150 million) and $1,675 million in callable capital (U.S. portion, $612 million). To obtain resources for its lending operations, the Bank, through June 30, 1965, had borrowed $285 million equivalent secured by its callable capital. In October 1964 the Bank borrowed $100 million in the United States, its third bond issue here, bringing to $225 million the total raised in U.S. markets. There were three Bank borrowings abroad in fiscal year 1965: A $15 million equivalent Deutsche Mark bond issue in Germany in July 1964; an $8.4 million equivalent sterling bond issue in the United Kingdom in September 1964; and a $12.5 million direct borrowing of U.S. dollars from the Government of Spain on March 30, 1965. Added to the $24.2 million Italian lira bond issue in April 1962, these Bank borrowings brought the total raised in foreign markets to the equivalent of $60 million.

On March 31, 1965, pursuant to recommendations of the fifth annual meeting of the Board of Governors of the IDB (see 1964 annual report, page 61), an expansion of the Fund for Special Operations by $900 million equivalent became effective. The U.S. share of the increase is $750 million, while the Latin American members are contributing $150 million in their national currencies. This is to provide sufficient funds for operations during the three years 1965–67. The contributions are to be paid in three equal installments, of which the first was paid by the United States before June 30, 1965, the second will be due before December 31, 1965, and the last will be due by the end of 1966.

The Social Progress Trust Fund was financed solely by the United States by appropriations of May 27, 1961, for $394 million and of January 6, 1964, for $131 million. This Trust Fund has never formed part of the Bank's resources, but has been administered by the Bank as trustee. The funds are now nearing exhaustion and the United States announced, in connection with the recent expansion of the Fund for Special Operations, that the United States will make no further contributions to the Social Progress Trust Fund. Its loan functions have been delegated by the Governors of the Bank to the expanded Fund for Special Operations.

Through June 30, 1965, the Bank had authorized 115 loans amounting to $583.7 million equivalent from its Ordinary Capital, 56 loans amounting to $192.4 million from the Fund for Special Operations, and 112 loans from the Social Progress Trust Fund amounting to $482.4 million—a total of 283 loans amounting to $1,258.5 million. Total disbursements from all three funds amounted to $602.1 million through the fiscal year 1965. Disbursements in the fiscal year 1965 roughly equaled those made during the entire prior period from the Bank's inception through June 30, 1964.

During the fiscal year, the Bank entered into two agreements with the Government of Canada which provided 25 million Canadian dollars for loans to Latin American member countries for purchases in Canada. An agreement of December 1964, provided that 10 million Canadian dollars would be made available through the Bank by the Government of Canada at low or no interest and with maturities of up to 50 years. In the second agreement, the Canadian Government reserved an additional 15 million Canadian dollars through the Export Credits Insurance Corporation for credits of up to 20 years at commercial interest rates.

The Export-Import Bank.—During the fiscal year 1965 the Export-Import Bank authorized over $1.8 billion in loans, guaranties and export credit insurance to assist in financing the sale of American goods and services overseas. Authorizations for long-term capital loans totaled $435.2 million; and exporter credits and guaranties amounted to $282.9 million. Export credit insurance extended through the Foreign Credit Insurance Association (FCIA) amounted to $721.5 million in the fiscal year. Other authorizations included $340 million in emergency foreign trade credits, $76.3 million in commodity credits, and $3.1 million for insurance covering U.S. goods on consignment.

The bank disbursed $403.2 million in fiscal 1965. During the year, private participation in the Bank's loans totaled $614.7 million, of which $450 million represented sales of portfolio participation certificates to private financial institutions. The Bank earned $177.8 million in interest and fees, and paid $15.1 million in interest on funds borrowed from the Treasury. In addition, the Bank paid $44 million in interest on participation certificates and $.5 million in interest to commercial banks. A dividend of $50 million was declared on the stock of the Bank held by the Secretary of the Treasury. At the close of the fiscal year, the Bank's retained income reserve for contingencies amounted to $944 million, and its uncommitted lending authority was $3,299 million. Receipts of principal and interest on the Bank's outstanding credits during fiscal 1965 contributed over $553 million to the U.S. balance of international payments.

The Agency for International Development.—The Agency for International Development (AID) is responsible for the economic assistance activities of the United States. These include development lending, development grants and technical cooperation, supporting assistance, investment guaranties, surveys of investment opportunities and negotiation of loans involving U.S.-owned local currencies including those acquired under section 104(e) and 104(g) of Public Law 480, as amended. AID is also responsible for administering funds appropriated for development loans and grants for Latin America.

Total U.S. dollar commitments by AID during fiscal 1965 amounted to $2.2 billion, of which $1.2 billion, or 55 percent, was on a loan basis. The Near East and South Asia received $694 million, of which $605 million, or 87 percent, was in the form of loans; Latin America received $588 million, of which $454 million was on a loan basis; the Far East received $450 million; including $69 million in loans; and Africa received $164 million, of which $76 million was on a loan basis. The balance ($282 million) was utilized for nonregional programs such as U.N. Technical Assistance, the U.N. Children's Fund, plus general program support and administrative expenses. AID continued the policy of direct procurement in the United States to minimize the impact of its expenditures on the U.S. balance of payments. At the close of fiscal 1965, over 85 percent of all AID dollars were committed directly for the purchase of U.S. goods and services.

Annual meetings of international financial institutions

International Monetary Fund and International Bank.—The annual meetings of the Boards of Governors of the International Monetary Fund and of the International Bank for Reconstruction and Development and its affiliates were held in Tokyo in September 1964. The Governors adopted a resolution requesting the Executive Directors to report on the desirability of increasing Fund quotas. Subsequently, the Directors submitted a report proposing increases in Fund quotas generally by 25 percent, with special increases for certain countries whose economic positions had changed considerably since the last revision of the quotas. At the meeting of the Bank and its affiliates approval was given to certain changes in their lending policies, as well as a request to the Executive Directors of the Bank to draft a convention for the arbitration and conciliation of investment disputes.[1]

Inter-American Development Bank.—Mr. David E. Bell, Administrator of the Agency for International Development (AID), as Alternate U.S. Governor of the Bank, led the U.S. delegation to the Sixth Annual Meeting of the Bank held in Asuncion, Paraguay, in April 1965. The delegation also included Mr. Tom Killefer, U.S. Executive Director of the Bank, representatives of the agencies constituting the National Advisory Council on International Monetary and Financial Problems and Members of Congress.

The Governors concerned themselves principally with the problem of obtaining financial and technical resources from nonmember countries and emphasized the broadest possible support for the Bank's efforts to promote the process of Latin American integration.

Organization for Economic Cooperation and Development.—The fourth Ministerial Council Meeting of the Organization for Economic Cooperation and Development (OECD) met in Paris on December 2–3, 1964. Acting Assistant Secretary of the Treasury Merlyn N. Trued served as a member of the U.S. delegation. The Council of Ministers reaffirmed the target established in 1961 for expanding by 50 percent the combined output of the Organization's 21 member nations over the decade ending in 1970. Noting the satisfactory progress achieved thus far in meeting this objective, the Council approved a proposal for a comprehensive mid-term review in 1965. The Council called for a continuation of efforts within the OECD to improve the capital markets of member countries, both as a means of facilitating economic growth and of contributing to balance-of-payments equilibrium. Work on capital market development has continued in the Committee for Invisible Transactions (a Treasury official is the U.S. expert on this Committee), the body within the OECD primarily responsible for the progressive removal of restrictions on international movements of capital and services.

The Organization's Economic Policy Committee continued to meet regularly throughout the year to discuss the overall economic situation of the member countries. Under Secretary of the Treasury for Monetary Affairs Robert V. Roosa was a member of the U.S. delegation at the meetings early in the fiscal year, and his successor, Frederick L. Deming, served in that capacity at the later meetings. A Treasury official also served on the U.S. delegation to the Economic Policy Committee Working Party on Policies for the Promotion of Economic Growth (Working Party 2), which is concerned with implementing the collective growth target mentioned above.

---

[1] These meetings were discussed in the 1964 annual report pages 62–4. See also exhibits 32 and 33 in the 1964 annual report.

The Economic Policy Committee's Working Party on Policies for the Promotion of Better Payments Equilibrium (Working Party 3) met at intervals of four to six weeks over the past year, with the Under Secretary of the Treasury for Monetary Affairs as Chairman of the U.S. delegation. In addition to its reviews of the external payments situation of both surplus and deficit countries in which special attention has been devoted to the United Kingdom and its efforts to achieve coordinated action toward the goal of international monetary stability, the Working Party, at the request of the Group of Ten, began a study of the adjustment process and undertook a continuing multilateral surveillance of the ways and means of financing balance-of-payments disequilibrium.

As a part of the Trade Committee's continuing efforts to expand trade among nations, discussions were held on the changes in the U.S. antidumping regulations as well as on the antidumping laws and regulations in other member countries. The Assistant Secretary of the Treasury for International Affairs is the principal U.S. representative on the Trade Committee's Group on Export Credit Guarantees which met several times during the year to examine questions of mutual interest in this area of activity.

The Treasury Department provides the U.S. representation on the Fiscal Committee, which has been developing model income tax conventions, examining the estate tax field, and encouraging international cooperation in other tax policy areas. The Treasury representative is Vice Chairman of the Fiscal Committee and has headed a working committee which published a report on "Fiscal Incentives for Private Investment in Developing Countries" during the fiscal year.

The Development Assistance Committee (DAC) of the OECD continues to coordinate development aid policies of member countries to achieve a greater degree of harmonization of the programs of donor countries and more effective use of such aid. Assistant Secretary of the Treasury John C. Bullitt served as a senior member of the U.S. delegation to the DAC Ministerial meeting in July 1964. Austria and Sweden became members of DAC in 1965, bringing its membership to 15.

The Annual Aid Review of the DAC provides for careful study and examination of each member's program and permits a comparison of relative aid burdens and general aid policies. The review of the United States was held in May of 1965.

The Economic Development and Review Committee of the OECD reviews annually the economies of the member countries and issues a public report; the Treasury participated in the Committee's formal examination of the U.S. economy in November 1964. A Treasury observer regularly attended meetings of the Managing Board of the European Monetary Agreement.

The General Agreement on Tariffs and Trade.—The General Agreement (GATT) is the principal instrument used by the United States to reduce and eliminate obstacles to the expansion of international trade. In the framework of developing the policy of the U.S. Government in the trade field, the Treasury continued to participate in the work of the Trade Expansion Act Advisory Committee, the Trade Executive Committee, the Trade Staff Committee, and the Trade Information Committee.

The negotiating phase of the Kennedy round began on November 16, 1964, when the industralized countries in the GATT submitted their lists of items to be excepted from the 50 percent linear tariff cut. In the absence of an agreed set of rules to govern negotiations on agricultural products, the exceptions lists tabled on November 16 covered only industrial products. Insofar as agricultural products are concerned, the subsequent discussions in the Kennedy round forum have sought to clarify and identify the possible scope and content of future negotiations. September 16, 1965, was set as the date for the tabling of agricultural offers. The United States has made it clear that the ultimate Kennedy round agreement must include the liberalization of trade in agricultural products as well as industrial products.

Discussions were also initiated in the Kennedy round negotiations on nontariff barriers to trade. These covered both complaints by the United States on the practices of other countries and complaints by others on U.S. practices. The latter group included such issues as the use of the American selling price in determining the value of certain imports and the U.S. antidumping law and regulations; in the former group, the United States raised such issues as the assessment of road taxes that appeared to place a greater burden on U.S. automobiles than on other types of cars and quantitative restrictions on imports of U.S. goods.

During the year a Treasury representative was a member of the U.S. delegation to the annual meeting of the GATT Contracting Parties, to the GATT Committee on Balance-of-Payments Restrictions, and to the special GATT Working Party which consulted with the United Kingdom on its application of a 15 percent temporary surcharge on imports in order to safeguard its external financial position and to correct its balance of payments.

The United Nations Conference on Trade and Development.—The First Session of the Trade and Development Board of the Conference met in New York April 5-30, 1965. The Board held its Second Session in Geneva August 24 to September 15, 1965. During these Sessions, the Board gave shape and direction to the new U.N. economic machinery, approved by the General Assembly on December 30, 1964, to deal with a variety of problems involving the developing countries. It established terms of reference for four principal subsidiary committees (Commodities, Manufactures, Invisibles, and Financing Related to Trade and Shipping), elected the members of the Committees, established a work program for the Board, and adopted a set of rules of procedure. The Treasury continued to participate in this general framework of activity.

Lend-lease silver

The liquidation of all obligations on account of Treasury silver transferred to certain countries during World War II under the authority of the Lend-Lease Act of March 11, 1941, was completed by repayments during fiscal 1965. The Lend-Lease Silver Liability Account of the Government of India was settled and closed on the books of the Treasury Department upon receipt from that Government of 324,809.08 fine troy ounces of silver. A final cash payment of $137,-328.73, equivalent to 106,215.19 fine troy ounces of silver converted on the basis of the monetary value, was received from Pakistan and its account has also been settled and closed.

Lend-lease silver transactions as of June 30, 1965

[In millions of fine ounces except where otherwise specifically indicated]

	Silver transferred from the Treasury to lend-lease for account of foreign governments	Silver returned and taken into the account of the Treasurer of the United States	Silver being returned	Dollar repayments (millions)	Silver to be returned
Australia	11.8	11.8			
Belgium	.3	.3			
Ethiopia	5.4	5.4			
Fiji	.2	.2			
India	172.5	172.5			
Netherlands	56.7	56.7			
Pakistan	53.5	48.8		[1] $5.6	
Saudi Arabia	[2] 22.3	1.4		[3] 20.4	
United Kingdom	88.1	88.1			
Total	410.8	385.2		26.0	

[1] Equivalent to 4.7 million fine troy ounces of silver converted on the basis of the market price on dates of receipts, or the monetary value.
[2] Includes 1,031,250 ounces lost at sea while in transit.
[3] Equivalent to 19.9 million fine troy ounces of silver converted on basis of the market price on dates of receipts.

ADMINISTRATIVE REPORTS

Management Improvement Program

The Treasury Department's management improvement program seeks to insure maximum effectiveness in reducing costs, increasing productivity, and improving efficiency at all operating and staff levels.

During fiscal 1965, as a result of continued cost consciousness of employees throughout the Department, Treasury's management improvement program achieved another record. Savings resulting from the program were estimated at $24.2 million on an annual recurring basis, while one-time savings reached $14.8 million making a fiscal year total of $39.0 million. Of these amounts, $3,369,000 was the result of the incentive awards program and $788,000 was achieved in Coast Guard's military awards program.

The more significant management improvements of Treasury bureaus are highlighted in the administrative reports of the individual offices and bureaus which follow.

Special studies and projects

The final report of the survey of the mission, organization, and management of the Bureau of Customs begun in 1963 was issued in March 1965. Simultaneously the President submitted Reorganization Plan No. 1 of 1965 to the Congress. This plan, designed to streamline and improve the operation and management of the Customs service,[1] became law on May 25, 1965.

In conjunction with Secret Service personnel, staff of the Assistant Secretary for Administration participated in several studies which included a survey of the budgetary, manpower, and equipment resources required for Presidential protection and an examination of the overall management and organization of the Secret Service.

The staff also assisted the Bureau of the Mint in acquiring sufficient heavy manufacturing equipment to avert a critical coin shortage while the new mint in Philadelphia is under construction. From surplus or reserve equipment held by the General Services Administration and the Department of Defense, the Mint was able to obtain over $1 million worth of industrial presses, tools, and other equipment.

Financial management

The Office of Budget and Finance continued to provide staff support and direction for the Secretary in the financial management of the Department's operating funds.

Preparatory to presenting the 1967 operating expense budget, on the program or mission basis long sought by the Bureau of the Budget and the Department, Coast Guard revised its accounting and operational reporting systems to provide proper support. The 1966 budget was presented in both the conventional and revised formats and was well received. Provision was made for more precise distri-

---

See Bureau of Customs administrative report

bution of Coast Guard aircraft operating costs to the specific programs served by the aircraft.

Plans were made for the establishment of a computerized service-wide payroll service for reservists' drill pay and retirement point records at Coast Guard Headquarters. This centralization will result in personnel savings of approximately 16 man-years and $77,600.

The management reporting system for the expanded capital outlay program of the Coast Guard was redesigned to provide a more timely and coordinated flow of management planning and progress information.

Automated payroll operations

The continuing program for automation of payrolls resulted in converting two additional Treasury organizations to the IRS computer system. Plans were completed and the actual work of conversion was well underway at fiscal yearend for a third large bureau. By the close of fiscal 1965 five organizations had been converted and tests had been initiated for conversion of a sixth. Through this system the usual payroll operations are performed with magnetic tape records producing checks, savings bonds, personnel statistics, related accounting statements, and other information for each pay period. Benefits to the bureaus include reduction in manpower expended in payroll and related accounting functions.

The accounts maintained by IRS for employee payroll withholdings and employer contributions of Treasury bureau payrolls were consolidated into a single set of accounts. The reporting of the funds disbursed for these withholdings and contributions was also consolidated. This eliminated the maintenance of as many as 16 accounts for each bureau serviced by the Internal Revenue Service. Disbursement procedures from these funds require only one payment document for similar type transactions in place of one for each bureau.

Accounting systems

Improvement was made in the accrual accounting system of several bureaus as the result of the development of accounting manuals. Bureaus which developed and submitted manuals to the General Accounting Office for review were: the Bureau of Public Debt; the Bureau of Narcotics; and the Office of the Treasurer of the United States.

The Bureau of Accounts system of internal cost-based budgeting was initially adopted in the fiscal year 1964. Improvements in the system during fiscal 1965 provided a better basis for operational planning and control as well as a means to measure the attainment of self-imposed goals. The Bureau is modifying administrative accounting in regional offices so that actual and budgeted cost data may be computerized. The Bureau also prepares monthly cost reports showing actual progress compared to budget plans. These reports are tailored to management needs and provide a sounder basis for formulating operating cost budgeting forecasts.

A number of bureaus revised their systems for controlling and accounting for nonexpendable property. Generally these systems reduced the number of items on inventory through the establishment of a $50 minimum as the basis for capitalization and control. These simplified systems have reduced paperwork and facilitated the physical inventory process without eliminating essential controls.

Internal auditing

Internal auditing is handled through a departmental audit staff in the Office of the Secretary and the staffs in 12 bureaus and offices. In addition to performing audits relating to funds appropriated to the Office of the Secretary, the departmental audit staff periodically reviews the internal audit systems of other Treasury bureaus and offices. Such reviews emphasize the necessity for adequate audit coverage, audit work programs, and effective reporting as a constructive service to management.

During fiscal 1965, the departmental audit staff completed reviews and appraisals of the systems of internal auditing in two Treasury bureaus, and audited payrolls and other related administrative activities in the Office of the Secretary.

Although corrective actions taken by bureaus and offices as a result of internal audit recommendations can sometimes be stated in monetary terms, most 1965 actions resulted in intangible improvements. In most Treasury bureaus these benefits were confined primarily to the strengthening of internal controls, improvements in procedures, and better utilization of personnel and space. In the Internal Revenue Service, work of the internal audit staff also resulted in corrective actions which effected additional tax revenue, or other matters having an impact on the revenue, of about $30 million.

Personnel management

In fiscal 1965 major emphasis was placed on evaluating programs, implementing new Government-wide programs, and strengthening existing personnel programs.

A comprehensive personnel management review of the Bureau of Narcotics was initiated with visits to headquarters and 18 field offices; the report of the review is to be submitted to the Commissioner of Narcotics during the fiscal year 1966. Evaluations of the personnel programs in the Bureau of Accounts, the U.S. Coast Guard, the Internal Revenue Service, the Bureau of the Mint, and the Bureau of the Public Debt were in process at the end of fiscal 1965. The majority of these are cooperative efforts involving the Office of Personnel and the Civil Service Commission.

The Treasury Department was commended for its increased employment of the handicapped by the Chairman of the Civil Service Commission, the District of Columbia Commissioners' Committee on Employment of the Handicapped, and the President's Committee on the Employment of the Handicapped. A program for placing returning Peace Corps volunteers was successfully initiated, as was the nationwide youth opportunity corps in which Treasury exceeded its quota of 884 by over 52 percent. A new centralized summer employment program in the Washington area during the summer of 1965 resulted in less expenditure of manpower in handling summer employment and in hiring better quality personnel.

Comprehensive regulations were issued on premium pay and wage boards appeals. A supplementary guide for classification of criminal investigator positions was cleared with the Civil Service Commission and readied for issuance. The basis for pay of 1,700 noncraft employees in the Bureau of Engraving and Printing was revised to a modified version of the Army-Air Force Wage Board System, effective April 25, 1965, thus aligning pay scales with prevailing industrial rates in this area. A study was completed of the Bureau of the Mint wage-fixing system, which involved some 1,000 wage board employees.

Significant developments occurred in employee-management relations. An arbitrator ruled in favor of local units rather than the National Association of Internal Revenue Employees (NAIRE) proposed nationwide unit in Internal Revenue. Other activities included an impasse in negotiations and a charge of unfair labor practices. All of these cases reflected issues and changes in relationships brought about by Executive Order 10988 and the striving to establish a framework for improved relationships.

The Office of Personnel continued to stress the use of external as well as internal resources in meeting employee training needs effectively and economically. During fiscal 1965 it published and distributed a report on classroom training for the fiscal years 1962–64, which helped Treasury bureaus evaluate their training efforts. The report reflected a heavy emphasis on technical training in the Department, a steady growth in employee training in bureaus other than IRS, and a significant increase in training at other Government agencies and non-Government facilities by most Treasury bureaus.

Incentive awards program

In support of the President's program to reduce costs and improve productivity, all Treasury bureaus were encouraged to increase their emphasis on employee suggestions and all phases of the incentive awards program. Suggestions received in fiscal 1965 increased by 68 percent; adopted suggestions increased by 64 percent; and estimated first-year benefits from the suggestion program increased by 96 percent to a total of $1,182,835. The number of performance awards and quality pay increases also rose. Total estimated benefits from all phases of the incentive awards program amounted to over $3.3 million.

On September 2, 1964, the First Annual Treasury Awards Ceremony was held at which 236 employees were recognized for their outstanding service and significant contributions to Treasury operations during fiscal 1964. Treasury's two top awards, for Exceptional Service or Meritorious Service, went to 44 employees. Thirty-four employees received recognition for outstanding suggestions or service, and 144 in the Washington area were cited for more than 40 years of Federal service.

Property and facilities management

The number of excess real properties disposed of during the past year was the largest since the inception of the program. Title and descriptive data were transmitted to GSA regional offices on 41 excess real properties involving 442 acres of land with improvements and a total acquisition cost of $1,250,000. These properties will either be sold by GSA with the proceeds going into the Treasury, transferred to other Government departments for further use, or conveyed to the States for use by historical, educational, or health institutions.

Consolidation of space was achieved in a number of Treasury activities. In nine cities, single locations were established to eliminate a number of previously separated activities.

In 26 different locations offices were relocated from leased to Government-owned buildings, which will result in annual savings of $22,000. In addition, 26 offices were closed.

The Bureau of Narcotics and the Washington Secret Service Field Office were relocated into new quarters. Additional space was also obtained for the IRS National Training School and the Bureau of Customs headquarters.

Personal property determined excess during the fiscal year exceeded $9.4 million. During the same period, $559,000 of excess property was reassigned for further utilization within the Department. Property transferred to other Federal agencies totaled $3.2 million and, in turn, Treasury received $6.6 million of excess property from other Federal agencies without reimbursement.

Safety program

Figures for the calendar year 1964 indicated that Treasury's disabling injury frequency rate (the number of lost-time injuries per million man-hours worked) was somewhat higher than the rates of recent years. However, it still remains considerably below the all-Federal rate, indicating the continuing effectiveness of this program.

To maintain interest in the program, a safety emblem contest was sponsored by the Treasury Safety Council with 532 Treasury employees submitting 1,150 different designs. An emblem was selected and has been adopted by the Treasury Safety Council for use in promoting safety awareness throughout the Department.

On February 24, 1965, the Secretary of the Treasury issued Administrative Circular No. 125, transmitting President Johnson's memorandum of February 16, 1965, announcing the initiation of *Mission SAFETY–70*. This is a new program to reduce Federal work injuries and costs, year by year, until a total 30 percent reduction is achieved by 1970. On May 7, 1965, Secretary Fowler met with the heads of Treasury bureaus to discuss their plans to implement *Mission SAFETY–70*. At the meeting bureau heads reported to the Secretary on their plans for the balance of calendar year 1965. The Secretary stated that he had assured the President that Treasury would achieve a 2.6 injury frequency rate by 1970 and that he expected the support of each bureau in this achievement.

Office of the Comptroller of the Currency

The Comptroller of the Currency, as the Administrator of the National Banking System, is charged with the responsibility of maintaining the public's confidence in the System by sustaining the banks' solvency and liquidity. An equally important public objective is to fashion the controls over banking so that banks may have the discretionary power to adapt their operations sensitively and efficiently to the needs of a growing economy.

The banking structure that is most ideal in terms of the public need will vary with the changing requirements for banking services and facilities. In our prosperous society these changes are constant, far-reaching, and of compelling importance. Increases in personal income and population affect the volume of savings seeking productive uses. The growth of capital and advances in technology bring new products and new industries. These, in turn, often give rise to new communities and shifts of population. Population movements are further accelerated as income levels rise and permit the purchase of new homes. All of these factors have worked to produce demands for additional types of banking services and for banking facilities at new locations.

During the period from 1961 to mid-1965, the Nation enjoyed its longest peacetime economic expansion in history. Real gross national product was 17 percent higher in 1964 than in 1960. Population continued to grow at a much higher rate than during the economically depressed 1930's.

The number of commercial banking offices increased by 18.5 percent during the years 1961–64, compared with a 12.9 percent increase in 1957–60, and an 8.7 percent increase in 1953–56. The 1961–64 expansion occurred in response to the banking needs generated by the economic growth of the years.

The *102d Annual Report of the Comptroller of the Currency* contains a statement of policy on the evolution of the banking structure, the texts of merger decisions, and summaries of litigation. Information relating to administrative matters, including a comparative statement of assessment and other operating income, and of financial operations, from 1958–64 is also given. The 1964 report continues the innovations of the 1963 report by presenting the Comptroller's principal addresses, his testimony before congressional committees, selected correspondence, and new rulings and interpretations.

Management improvement

Where economy or effectiveness warrants, the policy of decentralization of duties has been continued. The 14 regional comptrollers were given additional discretionary functions formerly reserved to the Washington office. Attorneys were assigned to several regional headquarters, resulting in more immediate and frequent transmission of Office opinion to bankers and other interested parties. The regional offices have assumed the responsibility for examining travel vouchers and reviewing certain aspects of bank examination reports. The performance of these functions was improved by their allocation to points closer to the traveling force and the bankers, and effected a substantial saving in time and money. New travel regulations, providing more equitable reimbursement to the force, also yielded considerable savings.

The Office conducted a one-week program in which regional personnel were instructed in the performance of their new duties. An illuminating side effect of this school was the discussion of problems common to both Washington and regional personnel. In addition, increased Washington-region communication at the highest levels has succeeded in establishing a common concern for efficiency. Regional visits by high-echelon members of the Washington staff, including Deputy Comptrollers, economists, and attorneys, as well as regional comptrollers' conferences, have been successful in bringing about this objective.

The Bureau of Accounts Audit Staff conducted an independent audit of the financial statements and supporting records of the Office of the Comptroller of the Currency for the calendar year 1963, and one for 1964 was in progress at the end of the fiscal year.

Status of national banks

The result of the effort to broaden the opportunities for national banks and enable them to meet the demands of commerce and industry is shown in the accompanying record of bank performance. In December 1964, there were 4,780 commercial banks under the supervision of the Comptroller of the Currency, including 7 nonnational banks in the District of Columbia, an increase of 3.4 percent since 1963. During the year there were 232 national bank charters issued, of which 205 were primary organizations and 27 were conversions from State banks; 782 branches were opened of which 60.6 percent, or 474, were located in communities with a population of less than 25,000, and 30.6 percent, or 239, belonged to banks with total resources of less than $25 million.

The assets of national banks grew 11.7 percent. Loans and discounts registered a 14.6 percent increase over 1963 and grew from 49.0 percent to 50.3 percent of the total assets. Securities displayed an increment of 4.2 percent but as a percentage of total assets, securities dropped from 30.6 in 1963 to 28.6 in 1964. U.S. Government securities increased 0.4 percent; however, their percentage of total assets decreased from 19.6 to 17.6. On the other hand, State and local obligations rose from 9.6 percent to 9.8 percent of total assets. This increase in loans and discounts, as contrasted with the relative decrease in securities holdings, reflected the brisk demand for loans from the private sector of the economy.

Number of national banks and banking offices, by States, June 30, 1965

State	National banks			Number of branches of national banks	Number of national banking offices [1]
	Total	Unit	With branches		
United States [2]	4,803	3,521	1,282	8,254	13,057
Alabama	84	59	25	110	194
Alaska	5	0	5	38	43
Arizona	4	1	3	168	172
Arkansas	65	40	25	53	118
California	94	60	34	1,681	1,775
Colorado	117	117	0	0	117
Connecticut	27	11	16	158	185
Delaware	5	3	2	4	9
District of Columbia	8	0	8	46	54
Florida	192	192	0	0	192
Georgia	54	30	24	103	157
Hawaii	2	0	2	39	41
Idaho	9	3	6	91	100
Illinois	415	415	0	0	415
Indiana	125	64	61	247	372
Iowa	102	80	22	24	126
Kansas	170	146	24	24	194
Kentucky	81	40	41	117	198
Louisiana	47	17	30	127	174
Maine	21	8	13	65	86
Maryland	50	24	26	177	227
Massachusetts	94	33	61	312	406
Michigan	97	42	55	377	474
Minnesota	193	191	2	6	199
Mississippi	34	9	25	48	82
Missouri	96	82	14	14	110
Montana	48	48	0	0	48
Nebraska	125	108	17	17	142
Nevada	3	1	2	32	35
New Hampshire	50	32	18	22	72
New Jersey	147	52	95	406	553
New Mexico	34	16	18	49	83
New York	198	105	93	792	990
North Carolina	30	9	21	256	286
North Dakota	42	37	5	5	47
Ohio	223	97	126	489	712
Oklahoma	222	197	25	25	247
Oregon	12	7	5	203	215
Pennsylvania	377	230	147	752	1,129
Rhode Island	4	0	4	53	57
South Carolina	24	5	19	168	192
South Dakota	33	28	5	35	68
Tennessee	75	28	47	185	260
Texas	544	544	0	0	544
Utah	13	9	4	54	67
Vermont	27	18	9	27	54
Virginia	121	53	68	299	420
Washington	31	14	17	330	361
West Virginia	79	79	0	0	79
Wisconsin	110	98	12	24	134
Wyoming	39	39	0	0	39
Virgin Islands	1	0	1	2	3
D.C.—all [4]	15	1	14	81	96

[1] Number of banking offices is the sum of total national banks and number of branches of national banks.
[2] Includes Virgin Islands.
[3] Includes Deposit Insurance National Bank of Dell City, Tex., and Deposit Insurance National Bank of Newport News, Va.—organized under Section 11 of the Federal Deposit Insurance Act—to operate no longer than a two-year period.
[4] Includes national and nonnational banks in the District of Columbia, all of which are supervised by the Comptroller of the Currency.

Assets, liabilities, and capital accounts of national banks on June 30, 1964, December 31, 1964, and June 30, 1965

[In millions of dollars]

Item	June 30, 1964 (4,702 banks)	Dec. 31, 1964 (4,773 banks)	June 30, 1965 (4,803 banks)
ASSETS			
Loans and discounts	88,519	95,577	102,059
U.S. Government securities, direct and guaranteed	31,551	33,537	30,323
Securities of States and political subdivisions	17,591	18,592	20,460
Other bonds, notes, and debentures	2,191	2,237	2,439
Total loans and securities	139,852	149,943	155,281
Federal funds sold	761	821	1,059
Direct lease financing	47	81	188
Balances with other banks, and cash items in process of collection	29,513	34,066	31,595
Fixed assets	2,683	2,789	2,893
Customers' liability on acceptances outstanding	609	652	723
Other assets	1,642	1,760	1,860
Total assets	175,107	190,113	193,599
LIABILITIES			
Demand deposits of individuals, partnerships, and corporations	66,030	74,200	68,987
Time and savings deposits of individuals, partnerships, and corporations	61,000	64,763	69,931
Deposits of U.S. Government	5,999	3,787	6,912
Deposits of States and political subdivisions	12,228	13,647	13,941
Deposits of banks	8,648	10,733	9,408
Certified and officers' checks	2,075	2,486	2,349
Total deposits	155,980	169,617	171,528
Demand deposits	89,681	98,660	94,826
Time and savings deposits	66,299	70,957	76,702
Rediscounts and other liabilities for borrowed money	79	299	603
Federal funds purchased	787	827	959
Acceptances executed by or for account of banks and outstanding	620	666	732
Other liabilities	3,344	3,656	3,924
Total liabilities	160,810	175,065	177,746
CAPITAL ACCOUNTS			
Debentures	304	475	814
Capital stock, total	4,190	4,314	4,607
Common stock	4,162	4,286	4,578
Preferred stock	28	28	29
Surplus	6,950	7,207	7,311
Undivided profits	2,491	2,657	2,741
Reserves	362	393	380
Total capital accounts	14,297	15,048	15,853
Total liabilities and capital accounts	175,107	190,113	193,599

Bureau of Customs

The major responsibility of the Bureau of Customs is to administer the Tariff Act of 1930, as amended. Primary duties include the assessment and collection of all duties, taxes, and fees on imported merchandise, the enforcement of customs and related laws, and the administration of certain navigation laws and treaties. As an enforcement organization, it engages in combating smuggling and frauds on the revenue and enforces the regulations of numerous other Federal agencies.

Management improvement program

Special search for economies.—During fiscal 1965, intensive efforts were made to initiate improvements to cope with increasing workloads. These improvements, when fully effective, are expected to result in savings and cost avoidance estimated at more than $1,204,700. Over 40 percent of the total savings realized resulted from progressive policies and measures for reducing backlogs. One substantial reduction, amounting to a cost avoidance of approximately $350,000 was effected by special administrative instructions concerning unappraised invoices on hand over 30 days and filed prior to August 31, 1963.

Management surveys.—*An Evaluation of Mission, Organization and Management of the Bureau of Customs*, a major management survey, was released on March 21, 1965. In the implementation of recommendations in this report, the President on March 25, 1965, submitted Reorganization Plan Number One of 1965 to the Congress. Under this plan which became effective May 25, 1965, all positions previously filled by Presidential appointment in the Bureau of Customs are to be abolished.

The President's plan permits a major reorganization of the customs field structure during the coming year in which administrative and some supervisory functions will be consolidated in nine regional headquarters. This will result in a reduction in the number of district offices and release their personnel to provide improved service to the importing and traveling public. The reorganization, begun in fiscal 1965, is essential because of the Bureau's expanding workload from increased trade and travel.

Much of the management activity throughout the year was concentrated on implementing Treasury Order No. 165-15, effective October 1, 1964[1]. Better functional supervision of the major field programs was achieved by Bureau headquarters reorganization which established four major offices in lieu of seven divisions; and by certain transfers of functions and delineations of responsibilities to improve operational direction and technical advice to field offices. A savings of $75,000 was realized by the adoption of random sampling to verify liquidated formal entries and by improving the review of these entries under an internal check system in the collectors offices.

Essential features of an improved and expanding Training and Career Development Program adopted recently include: A Training and Career Development Council in Bureau headquarters to assist

---

[1] See exhibit 70.

in planning and carrying out a Bureauwide Career Development and Executive Development Program; an Executive Evaluation Board to review the qualifications of applicants for middle management and executive positions; a Servicewide Management Intern Training Program to provide trained people for future assignments; and an intensified Reports Analysis Program in the Bureau headquarters which will be a continuing program covering all customs field activity reports which are prepared to identify, correct, or eliminate weaknesses and problems in field activities. Significant management improvements made at local offices and having possible application at other ports are given servicewide circulation through the periodical "Management Progress Digest." This digest summarizes local improvements and makes provision for furnishing more detailed information to interested offices.

Liquidation of entries.—During fiscal 1965, for the fourth consecutive year, the backlog of formal entries ready for tentative liquidation was reduced very substantially. The number of entries decreased 50.7 percent from 1964 to 144,000 on June 30, 1965. This reduction was achieved by introducing new simplified liquidating procedures and by reassigning entries to districts where the backlog had been eliminated.

Facilitation of international trade.—The number of ports designated for entering antique furniture, claimed free of duty for consumption, has been increased from 10 ports to all ports in 24 collection districts. The designation of these additional ports by the Secretary of the Treasury improves customs service to the importing public and better equalizes the examination workload of customs officers.

The sections of the Customs Regulations pertaining to the administration of the Antidumping Act of 1921 have been amended. The amended regulations make Government policy on antidumping claims more explicit and provide exporters, importers, and domestic industry representatives with additional information regarding evidence produced by interested persons to show either the existence or nonexistence of sales at less than fair value.

An intransit manifest developed jointly by Customs officials of the United States and Canada, may now be used to document merchandise moving in bond from the port of origin to the port of destination through either country. The new procedures permit bonded shipments to transit either country two or more times without additional documentation if the movement is continuous from the original port of entry to the ultimate destination.

Delegations of authority.—The authority of the Commissioner of Customs to sign any decision with respect to claims, fines, or penalties (including forfeitures) arising from violations of Customs laws was increased from $20,000 to $100,000, by a recent Treasury Decision. This permits more expeditious settlement of many major penalty cases and reduces the number of cases referred to the Secretary's office for decision.

To improve and facilitate administration of vessels documented in the United States, collectors of customs have been authorized to delegate authority to deputy collectors in charge of ports of entry to waive requirement for production of recordable instruments of conveyance and approve designation of home ports.

Collectors of customs also were granted authority to satisfy claims of error in admeasurement procedure when the claimant and the collector are in agreement with respect to: The error; the assigned tonnage; and the action to be taken. When there is an unresolved question, the Commissioner of Customs will make the decision. This change will expedite processing claims of error and adjustment of tonnage without jeopardizing the claimant's right to appeal when there is a disagreement.

Legislation.—On June 30, 1965, the Congress enacted major changes[1] in the tourist exemption law for returning residents to be effective on October 1, 1965. The amendments include: The elimination of the privilege of allowing "articles to follow," declared at the time the traveler returns to the United States, to be later admitted free of duty within his exemption; retention of the returning resident's exemption in the amount of $100 based on the aggregate fair retail value of the articles rather than on wholesale value; a provision for a $200 exemption in the case of residents arriving from American Samoa, Guam, and the Virgin Islands of the United States of which no more than $100 may be acquired elsewhere than in the islands; a reduction from one gallon of alcoholic beverages per person to one quart per adult resident with the exception of residents returning from specified insular possessions who retain the one gallon exemption provided that no more than one quart is acquired elsewhere than in the islands; and a provision that the dollar value of the exemptions allowable under the $10 gift section of the tariff act be computed on the basis of the aggregate fair retail value in the country of shipment of the articles.

The elimination of the "articles to follow" privilege will result in some savings to Customs.

Fees and charges.—As part of the program to insure that special services are as self-sustaining as possible, the fees charged for such services were reviewed. As a result, it was determined that three fees were no longer adequate to recover the cost of the services and were increased.

A $6.00 fee was set to recover the administrative and overhead costs involved in processing and issuing a yacht commission. Formerly, any vessel belonging to a regularly organized and incorporated yacht club, licensed as a yacht, and meeting certain other requirements could, upon application, receive a free commission which identified the yacht and its owner during one foreign voyage.

Training and orientation.—During fiscal 1965 technical training was provided to inspectors, examiners, agents, and port investigators in field procedures as well as to management officials in the Bureau headquarters. Within the orientation program, 22 new headquarters employees participated.

As part of the development and refinement of a servicewide training course for all new customs inspectors, a permanent staff of instructors was recruited and trained. The course was shortened from 6 weeks to 4 weeks primarily by providing orientation material to participants before the course began.

---

[1] Public law 89–62.

Forms management.—During fiscal 1965, 31 customs forms were revised, 4 new ones established, 4 consolidated, and 4 abolished. A program is underway to revamp the local forms program in each field office, to reduce their number and to eliminate unnecessary duplication. Based on the special review completed during fiscal 1965 of 156 reporting requirements imposed on the public, 102 forms are being simplified or eliminated. All saleable customs forms are being reviewed to determine whether current prices are adequate to cover costs to the Bureau.

Incentive awards.—To improve the effectiveness of employee participation in the Bureau of Customs Incentive Awards Program several innovations were made. The Customs Regulations were revised to increase the authority of field officers to consider and evaluate local employee suggestions; the average time required to take action on suggestions in the Bureau was reduced from 90 to 60 days; and a followup system was established to insure implementation of adopted suggestions. Tangible savings for fiscal 1965 resulting from adopted suggestions were approximately $72,000, an increase of about 250 percent over fiscal 1964.

Customs cooperation with the Agency for International Development.— The Bureau of Customs and the AID on May 11, 1965, signed a Participating Agency Service Agreement (PASA) for a customs technical assistance corps. Under the terms of the agreement, AID will reimburse Customs for the costs of recruiting and training 12 customs employees for overseas technical assistance assignments and for the costs of program direction and support for the AID assistance projects. The training period will be for approximately one year and those who successfully complete the course will be expected to serve in overseas assignments for a minimum of four years. Prior to the establishment of this program, each request from AID for customs personnel was advertised throughout the Customs Service and the chosen candidate was indoctrinated by AID before reporting overseas. Under this program, Customs will be able to provide well-qualified and trained Customs employees upon request by AID, without the delays formerly encountered.

During the fiscal year, in cooperation with AID, 71 customs officials from 19 foreign countries participated in a Bureau of Customs program of training which included meetings with key officials in Bureau headquarters to discuss management and technical subjects and visits to field offices to observe customs operations.

Work related to cotton textiles.—Upon receipt of directives issued by the President's Cabinet Textile Advisory Committee under the Long-Term Cotton Textile Arrangement, Customs implemented and administered 153 import quotas on cotton textiles and cotton textile products manufactured or produced in various countries; in addition, special visaed invoice requirements were enforced on cotton textiles in specific categories from 3 countries, all 64 categories in the case of 1 country and 1 category each in the case of 2 other countries. Weekly status reports on all the quotas and weekly cumulative import statistics on merchandise in nine categories under observation were furnished the Interagency Textile Administrative Committee for its use.

Collections

Revenue collected by the Customs Service during fiscal 1965, reached an alltime high of $2,062 million, including customs duty collections, excise taxes on imported merchandise collected for the Internal Revenue Service, and certain miscellaneous collections. Larger customs collections than in 1964 were reported by 39 out of the 45 customs districts. Collections and payments by customs districts are shown in table 24. The major classes of all collections by the Customs Bureau are shown in table 25.

More than 36 percent of all imports into the United States during fiscal 1965 were duty free and included commodities imported free for Government stockpile purposes or authorized by special acts of Congress for free entry. The remaining 64 percent constituted the basis of customs duties on imports.

Bureau operations

Carriers and persons entering.—More than 181 million persons were subject to customs inspection in fiscal 1965, a 5.7 percent increase in carriers, and a 4 percent increase in persons entering the United States. as shown in tables 87 and 88.

Entries of merchandise.—The volume and value of imports into the United States continued their rise in fiscal 1965, with total value reaching $19.7 billion. The volume and type of entries handled during the past two years are shown in table 85.

Drawback transactions.—Drawback allowance on the exportation of merchandise manufactured from imported materials and for certain other export transactions usually amounts to 99 percent of the customs duties paid at the time the goods are entered. The total drawback paid in fiscal 1965 as reflected in table 86 by principal commodities was $17,585,376.

Appraisement of merchandise (including Customs Information Exchange).—Invoices filed during fiscal 1965 amounted to 2,841,601, while the number of packages examined by appraisers' personnel totaled 1,875,027.

The backlog of unappraised invoices more than 30 days old declined to 413,829, a decrease of 24.8 percent from fiscal 1964. During the year, 3,203,000 individual line items were verified, each requiring a verification of four factors. Of these, changes were made in roughly 59 percent of the verified elements, a substantial portion of which were of an editorial nature. Substantive changes were necessary in approximately 20 percent of the reports.

Under the Antidumping Act of 1921, as amended (19 U.S.C. 160–171), 22 complaints were received, compared with 27[r] in fiscal 1964. The disposal of 30 cases left 21 under investigation at the end of fiscal 1965. Five cases were referred to the U.S. Tariff Commission for a determination as to possible injury to American industry. Two findings of dumping were made. Two new cases of countervailing duty were received, and three were closed.

---

[r] Revised.

One new case involving convict labor was received during this year and none were closed.

The activities of the Customs Information Exchange in New York, N.Y., continued at approximately the same high level as that of 1964. Appraisers' reports of classification and value, covering a cross section of imported merchandise received at each port, totaled 83,146 compared with 79,000 in 1964.

There were 6,889 reports of value differences during fiscal 1965 as compared with 6,091 in 1964. Differences in classification totaled 7,000 during 1965 compared with 6,947, in 1964, indicating an increase in new commodities received.

Detailed investigations abroad to obtain information for appraisement increased to 231 in fiscal 1965.

Technical services.—The 9 district laboratories and 1 branch laboratory of the Division of Technical Services analyzed over 129,000 samples in fiscal 1965. Despite changes brought about by Tariff Schedules of the United States and an extensive shipping strike, the laboratories analyzed almost 3,000 more samples than during the previous year. Most of these were submitted to the laboratories to assist in appraisement and tariff classification. Other classes analyzed were seizures (mainly narcotics and other prohibited merchandise), samples tested for other Government agencies, and preshipment samples (submitted by importers when requesting the rate of duty on a prospective import). Extensive research was carried out on tests for rubber and fluorspar.

The Division of Technical Services also analyzed cargo sample weighing data to assure accuracy and precision within statistical control limits.

Final approval was made of one bulk weighing and sampling equipment installation and tentative approval given for another. Installation of one truck scale was completed and another is in progress at Boston, Mass. Another was being installed in New York, N.Y., at the end of the fiscal year.

The improvement of U.S. border stations in cooperation with the Immigration and Naturalization Service was continued. Three new stations were completed, two occupied, three under construction, and contracts awarded for seven others during the fiscal year. Construction plans prepared by the General Services Administration for 19 major projects, providing space for Customs, were reviewed and appropriate changes recommended. Such facilities were completed at three locations.

Export control.—The following table compares export control activities in the fiscal years 1964 and 1965.

Activity	1964	1965	Percentage increase, or decrease (−)
Export declarations authenticated	5, 065, 217	5, 308, 272	4. 8
Shipments examined	359, 097	465, 226	29. 6
Number of seizures	403	360	−10. 7
Value of seizures	$421, 778	$336, 105	−20. 3
Export control employees	218	245	12. 4

Protests and appeals.—Protests filed by importers against the rate and amount of duty assessed and appeals for reappraisement filed by importers who did not agree with appraisers as to the value of merchandise are shown in the following table.

Protests and appeals	1964	1965	Percentage increase, or decrease (−)
Protests:			
Filed with collectors by importers (formal)	37, 050	47, 445	28. 1
Filed with collectors by importers (informal)	57, 586	61, 010	5. 9
Appeals for reappraisement filed with collectors	25, 700	24, 071	−6. 3

Marine activities.—During fiscal 1965 one meeting of the Subcommittee on Tonnage Measurement of the Maritime Safety Committee of the Intergovernmental Maritime Consultative Organization (IMCO) and one meeting of its working group were held in London to consider matters affecting the international tonnage measurement of ships. The U.S. delegation to each meeting was led by a Customs representative. The working group initiated and the Subcommittee approved a computer study for assessing parameters proposed by various nations for bases for a universal system of tonnage measurement of ships.

A customs representative, an observer for the United States, attended the first full conference of the Convention for a Uniform System of Tonnage Measurement of Ships since that convention was signed at Oslo on June 10, 1947. The conference, held at Oslo in May, was attended by member delegations from Denmark, the Federal Republic of Germany, Finland. France, Iceland, Israel, the Netherlands, Norway, Poland, and Sweden. Observers represented Italy, Japan, and the United Kingdom, as well as the United States; IMCO, the Panama Canal, and five classification societies were also represented by observers.

The primary purpose of the conference was to amend the tonnage measurement regulations to implement the recommendations on the treatment of shelter-deck and other "open" spaces adopted by the Third Assembly of IMCO. Identical bills, S. 906 and H.R. 3351, sponsored by the Treasury Department were introduced in the 89th Congress to implement the recommendations in the United States.

The United States was particularly interested in the consideration given to the possible relaxing of the 19-percent limit in the Oslo Rules for deductible water-ballast space.

A customs representative again participated in the work of the Group of Experts established by IMCO to study measures to facilitate maritime travel and the transport of goods by sea at its fifth and final session, January 18–22, 1965. The group considered the comments and proposals made by governments concerning a draft Convention on Facilitation of Maritime Traffic, a draft annex to that Convention, and certain draft resolutions.

The draft Convention is intended as the legal foundation for the annex, which contains a number of detailed technical provisions to facilitate maritime traffic and prevent unnecessary delays to ships, passengers, crews, cargoes, and baggage by reducing to a minimum the formalities, documentary requirements, and procedures required in connection with arrivals and departures of ships engaged in international travel.

The group prepared reports on the drafts for the International Conference on Facilitation of Maritime Travel and Transport.

The International Conference on Facilitation of Maritime Travel and Transport, under the auspices of IMCO, convened in London on March 24, 1965. It established and opened for acceptance and signature the Convention and annex referred to in the paragraph above. The annex consists of standards and recommended practices to be followed by governmental authorities with a view to facilitating maritime traffic and simplification of the formalities, documentary requirements, and procedures in connection with arrivals and departures of ships on international voyages. The Conference was attended by delegates from 57 countries, observers from 11, as well as representatives from various intergovernmental and nongovernmental organizations. The 18-member U.S. delegation was led by a Customs representative and included other Treasury and congressional representatives.

The Conference adopted various recommendations designed to furthur the purposes of the Convention and its annex and to provide for future work in facilitating maritime traffic.

A Customs representative also led the U.S. delegation to a meeting of the Group of Experts on Facilitation of International Waterborne Transportation under the auspices of the Organization of American States (OAS) at Lima, Peru, from April 20–24, 1965. After consideration of the comments submitted by various Governments on a preliminary draft of an annex to the Convention of Mar del Plata signed June 7, 1963, by a number of countries including the United States, the Group prepared the final draft. This draft followed the pattern of the annex adopted by the IMCO council mentioned above.

The Permanent Technical Committee on Ports met following the meeting of the Group of Experts and adopted the draft annex. This Committee proposed that a special Inter-American Port and Harbor Conference be convened to consider and act upon their recommendations on the proposed annex, as soon as the Secretary-General of the OAS determines that enough member governments are willing to participate.

Admeasurement.—A total of 4,410 admeasurements of vessels of all sizes and types for all ports were completed during fiscal 1965. In addition there were 360 readmeasurements and adjustments of tonnages of vessels. The total admeasurements for the 2 years were 4,770 and 4,544, respectively.

At the end of fiscal 1965, there were 343 pending applications for measurements of commercial vessels and 310 pending applications for yachts.

Documentation.—Vessels in the American merchant marine documented for commercial use increased to 46,604 in fiscal 1965 while those documented as yachts rose to 12,344. The following table compares the volume of marine documentation during fiscal years 1964 and 1965.

Activity	1964	1965	Percentage increase
Total vessels documented at end of year	56, 549	58, 948	4. 2
Documents issued (registers, enrollments, and licenses)	18, 984	19, 205	1. 2
Licenses renewed and changes of master endorsed	52, 324	53, 841	2. 9
Mortgages, satisfactions, notices of lien, bills of sale, abstracts of title, and other instruments of title recorded	16, 503	17, 542	6. 3
Abstracts of title and certificates of ownership issued	7, 311	7, 744	5. 9
Certificates and permits	1, 550	1, 632	5. 3
Name changes	1, 515	1, 536	1. 4

Legislation.—Treasury Department sponsored bills were introduced in the 89th Congress to simplify the admeasurement of small vessels and to amend the laws relating to admeasurement to permit implementation by the United States of the recommendations adopted by the Assembly of the IMCO on the treatment of shelter-deck and other "open" spaces.

Legislation was again proposed to repeal and amend certain statutes to permit the fixing of charges for various services rendered the public under the navigation laws on the basis of cost to the Government. No action had been taken on these bills at the close of the fiscal year.

The Marine Section in fiscal 1965 began a revision of the codification of the navigation laws in title 46, United States Code, which the Bureau of Customs administers.

Tonnage taxes.—Cyprus and Monaco were added to the list of nations which are exempt from the payment of special tonnage tax and light money.

Waivers.—In a few instances waivers of the coastwise shipping laws and other navigation laws in the interest of national defense were issued upon the request of the Assistant Secretary of Defense or the heads of other agencies of the Government. Novel among these was a waiver of certain of the navigation laws upon request of the Assistant Secretary of Defense to permit the experimental use of two foreign-built hovercraft by the City of Oakland, Calif., between points in the San Francisco Bay area for a period of 20 months.

Entry, clearance, and use of vessels.—Appropriate instructions were issued: To insure observance of the time limitations for the filing of applications for relief from duties assessed on the costs of repairs to and equipment for vessels of the United States obtained in foreign countries; to restate the requirements applicable to the landing of fish by foreign-flag vessels in U.S. ports in certain circumstances; to update and combine in one circular the list of countries having ratified and acceded to the International Load Line Convention of 1930; and to restate the requirement that an unmanned barge under American registry must be accompanied on a foreign voyage by the master whose name is endorsed on its register.

The following table compares entrances and clearances of vessels in fiscal year 1965 with 1964.

Vessel movements	1964	1965	Percentage increase, or decrease (−)
Entrances:			
Direct from foreign ports	48,651	49,426	1.6
Via other domestic ports	40,172	38,071	−5.2
Total	88,823	87,497	−1.5
Clearances:			
Direct to foreign ports	47,386	47,954	1.2
Via other domestic ports	40,091	37,936	−5.4
Total	87,477	85,890	−1.8

Law enforcement and investigative activities

On May 20, 1964, legislation was enacted (16 U.S.C. 1081–1085) "To prohibit fishing in territorial waters of the United States and in certain other areas by vessels other than vessels of the United States and by persons in charge of such vessels." Interim procedures for the enforcement of this law were issued by the Bureau of Customs during fiscal 1965.

Investigations completed.—The Customs Agency Service completed 21,019 investigations during fiscal 1965. The number and types of cases investigated during fiscal years 1964 and 1965 under customs, navigation, and related laws administered and enforced by Customs are shown in table 90.

The most active enforcement regions were: Western (headquarters at Los Angeles, Calif.), with 1,163 arrests and 591 convictions; Southwestern (headquarters at Houston, Tex.), with 616 arrests and 258 convictions; and Northeastern (headquarters at New York, N.Y.), with 284 arrests and 34 convictions.

The following table shows the number of arrests and dispositions thereof during fiscal years 1964 and 1965.

Activity	1964	1965	Percentage increase, or decrease (−)
Under or awaiting indictment at beginning of year	ʳ 620	768	23.9
Arrests	1,801	2,205	22.4
Turned over to other agencies	386	412	6.7
Prosecutions declined	338	354	4.7
Not indicted	14	2	−85.7
Convictions	780	944	21.0
Dismissals and acquittals	115	123	7.0
Nolle prossed	ʳ 20	29	45.0
Under or awaiting indictment at end of year	ᶻ 768	1,109	44.4

ʳ Revised.

Cooperation with other officers.—Officers of the Customs Agency Service cooperated with Federal, State, and local law enforcement agencies and with officials of foreign governments in 7,769 cases compared with 5,470ʳ last year.

ʳRevised.

Seizures, general.—A total of 7,836 seizures (aside from those of narcotics and other drugs) was made by the Customs Agency Service in fiscal 1965, having an appraised value of $16,827,588, while fines and penalties associated with the seizures amounted to $19,441,763.

Seizures, narcotic and other drugs.—The substantial increase in marihuana seizures was concentrated on the California border and involved gangs of Cuban refugees who were engaged in supplying the eastern market tributary to New York City, N.Y., and Miami, Fla.

A record 22 pounds (9,979.20 grams) of cocaine from Chile was seized at New York which led to the ultimate arrest of seven violators in this country and four in Chile. Two seizures of cocaine made at Miami were traced back to a violator who had jumped bail in that city after being convicted in 1961.

The largest seizure (34,629.53 grams) of French heroin ever recorded on the Mexican border by customs officers at Laredo, Tex., was reported in the 1964 annual report, page 89. That offense implicated the head of a gang with powerful political connections who made every effort to obstruct justice and eventually escaped from jail. However, he was recaptured and with three associates extradited to the United States where trial of the four was pending at the end of fiscal 1965.

The following table compares seizures of narcotic drugs and marihuana in 1965 with 1964.

Drug seizures	Fiscal years		Percentage increase, or decrease (−)
	1964	1965	
Narcotic drugs (weight in grams):			
Heroin	ʳ 41, 774. 73	11, 029. 24	−73. 6
Number of seizures	ʳ 210	238	13. 3
Raw opium	13, 021. 71	15, 511. 12	19. 1
Number of seizures	8	11	37. 5
Smoking opium	32, 734. 33	15, 588. 26	−52. 4
Number of seizures	17	16	−5. 9
Others	12, 919. 87	16, 706. 37	29. 3
Number of seizures	ʳ 325	232	−28. 6
Marihuana:			
Bulk (weight in kilograms)	ʳ 3, 200. 726	4, 339. 897	35. 6
Number of seizures	ʳ 584	678	16. 1
Cigarettes (number)	944	841	−10. 9
Number of seizures	ʳ 142	179	26. 1

ʳ Revised.

Work of foreign offices.—European offices of the Bureau supplied 291 information leads which resulted in 98 seizures having an appraised value of $136,000, and fines and penalties amounting to $294,000. Customs offices in the Far East are credited with 31 seizures having an appraised value of $825,000 and fines and penalties totaling $563,000.

A principal activity of all the foreign offices was the investigation of valuation frauds. Especially common in the Far East was the overstating of nondutiable components of inclusive prices, or inventing fictitious nondutiable components. Other violations included failure to declare purchases of expensive jewelry and clothing and the widespread practice by which foreign sellers declare goods sold to tourists as unsolicited gifts.

A significant occurrence during fiscal 1965 was the trial at Los Angeles, Calif., of a firm which had grossly undervalued over 30,000 transistor radios imported from Japan and Okinawa. Government agents and other witnesses were brought from Japan, New York, and Chicago. Both the firm and its vice president were found guilty and fined on 12 counts.

Other irregularities included misdeclarations of national origin, involving such commodities as stockings from Yugoslavia, mink skins from Russia, and jade articles from Communist China. Customs bureau disclosure of abuses with jade articles caused Hong Kong authorities to suspend the issuance of certificates of origin covering this item.

Our Tokyo office reported that while only two new dumping inquiries were initiated during the year, extreme interest in the subject was shown by the Japanese press, industry, and officials, in connection with new customs regulations. A finding of dumping promulgated as the result of an earlier investigation is believed to be the first ever made on a Japanese product.

Customs seizures of merchandise throughout the country during fiscal 1965 for violation of laws enforced by the Customs Service showed an increase of 2.6 percent in the number of seizures and a decrease of 44.1 percent in the appraised value, as compared with fiscal 1964. Details of these seizures by number and value are shown in table 89.

Foreign trade zones

During fiscal 1965 the number of entries received in Foreign Trade Zone No. 1, New York, N.Y., were 6.1 percent less than in fiscal 1964. Other activities in the zone also decreased. Large quantities of dates, machinery, zinc and lead ingots, wool and cotton piece goods, bottled and bulk liquors, chemicals, radios, cameras, Brazil nuts, alligator skins, caviar, talc, and tungsten ore were stored and approximately 7,000 manipulations operations were performed. Thirteen ships used the zone facilities for discharging cargo from foreign countries.

The number of entries received in Foreign Trade Zone No. 2 at New Orleans, La., increased 1.2 percent over last year. The following manipulations operations were performed in the zone: Fumigation of 17 different commodities, commingling, grinding and rebagging of casein, manufacture of lead and lead oxide into battery plates and storage batteries, marking of country of origin on musical instruments, sampling and affixing city and State stamps on whiskey and wine, repackaging of twist drills and packaging of personal and household effects for export, manufacture of wire rope into bridles, cutting of galvanized chain into various lengths, repackaging of bird seed, and destroying of chemical compounds.

Entries received in Foreign Trade Zone No. 3 at San Francisco, Calif., increased 2.8 percent over fiscal 1964, while long tons received in the zone increased 65.4 percent and their value 6.2 percent. There were 933 manipulations operations performed in the zone, an increase of 58.1 percent over last year.

Fiscal 1965 was the first full year of operation for Foreign Trade Subzone No. 3-A, at San Francisco, Calif. This subzone contains a manufacturing plant for the production of semifinished and finished wearing apparel from imported woven wool fabric. Semifinished apparel is cut to pattern and entered into U.S. Customs territory and transferred to a nearby plant operated by this firm where finished apparel is produced for domestic and foreign markets.

Although the number of entries received in Foreign Trade Zone No. 5 at Seattle, Wash., during fiscal 1965, decreased 7.3 percent from the year before, there were substantial increases in the following activities: Long tons received, 127.9 percent; value of goods entering the zone, 108.5 percent; long tons delivered from the zone, 138.1 percent; value of goods delivered from the zone, 135.5 percent; and duties and internal revenue taxes collected, 8.1 percent. Manipulations operations in the zone consisted of converting trucks into campers, cutting steel piling and woolen fabrics into lengths, replacing gaskets and tuning diesel engines, testing and repacking tape recorders, repacking salmon roe, compasses, and microscope parts.

There were substantial increases in the following activities at Foreign Trade Zone No. 7, at Mayaguez, P.R.: Entries received, 318.2 percent; long tons received, 60 percent; value of long tons received, 68.2 percent; long tons delivered from the zone, 153.8 percent; and value of goods delivered from the zone, 231 percent.

The number of entries received at subzone No. 7–A, Penuelas, P.R., during fiscal 1965 increased 200 percent over fiscal 1964. Thirteen ships used the zone facilities for discharging cargo from foreign countries and 10 ships berthed in the zone to lade domestic ship cargo.

There were decreases in all activities at Foreign Trade Zone No. 8, at Toledo, Ohio, with the exception of duties and internal revenue taxes collected which showed an increase of 21.7 percent. Operations in the zone consisted of public warehousing, converting panel trucks to campers, sorting and repacking twist drills, and combining cartons of alcoholic beverages for shipment and recoopering.

The following table summarizes foreign trade zone operations during fiscal 1965.

Trade zone	Number of entries	Received in zone		Delivered from zone		Duties and internal revenue taxes collected
		Long tons	Value	Long tons	Value	
New York	4,965	25,156	$34,804,505	32,354	$32,952,408	$6,555,718
New Orleans	3,038	24,742	10,700,611	25,368	10,781,677	1,247,926
San Francisco	6,689	2,305	3,176,629	2,276	2,568,667	675,372
San Francisco (subzone)	356	170	1,169,970	229	770,655	230,942
Seattle	1,039	1,055	2,466,791	1,055	2,444,229	178,197
Mayaguez	92	24	54,766	33	143,426	2,981
Penuelas (subzone)	36	232,253	3,917,061	133,771	8,365,404	125,941
Toledo	452	14,561	7,923,923	17,363	12,100,535	1,283,635

Customs ports of entry, stations, and airports

The limits of the ports of Aberdeen, Wash.; Muskegon, Mich.; Pascagoula, Miss.; Wrangell, Alaska; and Port Allen, Kauai, Hawaii, were extended and redescribed to include areas not heretofore covered. Changes in customs stations during the year included the designation of Wild Horse, Mont., and Willow Creek, Mont., and the revocation of Havre, Mont. The official port name of Los Angeles, Calif., was changed to Los Angeles-Long Beach, Calif.; and Port Allen, Kauai, Hawaii, was changed to Nawiliwili-Port Allen, Kauai, Hawaii. The designation of the Malone-Dufort Airport, Malone, N.Y., as an international airport was revoked.

Cost of administration

Customs operating expenses amounted to $82,289,912, including export control expenses and the cost of additional inspection reimbursed by the Department of Agriculture.

The following table shows man-year employment data in the fiscal years 1964 and 1965.

Operation	Man-years 1964	Man-years 1965	Percentage increase
Regular customs operations:			
Nonreimbursable	7,792	7,939	1.9
Reimbursable [1]	351	369	5.1
Total regular customs employment	8,143	8,308	2.0
Export control	218	245	12.4
Additional inspection for Department of Agriculture	228	236	3.5
Total employment	8,589	8,789	2.3

[1] Salaries reimbursed to the Government by the private firms who received the exclusive services of these employees.

Office of the Director of Practice

The Office of the Director of Practice is a part of the Office of the Secretary of the Treasury, under the immediate supervision of the General Counsel.

The Director of Practice receives and acts upon applications for enrollment to practice as attorneys or agents before the Internal Revenue Service; institutes and provides for the conduct of disciplinary proceedings relating to enrolled attorneys and agents; makes inquiries with respect to matters under his jurisdiction; and performs such other duties as are necessary or appropriate, or as are prescribed by the Secretary of the Treasury.

Internal reorganization of the Office of the Director of Practice was effected within the fiscal year, with the simultaneous transfer of the functions of the former Enrollment Section into the functionally enlarged and concurrently established Applications Section, which is under the general supervision of an attorney advisor.

During the year the Office put into operation an electronic data processing (magnetic tape) system, for the purpose of maintaining its enrollment and related rosters. This Director of Practice EDP system is being coordinated and further implemented through facilities of the Office of the Treasurer of the United States.

Applications for enrollment approved this year totaled 7,650 (4,098 attorneys and 3,552 agents, consisting of certified public accountants, successful Special Enrollment Examination candidates, and former Internal Revenue Service employees). Approximately 89,000 attorneys and agents were enrolled to practice before the Service at the end of fiscal 1965. Renewed cards issued during the year totaled 6,124, consisting of 2,826 to attorneys and 3,298 to agents.

The Special Enrollment Examination, held in Internal Revenue Service district offices in September 1964, was taken by 797 persons, of whom 480 achieved passing grades. During the year 424 successful examination candidates were enrolled to practice. Examinees have a period of three years in which to file for enrollment after notification of their successful completion of the examination.

The Office processed and closed 362 derogatory information cases during the fiscal year, and had 259 cases under review on June 30, 1965, 89 relating to attorneys, and 170 relating to agents. There were also 173 cases under investigation at the close of the fiscal year, 60 relating to attorneys and 113 relating to agents.

During the year there were 107 cases in which a discipline was imposed by this Office, or from which a related action resulted, such as the withdrawal or abandonment of an application for enrollment while under evaluation, or the acceptance of a resignation from enrollment. In addition, and as a result of disciplinary proceedings instituted by this Office, a hearing examiner imposed two disbarments and one suspension for four months. At the end of the fiscal year one additional case was awaiting trial before a hearing examiner.

Each district director of the Internal Revenue Service has authority to determine that a particular unenrolled person who signs a tax return as preparer is ineligible to exercise the privilege of limited practice without enrollment if the preparer is not of good character or reputation, or if the preparer conducts his practice in an unethical manner. The scope of requirements concerning limited practice without enrollment, applicable to those who prepare and sign Federal income tax returns, is set forth in Revenue Procedure 64-47, which became effective November 1, 1964. A district director's decision of ineligibility under this procedure may be appealed by the unenrolled preparer to the Director of Practice. During the fiscal year 11 such appeals were filed with the Director of Practice by unenrolled preparers of tax returns. In eight of these cases, the district director's decision was affirmed; in one case the decision was modified and affirmed; in one case the decision was reversed; and one appeal is awaiting final action.

Office of Domestic Gold and Silver Operations

The Office of Domestic Gold and Silver Operations, in the Office of the Under Secretary for Monetary Affairs, assists the Under Secretary in the formulation, execution, and coordination of policies and programs relating to gold and silver in both their monetary and commercial aspects. The Office administers the Treasury Department Gold Regulations relating to the purchase, sale, and control of industrial gold, gold coin, and gold certificates; issues licenses and other authorizations for the use, import and export of gold, and for the importation and exportation of gold coin; receives and examines reports of operations; and investigates and supervises the activities of users of gold. Investigations into possible violations of the Gold Regulations are coordinated with the U.S. Secret Service, the Bureau of Customs, and other enforcement agencies.

Gold controls

The comprehensive examination of gold reports, verification of records, and field inspections have been continued.

Purchases of gold for industrial use from the Treasury.—The gross sales of gold for industrial use by the Treasury increased in the calendar year 1964 to 3,665,245 fine troy ounces, as compared with 3,068,345 ounces in calendar year 1963, and 2,746,046 ounces in calendar 1962. Examinations of the books and reports of the gold users, however, continue to show no indication of hoarding or excessive inventories.

Gold coin licensing.—The volume of requests for the importation of gold coin and the cases involving coins acquired abroad without a license by uninformed tourists, continued at a high rate. Their settlement has been expedited to a large extent by the use of form letters and circulars which set forth the conditions governing the importation of gold coins.

End uses of gold.—End-Use Certificates with detailed information concerning the end use of gold were in effect throughout the calendar year 1964. The estimated allocation by use for 1964 is shown in the table below.

Estimated allocation of gold by use for the year 1964

End use	Fine ounces	Dollars, based on $35 per ounce	Percent
Jewelry and arts	2,664,274	$93,249,590	63.39
Dental	550,171	19,255,985	13.09
Space and defense, electrical and electronics	282,020	9,870,700	6.71
Space and defense, other	23,957	838,495	.57
Industrial, electrical, and electronics	432,908	15,151,780	10.30
Industrial, other	249,657	8,737,995	5.94
Total	4,202,987	147,104,545	100.00

Silver legislation

On June 3, 1965, the *Treasury Staff Study of Silver and Coinage* was released reviewing the increasing imbalance between silver supplies and uses and possible alternatives to our present silver coinage. The President transmitted to the Congress a bill providing for a new metallic composition of the 10 cent, 25 cent, and 50 cent pieces; for the purchase of newly-mined domestic silver should the price drop below the monetary price; and for certain standby authorities for the prevention of melting and hoarding of silver coins. Hearings were held on this bill in June 1965 [1] and legislation was enacted on July 23, 1965.[2] The elimination of silver from the 10 cent and 25 cent pieces and the sharply reduced silver content of the 50 cent piece authorized by this legislation will assure maintenance of an ample supply of coinage in the years ahead.

Bureau of Engraving and Printing

The Bureau of Engraving and Printing designs, engraves, and prints U.S. currency, Federal Reserve notes, securities, postage and revenue stamps, and various commissions, certificates, and other forms of engraved work for U.S. Government agencies, as well as bonds and postage and revenue stamps for the governments of various territories administered by the United States.

---

[1] See exhibits 21 and 22.
[2] See exhibit 23.

Management attainments

Throughout the year, the Bureau concentrated on expanding the conversion from wet to dry intaglio printing of currency. A second area for the production of currency, similar to the existing rotary currency area, has been set up. Four new four-plate, sheet-fed rotary intaglio presses of ultramodern design, embodying the latest engineering principles, have been purchased and put into production. Bureau personnel are currently making studies, adjustments, and modifications, as needed, to improve the operating characteristics of the presses and to correct mechanical deficiencies. Associated overprinting presses, processing machines, and equipment have been relocated in this area and are now in operation. Production and processing operations are continually reviewed in an effort to keep production costs to a minimum. A comparison of the base manufacturing cost rate for producing currency 18 subjects to a sheet with a projected rate for producing currency 32 subjects to the sheet on the new presses indicates that annual recurring savings estimated at approximately $3,200,000 will be realized.

In fiscal 1965, there were 632,691 people escorted on guided tours of Bureau operations. To accommodate visitors, the Bureau, over a period of years, has used a trained guide force of as many as 30 employees, most of whom were detailed from the production divisions during the busy tourist season from April to September. Concurrent with the installation of the four new sheet-fed rotary intaglio currency presses and the planning for related processing functions adjacent to these presses, a new and improved tour facility was constructed in which production operations will be described by audio-visual methods. Under the new arrangement, visitors will reach and leave the gallery by means of escalators eliminating the need for personal guide service. It is expected that the installation of this facility will preclude the necessity for detailing employees to the guide force during the tourist season, with a reduction in associated personnel costs of approximately $70,000 annually for the operation of this facility.

In the interest of maintaining efficient and economical operations, the Bureau has carried on intensive research, engineering, and development activities and a continuing program of production and quality control studies.

Financial and management type audits made by the Bureau's internal auditors indicate that Bureau policies have been effectively carried out. There were 25 recommendations outstanding on July 1, 1964. During fiscal 1965, 72 reports of audit, containing 46 additional recommendations, were released. Thirty-six recommendations were outstanding at the close of the year.

Through the excess property program, the Bureau received $2,634 from the sale of obsolete equipment and material declared excess to Bureau needs; and obtained equipment and furniture valued at $25,403 at no charge, through the Federal excess property utilization program.

The Bureau was awarded a certificate of achievement by the National Safety Council for the largest percentage reduction in the 1964 injury frequency rate among 26 printing and publishing establishments. In fiscal 1965, the Bureau initiated a program of offering prescription safety eyeglasses to maintenance employees who require prescription-ground glasses.

Employees were continuously urged to make suggestions for improvements in work processes as an effort toward accomplishment of the President's program to reduce costs and improve productivity. Estimated annual recurring savings of $17,396 and a one-time savings of $1,415 will accrue to the Bureau as a result of suggestions adopted through the incentives award program in fiscal 1965.

During the year, 293 Bureau employees participated in 27 Bureau training sessions; 100 employees completed 46 courses conducted by other Government agencies; and 46 employees attended seminars and training classes sponsored by non-Government organizations.

Estimated savings resulting from management improvements during fiscal 1965 totaled 6 man-years and approximately $88,000 on a recurring annual basis. All savings realized were applied against production costs and were reflected in the Bureau's billing rates to customer agencies.

New issues of postage stamps and deliveries of finished work

New issues of postage stamps delivered by the Bureau in fiscal 1965 are shown in table 91. A comparative statement of deliveries of finished work for the fiscal year 1964 and 1965 appears in table 92.

Finances

Bureau operations are financed by reimbursements to the Bureau of Engraving and Printing fund, as authorized by law. Comparative financial statements follow.

Statement of financial condition June 30, 1965 and 1964

Assets	June 30, 1965	June 30, 1964
Current assets:		
Cash:		
On hand	$824	$12
With the Treasury	4,427,824	5,333,878
Accounts receivable [1]	4,215,264	2,564,730
Inventories: [2]		
Finished goods	1,238,819	1,940,984
Work in process	3,412,963	3,649,869
Raw materials	684,501	969,258
Stores	1,021,704	1,044,655
Prepaid expenses	83,493	57,176
Total current assets	15,085,392	15,560,562
Fixed assets: [3]		
Plant machinery and equipment	21,767,112	20,116,698
Motor vehicles	160,616	146,665
Office machines	259,173	251,174
Furniture and fixtures	489,607	468,778
Dies, rolls, and plates	3,955,961	3,955,961
Building appurtenances	3,143,755	2,676,807
Fixed assets under construction	410,342	295,267
	30,186,566	27,911,350
Less accumulated depreciation	14,980,051	13,730,821
	15,206,515	14,180,529
Excess fixed assets (written down to 20% and 10% of book value, 1965 and 1964, respectively)	4,466	455
Total fixed assets	15,210,981	14,180,984
Deferred charges	156,050	147,119
Total assets	30,452,423	29,888,665

Footnotes at end of table.

Statement of financial condition June 30, 1965 and 1964—Continued

Liabilities and investment of the United States	June 30, 1965	June 30, 1964
Liabilities:		
Accounts payable	$736, 851	$1, 116, 028
Accrued liabilities:		
Payroll [4]	1, 919, 346	1, 142, 553
Accrued leave	1, 821, 655	1, 685, 726
Other	214, 307	136, 905
Trust and deposit liabilities	800, 453	624, 930
Other liabilities [4]	11, 510	307
Total liabilities [5]	5, 504, 122	4, 706, 449
Investment of the U.S. Government:		
Appropriation from U.S. Treasury	3, 250, 000	3, 250, 000
Donated assets, net [3]	22, 000, 930	22, 000, 930
	25, 250, 930	25, 250, 930
Accumulated earnings, or deficit (−) [6]	−302, 629	−68, 714
Total investment of the U.S. Government	24, 948, 301	25, 182, 216
Total liabilities and investment of the U.S. Government	30, 452, 423	29, 888, 665

[1] Accounts receivable at June 30, 1965, include $134,242 representing the value of finished goods and work in process inventories destroyed as a result of a fire as well as miscellaneous expenses incurred in connection thereto. A claim of negligence assessed against the contractor engaged in a construction project at the time of the fire was pending at the close of the fiscal year.

[2] Finished goods and work in process inventories are valued at cost, including administrative and service overhead. Except for the distinctive paper which is valued at the acquisition cost, raw materials and stores inventories are valued at the average cost of the materials and supplies on hand.

[3] Plant machinery and equipment, furniture and fixtures, office machines, and motor vehicles acquired on or before June 30, 1950, are stated at appraised values. Additions since June 30, 1950, and all building appurtenances are valued at acquisition cost. The Act of Aug. 4, 1950 (31 U.S.C. 181a) which established the Bureau of Engraving and Printing fund specifically excluded land and buildings valued at about $9,000,000 from the assets of the fund. Also excluded are appropriated funds of about $6,765,000 expended or transferred to GSA for extraordinary expenses in connection with uncapitalized building repairs and air conditioning. Dies, rolls, and plates were capitalized at July 1, 1951, on the basis of average unit costs of manufacture, reduced to recognize their estimated useful life. Since July 1, 1951, all costs of dies, rolls, and plates have been charged to operations in the year acquired.

[4] Accrued payroll and other liabilities at June 30, 1965, include $207,211 and $9,113, respectively, for claimed retroactive overtime pay due building guards or the estates of deceased building guards for services performed during the period October 1954–October 1964 in accordance with Comptroller General's Decision B–155197, dated Oct. 8, 1964, and Mar. 17, 1965. A contingent liability of an undetermined amount exists for former guards who may file claims.

[5] In addition, outstanding commitments with suppliers for unperformed contracts and undelivered purchase orders totaled $7,264,767 as of June 30, 1965, as compared with $7,906,174 at June 30, 1964; unperformed contracts at both dates include $2,177,087, representing the balance due for a prototype multicolor postage stamp web-fed intaglio printing press to be delivered in fiscal year 1966. The balance for the most part represents annual term contracts for materials and supplies for delivery in the ensuing fiscal year

[6] See following page, footnote 3.

Statement of income and expense, fiscal years 1965 and 1964

Income and expense	1965	1964
Operating revenue: Sales of engraving and printing	$31,028,383	$26,424,992
Operating costs:		
Cost of sales:		
Direct labor	12,004,970	10,099,336
Direct materials used	4,852,260	4,242,064
Prime cost	16,857,230	14,341,400
Overhead costs:		
Salaries and indirect labor [1]	8,968,383	8,165,638
Factory supplies	1,188,731	1,191,023
Repair parts and supplies	316,596	310,949
Employer's share personnel benefits	1,458,417	1,386,242
Rents, communications, and utilities	528,105	503,736
Other services	319,651	253,081
Depreciation and amortization	1,706,814	1,601,022
Gains (−), or losses on disposal or retirement of fixed assets	29,675	−2,634
Sundry expense (net)	56,037	46,531
Total overhead	14,572,409	13,455,588
Total costs [2]	31,429,639	27,796,988
Less:		
Nonproduction costs:		
Shop costs capitalized	424,564	369,331
Cost of miscellaneous services rendered other agencies	547,606	479,177
Cost of special services rendered—fire	2,242	
	974,412	848,508
Cost of production	30,455,227	26,948,480
Net increase (−), or decrease in finished goods and work in process inventories from operations	807,071	−490,894
Cost of sales	31,262,298	26,457,586
Operating profit, or loss (−)	−233,915	−32,594
Nonoperating revenue:		
Operation and maintenance of incinerator and space utilized by other agencies	469,767	421,323
Other direct charges for miscellaneous services	77,839	57,854
Claim receivable for fire loss	134,242	
	681,848	479,177
Nonoperating costs:		
Cost of miscellaneous services rendered other agencies	547,606	479,177
Cost of special services rendered—fire	2,242	
Work in process and finished goods inventory loss due to fire	132,000	
	681,848	479,177
Net profit, or loss (−) for the year [3]	−233,915	−32,594

[1] Includes $216,324 in 1965 to cover the cost of retroactive overtime pay for building guards, most of which was applicable to prior years.

[2] No amounts are included in the accounts of the fund for (1) interest on the investment of the Government in the Bureau of Engraving and Printing fund, (2) depreciation on the Bureau's buildings excluded from the assets of the fund by the Act of Aug. 4, 1950, and (3) certain costs of services performed by other agencies on behalf of the Bureau.

[3] The Act of Aug. 4, 1950, provided that customer agencies make payment to the Bureau at prices deemed adequate to recover all costs incidental to performing work or services requisitioned. Any surplus accruing to the fund in any fiscal year is to be paid into the general fund of the Treasury as miscellaneous receipts except that any surplus is applied first to restore any impairment of capital by reason of variations between prices charged and actual costs.

Statement of source and application of funds, fiscal years 1965 and 1964

Funds provided and applied	1965	1964
Funds provided:		
Sales of engraving and printing	$31, 028, 383	$26, 424, 992
Operation and maintenance of incinerator and space utilized by other agencies	469, 767	421, 323
Other direct charges for miscellaneous services	77, 839	57, 854
Claim receivable for fire loss	134, 242	
	31, 710, 231	26, 904, 169
Less cost of sales and service (excluding depreciation and other charges not requiring expenditure of funds: Fiscal year 1965, $1,736,489; fiscal year 1964, $1,598,388)	30, 207, 657	25, 338, 375
	1, 502, 574	1, 565, 794
Sale of surplus equipment	6, 430	17, 810
Decrease in working capital	1, 272, 843	734, 551
Total funds provided	2, 781, 847	2, 318, 155
Funds applied:		
Acquisition of fixed assets	2, 706, 967	2, 245, 012
Acquisition of experimental equipment; and plant repairs and alterations to be charged to future operations	74, 880	73, 143
Total funds applied	2, 781, 847	2, 318, 155

Fiscal Service

BUREAU OF ACCOUNTS

Functions of the Bureau of Accounts have Government-wide scope. They include central accounting and financial reporting; disbursing for virtually all civilian agencies; supervising the Government's depositary system; determining qualifications of insurance companies to do surety business with Government agencies; a variety of fiscal activities such as investment of trust funds, agency borrowings from the Treasury, and international claims and indebtedness; and Treasury staff representation in the Joint Financial Management Improvement Program.

Management improvement

Annual recurring savings of $1,056,000 were realized from the continuing management improvement program during fiscal 1965, attributable to further improvements in technology and systems, major realignments of organization and staffing, and the fruits of the continuing programs for the development of people in management skills at all levels.

Systems improvement

Bureau staff continued to represent Treasury on the steering committee and survey teams of the Joint Financial Management Improvement Program. Primary attention was given to assisting Government agencies to improve advance financing practices through letters of credit, pursuant to Department Circular No. 1075. (For details on the purpose of this circular, see 1964 annual report, page 101.)

More than 1,500 letters of credit were issued in fiscal year 1965 by the Departments of Agriculture; Labor; and Health, Education, and Welfare; Office of Economic Opportunity; National Aeronautics and Space Administration; National Science Foundation; Agency for International Development; and Atomic Energy Commission. Letters of credit were also utilized by the Treasury Department in making U.S. subscriptions to the International Monetary Fund and contributions to programs of the Inter-American Development Bank. Total disbursements drawing down letters of credit in fiscal 1965 exceeded $1.3 billion. The Office of Civil Defense, the State Department, and the Department of the Interior plan to use the procedure in fiscal 1966.

Department Circular No. 918, which regulates the withholding of State income taxes by Federal agencies, was supplemented to modify timing of payments and filing of tax returns. Agreements for withholding taxes were concluded with Arkansas, Kansas, and Rhode Island. These cooperative arrangements are now in effect for 30 States, including the District of Columbia.

Other systems work during the year included various studies to improve central accounting operations, administrative accounting procedures, and internal financial reporting. At the end of fiscal 1965, work was in process on a consolidated manual of all Treasury regulations on central accounting, reporting, and other fiscal matters, for the guidance of all Federal agencies. This manual covers certain prescribed forms and procedures which have been, or will be, dropped from titles 6 and 7 of the *General Accounting Office Policy and Procedures Manual for Guidance of Federal Agencies.*

Central accounting and reporting

Consolidation of the central accounting and central reporting organizations in April 1964 was instrumental in achieving considerable progress during fiscal 1965 toward maximum integration of the central accounting and reporting operations by use of the Bureau's EDP equipment originally acquired for disbursing work. The central accounts are now entirely in the computer system. A number of financial report operations have been so converted, including several tables in the monthly statement of receipts and expenditures. Computer programs for other tables appearing in this monthly report and other reports are expected to be developed and installed in fiscal year 1966. This looks to the capability for computer printouts of "camera" copies, for use in reproducing certain major Government-wide financial reports.

Department Circular No. 966, which covers business-type financial statements, was revised to update Treasury requirements for descriptive narrative submissions on the source of data included in statements; an explanation of accounting bases, principles, and standards; and the nature of underlying assets and liabilities. A completely new set of regulations was in process at the end of fiscal 1965 and is targeted for completion in fiscal 1966, to amalgamate all prior modifications, define terms more precisely, and achieve greater conformity between the agencies, the Bureau of the Budget, and the Treasury in the treatment of a wide variety of accounting transactions.

The reservation of foreign currencies on an unfunded basis continued to yield benefits to the Government through its favorable impact on cash financing costs and the balance of payments.   Amendment No. 1 to Department Circular 930, Revised, establishing regulations for further unfunding of foreign currencies, was issued during the year.

A total of 3,528,041 accounting items was processed by the central and regional offices through the central accounting system during fiscal 1965, a slight increase over the preceding year.

Internal auditing

Twenty audits of Bureau and nonbureau activities were begun during the fiscal year; two were in progress at yearend.   Thirteen of these audits were of fiscal functions, five of management operations, and two included both areas.

General coordination and staff assistance were furnished for the annual audit of the Exchange Stabilization Fund.   Also, an auditor was loaned to the Internal Audit Division, Office of the Secretary, for their audit of the administrative accounts of the Office of the Secretary.

Disbursing operations

The average unit cost for all disbursing operations reached a low of 2.98 cents in fiscal 1965; the unit cost in fiscal 1964 was 3.05 cents.[1] These figures cover the cost of all goods and services consumed in the central disbursing function, including depreciation of owned equipment in relation to the quantities of checks and savings bonds produced. (It does not include the cost of postage, which has no bearing on operational efficiency in the disbursing functions.)   Productivity per employee increased by 10 percent in 1965 over 1964.

During the year 11 regional disbursing offices were in operation, servicing over 1,500 offices of agencies.   Certain foreign service posts in Central and South America and the Far East also received disbursing services from the Washington and Manila regional offices, respectively.

More than 93 percent of all of the Bureau's checks and bonds were produced on computers, as conversions of payments to electronic data processing continued during the year.

A centralized electronic microfilm system was installed in the Chicago regional office, resulting in considerable savings.   This system produces microfilm records directly from data on magnetic tapes generated by the six largest regional disbursing offices.

Special machines for preparing checks for miscellaneous payments, using a heat transfer process, which imprint payee information on checks directly from vouchers submitted by the agencies, were installed in the 8 regional disbursing offices within the 48 contiguous States. Substantial savings result from the elimination of check typing and proofreading work in this area of the Division of Disbursement's operations.

---

[1] The unit cost of 3 11 cents shown in the 1964 annual report, page 102, did not include disbursing activities financed by reimbursements from certain agencies.

There follows a comparision of the fiscal year 1964 with the 1965 workload.

Classification	Volume	
	1964	1965
Operations financed by appropriated funds:		
Checks:		
Social security benefits	189, 431, 084	198, 593, 859
Veterans' benefits	62, 721, 888	68, 976, 138
Income tax refunds	42, 353, 609	39, 841, 453
Veterans' national service life insurance dividends	4, 406, 015	4, 279, 794
Other	45, 932, 888	40, 209, 189
Savings bonds issued	5, 087, 062	5, 500, 741
Adjustments and transfers	111, 758	54, 371
Total workload financed by appropriated funds	350, 049, 304	357, 455, 545
Operations financed by reimbursements:		
Railroad Retirement Board	12, 267, 997	12, 153, 862
Department of Agriculture (ACP)	360, 615	
Bureau of the Public Debt (certain savings bonds)	798, 670	850, 453
Total workload-reimbursable items	13, 427, 282	13, 004, 315
Total workload	363, 476, 586	370, 459, 860

Deposits, investments, and related activities

Federal depositary system.—The types of depositary services and number of commercial banking institutions authorized to provide each service, as of June 30, 1965, are shown in the following table.

Type of service provided by depositaries	Number of banking institutions
Receive proceeds of deposits by taxpayers and from sale of public debt securities, for credit in Treasury tax and loan accounts	12, 186
Receive deposits from district directors of internal revenue, military finance officers, and other Government officers	1, 036
Maintain official checking accounts of postmasters, clerks of U.S. courts, and other Government officers	5, 780
Furnish bank drafts to Government officers in exchange for collections	2, 250
Service State unemployment compensation benefit payments and clearing accounts	56
Operate limited banking facilities at military installations:	
In the United States and its outlying areas	274
Foreign	153

Investments.—Government trust funds are invested in marketable U.S. securities and special securities issued for purchase by the major trust funds as authorized by law. During the year legislation was enacted to authorize the Secretary of the Treasury to invest two additional funds.

Legislation approved October 13, 1964 (38 U.S.C. 725(b)), established the veterans' reopened insurance fund, which permits certain veterans to reinstate national service life insurance, and authorizes the Secretary of the Treasury to sell to the fund special interest-bearing securities of the United States. These special securities bear interest at a rate equal to the average market yield on marketable U.S. securities not due or callable until after the expiration of four years.

The District of Columbia judicial retirement and survivors annuity fund was established under legislation approved October 13, 1964 (78 Stat. 1061). The Secretary of the Treasury is authorized to invest this fund in interest-bearing securities of the United States or Federal farm loan bonds.

Table 66 shows the holdings of public debt and agency securities by Government agencies and accounts.

Loans by the Treasury.—The Bureau administers loan agreements with those Government corporations and agencies that have authority to borrow from the Treasury to finance certain programs. Legislation was enacted during the year authorizing borrowing to finance parking facilities for the John F. Kennedy Center for the Performing Arts, established January 23, 1964 (78 Stat. 5). The Board of Regents of the Smithsonian Institution is authorized to sell to the Secretary of the Treasury revenue bonds which are to be retired by the Board from parking facility revenues. Tables 108, 109, and 110 show the status of Treasury loans to Government corporations and agencies as of June 30, 1965.

Surety bonds.—Executive agencies are required by law to obtain blanket, position schedule, or other types of surety bonds covering those employees required to be bonded. Legislative and judicial branches are permitted by law to follow the same procedure. The Secretary of the Treasury issues certificates of authority, renewable each June 1, to corporate sureties that are qualified to execute bonds in favor of the United States. A total of 259 companies held such certificates as of June 30, 1965 (published annually in the *Federal Register* in relation to Department Circular 570, Revised). A summary of bonding activities of Government agencies follows:

Number of officers and employees covered on June
30, 1965_____   976,961
Aggregate penal sums of bonds procured_____ $3,511,234,300
Total premiums paid by Government in fiscal year
1965 _____ $229,997
Administrative expenses in fiscal year 1965_____ $45,932

Foreign indebtedness

World War I.—Following an agreement with the Government of Greece on May 28, 1964, legislation was introduced to authorize the acceptance of a settlement of the World War I indebtedness of Greece and the use of the payments to finance a mutual cultural and educational exchange program. The legislative proposal was pending in the Congress at yearend.

The Government of Finland made total payments of $374,645 during fiscal 1965, which were used to finance educational exchange programs with that Government (22 U.S.C. 2455(e)). For the status of all World War I indebtedness see tables 103 and 104.

World War II.—U.S. dollar payments of $49 million (including the U.S. dollar value of returned lend-lease silver) and the equivalent of $13 million in local currencies were received from debtor governments, under lend-lease and surplus property sales agreements. See table 106 for the status of the lend-lease and surplus property accounts administered by the Treasury.

Credit to the United Kingdom.—Although there was a deferral of the principal and interest installment due December 31, 1964 (under the financial aid agreement of December 6, 1945, as amended March 6, 1957) the United Kingdom paid previously deferred principal and interest installments, and interest thereon, totaling $3.8 million. Cumulative payments total $1,389.6 million, of which $788.7 million is interest. The unmatured principal balance is $3,149.1 million; deferred interest installments outstanding amount to $201.8 million.

Payment of claims against foreign governments

Mixed Claims Commission, U.S. and Germany.—The Federal Republic of Germany paid $4 million during the year under the agreement of February 27, 1953, enabling a further distribution to be made to holders of awards certified by the Mixed Claims Commission on claims arising from World War I. Table 93 shows the status of the claims fund.

Foreign Claims Settlement Commission.—The fifth installment of $2 million was received from the Polish Government under the July 16, 1960, agreement. These payments will be used to settle claims of American nationals against Poland which have been adjudicated by the Foreign Claims Settlement Commission. The Commission expects to complete adjudication of these claims by March 31, 1966. Payments up to $1,000 were made during the year on each award certified to the Treasury by the Commission.

During the year the Commission began certifying to the Treasury those claims filed under the War Claims Act of 1948, as amended. The Treasury received $75 million for payment of these awards; additional amounts will become available through the U.S. sale of seized assets of German and Japanese nationals, including substantial sums realized from the sale of General Aniline and Film Corp. stock. The deadline for filing claims with the Commission was January 15, 1965. Payments of awards made due to death and personal injury were authorized and begun in fiscal 1965. See table 94.

Defense lending

Effective with the close of fiscal year 1964, the Office of Defense Lending was abolished and its functions transferred to the Commissioner of Accounts, pursuant to Treasury Department Order No. 185-2, dated June 24, 1964.[1]

Defense Production Act.—No new loans to private businesses were made during the year under section 302 of the Defense Production Act of 1950, as amended. Loans outstanding were reduced from $17.9 million to $16.7 million during fiscal 1965. Further transfers of $1.7 million were made to the account of General Services Administration, Revolving Fund, Defense Production Act, from the net earnings accumulated since inception of the program, bringing the total of these transfers to $16.5 million.

Federal Civil Defense Act.—The remaining deferred participation commitments under section 409 of the Federal Civil Defense Act were liquidated during fiscal 1965 and outstanding loans reduced to $509,-994. Notes payable to the Treasury were reduced $71,091 to a total of $33,909, and interest payments of $3,246 were made during the year.

---

[1] See 1964 annual report, exhibit 54, p. 374.

Liquidation of Reconstruction Finance Corporation assets.—The Secretary of the Treasury's responsibility in the liquidation of RFC assets relates to completing the liquidation of business loans and securities with individual balances of $250,000 or more as of June 30, 1957, securities of and loans to railroads, securities of financial institutions, and the windup of corporate affairs. Net income and proceeds of liquidation amounting to $606,134 were paid into the Treasury as miscellaneous receipts in fiscal 1965, making a cumulative total of $53.7 million since July 1, 1957. Total unliquidated assets as of June 30, 1965, had a gross book value of $5.5 million.

Depositary receipts

The following table shows the volume of depositary receipts for the fiscal years 1960–65. A description of the depositary receipt procedure is contained on page 141 of the 1962 annual report.

Fiscal year	Income and social security	Railroad retirement taxes	Federal excise taxes	Total
1960	9,469,057	10,625	598,881	10,078,563
1961	9,908,068	10,724	618,971	10,537,763
1962	10,477,119	10,262	610,026	11,097,407
1963	11,161,897	9,937	619,519	11,791,353
1964	11,729,243	9,911	633,437	12,372,591
1965	12,012,385	9,859	644,753	12,666,997

NOTE.—Comparable data for 1944–59 will be found in the 1962 annual report, page 141.

Government losses in shipment

Claims totaling $44,210.04 were paid from the revolving fund established by the Government Losses in Shipment Act, as amended. Details of operations under this act are shown in table 114.

Other operations

Withheld foreign checks.—On November 9, 1964, Department Circular 655 was completely revised to incorporate into one document the original circular dated March 19, 1941, and the 14 later supplements.

Donations and contributions.—Bureau receipts deposited into the Treasury during the year as "conscience fund" contributions amounted to $18,441.15. Other unconditional donations totaled $651,863.05; such receipts by other Government agencies amounted to $9,479.77. Conditional gifts to further the defense effort amounted to $150,822.19. Gifts of money and the proceeds of real or personal property donated in fiscal 1965 for the purpose of reducing the public debt amounted to $709,777.35, of which $706,707.35 was used to purchase and retire public debt securities.

BUREAU OF THE PUBLIC DEBT

The Bureau of the Public Debt, in support of the management of the public debt, has responsibility for the preparation of Treasury Department circulars offering public debt securities, the direction of the handling of subscriptions and making allotments, the formulation of instructions and regulations pertaining to each security issue, the issuance of the securities, and the conduct or direction of transactions in those outstanding. The Bureau is responsible for the final audit and custody of retired securities, the maintenance of the control accounts covering all public debt issues, the keeping of individual accounts with owners of registered securities and authorizing the issue of checks in payment of interest thereon, and the handling of claims on account of lost, stolen, destroyed, or mutilated securities.

The Bureau's principal office and headquarters is in Washington, D.C. Offices also are maintained in Chicago, Ill., and Parkersburg, W. Va., where most Bureau operations related to U.S. savings bonds are handled. Under Bureau supervision many transactions in public debt securities are conducted by the Federal Reserve banks and their branches as fiscal agents of the United States. Selected post offices, private financial institutions, industrial organizations, and others (approximately 19,200 in all) cooperate in the issuance of savings bonds.

Management improvement

The EDP system in the Parkersburg office was expanded and updated by the acquisition of two new system components, which have increased efficiency and permitted the conversion to electronics of operations previously performed either manually or on other types of equipment.

The fees due paying agents who redeem savings bonds are now being computed electronically, and check issue information is supplied to the Regional Disbursing Office on magnetic tape. Statistical reports of employee participation in company-operated payroll savings plans are also being developed electronically. Both of these operations were previously performed on conventional tabulating equipment in the Washington office.

Accounting and statistical documents now prepared on the computer include the permanent receipts for shipments of stubs and bonds, advices of adjustment covering individual differences disclosed in the audit of stub and bond transmittals, certain machine utilization and personnel production reports, and cash accounting reports.

An EDP programming refinement has substantially reduced tape requirements for the maintenance of the consolidated file reflecting alphabetic data and bond identification data, both of which are compacted under a new tape format. This permits more frequent inquiry searches with no increase in machine time.

Additional operating economies were effected in the Parkersburg office through the installation of a revised procedure for correcting mispunched registration stubs, the replacement of manual film readers with automatic reader-printers, and a revision in the stub adjustment procedure which eliminated the typing of substitute registration stubs.

Joint projects were instituted with three large Government issuing agents using computers to inscribe Series E savings bonds, with a view to having these agents furnish issue data on magnetic tape and microfilm, rather than through the submission of registration stubs. Following a successful trial period, the Navy Department, Bureau of Supplies and Accounts will convert to this system early in fiscal 1966. The projects with the other agents are being continued.

Authority was delegated to the Federal Reserve banks and branches to redeem bearer Treasury bonds of eligible issues presented in payment of Federal estate taxes and to remit the proceeds to the appropriate district director of Internal Revenue. This decentralization will result in operating economies as well as improved service to the public.

The accounting records of the Division of Retired Securities were revised to eliminate certain control accounts and reduce maintenance detail by more extensively using basic data in the public debt accounts. Changes were also made in the method of preparation and the arrangement of destruction schedules, thereby facilitating the preparation of the schedules and the selection of items to be destroyed.

Bureau operations

The extent of the change in the composition of the public debt is one measure of the Bureau's work. The debt falls into two broad categories: public issues and special issues. Public issues consist of marketable Treasury bills, certificates of indebtedness, notes, and bonds; and nonmarketable securities, chiefly U.S. savings bonds and Treasury bonds of the investment series. Special issues of certificates, notes, and bonds are made by the Treasury directly to various Government trust and certain other accounts and are payable only for these accounts.

During the year, 24,297 individual accounts covering publicly held registered securities other than U.S. savings bonds and retirement plan bonds were opened and 32,510 were closed. This reduced the number of open accounts to 215,020 covering registered securities in the principal amount of $12,559 million. There were 410,913 interest checks with a value of $409,373,018 issued during the year.

Redeemed and canceled securities other than savings bonds and retirement plan bonds received for audit included 5,517,912 bearer securities and 711,609 registered securities. Coupons totaling 17,471,487 were received.

A summary of public debt operations handled by the Bureau appears on pages 17 to 29 of this report and in tables 29–57.

U.S. savings bonds.—The issuance and redemption of savings bonds results in a heavy administrative burden for the Bureau of the Public Debt, involving: Maintenance of alphabetical and numerical ownership records for the 2.7 billion bonds issued since 1935; adjudication of claims for lost, stolen, and destroyed bonds (which totaled 2.0 million pieces on June 30, 1965); and the handling and recording of retired bonds.

Detailed information on sales, accrued discount, and redemption of savings bonds will be found in tables 48 to 50, inclusive.

There were 98.4 million stubs representing the issuance of Series E bonds received for registration, making a grand total of 2,649.6 million, including reissues, received through June 30, 1965.

All registration stubs of Series E savings bonds and all retired Series E savings bonds are microfilmed, audited, and destroyed, after required permanent record data are prepared by an EDP system in the Parkersburg office. Prior to the establishment of that office these savings bond operations were performed in several Bureau offices manually and on tabulating equipment. The following table shows the status of processing operations in the Parkersburg office.

Fiscal year	Received	Microfilmed	Keypunched	Converted to magnetic tape	Audited and classified	Destroyed	Balance			
							Unfilmed	Not keypunched	Not converted to magnetic tape	Unaudited
Stubs of issued card type Series E savings bonds [in millions of pieces]										
1958-60	234.2	230.7	227.4	227.2	225.2	58.3	3.5	6.8	7.0	9.0
1961	88.7	90.7	92.4	92.2	92.9	154.4	1.5	3.1	3.5	4.8
1962	91.0	90.2	88.7	89.1	88.9	154.1	2.3	5.4	5.4	6.9
1963	94.3	93.9	95.0	95.0	93.0	69.6	2.7	4.7	4.7	8.2
1964	100.1	98.2	97.6	97.6	98.4	96.2	4.6	7.2	7.2	9.9
1965	98.4	100.7	101.1	101.1	101.7	123.7	2.3	4.5	4.5	6.6
Total	706.7	704.4	702.2	702.2	700.1	656.3	---------	-----------	-----------	---------
Retired card type Series E savings bonds [in millions of pieces]										
1958-60	117.9	116.5	114.4	113.3	112.5	20.6	1.4	3.5	4.6	5.4
1961	59.7	60.6	61.5	62.4	62.8	93.0	.5	1.7	1.9	2.3
1962	62.4	61.3	61.1	61.1	60.3	95.0	1.6	3.0	3.2	4.4
1963	64.9	64.3	64.1	64.3	63.5	48.3	2.2	3.8	3.8	5.8
1964	70.1	70.0	68.9	68.9	69.1	83.4	2.3	5.0	5.0	6.8
1965	75.3	75.9	77.1	76.8	76.9	59.8	1.7	3.2	3.5	5.2
Total	450.3	448.6	447.1	446.8	445.1	400.1	---------	-----------	-----------	---------
Retired paper type Series E savings bonds [in millions of pieces]										
1962	0.8	0.8	0.7	0.7	0.7	--------		0.1	0.1	0.1
1963	21.8	21.2	20.8	20.8	19.9	5.1	0.6	1.1	1.1	2.0
1964	22.4	22.4	22.1	22.1	22.3	23.4	.6	1.4	1.4	2.1
1965	20.4	20.5	21.0	20.9	21.2	11.0	.5	.8	.9	1.3
Total	65.4	64.9	64.6	64.5	64.1	39.5	---------	-----------	-----------	---------

Of the 91.3 million Series A-E savings bonds redeemed and received by the Bureau during the year, 89.0 million (97.4 percent) were redeemed by approximately 16,200 authorized paying agents. These agents were reimbursed quarterly at the rate of 15 cents each for the first 1,000 bonds paid and 10 cents each for all over the first 1,000, for a total of $11,522,472 and an average of 12.95 cents per bond.

The following table shows the number of savings bonds outstanding as of June 30, 1965, by series and denomination.

Series [1]	Total	Denomination (in thousands of pieces)										
		$10	$25	$50	$75	$100	$200	$500	$1,000	$5,000	$10,000	$100,000
E	467,158	716	247,381	106,480	1,030	78,730	8,051	12,013	12,709	------	46	2
H	6,884							2,634	3,832	324	95	
A	2		1	(*)		1		(*)	(*)			
B	3		1	1		1		(*)	(*)			
C	9		3	2		3		1	1			
D	46		17	9		13		3	4			
F	49		21			15		4	8	1	(*)	
G	120					59		23	36	2	(*)	
J	332		60			115		34	89	13	20	(*)
K	366							95	204	32	34	1
Total	474,969	716	247,484	106,492	1,030	78,937	8,051	14,807	16,883	372	195	3

* Less than 500 pieces.
[1] Currently only bonds of Series E and H are on sale.

The following table shows the number of issuing and paying agents for Series A–E savings bonds by classes.

June 30	Post offices [1]	Banks	Building and savings and loan associations	Credit unions	Companies operating payroll plans	All others	Total
			Issuing agents				
1945	24,038	15,232	3,477	2,081	[2] 9,605	(2)	54,433
1950	25,060	15,225	1,557	522	3,052	550	45,966
1955	2,476	15,692	1,555	428	2,942	588	23,681
1960	1,093	16,436	1,851	320	2,352	643	22,695
1961	1,061	13,505	1,617	285	2,045	590	[3] 19,103
1962	1,046	13,559	1,670	281	1,978	573	19,107
1963	1,011	13,644	1,679	269	1,857	560	19,020
1964	977	13,908	1,702	252	1,783	528	19,150
1965	943	14,095	1,702	246	1,695	510	19,191
			Paying agents				
1945		13,466					13,466
1950		15,623	874	137		57	16,691
1955		16,269	1,188	139		56	17,652
1960		17,127	1,797	169		60	19,153
1961		13,670	1,605	158		16	[3] 15,449
1962		13,687	1,690	160		16	15,553
1963		13,826	1,739	155		15	15,735
1964		14,039	1,779	158		15	15,991
1965		14,190	1,816	157		15	16,178

[1] Estimated by the Post Office Department for 1955 and thereafter. Sale of Series E savings bonds was discontinued at post offices at the close of business on Dec. 31, 1953, except in those localities where no other public facilities for their sale were available.
[2] "All others" included with companies operating payroll plans.
[3] Substantial reduction due to reclassification by Federal Reserve banks effective Dec. 31, 1960, to include only the actual number of entities currently qualified.

Interest checks issued on current income type savings bonds (Series H and K) during the year totaled 5,217,914 with a value of $323,033,-173. New accounts established for Series H bonds, the only current income type savings bond presently on sale, totaled 142,214, while accounts closed for Series H bonds totaled 131,553, an increase of 10,661 accounts.

Applications received during the year for the issue of duplicates of savings bonds lost, stolen, or destroyed after receipt by the registered owner or his agent totaled 34,439. In 22,720 of these cases the issuance of duplicate bonds was authorized. In addition, 12,735 applications for relief were received in cases where the original bonds were reported as not being received after having been mailed to the registered owner or his agent.

OFFICE OF THE TREASURER OF THE UNITED STATES

The Treasurer of the United States is responsible for the receipt, custody, and disbursement, upon proper order, of the public moneys and for maintaining records of the source, location, and disposition of these funds. Federal Reserve banks as fiscal agents of the United States perform many functions for the Treasurer. These include: The verification and destruction of U.S. paper currency; the redemption of public debt securities; the keeping of cash accounts in the name of the Treasurer; the acceptance of deposits made by Government officers for credit; and the custody of bonds held to secure public deposits in commercial banks.

Commercial banks qualifying as depositaries provide banking facilities for the Government in the United States and in foreign countries. Data on the transactions handled for the Treasurer by Federal Reserve banks and commercial banks are reported daily to the Treasurer and are entered in the Treasurer's general accounts.

The Treasurer maintains current summary accounts of all receipts and expenditures; pays the principal and interest on the public debt; provides checking account facilities for Government disbursing officers, corporations, and agencies; pays checks drawn on the Treasurer of the United States and reconciles the checking accounts of the disbursing officers; procures, stores, issues, and redeems U.S. currency; audits redeemed Federal Reserve currency; examines and determines the value of mutilated currency; and acts as special agent for the payment of principal and interest on certain securities of U.S. Government corporations and on certain securities issued by Puerto Rico on or before January 1, 1940.

The Office of the Treasurer maintains facilities at the Treasury to: Accept deposits of public moneys by Government officers; cash U.S. savings bonds and checks drawn on the Treasurer; receive excess and unfit currency and coins; and conduct transactions in both marketable and nonmarketable public debt securities. The Office also prepares the *Daily Statement of the United States Treasury* and the monthly *Circulation Statement of United States Money*.

Under the authority delegated by the Comptroller General of the United States, the Treasurer processes claims arising from forged endorsements and other irregularities involving checks paid by the Treasurer and passes upon claims for substitute checks to replace lost or destroyed unpaid checks.

The Treasurer of the United States is Treasurer of the Board of Trustees of the Postal Savings System. She is also custodian of bonds held to secure public deposits in commercial banks, bonds held to secure postal savings on deposit in banks, and miscellaneous securities held for other agencies.

Management improvement

This year's management improvements were concentrated in the areas of better utilization of personnel and other resources, motivating employees to increase their proficiency and usefulness to the bureau, and more effective organizational structure. Nine incentive awards were given to keypunch operators in recognition of their noteworthy proficiency.

In other data processing operations, certain reports, records, and procedural steps were eliminated, thus freeing personnel and machines for additional services to other Treasury offices.

Reorganizations included a change in the check claims activity designed to eliminate bottlenecks in the review process by expanding top level review capabilities, facilitating and unifying claims examiner training, and providing greater staffing flexibility.

Assets and liabilities in the Treasurer's account

A summary of the assets and liabilities in the Treasurer's account at the close of the fiscal years 1964 and 1965 is shown in table 58.

The assets of the Treasurer consist of gold and silver bullion, coin and paper currency, deposits in Federal Reserve banks, and deposits in commercial banks designated as Government depositaries.

Gold.—The Treasurer's gold assets declined during fiscal 1965 for the eighth consecutive year. The net reduction of $1,527.2 million, daily Treasury statement basis, shown in table 58, includes a payment of $258.8 million on June 30, 1965, for 25 percent of the increase in the quota of the United States in the International Monetary Fund and other disbursements of $1,755.1 million, offset by receipts of $486.6 million.

Silver.—The Treasurer's Office continued the policy of reducing the amount of silver certificates outstanding so that silver bullion securing such certificates could be released to the Bureau of the Mint for coinage. Commercial demands for silver were met by exchanging bullion for silver certificates at the New York and San Francisco assay offices under instructions issued by the Secretary on July 22, 1963 (28 F.R. 7530).

The results achieved for the fiscal year are shown below on the basis of the daily Treasury statement.

Silver bullion		Value at $1.29+ per oz. (In millions)
Available for release at beginning of fiscal year 1965 [1]		$27.2
Increase from reduction in silver certificates outstanding [1]		933.8
Total available for all purposes during the year		961.0
Disposition:		
Exchanged for silver certificates	$213.5	
Released for coinage, etc., at request of Bureau of the Mint	365.9	−579.4
Balance available at end of fiscal year 1965 [1]		381.6

[1] See table 58.

The following table also on the basis of the *Daily Statement of the United States Treasury* summarizes transactions in silver bullion of all types during fiscal 1965.

Fiscal year 1965	Held to secure silver certificates	Held for coinage, etc.		
	Monetary value	Monetary value	Cost value	Recoinage value
	(In millions)			
On hand July 1, 1964	$1,846.8	$1.4	$10.2	ʳ $0.1
Received(+), or disbursed(−), net		−3.1	−1.4	+.5
Exchanged for silver certificates	−213.5			
Released for coinage	−365.9	+365.9		
Used in coinage		−354.3		−.6
On hand June 30, 1965	1,267.4	9.9	8.8	

ʳ Revised.

Balances with depositaries.—The following table shows the number of each class of depositaries and balances on June 30, 1965.

Class	Number of accounts with depositaries [1]	Deposits to the credit of the Treasurer of the United States June 30, 1965
Federal Reserve banks and branches	36	[2] $905,499,624
Other domestic depositaries reporting directly to the Treasurer	47	38,604,737
Depositaries reporting through Federal Reserve banks:		
General depositaries, etc	1,946	224,960,022
Special depositaries, Treasury tax and loan accounts	12,186	10,688,996,287
Foreign depositaries [3]	62	56,118,925
Total	14,277	11,914,179,595

[1] Includes only depositaries having balances with the Treasurer of the United States on June 30, 1965. Excludes depositaries duly designated for this purpose but having no balances on that date and those designated to furnish official checking account facilities or other services to Government officers, but which are not authorized to maintain accounts with the Treasurer. Banking institutions designated as general depositaries are also frequently designated as special depositaries, hence the total number of accounts exceeds the number of institutions involved.
[2] Includes checks for $233,455,909 in process of collection.
[3] Principally branches of U.S. banks and of the American Express Co., Inc.

Bureau operations

Receiving and disbursing public moneys.—Government officers deposit moneys collected to the credit of the Treasurer of the United States, either with the Treasurer at Washington, with Federal Reserve banks, or at designated Government depositaries, domestic or foreign. All payments are withdrawn from the Treasurer's account. Moneys deposited and withdrawn in the fiscal years 1964 and 1965, exclusive of certain intragovernmental transactions, are shown in the following table on the daily Treasury statement basis.

Deposits, withdrawals, and balances in the Treasurer's account	1964	1965
Balance at beginning of fiscal year	$12,116,176,163	$11,035,731,209
Cash deposits:		
Internal revenue, customs, trust fund, and other collections	121,581,066,544	125,464,340,732
Public debt receipts [1]	230,012,138,001	239,286,169,978
Less:		
Accrued discount on savings bonds and Treasury bills	−3,372,296,050	−3,717,131,345
Purchases by Government agencies	−51,118,494,823	−49,395,891,396
Sales of securities of Government agencies in market	8,917,936,633	10,676,163,749
Total deposits	306,020,350,305	322,313,651,718
Cash withdrawals:		
Budget and trust accounts, etc	124,065,882,136	126,395,262,802
Public debt redemptions [1]	224,158,871,740	233,725,170,252
Less:		
Redemptions included in budget and trust accounts	−2,273,223,086	−3,467,431,831
Redemptions by Government agencies	−48,373,355,385	−46,973,403,368
Redemptions of securities of Government agencies in market	8,031,959,150	10,475,544,025
Total withdrawals	305,610,134,555	320,155,141,880
Change in clearing accounts (checks outstanding, deposits in transit, unclassified transactions, etc.), net deposits, or withdrawals (−)	−1,490,660,704	−583,976,412
Balance at close of fiscal year	11,035,731,209	12,610,264,635

[1] For details see table 41.

Issuing and redeeming paper currency.—By law the Treasurer is the agent for the issue and redemption of U.S. paper currency. The Treasurer's Office procures all U.S. paper currency from the Bureau of Engraving and Printing and places it in circulation as needed, chiefly through the facilities of the Federal Reserve banks and their branches.

The Federal Reserve banks and branches, as agents of the Treasury, redeem and destroy the major portion of the U.S. currency as it becomes unfit for circulation. A small amount is handled directly by the Treasurer's Office.

Federal Reserve banks issue Federal Reserve notes; they also redeem these notes, cut them in half, and forward the halves separately to Washington where the Currency Redemption Division of the Treasurer's Office verifies the lower halves and the Office of the Comptroller of the Currency verifies the upper halves. Both halves are then destroyed under the direction of a special committee.

The Currency Redemption Division also redeems unfit paper currency all types received from local sources in Washington and from Government officers abroad; and examines and identifies for lawful redemption all burned and mutilated currency received from any source. During fiscal 1965 the Division examined such currency for 46,692 claimants and made payments totaling $12,899,447.

A comparison of the paper currency of all classes, including Federal Reserve notes, issued, redeemed, and outstanding during the fiscal years 1964 and 1965 follows.

	Fiscal year 1964		Fiscal year 1965	
	Pieces	Amount	Pieces	Amount
Outstanding July 1_____	3,920,084,726	$37,484,776,160	4,116,908,485	$39,559,128,671
Issues during year_____	1,866,174,623	10,239,966,528	1,985,469,083	9,826,962,793
Redemptions during year_____	1,669,350,864	8,165,614,017	1,560,382,209	10,721,313,796
Outstanding June 30_____	4,116,908,485	39,559,128,671	4,541,995,359	38,664,777,668

Table 65 shows by class and denomination the value of paper currency issued and redeemed during the fiscal year 1965 and the amounts outstanding at the end of the year. Tables 60 through 64 give further details on the stock and circulation of money in the United States.

Paying grants through letters of credit.—Treasury Department Circular No. 1075 dated May 28, 1964, established a procedure "to preclude withdrawals from the Treasury any sooner than necessary" in cases where Federal programs are financed by grants or other payments to State or local governments or to educational or other institutions. Under this procedure Government departments and agencies issue letters of credit which permit grantees to make withdrawals from the account of the Treasurer of the United States as they need funds to accomplish the object for which a grant has been awarded.

By the close of fiscal 1965, more than 1,500 letters of credit had been issued by the nine Government departments and agencies which had put this procedure into effect for one or more of their programs. A total of 5,065 withdrawal transactions, under letters of credit, involving $1,549.2 million, had been processed by June 30, 1965.

Checking accounts of disbursing officers and agencies.—As of June 30, 1965, the Treasurer maintained 2,145 checking accounts, compared with 2,174 the year before. The number of checks paid by categories of disbursing officers during fiscal 1964 and 1965 follows.

Disbursing officers	Number of checks paid	
	1964	1965
Treasury	355, 813, 618	362, 071, 237
Army	27, 813, 399	28, 418, 544
Navy	33, 034, 809	33, 303, 977
Air Force	33, 340, 716	34, 557, 707
Other	24, 244, 516	24, 259, 758
Total	474, 247, 058	482, 611, 223

Settling check claims.—The Treasurer processed 393,000 requests to stop payment on Government checks, and 21,000 requests for information and for photostatic copies of paid checks during the fiscal year. Sixty-six thousand requests for removal of stop payments were processed.

The Treasurer acted upon 229,000 paid check claims including those involving the forgery, alteration, counterfeiting, or fraudulent issuance and negotiation of Government checks which were referred to the U.S. Secret Service for investigation. Reclamation was requested from those having liability to the United States on 33,459 claims, and $3,672,329 was recovered. Settlements and adjustments were made on 26,480 forgery cases totaling $3,736,798. Payments from the check forgery insurance fund, established to enable the Treasurer to expedite settlement of check claims, totaled $675,628. As recoveries are made, these moneys are restored to the fund. Settlements totaling $4,535,198 have been made from the check forgery insurance fund since its establishment in 1941.

Claims by payees and others involving 114,000 outstanding checks were acted upon. Of these, 98,000 were certified for issuance of substitute checks valued at $30,370,000 to replace checks not received, i.e., lost, stolen, or destroyed.

Collecting checks deposited.—Government officers during the year deposited more than 7,202,000 commercial checks, drafts, money orders, etc., with the Cash Division in Washington for collection.

Custody of securities.—The face value of securities held in the custody of the Treasurer as of June 30, 1964, and June 30, 1965, is shown below.

Purpose for which held	June 30	
	1964	1965
As collateral:		
To secure deposits of public moneys in depositary banks	$118, 313, 100	$75, 223, 100
To secure postal savings funds	16, 927, 000	18, 917, 000
In lieu of sureties	6, 591, 000	4, 057, 500
In custody for Government officers and others:		
For the Secretary of the Treasury [1]	35, 609, 163, 447	34, 908, 409, 499
For Board of Trustees, Postal Savings System	432, 079, 000	355, 579, 000
For the Comptroller of the Currency	14, 790, 000	16, 388, 500
For the Federal Deposit Insurance Corporation	1, 142, 077, 900	1, 169, 148, 000
For the Rural Electrification Administration	125, 639, 626	124, 368, 030
For the District of Columbia	130, 646, 529	140, 849, 297
For the Commissioner of Indian Affairs	35, 800, 800	35, 016, 075
Foreign securities [2]	12, 056, 059, 132	12, 051, 630, 530
Other [3]	79, 604, 970	69, 895, 011
For Government security transactions:		
Unissued bearer securities	1, 630, 409, 950	1, 758, 882, 800
Total	51, 398, 102, 454	50, 728, 364, 342

[1] Includes those securities listed in table 108 as in custody of the Treasury.
[2] Issued by foreign governments to the United States for indebtedness arising from World War I.
[3] Includes U.S. savings bonds in safekeeping for individuals.

Servicing securities for Federal agencies and for certain other governments.—In accordance with agreements between the Secretary of the Treasury and various Government corporations and agencies and Puerto Rico, the Treasurer of the United States acts as special agent for the payment of principal of and interest on their securities. The amounts of these payments during the fiscal year 1965, on the daily Treasury statement basis, follow.

Payment made for	Principal	Interest paid with principal	Registered interest [1]	Coupon interest
Banks for cooperatives	$1,250,860,000	$24,651,751		
District of Columbia Armory Board				$829,227
Federal home loan banks	3,801,345,000	111,956,982		40,677,904
Federal Housing Administration	782,312,950	11,423,748	$34,832,762	
Federal intermediate credit banks	2,977,095,000	88,864,417		
Federal land banks	566,624,600	15,705		119,925,542
Federal National Mortgage Association	346,898,000		9,325,868	67,253,315
Puerto Rico	210,500			57,548
Others	23,475	8		2,924
Total	9,725,369,525	236,912,612	44,158,630	228,746,460

[1] On the basis of checks issued.

Office of Foreign Assets Control

The Office of Foreign Assets Control is responsible for administering the Treasury Department's freezing controls under section 5(b) of the Trading with the Enemy Act. The controls under the Foreign Assets Control Regulations with respect to trade and financial transactions with, and assets in the United States of Communist China, North Korea, North Vietnam and their nationals were continued during the 1965 fiscal year. The prohibitions under the regulations relating to the purchase and importation of Communist Chinese, North Korean, and North Vietnamese merchandise and the procedures for specified commodities of types principally imported from mainland China prior to the regulations also remained relatively unchanged. The enforcement measures taken by the Control during fiscal 1965 included, in addition to $151,907 in fines and forfeitures collected, one successful criminal prosecution and one indictment.

The Cuban Assets Control Regulations were also continued. These regulations were issued under section 5(b) of the Trading with the Enemy Act and also under section 620(a) of the Foreign Assistance Act of 1961. They apply to Cuba and nationals thereof and are of the same nature as the controls applied to China, North Korea, and North Vietnam under the Foreign Assets Control Regulations. That is, they block all Cuban assets in the United States and prohibit all unlicensed financial and commercial transactions by Americans with Cuba or nationals thereof.

The Office of Foreign Assets Control also administers the Transaction Control Regulations which supplement the export controls exercised by the Department of Commerce over direct exports from the United States to the Soviet bloc. The Transaction Control Regulations prohibit, unless licensed, any person within the United States from purchasing or selling or arranging the purchase or sale of internationally controlled strategic commodities located outside the United

States for ultimate delivery to the Soviet bloc. As in the case of both the Foreign Assets and Cuban Assets Control Regulations, the prohibitions apply not only to domestic American companies but also to foreign firms owned or controlled by persons within the United States.

Internal Revenue Service [1]

The Internal Revenue Service administers the internal revenue laws embodied in the Internal Revenue Code (Title 26 U.S.C.) and certain other statutes, including the Federal Alcohol Administration Act (27 U.S.C. 201–212), the Liquor Enforcement Act of 1936 (18 U.S.C. 1261, 1262, 3615), and the Federal Firearms Act (15 U.S.C. 901–909). It is the mission of the Service to encourage and achieve the highest possible degree of voluntary compliance with the tax laws and regulations and to maintain the highest degree of public confidence in the integrity and efficiency of the Service.

Major management improvements

The Service compiled its most impressive record in improving operations and reducing costs during the fiscal year 1965. Recurring, onetime, and incentive awards savings from cost reduction and management improvements totaled $17.1 million, an increase of 47 percent over the previous high of $11.6 million in fiscal 1963. Twenty-five individual management improvement and cost reduction actions, each of which produced, or will produce annual savings in excess of $100,000, made a substantial contribution to the total savings. Only 11 comparable actions were completed in 1964.

Major systems and procedural changes.—The following are examples of the changes made during fiscal 1965 to effect optimum utilization of resources: (1) A new system which transfers data directly from magnetic tape to microfilm has been adopted for production of final printed computer outputs such as indexes and settlement registers for use in district offices and service centers. The small volume of microfilm contrasts sharply with the great volume of paper outputs previously necessary. Savings in manpower (four man-years), space, paper, and computer printout time are estimated at $298,700 annually beginning in 1966. (2) A computerized tape library system was devised which enabled the Service to defer additional tape purchases estimated at $303,000. (3) Simplified key punching procedures resulted in first year savings of 136 man-years and $542,800 during fiscal 1965. (4) Purchasing rather than leasing computers and certain other ADP equipment was found to be to the Government's advantage. Nonrecurring savings to be realized through this change are estimated at $1 million over the next three years. (5) Issuance by service centers of followup notices on individual income tax accounts completes the mechanization of all major collection notices to the taxpayer. This changeover will result in savings of 128 man-years and $587,000 in fiscal 1966 and ensuing years. (6) Section 6405 of the Internal Revenue Code of 1954 requires reports to the Joint Committee on Internal Revenue taxation of all refunds and credits of income,

---

[1] Additional information will be found in the separate *Annual Report of the Commissioner of Internal Revenue.*

war profits, excess profits, and estate and gift tax in excess of $100,000. Simplification of the processing of these cases will produce substantial benefits including savings on interest payments estimated at $2.0 million annually. (7) Authority has been obtained from the Joint Committee on Printing to decentralize reprints of tax forms for all regions. This authority provides a means for obtaining emergency supplies of tax forms from commercial or GPO plants; other refinements in estimation of requirements were made, resulting in estimated annual savings of $350,000.

Management of manpower resources.—A few examples of the many actions taken by the Service during the year to improve manpower utilization are described below:

A survey to evaluate the utilization of manpower assigned to alcohol and tobacco tax enforcement was completed. It involved a comprehensive appraisal and assessment of the enforcement organization and operations in each region to determine what steps could be taken at regional, branch, and post-of-duty levels to achieve more effective and efficient utilization of investigative manpower. Implementation of survey recommendations resulted in a net reduction of 35 man-years in enforcement manpower valued at $260,000.

Extensive revision, including the development of improved training materials, of the classroom portion of revenue officer training was completed. The new shortened course will enable trainees to work independently sooner than was previously possible. Total annual estimated savings of 28 man-years and $223,000 are anticipated.

Staffing of 206 selected local offices with 271 full-time personnel to assist taxpayers was undertaken to provide year-round assistance, thereby releasing higher paid revenue agents and officers for enforcement work. Estimated annual savings of $250,000 are based on the improved utilization of manpower.

Several major organizational changes were made to improve operations and increase efficiency. Among other benefits, most improvements resulted in supervisory and other overhead positions being diverted to direct enforcement work, thereby reducing requirements for additional manpower to meet increasing workloads. Following are some of the most significant changes.

Consolidation of New York and Northeast regions.—Effective January 4, 1965, by authority of Treasury Department Order No. 150–65,[1] the New York and Northeast regions were consolidated into a single region, the North-Atlantic Region, with headquarters in New York City. The purpose of this consolidation was to bring about a better balance between the various Internal Revenue Service regions and to reduce overhead supervisory expenses.

Consolidation of Office Collection Force (OCF) organizations.— Consolidating OCF organizations in large metropolitan areas permitted centralization of nontechnical functions and released supervisory revenue officers for direct enforcement work. Savings of 19.6 man-years and $136,000 were realized during the year.

Technical Division reorganized.—The structure of the technical organization in the National Office was realigned by type of tax rather

---

[1] See exhibit 70.

than by function. The new organization, fully implemented in July 1965, is designed to more effectively utilize manpower and improve service to taxpayers.

Chief Counsel's office.—The office of the Chief Counsel was reorganized by the addition of the position of Deputy Chief Counsel and the establishment of a new division, to provide for a more efficient performance of administrative and nontax legal functions.

Personnel

A major step in the personnel program of the Service in fiscal 1965 was participation in the development of an improved position management and control system, to coordinate manpower cost reduction efforts of line managers at every level with those of support staff organizations. Other highlights of the 1965 program included the first substantive collective bargaining agreement negotiated between the Service and an employee organization; attitude surveys decentralized to the regions and conducted in nine different districts; outstanding gains in the suggestions and awards program, signaling increased recognition of employee contributions to good management; and further progress in the recruitment and redeployment problems associated with the continuing conversion from manual processing and revenue accounting methods to ADP.

Executive selection and development.—The executive selection and development program, established in 1955, has progressed to where it now represents the route to the Service's top level executive positions and is the means through which the Service seeks to assure itself a staff of first-rate career executives. Among the program's 120 graduates, for example, are 34 assistant district directors, 33 district directors, 7 assistant service center directors, 3 service center directors, 20 assistant regional commissioners, and 11 National Office executives.

Incentive awards program.—Outstanding progress was made in fulfilling President Johnson's expressed desire for a stronger incentive awards program throughout the Federal Government. Fiscal year 1965 set an all-time Service high for suggestion program results with an increase of more than 50 percent in suggestions received, adopted, and in estimated savings. At the same time, there were noteworthy increases in the number of honor and performance awards presented for services of an exceptional nature.

The highlight of the year's program was the Civil Service Commission's Tenth Anniversary Awards Ceremony on December 4, 1964, at which President Johnson honored 30 top cost-cutters in the Federal Service, of whom 5 were Service employees who comprised a task force which initiated savings of over $900,000 annually.

Equal employment program.—The Service continued to place special emphasis upon the nondiscrimination program—the employment of minority group members, women, the physically handicapped, and the mentally retarded.

Minority group members were employed in fiscal 1965 in areas and job categories which heretofore had not been open to them. The appointment of two minority group members to the 1965 Executive Selection and Development Program was an indication of the progress of this program within the Service.

The Service continued to employ many handicapped persons ranging from those of limited mental ability through highly skilled professional employees with physical handicaps.

Training

It has been demonstrated that training programs to develop better management result in improved service to the public and the maintenance of the highest standards of personal integrity, therefore the supervisory and management development program was strengthened. The number of supervisors and managers selected for training was increased, and laboratory-type sessions, IRS case study material, and other improved techniques were added to the general supervisory and managerial training courses.   Management training was broadened by: early identification and training of potential first-line supervisors and managers; strengthening training of supervisors of processing operations; and separate programs focusing on problems of supervision in individual functions.

Changes in tax laws, techniques for their administration, and the continuing effort of the Service to assure that its employees develop the highest possible skills in administering and interpreting the laws and in dealing with taxpayers requires that operational training programs be reexamined, modified, and broadened.   Accordingly, several significant actions were taken in operational areas during the year, including, for example, the orientation courses in ADP for alcohol and tobacco tax, audit, and intelligence personnel.

Interpretation and communication of tax law to taxpayers

To promote voluntary compliance, the foundation of our unique self-assessment system, the Service strives to keep the public well-informed and to accommodate administrative practices and procedures for the convenience of taxpayers.   Programs directed toward the accomplishment of these objectives include: Publication of numerous tax guides covering a wide variety of separate tax situations; dissemination of information through news media by a broad public information program; providing direct personal taxpayer assistance in local offices; and the preparation and distribution of educational materials, tax forms and instructions, regulations, and rulings.

Public information program.—Major changes in the tax law and in administrative procedures led to an increase in the volume and variety of information supplied to mass communications media during 1965. The provisions of the 1964 tax reduction law were emphasized in all materials distributed to the mass media during the income tax filing season.   These included news releases, magazine features, television and movie films, radio scripts and spot announcements.   In addition, exhibits, displays, and related items were prepared to augment filing season communication.

The extension of the automatic data processing system required the dissemination of special information to familiarize taxpayers with the system.   As an illustration, an optional filing procedure for individual income taxpayers filing refund returns was initiated in the Southeast Region.   Taxpayers were informed through newspaper, television, and radio publicity that they could speed up their refunds and facilitate returns processing by sending their returns direct to the service center at Chamblee, Ga., instead of to their district office. The response was very substantial.

Taxpayer assistance program.—The taxpayer assistance program initiated in fiscal 1964 on a year-round basis, provides the type and degree of information assistance taxpayers need to fulfill their tax obligations at a minimum of inconvenience to them through a method most efficient and economical to the Government.

Nationwide, more than 25 million taxpayers received assistance during the year, about 2 million more than in fiscal 1964. Approximately 16.2 million taxpayers were assisted through telephone contacts, which is stressed as an effective as well as inexpensive method of providing assistance for both the taxpayer and the Government. For the nine million taxpayers visiting Service offices, continued emphasis was placed on the self-help method.

Tax-return forms.—The enactment of the Revenue Act of 1964 required the revision of the tax rate tables of all income tax returns, both individual and corporation. The Excise Tax Reduction Act of 1965 will necessitate the elimination of one and revision of several other excise tax forms. Altogether, over 250 forms, instructions, and related documents were revised or reviewed during fiscal 1965.

Tax rulings.—The National Office issues rulings to answer inquiries of individuals and organizations as to their status for tax purposes and the tax effect of their acts or transactions. Rulings are written statements issued to taxpayers which interpret or apply the tax laws to a specific set of facts. During the year, 34,345 requests (31,255 from taxpayers and 3,090 from field offices) for technical advice were processed. At the close of the year, 5,922 requests for rulings and technical advice were on hand, excluding a relatively small number relating to alcohol and tobacco taxes.

In addition, 6,892 formal and informal technical conferences were held with taxpayers and their representatives.

Regulations program.—During the fiscal year 1965, 85 final regulations, 61 notices of proposed rulemaking, and 13 Executive orders were published in the *Federal Register*. Three notices and eight final regulations were in connection with alcohol and tobacco tax administration.

Fifteen of the final regulations and nine notices of proposed rulemaking related to the Revenue Act of 1964. Fourteen final regulations and six notices related to the Revenue Act of 1962. Several final regulations resulted from other revenue acts while others were written pursuant to administrative decisions.

Internal revenue, collections and refunds

Gross collections.—Internal revenue collections totaled $114.4 billion in fiscal 1965, an increase of $2.2 billion over 1964 collections. The decrease of nearly $1 billion from 1964 in individual income tax collections was due to the lower tax rates in effect during fiscal 1965 under the Revenue Act of 1964. This decrease was more than offset by collections of corporation income taxes which increased $1.8 billion. Some of this increase is accounted for by the higher proportion of corporation income tax prepaid through estimated payments pursuant to the Revenue Act of 1964.

Employment tax collections exceeded the 1964 total by $42.8 million, reflecting the higher employment level throughout 1965. Excise tax collections increased 6.1 percent over 1964. The Excise Tax Reduction Act of 1965 [1] enacted in June 1965 did not affect excise tax collections during fiscal year 1965.

A comparison of gross collections in the fiscal years 1964 and 1965 by principal types of tax is shown below. Collections from 1936–65 by detailed categories are given in table 21.

Source	In thousands of dollars	
	1964	1965
Income taxes:		
Corporation_____	24, 300, 863	26, 131, 334
Individual:		
Withheld by employers_____	39, 258, 881	36, 840, 394
Other_____	15, 331, 473	16, 820, 288
Total individual income taxes_____	54, 590, 354	53, 660, 683
Total income taxes_____	78, 891, 218	79, 792, 016
Employment taxes:		
Old-age and disability insurance_____	15, 557, 783	15, 846, 073
Unemployment insurance_____	850, 858	622, 499
Railroad retirement_____	593, 864	635, 734
Total employment taxes_____	17, 002, 504	17, 104, 306
Estate and gift taxes_____	2, 416, 303	2, 745, 532
Excise taxes:		
Alcohol_____	3, 577, 499	3, 772, 638
Tobacco_____	2, 052, 545	2, 148, 594
Other excise_____	8, 320, 188	8, 871, 547
Total excise taxes_____	13, 950, 232	14, 792, 779
Total collections_____	112, 260, 257	114, 434, 634

Refunds.—Refunds of internal revenue, comprising both principal and interest, totaled $6.1 billion in fiscal 1965, compared with the $7.2 billion refunded in 1964. This was due primarily to the fact that the Revenue Act of 1964 provided for a greater rate of reduction in taxes withheld than the tax rate for the calendar year 1964. Consequently, for many individual taxpayers withholding was insufficient to meet their tax liability. The second-stage decrease in tax rates, effective for taxable years beginning after December 31, 1964, brings the tax and withholding more in line.

Receipt and processing of returns

Number of returns filed.—A total of 102.5 million tax returns were filed in fiscal 1965, an increase of 2.4 million over 1964. Individual income tax returns rose 1.7 million to 65.9 million in 1965. Corporation income tax returns increased 53,000 to 1,420,000. Approximately 340 million information documents, including employers' copies of Forms W–2 and copies attached to employees' returns, were filed.

[1] See exhibits 30, 31, and 32.

Automatic data processing.—At the beginning of fiscal 1965, four service centers serving the Mid-Atlantic, Central, Southeast, and Southwest regions were processing business returns under the ADP master file concept. On January 1, 1965, as scheduled, the service centers, at Lawrence, Mass., serving the North-Atlantic Region, at Kansas City, Mo., serving the Midwest Region, and at Ogden, Utah, serving the Western Region began processing business returns completing installation of the system for business returns. At the end of fiscal 1965 the Business Master File, with the addition of accounts for these three regions, contained over 5.0 million taxpayer accounts. In the first half of fiscal 1965, when only four regions were on the Business Master File, nearly 4.2 million returns and declarations of estimated tax were posted to the file. Over 8.4 million returns were posted during the second half of the year making a total of 12.6 million.

During fiscal 1965, the Southeast Service Center, Chamblee, Ga., was in its fourth year of processing business returns and in its third year of processing individual returns. The Mid-Atlantic Service Center was in its third year of processing business returns, and began processing individual returns on January 1, 1965. With the addition of the Mid-Atlantic Region, the Individual Master File now contains approximately 18 million accounts. In fiscal 1965, about 19 million returns and estimated tax declarations were posted to these accounts. These totals for the Southeast and Mid-Atlantic Regions represent approximately 26.4 percent of individual income tax returns and declarations filed nationwide. The other five regional service centers will begin processing individual returns in 1966 and 1967. Thereafter, data from the Federal tax returns of all of the nation's taxpayers, business and individual alike, will be recorded on the master file. Actually, all taxpayers will be under ADP beginning on January 1, 1966, since all taxpayer transactions after December 31, 1965, will be shown on returns filed in 1967 and subsequent processing years.

From the beginning of ADP, it was apparent that the most efficient and economical regional operation would be dependent upon returns being filed directly with the service centers. After three years' experience in processing business returns, and two in processing individual returns, the Southeast Service Center began to test the direct filing plan on January 1, 1965. Taxpayers in that region were given the option of filing their individual income tax returns directly with the center if they were to receive a refund. About 4.3 million taxpayers in the seven State area exercised this option. This test proved that preliminary processing operations can be performed more economically at the service centers. The option will be continued in the Southeast Region and extended to taxpayers in the Mid-Atlantic Region during the 1966 filing period.

The IRS Data Center, operating independently of the basic ADP system, will be located in Detroit, Mich. Beginning January 1, 1966, the Data Center will assume all data processing activities of the service centers not directly related to the ADP master file.

Enforcement activities

To preserve and strengthen the voluntary compliance system, the Service, through a comprehensive enforcement program, seeks to assure that all taxpayers pay only their just share and, where warranted, prosecutes taxpayers who ignore or seek to evade their tax responsibilities.

Examination of returns.—During fiscal 1965, 3.5 million returns were examined. This decrease of 4 percent from 1964 reflects a continuation of the cutback planned in fiscal 1963 to provide a more balanced program by shifting emphasis from the examination of low income nonbusiness returns to that of higher income nonbusiness returns and small business returns. The number of returns examined during the last two fiscal years is shown in the following table.

Type of return	In thousands of returns	
	1964	1965
Income tax:		
Corporation	163	164
Individual and fiduciary	3,236	3,092
Exempt organizations	10	12
Total income tax	3,409	3,268
Estate and gift taxes	31	35
Excise and employment taxes	180	1 169
Grand total	3,620	1 3,472

¹Includes 623 interest equalization tax returns examined.

A total of $2,729 million in additional tax and penalties was recommended on returns examined in fiscal 1965. This was an increase of $179 million over the previous high of $2,550 million in fiscal 1964. Gains of $149 million and $47 million over 1964 occurred in the individual and corporation tax areas, respectively. The estate, gift, excise, and employment tax areas showed a net decline of $15.9 million.

The interest equalization tax, Public Law 88–563, approved September 2, 1964, imposed an excise tax on the acquisition by American citizens of certain foreign securities from a foreign person. In the 1965 fiscal year $2.1 million in additional tax and penalties were recommended as a consequence of examining interest equalization tax returns.

The Service in recent years expanded its exempt organization audit program, developed specialized training programs, and instituted studies into tax abuses in this area. Data processing techniques are also being applied to improve compliance. One example is the establishment of a master file of exempt organizations.

In addition to the increases in taxes and penalties recommended, district audit personnel determined that some taxpayers had overstated their tax liabilities by $144.6 million exclusive of claims for refund.

Mathematical verification.—During fiscal year 1965, 62.9 million individual income tax returns were mathematically verified. There were 3.9 million taxpayer errors discovered, an increase of 49 percent over fiscal 1964. This was due primarily to taxpayers' misinterpretation of the use of the minimum standard deduction incorporated into law beginning with the calendar year 1964.

The $99.9 million in net yield—the potential additional revenue accruing from the difference between the taxpayer errors increasing revenue and the taxpayer errors decreasing revenue—exceeded the fiscal 1964 net yield by 7.5 percent.

Delinquent returns.—The Service secured 1.2 million delinquent returns representing $281.3 million in unreported tax, interest, and penalties during fiscal 1965. About 100,000 of these returns, representing $61.1 million in unreported liabilities were secured by district audit divisions incidental to the examination of returns. The bulk, approximately 1.1 million returns representing $220.2 million, was secured through the established delinquent returns program.

Summary of additional tax from direct enforcement.—A detailed comparison of additional tax assessments from direct enforcement during the last two fiscal years follows.

Sources	In thousands of dollars	
	1964	1965
Additional tax, interest, and penalties resulting from examination	2, 062, 008	2, 151, 187
Increases in individual income tax resulting from mathematical verification	165, 501	194, 086
National Identity File [1]	ʳ 2, 654	3, 374
Tax, interest, and penalties on delinquent returns	275, 480	²281, 278
Total additional tax, interest, and penalties	ʳ 2, 505, 642	² 2, 629, 925
Claims disallowed	445, 556	278, 795

ʳ Revised.

[1] An interim computer procedure established in regions processing individual income tax returns to identify taxpayers filing more than one return. When the Individual Master File is operative nationwide this procedure will no longer be necessary.

² Includes 111 returns with additional tax and penalties of $2,030,558 (interest equalization tax).

Tax fraud investigations, indictments and convictions.—As part of the Government's drive on organized crime, the Service continued to give top priority to the investigation of the tax affairs of major racketeers. During fiscal 1965 many racketeers were brought before the courts for tax evasion. The fact that this type of investigation requires more manpower per case than other fraud investigations, contributed to the decline in the number of full-scale investigations completed and prosecution recommendations. Full-scale investigations totaled 3,643, while prosecution was recommended in 2,382 cases. Preliminary investigations rose from 9,846 in fiscal 1964 to 10,520 in fiscal 1965.

Indictments were returned against 1,919 defendants, an increase of 342 over fiscal 1964. In cases reaching the courts, 1,251 defendants entered pleas of guilty or *nolo contendere*, 200 were convicted, 86 acquitted, and 195 cases were nol-prossed or dismissed. Convictions for fraud during the fiscal year 1965 totaled 1,451, well above the past ten years' average of 1,251.

Alcohol and tobacco tax administration.—The illicit liquor traffic concentrated in the Southern States continues to be the major enforcement problem of alcohol and tobacco tax investigators. To cope with this problem with greater success, particular emphasis is being given to the perfection of cases against violators posing the greatest threat to the revenue and the development of evidence to withstand the test of trial action.

The soundness of this approach was reflected in the increasingly receptive attitude of United States attorneys toward such cases, and the more severe sentences imposed by the courts. Results of this firmer attitude were apparent in the length of prison sentences which averaged 449 days in fiscal 1965, compared to 403 days in fiscal 1964. Even more encouraging was the result of trial actions in conspiracy and other major cases in which sentences increased from an average of 584 days in fiscal 1964 to 1,165 days (more than three years) in fiscal 1965.

Data on seizures and arrests resulting from investigative work during the last 10 fiscal years follows.

Fiscal year	Number of stills seized	Gallons of mash seized	Number of arrests made [1]
1956	14,499	8,643,200	11,380
1957	11,820	6,756,600	11,513
1958	9,272	5,140,800	11,631
1959	9,225	4,655,600	10,912
1960	8,290	4,274,400	10,376
1961	6,826	3,669,500	9,503
1962	6,886	3,424,500	9,126
1963	6,213	3,092,600	8,507
1964	6,837	3,123,800	8,198
1965	7,432	3,637,900	7,426

[1] Includes arrests for firearms violations and tobacco tax violations, which numbered 254 and 1, respectively, during 1965.

A total of 30,552 on-site inspections of plants and permittees was completed in fiscal year 1965. The decrease of about 1,000 from 1964 reflected a planned reduction to offset the additional time required for more comprehensive evaluations of proprietors' operations under the audit-type approach.

Firearms law enforcement.—In the fiscal year 1965 investigations of violations of the National and Federal firearms acts resulted in the perfection of 394 criminal cases, 254 arrests, and the seizure of 94 vehicles and 4,050 firearms. Comparative figures for 1964 were the perfection of 373 criminal cases, 300 arrests, and the seizure of 94 vehicles and 3,567 firearms.

Collection of past-due accounts.—There were 2.4 million accounts that became past due in fiscal 1965. Although this was a decrease of 21 percent from the number of accounts established in 1964, the $1,551 million of delinquent tax involved was $88 million more, as a result of a few unusually large accounts. The decline in new accounts was largely attributable to the initiation of a new "followup notice" procedure that eliminated the need for further enforcement action on some accounts and deferred action on the remainder until early in the next fiscal year. Other factors that were responsible for the decrease of new past-due accounts compared with last year were: (1) increased activity at the service centers in June 1964 which resulted in the establishment of many accounts which would normally have been established in fiscal 1965, and (2) the salutary effects of intensified enforcement.

Progress continued to be made in the program emphasized in fiscal 1964 to reduce the inventory of past-due accounts. Over 2.8 million accounts were closed during fiscal 1965 resulting in an all-time low inventory of 530,000 accounts, almost 45 percent below the balance at the close of fiscal 1964. Because a few of the new past-due accounts involved unusually large amounts, total taxes due in the accounts pending at the end of the year aggregated $1,182 million, $84 million more than last year.

The Service continued to make immediate contacts with employers and excise taxpayers who failed to pay withholding and similar trust fund taxes when due. For the first time since the program began there was a decline in this activity in fiscal 1965, indicating improved taxpayer compliance. The total of 148,000 notices on trust fund and dishonored check accounts was 57,000 fewer than in 1964. Of these 104,000, or 70 percent, were closed while in notice status. The amount collected was $217 million, compared to $247 million in 1964.

Appeals and civil litigation.—Case referrals from district audit divisions to regional appellate divisions were 22 percent higher in fiscal year 1965 than in 1964. Partially offsetting the impact of this increase in appeals was a nine percent rise in the cases disposed of by appellate divisions, resulting principally from more effective use of manpower. While the inventory on June 30, 1965, was 22 percent above a year ago, anticipated improvement in manpower utilization in areas with the heaviest workloads are expected to permit the continued timely handling of the larger caseload. Petitions filed with the Tax Court of the United States numbered 6,852.

The status of civil cases in the trial courts won or partially won by the Government during fiscal 1965 was as follows: In the Tax Court, 83 percent; in the Court of Claims, 81 percent; and in the U.S. district courts, 64 percent. Comparable percentages for the preceding year were 81 percent for the Tax Court, 58 percent for the Court of Claims, and 60 percent in the district courts.

The Government won 16 and lost 6 of the 22 civil tax cases decided by the Supreme Court in fiscal 1965. Last year the Court sustained the Government in five such cases and decided against it in two. The Government also won, in whole or in part, 302 (79 percent) of the 381 civil tax cases decided by courts of appeal (exclusive of collection litigation and alcohol and tobacco tax legal matters).

International activities

The overseas affairs of the Service include the administration of the tax laws as they apply to U.S. citizens and businesses abroad, participation in the negotiation of tax conventions and preparation of regulations under these pacts, and the furnishing of technical assistance to developing countries.

International operations.—In the 1965 fiscal year 454,717 returns were filed with the Office of International Operations, 7,279 more than in the preceding year. Added to the full range of audit and collection activity with respect to these returns are many special problems not usually encountered in domestic returns. Such problems are attributable to the complexity of the laws pertaining to international taxation and to the special treatment of income under the respective tax treaties. As a consequence, the error rate on returns examined is greater than the rate applicable to domestic returns. A total of 22,104 returns were examined, and deficiencies and penalties recommended amounted to $57.9 million. Collections against 18,753 past-due accounts of taxpayers totaled $6.4 million.

In conducting the annual overseas taxpayer assistance and education program, assistance was given to 45,131 U.S. taxpayers through personal and telephone contact and through correspondence. Also, 14 schools were conducted for military tax instructors assigned to assist armed forces personnel abroad in the preparation of their tax returns.

Tax conventions.—Discussions took place in Washington with three countries and abroad with seven countries with a view to the conclusion of four new income tax conventions, five protocols supplementing those already in existence, and one tax convention replacing an existing one.[1]

Foreign tax assistance.—The Service's foreign tax assistance program meets requests for technical assistance in tax administration from developing countries of the free world. The program is administered by the Foreign Tax Assistance Staff, an integral part of the Commissioner's office.

Long-range tax modernization teams were established in eight more countries in fiscal 1965: Bolivia, Brazil, Costa Rica, Dominican Republic, India, Panama, Paraguay, and Uruguay. Seventeen such teams now are active overseas. Previously established teams are located in Chile, Colombia, Ecuador, El Salvador, Guatemala, South Korea, Nicaragua, Peru, and the Republic of the Philippines.

The Service was host to 319 foreign officials and students from 54 countries including the chief tax officers from Brazil, France, Nicaragua, and Uruguay. A majority of the visitors received special orientation or training in National Office and field operations.

It has become increasingly clear that one of the most urgent needs of the developing countries is trained personnel. Two pilot programs were introduced this year—a course for audit supervisors from Spanish speaking Latin American countries, held at the Albuquerque District Office and mobile training teams. The Albuquerque course was taught entirely in Spanish by Spanish-speaking Service personnel. This innovation in AID-sponsored training permitted the selection of participants solely on the basis of their abilities in tax administration. The mobile training teams traveled in various Latin American countries and were prepared to teach courses ranging from basic accounting to advanced audit techniques depending on the capacity of host country trainees.

Planning activities

The planning activities of the Service embrace short and long-range estimates and forecasts, a current program of research, organizational planning, statistical reporting, and systems development.

Long-range planning.—The long-range plan of the Service provides an essential management and planning tool for establishing goals, forecasting future needs, and assuring that current programs are

---

[1] See pages 47–48.

designed to meet established goals. The prime objective is to maintain a low-cost Federal tax administration system by maintaining and extending high levels of voluntary compliance with tax law requirements. The achievement of this objective requires the continuous evaluation of every phase of Service operations in order to forecast basic growth needs and to identify opportunities for improvements in taxpayer compliance and in the utilization of resources. The needs and opportunities thus identified are carefully reviewed in terms of available alternatives, overriding priorities, and practical resource limitations. Upon passing these tests, they provide the basis for the operational goals and the program guidelines in the long-range plan.

The most important workload indicator used by long-range planners is the forecast of tax returns filing. The volume of returns filed in recent years has been steadily increasing and the outlook for continued growth in the nation's population, labor force, and economy indicates further substantial gains in the number of returns. Recently prepared projections indicate that the number of returns filed will reach 111 million by 1970.

Short-range operational planning.—Planning for the current year is based on the portions of the long-range plan which can realistically be attained in a relatively short period of time. Budget requests for the coming year are based directly upon the plan. After enactment of congressional appropriations, appropriate adjustments are made and resources are allocated to the various activities of the Service through an approved financial plan.

Current goals, workloads, and performance measurements in the principal activities are provided by detailed work planning and control systems and by integrated reporting requirements.

Current research program.—Research activities were conducted throughout fiscal 1965 relating to changes in the excise tax laws, the 1964 changes in the Internal Revenue Code, the increased scope of data processing, the Service's emphasis on improving operations and taxpayer compliance, and inquiries by congressional committees, academic institutions, other Government agencies, and State and local governments.

A substantial part of research resources was expended on studies to determine the administrative effect of proposed legislative changes. An estimate of the costs related to the administration of the various excise taxes was one of the most important studies during fiscal 1965. Another significant study involved the drawing of nationwide samples on the degree of taxpayer compliance in reporting interest from Series E and H savings bonds and the comparability of other interest income and dividends as shown on tax returns with the amounts given on information returns.

The Taxpayer Compliance Measurement Program (TCMP) is already producing tangible results. For example, data obtained through TCMP's Phase I on delinquent accounts indicate that a significant portion of these accounts are closed by correspondence when referred to local offices for collection. Accordingly, a new procedure provides for the expanded use of ADP in the mailing of followup notices and in the related processing operations on these accounts. Thus local offices are relieved of a substantial clerical operation and the new procedure is expected to reduce delinquent account issuances by about 500,000 annually.

Expected short-run operational benefits from TCMP can be summarized as: (1) establishing the extent of potential savings from revised collection programs based on greater use of data processing procedures and lesser use of enforcement manpower; (2) determination of the level of adequacy of the Business Master File as a delinquent returns check; (3) disclosures of pockets of delinquent returns noncompliance for systematic follow-through by enforcement personnel, and the use of educational programs and other indicated tax administration methods; and (4) development of an effective ADP procedure for selecting the individual returns most urgently in need of examination.

Over a longer period, TCMP will indicate whether current tax administration procedures are reducing, increasing, or maintaining the willingness and ability of taxpayers to comply with the Federal tax laws.

Systems development.—Action taken in this area was directed toward achieving four broad objectives:

(1) Reducing costs and increasing efficiency of computer configurations already in place or scheduled for installation in service centers and the National Computer Center. (Results are reported under Management Improvement, above.)

(2) Reducing costs and increasing efficiency in input preparation in service centers. The principal achievement in this area was the development of simplified key-punching procedures (see Management Improvement, above).

(3) Improving and developing information systems for program managers responsible for the coordination and control of the Service's resources. For example, a system which assists attorneys in coordinating pending cases to insure that consistent positions are being taken on similar issues is currently operating in Chief Counsel offices.

(4) Developing a future ADP systems concept that will take advantage of technological advances. Major improvements in data bank storage along with developments in high-speed communications suggest that research studies are needed to determine the potential utilization of these developments in the Service's data processing and other functional areas. Development of the specific definition and scope of this project was started in fiscal 1965.

Inspection activities

Within the Service an inspection function is performed by an independent fact-finding body reporting directly to the Commissioner. This activity, headed by an Assistant Commissioner, encompasses the internal audit and internal security areas. Major investigations, such as those involving fraud on the revenue, are subject to close interfunctional coordination.

Internal audit.—The Service's internal audit program, an integral part of its management control system, provides for an annual independent review and appraisal of Service operations for the Commissioner and all other levels of management. This program covers all

Service field organizations and activities and includes a determination of whether the policies, practices, procedures, and controls adequately protect the revenue and are carried out effectively.

Internal audit examinations disclosed certain conditions requiring correction by management. Some of the actions taken are measurable in terms of additional revenues collected or savings effected. A conservative estimate of the results of these actions during fiscal 1965 totals more than $30 million. Included are such items as management's action on specific tax cases, interest and penalties not properly assessed, and accelerated collection actions.

Internal security.—The aid management in maintaining public confidence in the integrity and impartiality of the officers and employees of the Service, internal security investigators provide management with information on any matter that represents a potential threat to the integrity standards of the Service. During fiscal 1965 the services performed by internal security inspectors included: Background investigations of new employees; investigations of employee breaches of integrity; investigations of taxpayers' attempts to bribe employees; and assistance to other Government agencies (also performed by the Service's internal audit inspectors).

Internal security investigations of all types completed during the year totaled 8,825. In addition, police checks were made on 6,510 employees considered for short-term appointments, compared with 5,075 checks made during fiscal year 1964.

Office of the Assistant Secretary for International Affairs

Treasury Department Order No. 202, effective October 14, 1964 (see exhibit 70), transferred to the Office of the Assistant Secretary for International Affairs the constituent units which had been established as the Office of International Affairs by Treasury Department Order No. 198, dated October 15, 1962.

By direction of the Secretary, the responsibilities of the Office of the Assistant Secretary for International Affairs include the Treasury's activities in relation to international financial and monetary problems, covering such matters as the U.S. balance of payments, the convertibility of currencies, exchange rates and restrictions, the operation of the U.S. $E_{xch}ang_e$ Stabilization Fund and the extension of stabilization credits; international aspects of gold and silver policy; the Bretton Woods Agreements Act, and the operations of the International Monetary Fund, the International Bank for Reconstruction and Development, the International Finance Corporation, the International Development Association, and the Inter-American Development Bank; foreign lending and assistance; the Organization for Economic Cooperation and Development and its committees, and the North Atlantic Treaty Organization.

The responsibilities of the Office of the Assistant Secretary for International Affairs also include activities of the Treasury in relation to the National Advisory Council on International Monetary and Financial Problems. The Secretary of the Treasury is Chairman of the Council, which was established in 1945 by the Bretton Woods Agreements Act (22 U.S.C. 286b)[1] in order to coordinate the policies and operations of the U.S. representatives on the International Monetary Fund, and the International Bank, and of all agencies of the Government which make or participate in making foreign loans or which engage in foreign financial, exchange, or monetary transactions. The acts authorizing U.S. membership in the International Finance Corporation, the International Development Association, and the Inter-American Development Bank also provide for the coordination by the National Advisory Council of the policies and operations of the U.S. representatives to these institutions.

The Office also acts for the Treasury on the financial aspects of international treaties, agreements, and organizations in which the United States participates, and takes part in negotiations with foreign governments with regard to matters included within its responsibilities. It assists the Secretary on the financial aspects of international trade matters.

The Office of the Assistant Secretary for International Affairs advises Treasury officials and other departments and agencies of the Government concerning exchange rates and other financial problems encountered in operations involving foreign currencies. In particular, it advises the Department of State and the Department of Defense on financial matters related to their normal operations in foreign countries and on the special financial problems arising from defense preparation and military operations. In conjunction with its other activities the Office studies the financial policies of foreign countries, their exchange rates, balances of payments, capital flows, and other related problems. It assists the Secretary, in his capacity as Chairman of the Cabinet Committee on the Balance of Payments, in review for the President of the entire range of administration programs and policies for achieving a lasting equilibrium in the U.S. balance of payments and for assuring a strong international payments system, and prepares reports to the President on the balance-of-payments situation and on administration measures in this area.

The Office administers the Treasury foreign exchange reporting system. The reporting system collects through the Federal Reserve banks statistical data on capital movements between the United States and foreign countries.

Bureau of the Mint [2]

The Bureau of the Mint, with headquarters in Washington, D.C., operates four mints and assay offices which are located in Denver, Philadelphia, San Francisco, and New York City. Two bullion depositories, in Fort Knox, Ky., and West Point, N.Y., are maintained for the storage of values.

---

[1] Reorganization Plan No. 4 of 1965, dated May 27, 1965, and effective July 26, 1965, abolished the National Advisory Council as a statutory body and transferred its functions to the President. By an interim Executive Order dated July 28, 1965, and effective July 27, a new National Advisory Council on International Monetary and Financial Problems was established, with "the same membership, functions, and status" as its predecessor. It is contemplated that a further Executive Order relating to the Council will be issued before the present order terminates on Jan. 1, 1966.

[2] Additional information is contained in the separate *Annual Report of the Director of the Mint.*

The Mint manufactures and distributes all coins of the United States; redeems uncurrent and mutilated coins that are withdrawn from circulation; and, as production schedules permit, manufactures foreign coins and coinage dies on a reimbursable basis for other governments.

In addition to the coinage function, the Mint receives deposits of gold and silver bullion in unrefined and refined forms for which payments, either in fine bars of gold or silver, or by check, are made on the basis of mint assays. Sources of deposits, both domestic and foreign, include those of individuals, private companies, central banks, other Government agencies, and international monetary institutions.

The Mint melts and refines gold and silver, and also the platinum group metals; manufactures gold and silver bars for "good delivery," issue, or storage; and disburses gold and silver bullion for authorized monetary and industrial purposes.

Related activities involve the continuous safeguarding of the monetary metals and other values in custody, including coins in various processing stages until finished and released for circulation.

Medallic work comprises the production of national medals authorized by special acts of Congress, and medals and other distinguishing decorations for U.S. Government agencies.

The Mint conducts metallurgical investigations, performs chemical and metallurgical analyses, and other technical services.

Domestic coinage

Coinage legislation of 1965.—President Johnson proposed legislation to provide for the coinage of the United States in a special message to Congress on June 3, 1965. (See exhibit 20.) Following this, public hearings were held before the Banking and Currency committees of the House of Representatives [1] and the Senate. The Coinage Act of 1965, Public Law 89–81, was signed by President Johnson on July 23, 1965. (See exhibit 23.)

The act authorizes the minting and issuance of a new type of three-layer composite coin for the half dollar, quarter dollar, and dime which reflect the latest developments in modern technology. No changes were made in the silverpdollar, the cupronickel 5-cent piece, or the bronze 1-cent piece.

The new half dollar will contain an overall silver content of 40 percent and be nearly indistinguishable in appearance from the present homogeneous alloy of 90 percent silver and 10 percent copper. The cladding alloy of the outside layers will be 80 percent silver and 20 percent copper, with an inner core of approximately 21 percent silver and 79 percent copper.

Silver will be eliminated from the quarter dollar and dime. The cladding alloy of the outside layers will be 75 percent copper and 25 percent nickel; an inner core of pure copper will give the coins a distinctive feature—a copper edge. Except for the edge, the outward appearance of the quarter and dime will resemble the cupronickel 5-cent piece.

See exhibit 21, statement by Secretary Fowler before the House committee

The new series of subsidiary coins will have the same diameters, designs, and inscriptions as the present series.

For several years before the selection of composite coins, the Mint conducted extensive metallurgical and technical experiments and investigations of materials which could be considered as possible substitutes for the existing coins of high silver fineness. Many practical requirements entered into the studies since coins serve the public in a dual capacity, as a medium of exchange and as technical merchandising instruments for use in coin-operated machines.

Metals included a range of silver alloys of varying finenesses; also all other traditional coinage metals in either pure or alloyed forms; and the "newer" metals. Recent scientific developments and improved methods of metal processing in the industrial field were tested and evaluated for coinability and full-scale minting operations.

During the fiscal year 1965, the Mint's program was supplemented by the independent study of a private metallurgical research institute. Results of the complete survey were incorporated into the overall *Treasury Staff Study of Silver and Coinage.*

Accelerated production program.—An accelerated coinage program designed to overcome the general coin shortage was announced by the Treasury before the close of the fiscal year 1964. Accordingly, the Mint's "crash program" was initiated in July 1964, and it progressed steadily month by month throughout fiscal 1965. The year's total production of over 7.2 billion coins was more than two-thirds greater than the 1964 output. Monthly production, ranging from 458 million pieces to over 700 million, reached a peak of 738.7 million pieces in April 1965. This unprecedented record was due in part to the following measures adopted under the crash program:

1. Purchased from private industry minor coinage metals in the form of bronze and cupronickel strip for the one and five cent denominations.

2. Purchased new coin and blanking presses, and other operative equipment; arranged for the return of Mint presses on loan to museums and converted them for current use.

3. Acquired from the Department of Defense and the General Services Administration surplus machines which could be converted to mint blanking and stamping operations.

4. Suspended proof coin production at Philadelphia after December 1964; converted suitable proof coin presses for high speed production of regular coinage; and transferred proof coin personnel to regular coinage operations.

5. Utilized the Frankford Arsenal of the Department of Defense in Philadelphia for annealing and cleaning bronze blanks for the Philadelphia Mint.

6. Reacquired space in the San Francisco facility which had been occupied by other Government agencies after coinage operations were discontinued in 1955; reactivated the space, installing machinery for the blanking, annealing, cleaning, and upsetting of bronze and cupronickel planchets for final stamping at the Denver Mint. By the spring of 1965, San Francisco was supplying Denver with all of their one and five cent blanks.

Activities of the San Francisco Assay Office will continue to expand under the Coinage Act of 1965 which authorizes the temporary use of the institution for full-scale minting operations. The act also provides for the refining of precious metals.

7. Hired additional personnel and operated on a 24-hour day, 7 days a week schedule.

8. Renovated space in Denver and Philadelphia for expanded coinage operations. In Denver, a vacant building adjacent to the Mint was remodeled by the General Services Administration for additional coinage presses. A total of 99 presses were in operation at the two mints on June 30, 1965, compared with 60 on June 30, 1964.

9. Retained the "1964" date on coins manufactured after January 1, 1965. Public Law 88–580, enacted on September 3, 1964, provided the Mint with the authority to inscribe the figure "1964" on all coins minted until adequate supplies are available. This measure was designed to eliminate the incentive for keeping 1964 coins out of circulation for speculative purposes.

10. The Mint accepted no foreign coinage orders during fiscal 1965, utilizing all facilities for production of domestic coins.

As rapidly as the coins were finished they were shipped to the Federal Reserve banks and branches, and the Treasury in Washington, D.C., for immediate circulation in the denominations indicated below.

Production and issue of U.S. coins, fiscal year 1965 [1]

Denomination	Number of pieces [2]	Face value	Distribution (based on pieces)	Metallic composition
	In millions		Percent	
1-cent pieces	3,717.2	$37.2	51.3	95% copper, 5% zinc.
5-cent pieces	1,578.0	78.9	21.8	75% copper, 25% nickel.
Dimes	1,036.2	103.6	14.3	900 parts silver, 100 parts copper.
Quarter dollars	715.8	179.0	9.9	Do.
Half dollars	194.6	97.3	2.7	Do.
Total	7,241.8	496.0	100.0	

[1] All coins struck during fiscal 1965 were dated 1964. The unrounded data for production and issue will vary slightly.
[2] The standard gross weight totaled approximately 31,900 short tons, as follows: 1-cent pieces, 12,700 tons; 5-cent pieces, 8,700 tons; dimes, 2,900 tons; quarter dollars, 4,900 tons; and half dollars, 2,700 tons.

A nationwide inquiry relative to the shortage of coins in circulation was made by the Legal and Monetary Affairs Subcommittee of the Committee on Government Operations, House of Representatives. Public hearings were held in two sessions: the first on June 30, July 1, and 2, 1964; and the second on February 16 and 17, 1965. In response to the committee's request, information was furnished by members of Congress, Government officials, commercial bankers, representatives of business concerns dealing with large quantities of coins, trade associations, and other interested citizens. Treasury officials presented comprehensive information on coinage production and distribution.

Stock.—The total face value of U.S. coins held in the Treasury, Federal Reserve banks, commercial banks, and in the hands of the public is compared below for the close of the fiscal years 1964 and 1965.

Stock of U.S. coins	Face Value (in millions)		
	June 30, 1964	June 30, 1965	Increase
Minor coins	$737.7	$853.4	$115.7
Subsidiary silver coins	1,999.5	2,375.3	375.9
Silver dollars	484.7	484.7	
Total	3,221.9	3,713.4	491.6

Gold activities

The gold bullion activity at the mints, assay offices, and the Fort Knox Depository included receipts of $208.2 million, issues of $1,688.2 million, and transfers between Mint institutions valued at $1,524.6 million during 1965. The sources of receipts, the disposition, and the total held in custody on June 30, 1964, and June 30, 1965, are shown in the following table.

Gold holdings and transactions (excluding intermint transfers [1])	Quantity		Value at $35 per ounce
	Short tons	Fine ounces	
			In millions
Holdings on June 30, 1964	14,824	432.4	$15,132.9
Receipts in fiscal year 1965:			
Newly mined domestic gold	24	0.7	24.9
Scrap gold from domestic sources	19	.5	19.0
Foreign and other miscellaneous deposits	161	4.7	164.3
Total receipts	204	5.9	208.2
Issues in fiscal year 1965:			
Sales for domestic industrial, professional, and artistic use	139	4.1	141.9
Exchanges for scrap gold	3	.1	3.2
Exchanges for other than scrap gold	28	.8	28.6
Other monetary issues	1,484	43.3	1,514.5
Total issues	1,654	48.2	1,688.2
Holdings on June 30, 1965	13,374	390.1	13,652.9

[1] Intermint transfers amounted to 43.6 million fine ounces (1,494 tons) valued at $1,524.6 million in fiscal 1965.

Silver activities

During fiscal 1965, deposits of 4.4 million fine ounces of unrefined silver were added to the stock of 1,378.5 million ounces held by the Mint on June 30, 1964. The principal use of silver in 1965 was the manufacture of 274.5 million ounces into U.S. coins in the half dollar, quarter dollar, and dime denominations. This was the largest amount of silver ever minted in a single year.

In millions

Number of silver coins manufactured _____ 1,946.6
Face value _____ $379.9
Silver content, fine ounces _____ [1] 274.5

[1] Includes 0.5 million ounces of recoinage bullion from the normal melting of uncurrent (worn) coins withdrawn from circulation.

Silver bullion issued to other U.S. Government agencies and the public amounted to 173.3 million ounces. Further details are given in the table below.

Silver bullion holdings and transactions (excluding intermint transfers)	Quantity [1]	
	Fine ounces (in millions)	Short tons
Holdings on June 30, 1964	1,378.5	47,263.3
Receipts in fiscal year 1965:		
Newly mined domestic silver	(*)	0.4
Recoinage bullion from uncurrent silver coins	0.4	12.1
Deposits in exchange for fine bars	3.3	113.8
Other miscellaneous receipts	.7	23.0
Total receipts	4.4	149.3
Issues in fiscal year 1965		
Manufactured into U.S. subsidiary silver coins	274.5	9,410.0
Bars issued in exchange for deposits	3.3	113.8
Bars issued in exchange for silver certificates [2]	165.1	5,660.6
Other miscellaneous issues	4.9	168.2
Total issues	447.8	15,352.6
Holdings on June 30, 1965	935.1	32,060.0

*Less than 50,000 ounces.
[1] Excludes 64.7 million fine ounces (2,220 tons) of Treasury silver held by other agencies of the U.S. Government.
[2] Issued pursuant to Instructions of Secretary of the Treasury, July 22, 1963, as provided under section 2 of the act of June 4, 1963 (31 U.S.C. 405a-1).

Revenue deposited into the general fund of the Treasury

The Bureau of the Mint deposited $114.3 million into the general fund of the Treasury in 1965. Seigniorage resulting from the manufacture of the domestic coins reflected a gain of 64 percent over that of 1964. Other revenue, included profit on the sale of silver bullion, handling charges on gold bullion, other bullion charges, sale of equipment, scrap, and salvage materials, and miscellaneous fees, etc. A comparison of the fiscal years 1964 and 1965 follows.

Revenue deposited into the general fund of the Treasury	In millions	
	1964	1965
Seigniorage on subsidiary silver coinage	$21.0	$21.9
Seigniorage on minor coinage	47.8	91.1
	68.7	113.0
All other	2.1	1.3
Total	70.8	114.3

Monetary assets and liabilities

The total monetary assets and liabilities of the mints, assay offices, and bullion depositories for June 30, 1964, and June 30, 1965, are set forth in the following statement.

Item	In millions	
	June 30, 1964	June 30, 1965
ASSETS		
Gold bullion	$15,132.9	$13,652.9
Silver bullion	1,774.8	1,202.5
Silver coin	2.7	.1
Minor coin	.2	(*)
Minor coinage metal, etc	.7	11.0
Total assets	16,911.4	14,866.5
LIABILITIES		
Bullion fund	16,910.5	14,855.5
Minor coinage metal fund	(*)	2.6
All other	.9	8.4
Total liabilities	16,911.4	14,866.5

*Less than $50,000.

Gold and silver production and consumption in the United States

Statistics on the domestic refinery production and industrial consumption of gold and silver are compiled on a calendar year basis by the Office of the Director of the Mint.

Production data are based on the deposits of newly mined material received by U.S. mints and assay offices and privately owned refineries. The deposits are traced back through the various refining processes to determine the States where the ores were mined. In 1965, South Dakota, ranking first in gold production, accounted for 42 percent of the output among 15 producing States. Next in order were Utah, Arizona, Washington, and Nevada, whose combined output was 43 percent of the total.

Among the 16 silver producing States, Idaho ranked first with 45 percent of the total output. Arizona in second place with 16 percent, was followed by Montana, 15 percent; Utah, 12 percent; and Colorado, 7 percent. Total production for 1963 and 1964 was as follows:

	U.S. gold production		U.S. silver production	
Calendar year	Fine ounces	Value at $35 per ounce	Fine ounces	Value
	In millions			
1963	1.5	$51.4	35.0	[1] $44.8
1964	1.5	51.4	37.0	[2] 47.9

[1] Valued at $1.2804, the equivalent of the annual average in New York of $1.27912 for refined bar silver 999/1000 fine.

[2] Valued at $1.29429, the equivalent of $1.293 for refined bar silver 999/1000 fine. This quotation has been unchanged from Sept. 9, 1963.

Consumption data represent the net amount of gold and silver issued for industrial, professional, and artistic use by Mint institutions, private refiners, and dealers. Net issues are obtained by deducting from gross issues, the amount of gold and silver contained in secondary material (scrap) received by the same concerns during the year. Data for 1963 and 1964, as described above, are summarized in the following table.

Item	U.S. gold consumption		U.S. silver consumption [1]	
	1963	1964	1963	1964
	Fine ounces (in millions)			
Total issues of bullion in various forms_____	4.3	5.9	204.5	196.6
Returns of secondary materials (scrap) [3]_____	1.3	1.1	94.5	76.1
Net issues [3]_____	2.9	4.8	110.0	120.5

[1] Does not include silver used in coinage.
[2] Does not include coin or coinage scrap.
[3] The equivalent of domestic industrial consumption.

Bureau of Narcotics [1]

The Bureau of Narcotics administers Federal laws controlling narcotic drugs and marihuana and carries out the responsibilities of the Government under the international conventions and protocols relating to these drugs.

Bureau responsibility for regulating the legitimate supplies of narcotic drugs for medical and scientific purposes involves supervision of U.S. imports and exports of these drugs, and control of the manufacture and domestic trade in them to prevent diversion into illicit channels. Enforcement duties include apprehension of interstate and international violators of narcotic laws and cooperation with State and local law enforcement agencies. At the request of foreign police authorities, Bureau agents assist in mutually beneficial investigations of international narcotic traffickers. The recently expanded program in cooperation with foreign countries has greatly curtailed smuggling of narcotic drugs into the United States.

Management improvement

Several significant management actions were taken. Automatic data processing equipment was used more effectively. Statistics relating to convicted violators of the Federal narcotic and marihuana laws were converted to ADP, thus effecting an estimated saving of one-half a man-year and making current data available more promptly. A study was in process at the end of fiscal 1965 to determine the feasibility of automating registrant returns to expedite their audit and to promote overall improvement in the control of the legitimate trade in narcotic drugs.

---

[1] For further information see the separate Bureau of Narcotics report, *Traffic in Opium and Other Dangerous Drugs for the Year Ended December 31, 1964.*

Pursuant to a recommendation of the President's Advisory Commission on Narcotic and Drug Abuse, a brochure dealing with the preparation of addiction reports was distributed to Federal, State, and local law enforcement agencies, as well as proprietary groups who report information on addiction to the Bureau. This has been beneficial in improving the accuracy and quality of reports on addiction received by the Bureau. The President's Commission also recommended that the Bureau substantially increase the number of agents assisting foreign law enforcement officers under the expanded foreign program.

Training schools

The Bureau of Narcotics Training School held nine two-week sessions during fiscal 1965 and graduated 375 students: 46 Bureau agents; 256 State and local police officers; 54 military investigative personnel; and 19 foreign law enforcement officials. One of the sessions was conducted at Pasadena, Calif., for 127 law enforcement students from seven Western States in that area.

On-the-job training was provided for 20 foreign police officers from 9 countries. Short seminars or conferences were arranged for 46 other visiting foreign officials. A pilot study of an on-the-job training project for Bureau agents was made during fiscal 1965; this training is scheduled to continue as a permanent part of the Bureau program.

The Bureau school, together with district offices, initiated a program of three-day seminars on narcotics, which in fiscal 1965 were held in New York City, Pittsburgh, and Oklahoma City, to assist State and local enforcement officers in conducting narcotic investigations.

School staff members participated in the programs of the Office of Special Investigations, U.S. Air Force School, the FBI National Academy, and the International Police Academy.

The Director of Training participated in the United Nations Seminar on Narcotics Control for Enforcement Officers held at Manila, Philippines, January 20–February 3, 1965, as well as in the following seminars: Frances Glessner Lee Seminar in Homicide Investigation, Harvard Medical School; Washington Institute of Scientific Studies for the Prevention of Alcoholism; and the Fifteenth Annual Law Enforcement Institute, of the University of Maryland. The Director of Training in April 1965, in response to the request of the Puerto Rican Government, conducted a three-day seminar on narcotics for 30 narcotic enforcement officers in San Juan, Puerto Rico.

During the fiscal year 35 narcotic agents attended the five-week basic course of the Treasury Law Enforcement School. Four narcotic agents attended the three-week course of the Technical Investigative Aids School.

The Bureau of Narcotics participated in interagency training facilities, especially those offered by the Civil Service Commission in supervision and group performance, interrelationships in administration and international relations, and executive leadership. The benefits derived from the Civil Service Commission program were reflected in the more effective and meaningful annual Conference of District Supervisors, held in May 1965. Most of the conference program dealt with leadership and group performance with Civil Service Commission, Department, and Bureau officials addressing the group.

The Bureau provides training materials for district supervisors to use in their weekly staff refresher courses.

Enforcement activities

The noticeable increase in the number of joint investigations and the quantities of narcotic drugs seized by foreign police officers assisted by Bureau agents reflected the success of the accelerated foreign enforcement program. Selected examples of such cooperation follow.

An investigation begun in Chicago led to the seizure in Guadalajara, Mexico, of a heroin-conversion laboratory and the arrests of five defendants. Several years of investigation coordinated with the New York City Police Department, Honduran, and Mexican authorities culminated in the seizure of more than two kilograms of heroin and the arrests of three members of a large illicit heroin and cocaine trafficking organization. Other investigations with Mexican authorities included one in Montemorelos, Mexico, where Mexican police officers engaged in a gun battle in which one trafficker was killed, five others arrested, and a half ton of marihuana seized; in another, at San Luis Potosi, Mexico, 700 kilograms of marihuana and 6 pistols were seized.

The largest French heroin-conversion laboratory ever uncovered, including 105 kilograms of heroin and 68 kilograms of morphine base, was seized near Aubagne, France; its operator and several other defendants were arrested, six of whom have been convicted and sentenced.

Investigation of an international conspiracy involving employees of a French international airline who had been delivering heroin in lots of 20 kilograms to 40 kilograms to Anchorage, Alaska, and Montreal, Canada, resulted in several arrests by the Royal Canadian Mounted Police at Montreal, Canada, and by the French Surete Nationale at Paris and the seizure of 62 pounds of heroin.

At La Paz, Bolivia, a physician and two associates, who were major suppliers of cocaine to New York City traffickers, were arrested and one kilogram of cocaine seized.

In the Middle East, Turkish police officers at Dursunbey, following a gun battle, seized 45 kilograms of morphine base and arrested the leader and two associates of a large Turkish international trafficking organization.

Police officers at Damascus, Syria, and Beirut, Lebanon, simultaneously arrested five traffickers and seized 20 kilograms of morphine base. This group had obtained the narcotic in Syria and transported it through Beirut, Lebanon, to France for conversion to heroin destined primarily for distribution in the United States.

Singapore authorities seized more than 1 kilogram of "999" brand morphine base and arrested three defendants.

In Bangkok, Thailand, a joint investigation of Bureau agents with the U.S. Air Force Office of Special Investigations and Thai authorities netted over 12 kilograms of "999" brand morphine base, one-half kilogram of heroin, and more than 6 kilograms of morphine base powder. A Royal Thai Air Force captain, a master sergeant, and three civilians were arrested.

Bureau agents working with Hong Kong Narcotics Bureau officers learned of the seizure there of 1,363 kilograms of raw opium and more than 81 kilograms of "999" brand morphine base. The joint investigation continued and led to the arrest of 3 suspects and the seizure of 818 kilograms of raw opium and more than 90 kilograms of morphine base concealed in bamboo poles which had arrived in Hong Kong aboard a British freighter from Bangkok. The source of the drugs in Bangkok had not been determined by the end of fiscal 1965.

For several years a large-scale narcotic trafficking syndicate had been importing heroin in lots of 50 kilograms to 100 kilograms into New York City from France. Following the seizure of 44 kilograms of heroin from several suspects in 1962, Bureau agents and New York City police officers continued their undercover investigation and surveillance of this group. In February 1965 they began a series of 18 arrests of Cosa Nostra members.

Bureau agents also in New York City, arrested a member of the notorious Mulberry Street Mob, as he delivered about one-half pound of heroin to a well-known narcotic violator.

During fiscal 1965 the Bureau seized a total of 58,321 grams of narcotics, principally heroin, in the illicit traffic, while seizures of marihuana amounted to 1,284,386 grams bulk.

The number of violators of the narcotic laws reported by Federal narcotic enforcement officers is shown in the accompanying table.

Number of violators of the narcotic and marihuana laws prosecuted during the fiscal year 1965 with their dispositions and penalties

	Narcotic laws				Marihuana laws	
	Registered persons		Nonregistered persons		Nonregistered persons	
	Federal court	State court	Federal court	State court	Federal court	State court
Convicted	3	1	814	324	110	74
Acquitted			34	9	7	4
Total [1]	4		1,181		195	

	Yrs.	Mos.	Yrs.	Mos.	Yrs.	Mos.	Yrs.	Mos.	Yrs.	Mos.	Yrs.	Mos.
Sentences imposed			4		4,097	3	1,077	3	444	6	301	10
Fines imposed					$225,610		$8,515		$11,010		$1,060	

	Yrs.	Mos.	Yrs.	Mos.	Yrs.	Mos.	Yrs.	Mos.	Yrs.	Mos.	Yrs.	Mos.
Average sentence per conviction:												
1965			4		5		3	3	4		4	1
1964	4	2			5	6	4		4	3	3	6
Average fine per conviction:												
1965					$277		$26		$100		$14	
1964	$125				135		59		109		51	

[1] Some cases tried in Federal courts and some cases tried in State courts are made by Federal and State officers working in cooperation.

Control of manufacture and medical distribution

The Bureau issues permits for imports of the crude materials, for exports of finished drugs, and for the intransit movement of narcotic drugs and preparations through the United States from one foreign country to another. It supervises the manufacture and distribution of narcotic medicines within the United States and has authority to license the growing of opium poppies to meet the medicinal needs of the country if and when their production might become necessary in the public interest.

The operational authority of the Bureau derives from the following statutes: 5 U.S.C. 258a, 282–282c; 18 U.S.C. 1401–1407; 21 U.S.C. 171–184a, 188–188n, 197–199, 501–517; 26 U.S.C. 4701–4762, 4771–4774, 7237, and 7607; 49 U.S.C. 781–788; and 78 Stat. 367.

During fiscal 1965, 200,920 kilograms of raw opium were imported from India and Turkey and 294,190 kilograms of coca leaves were imported from Bolivia and Peru to meet medical requirements for opium derivatives and cocaine and to supply nonnarcotic coca flavoring extracts. The latter were obtained as a byproduct from the same leaves from which the cocaine was simultaneously extracted.

The quantity of narcotic drugs exported during 1965 increased to 1,084 kilograms 856 grams from 836 kilograms 94 grams exported during the previous year.

There were 2,194 thefts of narcotics, amounting to 115,899 grams, reported during 1965 from persons authorized to handle the drugs, compared with 1,580 thefts amounting to 74,348 grams in 1964.

Approximately 367,840 persons were registered to engage in lawful narcotic and marihuana activities during fiscal 1965.

International control and cooperation

Opium, coca leaves, marihuana, and their more important derivatives have been internationally controlled by the terms of the Opium Conventions of 1912, 1925, and 1931. Under Article II of the 1931 Convention and the international Protocol of November 19, 1948, 12 secondary derivatives of opium and 59 synthetic drugs have been found by the World Health Organization to have addicting qualities similar to morphine or cocaine and have been brought under the controls provided by the treaties. For further details concerning international control and cooperation, see the 1963 annual report, page 156.

The Single Convention on Narcotic Drugs, 1961, came into force December 13, 1964. By June 30, 1965, it had been ratified by 47 countries. The U.S. Government will not ratify the Single Convention unless and until it is amended to rectify certain provisions which it believes would weaken international control of opium production.

Cooperation with States, counties, and local authorities

Excellent cooperation among Federal, State, and local narcotic law enforcement agencies continued in free exchange of information, in coordinating the investigation and prosecution of minor violations and routine inspections by State and local authorities. There has also been a notable improvement in the quality of addiction reports, as indicated above under Management Improvement.

Drug addiction

The Bureau recorded 55,695 active addicts, as of June 30, 1965, compiled from reports received from Federal, State, local, and private agencies.

United States Coast Guard

The Coast Guard is responsible for enforcing or assisting in the enforcement of Federal laws on the high seas and waters subject to the jurisdiction of the United States. These laws govern navigation, shipping and other maritime operations, and the related protection of life and property. The Service also coordinates and provides maritime search and rescue facilities for marine and air commerce and the Armed Forces. Other functions include promoting the safety of merchant vessels, conducting oceanographic research, furnishing ice breaking services, and developing, installing, maintaining, and operating aids to maritime navigation. The Coast Guard has a further responsibility for maintaining a state of readiness to function as a specialized service of the Navy in time of war or national emergency.

Management improvement

During fiscal 1965 management improvement and cost reduction actions in the Coast Guard brought savings in excess of $16 million, more than double that of any previous year. In the area of manpower utilization, significant gains resulted from the automation of previously manned light stations; the replacement of two lightships by fixed light structures; the disestablishment of one loran station and the transfer of three others for operation by the Japanese Government; and the collocation of three loran-A with three loran-C stations in the Western Pacific.

To obtain billets urgently needed to extend the Automated Merchant Vessel Reporting System (AMVER) to the Pacific Ocean—scheduled to begin operation on July 1, 1965—the Coast Guard carried out studies of manpower utilization and workload distribution which resulted in the reassignment of 44 enlisted and warrant radiomen to the new program. Additional savings in manpower and equipment costs were realized by expanding the capacity of the East Coast AMVER Computer Center in New York to handle the data processing workload of the west coast system, thus eliminating the need for the acquisition of a second computer and an estimated 19 additional men to operate it.

Some $600,000 in manufacturing costs and $78,000 in annual operating expenses were saved by building three 75-foot buoy tenders in place of three larger tenders approved previously in the construction program. The substitution of the smaller tenders was made possible by reassignment of existing vessels. The Coast Guard also eliminated an estimated expenditure of about $856,000 by deleting pulling boats from vessel allowance lists. Most of these boats would have required major repairs or replacement.

The Coast Guard conducted three management seminars during fiscal 1965, designed to improve the management capabilities of officers presently—or likely to be—assigned to executive positions. Several meetings and lecture-discussions were also held to improve coordination and teamwork between military and civilian personnel. These sessions, attended by those in the middle and higher management brackets, were intended to clarify the interrelationship and interdependency of military and civilian positions, thereby furthering management effectiveness.

Coast Guard patrol boats assist Navy in Vietnam

Seventeen Coast Guard 82-foot patrol boats have been deployed to South Vietnam to assist in halting communist infiltration by sea of men, weapons, and other materials into the hands of the Viet Cong guerillas. The Coast Guard squadron, specially trained and equipped will board and inspect junks and other craft for contraband cargo. Under the operational control of the Navy's 7th Fleet, these are the first Coast Guard vessels to be used in a combat situation since World War II.

Search and rescue

During the last five years, Coast Guard response to calls for assistance has increased by 29 percent, an additional workload which has been met, in part, by increased operating efficiency. As part of a long-range plan to develop more effective search and rescue techniques, a new electronic Datum Marker Buoy is under operational evaluation. Dropped at the best position of a distress case, it drifts at the same rate as a man in the water and emits a radio signal for 48 hours that can be picked up by SAR units as far away as 70 miles. The first operational uses have been highly successful.

The use of helicopters operating from the new *Reliance*-class cutters has opened a new horizon in search operations. Helicopters refueling from these small vessels are able to search an area with far greater effectiveness than fixed-wing aircraft alone. Two of these new cutter-helicopter teams participated in the GT-3 shot of the Gemini Space Shot series, and a helicopter from *Diligence* was the first aircraft to reach the downed capsule.

The Automated Merchant Vessel Reporting System (AMVER) continued to coordinate the services of merchant ships in search and rescue cases, plotting the movements of some 1,000 vessels daily in the Atlantic. The system is being extended to the Pacific in fiscal 1966.

Some typical examples of Coast Guard assistance rendered during fiscal 1965 are summarized below.

Ship disaster.—On December 20, 1964, the United States M/V *Smith Voyager*, while approximately 800 miles east-southeast of Bermuda in heavy weather, broadcast a distress message after shifting cargo caused a 30-degree list and a loss of power. Three merchant vessels, three Coast Guard cutters, and Coast Guard and Air Force aircraft diverted to assist the 42 persons on board. Thirty-eight persons were rescued and four bodies recovered despite adverse weather and sea conditions. This was but one of nine major ship disasters at sea during the winter of 1964–65.

Airline crash.—On February 9, 1965, a commercial DC–7 exploded in midair off Jones Beach, Long Island, with 84 persons on board. An extensive search utilizing 7 Coast Guard cutters, 6 Coast Guard aircraft, and a Navy tug recovered 9 bodies and various pieces of debris. There were no survivors.

Midwest floods.—During April 1965, rain and melting snow in southern Minnesota and northern Iowa caused record floods along the Mississippi and Red Rivers. Coast Guard flood relief teams preceded the crests downriver, strengthening dikes, and evacuating persons in danger. Where the dikes did not hold, whole towns and tens of thousands of square miles were completely inundated. Coastguardsmen in small boats and helicopters evacuated over 3,000 stranded persons.

Medical evacuation.—Medical assistance was rendered to the Indian M/V *Kaksami Jayanti* when her chief officer was severely injured. A Coast Guard helicopter and fixed-wing aircraft, escorted by a 95-foot WPB and a 40-foot utility boat, rendezvoused with the ship 240 miles northwest of Queen Charlotte, Alaska. The patient was airlifted to an ambulance for transfer to a hospital.

A tabulation of search and rescue assistance for fiscal year 1965 follows.

Operations	Response by—			
	Aviation units	Ships	Shore units	Total
ASSISTANCE CALLS RESPONDED TO FOR				
Private vessels	2,202	2,620	18,950	23,772
Commercial fishing vessels	621	1,433	2,792	4,846
Other commercial vessels	293	599	1,757	2,649
Government vessels	55	100	258	413
Private aircraft	263	59	183	505
Commercial aircraft	70	25	39	134
Military aircraft	414	87	59	560
Other aircraft	9	4	10	23
Personnel only	1,224	437	2,112	3,773
Miscellaneous	405	292	1,214	1,911
Total	5,556	5,656	27,374	38,586
MAJOR TYPE OF ASSISTANCE RENDERED				
Located	1,179	255	898	2,332
Refloated	30	151	2,220	2,401
Towed	306	2,488	14,471	17,265
Aircraft escorted	264			264
Fueled or repaired	17	134	175	326
Medical	685	273	1,187	2,145
Personnel rescued	147	77	297	521
Searches	937	575	1,998	3,510
Attempts to assist	1,308	923	3,664	5,895
Other assistance	915	947	3,970	5,832
Total	5,788	5,823	28,880	40,491
PERSONS INVOLVED IN ASSISTANCE CASES				
Lives saved	616	346	1,022	1,984
Medical assistance rendered	825	365	1,365	2,555
Otherwise assisted	13,233	17,518	68,317	99,068
Total assisted	16,074	20,329	72,004	103,607
VALUE OF PROPERTY INVOLVED INCLUDING CARGO				
Vessels				$1,197,151,700
Aircraft				640,229,900
Miscellaneous				36,292,000
Total				1,873,673,600

Marine inspection and allied safety measures

There were 4,432 marine casualties reported during fiscal 1965, four of which were major and required marine boards of investigation. Inquiries revealed that 125 lives were lost from vessel casualties, 178 from personal accidents, and 225 deaths were due to miscellaneous causes. (These figures exclude pleasure craft covered by the Federal Boating Act of 1958.)

Of the four casualties investigated by marine boards, foremost was the foundering of the wheat laden SS *Smith Voyager* in the Atlantic Ocean on December 20, 1964. Four crewmembers lost their lives while abandoning the vessel which later sank while under tow. Another accident involved the American tanker *Santa Maria* which collided with the Norwegian tanker *Sirrah* off Anchorage, Alaska, on October 19, 1964, causing one fatality and extensive damage to both vessels. Another inquiry concerned the collision of the American freighter *Cedarville* and the Norwegian freighter *Topdalsfjord* near the Straits of Mackinac on May 7, 1965. The *Cedarville* sank with 10 crewmen aboard. The fourth casualty investigated was the flooding of the Panamanian tanker *Daniel Pierce* which resulted in its cargo, sulfuric acid, contaminating the Port of Guanica, Puerto Rico, on July 13, 1964. The harbor was closed to all traffic and the town partially evacuated. There were no fatalities.

The International Convention for Safety of Life at Sea, 1960 (SOLAS), became effective on May 26, 1965. Safety certificates in accord with the new standards will now be issued to passenger, cargo, and tank vessels as they come up for initial inspections or reinspections.

Recreational boating.—The phenomenal growth in recreational boating is continuing, with more than 7,750,000 pleasure craft estimated to have been in use in the United States during calender 1964. To cope with this activity several innovations were made by the Coast Guard. For example, safety patrols are to be used to deter, detect, and report unsafe boating practices. Under this program, law enforcement in general should be improved *t*hrough better coverage of boating areas although fewer boats than in the past will be routinely stopped and examined. A Boarding Officers' Instructor Indoctrination Course was conducted by the Coast Guard to promote uniform enforcement by States. Greater emphasis is being placed on dissemination of safety information to the boating public and to boat manufacturers and dealers.

As of December 31, 1964, there were 3,763,469 pleasure craft numbered, 183,043 by the Coast Guard and the remainder by the 45 States and the Virgin Islands which have numbering systems approved by the Coast Guard. During calendar 1964, 5,036 vessels were involved in 3,912 boating accidents which resulted in 1,192 fatalities, 1,193 injuries, and property damage estimated at $5,171,600. Capsizing continued to be a major cause of fatalities while collisions accounted for 42 percent of all boating accidents. Fires and explosions were the cause of 44 percent of the reported property damage.

Merchant marine technical activities.—In the commercial shipbuilding field, considerable interest is being shown in submarine tankers, ground effect machines, hydrofoils, exotic research vessels, chemical carriers, etc. In many cases the development of completely new concepts or criteria for evaluating safety of design and operation is required of the Coast Guard. In conjunction with these new designs some of the special areas requiring detailed consideration include the use of high strength steel, aluminum, newly developed insulation, and the arrangement of spaces and equipment.

The nuclear-powered N.S. *Savannah* is now in operation, and the U.S. Army MH-1A floating nuclear power plant is to be certificated by the Coast Guard during 1966. These vessels have given the Coast Guard practical experience in the construction and operation of pressurized water reactors in the marine environment.

Approximately 24 passenger hydrofoils, representing three different designs, have been certificated to date by the Coast Guard, and two passenger-carrying Ground Effect Machines (GEMs) for use in the San Francisco Bay area are being evaluated.

The Coast Guard published a book entitled *Chemical Data Guide for Bulk Shipments by Water*, believed to be the first publication dealing with the hazards of transporting chemicals by water. It should assist in dealing with emergencies and prove useful as a reference manual for marine inspectors.

Although not required by law, several Federal agencies are availing themselves of Coast Guard knowledge and experience to assist in the construction of safe and seaworthy vessels, ranging from oceanographic research vessels to satellite tracking ships.

Tabulated below are certain of the marine inspection functions of the Coast Guard, comparing the workload for the fiscal years 1964 and 1965.

Inspection activities	Number		Gross tonnage	
	1964	1965	1964	1965
Vessels inspected for certification [1]	5,644	5,343	9,604,360	11,765,913
Vessels reinspected	6,134	5,003	12,584,433	9,606,985
Drydock inspections	5,882	5,798	13,757,828	13,868,000
Equipment inspected at factory	1,251,350	1,128,917		
Miscellaneous vessel inspections	27,886	26,329		
Violations of navigation and inspection laws (administrative action completed)	54,759	38,128		
Inspection of foreign vessels		1,428		13,982,117
Merchant vessel plans reviewed	36,605	40,641		
Structures inspected (Outer Continental Shelf Lands Act)		52		

[1] Includes initial inspections.

Meetings, conferences, and publications.—The Merchant Marine Council held four regular and two special committee meetings, one public hearing and an executive session to consider proposed amendments to regulations.

The Coast Guard participated in numerous meetings and conferences held in the United States to promote maritime safety, and was actively or indirectly concerned with 27 international meetings held in London by the Intergovernmental Maritime Consultative Organization (IMCO).

The Coast Guard continued to distribute the publications, *Pleasure Craft, Recreational Boating Guide,* and the *Proceedings of the Merchant Marine Council* to promote greater safety in recreational boating and in the maritime industry.

Merchant marine personnel.—Merchant marine personnel were issued 67,818 documents during the fiscal year. Coast Guard shipping commissioners processed 7,703 sets of shipping articles involving 486,576 individual transactions relating to the shipment and discharge of seamen. Merchant marine investigating sections in major U.S. ports and merchant marine details in certain foreign ports investigated 17,310 cases involving negligence, incompetence, and misconduct. Charges were preferred and hearings held on 1,067 cases before civilian examiners. Security checks were made of 19,987 persons desiring employment on merchant vessels.

Law enforcement

Patrols of the Florida Straits and Bahama Islands were continued as high priority projects, since Cuban refugee action, enforcement of neutrality, and fishing vessel movements require constant surveillance. Enforcement of international fisheries conventions also assumed a role of major importance as foreign fishing fleets have set up large scale operations off U.S. shores. The Alaska Patrol required the temporary redeployment of six cutters to enforce international fishery conservation treaties during fiscal 1965. The Coast Guard's role in the enforcement of water pollution laws continued to grow because of national concern with the increased pollution by oil and other materials.

Port Security.—Fifty-three captains of the port enforce Port Security and Dangerous Cargo Regulations throughout the United States. During the past 10 years production and water transportation of industrial chemicals has tripled, resulting in increased Coast Guard responsibilities under the Dangerous Cargo Act. In addition to the safety aspects of the Port Security Program, the Coast Guard is charged with protecting U.S. ports and harbors against sabotage. This required special attention for certain vessels making a total of 265 port entries (1,259 days in port) during the fiscal year. The following table illustrates the workload in the major enforcement areas for fiscal year 1965.

Enforcement work	Number
	1965
Motorboats boarded	121,892
Waterfront facilities inspected	30,777
Reported Violations of:	
Motorboat Act	39,857
Port security regulations	4,137
Oil Pollution Act	617
Other laws	487
Explosives:	
Loading permits issued	519
Loadings supervised	640
Other hazardous cargoes inspected	9,623

Military readiness

As part of the Coast Guard military readiness program, 30 ships participated in Navy refresher training and three ships in shakedown training during the fiscal year. The Navy-Coast Guard class improvement plan for installing new military readiness equipment on high endurance cutters is approximately 20 percent complete. Coast Guard units participated in a number of joint military training exercises. As reported above, 17 Coast Guard patrol craft were sent to South Vietnam for surveillance of the coastal sea routes.

Aids to navigation

During fiscal 1965 the Frying Pan Shoals, N.C., lightship and the Savannah, Ga., lightship were replaced by newly constructed fixed light structures. Nine manned light stations were converted to automatic operation to reduce costs without reduction of service. The revision of the radiobeacon system was completed in the Great Lakes as part of a coordinated program with the Canadian Department of Transport. On July 1, 1964, three loran stations in Japan were transferred to the Japanese Maritime Safety Agency, and the station in Pusan, Korea, was discontinued. Japan established another station at Tsushima in order to maintain service in the area.

The volume of aids to navigation maintained by the Coast Guard as of March 31, 1965, follows.

Navigational aids	Number
	1965
Loran transmitters	64
Radiobeacons	189
Fog signals (except sound buoys)	583
Lights (including lightships)	11,084
Daybeacons	7,193
Buoys:	
Lighted (including sound)	3,642
Unlighted sound	336
Unlighted	10,959
River type	7,728
Total	41,778

Ocean stations

The Coast Guard continued its operation of four ocean stations in the North Atlantic and two in the North Pacific. These ships, spending 78,420 operating hours on patrol, provided meteorological, navigational, communications, and rescue services for air and marine commerce and collected various scientific data.

Oceanography

Progress continued toward full participation in the National Oceanographic Program. Twenty-nine ships have now been outfitted for oceanographic surveys, and programs of routine time-series observations on ocean stations *Bravo, Charlie,* and *Victor* were initiated. A shipboard computer on board the oceanographic ship USCGC *Evergreen* has improved the quality of its surveys. The USCGC *Woodrush* conducted extensive seismic experiments in Lake Superior in support of a joint United States/Canadian Study of the North American Crustal Structure.

Coast Guard intelligence

During the fiscal year, 2,439 internal security and criminal investigations were made, as well as 12,052 national agency checks. In addition, 23,486 merchant mariners and 7,658 applicants for port security cards were screened to determine whether documents should be issued.

Operational facilities

The following table shows the distribution of operating hours for the major functions of Coast Guard vessels, aviation units, and shore units (including small boats) for the fiscal year 1965.

Workload distribution, fiscal 1965

Activity	Vessels (operating hours)	Aviation units (flight hours)	Shore units (operating hours)
Law enforcement	51,133	5,805	68,206
Search and rescue	106,223	26,190	86,913
Aids to navigation	209,081	8,084	87,067
Reserve training	12,693	24	2,078
Ice breaking	14,004	192	531
Oceanography	7,011	572	106
Military readiness	29,217	243	3,198
Cooperation with other agencies	18,270	2,378	4,816
Port security	16,222	472	39,671
Training of cadets and officer candidates	4,916		91
Ocean stations	78,420		
Nonmission movement	43,991		19,328
Proficiency training [1]		27,551	
Ferry [1]		1,704	
Tests [1]		1,605	
Administrative [1]		6,413	
Total	591,181	81,233	312,005

[1] Applies to aircraft only.

Floating units.—As part of the continuing program to replace overage and obsolete ships, the second and third 210-foot WPC-class medium endurance cutters were completed in fiscal 1965, and construction of the first of the newly-designed 378-foot WPG-class high endurance cutters neared the midpoint. Three 157-foot coastal buoy tenders and several smaller vessels were also completed, and a 221-foot reserve training vessel acquired from the Navy was commissioned. On June 30, 1965, the Service had 323 ships in active commission.

Shore units.—Fourteen facilities, including light attendant stations, loran transmitting stations, and inspector offices, were disestablished, while 17 new facilities were established and 11 were reorganized.

Aviation and aircraft.—The Coast Guard operated 153 aircraft, including 57 helicopters, during fiscal 1965. Seven turbine-powered amphibian helicopters replaced overage models and a new helicopter station was commissioned at Astoria, Oreg. Additional helicopters were assigned to the Annette Air Station, Alaska, to augment service at that activity.

Communications.—Major Coast Guard commands have been included in the Defense Communication Agency's Automatic Voice Network (AUTOVON) and Automatic Digital Network (AUTODIN) expansion program.   Additional communication circuits for search and rescue were added, and the SARLANT teletypewriter circuit which serves major search and rescue commands on the east coast was converted to an automatic 83B3 selective calling system.   In November 1964, the President approved the inclusion of Coast Guard landline circuits with those of the National Communications System.

Engineering developments

Civil engineering.—A new search and rescue station was completed at Brookings, Oreg., and the construction of a new air station at Selfridge Air Base near Detroit, Mich., begun.   The construction of a new replacement runway at the Elizabeth City, N.C., Air Base was near completion at the close of the fiscal year; and work had been started on a new field house at the Coast Guard Academy.

Rechargeable lead acid batteries and electric-motor flashers on minor lighted aids to navigation are being replaced with more economical and reliable single cycle air depolarized batteries and solid state electronic flashers.   Standardized day marks have been designed to facilitate mass production of low cost uniform signal marks for identification of aids to navigation structures.

Electronics engineering.—The Coast Guard completed a series of flight tests of the engineering model of a loran-C coordinate converter, which demonstrated the feasibility of loran-C as a highly accurate enroute and terminal air navigation system.   A lightweight UHF/VHF homing device was developed for the HH–52A helicopter, enabling faster location of any distressed vessel, aircraft, or emergency beacon capable of transmitting in the UHF/VHF frequency range.

Two new schools to improve the training of Coast Guard aviation electronics technicians have been opened at the Aircraft Repair and Supply Center, Elizabeth City, N.C.

The MK–56 Gun Fire Control System to be used aboard large cutters is to be modified to enable its use for tracking high altitude weather balloons, thus eliminating the need for separate special purpose equipment.

The new primary radio station at Miami was put into operation this year.   This is another step in a modernization program, which will improve communications reliability through use of the most up-to-date equipment.

Naval engineering.—Several large vessels and a number of smaller ones were completed during the fiscal year (See *Floating units* above for further details).   Contracts were let and initial construction begun on 13 smaller vessels.   Contracts were awarded for the construction of the second 378-foot high endurance cutter and five 210-foot medium endurance cutters.   Multiyear contracts are now being employed, where practicable, to reduce construction costs.   Standard boatbuilding construction continued during the year with the production of thirteen 44-foot motor life boats, eleven 40-foot utility boats, and twenty-seven 25-foot motor selfbailing surfboats. Thirteen 19-foot boats, capable of being towed on and launched from trailers, were placed in use for servicing navigational aids on intercoastal waterways.

Aeronautical engineering.—Flotation equipment was developed and installed on inservice and production HH–52 helicopters to improve the waterborne stability of the aircraft with the rotors stopped. This will increase personnel safety and reduce the cost of crash damage repairs. The program to improve the engine reliability of HU–16E aircraft was also completed.

Testing and development.—Advances were made in the development of equipment and techniques to accelerate the automation of manned light stations. A simple radio remote control system, designed for point-to-point control of a single small light station, has been in use for 16 months. A more sophisticated system has successfully exercised experimental control over a major light/fog signal/radiobeacon station. This complex system, capable of controlling a network of six major light stations, will be tested in the western Long Island Sound area early in fiscal 1966.

Baltimore Light, the world's first nuclear-powered lighthouse, completed one year of successful operation in May 1965. The SNAP-7B generator, developed under AEC sponsorship, has proved to be a reliable power source, but isotopic power is not now economically competitive with more conventional energy sources for aids to navigation.

A Coast Guard 30-foot utility boat has been equipped with hydrofoils to study the advantages and liabilities of hydrofoil craft as search and rescue vehicles.

Coast Guard reserve

Reserve training cruises were conducted on the east coast by the USCGC *Tanager* for 1,484 reservists. Active duty training courses for reservists on the West Coast were instituted at the Coast Guard Base, Alameda, Calif., during the summer months.

The first group of women recruits (SPARs) since World War II entered on active duty for one year of training, after which they will be assigned to organized reserve training units. A limited pilot enlistment program, consisting of four months instead of six months initial active duty for training, was commenced for port security personnel in certain areas. If successful, the program will be expanded, thus saving two months of active duty training time for personnel entering the port security rating.

Personnel

The Continuation Boards required by the interim provisions of legislation approved in September 1963 (14 U.S.C. 211 *et seq.*) to reduce the officer personnel hump in the grades of commander and captain were completed. A total of 12 captains and 73 commanders are being retired as they reach minimum eligibility. The personnel strength of the Coast Guard as of June 30, 1964 and 1965 is shown in the following table.

Personnel	Number	
	1964	1965
Military personnel:		
Commissioned officers	3,293	3,388
Commissioned warrant officers	867	844
Warrant officers	207	244
Cadets	385	440
Enlisted men	r 27,509	26,860
Total	r 32,261	31,776
Civilian personnel:		
Salaried (General Service)	2,757	2,856
Wageboard	2,292	2,308
Lamplighters	180	158
Total (exclusive of vacancies)	5,229	5,322
Ready reservists:		
Officers	3,620	3,796
Enlisted	24,286	26,446
Total	27,906	30,242

r Revised.

The table below reflects the changes in the number of officers on active duty as of June 30, 1964 and 1965.

Officers	Number	
	1964	1965
Additions of commissioned officers:		
Coast Guard Academy graduates	109	114
Reserve officers called to active duty	24	55
Former merchant marine officers appointed	0	2
Officer Candidate School graduates	221	244
Total	354	415
Losses of commissioned officers:		
Regular [1]	143	178
Reserve on completion of obligated service	103	145
Total	246	323
Net gain	108	92

[1] Through retirements, resignations, revocations, and deaths.

Recruiting and training.—Fifty-nine main recruiting stations and 50 substations were manned by 257 recruiters during the fiscal year. There were 11,749 applicants for enlistment in the regular Coast Guard and 4,914 were enlisted. The Reserve received 6,711 applications and enlisted 3,565.

A Coast Guard aviation cadet program was begun during the year with 10 enlisted applicants selected. Under another new program, direct commissions as Lt.(jg.) in the U.S. Coast Guard Reserve will be offered to law school graduates, who would spend three years on active duty. The first of this group will be commissioned during the fiscal year 1966.

Coast Guard education program.—The education and training programs sponsored by and participated in by the Service are summarized for the fiscal years 1964 and 1965 as follows.

Education and training programs	Number	
	1964	1965
Coast Guard Academy:		
Applications	3,941	3,745
Applications approved	2,761	2,706
Appointments accepted	275	1 280
Cadets	548	597
Graduates (Bachelor of Science degree)	109	114
Officer training completed:		
Officer Candidate School graduates	221	244
Postgraduate	63	67
Flight training	31	28
Helicopter training	22	25
C-130 B aircraft training	23	13
Short-term specialized courses	588	690
Off-duty courses at civilian schools	594	575
Enlisted training completed:		
Recruit training:		
Regular	3,107	3,295
Reserve	2,120	2,401
Coast Guard basic petty officer schools	1,447	1,407
Navy basic petty officer schools	385	324
Advanced schools (Navy and Coast Guard)	76	101
Specialized courses (Service and civilian)	1,687	2,573
Off-duty education (civilian schools)	238	390
Correspondence courses completed:		
Coast Guard Institute	9,858	8,996
U.S. Armed Forces Institute	249	301
U.S. Naval Correspondence Course Center	11,480	13,210

1 Estimated.

Coast Guard Auxiliary

The Auxiliary, a voluntary nonmilitary organization functioning in 686 communities, conducted public instruction courses in safe boating which were attended by 137,395 persons in fiscal 1965. Courtesy examinations of the safety equipment of some 183,000 motorboats were made by specially qualified Auxiliarists. The Auxiliary also cooperated with the regular Coast Guard in making 2,875 regatta patrols, and participated in 5,985 assistance missions which were instrumental in saving 161 lives. As of June 30, 1965, this organization had 23,004 members, including 5,860 instructors and 8,197 inspector-examiners. The membership operated 14,966 facilities, consisting of boats, aircraft, and radio stations.

Fiscal and supply management

Contracts for the construction of high endurance and medium endurance cutters awarded during fiscal 1965 contained options for the procurement of additional vessels which were programmed in the Coast Guard budget estimates for the fiscal year 1966. These multi-year procurements are expected to save $1,350,000 in total contract prices. This procurement policy will be utilized in the future whenever feasible.

The Coast Guard cost accounting and operational data reporting systems were revised to produce the financial information and operational performance statistics required for the distribution of operating costs to Coast Guard programs. The Coast Guard budget presentation for fiscal 1967 will be program-oriented, using actual accounting and performance data collected during fiscal year 1965.

Coast Guard operating units have been provided an improved level of direct retail supply support by stores issuing activities of the Department of Defense and the General Services Administration. This has enabled a corresponding reduction in Coast Guard inventories.

Funds available, obligations, and balances

The following table shows the amount of funds available for the Coast Guard during fiscal 1965 and the amounts of obligations and unobligated balances.

	Funds available [1]	Net total obligations	Unobligated balance [2]
Appropriated funds:			
Operating expenses	$273,748,504	$273,691,046	$57,458
Reserve training	20,939,000	20,858,889	80,111
Retired pay	36,961,000	36,958,434	2,566
Acquisition, construction, and improvement	92,616,446	78,970,471	13,819,864
Total appropriated funds	424,264,950	410,478,840	13,959,999
Reimbursements:			
Operating expenses	14,220,342	14,220,342	
Acquisition, construction, and improvements	14,327,986	6,876,030	7,477,789
Total reimbursements	28,548,328	21,096,372	7,477,789
Trust fund, U.S. Coast Guard gift fund	43,458	4,737	38,721
Grand total	452,856,736	431,579,949	21,476,510

[1] Funds available include unobligated balances brought forward from prior year appropriation as follows: Acquisition, construction, and improvements:

Appropriated funds	$7,186,446
Reimbursements	14,068,557
U.S. Coast Guard gift fund	15,415

[2] Unobligated balance of $21,297,653 under the acquisition, construction, and improvements appropriation remains available for obligation in fiscal year 1966. These funds are programmed for obligation in fiscal 1966 for the following general purposes:

	Coast Guard projects	Department of Defense projects
For projects deferred in fiscal 1965 to be subsequently accomplished	$4,575,000	
For completion of projects started in fiscal 1965	9,244,864	$7,477,789
	13,819,864	7,477,789

United States Savings Bonds Division

The primary responsibility of the U.S. Savings Bonds Division is to promote the sale and retention of savings bonds and the sale of savings stamps. The savings bonds program makes a vital contribution to Government financing and debt management policy as one of the most significant means through which the Treasury achieves the broadest possible ownership of the public debt.

Management improvement

The Savings Bonds Division is headed by a National Director and Assistant National Director and consists of two principal branches: Sales, and Advertising and Promotion. The branch chiefs, together with the National Director and Assistant National Director, make up the Division's Management Committee, whose main purpose is continuing improvement of the Division's services.

The Division has 6 regional offices and offices in the 50 States and the District of Columbia through which sales materials are disseminated. A relatively small sales and service staff recruits, trains, and services a large volunteer savings bonds sales corps. Liaison is maintained with all types of financial, business, labor, agricultural, and educational institutions, as well as with other civic organizations. Their volunteer services are enlisted to sell savings bonds at banks, savings and loan associations, credit unions, certain post offices (those in communities where there is no other sales outlet), and business establishments operating the payroll savings plan.

In October 1964 a quarterly management improvement report was initiated under which State offices reported management activities to the headquarters staff. The new system is still in an experimental stage, but has served to make the field staff more management conscious, and has increased headquarters staff information on the way in which State offices are administered.

In February 1965 a *Field Communications Guide* was issued as a manual for communications between the field and headquarters offices. The guide has been well received as a reference work and as a training guide.

During fiscal 1965, six States transferred their addressograph operations to the Distribution Center. Of these States, five were able to declare their addressograph equipment surplus. Indirect savings were made by the release of clerical time for more gainful activity.

Newsette, a Division publication, initiated in May 1965, is designed to keep all Division employees informed about the Federal Government, the Treasury Department, and the entire Savings Bonds Division. The Division plans to consolidate its administrative information in this publication, thereby substantially reducing the employees' required reading material.

Programming has been completed for the conversion of payroll savings reporting to an EDP system using the facilities of the Parkersburg office of the Bureau of the Public Debt. First reports under the new system were mailed to 37,000 business firms during the week of July 5, 1965.

The new equipment has been programmed to produce a number of highly useful operating reports at minor cost which had not been possible under the previous system.

In addition, steps are under way to handle the allocation of sales credits by large interstate companies based on the actual payroll savings participants in each State.

Stepped-up servicing of publicity media such as providing live radio spots to local radio stations and negatives for offset service to newspapers and periodicals are further examples of the continuing effort of the Division in the area of management improvement.

Promotional activities

A "Red, White, and Blue" plan for all Americans set the pace for savings bond promotions in the fiscal year 1965, the program's "Star-Spangled Savings Bonds Year."

May, the anniversary month of the popular Series E Bond, was selected for "Star-Spangled Security Month."

To launch the campaign within industry and outline its goals, the 1965 U.S. Industrial Payroll Savings Committee, a volunteer committee appointed by the Treasury Department, met in Washington on January 12. Twenty-seven business and industrial leaders, each representing a major metropolitan market area, comprised the Committee, headed by Elmer W. Engstrom, president, Radio Corporation of America. Secretary of the Treasury Fowler serves as the Committee's Honorary General Chairman. Members-at-large are Frank R. Milliken, president of Kennecott Copper Corporation, and Harold S. Geneen, chairman and president of International Telephone and Telegraph Corporation, chairmen of the 1964 and 1963 committees, respectively.

Locally, metropolitan chairmen organize, lead, and encourage business and industrial leaders to conduct intensive payroll savings campaigns in their own companies.

During January–July 1965, more than 8,000 business firms promoted payroll savings. By July 31, 74 percent of the Committee's goal of 1,100,000 new "sign-ups" had been attained. The 809,756 new enrollments represented a gain of 14 percent over the corresponding months of 1964. In addition to the new "sign-ups," thousands of employees already participating in the plan increased their regular bond savings. Sales of the small-denomination Series E bonds (bought chiefly by payroll savers) registered peacetime records in fiscal 1965.

Organized labor gave its full cooperation to payroll savings campaigns in industry. Through the National Labor Advisory Committee for Savings Bonds, the sales program was successfully publicized by national unions among their members.

The 1965 "Star-Spangled Savings Plan for All Americans" was also marked by highly effective campaigns within the Federal Government. Led by the Interdepartmental Savings Bond Committee, under the Chairman of the Civil Service Commission, John W. Macy, Jr., this campaign raised the number of civilian and military employees enrolled in the payroll savings plan to 2,398,825 at the end of the year, an increase of 39,460 participants.

Besides these concerted campaigns, the Division coordinated numerous individual drives to promote the sale of E and H bonds with the aid of national organizations and community institutions. To organize and direct the campaigns, under the chairmanship of Bernard B. Burford, secretary-treasurer of Optimist International, executives of the major national organizations, with more than 60 million members, met in Chicago in January 1965 and in Washington in February. "Community Bond Campaigns," designed to encourage American families to buy at least a bond a year, were held in many of the Nation's cities and towns during the fiscal year.

During fiscal 1965 the motion picture industry produced a new 20-minute color short, "The Land We Love," to assist the Division in promoting the sale of savings bonds. Ten motion picture companies contributed footage; Warner Brothers Studio donated its full facilities. The Department of Defense and the Treasury Department's Coast Guard cooperated by "shooting" some of the scenes. This film is a splendid example of the volunteer contributions of the American public in support of the U.S. savings bonds program.

The women's organizations of the Nation act as volunteer leaders in the promotion of U.S. savings stamps sales. Stamps are sold primarily in the Nation's schools. The "Junior Astronaut" program initiated during academic year 1962–63 continued in fiscal year 1965, with more than 5,000,000 student stamp buyers receiving a certificate signed by the Nation's 7 original astronauts designating each one as a "Junior Astronaut." The sale of 115 million savings stamps in 1965 was the largest number sold in any peacetime year.

The voluntary assistance provided by the Advertising Council and its task force agencies who prepare and donate advertising and promotional material are of major importance to all campaigns and promotional activities undertaken by the U.S. Savings Bonds Division. Also of immeasurable value to the sales program are the contributions and cooperation of banks and other financial institutions, as well as of industry and community volunteers, whose efforts continued at high levels throughout fiscal 1965.

Donated advertising time and space alone is conservatively estimated at a value of more than $50 million annually. Because of this support, the costs to the Government of promoting the sale of Series E and H bonds are held to a minimum and average approximately one-tenth of one percent of annual sales.

Sales of E and H savings bonds during fiscal 1965 totaled $4.5 billion. Details of sales, redemptions, and amount outstanding will be found in tables 48–50.

United States Secret Service

Principal functions of the U.S. Secret Service are the protection of the President of the United States, the members of his immediate family, the President-elect, the Vice President or other officer next in order of succession to the office of President, and the Vice-President-elect; the protection of a former President, at his request, for a reasonable period after he leaves office; the detection and arrest of persons committing any offenses against the laws of the United States relating to obligations and securities of the United States and of foreign governments; and the detection and arrest of persons violating certain laws relating to the Federal Deposit Insurance Corporation, Federal land banks, and Federal land bank associations. The duties of the Service are defined by section 3056, title 18, United States Code.

Management improvement

During the fiscal year 1965 the management improvement program of the Service gave increased attention to cost reduction, economy of operations, and increased productivity. The Inspection Staff continued to analyze procedures and methods at the time of each field office and Headquarters section inspection, and to make suggestions for improvements.

An advisory committee was formed to study the application of data processing to the huge volume of letters and reports handled in connection with the protection responsibilities of the Service.

Studies of new techniques and methods to expedite criminal investigations continued. During fiscal 1965 a procedural change was made in the submission of settlement reports in cases of forged Government checks, where the forger had already been identified before receipt of the check for investigation. The reports are now submitted by the Headquarters Forgery Section to the Treasurer of the United States when the case is received instead of by Secret Service field offices. This benefits the payee who receives a duplicate check earlier while reducing work in the Office of the Treasurer and in the Secret Service.

The Counterfeit Note Index, a necessary operating document in each field office, was revised and computer programmed to produce a more effective index.

Participation in the incentive awards program was improved during fiscal 1965, with the number of suggestions increasing more than 55 percent. The number of quality pay increases rose 700 percent.

Training

Training activities of the Service were expanded during the year. Seven Secret Service Training Schools, one Treasury Guard Force School, and various types of other Service schools were conducted. In addition, an Administration and Management Institute was organized for first line supervisors. Outside training included attendance at the FBI Foreign Language School, the FBI Academy, Brookings Institution, American University, GSA Secretarial Courses, GSA Institute Course on Small Purchases, Department of Defense Crypto Schools, and firearms instructions courses by the Colt Co. and Smith and Wesson Co.

Protective and security activities

The protection of the First Family and the Vice President, and the widow and minor children of the late President Kennedy continued to be the most important responsibility of the Secret Service.

Investigations concerning protective activities increased from 2,020 in 1964 to 2,428 in 1965, or 20.2 percent. There were 288 cases pending at the close of the fiscal year, representing a 14.3 percent increase from the end of fiscal 1964.

Enforcement activities

Counterfeiting continued to be a major concern. However, the large seizures in the previous year of illicit plants for the manufacture of counterfeit money was reflected in some reduction in the number of plants and the amount in counterfeit money seized this fiscal year.

During fiscal 1965, 36 plants for the manufacture of counterfeit money were seized, a decrease of 18.2 percent from 1964. There were 484 new issues of counterfeit notes seized and 723 persons arrested for counterfeiting offenses during the year. Counterfeit money received decreased 56.6 percent to $3,363,809. The loss to the public amounted to $846,213 because Secret Service agents seized $2,517,596 before it could be passed. The majority of the notes passed on the public came from large organized groups of offenders in the New York-Newark and Cleveland-Chicago areas.

During April 1965 four men were arrested in San Francisco for passing counterfeit $20 notes on the Federal Reserve Bank of San Francisco. Following the arrest, $100,000 in the notes was seized from a room occupied by two of the men and another $156,000 was found in safe deposit boxes rented by the defendants in two Los Angeles banks.

The defendants admitted manufacturing the notes in a printing shop operated by one of them in Portland, Oreg.

In December 1964, the owner of a printing shop in Allston, Mass., and an associate printed $150,000 in counterfeit $20 Federal Reserve notes. Although they solicited underworld contacts to arrange for the sale of the notes, the buyer they found was actually an undercover Secret Service agent. The group was arrested and their equipment and counterfeits, including a quantity of counterfeit American Express checks, seized before any could be passed.

During August 1964 special agents in Cleveland began investigating the purchase of certain materials which could be used for counterfeiting. By December the investigation had progressed sufficiently to secure a Federal search warrant for the home of a principal suspect who was apprehended there. Special agents found a press and other paraphernalia as well as $50,000 in new counterfeit $20 and $100 Federal Reserve notes. The suspect escaped his guard, leaped through a glass door and fired four shots at the pursuing agents as he ran, using a gun handed to him by a woman who had concealed it in a blanket covering her baby. The agents returned the fire and wounded the suspect. The subject, a notorious hoodlum on the "Ten Most Wanted List" of the FBI, was persuaded to surrender and was hospitalized. He escaped from the hospital, was recaptured the same day, and is now serving a life sentence.

During February 1965 South African police arrested two men in Johannesburg, for possession of a suitcase containing $495,000 in counterfeit $5 notes, drawn on the Federal Reserve Bank of San Francisco. One of the men had manufactured the notes in a printing shop in Johannesburg, where he was employed.

Close and effective work by special agents assigned to the Paris-office and the Italian Police resulted in the arrest of 11 persons in Italy during June 1965. The authorities seized $7,100 in counterfeit $50 and $100 U.S. Federal Reserve notes, issued on various Federal Reserve banks. These arrests halted a large criminal operation responsible for the distribution of stolen diamonds and automobiles, illegally possessed gold and arms, and many varieties of smuggled goods.

During August 1964 a man was arrested in San Francisco and approximately $20,000 in counterfeit notes and negatives for four different types of notes drawn on the Federal Reserve banks of New York, Boston, and Chicago seized. As a result of that arrest, two trunks containing $716,000 in counterfeits were seized from a warehouse near Hartford, Conn. Another man was arrested and both defendants were convicted. Less than $400 in the notes was passed on the public.

The alterations of U.S. coins to enhance their numismatic value increased during the fiscal year. This problem has grown rapidly in the past two years. One case involved the purchase for $25,000 by a Virginia coin dealer of a roll of silver dollars dated 1893. The mint mark on each coin had been altered so expertly that a reputable and experienced numismatic firm had judged them to be genuine.

Counterfeit U.S. currency continued to be a problem in foreign countries. During fiscal 1965, $951,595 was received as compared with $157,740 in the previous fiscal year. Since a great deal of such activity does not come to the attention of the Secret Service, despite mutual agreements, these figures undoubtedly represent a relatively small part of the amount manufactured and/or circulated. Close liaison with Interpol as well as with police officials throughout the world has been very fruitful in improving this phase of the Service's operations. Police officials from many countries receive instructions on detection of counterfeits from the Service, both when they visit Washington and when Service employees are traveling in their countries on other assignments. Particularly effective cooperation exists with authorities in Canada and Mexico. Notices of U.S. counterfeits in circulation are regularly furnished to finance officers and employees of our Defense establishments overseas with whom the Secret Service maintains excellent liaison. Close contact is also maintained with State Department representatives throughout the world on counterfeiting and protective matters. Liaison with nations in the Far East is handled through the office in Hawaii and with nations in Europe, the Middle East, and Africa from the Paris office.

Secret Service responsibility extends to the counterfeiting in the United States of money of other countries. During fiscal 1965, the Service seized 1,897 pieces of counterfeit foreign currency in this country.

The following table summarizes receipts of counterfeit money during the fiscal years 1964 and 1965.

Counterfeit money received, fiscal years 1964 and 1965

Receipts of counterfeit currency and coins	1964	1965	Percentage increase, or decrease (−)
Counterfeit money received in the United States:			
Loss to the public	$530, 434. 45	$846, 213. 30	59. 5
Seized before circulation	7, 222, 015. 78	2, 517, 596. 27	−65. 2
Total	7, 752, 450. 23	3, 363, 809. 57	−56. 6
Counterfeit U.S. currency received in foreign countries	157, 740	951, 595	503. 3
Pieces of counterfeit currency of other nations received in the United States	246, 010	1, 897	−99.0

Although there has been a slight decline in the number of forged Government checks received, this continues to be a major problem. During the past fiscal year, 39,399 cases involving a face amount of $3,967,777.04 were investigated. A total of 2,720 persons were arrested for check forgery in 1965.

In fiscal 1965, 5,586 cases involving the forgery of U.S. savings bonds with a face amount of $605,980.93 were investigated; arrests for bond forgery offenses totaled 69.

The decline in the number of check and bond forgery cases may be attributable to improved investigative techniques as well as a continued healthy economic climate. It is significant that the decrease in these cases occurred despite a continuing increase in the number of checks issued and a general rise in criminal activity.

The following are representative of the cases involving large scale multiple forgers of checks and bonds.

In August 1964 a man was arrested for forging about 130 U.S. Treasury checks at various places in Pennsylvania, Ohio, Virginia, New York, Connecticut, and Delaware. In 1959 he had been released from a penitentiary where he had been incarcerated for previous counterfeiting offenses. He estimated that he had forged and negotiated from $75,000 to $100,000 worth of various types of negotiable instruments since 1959. He was sentenced for 15 years.

Four persons who stole and forged approximately 70 U.S. Treasury checks in Florida during 1964 have been convicted.

A husband and wife team stole and forged more than 60 checks during 1964 throughout the New England States. Both have been sentenced. The successful investigation and prosecution in this case was at least partially due to use of the ninhydrin identification process, now widely used in the Service.

During 1965 a man was arrested in California while attempting to redeem 156 U.S. savings bonds. At the time he was free on bond awaiting sentence for the forgery of a stolen U.S. Treasury check.

During this fiscal year, two men were arrested in Florida for forging 361 savings bonds, which had been received from a "fence" in New York and Miami, Fla. When arrested one of them was administering narcotics to himself.

Gold Reserve Act violations required a great deal of investigative time, with 137 cases handled during the year. Such cases are usually complex and time consuming. Conferences were held with the Customs Agency Service and the Office of Domestic Gold and Silver Operations to effect closer coordination in the handling of gold cases.

The following tables show the number of criminal and noncriminal investigations completed and arrests made by the Secret Service in fiscal years 1964 and 1965.

Criminal and noncriminal cases investigated, fiscal years 1964 and 1965

Cases investigated	1964	1965	Percentage increase, or decrease (−)
Counterfeiting	12,166	16,213	33.3
Forged Government checks	41,236	39,399	−4.5
Forged Government bonds	5,795	5,586	−3.6
Miscellaneous criminal	2,217	2,903	30.9
Miscellaneous noncriminal	10,601	13,542	27.7
Total	72,015	77,643	7.8

Number of arrests, fiscal years 1964 and 1965

Offenses	1964	1965	Percentage increase, or decrease (−)
Counterfeiting	737	723	−1.9
Forged Government checks	3,192	2,720	−14.8
Forged or stolen bonds	74	69	−6.8
Miscellaneous	171	249	45.6
Total	4,174	3,761	−9.9

Cases of all types investigated by the Service during fiscal 1965 totaled 77,643, while 3,761 persons were arrested.

Offenses investigated by the Secret Service resulted in the conviction of 3,182 persons, 97.5 percent of the cases brought to trial during the year.

The trends in crimes over which this Service has jurisdiction remain generally consistent with nationwide trends in other crimes.

Cooperation with State, county, local authorities, and industry

The Secret Service has a fine record built up over many decades of cooperation and coordination with all local and Federal authorities. During the current fiscal year, special emphasis was given to maintaining and improving this record, with particular attention to protective activities. The Service continued the program developed over many years of fostering close cooperation with all segments of industry which are concerned with the laws enforced by the Service.

EXHIBITS

Public Debt Operations, Calls of Guaranteed Securities, Regulations, and Legislation

Treasury Notes and Treasury Bonds Offered and Allotted

Exhibit 1.—Treasury notes

Two Treasury circulars, one containing an exchange offering and the other containing a cash offering, are reproduced in this exhibit. Circulars pertaining to the other note offerings during the fiscal year 1965 are similar in form and therefore are not reproduced in this report. However, the essential details for each offering are summarized in the first table following the circulars and the final allotments of the new notes are shown in the second table.

DEPARTMENT CIRCULAR NO. 1-65. PUBLIC DEBT

TREASURY DEPARTMENT,
Washington, January 28, 1965.

I. OFFERING OF NOTES

1. The Secretary of the Treasury, pursuant to the authority of the Second Liberty Bond Act, as amended, offers $2,170,000,000, or thereabouts, of notes of the United States, designated 4 percent Treasury notes of Series E–1966, at 99.85 percent of their face value and accrued interest. The 2⅝ percent Treasury bonds of 1965, maturing February 15, 1965, will be accepted at par in payment or exchange, in whole or in part, to the extent subscriptions are allotted by the Treasury. The books will be open only on February 1, 1965, for the receipt of subscriptions.

II. DESCRIPTION OF NOTES

1. The notes will be dated February 15, 1965, and will bear interest from that date at the rate of 4 percent per annum, payable on a semiannual basis on May 15 and November 15, 1965, and on May 15 and November 15, 1966. They will mature November 15, 1966, and will not be subject to call for redemption prior to maturity.

2. The income derived from the notes is subject to all taxes imposed under the Internal Revenue Code of 1954. The notes are subject to estate, inheritance, gift, or other excise taxes, whether Federal or State, but are exempt from all taxation now or hereafter imposed on the principal or interest thereof by any State, or any of the possessions of the United States, or by any local taxing authority.

3. The notes will be acceptable to secure deposits of public moneys. They will not be acceptable in payment of taxes.

4. Bearer notes with interest coupons attached, and notes registered as to principal and interest, will be issued in denominations of $1,000, $5,000, $10,000, $100,000, $1,000,000, $100,000,000, and $500,000,000. Provision will be made for the interchange of notes of different denominations and of coupon and registered notes, and for the transfer of registered notes, under rules and regulations prescribed by the Secretary of the Treasury.

5. The notes will be subject to the general regulations of the Treasury Department, now or hereafter prescribed, governing United States notes.

III. SUBSCRIPTION AND ALLOTMENT

1. Subscriptions accepting the offer made by this circular will be received at the Federal Reserve banks and branches and at the Office of the Treasurer of the United States, Washington, D.C., 20220. Only the Federal Reserve

banks and the Treasury Department are authorized to act as official agencies. Commercial banks, which for this purpose are defined as banks accepting demand deposits, may submit subscriptions for account of customers provided the names of the customers are set forth in such subscriptions. Others than commercial banks will not be permitted to enter subscriptions except for their own account. Subscriptions from commercial banks for their own account will be restricted in each case to an amount not exceeding 50 percent of the combined capital (not including capital notes or debentures), surplus and undivided profits of the subscribing bank. Subscriptions will be received without deposit from banking institutions for their own account, federally-insured savings and loan associations, States, political subdivisions, or instrumentalities thereof, public pension and retirement and other public funds, international organizations in which the United States holds membership, foreign central banks and foreign States, dealers who make primary markets in Government securities and report daily to the Federal Reserve Bank of New York their positions with respect to Government securities and borrowings thereon, Federal Reserve banks and Government investment accounts. Subscriptions from all others must be accompanied by payment (in cash or in Treasury bonds of 1965, maturing February 15, 1965, which will be accepted at par) of 2 percent of the amount of notes applied for, not subject to withdrawal until after allotment. Registered bonds submitted as deposits should be assigned as provided in section V hereof. Following allotment, any portion of the 2 percent payment in excess of 2 percent of the amount of notes allotted may be released upon the request of the subscribers.

2. All subscribers requesting registered notes will be required to furnish appropriate identifying numbers as required on tax returns and other documents submitted to the Internal Revenue Service, i.e., an individual's social security number or an employer identification number.

3. All subscribers are required to agree not to purchase or to sell, or to make any agreements with respect to the purchase or sale or other disposition of any notes of this issue at a specific rate or price, until after midnight February 1, 1965.

4. Commercial banks in submitting subscriptions will be required to certify that they have no beneficial interest in any of the subscriptions they enter for the account of their customers, and that their customers have no beneficial interest in the banks' subscriptions for their own account.

5. Under the Second Liberty Bond Act, as amended, the Secretary of the Treasury has the authority to reject or reduce any subscription, to allot less than the amount of notes applied for, and to make different percentage allotments to various classes of subscribers when he deems it to be in the public interest; and any action he may take in these respects shall be final. Subject to the exercise of that authority, subscriptions will be allotted (1) in full for any State, political subdivision or instrumentality thereof, public pension and retirement and other public fund, international organization in which the United States holds membership, foreign central bank and foreign State, Federal Reserve bank, or Government investment account that certifies in writing that at 4 p.m., eastern standard time, January 27, 1965, it owned or had contracted to purchase for value 2⅝ percent Treasury bonds of 1965 in an amount equal to or greater than the amount of its subscription (if the certification is not made, none of such subscriber's subscription shall be subject to a preferred full allotment) and (2) for all others as publicly announced. Allotment notices will be sent out promptly upon allotment.

IV. PAYMENT

1. Payment at 99.85 percent of their face value and accrued interest, if any, for notes allotted hereunder must be made or completed on or before February 15, 1965, or on later allotment. Payment will not be deemed to have been completed where registered notes are requested if the appropriate identifying number, as required by paragraph 2 of section III hereof, has not been furnished; provided, however, if a subscriber has applied for but is unable to furnish the identifying number by the payment date only because it has not been issued, he may elect to receive, pending the furnishing of the identifying number, interim receipts and in this case payment will be deemed to have been completed. In every case where full payment is not completed, the payment with application up to 2 per-

cent of the amount of notes allotted shall, upon declaration made by the Secretary of the Treasury in his discretion, be forfeited to the United States. Payment may be made for any notes allotted hereunder in cash or by exchange of 2⅝ percent Treasury bonds of 1965, which will be accepted at par. A cash adjustment will be made for the difference ($1.50 per $1,000) between the par value of maturing bonds accepted in exchange and the issue price of the notes. The payment will be made in the case of bearer bonds following their acceptance and in the case of registered bonds following discharge of registration. In the case of registered bonds, the payment will be made by check drawn in accordance with the assignments on the bonds surrendered or by credit in any account maintained by a banking institution with the Federal Reserve bank of its district. Where payment is made with bonds in bearer form, coupons dated February 15, 1965, should be detached and cashed when due. In the case of registered bonds, the final interest due on February 15, 1965, will be paid by issue of interest checks in regular course to holders of record on January 15, 1965, the date the transfer books closed.

V. ASSIGNMENT OF REGISTERED BONDS

1. Treasury bonds of 1965 in registered form tendered as deposits and in payment for notes allotted hereunder should be assigned by the registered payees or assignees thereof, in accordance with the general regulations of the Treasury Department, in one of the forms hereafter set forth. Bonds tendered in payment should be surrendered to a Federal Reserve bank or branch or to the Office of the Treasurer of the United States, Washington, D.C., 20220. The bonds must be delivered at the expense and risk of the holder. If the notes are desired registered in the same name as the bonds surrendered, the assignment should be to "The Secretary of the Treasury for 4 percent Treasury Notes of Series E–1966"; if the notes are desired registered in another name, the assignment should be to "The Secretary of the Treasury for 4 percent Treasury Notes of Series E–1966 in the name of _____"; if notes in coupon form are desired, the assignment should be to "The Secretary of the Treasury for 4 percent Treasury Notes of Series E–1966 in coupon form to be delivered to _____."

VI. GENERAL PROVISIONS

1. As fiscal agents of the United States, Federal Reserve banks are authorized and requested to receive subscriptions, to make such allotments as may be prescribed by the Secretary of the Treasury, to issue such notices as may be necessary, to receive payment for and make delivery of notes on full-paid subscriptions allotted, and they may issue interim receipts pending delivery of the definitive notes.

2. The Secretary of the Treasury may at any time, or from time to time, prescribe supplemental or amendatory rules and regulations governing the offering, which will be communicated promptly to the Federal Reserve banks.

DOUGLAS DILLON,
Secretary of the Treasury.

DEPARTMENT CIRCULAR NO. 2–65. PUBLIC DEBT

TREASURY DEPARTMENT,
Washington, April 29, 1965.

I. OFFERING OF NOTES

1. The Secretary of the Treasury, pursuant to the authority of the Second Liberty Bond Act, as amended, offers notes of the United States, designated 4 percent Treasury notes of Series A–1966, at 99.85 percent of their face value and accrued interest, in exchange for the following notes maturing May 15, 1965:

4⅝ percent Treasury notes of Series A–1965; or
3⅞ percent Treasury notes of Series C–1965.

A cash payment will be due from subscribers as set forth in section IV hereof. The amount of this offering will be limited to the amount of eligible notes tendered in exchange. The books will be open only on May 3 through May 5, 1965, for the receipt of subscriptions.

2. In addition, holders of the notes enumerated in paragraph 1 of this section are offered the privilege of exchanging all or any part of such notes for 4¼ percent Treasury bonds of 1974, which offering is set forth in Department Circular, Public Debt Series—No. 3-65, issued simultaneously with this circular.

II. DESCRIPTION OF NOTES

1. The notes now offered will be identical in all respects with the 4 percent Treasury notes of Series A–1966 issued pursuant to Department Circulars, Public Debt Series—Nos. 3-62 and 4-64, dated February 5, 1962, and January 31, 1964, respectively, except that interest will accrue from May 15, 1965. With this exception the notes are described in the following quotation from Department Circular No. 3-62:

"1. The notes will be dated February 15, 1962, and will bear interest from that date at the rate of 4 percent per annum, payable semiannually on August 15, 1962, and thereafter on February 15 and August 15 in each year until the principal amount becomes payable. They will mature August 15, 1966, and will not be subject to call for redemption prior to maturity.

"2. The income derived from the notes is subject to all taxes imposed under the Internal Revenue Code of 1954. The notes are subject to estate, inheritance, gift, or other excise taxes, whether Federal or State, but are exempt from all taxation now or hereafter imposed on the principal or interest thereof by any State, or any of the possessions of the United States, or by any local taxing authority.

"3. The notes will be acceptable to secure deposits of public moneys. They will not be acceptable in payment of taxes.

"4. Bearer notes with interest coupons attached, and notes registered as to principal and interest, will be issued in denominations of $1,000, $5,000, $10,000, $100,000, $1,000,000, $100,000,000, and $500,000,000. Provision will be made for the interchange of notes of different denominations and of coupon and registered notes, and for the transfer of registered notes, under rules and regulations prescribed by the Secretary of the Treasury.

"5. The notes will be subject to the general regulations of the Treasury Department, now or hereafter prescribed, governing United States notes."

III. SUBSCRIPTION AND ALLOTMENT

1. Subscriptions accepting the offer made by this circular will be received at the Federal Reserve banks and branches and at the Office of the Treasurer of the United States, Washington, D.C., 20220. Banking institutions generally may submit subscriptions for account of customers, but only the Federal Reserve banks and the Treasury Department are authorized to act as official agencies.

2. All subscribers requesting registered notes will be required to furnish appropriate identifying numbers as required on tax returns and other documents submitted to the Internal Revenue Service, i.e., an individual's social security number or an employer identification number.

3. Under the Second Liberty Bond Act, as amended, the Secretary of the Treasury has the authority to reject or reduce any subscription, and to allot less than the amount of notes applied for when he deems it to be in the public interest; and any action he may take in these respects shall be final. Subject to the exercise of that authority, all subscriptions will be allotted in full.

IV. PAYMENT

1. Payment for the face amount of notes allotted hereunder together with a cash payment of $8.33425 per $1,000 (the difference between $9.83425 per $1,000 payable by the subscriber for accrued interest from February 15 to May 15, 1965, and $1.50 per $1,000 payable to the subscriber on account of the issue price, of the notes allotted) must be made on or before May 17, 1965, or on later allotment. Payment for the face amount of the notes allotted may be made only in a like face amount of notes of the two issues enumerated in paragraph 1 of section

I hereof, which together with the cash payment referred to in the preceding sentence should accompany the subscription. Payment will not be deemed to have been completed where registered notes are requested if the appropriate identifying number, as required by paragraph 2 of section III hereof, has not been furnished; provided, however, if a subscriber has applied for but is unable to furnish the identifying number by the payment date only because it has not been issued, he may elect to receive, pending the furnishing of the identifying number, interim receipts and in tnis case payment will be deemed to have been completed. When payment is made with notes in bearer form, coupons dated May 15, 1965, should be detached and cashed when due. When payment is made with registered notes, the final interest due on May 15, 1965, will be paid by issue of interest checks in regular course to holders of record on April 15, 1965, the date the transfer books closed.

V. ASSIGNMENT OF REGISTERED NOTES

1. Treasury notes of Series A–1965 and Series C–1965 in registered form tendered in payment for notes offered hereunder should be assigned by the registered payees or assignees thereof, in accordance with the general regulations of the Treasury Department governing assignments for transfer or exchange, in one of the forms hereafter set forth, and thereafter should be surrendered with the subscription to a Federal Reserve bank or branch or to the Office of the Treasurer of the United States, Washington, D.C., 20220. The maturing notes must be delivered at the expense and risk of the holder. If the new notes are desired registered in the same name as the notes surrendered, the assignment should be to "The Secretary of the Treasury for exchange for 4 percent Treasury Notes of Series A–1966"; if the new notes are desired registered in another name, the assignment should be to "The Secretary of the Treasury for exchange for 4 percent Treasury notes of Series A–1966 in the name of _____"; if new notes in coupon form are desired, the assignment should be to "The Secretary of the Treasury for exchange for 4 percent Treasury notes of Series A–1966 in coupon form to be delivered to _____."

VI. GENERAL PROVISIONS

1. As fiscal agents of the United States, Federal Reserve banks are authorized and requested to receive subscriptions, to make such allotments as may be prescribed by the Secretary of the Treasury, to issue such notices as may be necessary, to receive payment for and make delivery of notes on full-paid subscriptions allotted, and they may issue interim receipts pending delivery of the definitive notes.

2. The Secretary of the Treasury may at any time, or from time to time, prescribe supplemental or amendatory rules and regulations governing the offering, which will be communicated promptly to the Federal Reserve banks.

HENRY H. FOWLER,
Secretary of the Treasury.

Summary of information pertaining to Treasury notes issued during the fiscal year 1965

Date of preliminary announcement	Department circular Number	Department circular Date	Concurrent offering circular number	Treasury notes issued for exchange or for cash	Date of issue	Date of maturity	Date subscription books closed	Allotment payment date on or before (or on later allotment)
1964	*1964*				*1964*	*1966*	*1964*	*1964*
July 29	11-64	July 30	--------	3⅞ percent Series C-1966 issued at par for cash [1]	Aug. 15	Feb. 15	Aug. 3	Aug. 17
Oct. 28	12-64	Oct. 29	--------	4 percent Series D-1966 issued at par for cash [2]	Nov. 15	May 15	Nov. 2	Nov. 16
1965	*1965*				*1965*		*1965*	*1965*
Jan. 27	1-65	Jan. 28	--------	4 percent Series E-1966 issued at 99.85 for cash [3]	Feb. 15	Nov. 15	Feb. 1	Feb. 15
Apr. 28	2-65	Apr. 29	3-65	4 percent Series A-1966 issued at 99.85 in exchange for—4⅜ percent Series A-1965 notes maturing May 15, 1965; 3⅞ percent Series C-1965 notes maturing May 15, 1965.	[4] Feb. 15 *1962*	Aug. 15	May 5	[5] May 17

[1] ... of 5 ... pcnt Treasury notes of Series B-1964, ... and 3¾ percent ... notes of Series ... 1964, ... were not offered preemptive rights to exchange their holdings for the new notes. Payment for cash subscriptions allotted could be made in whole or in part by exchange at par of the notes of Series B-1964 and ...; ... dated Aug. 15, 1964, were detached from such notes in bearer form and cashed when due.

[2] ... of 4⅞ percent ... notes of Series C-1964 and 3¾ percent ... notes of Series ... 1964, were not ... two rights to ... their holdings for the new notes. Payment for cash ... made in whole or in part by exchange at par of the notes of Series C-1964 and F-1964; ... dated Nov. 15 1964 were detached from such notes in bearer form and

[3] Holders of 2⅝ percent Treasury bonds of 1965, which matured Feb. 15, 1965, were not offered preemptive rights to exchange their holdings for the new notes. See Department Circular No. 1-65 in this exhibit for provisions for subscription and payment.

[4] Interest payable from May 15, 1965.

[5] See Department Circular No. 2-65 in this exhibit for provisions for subscription and payment.

Allotments of Treasury notes issued during the fiscal year 1965, by Federal Reserve districts

[In thousands]

Federal Reserve district	3⅝ percent Series C-1966 notes [1]	4 percent Series D-1966 notes [2]	4 percent Series E-1966 notes [1]	4 percent Series A-1966 notes issued in exchange for—[3]		Total issued
				4⅝ percent Series A-1965 Treasury notes maturing May 15, 1965 [4]	3⅞ percent Series C-1965 Treasury notes maturing May 15, 1965 [4]	
Boston	$81,488	$132,622	$77,262	$22,337	$46,195	$68,532
New York	2,850,455	7,576,837	1,169,234	462,915	4,435,169	4,898,084
Philadelphia	44,272	78,274	54,708	14,783	23,771	38,554
Cleveland	124,018	183,453	103,888	36,939	68,473	105,412
Richmond	55,530	99,938	56,195	13,078	37,660	50,747
Atlanta	98,560	157,659	90,978	23,899	56,557	80,456
Chicago	273,940	491,421	327,143	100,057	180,864	280,921
St. Louis	60,570	125,160	61,846	21,882	65,918	87,800
Minneapolis	35,977	62,552	42,107	19,720	39,067	58,787
Kansas City	83,884	121,836	55,169	26,706	32,403	59,109
Dallas	46,479	90,630	35,726	12,006	34,612	46,618
San Francisco	278,440	392,615	179,066	35,857	66,093	101,950
Treasury	6,305	5,945	439	12,476	14,796	27,272
Total note allotments	4,039,918	9,518,942	2,253,821	802,655	5,101,587	5,904,242
Securities eligible for exchange:						
Exchanged in concurrent offerings				732,389	1,329,296	2,061,685
Total exchanged				1,535,044	6,430,883	7,965,927
Not submitted for exchange				280,666	189,234	469,900
Total securities eligible for exchange				1,815,710	6,620,117	8,435,827

[1] Subscriptions from States, political subdivisions or instrumentalities thereof, public pension and retirement and other public funds, international organizations in which the United States holds membership, foreign central banks and foreign States, Government investment accounts, and the Federal Reserve banks were allotted in full if the subscriber certified that it owned a like or greater amount of securities that could be used in payment for the notes. Subscriptions from all others in amounts up to $100,000 were allotted in full; amounts over $100,000 were allotted 15 percent, but not less than $100,000 to any one subscriber.

[2] Subscriptions from States, political subdivisions or instrumentalities thereof, public pension and retirement and other public funds, international organizations in which the United States holds membership, foreign central banks and foreign States, Government investment accounts, and the Federal Reserve banks were allotted in full if the subscriber certified that it owned a like or greater amount of securities that could be used in payment for the notes. Subscriptions from all others in amounts up to $100,000 were allotted in full; amounts over $100,000 were allotted 16.5 percent, but not less than $100,000 to any one subscriber.

[3] Subscriptions were allotted in full.

[4] 4¼ percent Treasury bonds of 1974 were also offered in exchange for this security.

Exhibit 2.—Treasury bonds

Two Treasury circulars, one containing an exchange offering for maturing issues and the other containing an advance refunding exchange offering, are reproduced in this exhibit. Circulars pertaining to the other bond offerings during the fiscal year 1965 are similar in form and therefore are not reproduced in this report. However, the essential details for each offering are summarized in the first table following the circulars and the final allotments of the new bonds are shown in the second table.

DEPARTMENT CIRCULAR NO. 10–64.   PUBLIC DEBT

TREASURY DEPARTMENT,
Washington, July 9, 1964.

I. OFFERING OF BONDS

1. The Secretary of the Treasury, pursuant to the authority of the Second Liberty Bond Act, as amended, invites subscriptions from the people of the United States for bonds of the United States, designated 4¼ percent Treasury bonds of 1987–92:

(1) at 100.10 percent of their face value in exchange for 3¾ percent Treasury notes of Series E–1964, dated August 1, 1961, due August 15, 1964;

(2) at 99.95 percent of their face value in exchange for 5 percent Treasury notes of Series B–1964, dated October 15, 1959, due August 15, 1964;

(3) at 99.95 percent of their face value in exchange for 3¾ percent Treasury notes of Series F–1964, dated August 15, 1963, due November 15, 1964;

(4) at 99.60 percent of their face value in exchange for 4⅞ percent Treasury notes of Series C–1964, dated February 15, 1960, due November 15, 1964;

(5) at 99.90 percent of their face value in exchange for 3⅞ percent Treasury notes of Series C–1965, dated November 15, 1963, due May 15, 1965;

(6) at 100.30 percent of their face value in exchange for 3⅝ percent Treasury notes of Series B–1966, dated May 15, 1962, due February 15, 1966;

(7) at 100.15 percent of their face value in exchange for 3¾ percent Treasury bonds of 1966, dated November 15, 1960, due May 15, 1966;

(8) at 99.75 percent of their face value in exchange for 4 percent Treasury notes of Series A–1966, dated February 15, 1962, due August 15, 1966; or

(9) at 100.70 percent of their face value in exchange for 3⅝ percent Treasury notes of Series B–1967, dated March 15, 1963, due February 15, 1967.

Interest adjustments as of July 22, 1964, and the cash payments on account of the issue prices of the new bonds will be made as set forth in section IV hereof. The amount of the offering under this circular will be limited to the amount of eligible securities tendered in exchange and accepted. Delivery of the new bonds will be made on July 24, 1964. The books will be open only on July 13 through July 16, 1964, for the receipt of subscriptions for this issue.

2. In addition to the offering under this circular, holders of securities of the issues enumerated in paragraph 1 of this section are offered the privilege of exchanging all or any part of such securities for 4 percent Treasury bonds of 1969 (Oct.), or 4⅛ percent Treasury bonds of 1973, which offerings are set forth in Department Circulars, Public Debt Series Nos. 8–64 and 9–64, respectively, issued simultaneously with this circular.

3. *Nonrecognition of gain or loss for Federal income tax purposes.*[1]—Pursuant to the provisions of section 1037(a) of the Internal Revenue Code of 1954 as added by Public Law 86–346 (approved September 22, 1959), the Secretary of the Treasury hereby declares that no gain or loss shall be recognized for Federal income tax purposes upon the exchange with the United States of the

3⅞ percent Treasury notes of Series C–1965,
3⅝ percent Treasury notes of Series B–1966,
3¾ percent Treasury bonds of 1966,
4 percent Treasury notes of Series A–1966, or
3⅝ percent Treasury notes of Series B–1967,

solely for the 4¼ percent Treasury bonds of 1987–92. Section 1031(b) of the Code, however, requires recognition of any gain realized on the exchange to the

---

[1] Gain or loss, if any, upon the exchange of the securities of the first four issues listed in paragraph 1 of this section, must be fully recognized under the Code.

extent that money is received by the security holder in connection with the exchange. To the extent not recognized at the time of the exchange, gain or loss, if any, upon the obligations surrendered in exchange will be taken into account upon the disposition or redemption of the new obligations.

II. DESCRIPTION OF BONDS

1. The bonds now offered will be identical in all respects with the 4¼ percent Treasury bonds of 1987–92 issued pursuant to Department Circular, Public Debt Series No. 14–62, dated July 30, 1962, except that interest will accrue from July 22, 1964. With this exception the bonds are described in the following quotation from Department Circular No. 14–62:

"1. The bonds will be dated August 15, 1962, and will bear interest from that date at the rate of 4¼ percent per annum payable semiannually on February 15 and August 15 in each year until the principal amount becomes payable. They will mature August 15, 1992, but may be redeemed at the option of the United States on and after August 15, 1987, in whole or in part, at par and accrued interest, on any interest day or days, on 4 months' notice of redemption given in such manner as the Secretary of the Treasury shall prescribe. In case of partial redemption the bonds to be redeemed will be determined by such method as may be prescribed by the Secretary of the Treasury. From the date of redemption designated in any such notice, interest on the bonds called for redemption shall cease.

"2. The income derived from the bonds is subject to all taxes imposed under the Internal Revenue Code of 1954. The bonds are subject to estate, inheritance, gift, or other excise taxes, whether Federal or State, but are exempt from all taxation now or hereafter imposed on the principal or interest thereof by any State, or any of the possessions of the United States, or by any local taxing authority.

"3. The bonds will be acceptable to secure deposits of public moneys.

"4. Bearer bonds with interest coupons attached, and bonds registered as to principal and interest, will be issued in denominations of $500, $1,000, $5,000, $10,000, $100,000, and $1,000,000. Provision will be made for the interchange of bonds of different denominations and of coupon and registered bonds, and for the transfer of registered bonds, under rules and regulations prescribed by the Secretary of the Treasury.

"5. Any bonds issued hereunder which upon the death of the owner constitute part of his estate, will be redeemed at the option of the duly constituted representatives of the deceased owner's estate, at par and accrued interest to date of payment,[1] provided:

(a) that the bonds were actually owned by the decedent at the time of his death; and

(b) that the Secretary of the Treasury be authorized to apply the entire proceeds of redemption to the payment of Federal estate taxes.

Registered bonds submitted for redemption hereunder must be duly assigned to 'The Secretary of the Treasury for redemption, the proceeds to be paid to the District Director of Internal Revenue at _____ for credit on Federal estate taxes due from estate of _____.' Owing to the periodic closing of the transfer books and the impossibility of stopping payment of interest to the registered owner during the closed period, registered bonds received after the closing of the books for payment during such closed period will be paid only at par with a deduction of interest from the date of payment to the next interest payment date;[2] bonds received during the closed period for payment at a date after the books reopen will be paid at par plus accrued interest from the reopening of the books to the date of payment. In either case checks for the full six months' interest due on the last day of the closed period will be forwarded to the owner in due course. All bonds submitted must be accompanied by Form PD 1782,[3] properly completed, signed and certified, and by proof of the representa-

---

[1] An exact half-year's interest is computed for each full half-year period irrespective of the actual number of days in the half year. For a fractional part of any half year, computation is on the basis of the actual number of days in such half year.
[2] The transfer books are closed from January 16 through February 15, and from July 16 through August 15 (both dates inclusive) in each year.
[3] Copies of Form PD 1782 may be obtained from any Federal Reserve bank or from the Treasury Department, Washington, D.C., 20226.

tives' authority in the form of a court certificate or a certified copy of the representatives' letters of appointment issued by the court. The certificate, or the certification to the letters, must be under the seal of the court, and except in the case of a corporate representative, must contain a statement that the appointment is in full force and be dated within six months prior to the submission of the bonds, unless the certificate or letters show that the appointment was made within one year immediately prior to such submission. Upon payment of the bonds appropriate memorandum receipt will be forwarded to the representatives, which will be followed in due course by formal receipt from the district director of Internal Revenue.

"6· The bonds will be subject to the general regulations of the Treasury Department, now or hereafter prescribed, governing United States bonds."

III. SUBSCRIPTION AND ALLOTMENT

1. Subscriptions will be received at the Federal Reserve banks and branches and at the Office of the Treasurer of the United States, Washington, D.C., 20220. Banking institutions generally may submit subscriptions for account of customers, but only the Federal Reserve banks and the Treasury Department are authorized to act as official agencies.

2. All subscribers requesting registered bonds will be required to furnish appropriate identifying numbers as required on tax returns and other documents submitted to the Internal Revenue Service, i.e., an individual's social security number or an employer identification number.

3. The Secretary of the Treasury reserves the right to reject or reduce any subscription, and to allot less than the amount of bonds applied for; and any action he may take in these respects shall be final. Subject to these reservations, all subscriptions will be allotted in full. Allotment notices will be sent out promptly upon allotment.

IV. PAYMENT

1. Payment for the face amount of bonds allotted hereunder must be made on or before July 24, 1964, or on later allotment, and may be made only in a like face amount of securities of the nine issues enumerated in paragraph 1 of section I hereof, which should accompany the subscription. Payment will not be deemed to have been completed where registered bonds are requested if the appropriate identifying number, as required by paragraph 2 of section III hereof, has not been furnished; provided, however, if a subscriber has applied for but is unable to furnish the identifying number by the payment date only because it has not been issued, he may elect to receive, pending the furnishing of the identifying number, interim receipts and in this case payment will be deemed to have been completed. Cash payments due from subscribers (paragraphs 2, 4, 5, 6, 7, 8, and 10 below) should accompany the subscription. Cash payments due to subcribers (paragraphs 3 and 9 below) will be made in the case of bearer securities following their acceptance and in the case of registered securities following discharge of registration. In the case of registered securities, the payment will be made by check drawn in accordance with the assignments on the securities surrendered or by credit in any account maintained by a banking institution with the Federal Reserve bank of its district.

2. *3¾ percent notes of Series E–1964.*—Coupons dated August 15, 1964, must be attached to the notes in bearer form when surrendered. Accrued interest from February 15 to July 22, 1964 ($16.27747 per $1,000) will be credited, accrued interest from February 15 to July 22, 1964 ($18.44780 per $1,000) on the bonds to be issued plus the payment ($1.00 per $1,000) due the United States on account of the issue price of the bonds will be charged, and the difference ($3.17033 per $1,000) must be paid by subscribers.

3. *5 percent notes of Series B–1964.*—Coupons dated August 15, 1964, must be attached to the notes in bearer form when surrendered. Accrued interest from February 15 to July 22, 1964 ($21.70330 per $1,000) plus the payment ($0.50 per $1,000) due to the subscriber on account of the issue price of the bonds will be credited, accrued interest from February 15 to July 22, 1964 ($18.44780 per $1,000) on the bonds to be issued will be charged, and the difference ($3.75550 per $1,000) will be paid to subscribers.

3¾ percent notes of Series F–1964.—Coupons dated November 15, 1964, must be attached to the notes in bearer form when surrendered. Accrued interest from May 15 to July 22, 1964 ($6.92935 per $1,000) plus the payment ($0.50 per $1,000) due to the subscriber on account of the issue price of the bonds will be credited, accrued interest from February 15 to July 22, 1964 ($18.44780 per $1,000) on the bonds to be issued will be charged, and the difference ($11.01845 per $1,000) must be paid by subscribers.

5. *4⅞ percent notes of Series C–1964.*—Coupons dated November 15, 1964, must be attached to the notes in bearer form when surrendered. Accrued interest from May 15 to July 22, 1964 ($9.00815 per $1,000) plus the payment ($4.00 per $1,000) due to the subscriber on account of the issue price of the bonds will be credited, accrued interest from February 15, to July 22, 1964 ($18.44780 per $1,000) on the bonds to be issued will be charged, and the difference ($5.43965 per $1,000) must be paid by subscribers.

6. *3⅞ percent notes of Series C–1965.*—Coupons dated November 15, 1964, and May 15, 1965, must be attached to the notes in bearer form when surrendered. Accrued interest from May 15 to July 22, 1964 ($7.16033 per $1,000) plus the payment ($1.00 per $1,000) due to the subscriber on account of the issue price of the bonds will be credited, accrued interest from February 15 to July 22, 1964 ($18.44780 per $1,000) on the bonds to be issued will be charged, and the difference ($10.28747 per $1,000) must be paid by subscribers.

7. *3⅝ percent notes of Series B–1966.*—Coupons dated August 15, 1964, and all subsequent coupons, must be attached to the notes in bearer form when surrendered. Accrued interest from February 15 to July 22, 1964 ($15.73489 per $1,000) will be credited, accrued interest from February 15 to July 22, 1964 ($18.44780 per $1,000) on the bonds to be issued plus the payment ($3.00 per $1,000) due the United States on account of the issue price of the bonds will be charged, and the difference ($5.71291 per $1,000) must be paid by subscribers.

8. *3¾ percent bonds of 1966.*—Coupons dated November 15, 1964, and all subsequent coupons must be attached to the bonds in bearer form when surrendered. Accrued interest from May 15 to July 22, 1964 ($6.92935 per $1,000) will be credited, accrued interest from February 15 to July 22, 1964 ($18.44780 per $1,000) on the bonds to be issued plus the payment ($1.50 per $1,000) due the United States on account of the issue price of the new bonds will be charged, and the difference ($13.01845 per $1,000) must be paid by subscribers.

9. *4 percent notes of Series A–1966.*—Coupons dated August 15, 1964, and all subsequent coupons, must be attached to the notes in bearer form when surrendered. Accrued interest from February 15 to July 22, 1964 ($17.36264 per $1,000) plus the payment ($2.50 per $1,000) due to the subscriber on account of the issue price of the bonds will be credited, accrued interest from February 15 to July 22, 1964 ($18.44780 per $1,000) on the bonds to be issued will be charged, and the difference ($1.41484 per $1,000) will be paid to subscribers.

10. *3⅝ percent notes of Series B–1967.*—Coupons dated August 15, 1964, and all subsequent coupons, must be attached to the notes in bearer form when surrendered. Accrued interest from February 15 to July 22, 1964 ($15.73489 per $1,000) will be credited, accrued interest from February 15 to July 22, 1964 ($18.44780 per $1,000) on the bonds to be issued plus the payment ($7.00 per $1,000) due the United States on account of the issue price of the bonds will be charged, and the difference ($9.71291 per $1,000) must be paid by subscribers.

V. ASSIGNMENT OF REGISTERED SECURITIES

1. Eligible Treasury securities in registered form tendered in payment for bonds offered hereunder should be assigned by the registered payees or assignees thereof, in accordance with the general regulations of the Treasury Department governing assignments for transfer or exchange, in one of the forms hereafter set forth, and thereafter should be surrendered with the subscription to a Federal Reserve bank or branch or to the Office of the Treasurer of the United States, Washington, D.C., 20220. The securities must be delivered at the expense and risk of the holder. If the new bonds are desired registered in the same name as the securities surrendered, the assignment should be to "The Secretary of the Treasury for exchange for 4¼ percent Treasury bonds of 1987–92"; if the new bonds are desired registered in another name, the assignment should be to "The Secretary of the Treasury for exchange for 4¼ percent Treasury Bonds of 1987–92 in the name of _____"; if new bonds in coupon form are desired, the assignment should be to "The Secretary of the

Treasury for exchange for 4¼ percent Treasury Bonds of 1987–92 in coupon form to be delivered to _____."

VI. GENERAL PROVISIONS

1. As fiscal agents of the United States, Federal Reserve banks are authorized and requested to receive subscriptions, to make allotments on the basis and up to the amounts indicated by the Secretary of the Treasury to the Federal Reserve banks of the respective districts, to issue allotment notices, to receive payment for bonds allotted, to make delivery of bonds on full-paid subscriptions allotted, and they may issue interim receipts pending delivery of the definitive bonds.

2. The Secretary of the Treasury may at any time, or from time to time, prescribe supplemental or amendatory rules and regulations governing the offering, which will be communicated promptly to the Federal Reserve banks.

DOUGLAS DILLON,
Secretary of the Treasury.

DEPARTMENT CIRCULAR NO. 3–65. PUBLIC DEBT

TREASURY DEPARTMENT,
Washington, April 29, 1965.

I. OFFERING OF BONDS

1. The Secretary of the Treasury, pursuant to the authority of the Second Liberty Bond Act, as amended, offers bonds of the United States, designated 4¼ percent Treasury bonds of 1974, at 100.25 percent of their face value, in exchange for the following notes maturing May 15, 1965:

4⅝ percent Treasury notes of Series A–1965; or
3⅞ percent Treasury notes of Series C–1965.

The amount of this offering will be limited to the amount of eligible notes tendered in exchange. The books will be open only on May 3 through May 5, 1965, for the receipt of subscriptions.

2. In addition, holders of the notes enumerated in paragraph 1 of this section are offered the privilege of exchanging all or any part of such notes for 4 percent Treasury notes of Series A–1966, which offering is set forth in Department Circular, Public Debt Series–No. 2–65, issued simultaneously with this circular.

II. DESCRIPTION OF BONDS

1. The bonds now offered will be identical in all respects with the 4¼ percent Treasury bonds of 1974 issued pursuant to Department Circular, Public Debt Series No. 7–64, dated April 30, 1964, except that interest will accrue from May 15, 1965. With this exception the bonds are described in the following quotation from Department Circular No. 7–64:

"1. The bonds will be dated May 15, 1964, and will bear interest from that date at the rate of 4¼ percent per annum, payable semiannually on November 15, 1964, and thereafter on May 15 and November 15 in each year until the principal amount becomes payable. They will mature May 15, 1974, and will not be subject to call for redemption prior to maturity.

"2. The income derived from the bonds is subject to all taxes imposed under the Internal Revenue Code of 1954. The bonds are subject to estate, inheritance, gift, or other excise taxes, whether Federal or State, but are exempt from all taxation now or hereafter imposed on the principal or interest thereof by any State, or any of the possessions of the United States, or by any local taxing authority.

"3. The bonds will be acceptable to secure deposits of public moneys.

"4. Bearer bonds with interest coupons attached, and bonds registered as to principal and interest, will be issued in denominations of $500, $1,000, $5,000, $10,000, $100,000, and $1,000,000. Provision will be made for the interchange of bonds of different denominations and of coupon and registered bonds, and for the transfer of registered bonds, under rules and regulations prescribed by the Secretary of the Treasury.

"5. Any bonds issued hereunder which are owned by a decedent at the time of his death and thereupon constitute a part of his estate will be redeemed at par and accrued interest prior to maturity, provided the Secretary of the Treasury is authorized by the representative of the estate to apply the entire proceeds of redemption to payment of the decedents Federal estate taxes.

"6. The bonds will be subject to the general regulations of the Treasury Department, now or hereafter prescribed, governing United States bonds."

III. SUBSCRIPTION AND ALLOTMENT

1. Subscriptions accepting the offer made by this circular will be received at the Federal Reserve banks and branches and at the Office of the Treasurer of the United States, Washington, D.C., 20220. Banking institutions generally may submit subscriptions for account of customers, but only the Federal Reserve banks and the Treasury Department are authorized to act as official agencies.

2. All subscribers requesting registered bonds will be required to furnish appropriate identifying numbers as required on tax returns and other documents submitted to the Internal Revenue Service, i.e., an individual's social security number or an employer identification number.

3. Under the Second Liberty Bond Act, as amended, the Secretary of the Treasury has the authority to reject or reduce any subscription, and to allot less than the amount of bonds applied for when he deems it to be in the public interest; and any action he may take in these respects shall be final. Subject to the exercise of that authority, all subscriptions will be allotted in full.

IV. PAYMENT

1. Payment for the face amount of bonds allotted hereunder must be made on or before May 17, 1965, or on later allotment, and may be made only in a like face amount of notes of the two issues enumerated in paragraph 1 of section I hereof, which should accompany the subscription. A cash payment of $2.50 per $1,000 on account of the issue price of the new bonds must be paid by subscribers and should accompany the subscription. Payment will not be deemed to have been completed where registered bonds are requested if the appropriate identifying number, as required by paragraph 2 of section III hereof, has not been furnished; provided, however, if a subscriber has applied for but is unable to furnish the identifying number by the payment date only because it has not been issued, he may elect to receive, pending the furnishing of the identifying number, interim receipts and in this case payment will be deemed to have been completed. When payment is made with notes in bearer form, coupons dated May 15, 1965, should be detached and cashed when due. When payment is made with registered notes, the final interest due on May 15, 1965, will be paid by issue of interest checks in regular course to holders of record on April 15, 1965, the date the transfer books closed.

V. ASSIGNMENT OF REGISTERED NOTES

1. Treasury Notes of Series A–1965 and Series C–1965 in registered form tendered in payment for bonds offered hereunder should be assigned by the registered payees or assignees thereof, in accordance with the general regulations of the Treasury Department governing assignments for transfer or exchange, in one of the forms hereafter set forth, and thereafter should be surrendered with the subscription to a Federal Reserve bank or branch or to the Office of the Treasurer of the United States, Washington, D.C., 20220. The notes must be delivered at the expense and risk of the holder. If the bonds are desired registered in the same name as the notes surrendered, the assignment should be to "The Secretary of the Treasury for exchange for 4¼ percent Treasury Bonds of 1974"; if the bonds are desired registered in another name, the assignment should be to "The Secretary of the Treasury for exchange for 4¼ percent Treasury Bonds of 1974 in the name of _____";
if bonds in coupon form are desired, the assignment should be to "The Secretary of the Treasury for exchange for 4¼ percent Treasury Bonds of 1974 in coupon form to be delivered to _____"

VI. GENERAL PROVISIONS

1. As fiscal agents of the United States, Federal Reserve banks are authorized and requested to receive subscriptions, to make such allotments as may be prescribed by the Secretary of the Treasury, to issue such notices as may be necessary, to receive payment for and make delivery of bonds on full-paid subscriptions allotted, and they may issue interim receipts pending delivery of the definitive bonds.

2. The Secretary of the Treasury may at any time, or from time to time, prescribe supplemental or amendatory rules and regulations governing the offering, which will be communicated promptly to the Federal Reserve banks.

HENRY H. FOWLER,
Secretary of the Treasury.

Summary of information pertaining to Treasury bonds issued during the fiscal year 1965

Date of preliminary announcement	Department circular		Concurrent offering circular number	Treasury bonds issued for exchange	Date of issue	Date of maturity	Date subscription books closed	Allotment payment date on or before (or on later allotment)
	Number	Date						
1964 July 8	8–64	*1964* July 9	9–64, 10–64	4 percent of 1969 issued at prices indicated below in exchange for— 3¾ percent Series E–1964 notes maturing Aug. 15, 1964 (99.70);[4] 5 percent Series B–1964 notes maturing Aug. 15, 1964 [illegible];[4] 3¾ percent Series F–1964 notes maturing Nov. 15, 1964 (99.55);[4] 4⅞ percent Series C–1964 notes maturing Nov. 15, 1964 (99.20);[4] 3⅞ percent Series C–1965 notes maturing May 15, 1965 [illegible]; 3⅝ percent Series B–1966 notes maturing Feb. 15, 1966 [illegible]; 3¾ percent Treasury bonds of 1966 maturing May 15, 1966 (99.75); 4 percent Series A–1966 notes maturing Aug. 15, 1966 (99.35); 3⅝ percent Series B–1967 notes maturing Feb. 15, 1967 (100.30).	*1957* [1] Oct. 1	*1969* Oct. 1	*1964* July 16	*1964* [2, 3] July 24
July 8	9–64	July 9	8–64, 10–64	4⅛ percent of 1973 issued at prices indicated below in exchange for— 3¾ percent Series E–1964 notes maturing Aug. 15, 1964 (99.25);[4] 5 percent Series B–1964 notes maturing Aug. 15, 1964 (99.10);[4] 3¾ percent Series F–1964 notes maturing Nov. 15, 1964 (99.90);[4] 4⅞ percent Series C–1964 notes maturing Nov. 15, 1964 (99.95);[4] 3⅞ percent Series C–1965 notes maturing May 15, 1965 (99.05); 3⅝ percent Series B–1966 notes maturing Feb. 15, 1966 (99.45); 3¾ percent Treasury bonds of 1966 maturing May 15, 1966 (99.30); 4 percent Series A–1966 notes maturing Aug. 15, 1966 (99.90); 3⅝ percent Series B–1967 notes maturing Feb. 15, 1967 (99.85).	*1964* July 22	*1973* Nov. 15	July 16	[2, 5] July 24
July 8	10–64	July 9	8–64, 9–64	4¼ percent of 1987–92 issued at prices indicated below in exchange for— 3¾ percent Series E–1964 notes maturing Aug. 15, 1964 (100.10);[4] 5 percent Series B–1964 notes maturing Aug. 15 1964 (99.95);[4] 3¾ percent Series F–1964 notes maturing Nov. 15, 1964 (99.95);[4] 4⅞ percent Series C–1964 notes maturing Nov. 15, 1964 (99.60);[4] 3⅞ percent Series C–1965 notes maturing May 15, 1965 (99.90); 3⅝ percent Series B–1966 notes maturing Feb. 15, 1966 (100.30); 3¾ percent Treasury bonds of 1966 maturing May 15, 1966 (100.15) 4 percent Series A–1966 notes maturing Aug. 15, 1966 (99.75); 3⅝ percent Series B–1967 notes maturing Feb. 15, 1967 (100.70).	*1962* [1] Aug. 15	*1992* Aug. 15	July 16	[6] July 24

Footnotes at end of table.

Summary of information pertaining to Treasury bonds issued during the fiscal year 1965—Continued

Date of preliminary announcement	Department circular: Number	Department circular: Date	Concurrent offering circular number	Treasury bonds issued for exchange	Date of issue	Date of maturity	Date subscription books closed	Allotment payment date on or before (or on later allotment)
Dec. 30	13-64	Dec. 31	14-64, 15-64	4 percent of 1970 issued at prices indicated below in exchange for—	*1965* Jan. 15	*1970* Feb. 15	*1965* Jan. 8	*1965* [7] [8] Jan. 19
				2⅝ percent Treasury bonds of 1965 maturing Feb. 15, 1965 (99.40);[4]				
				3½ percent Series B-1965 notes maturing Nov. 15, 1965 (99.55);				
				4 percent Series E-1965 notes maturing Nov. 15, 1965 (99.19);				
				3⅝ percent Series B-1966 notes maturing Feb. 15, 1966 (99.60);				
				3⅞ percent Series C-1966 notes maturing Feb. 15, 1966 (99.30);				
				3¾ percent Treasury bonds of 1966 maturing May 15, 1966 (99.50);				
				3¾ percent Series A-1967 notes maturing Aug. 15, 1967 (99.95);				
				3⅝ percent Treasury bonds of 1967 maturing Nov. 15, 1967 (100.30).				
Dec. 30	14-64	Dec. 31	13-64, 15-64	4⅛ percent of 1974 issued at prices indicated below in exchange for—	Jan. 15	*1974* Feb. 15	Jan. 8	[7] [9] Jan. 19
				2⅝ percent Treasury bonds of 1965 maturing Feb. 15, 1965 (99.35);[4]				
				3½ percent Series B-1965 notes maturing Nov. 15, 1965 (99.50);				
				4 percent Series E-1965 notes maturing Nov. 15, 1965 (99.05);				
				3⅝ percent Series B-1966 notes maturing Feb. 15, 1966 (99.55);				
				3⅞ percent Series C-1966 notes maturing Feb. 15, 1966 (99.25);				
				3¾ percent Treasury bonds of 1966 maturing May 15, 1966 (99.45);				
				3¾ percent Series A-1967 notes maturing Aug. 15, 1967 (99.90);				
				3⅝ percent Treasury bonds of 1967 maturing Nov. 15, 1967 (100.25).				
Dec. 30	15-64	Dec. 31	13-64, 14-64	4¼ percent of 1987-92 issued at prices indicated below in exchange for—	*1962* [10] Aug. 15	*1992* Aug. 15	Jan. 8	[7] [11] Jan. 19
				2⅝ percent Treasury bonds of 1965 maturing Feb. 15, 1965 (100.25);[4]				
				3½ percent Series B-1965 notes maturing Nov. 15, 1965 (100.40);				
				4 percent Series E-1965 notes maturing Nov. 15, 1965 (99.95);				
				3⅝ percent Series B-1966 notes maturing Feb. 15, 1966 (100.45);				
				3⅞ percent Series C-1966 notes maturing Feb. 15, 1966 (100.15);				
				3¾ percent Treasury bonds of 1966 maturing May 15, 1966 (100.35);				
				3¾ percent Series A-1967 notes maturing Aug. 15, 1967 (100.80);				
				3⅝ percent Treasury bonds of 1967 maturing Nov. 15, 1967 (101.15).				
1965 Apr. 28	3-65	*1965* Apr. 29	2-65	4¼ percent of 1974 issued at prices indicated below in exchange for—	*1964* [12] May 15	*1974* May 15	May 5	[13] May 17
				4⅝ percent Series A-1965 notes maturing May 15, 1965 (100.25);				
				3⅞ percent Series C-1965 notes maturing May 15, 1965 (100.25).				

[1] Interest payable from July 22, 1964.

[2] All coupons dated subsequent to the payment date were required to be attached to bearer securities submitted in exchange and interest was adjusted on all securities as of July 22, 1965.

[3] Accrued interest on old security (Col. 2) and amount due subscriber on account of issue price of new bond (Col. 3) were credited to subscriber, accrued interest on new bond (Col. 4) and amount due from subscriber on account of issue price of new bond (Col. 5) were charged to subscriber, and difference paid to subscriber (Col. 6) or collected from subscriber (Col. 7) as follows (per $1,000):

Security	Col. 2	Col. 3	Col. 4	Col. 5	Col. 6	Col. 7
3¾% Note E-1964	$16.27747	$[illegible].00	$12.24044	-----	$7.03703	--------
4% Note B-1964	21. [illegible]	4.50	12.24044	-----	13.92286	--------
[illegible] Note [illegible]-[illegible]64	6. [illegible]	4.50	12.24044	-----	--------	$0.81109
4[illegible]% Note [illegible]64	9. [illegible]	8.00	12.24044	-----	4.76771	--------
3⅞% Note [illegible]65	7. [illegible]	5.00	12.24044	-----	--------	0.08011
3⅝% Note B-1966	15. [illegible]	1.00	12.24044	-----	4.49445	--------
3¾% Bond [illegible]	6. [illegible]	2.50	12.24044	-----	--------	2.81109
4% Note [illegible]66	17. [illegible]	6.50	12.24044	-----	11.62220	--------
3⅝% Note [illegible]	15.73489	-----	12.24044	$[illegible].00	0.49445	--------

[4] Holders of [illegible] were not [illegible] the nontaxable [illegible] privil[illegible].

[5] [illegible] were made to [illegible] as [illegible] (per $1,000):

Security	Accrued interest on old security	Paid on account of issue price of [illegible]	Total
3[illegible]% Note E-1964	$16.27747	$7.50	$[illegible].77747
[illegible]% Note B-[illegible]	[illegible].[illegible]	9.00	30.70330
3¾% Note F-[illegible]	6.2935	9.00	15.2935
[illegible]% Note C-1964	9.[illegible]	12.50	[illegible].[illegible]
3⅞% Note C-1965	7.[illegible]	9.50	16.[illegible]
[illegible]% Note B-[illegible]	15.73489	5.50	21.23489
3[illegible]% Bond 1966	6.2935	7.00	13.2935
[illegible]% Note A-1966	17.[illegible]	11.00	28.[illegible]
[illegible]% Note B-1967	15.[illegible]	1.50	17.[illegible]

[6] See Department Circular No. [illegible] in this exhibit for [illegible] and [illegible].

[7] All [illegible] to the [illegible] were [illegible] to be [illegible] to [illegible] in [illegible] and [illegible] was [illegible] on all [illegible]rities as of [illegible]. 15, [illegible].

[8] [illegible] interest on old [illegible] was [illegible] to [illegible] (Col. 2) and amount due to [illegible] (Col. 3) or due from [illegible] (Col. 4) on [illegible] of issue price of new [illegible] was [illegible] or [illegible] and the net [illegible] was paid to [illegible] (Col. 5) as fo[illegible] (per $1,000):

Security	Col. 2	Col. 3	Col. 4	Col. 5
2⅝% Bond [illegible]	1[illegible].[illegible]	$6.00	-----	$16.[illegible]
[illegible]% Note B-1965	5.[illegible]	4.50	-----	10.[illegible]
[illegible]% Note E-1965	6.[illegible]	9.00	-----	15.[illegible]
[illegible]% Note B-1966	15.07133	4.00	-----	19.07133
[illegible]% Note [illegible]	16.[illegible]	7.00	-----	[illegible].[illegible]
[illegible]% Bond [illegible]	[illegible]	5.00	-----	11.[illegible]
3¾% Note [illegible]67	15.[illegible]	0.50	-----	16.[illegible]
[illegible]% Bond [illegible]	6.10843	-----	$[illegible].00	3.[illegible]

[9] [illegible] interest on old [illegible] was [illegible] to [illegible] (Col. 2) and [illegible] due to [illegible] (Col. 3) or due from [illegible] (Col. 4) on [illegible] of issue price of new [illegible] was [illegible] or charged and the net amount was paid to [illegible] (Col. 5) as [illegible] (per [illegible]):

Security	Col. 2	Col. 3	Col. 4	Col. 5
[illegible]% Bond 1965	1[illegible].[illegible]	$6.50	-----	$17.41372
[illegible]% Note B-[illegible]	5.89779	5.00	-----	[illegible]
[illegible]% Note E-[illegible]	6.74033	9.50	-----	16.24033
[illegible]% Note B-[illegible]	15.07133	4.50	-----	[illegible]
[illegible]% Note C-[illegible]	16.11073	7.50	-----	[illegible]
[illegible]% Bond 1966	6.31906	5.50	-----	11.[illegible]
[illegible]% Note A-[illegible]	15.59103	1.00	-----	[illegible]
3⅝% Bond 1967	6.10843	-----	$2.50	3.60843

[10] Interest payable from [illegible]. [illegible], [illegible].

[11] [illegible] interest on old security (Col. 2) and [illegible] due [illegible] on account of issue price of new bond (Col. 3) were [illegible] to [illegible], [illegible] on new bond (Col. 4) and [illegible] due from [illegible] on [illegible] of issue price of new bond (Col. 5) were charged to [illegible] and the [illegible] (Col. 6) was [illegible] from sub[illegible] as [illegible] (per $1,000):

[illegible]	Col. 2	Col. 3	Col. 4	Col. 5	Col. 6
[illegible]% Bond 1965	$10.91[illegible]	-----	$17.66984	$2.50	$9.25612
[illegible]% Note B-[illegible]	5.89779	$0.50	17.66984	-----	15.77205
[illegible]% Note E-1965	[illegible]	-----	17.66984	4.00	10.42951
[illegible]% Note B-1966	15.07133	-----	17.66984	4.50	7.09851
[illegible]% Note C-1966	16.11073	-----	17.66984	1.50	3.05911
[illegible]% Bond [illegible]	6.31906	-----	17.66984	3.50	14.85078
3¾% Note A-1967	15.59103	-----	17.66984	8.00	10.07881
[illegible]% Bond 1967	6.10843	-----	17.66984	1[illegible]	23.06141

[12] [illegible] payable from May 15, [illegible].

[13] See Department [illegible] No. 3-65 in this exhibit for [illegible] for [illegible] and payment.

Allotments of Treasury bonds issued during the fiscal year 1965, by Federal Reserve districts

[In thousands]

Federal Reserve district	3¾ percent Series E-1964 Treasury notes maturing Aug. 15, 1964 [2]	5 percent Series B-1964 Treasury notes maturing Aug. 15, 1964 [2]	3¾ percent Series F-1964 Treasury notes maturing Nov. 15, 1964 [2]	4⅞ percent Series C-1964 Treasury notes maturing Nov. 15, 1964 [2]	3⅞ percent Series C-1965 Treasury notes maturing May 15, 1965 [2]	3⅝ percent Series B-1966 Treasury notes maturing Feb. 15, 1966 [2]	3¾ percent Treasury bonds of 1966 maturing May 15, 1966 [2]	4 percent Series A-1966 Treasury notes maturing Aug. 15, 1966 [2]	3⅝ percent Series B-1967 Treasury notes maturing Feb. 15, 1967 [2]	Total issued
						4 percent Treasury bonds of 1969 issued in exchange for— [1]				
Boston	$19,219	$6,027	$4,726	$4,225	$18,338	$28,180	$13,565	$4,815	$13,462	$112,557
New York	265,551	186,062	49,830	182,368	212,151	392,173	85,003	77,447	266,168	1,716,753
Philadelphia	21,328	8,397	5,182	3,363	4,307	19,613	10,142	3,234	11,068	86,634
Cld.	50,126	7,839	13,539	6,821	34,253	90,978	15,887	8,777	40,557	268,777
Richmond	15,536	5,672	1,478	1,019	7,383	19,339	4,765	1,196	37,405	93,793
Atlanta	22,474	7,395	6,295	2,494	13,142	39,453	6,587	14,925	25,263	138,028
Chicago	125,276	25,987	28,044	18,285	57,700	188,757	77,082	37,314	76,707	635,152
St. Louis	27,708	8,877	7,687	5,872	19,334	30,810	16,157	6,555	45,373	168,373
Minneapolis	18,070	5,832	8,622	8,113	6,181	21,247	11,227	2,812	8,588	90,692
Kansas City	37,569	14,322	11,028	8,264	9,728	33,173	20,248	9,430	15,377	159,139
Dallas	17,150	3,993	8,290	3,451	4,614	45,424	21,940	3,853	12,542	121,257
San Francisco	14,131	4,555	16,333	4,146	11,735	31,962	10,957	7,936	24,131	125,876
Treasury	593	1,583	297	1,237	522	883	723	435	2,287	8,560
Total bond allotments	634,731	286,541	161,341	249,658	399,388	941,992	294,283	178,729	578,928	3,725,591
Securities eligible for exchange: Exchanged in concurrent offerings	539,801	559,210	357,632	350,212	957,311	1,450,444	317,654	485,014	538,269	5,555,547
Total exchanged	1,174,532	845,751	518,973	599,870	1,356,609	2,392,436	611,937	663,743	1,117,197	9,281,138
Not submitted for exchange	2,911,622	1,199,502	5,442,250	3,267,326	6,620,117	3,260,303	2,250,086	5,156,228	2,357,648	32,465,082
Total securities eligible for exchange	4,086,154	2,045,253	5,961,223	3,867,196	7,976,816	5,652,739	2,862,023	5,819,971	3,474,845	41,746,220

Footnotes at end of table.

Allotments of Treasury bonds issued during the fiscal year 1965, by Federal Reserve districts—Continued

[In thousands]

Federal Reserve district	3¾ percent Series E-1964 Treasury notes maturing Aug. 15, 1964 [3]	5 percent Series B-1964 Treasury notes maturing Aug. 15, 1964 [3]	3¾ percent Series F-1964 Treasury notes maturing Nov. 15, 1964 [3]	4⅞ percent Series C-1964 Treasury notes maturing Nov. 15, 1964 [3]	3⅞ percent Series C-1965 Treasury notes maturing May 15, 1965 [3]	4⅛ percent Treasury bonds of 1973 issued in exchange for— [1] 3⅝ percent Series B-1966 Treasury notes maturing Feb. 15, 1966 [3]	3¾ percent Treasury bonds of 1966 maturing May 15, 1966 [3]	4 percent Series A-1966 Treasury notes maturing Aug. 15, 1966 [3]	3⅝ percent Series B-1967 Treasury notes maturing Feb. 15, 1967 [3]	Total issued
Boston	$8,813	$52,405	$3,560	$29,841	$61,670	$31,947	$14,392	$25,103	$18,610	$246,341
New York	151,132	134,691	96,277	105,424	447,475	664,788	106,565	147,991	233,749	2,088,092
Philadelphia	4,670	65,376	15,730	3,667	4,368	18,269	15,984	6,004	20,464	154,532
Cleveland	4,939	17,662	13,628	5,735	21,146	18,273	39,112	7,817	11,967	140,279
Richmond	3,911	6,259	1,045	2,240	4,524	8,450	5,597	636	12,337	44,999
Atlanta	11,296	5,390	2,838	7,526	5,235	6,968	6,193	9,006	8,746	63,188
Chicago	68,777	33,102	47,772	24,512	61,395	162,816	52,891	84,390	87,011	622,636
St. Louis	6,904	7,874	4,521	4,420	21,428	13,014	7,191	12,830	10,877	89,059
Minneapolis	9,456	7,409	7,457	5,730	6,984	46,082	10,043	6,103	11,218	110,482
Kansas City	14,089	12,226	3,761	6,513	10,000	27,913	12,062	9,626	23,038	119,228
Dallas	19,344	5,336	3,405	5,135	5,891	47,218	11,275	6,330	10,693	114,627
San Francisco	39,690	12,409	12,323	31,029	118,165	255,138	14,758	13,420	49,846	546,778
	804	2,155	304	390	1,023	1,892	788	4,829	4,785	16,970
Total bond allotments	343,825	362,294	212,621	232,162	769,304	1,302,758	296,851	334,055	503,341	4,357,211
Securities eligible for exchange: Exchanged in concurrent offerings	830,707	483,457	306,352	367,708	587,395	1,089,678	315,086	329,688	613,856	4,923,927
Total exchanged	1,174,532	845,751	518,973	599,870	1,356,699	2,392,436	611,937	663,743	1,117,197	9,281,138
Not submitted for exchange	2,911,622	1,199,502	5,442,250	3,267,326	6,620,117	3,260,303	2,250,086	5,156,228	2,357,648	32,465,082
Total securities eligible for exchange	4,086,154	2,045,253	5,961,223	3,867,196	7,976,816	5,652,739	2,862,023	5,819,971	3,474,845	41,746,220

Footnotes at end of table.

Allotments of Treasury bonds issued during the fiscal year 1965, by Federal Reserve districts—Continued

[In thousands]

Federal Reserve district	4¼ percent Treasury bonds of 1987-92 issued in exchange for—[1]									Total issued
	3¾ percent Series E-1964 Treasury notes maturing Aug. 15, 1964 [4]	5 percent Series B-1964 Treasury notes maturing Aug. 15, 1964 [4]	3¾ percent Series F-1964 Treasury notes maturing Nov. 15, 1964 [4]	4⅞ percent Series C-1964 Treasury notes maturing Nov. 15, 1964 [4]	3⅞ percent Series C-1965 Treasury notes maturing May 15, 1965 [4]	3⅝ percent Series B-1966 Treasury notes maturing Feb. 15, 1966 [4]	3¾ percent Treasury bonds of 1966 maturing May 15, 1966 [4]	4 percent Series A-1966 Treasury notes maturing Aug. 15, 1966 [4]	3⅝ percent Series B-1967 Treasury notes maturing Feb. 15, 1967 [4]	
Boston	$550	$14,353	$4,335	$7,307	$15,651	$1,319	$1,545	$10,917	$1,302	$57,279
New York	167,616	146,113	137,895	80,510	114,132	88,590	16,898	95,979	25,762	873,495
Philadelphia	1,008	1,275	16	164	113	30	67	15	100	2,788
Cleveland	158	13,021	362	1,076	1,675	1,024	148	193	50	17,607
Richmond	165	440	1	134	125	1,079				1,944
Atlanta	110	442	200	18,581	111	100	35	112	20	19,711
Chicago	4,147	5,363	115	5,186	10,183	8,406	811	38,757	2,827	75,795
St. Louis	451	1,206	415	475	1,835	1,339	128	983	106	6,938
Minneapolis		400		2,905	490	25	204	2,550	110	6,684
Kansas City	289	777	18	68	266	51	256	322	2	2,049
Dallas	1,500	753	780	265	20	110		268	10	3,706
San Francisco	19,982	12,635	874	1,216	43,506	45,507	711	415	4,139	128,985
[illegible]		138		163		106		448	500	1,355
Total bond allotments	196,976	196,916	145,011	118,050	188,007	147,686	20,803	150,959	34,928	1,198,336
Securities eligible for exchange:										
Exchanged in concurrent offerings	978,556	648,835	373,962	481,820	1,168,692	2,244,750	591,134	512,784	1,082,269	8,082,802
Total exchanged	1,174,532	845,751	518,973	599,870	1,356,699	2,392,436	611,937	663,743	1,117,197	9,281,138
Not submitted for exchange	2,911,622	1,199,502	5,442,250	3,267,326	6,620,117	3,260,303	2,250,086	5,156,228	2,357,648	32,465,082
Total securities eligible for exchange	4,086,154	2,045,253	5,961,223	3,867,196	7,976,816	5,652,739	2,862,023	5,819,971	3,474,845	41,746,220

Footnotes at end of table.

Allotments of Treasury bonds issued during the fiscal year 1965, by Federal Reserve districts—Continued

[In thousands]

Federal Reserve district	4 percent Treasury bonds of 1970 issued in exchange for—[1]								
	2⅝ percent Treasury bonds of 1965 maturing Feb. 15, 1965 [5]	3½ percent Series B–1965 Treasury notes maturing Nov. 15, 1965 [5]	4 percent Series E–1965 Treasury notes maturing Nov. 15, 1965 [5]	3⅝ percent Series B–1966 Treasury notes maturing Feb. 15, 1966 [5]	3⅞ percent Series C–1966 Treasury notes maturing Feb. 15, 1966 [5]	3¾ percent Treasury bonds of 1966 maturing May 15, 1966 [5]	3¾ percent Series A–1967 Treasury notes maturing Aug. 15, 1967 [5]	3⅝ percent Treasury bonds of 1967 maturing Nov. 15, 1967 [5]	Total issued
Boston	$8, 594	$13, 584	$21, 416	$12, 134	$13, 850	$5, 233	$18, 199	$25, 126	$118, 136
New York	266, 311	189, 837	51, 581	323, 310	221, 555	148, 591	434, 633	208, 643	1, 844, 461
Philadelphia	9, 522	36, 717	3, 922	27, 291	8, 057	7, 900	16, 048	17, 711	127, 168
Cleveland	39, 992	62, 185	15, 142	40, 222	65, 029	14, 063	69, 953	36, 196	342, 782
Richmond	11, 807	20, 693	3, 375	13, 323	5, 390	5, 697	25, 450	24, 853	110, 588
Atlanta	29, 779	32, 558	6, 267	20, 542	3, 098	6, 747	29, 824	23, 112	151, 927
Chicago	129, 360	140, 170	30, 133	80, 571	37, 742	52, 882	168, 948	134, 751	774, 557
St. Louis	30, 612	25, 956	11, 540	16, 583	7, 346	11, 303	26, 274	27, 795	157, 409
Minneapolis	21, 831	24, 349	9, 375	8, 552	2, 947	14, 366	15, 269	17, 575	114, 264
Kansas City	42, 275	23, 850	9, 012	17, 280	3, 632	13, 658	23, 824	29, 743	163, 274
Dallas	15, 760	22, 914	8, 733	9, 506	6, 079	8, 959	39, 939	25, 738	137, 628
San Francisco	66, 666	43, 002	3, 035	13, 696	3, 941	9, 767	30, 948	124, 910	295, 965
Treasury	1, 122	3, 686	2, 141	4, 534	144	383	3, 518	27, 733	43, 261
Total bond allotments	673, 631	639, 501	175, 672	587, 544	378, 810	299, 549	902, 827	723, 886	4, 381, 420
Securities eligible for exchange:									
Exchanged in concurrent offerings	1, 134, 690	697, 699	285, 041	477, 692	1, 064, 513	262, 990	601, 027	861, 118	5, 384, 770
Total exchanged	1, 808, 321	1, 337, 200	460, 713	1, 065, 236	1, 443, 323	562, 539	1, 503, 854	1, 585, 004	9, 766, 190
Not submitted for exchange	2, 167, 447	1, 616, 604	8, 099, 286	2, 195, 067	2, 596, 595	1, 687, 548	2, 929, 360	2, 018, 540	23, 310, 447
Total securities eligible for exchange	3, 975, 768	2, 953, 804	8, 559, 999	3, 260, 303	4, 039, 918	2, 250, 087	4, 433, 214	3, 603, 544	33, 076, 637

Footnotes at end of table.

Allotments of Treasury bonds issued during the fiscal year 1965, by Federal Reserve districts—Continued

[In thousands]

Federal Reserve district	4⅛ percent Treasury bonds of 1974 issued in exchange for—[1]								
	2⅝ percent Treasury bonds of 1965 maturing Feb. 15, 1965[6]	3½ percent Series B-1965 Treasury notes maturing Nov. 15, 1965[6]	4 percent Series E-1965 Treasury notes maturing Nov. 15, 1965[6]	3⅝ percent Series B-1966 Treasury notes maturing Feb. 15, 1966[6]	3⅞ percent Series C-1966 Treasury notes maturing Feb. 15, 1966[6]	3¾ percent Treasury bonds of 1966 maturing May 15, 1966[6]	3¾ percent Series A-1967 Treasury notes maturing Aug. 15, 1967[6]	3⅝ percent Treasury bonds of 1967 maturing Nov. 15, 1967[6]	Total issued
Boston	$2, 070	$10, 225	$4, 496	$18, 483	$4, 008	$1, 608	$18, 374	$22, 021	$81, 285
New York	271, 972	165, 551	81, 211	236, 579	318, 328	79, 915	152, 894	233, 252	1, 539, 702
Philadelphia	7, 620	7, 300	4, 161	3, 280	4, 528	3, 983	16, 680	24, 054	71, 606
Cleveland	15, 628	6, 071	3, 989	5, 656	24, 066	3, 844	15, 862	40, 757	115, 873
Richmond	3, 343	6, 658	1, 988	11, 848	1, 727	1, 628	6, 668	21, 874	55, 734
Atlanta	6, 344	12, 470	1, 562	1, 531	2, 207	2, 284	8, 915	24, 911	60, 224
Chicago	97, 364	128, 411	20, 563	25, 727	11, 161	33, 128	64, 228	114, 797	495, 379
St. Louis	5, 647	2, 960	3, 951	3, 447	2, 268	3, 363	7, 845	21, 317	50, 798
Minneapolis	4, 678	16, 845	3, 531	4, 391	5, 085	4, 499	10, 952	28, 620	78, 601
Kansas City	9, 974	2, 586	8, 927	5, 749	6, 045	4, 411	9, 904	17, 999	65, 595
Dallas	5, 828	4, 165	2, 417	5, 607	1, 643	4, 074	22, 105	21, 892	67, 731
San Francisco	62, 752	52, 300	3, 260	11, 444	12, 843	4, 149	126, 286	46, 397	319, 431
Treasury	242	200	270	18	6, 050	31	576	121, 028	128, 415
Total bond allotments	493, 462	415, 742	140, 326	333, 760	399, 959	146, 917	461, 289	738, 919	3, 130, 374
Securities eligible for exchange:									
Exchanged in concurrent offerings	1, 314, 859	921, 458	320, 387	731, 476	1, 043, 364	415, 622	1, 042, 565	846, 085	6, 635, 816
Total exchanged	1, 808, 321	1, 337, 200	460, 713	1, 065, 236	1, 443, 323	562, 539	1, 503, 854	1, 585, 004	9, 766, 190
Not submitted for exchange	2, 167, 447	1, 616, 604	8, 099, 286	2, 195, 067	2, 596, 595	1, 687, 548	2, 929, 360	2, 018, 540	23, 310, 447
Total securities eligible for exchange	3, 975, 768	2, 953, 804	8, 559, 999	3, 260, 303	4, 039, 918	2, 250, 087	4, 433, 214	3, 603, 544	33, 076, 637

Footnotes at end of table.

Allotments of Treasury bonds issued during the fiscal year 1965, by Federal Reserve districts—Continued

[In thousands]

Federal Reserve district	4¼ percent Treasury bonds of 1987–92 issued in exchange for—[1]								
	2⅝ percent Treasury bonds of 1965 maturing Feb. 15, 1965 [7]	3½ percent Series B–1965 Treasury notes maturing Nov. 15, 1965 [7]	4 percent Series E–1965 Treasury notes maturing Nov. 15, 1965 [7]	3⅝ percent Series B–1966 Treasury notes maturing Feb. 15, 1966 [7]	3⅞ percent Series C–1966 Treasury notes maturing Feb. 15, 1966 [7]	3¾ percent Treasury bonds of 1966 maturing May 15, 1966 [7]	3¾ percent Series A–1967 Treasury notes maturing Aug. 15, 1967 [7]	3⅝ percent Treasury bonds of 1967 maturing Nov. 15, 1967 [7]	Total issued
Boston	$4, 859	$2, 316	$2, 305	$954	$12, 783	$1, 458	$16, 106	$11, 459	$52, 240
New York	494, 999	245, 706	130, 412	112, 148	568, 726	72, 663	53, 700	62, 499	1, 740, 853
Philadelphia	6	70	204	27	102	46	84	3, 011	3, 550
Cleveland	2, 568	376	158	143	185	29, 731	50, 799	2, 609	86, 569
Richmond	10, 241		5, 300	2, 020				108	17, 669
Atlanta	134	545	340	50	287		84	535	1, 975
Chicago	45, 846	4, 755	2, 231	13, 295	39, 058	1, 723	9, 090	18, 819	134, 817
St. Louis	1, 779	148	38	268	3, 137	38	330	2, 119	7, 857
Minneapolis	340	2, 390	890	50	100	668	131	1, 113	5, 682
Kansas City	589	208	50	121	2, 185	160	55	1, 233	4, 601
Dallas	170	306	1, 630	3, 445	318	9, 327	429	9, 497	25, 122
San Francisco	79, 697	25, 117	1, 139	9, 511	37, 167	258	8, 822	8, 657	170, 368
Treasury		20	18	1, 900	506	1	108	540	3, 093
Total bond allotments	641, 228	281, 957	144, 715	143, 932	664, 554	116, 073	139, 738	122, 199	2, 254, 396
Securities eligible for exchange:									
Exchanged in concurrent offerings	1, 167, 093	1, 055, 243	315, 998	921, 304	778, 769	446, 466	1, 364, 116	1, 462, 805	7, 511, 794
Total exchanged	1, 808, 321	1, 337, 200	460, 713	1, 065, 236	1, 443, 323	562, 539	1, 503, 854	1, 585, 004	9, 766, 190
Not submitted for exchange	2, 167, 447	1, 616, 604	8, 099, 286	2, 195, 067	2, 596, 595	1, 687, 548	2, 929, 360	2, 018, 540	23, 310, 447
Total securities eligible for exchange	3, 975, 768	2, 953, 804	8, 559, 999	3, 260, 303	4, 039, 918	2, 250, 087	4, 433, 214	3, 603, 544	33, 076, 637

Footnotes at end of table.

Allotments of Treasury bonds issued during the fiscal year 1965, by Federal Reserve districts—Continued

[In thousands]

Federal Reserve district	4¼ percent Treasury bonds of 1974 issued in exchange for—[3]		Total issued
	4⅝ percent Series A–1965 Treasury notes maturing May 15, 1965 [9]	3⅞ percent Series C–1965 Treasury notes maturing May 15, 1965 [9]	
Boston	$52,708	$31,378	$84,176
New York	375,311	827,761	1,203,072
Philadelphia	7,766	15,493	23,259
Cleveland	26,980	62,127	89,107
Richmond	8,637	7,177	15,814
Atlanta	19,907	21,833	41,740
Chicago	88,461	154,315	242,776
St. Louis	14,706	24,770	39,476
Minneapolis	13,485	20,352	33,837
Kansas City	22,420	12,313	34,733
Dallas	11,722	14,978	26,700
San Francisco	88,389	113,112	201,501
Treasury	1,807	23,687	25,494
Total bond allotments	732,389	1,329,296	2,061,685
Securities eligible for exchange:			
Exchanged in concurrent offerings	802,655	5,101,587	5,904,242
Total exchanged	1,535,044	6,430,883	7,965,927
Not submitted for exchange	280,666	189,234	469,900
Total securities eligible for exchange	1,815,710	6,620,117	8,435,827

[1] Advance refunding; all subscriptions were allotted in full.
[2] 4⅛ percent Treasury bonds of 1973 and 4¼ percent Treasury bonds of 1987–92 were also offered in exchange for this security.
[3] 4 percent Treasury bonds of 1969 and 4¼ percent Treasury bonds of 1987–92 were also offered in exchange for this security.
[4] 4 percent Treasury bonds of 1969 and 4⅛ percent Treasury bonds of 1973 were also offered in exchange for this security.
[5] 4⅛ percent Treasury bonds of 1974 and 4¼ percent Treasury bonds of 1987–92 were also offered in exchange or this security.

[6] 4 percent Treasury bonds of 1970 and 4¼ percent Treasury bonds of 1987–92 were also offered in exchange for this security.
[7] 4 percent Treasury bonds of 1970 and 4⅛ percent Treasury bonds of 1974 were also offered in exchange for this security.
[8] All subscriptions were allotted in full.
[9] 4 percent Treasury notes of Series A–1966 were also offered in exchange for this security.

Treasury Bills Offered and Tenders Accepted

Exhibit 3.—Treasury bills

During the fiscal year 1965 there were 52 weekly issues each of 13-week and 26-week Treasury bills (the 13-week bills represent additional issues of bills with an original maturity of 26 weeks), 13 one-year issues, 4 issues of tax anticipation series and one issue of a strip of weekly bills consisting of additional amounts of 10 series of outstanding bills. Four press releases inviting tenders, which are representative of the four types of bill issues, are reproduced in this exhibit as follows: strip of issues, July 20, 1964; tax anticipation series, November 10, 1964; weekly issues, April 14, 1965; and one-year issues, April 19, 1965. Also reproduced is the press release of April 19, 1965, which is representative of the releases announcing the acceptance of tenders for all types of issues. Following the press releases is a summary table of data for each issue.

PRESS RELEASE OF JULY 20, 1964

The Treasury Department, by this public notice, invites tenders for additional amounts of ten series of Treasury bills to an aggregate amount of $1,000,000,000, or thereabouts, for cash. The additional bills will be issued July 29, 1964, will be in the amounts, and will be in addition to the bills originally issued and maturing, as follows:

Amount of additional issue	Original issue dates 1964	Maturity dates 1964	Days from July 29, 1964, to maturity	Amount currently outstanding (in millions)
$100,000,000	April 16	October 15	78	$2,102
100,000,000	April 23	October 22	85	901
100,000,000	April 30	October 29	92	900
100,000,000	May 7	November 5	99	900
100,000,000	May 14	November 12	106	900
100,000,000	May 21	November 19	113	900
100,000,000	May 28	November 27	121	900
100,000,000	June 4	December 3	127	905
100,000,000	June 11	December 10	134	901
100,000,000	June 18	December 17	141	901
1,000,000,000				

The additional and original bills will be freely interchangeable.

Each tender submitted must be in the amount of $10,000, or an even multiple thereof, and the amount tendered will be applied to each of the above series of bills on the basis of the ratio of each series to the total of all series. (For example, an accepted tender for $50,000 will be applied $5,000 to the issue with original date of April 16, 1964, and $5,000 to each of the additional weekly issues through the issue with original date of June 18, 1964.)

The bills offered hereunder will be issued on a discount basis under competitive and noncompetitive bidding as hereinafter provided, and at maturity their face amount will be payable without interest. They will be issued in bearer form only, and in denominations of $1,000, $5,000, $10,000, $50,000, $100,000, $500,000, and $1,000,000 (maturity value).

Tenders will be received at Federal Reserve banks and branches up to the closing hour, one-thirty p.m., eastern daylight saving time, Friday, July 24, 1964. Tenders will not be received at the Treasury Department, Washington. In the case of competitive tenders the price offered must be expressed on the basis of 100, with not more than three decimals, e.g., 99.925. Fractions may not be used. A single price must be submitted for each unit of $10,000, or even multiple thereof. A unit represents $1,000 face amount of each issue of bills offered hereunder, as previously described. It is urged that tenders be made on the printed forms and forwarded in the special envelopes which will be supplied by Federal Reserve banks and branches on application therefor.

Banking institutions generally may submit tenders for account of customers provided the names of the customers are set forth in such tenders. Others than banking institutions will not be permitted to submit tenders except for their own account. Tenders will be received without deposit from incorporated banks and trust companies and from responsible and recognized dealers in investment securities. Tenders from others must be accompanied by payment of 2 percent of the face amount of Treasury bills applied for, unless the tenders are accompanied by an express guaranty of payment by an incorporated bank or trust company.

Immediately after the closing hour, tenders will be opened at the Federal Reserve banks and branches, following which public announcement will be made by the Treasury Department of the amount and price range of accepted bids. Those submitting tenders will be advised of the acceptance or rejection thereof. The Secretary of the Treasury expressly reserves the right to accept or reject any or all tenders, in whole or in part, and his action in any such respect shall be final. Noncompetitive tenders for $100,000 or less (in even multiples of $10,000) without stated price from any one bidder will be accepted in full at the average price (in three decimals) of accepted competitive bids, provided, however, that if the total of noncompetitive tenders exceeds $200,000,000, the Secretary of the Treasury reserves the right to allot less than the amount applied for on a straight percentage basis with adjustments where necessary to the next higher multiple of $10,000. Settlement for accepted tenders in accordance with the bids must be made or completed at the Federal Reserve bank or branch in cash or other immediately available funds on July 29, 1964.

The income derived from Treasury bills, whether interest or gain from the sale or other disposition of the bills, does not have any exemption, as such, and loss from the sale or other disposition of Treasury bills does not have any special treatment, as such, under the Internal Revenue Code of 1954. The bills are subject to estate, inheritance, gift, or other excise taxes, whether Federal or State, but are exempt from all taxation now or hereafter imposed on the principal or interest thereof by any State, or any of the possessions of the United States, or by any local taxing authority. For purposes of taxation the amount of discount at which Treasury bills are originally sold by the United States is considered to be interest.

Under sections 454(b) and 1221(5) of the Internal Revenue Code of 1954 the amount of discount at which bills issued hereunder are sold is not considered to accrue until such bills are sold, redeemed, or otherwise disposed of, and such bills are excluded from consideration as capital assets. Accordingly, the owner of Treasury bills (other than life insurance companies) issued hereunder need include in his income tax return only the difference between the price paid for such bills, whether on original issue or on subsequent purchase, and the amount actually received either upon sale or redemption at maturity during the taxable year for which the return is made, as ordinary gain or loss. Purchasers of a strip of the bills offered hereunder should, for tax purposes, take such bills on to their books on the basis of their purchase price prorated to each of the ten outstanding issues using as a basis for proration the closing market prices for each of the issues on July 29, 1964. (Federal Reserve banks will have available a list of these market prices, based on the mean between the bid and asked quotations furnished by the Federal Reserve Bank of New York.)

Treasury Department Circular No. 418, Revised, and this notice, prescribe the terms of the Treasury bills and govern the conditions of their issue. Copies of the circular may be obtained from any Federal Reserve bank or branch.

PRESS RELEASE OF NOVEMBER 10, 1964

The Treasury Department, by this public notice, invites tenders for $1,500,-000,000, or thereabouts, of 210-day Treasury bills, to be issued on a discount basis under competitive and noncompetitive bidding as hereinafter provided. The bills of this series will be designated tax anticipation series, they will be dated November 24, 1964, and they will mature June 22, 1965. They will be accepted at face value in payment of income taxes due on June 15, 1965, and to the extent they are not presented for this purpose the face amount of these bills will be payable without interest at maturity. Taxpayers desiring to apply these bills in payment of June 15, 1965, income taxes have the privilege of surrendering them to any Federal Reserve bank or branch or to the Office of the Treasurer of the United States, Washington, not more than 15 days before June 15, 1965, and receiving receipts therefor showing the face amount of the bills so surrendered. These receipts may be submitted in lieu of the bills on or before June 15, 1965, to the District Director of Internal Revenue for the District in which such taxes are payable. The bills will be issued in bearer form only, and in denominations of $1,000, $5,000, $10,000, $50,000, $100,000, $500,000, and $1,000,000 (maturity value).

Tenders will be received at Federal Reserve banks and branches up to the closing hour, one-thirty p.m., eastern standard time, Tuesday, November 17, 1964. Tenders will not be received at the Treasury Department, Washington. Each tender must be for an even multiple of $1,000, and in the case of competitive tenders the price offered must be expressed on the basis of 100, with not more than three decimals, e.g., 99.925. Fractions may not be used. It is urged that tenders be made on the printed forms and forwarded in the special envelopes which will be supplied by Federal Reserve banks or branches on application therefor.

Banking institutions generally may submit tenders for account of customers provided the names of the customers are set forth in such tenders. Others than banking institutions will not be permitted to submit tenders except for their own account. Tenders will be received without deposit from incorporated banks and trust companies and from responsible and recognized dealers in investment securities. Tenders from others must be accompanied by payment of 2 percent of the face amount of Treasury bills applied for, unless the tenders are accompanied by an express guaranty of payment by an incorporated bank or trust company.

All bidders are required to agree not to purchase or to sell, or to make any agreements with respect to the purchase or sale or other disposition of any bills of this issue at a specific rate or price, until after one-thirty p.m., eastern standard time, Tuesday, November 17, 1964.

Immediately after the closing hour, tenders will be opened at the Federal Reserve banks and branches, following which public announcement will be made by the Treasury Department of the amount and price range of accepted bids. Those submitting tenders will be advised of the acceptance or rejection thereof. The Secretary of the Treasury expressly reserves the right to accept or reject any or all tenders, in whole or in part, and his action in any such respect shall be final. Subject to these reservations, noncompetitive tenders for $200,000 or less without stated price from any one bidder will be accepted in full at the average price (in three decimals) of accepted competitive bids. Payment of accepted tenders at the prices offered must be made or completed at the Federal Reserve bank in cash or other immediately available funds on November 24, 1964, provided, however, any qualified depositary will be permitted to make payment by credit in its Treasury tax and loan account for not more than 50 percent of the amount of Treasury bills allotted to it for itself and its customers up to any amount for which it shall be qualified in excess of existing deposits when so notified by the Federal Reserve bank of its district.

The income derived from Treasury bills, whether interest or gain from the sale or other disposition of the bills, does not have any exemption, as such, and loss from the sale or other disposition of Treasury bills does not have any special treatment, as such, under the Internal Revenue Code of 1954. The bills are subject to estate, inheritance, gift, or other excise taxes, whether Federal or State, but are exempt from all taxation now or hereafter imposed on the principal or interest thereof by any State, or any of the possessions of the United States, or by any local taxing authority. For purposes of taxation the amount of discount at which Treasury bills are originally sold by the United States is considered to be interest. Under sections 454(b) and 1221(5) of the Internal Revenue Code of 1954 the amount of discount at which bills issued hereunder are sold is not considered to accrue until such bills are sold, redeemed, or otherwise disposed of, and such bills are excluded from consideration as capital assets. Accordingly, the owner of Treasury bills (other than life insurance companies) issued hereunder need include in his income tax return only the difference between the price paid for such bills, whether on original issue or on subsequent purchase, and the amount actually received either upon sale or redemption at maturity during the taxable year for which the return is made, as ordinary gain or loss.

Treasury Department Circular No. 418 (current revision) and this notice, prescribe the terms of the Treasury bills and govern the conditions of their issue. Copies of the circular may be obtained from any Federal Reserve bank or branch.

PRESS RELEASE OF APRIL 14, 1965

The Treasury Department, by this public notice, invites tenders for two series of Treasury bills to the aggregate amount of $2,200,000,000, or thereabouts, for cash and in exchange for Treasury bills maturing April 22, 1965, in the amount of $2,201,051,000, as follows:

91-day bills (to maturity date) to be issued April 22, 1965, in the amount of $1,200,000,000, or thereabouts, representing an additional amount of bills dated January 21, 1965, and to mature July 22, 1965, originally issued in the amount of $1,001,051,000, the additional and original bills to be freely interchangeable.

182-day bills, for $1,000,000,000, or thereabouts, to be dated April 22, 1965, and to mature October 21, 1965.

The bills of both series will be issued on a discount basis under competitive and noncompetitive bidding as hereinafter provided, and at maturity their face amount will be payable without interest. They will be issued in bearer form only, and in denominations of $1,000, $5,000, $10,000, $50,000, $100,000, $500,000, and $1,000,000 (maturity value).

Tenders will be received at Federal Reserve banks and branches up to the closing hour, one-thirty p.m., eastern standard time, Monday, April 19, 1965. Tenders will not be received at the Treasury Department, Washington. Each tender must be for an even multiple of $1,000, and in the case of competitive tenders the price offered must be expressed on the basis of 100, with not more than three decimals, e. g., 99.925. Fractions may not be used. It is urged that tenders be made on the printed forms and forwarded in the special envelopes which will be supplied by Federal Reserve banks or branches on application therefor.

Banking institutions generally may submit tenders for account of customers provided the names of the customers are set forth in such tenders. Others than banking institutions will not be permitted to submit tenders except for their own account. Tenders will be received without deposit from incorporated banks and trust companies and from responsible and recognized dealers in investment securities. Tenders from others must be accompanied by payment of 2 percent of the face amount of Treasury bills applied for, unless the tenders are accompanied by an express guaranty of payment by an incorporated bank or trust company.

Immediately after the closing hour, tenders will be opened at the Federal Reserve banks and branches, following which public announcement will be made by the Treasury Department of the amount and price range of accepted bids. Those submitting tenders will be advised of the acceptance or rejection thereof. The Secretary of the Treasury expressly reserves the right to accept or reject any or all tenders, in whole or in part, and his action in any such respect shall be final. Subject to these reservations noncompetitive tenders for each issue for $200,000 or less without stated price from any one bidder will be accepted in full at the average price (in three decimals) of accepted competitive bids for the respective issues. Settlement for accepted tenders in accordance with the bids must be made or completed at the Federal Reserve banks on April 22, 1965, in cash or other immediately available funds or in a like face amount of Treasury bills maturing April 22, 1965. Cash and exchange tenders will receive equal treatment. Cash adjustments will be made for differences between the par value of maturing bills accepted in exchange and the issue price of the new bills.

The income derived from Treasury bills, whether interest or gain from the sale or other disposition of the bills, does not have any exemption, as such, and loss from the sale or other disposition of Treasury bills does not have any special treatment, as such, under the Internal Revenue Code of 1954. The bills are subject to estate, inheritance, gift, or other excise taxes, whether Federal or State, but are exempt from all taxation now or hereafter imposed on the principal or interest thereof by any State, or any of the possessions of the United States, or by any local taxing authority. For purposes of taxation the amount of discount at which Treasury bills are originally sold by the United States is considered to be interest. Under sections 454(b) and 1221(5) of the Internal Revenue Code of 1954 the amount of discount at which bills issued hereunder are sold is not considered to accrue until such bills are sold, redeemed, or otherwise disposed of, and such bills are excluded from consideration as capital assets. Accordingly, the owner of Treasury bills (other than life insurance companies) issued hereunder need include in his income tax return only the difference between the price paid for such bills, whether on original issue or on subsequent purchase, and the amount actually received either upon sale or redemption at maturity during the taxable year for which the return is made, as ordinary gain or loss.

Treasury Department Circular No. 418 (current revision) and this notice prescribe the terms of the Treasury bills and govern the conditions of their issue. Copies of the circular may be obtained from any Federal Reserve bank or branch.

<hr>

PRESS RELEASE OF APRIL 19, 1965

The Treasury Department, by this public notice, invites tenders for $1,000,-000,000, or thereabouts, of 365-day Treasury bills, for cash and in exchange for Treasury bills maturing April 30, 1965, in the amount of $1,001,439,000, to be issued on a discount basis under competitive and noncompetitive bidding as hereinafter provided. The bills of this series will be dated April 30, 1965, and will mature April 30, 1966, when the face amount will be payable without interest. They will be issued in bearer form only, and in denominations of $1,000, $5,000, $10,000, $50,000, $100,000, $500,000, and $1,000,000 (maturity value).

Tenders will be received at Federal Reserve banks and branches up to the closing hour, one-thirty p.m., eastern standard time, Friday, April 23, 1965. Tenders will not be received at the Treasury Department, Washington. Each tender must be for an even multiple of $1,000, and in the case of competitive tenders the price offered must be expressed on the basis of 100, with not more than three decimals, e. g., 99.925. Fractions may not be used. (Notwithstanding the fact that these bills will run for 365 days, the discount rate will be computed on a bank discount basis of 360 days, as is currently the practice on all issues of Treasury bills.) It is urged that tenders be made on the printed forms and forwarded in the special envelopes which will be supplied by Federal Reserve banks or branches on application therefor.

Banking institutions generally may submit tenders for account of customers provided the names of the customers are set forth in such tenders. Others than banking institutions will not be permitted to submit tenders except for their own account. Tenders will be received without deposit from incorporated banks and trust companies and from responsible and recognized dealers in investment securities. Tenders from others must be accompanied by payment of 2 percent of the face amount of Treasury bills applied for, unless the tenders are accompanied by an express guaranty of payment by an incorporated bank or trust company.

Immediately after the closing hour, tenders will be opened at the Federal Reserve banks and branches, following which public announcement will be made by the Treasury Department of the amount and price range of accepted bids. Those submitting tenders will be advised of the acceptance or rejection thereof. The Secretary of the Treasury expressly reserves the right to accept or reject any or all tenders, in whole or in part, and his action in any such respect shall be final. Subject to these reservations, noncompetitive tenders for $200,000 or less without stated price from any one bidder will be accepted in full at the average price (in three decimals) of accepted competitive bids. Settlement for accepted tenders in accordance with the bids must be made or completed at the Federal Reserve bank on April 30, 1965, in cash or other immediately available funds or in a like face amount of Treasury bills maturing April 30, 1965. Cash and exchange tenders will receive equal treatment. Cash adjustments will be made for differences between the par value of maturing bills accepted in exchange and the issue price of the new bills.

The income derived from Treasury bills, whether interest or gain from the sale or other disposition of the bills, does not have any exemption, as such, and loss from the sale or other disposition of Treasury bills does not have any special treatment, as such, under the Internal Revenue Code of 1954. The bills are subject to estate, inheritance, gift, or other excise taxes, whether Federal or State, but are exempt from all taxation now or hereafter imposed on the principal or interest thereof by any State, or any of the possessions of the United States, or by any local taxing authority. For purposes of taxation the amount of discount at which Treasury bills are originally sold by the United States is considered to be interest. Under sections 454(b) and 1221(5) of the Internal Revenue Code of 1954 the amount of discount at which bills issued hereunder are sold is not considered to accrue until such bills are sold, redeemed, or otherwise disposed of, and such bills are excluded from consideration as capital assets. Accordingly, the owner of Treasury bills (other than life insurance companies) issued hereunder need include in his income tax return only the difference between the price paid for such bills, whether on original issue or on subsequent purchase, and the amount actually received either upon sale or redemption at maturity during the taxable year for which the return is made, as ordinary gain or loss.

Treasury Department Circular No. 418 (current revision) and this notice, prescribe the terms of the Treasury bills and govern the conditions of their issue. Copies of the circular may be obtained from any Federal Reserve bank or branch.

PRESS RELEASE OF APRIL 19, 1965

The Treasury Department announced last evening that the tenders for two series of Treasury bills, one series to be an additional issue of the bills dated January 21, 1965, and the other series to be dated April 22, 1965, which were offered on April 14, were opened at the Federal Reserve banks on April 19. Tenders were invited for $1,200,000,000, or thereabouts, of 91-day bills and for $1,000,000,000, or thereabouts, of 182-day bills. The details of the two series are as follows:

Range of accepted competitive bids	91-day Treasury bills maturing July 22, 1965		182-day Treasury bills maturing Oct. 21, 1965	
	Price	Approximate equivalent annual rate	Price	Approximate equivalent annual rate
High	99.006	3.932%	[1] 97.978	4.000%
Low	99.001	3.952%	97.971	4.013%
Average	99.003	[2] 3.946%	97.974	[2] 4.008%

[1] Excepting 3 tenders totaling $1,534,000.
[2] On a coupon issue of the same length and for the same amount invested, the return on these bills would provide yields of 4.04%, for the 91-day bills, and 4.15%, for the 182-day bills. Interest rates on bills are quoted in terms of bank discount with the return related to the face amount of the bills payable at maturity rather than the amount invested and their length in actual number of days related to a 360-day year. In contrast, yields on certificates, notes, and bonds are computed in terms of interest on the amount invested, and relate the number of days remaining in an interest payment period to the actual number of days in the period, with semiannual compounding if more than one coupon period is involved.

NOTE.—62 percent of the amount of 91-day bills bid for at the low price was accepted. 5 percent of the amount of 182-day bills bid for at the low price was accepted.

Total tenders applied for and accepted by Federal Reserve districts

District	Applied for	Accepted	Applied for	Accepted
Boston	$15,923,000	$15,923,000	$25,935,000	$25,935,000
New York	1,490,917,000	739,697,000	1,337,392,000	681,792,000
Philadelphia	28,232,000	15,232,000	16,436,000	6,916,000
Cleveland	26,137,000	26,137,000	37,899,000	23,149,000
Richmond	14,867,000	14,567,000	4,056,000	4,056,000
Atlanta	41,704,000	32,614,000	29,116,000	24,166,000
Chicago	291,551,000	136,431,000	267,813,000	112,513,000
St. Louis	53,705,000	44,679,000	13,446,000	11,946,000
Minneapolis	25,667,000	19,527,000	11,474,000	9,024,000
Kansas City	27,707,000	25,567,000	19,374,000	16,574,000
Dallas	28,348,000	20,968,000	23,394,000	7,969,000
San Francisco	203,307,000	110,071,000	135,009,000	77,272,000
Total	2,248,065,000	[1] 1,201,413,000	1,921,344,000	[2] 1,001,312,000

[1] Includes $260,097,000 noncompetitive tenders accepted at the average price of 99.003.
[2] Includes $108,127,000 noncompetitive tenders accepted at the average price of 97.974.

Summary of information pertaining to Treasury bills issued during the fiscal year 1965

[Dollar amounts in thousands]

Date of issue	Date of maturity	Days to maturity [1]	Maturity value — Total applied for	Tenders accepted — Total accepted	Tenders accepted — On competitive basis	Tenders accepted — On noncompetitive basis	For cash	In exchange	Total bids accepted — Average price per hundred	Total bids accepted — Equivalent average rate (percent)	Competitive bids accepted — High — Price per hundred	High — Equivalent rate (percent)	Low — Price per hundred	Low — Equivalent rate (percent)	Amount maturing on issue date of new offering
						Regular Weekly									
1964 July 2	Oct. 1, 1964	91	$1,913,700	$1,200,167	$993,055	$207,112	$1,036,198	$163,969	99.121	3.479	99.124	3.465	99.118	3.489	$1,300,560
2	Dec. 31, 1964	182	1,680,520	900,402	849,295	51,107	807,994	92,408	98.217	3.528	98.220	3.521	98.214	3.533	800,466
9	Oct. 8, 1964	91	2,178,912	1,201,238	965,167	236,071	1,029,092	172,146	99.117	3.544	99.121	3.477	99.115	3.501	1,300,592
9	Jan. 7, 1965	182	2,414,326	900,046	839,956	60,090	848,591	51,455	98.208	3.544	98.217	3.527	98.200	3.560	800,403
16	Oct. 15, 1964	91	2,122,719	1,201,549	878,501	323,048	1,185,099	16,450	99.128	3.448	99.134	3.426	99.126	3.458	1,200,506
16	Jan. 14, 1965	182	2,409,225	902,495	810,219	92,276	898,097	4,398	98.206	3.549	98.216	3.529	98.198	3.564	800,444
23	Oct. 22, 1964	91	2,069,809	1,200,735	963,315	237,420	928,745	271,990	99.115	3.502	99.128	3.450	99.112	3.513	1,200,078
23	Jan. 21, 1965	182	1,332,877	899,827	839,486	60,341	787,923	111,904	98.170	3.619	98.182	3.596	98.159	3.642	800,615
29 [3]	Oct. 15, 1964 Oct. 22, 1964 Oct. 29, 1964 Nov. 5, 1964 Nov. 12, 1964 Nov. 19, 1964 Nov. 27, 1964 Dec. 3, 1964 Dec. 10, 1964 Dec. 17, 1964	78 85 92 99 106 113 121 127 134 141	2,147,330	1,000,860	996,830	4,030	1,000,860	---	98.933	3.505	98.941	3.478	98.929	3.518	---
30	Oct. 29, 1964	91	2,203,740	1,200,736	987,032	213,704	993,487	207,249	99.122	3.475	99.124	3.465	99.119	3.485	1,201,283
30	Jan. 28, 1965	182	1,889,232	901,969	844,449	57,520	790,410	111,559	98.184	3.591	98.188	3.584	98.182	3.596	800,267
Aug. 6	Nov. 5, 1964	91	2,389,381	1,200,441	966,679	233,762	1,010,563	189,878	99.118	3.489	99.122	3.473	99.116	3.497	1,200,271
6	Feb. 4, 1965	182	1,750,965	900,616	842,322	58,294	788,675	11,941	98.186	3.588	98.192	3.576	98.184	3.592	900,431
13	Nov. 12, 1964	91	2,092,368	1,196,793	937,860	257,933	1,128,930	66,863	99.113	3.510	99.118	3.489	99.111	3.517	1,200,553
13	Feb. 11, 1965	182	1,597,308	901,846	838,173	63,673	848,664	53,182	98.174	3.512	98.186	3.588	98.170	3.620	900,881
20	Nov. 19, 1964	91	1,597,365	1,200,177	954,040	246,137	931,492	268,685	99.115	3.111	99.115	3.501	99.111	3.517	1,202,081
20	Feb. 18, 1965	182	2,070,777	901,346	838,613	62,733	779,053	122,293	98.163	3.634	98.171	3.618	98.161	3.638	900,955
27	Nov. 27, 1964	92	2,049,191	1,201,538	980,095	221,443	967,300	234,238	99.102	3.513	99.106	3.608	99.100	3.522	1,199,984
27	Feb. 25, 1965	182	1,962,121	902,006	845,876	56,130	789,900	112,106	98.160	3.639	98.166	3.628	98.158	3.644	901,802

F Footnotes at end of table.

Summary of information pertaining to Treasury bills issued during the fiscal year 1965—Continued

Regular Weekly—Continued

| Date of issue | Date of maturity | Days to maturity [1] | Total applied for | Maturity value — Tenders accepted | | | | | Total bids accepted | | Competitive bids accepted | | | | Amount maturing on issue date of new offering |
| | | | | Total accepted | On competitive basis | On noncompetitive basis | For cash | In exchange | Average price per hundred | Equivalent average rate (percent) | High | | Low | | |
											Price per hundred	Equivalent rate (percent)	Price per hundred	Equivalent rate (percent)	
1964															
Sept. 3	Dec. 3, 1964	91	$2,129,431	$1,200,678	$963,450	$237,228	$978,370	$222,308	99.112	3.512	99.115	3.501	99.110	3.521	$1,201,964
3	Mar. 4, 1965	182	1,522,489	900,287	836,825	63,462	784,862	115,425	98.165	3.629	98.171	3.618	98.161	3.638	902,448
10	Dec. 10, 1964	91	2,169,481	1,301,783	1,064,472	237,311	1,220,814	80,969	99.112	3.514	99.117	3.493	99.109	3.525	1,201,130
10	Mar. 11, 1965	182	1,463,946	900,822	839,589	61,233	868,644	32,178	98.155	3.649	98.162	3.636	98.149	3.661	900,265
17	Dec. 17, 1964	91	2,082,514	1,301,621	1,021,542	280,079	1,162,969	138,652	99.105	3.541	99.114	3.505	99.103	3.549	1,200,661
17	Mar. 18, 1965	182	1,474,395	900,020	825,345	74,675	836,192	63,828	98.140	3.693	98.140	3.679	98.129	3.701	898,804
24	Dec. 24, 1964	91	2,200,319	1,301,980	1,055,764	246,216	1,139,536	162,444	99.105	3.542	99.108	3.529	99.103	3.549	1,201,309
24	Mar. 25, 1965	182	1,623,973	900,644	834,934	65,710	816,010	84,634	98.133	3.692	98.136	3.687	98.131	3.697	900,302
Oct. 1	Dec. 31, 1964	91	2,085,860	1,300,880	1,065,802	235,078	1,140,477	160,403	99.101	3.555	99.106	3.537	99.100	3.560	1,200,167
1	Apr. 1, 1965	182	1,450,772	900,333	828,957	71,376	827,168	73,165	98.124	3.711	98.134	3.691	98.120	3.719	901,457
1965															
Jan. 8	Jan. 7	91	1,912,812	1,200,292	959,909	240,383	1,041,049	159,243	99.094	3.583	99.098	3.568	99.091	3.596	1,201,238
8	Apr. 8	182	1,634,687	901,176	822,994	78,182	828,046	73,130	98.107	3.744	98.110	3.738	98.105	3.748	900,029
15	Jan. 14	91	2,163,822	1,211,565	937,455	274,110	1,197,760	13,805	99.095	3.580	99.098	3.568	99.093	3.588	1,201,549
15	Apr. 15	182	2,095,533	1,004,483	914,536	89,947	998,864	5,619	98.118	3.726	98.118	3.723	98.115	3.729	900,050
22	Jan. 21	91	2,170,090	1,202,917	949,134	253,783	1,009,532	193,385	99.092	3.592	99.094	3.584	99.091	3.596	1,200,735
22	Apr. 22	182	1,725,361	1,000,769	917,234	83,485	886,597	114,172	98.110	3.738	98.118	3.723	98.106	3.746	900,793
29	Jan. 28	91	2,204,764	1,200,175	966,494	233,681	985,055	215,120	99.098	3.568	99.101	3.556	99.097	3.572	1,200,736
29	Apr. 29	182	1,902,159	1,002,754	931,307	71,447	900,052	102,702	98.117	3.724	98.121	3.717	98.116	3.727	900,482
Nov. 5	Feb. 4	91	2,106,301	1,200,577	955,661	244,916	995,324	205,253	99.100	3.561	99.105	3.541	99.098	3.568	1,200,441
5	May 6	182	1,650,175	999,960	928,425	71,535	886,613	113,347	98.120	3.718	98.124	3.711	98.116	3.727	900,393
12	Feb 11	91	2,029,151	1,199,941	944,803	255,138	1,050,278	149,663	99.097	3.574	99.100	3.560	99.095	3.580	1,195,793
12	May 13	182	1,742,422	1,000,317	912,712	87,605	926,016	74,301	98.108	3.742	98.115	3.729	98.106	3.748	900,452
19	Feb. 18	91	2,158,178	1,201,041	938,565	262,476	970,821	230,220	99.090	3.600	99.093	3.588	99.089	3.604	1,200,177
19	May 20	182	1,812,350	1,000,823	923,983	76,840	867,498	133,325	98.093	3.772	98.098	3.762	98.090	3.778	900,490
27	Feb. 25	90	2,638,731	1,200,195	980,350	219,846	982,364	217,832	99.061	3.757	99.068	3.728	99.054	3.784	1,201,538
27	May 27	181	1,937,757	1,000,102	931,676	68,426	877,363	122,739	98.018	3.942	98.040	3.898	98.000	3.978	900,091
Dec. 3	Mar. 4	91	2,042,564	1,200,224	962,662	237,562	1,007,569	192,655	99.022	3.868	99.030	3.837	99.016	3.893	1,200,678
3	June 3	182	1,835,321	1,000,051	932,635	67,416	867,826	132,225	97.962	4.030	97.973	4.009	97.95	4.04	904,729

1,301,783	3.873	99.021	3.750	99.052	3.815	99.036	15,120	1,285,897	258,475	1,042,542	1,301,017	1,829,067	91	Mar. 11	10
900,518	3.972	97.992	3.916	98.020	3.944	98.006	4,997	995,581	91,489	909,089	1,000,578	1,672,878	182	June 10	10
1,301,621	3.881	99.019	3.841	99.029	3.864	99.023	17,974	1,282,866	276,391	1,024,449	1,300,840	2,324,666	91	Mar. 18	17
4,901,049	3.974	97.991	3.948	98.004	3.965	97.996	7,453	993,151	113,621	886,983	1,000,604	2,097,454	182	June 17	7
1,301,980	3.877	99.020	3.857	99.025	3.868	99.022	192,212	1,015,884	126,032	993,064	1,208,096	2,109,531	91	Mar. 25	24
900,065	3.964	97.996	3.952	98.002	3.960	97.998	134,800	870,107	215,032	904,322	1,004,907	2,189,011	182	June 24	24
900,880	3.873	99.021	3.853	99.026	3.866	99.023	201,670	998,184	100,585	967,158	1,199,854	2,264,222	91	Apr. 1	31
900,402	3.960	97.998	3.948	98.004	3.957	97.999	123,513	878,464	232,696	904,385	1,001,977	2,038,711	182	July 1	31
1965															
1,200,292	3.833	99.031	3.814	99.036	3.829	99.032	213,375	888,465	239,993	861,847	1,101,840	1,986,695	91	Apr. 8	7
900,046	3.928	98.014	3.916	98.020	3.927	98.015	85,452	85,910	86,651	916,711	1,003,362	2,020,324	182	July 8	7
1,211,565	3.822	99.034	3.790	99.042	3.814	99.036	181,686	917,948	312,380	787,254	1,099,634	2,171,205	91	Apr. 15	15
902,495	3.952	98.002	3.928	98.015	3.942	98.007	95,080	905,987	126,213	874,854	1,000,847	1,811,184	182	July 22	14
1,202,917	3.833	99.031	3.806	99.038	3.821	99.034	199,823	1,000,459	260,272	940,010	1,200,282	1,099,469	91	Apr. 21	22
899,827	3.962	97.997	3.833	98.000	3.960	97.998	123,120	877,931	98,055	902,497	1,001,051	1,475,013	182	July 21	22
1,200,175	3.857	99.025	3.833	99.031	3.848	99.027	213,152	989,713	225,368	977,497	1,202,865	1,485,324	91	Apr. 28	28
901,969	3.948	98.004	3.936	98.010	3.946	98.005	132,035	871,198	98,228	905,005	1,003,233	2,226,134	182	July 28	28
1,200,577	3.893	99.016	3.865	99.023	3.888	99.017	242,072	980,445	230,452	902,517	1,003,580	2,469,650	91	May 6	4
1,199,941	3.972	97.994	3.960	98.005	3.888	97.994	133,651	869,929	89,663	913,917	1,003,517	2,226,693	182	Aug. 5	4
901,846	3.913	99.011	3.893	99.016	3.908	99.013	133,629	1,020,728	252,352	948,005	1,003,357	2,241,693	91	May 13	6
901,041	3.990	97.983	3.960	97.990	3.987	97.984	132,922	888,314	92,424	908,812	1,001,236	2,448,440	182	Aug. 12	13
1,201,346	3.952	97.983	3.976	98.010	3.903	97.984	12,338	1,187,733	253,685	907,200	1,000,071	2,073,818	91	May 20	12
1,200,196	4.019	97.908	3.994	97.981	3.936	9.920	1,847	998,511	93,158	907,246	1,000,358	2,161,767	182	Aug. 19	20
902,006	3.996	97.955	3.933	98.995	4.015	98.992	234,346	966,571	206,803	927,246	1,000,917	2,327,347	91	May 27	18
900,224	3.988	97.958	3.976	97.961	4.043	97.956	142,991	860,395	76,140	961,993	1,003,386	2,503,559	182	Aug. 25	25
1,200,287	4.039	97.978	4.033	97.961	4.037	97.959	228,334	971,663	94,770	905,529	1,000,299	2,358,807	91	June 3	25
1,301,017	3.956	98.005	3.988	97.984	3.948	99.006	135,465	864,834	255,859	944,895	1,000,754	2,303,530	182	Sept. 2	4
900,822	3.928	98.000	3.901	99.004	4.001	99.002	184,384	1,016,370	95,541	900,814	1,200,355	2,151,455	91	Sept. 2	4
1,300,840	3.992	98.010	3.986	97.985	3.917	99.004	75,876	924,479	276,661	924,332	1,200,993	1,880,194	182	Sept. 9	11
900,020	3.928	99.007	3.916	99.010	3.990	99.009	188,121	1,012,872	102,656	899,870	1,002,526	2,248,707	91	June 17	11
1,208,096	3.990	99.010	3.978	99.014	3.922	99.009	54,174	948,352	238,690	964,064	1,002,754	2,331,424	182	Sept. 16	18
900,644	3.932	99.006	3.901	99.006	3.984	99.986	166,420	1,036,334	91,607	908,850	1,000,457	2,367,963	91	June 24	18
1,199,854	.000	99.978	3.980	97.989	3.921	99.981	140,541	859,616	230,712	969,454	1,000,166	2,023,932	182	Sept. 23	25
900,333	3.948	99.002	3.928	99.007	3.993	99.004	198,776	1,001,390	102,810	899,253	1,002,063	2,061,246	91	July 1	25
1,101,840	3.996	97.980	3.988	99.007	3.942	97.981	144,444	857,619	242,938	958,881	1,201,819	1,937,578	182	Sept. 30	1
901,176	3.944	99.003	3.928	99.005	3.993	97.981	191,332	1,010,487	96,857	904,404	1,201,261	2,280,698	91	July 8	1
1,099,634	3.998	97.979	3.978	99.006	3.991	97.983	92,530	908,731	298,320	902,348	1,200,668	2,188,024	182	Oct. 7	8
1,004,483	3.952	99.001	3.928	99.003	3.946	97.974	171,422	1,029,246	124,443	876,256	1,000,699	1,832,482	91	July 15	8
1,200,282	4.013	97.971	3.932	99.006	4.008	97.003	86,422	914,277	260,248	941,316	1,201,564	2,248,216	182	Oct. 14	15
1,000,769	3.920	99.009	3 .000	97.978	3.916	97.974	219,233	982,331	234,626	893,185	1,201,522	1,921,554	91	July 22	15
1,202,865	3.980	97.988	3.970	97.993	3.978	99.989	155,258	995,602	108,337	966,472	1,201,098	2,267,394	182	Oct. 21	22
1,002,754							153,200	850,075	92,606	910,669	1,003,275	2,210,644	182	Oct. 28	29

Footnotes at end of table.

Summary of information pertaining to Treasury bills issued during the fiscal year 1965—Continued

Date of issue	Date of maturity	Days to maturity [1]	Total applied for	Total accepted	On competitive basis	On noncompetitive basis	For cash	In exchange	Average price per hundred	Equivalent average rate (percent)	High Price per hundred	High Equivalent rate (percent)	Low Price per hundred	Low Equivalent rate (percent)	Amount maturing on issue date of new offering
							Regular Weekly—Continued								
1965	*1965*														
May 6	Aug. 5	91	$2,073,412	$1,200,536	$973,517	$227,019	$971,271	$229,265	99.014	3.901	99.016	3.893	99.012	3.909	$1,202,817
May 6	Nov. 4	182	1,958,383	1,000,414	909,037	91,377	838,522	161,892	98.003	3.950	98.004	3.948	98.001	3.954	999,960
May 13	Aug. 12	91	2,246,167	1,200,969	962,949	288,020	977,871	223,098	99.016	3.893	99.020	3.877	99.015	3.897	1,200,357
May 13	Nov. 12	183	1,871,725	1,200,857	902,358	98,499	866,647	134,210	97.992	3.893	97.998[2]	3.938	97.990	3.954	1,000,317
May 20	Aug. 19	91	1,952,704	1,200,891	963,164	237,727	1,013,276	187,615	99.015	3.897	99.018	3.885	99.012	3.909	1,200,071
May 20	Nov. 18	182	2,041,003	1,001,778	898,860	102,918	896,771	105,007	98.000	3.955	98.003	3.950	99.015	3.960	1,000,823
May 27	Aug. 26	91	2,090,782	1,199,660	984,208	215,452	963,121	216,539	99.017	3.889	99.020	3.877	97.994	3.897	1,200,917
May 27	Nov. 26	183	2,001,200	1,000,785	916,036	84,749	857,411	143,374	97.945	3.944	97.998[2]	3.938	99.020	3.946	1,000,102
June 3	Sept. 2	91	2,206,827	1,202,352	991,672	210,680	975,008	227,344	99.022	3.870	99.026	3.853	99.026	3.877	1,000,197
June 3	Dec. 2	182	1,992,142	1,001,177	917,560	83,617	884,850	116,327	98.016	3.924	98.023	3.911	98.013	3.930	1,000,051
June 10	Sept. 9	91	1,932,400	1,200,254	954,506	245,748	1,024,630	175,624	99.044	3.781	99.049	3.762	99.049	3.869	1,200,754
June 10	Dec. 9	182	1,846,257	1,000,294	896,138	104,156	896,155	104,139	98.047	3.863	98.054	3.849	98.044	3.806	1,000,578
June 17	Sept. 16	91	2,039,887	1,200,670	954,906	245,764	1,015,367	185,303	99.040	3.799	98.045	3.786	98.041	3.875	1,200,993
June 17	Dec. 16	182	2,302,842	1,001,469	899,027	102,442	886,590	114,879	98.042	3.873	98.045	3.867	99.042	3.790	1,000,604
June 24	Sept. 23	91	2,221,341	1,205,281	970,213	235,068	1,001,183	204,098	99.042	3.789	99.047	3.770	99.042	3.790	1,202,754
June 24	Dec. 23	182	2,340,802	1,001,519	891,448	110,071	914,899	86,620	98.063	3.831	98.068	3.822	98.062	3.833	1,004,907
							Tax Anticipation								
1964	*1965*														
Sept. 2	Mar. 22	201	$2,234,994	$1,000,965	$971,771	$29,194	$1,000,965	------	98.001	3.580	98.012[2]	3.561	97.998	3.586	------
Oct. 26	Mar. 22	147	3,188,232	1,503,195	1,299,263	203,932	1,503,195	------	98.564	3.518	98.575	3.490	98.559	3.529	------
Nov. 24	June 22	210	3,703,119	1,504,489	1,298,870	205,619	1,504,489	------	97.877	3.639	97.895[2]	3.609	97.874	3.645	------
1965															
Jan. 18	June 22	155	4,044,947	1,758,347	1,517,200	241,147	1,758,347	------	98.402	3.711	98.411[2]	3.691	98.399	3.718	------

One-Year

1964	1965														
July 7	June 30	358	$2,393,266	$1,001,222	$979,820	$21,402	$1,001,222		96.329	3.691	96.336	3.684	96.327	3.694	
Aug. 4	July 31	361	2,080,052	1,000,462	979,275	21,187	1,000,462		96.346	3.644	96.362	3.628	96.339	3.651	
Aug. 31	Aug. 31	365	1,940,279	1,000,439	960,205	40,234	973,989	$26,450	96.260	3.688	96.270	3.679	96.252	3.697	$1,001,143
Sept. 30	Sept. 30	365	1,849,028	1,000,539	947,691	52,848	982,146	18,393	96.174	3.773	96.189	3.759	96.169	3.779	1,000,960
Oct. 31	Oct. 31	365	2,349,703	989,950	954,691	45,259	896,159	103,791	95.876	3.790	96.168	3.780	96.154	3.793	1,000,273
Nov. 30	Nov. 30	365	2,496,632	1,000,542	948,419	52,123	937,414	63,128	95.972	4.068	95.944	4.000	95.855	4.088	1,004,801
Dec. 31	Dec. 31	365	2,310,836	1,002,951	957,341	45,610	976,694	26,257	95.972	3.972	95.987	3.958	95.965	3.980	1,000,309
1965	**1966**														
Jan. 31	Jan. 31	365	2,907,878	1,000,387	947,866	52,521	897,633	102,754	96.000	3.945	[2] 96.007	3.938	95.998	3.947	1,000,393
Feb. 28	Feb. 28	365	2,023,196	1,000,705	965,677	35,028	964,106	36,599	95.882	4.062	95.904	4.040	95.873	4.070	1,000,520
Mar. 31	Mar. 31	365	2,241,262	1,000,304	946,618	53,686	950,986	49,318	95.957	3.987	95.973	3.972	95.950	3.995	1,001,464
Apr. 30	Apr. 30	365	2,573,194	1,001,162	964,100	37,062	880,278	120,884	95.949	3.996	95.951	3.994	95.945	3.999	1,001,439
May 31	May 31	365	2,751,993	1,000,886	969,510	31,376	900,604	100,282	95.991	3.954	95.994	3.951	95.991	3.954	1,000,141
June 30	June 30	356	2,190,847	1,000,647	953,065	47,582	938,546	62,101	96.140	3.807	[2] 96.157	3.790	96.126	3.821	1,001,222

[1] The 13-week bills ... that the issue of ... ept. that the issue of ... ally small ... maturity of one year.

[1] Total issues of bills with an original maturity of ... for 1 ... was an ... se of bills with an orig ...

NOTE.—The usual timing with respect to weekly issues of Treasury bills is: Press release inviting tenders, 8 days before date of issue; closing date on which tenders are accepted, 3 days before date of issue; and press release announcing acceptance of tenders, 2 days before date of issue.

Guaranteed Debentures Called

Exhibit 4.—Calls for partial redemption, before maturity, of insurance fund and home improvement account debentures

During the fiscal year 1965, there were 32 calls for partial redemption, before maturity, of insurance fund debentures, and one call of home improvement account debentures, 22 dated September 23, 1964, and 11 dated March 25, 1965. The notices of call were published in the *Federal Register* of September 29, 1964, and March 31, 1965. The notice covering the call of the 3¾ percent servicemen's mortgage insurance fund debentures Series EE, is shown in this exhibit. Since the other notices of call are similar to this notice, they have been omitted, but the essential details are summarized in the table following the notice of call.

NOTICE OF CALL. FEDERAL REGISTER OF MARCH 31, 1965

To Holders of 3¾ Percent Servicemen's Mortgage Insurance Fund Debentures, Series EE:

NOTICE OF CALL FOR PARTIAL REDEMPTION, BEFORE MATURITY, OF 3¾ PERCENT SERVICEMEN'S MORTGAGE INSURANCE FUND DEBENTURES, SERIES EE

Pursuant to the authority conferred by the National Housing Act (48 Stat. 1246; U.S.C., title 12, sec. 1701 *et seq.*) as amended, public notice is hereby given that Servicemen's Mortgage Insurance Fund Debentures, Series EE, bearing interest at 3¾ percent as designated below are hereby called for redemption, at par and accrued interest, on July 1, 1965, on which date interest on such debentures shall cease:

3¾ Percent Servicemen's Mortgage Insurance Fund Debentures, Series EE

Denomination	Range of inclusive serial numbers within which called debentures fall
$50	3,397 to 3,912
100	{ 25,344 to 25,347 and
	{ 25,937 to 30,201
500	6,247 to 7,228
1,000	{ 19,918 to 22,822 and
	{ 22,918
5,000	3,442 to 3,911
10,000	3,839 to 4,288

Although the above inclusive serial numbers include Series EE debentures bearing other rates, only those bearing interest at the rate of 3¾ percent, listed above, are included in this call, together with certain other debentures bearing the same rate and registered in the name of the Federal National Mortgage Association.

No transfers or denominational exchanges in debentures covered by the foregoing call will be made on the books maintained by the Treasury Department on or after April 1, 1965. This does not affect the right of the holder of a debenture to sell and assign the debenture on or after April 1, 1965, and provision will be made for the payment of final interest due on July 1, 1965, with the principal thereof to the actual owner, as shown by the assignments thereon.

The Commissioner of the Federal Housing Administration hereby offers to purchase any debentures included in this call at any time from April 1, 1965, to June 30, 1965, inclusive, at par and accrued interest, to date of purchase.

Instructions for the presentation and surrender of debentures for redemption on or after July 1, 1965, or for purchase prior to that date will be given by the Secretary of the Treasury.

P. N. BROWNSTEIN,
Federal Housing Commissioner.

APPROVED: *March 26, 1965.*
JOHN K. CARLOCK,
Fiscal Assistant Secretary of the Treasury.

Summary of information contained in the notices of call for partial redemption of insurance fund debentures during the fiscal year 1965

	3¾ percent mutual mortgage insurance fund debentures, Series AA	3⅞ percent mutual mortgage insurance fund debentures, Series AA	4 percent mutual mortgage insurance fund debentures, Series AA	4⅛ percent mutual mortgage insurance fund debentures, Series AA	4¼ percent mutual mortgage insurance fund debentures, Series AA
Notice of call	Mar. 25, 1965	Mar. 25, 1965	Mar. 25, 1965	Sept. 23, 1964	Mar. 25, 1965.
Redemption date	July 1, 1965	July 1, 1965	July 1, 1965	Jan. 1, 1965	July 1, 1965.
Serial numbers called by denominations:					
$50	13941–21185	15324, 16339–70643, 70652–70653.	24779, 26055–70641	25399–55457, 55534, 55718–55721.	55461–70640, 70852, 70934, 70988.
100	63646–115199	65349–500571, 500760–500768, 500791–500794, 501606, 502033–502034, 502040–502044.	104019–500566, 501605.	148308–148571, 149603–379511, 379752, 379966–379976, 380392, 380418, 380805–380807, 380847–780845, 380881–380883, 38876–95096, 95242, 95329, 95337, 95430.	379512–500581, 501034–501038, 501904–501906, 502032, 503040–503041.
500	16912–30601	17238, 17382–124962, 125020, 125023, 125145–125146, 125328.	26256, 27764, 30786, 32494, 33372–124967.	38876–95096, 95242, 95329, 95337, 95430.	95098–1249070, 125081, 125219.
1,000	52497–99946	54075–380819, 380970–380973, 380978–380981, 381008, 381396–381399.	90524, 101112, 110300–380817, 381011.	127550–293376, 293547, 293835–293841, 293909, 294468–294469, 294484, 294791–294792, 294840–294842.	293390–380815, 381009–381010, 381617–381621–381766, 381768, 382389, 382570–382571.
5,000	15064–22960, 23325, 23328, 23337.	15534–74225, 74257, 74259, 74421.	25196, 25545, 26325–74224, 74362.	27589–58387, 58483, 58506–58507, 58569.	58398–74222, 74268.
10,000	9977, 10023–14822	10032–62739	13363, 13962, 15183–62721	18486–46958	46962–62741, 62873, 62927, 63043, 63232.
Final date for transfers or deliveries (but not for sale or assignment).	Apr. 1, 1965	Apr. 1, 1965	Apr. 1, 1965	Oct. 1, 1964.	Apr. 1, 1965.
Redemption on call date, amount of int. per $500 paid in full with principal.	$18.75	$19.375	$20.00	$20.625	$20.625
Presentation for purchase prior to call date:					
Period.	Apr. 1–July 1, 1965.	Apr. 1–July 1, 1965.	Apr. 1–July 1, 1965.	Oct. 1–Dec. 31, 1964.	Apr. 1–July 1, 1965.
Amount of medi... int. per $1,000 per day paid with principal.	$0.103591160 from Jan. 1, 1965, to date of purchase.	$0.107044199 from Jan. 1, 1965, to date of purchase.	$0.110497238 from Jan. 1, 1965, to date of purchase.	$0.11209276 from July 1, 1964, to date of purchase.	$0.113950276 from Jan. 1, 1965, to date of purchase.

Summary of information contained in the notices of call for partial redemption of insurance fund debentures during the fiscal year 1965—Con.

	3⅞, 4, and 4⅛ percent housing insurance fund debentures, Series BB	3⅞ percent housing insurance fund debentures, Series BB	4 percent housing insurance fund debentures, Series BB	4⅛ percent housing insurance fund debentures, Series BB
Notice of call	Sept. 23, 1964	Mar. 25, 1965	Mar. 25, 1965	Mar. 25, 1965.
Redemption date	Jan. 1, 1965	July 1, 1965	July 1, 1965	July 1, 1965.
Serial numbers called by denominations:				
$50	480–1580	1591–1659, 1667	1581–1657	1582–1663.
100	1968–12853	12932–13719	12868–13681	12865–13718.
500	639–3393	3475–3644, 3646	3395–3638	3396–3645, 3659.
1,000	2317–11837	11881–12559	11840–12535	11839–12558.
5,000	647–1586	1589–1729	1603–1743	1604–1744.
10,000	5498–22170	22394–28190	22171–28630	22377–28619.
Final date for transfers or denominational exchanges (but not for sale or assignment).	Oct. 1, 1964	Apr. 1, 1965	Apr. 1, 1965	Apr. 1, 1965.
Redemption on call date, amount of interest per $1,000 paid in full with principal.	$19.375 for 3⅞%, $20.00 for 4%, $20.625 for 4⅛%.	$19.375	$20.00	$20.625.
Presentation for purchase prior to call date:				
Period	Oct. 1, 1964–Jan. 1, 1965	Apr. 1–July 1, 1965	Apr. 1–July 1, 1965	Apr. 1–July 1, 1965.
Amount of accrued interest per $1,000 per day paid with principal.	$0.105299 for 3⅞%, $0.108696 for 4%, $0.112092 for 4⅛%, from July 1, 1964, to date of purchase.	$0.107044199 from Jan. 1, 1965, to date of purchase.	$0.110497238 from Jan. 1, 1965, to date of purchase.	$0.113950276 from Jan. 1, 1965, to date of purchase.

	3¾ percent section 220 housing insurance fund debentures, Series CC	3⅞ percent section 220 housing insurance fund debentures, Series CC	4⅛ percent section 220 housing insurance fund debentures, Series CC	4⅛ percent section 220 housing insurance fund debentures, Series CC
Notice of call	Mar. 25, 1965	Mar. 25, 1965	Sept. 23, 1964	Mar. 25, 1965.
Redemption date	July 1, 1965	July 1, 1965	Jan. 1, 1965	July 1, 1965.
Serial numbers called by denominations:				
$50	41, 43			51.
10	184–193	232	217–228	233–237.
500	56	70	67	71.
1,000	157, 158	193–195	186–192	196–197.
10,000	5680–6062			6751.
Final date for transfers or denominational exchanges (but not for sale or assignment).	Apr. 1, 1965	Apr. 1, 1965	Oct. 1, 1964	Apr. 1, 1965.
Redemption on call date, amount of interest per $1,000 paid in full with principal.	$18.75	$19.375	$20.625	$20.625.
Presentation for purchase prior to call date:				
Period	Apr. 1–July 1, 1965	Apr. 1–July 1, 1965	Oct. 1–Dec. 31, 1964	Apr. 1–July 1, 1965.
Amount of accrued interest per $1,000 per day paid with principal.	$0.103591160 from Jan. 1, 1965, to date of purchase.	$0.107044199 from Jan. 1, 1965, to date of purchase.	$0.112092 from July 1, 1964, to date of purchase.	$0.113950276 from Jan. 1, 1965, to date of purchase.

	3¾ percent section 221 housing insurance fund debentures, Series DD	3⅞ percent section 221 housing insurance fund debentures, Series DD	4 and 4⅛ percent section 221 housing insurance fund debentures, Series DD
Notice of call			
Redemption date	Mar. 25, 1965	Mar. 25, 1965	Sept. 23, 1964.
Serial numbers called by	July 1, 1965	July 1, 1965	Jan. 1, 1965.
$50	1005–2847	465–2885,	1336–2752.
100	1856–19801	2280–21186.	5966–20232.
500	1546–6145.	768–5463.	2657–5248.
1,000	...2145,	2584–19126.	6026–18499.
1,000	1412–5397	1048–5970, 5975.	2018–5820.
	30– ... 63	1403–7482	1893–7404.
Final date for transfers or denominational exchanges (but not for sale or assignment)	Apr. 1, 60	Apr. 1, 60	Oct. 1, 1964.
Redemption on call date, amount of principal paid in full with principal	$18.75	$19.375	$20.00 for 4%, $20.625 for 4⅛%.
Period of accrued interest per $1,000 per day paid with principal	Apr. 1–July 1, 1965. $0.103591160 from Jan. 1, 1965, to date of purchase.	Apr. 1–July 1, 1965. $0.107044199 from Jan. 1, 1965, to date of purchase.	Oct. 1, 1964–Jan. 1, 1965. $0.108696 for 4%, $0.112002 for 4⅛%, from July 1, 1964, to date of purchase.

	4 percent section 221 housing insurance fund debentures, Series DD	4⅛ percent section 221 housing insurance fund debentures, Series DD	3¾, 3⅞, 4, and 4⅛ percent servicemen's mortgage insurance fund debentures, Series EE
Notice of call			
Redemption date	Mar. 25, 1965	Mar. 25, 60	Sept. 23, 1964.
Serial numbers called by	July 1, 1965	July 1, 60	Jan. 1, 1965.
$50	2754–2888, 2894.	2776–2887.	584–3394.
100	20234–21189, 21215	20331–21181	4098–25913.
500	5249–5465.	5265–5460	1078–6243.
1,000	18502–19127	...918	3855–19906.
5,000	5822–5962	5826–5965, 5976.	880–3439.
10,000	7407–7479	7466–7475.	698–3333.
Final date for transfers or denominational exchanges (but not for sale or assignment)	Apr. 1, 1965	Apr. 1, 1 65	Oct. 1, 1964.
Redemption on call date, amount of principal paid in full with principal	$20.00.	$20.625	$18.75 for 3¾%, $19.375 for 3⅞%, $20.00 for 4%, $20.625 for 4⅛%.
Presentation for purchase prior to call date: Period of accrued interest per $1,000 per day paid with principal	Apr. 1–July 1, 1965. $0.110497238 from Jan. 1, 1965, to date of purchase.	Apr. 1–July 1, 1965. $0.113950276 from Jan. 1, 1965, to date.	Oct. 1, 1964–Jan. 1, 1965. $0.101962 for 3¾%, $0.105299 for 3⅞%, $0.108696 for 4%, $0.112002 for 4⅛%, from July 1, 1964, to date of purchase.

Summary of information contained in the notices of call for partial redemption of insurance fund debentures during the fiscal year 1965—Con.

	3¾ percent servicemen's mortgage insurance fund debentures, Series EE	3⅞ percent servicemen's mortgage insurance fund debentures, Series EE	4 percent servicemen's mortgage insurance fund debentures, Series EE
Notice of call			
Redemption date	Mar. 25, 1965.	Mar. 25, 1965.	Mar. 25, 1965.
	July 1, 1965.	July 1, 1965.	July 1, 1965.
Serial numbers called by denominations:			
$50	3397–3912.	3396–3905.	3400–3914.
100	25344–25347, 25937–30201.	25914–30175.	25925–30217.
500	6247–7228.	6255–7222, 7269.	6245–7231.
1,000	19918–22822, 22918.	19907–22802, 22889.	19942–22829, 22887.
	3442–3911.	3440–3907.	3451–3912.
0,000	3839–4288.	3835–4281.	3336–4282.
Final date for transfers or denominational exchanges (but not for sale or assignment).	Apr. 1, 1965.	Apr. 1, 1965.	Apr. 1, 1965.
Redemption on call date, amount of interest per $1,000 paid in full with principal.	$18.75.	$19.375.	$20.00.
Presentation for purchase prior to call date:			
Period	Apr. 1–July 1, 1965.	Apr. 1–July 1, 1965.	Apr. 1–July 1, 1965.
Amount of accrued interest per $1,000 per day paid with principal.	$0.103591160 from Jan. 1, 1965, to date of purchase.	$0.107044199 from Jan. 1, 1965, to date of purchase.	$0.110497238 from Jan. 1, 1965, to date of purchase.

	4⅛ percent servicemen's mortgage insurance fund debentures, Series EE	3¾, 3⅞, 4, and 4⅛ percent armed services housing mortgage insurance fund debentures, Series FF	3¾ percent armed services housing mortgage insurance fund debentures, Series FF
Notice of call			
Redemption date	Mar. 25, 1965.	Sept. 23, 1964.	Mar. 25, 1965.
	July 1, 1965.	Jan. 1, 1965.	July 1, 1965.
Serial numbers called by denominations:			
$50	3395–3911.	115–214.	2483–2590.
100	25919–30213, 30308–30313.	1430–2471.	564.
500	6244–7230, 7254.	319–538.	2637–2661.
1,000	19912–22826.	1787–2567.	550.
5,000	3444–3910.	358–524.	9861.
10,000	3837–4288.	9408–9859.	
Final date for transfers or denominational exchanges (but not for sale or assignment).	Apr. 1, 1965.	Oct. 1, 1964.	Apr. 1, 1965.
Redemption on call date, amount of interest per $1,000 paid in full with principal.	$20.625.	$18.75 for 3¾%, $19.375 for 3⅞%, $20.00 for 4%, $20.625 for 4⅛%.	$18.75.
Presentation for purchase prior to call date:			
Period	Apr. 1–July 1, 1965.	Oct. 1, 1964–Jan. 1, 1965.	Apr. 1–July 1, 1965.
Amount of accrued interest per $1,000 per day paid with principal.	$0.113950276 from Jan. 1, 1965, to date of purchase.	$0.101902 for 3¾%, $0.105299 for 3⅞%, $0.108696 for 4%, $0.112092 for 4⅛%, from July 1, 1964, to date of purchase.	$0.103591160 from Jan. 1, 1965, to date of purchase.

	3⅞ percent armed services housing mortgage insurance fund debentures, Series FF	4 percent armed services housing mortgage insurance fund debentures, Series FF	4⅛ percent armed services housing mortgage insurance fund debentures, Series FF	2½ percent war housing insurance fund debentures, Series H
Date of call				
Redemption date	Mar. 25, 1965 / July 1, 1965	Mar. 25, 1965 / July 1, 1965	Mar. 25, 1965 / July 1, 1965	Sept. 23, 1964 / Jan. 1, 1965
Serial numbers called by denominations:				
$50	225, 227	226	215–216	4996–5017,
100	2515–2607	2527–2605	2479–2586	19224–19225, 19231–19389.
500	553–554	548–566	549–559	5531–5565.
1,000	2573–2673	2615–2671	2575–2656	22856, 22861–22993.
			545	5237, 5243–5262.
				53129–53262.
Final date for transfers or denominational exchanges (but not for sale or assignment).	9864–9920 / Apr. 1, 1965	9866–9923 / Apr. 1, 1965	9862–9863 / Apr. 1, 1965	53129–53623. / Oct. 1, 1964.
Redemption on call date, amount of interest per $1,000 paid in full with principal.	$19.375	$20.00	$20.625	$12.6
Presentation for purchase prior to call date: Period	Apr. 1–July 1, 19__	Apr. 1–July 1, 1965	Apr. 1–July 1, 1965	Oct. 1–Dec. 31, 1964.
Amount of accrued interest per $1,000 paid with principal also.	$0.0?9 from Jan. 1, 1965, to date of purchase.	$0.10497238 from Jan. 1, 1965, to date of purchase.	$0.11395276 from Jan. 1, 1965, to date of purchase.	$0.067935 from July 1, 1964, to date of purchase.

	4 percent section 203 home improvement account debentures, Series HH	2½ percent Title I housing insurance fund debentures, Series L	2¾ percent Title I housing insurance fund debentures Series R	3 percent Title I housing insurance fund debentures, Series T
Date of call				
Redemption date	Sept. 23, 1964 / Jan. 1, 1965	Sept. 23, 1964 / Jan. 1, 1965	Sept. 23, 1964 / Jan. 1, 1965	Sept. 23, 1964 / Jan. 1, 1965
Serial numbers called by denominations:				
$50		212–215, 261	559–565	624–643.
100		564–596	1564–1634	2533–2686.
60		204–209	384–396	773–819.
1,000		693–710	858–925	1904–2031.
50			260–261	
Final date for transfers or denominational exchanges (but not for sale or assignment).	Oct. 1, 1964	Oct. 1, 1964	Oct. 1, 1964	Oct. 1, 1964.
Redemption on call date, amount of interest per $1,000 paid in full with principal.	$20.00	$12.50	$13.75	$15.00.
Presentation for purchase prior to call date: Period	Oct. 1–Dec. 31, 1964.	Oct. 1–Dec. 31, 1964.	Oct. 1–Dec. 31, 1964.	Oct. 1–Dec. 31, 1964.
Amount of accrued interest per $1,000 paid with principal.	$0.108696 from July 1, 1964, to date of purchase.	$0.067935 from July 1, 1964, to date of purchase.	$0.074728 from July 1, 1964, to date of purchase.	$0.081522 from July 1, 1964, to date of purchase.

Regulations

Exhibit 5.—Revision, December 4, 1964, of Department Circular No. 853, regulations governing restrictive endorsements of United States bearer securities

TREASURY DEPARTMENT,
Washington, December 4, 1964.

Department Circular No. 853, dated October 5, 1949, is hereby amended and issued as Department Circular No. 853, Revised.

AUTHORITY: Secs. 328.1 to 328.9 issued under R.S. 161, as amended (5 U.S.C. 22); Second Liberty Bond Act, as amended (31 U.S.C. 752, 753, 754, 754b).

Sec. 328.1. *Scope of regulations.*—These regulations are applicable only to United States bearer securities[1] presented (a) by or through banks for payment at or after their maturity or call date, or in exchange for any securities under any exchange offering, (b) by or through banks at any time prior to their maturity or call date for redemption at par and application of the proceeds in payment of Federal estate taxes, provided said securities by the terms of their issue are eligible for such redemption, and (c) by district directors, Internal Revenue Service, for redemption, with the proceeds to be applied to payment of taxes (other than securities presented under (b) above). These regulations do not apply to bearer securities presented for any other transaction, or to registered securities assigned in blank, or to bearer, or so assigned as to become, in effect, payable to bearer.

Sec. 328.2. *Definitions.*—Certain words and terms, as used in these regulations, are defined as follows:

(a) "Banks" refer to, and include, incorporated banks (i.e., banks doing a general commercial banking business), incorporated trust companies (i.e., trust companies doing either a general banking business or general trust business), and savings banks (whether or not mutual).

(b) "Bearer securities" or "securities" are those which are payable on their face to "bearer," the ownership of which is not recorded. They include "Treasury bonds," "Treasury notes," "Treasury certificates of indebtedness," and "Treasury bills."

Sec. 328.3. *Authorization for restrictive endorsements.*—(a) *By banks.* Banks are authorized, under the conditions and in the form hereinafter provided, to place restrictive endorsements upon the face of bearer securities owned by themselves or their customers for the purpose of presentation to Federal Reserve banks or branches, or to the Treasurer of the United States, as follows:

(1) *For payment or redemption*—at any time within one calendar month prior to their maturity date, or the date on which they become payable pursuant to a call for redemption, or at any time after their maturity or call date;

(2) *For exchange*—during any period for their presentation pursuant to an exchange offering; and

(3) *For redemption at par in payment of Federal estate taxes (only eligible securities)*—at any time prior to their maturity or call redemption date.

(b) *By district directors, Internal Revenue Service.* District directors, Internal Revenue Service, are authorized, under the conditions and in the form hereinafter provided, to place restrictive endorsements upon the face of bearer securities for the purpose of presentation to Federal Reserve banks or branches, or to the Treasurer of the United States, for redemption and application of the proceeds in payment of taxes (other than securities presented for redemption at par and application of the proceeds in payment of Federal estate taxes).

(c) *Instructions from Federal Reserve banks.* Federal Reserve banks will inform eligible banks and district directors of the Internal Revenue Service in their respective districts as to the procedure to be followed under the authority granted by these regulations. No bank or district director should imprint restrictive endorsements on securities until such information is received from the Federal Reserve bank.

Sec. 328.4. *Effect of restrictive endorsements.*—Bearer securities bearing restrictive endorsements as herein provided will thereafter be nonnegotiable and

---

[1] These regulations may also apply to securities issued by certain agencies of the United States and the former Government of Puerto Rico for which the Treasury Department of the United States acts as transfer agency, provided the issuing authorities for such securities have adopted by appropriate regulations the provisions of this circular.

payment, redemption, or exchange will be made only as provided in such endorsements.

Sec. 328.5. *Forms of endorsement.*—(a) *When presented by banks*—

(1) *For payment or exchange.* The endorsement placed on a bearer security presented for payment or exchange by a bank should be in the following form:

For presentation to the Federal Reserve Bank of _____, Fiscal Agent of the United States, for redemption or in exchange for securities of a new issue, in accordance with written instructions submitted by _____.

(Insert name of presenting bank)

ABA No. _____

(2) *For redemption at par.* The endorsement placed on a bearer security presented for redemption at par in payment of Federal estate taxes should be in the following form:

For presentation to the Federal Reserve Bank of _____, Fiscal Agent of the United States, for redemption at par in payment of Federal estate taxes, in accordance with written instructions submitted by _____.

(Insert name of presenting bank)

ABA No. _____

(b) *When presented by district directors, Internal Revenue Service.* The endorsement placed on a bearer security by a district director, Internal Revenue Service, should be in the following form:

For presentation to the Federal Reserve Bank of _____, Fiscal Agent of the United States, for redemption, the proceeds to be credited to the account of the district director, Internal Revenue Service at _____, for credit on the Federal _____ taxes due from _____

Income, gift, or other (Name and address)

Sec. 328.6. *Requirements for endorsements.*—(a) *On bearer securities.* The endorsement must be imprinted in the left-hand portion of the face of each security with the first line thereof parallel to the left edge of the security and in such manner as to be clearly legible and in such position that it will not obscure the serial number, series designation or other identifying data, and cover the smallest possible portion of the text on the face of the security. The dimensions of the endorsement should be approximately four inches in width and one and one-half inches in height, and must be imprinted by stamp or plate of such character, with a carbon pigment ink, and by such means, as will render the endorsement substantially ineradicable. In cases where the endorsement is being made by a bank, immediately below and as part of the endorsement the ABA code number of the presenting bank must be perforated in figures approximately one-fourth to one-half inch in height. The perforations should be placed as nearly as possible beneath the endorsement without obliterating any of the identifying data. The name of the Federal Reserve bank of the district must appear on the plate or stamp used for the imprinting of the endorsement, and presentation to the appropriate branch of the Federal Reserve bank named will be considered as presentation to the bank. When securities are to be presented to the Treasurer of the United States, the words "Treasurer of the United States" should be used in lieu of the words "Federal Reserve Bank of _____, Fiscal Agent of the United States." No subsequent endorsement will be permitted and no other form of endorsement may be made.

(b) *On coupons.* Unmatured coupons attached to restrictively endorsed securities should be cancelled by imprinting the prescribed endorsement in such manner that a substantial portion of the endorsement will appear on each such coupon. Where such endorsements are made by a bank, its ABA code number should not be perforated on the coupons. If any such coupons are missing, deduction of their face amount will be made in cases of redemption, and in cases of exchange, remittance equal to the face amount of the missing coupons must accompany the securities. All matured coupons, including coupons which will mature on or before the date of redemption or exchange (except as otherwise specifically provided in an announcement of an exchange offering), should be detached from securities upon which restrictive endorsements are to be imprinted.

Sec. 328.7. *Shipment of securities.*—Securities bearing restrictive endorsements may be shipped, at the risk and expense of the shipper, by registered mail, messenger, armored car service, or express to the Federal Reserve bank of the district in which the presenting bank or district director, Internal Revenue Service, is located, or to the appropriate branch of such Federal Reserve bank.

Shipments to the Treasurer of the United States, Washington, D.C., should be made by messenger or armored car.

Sec. 328.8. *Loss, theft, or destruction of securities bearing restrictive endorsements.*—(a) *General.* Relief will be provided on account of securities bearing restrictive endorsements proved to have been lost, stolen or destroyed, upon the owner's application, in the same manner as registered securities which have not been assigned. (See Subpart N of the current revision of Department Circular No. 300,[1] the general regulations with respect to United States securities.) Except for bearer securities submitted for redemption at par in payment of Federal estate taxes, a bank will be considered the owner of securities handled on behalf of customers unless it otherwise requests. The application for relief (Form PD 2211) and instructions will be furnished by the Federal Reserve banks.

(b) *Bond of indemnity.* Where securities bearing restrictive endorsements shipped by a bank have been lost, stolen, or destroyed, a bond of indemnity with surety satisfactory to the Secretary of the Treasury will be required from the owner. If such bond is executed by a bank or other corporation, the execution must be authorized by general or special resolution of the board of directors, or other body exercising similar functions under its bylaws. Ordinarily, no surety will be required on a bond executed by a presenting bank. The Secretary of the Treasury reserves the right, however, to require a surety in any case in which he considers such action necessary for the protection of the United States.

Sec. 328.9. *Miscellaneous.*—The provisions of this circular are subject to the current revision of Department Circular No. 300. The Secretary of the Treasury reserves the right at any time to amend, supplement, or withdraw any or all of the provisions of these regulations.

JOHN K. CARLOCK,
Fiscal Assistant Secretary.

Exhibit 6.—Third revision, December 23, 1964, of Department Circular No. 300, general regulations with respect to United States securities

TREASURY DEPARTMENT,
Washington, December 23, 1964.

Department Circular No. 300, Second Revision, dated April 19, 1963 (31 CFR 306), is hereby amended and issued as the Third Revision.

AUTHORITY: Secs. 306.0 to 306.118 issued under R.S. 3706, 40 Stat. 288, 290, 1309, 48 Stat. 343, and 50 Stat. 481; 31 U.S.C. 738a, 739, 752, 752a, 753, 754, 754a, and 754b.

SUBPART A—GENERAL INFORMATION

Sec. 306.0. *Applicability of regulations.*—These regulations apply to all United States transferable and nontransferable securities,[2] other than United States savings bonds, to the extent specified in these regulations, the offering circulars or special regulations governing such securities.

Sec. 306.1. *Official agencies.*

(a) *Subscriptions–tenders–bids.*—Securities subject to these regulations are issued from time to time pursuant to public offerings by the Secretary of the Treasury, through the Federal Reserve banks, fiscal agents of the United States, and the Treasurer of the United States. Only the Federal Reserve banks and branches and the Treasury Department are authorized to act as official agencies, and subscriptions for securities, tenders for Treasury bills, and bids, to the extent provided in the regulations governing the sale of Treasury bonds through competitive bidding, may be made direct to them; however, banking institutions may assist customers with their subscriptions, tenders or bids.

---

[1] See exhibit 6.
[2] Bonds and other securities issued by certain agencies of the United States and the former government of Puerto Rico are subject to these regulations, so far as applicable, under special arrangements with the issuing authorities. Information as to their application to any particular transaction in any designated security will be furnished by the Bureau of the Public Debt, Division of Loans and Currency, Washington, D.C., 20226, upon request.

(b) *Transactions after issue.*—The Bureau of the Public Debt, Treasury Department, is charged with matters relating to transactions in securities after original issue. Correspondence concerning such transactions and requests for appropriate forms may be addressed to (1) the Federal Reserve bank or branch of the district in which the correspondent is located, or (2) the Bureau of the Public Debt, Division of Loans and Currency, Washington, D.C., 20226, or (3) the Office of the Treasurer of the United States, Securities Division, Washington, D.C., 20220, except where specific instructions are otherwise given in these regulations. The addresses of the Federal Reserve banks and branches are:

Federal Reserve Bank of Boston, Boston, Mass. 02106.
Federal Reserve Bank of New York, New York, N.Y. 10045.
    Buffalo Branch, Buffalo, N.Y. 14240.
Federal Reserve Bank of Philadelphia, Philadelphia, Pa. 19101.
Federal Reserve Bank of Cleveland, Cleveland, Ohio 44101.
    Cincinnati Branch, Cincinnati, Ohio 45201.
    Pittsburgh Branch, Pittsburgh, Pa. 15230.
Federal Reserve Bank of Richmond, Richmond, Va. 23213.
    Baltimore Branch, Baltimore, Md. 21203.
    Charlotte Branch, Charlotte, N.C. 28201.
Federal Reserve Bank of Atlanta, Atlanta, Ga. 30303.
    Birmingham Branch, Birmingham, Ala. 35202.
    Jacksonville Branch, Jacksonville, Fla. 32201.
    Nashville Branch, Nashville, Tenn. 37203.
    New Orleans Branch, New Orleans, La. 70160.
Federal Reserve Bank of Chicago, P.O. Box 834, Chicago, Ill. 60690.
    Detroit Branch, P.O. Box 1059, Detroit, Mich. 48231.

Federal Reserve Bank of St. Louis, P.O. Box 442, St. Louis, Mo. 63166.
    Little Rock Branch, P.O. Box 1261, Little Rock, Ark. 72203.
    Louisville Branch, P.O. Box 899, Louisville, Ky. 40201.
    Memphis Branch, P.O. Box 407, Memphis, Tenn. 38101.
Federal Reserve Bank of Minneapolis, Minneapolis, Minn. 55440.
    Helena Branch, Helena, Mont. 59601.
Federal Reserve Bank of Kansas City, Kansas City, Mo. 64106.
    Denver Branch, Denver, Colo. 80217.
    Oklahoma City Branch, Oklahoma City, Okla. 73101.
    Omaha Branch, Omaha, Nebr. 68102.
Federal Reserve Bank of Dallas, Station K, Dallas, Tex. 75222.
    El Paso Branch, P.O. Box 100, El Paso, Tex. 79999.
    Houston Branch, P.O. Box 2578, Houston, Tex. 77001.
    San Antonio Branch, P.O. Box 1471, San Antonio, Tex. 78206.
Federal Reserve Bank of San Francisco, San Francisco, Calif. 94120.
    Los Angeles Branch, P.O. Box 2077, Los Angeles, Calif. 90054.
    Portland Branch, P.O. Box 3456, Portland, Oreg. 97208.
    Salt Lake City Branch, P.O. Box 780, Salt Lake City, Utah 84110.
    Seattle Branch, P.O. Box 3567, Seattle, Wash. 98124.

Sec. 306.2. *Definitions of words and terms as used in these regulations.*

(a) "Advance refunding offer" is an offer to a holder of a security, in advance of its call or maturity, to exchange it for another security.

(b) "Bearer securities" are those which are payable on their face at maturity or call for redemption before maturity in accordance with their terms to "bearer," the ownership of which is not recorded. Title to such securities may pass by delivery without endorsement and without notice. "Coupon securities" are bearer securities which are issued with interest coupons attached.

(c) "Bureau" refers to the Bureau of the Public Debt, Division of Loans and Currency, Washington, D.C., 20226.

(d) "Call date" or "date of call" is the date fixed in the official notice of call published in the *Federal Register* as the date on which the obligor will make payment of the security before maturity in accordance with its terms.

(e) "Court" means one which has jurisdiction over the parties and the subject matter.

(f) 'Department" refers to the Treasury Department.

(g) "Face maturity date" is the payment date specified in the text of a security.

(h) "Incompetent" refers to a person under any legal disability except minority.

(i) "Joint owner" and "joint ownership" refer to any permitted form of ownership by two or more persons.

(j) "Nontransferable securities" are those issued only in registered form which according to their terms are payable only to the registered owners or recognized successors in title to the extent and in the manner provided in the offering circulars or special applicable regulations.

(k) "Payment" and "redemption," unless otherwise indicated by the context, are used interchangeably for payment at maturity or payment before maturity pursuant to a call for redemption in accordance with the terms of the securities.

(l) "Redemption-exchange" is any authorized redemption of securities for the purpose of applying the proceeds in payment for other securities offered in exchange.

(m) "Registered securities" refers to securities payable on their face at maturity or call for redemption before maturity in accordance with their terms to the persons whose names are inscribed thereon.

(n) "Securities assigned in blank" or "securities so assigned as to become, in effect, payable to bearer" refers to registered securities which are assigned by the owner or his authorized representative without designating the assignee. Registered securities assigned simply to "The Secretary of the Treasury" or in the case of Treasury Bonds, Investment Series B–1975–80, to "The Secretary of the Treasury for exchange for the current Series EA or EO Treasury notes" are considered to be so assigned as to become, in effect, payable to bearer.

(o) "Taxpayer identifying number" means the appropriate identifying number as required on tax returns and other documents submitted to the Internal Revenue Service, i.e., an individual's social security account number or an employer identification number. A social security account number is composed of nine digits separated by two hyphens, for example, 123–45–6789; an employer identification number is composed of nine digits separated by one hyphen, for example, 12–3456789. The hyphens are an essential part of the numbers and must be included.

(p) "Transferable securities," which may be in either registered or bearer form, refers to securities which may be sold on the market and transfer of title accomplished by assignment and delivery if in registered form, or by delivery only if in bearer form.

(q) "Treasurer's Office" refers to the Office of the Treasurer of the United States, Securities Division, Washington, D.C., 20220.

(r) "Treasury securities," "Treasury bonds," "Treasury notes," "Treasury certificates of indebtedness," and "Treasury bills," or simply "securities," "bonds, "notes," "certificates," and "bills," unless otherwise indicated by the context, refer only to transferable securities.

Sec. 306.3. *Transportation charges and risks in the shipment of securities.*— The following rules will govern transportation to, from and between the Treasury Department and the Federal Reserve banks and branches of securities issued on or presented for authorized transactions:

(a) The securities may be presented or received by the owners or their agents in person.

(b) Securities issued *on original issue*, unless delivered in person, will be delivered by registered mail or by other means at the risk and expense of the United States.

(c) The United States will assume the risk and expense of any transportation of securities which may be necessary between the Federal Reserve banks and branches and the Treasury.

(d) Securities submitted for any transaction after original issue, if not presented in person, must be forwarded at the owner's risk and expense.

(e) *Bearer securities* issued on transactions other than original issue will be delivered by registered mail, covered by insurance, at the owner's risk and expense, unless called for in person by the owner or his agent. *Registered securities* issued on such transactions will be delivered by registered mail at the risk of, but without expense to, the registered owner. Should delivery by other means he desired, advance arrangements should be made with the official agency to which the original securities were presented.

SUBPART B—REGISTRATION

Sec. 306.10. *General.*—The registration used must express the actual ownership of a security, and may not include any restriction on the authority of the owner to dispose of it in any manner, except as otherwise specifically provided in these regulations. The Treasury Department reserves the right to treat the registration as conclusive of ownership. Requests for registration should be clear, accurate, and complete, conform with one of the forms set forth in this subpart, and include appropriate taxpayer identifying numbers.[1] The registration of all bonds owned by the same person, organization, or fiduciary should be uniform with respect to the name of the owner and, in the case of a fiduciary, the description of the fiduciary capacity. Individual owners should be designated by the names by which they are ordinarily known or under which they do business, preferably including at least one full given name. The name of an individual may be preceded by any applicable title, such as "Dr." or "Rev.," or followed by "M.D.," "D.D." or other similar designation. "Sr." or "Jr." or any other similar suffix should be included when ordinarily used or when necessary to distinguish the owner from a member of his family. The name of a woman must be preceded by "Miss" or "Mrs.," unless some other applicable title or designation is used. A married woman's own given name, not that of her husband, must be used, for example, "Mrs. Mary A. Jones," NOT "Mrs. Frank B. Jones." The address should include, where appropriate, the number and street, route, or any other local feature and the ZIP Code.

Sec. 306.11. *Forms of registration for transferable securities.*—The forms of registration described below are authorized for transferable securities:

(a) *Natural persons in their own right.*—In the names of natural persons who are not under any legal disability, in their own right, substantially as follows:

(1) *One person.*—In the name of one individual. Examples:

John A. Doe (123–45–6789)
Mrs. Mary C. Doe (123–45–6789)
Miss Elizabeth Jane Doe (123–45–6789)

An individual who is sole proprietor of a business conducted under a trade name may include a reference to the trade name. Examples:

John A. Doe, doing business as Doe's Home Appliance Store (12–3456789)
John A. Doe (123–45–6789), d/b/a Doe's Home Appliance Store

(2) *Two or more persons—general.*—Securities will not be registered in the name of one person payable on death to another, or in any form which purports to authorize transfer by less than all the persons named in the registration (or all the survivors).[2] Securities will not be registered in the forms "John A. Doe and Mrs. Mary C. Doe, or either of them" or "William C. Doe or Henry J. Doe, or either of them" and securities so assigned will be treated as though the words "or either of them" do not appear in the assignments. The taxpayer identifying number of any of the joint owners may be shown on securities registered in joint ownership form. However, if such owners are husband and wife, the husband's number should be shown. If the joint owners are a minor and an adult, the adult's number should be shown.

(i) *With right of survivorship.*—In the names of two or more individuals with right of survivorship. Examples:

John A. Doe (123–45–6789) or Mrs. Mary C. Doe or the survivor
Mrs. Mary C. Doe and John A. Doe (123–45–6789) or the survivor

---

[1] Taxpayer identifying numbers are not required for foreign governments, nonresident aliens not engaged in trade or business within the United States, international organizations and foreign corporations not engaged in trade or business and not having an office or place of business or a financial or paying agent within the United States, and other persons or organizations as may be exempted from furnishing such numbers under regulations of the Internal Revenue Service.

[2] WARNING: DIFFERENCE BETWEEN TRANSFERABLE TREASURY SECURITIES REGISTERED IN THE NAMES OF TWO OR MORE PERSONS AND UNITED STATES SAVINGS BONDS IN COOWNERSHIP FORM. The effect of registering Treasury securities to which these regulations apply in the names of two or more persons differs decidedly from registration of savings bonds in coownership form. Savings bonds are virtually redeemable on demand at the option of either coowner on his signature alone. Transferable Treasury securities are redeemable only at maturity or upon prior call by the Secretary of the Treasury. Accordingly, if cash is needed before such time, it can be realized only by sale on the market. This involves a transfer of ownership which can be accomplished only upon proper assignment by or in behalf of all owners.

John A. Doe (123–45–6789) or Mrs. Mary C. Doe or Miss Mary Ann Doe or the survivors or survivor
John A. Doe (123–45–6789) or Mrs. Mary C. Doe
John A. Doe (123–45–6789) and Mrs. Mary C. Doe

(ii) *Without right of survivorship.*—In the names of two or more individuals in such manner as to preclude the right of survivorship. Examples:

John A. Doe (123–45–6789) and William A Doe as tenants in common
John A. Jones as natural guardian of Henry B. Jones, a minor, or Robert C. Jones (123–45–6789), without right of survivorship

(b) *Minors and incompetents.*—(1) *Natural guardians of minors.*—A security may be registered in the name of a natural guardian of a minor for whose *estate* no legal guardian or similar representative has legally qualified. Example:

John R. Jones as natural guardian of Henry M. Jones, a minor (123–45–6789)

Either parent with whom the minor resides, or if he does not reside with either parent, the person who furnishes his chief support, will be recognized as his natural guardian and will be considered a fiduciary. Registration in the name of a minor in his own right as owner or as joint owner is not authorized. Securities so registered, upon qualification of the natural guardian, will be treated as though registered in the name of the natural guardian in that capacity.

(2) *Custodian under statute authorizing gifts to minors.*—A security may be purchased as a gift to a minor under a gifts to minor statute in effect in a State in which either the donor or the minor resides, in which case the security should be registered as provided in the statute, with the addition of a parenthetical reference identifying the statute if the registration does not clearly identify it. Examples:

William C. Jones, as custodian for John A. Smith, a minor (123–45–6789), under the California Uniform Gifts to Minors Act
Robert C. Smith, as custodian for Henry L. Brown, a minor (123–45–6789), under the laws of Georgia (Ch. 48–3, Code of Ga. Anno.)

(3) *Incompetents not under guardianship.*—Registration in the form "John A. Brown, an incompetent (123–45–6789), under voluntary guardianship," is permitted only on reissue after a voluntary guardian has qualified for the purpose of collecting interest. (See secs. 306.37(c)(2) and 306.57(c)(2).) Otherwise, registration in the name of an incompetent not under legal guardianship is not authorized.

(c) *Executors, administrators, guardians, and similar representatives or fiduciaries.*—A security may be registered in the names of legally qualified executors, administrators, guardians, conservators, or similar representatives or fiduciaries of a single estate. The names and capacities of all the representatives or fiduciaries, as shown in their letters of appointment, must be included in the registration and must be followed by an adequate identifying reference to the estate. Examples:

John Smith, executor of the will (or administrator of the estate) of Henry J. Jones, deceased (123–45–6789)
William C. Jones, guardian (or conservator, etc.) of the estate of James D. Brown, a minor (or an incompetent) (123–45–6789)

(d) *Private trust estates.*—A security may be registered in the name and title of the trustee or trustees of a single duly constituted private trust, followed by an adequate identifying reference to the authority governing the trust. Examples:

John Jones and Blank Trust Company, Albany, N.Y., trustees under the will of Sarah Jones, deceased (12–3456789)
John Doe and Richard Roe, trustees under agreement with Henry Jones dated 2/9/50 (12–3456789)

The names of all trustees, in the form used in the trust instrument, must be included in the registration, except as follows:

(1) If there are several trustees designated as a board or authorized to act as a unit, their names should be omitted and the words "Board of Trustees" should be substituted for the word "trustees." Example:

> Board of Trustees of Blank Company Retirement Fund under collective bargaining agreement dated 6/30/50 (12–3456789)

(2) If the trustees do not constitute a board or otherwise act as a unit, and are either too numerous to be designated in the inscription by names and title, or serve for limited terms, some or all of the names may be omitted. Examples:

> John Smith, Henry Jones, et al., trustees under the will of Henry J. Smith, deceased (12–3456789)
> Trustees under the will of Henry J. Smith, deceased (12–3456789)
> Trustees of Retirement Fund of Industrial Manufacturing Co., under directors' resolution of 6/30/50 (12–3456789)

(e) *Private organizations (corporations, unincorporated associations, and partnerships).*—A security may be registered in the name of any private corporation, unincorporated association, or partnership. The full legal name of the organization, as set forth in its charter, articles of incorporation, constitution, partnership agreement, or other authority from which its powers are derived, must be included in the registration, and may be followed, if desired, by a parenthetical reference to a particular account or fund other than a trust fund, in accordance with the rules and examples given below:

(1) *A corporation.*—The name of a business, fraternal, religious, or other private corporation must be followed by descriptive words indicating the corporate status unless the term "corporation" or the abbreviation "Inc." is part of the name or the name is that of a corporation or association organized under Federal law, such as a national bank or Federal savings and loan association. Examples:

> Smith Manufacturing Company, a corp. (12–3456789)
> The Standard Manufacturing Corp. (12–3456789)
> Jones & Brown, Inc. (12–3456789) (Depreciation Acct.)
> First National Bank of _____ (12–3456789)

(2) *An unincorporated association.*—The name of a lodge, club, labor union, veterans' organization, religious society, or similar self-governing organization which is not incorporated (whether or not it is chartered by or affiliated with a parent organization which is incorporated) must be followed by the words "an unincorporated association." Examples:

> American Legion Post No. _____, Department of the D.C., an unincorporated assn. (12–3456789)
> Local Union No. 100, Brotherhood of Locomotive Engineers, an unincorporated association (12–3456789)

Securities should not be registered in the name of an unincorporated association if the legal title to its property in general, or the legal title to the funds with which the securities are to be purchased, is held by trustees. In such a case the securities should be registered in the title of the trustees in accordance with (d) of this section. The term "unincorporated association " should not be used to describe a trust fund, a partnership, or a business conducted under a trade name.

(3) *A partnership.*—The name of a partnership must be followed by the words "a partnership." Examples:

> Smith & Brown, a partnership (12–3456789)
> Acme Novelty Co., a limited partnership (12–3456789)

(f) *States, public bodies and corporations, and public officers.*—A security may be registered in the name of a State or county, city, town, village, school district, or other political entity, public body or corporation established by law (including a board, commission, administration, authority, or agency) which is the owner or official custodian of public funds, *other than trust funds*, or in the full legal title of the public officer having custody. Examples:

State of Maine
Town of Rye, N.Y.
Maryland State Highway Commission
Treasurer, City of Springfield, Ill.
Treasurer of Rhode Island (State Forestry Fund)

(g) *States, public officers, corporations, or bodies as trustees.*—A security may be registered in the title of a public officer or in the name of a State or county, a public corporation or public body acting as trustee under express authority of law, followed by appropriate reference to the statute creating the trust. Examples:

Insurance Commissioner of Pennsylvania, trustee for the benefit of the policyholders of the Blank Insurance Co. (12–3456789), under Sec. _____, Penna. Stats.
Rhode Island Sinking Fund Commission, trustee of the General Sinking Fund under Ch. 35, Gen. Laws of R.I.

Sec. 306.12. *Errors in registration.*—If an erroneously inscribed security is received it should not be altered in any respect, but the Bureau, a Federal Reserve bank or branch, or the Treasurer's Office should be furnished full particulars concerning the error and asked to furnish instructions.

Sec. 306.13. *Nontransferable securities.*—Upon authorized reissue, Treasury Bonds, Investment Series B–1975–80, may be registered in the forms set forth in sec. 306.11.

SUBPART C—TRANSFERS, EXCHANGES, AND REISSUES

Sec. 306.15. *Transfers and exchanges of securities—closed periods.*

(a) *General.*—The transfer of registered securities should be made by assignment in accordance with Subpart F. Transferable registered securities are eligible for denominational exchange and exchange for bearer securities. Bearer securities are eligible for denominational exchange, and when so provided in the offering circular, are eligible for exchange for registered securities. Specific instructions for issuance and delivery of the new securities, signed by the owner or his authorized representative must accompany the securities presented. (Form PD 1642, 1643, 1644, or 1827, as appropriate, may be used.) Denominational exchanges, exchanges of Treasury Bonds, Investment Series B–1975–80, for the current series of EA or EO 1½ percent 5-year Treasury notes, and optional redemption of bonds at par as provided in sec. 306.28 may be made at any time. Securities presented for transfer or for exchange for bearer securities of the same issue must be received by the Bureau not less than one full month before the date on which the securities mature or become redeemable pursuant to a call for redemption before maturity, and any security so presented which is received too late to comply with this provision will be accepted for payment only.

(b) *Closing of transfer books.*—The transfer books are closed for one full month preceding interest payment dates and call or maturity dates. If the date set for closing of the transfer books falls on Saturday, Sunday, or a legal holiday, the books will be closed as of the close of business on the last business day preceding that date. If registered securities which have not matured or been called are received by the Bureau for transfer, reissue, or exchange for coupon securities, or coupon securities which have not matured or been called are received for exchange for registered securities during the time the books for that loan are closed, the transaction will not be completed until the first business day following the date on which interest falls due, when such books are reopened. If registered securities are received for transfer or exchange for bearer securities, or coupon securities are received for exchange for registered securities, during the time the books are closed for payment of final interest at maturity or call, unless otherwise provided in the offering circular or notice of call, the following action will be taken:

(1) Payment of final interest will be made to the registered owner of record on the date the books were closed.

(2) Payment of principal will be made to (i) the assignee under a proper assignment of the securities, or (ii) if the securities have been assigned for

exchange for bearer securities, to the registered owner of record on the date the books were closed.

Sec. 306.16. *Denominational exchanges of registered securities.*—No assignment will be required for the authorized exchange of registered securities for like securities in the same names in other authorized denominations.

Sec. 306.17. *Exchanges of registered securities for coupon securities.*—Registered securities submitted for exchange for coupon securities should be assigned to "The Secretary of the Treasury for exchange for coupon securities to be delivered to (inserting the name and address of the person to whom delivery of the coupon securities is to be made)." Assignments to "The Secretary of the Treasury for exchange for coupon securities," or assignments in blank will also be accepted. The coupon securities issued upon exchange will have all unmatured coupons attached.

Sec. 306.18. *Exchange of coupon securities for registered securities.*—Coupon securities presented for exchange for registered securities should have all matured interest coupons detached. All unmatured coupons should be attached, except that if presented when the transfer books are closed (in which case the exchange will be effected on or after the date on which the books are reopened), the next maturing coupons should be detached and held for collection in ordinary course when due. If any coupons which should be attached are missing, the securities must be accompanied by a remittance in an amount equal to the face amount of the missing coupons. The new registered securities will bear interest from the interest payment date next preceding the date on which the exchange is made.

Sec. 306.19. *Denominational exchanges of coupon securities.*—All matured interest coupons and all unmatured coupons likely to mature before an exchange can be completed should be detached from securities presented for denominational exchange. All unmatured coupons should be attached. If any are missing, the securities must be accompanied by a remittance in an amount equal to the face amount of the missing coupons. The new coupon securities will have all unmatured coupons attached.

Sec. 306.20. *Reissue of registered transferable securities.*—Assignments are not required for reissue of registered transferable securities in the name(s) of (a) the surviving joint owner(s) of securities registered in the names of or assigned to two or more persons, unless the registration or assignment includes words which preclude the right of survivorship, (b) a succeeding fiduciary or other lawful successor, (c) an individual, corporation or unincorporated association whose name has been legally changed, (d) a corporation or unincorporated association, which is the lawful successor to another corporation or unincorporated association, and (e) a successor in title to a public officer or body. Evidence of survivorship, succession, or change of name, as appropriate, must be furnished. The appropriate taxpayer identifying number also must be furnished if the registration of the securities submitted does not include such number for the person(s) or organization to be named on the reissued securities.

Sec. 306.21. *Reissue of nontransferable securities.*

(a) *Treasury Bonds, Investment Series A–1965.*—Bonds of this series may be reissued only when (1) the name of an owner has been changed, (2) the trustees in whose names the bonds are registered have been succeeded by other trustees, and (3) the corporation, unincorporated association, or fund in whose name the bonds are registered has been succeeded by another corporation or unincorporated association or fund, by operation of law or otherwise, whereby the business or activities of the original organization or fund are continued without substantial change in the successor. Bonds presented for reissue must be accompanied by pertinent evidence and an appropriate request for reissue. (Form PD 2168 should be used.)

(b) *Treasury Bonds, Investment Series B–1975–80.*—Bonds of this series may be reissued only in the names of (1) lawful successors in title, (2) the legal representatives or distributees of a deceased owner's estate, or the distributees of a trust estate, and (3) State supervisory authorities in pursuance of any pledge required of the owner under State law, or upon termination of the pledge in the names of the pledgors or their successors. Bonds presented for reissue must be accompanied by evidence of entitlement.

Sec. 306.22. *Exchange of Treasury Bonds, Investment Series B–1975–80.*—
Bonds of this series presented for exchange for 1½ percent 5-year Treasury notes must bear duly executed assignments to "The Secretary of the Treasury for

exchange for the current series of EA or EO Treasury notes to be delivered to (inserting the name and address of the person to whom the notes are to be delivered)." The notes will bear the April 1 or October 1 date next preceding the date the bonds, duly assigned with supporting evidence, if necessary, are received by the Bureau or a Federal Reserve bank or branch. Interest accrued at the rate of 2¾ percent on the bonds surrendered from the next preceding interest payment date to the date of exchange will be credited, and interest at the rate of 1½ percent on the notes for the same period will be charged and the difference will be paid to the owner.

SUBPART D—REDEMPTION OR PAYMENT

Sec. 306.25. *Presentation and surrender.*

(a) *General.*—Securities, whether in registered or bearer form, are payable in regular course of business at maturity unless called for redemption before maturity in accordance with their terms, in which case they will be payable in regular course of business on the date of call. The Secretary of the Treasury may provide for the exchange of maturing or called securities, or in advance of call or maturity, may afford owners the opportunity of exchanging a security for another security pursuant to an advance refunding offer. Registered securities should be presented and surrendered for redemption to the Bureau, a Federal Reserve bank or branch, or the Treasurer's Office, and bearer securities to a Federal Reserve bank or branch or the Treasurer's Office.[1] If securities are registered in the name of, or assigned to (1) a State or other political entity, (2) a corporation, or (3) a board, committee or other body authorized to act as a unit and which is the fiduciary of a public or private trust estate, no evidence will be required in support of an assignment by an officer of the registered owner or assignee for redemption for its account. Under the same circumstances, no evidence will be required for an assignment for redemption-exchange, or exchange pursuant to an advance refunding offer, if the new securities are to be registered exactly the same as the registration or assignment of the securities surrendered. To the extent appropriate, these rules also apply to securities registered in the title of a public officer who is the official custodian of public funds.

(b) *"Overdue" securities.*—If a bearer security or a registered security assigned in blank, or to bearer or so assigned as to become, in effect, payable to bearer, is presented and surrendered for redemption after it has become overdue, the Secretary of the Treasury may require satisfactory proof of ownership. (Form PD 1071 may be used.) A security shall be considered to be overdue after the lapse of the following periods of time from its face maturity:

(1) One year for Treasury bonds.
(2) Six months for Treasury notes and certificates of indebtedness.
(3) Three months for Treasury bills.
(4) Other securities:
    (i) One year for securities issued for a term of five years or longer.
    (ii) Six months for securities issued for a term of one year or more but less than five years.
    (iii) Three months for securities issued for a term of less than one year.

Sec. 306.26. *Redemption of registered securities at maturity, upon prior call, or for advance refunding.*—Registered securities presented and surrendered for redemption at maturity or pursuant to a call for redemption before maturity should be assigned to "The Secretary of the Treasury for redemption," unless the assignor desires that payment be made to some other person, in which case the assignments should be made to "The Secretary of the Treasury for redemption for the account of (inserting name and address of person to whom payment is to be made)." Assignments in blank or other assignments having a similar effect will be accepted but specific instructions for the issuance and delivery of the redemption check, signed by the owner or his authorized representative, must accompany the securities, unless included in the assignment. (Form PD 1705 may be used.) Payment of the principal will be made either (a) by check drawn on the Treasurer of the United States to the order of the person

---

[1] See sec. 306.28 for presentation and surrender of securities eligible for use in payment of Federal estate taxes.

entitled and mailed in accordance with the instructions received, or (b) upon appropriate request, by crediting the amount in a member bank's account with the Federal Reserve bank of its district. Securities presented for advance refunding should be assigned as provided in the advance refunding offer.

Sec. 306.27. *Redemption of bearer securities at maturity, upon prior call, or for advance refunding.*—All interest coupons due and payable on or before the date of maturity or date fixed in the call for redemption before maturity should be detached from coupon securities presented for redemption and should be collected separately in regular course. All coupons bearing dates subsequent to a date fixed in a call for redemption, or an offer of advance refunding, should be left attached to the securities. If any such coupons are missing the full face amount thereof will be deducted from the payment to be made upon redemption or the advance refunding adjustment unless satisfactory evidence of their destruction is submitted. Any amounts so deducted will be held in the Department to provide for adjustments or refunds in the event that the missing coupons should be subsequently presented or their destruction is later satisfactorily established. In the absence of other instructions, payment of bearer securities will be made by check drawn to the order of the person presenting and surrendering the securities and mailed to him at his address, as given in the advice which should accompany the securities. (Form PD 1704 may be used.) A Federal Reserve bank, upon appropriate request, may make payment to a member bank from which bearer securities are received by crediting the amount in the member bank's account.

Sec. 306.28. *Optional redemption of Treasury bonds at par (before maturity or call redemption date) and application of the proceeds in payment of Federal estate taxes.*

(a) *General.*—All Treasury bonds to be redeemed at par for the purpose of applying the proceeds to payment of Federal estate taxes on a decedent's estate [1] must be presented and surrendered to a Federal Reserve bank or branch or the Bureau. They should be accompanied by Form PD 1782, fully completed and duly executed in accordance with the instructions on the form, and evidence as described therein. Redemption will be made at par plus accrued interest from the last preceding interest payment date to the date of redemption, except that if registered bonds are received by a Federal Reserve bank or branch or the Bureau within one month preceding an interest payment date for redemption before that date a deduction will be made for interest from the date of redemption to the interest payment date, and a check for the full six months' interest will be paid in due course. The proceeds of redemption will be deposited to the credit of the district director, Internal Revenue Service, designated in Form PD 1782, the representative of the estate will be notified of the deposit, and the district director will forward a formal receipt.

(b) *Conditions.*—The bonds presented for redemption under this section must have (1) been owned by the decedent at the time of his death and (2) thereupon constituted part of his estate, as determined by the following rules in the case of joint ownership, partnership, and trust holdings:

(i) *Joint ownerships.*—Bonds held by the decedent at the time of his death in joint ownership with another person or persons will be deemed to have met the above conditions either (a) to the extent to which the bonds actually became the property of the decedent's estate, or (b) in an amount not to exceed the amount of the Federal estate taxes which the surviving joint owner or owners are required to pay on account of such bonds and other jointly-held property. [2]

(ii) *Partnerships.*—Bonds held at the time of the decedent's death by a partnership in which he had an interest will be deemed to have met the above conditions to the extent of his fractional share of the bonds so held proportionate to his interest in the assets of the partnership.

---

[1] Certain issues of Treasury bonds are redeemable at par and accrued interest upon the death of the owner, at the option of the representative of, or if none, the persons entitled to, his estate, for the purpose of having the entire proceeds applied in payment of the Federal estate taxes on the decedent's estate, in accordance with the terms of the offering circulars cited on the face of the bonds. A current list of eligible issues may be obtained from any Federal Reserve bank or branch, the Bureau of the Public Debt, or the Treasurer's Office.

[2] Substantially the same rule applies to community property except that upon the death of either spouse bonds which constitute part of the community estate are deemed to meet the required conditions to the extent of *one-half of each loan and issue of bonds.*

(iii) *Trusts.*—Bonds held in trust at the time of the decedent's death will be deemed to have met the above conditions in an amount not to exceed the amount of the Federal estate taxes if (a) the trust actually terminated in favor of the decedent's estate, or (b) the trustee as such is required to pay the decedent's Federal estate taxes under the terms of the trust instrument or otherwise, or (c) the debts of the decedent's estate, including costs of administration, State inheritance and Federal estate taxes, exceed the assets of his estate without regard to the trust estate.

(c) *Transactions after owner's death.*—No transactions involving changes of ownership may be conducted after an owner's death without affecting the eligibility of the bonds for redemption at par for application of the proceeds to payment of Federal estate taxes. Transactions, involving no changes of ownership, which may be conducted without affecting eligibility are (1) exchange of bonds for those of lower denominations where the bonds exceed the amount of the taxes and are not in the lowest authorized denominations, (2) exchange of registered bonds for coupon bonds, (3) exchange of coupon bonds for bonds registered in the names of the representatives of the estate, and (4) transfer to the names of the representatives of the owner's estate. However, any such transactions must be explained on Form PD 1782 or in a supplemental statement.

SUBPART E—INTEREST

Sec. 306.35. *Computation of interest.*—The interest on Treasury securities accrues and is payable on a semiannual basis unless otherwise provided in the circular offering them for sale or exchange. If the period of accrual is an exact six months, the interest accrual is an exact one-half year's interest, without regard to the number of days in the period. If the period of accrual is less than an exact six months, the accrued interest is computed by determining the daily rate of accrual on the basis of the exact number of days in the full interest period and multiplying the daily rate by the exact number of days in the fractional period for which interest has actually accrued. A full interest period does not include the day as of which the securities were issued or the day on which the last preceding interest became due, but does include the day on which the next succeeding interest payment is due. A fractional part of an interest period does not include the day as of which the securities were issued or the day on which the last preceding interest payment became due, but does include the day as of which the transaction terminating the accrual of interest is effected. The 29th of February in a leap year is included whenever it falls within either a full interest period or a fractional part thereof.[1]

Sec. 306.36. *Termination of interest.*—Securities will cease to bear interest on the date of their maturity unless they have been called for redemption before maturity in accordance with their terms, in which case they will cease to bear interest on the date of call.

Sec. 306.37. *Interest on registered securities.*

(a) *Method of payment.*—The interest on registered securities is payable by checks drawn on the Treasurer of the United States to the order of the registered owners, except as otherwise provided herein. Interest checks are prepared by the Department in advance of the interest payment date and are ordinarily mailed in time to reach the addressees on that date. Interest on a registered security which has not matured or been called and which is presented for any transaction during the period the books for that loan are closed will be paid by check drawn to the order of the registered owner of record. Upon receipt of notice of the death or incompetency of an individual named as registered owner, a change in the name or in the status of a partnership, corporation, or unincorporated association, the removal, resignation, succession, or death of a fiduciary or trustee, delivery of interest checks will be withheld pending receipt and approval of evidence showing who is entitled to receive the interest checks. If the inscriptions on securities do not clearly identify the owners, delivery of interest checks will be withheld pending reissue of the securities in the correct registration. The final installment of interest, unless otherwise provided in the offering

---

[1] The Appendix to these regulations contains a complete explanation of the method of computing interest on a semiannual basis on Treasury bonds, notes, and certificates of indebtedness, and an outline of the method of computing the discount rates on Treasury bills. Also included are tables of computation of interest on quarterly and annual bases.

circular or notice of call, will be paid by check drawn to the order of the registered owner of record and mailed in advance of the interest payment date in time to reach the addressee on or about that date.[1] Interest on securities presented for advance refunding will be adjusted as provided in the advance refunding offer.

(b) *Change of address.*—To assure timely delivery of interest checks, owners should promptly notify the Bureau of any change of address. (Form PD 345 may be used.) The notification must be signed by the registered owner or a joint owner or an authorized representative, and should show the old and new addresses, the serial number and denomination of each security, the titles of the securities (for example 3¼ percent Treasury Bonds of 1978–83, dated May 1, 1953), and the registration of each security. Notifications by attorneys in fact, trustees, or by the legal representatives of the estates of deceased, incompetent, or minor owners should be supported by proof of their authority, unless in the case of trustees or legal representatives, they are named in the registration.

(c) *Collection of interest checks.*

(1) *General.*—Interest checks may be collected in accordance with the regulations governing the endorsement and payment of Government warrants and checks, which are contained in Department Circular No. 21, Revised, as amended (31 CFR 360).

(2) *By voluntary guardians of incompetents.*—Interest checks drawn to the order of a person who has become incompetent and for whose estate no legal guardian or similar representative has been appointed should be returned to the Bureau with a full explanation of the circumstances. For collection of interest, the Department will recognize the relative responsible for the incompetent's care and support or some other person as voluntary guardian for the incompetent. (Application may be made on Form PD 1461.)

(d) *Nonreceipt, loss, theft, or destruction of interest checks.*—If an interest check is not received within a reasonable period after an interest payment date the Bureau should be notified. Should a check be lost, stolen, or destroyed after receipt, the Office of the Treasurer of the United States, Check Claims Division, Washington, D.C., 20226, should be notified. Notification should include the name and address of the owner, the serial number, denomination, and title of the security upon which the interest was payable. If the check is subsequently received or recovered the latter office should also be advised.

Sec. 306.38. *Interest on bearer securities.*—Unless the offering circular and notice of call provide otherwise, interest on coupon securities is payable in regular course of business upon presentation and surrender of the interest coupons as they mature. Such coupons are payable at any Federal Reserve bank or branch, or the Treasurer's Office.[2] Interest on Treasury bills, and any other bearer securities which may be sold and issued on a discount basis and which are payable at par at maturity, is represented by the difference between the purchase price and the par value, and no coupons are attached.

SUBPART F—ASSIGNMENTS OF REGISTERED SECURITIES—GENERAL

Sec. 306.40. *Execution of assignments or special endorsements.*

(a) *Execution of assignments.*—The assignment of a registered security should be executed by the owner or his authorized representative in the presence of an officer authorized to certify assignments. All assignments must be made on the backs of the securities, unless otherwise authorized by the Bureau, a Federal Reserve bank or branch, or the Treasurer of the United States. An assignment by mark (X) must be witnessed not only by a certifying officer but also by at least one other person, who should add an endorsement substantially as follows: "Witness to signature by mark," followed by his signature and address.

(b) *Special endorsements in lieu of assignments.*—A security may be presented without assignment for any authorized transaction by a financial institution which is (1) a member of the Federal Reserve System, (2) a member of the Federal Home Loan Bank System, or (3) insured by the Federal Deposit

---

[1] The final installment of interest on securities which matured or were called before the effective date of these regulations will be paid with the principal upon presentation of the securities unless otherwise provided in the offering circular or notice of call. See sec. 306.15(b) for presentation of securities during periods transfer books are closed.
[2] Banking institutions will usually cash the coupons without charge as an accommodation to their customers.

Insurance Corporation, provided full instructions are furnished as to the transaction desired and the security bears the endorsement, *under the official seal of the institution, as follows:*

Presented in accordance with instructions of the owner(s).
Absence of assignment guaranteed.

\-
(Name of financial institution)

By \-
(Signature and title of officer)

This form of endorsement will be an unconditional guarantee to the Treasury Department that the institution is acting as attorney in fact for the owner(s) of the security under proper authorization and that the officer is duly authorized to act.

Sec. 306.41. *Form of assignment.*—Registered securities may be assigned in blank, to bearer, to a specified transferee, to the Secretary of the Treasury for exchange for coupon securities, or to the Secretary of the Treasury for redemption or for exchange for other securities offered at maturity, upon call or pursuant to an advance refunding offer. Assignments to "The Secretary of the Treasury," "The Secretary of the Treasury for transfer," or "The Secretary of the Treasury for exchange" will not be accepted, unless supplemented by specific instructions by or in behalf of the owner.

Sec. 306.42. *Alterations and erasures.*—If an alteration or erasure has been made in an assignment, the assignor should appear before an authorized certifying officer and execute a new assignment to the same assignee. If the new assignment is to other than the assignee whose name has been altered or erased, a disclaimer from the first-named assignee should be obtained. Otherwise, an affidavit of explanation by the person responsible for the alteration or erasure should be submitted for consideration.

Sec. 306.43. *Voidance of assignments.*—An assignment of a security to or for the account of another person, not completed by delivery, may be voided by a disclaimer of interest from that person. The disclaimer should be executed in the presence of an officer authorized to certify assignments of securities. Unless otherwise authorized by the Bureau, a Federal Reserve bank or branch, or the Treasurer of the United States, the disclaimer must be written, typed, or stamped on the back of the security in substantially the following form:

The undersigned as assignee of this security hereby disclaims any interest herein.

\-
(Signature)

I certify that the above-named person as described, whose identity is well known or proved to me, personally appeared before me the _____ day of _____ at _____ and signed the above
(Month and year)   (Place)
disclaimer of interest.
(SEAL)

\-
(Signature and official designation
of certifying officer)

In the absence of a disclaimer, an affidavit or affidavits should be submitted for consideration explaining why a disclaimer cannot be obtained, reciting all other material facts and circumstances relating to the transaction, including whether or not the security was delivered to the person named as assignee and whether or not the affiants know of any basis for the assignee claiming any right, title or interest in the security. After an assignment has been voided, in order to dispose of the security, an assignment by or on behalf of the owner will be required.

Sec. 306.44. *Discrepancies in names.*—The Department will ordinarily require an explanation of discrepancies in the names which appear in inscriptions, assignments, supporting evidence, or in the signatures to any assignments. (Form PD 385 may be used for this purpose.) However, where the variations in the name of the registered owner, as inscribed on securities of the same or different issues, are such that both may properly represent the same person, for example, "J. T. Smith" and "John T. Smith," no proof of identity will be required *if the assignments are signed exactly as the securities are inscribed and are duly certified by the same certifying officer.*

Sec. 306.45. *Officers authorized to certify assignments.*

(a) *Officers authorized generally.*—Officers authorized to certify assignments include:

(1) Officers and employees of banks and trust companies chartered by or incorporated under the laws of the United States or those of any State, commonwealth or territory of the United States, and Federal savings and loan associations, or other organizations which are members of the Federal Home Loan Bank System, who have been authorized to (i) generally bind their respective institutions by their acts, (ii) unqualifiedly guarantee signatures to assignments of securities, or (iii) expressly certify assignments of securities.

(2) Officers of Federal Reserve banks and branches.

(3) Officers of Federal land banks, Federal intermediate credit banks and banks for cooperatives, the central bank for cooperatives, and Federal home loan banks.

(4) United States attorneys, collectors of customs, and regional commissioners and district directors, Internal Revenue Service.

(5) Judges and clerks of United States courts.

(b) *Authorized officers in foreign countries.*—The following officers are authorized to certify assignments in foreign countries:

(1) United States diplomatic or consular representatives.

(2) Managers, assistant managers, and other officers of foreign branches of banks or trust companies chartered by or incorporated under the laws of the United States or any State, commonwealth or territory of the United States.

(3) Notaries public and other officers authorized to administer oaths. The official position and authority of any such officer must be certified by a United States diplomatic or consular representative under seal of his office.

(c) *Officers having limited authority.*—The following officers are authorized to certify assignments to the extent set forth in connection with each class of officers:

(1) Postmasters, acting postmasters, assistant postmasters, inspectors-in-charge, chief and assistant chief accountants, and superintendents of stations of any post office, notaries public, and justices of the peace in the United States, its territories and possessions, the Commonwealth of Puerto Rico and the Canal Zone, but only for assignment of securities for redemption for the account of the assignor, or for redemption-exchange, or pursuant to an advance refunding offer for other securities to be registered in his name, or in his name with a joint owner. The signature of any post office official, other than a postmaster, must be in the following form: "John A. Doe, Postmaster, by Richard B. Roe, Superintendent of Station."

(2) Commissioned officers and warrant officers of the Armed Forces of the United States for assignments of securities of any class for any authorized transaction, but only with respect to assignments executed by (i) Armed Forces personnel and civilian field employees, and (ii) members of the families of such personnel or civilian employees.

(d) *Special provisions for certifying assignments.*—The Commissioner of the Public Debt, the Chief of the Division of Loans and Currency, any Federal Reserve bank or branch, or the Treasurer of the United States, is authorized to make special provisions for any case or class of cases.

Sec. 306.46. *Duties and responsibilities of certifying officer.*—A certifying officer must require execution of an assignment, or a form with respect to securities, in his presence after he has established the identity of the assignor and before he certifies the signature. He must then complete the certification. An employee who is not an officer should insert "Authorized signature" in the space provided for the title. However, an assignment of a security need not be executed in the presence of the certifying officer if he unqualifiedly guarantees the signature thereto, in which case he must place his endorsement on the security, following the signature, in the form "Signature guaranteed, First National Bank of Jonesville, N.H., by A. B. Doe, President." The certifying officer and, if he is an officer or employee of an organization, the organization will be held responsible for any loss the United States may suffer as the result of his fault or negligence.

Sec. 306.47. *Evidence of certifying officer's authority.*—The authority of an individual to act as a certifying officer is established by affixing to a certification of an assignment, or a form with respect to securities, or an unqualified guarantee of a signature to an assignment, either (a) the official seal of the organization, or (b) a legible imprint of the issuing agent's dating stamp, if the organization is an authorized issuing agent for United States savings bonds of Series E. Use of such stamp shall result in the same responsibility on the part of the organization as if its official seal were used. If the certifying officer does not have access to the seal or issuing agent's dating stamp, his authority to act as a certifying officer must be certified, under official seal or stamp, to the Bureau by an officer having access to the organization's records and will be recognized until evidence is received that his authority has been terminated. (Form PD 835 may be used.) Any post office official must use the official stamp of his office. A commissioned or warrant officer of any of the armed forces of the United States should indicate his rank and state that the person executing the assignment is one of the class whose signature he is authorized to certify. A judge or clerk of court must use the seal of the court. Any other certifying officer must use his official seal or stamp, if any, but, if he has neither, his official position and a specimen of his signature must be certified by some other authorized officer under official seal or stamp or otherwise proved to the satisfaction of the Department.

Sec. 306.48. *Interested persons not to act as certifying officer or witness.—* Neither the assignor, the assignee, nor any person having an interest in a security may act as a certifying officer, or as a witness to an assignment by mark. However, a bank officer may certify an assignment to the bank, or an assignment executed by another officer in its behalf.

Sec. 306.49. *Nontransferable securities.—*The provisions of this subpart, so far as applicable, govern transactions in Treasury Bonds, Investment Series B—1975–80.

SUBPART G—ASSIGNMENTS BY OR IN BEHALF OF INDIVIDUALS

Sec. 306.55. *Signatures, minor errors, and change of name.—*The owner's signature to an assignment should be in the form in which the security is inscribed or assigned, unless such inscription or assignment is incorrect or the name has since been changed. In case of a change of name, the signature to the assignment should show both names and the manner in which the change was made, for example, "John Young, changed by order of court from Hans Jung." Evidence of the change will be required. However, no evidence is required to support an assignment if the change resulted from marriage and the signature, which must be duly certified by an authorized officer, is written to show that fact, for example, "Mrs. Mary J. Brown, changed by marriage from Miss Mary Jones."

Sec. 306.56. *Assignment of securities registered in the names of or assigned to two or more persons.*

(a) *For transfer or exchange.—*Securities registered in the names of or assigned to two or more persons may be transferred or exchanged during the lives of all the joint owners only upon assignments by all or on their behalf by authorized representatives. Upon proof of the death of one, the Department will accept an assignment by or in behalf of the survivor or survivors, unless the registration or assignment includes words which preclude the right of survivorship. In the latter case, in addition to assignment by or in behalf of the survivor or survivors, an assignment in behalf of the decedent's estate will be required.

(b) *For advance refunding exchanges.—*Securities registered in the names of or assigned to two or more persons, whether jointly or in the alternative, may be assigned by one where the securities to be received in exchange are to be registered in the same names and form. If bearer securities or securities in a different form are to be issued, all persons named must assign, except that in case of death paragraph (a) of this section shall apply.

(c) *For redemption or redemption-exchange.*

(1) *Alternative registration or assignment.—*Securities registered in the names of or assigned to two or more persons *in the alternative*, for example, "John B. Smith or Mrs. Mary J. Smith" or "John B. Smith or Mrs. Mary J. Smith or the survivor," may be assigned by one of them at maturity or upon call, for redemption or redemption-exchange, for his own account or otherwise, whether or not the other joint owner or owners are deceased.

(2) *Joint registration or assignment.—*Securities registered in the names of or assigned to two or more persons *jointly*, for example, "John B. Smith and Mrs. Mary J. Smith," "John B. Smith and Mrs. Mary J. Smith or the survivor," or "John B. Smith and Mrs. Mary J. Smith as tenants in common," may be as-

signed by one of them during the lives of all only for (i) redemption at maturity or upon call, *and then only for redemption for the account of all,* or (ii) redemption-exchange for securities to be registered in their names in the same form as appears in the registration or assignment of the securities surrendered. Upon proof of the death of one of the joint owners, the survivor or survivors may assign securities so registered or assigned for redemption or redemption-exchange for any account, except that, if the words "as tenants in common" or other words which preclude the right of survivorship appear in the registration or assignment, assignment in behalf of the decedent's estate also will be required.

Sec. 306.57. *Minors and incompetents.*

(a) *Assignments of securities registered in name of minor.*

(1) *By minor.*—Securities registered in the name of a minor for whose estate no guardian or similar representative is legally qualified may be assigned by the minor at maturity or call for redemption if the total face amount of the matured or called securities so registered does not exceed $500, and if the minor, in the opinion of the certifying officer, is of sufficient competency to execute the assignments and understand the nature of the transaction.

(2) *By natural guardian.*—Securities registered in the name of a minor for whose estate no legal guardian or similar representative has qualified may be assigned by the natural guardian upon qualification. (Form PD 2481 may be used for this purpose.)

(b) *Assignments of securities registered in name of natural guardian of minor.*—Securities registered in the name of a natural guardian of a minor may be assigned by the natural guardian for any authorized transaction except one for the apparent benefit of the natural guardian. If the natural guardian in whose name the securities are registered is deceased or is no longer qualified to act as natural guardian, the securities may be assigned by the person then acting as natural guardian. The assignment by the new natural guardian should be supported by proof of the death or disqualification of the former natural guardian and by evidence of his own status as natural guardian. (Form PD 2481 may be used for this purpose.) No assignment by a natural guardian will be accepted after receipt of notice of the minor's attainment of majority, removal of his disability of minority, disqualification of the natural guardian to act as such, qualification of a legal guardian or similar representative, or the death of the minor.

(c) *Assignments by voluntary guardians of incompetents.*—Registered securities belonging to an incompetent for whose estate no legal guardian or similar representative is legally qualified may be assigned by the relative responsible for his care and support or some other person as voluntary guardian:

(1) For redemption or exchange for bearer securities, if the proceeds of the securities are needed to pay expenses already incurred, or to be incurred during any 90-day period, for the care and support of the incompetent or his legal dependents and the total face amount of such securities for which redemption or exchange is requested does not exceed $1,000.

(2) For redemption-exchange, if the securities are matured or have been called, or pursuant to an advance refunding offer, for reinvestment in other securities to be registered in the form "A, an incompetent (123–45–6789) under voluntary guardianship."

An application on Form PD 1461 by the person seeking authority to act as voluntary guardian will be required.

(d) *Assignments by legal guardians of minors or incompetents.*—Securities registered in the name and title of the legal guardian or similar representative of the estate of a minor or incompetent may be assigned by the representative for any authorized transaction without proof of his qualification. Assignments by a representative of any other securities belonging to a minor or incompetent must be supported by properly certified evidence of qualification. The evidence must be dated not more than one year before the date of the assignments and must contain a statement showing the appointment is in full force unless it shows the appointment was made not more than one year before the date of the assignment or the representative or a corepresentative is a corporation. An assignment by the representative will not be accepted after receipt of notice of termination of the guardianship, except for transfer to the former ward.

Sec. 306.58. *Nontransferable securities.*—The provisions of this subpart, so far as applicable, govern transactions in Treasury Bonds, Investments Series B–1975–80.

SUBPART H—ASSIGNMENTS IN BEHALF OF ESTATES OF DECEASED OWNERS

Sec. 306.65. *Special provisions applicable to small amounts of securities, interest checks, or redemption checks.*—Entitlement to, or the authority to dispose of, a small amount of securities and checks issued in payment thereof or in payment of interest thereon, belonging to the estate of a decedent, may be established through the use of certain short forms, according to the aggregate amount of securities and checks involved (excluding checks representing interest on the securities), as indicated by the following table:

Amount	Circumstances	Form	To be executed by—
$100	No administration	PD 2216	Person who paid burial expenses.
500	Estate being administered	PD 2488	Executor or administrator
500	Estate settled	PD 2458-1	Former executor or administrator, attorney, or other qualified person.

Sec. 306.66. *Estates—administration.*

(a) *Temporary or special administrators.*—Temporary or special administrators may assign securities for any authorized transaction within the scope of their authority. The assignments must be supported by:

(1) *Temporary administrators.*—A certificate, under court seal, showing the appointment in full force within thirty days preceding the date of receipt of the securities.

(2) *Special administrators.*—A certificate, under court seal, showing the appointment in full force within 6 months preceding the date of receipt of the securities. Authority for assignments for transactions not within the scope of appointment must be established by a duly certified copy of a special order of court.

(b) *In course of administration.*—A security belonging to the estate of a decedent which is being administered by a duly qualified executor or general administrator will be accepted for any authorized transaction upon assignment by such representative. (See sec. 306.77.) Unless the security is registered in the name of and shows the capacity of the representative, the assignment must be supported by a certificate or a copy of the letters of appointment, certified under court seal. The certificate or certification, if required, must be dated not more than six months before the date of the assignment and must contain a statement that the appointment is in full force, unless (1) it shows the appointment was made not more than one year before the date of the assignment, or (2) the representative or a corepresentative is a corporation, or (3) redemption is being made for application of the proceeds in payment of Federal estate taxes as provided by sec. 306.28.

(c) *After settlement through court proceedings.*—Securities belonging to the estate of a decedent which has been settled in court will be accepted for any authorized transaction upon assignments by the person or persons entitled, as determined by the court. The assignments should be supported by a copy, certified under court seal, of the decree of distribution, the representative's final account as approved by the court, or other pertinent court records.

Sec. 306.67. *Estates not administered.*

(a) *Special provisions under State laws.*—If, under State law, a person has been recognized or appointed to receive or distribute the assets of a decedent's estate without regular administration, his assignment of securities belonging to the estate will be accepted provided he submits appropriate evidence of his authority.

(b) *Agreement of persons entitled.*—When it appears that no legal representative of a decedent's estate has been or is to be appointed, securities belonging to the estate may be duly disposed of pursuant to an agreement and assignment by all persons entitled to share in the decedent's personal estate. (Form PD 1646 may be used.) However, all debts of the decedent and his estate must be paid or provided for and the interests of any minors or incompetents must be protected.

Sec. 306.68. *Nontransferable securities.*—The provisions of this subpart, so far as applicable, govern transactions in Treasury Bonds, Investment Series B-1975-80.

SUBPART I—ASSIGNMENTS BY OR IN BEHALF OF TRUSTEES AND SIMILAR FIDUCIARIES

Sec. 306.75. *Individual fiduciaries.*—Securities registered in, or assigned to, the names and titles of individual fiduciaries will be accepted for any authorized transaction upon assignment by the designated fiduciaries without proof of their qualification. If the fiduciaries in whose names the securities are registered, or to whom they have been assigned, have been succeeded by other fiduciaries, evidence of successorship must be furnished. If the appointment of a successor is not required under the terms of the trust instrument or otherwise and is not contemplated, assignments by the surviving or remaining fiduciary or fiduciaries must be supported by appropriate proof. This requires (a) proof of the death, resignation, removal, or disqualification of the former fiduciary and (b) evidence that the surviving or remaining fiduciary or fiduciaries are fully qualified to administer the fiduciary estate, which may be in the form of a certificate by them showing the appointment of a successor has not been applied for, is not contemplated, and is not necessary under the terms of the trust instrument or otherwise. Assignments of securities registered in the titles, without the names of the fiduciaries, for example, "Trustees of the George E. White Memorial Scholarship Fund under deed of trust dated 11/10/40, executed by John W. White," must be supported by proof that the assignors are the qualified and acting trustees of the designated trust estate, unless they are empowered to act as a unit in which case the provisions of sec. 306.76 shall apply. (Form PD 2446 may be used to furnish proof of incumbency of fiduciaries.) Assignments by fiduciaries of securities not registered or assigned in such manner as to show that they belong to the estate for which the assignors are acting must also be supported by evidence that the estate is entitled to the securities.

Sec. 306.76. *Fiduciaries acting as a unit.*—Securities registered in the name of or assigned to a board, committee, or other body authorized to act as a unit for any public or private trust estate may be assigned for any authorized transaction by anyone authorized to act in behalf of such body. Except as otherwise provided in this section, the assignments must be supported by a copy of a resolution adopted by the body, properly certified under its seal, or, if none, sworn to by a member of the body having access to its records. (Form PD 2495 may be used.) If the person assigning is designated in the resolution by title only, his incumbency must be duly certified by another member of the body. (Form PD 2446 may be used.) If the fiduciaries of any trust estate are empowered to act as a unit, although not designated as a board, committee, or other body, securities registered in their names or assigned to them as such, or in their titles without their names, may be assigned by anyone authorized by the group to act in its behalf. Such assignments may be supported by a sworn copy of a resolution adopted by the group in accordance with the terms of the trust instrument, and proof of their authority to act as a unit may be required. As an alternative, assignments by all the fiduciaries, supported by proof of their incumbency if not named on the securities, will be accepted.

Sec. 306.77. *Corepresentatives and fiduciaries.*—If there are two or more executors, administrators, guardians, or similar representatives, or trustees of an estate, all must unite in the assignment of any securities belonging to the estate. However, when a statute, a decree of court, or the instrument under which the representatives or fiduciaries are acting provides otherwise, assignments in accordance with their authority will be accepted. If the securities have matured or been called and are submitted for redemption for the account of all, or for redemption-exchange or pursuant to an advance refunding offer and the securities offered in exchange are to be registered in the names of all, only one representative or fiduciary need execute the assignment.

Sec. 306.78. *Nontransferable securities.*—The provisions of this subpart, so far as applicable, govern assignments of Treasury Bonds, Investment Series B–1975–80.

SUBPART J—ASSIGNMENTS IN BEHALF OF PRIVATE OR PUBLIC ORGANIZATIONS

Sec. 306.85. *Private corporations and unincorporated associations.*—Securities registered in the name of, or assigned to, an unincorporated association, or a private corporation in its own right or in a representative or fiduciary capacity, may be assigned in its behalf for any authorized transaction by any duly authorized officer or officers. Evidence, in the form of a resolution of the governing body, authorizing the assigning officer to assign, or to sell, or to otherwise dispose of the securities will ordinarily be required to support assignments. Resolutions may relate to any or all registered securities owned by the organization or held by it in a representative or fiduciary capacity. (Form PD 1010, or any substantially similar form, may be used when the authority relates to specific securities; Form PD 1011, or any substantially similar form, may be used for securities generally.) If the officer or officers derive their authority from the charter, constitution or bylaws, a copy or a pertinent extract therefrom, properly certified, will be required in lieu of a resolution. If the resolution or other supporting document shows the title of an authorized officer, without his name, it must be supplemented by a certificate of incumbency. (Form PD 1014 may be used.)

Sec. 306.86. *Change of name and succession of private organizations.*—If a private corporation or unincorporated association changes its name or is lawfully succeeded by another corporation or unincorporated association, its securities may be assigned in behalf of the organization in its new name or that of its successor by an authorized officer in accordance with sec. 306.85. The assignment must be supported by evidence of the change of name or successorship.

Sec. 306.87. *Partnerships.*—An assignment of a security registered in the name of or assigned to a partnership must be executed by a general partner. Upon dissolution of a partnership, assignment by all living partners and by the persons entitled to assign in behalf of any deceased partner's estate will be required unless the laws of the jurisdiction authorize a general partner to bind the partnership by any act appropriate for winding up partnership affairs. In those cases where assignments by or in behalf of all partners are required this fact must be shown in the assignment; otherwise, an affidavit by a former general partner must be furnished identifying all the persons who had been partners immediately prior to dissolution. Upon voluntary dissolution, for any jurisdiction where a general partner may not act in winding up partnership affairs, an assignment by a liquidating partner, as such, must be supported by a duly executed agreement among the partners appointing the liquidating partner.

Sec. 306.88. *Political entities and public corporations.*—Securities registered in the name of, or assigned to, a State, county, city, town, village, school district, or other political entity, public body or corporation, may be assigned by a duly authorized officer, supported by evidence of his authority.

Sec. 306.89. *Public officers.*—Securities registered in the name of, or assigned to, a public officer designated by title may be assigned by such officer, supported by evidence of incumbency. Assignments for the officer's own apparent individual benefit will not be recognized.

Sec. 306.90. *Nontransferable securities.*—The provisions of this subpart apply to Treasury Bonds, Investment Series B–1975–80.

SUBPART K—ATTORNEYS IN FACT

Sec. 306.91. *Attorneys in fact.*

(a) *General.*—Assignments by an attorney in fact will be recognized if supported by an adequate power of attorney. Every power must be executed in the presence of an authorized certifying officer under the conditions set out in sec. 306.45 for certification of assignments. Powers need not be submitted in support of assignments for redemption-exchange or exchanges pursuant to advance refunding offers where the securities to be issued are to be registered in the same names and forms as appear in the inscriptions or assignments of the securities surrendered, and such securities are registered in the names of or assigned to (1) corporations, unincorporated associations, lodges, societies, or similar organizations, or their legal successors, or (2) individuals, and the assignments are executed on their behalf by corporate attorneys in fact. In all other cases, the original power, or a photocopy showing the grantor's autograph signature, properly certified, must be submitted, together with the security assigned on the owner's behalf by the attorney in fact.

An assignment by a substitute attorney in fact must be supported by an authorizing power of attorney and power of substitution. An assignment by an attorney in fact or a substitute attorney in fact for the apparent benefit of either will not be accepted unless expressly authorized. (Form PD 1001, 1002, 1003, or 1004, as appropriate, may be used to appoint an attorney in fact. An attorney in fact may use Form PD 1006 or 1008 to appoint a substitute. However, any form sufficient in substance may be used.)

If there are two or more joint attorneys in fact or substitutes, all must unite in an assignment. However, less than all may assign if the power authorizes less than all to act, or the assignment is for redemption for the account of the owner, or for redemption-exchange or pursuant to an advance refunding offer and the new securities are to be registered in the owner's name. A power of attorney or of substitution not coupled with an interest will be recognized until the Bureau receives proof of revocation or proof of the grantor's death or incompetency.

(b) *For legal representatives and fiduciaries.*—Assignments by an attorney in fact or substitute attorney in fact for a legal representative or fiduciary, in addition to the power of attorney and of substitution, must be supported by evidence, if any, as required by secs. 306.57(d), 306.66(b), 306.75, and 306.76. Powers must specifically designate the securities to be assigned.

(c) *For corporations or unincorporated associations.*—Assignments by an attorney in fact or a substitute attorney in fact in behalf of a corporation or unincorporated association, in addition to the power of attorney and power of substitution, must be supported by one of the following documents certified under seal of the organization, or, if it has no seal, sworn to by an officer who has access to the records:

(1) A copy of the resolution of the governing body authorizing an officer to appoint an attorney in fact, with power of substitution if pertinent, to assign, or to sell, or to otherwise dispose of, the securities, or

(2) A copy of the charter, constitution, or bylaws, or a pertinent extract therefrom, showing the authority of an officer to appoint an attorney in fact, or

(3) A copy of the resolution of the governing body directly appointing an attorney in fact.

If the resolution or other supporting document shows only the title of the authorized officer, without his name, a certificate of incumbency must also be furnished. (Form PD 1014 may be used.) The power may not be broader than the resolution or other authority.

(d) *For public corporations.*—A general power of attorney in behalf of a public corporation will be recognized only if it is authorized by statute.

Sec. 306.92. *Nontransferable securities.*—The provisions of this subpart shall apply to nontransferable securities, subject only to the limitations imposed by the terms of the particular issues.

SUBPART L—TRANSFER THROUGH JUDICIAL PROCEEDINGS

Sec. 306.95. *Transferable securities.*—The Department will recognize valid judicial proceedings affecting the ownership of or interest in transferable securities, *upon presentation of the securities together with evidence of the proceedings.* In the case of securities registered in the names of two or more persons, the extent of their respective interests in the securities must be determined by the court in proceedings to which they are parties or must otherwise be validly established.[1]

Sec. 306.96. *Evidence required.*—Copies of a final judgment, decree, or order of court and of any necessary supplementary proceedings must be submitted. Assignments by a trustee in bankruptcy or a receiver of an insolvent's estate must be supported by evidence of his qualification. Assignments by a receiver in equity or a similar court officer must be supported by a copy of an order authorizing him to assign, or to sell, or to otherwise dispose of, the securities. Where the documents are dated more than six months prior to presentation of the securities, there must also be submitted a certificate dated within six months of presentation of the securities, showing the judgment, decree or order, or evidence of qualification, is in full force. Any such evidence must be certified under court seal.

Sec. 306.97. *Nontransferable securities.*

(a) *Treasury Bonds, Investment Series A–1965.*—The provisions of this subpart shall apply to bonds of this series, except that reference to assignments shall be deemed only to refer to requests for payment. With the exception of a trustee in bankruptcy or a receiver of an insolvent's estate, payment will

---

[1] A finder claiming the ownership of a bearer security or a registered security assigned in blank or so assigned as to become, in effect, payable to bearer, must perfect his title in accordance with the provisions of State law. If there are no such provisions, the Department will not recognize his title to the security.

be limited to the redemption value current thirty days after termination of the judicial proceedings or current at the time the bonds are surrendered for redemption, which ever is less. No judicial proceedings will be recognized if they would give effect to an attempted voluntary transfer inter vivos of the bonds.

(b) *Treasury Bonds, Investment Series B–1975–80.*—The provisions of this subpart shall apply to bonds of this series, except that prior to maturity any reference to assignments shall be deemed to refer to assignments of the bonds for exchange for the current series of 1½ percent 5-year EA or EO Treasury notes.

SUBPART M—REQUESTS FOR SUSPENSION OF TRANSACTIONS

Sec. 306.100. *Requests for suspension of transactions in securities.*

(a) *Registered securities.*

(1) *Reports of loss, theft, or destruction of registered securities.*—Reports of lost, stolen, or destroyed registered securities not so assigned as to become, in effect, payable to bearer, will be accepted from the owner or his authorized agent at any time and records will be maintained of the reports. If such a registered security is presented to the Department, the owner will be duly advised and given all available information.

(2) *Reports of assignments affected by fraud.*—The Department reserves the right to suspend any transaction in a registered security bearing an apparently valid assignment, if prior to the time it is received in the Department a report is received from and a claim is filed by an assignor that his assignment was affected by fraud. The interested parties will be notified of the suspension and given a reasonable period of time within which to effect settlement by agreement or institute judicial proceedings. If subsequent to the time the Department has transferred, exchanged, or redeemed a registered security in reliance on an apparently valid assignment, a report or claim is received that the assignment was affected by fraud, the Department will undertake only to furnish all available information.

(3) *Reports of forged assignments.*—If it is claimed that the assignment of a registered security is a forgery, the Department will investigate the matter and if it is established that the assignment was forged and the owner did not authorize or ratify the assignment, or receive any benefits therefrom, the Department will recognize his ownership and grant appropriate relief.

(b) *Bearer securities or registered securities so assigned as to become, in effect, payable to bearer.*

(1) *Securities not overdue.*—Neither the Department nor any of its agents will accept notice of any claim or of pending judicial proceedings by any person for the purpose of suspending transactions in bearer securities, or registered securities so assigned as to become, in effect, payable to bearer which are not overdue as defined in sec. 306.25.[1] However, if the securities are received and retired, the Department will undertake to notify persons who appear to be entitled to any available information concerning the source from which the securities were received.

(2) *Overdue securities.*—Reports that bearer securities, or registered securities so assigned as to become, in effect, payable to bearer, were lost, stolen or possibly destroyed after they became overdue as defined in sec. 306.25 will be accepted by the Bureau for the purpose of suspending redemption of the securities if the claimant establishes his interest. If the securities are presented, their redemption will be suspended and the presenter and the claimant will each be given an opportunity to establish ownership.

---

[1] It has been the longstanding policy of the Department to assume no responsibility for the protection of bearer securities not in the possession of persons claiming rights therein and to give no effect to any notice of such claims. This policy was formalized on Apr. 27, 1867, when the Secretary of the Treasury issued the following statement:

"In consequence of the increasing trouble, wholly without practical benefit, arising from notices which are constantly received at the Department respecting the loss of coupon bonds, which are payable to bearer, and of Treasury notes issued and remaining in blank at the time of loss, it becomes necessary to give this public notice, that the Government cannot protect and will not undertake to protect the owners of such bonds and notes against the consequences of their own fault or misfortune.

"Hereafter all bonds, notes, and coupons, payable to bearer, and Treasury notes issued and remaining in blank, will be paid to the party presenting them in pursuance of the regulations of the Department, in the course of regular business; and no attention will be paid to caveats which may be filed for the purpose of preventing such payment."

Sec. 306.105. *Statutory authority and requirements.*—Section 8 of the Act of July 8, 1937 (50 Stat. 481), as amended (31 U.S.C. 738a), provides for relief, under certain conditions, on account of the loss, theft, destruction, multilation, or defacement of United States interest-bearing securities. To obtain relief the security must be fully identified and the pertinent facts proved to the satisfaction of the Secretary of the Treasury, and generally, a bond of indemnity in such form and with such surety, sureties or security as may be required to protect the interest of the United States, must be filed.

Sec. 306.106. *Reports of loss, theft, destruction, multilation, or defacement of securities.*

(a) *Loss or theft.*—Report of the loss or theft of a security should be made promptly to the Bureau. The report should include :

(1) The name and present address of the owner, and his address at the time the security was issued, and, if the report is made by any other person, the capacity in which he represents the owner ;

(2) The identification of the security by title of loan, issue date, interest rate, serial number, and denomination, and in the case of a registered security, the exact form of inscription and a full description of any assignment, endorsement or other writing thereon ; and

(3) A statement of the circumstances.

(b) *Destruction, mutilation, or defacement.*—If a security is destroyed, or becomes so mutilated or defaced as to impair its value to the owner, a report of the circumstances, as outlined in paragraph (a), must be made to the Bureau. All available portions of the multilated or defaced security must also be submitted. In any appropriate case, a form for use in applying for relief will be furnished.

Sec. 306.107. *Relief authorized for lost, stolen, destroyed, multilated, or defaced securities.*

(a) *Registered securities.*—Relief is authorized for a registered security not assigned in blank or not so assigned as to become, in effect, payable to bearer, when it has been established that the security has been lost, stolen, destroyed, multilated, or defaced. Relief is available in the same manner for bearer securities restrictively endorsed in accordance with the provisions of Department Circular No. 853, current revision (31 CFR 328).

(b) *Bearer securities or registered securities so assigned as to become, in effect, payable to bearer.*—Relief is authorized for bearer securities and registered securities so assigned as to become, in effect, payable to bearer, proved to have been destroyed, multilated, or defaced. Relief will also be granted for such securities if they were lost or stolen under such circumstances and have been missing for such period of time after they have matured or become redeemable pursuant to a call for redemption as in the judgment of the Secretary of the Treasury establishes that they (1) have been destroyed or have become irretrievably lost (2) are not held by any person as his own property and (3) will never become the basis of a valid claim against the United States.

(c) *Interest coupons.*—Relief is authorized for interest coupons if it is established they were attached to a security at the time they were destroyed, mutilated, or defaced.

Sec. 306.108. *Type of relief granted.*—When relief is granted for a lost, stolen, destroyed, mutilated, or defaced security, it will be in the form of either (a) a substitute security marked "Duplicate," bearing the same issue date and showing the serial number of the original security, if the security for which relief is being granted has not matured or become redeemable pursuant to a call for redemption before maturity in accordance with its terms, or (b) payment, if the security has matured or become redeemable pursuant to a call. When a substitute is issued to replace a destroyed, mutilated, or defaced coupon security it will have attached all coupons corresponding to those proved to have been attached thereto at the time of the mishap, except that any matured coupons will not be attached but will be paid by check. Relief will not be granted in any case before the expiration of six months from date of loss or theft.

Sec. 306.109. *Nontransferable securities.*—The provisions of this subpart shall apply to all nontransferable securities, other than United States savings bonds, subject only to the limitations imposed by the terms of the particular issues.

SUBPART O—MISCELLANEOUS PROVISIONS

Sec. 306.115. *Additional requirements.*—In any case or any class of cases arising under these regulations the Secretary of the Treasury may require such additional evidence and a bond of indemnity with or without surety, as may in his judgment be necessary for the protection of the interests of the United States.

Sec. 306.116. *Waiver of regulations.*—The Secretary of the Treasury reserves the right, in his discretion, to waive or modify any provision or provisions of these regulations in any particular case or class of cases for the convenience of the United States or in order to relieve any person or persons of unnecessary hardship, if such action is not inconsistent with law, does not impair any existing rights, and he is satisfied that such action would not subject the United States to any substantial, expense or liability.

Sec. 306.117. *Preservation of existing rights.*—Nothing contained in these regulations shall limit or restrict existing rights which holders of securities heretofore issued may have acquired under the circulars offering such securities for sale or under the regulations in force at the time of acquisition.

Sec. 306.118. *Supplements, amendments, or revisions.*—The Secretary of the Treasury may at any time, or from time to time, prescribe additional, supplemental, amendatory or revised regulations with respect to United States securities.

JOHN K. CARLOCK,
Fiscal Assistant Secretary of the Treasury.

Appendix.—Computation of Interest on Treasury Bonds, Treasury Notes, and Treasury Certificates of Indebtedness, and Computation of Discount on Treasury Bills

TREASURY BONDS, TREASURY NOTES, AND TREASURY CERTIFICATES OF INDEBTEDNESS

COMPUTATION OF INTEREST ON AN ANNUAL BASIS ONE DAY'S INTEREST IS 1/365 OR 1/366 OF 1 YEAR'S INTEREST

Computation of interest will be made on an annual basis in all cases where interest is payable in one amount for the full term of the security, unless such term is an exact quarter-year (3 months) or an exact half-year (6 months), when it is provided that interest shall be computed on a quarterly or semiannual basis, respectively.

If the term of the securities is exactly one year, the interest is computed for the full period at the specified rate, regardless of the number of days in such period.

If the term of the securities is less than one full year, the annual interest period for purposes of computation is considered to be the full year from but not including the date of issue to and including the anniversary of such date.

If the term of the securities is more than one full year, computation is made on the basis of one full annual interest period, ending with the maturity date, and a fractional part of the preceding full annual interest period.

The computation of interest for any fractional part of an annual interest period is made on the basis of 365 actual days in any such period, or 366 days if February 29 falls within such annual period.

COMPUTATION OF INTEREST ON A SEMIANNUAL BASIS ONE DAY'S INTEREST IS 1/181, 1/182, 1/183, OR 1/184 OF 1/2 YEAR'S INTEREST

Computation of interest will be made on a semiannual basis in all cases where interest is payable for one or more full half-year (6 months) periods, or for one or more full half-year periods and a fractional part of a half-year period. A semiannual interest period is an exact half-year or 6 months, for computation purposes, and may comprise 181, 182, 183, or 184 actual days.

An exact half-year's interest at the specified rate is computed for each full period of exactly 6 months, irrespective of the actual number of days in the half-year.

If the initial interest covers a fractional part of a half-year, computation is made on the basis of the actual number of days in the half-year (exactly 6 months) ending on the day such initial interest becomes due. If the initial interest covers a period in excess of 6 months, computation is made on the basis of one full half-year period, ending with the interest due date, and a fractional part of the preceding full half-year period.

Interest for any fractional part of a full half-year period is computed on the basis of the exact number of days in the full period, including February 29 whenever it falls within such a period.

The number of days in any half-year period is shown in the following table:

For the half-year		Number of days	
Beginning from the 1st or 15th day of—	Ending on the 1st or 15th day of—	Regular year	Leap year
January	July	181	182
February	August	181	182
March	September	184	184
April	October	183	183
May	November	184	184
June	December	183	183
July	January	184	184
August	February	184	184
September	March	181	182
October	April	182	183
November	May	181	182
December	June	182	183
One year (any 2 consecutive half-years)		365	366

COMPUTATION OF INTEREST ON A QUARTERLY BASIS ONE DAY'S INTEREST IS 1/89, 1/90, 1/91, OR 1/92 OF 1/4 YEAR'S INTEREST

Computation of interest will be made on a quarterly basis in all cases where interest is payable for one or more full quarter-year periods, or for one or more full quarter-year periods and a fractional part of a quarter-year period.

A quarter-year interest period is an exact quarter-year of three months, and may comprise 89, 90, 91, or 92 days. An exact quarter-year's interest is computed for each full quarter-year period irrespective of the actual number of days in the quarter-year. For a fractional part of any quarter-year computation is on the basis of the actual number of days in such quarter-year (February 29 being included if it falls within any such quarter-year). If the initial interest covers a fractional part of a quarter-year (preceding a full quarter-year period), computation is on the basis of the actual number of days in the quarter-year (exactly 3 months) ending on the day such initial interest becomes due: if the final interest covers a fractional part of a quarter-year (following a full quarter-year period), computation is on the basis of the actual number of days in the quarter-year beginning on the day such final interest begins to accrue and ending exactly three months thereafter. The number of days in any quarter-year period is shown in the following table:

For the quarter-year		Number of days	
Beginning from the 1st or 15th day of—	Ending on the 1st or 15th day of—	Regular year	Leap year
January	April	90	91
February	May	89	90
March	June	92	92
April	July	91	91
May	August	92	92
June	September	92	92
July	October	92	92
August	November	92	92
September	December	91	91
October	January	92	92
November	February	92	92
December	March	90	91
One year (any 4 consecutive quarters)		365	366

Use of Interest Tables

In the appended tables decimals are set forth for use in computing interest for fractional parts of interest periods. The decimals cover interest on $1,000 for one day in each possible quarterly (table I), semiannual (table II), and annual (table III) interest period, at all rates of interest, in steps of ⅛ percent, from ⅛ to 6 percent. The amount of interest accruing on any date (for a fractional part of an interest period) on $1,000 face amount of any issue of Treasury bonds, Treasury notes, or Treasury certificates of indebtedness may be ascertained in the following way:

(1) The date of issue, the dates for the payment of interest, the basis (quarterly, semiannual, or annual) upon which interest is computed, and the rate of interest (percent per annum) may be determined from the text of the security, or from the official circular governing the issue.

(2) Determine the interest period of which the fraction is a part, and calculate the number of days in the full period to determine the proper column to be used in selecting the decimal for one day's interest.

(3) Calculate the actual number of days in the fractional period *from* but not including the date of issue or the day on which the last preceding interest payment was made, *to* and including the day on which the next succeeding interest payment is due or the day as of which the transaction which terminates the accrual of additional interest is effected.

(4) Multiply the appropriate decimal (one day's interest on $1,000) by the number of days in the fractional part of the interest period. The appropriate decimal will be found in the appended table for interest payable quarterly, semiannually, or annually, as the case may be, opposite the rate borne by the security, and in the column showing the full interest period of which the fractional period is a part. (For interest on any other amount, multiply the amount of interest on $1,000 by the other amount expressed as a decimal of $1,000.)

TREASURY BILLS

The methods of computing discount rates on U.S. Treasury bills are given below:

Computation will be made on an annual basis in all cases. The annual period for bank discount is a year of 360 days, and all computations of such discount for a fractional part of the year will be made on that basis. The annual period for true discount is one full year from but not including the date of issue to and including the anniversary of such date. Computation of true discount for a fractional part of a year will be made on the basis of 365 days in the year, or 366 days if February 29 falls within the year.

BANK DISCOUNT

The bank discount rate on a Treasury bill may be ascertained by (1) subtracting the sale price of the bill from its face value to obtain the amount of discount; (2) dividing the amount of discount by the number of days the bill is to run to obtain the amount of discount per day; (3) multiplying the amount of discount per day by 360 (the number of days in a commercial year of 12 months of 30 days each) to obtain the amount of discount per year; and (4) dividing the amount of discount per year by the face value of the bill to obtain the bank discount rate.

For example:
91-day bill—dated April 1, 1954—due July 1, 1954 :

Principal amount—maturity value	$100. 00
Price at issue—amount received	99. 50
Amount of discount	. 50

$0.50 ÷ 91 × 360 ÷ $100 = 1.978 percent.

TRUE DISCOUNT

The true discount rate on a Treasury bill of not more than one-half year in length may be ascertained by (1 and 2) obtaining the amount of discount per day by following the first two steps described under "Bank Discount;" (3) multiplying the amount of discount per day by the actual number of days in the year from the date of issue (365 ordinarily, but 366 if February 29 falls within the year from date of issue) to obtain the amount of discount per year ; and (4) dividing the amount of discount per year by the sale price of the bill to obtain the true discount rate.

For example :
91-day bill—dated April 1, 1954—due July 1, 1954 :

Principal amount—maturity value	$100.00
Price at issue—amount received	99.50
Amount of discount	.50

$0.50 \div 91 \times 365 \div $99.50 = 2.016$ percent.

TABLE I.—*Decimal for one day's interest on $1,000 at various rates of interest, payable quarterly, or on a quarterly basis, in regular years of 365 days and in leap years of 366 days*

Rate per annum	Interest period ending on the 1st or 15th of—			
	Quarter-year of 92 days Regular year: January, February, June, August, September, October, November	Quarter-year of 91 days Regular year: July, December Leap year: March, April	Quarter-year of 90 days Regular year: March, April Leap year: May	Quarter-year of 89 days Regular year: May
Percent				
⅛	$0.003 396 739	$0.003 434 066	$0.003 472 222	$0.003 511 236
¼	.006 793 478	.006 868 132	.006 944 444	.007 022 472
⅜	.010 190 217	.010 302 198	.010 416 667	.010 533 708
½	.013 586 957	.013 736 264	.013 888 889	.014 044 944
⅝	.016 983 696	.017 170 330	.017 361 111	.017 556 180
¾	.020 380 435	.020 604 396	.020 833 333	.021 067 416
⅞	.023 777 174	.024 038 462	.024 305 556	.024 578 652
1	.027 173 913	.027 472 527	.027 777 778	.028 089 888
1⅛	.030 570 652	.030 906 593	.031 250 000	.031 601 124
1¼	.033 967 391	.034 340 659	.034 722 222	.035 112 360
1⅜	.037 364 130	.037 774 725	.038 194 444	.038 623 596
1½	.040 760 870	.041 208 791	.041 666 667	.042 134 831
1⅝	.044 157 609	.044 642 857	.045 138 889	.045 646 067
1¾	.047 554 348	.048 076 923	.048 611 111	.049 157 303
1⅞	.050 951 087	.051 510 989	.052 083 333	.052 668 539
2	.054 347 826	.054 945 055	.055 555 556	.056 179 775
2⅛	.057 744 565	.058 379 121	.059 027 778	.059 691 011
2¼	.061 141 304	.061 813 187	.062 500 000	.063 202 247
2⅜	.064 538 043	.065 247 253	.065 972 222	.066 713 483
2½	.067 934 783	.068 681 319	.069 444 444	.070 224 719
2⅝	.071 331 522	.072 115 385	.072 916 667	.073 735 955
2¾	.074 728 261	.075 549 451	.076 388 889	.077 247 191
2⅞	.078 125 000	.078 983 516	.079 861 111	.080 758 427
3	.081 521 739	.082 417 582	.083 333 333	.084 269 663
3⅛	.084 918 478	.085 851 648	.086 805 556	.087 780 899
3¼	.088 315 217	.089 285 714	.090 277 778	.091 292 135
3⅜	.091 711 957	.092 719 780	.093 750 000	.094 803 371
3½	.095 108 696	.096 153 846	.097 222 222	.098 314 607
3⅝	.098 505 435	.099 587 912	.100 694 444	.101 825 843
3¾	.101 902 174	.103 021 978	.104 166 667	.105 337 079
3⅞	.105 298 913	.106 456 044	.107 638 889	.108 848 315
4	.108 695 652	.109 890 110	.111 111 111	.112 359 551
4⅛	.112 092 391	.113 324 176	.114 583 333	.115 870 787
4¼	.115 489 130	.116 758 242	.118 055 556	.119 382 022
4⅜	.118 885 870	.120 192 308	.121 527 778	.122 893 258
4½	.122 282 609	.123 626 374	.125 000 000	.126 404 494
4⅝	.125 679 348	.127 060 440	.128 472 222	.129 915 730
4¾	.129 076 087	.130 494 505	.131 944 444	.133 426 966
4⅞	.132 472 826	.133 928 571	.135 416 667	.136 938 202
5	.135 869 565	.137 362 637	.138 888 889	.140 449 438
5⅛	.139 266 304	.140 796 703	.142 361 111	.143 960 674
5¼	.142 663 043	.144 230 769	.145 833 333	.147 471 910
5⅜	.146 059 783	.147 664 835	.149 305 556	.150 983 146
5½	.149 456 522	.151 098 901	.152 777 778	.154 494 382
5⅝	.152 853 261	.154 532 967	.156 250 000	.158 005 618
5¾	.156 250 000	.157 967 033	.159 722 222	.161 516 854
5⅞	.159 646 739	.161 401 099	.163 194 444	.165 028 090
6	.163 043 478	.164 835 165	.166 666 667	.168 539 326

TABLE II.—*Decimal for one day's interest on $1,000 at various rates of interest, payable semiannually or on a semiannual basis, in regular years of 365 days and in leap years of 366 days*

Rate per annum	Interest period ending on the 1st or 15th of—			
	Half-year of 184 days Regular year: January, February, September, November	Half-year of 183 days Regular year: October, December Leap year: April, June	Half-year of 182 days Regular year: April, June Leap year: March, May, July, August	Half-year of 181 days Regular year: March, May, July, August
Percent				
⅛	$0.003 396 739	$0.003 415 301	$0.003 434 066	$0.003 453 039
¼	.006 793 478	.006 830 601	.006 868 132	.006 906 077
⅜	.010 190 217	.010 245 902	.010 302 198	.010 359 116
½	.013 586 957	.013 661 202	.013 736 264	.013 812 155
⅝	.016 983 696	.017 076 503	.017 170 330	.017 265 193
¾	.020 380 435	.020 491 803	.020 604 396	.020 718 232
⅞	.023 777 174	.023 907 104	.024 038 462	.024 171 271
1	.027 173 913	.027 322 404	.027 472 527	.027 624 309
1⅛	.030 570 652	.030 737 705	.030 906 593	.031 077 348
1¼	.033 967 391	.034 153 005	.034 340 659	.034 530 387
1⅜	.037 364 130	.037 568 306	.037 774 725	.037 983 425
1½	.040 760 870	.040 983 607	.041 208 791	.041 436 464
1⅝	.044 157 609	.044 398 907	.044 642 857	.044 889 503
1¾	.047 554 348	.047 814 208	.048 076 923	.048 342 541
1⅞	.050 951 087	.051 229 508	.051 510 989	.051 795 580
2	.054 347 826	.054 644 809	.054 945 055	.055 248 619
2⅛	.057 744 565	.058 060 109	.058 379 121	.058 701 657
2¼	.061 141 304	.061 475 410	.061 813 187	.062 154 696
2⅜	.064 538 043	.064 890 710	.065 247 253	.065 607 735
2½	.067 934 783	.068 306 011	.068 681 319	.069 060 773
2⅝	.071 331 522	.071 721 311	.072 115 385	.072 513 812
2¾	.074 728 261	.075 136 612	.075 549 451	.075 966 851
2⅞	.078 125 000	.078 551 913	.078 983 516	.079 419 890
3	.081 521 739	.081 967 213	.082 417 582	.082 872 928
3⅛	.084 918 478	.085 382 514	.085 851 648	.086 325 967
3¼	.088 315 217	.088 797 814	.089 285 714	.089 779 006
3⅜	.091 711 957	.092 213 115	.092 719 780	.093 232 044
3½	.095 108 696	.095 628 415	.096 153 846	.096 685 083
3⅝	.098 505 435	.099 043 716	.099 587 912	.100 138 122
3¾	.101 902 174	.102 459 016	.103 021 978	.103 591 160
3⅞	.105 298 913	.105 874 317	.106 456 044	.107 044 199
4	.108 695 652	.109 289 617	.109 890 110	.110 497 238
4⅛	.112 092 391	.112 704 918	.113 324 176	.113 950 276
4¼	.115 489 130	.116 120 219	.116 758 242	.117 403 315
4⅜	.118 885 870	.119 535 519	.120 192 308	.120 856 354
4½	.122 282 609	.122 950 820	.123 626 374	.124 309 392
4⅝	.125 679 348	.126 366 120	.127 060 440	.127 762 431
4¾	.129 076 087	.129 781 421	.130 494 505	.131 215 470
4⅞	.132 472 826	.133 196 721	.133 928 571	.134 668 508
5	.135 869 565	.136 612 022	.137 362 637	.138 121 547
5⅛	.139 266 304	.140 027 322	.140 796 703	.141 574 586
5¼	.142 663 043	.143 442 623	.144 230 769	.145 027 624
5⅜	.146 059 783	.146 857 923	.147 664 835	.148 480 663
5½	.149 456 522	.150 273 224	.151 098 901	.151 933 702
5⅝	.152 853 261	.153 688 525	.154 543 967	.155 386 740
5¾	.156 250 000	.157 103 825	.157 967 033	.158 839 779
5⅞	.159 646 739	.160 519 126	.161 401 099	.162 292 818
6	.163 043 478	.163 934 426	.164 835 165	.165 745 856

TABLE III.—*Decimal for one day's interest on $1,000 at various rates of interest, payable annually or on an annual basis, in regular years of 365 days and in leap years of 366 days.*

Rate per annum	Regular year, 365 days	Leap year, 366 days
Percent		
⅛	$0.003 424 658	$0.003 415 301
¼	.006 849 315	.006 830 601
⅜	.010 273 973	.010 254 902
½	.013 698 630	.013 661 202
⅝	.017 123 288	.017 076 503
¾	.020 547 945	.020 491 803
⅞	.023 972 603	.023 907 104
1	.027 397 260	.027 322 404
1⅛	.030 821 918	.030 737 705
1¼	.034 246 575	.034 153 005
1⅜	.037 671 233	.037 568 306
1½	.041 095 890	.040 983 607
1⅝	.044 520 548	.044 398 907
1¾	.047 945 205	.047 814 208
1⅞	.051 369 863	.051 229 508
2	.054 794 521	.054 644 809
2⅛	.058 219 178	.058 060 109
2¼	.061 643 836	.061 475 410
2⅜	.065 068 493	.064 890 710
2½	.068 493 151	.068 306 011
2⅝	.071 917 808	.071 721 311
2¾	.075 342 466	.075 136 612
2⅞	.078 767 123	.078 551 913
3	.082 191 781	.081 967 213
3⅛	.085 616 438	.085 382 514
3¼	.089 041 096	.088 797 814
3⅜	.092 465 753	.092 213 115
3½	.095 890 411	.095 628 415
3⅝	.099 315 068	.099 043 716
3¾	.102 739 762	.102 459 016
3⅞	.106 164 384	.105 874 317
4	.109 589 041	.109 289 617
4⅛	.113 013 699	.112 704 918
4¼	.116 438 356	.116 120 219
4⅜	.119 863 014	.119 535 519
4½	.123 287 671	.122 950 820
4⅝	.126 712 329	.126 366 120
4¾	.130 136 986	.129 781 421
4⅞	.133 561 644	.133 196 721
5	.136 986 301	.136 612 022
5⅛	.140 410 959	.140 027 322
5¼	.143 835 616	.143 442 623
5⅜	.147 260 274	.146 857 923
5½	.150 684 932	.150 273 224
5⅝	.154 109 589	.153 688 525
5¾	.157 534 247	.157 103 825
5⅞	.160 958 904	.160 519 126
6	.164 383 562	.163 934 426

Exhibit 7.—Ninth revision, December 23, 1964, of Department Circular No. 530, regulations governing United States savings bonds

TREASURY DEPARTMENT,
Washington, December 23, 1964.

Department Circular No. 530, Eighth Revision, dated December 26, 1957, as amended (31 CFR 315), is hereby further amended and issued as the Ninth Revision.

AUTHORITY: Secs. 315.0 to 315.93 issued under authority of sections 22 and 25 of the Second Liberty Bond Act, as amended, 49 Stat. 21, as amended, 73 Stat. 621 (31 U.S.C. 757c, 757c–1).

SUBPART A—GENERAL INFORMATION

Sec. 315. *Applicability of regulations.*—These regulations apply to all United States savings bonds of whatever series designation (hereinafter referred to as "savings bonds" or "bonds") bearing any issue dates whatever, to the extent specified herein and in the offering circulars governing such bonds. The provisions of these regulations with respect to bonds registered in the names of certain classes of individuals, fiduciaries, and organizations are equally applicable to bonds to which such individuals, fiduciaries, and organizations are otherwise shown to be entitled under these regulations. The provisions of Department Circular No. 300, current revision (31 CFR 306), have no application to savings bonds.

Sec. 315.1 *Official agencies.*—The Bureau of the Public Debt of the Treasury Department is charged with matters relating to savings bonds. Correspondence concerning transactions after original issue and requests for appropriate forms should be addressed to (1) the Federal Reserve bank or branch of the district in which the correspondent is located, or (2) the Bureau of the Public Debt, Division of Loans and Currency Branch, 536 South Clark Street, Chicago, Ill. 60605, or (3) the Office of the Treasurer of the United States, Securities Division, Washington, D.C. 20220, except where specific instructions are otherwise given in these regulations. Notices or documents not filed in accordance with instructions in these regulations will not be recognized. The addresses of the Federal Reserve banks and branches are:

Federal Reserve Bank of Boston, Boston, Mass. 02106.

Federal Reserve Bank of New York, New York, N.Y. 10045.
　Buffalo Branch, Buffalo, N.Y. 14240.

Federal Reserve Bank of Philadelphia, Philadelphia, Pa. 19101.

Federal Reserve Bank of Cleveland, Cleveland, Ohio 44101.
　Cincinnati Branch, Cincinnati, Ohio 45201.
　Pittsburgh Branch, Pittsburgh, Pa. 15230.

Federal Reserve Bank of Richmond, Richmond, Va. 23213.
　Baltimore Branch, Baltimore, Md. 21203.
　Charlotte Branch, Charlotte, N.C. 28201.

Federal Reserve Bank of Atlanta, Atlanta, Ga. 30303.
　Birmingham Branch, Birmingham, Ala. 35202.
　Jacksonville Branch, Jacksonville, Fla. 32201.
　Nashville B r a n c h, Nashville, Tenn. 37203.

Federal Reserve Bank of Atlanta, Atlanta, Ga. 30303—Continued
　New Orleans Branch, New Orleans, La. 70160.

Federal Reserve Bank of Chicago, P.O. Box 834, Chicago, Ill. 60690.
　Detroit Branch, P.O. Box 1059, Detroit, Mich. 48231.

Federal Reserve Bank of St. Louis, P.O. Box 442, St. Louis, Mo. 63166.
　Little Rock Branch, P.O. Box 1261, Little Rock, Ark. 72203.
　Louisville Branch, P.O. Box 899, Louisville, Ky. 40201.
　Memphis Branch, P.O. Box 407, Memphis, Tenn. 38101.

Federal Reserve Bank of Minneapolis, Minneapolis, Minn. 55440.
　Helena Branch, Helena, Mont. 59601.

Federal Reserve Bank of Kansas City, Kansas City, Mo. 64106.
　Denver Branch, Denver, Colo. 80217.
　Oklahoma City Branch, Oklahoma City, Okla. 73101.
　Omaha Branch, Omaha, Nebr. 68102.

Federal Reserve Bank of Dallas, Station K, Dallas, Tex. 75222.
El Paso Branch, P.O. Box 100, El Paso, Tex. 79999.
Houston Branch, P.O. Box 2578, Houston, Tex. 77001.
San Antonio Branch, P.O. Box 1471, San Antonio, Tex. 78206.

Federal Reserve Bank of San Francisco, San Francisco, Calif. 94120.
Los Angeles Branch, P.O. Box 2077, Los Angeles, Calif. 90054.
Portland Branch, P.O. Box 3456, Portland, Oreg. 97208.
Salt Lake City Branch, P.O. Box 780, Salt Lake City, Utah 84110.
Seattle Branch, P.O. Box 3567, Seattle, Wash. 98124.

Sec. 315.2. *Definition of words and terms as used in these regulations.*

(a) "Authorized issuing agent" means an incorporated bank, trust company, savings bank, savings and loan association, other organization, or instrumentality of the United States, qualified as an issuing agent under the provisions of Department Circular No. 657, current revision (31 CFR 317).

(b) "Authorized paying agent" means an incorporated bank, trust company, savings bank, savings and loan association, or other organization qualified as a paying agent under the provisions of Department Circular No. 750, current revision (31 CFR 321).

(c) "Court" means one which has jurisdiction over the parties and subject matter.

(d) "Extended maturity date" is the date on which a bond will mature and cease to bear interest under applicable optional extension provisions.

(e) "Extended maturity value" is the value of a bond at maturity under applicable optional extension provisions.

(f) "Face value" of a bond refers to the value of the bond as shown on the face thereof.

(g) "Incompetent" refers to a person under any legal disability except minority.

(h) "Maturity date" means the date on which the bond will mature by the terms of the circular offering it for sale without regard to any optional extension period.

(i) "Optional extension period" [1] means any period after maturity date which the owner may retain the bonds and continue to earn interest on the maturity value in accordance with the terms of the circular offering such bonds for sale.

(j) "Payment" and "redemption" are used interchangeably, unless otherwise indicated. They refer to payment of a bond in accordance with these regulations.

(k) "Personal trust estate" means a trust estate established by natural persons in their own right for the benefit of themselves or other natural persons in whole or in part, and common trust funds comprised in whole or in part of such trust estates.

(l) "Presented and surrendered" and "presentation and surrender" mean the actual receipt of a bond, with an appropriate request for the particular transaction, by the Bureau of the Public Debt, Chicago or Washington office, the Office of the Treasurer of the United States, Securities Division, or a Federal Reserve bank or branch, or, if the transaction is one which an authorized paying agent may handle, receipt by such authorized paying agent.

(m) "Representative of the estate of a minor, incompetent, aged person, absentee, etc.," means a guardian, conservator, or similar representative appointed by a court or otherwise legally qualified, regardless of the title by which designated. These terms do not refer to a voluntary guardian recognized under sec. 315.53, to a natural guardian, such as a parent, including a parent to whom custody of a child has been awarded through divorce proceedings or a parent by adoption, or to the executor or administrator of the estate of a decedent.

(n) "Reissue" means the cancellation and retirement of a bond and issue of a new bond or bonds of the same series, amount (face value) (or the remainder thereof in case of partial redemption), and issue date.

(o) "Taxpayer identifying number" means the appropriate identifying number as required on tax returns and other documents submitted to the Internal

---

[1] All Series E bonds have a 10-year optional extension period. Those bearing issue dates of May 1, 1941, through May 1, 1949, have a second 10-year optional extension period. Series H bonds bearing issue dates of June 1, 1952, through Jan. 1, 1957, have a 10-year optional extension period. Other bonds do not have this feature.

Revenue Service, i.e., an individual's social security account number or an employer identification number. The social security account number is composed of nine digits separated by two hyphens, for example, 123–45–6789; the employer identification number is composed of nine digits separated by one hyphen, for example, 12–3456789. The hyphens are an essential part of the numbers and must be included.

SUBPART B—REGISTRATION

Sec. 315.5 *General.*—Savings bonds are issued only in registered form. The registration used on issue or reissue must express the actual ownership of and interest in the bond and, except as otherwise specifically provided in Subpart E and section 315.48 of Subpart J of these regulations, will be considered as conclusive of such ownership and interest. No designation of an attorney, agent, or other representative to request or receive payment on behalf of the owner or a coowner, nor any restriction on the right of the owner or a coowner to receive payment of the bond or interest, except as provided in the regulations, may be made in the registration or otherwise. Registrations requested in applications for purchase or requests for reissue should be clear, accurate, and complete, conform with one of the forms set forth in this subpart, and include the appropriate taxpayer identifying number.[1] The registration of all bonds owned by the same person, organization, or fiduciary should be uniform with respect to the name of the owner and, in the case of a fiduciary, the description of the fiduciary capacity. The owner, coowner, or beneficiary should be designated by the name by which he is ordinarily known or the one under which he does business, including preferably at least one full given name. The name may be preceded by any applicable title, such as "Dr." or "Rev.," or followed by "M.D.," "D.D.," or other similar designation. "Sr." or "Jr." or a similar suffix should be included, when ordinarily used or when necessary to distinguish the owner from a member of his family. The name of a woman must be preceded by "Miss" or "Mrs.," unless some other applicable title or designation is used. A married woman's own given name, not that of her husband, must be used, for example, "Mrs. Mary A. Jones," NOT "Mrs. Frank B. Jones." The post office address should include where appropriate, the number and street, route, or any other local feature, and the ZIP Code.

Sec. 315.6 *Restrictions on registration.*

(a) *Residence.*—Registration of bonds is restricted on original issue, but not on authorized reissue, to persons (whether natural persons or others) who are:

(1) residents of the United States, its territories and possessions, the Commonwealth of Puerto Rico, and the Canal Zone;

(2) citizens of the United States temporarily residing abroad; and

(3) civilian employees of the United States or members of its Armed Forces, regardless of their residence or citizenship.

However, other natural persons may be designated as coowners or beneficiaries with natural persons of the above classes, whether on original issue or reissue, except that registration is not permitted in any form which includes the name of any alien who is resident of any area with respect to which the Treasury Department restricts or regulates the delivery of checks drawn against funds of the United States or any agency or instrumentality thereof.[2]

(b) *Minority.*—Bonds purchased by another person with funds belonging to a minor should be registered in the name of the minor without a coowner or

---

[1] It is not mandatory to include taxpayer identifying numbers in registrations of Series E bonds. Issuing agents for Series E bonds issued under payroll savings plans who desire to place such numbers on the bonds should obtain instructions from the Bureau of the Public Debt, Washington, D.C. 20220. As the numbers must be included in Series H bond registrations, except with respect to such persons and organizations as may be exempt from furnishing such numbers under the regulations of the Internal Revenue Service, they are shown in the examples in sec. 315.7 for guidance. Series H bonds inscribed in the name of an individual, with or without a beneficiary, must show the individual's social security account number. The social security account number of either coowner may be shown on bonds registered in coownership form, except that if the coowners are husband and wife, the husband's number should be shown. If the coowners are a minor and an adult, the adult's number should be shown. Questions concerning taxpayer identifying numbers and correct forms of registration should be submitted to the Federal Reserve bank or branch of the appropriate district, or to the Bureau of the Public Debt, Division of Loans and Currency Branch, 536 South Clark Street, Chicago, Ill. 60605, or to the Office of the Treasurer of the United States, Securities Division, Washington, D.C. 20220.

[2] See Department Circular No. 655, current revision (31 CFR 211).

beneficiary. A minor may name a coowner or beneficiary on bonds he purchases with his wages, earnings, or other funds belonging to him and under his control. A minor, whether or not under legal guardianship, may be named as owner, co-owner, or beneficiary on bonds purchased by another individual with funds other than those belonging to the minor.

If there is a representative of a minor's estate, bonds should be registered in the name of the minor, or in the name of the representative, followed in either case by an appropriate reference to the guardianship. Bonds purchased by a representative of two or more minors, even though appointed in a single proceeding, should be registered separately in a form to show each guardianship estate. A bond may be purchased as a gift to a minor under a gifts to minors statute in effect in a State in which either the donor or the minor resides, in which case the bond should be registered as provided in the statute, with the addition of a parenthetical reference identifying the statute if the registration does not clearly identify it. Registration in the name of a natural guardian is not authorized. See examples of forms of registration under sec. 315.7(b).

(c) *Incompetency.*—Bonds should not be registered in the name of an incompetent unless there is a legal representative of his estate, except under the provisions of sec. 315.53. If there is a legal representative, the provisions of paragraph (b) of this section apply as to registration in the name of the legal representative or in the name of the incompetent followed by reference to the guardianship.

Sec. 315.7. *Authorized forms of registration.*—Subject to any limitations or restrictions contained in these regulations on the right of any person to be named as owner, coowner, or beneficiary, bonds may be registered in the following forms: [1]

(a) *Natural persons.*—In the names of natural persons in their own right.

(1) *Single owner.* Example: John A. Jones 123–45–6789.

(2) *Coownership form—two persons (only).* In the alternative as coowners.

Examples:

John A. Jones 123–45–6789 or Mrs. Ella S. Jones.
Mrs. Ella S. Jones or John A. Jones 123–45–9876.

No other form of registration establishing coownership is authorized.

(3) *Beneficiary form—two persons (only).* Examples:
John A. Jones 123–45–6789 payable on death to Mrs. Ella S. Jones.
John A. Jones 123–45–6789 P.O.D. Mrs. Ella S. Jones.

"Payable on death" may be abbreviated to "P.O.D." as indicated in the last example. The first person named is hereinafter referred to as the owner and the second named person as the beneficiary.

(b) *Fiduciaries and private or public organizations.*—Only the single owner form of registration is available for bonds owned by other than natural persons, and the registration must conform to the forms authorized in this subsection.

(1) *Fiduciaries.*—In the names of any persons or organizations, public or private, as fiduciaries, but not where the fiduciary would hold the bonds merely or principally as security for the performance of a duty, obligation, or service.

(i) *Guardians, custodians, conservators, etc.*—In the name and title or capacity of the legally appointed, designated, or authorized representative or representatives of the estate of a minor, incompetent, aged person, absentee, etc., or in the name of such individual, followed by an appropriate reference to the estate and showing the nature of the legal disability or referring to the applicable statute. Examples:

William C. Jones, guardian (or conservator, trustee, etc.) of the estate of James F. Brown 123–45–6789, a minor (or an incompetent, aged person, infirm person, or absentee).

John Smith 123–45–6789, a minor (or an incompetent, aged person, infirm person, or absentee) under legal guardianship (or conservatorship or trusteeship, etc.) of Henry C. Smith.

John Smith 123–45–6789, an adult under conservatorship of Henry Smith pursuant to sec. 572, 1963 Iowa Probate Code.

John Smith 123–45–6789, a minor (or incompetent) under custodianship by designation of the Veterans Administration.

---

[1] See Department Circular No. 655, current revision (31 CFR 211).

John Smith 123–45–6789, an incompetent for whom Henry C. Smith has been designated trustee by the Department of the Army pursuant to 37 U.S.C. 351–354.

William C. Jones, as custodian for John Smith 123–45–6789, under the California Uniform Gifts of Securities to Minors Act.

William C. Jones, as custodian for John Smith 123–45–6789, a minor, under the laws of Georgia (Chapter 48–3, Code of Ga. Ann.).

Richard Roe 123–45–6789, a minor (or an incapacitated adult) beneficiary for whom Reva Roe has been designated representative payee by the Secretary of Health, Education, and Welfare, pursuant to 42 U.S.C. 405(j).

(ii) *Executors, administrators, etc.*

(a) In the name of the representative or representatives of the estate of a decedent appointed by a court or otherwise legally qualified. The registration should include the name of the decedent and the name or names of all representatives. The name and title of the representative must be followed by adequate identifying reference to the estate. Example:

John Smith, executor of the will (or administrator of the estate) of Henry J. Smith, deceased 12–3456789.

(b) In the name of an executor authorized to administer a trust under the terms of a will although he is not named as trustee. Example:

John Smith, executor of the will of Henry J. Smith, deceased, in trust for Mrs. Jane Smith, with remainder over 12–3456789.

(iii) *Trustees.*—In the name and title or capacity (or title or capacity alone where hereinafter provided) of the trustee or trustees of a single duly constituted trust estate (which will be considered as an entity), substantially in accordance with the examples set forth in this paragraph. Unless otherwise indicated, an adequate identifying reference should be made to the trust instrument or other authority creating the trust. A common trust fund established and maintained according to law by a financial institution duly authorized to act as a fiduciary will be considered as a single duly constituted trust estate within the meaning of these regulations.

(a) *Will, deed of trust, agreement, or similar instrument.*—Examples:

John Smith and the First National Bank, trustees under the will of Henry J. Smith deceased 12–3456789.

The Second National Bank, trustee under an agreement with George E. White, dated February 1, 1935, 12–3456789.

If the authority creating the trust designates by title only an officer of a board or an organization as trustee, only the title of the officer should be used in the registration. Example:

Chairman, Board of Trustees, First Church of Christ, Scientist, of Chicago, Ill., in trust under the will of Henry J. Smith, deceased 12–3456789.

If the trustees are too numerous to be designated in the inscription by names and capacity, the names or some of the names may be omitted. Examples:

John Smith, Henry Jones, et al., trustees under the will of Henry J. Smith, deceased 12–3456789.

Trustees under the will of Henry J. Smith, deceased 12–3456789.

(b) *Pension, retirement, or similar fund, or employees' savings plans.*—In the name and title (or title alone) of the trustee or trustees of a pension, retirement, or similar fund, or an employees' savings plan. If the instrument creating the trust provides that the trustees shall serve for a limited term, the names of the trustees may be omitted. Examples:

First National Bank and Trust Company, trustee of the Employees' Savings Plan of Jones Company, Inc., U/A dated Jan. 17, 1959, 12–3456789.

Trustees of the Employees' Savings Plan of Johnson Company, Inc., U/A dated Jan. 20, 1964, 12–3456789.

First National Bank, trustee of pension fund of Industrial Manufacturing Company, under agreement with said company dated Mar. 31, 1949, 12–3456789.

Trustees of Retirement Fund of Industrial Manufacturing Company, under resolution adopted by its board of directors on Mar. 31, 1949, 12–3456789.

(c) *Funds of a lodge, church, society, or similar organization.*—If the funds of a lodge, church, society, or similar organization, whether incorporated or not, are held in trust by a trustee or trustees or a board of trustees, only the capacity should be used in the registration. Examples:

Trustees of the First Baptist Church, Akron, Ohio, acting as a Board under section 15 of its by-laws, 12–3456789.

Trustees of Jamestown Lodge No. 1,000, Benevolent and Protective Order of Elks, under section 10 of its by-laws, 12–3456789.

Board of Trustees of the Lotus Club, Washington, Ind., under Article X of its constitution, 12–3456789.

(d) *Public officers, corporations, or bodies.*—If a public officer, public corporation, or public body acts as trustee under express authority of law, only the title should be used in the registration. Examples:

Rhode Island Sinking Fund Commission, trustee of the General Sinking Fund, under Ch. 35, Gen. Laws of R.I.

Superintendent of the Confederate Home for Men, in trust for the Benefit Fund, under sec. 3183c, Vernon's Civil Stats. of Texas Ann.

(e) *School, class, or activity fund.*—If the principal or other officer of a public, private, or parochial school acts as trustee for the benefit of the student body or a class, group, or activity thereof, only the title should be used in the registration, and if the amount purchased for any one fund does not exceed $500 (face value), no reference need be made to a trust instrument. Examples:

Principal, Western High School, in trust for Class of 1955 Library Fund 12–3456789.

Director of Athletics, Western High School, in trust for Student Activities Association under resolution adopted May 12, 1955, 12–3456789.

(iv) *Life tenants.*—In the name of a life tenant, followed by adequate identifying reference to the instrument creating the life tenancy. Example:

Mrs. Jane Smith, life tenant under the will of Henry J. Smith, deceased 12–3456789.

(v) *Investment agents.*—In the name of a bank, trust company, or other financial institution, or individual, holding funds of a religious, educational, charitable, or nonprofit organization, whether or not incorporated, as agent under an agreement with the organization for the sole purpose of investing and reinvesting the funds and paying the income to the organization. The name and designation of the agent should be followed by an adequate identifying reference to the agreement. Examples:

Black County National Bank, fiscal agent 12–3456789, under agreement with the Evangelical Lutheran Church of The Holy Trinity, dated Dec. 28, 1949.

First National Bank and Trust Company, investment agent 12–3456789, under agreement dated Sept. 16, 1964, with Central City Post No. 1000, Department of Illinois, American Legion.

(2) *Private organizations (corporations, associations, and partnerships, etc.).*—In the name of any private organization, but not in the names of commercial banks, which are defined for this purpose as those accepting demand deposits. The full legal name of the organization, without mention of any officer or member by name or title, should be used as follows:

(i) *A corporation.*—A business, fraternal, religious, or other private corporation, followed preferably by the words "a corporation" (unless the fact of incorporation is shown in the name). Examples:

Smith Manufacturing Company, a corporation, 12–3456789.

Jones and Brown ,Inc. 12–3456789.

(ii) *An unincorporated association.*—An unincorporated lodge, society, or similar self-governing association, followed preferably by the words "an unincorporated association." The term "an unincorporated association" should not be used to describe a trust fund, a board of trustees, a partnership, or a business conducted under a trade name or as a sole proprietorship. If the association is chartered by or affiliated with a parent organization, the name or designation of the subordinate or local organization should be given first, followed by the name of the parent organization. The name of the parent or national organization may be placed in parentheses and, if it is well known, may be abbreviated. Examples:

The Lotus Club, an unincorporated association, 12–3456789.

Local 447, Brotherhood of Railroad Trainmen, an unincorporated association, 12–3456789.

782–556—66——16

Eureka Lodge No. 317 (A.F. & A.M.), an unincorporated association, 12–3456789.

(iii) *A partnership.*—A partnership (which will be considered as an entity), followed by the words "a partnership." Examples:

Smith and Brown, a partnership 12–3456789.

Acme Novelty Company, a partnership 12–3456789.

(iv) *Institutions (churches, hospitals, homes, schools, etc.).*—In the name of a church, hospital, home, school, or similar institution conducted by a private organization or by private trustees, regardless of the manner in which it is organized or governed or title to its property is held. Examples:

Shriners' Hospital for Crippled Children, St. Louis, Mo. 12–3456789.

St. Mary's Roman Catholic Church, Albany, N.Y. 12–3456789.

Rodeph Shalom Sunday School, Philadelphia, Pa. 12–3456789.

(3) *Government units, agencies, and officers.*—In the full legal name or title of the owner or official custodian of public funds, other than trust funds, as follows:

(i) Any governmental unit, as a State, county, city, town, village, or school district. Examples:

State of Maine.

Town of Rye, New York (Street Improvement Fund).

(ii) Any board, commission, government owned corporation, or other public body duly constituted by law. Example:

Maryland State Highway Commission.

(iii) Any public officer designated by title only. Example:

Treasurer, City of Chicago.

(c) *Treasurer of the United States as coowner or beneficiary.*—Those who desire to do so may make gifts to the United States by designating the Treasurer of the United States as coowner or beneficiary. Bonds so registered may not be reissued to change the designation. Examples:

John A. Jones 123–45–6789 or the Treasurer of the United States of America.

John A. Jones 123–45–6789 P.O.D. the Treasurer of the United States of America.

Sec. 315.8. *Unauthorized registration.*—A savings bond inscribed in a form not substantially in agreement with one of those authorized by this subpart will not be considered as validly issued, except that once it is established that the bond can be reissued in a form of registration which is valid under these regulations it will be considered as having been validly issued from the date of original issue.

SUBPART C—LIMITATIONS ON HOLDINGS

Sec. 315.10. *Amount which may be held.*—The amounts of savings bonds of each series, issued in any one calendar year, which may be held by any one person at any one time, computed in accordance with the provisions of sec. 315.11, are limited as follows:[1]

(a) *Series E.*—$5.000 (face value) for each calendar year up to and including the calendar year 1947; $10,000 (face value) for the calendar years 1948 to 1951, inclusive; $20,000 (face value) for the calendar years 1952 to 1956, inclusive; $10,000 (face value) for the calendar year 1957[2] and each calendar year thereafter; except that trustees of an employees' saving plan (as defined in Department Circular No. 653, current revision) may purchase $2,000 (face value) multiplied by the highest number of employees participating in the plan at any time during the calendar year in which the bonds are issued.

(b) *Series H.*—$20,000 (face value) for each calendar year up to and including the calendar year 1956; $10,000 (face value) for the calendar years 1957[2]

---

[1] Bonds of Series F, G, J, and K, no longer available for purchase, are subject to the limitations on holdings and rules for computation of holdings set forth in secs. 315.8 and 315.9 of Department Circular No. 530, Seventh Revision.

[2] Effective May 1, 1957. Accordingly, investors who purchased $20,000 (face value) of bonds of Series E bearing issue dates of January 1 through April 1 were not entitled to purchase additional bonds of that series during 1957. The same limitation applies to bonds of Series H bearing those issue dates. Investors who purchased less than $10,000 (face value) of bonds of either series prior to May 1 were entitled only to purchase enough of either series to bring their total for that series for 1957 to $10,000 (face value).

to 1961, inclusive; $20,000 (face value) for the calendar year 1962 and each calendar year thereafter.

Sec. 315.11. *Computation of amount.*

(a) *Definition of "person."*—The term "person" for purposes of this section shall mean any legal entity and shall include but not be limited to natural persons, corporations (public or private), partnerships, unincorporated associations, and trust estates. The holdings of each person individually and his holdings in any fiduciary capacity authorized by these regulations, such as, for example, his holdings as a guardian of the estate of a minor, as a life tenant, or as trustee under a will or deed of trust, shall be computed separately. A pension or retirement fund or an investment, insurance, annuity, or similar fund or trust will be regarded as an entity regardless of the number of beneficiaries or the manner in which their respective interests are established or determined. Segregation of individual shares as a matter of bookkeeping or as a result of individual agreements with beneficiaries or the express designation of individual shares as separate trusts will not operate to constitute separate trusts under these regulations.

(b) *Bonds that must be included in computation.*—Except as provided in paragraph (c) of this section, there must be taken into account in computing the holdings of each person:

(1) All bonds registered in the name of that person alone;

(2) All bonds registered in the name of the representative of the estate of that person;

(3) All bonds originally registered in the name of that person as coowner or reissued at the request of the original owner to add the name of that person as coowner or to designate him as coowner instead of as beneficiary. However, the amount of bonds of Series E and H held in coownership form may be applied to the holdings of either of the coowners but will not be applied to both, or the amount may be apportioned between them.

(c) *Bonds that may be excluded from computation.*—There need not be taken into account:

(1) Bonds on which that person is named beneficiary;

(2) Bonds in which his interest is only that of a beneficiary under a trust;

(3) Bonds to which he has become entitled under sec. 315.66 as surviving beneficiary upon the death of the registered owner as an heir or legatee of the deceased owner, or by virtue of the termination of a trust or the happening of any other event;

(4) Bonds of Series E purchased with the proceeds of matured bonds of Series A, C–1938, and D, where such matured bonds were presented for that purpose;

(5) Bonds of Series E bearing issue dates from May 1, 1941, to Dec. 1, 1945, inclusive, held by individuals in their own right which are not more than $5,000 (face value) in excess of the prescribed limit;

(6) Bonds of Series E or H reissued under sec. 315.61(a)(1);

(7) Bonds of Series E or H reissued in the name of a trustee of a personal trust estate which did not represent excess holdings prior to such reissue;

(8) Bonds of Series E or H purchased with the proceeds of bonds of Series F, G, J, or K, at or after maturity, where such matured bonds are presented for that purpose in accordance with the provisions of Department Circulars Nos. 653, current revision (31 CFR 316), offering bonds of Series E, and 905, current revision (31 CFR 332), offering bonds of Series H;

(9) Bonds of Series H issued in exchange for bonds of Series E, F, or J under the provisions of Department Circular No. 1036, as amended.

Sec. 315.12. *Disposition of excess.*—If any person at any time acquires savings bonds issued during any one calendar year in excess of the prescribed amount, the excess must be immediately surrendered for refund of the purchase price, less (in the case of current income bonds) any interest which may have been paid thereon, or for such other adjustment as may be possible. For good cause found the Secretary of the Treasury may permit excess holdings to stand in any particular case or class of cases.

SUBPART D—LIMITATION ON TRANSFER OR PLEDGE

Sec. 315.15. *Limitation on transfer or pledge.*—Savings bonds are not transferable and are payable only to the owners named thereon, except as specifically provided in these regulations, and then only in the manner and to the extent so provided. A savings bond may not be hypothecated, pledged as collateral, or used as security for the performance of an obligation, except as provided in sec. 315.16.

Sec. 315.16 *Pledge under Department Circulars Nos. 154 and 657.*—A bond may be pledged by the registered owner in lieu of surety under the provisions of Department Circular No. 154, current revision (31 CFR 225), if the bond approving officer is the Secretary of the Treasury, in which case an irrevocable power of attorney shall be executed authorizing the Secretary of the Treasury to request payment. A bond may also be deposited as security with a Federal Reserve bank under the provisions of Department Circular No. 657, current revision (31 CFR 317), by an institution certified under that circular as an issuing agent for Series E bonds.

SUBPART E—LIMITATION ON JUDICIAL PROCEEDINGS—NO STOPPAGE OR CAVEATS PERMITTED

Sec. 315.20. *General.*—No judicial determination will be recognized which would give effect to an attempted voluntary transfer inter vivos of a bond or would defeat or impair the rights of survivorship conferred by these regulations upon a surviving coowner or beneficiary, and all other provisions of this subpart are subject to this restriction. Otherwise, a claim against an owner or coowner of a savings bond and conflicting claims as to ownership of, or interest in, such bond as between coowners or between the registered owner and beneficiary will be recognized, when established by valid judicial proceedings, upon presentation and surrender of the bond, but only as specifically provided in this subpart.

Neither the Treasury Department nor any agency for the issue, reissue, or redemption of savings bonds will accept notices of adverse claims of or pending judicial proceedings or undertake to protect the interests of litigants who do not have possession of a bond.

Sec. 315.21. *Payment to judgment creditors.*

(a) *Creditors.*—Payment (but not reissue) of a savings bond registered in single ownership, coownership, or beneficiary form will be made to the purchaser at a sale under a levy or to the officer authorized to levy upon the property of the registered owner or coowner under appropriate process to satisfy a money judgment. Payment will be made to such purchaser or officer only to the extent necessary to satisfy the judgment and will be limited to the redemption value current sixty days after the termination of judicial proceedings. Payment of a bond registered in coownership form pursuant to a judgment or levy against only one of the coowners will be limited to the extent of that coowner's interest in the bond; this interest may be established by an agreement between the coowners or by a judgment, decree, or order of court entered in a proceeding to which both coowners are parties.

(b) *Trustees in bankruptcy and receivers.*—Payment of a savings bond will be made to a trustee in bankruptcy, a receiver of an insolvent's estate, a receiver in equity or a similar officer of the court, under the applicable provisions of subsection (a) of this section, except that payment will be made at the redemption value current on the date of payment.

Sec. 315.22. *Payment or reissue pursuant to judgment.*

(a) *Divorce.*—A decree of divorce ratifying or confirming a property settlement agreement or otherwise settling the respective interests of the parties in a bond will not be regarded as a proceeding giving effect to an attempted voluntary transfer under the provisions of sec. 315.20. Consequently, reissue of a savings bond may be made to eliminate the name of one spouse as owner, coowner, or beneficiary, or to substitute the name of one spouse for that of the other as owner, coowner, or beneficiary pursuant to such a decree. The evidence required under sec. 315.23 must be submitted in any case. Where the decree does not set out the terms of the property settlement agreement a certified copy of the agreement must also be submitted. If bonds are registered with a person other than one of the spouses as owner or coowner there must be submitted either a request for reissue by such person or a certified copy of a judgment, decree, or order of court entered in a proceeding to which he was a party, determining the extent of the interest in the bond held by the spouse whose name is to be eliminated, and reissue will be permitted only to the extent of the spouse's interest in the bonds. Payment rather than reissue will be made if requested.

(b) *Gifts causa mortis.*—A bond belonging solely to one person will be paid or reissued on the request of the person found by a court to be entitled thereto by reason of a gift *causa mortis* by the sole owner.

(c) *Date for determining rights.*—For the purpose of determining whether or not reissue shall be made under this section pursuant to judicial proceedings, the rights of all parties involved shall be those existing under these regulations at the time of the entry of the final judgment, decree, or order.

Sec. 315.23. *Evidence necessary.*— To establish the validity of judicial proceedings, there must be submitted certified copies of a final judgment, decree, or order of court and of any necessary supplementary proceedings. If the judgment, decree, or order of court was rendered more than six months prior to the presentation of the bond, there must also be submitted a certificate from the clerk of the court, under its seal, dated within six months of the presentation of the bond showing that the judgment, decree, or order of court is in full force. A request for payment by a trustee in bankruptcy must be supported by duly certified evidence of his appointment and qualification. A request for payment by a receiver of an insolvent's estate must be supported by a copy of the order appointing him, certified by the clerk of the court, under its seal, as being in full force on a date not more than six months prior to the date of the presentation of the bond. A request for payment by a receiver in equity or a similar officer of the court, other than a receiver of an insolvent's estate, must be supported by a copy of an order authorizing him to present the bond for redemption, certified by the clerk of the court, under its seal, as being in full force on a date not more than six months prior to the presentation of the bond.

SUBPART F.—RELIEF FOR LOSS, THEFT, DESTRUCTION, MUTILATION, DEFACEMENT, OR NONRECEIPT OF BONDS

Sec. 315.25. *After receipt by owner or his representative.*—Relief, either by the issue of a substitute bond marked "DUPLICATE" or by payment, may be given under section 8 of the Act of July 8, 1937, as amended (50 Stat. 481, as amended; 31 U.S.C. 738a) for the loss, theft, destruction, mutilation, or defacement of a bond after receipt by the owner or his representative. In granting relief under the act, the Secretary of the Treasury may require a bond of indemnity in such form and with such surety as may be deemed necessary for the protection of the United States of America. In all cases the bond must be identified and the applicant must submit satisfactory evidence of loss, theft, or destruction, or a satisfactory explanation of the mutilation or defacement. Relief on account of loss or theft ordinarily will not be granted until six months after the date of receipt by the Bureau of the Public Debt of the notice of such loss or theft.

Sec. 315.26. *Procedure to be followed.*—Immediate notice of the facts concerning the loss, theft, destruction, mutilation, or defacement of a bond, together with its complete description (series, year and month of issue, serial number, name and address of the registered owner or coowners), should be given to the Bureau of the Public Debt, Division of Loans and Currency Branch. Defaced bonds and all available fragments of mutilated bonds in any form whatsoever should be submitted. That office will furnish the proper application form and instructions.

The application must be made by the person or persons (including both coowners, if living), authorized under these regulations to request payment of the bond, except as follows:

(1) If the bond is in beneficiary form and the owner and beneficiary are both living, both ordinarily will be required to join in the application.

(2) If a minor named on a bond as owner, coowner, or beneficiary is not of sufficient competency and understanding to request payment, both parents ordinarily will be required to join in the application.

Sec. 315.27. *Nonreceipt of bond.*—If a bond, on original issue or on reissue, is not received from the issuing agent by the registered owner or other person to whom delivery of the bond was directed, the issuing agent should be notified as promptly as possible and given all information available about the transaction. The agent will then obtain appropriate instructions and forms. After approval of the application for relief, relief will be granted by the issuance of a bond, bearing the same issue date as the bond which was not received.

Sec. 315.28. *Recovery or receipt of bonds reported lost, stolen, destroyed or not received.*—If a bond reported lost, stolen, destroyed, or not received, is recovered or received before relief is granted, the Bureau of the Public Debt, Division of Loans and Currency Branch, should be notified promptly. If recovered or received after relief is granted, the bond should be surrendered promptly to the same office for cancellation.

SUBPART G.—INTEREST

Sec. 315.30. *General.*—Savings bonds are issued in two forms: (1) appreciation bonds, issued on a discount basis and redeemable before final maturity at increasing fixed redemption values; and (2) current income bonds, issued at par, bearing interest payable semiannually [1] and redeemable before final maturity at par or at fixed redemption values less than par.

Sec. 315.31. *Appreciation bonds.*—Bonds issued on a discount basis increase in redemption value at the end of the first half-year from issue date and at the end of each successive half-year period thereafter until their maturity date, when the full face amount becomes payable.[2] Bonds of Series E bearing issue dates of May 1, 1941, through May 1, 1949, will continue to increase in redemption value after the maturity date for twenty years and those bearing issue dates beginning with June 1, 1949, for ten years after the maturity date, in accordance with the provisions of Department Circular No. 653, current revision.[3] The increment in value (interest) on appreciation bonds is payable only on redemption of the bonds.

Sec. 315.32. *Current income bonds.*

(a) *Interest rates.*—The interest payable on a current income bond is fixed by the provisions of the Department circular offering the particular series of bonds to the public.[1]

(b) *Method of interest payments.*—Interest due on a current income bond is payable semiannually beginning six months from its issue date and will be paid on each interest payment date by check drawn to the order of the person or persons in whose names the bond is inscribed, in the same form as their names appear in the inscription on the bond, and mailed to the address of record (that given for the delivery of interest checks in the application for purchase or the request for reissue or, if no instruction is given as to the delivery of interest checks, the address given for the owner or the first-named coowner), except that:

(1) In the case of a bond registered in the form "A payable on death to B" the check will be drawn to the order of "A" alone until the Bureau of the Public Debt, Division of Loans and Currency Branch, receives notice of A's death, from which time the payment of interest will be suspended, until the bond is presented for payment or reissue. Interest so withheld will be paid to the person found to be entitled to the bond.

(2) Upon receipt of notice of the death of the coowner to whom interest is being mailed, payment of interest will be suspended until a request for change of address is received from the other coowner, if living, or, if not, until satisfactory evidence is submitted as to who is authorized to endorse and collect such checks on behalf of the estate of the last deceased coowner, in accordance with the provisions of Subpart O.

(3) Upon receipt of notice of the death of the owner of a bond, payment of interest on the bond will be suspended until satisfactory evidence is submitted as to who is authorized to endorse and collect such checks on behalf of the estate of the decedent, in accordance with the provisions of Subpart O.

---

[1] The final interest on bonds of Series H bearing issue dates of June 1, 1952, through Jan. 1, 1957, covers a period of two months, from 9½ years to 9 years, 8 months. Bonds so dated will continue to earn interest for a 10-year optional extension period, during which time interest will accrue and be paid beginning six months from the original maturity date, in accordance with the provisions of Department Circular No. 905, current revision. Since May 1, 1957, the only current income bonds on sale are those of Series H. See Department Circulars Nos. 654, Third Revision, as amended, for Series G, and 906, as amended, for Series K.

[2] Series E bonds issued on or before Apr. 30, 1952, and Series F bonds, the sale of which was terminated Apr. 30, 1952, increased in redemption value at the end of the first year from issue date; Series E bonds issued on and after May 1, 1952, and Series J bonds, the sale of which began on May 1, 1952, increased in redemption value at the end of the first half-year from issue date. The last increase in redemption value of Series E bonds issued on or after May 1, 1952, prior to the start of the 10-year optional extension period covers these periods: two months, from 9½ years through 9 years, 8 months, for bonds issued before Feb. 1, 1957; five months, from 8½ years through 8 years, 11 months, for bonds issued on or after Feb. 1, 1957, but before June 1, 1959; and three months, from 7½ years through 7 years 9 months, for bonds issued on or after June 1, 1959.

[3] See Tables of Redemption Values of that circular for extended maturity values.

(4) Whenever practicable the accounts for all current income bonds of the same series, with the same inscription, on which interest is payable on the same dates, will be consolidated and a single check will be issued on each interest payment date for interest on all such bonds. The check inscription may vary from the inscriptions on the bonds in cases of very long inscriptions or where there is lack of uniformity in the inscriptions on the bonds.

(5) The interest due at maturity in the case of bonds for which an optional extension privilege has not been granted and at the extended maturity date for all bonds for which an optional extension privilege has been granted will be paid with the principal and in the same manner. However, if the registered owner of a bond in beneficiary form dies on or after the due date without having presented and surrendered the bond for payment or authorized reissue, and is survived by the beneficiary, the interest may be paid to the legal representative of or the person entitled to the registered owner's estate. To obtain such payment, the bond with a request therefor by the beneficiary should be submitted together with evidence as required in Subpart O.

(c) *Notices affecting delivery of interest checks.*—Notices affecting the delivery of interest checks, including changes in addresses, should be sent to the Bureau of the Public Debt, Division of Loans and Currency Branch, 536 South Clark Street, Chicago, Ill. 60605. Each bond should be described in the notice by issue date, serial number, series (including year of issue), and inscription appearing on the face of the bond. The bonds should not be submitted. The notice must be signed by the owner or a coowner, or in the case of a minor or incompetent as provided in (d) or (e) of this section. A notice which would affect delivery of an interest check will be acted upon as rapidly as possible, but if the notice is not received at least one month before an interest payment date, no assurance can be given that action can be taken in time to make the change, or suspend the mailing of the interest due on that date.

(d) *Representative appointed for the estate of a minor, incompetent, absentee, etc.*—Interest on current income bonds will be paid to the representative appointed for the estate of the owner of such bonds who is a minor, incompetent, absentee, etc., in accordance with the provisions of sec. 315.50 relating to payment of the bonds. However, if the registration of the bonds does not include reference to the owner's status, the bonds should be submitted to the Bureau of the Public Debt, Division of Loans and Currency Branch, at the address shown in (c) of this section, or to a Federal Reserve bank for appropriate reissue so that interest checks may be properly drawn and delivered. They must be accompanied by the proof of appointment required by sec. 315.50.

(e) *Adult incompetent's estate having no representative.*—If an adult owner of a current income bond is incompetent to endorse and collect the interest checks and no legal guardian or similar representative is legally qualified to do so, the relative responsible for his care and support, or some other appropriate person, may apply to the Bureau of the Public Debt, Division of Loans and Currency Branch, for recognition as voluntary guardian for the purpose of receiving, endorsing, and collecting the checks. Form PD 2513 should be used in making application for this purpose.

(f) *Reissue during interest period.*—Physical reissue of a bond will be made as soon as practicable without regard to interest payment dates. If a current income bond is reissued between interest payment dates, interest for the entire period will ordinarily be paid on the next interest payment date, by check drawn to the order of the person in whose name the bond is reissued. However, if reissue is made during the month preceding an interest payment date, the interest due on the first day of the next month may in some cases be paid to the former owner or the representative of his estate.

(g) *Termination of interest.*—Interest on current income bonds will cease at maturity, or extended maturity in the case of bonds for which an optional extension period has been granted, or in case of redemption prior to maturity, on the last day of the interest period immediately preceding the date of redemption, except that, if the date of redemption falls on an interest payment date, interest will cease on that date. For example, if a bond on which interest is payable on January 1 and July 1 is redeemed on September 1, interest will cease on the preceding July 1, and no adjustment of interest will be made for the period from July 1 to September 1. The same rules apply in case of partial redemption with respect to the amount redeemed.

(h) *Endorsement of checks.*—Interest checks may be collected upon the endorsement of the payee or his authorized representative in accordance with the regulations governing the endorsement and payment of Government warrants and checks, which are contained in Department Circular No. 21, current revision (31 CFR 360). A form for the appointment of an attorney in fact for this purpose may be obtained from the Office of the Treasurer of the United States or from any Federal Reserve bank. If the owner is incompetent or deceased and no legal representative of his estate has been or will be appointed, the Bureau of the Public Debt, Division of Loans and Currency Branch (address given in (c) of this section), or a Federal Reserve bank will furnish instructions upon request.

(i) *Nonreceipt or loss of check.*—If an interest check is not received or is lost after receipt, the Bureau of the Public Debt, Division of Loans and Currency Branch, should be notified of the facts and given information concerning the amount, number, and inscription of the bonds, as well as a description of the check, if possible.

SUBPART H—GENERAL PROVISIONS FOR PAYMENT AND REDEMPTION

Sec. 315.35. *Provisions applicable both before and after maturity.*[1]—Payment of a savings bond will be made to the person or persons entitled thereto under the provisions of these regulations upon presentation and surrender of the bond with an appropriate request for payment, except that checks in payment will not be delivered to addressees in areas with respect to which the Treasury Department restricts or regulates the delivery of checks drawn against funds of the United States or any agency or instrumentality thereof.[2] Payment will be made without regard to any notice of adverse claims to a bond and no stoppage or caveat against payment in accordance with the registration will be entered.

Sec. 315.36. *Before maturity.*

(a) *At option of owner.*—Pursuant to its terms, a savings bond may not be called for redemption by the Secretary of the Treasury prior to maturity date, or extended maturity date in case of bonds for which an optional extension period has been granted, but may be redeemed in whole or in part at the option of the owner prior to maturity, or extended maturity, under the terms and conditions set forth in the offering circular for each series and in accordance with the provisions of these regulations, following presentation and surrender as provided in this subpart.

(b) *Series E.*—A bond of Series E will be redeemed at any time after two months from issue date without advance notice, at the appropriate redemption value as shown in the revision of Department Circular No. 653 current at the time of redemption.

(c) *Series H, J, and K.*—A bond of Series J or K will be redeemed on one calendar month's notice and a bond of Series H will be redeemed after six months from issue date on one calendar month's notice to a Federal Reserve bank or branch, or the Bureau of the Public Debt, Division of Loans and Currency Branch, or the Office of the Treasurer of the United States, Securities Division. Such notice may be given separately in writing or by presenting and surrendering the bond with a duly executed request for payment. Payment will be made as of the first day of the first month following by at least one full calendar month the date of receipt of notice. For example, if notice is received on June 1, payment will be made as of July 1, but if notice is received between June 2 and July 1, inclusive, payment ordinarily will be made as of August 1. If notice is given separately, the bond must be presented and surrendered with a duly executed request for payment to the same agency to which notice is given, not less than 20 days before the date on which payment is to be made. For example, if notice is received on June 15, the bond should be received not later than July 12. (See sec. 315.32(g) for provisions as to interest on current income bonds redeemed prior to maturity.) A bond of Series H will be redeemed at PAR. A bond of Series J or K will be redeemed at the appropriate redemption value as shown in the table printed on the bond, except as provided

---

[1] Bonds of Series A through D and Series F and G have all now matured. They earn no interest after maturity. Any such bonds which have not been redeemed should be presented for payment.

[2] See Department Circular No. 655, current revision (31 CFR 211).

in (d), below. (See sec. 315.37 for provisions as to notice to redeem current income bonds for which an optional extension period has been granted.)

(d) *Series K: Redemption at par.*

(1) A bond of Series K issued in exchange for matured bonds of Series E under the provisions of Department Circular No. 906 is payable at par.

(2) A bond of Series K registered in the name of a natural person or persons in their own right will be paid at par upon the request of the person entitled to the bond upon the death of the owner or either coowner.

(3) A bond of Series K held by a trustee, life tenant, or other fiduciary (exclusive of trustees of a pension, retirement, investment, insurance, annuity or similar fund, or employees' savings plan) will be paid at par upon appropriate request upon the termination, in whole or in part, of a trust, life tenancy, or other fiduciary estate by reason of the death of a natural person, but in the case of partial termination, redemption at par will be made to the extent of not more than the pro rata portion of the trust or fiduciary estate so terminated. Bonds of Series K held by a financial institution in its name as trustee of its common trust fund will be paid at par upon the request of the fiduciary upon the termination, in whole or in part, of a participating trust by reason of the death of a natural person, to the extent of not more than the pro rata portion of the common trust fund so terminated.

The option to receive payment at par under subparagraph (d) (2) and (3) of this section may be exercised by a signed request for payment or by express written notice, in either case specifying that redemption at par is desired. Payment may be postponed to the second interest payment date following the date of death, if so requested; otherwise, payment will be made in regular course. A death certificate or other acceptable evidence of death must be submitted. *In no case of redemption at par before maturity under subparagraph (d) (2) and (3) will interest be payable beyond the second interest payment date following the date of death.*

(e) *Withdrawal of request for redemption.*—An owner who has presented and surrendered a savings bond to the Treasury Department or a Federal Reserve bank or branch, or an authorized paying agent, for payment, with an appropriate request for payment, may withdraw such request if notice of intent to withdraw is given to and received by the same agency to which the bond was presented prior to the issuance of a check in payment by the Treasury Department or a Federal Reserve bank, or payment by the authorized paying agent. Such request may be withdrawn under the same conditions by the executor or administrator of the estate of a deceased owner, or by the person or persons entitled to the bond under Subpart O, or by the representative of the estate of a person under legal disability, unless presentation and surrender of the bond have cut off rights of survivorship under the provisions of Subpart M or Subpart N.

Sec. 315.37. *At or after maturity.*—Pursuant to its terms, a savings bond of any series will be paid at or after maturity at the maturity value fixed by the terms of the Department Circular offering the particular series of bonds to the public, current at the time of redemption, and in no greater amount. No advance notice will be required for the redemption of matured savings bonds except that any current income bond for which an optional extension period has been provided will, beginning with the first day of the third calendar month following the calendar month in which the bond originally matured, be regarded as unmatured until it reaches its extended maturity date, and the same notice prior to redemption will be required for it as required for bonds of the same series which have not reached original maturity.

Sec. 315.38. *Requests for payment.*

(a) *Form and execution of requests.*—A request for payment of a bond must be executed on the form appearing on the back of the bond unless (1) the bond is accepted by an authorized paying agent for payment or for presentation to a Federal Reserve bank for payment without the owner's signature to the request for payment under the provisions of Department Circular No. 888, current revision (31 CFR 330), or (2) authority is given for the execution of a separate or detached request.

(b) *Date of request.*—Ordinarily, requests executed more than six months before the date of receipt of a bond for payment will not be accepted; nor will a bond ordinarily be accepted for redemption more than three calendar months prior to the date redemption is requested under these regulations.

(c) *Identification and signature of owner.*—Unless the bond is presented under the provisions of paragraph (a) of this section or sec. 315.39(b), an owner in whose name the bond is inscribed or other person entitled to payment under the provisions of these regulations must appear before and establish his identity to an officer authorized to certify requests for payment (see Subpart I), and in the presence of such officer sign the request for payment in ink, adding in the space provided the address to which the check issued in payment is to be mailed. A signature made by mark (X) must be witnessed by at least one disinterested person in addition to the certifying officer and must be attested by endorsement in the blank space, substantially as follows: "Witness to the above signature by mark," followed by the signature and address of the witness. If the name of the owner or other person entitled to payment as it appears in the registration or in evidence on file in the Bureau of the Public Debt, Division of Loans and Currency Branch, has been changed by marriage or in any other legal manner, the signature to the request for payment should show both names and the manner in which the change was made, for example, "Mrs. Mary T. Jones Smith (Mrs. Mary T. J. Smith or Mrs. Mary T. Smith), changed by marriage from Miss Mary T. Jones," or "John R. Young, changed by order of court from Hans R. Jung." (See sec. 315.49.) No request signed in behalf of the owner or person entitled to payment by an agent or a person acting under a power of attorney will be recognized by the Treasury Department, except when the bond has been pledged in lieu of surety under Department Circular No. 154, current revision (31 CFR 225), as provided in sec. 315.16.

(d) *Certification of request.*—After the request for payment has been signed by the owner, the certifying officer should complete and sign the certificate following the request for payment and the bond should then be presented and surrendered as provided in Sec. 315.39(a).

Sec. 315.39. *Presentation and surrender.*

(a) *All series.*—Except for cases coming within the provisions of paragraph (b) of this section, after the request for payment has been duly signed by the owner and certified as provided in Subpart I, the bond should be presented and surrendered to (1) a Federal Reserve bank or branch, (2) the Bureau of the Public Debt, Division of Loans and Currency Branch, or (3) the Office of the Treasurer of the United States, Securities Division. Usually payment will be expedited by surrender to a Federal Reserve bank or branch. In all cases presentation will be at the expense and risk of the owner. Payment will be made by check drawn to the order of the registered owner or other person entitled and mailed to the address given in the request for payment or, if no address is given, to the address shown in instructions accompanying the bond.

(b) *Optional procedure limited to bonds of Series A to E, inclusive, in the names of individual owners or coowners only.*—A natural person whose name is inscribed on the face of a bond of Series A, B, C, D, or E, either as owner or coowner in his own right, may present such bond for redemption to an authorized paying agent. If such a person is not known to the paying agent, he must establish his identity to the agent. (See sec. 315.43.) Such owner or coowner must sign the request for payment, and add his home or business address. Even though the request for payment may have been signed, or signed and certified, before presentation of the bond, the representative of the paying agent must be satisfied that the person presenting the bond for payment is the owner or coowner and may require him to sign the request for payment again. If the bond is in order for payment, the paying agent will make immediate payment at the appropriate redemption value without charge to the owner or coowner. This procedure is not applicable to partial redemption cases, or deceased owner cases, or other cases in which documentary evidence is required.

Sec. 315.40. *Partial redemption.*—A bond of any series may be redeemed in part at current redemption value, but only in amounts corresponding to authorized denominations, upon presentation and surrender of the bond in accordance with sec. 315.39(a). In any case in which partial redemption is authorized before the request for payment is signed the phrase "to the extent of $_____ (face value) and reissue of the remainder" should be added to the first sentence of the request. Upon partial redemption of the bond, the remainder will be reissued as of the original issue date, as provided in Subpart J. For payment of interest on current income bonds in case of partial redemption, see Subpart G.

Sec. 315.41. *Nonreceipt or loss of checks issued in payment.*—In case a check in payment of a bond surrendered for redemption is not received within a reasonable time or in case such check is lost after receipt, notice should be given to the same agency to which the bond was surrendered for payment, accompanied by a description of the bond by series, denomination, serial number, and registration. The notice should state whether or not the check was received and should give the date upon which the bond was surrendered for payment.

SUBPART I—CERTIFYING OFFICERS

Sec. 315.42. *Persons who may certify.*—The following persons are authorized to act as certifying officers for the purpose of certifying requests for payment and forms with respect to bonds:

(a) *At United States post offices.*—Any postmaster, acting postmaster, or inspector in charge or other post office official or clerk designated for that purpose. One or more of these officials will be found at every United States post office, classified branch, or station. A post office official or clerk other than a postmaster, acting postmaster, or inspector in charge should certify in the name of the postmaster or acting postmaster, followed by his own signature and official title, for example, "John Doe, postmaster, by Richard Roe, postal cashier." Signatures of these officers should be authenticated by a legible imprint of the post office dating stamp.

(b) *At banks, trust companies, and branches.*—Any officer of any bank or trust company incorporated in the United States (including for this purpose its territories and possessions and the Commonwealth of Puerto Rico) or domestic or foreign branch of such bank or trust company; any officer of a Federal Reserve bank, Federal land bank, and Federal home loan bank; any employee of any such bank or trust company expressly authorized by the corporation for that purpose, who should sign over the title "Designated Employee"; and Federal Reserve agents and assistant Federal Reserve agents located at the several Federal Reserve banks. Certifications by any of these officers or designated employees should be authenticated by either a legible impression of the corporate seal of the bank or trust company or, in the case of banks or trust companies and their branches which are authorized issuing agents for bonds of Series E, by a legible imprint of the issuing agent's dating stamp.

(c) *Issuing agents not banks or trust companies.*—Any officer of a corporation not a bank or trust company and of any other organization which is an authorized issuing agent for bonds of Series E. All certifications by such officers must be authenticated by a legible imprint of the issuing agent's dating stamp.

(d) *Commissioned and warrant officers of Armed Forces.*—Commissioned and warrant officers of any of the Armed Forces of the United States, but only for members and the families of members of their respective services and civilian employees at posts or bases or stations. Such certifying officer should indicate his rank and state that the person signing the request is one of the class whose request he is authorized to certify.

(e) *United States officials.*—Judges, clerks, and deputy clerks of United States courts, including United States courts for the territories, possessions, the Commonwealth of Puerto Rico, and the Canal Zone; United States commissioners; United States attorneys; United States collectors of customs and their deputies; Regional commissioners and district directors of Internal Revenue and Internal Revenue agents; the officer in charge of any home, hospital, or other facility of the Veterans Administration, but only for patients and employees of such facilities; certain officers of Federal penal institutions designated for that purpose by the Secretary of the Treasury; certain officers of the United States Public Health Service Hospitals at Lexington, Ky., and Fort Worth, Tex., and of United States Marine Hospitals at Fort Stanton, N. Mex., and Carville, La., designated for that purpose by the Secretary of the Treasury (in each case, however, only for inmates or employees of the institution involved).

(f) *Officers authorized in particular localities.*—Certain designated officers in the Treasury Department; the Governor and Treasurer of Puerto Rico; the Governor and Commissioner of Finance of the Virgin Islands; the Governor and Director of Finance of Guam; the Governor and Director of Administrative Services of American Samoa; the Governor, paymaster, or acting paymaster and collector or acting collector of the Panama Canal; and postmasters and acting postmasters of the Bureau of Posts of the Canal Zone.

(g) *In foreign countries.*—In a foreign country requests for payment may be signed in the presence of and be certified by any United States diplomatic or consular representative, or the manager or other officer of a foreign branch of a bank or trust company incorporated in the United States whose signature is attested by an impression of the corporate seal or is certified to the Treasury Department. If such an officer is not available, requests for payment may be signed in the presence of and be certified by a notary or other officer authorized to administer oaths, but his official character and jurisdiction should be certified by a United States diplomatic or consular officer under seal of his office.

(h) *Special provisions.*—In the event none of the officers authorized to certify requests for payment of bonds is readily accessible, the Commissioner of the Public Debt, the Deputy Commissioner of the Public Debt in Charge of the Chicago Office, the Treasurer of the United States, or any Federal Reserve bank or branch is authorized to make special provision for any particular case.

Sec. 315.43. *General instructions to certifying officers.*—A certifying officer should require that a person presenting bonds, or forms with respect thereto, establish his identity by positive and reliable evidence before the bonds or forms are signed, unless the presenter is personally well known to the officer. Such officer and, if he is an officer or employee of an organization, the organization will be held fully responsible for the adequacy of the identification. The certifying officer should place an adequate notation on the back of the bond or form, or on a separate record, showing exactly how identification was established. The certifying officer must affix to the certification his official signature, title, seal or dating stamp, address (if not shown in the seal or stamp), and the date of execution. Officers of Veterans Administration facilities, Public Health Service hospitals, Marine hospitals, and Federal penal institutions should use the seal of the particular institution or service, where such seal is available. A certifying officer other than a post office official, officer of a bank or trust company, or officer of an issuing agent who does not possess an official seal should add a statement to that effect to his certification.

Sec. 315.44. *Interested person not to certify.*—A certifying officer may not certify a request for payment of a bond, or a form with respect to a bond, in which he has or is acquiring an interest, either in his own right or in a representative capacity.

SUBPART J—REISSUE AND DENOMINATIONAL EXCHANGE

Sec. 315.45. *General.*—Reissue of a bond may be made only under the conditions specified in these regulations. Reissue is not authorized solely for the purpose of effecting an exchange as between authorized denominations, but in case of authorized reissue the new bond or bonds may be issued in any authorized denomination or denominations.

Reissue will not be made if the request therefor is received less than one full calendar month before the maturity date, except for bonds of Series E and H for which optional extension periods have been provided in Department Circulars Nos. 653 and 905, current revisions (31 CFR 316 and 332). In the case of such bonds, reissue will not be made if the request is received less than one full month before the extended maturity date. However, a request for reissue of a bond received prior to its maturity, or its extended maturity date, will be effective to establish ownership as though the requested reissue had been made.

A request for reissue of a bond received on or after its maturity, or its extended maturity date, will not be effective to name a coowner or beneficiary or to promote a beneficiary to a coowner, but requests for reissue in the names of persons who have become entitled by operation of law will be recognized as establishing the right of those persons to receive payment.

Reissues under the provisions of this subpart may be made only at (1) a Federal Reserve bank or branch, (2) the Bureau of the Public Debt, Division of Loans and Currency Branch, or (3) the Office of the Treasurer of the United States, Securities Division.

Sec. 315.46. *Requests for reissue.*—A request for reissue should be made on the prescribed form by the person authorized under these regulations to make such request. Appropriate forms may be obtained from any Federal Reserve bank, the Office of the Treasurer of the United States, or the Bureau of the Public Debt, Division of Loans and Currency Branch.

Sec. 315.47. *Effective date.*—In any case of authorized reissue, the Treasury Department will treat the receipt by (1) a Federal Reserve bank or branch, or (2) the Bureau of the Public Debt, Division of Loans and Currency Branch, or (3) the Office of the Treasurer of the United States, Securities Division, of a bond and an appropriate request for reissue thereof as determining the date upon which the reissue is effective. If the owner or either coowner of a bond dies after he has presented and surrendered the bond for authorized reissue, the bond will be regarded as though reissued in the decedent's lifetime.

Sec. 315.48. *Correction of errors.*—Reissue of a bond may be made to correct an error in the original issue, upon appropriate request supported by satisfactory proof of the error.

Sec. 315.49. *Change of name.*—An owner, coowner, or beneficiary whose name is changed by marriage, divorce, annulment, order of court, or in any other legal manner after the issue of a bond should submit the bond with a request on Form PD 1474 for reissue to substitute the new name for the name inscribed on the bond. The signature to the request for reissue should show the new name, the manner in which the change was made and the former name. If the change of name was made other than by marriage, the request must be supported by satisfactory proof of the change.

SUBPART K—MINORS, INCOMPETENTS, AGED PERSONS, ABSENTEES, ETC.

Sec. 315.50. *Payment to representative of estate.*—If the form of registration of a savings bond indicates that the owner is a minor, an incompetent, aged person, absentee, etc., and that there is a representative of his estate, payment will be made to such representative. During the lifetime of such owner, the representative of his estate will be recognized as entitled to obtain payment of a bond registered in the name of the ward as owner or coowner, or of a bond to which the ward has become entitled. After the death of such owner, his representative, so long as he is authorized to act for the estate, will be entitled to obtain payment of a bond to which the ward was solely entitled. If the form of registration does not indicate there is a representative of the estate of a minor owner or coowner, a notice that there is such a representative will not be accepted for the purpose of preventing payment to the minor or to a parent or other person on behalf of the minor, as provided in secs. 315.51 and 315.52.

The request for payment appearing on the back of a bond should be signed by the representative as such, for example, "John A. Jones, guardian (committee) of the estate of Henry W. Smith, a minor (an incompetent)." Unless the form of registration gives the name of the representative requesting payment, a certificate, or a certified copy of the letters of appointment, from the court making the appointment, under court seal, or other proof of qualification if not appointed by a court, should be submitted with the bond.

Sec. 315.51. *Payment to minors.*—If the owner of a savings bond is a minor and the form of registration does not indicate that there is a representative of his estate, payment will be made to him upon his request, provided he is of sufficient competency to sign his name to the request for payment and to understand the nature of the transaction. In general, the fact that the request for payment has been signed by a minor and duly certified will be accepted as sufficient proof of competency and understanding.

Sec. 315.52. *Payment to a parent or other person on behalf of a minor.*—If the owner of a savings bond is a minor and the form of registration does not indicate that there is a representative of his estate, and if such minor owner is not of sufficient competency to sign his name to the request for payment and to understand the nature of the transaction, payment will be made to either parent of the minor with whom he resides or, if the minor does not reside with either parent, then to the person who furnishes his chief support. His parent or the person furnishing his chief support should execute the request for payment and furnish a certificate, which may be typed or written on the back of the bond, as to his right to act for the minor. If a parent signs the request, the certificate and signature thereto should be in substantially the following form:

"I certify that I am the mother (or father) of John C. Jones and the person with whom he resides. He is _____ years of age and is not of sufficient competency and understanding to make this request.

"Mrs. Mary Jones on behalf of John C. Jones."

If a person other than a parent signs the request, the certificate and signature thereto, including a reference to the person's relationship, if any, to the minor, should be in substantially the following form:

"I certify that John C. Jones does not reside with either parent and that I furnish his chief support. He is _____ years of age and is not of sufficient competency and understanding to make this request.

"Mrs Alice Brown, grandmother, on behalf of John C. Jones."

Sec. 315.53. *Payment or reinvestment upon request of voluntary guardian of incompetent.*—If the adult owner of bonds is incompetent to request and receive payment thereof and no other person is legally qualified to do so, the relative responsible for his care and support or some other person may submit an application as voluntary guardian for redemption of the bonds in the following cases:

(a) Where the proceeds of the bonds are needed to pay expenses already incurred, or to be incurred during any 90-day period, for the support of the incompetent or his legal dependents, bonds belonging to the incompetent, not exceeding $1,000 (face value), may be submitted for redemption;

(b) Where the bond has matured and it is desired to redeem it and reinvest the proceeds in savings bonds. The proceeds of any matured appreciation type bonds ordinarily will be required to be reinvested in Series E bonds. The proceeds of matured current income bonds may be invested in Series H or Series E bonds. The new bonds must be registered in the name of the incompetent followed by the words "an incompetent." A living coowner or beneficiary named on the matured bond must be designated on the new bonds unless he is a competent adult and furnishes a certified statement consenting to omission of his name. If an amount insufficient to purchase an additional bond of any authorized denomination of any series remains after the reinvestment, the voluntary guardian may, if he so desires, furnish additional funds sufficient to purchase another bond of either series in the lowest available denomination. If additional funds are not furnished, the remaining amount will be paid to the voluntary guardian for the use and benefit of the incompetent.

Sec. 315.54. *Reissue.*—A bond of which a minor or other person under legal disability is the owner or in which he has an interest may be reissued upon an authorized reissue transaction under the following conditions:

(a) A minor of sufficient competency to sign his name to the request and to understand the nature of the transaction may request reissue to add a coowner or beneficiary to a bond registered in his name alone or to which he is entitled in his own right.

(b) A bond on which a minor is named as beneficiary or coowner may be reissued in the name of a custodian for the minor under a statute authorizing gifts to minors upon the request of the adult whose name appears on the bond as owner or coowner.

(c) Except to the extent provided in (a) and (b) of this section, reissue will be restricted to a form of registration which does not adversely affect the existing ownership or interest of the minor or such other person. Requests for reissue should be executed by the person authorized to request payment under secs. 315.50 and 315.52, or who may request recognition as a voluntary guardian under sec. 315.53 and in the same manner.

SUBPART L—NATURAL PERSON AS SOLE OWNER

Sec. 315.55. *Payment.*—A savings bond registered in the name of a natural person in his own right, without a coowner or beneficiary, will be paid to him during his lifetime under Subpart H. Upon the death of the owner such bond will be considered as belonging to his estate and will be paid under Subpart O, except as otherwise provided in these regulations.

Sec. 315.56. *Reissue for certain purposes.*—A savings bond registered in the name of a natural person in his own right may be reissued upon appropriate request by him (subject to the provisions of sec. 315.54), upon presentation and surrender during his lifetime, for the following purposes:

(a) *Addition of a coowner or beneficiary.*—To name another natural person as coowner or as beneficiary. Form PD 1787 should be used.

(b) *Divorce or annulment.*—To name as registered owner the other party to a divorce or annulment occurring after issue of the bond. Form PD 3360 should be used.

(c) *Certain degrees of relationship.*—To name as registered owner a person related to the owner as provided in sec. 315.61(a)(1)(i), with a beneficiary or coowner, if so desired. Form PD 3360 should be used.

(d) *Trustees.*—To name the trustee of (1) a personal trust estate created by the owner, or (2) a personal trust estate created by other than the owner if a beneficiary of the trust and the owner are related as provided in sec. 315.61(a) (1)(i). Form PD 1851 should be used.

SUBPART M—TWO NATURAL PERSONS AS COOWNERS

Sec. 315.60. *Payment during the lives of both coowners.*—A savings bond registered in coownership form, for example, "John A. Jones or Mrs. Mary C. Jones," will be paid to either upon his separate request, and upon payment to him the other shall cease to have any interest in the bond. If both request payment jointly, payment will be made by check drawn to their order jointly, for example, "John A. Jones AND Mrs. Mary C. Jones."

Sec. 315.61. *Reissue during the lives of both coowners.*

(a) *General.*—A bond registered in coownership form may be reissued upon its presentation and surrender during the lifetime and competency of both coowners, upon the request of both, as follows:

(1) In the name of either coowner, alone or with a new coowner or beneficiary—

(i) If the coowner whose name is to remain on the bond is related to the coowner whose name is to be eliminated as: husband, wife; parent, child (including stepchild); brother, sister (including the half blood, stepbrother, stepsister, or brother or sister through adoption); grandparent, grandchild; great grandparent, great grandchild; uncle, aunt, nephew, niece (including a child of a brother or sister of the present spouse); granduncle, grandaunt, grandnephew, grandniece; father-in-law, mother-in-law, son-in-law, daughter-in-law, brother-in-law, sister-in-law.

(ii) If one of them marries after issue of the bond.

(iii) If they are divorced or legally separated from each other, or their marriage is annulled, after issue of the bond.

(2) In the name of a third person related to either coowner, as provided in (a)(1)(i) of this section, with a coowner or beneficiary, if so desired. (Form PD 1938 should be used for any of the above classes.)

(3) In the name of a trustee of (i) a personal trust estate created by either coowner, or (ii) a personal trust estate created by other than a coowner if a beneficiary of the trust is related to either coowner as provided in (a)(1)(i) of this section.

Form PD 1851 should be used.

(b) *Minor coowners.*—A request for reissue signed by a minor coowner of sufficient competency to sign his name to the request and understand the nature of the transaction, and for whose estate no representative has been appointed, will be recognized if the bond is to be reissued in his name alone, or in his name with a new coowner or beneficiary. A request for reissue to eliminate the other coowner, signed in behalf of a minor coowner by the representative of his estate will be recognized; however, a request to eliminate the name of the minor will be recognized only if supported by evidence that a court has ordered the representative to request such reissue (see sec. 315.23). A minor coowner for whose estate no representative has been appointed may be promoted to sole owner upon the request of the competent coowner. A competent coowner may, upon his own request, have the bond reissued to remove his name and name a custodian for the minor under a statute authorizing gifts to minors.

(c) *Incompetent coowners.*—Reissue will not be made if one coowner is incompetent and a representative of the incompetent's estate has not been appointed, except to add "an incompetent" after his name or to eliminate the other coowner from the registration. If there is a representative, the provisions of paragraph (b) of this section apply as to his execution of a request for reissue.

Sec. 315.62. *After the death of one or both coowners.*—If either coowner dies without the bond having been presented and surrendered for payment or authorized reissue, the survivor will be recognized as the sole and absolute owner. Thereafter, payment or reissue will be made as though the bond were registered in the name of the survivor alone (see Subpart L), except that a request for reissue by him must be supported by proof of death of the other coowner, and except further that after the death of the survivor proof of death of both coowners and of the order in which they died will be required. The presentation and surrender of a bond by one coowner for payment establishes his right to receive the proceeds of the bond, and if he should die before the transaction is completed, payment will be made to the legal representative of, or persons entitled to, his estate in accordance with the provisions of Subpart O. If either coowner dies after the bond has been presented and surrendered for authorized reissue (see sec 315.47), the bond will be regarded as though reissued during his lifetime.

Sec. 315.63. *Upon death of both coowners in a common disaster, etc.*—If both coowners die under such conditions that it cannot be established either by presumption of law or otherwise which died first, the bond will be considered as belonging to the estates of both equally, and payment or reissue will be made accordingly. (See Subpart O.)

SUBPART N—TWO NATURAL PERSONS AS OWNER AND BENEFICIARY

Sec. 315.65. *During the lifetime of the registered owner.*—A savings bond registered in beneficiary form, for example, "John A. Jones payable on death to Mrs. Mary C. Jones," will be paid or reissued upon presentation and surrender during the lifetime of the registered owner, as follows:

(a) *Payment.*—The bond will be paid to the registered owner during his lifetime upon his properly executed request as though no beneficiary had been named in the registration. The presentation and surrender of the bond by the registered owner for payment establishes his exclusive right to the proceeds of the bond, and if he should die before the transaction is completed, payment will be made to the legal representative of, or the persons entitled to, his estate upon receipt of proof of the appointment and qualification of the representative or the identity of the persons entitled, in accordance with the provisions of Subpart O.

(b) *Reissue.*

(1) The bond will be reissued on a duly certified request of the owner:

(i) To name the beneficiary designated on the bond as coowner. Form PD 1787 should be used.

(ii) To eliminate his name as owner and to name as owner a custodian for the beneficiary, if a minor, under a statute authorizing gifts to minors. Form PD 3360 should be used.

(iii) To eliminate the beneficiary, to substitute another person as beneficiary, or to name another person as coowner, if the request of the owner is supported by the beneficiary's duly certified consent to elimination of his name or by proof of his death.[1] Form PD 1787 should be used.

(iv) In the name of a trustee of (1) a personal trust estate created by the owner, or (2) a personal trust estate created by other than the owner if the owner and a beneficiary of the trust are related as provided in sec. 315.61(a) (1)(i), and the request of the owner is supported by the duly certified consent of the beneficiary, or by proof of his death.[1] Form PD 1851 should be used by the owner and the beneficiary.

Sec. 315.66. *After the death of the registered owner.*—If the registered owner dies without the bond having been presented and surrendered for payment or authorized reissue and is survived by the beneficiary, upon proof of death of the owner the beneficiary will be recognized as the sole and absolute owner, and payment or reissue will be made as though the bond were registered in his name alone (see Subpart L).

SUBPART O—DECEASED OWNERS

Sec. 315.70. *General.*—Upon the death of the owner of a savings bond who is not survived by a coowner or designated beneficiary and who had not during his lifetime presented and surrendered the bond for payment or an authorized reissue, the bond will be considered as belonging to his estate and will be paid or reissued accordingly as hereinafter provided, except that reissue under this subpart will not be permitted if otherwise in conflict with these regulations. If

---

[1] The provisions of this section do not apply to bonds on which the Treasurer of the United States of America is named as beneficiary.

the person entitled is an alien who is a resident of an area with respect to which the Treasury Department restricts or regulates the delivery of checks drawn against funds of the United States of America or any agency or instrumentality thereof, payment of, and interest on, a bond will not be made so long as the restriction applies.[1] A creditor is entitled only to payment of a bond to the extent of not more than his claim.

Sec. 315.71. *Special provisions applicable to small amounts of savings bonds, interest checks or redemption checks.*—Entitlement to, or the authority to dispose of, a small amount of bonds and checks issued in payment thereof or in payment of interest thereon, belonging to the estate of a decedent, may be established through the use of certain short forms, according to the aggregate face amount of bonds and checks involved (excluding checks representing interest on the bonds), as indicated by the following table:

Amount	Circumstances	Form	To be executed by—
$100	No administration	PD 2216	Person who paid burial expenses.
500	Estate being administered	PD 2488-1	Executor or administrator.
500	Estate settled	PD 2458	Former executor or administrator, attorney, or other qualified person.

Sec. 315.72. *Estates administered.*

(a) *In course of administration.*—If the estate of a decedent is being administered in court, the bond will be paid to the duly qualified representative of the estate or will be reissued in the names of the persons entitled to share in the estate, upon the request of the representative and compliance with the following requirements:

(1) Where there are two or more legal representatives, all must join in the request for payment or reissue, except as provided in secs. 315.77 and 315.78.

(2) The request for payment or reissue should be signed in the form, for example, "John A. Jones, administrator of the estate (or executor of the will) of Henry W. Jones, deceased," and must be supported by proof of the representative's authority in the form of a court certificate or a certified copy of the representative's letters of appointment. The certificate or the certification to the letters must be under seal of the court and, except in the case of a corporate representative, must contain a statement that the appointment is in full force and should be dated within six months of the date of presentation of the bond, unless the certificate or letters show that the appointment was made within one year immediately prior to such presentation.

(3) In case of reissue the legal representative of the estate should certify that each person in whose name reissue is requested is entitled to the extent specified for each and has consented to such reissue. A request for reissue by the legal representative should be made on Form PD 1455. If a person in whose name reissue is requested desires to name a coowner or beneficiary, such person should execute an additional request for that purpose, using Form PD 1787.

(b) *After settlement through court proceedings.*—If the estate of the decedent has been settled in court, the bond will be paid to, or reissued in the name of, the person entitled thereto as determined by the court. The request for payment or reissue should be made by the person shown to be entitled, supported by a duly certified copy of the representative's final account as approved by the court, decree of distribution, or other pertinent court records, supplemented, if there are two or more persons having an apparent interest in the bond, by an agreement executed by them concerning the disposition of the bond. Form PD 1787 should be used by the person entitled if he wishes to name a coowner or beneficiary.

Sec. 315.73. *Estates not administered.*

(a) *Special provisions under State laws.*—If, under State law, a person has been recognized or appointed to receive or distribute the assets of a decedent's estate without regular administration, his request for payment or reissue of a bond to the person or persons entitled will be accepted provided he submits appropriate evidence of his authority.

---

[1] See Department Circular No. 655, current revision (31 CFR 211).

(b) *Agreement of persons entitled.*—When it appears that no legal representative of a decedent's estate has been or will be appointed, the bond will be paid to, or reissued in the name of, the person or persons entitled, including those entitled as donees of a gift *causa mortis*, pursuant to an agreement and request by all persons entitled to share in the decedent's personal estate. A form of agreement for settlement without administration, Form PD 1946–1, should be used for cases in which the total face amount of bonds and redemption and interest checks belonging to the decedent's estate is in excess of $500. Where the total face amount does not exceed $500, Form PD 1946 may be used. If the persons entitled to share in the personal estate include minors or incompetents, payment or reissue of the bond will not be permitted without administration except to them or in their names unless their interests are otherwise protected to the satisfaction of the Treasury Department.

SUBPART P—FIDUCIARIES

Sec. 315.75. *Payment.*—A savings bond registered in the name of a fiduciary or otherwise belonging to a fiduciary estate will be paid to the fiduciary or fiduciaries in accordance with the provisions of secs. 315.77 and 315.78.

Sec. 315.76. *Reissue.*

(a) *In the name of person entitled.*

(1) *Distribution of trust estate in kind.*—A bond to which a beneficiary of a trust estate has become lawfully entitled in his own right or in a fiduciary capacity, in whole or in part, under the terms of a trust instrument, will be reissued in his name to the extent of his interest, upon the request of the trustee or trustees and their certification that such person is entitled and has agreed to reissue in his name.

(2) *After termination of trust estate.*—If the person who would be lawfully entitled to a bond upon the termination of a trust does not desire to have distribution made to him in kind, as provided in paragraph (1) above, the trustee or trustees should present the bond for payment before the estate is terminated. If, however, the estate is terminated without such payment or reissue having been made, the bond will thereafter be paid to or reissued in the name of the person lawfully entitled upon his request and satisfactory proof of ownership, supplemented, if there are two or more persons having any apparent interest in the bond, by an agreement executed by all such persons concerning the disposition of the bond.

(3) *Upon termination of guardianship estate.*—If the estate of a minor or incompetent or of an absentee is terminated, during the ward's lifetime, a bond registered to show that there is a representative of the estate will be reissued in the name of the former ward upon the representative's request and certification that the former ward is entitled and has agreed to reissue in his name (Form PD 1455 should be used), or will be paid to or reissued in the name of the former ward upon his own request, supported in either case by satisfactory evidence that his disability has been removed or that an absentee has returned to claim his property. Certification by the representative that a former minor has attained his majority, that a former incompetent has been legally restored to competency, that a legal disability of a female ward has been removed by marriage, if the State law so provides, or that an absentee has appeared to claim his property, will ordinarily be accepted as sufficient (see sec. 315.77 if the representative's name is not shown in the registration). Upon the termination of the estate as the result of the death of the ward, a bond registered to show that there is a representative of his estate will be reissued in accordance with the provisions of Subpart O.

(4) *Upon termination of life estate.*—Upon the death of a life tenant, a bond registered in his name as life tenant may be reissued in the name of the person or persons entitled pursuant to an agreement and request of all of the persons having an interest in the remainder.

(b) *In the name of a succeeding fiduciary.*—If a fiduciary in whose name a bond is registered has been succeeded by another, the bond will re reissued in the name of the succeeding fiduciary upon appropriate request and satisfactory evidence of successorship. Form PD 1455 should be used.

(c) *In the name of financial institution as trustee of common trust fund.*—A bond held by a bank, trust company, or other financial institution as a trustee, guardian or similar representative, executor or administrator may be reissued in its name as trustee of its common trust fund to the extent that participation therein by the institution in such capacity is authorized by law or applicable regulations. A request for reissue to the institution as trustee of its common trust fund should be executed on its behalf in the capacity in which the bond is held and by the cofiduciary, if any. Form PD 1455 should be used.

Sec. 315.77. *Requests for reissue or payment prior to maturity or extended maturity.*—The following rules apply to both requests for reissue and payment by fiduciaries: A request for reissue or payment prior to maturity, or extended maturity for bonds for which an optional extension period has been provided, must be signed by all acting fiduciaries unless by express statute, decree of court, or the terms of the instrument under which the fiduciaries are acting, some one or more of them may properly execute the request. If the fiduciaries named in the registration are still acting, no further evidence of authority will be required. Otherwise, a request must be supported by evidence as specified below:

(a) *Fiduciaries by title only.*—If the bond is registered in the titles, without the names, of fiduciaries not acting as a board, satisfactory evidence of their incumbency must be furnished. except in the case of bonds registered in the title of public officers as trustees.

(b) *Succeeding fiduciaries.*—If the fiduciaries in whose names the bond is registered have been succeeded by other fiduciaries, satisfactory evidence of successorship must be furnished.

(c) *Boards, committees, etc.*—A savings bond registered in the name of a board, committee, commission, or other body, empowered to act as a unit and to hold title to the property of a religious, educational, charitable, or nonprofit organization or public corporation will be paid upon a request for payment signed in the name of the board or other body by an authorized officer thereof. A request so signed and duly certified will ordinarily be accepted without further evidence of the officer's authority. The check in payment of the bond will be drawn in the name of the board or other body as fiduciary for the organization named in the registration or shown by satisfactory evidence to be entitled as successor thereto.

(d) *Corporate fiduciaries.*—If a public or private corporation or a political body, such as a State or county, is acting as a fiduciary, a request must be signed in the name of the corporation or other body in the fiduciary capacity in which it is acting, by an authorized officer thereof. A request so signed and duly certified will ordinarily be accepted without further evidence of the officer's authority.

(e) *Registration not disclosing trust or other fiduciary estate.*—If the registration of the bond does not show that it belongs to a trust or other fiduciary estate or does not identify the estate to which it belongs, satisfactory evidence of ownership must be furnished in addition to any other evidence required by this section.

Sec. 315.78. *Requests for payment at or after maturity.*—A request for payment at or after the maturity date, or extended maturity date for bonds for which an optional extension period has been provided, signed by any one or more acting fiduciaries, will be accepted. Payment ordinarily will be made by check drawn as the bond is inscribed.

SUBPART Q—PRIVATE ORGANIZATIONS (CORPORATIONS, ASSOCIATIONS, PARTNERSHIPS, ETC.) AND GOVERNMENTAL AGENCIES, UNITS, AND OFFICERS

Sec. 315.80. *Payment to corporations or unincorporated associations.*—A savings bond registered in the name of a private corporation or an unincorporated association will be paid to the corporation or unincorporated association upon request for payment on its behalf by a duly authorized officer thereof. The signature to the request should be in the form, for example, "The Jones Coal Company, a corporation, by John Jones, President," or "The Lotus Club, an unincorporated association, by William A. Smith, Treasurer." A request for payment so signed and duly certified will ordinarily be accepted without further evidence of the officer's authority.

Sec. 315.81. *Payment to partnerships.*—A savings bond registered in the name of an existing partnership will be paid upon a request for payment signed by a general partner. The signature to the request should be in the form, for example, "Smith and Jones, a partnership, by John Jones, a general partner." A request for payment so signed and duly certified will ordinarily be accepted as sufficient evidence that the partnership is still in existence and that the person signing the request is duly authorized.

Sec. 315.82. *Reissue or payment to successors of corporations, unincorporated associations, or partnerships.*—A savings bond registered in the name of a private corporation, an unincorporated association, or a partnership which has been succeeded by another corporation, unincorporated association, or partnership by operation of law or otherwise, as the result of merger, consolidation, incorporation, reincorporation, conversion, or reorganization, or which has been lawfully succeeded in any manner whereby the business or activities of the original organization are continued without substantial change, will be paid to or reissued in the name of the succeeding organization upon appropriate request on its behalf, supported by satisfactory evidence of successorship.   Form PD 1540 should be used.

Sec. 315.83. *Reissue or payment on dissolution of corporation or partnership.*

(a) *Corporations.*—A savings bond registered in the name of a private corporation which is in the process of dissolution will be paid to the authorized representative of the corporation upon a duly executed request for payment, supported by satisfactory evidence of the representative's authority.   Upon the termination of dissolution proceedings, the bond may be reissued in the names of those persons, other than creditors, entitled to the assets of the corporation, to the extent of their respective interests.   Reissue under this subsection will be made upon the duly executed request of the authorized representative of the corporation and upon proof that all statutory provisions governing the dissolution of the corporation have been complied with and that the persons in whose names reissue is requested are entitled and have agreed to the reissue. If the dissolution proceedings are under the direction of a court, a certified copy of an order of the court, showing the authority of the representative to make the distribution requested, must be furnished.

(b) *Partnerships.*—A savings bond registered in the name of a partnership which has been dissolved by death or withdrawal of a partner, or in any other manner, will be paid upon a request for payment by any partner or partners authorized by law to act on behalf of the dissolved partnership, or will be paid to or reissued in the names of the persons, other than creditors, entitled thereto as the result of such dissolution to the extent of their respective interests, upon their request supported by satisfactory evidence of their title, including proof that the debts of the partnership have been paid or properly provided for.   Form PD 2514 should be used.

Sec. 315.84. *Payment to institutions (churches, hospitals, homes, schools, etc.).*—A savings bond registered in the name of a church, hospital, home, school, or similar institution without reference in the registration to the manner in which it is organized or governed or to the manner in which title to its property is held will be paid upon a request for payment signed on behalf of such institution by an authorized representative.   For the purpose of this section, a request for payment signed by a pastor of a church, superintendent of a hospital, president of a college, or by any official generally recognized as having authority to conduct the financial affairs of the particular institution will ordinarily be accepted without further proof of his authority.   The signature to the request should be in the form, for example, "Shriners' Hospital for Crippled Children, St. Louis, Mo., by William A. Smith, superintendent," or "St. Mary's Roman Catholic Church, Albany, N.Y., by John Jones, pastor."

Sec. 315.85. *Reissue in name of trustee or agent for investment purposes.*— A savings bond registered in the name of a religious, educational, charitable, or nonprofit organization, whether or not incorporated, may be reissued in the name of a bank, trust company, or other financial institution, or an individual, as trustee or agent under an agreement with the organization under which the trustee or agent holds funds of the organization, in whole or in part, for the purpose of investing and reinvesting the principal and paying the income to the organization.   Form PD 2177 should be used and should be signed on behalf of the organization by an authorized officer.

Sec. 315.86. *Reissue upon termination of investment agency.*—A savings bond registered in the name of a bank, trust company, or other financial institution, or individual, as agent for investment purposes only, under an agreement with a religious, educational, charitable, or nonprofit organization, may be reissued in the name of the organization upon termination of the agency.   The former agent should request such reissue and should certify that the organization is entitled by reason of the termination of the agency, using Form PD 1455. If such request and certification are not obtainable, the bond will be reissued in the name of the organization upon its own request, supported by satisfactory evidence of the termination of the agency.

Sec. 315.87. *Payment to governmental agencies and units.*—A savings bond registered in the name of a State, county, city, town, or village, or in the name of a Federal, State, or local governmental agency such as a board, commission, or corporation, will be paid upon a request signed in the name of the governmental agency or unit by a duly authorized officer thereof. A request for payment so signed and duly certified will ordinarily be accepted without further proof of the officer's authority.

Sec. 315.88. *Payment to Government officers.*—A savings bond registered in the official title of an officer of a Government agency or unit will be paid upon a request for payment signed by the designated officer. The fact that the request for payment is so signed and duly certified will ordinarily be accepted as proof that the person signing is the incumbent of the designated office.

SUBPART R—MISCELLANEOUS PROVISIONS

Sec. 315.90. *Waiver of regulations.*—The Secretary of the Treasury reserves the right, in his discretion, to waive or modify any provision or provisions of these regulations in any particular case or class of cases for the convenience of the United States of America or in order to relieve any person or persons of unnecessary hardship, if such action would not be inconsistent with law and would not impair any existing rights, and if he is satisfied that such action would not subject the United States of America to any substantial expense or liability.

Sec. 315.91. *Additional requirements; bond of indemnity; taxpayer identifying numbers.*—The Secretary of the Treasury may require (a) such additional evidence as he may consider necessary or advisable, (b) a bond of indemnity, with or without surety, in any case where he may consider such a bond necessary for the protection of the interests of the United States of America, and (c) without prior notice, that appropriate taxpayer identifying numbers be furnished for issue, reissue, or payment of any savings bond.

Sec. 315.92 *Preservation of rights.*—Nothing contained in these regulations shall be construed to limit or restrict existing rights which holders of savings bonds heretofore issued may have acquired under the circulars offering the bonds for sale or under the regulations in force at the time of purchase.

Sec. 315.93. *Supplements, amendments, or revisions.*—The Secretary of the Treasury may at any time, or from time to time, prescribe additional, supplemental, amendatory, or revised rules and regulations governing United States savings bonds.

JOHN K. CARLOCK,
Fiscal Assistant Secretary of the Treasury.

Exhibit 8.—Sixth revision, December 23, 1964, of Department Circular No. 653, offering of United States savings bonds, Series E

TREASURY DEPARTMENT,
Washington, December 23, 1964.

Department Circular No. 653, Fifth Revision, dated September 23, 1959, as amended (31 CFR 316), is hereby further amended and issued as the Sixth Revision.[1]

AUTHORITY: Secs. 316.1 to 316.14 issued under authority of sections 22 and 25 of the Second Liberty Bond Act, as amended, 49 Stat. 21, as amended, and 73 Stat. 621 (31 U.S.C. 757c, 757c–1).

Sec. 316.1 *Offering of bonds.*—The Secretary of the Treasury offers for sale to the people of the United States, United States savings bonds of Series E, hereinafter generally referred to as Series E bonds. These bonds are substantially

---

[1] The basic terms of the bonds offered under the Fifth Revision have not been changed. The material in the Fifth Revision and its three amendments has been reorganized and edited in connection with the publication of the 1965 edition of Title 31 of the Code of Federal Regulations.

a continuation of the Series E bonds heretofore available. This offering of bonds will continue until terminated by the Secretary of the Treasury.

Sec. 316.2. *Description of bonds currently offered.*—(a) *General.*—Series E bonds bear a facsimile of the signature of the Secretary of the Treasury and of the Seal of the Treasury Department. The bonds are issued only in registered form and are nontransferable.

(b) *Denominations and prices.*—Series E bonds are issued on a discount basis at 75 percent of their face values. The denominations and issue prices are:

Denomination (face value)	Issue (purchase) price
$25	$18.75
50	37.50
75	56.25
100	75.00
200	150.00
500	375.00
1,000	750.00
10,000	7,500.00
100,000 [1]	75,000.00

(c) *Inscription and issue.*—At the time of issue the issuing agent will (1) inscribe on the face of each Series E bond the name and address of the owner, and the name of the beneficiary, if any, or the name and address of one coowner, and the name of the other coowner, (2) enter in the upper right-hand portion of the bond the issue date, and (3) imprint the agent's dating stamp in the lower right-hand portion to show the date the bond is actually inscribed. A Series E bond shall be valid only if an authorized issuing agent receives payment therefor and duly inscribes, dates, stamps, and makes delivery of the bond in accordance with the purchaser's instructions. The Treasury Department may require, without prior notice, that the appropriate identifying number as required on tax returns and other documents submitted to the Internal Revenue Service be furnished for inclusion in the inscription.

(d) *Term.*—A Series E bond shall be dated as of the first day of the month in which payment of the issue price is received by an agent authorized to issue such bonds. This date is the issue date and the bond will mature and be payable at face value 7 years and 9 months from such issue date. The bond may not be called for redemption by the Secretary of the Treasury prior to maturity or the end of the extended maturity period (see sec. 316.8(a)(1)). The bond may be redeemed at the owner's option at any time after two months from issue date at fixed redemption values; however, the Treasury Department may require reasonable notice of presentation of a bond for redemption prior to maturity. The owner has the option of continuing to hold the bond for an extended maturity period at a rate of interest to be determined prior to the original maturity of such bond.

(e) *Investment yield (interest).*—The investment yield (interest) on a Series E bond will be approximately 3.75 percent per annum compounded semiannually if the bond is held to maturity; [2] but the yield will be less if the bond is redeemed prior to maturity. The interest will be paid as a part of the redemption value. During the first six months from issue date the bonds will be redeemable only at issue price. The redemption value will increase at the end of the first half-year period from issue date and successive periods thereafter (see Table I).

Sec. 316.3. *Governing regulations.*—Series E bonds are subject to the regulations of the Treasury Department, now or hereafter prescribed, governing United States savings bonds, contained in Department Circular No. 530, current revision (31 CFR 315).[3]

---

[1] The $100,000 denomination is available only for purchase by trustees of employees' savings plans as described in section 316.5(c).

[2] Under authority of section 25, 73 Stat. 621 (31 U.S.C. 757c–1), the President of the United States on Sept. 22, 1959, concluded that with respect to Series E bonds it was necessary in the national interest to exceed the maximum interest rate and investment yield prescribed by section 22 of the Second Liberty Bond Act, as amended (31 U.S.C. 757c).

[3] Copies may be obtained from any Federal Reserve bank or branch, or the Bureau of the Public Debt, Washington, D.C. 20220, or its Chicago Office, 536 South Clark Street, Chicago, Ill. 60605. (See exhibit 7.)

Sec. 316.4 *Registration.—(a) General.*—Generally, only residents of the United States, its territories and possessions, the Commonwealth of Puerto Rico, the Canal Zone and citizens of the United States temporarily residing abroad are eligible to be named as owners of Series E bonds. The bonds may be registered in the names of natural persons in their own right as provided in (b) of this section, and in the names and titles or capacities of fiduciaries and organizations as provided in (c) of this section. Full information regarding authorized forms of registration and restrictions with respect thereto will be found in the governing regulations.

(b) *Natural persons in their own right.*—The bonds may be registered in the names of natural persons (whether adults or minors) in their own right, in single ownership, coownership, and beneficiary forms.

(c) *Others.*—The bonds may be registered in single ownership form in the names of fiduciaries and private and public organizations, as follows:

(1) *Fiduciaries.*—In the names of and showing the titles or capacities of any persons or organizations, public or private, as fiduciaries (including trustees, legal guardians or similar representatives, and certain custodians), but not where the fiduciary would hold the bonds merely or principally as security for the performance of a duty, obligation, or service.

(2) *Private and public organizations.*—In the names of private or public organizations (including private corporations, partnerships, and unincorporated associations, and States, counties, public corporations, and other public bodies) in their own right, but not in the names of commercial banks.[1]

Sec. 316.5. *Limitations on holdings.*—The amount of Series E bonds originally issued during any one calendar year that may be held by any one person, at any one time, computed in accordance with the governing regulations, is limited, as follows:

(a) *General limitation.*—$10,000 (face value) for the calendar year 1959 and each calendar year thereafter.

(b) *Special limitation for owners of savings bonds of Series F, G, J, and K.*— Owners, except commercial banks[1] in their own right (as distinguished from a representative or fiduciary capacity), of outstanding bonds of Series F and G, all of which are now matured, and bonds of Series J and K, at or after maturity, may purchase Series E bonds with the proceeds of redemption without regard to the general limitation on holdings, under the following restrictions and conditions:

(1) The bonds must be presented to a Federal Reserve bank or branch, the Office of the Treasurer of the United States, Securities Division, or the Bureau of the Public Debt, Division of Loans and Currency Branch, for the specific purpose of taking advantage of this privilege. The Series E bonds will be dated as of the first day of the month in which the bonds presented are received by the agency.

(2) Series E bonds may be purchased with the proceeds of the bonds presented only up to the denominational amounts that the proceeds thereof will fully cover. Any difference between such proceeds and the purchase price of the Series E bonds will be paid to the owner.

(3) The Series E bonds will be registered in the name of the owner in any authorized form of registration, subject to the restrictions prescribed by the governing regulations.

(4) This privilege will continue until terminated by the Secretary of the Treasury.

(c) *Special limitation for employees' savings plans.*—$2,000 (face value) multiplied by the highest number of participants in an employees' savings plan, as defined in (1) of this paragraph, at any time during the year in which the bonds are issued.[2]

(1) *Definition of plan and conditions of eligibility.*—

(i) The employees' savings plan must have been established by the employer for the exclusive and irrevocable benefit of his employees or their beneficiaries,

---

[1] Commercial banks, as defined in section 315.7(d)(2) of Department Circular No. 530, current revision, the governing regulations, for this purpose are those accepting demand deposits.

[2] Savings and vacation plans may be eligible for this special limitation. Questions concerning eligibility of such plans should be addressed to the Bureau of the Public Debt, Division of Loans and Currency Branch, 536 South Clark Street, Chicago, Ill. 60605.

afford employees the means of making regular savings from their wages through payroll deductions, and provide for employer contributions to be added to such savings.

(ii) The entire assets thereof must be credited to the individual accounts of participating employees and assets credited to the account of an employee may be distributed only to him or his beneficiary, except as otherwise provided herein.

(iii) Series E bonds may be purchased only with assets credited to the accounts of participating employees and only if the amount taken from any account at any time for that purpose is equal to the purchase price of a bond or bonds in an authorized denomination or denominations, and shares therein are credited to the accounts of the individuals from which the purchase price thereof was derived, in amounts corresponding with their shares. For example, if $37.50 credited to the account of John Jones is commingled with funds credited to the accounts of other employees to make a total of $7,500, with which a Series E bond in denomination of $10,000 (face value) is purchased in January 1965 and registered in the name and title of the trustee or trustees, the plan must provide, in effect, that John Jones' account shall be credited to show that he is the owner of a Series E bond in the denomination of $50 (face value) bearing the issue date of January 1, 1965.

(iv) Each participating employee shall have an irrevocable right at any time to demand and receive from the trustee or trustees all assets credited to his account or the value thereof, if he so prefers, without regard to any condition other than the loss or suspension of the privilege of participating further in the plan, except that a plan will not be deemed to be inconsistent herewith if it limits or modifies the exercise of any such right by providing that the employer's contribution does not vest absolutely until the employee shall have made contributions under the plan in each of not more than 60 calendar months succeeding the month for which the employer's contribution is made.

(v) Upon the death of an employee, his beneficiary shall have the absolute and unconditional right to demand and receive from the trustee or trustees all the assets credited to the account of the employee, or the value thereof, if he so prefers.

(vi) When settlement is made with an employee or his beneficiary with respect to any Series E bond registered in the name and title of the trustee or trustees in which the employee has a share (see (ii) hereof), the bond must be submitted for redemption or reissue to the extent of such share; if an employee or his beneficiary is to receive distribution in kind, bonds bearing the same issue dates as those credited to the employee's account will be reissued in the name of the distributee to the extent to which he is entitled, in authorized denominations, in any authorized form of registration, upon the request and certification of the trustee or trustees in accordance with the regulations governing United States savings bonds.

(2) *Definitions of terms used in this section and related provisions.—*

(i) The term "savings plan" includes any regulations issued under the plan with regard to Series E bonds; a copy of the plan and any such regulations, together with a copy of the trust agreement certified by a trustee to be true copies, must be submitted to the Federal Reserve bank of the district in order to establish the eligibility of the trustee or trustees to purchase bonds in excess of the general limitation in any calendar year.

(ii) The term "assets" means all funds, including the employees' contributions and employer's contributions and assets purchased therewith as well as accretions thereto, such as dividends on stock, the increment in value on bonds and all other income; but, notwithstanding any other provision of this section, the right to demand and receive "all assets" credited to the account of an employee shall not be construed to require the distribution of assets in kind when it would not be possible or practicable to make such distribution; for example, Series E bonds may not be reissued in unauthorized denominations, and fractional shares of stock are not readily distributable in kind.

(iii) The term "beneficiary" means the person or persons, if any, designated by the employee in accordance with the terms of the plan to receive the benefits of the trust upon his death or the estate of the employee, and the term "distributee" means the employee or his beneficiary.

Sec. 316.6 *Purchase of bonds.*—Series E bonds may be purchased, as follows:
(a) *Over-the-counter for cash.*

(1) *Bonds registered in names of natural persons in their own right only.*—
At such incorporated banks, trust companies, and other agencies as have been duly qualified as issuing agents and at selected United States post offices.

(2) *Bonds registered in all authorized forms.*—At Federal Reserve banks and branches and at the Office of the Treasurer of the United States, Securities Division, Washington, D.C. 20220.

(b) *On mail order.*—By mail upon application to any Federal Reserve bank or branch or to the Office of the Treasurer of the United States, Securities Division, D.C. 20220, accompanied by a remittance to cover the issue price. Any form of exchange, including personal checks, will be accepted subject to collection. Checks or other forms of exchange should be drawn to the order of the Federal Reserve bank or the Treasurer of the United States, as the case may be. Checks payable by endorsement are not acceptable. Any depositary qualified pursuant to the provisions of Treasury Department Circular No. 92, current revision (31 CFR 203), will be permitted to make payment by credit for bonds applied for on behalf of its customers up to any amount for which it shall be qualified in excess of existing deposits, when so notified by the Federal Reserve bank of its district.

(c) *Savings stamps.*—Savings stamps, in authorized denominations may be purchased at most post offices and at such other agencies as may be designated from time to time. The stamps may be used to accumulate credits for the purchase of Series E bonds. Albums for affixing the stamps will be available without charge, and such albums will be receivable by any authorized issuing agent in the amount of the affixed stamps on the purchase price of the bonds.

Sec. 316.7. *Delivery of bonds by mail.*—Issuing agents are authorized to deliver Series E bonds by mail at the risk and expense of the United States, at the address given by the purchaser, but only within the United States, its territories and possessions, the Commonwealth of Puerto Rico, and the Canal Zone. No mail deliveries elsewhere will be made. If purchased by citizens of the United States temporarily residing abroad, the bonds will be delivered at such address in the United States as the purchaser directs.

Sec. 316.8. *Extended terms and improved yields for outstanding bonds.*—
(a) *Optional extension privileges.*

(1) *General.*—The term "optional extension privilege," when used herein, means the privilege of retaining Series E bonds after maturity for a period, known as the "extended maturity period," or as the "second extended maturity period," and of earning interest *upon the maturity values or extended maturity values thereof,* as the case may be.[1] The tables at the end of this circular, which are incorporated herein, show current redemption values and investment yields. No special action is required of owners desiring to take advantage of any optional extension privilege. Merely by continuing to hold their bonds after maturity, they will continue to earn further interest. Interest will accrue at the end of the first half-year period following maturity or extended maturity and at the end of each successive half-year period thereafter until final maturity.

(2) *For bonds with issue dates of May 1, 1941, through May 1, 1949.*—Owners of Series E bonds with issue dates of May 1, 1941, through May 1, 1949, have the option of retaining their bonds for a second extended maturity period of ten years.

(3) *For bonds with issue dates of June 1, 1949, through April 1, 1957.*—Owners of Series E bonds with issue dates of June 1, 1949, through April 1, 1957, have the option of continuing to hold their bonds for an extended maturity period of ten years.

(4) *For bonds with issue date of May 1, 1957, or thereafter.*—Owners of Series E bonds with issue date of May 1, 1957, or thereafter have the option of continuing to hold such bonds for an extended maturity period of ten years at rates of interest to be determined prior to the original maturity of such bonds.

(b) *Improved yields.*

(1) *For bonds with issue dates of May 1, 1941, through May 1, 1949.*—The investment yields on outstanding Series E bonds with issue dates of May 1,

---

[1] The redemption value of any bond at original maturity is the base upon which interest will accrue during the extended maturity period. The redemption value of any bond at the end of the extended maturity period is the base upon which interest accrues during the second extended maturity period.

1941, through May 1, 1949, were increased for the remaining period of their extended maturity: (i) by not less than six-tenths of one percent per annum on bonds with issue dates of May 1, 1941, through April 1, 1942; and (ii) five-tenths of one percent per annum on bonds with issue dates of May 1, 1942, through May 1, 1949, if held to the end of the extended maturity period, and by lesser amounts if redeemed earlier.[1] The improvement in investment yields started on June 1, 1959, for bonds with the issue months of June or December and on the date of the first increase in redemption value after June 1, 1959, for a bond with any other issue month. The resulting yields are in terms of rate percent per annum, compounded semiannually. See tables 2 through 19[2] for current redemption values and investment yields.

(2) *For bonds with issue dates of June 1, 1949, through April 1, 1957.*[3]— The investment yields on outstanding Series E bonds with issue dates of June 1, 1949, through April 1, 1957, were increased for the extended maturity period by approximately three-fourths of one percent per annum, compounded semi-annually for bonds held at the end of that period and by lesser amounts if redeemed earlier. See tables 20 through 37[2] for current redemption values and investment yields.

(3) *For bonds with issue dates of May 1, 1957, through May 1, 1959.*[3]—The investment yields on outstanding Series E bonds with issue dates of May 1, 1957, through May 1, 1959, were increased beginning June 1, 1959, by five-tenths of one percent per annum if held to original maturity and by lesser amounts if redeemed earlier. The improvement in investment yields started on June 1, 1959, for bonds with the issue months of June or December and on the date of the first increase in redemption value after June 1, 1959, for a bond with any other issue month. The resulting yields are in terms of rate percent per annum, compounded semiannually. See tables 38 through 42[2] for current redemption values and investment yields.

Sec. 316.9. *Taxation.*—(a) *General.*—For the purpose of determining taxes and tax exemptions, the increment in value represented by the difference between the price paid for Series E bonds (which are issued on a discount basis) and the redemption value received therefor shall be considered as interest. Such interest is subject to all taxes imposed under the Internal Revenue Code of 1954. The bonds are subject to estate, inheritance, gift, or other excise taxes, whether Federal or State, but are exempt from all taxation now or hereafter imposed on the principal or interest thereof by any State, or any of the possessions of the United States, or by any local taxing authority.

(b) *Federal income tax on Series E bonds.*—An owner of Series E bonds who is a cash basis taxpayer and accordingly not required to report the increase in redemption value of his bonds each year as it accrues is required to include such amount in gross income for Federal income tax purposes for the taxable year of final maturity, actual redemption, or other disposition, whichever is earlier. An owner not reporting the increase in redemption value of such bonds currently for income tax purposes may elect in any year prior to final maturity, subject to the provisions of section 454 of the Internal Revenue Code of 1954 and the regulations prescribed thereunder, for such year and subsequent years to report such income annually. An owner who is required, or chooses, to report the increase in redemption value of his bonds each year as it accrues must continue to do so so long as he retains the bonds, unless in accordance with the income tax regulations he obtains permission from the Internal Revenue Service to change to a different method of reporting income from such obligations. In-

---

[1] The investment yields *for the full extended maturity period* of the bonds referred to in section 316.8(a)(2) and (b)(1) were, according to issue dates, as follows:

May 1, 1941, through Apr. 1, 1942	2.90
May 1, 1942, through May 1, 1949	3.00

percent per annum, compounded semiannually.

[2] See "Note" at end of this exhibit.

[3] The investment yields *for the full original maturity period* of bonds referred to in section 316.8(b)(2) and (3), were, according to issue dates, as follows:

Dec. 1, 1949, through Apr. 1, 1952	2.90
May 1, 1952, through Jan. 1, 1957	3.00
Feb. 1, 1957, through May 1, 1959	3.25

These yields were increased, effective one-half year from the next date after June 1, 1959, on which the redemption value increased, by not less than six-tenths of one percent for bonds with issue dates of Dec. 1, 1949, through Apr. 1, 1952, and by five-tenths of one percent for bonds with issue dates of May 1, 1952, through May 1, 1959. All of these yields are in terms of rate percent per annum, compounded semiannually.

quiry concerning further information on Federal taxes should be addressed to the district director, Internal Revenue Service, of the taxpayer's district, or the Internal Revenue Service, Washington, D.C., 20224.

Sec. 316.10. *Payment or redemption.*—(a) *General.*—A Series E bond may be redeemed in accordance with its terms at the appropriate redemption value as shown in the applicable tables hereof for bonds bearing various issue dates back to May 1, 1941. The redemption values of bonds in the denomination of $100,000 [1] (which was authorized as of January 1, 1954) are not shown in the tables. However, the redemption values of bonds in that denomination will be equal to the total redemption values of ten $10,000 bonds bearing the same issue dates. A Series E bond in a denomination higher than $25 (face value) may be redeemed in part but only in the amount of an authorized denomination or multiple thereof.

(b) *Federal Reserve banks and branches and Treasurer of the United States.*—Owners of Series E bonds may obtain payment upon presentation and surrender of the bonds to a Federal Reserve bank or branch or to the Office of the Treasurer of the United States, Securities Division, Washington, D.C., 20220, with the requests for payment on the bonds duly executed and certified in accordance with the governing regulations.

(c) *Incorporated banks, trust companies, and other financial institutions.*—An individual (natural person) whose name is inscribed on a Series E bond either as owner or coowner in his own right may also present such bond to any incorporated bank or trust company or other financial institution which is qualified as a paying agent under Department Circular No. 750, current revision (31 CFR 321). If such bond is in order for payment by the paying agent, the owner or coowner, upon establishing his identity to the satisfaction of the agent and upon signing the request for payment and adding his home or business address, may receive immediate payment of the current redemption value.

Sec. 316.11. *Reservation as to issue of bonds.*—The Secretary of the Treasury reserves the right to reject any application for Series E bonds, in whole or in part, and to refuse to issue or permit to be issued hereunder any such bonds in any case or any class or classes of cases if he deems such action to be in the public interest, and his action in any such respect shall be final.

Sec. 316.12. *Preservation of rights.*—Nothing contained herein shall limit or restrict rights which owners of Series E bonds heretofore issued have acquired under offers previously in force.

Sec. 316.13. *Fiscal agents.*—Federal Reserve banks and branches, as fiscal agents of the United States, are authorized to perform such services as may be requested of them by the Secretary of the Treasury in connection with the issue, delivery, redemption, and payment of Series E bonds.

Sec. 316.14. *Reservations as to terms of offer.*—The Secretary of the Treasury may at any time or from time to time supplement or amend the terms of this offering of bonds (31 CFR 316), or of any amendments or supplements thereto.

JOHN K. CARLOCK,
Fiscal Assistant Secretary of the Treasury.

---

[1] The $100,000 denomination is only available for purchase by trustees of employees' savings plans as described in section 316.5(c).

TABLES OF REDEMPTION VALUES AND INVESTMENT YIELDS FOR UNITED STATES SAVINGS BONDS OF SERIES E

Each table shows: (1) How bonds of Series E bearing the issue dates covered by the table, by denominations, increase in redemption value for each successive half-year period (a) following the date of issue for bonds bearing issue dates beginning Dec. 1, 1954; (b) following original maturity for bonds bearing issue dates of Dec. 1, 1944, through Nov. 1, 1954 (c) following first extended maturity for bonds bearing issue dates of May 1, 1941, through Nov. 1, 1944 (for the latest revised redemption values and investment yields during original maturity and first extended maturity periods not shown in these tables see Department Circular 653, Fifth Revision, dated Sept. 23, 1959); (2) the approximate investment yield on the purchase price from issue date to the beginning of each half-year period shown on the table; and (3) the approximate investment yield on the current redemption value from the beginning of each half-year period shown on the table to maturity. Yields are expressed in terms of rate percent per annum, compounded semiannually.

TABLE I.—*Bonds bearing issue dates beginning June 1, 1959*

Period after issue date	$18.75 / 25.00	$37.50 / 50.00	$56.25 / 75.00	$75.00 / 100.00	$150.00 / 200.00	$375.00 / 500.00	$750.00 / 1,000.00	$7,500 / 10,000	Approximate investment yield [1] (2) On purchase price from issue date to beginning of each half-year period [1]	(3) On current redemption value from beginning of each half-year period [2] to maturity
	(1) Redemption values during each half-year period [2] (values increase on first day of period shown)								*Percent*	*Percent*
First ½ year	$18.75	$37.50	$56.25	$75.00	$150.00	$375.00	$750.00	$7,500	0.00	3.75
½ to 1 year	18.91	37.82	56.73	75.64	151.28	378.20	756.40	7,564	1.71	3.89
1 to 1½ years	19.19	38.38	57.57	76.76	153.52	383.80	767.60	7,676	2.33	3.96
1½ to 2 years	19.51	39.02	58.53	78.04	156.08	390.20	780.40	7,804	2.67	4.01
2 to 2½ years	19.90	39.80	59.70	79.60	159.20	398.00	796.00	7,960	3.00	4.01
2½ to 3 years	20.28	40.56	60.84	81.12	162.24	405.60	811.20	8,112	3.16	4.03
3 to 3½ years	20.66	41.32	61.98	82.64	165.28	413.20	826.40	8,264	3.28	4.05
3½ to 4 years	21.07	42.14	63.21	84.28	168.56	421.40	842.80	8,428	3.36	4.06
4 to 4½ years	21.50	43.00	64.50	86.00	172.00	430.00	860.00	8,600	3.45	4.06
4½ to 5 years	21.95	43.90	65.85	87.80	175.60	439.00	878.00	8,780	3.53	4.04
5 to 5½ years	22.40	44.80	67.20	89.60	179.20	448.00	896.00	8,960	3.59	4.03
5½ to 6 years	22.86	45.72	68.58	91.44	182.88	457.20	914.40	9,144	3.64	4.02
6 to 6½ years	23.32	46.64	69.96	93.28	186.56	466.40	932.80	9,328	3.67	4.01
6½ to 7 years	23.79	47.58	71.37	95.16	190.32	475.80	951.60	9,516	3.70	4.01
7 to 7½ years	24.27	48.54	72.81	97.08	194.16	485.40	970.80	9,708	3.72	3.99
7½ years to 7 years and 9 months	24.75	49.50	74.25	99.00	198.00	495.00	990.00	9,900	3.74	4.06
MATURITY VALUE (7 years and 9 months from issue date)	25.00	50.00	75.00	100.00	200.00	500.00	1,000.00	10,000	3.75	

[1] Calculated on basis of $1,000 bond (face value).
[2] 3-month period in the case of the 7½ year to 7 year and 9 month period.
[3] Approximate investment yield for entire period from issuance to maturity.

NOTE.—The other tables are not reproduced in this exhibit as the redemption values and approximate investment yields shown in those tables are the same as those published in previous annual reports as follows: tables 2–19 cover bonds bearing issue dates from May 1, 1941, through May 1, 1949, and appear as tables I–XVIII, respectively, on pages 275–292 of the 1961 annual report; and tables 20–42 cover bonds bearing issue dates from June 1, 1949, through May 1, 1959, which appear on pages 232–254 of the 1960 annual report.

Exhibit 9.—Fifth amendment, December 23, 1964, of Department Circular No. 750, regulations governing payments by banks and other financial institutions in connection with the redemption of United States savings bonds

TREASURY DEPARTMENT,
Washington, December 23, 1964.

Subsection (a) of section 321.4 Department Circular No. 750, Revised, dated June 30, 1945, as amended and supplemented (31 CFR, Part 321), is hereby further amended as follows:

Sec. 321.4. *Meaning of terms in this circular* * * *

(a) "Paying agent(s)" or "agent(s)" shall mean (1) any eligible financial institution duly qualified pursuant to the provisions of this circular (31 CFR 321) to make payments in connection with the redemption and redemption-exchange of the United States savings bonds hereinafter specified, including branches of such institutions located within the United States, its territories and possessions, the Commonwealth of Puerto Rico and the Canal Zone, and (2) banking facilities of such institutions established at Armed Forces installations and other places with the specific approval of the Treasury Department.

JOHN K. CARLOCK,
Fiscal Assistant Secretary of the Treasury.

Exhibit 10.—Third revision, December 23, 1964, of Department Circular No. 905, offering of United States savings bonds, Series H

TREASURY DEPARTMENT,
Washington, December 23, 1964.

Department Circular No. 905, Second Revision, dated September 23, 1959, as amended (31 CFR 332), is hereby further amended and issued as the Third Revision.[1]

AUTHORITY: Secs. 332.1 to 332.14 issued under authority of sections 22 and 25 of the Second Liberty Bond Act, as amended, 49 Stat. 21, as amended, and 73 Stat. 621 (31 U.S.C. 757c, 757c–1).

Sec. 332.1. *Offering of bonds.*—The Secretary of the Treasury offers for sale to the people of the United States, United States savings bond of Series H, hereinafter generally referred to as Series H bonds. These bonds are substantially a continuation of the Series H bonds heretofore available. This offering of bonds will continue until terminated by the Secretary of the Treasury.

Sec. 332.2. *Description of bonds currently offered.*—(a) *General.*—Series H bonds bear a facsimile of the signature of the Secretary of the Treasury and of the Seal of the Treasury Department. The bonds are issued only in registered form and are nontransferable.

(b) *Denominations and prices.*—Series H bonds are issued at par and are available in denominations of $500, $1,000, $5,000, and $10,000.

(c) *Inscription and issue.*—At the time of issue the issuing agent will (1) inscribe on the face of each Series H bond the name, taxpayer identifying number,[2] and address of the owner, and the name of the beneficiary, if any, or the names of the coowners, the taxpayer identifying number of one coowner,[2] and the address of one coowner, (2) enter in the upper right-hand portion of the bond the issue date, and (3) imprint the agent's dating stamp in the lower right-hand portion to show the date the bond is actually inscribed. A Series H bond shall be valid only if an authorized issuing agent receives payment therefor and duly inscribes, dates, stamps, and makes delivery of the bond in accordance with the purchaser's instructions.

---

[1] The basic terms of the bonds offered under the Second Revision have not been changed. The material in the Second Revision and its four amendments has been reorganized and edited in connection with the publication of the 1965 edition of Title 31 of the Code of Federal Regulations.

[2] The number required to be used on tax returns and other documents submitted to the Internal Revenue Service (an individual's social security account number or employer identification number). If the coowners are husband and wife, the husband's number should be furnished. If the coowners are a minor and an adult, the adult's number should be furnished.

(d) *Terms.*—A Series H bond will be dated as of the first day of the month in which payment therefor is received by an agent authorized to issue such bonds. This date is the issue date and the bond will mature and be payable ten years from such issue date. The bond may not be called for redemption by the Secretary of the Treasury prior to maturity, but may be redeemed, AT PAR after six months from issue date, at the owner's option, but only upon one calendar month's notice as provided in sec. 332.10.

(e) *Interest (investment yield).*—The interest on a Series H bond will be paid semiannually by check drawn to the order of the registered owner or co-owners, beginning six months from issue date. Interest payments will be on a graduated scale, fixed to afford an investment yield of approximately 3.75 percent per annum, compounded semiannually if the bond is held to maturity;[1] but the yield will be less if the bond is redeemed prior to maturity. (See table I of the tables at the end of this circular, which are incorporated herein.) Interest will cease at maturity, or in the case of redemption before maturity, at the end of the interest period next preceding the date of redemption, except that if the date of redemption falls on an interest payment date, interest will cease on that date.

Sec. 332.3. *Governing regulations.*—Series H bonds are subject to the regulations of the Treasury Department, now or hereafter prescribed, governing United States savings bonds, contained in Department Circular No. 530, current revision (31 CFR 315).[2]

Sec. 332.4. *Registration.*—(a) *General.*—Generally, only residents of the United States, its territories and possessions, the Commonwealth of Puerto Rico, the Canal Zone and citizens of the United States temporarily residing abroad are eligible to be named as owners of Series H bonds. The bonds may be registered in the names of natural persons in their own right as provided in (b) of this section, and in the names and titles or capacities of fiduciaries and organizations as provided in (c) of this section. Full information regarding authorized forms of registration and restrictions with respect thereto will be found in the governing regulations.

(b) *Natural persons in their own right.*—The bonds may be registered in the names of natural persons (whether adults or minors) in their own right, in single ownership, coownership, and beneficiary forms.

(c) *Others.*—The bonds may be registered in single ownership form in the names of fiduciaries and private and public organizations, as follows:

(1) *Fiduciaries.*—In the names of and showing the titles or capacities of any persons or organizations, public or private, as fiduciaries (including trustees, legal guardians or similar representatives, and certain custodians) but not where the fiduciary would hold the bonds merely or principally as security for the performance of a duty, obligation, or service.

(2) *Private and public organizations.*—In the names of private or public organizations (including private corporations, partnerships, and unincorporated associations, and States, counties, public corporations, and other public bodies), in their own right, but not in the names of commercial banks.[3]

Sec. 332.5. *Limitations on holdings.*—The amount of Series H bonds originally issued during any one calendar year that may be held by any one person at any one time, computed in accordance with the governing regulations, is limited, as follows:

(a) *General limitation.*—$20,000 (face value) for the calendar year 1962 and each calendar year thereafter.

(b) *Special limitation for owners of savings bonds of Series F, G, J, and K.*—Owners, except commercial banks[3] in their own right (as distinguished from a representative or fiduciary capacity), of outstanding bonds of Series F and G,

---

[1] Under authority of section 25, 73 Stat. 621 (31 U.S.C. 757c–1), the President of the United States on Sept. 22, 1959, concluded that with respect to Series H bonds it was necessary in the national interest to exceed the maximum interest rate and investment yield prescribed by section 22 of the Second Liberty Bond Act, as amended (31 U.S.C. 757c).

[2] Copies may be obtained on application to any Federal Reserve bank or branch or the Bureau of the Public Debt, Washington, D.C., 20220, or its Chicago Office, 536 South Clark Street, Chicago, Ill., 60605. (See exhibit 7.)

[3] Commercial banks as defined in section 315.7(d)(2) of Department Circular No. 530, current revision, the governing regulations, for this purpose are those accepting demand deposits.

all of which are now matured, and bonds of Series J and K, at or after maturity may apply the proceeds of such bonds to the purchase of Series H bonds without regard to the general limitation on holdings, under the following restrictions and conditions:

(1) The bonds must be presented to a Federal Reserve bank or branch, the Office of the Treasurer of the United States, Securities Division, or the Bureau of the Public Debt, Division of Loans and Currency Branch, for the specific purpose of taking advantage of this privilege. The Series H bonds will be dated as of the first day of the month in which the bonds presented are received by the issuing agent.

(2) Series H bonds may be purchased with the proceeds of the bonds presented only up to the denominational amounts that the proceeds thereof will fully cover. Any difference between such proceeds and the purchase price of the Series H bonds will be paid to the owner.

(3) The Series H bonds will be registered in the name of the owner in any authorized form of registration subject to the restrictions prescribed by the governing regulations.

(4) This privilege will continue until terminated by the Secretary of the Treasury.

(c) *Exchanges pursuant to Department Circular No. 1036, as amended.*—Series H bonds issued in exchange for bonds of Series E, Series F, or Series J under the provisions of Department Circular No. 1036, as amended (31 CFR 339), are exempt from the annual limitation.

Sec. 332.6 *Purchase of bonds.*—(a) *Agents.*—Only the Federal Reserve banks and branches and the Treasury Department are authorized to act as official issuing agents for the sale of Series H bonds. However, commercial banks and trust companies may forward applications for purchase of the bonds. The date of receipt of the application and payment to an issuing agent will govern the issue date of the bonds purchased.

(b) *Application for purchase and remittance.*—The applicant for purchase of Series H bonds should furnish (1) instructions for registration of the bonds to be issued, which must be in an authorized form, (2) the appropriate taxpayer identifying number or numbers,[1] (3) the post office address of the owner or a coowner (preferably the first-named), (4) the address for delivery of the bonds, and (5) the address for mailing checks in payment of interest. The application should be forwarded to a Federal Reserve bank or branch or the Office of the Treasurer of the United States, Securities Division, Washington, D.C., 20220, accompanied by a remittance to cover the purchase price. Any form of exchange including personal checks will be accepted subject to collection. Checks or other forms of exchange should be drawn to the order of the Federal Reserve bank or Treasurer of the United States, as the case may be. Checks payable by endorsement are not acceptable. Any depositary qualified pursuant to Treasury Department Circular No. 92, current revision (31 CFR 203), will be permitted to make payment by credit for bonds applied for on behalf of its customers up to any amount for which it shall be qualified in excess of existing deposits, when so notified by the Federal Reserve bank of its district.

Sec. 332.7. *Delivery of bonds.*—Authorized issuing agents will deliver the Series H bonds either in person, or by mail at the risk and expense of the United States at the address given by the purchaser, but only within the United States, its territories and possessions, the Commonwealth of Puerto Rico, and the Canal Zone. No mail deliveries elsewhere will be made. If purchased by citizens of the United States temporarily residing abroad, the bonds will be delivered at such address in the United States as the purchaser directs.

Sec. 332.8. *Improved yield and extension of term for outstanding bonds.*—(a) *Improved yield to maturity for outstanding bonds with issue dates of June 1, 1952, through May 1, 1959.*—The investment yields on all outstanding Series H bonds with issue dates prior to June 1, 1959, were increased, beginning on and after June 1, 1959, as described below, for the remaining period to maturity,

---

[1] The number required to be used on tax returns and other documents submitted to the Internal Revenue Service (an individual's social security account number or employer identification number). If the coowners are husband and wife, the husband's number should be furnished. If the coowners are a minor and an adult, the adult's number should be furnished.

by not less than one-half of one percent, and by lesser amounts if redeemed earlier.[1] The resulting yields are in terms of rate percent per annum, compounded semiannually. See Tables 2 through 16[2] for current schedules of interest payments and investment yields. This increase became effective beginning with interest payments due December 1, 1959, for bonds with the issue month of June or December of any year prior to 1950, and for all other bonds on the next interest payment date after December 1, 1959.

(b) *Extended maturity period for bonds with issue dates of June 1, 1952, through January 1, 1957.*—Owners of Series H bonds with these issue dates have the option of continuing to hold such bonds for an extended maturity period of ten years with an investment yield of approximately 3.75 percent payable semiannually. Bonds held after maturity will earn further interest which will accrue and be paid semiannually by check drawn to the order of the owner or coowners beginning six months from the original maturity dates. Interest payments will be made in the amounts shown in Tables 2 through 11.[2]

Sec. 332.9 *Taxation.*—The income derived from Series H bonds is subject to all taxes imposed under the Internal Revenue Code of 1954. The bonds are subject to estate, inheritance, gift, or other excise taxes, whether Federal or State, but are exempt from all taxation now or hereafter imposed on the principal or interest thereof by any State, by any of the possessions of the United States or by any local taxing authority.

Sec. 332.10. *Payment or redemption.*—(a) *Prior to maturity.*—Prior to maturity a Series H bond will be redeemed AT PAR, in whole or in part, in the amount of an authorized denomination or multiple thereof, at the option of the owner, after six months from the issue date upon one calendar month's notice to (1) a Federal Reserve bank or branch, (2) the Office of the Treasurer of the United States, Securities Division, Washington, D.C., 20220, or (3) the Bureau of the Public Debt, Division of Loans and Currency Branch, 536 South Clark Street, Chicago, Ill., 60605. Such notice may be given separately, in writing, or by presenting and surrendering the bond with a duly executed request for payment. If notice is given separately, the bond must be presented with a duly executed request for payment to the same agent not less than twenty days before the redemption date fixed by the notice. Payment will be made as of the first day of the first month following by at least one full calendar month the date of the receipt of notice.

(b) *At maturity.*—Upon maturity a Series H bond will be redeemed at par upon presentation of the bond with a duly executed request for payment to one of the agents designated in (a) of this section. Any Series H bond having an extended maturity period will be redeemed at par upon original maturity and for two calendar months following the month in which the bond originally matures without advance notice.[3]

(c) *During extended maturity period.*—A Series H bond having an extended maturity period will, beginning with the first day of the third calendar month following the calendar month in which the bond originally matures, be regarded as unmatured until it reaches its final maturity date and may be redeemed in the same manner and subject to the same notice for redemption as provided in (a) of this section.

Sec. 332.11. *Reservation as to issue of bonds.*—The Secretary of the Treasury reserves the right to reject any application for Series H bonds, in whole or in part, and to refuse to issue or permit to be issued hereunder any such bonds in any case or any class or any classes of cases if he deems such action to be in the public interest, and his action in any such respect shall be final.

Sec. 332.12. *Preservation of rights.*—Nothing contained herein shall limit or restrict rights which owners of Series H bonds heretofore issued have acquired under offers previously in force.

---

[1] The investment yield to maturity heretofore prescribed for the bonds referred to in section 332.8(a) were (according to issue dates), as follows:

June 1, 1952, through Jan. 1, 1957_____	3.00
Feb. 1, 1957, through May 1, 1959_____	3.25

percent per annum compounded semiannually.

[2] See "Note" at end of this exhibit.

[3] For example, if a bond is dated June 1, 1955, the date of original maturity is Feb. 1, 1965. The date on which the right to payment without advance notice will be suspended is May 1, 1965.

Sec. 332.13. *Fiscal agents.*—Federal Reserve banks and branches, as fiscal agents of the United States, are authorized to perform such services as may be requested of them by the Secretary of the Treasury in connection with the issue, delivery, redemption and payment of Series H bonds.

Sec. 332.14. *Reservation as to terms of offer.*—The Secretary of the Treasury may at any time or from time to time supplement or amend the terms of this offering of bonds (31 CFR 332), or of any amendments or supplements thereto.

JOHN K. CARLOCK,
Fiscal Assistant Secretary of the Treasury.

TABLES OF CHECKS ISSUED AND INVESTMENT YIELDS FOR UNITED STATES SAVINGS BONDS OF SERIES H

Each table shows: (1) Amounts of interest checks paid on United States savings bonds of Series H bearing issue dates covered by the table, by denominations, on each interest payment date (a) following the date of issue for bonds bearing issue dates beginning Dec. 1, 1954; (b) following original maturity date for bonds bearing issue dates of June 1, 1952, through Nov. 1, 1954 (for the latest revised amounts of interest checks and investment yields during the original maturity period not shown in these tables, see Department Circular 905, Second Revision, dated Sept. 23, 1959); (2) the approximate investment yield on the face value from issue date to each interest payment date; and (3) the approximate investment yield on the face value from each interest payment date to maturity. Yields are expressed in terms of rate percent per annum, compounded semiannually.

TABLE I.—*Bonds bearing issue dates, beginning June 1, 1959*

Face value { Issue price / Redemption [1] and maturity value	$500 / 500	$1,000 / 1,000	$5,000 / 5,000	$10,000 / 10,000	Approximate investment yield on face value [2]	
					(2) From issue date to each interest payment date	(3) From each interest payment date to maturity [3]
Period of time bond is held after issue date	(1) Amounts of interest checks for each denomination					
					Percent	*Percent*
½ year	$4.00	$8.00	$40.00	$80.00	1.60	3.88
1 year	7.25	14.50	72.50	145.00	2.25	3.95
1½ years	8.00	16.00	80.00	160.00	2.56	4.00
2 years	10.00	20.00	100.00	200.00	2.91	4.00
2½ years	10.00	20.00	100.00	200.00	3.12	4.00
3 years	10.00	20.00	100.00	200.00	3.26	4.00
3½ years	10.00	20.00	100.00	200.00	3.44	4.00
4 years	10.00	20.00	100.00	200.00	3.49	4.00
4½ years	10.00	20.00	100.00	200.00	3.54	4.00
5 years	10.00	20.00	100.00	200.00	3.58	4.00
5½ years	10.00	20.00	100.00	200.00	3.61	4.00
6 years	10.00	20.00	100.00	200.00	3.64	4.00
6½ years	10.00	20.00	100.00	200.00	3.66	4.00
7 years	10.00	20.00	100.00	200.00	3.68	4.00
7½ years	10.00	20.00	100.00	200.00	3.70	4.00
8 years	10.00	20.00	100.00	200.00	3.71	4.00
8½ years	10.00	20.00	100.00	200.00	3.72	4.00
9 years	10.00	20.00	100.00	200.00	3.74	4.00
9½ years	10.00	20.00	100.00	200.00	3.74	4.00
10 years (maturity)	10.00	20.00	100.00	200.00	3.75	----------

[1] At all times, except that bond is not redeemable during first 6 months.
[2] Calculated on the basis of $1,000 bond.
[3] Approximate investment yield for entire period from issuance to maturity is 3.75 percent per annum.

NOTE.—The other tables are not reproduced in this exhibit as the amounts of interest checks and approximate investment yields shown in those tables are the same as those published in previous annual reports as follows: tables 2–11 cover bonds bearing issue dates from June 1, 1952, through January 1, 1957, and appear as tables I–X, respectively, on pages 260–269 of the 1962 annual report; and tables 12–16 cover bonds bearing issue dates from February 1, 1957, through May 1, 1959, which appear on pages 270–274 of the 1960 annual report.

Legislation

Exhibit 11.—An act to provide for a temporary increase in the public debt limit set forth in section 21 of the Second Liberty Bond Act

[Public Law 89–49, 89th Congress, H.R. 8464, June 24, 1965]

Be it enacted by the Senate and House of Representatives of the United States of America in Congress assembled, That, during the period beginning on July 1, 1965, and ending on June 30, 1966, the public debt limit set forth in the first sentence of section 21 of the Second Liberty Bond Act, as amended (31 U.S.C. 757b), shall be temporarily increased to $328,000,000,000.

Public debt limit. Temporary increase. 78 Stat. 225.

Approved June 24, 1965.

Financial Policy

Exhibit 12.—Statement by Secretary of the Treasury Dillon, February 22, 1965, before the Joint Economic Committee

We meet after a year of substantial progress and accomplishment. But we have no cause for complacency.

At home too many of our workers—particularly younger people just entering their productive years and those who suffer from inexperience, lack of education, and racial prejudice—are without jobs. As we enter the fifth consecutive year of economic advance, we must be alert both to the dangers of price pressures and of any flagging in the forces of expansion.

At the same time, our balance of payments has not shown the improvement we must have. Further action, as outlined by President Johnson in his Message on the Balance of Payments, is essential to the continued strength of the dollar. And, on that solid foundation, we must press forward, in cooperation with our friends and trading partners, with our effort to assure the capacity of the international monetary system over the years ahead to provide the reserves and credit facilities needed to support the vigorous and balanced growth of the free world economy.

Fiscal policy and a progressive economy

Maintenance of a healthy rate of domestic economic expansion, free from inflation, will continue to require the coordinated use of the tools of fiscal, monetary, and debt management policy. But, within that framework, fiscal policy, and particularly tax policy, has unquestionably come to assume a more crucial role than ever before in sustaining our forward momentum and carrying out the mandate of the Employment Act of 1946.

The first important steps to spur more rapid growth through tax policy were taken in 1962. The Revenue Act of 1962, you will recall, provided for a tax credit of 7 percent on new investment in machinery and equipment, and in the same year the Treasury reformed and liberalized the tax treatment of depreciation, bringing up to date badly outmoded procedures that served as a drag on new investment. Coupled with the two-stage reduction in the corporate tax rate contained in the Revenue Act of 1964, these measures provided a powerful stimulus to business investment in plant and equipment, increasing the profitability of a typical investment in new equipment by more than 30 percent.

Just last week we improved and liberalized the reserve ratio test procedures that accompanied the 1962 liberalization of depreciation. This action was taken after extensive studies. It will make certain that businesses which truly wish to adapt their replacement practices to the new shorter lives announced in 1962 can obtain the full tax benefits of the 1962 guidelines. For 1965 it will mean that additional taxes will amount to a maximum of $100 million rather than the $800 million that would have been the case under the original 1962 reserve ratio test procedures.

The response of private investment to tax incentives and to expanding sales and profits has been remarkable indeed. Producers' outlays on durable equipment, after correction for price change, amounted to $26 billion in 1961, as compared to $26.6 billion in 1952. But in the three years since 1961, those same outlays, again corrected for price change, have risen to $35.1 billion, an increase of over one-third in the space of only three years. Yet, the expansion of investment has been closely geared to requirements for new productive capacity and no unsustainable capital goods boom on the 1956–57 model has been allowed to develop.

Along with the invigoration of private investment that is so basic for long-run growth, the individual tax reduction of 1964, as it becomes fully effective, is releasing $11 billion of consumer purchasing power at 1965 levels of income. The size, composition, and timing of last year's tax cut were carefully planned, and the results were almost exactly as predicted in the 1964 Economic Report of the President.

A year ago that report projected a gross national product of $623 billion as the midpoint within a $10 billion range. The actual result is now estimated at $622.6 billion. A year ago the report estimated that with tax reduction the unemployment rate could be expected to fall to approximately 5 percent at the end of the year, as it actually did, before falling even further to 4.8 percent in January. The behavior of personal income, corporate profits, and other measures was also in line with our expectations.

The tax reduction enacted last year continues to spur consumer and business spending, although the large initial thrust is now behind us. Later this year we will further improve the tax system, encourage price declines, and give the economy another measured and timely stimulus through the reduction and elimination of some of our excise taxes. The President's budget provides for excise tax reductions effective on July 1 that will total $1.75 billion a year when fully effective. The President will spell out the details of this program in ample time to permit consideration by the Congress before midyear.

Over the past four years, as this record suggests, we have come to a far greater appreciation of how fiscal and tax policy can help achieve our economic goals. But much remains to be done before we can be satisfied that this policy tool can be used with the flexibility that is essential should recessionary tendencies gather force.

To meet that need, the President has urged that the Congress review its own procedures to assure prompt action on temporary tax cuts, if and when required. The lengthy and painstaking deliberations by the Congress, which are entirely necessary and appropriate before undertaking a lasting structural change in the tax structure, are not relevant to purely temporary, across-the-board, antirecessionary cuts.

We simply must be able to count on procedures that insure an early decision in response to a Presidential proposal, or else we must give up the strongest antirecessionary weapon in our arsenal.

At the same time, we must, of course, develop programs that will attack structural problems of unemployment and depressed areas at their roots and solve them within a framework of overall price stability. These deep-seated problems will only yield to a concerted attack aimed directly at their causes. We are mounting just such an attack.

In a modern industrial society, those without skills, or with skills no longer in demand, suffer a heavy disadvantage. Training programs such as those now being conducted under both the Manpower Development and Training Act and the Economic Opportunity Act can make a key contribution to individual and national welfare. The Appalachia program, now under congressional consideration, is an ambitious effort to deal in a coordinated way with a particular depressed area problem. An improved Area Redevelopment Act would be helpful in spurring growth. Carefully designed programs such as these will play a steadily increasing role in reducing unemployment and widening job opportunities.

Monetary and debt management policies

The timely use of fiscal policy enables us to make far more effective use of the tools of monetary and debt management policies in meeting our internal and external economic goals. For instance, the stimulus from tax reduction, by lifting some of the burden for promoting economic expansion from monetary policy, has made extremely easy money policies at home unnecessary, policies that would have been totally out of keeping with our balance-of-payments problem.

The fact is that, in a world of increasingly free trade and payments, we cannot expect to insulate our domestic money and capital markets entirely from those of other countries, nor would that be consistent with our longer-range goals of a liberal world economic order. As the President emphasized in his Economic Report, monetary policy must and will remain free to respond if the stability of the dollar is threatened, either from domestic inflation as a result of excessive demand, or from outflows of money and capital that undermine our balance of payments. But, if monetary policy is to play that role effectively, and without potential damage to the internal economy, we must also recognize the corollary need for dynamic, flexible fiscal policies in promoting domestic prosperity.

So long as we are willing in the future, as during the past few years, to use all the varied tools of financial policy flexibly, and in complementary ways, intolerable conflicts need not arise between our commitment to defend the dollar and our commitment to sustained domestic growth and prosperity. Effective economic policy does not require that every tool be pushed hard in the same direction and at the same time. What is required is that, in seeking our varied goals, we achieve a blend and a balance among our policy tools—taking advantage of the strong points of each—that will permit progress in several directions simultaneously.

The debt management record

The use of our policy instruments in the pursuit of multiple objectives is well illustrated in an area for which I have had direct responsibility and which affects the economy almost daily: the management of the public debt.

Debt management has in recent years helped keep our market interest rates in the short-term area reasonably competitive with rates in major foreign money centers, thus minimizing interest rate incentives to the transfer of short-term funds abroad. Thus, we increased the volume of Treasury bills $5.0 billion further during 1964, helping to raise the three-month bill rate from about $3\frac{1}{2}$ percent at the close of 1963 to just under 4 percent today.

At the same time, however, it has been important to insure that this action, undertaken for balance-of-payments reasons, did not clash with other objectives. With persistent unemployment and unused industrial capacity, we have wanted to avoid upward pressures on the structure of long-term interest rates, and to assure the availability of investment funds adequate to support the steady rise in domestic investment and economic activity.

In addition, the Treasury also has continuously before it the need to maintain a well-balanced maturity structure in the national debt, a prerequisite for flexibility in its financing decisions. This requires sizeable placements of new intermediate and longer-term securities in the market in order to offset the shortening effect of the passage of time on the term to maturity of outstanding issues. Otherwise, debt would soon pile up in the short-term area, not only risking an inflationary potential but also straining that sector of the market and using up some or all of the short-term borrowing capacity which it is prudent to hold in reserve for emergencies.

To achieve this balanced debt structure and avoid any excessive buildup of liquidity, the Treasury last year reduced outstanding short-term debt other than Treasury bills by an even larger amount than the rise in the volume of bills. As a result, the total marketable debt due within one year actually declined by $1.0 billion. And, as in the preceding year, the Treasury's borrowing was done, on balance, without recourse to the commercial banking system, making it the third successive year in which bank holdings of Treasury securities showed no increase. Actually, commercial bank holdings of Government debt as shown in the attached table were slightly lower at the end of January than they were four years earlier. Thus, all of the large increase in bank credit over the past four years has been used to finance private borrowers and State and local governments.

The great bulk of the Treasury's debt extension has continued to be achieved through advance refundings, a technique initiated during the preceding Administration and further developed and extensively utilized during the past four years. One important advantage of this technique is that it minimizes the impact on the market and on interest rates of our debt extension operations. Investors responded to 3 advance refunding offers, in January and July 1964 and January 1965, by exchanging existing short-term holdings for $4.2 billion of bonds maturing in 20 years or more, for $7.5 billion of bonds maturing in about 9 years, and for $10.3 billion of bonds maturing in 5 to 7 years. An additional $1.5 billion of 10-year bonds was issued in the regular refunding in May 1964.

Reflecting these operations, the marketable debt due in 5 years or more rose $7.1 billion in the 12 months that ended on January 31, exceeding the $5.8 billion increase in the entire marketable debt over this period. As the attached table indicates, an amount larger than the entire $25.1 billion increase in the marketable debt since January 1961 has been financed over that period in longer-term issues; marketable debt due in 5 years or more is up $26.9 billion. Accordingly, the average maturity of the marketable debt as of January 31, 1965, was 5 years 5 months longer than its year-ago level and 11 months longer than in January 1961.

Moreover, if we add the $2.6 billion increase in the outstanding volume of savings bonds since January 1961 to the $26.9 billion increase in the portion of the marketable debt due in 5 years or more, we get a total of $29.5 billion, well beyond the $28.4 billion rise in the entire public debt over these 4 years. This is a clear record of noninflationary finance not often recognized by those who like to talk of loose fiscal policies in Washington.

It is noteworthy that these efforts to finance the Government at long-term have been achieved without any noticeable upward pressure on long-term yields. Most long-term interest rates important to private economic activity are now well below the levels touched in 1961: Average conventional mortgage rates are currently 5.8 percent, down nearly ⅜ percent; offering yields on new high-grade corporate bonds have recently been under 4½ percent, ⅛ percent or more below levels of the spring of 1961; and a widely-used municipal bond yield average which was as high as 3.55 percent in 1961 is currently 3.10 percent.

This is an impressive record when one considers the increase of about 1¾ percent in short-term yields that has taken place since the lows of early 1961, as well as the record demand for funds. The volume of funds raised during the past 4 years totals about $240 billion, nearly 50 percent higher than the total of the preceding 4 years. A major part of the explanation lies, of course, in the high and rising flow of savings for longer-term investment generated out of the steadily rising incomes that have accompanied our prosperity. The smooth flow of these savings into investment has been greatly assisted and encouraged by confidence in continuing price stability and by the increases in interest rates paid by savings institutions and commercial banks.

Clearly, the Treasury's program of noninflationary debt management has been entirely consistent with full availability of credit to private borrowers at stable or declining long-term interest rates.

Importance of cost-price stability

Fiscal incentives and sound financing of the national debt have helped account for the remarkable degree of price stability that has accompanied our vigorous expansion. In contrast, earlier postwar expansions have typically been marred, after the initial recovery period, by rapid increases in costs and narrowing profit margins. The bidding up of prices and costs dissipated the forces for expansion; maladjustments and distortions soon developed, and recessionary forces gathered strength.

We have avoided that pattern during the present expansion. The rise in productivity associated with more rapid growth and an expanded scale of investment, along with moderation in wage demands, has caused manufacturing labor costs per unit of output to decline more or less steadily throughout the current expansion. As a result, there has been no squeeze on profit margins and little upward pressure on prices. With costs and prices stable, and productivity rising steadily, we have maintained a good balance throughout the economy and no drastic tightening of money has been necessary to curb over-exuberance.

We must not allow the dismal cycle of inflation and recession of the earlier postwar period to reappear. The challenge is clear, for experience shows that the task of maintaining cost-price stability becomes more difficult as expansion whittles away margins of unused plant capacity and selective labor shortages begin to appear. Moreover, some signs of price pressures—fortunately confined to limited sectors of the economy and in some cases reflecting temporary interruptions in the flow of raw materials from abroad—were apparent in the closing months of 1964.

These pressures by no means signify that our long period of price stability is ending. They do, however, reemphasize the need for vigilance.

Our financial policies afford assurance that total demand will remain well within our growing capacity to produce, and we do not face excess demand inflation. But, in addition, we must recognize that, even at a time when overall demand is not excessive, costs and prices may be pushed up by pressures of wage bargaining and the pricing policies of large firms.

The record of labor and industry in recent years in this respect has been good, although we are all aware, I think, that it has not been in every instance as good as it could have been. The price-wage guideposts, endorsed by both President Kennedy and President Johnson, point unambiguously to the responsibilities of both labor and management if key wage settlements and pricing decisions are to serve the public interest. The acceptance by all sectors of our economy of their continuing responsibility for noninflationary policies is the key to steady expansion at home and a stronger competitive position abroad.

Balance of payments

Cost-price stability has contributed to a marked improvement in our already favorable balance of trade. Commercial exports, excluding those financed by the Government, rose to $22.4 billion in 1964, an increase of 16 percent over 1963, and fully 28 percent over 1960 levels. As a result, our commercial trade surplus widened from 1963's $2.3 billion to an estimated $3.7 billion in 1964, despite the larger demand for imports generated by our rising levels of economic activity.

The 1964 results were, of course, aided by the special grain sales to both Eastern and Western Europe early in the year, and we cannot count on equally favorable overall trends in 1965. But, there can be little doubt that the relative stability of our own costs and prices since 1958, while most foreign costs and prices have been rising more or less steadily, is at last beginning to count in our favor.

Our improved trade balance has been paralleled by further savings in net Government spending overseas, and by an unprecedented increase in income from our rising volume of foreign investments. These factors combined to reduce our deficit on regular transactions to an annual rate of about $2 billion over the first three quarters of 1964, about in line with earlier expectations despite rising levels of capital outflows.

However, as you know, progress in reducing our deficit for the year as a whole was disappointing. A sharp deterioration during the fourth quarter pushed our deficit on regular transactions up to $3.0 billion for the year as a whole. While some of the fourth quarter results can be traced to temporary factors, analysis of the results for the year made it perfectly clear that new measures needed to be taken to achieve a more rapid reduction in the underlying deficit and to maintain the international strength and stability of the dollar unquestioned.

As a consequence, President Johnson has announced a 10-point program to intensify our effort to reach an early balance. Export promotion will be pressed even harder and the overseas dollar cost of Government programs will be reduced even further. In addition, legislation will be sought to narrow the gap on tourist expenditures by reducing the duty-free exemption on our returning tourists and our "See the U.S.A." program will be greatly intensified. But, the major thrust of the President's program is in the area of capital movements.

The reason is simple. The bulk of our difficulty can be traced to accelerating outflows of American investment and loan funds to a rapidly growing outside world that desires capital and that apparently is still incapable of mobilizing its own savings with full effectiveness. Since 1960, gains in our trade balance, net savings in our aid and military programs overseas, and rising investment income have benefited our balance of payments by about $3.9 billion. But over that same period, private capital flows abroad increased by about $2½ billion to a record $6.3 billion, washing away most of the gains in other sectors of our accounts.

This huge capital outflow is in one sense a reflection of our basic strength as a nation, the huge savings we are capable of generating, the steady increase in our holdings of productive and profitable assets abroad, and the worldwide usefulness of the dollar. But, at this point in time, it is also evident that our balance-of-payments position cannot afford accelerating outflows of capital at the expense of our international liquidity. Nor can we afford a heavy outflow of the gold that stands behind our pledge to maintain the value of the dollar at $35 an ounce.

And just such an outflow is inevitable unless we take the steps that will hold the outflows of capital within our capacity as a nation to finance them.

The success of this program rests on the cooperation of the business and financial communities in a voluntary program to limit the flow of dollars abroad arising from their own operations. Such a voluntary program, designed in the public interest, can be an enormously effective instrument in assisting the early balance in our payments that is so urgently needed. Only last Thursday, the President, together with Secretary Connor, Chairman Martin, and I, outlined to a group of distinguished business and financial leaders the nature of this voluntary program. I am sure they will respond to the challenge quickly and effectively.

International financial cooperation

Early and decisive reductions in our balance-of-payments deficit are essential not only to protect the dollar, but also to permit calm and orderly study and appraisal of the most effective approaches toward assuring the adequacy of the international financial system to meet the needs of a growing world. The capacity of the present system to meet short-run strains has been impressively demonstrated, most recently when sterling came under heavy pressure. The massive credits extended to the British amounted to a collective endorsement—backed by $3 billion of hard cash—of existing exchange parities by the major industrial countries. The speed and effectiveness with which these credits could be assembled was a product of the close international financial cooperation built up over recent years.

Meanwhile, we are exploring with other leading nations how best to meet the longer-range needs of the world for international liquidity and for more effective processes of international balance-of-payments adjustment. These studies are complex and difficult, and it is not surprising that some differences of approach among the major countries are evident at this stage. Certainly, we cannot afford to look back nostalgically and seek a solution in the rigid mechanism of a pure gold standard, a mechanism that even in an earlier and simpler day was prone to breakdown and deflation. Instead, the challenge is to build upon the system that has served the world so well over the postwar years, with full awareness of its problems and shortcomings, to be sure, but also with healthy respect for its resiliency and flexibility in responding to varied and never fully predictable needs.

While this longrun effort is being pressed to a satisfactory conclusion, the planned expansion of IMF resources provides tangible assurance that the financial support needed to facilitate expansion in world trade and payments will be available.

The Executive Directors of the International Monetary Fund have agreed in principle to submit to member governments, proposals for a general increase of all quotas by 25 percent, plus special increases for a relatively small number of countries whose quotas are out of line with their economic importance. Together, these increases, if accepted by the member countries, would total $4.8 billion, and when completed would bring the total quotas of the Fund up to $20.9 billion, an overall rise of approximately 30 percent. The U.S. quota, which would be subject only to the 25-percent general increase, would rise from the present $4,125 million to $5,160 million. It is expected that legislation providing for this increase will be introduced next month; full provision for it has already been made in the President's budget.

The Fund proposals will provide that 25 percent of each country's quota increase must be paid in gold. The United States has been prepared at all times to pay this 25 percent from its own gold holdings, but we had been concerned that such payments by others would lead to large purchases of U.S. gold. I am glad to say that this possibility will be forestalled by measures agreed upon in the Fund. I believe that the understandings that have been reached will fully protect the interests of the United States, the payments system as a whole, the Fund, and its other members.

Conclusion

I have touched upon several key challenges for economic policy in 1965: Maintaining price stability while reducing unemployment; achieving a decisive reduction in our balance-of-payments deficit; and progress toward a stronger international payments system. Each of these problems we approach from a position of great strength.

Business is moving ahead with good momentum, but without inflationary pressures on supplies or speculative excesses. Our international competitive position is slowly but surely improving, and standing behind the dollar is the world's largest gold stock and a huge volume of foreign assets. The international financial system has withstood a series of shocks and strains, while demonstrating its ability to finance a further large increase in world trade.

Given a continued willingness to use all our tools of economic policy in flexible and imaginative ways—and with the vital support of industry, labor, and finance—I am confident that the challenges of today will become the successes of tomorrow.

The structure and ownership of the public debt January 1961 and January 1965

(In billions of dollars)

	January 1961	January 1965	Change
Debt structure:			
Marketable public debt:			
Due within 5 years	$146. 4	$144. 7	−$1. 8
Due after 5 years	42. 9	69. 7	+26. 9
Nonmarketable public debt:			
Savings bonds	47. 2	49. 8	+2. 6
Special issues and other	53. 6	54. 4	+0. 8
Total public debt	290. 2	318. 6	+28. 4
Ownership:			
Commercial banks	62. 7	ᵖ 62. 3	−0. 4
Other publicly-held debt ¹	146. 4	ᵖ 160. 5	+14. 1
Total publicly-held debt	209. 1	222. 8	+13. 7
Government investment accounts	54. 6	59. 1	+4. 5
Federal Reserve banks	26. 6	36. 7	+10. 2
Total public debt	290. 2	318. 6	+28. 4

ᵖ Preliminary.
¹ Includes State and local governments, individuals, private investment institutions, corporations, all other private holders.

Exhibit 13.—Remarks by Secretary of the Treasury Dillon, October 27, 1964, before the 90th annual convention of the American Bankers Association, on fiscal and economic policies

This is the third time in the past four years that I have had the privilege of appearing before you to discuss national economic policies. During those years the United States has faced serious economic challenges both at home and abroad.

At home the central challenge, after years of recurring recession and slow growth, was to bring our economic performance closer to our unmatched potential.

There is no better measure of our success than the 44 months of unbroken business advance that the nation has thus far achieved, a record of recovery unexcelled in our peacetime history.

That advance has added more than $100 billion in real terms, or roughly 20 percent, to our annual output. In the space of less than four years, the increase in our annual production alone has exceeded the total gross national product of any other nation of the free world. In more personal terms, disposable income of the average American household, when measured in constant dollars, has risen by well over $700 during the last four years, an increase greater than that during the preceding eight years.

At the same time, company after company is reporting record profits and enlarged capital spending programs. It is clear that sharply higher returns on invested capital are furnishing new and stronger incentives for investment in modern plant and equipment—investment which will provide new jobs, increase productivity, and spur future growth.

Abroad, we have made progress in closing the deficit in our balance of payments, assuring a stable dollar and, on that solid base, building a stronger payments system. Our payments deficit during the last fiscal year was cut to $1.7 billion, well under half of the 1958–60 average. Confidence in the dollar has reduced the pressure on our gold stock. As a result, in each of the past two months our total gold stock has actually shown a slight increase over the level of the preceding year, the first time that we have seen a year to year increase in our gold stock since the Suez crisis in 1957.

These gains, together with the economic gains we have achieved at home, make an impressive record. But continued prosperity at home and further progress abroad are not, and never can be, automatic. So today our concern must focus on the challenges that still lie ahead.

We cannot, of course, now anticipate every possible threat to stable and orderly economic growth that may arise over the coming years. The complexity of our own economy, and the impact of events in other parts of this swiftly changing world, will continue to place the highest premium on flexibility in the use of all our economic policy tools.

We long ago learned that timely shifts in monetary policy are essential both to sustain growth and to combat inflationary excesses as they emerge. But experience has also shown that monetary policy, no matter how flexibly and intelligently implemented, cannot, by itself, achieve our multiple goals. We cannot insist that large changes in interest rates and credit availability must carry the full burden of stabilizing the domestic economy, and at the same time rely on monetary policy as the primary means of bringing balance to our international accounts. Nor can we expect monetary policy to do either of those jobs effectively if, by neglect or misdirection, we allow other policy tools to operate at cross purposes.

Our needs require, and have received, a coordinated blend of financial and economic policies that can be adapted to both our internal and external circumstances. This blend, as you know, has meant a new and indispensable role for fiscal policy, complementing and reinforcing more traditional monetary policies. Building on this recent experience is the best way to cope promptly and effectively with new challenges no matter from what direction they come.

Let me, however, make one point crystal clear. An active, flexible fiscal policy should not, and does not, require any sacrifice of the basic principles of fiscal responsibility. I believe that the record of these recent years amply demonstrates that point.

President Johnson has given, and continues to give, his personal attention to making certain that tax reduction is coupled with the strictest vigilance in assuring a full dollar of value for every dollar spent.

It is true that our budget has increased appreciably during the past four years; expenditures for 1965 are expected to be between $15 billion and $16 billion higher than in 1961. But $5 billion of the rise from the fiscal 1961 to the fiscal 1965 budget is accounted for by the urgent national need to maintain defenses second to none. Our space program has also seen an increase of more than $4 billion, as it had to if we were not to abandon that new frontier to the Soviets. And more than $2 billion is accounted for by larger interest payments on the Federal debt.

The true test of our record in expenditure control lies not in these items but in what has happened to all other governmental expenditures, including welfare programs, domestic housekeeping, ordinary civilian services, agricultural payments, and all the rest. Annual expenditures on all of these programs combined have grown, over the four years, fiscal 1961–65, by something less than $4½ billion. That figure is more than 25 percent less than the increase in these same programs during the 1957–61 period when the previous Administration was doing its level best to hold down unnecessary expenditures. This 25-percent improvement is the fair measure of the effectiveness of the current Administration's cost control effort over the past four years.

During the current fiscal year we will achieve a year-to-year decline in total expenditures for only the second time since the end of the Korean War permitted a substantial, but nonrecurring, cut in defense spending. And this year's reduction is being accomplished despite the half billion dollar cost of the long overdue adjustment in Federal salaries, the new antipoverty program, higher interest costs, and other built-in increases.

This accomplishment is possible only because of a sustained drive for budgetary economies that, for sheer intensity and effectiveness, exceeds anything within my experience in Government. One result is that Federal employment has been cut below the level at the end of fiscal 1962, two and a quarter years ago. In fact, Federal civilian employment, as a proportion of the total national work force, has dropped to its lowest point since 1941.

Fiscal responsibility does not imply that urgent national needs must go unsatisfied. But it does require, in the face of almost limitless pressures for new and expanded programs, a zealous and never-ending search for economies in less urgent areas. The Government sector of the economy must be held to a size where the burden of taxes and debt can be carried by a growing economy, without inflationary pressures.

By this test, too, the record is clear. During the current fiscal year, despite the requirements of defense and space, budget expenditures will be lower relative to our gross national product than at any time in the past 13 years. The share of total personal income preempted by the Federal individual income tax will decline to 9 percent, smaller than in any fiscal year since 1951. And the Federal debt as a proportion of GNP, a realistic measure of its burden, will, by the end of this fiscal year, have dropped back to the levels prevailing at the very beginning of World War II.

These figures also underscore the fact that the basic economic strategy of this Administration has been to look to the private sector of the economy as the main engine for expansion. Government has had an essential role to play in this process, but this role was not simply to seek increases in its own spending. Rather, it was to provide, through its economic and financial policies, a favorable climate for business investment and private spending. It was to promote continued increases in efficiency and productivity, so essential both to sustained domestic growth and to our export effort. And all of this had to be done within a framework of price stability.

Monetary and debt management policies could do part of the job. We ruled out the extremes of easy money, even had they been otherwise desirable, because it was vital to our payments effort that we keep our money market rates roughly in equilibrium with those abroad. But consistent with that constraint, we developed techniques to assure an ample flow of credit to long-term borrowers. That was, of course, a process in which the banking community played an essential role by aggressively seeking out and mobilizing funds that could, in turn, be made available to businesses, homebuyers, and State and local governments.

We could not, however, meet our objectives with monetary policy alone. There was also a compelling need to cut through the inhibitions, lethargy, and maze of detail that for much too long had blocked sorely needed tax reduction and reform.

Because of tax reduction, we have had temporarily to accept somewhat larger budgetary deficits than we would otherwise have had. We have not sought those deficits. They are the price we had to pay for timely, effective tax and fiscal policy. The price is acceptable only because, under existing conditions and with prudent management of the debt, those deficits do not pose an inflationary problem. They are, instead, a transitional step toward our basic goal of a balanced budget in a healthy, full employment economy.

The choice we faced was not one between balanced budgets and tax reduction. An economy prone to recession and slow growth is also prone to deficits, for we cannot meet our essential spending needs from a shrunken tax base. We learned that lesson the hard way during the latter part of the 1950's, a lesson highlighted by the record $12 billion deficit that followed the 1958 recession. The ironic, but plain, fact was that our excessively high tax rates were themselves contributing to the sluggishness of the economy.

Carefully designed tax reduction offered the most promising way out of that impasse. By expanding incomes and profits, it promised to greatly widen the tax base, with the result that our revenues would rise despite the reduced rates.

That is not simply theory. It is now being confirmed every day by actual experience. With continued expenditure control, and an expanded tax base, we can look forward to the steady reduction and eventual elimination of our budgetary deficit in a vigorously expanding economy.

This bold and successful use of fiscal policy has important implications for the future. There is now a growing national consensus that the more active use of fiscal policy, together with responsible debt management and monetary policies, has a key role to play in achieving our economic objectives. There is also a growing understanding that a more flexible fiscal policy need not be associated with loose spending practices, and that the added revenues yielded by economic growth can offer further opportunities for tax reduction.

During the coming session of Congress, we should undertake the next priority item on our agenda: an overhauling of the crazy quilt of excise taxes that we have inherited in good part from past emergencies. The extensive studies that are needed to lay a responsible groundwork for such action have been underway for some time.

We must guard, however, against allowing the first glow of success to distort the developing consensus on the responsible use of fiscal policy into something quite different. In this uncertain world, we simply cannot responsibly schedule fixed tax reduction for years ahead in blithe ignorance of, or unconcern for, expenditure needs and the state of the economy. Changes in our tax system must be recognized for what they are: strong medicine, to be prescribed only after the most painstaking and careful diagnosis.

A budget deficit acceptable under conditions of excessive unemployment would be dangerously inflationary when production is straining at capacity. A willingness to use fiscal stimulus under one set of conditions must be matched by a willingness to accept restraint when needed. I need not emphasize to this audience, which is so well schooled in the principle and practice of flexible monetary policies, the dangers of a rigid commitment to particular policies for years ahead, no matter how enticing the prospect may appear today.

One factor that must always receive great weight in our policy decisions is the imperative need to maintain price stability. With industrial prices today averaging almost precisely the same as in 1958, we can look back on the longest period of sustained stability in many decades. Manufacturing labor costs per unit of output have actually declined during the current expansion, a reflection of our rapid gains in productivity and responsible wage bargaining. In both respects, our performance has been unmatched by any other major industrialized nation.

There has been no persuasive evidence of a prolonged buildup of excessive liquidity in our domestic economy. Increases in the money supply since 1960 have been relatively modest, at a rate well below the increase in production. Corporate cash flow has been expanding rapidly, but we have large investment and working capital needs. As a result, aggregate corporate balance sheets do not reflect an accumulation of liquid assets that might fuel an uncontrollable burst of spending. And slowly, but noticeably, bank liquidity has been reduced.

One important factor in maintaining this balance, and thereby easing the task of the monetary authorities, has been the steady progress in restructuring the national debt. Since early 1961 outstanding marketable Treasury securities maturing in more than 5 years have increased by more than $26 billion, an amount exceeding the entire growth in the public debt. In effect, our entire cumulative budget deficit has been financed at long-term, drawing upon the savings generated by a growing economy in ways that will not contribute to inflationary pressures. This has meant an increase in the average life of the national debt from 4 years 6 months in January 1961, to 5 years 3 months as of the end of last month. And, instead of the creation of bank credit to finance the Government, commercial bank holdings of Federal debt have declined.

Taking a broad look at the past four years, I am persuaded that monetary policy has made as great a contribution to the solution of our balance-of-payments problem as it appropriately could have done. A severe tightening of credit might, it is true, have reduced the outflow of short-term funds, and attracted some money from abroad. That approach would have had merit if our deficit had resulted from the classic problem of internal inflation with shortages of labor and industrial capacity. But that was clearly not the case. The basic solution to our balance-of-payments problem lay elsewhere: in spurring gains in efficiency of operation and in improving the investment climate so that our industry could better its position in world markets. In these circumstances tight money, while perhaps permitting us briefly to balance our external accounts, would have provided only a fleeting illusion of progress. By working at cross purposes to our fundamental needs to stimulate investment and productivity, it would surely have been self-defeating.

These judgments do not in any way imply that monetary policy should not be sensitive both to inflationary pressures at home and to any new difficulties in the balance of payments that may require a prompt and effective response. To the contrary, the importance of the tax reduction program lies in part in the fact that it has placed the monetary authorities in a stronger position to deal appropriately with such contingencies should they arise.

As our economy moves ahead over the coming weeks and months, the monetary authorities will certainly be watching closely for evidence, either in financial flows or elsewhere, of forces that could develop into a threat to either price stability or orderly expansion. But we must not assume that the maintenance of price stability is the responsibility of the monetary authorities alone. For the most difficult problem—and one with which the monetary authorities are ill-equipped to deal—would be spreading wage and cost pressures that industry could not absorb from rising productivity. Here the heaviest responsibility rests on both industry and labor to maintain a relationship between wages, productivity, and prices that can permit us to prolong our excellent record of cost and price stability.

For price stability today is imperative, not only to our domestic economy, but to our balance-of-payments position. In the past year, we have begun to see clear evidence that price stability is gradually improving our international competitive position. During fiscal year 1964 our commercial exports rose by 16 percent, far exceeding the 9-percent rise in imports that has been a natural consequence of our rising levels of business activity. As a result, our commercial trade balance increased by $1.4 billion, helping to cut our balance-of-payments deficit over the same period more than in half. And during the recent summer months our exports reached a new peak, despite expected declines in grain shipments from the exceptionally high levels of last winter.

Important savings have developed in other sectors of our international accounts. By midyear, the annual balance-of-payments costs of our aid and defense programs had been trimmed back by roughly $500 million from their 1962 levels. Further reductions already scheduled will next year bring those savings to approximately $1 billion. The dangerous threat to the dollar arising from last year's accelerating outflow of portfolio capital has been successfully braked through the interest equalization tax. As anticipated, that necessary, but temporary, measure is providing the breathing time we need until European capital markets are more fully developed and our other measures have had time to become fully effective.

The favorable influence of these factors on our balance of payments is frequently obscured by erratic fluctuations from month to month and quarter to quarter. For example, our payments deficit dropped abruptly during the first quarter of this year in response to an unusual combination of temporary factors, only to give way to a considerably larger deficit in the second quarter. The latest figures for the third quarter, while still fragmentary, indicate that the deficit will fall between those extremes, and confirm the prospects of substantial improvement for 1964 as a whole. Looked at in the longer view we are justified in taking real satisfaction from the substantial improvement in our international payments that has characterized the past 15 months.

I am not suggesting that our balance-of-payments problem is over. It clearly is not. In some ways, the hardest part of the job remains ahead. Moreover, in a world of convertible currencies, with trade and capital free to flow across national boundaries, it will never again be possible to take the relaxed attitude toward our international payments that characterized much of the period since World War II.

What I am saying is that I am confident that this challenge can be met, and that it can be met while reaching new peaks of prosperity at home. That confidence does not arise out of any false hope that we can simply ride on the momentum of the past into a new era of "painless prosperity." Rather, it arises from the fact that we have learned much in recent years about how to use and blend our varied tools of Government policy in new ways, always within a framework of free markets and fiscal responsibility. It arises because once again our system of free private enterprise has demonstrated its enormous capacity for growth and innovation in a climate of price stability and renewed incentives. These are the solid building blocks of which we can and will fashion a better future for all America.

Exhibit 14.—Remarks by Secretary of the Treasury Dillon, March 19, 1965, before the 13th annual monetary conference of the American Bankers Association, Princeton, New Jersey, on capital markets, interest rates, and balance of payments

This is the fourth year in which I have had the special privilege of addressing this Conference of distinguished leaders in the world of finance. These have been years of remarkable innovation in financial practices and policies, public and private, both within the United States and abroad. Internationally, we have fashioned a framework for mutual consultation and cooperation that—measured against our common objectives of steady growth and flourishing world trade, coupled with substantial price stability—has proved both durable and viable.

But, despite much excellent progress, our international financial system still suffers from a disturbing disequilibrium, one I have discussed with you on previous occasions. This is the seemingly chronic tendency for capital to flow between countries in directions and in amounts that impede the entire process of restoring balance in the payments of deficit and surplus countries alike.

The Group of Ten, in their recent study [1] of the international monetary system, concluded unanimously that ways must be found to improve the process of balance-of-payments adjustment. The United States wholeheartedly joined in that conclusion and welcomes the systematic studies of this matter now underway in Working Party III of the OECD. However, if these studies are to have truly useful results they must face up to the stubborn and extremely difficult problem posed by the deep structural imbalances in the world's capital markets that have enormously complicated the smooth functioning of the adjustment mechanism.

The nature of the problem is clearly illustrated by developments in our balance of payments last year. By 1964, the measure we had undertaken to improve our trade position and to reduce the balance-of-payments impact of our aid and defense programs had achieved visible and gratifying results. Yet, as you know, our deficit last year was once again disappointingly large, primarily because capital had poured out of the United States in unprecedented amounts—in significant part to the strong surplus countries of Western Europe. The recent Annual Report of the Monetary Commission of the European Economic Community highlighted this point, noting that an improvement of about $3 billion in U.S. transactions for goods and services and Government accounts had been largely offset by a $2 billion increase in private capital outflows.

Within the basic limitations set by the needs of an underemployed domestic economy, the United States throughout the last four years had been alert to the fact that excessively easy money at home could only aggravate the problem of capital outflows. By shifting much of the burden for promoting domestic expansion to fiscal policy and tax reduction, we have enabled our monetary authorities to move gradually, but steadily, to an essentially neutral monetary policy.

Our short-term market interest rates have climbed significantly since the 1960–61 recession, responding largely to two half point increases in the discount rate. With the discount rate now at 4 percent, Treasury bill yields are within one-half percent or so of their postwar high, a high reached only briefly during the period of very tight money in 1959. Loan/deposit ratios of banks have gradually climbed to a postwar peak, and other traditional measures of bank liquidity have confirmed a gradual tightening in their position. The Federal Reserve has rather steadily reduced the free reserves of the banking system, and, for the past month, the banks have actually operated with a small net borrowed reserve position. While corporate cash flow has remained high, liquidity ratios have reached the lowest levels in a quarter of a century.

Clearly, credit has remained readily available in the United States throughout this period, and our bank lending and long-term interest rates are still low relative to most other countries. But it is also a palpable fact that rising investment opportunities and credit demands at home, combined with increases in the Federal Reserve discount rate and greater restraint in the provision of bank reserves, have noticeably reduced the ease of our market. Yet, instead of declining in response to these developments, the capital outflow has accelerated.

---

[1] See 1964 annual report, exhibit 49.

This fact alone casts into doubt the thesis of those who view the problem almost entirely in terms of "excessive" domestic liquidity, with tighter monetary policy the simple, effective, and unique remedy. Naturally, if one defines an excess of liquidity as synonymous with an excessive capital outflow, I suppose that position would be unassailable. But that kind of analysis bears no realistic relationship to the difficulty we face today. All it does is to define away the substance of a very real and tough problem.

In my judgment, it is much more enlightening, although still not the entire answer, to analyze the problem in terms of differences in investment profitability, rather than in terms of liquidity. Consider, for example, the outflow of funds for direct investment abroad, which has continued to rise, reaching $2.3 billion in 1964. At the present time, many American firms clearly believe that a portion of their available resources can be most profitably invested in subsidiaries abroad. That calculation rests on a variety of familiar considerations: The more rapid growth of certain foreign markets; a desire to operate inside a wall of external tariffs; proximity to readily available raw materials; and lower production costs, to name some of the most obvious factors.

But perhaps most important of all is the fact that U.S. industrial development so far exceeds that of any other country. This has brought with it a degree of competition that is unknown anywhere else in the world. Add to this our enormous flow of savings, and it is not surprising to find a general acceptance of lower rates of return on capital in this country than prevail elsewhere, rates that only partially reflect differences in risks between investments here and abroad. At the same time, our businessmen and investors tend to place higher capital values on prospective earnings than is the case elsewhere, and our corporations at times find it attractive to pay higher prices in the acquisition of going concerns abroad than would seem reasonable to local investors.

Whatever the specific reason that particular direct investments abroad appear to a given company to be a more profitable use for its funds, the fact is that we cannot effectively influence this judgment by simply reducing liquidity and tightening credit at hom. So long as the basic difference in profitability remains, any gain in terms of reduced foreign investment will entail a substantially larger cost in terms of dampening domestic investment as well. There seems, therefore, little warrant either in theory or in practice for basing economic policy on a presumption that corporate managers will permit considerations of the rate and availability of bank credit to affect their decisions on foreign investment, while leaving the domestic economy untouched.

In the broadest sense, international differences in the rate of return on investment—as these differences are reflected in interest rates and the intensity of demands for credit—also lie behind the accelerating outflow of bank loans and other credits abroad. This structural imbalance forced us to propose the interest equalization tax during the summer of 1963. It effectively increased the cost of long-term portfolio credit to foreigners in developed countries. As a result the outflow of long-term portfolio capital in 1964 dropped back to the 1960 level.

The plain fact is that foreign borrowers are willing and able to pay higher rates than domestic borrowers of similar credit standing with free access to the vast resources of the American credit market, and foreign loans are thus in many instances more profitable to the lending banks. The same is true for the placement of liquid funds by our corporations. But the massive outflow of these types of credit is also related to other deepseated structural characteristics of American and foreign capital markets.

As you know, with rare exceptions, foreign financial markets, even in countries with the most highly developed economies, lack a large and fluid short-term money market. Long-term bond markets are usually even more constricted. As a result, in most other countries there is simply no effective mechanism by which private borrowers and lenders, and to a very considerable extent governments, can readily raise or dispose of large sums in short periods of time in the open market. Instead, the available funds within each country are channeled almost entirely through a relatively few big institutions dealing with individual customers on a personalized basis. These institutional markets are fairly well insulated from the short-term money market, and frequently respond only sluggishly if at all to the actions of the monetary authorities.

The fluidity and size of the market available to most private borrowers abroad is further impaired by the fact that many foreign governments preempt a very large fraction of the savings available for investment, or direct it into officially sanctioned uses, frequently with a sizeable subsidy for preferred borrowers added along the way. This is partly a natural result of basic social decisions to provide, through Government social insurance programs, the protection for citizens that we in the United States furnish to a much larger extent through private insurance and private industry. But, it is also a reflection, in many instances, of a conscious desire to provide special preferences to one major group of borrowers or another, and to maintain a high degree of Government control of national economic development. In either case, the natural result is to leave those businesses and other borrowers that must look to the remainder of the market more or less perpetually starved for funds, and with an impelling desire to seek needed capital from abroad.

All of these factors have contributed to a structure of long-term interest rates in Europe that, with only one or two exceptions, has remained throughout the postwar period at levels that, in the light of past history, are usually high. Official discount rates, and the money market rates more immediately influenced by the official rates, often bear little relationship to the loan charges payable by local borrowers. And, faced with constricted internal markets, and thus denied a full range of fiscal and monetary tools, the authorities themselves often find it essential to pursue essentially domestic credit objectives—and in some instances even to finance internal budgetary needs—through adjustments in external flows of funds. Sometimes this is done by borrowing directly from abroad and sometimes by seeking to influence the external borrowing or placement of funds by their commercial banks.

The sheer size of the U.S. economy and the tremendous volume of funds raised in our credit markets, estimated last year at over $70 billion, help account for the much greater fluidity of our markets and their ability to adjust to, and absorb, large domestic or foreign demands with relative ease. But it is not a question of size alone. The relative freedom of the market mechanism, and the intensity of competitive pressures among institutions with a wide variety of investment options, permit funds to flow promptly from one sector of our economy to another in response to changing demands. And, a long history of confidence in our currency, further fortified by the stability of our prices in recent years, has encouraged individuals and investment institutions to commit funds freely at long term.

As a result of the pressure of the huge volume of private savings seeking investment in our market, our long-term interest rate structure has remained essentially stable during the past four years, even though money market rates have risen by 1½ percent or more to a range of 4 to 4½ percent. As a result, the differential between short- and long-term rates has almost disappeared. Nevertheless, the bond market has continued to absorb a record volume of long-term financing at stable rate levels.

Another indication of the strength of our longer-term markets is that, over the past four years, they have not merely provided the vast amount of funds necessary to support high levels of homebuilding, a remarkable expansion in business investment, and the rapidly growing needs of our States and localities. They have also provided funds to the Government, equal to the entire $28.8 billion Federal deficit during the first four years of this Administration. During that period more than that amount was placed in savings bonds and marketable debt maturing in over five years. This achievement is reflected in the increase of almost one year or 20 percent in the average length of the marketable debt to a level last seen in mid-1956.

In this setting we could not expect moderately tighter monetary policies to bring the needed reduction in the outflow of long-term funds abroad. The disparities in the structure of the capital markets of our different countries are simply too great to permit us to rely heavily on that approach toward adjustment. Much more is needed to bring interest rates here and in other industrialized countries into the rough alignment that is surely necessary if we are to put a permanent end to the destabilizing capital flows that have characterized the past two years.

It might, of course, be argued that extremely tight money would be able to do the job if continued over a long enough period. Such a policy rests on the highly doubtful assumption that in spite of our huge volume of savings it would be technically feasible—perhaps by drastically reducing the money supply—

to raise the general level of our bank and long-term interest rates by the 1½ to 2 percent that would be needed to achieve interest rate parity with Europe.

But even granting that assumption, such a policy would surely be self-defeating. Before it could achieve the interest rate objective, the extreme restriction of credit would surely move us toward domestic recession, and at a time when our economy is already failing to use its resources to the full. A recession would, in turn, delay our fundamental aim of creating a more favorable climate for investment in the United States. At the same time, it would rapidly create forces for easy money that would be likely to prove irresistible. Thus the end result would not be an improvement but rather an aggravation of our balance-of-payments problem.

To cite these limitations and difficulties in the use of monetary policy is not, of course, to say that monetary policy does not have a useful and indeed essential role to play in helping the adjustment process in the United States, as in other countries. It has played such a role, is playing such a role now, and will continue to do so in the future. In fact, as I suggested earlier, one of our chief reasons for relying primarily upon fiscal policy to stimulate the domestic economy was to give monetary policy additional freedom in coping with our balance-of-payments problem. And I can assure you that monetary policy remains fully available for further use should the need arise. But I see no realistic prospect that the full burden for achieving a permanent international adjustment in capital flows can reasonably be thrust on American monetary policy alone either now or in the foreseeable future.

Instead, as I have suggested before to this group, the only really satisfactory long-range solution to our present problem of excessive capital outflows lies in achieving a more attractive environment for investment within the United States through tax reduction and sustained growth, together with the development of far larger, far more efficient, and far more flexible capital markets abroad. While there has been some encouraging progress in both of these directions, much more remains to be done.

These are, of course, longrun measures, and their influence on capital flows must be expected to emerge only slowly. For the time being, the existing disequilibrium, and the urgency of reducing our deficit, has required that we seek the cooperation of our banks and other financial institutions, as well as of our industrial firms, in voluntarily reducing the flow of capital abroad. The response of those asked to participate in this voluntary program has been most gratifying. The effects are already clearly visible both in the foreign exchange markets and in our preliminary payments statistics which point to a sharp and favorable change since mid-February. But two swallows don't make a summer. We need a considerable period of balance to offset the deficits of the past. We know we can count on your cooperation in achieving this vitally needed result.

But the success of our present program does not, of course, meet the basic problem. The nations of the free world, working together, must develop better means for influencing capital flows within a basic framework of free markets and national objectives, and without placing intolerable burdens either upon monetary policy or upon the resources of the international monetary system.

We must be under no illusion that a different or improved international monetary system could in any way eliminate the need for adjusting these flows. But these two questions are nonetheless related, for one of the basic functions of the international monetary system is to provide sufficient means for financing deficits and surpluses to permit the working out of an orderly process of adjustment.

This linkage between the process of adjustment and the international monetary system seems to me to be at the source of much of the confusion and difficulty evident in recent international efforts to develop a common approach toward the further evolution of the international payments system. All the major countries are fully agreed, I believe, on the need for developing an assured method of generating international liquidity in adequate, but not excessive, amounts as world trade and production increases over the years ahead. This much clearly emerged from the studies of the Group of Ten and the International Monetary Fund last year.

But in recent months, there has been little progress toward more concrete agreement on methods and approaches. The pronounced divergences in view that have been evident can, I believe, be traced in good part to quite different assumptions about the relationship of international monetary reform to the current U.S. payments deficit.

The overriding need, in one European view, is to develop a mechanism which would force a prompt end to our payments deficits. We fully agree with these European friends on the necessity for achieving early balance in our international accounts. And we intend to achieve this goal by our own actions, which now for the first time cover all aspects of our payments problem.

But, in assessing the problems of the international monetary system, our concern and that of a number of other countries has been to look toward the future, when there will no longer be an American payments deficit pumping dollars into the reserves of other countries. So the thrust of our thinking has been to find the best way of developing supplementary means of providing the liquidity that is likely to be needed. We feel that this can only be done gradually and by building on what we now have. And we emphatically disagree with the thesis recently propounded in some quarters which would turn back the clock and embrace an outmoded and highly restrictive system, a system that would surely cripple the growth of international trade and commerce as our deficit was ended.

Under the circumstances, with these broad differences of approach, any final resolution of the variety of issues that have been raised seems to me highly unlikely until the United States has brought its international payments into balance. As that is done it will become less and less easy to ignore the potential need for supplementary sources of reserve assets and international credit facilities. Meanwhile, difficult and time consuming technical studies are well underway under the auspices of the Group of Ten, helping to clarify the issues and to evaluate alternative techniques. These studies will, I believe, provide the basis for timely agreements on ways and means for improving the present monetary system well in advance of any urgent need.

In looking back on the past four years, and on the postwar period as a whole, there can be no question that the present system—anchored on gold and the dollar, and effectively supplemented by the International Monetary Fund—has served the world well. The extremes of inflation and deflation characteristic of other postwar periods have been avoided. Barriers to trade have been lowered or removed. And, in this environment, the vast productive capabilities of the free world have been released to the benefit of us all.

The challenge for the future is to build further on this system, recognizing its potential weaknesses and shortcomings, but preserving the elements of strength and flexibility that have contributed so much to our progress.

In this area, as in the area of adjusting capital flows, I have no fixed blueprint to offer to those who will share the responsibility for developing solutions. I remain confident, however, that solutions can and will be found, provided only that the United States discharges its own immediate responsibility to maintain the full strength of the dollar as the world's primary reserve currency by achieving an early balance in its international accounts. And with the help of you gentlemen that is exactly what we are going to do.

Exhibit 15.—Remarks by Secretary of the Treasury Dillon, March 26, 1965, before the American Bankers Association Symposium on Federal Taxation, on fiscal and tax policy

I am particularly pleased to make this, my last public speech as Secretary of the Treasury, before a group which has contributed so much to the better understanding of economic issues over the past four years.

In the light of our experience during those years, I would like to consider a few of the problems and prospects that may lie ahead.

Budgetary policy

I have no doubt that, despite our better understanding of economic realities, a great deal of discussion over the next few years will continue to center around the question of budget deficits and balanced budgets. There are still many who hold that the budget should be balanced every year or at least over some very short period of years, no matter what the circumstances. This view usually assumes that a balanced budget is entirely neutral in its economic impact, neither inflationary nor deflationary, and thus has no effect at all upon the private economy.

But when we examine the facts a little more carefully, we discover that some taxes are more deflationary than others and that some expenditures are less inflationary than others—that our economic performance is affected by the structure of taxes and expenditures as well as by their level.

When we scrutinize the administrative budget, which is the budget that most people want to balance, we find a whole host of disparate items. In that budget, a loan is treated as an expenditure in exactly the same manner as wages paid, and the repayment of a debt to the Federal Government is treated as a revenue receipt just as if it were a tax collection. It would certainly be surprising if the achievement of balance between the so-called expenditures and the so-called revenues of such a budget turned out to have a neutral effect upon the private economy.

A far more realistic approach to budget making is to consider first the essential needs that must be met by Federal expenditures. We can then estimate the impact of these expenditures on the economy in the light of foreseeable revenues. Finally, after considering the economic outlook, we can make whatever adjustments appear necessary and so put together a budget that both meets essential national needs and produces an economic impact appropriate to existing conditions.

In 1963, for example, when we first proposed the tax cut, and again in early 1964, when it was about to go into effect, our budgets reflected the imperative need for restraint in public expenditures at a time when we were giving expenditures in the private sector of our economy so large a stimulus through tax reduction.

And in his Budget Message of this year, President Johnson recognized that, if we are to continue our steady progress toward the twin goals of full employment and balanced budgets, we must move carefully. Thus, while the projected deficit of $5.3 billion for fiscal 1966 was $1 billion less than that projected for fiscal 1965, the President found room to include a prudent amount of excise tax reduction designed not only to remove inequities but also to insure the continued expansion of our economy.

This approach means, as President Johnson has amply demonstrated, that, while on the one hand, we must provide for essential national needs, whether they be economic, social, or defense, we must also rigorously, even ruthlessly, seek out and eliminate waste and inefficiency wherever we find them.

We see the success of this approach in the fact that, over the past four years we have achieved a substantial improvement in our employment situation at the same time that we have compiled an outstanding record of price stability: a record which stands in striking contrast to the pattern of steadily rising prices in other leading industrial nations.

A proper concern for the level of employment and for the requirements of the economy need not lead to continuing deficits. If we can keep our economy moving steadily ahead, it is perfectly feasible, even after allowing for increases in budget expenditures of about $3 billion a year to foresee a balanced budget in fiscal 1968, just three years from now.

In evaluating budget policy, past, present, and future we must always bear in mind that our stubborn balance-of-payments problems force us to rely less on monetary policy and more on fiscal policy in fostering economic growth. As you know, we are now well launched upon a program to bring our balance-of-payments deficits to a swift and sure end. But there is little likelihood that the success of that program will permit us to shift more of the burden of sustaining domestic economic advance to monetary policy. High interest rates abroad and other structural imbalances in the world's capital markets will force us to continue, for the foreseeable future, to place our chief reliance on fiscal policy to keep our economy healthy and strong.

Flexibility of tax rates

But fiscal policy will not fulfill, as it must, its potential as a force for strong and stable economic growth, until we can employ it as a weapon to forestall—and not merely react to—recession. Thus, the President recommended in his Economic Message that the Congress take steps to ensure "that its procedures will permit rapid action on temporary income tax cuts if recession threatens." This is a reasonable alternative to the recommendation made by the Commission on

Money and Credit that the President be given discretionary authority to reduce tax rates when recession threatens. For, it allows us to deal with the problem of rapid and temporary fiscal adjustments while maintaining unchanged our traditional congressional control over taxes. It requires only the assurance of a prompt congressional vote whenever a temporary tax cut proposal is made by the President. The Congress can adopt whatever procedures it believes necessary to assure prompt action. But prompt action is absolutely essential since delay in the face of oncoming recession could easily cost the Nation billions of dollars in production and hundreds of thousands, or even millions, of jobs.

Expenditure policy

No matter, however, how versatile and potent a weapon we make of fiscal policy, we will continue to face critical choices in actually bringing it to bear upon our economic needs and problems. No simple arbitrary formula can tell us how to make those choices. A growing economy inevitably brings rising government expenditures, and confronts us with difficult decisions on how those expenditures should be made. A normal year's economic growth, such as an increase of $40 billion in gross national product, means that total expenditures in our society will have grown by $40 billion. For that is just what GNP is— the sum of all the final expenditures in our economy. Much of this growth can and should be in the things we buy, privately and individually, for ourselves. But as our economy and our wealth expand, so does our need for public services, and so does the capacity of State, local, and Federal Government to meet these needs. We must decide, each year, how many of our urgent public needs we should meet out of our growing productive capacity, which programs deserve priority, and which can be cut back.

These choices inevitably involve tough decisions like those we have recently made on Navy yards, veterans' hospitals, and Customs collectors. They also involve programs of enormous promise, such as the Peace Corps, improved education, or the war on poverty. Too often in the past such decisions have simply been the accidental byproducts of a confrontation between an alliance of the advocates of various expenditure programs on the one side and the opponents of all expenditure programs on the other. I am not at all sure that this approach has been very effective in weeding out expenditure programs, and I particularly doubt that it has succeeded in weeding out the least worthy ones.

But here again there is an alternative approach, which is simply the careful analysis of costs and benefits in particular programs. This is the kind of analysis that has gone into the development of our defense programs, into the veterans' hospital program and that is now being used in evaluating the supersonic transport program. It is in this direction, rather than in arbitrary budget ceilings, that we must seek for solutions in trying to allocate expenditures between the public and the private sectors of our economy.

Apart from the economic aspect of our fiscal policy, we must also consider its human aspects. That is why we have emphasized both the incentive and the equity aspects of our tax proposals. What we have said about incentives has fallen on fertile soil, but what we have said about equity has often fallen on harder soil.

While we all agree that we should have a tax system that is progressive in its impact, we do not all agree on just how progressive it ought to be. This is not surprising, but it has its unfortunate aspects. For a great deal of our concern about this problem of progression, or "vertical equity" has unintentionally drawn attention away from the equally serious problem of "horizontal equity," the unfair tax treatment of different individuals at basically similar income levels.

Capital gains at death and the estate tax

Perhaps the most important problem in this area of horizontal equity lies in the treatment of capital gains at death. Under our present law, a man who accumulates wealth during his lifetime from earned income and dividends will pay substantial income taxes during his lifetime on this income and estate taxes will also be levied on what he has left. Yet a second man whose investment has been in low dividend, high growth stocks may accumulate the same amount of wealth through increasing stock values. If he keeps these securities for his entire lifetime, he will receive the same estate tax treatment as the first man, but will never have paid any income tax on the increase in his wealth.

I see no justification for such widely disparate tax treatment of two individuals who through choice or circumstance happen to follow a different financial strategy for making money. Such treatment distorts the natural pattern of investment by placing a high premium on tax advantage. Why sell an asset whose value has increased and thereby incur a capital gains tax, if that tax can be avoided by holding on to the asset until death? By thus interfering with the free flow of capital in the market we unintentionally sap the vitality of our free enterprise system and harm both the economy and the Nation. In addition, such treatment of capital gains erodes the tax base and increases the tax burden on all who cannot benefit from this provision.

In the light of the Administration's unsuccessful efforts to solve this problem in 1963, it seems likely that consideration of possible alternatives for providing more equitable treatment of capital gains at death should be coupled with a thorough review of our taxes on estates and gifts. These taxes have not been subjected to such a review for many years and their modernization deserves a high priority. For one thing, a thorough review of estate tax exemptions and rate schedules seems clearly in order.

Treatment of lower income taxpayers

On the problem of vertical equity, the treatment of taxpayers at different income levels, there has been much concern over how the tax burden is distributed between the very rich on the one hand and everyone else on the other. As a result, we have given little attention to the progressivity of our system in the middle- and lower-income groups, which include most of our citizens.

The fact is that our tax system involves very little progression between the lowest brackets and those of taxpayers with up to about $15,000 of income. Furthermore, whatever progressivity the individual income tax has at these levels is offset to a considerable extent by regressive taxes elsewhere in our tax system.

Clearly, we do not give adequate tax relief to those with very low incomes. For instance, the biggest jump in progressivity is at the start of the very first bracket, where we jump from a zero rate all the way to 14 percent.

Although it may be surprising to some, the fact is that, over time, the income tax bite increases more at low levels than it does at high levels. In 1955 the poorest one-fifth of American families had an average income tax rate of 2.9 percent. By 1961 this had risen to 3.6 percent. On the other hand, the 5 percent with the highest incomes had an effective tax rate of 18.9 percent in both years even though, in 1955, that 5 percent included all families with incomes of over $13,000, and in 1961 it only included families with incomes of over $16,400. Clearly an income tax with fixed rates and exemptions tends to become less and less progressive with the passage of time.

These considerations bear directly upon our current intention to reduce excise taxes, which are particularly regressive. In the longer run, they require that we give serious thought to the structure of our tax system at the lower income levels. We made a beginning in this direction in the Revenue Act of 1964 with the minimum standard deduction, a new method of lessening the tax burden of those who can least afford to carry it. But both interests of tax fairness, as well as the need to lighten the burden of true poverty, call for further action.

Relationship between the corporate and the individual income tax

The final issue of tax equity I would like to stress concerns the interrelationship between the corporate tax and the individual income tax. We often hear the claim that dividends are subject to double taxation. But if one devotes any time to this matter, it becomes quite clear that at some income levels and with some dividend distribution policies, the total tax burden on corporate income can be less than the total tax burden on income earned directly, say, through a proprietorship or a partnership.

One serious problem is the question of just who pays the corporate tax. There has been a great deal of theoretical speculation about this very complex problem. Yet even with the careful statistical analyses of recent years we are still far from agreement.

Should we eventually decide that the tax is largely borne by shareholders, the issue of the so-called double taxation of dividends must then be considered hand-in-hand with the issue of the appropriate treatment of retained earnings.

For retained earnings ultimately increase stock values and so contribute to capital gains, which brings us back full circle to issues such as the treatment of capital gains at death.

These, then, are some of the many problems and prospects that lie ahead in fiscal and tax policy. What is clear is that our problems are continually changing. If we are to keep up with the times we must continually attack them with the newest and best tools of analysis in a climate as free as possible of old prejudices. That is the unchanging challenge that is always before us.

Exhibit 16.—Remarks by Secretary of the Treasury Fowler, April 17, 1965, before the annual convention of the American Society of Newspaper Editors, on economic policy

I am particularly happy to make this, my first full-fledged speech as Secretary of the Treasury, before a group that plays so vital a role in informing the American public about the complex and critical issues that confront our nation.

As I do so I am conscious that I observe a precedent set four years ago when my distinguished predecessor and good friend, Douglas Dillon, made his maiden economic address as Secretary of the Treasury before this very same group.

In that address, he set forth a two-fold program to bring us closer to our economic goals: First, a complete overhaul of our tax system to augment incentive, initiative, and effort in the private sector of our economy; and, second, an overall monetary approach to assure the ample availability of long-term credit so essential to domestic growth while maintaining short-term rates at levels high enough to prevent any excessive outflow of dollars abroad. These policies, he declared, would lead us, and I quote, "to a period of growth and prosperity during the sixties such as this Nation has never known."

Next month, the economic expansion that began in February of 1961 will become the longest in the entire history of our nation, except for the expansion that included World War II. There could be no better testimony to the success of our economic policies over the past four years.

As Under Secretary of the Treasury I was privileged to participate in the first formation of those policies and to assist at every major stage of their development, adoption, and execution. I am convinced we must continue to build upon those policies, improving them as we can, and adapting them to meet new problems and new needs. But policies cannot be static in a world as rapidly changing as ours. The problems and prospects we face today could scarcely be more different from those we faced four years ago.

According to the Gallup Poll published yesterday, the American people consider economic problems the least important facing the Nation, in contrast to the people in many countries abroad who cite economic problems as their most important. And the latest quarterly report on consumer attitudes by the University of Michigan finds consumer confidence in the Nation's economic outlook at its highest level since 1956. The business community continues to demonstrate through its investment plans and behavior that it shares this same solid confidence in our economic prospects. But while our grounds for confidence are indeed firm, we must never make the cardinal mistake of taking continued progress as a foregone conclusion. For continued progress rests on the continued success of proper government policies and private effort. And to judge what those policies and that effort must be if we are to sustain the current upsurge, we must understand what they have been in the past, how the best features can be conserved and built upon for the future. It will be our purpose to appraise the past as a basis for the future.

Certainly, the expansion we now enjoy was far from a foregone conclusion four years ago.

Then we were just emerging from our fourth postwar recession, acutely aware that each of the three prior recessions had been followed by shorter and weaker recoveries, and that the previous recession had produced the largest peacetime budget deficit in our history. Unemployment was intolerably high. Business investment was far less than we needed to generate more vigorous and viable economic growth and maintain a strongly competitive position in world markets, including our own home market which was becoming increasingly open to import

competition. At the same time, a series of balance-of-payments deficits—aver·
aging, on the basis of regular transactions, almost $4 billion a year from 1958–60—
had made us vulnerable on the international front.

We were firmly convinced that the only final answer to our problems on both
the domestic and international fronts lay in reinvigorating the private sector as
the prime mover in the achievement of our economic goals.   The private economy
simply could not do its job as long as incentives were dulled and it continued
to labor under excessively high wartime tax rates, rates originally applied to
restrain strong inflationary pressures that accompanied wars and emergencies.

Our first step was to redouble the incentives for greater private domestic
investment in new plant and equipment—investment that had been lagging for
far too long and whose strength was essential if we were to have a firm foundation for sustaining uninterrupted economic growth for any long period of time.
The Revenue Act of 1962 granted a tax credit of 7 percent on new investment
in machinery and equipment, and in that same year the Treasury reformed and
liberalized the tax treatment of depreciation.   Together with the cut in the
corporate tax rate contained in the Revenue Act of 1964—amounting to some
$2.7 billion at current income levels—these measures have raised the profit-
ability of a typical investment in new equipment by more than one-third.

We complemented our initial move to accelerate private investment by reducing substantially personal income tax rates across the board, thereby cutting
more than $11 billion, at current income levels, from the tax load borne by
individual taxpayers, thus providing a massive increase in private demand.

To these tax measures for expanding the role of our private sector, we
joined a rigorous program of control over Government expenditures, a program
that has reached new heights of intensity and effectiveness under the leadership
of President Johnson.   In his administrative budgets thus far—those covering
fiscal years 1965 and 1966—President Johnson has held total expenditure
increases down to an average of $1 billion a year, $2 billion or two-thirds, less
than the average annual increase of $3 billion over the previous 10 years.

The response of the private economy to these policies has been magnificent.
From the first quarter of 1961 to the quarter just ended, our gross national
product has grown by an average of more than 5 percent a year, in constant
prices.   The unemployment rate has fallen from 6.9 percent in February of 1961
to 4.7 percent last month, a 7-year low.   At the same time, we have gained some
5 million jobs, including 1.7 million in the last 12 months.   Particularly significant is the 600,000 job gain in manufacturing over the last 12 months, bringing total manufacturing employment back around the peak level of 17½ million
for 1953, despite the tremendous technological advances in labor-saving devices
in this period.   Profits have reached new highs each year, for a total gain of
over 60 percent in profits after taxes.   Business investment in new plant and
equipment has recovered sharply from its tendency during the 1950's to lag
or decline.   This year's planned expenditures for plant and equipment stand,
according to the latest official survey, at $50.2 billion, or more than double the
level of a decade ago.   And the $14.5 billion growth in those expenditures for
the 5 years 1961–65 exceeds by $4.1 billion the increase for the entire decade
of the fifties.   And, after taxes and in constant dollars, average per capita
income has grown by an average of 3⅓ percent a year.   And these have been
real gains—preserved by a record of price stability—unmatched by that of any
other major industrial country.

Our resurgent economic performance since early 1961 has added more than
$100 billion in real terms to our national output, a total that far exceeds the
entire added output during the same period by all of Western Europe.   As a
yardstick, one might remember that this added slice on our national cake in
the last four years exceeds the entire gross national product of France and
Belgium.   In fact, the increase alone in our national output over the past four
years surpasses the total national output of any other nation of the free world,
and continues to widen the already enormous distance that separates our ability
to produce from that of the Soviet Union.

These are the gains, and the policies, upon which we must build, for they offer
us solid ground from which we can move confidently into the future.   These,
however, are not the only gains the past four years have brought us.   For
underlying all these is an achievement whose importance is impossible to
measure and equally impossible to overemphasize.

I speak of the remarkable degree of cooperation, understanding, and mutual confidence that has gradually emerged over the past 4 years between business and labor and Government. As we have pursued policies to fashion a better balance between the public and private sectors, business and labor and Government have moved together in a growing partnership for progress. They have discovered that by pulling together they can achieve much more than by pulling apart. They have become more concerned about working together toward greater abundance for all and less concerned about who receives the greater marginal advantage—and the result has been greater wage-income for the workingman, greater profits for the businessman and the investor, and greater revenues for meeting the demands on Government at lower tax rates for the taxpayer. And these results merely suggest what accomplishments the future may hold as, more and more, we bring to bear the full resources of this Nation in a concerted attack upon the problems that confront it. An essential ingredient in this better understanding between business, labor, and Government is national leadership. No man in our long national history has done more or labored with greater intensity to bring about this understanding than the man in the White House. He works at it night and day. And his example is one for all of us to follow if we are to sustain our recent advances and cope with the emergent problems of our time.

We are fortunate that the problems before us today are vastly different from those that loomed ahead four years ago. For those early problems, domestically, at least, were largely the product of our failure, while our problems today issue, in large part, from the very success of our labors over the last four years.

Despite the sure progress we have made in creating more jobs we have yet to reach our interim goal of 4-percent unemployment. To reach that goal, we must sustain a steady growth in demand, a growth to which Government fiscal policies have made, and will continue to make, a vital contribution.

The prudent amount of excise tax reduction we have scheduled for the last half of this year, while improving our tax structure, will also help sustain our economic momentum by expanding private purchasing power. At the same time, it will offer new incentives for price reductions. But the excise tax reduction must be a prudent amount, not an excessive one that will interrupt the movement of the last two years from large budget deficits towards balance as the economy moves forward to the objective of full employment with balanced budgets or surpluses.

While our economy is still not operating at full potential, we may approach the point where growing demand alone cannot make the inroads upon unemployment we want without undermining the gains in efficiency we need or exerting a strain upon our prices. This means growth in demand must be accompanied by a broad and growing attack on so-called hard core, or structural, unemployment. Through such programs as Manpower Retraining and the Job Corps we are just beginning to mount such an attack.

In addition to the compassion we share with all for those who lack opportunity, there are hard-bitten financial and economic reasons why the Treasury was and will continue to be in the forefront of those supporting the efforts of the Department of Labor and the Office of Economic Opportunity in this area.

The need to reduce structural unemployment and the need to preserve price stability are two of the paramount challenges we face in the domestic economic field. And any effective answer to these challenges cannot come from Government programs alone, it must come, on the contrary, from the joint effort of Government and the private sector. In this country we have long been familiar with private programs to train or retrain the unskilled and to place them in productive jobs. But surely there is enormous room, and need, for more programs of this kind. And most critical of all is the need for private industry to seek ways of synchronizing its recruitment policies with these retraining programs, whether public or private. The time has come for America to take the same private initiative and ingenuity that have fashioned the most powerful economic machine in history and apply them, more and more, to the task of helping the many poor or disadvantaged in our society who do not fully share in its abundant life.

At the same time, nothing could be so foolish or so wasteful as to expend our talents and our resources in trying to sustain our economic upsurge and extend its benefits to more and more of our citizens, if we fail to protect our hard-won gains against inflation. The policies of this Administration will continue to support strong and sound, but not excessive, growth in our economy and in the availability of credit essential to that kind of growth. For its part, the Treasury will continue to manage the public debt prudently, seeking to place any increase in that debt in the hands of private savers rather than in commercial banks, where it might contribute to inflation.

But continued wage and price stability must depend in the future, as it has in the past, upon the determination of American business and American labor to avoid wage rises that outdistance our gains in productivity and price rises not justified by actual cost increases. Wage and price stability is vital to both our balance of payments and our domestic economic progress, and it is to American business and American labor that we must look to maintain it.

On the international financial front, as in our home economy, we can meet the challenges before us with the full confidence that we deal from a position of growing strength. As President Johnson pointed out in his Balance-of-Payments Message earlier this year, we have the world's most productive and efficient economy, the world's largest supply of gold, the world's strongest creditor position, and—by virtue of our fine record of price stability—the world's most favorable trade position.

Therefore, let there be no confusion: our balance-of-payments problem bears no kinship to the classic pattern in which, because it cannot compete successfully, one country cannot sell as much goods and services as it buys. Our commercial trade surplus last year stood at $3.7 billion, over $1 billion larger than it was four years ago, and more than twice the size of West Germany's, the next largest in the world. And our private investments abroad exceed the total of foreign investment in the United States, plus all other liabilities to foreigners, by some $18 billion, a figure that grows larger every year.

Moreover, the hard-won improvement in our competitive position, the balance-of-payments measures that we have employed over the past four years, and our rising returns from private foreign investment, have brought us some $3.5 billion worth of balance-of-payments improvement, enough, all else aside, to have given us virtual balance in our payments last year.

In a climate of wage-price stability, our tax measures to heighten incentives and encourage greater productivity at home, along with numerous direct aids to exports, have helped make American business a formidable competitor indeed in markets abroad, as our huge trade surplus demonstrates.

We have also reduced by almost $500 million the annual balance-of-payments cost of a foreign aid program of far larger dollar dimensions. Today, 85 percent of our foreign aid commitments are spent for American goods and services. In spite of rising costs abroad, we have cut $700 million from our net military expenditures abroad.

Despite these improvements we had, as you know, a balance-of-payments deficit last year of $3 billion, largely the result of swelling private capital outflows that last year amounted to $6.4 billion, $2.5 billion more than in 1960, and $2.1 billion more than in 1963.

The President's new program calls for redoubling all our prior balance-of-payments efforts. But most important, it asks our businesses and banks to cut down on the flow of our capital abroad, until new arrangements in the international monetary system and improved capital markets abroad offer assurance that uninhibited capital flows will not endanger the dollar. Over the next few weeks we will have some first hard figures to show exactly how successful that voluntary effort has been thus far. But we have only to look abroad and see how much dearer and scarcer dollars have become to recognize what good results that effort has already yielded.

I have no doubt that this voluntary program will succeed. And surely there can now be no doubt in anyone's mind, here or abroad, that American Government and American business are determined to bring our balance-of-payments deficits to a swift and sure end. End them we must, and end them we shall.

We do not, however, conceive of the voluntary program as a final or fundamental solution to our balance-of-payments problem. Nor do we join with those who would have us hide within a tight protective shell of direct controls or rashly risk harm to our domestic economy by applying a hard brake to credit expansion. On the contrary, the more lasting solution to our balance-of-payments problem must continue to come from our unflagging efforts to make our economy continually more competitive in world markets and continually more attractive and more accessible to foreign capital. It must come, as well, from European efforts to improve their own capital markets, markets whose deficiencies become more apparent as our interim measures to halt excessive capital outflows take firmer and firmer hold.

Our very success in moving toward lasting balance in our payments has begun to throw into sharper relief a potential problem in our international payments system, a problem that will require concerted attention in the months ahead. For the United States can no longer afford to furnish steady increases in international liquidity through deficits in our international payments. As those deficits dwindle, it will become more and more urgent that we progress toward some agreement with our foreign friends on ways to strengthen the international monetary system and assure ample liquidity for expanding world trade.

Thus, on both the international and domestic economic fronts, we do not suffer from any lack of challenge, or any lack of opportunity. But there is no challenge and no opportunity before us which we are not far more able to meet than we were four years ago. If we continue to build upon the progress and the policies of those years, we can look forward in all sober confidence to sustained economic progress on all fronts far into the foreseeable future.

Our failures during the fifties taught us that we cannot fashion successful economic policies by remaining in thrall to some abstract theory, or by adhering to some doctrinaire dictum of the past. They taught us the folly of exclusive or excessive reliance upon one policy instrument for a single solution to all our problems.

The success of the past four years has demonstrated how our various instruments of economic policy—tax policy, expenditure policy, monetary policy, and many privately woven policies, as for example, the avoidance of unstabilizing action in the field of wages, prices, and inventories—can work together, in proper proportions and with sound balance, to move us simultaneously toward multiple economic goals. Each policy instrument has its strengths and its limitations under given conditions. The task is to coordinate these instruments in ways that respond to the needs of a complex and rapidly changing economic scene.

To succeed in that task requires that our approach be pragmatic rather than dogmatic, balanced rather than extreme, resilient rather than rigid. It requires that the public and the private sector of our economy work as partners in the pursuit of our national economic goals. We have seen what surpassing accomplishments can come from following this path. If we but continue to follow it, I see no end to those accomplishments.

Exhibit 17.—Other Treasury testimony published in hearings before congressional committees, July 1, 1964–June 30, 1965

Secretary of the Treasury Dillon

Statement on the budget for 1966, published in hearings before the Committee on Appropriations, House of Representatives, 89th Congress, 1st session, January 28, 1965, pages 30–35.

Monetary Developments

Exhibit 18.—Statement by Secretary of the Treasury Dillon, February 1, 1965, before the House Committee on Banking and Currency, on H.R. 3818, an act to eliminate the provision of existing law that Federal Reserve banks hold gold certificates equivalent to at least 25 percent of their own deposit liabilities

I welcome this opportunity to discuss H.R. 3818, which would implement a recommendation by the President in his Economic Message to adapt the gold reserve provisions of the Federal Reserve Act to the realities of present and prospective monetary requirements. This would be achieved by eliminating the provision of existing law that the Federal Reserve banks hold gold certificates equivalent to at least 25 percent of their own deposit liabilities. The similar requirement that a gold certificate reserve of 25 percent be maintained against Federal Reserve notes in circulation would not be affected.

The need for action

The need for this legislation does not arise from any sudden emergency or crisis, nor does it signal any prospective change in the economic and financial policies of the Administration or of the Federal Reserve System. In the future as in the past, our domestic monetary policies will be directed toward meeting the basic needs of our economy for adequate, but not excessive, amounts of money and credit. Gold will continue to be made freely available, at the fixed price of $35 per ounce, to meet the legitimate demands of foreign monetary authorities, a policy that is the basic foundation of the international monetary system. The purpose of this legislation is simply to eliminate any unnecessary questions or doubts about our ability to discharge these two fundamental responsibilities with full effectiveness over the years ahead.

Sustained, healthy growth at home—marred neither by inflationary excesses nor by widespread unemployment and wasted resources—must necessarily be supported by orderly growth in the volume of money and credit. This monetary expansion will, in turn, require a larger base of bank reserves, which are held largely in the form of deposits by the commercial banks at the Federal Reserve. It will also mean larger amounts of currency in circulation—currency consisting almost entirely of Federal Reserve notes—as the rising volume of trade generates additional demands for cash.

Under the provisions of present law, these expanding Federal Reserve note and deposit liabilities will in turn require that increasing amounts of our gold be set aside as part of the Federal Reserve banks' gold certificate reserves. But, the present operating margin of so-called free gold over and above existing requirements is already relatively small. The normal growth of our domestic money supply will exhaust this margin within a year or two, even without the outflow of a single ounce of gold.

Clearly, the capacity of the Federal Reserve to accommodate the monetary and credit needs of a strong and growing economy with stable prices must not be jeopardized. Equally clearly, our pledge to maintain the convertibility of the dollar into gold at $35 an ounce must not be cast into doubt by fear that our gold stock available for that purpose may be inadequate.

True enough, the emergency provisions of present law can be invoked if needed to suspend the gold cover requirement, but these provisions clearly are framed for temporary use rather than for long-range needs of growth. H.R. 3818 would meet this problem simply and straightforwardly, for as long ahead as anyone can now foresee, by immediately freeing almost $5 billion of gold presently held as reserves against Federal Reserve deposits. It will also permit us to avoid the present necessity of automatically setting aside additional gold as the growth of our economy enlarges the volume of bank deposits.

The present situation

At the end of 1964, the volume of Federal Reserve notes in circulation, which make up over 95 percent of our basic currency, totaled $35.3 billion. At the same time, Federal Reserve deposit liabilities amounted to $19.5 billion. Together, these Federal Reserve liabilities required a gold certificate reserve of $13.7 billion, absorbing for that purpose all but $1.4 billion of the gold certificates issued to the Federal Reserve against the Treasury gold stock. And since January 1st the Treasury gold stock has declined by $200 million as a result of sales to foreigners, with further losses to be expected.

In terms of ratios, gold certificate holdings had fallen to 27.5 percent of the note and deposit liabilities on December 31, 1964. This represented a decline of 2.2 percentage points in the ratio in the space of a year, and during that year our loss of gold to foreigners amounted to only $125 million. The decline in the ratio during 1964 was thus almost entirely accounted for by the needs of our domestic economy for additional money and bank credit and by the expansion in currency that is a normal reflection of growing trade and business turnover.

Looked at over a longer period of time, it is true that declines in our gold stock, as well as increases in Federal Reserve notes and deposits, have contributed to the declining ratio. These losses of gold to foreigners are, of course, closely connected to the balance-of-payments deficits we have run over the past 15 years.

It is essential that the vigorous effort launched in 1961 to reduce and eliminate that deficit and to stem the gold loss be continued and reinforced until equilibrium is restored. The Administration, as you know, attaches the highest priority to that effort, and the President will shortly review our entire balance-of-payments program in a special message to the Congress.

However, it is abundantly clear that the U.S. cannot expect to support its own long-term monetary expansion—an expansion that will inevitably be associated with the continued growth of our domestic economy—by attracting to this country a disproportionate share of world gold reserves. The fact is that, even after the large gold outflow of the past decade or more, the United States still holds some 35 percent of the monetary gold of the entire free world. Certainly, it is essential that this country, with the dollar playing a key role as a world reserve and trading currency, continue to hold a large gold stock, and our policies are directed toward that end. Moreover, as our balance-of-payments deficit is ended, some reflux of gold from abroad could be a normal and healthy development. But, it would be shortsighted and self-defeating to attempt deliberately to draw in from abroad the billions of dollars of gold that would be necessary over the years simply to meet the mechanical requirements of present law as our economy grows.

During the past year, Federal Reserve notes in circulation increased by $2,466 million. Of this, $662 million resulted from a decline of the same amount in the circulation of silver certificates. Meanwhile deposits of member banks, representing their required serves, also grew $1,037 million during 1964. Thus, disregarding the temporary, one-time impact of the retirement of silver certificates, it was necessary under present law to add over $700 million of gold to the reserves required against Federal Reserve notes and deposits. This amount is more than the average annual increase over recent years in monetary stocks of gold in the entire free world.

If we attempted to drain gold from abroad year after year in the amounts needed to meet the essentially arbitrary and outmoded gold cover provisions of present law, the only result would be a drive by other countries to protect their own gold by controls and restrictions that would sacrifice all the progress that has been made toward freer trade and payments among the nations of the free world. Far from looking toward future increases in our gold stock adequate to meet the gold cover requirement, the hard fact is that until our own balance of payments can be brought into equilibrium, we must be prepared for further outflows.

The purpose and effectiveness of the gold reserve requirement

The current gold cover requirement is an outgrowth of a much earlier period in our monetary history, and can be fully understood only in the context of circumstances that have long since vanished. Prior to the establishment of the Federal Reserve System in 1913, the several kinds of paper currency then in use circulated alongside gold coins domestically, and were freely convertible, directly or indirectly, into gold. In an effort to protect this convertibility, a variety of devices was used at various times to maintain the note circulation in a fixed relationship to gold and to provide assured redemption facilities. One result was that the supply of currency was not responsive to the changing needs of the economy, and this so-called inelasticity, combined with deficiencies in the banking structure, helped make the economy prone to recurrent bouts of inflation and panic.

The Federal Reserve System was designed to eliminate these defects by providing a means for adjusting the supply of currency, deposits, and credit flexibly to the needs of commerce and business. At the same time, however, our currency, including the new Federal Reserve notes, remained convertible into gold. Under these circumstances it was entirely natural that those framing the Federal Reserve Act included a provision that the Federal Reserve banks maintain certain minimum reserves of gold in relation to their note and deposit liabilities, even though the passage of the Federal Reserve Act clearly recognized that the supply of money and credit should be adjusted to the needs of the economy rather than set in some fixed relationship to gold. These minimum requirements were apparently considered desirable largely to encourage full public confidence in the new institutions; to assure acceptability of the newly introduced Federal Reserve notes alongside gold; and finally to provide some ultimate limit to the expansion of Federal Reserve credit.

It is also worthy of mention that the original Federal Reserve Act treated reserves against deposits in a different manner than reserves against Federal

Reserve currency. In the first place the reserves against deposits were originally set at 35 percent while those against notes were set at 40 percent. Possibly more significant is the fact that the original Federal Reserve Act provided for reserves against notes to be held only in gold, but permitted either gold or "lawful money" to serve as reserves behind deposit liabilities. Only since 1945, when the current 25 percent requirement was established, have note and deposit liabilities been treated in the same fashion. Thus there is clear precedent for treating deposit liabilities in a different fashion from Federal Reserve notes as far as reserves are concerned.

I believe the record of the past half century makes it amply clear that the provision of Federal Reserve credit, and the associated increase in its note and deposit liabilities, has, quite properly, been related to the needs of the economy rather than to the reserve requirements specified by law.

During the first two decades of the Federal Reserve System, when our currency was still redeemable in gold domestically, the level of Federal Reserve bank deposits and currency typically fluctuated far below the limits set by the gold reserve requirement. As shown by the table attached to my statement, this remained the pattern during the 1930's and early 1940's, after the convertibility of our currency into gold by American residents was ended. At one time, in 1940, the ratio actually rose as high as 91 percent.

Toward the end of World War II, there was concern that the vast expansion of money and credit required by wartime financing might exhaust the "free gold" held in excess of legal requirements, thus hampering the war effort. Congress consequently reduced the reserve requirements set by the original Federal Reserve Act to the present uniform requirement of 25 percent in gold against both notes and deposits. As it turned out, of course, the war was soon over, and the actual ratio remained over 40 percent until 1959. This experience clearly demonstrates that the release of gold from the legal requirement in excess of the needs that actually materialized did not become a basis for an unwarranted expansion in Federal Reserve credit.

Today, the strong probability that the present margin of gold over the 25 percent requirement will be exhausted within a relatively short time no more indicates a need for domestic monetary restriction than the existence of a wide margin of "free gold" in the past provided a useful signal or excuse for monetary expansion. The fact is that, the Federal Reserve, in discharging the fundamental responsibility delegated to it by the Congress for regulating the supply of money and credit in accord with the needs of the economy, must not be constricted by an arbitrary formula designed for another time.

While the desirability of eliminating the gold reserve requirement against Federal Reserve bank deposits appears to me beyond dispute, I recognize that the purpose of any change in a requirement of this kind that has lingered on for many years can easily be misunderstood and misconstrued. There may be some, for instance, who fear that this action may in some fashion imply a departure from the Administration's firm policy of maintaining the stability of the dollar both at home and internationally. Let me, therefore, make it crystal clear that I am most keenly aware of the dangers that can come from an undisciplined expansion of credit. The proposal before you does not carry this danger.

In the future, as in the past, the best assurance we can have that the supply of bank reserves will be neither so little as to stifle growth nor so large as to fuel inflation lies in a responsible and independent Federal Reserve System, functioning within a framework of responsible Government. For our part, this Administration has and will continue to work in close cooperation with the Federal Reserve in developing an effective financial program, while fully respecting its unique place within our structure of Government and its special responsibility for developing informed, independent judgments concerning monetary policy.

International implications

President Johnson has recently reiterated the fixed policy of the United States to defend the present gold value of the dollar "with every resource at our command." The Chairman of the Federal Reserve Board has repeatedly made it clear that the existing gold reserve requirement need be no bar to our making good on that pledge. Present law provides that the gold requirement can be suspended, initially for 30 days, and subsequently for intervals of 15 days. It should be clearly understood by all that that provision of law could and would be invoked if required to meet foreign demands, and that the suspension would be renewed as long as needed.

It would clearly be incongruous, however, to fall back on special and easily misunderstood powers for temporary suspension at a time when we are dealing with basic long-term problems rather than with a passing emergency. Reliance on a temporary arrangement can give rise to totally unwarranted doubts at home and abroad over the extent of our commitment to the international stability of the dollar, and over our ability fully to support that commitment. Without question, prompt passage of the measure before you, unequivocally releasing some $5 billion of gold from the present requirement, will reinforce confidence in the stability and strength of the dollar by placing beyond any doubt the willingness of both the executive and legislative branches to make our gold fully available in its defense.

In this connection, it is worth emphasizing that almost all industrially important foreign countries have long since abandoned any rigid tie between their gold holdings and the domestic monetary system. One relatively small country, Belgium, fixes a minimum legal ratio between gold and central bank note and deposit liabilities. One other country, Switzerland, has retained a link to the note issue (as would H.R. 3818), but it has no requirement against other central bank liabilities. In the Netherlands, the comparable reserve requirement can be met by holdings of foreign exchange as well as gold. South Africa, which accounts for 70 percent of the free world production of gold, also, and understandably, has a gold reserve requirement very similar to our own present requirement. In every other instance, among the leading financial powers of the free world, gold holdings are unequivocally available for international use.

Conclusion

H.R. 3818 represents an essentially modest step to bring our gold reserve requirement into line with present needs. Its implications for our economic well being are, however, important.

You will find, I am sure, that this bill has broad support among informed banking and financial circles in this country. As a further indication of our firm intent to defend the gold value of the dollar against any potential pressure, it will help reinforce confidence in the dollar abroad, and I am certain it will be warmly welcomed by foreign monetary officials. I urge that you promptly report the bill favorably to the House and speed its passage.

Ratio of gold certificate reserves to deposit and Federal Reserve note liabilities combined

Yearend	Percent	Yearend	Percent
1932	62.9	1949	54.7
1933	63.8	1950	49.4
1934	70.8	1951	46.4
1935	77.6	1952	46.2
1936	80.1	1953	44.5
1937	79.9	1954	45.1
1938	83.7	1955	44.4
1939	86.7	1956	44.6
1940	90.8	1957	46.3
1941	90.8	1958	42.1
1942	76.3	1959	39.9
1943	62.6	1960	37.4
1944	49.0	1961	34.8
1945	41.7	1962	31.8
1946	43.5	1963	29.7
1947	48.3	1964	27.5
1948	48.9		

SOURCE.—*Federal Reserve Bulletin.*

Exhibit 19.—An act to eliminate the requirement that Federal Reserve banks maintain certain reserves in gold certificates against deposit liabilities

[Public Law 89–3, 89th Congress, H.R. 3818, March 3, 1965]

Be it enacted by the Senate and House of Representatives of the United States of America in Congress assembled, That the first sentence of the third paragraph of section 16 of the Federal Reserve Act, as amended (12 U.S.C. 413), is further amended by striking out "reserves in gold certificates of not less than 25 per centum against its deposits and".

79 Stat. 5,
Federal Reserve banks.
Gold certificates.
40 Stat. 236.

SEC. 2. The eighteenth paragraph of section 16 of the Federal Reserve Act, as amended (12 U.S.C. 467), is further amended by substituting a period for the comma after the word "notes" and striking out the remainder of the paragraph.

Approved March 3, 1965.

Exhibit 20.—Message from the President, June 3, 1965, relative to the coinage program

To the Congress of the United States:

From the early days of our independence the United States has used a system of coinage fully equal in quantity and in quality to all the tasks imposed upon it by the Nation's commerce.

We are today using one of the few existing silver coinages in the world. Our coins, in fact, are little changed from those first established by the Mint Act of 1792. For 173 years, we have maintained a system of abundant coins that with the exception of pennies and nickels is nearly pure silver.

The long tradition of our silver coinage is one of the many marks of the extraordinary stability of our political and economic system.

Continuity, however, is not the only characteristic of a great nation's coinage. We should not hesitate to change our coinage to meet new and growing needs. I am, therefore, proposing certain changes in our coinage system—changes dictated by need—which will help Americans to carry out their daily transactions in the most efficient way possible.

There has been for some years a worldwide shortage of silver. The United States is not exempt from that shortage—and we will not be exempt as it worsens. Silver is becoming too scarce for continued large scale use in coins. To maintain unchanged our high silver coinage in the face of this stark reality would only invite a chronic and growing scarcity of coins.

We expect to use more than 300 million troy ounces—over 10 thousand tons— of silver for our coinage this year. That is far more than total new production of silver expected in the entire free world this year. Although we have a large stock of silver on hand we cannot continue indefinitely to make coins of a high silver content—in the required quantity—in the face of such an imbalance in the production of silver and the demand for it.

We must take steps to maintain an adequate supply of coins, or face chaos in the myriad transactions of our daily life—from using pay telephones to parking in a metered zone to providing our children with money for lunch at school.

The legislation I am sending to the Congress with this Message will ensure a stable and dignified coinage, fully adequate in quantity and in its specially designed technical characteristics to the needs of our twentieth century life. It can be maintained indefinitely, however much the demand for coin may grow.

Much as we all would prefer to retain the silver coins now in use, there is no practical alternative to a new coinage based on materials in adequate supply.

THE NEW COINAGE

I propose no change in either the penny or the nickel.

The new dime and the quarter—while remaining the same size and design as the present dime and quarter—will be composite coins. They will have faces of the same copper-nickel alloy used in our present five-cent piece, bonded to a core of pure copper. The new dime and quarter will, therefore, outwardly resemble the nickel, except in size and design, but with the further distinction that their copper core will give them a copper edge.

This type of coin was selected because, alone among practical alternatives, it can be used together with our existing silver coins in the millions of coin-operated devices that Americans now depend upon heavily for many kinds of food and other goods.

THE HALF DOLLAR

Our new half dollar will be nearly indistinguishable in appearance from the present half dollar.

It will continue to be made of silver and copper, but the silver content will be reduced from 90 percent to 40 percent. It will be faced with an alloy of 80-percent silver and 20-percent copper, bonded to a core of 21-percent silver and 79-percent copper. The new half dollar will continue to be minted with the image of President Kennedy. Its size will be unchanged.

THE SILVER DOLLAR

No change in this famous old coin, or plans for additional production, are proposed at this time. It is possible that implementation of the new coinage legislation that I am proposing, greatly reducing the requirement for silver in our subsidiary coinage, will actually make feasible the minting of additional silver dollars in the future. Certainly, without this change in the silver content of the subsidiary coinage, further minting of the silver dollar would be forever foreclosed.

It is our intention that the new coinage circulate side-by-side with our existing coinage. We plan to continue the minting of our current silver coins while the new coinage is brought into quantity production.

The new coins will be placed in circulation some time in 1966.

In terms of the present pattern of coin usage, adoption of the new coinage will permit a saving of some 90 percent of the silver we are now putting into coins annually.

I want to make it absolutely clear that these changes in our coinage will have no effect on the purchasing power of our coins. The new ones will be exchanged at full face value for the paper currency of the United States. They will be accepted by the Treasury and by the Federal Reserve banks for any of the financial obligations of the United States. The legislation I am proposing expressly recognizes the new coins as legal tender.

It is of primary importance, of course, that our new coins be specifically designed to serve our modern, technological society. In the early days of the Republic, silver coins served well because the value of a coin could only be measured by the value of the precious metal contained in it. For many decades now the value of a particular coin has depended not on the value of the metal in it, but on the face value of the coin. Today's coinage must primarily be utilitarian. The new coinage will meet this requirement fully, while dispensing with the idea that it contain precious metal.

It is, above all, practical. It has been specifically designed to function, without causing delays or disruptions of service, in coin-operated merchandising machines.

Furthermore, it is composed of materials low enough in value and readily enough available to insure that we can have as many coins as we need.

The legislation I am proposing also contains these additional recommendations:

OTHER AUTHORITY REQUESTED

First—As a useful precautionary measure, I request standby authority to institute controls over the melting and export of coins to assist the protection of our existing and our new silver coinage.

Second—I request authority to purchase domestically mined silver at not less than $1.25 per ounce.

Third—I am asking for authority to reactivate minting operations temporarily at the San Francisco Assay Office.

Fourth—As a safeguard for assured availability of the new coinage, I am asking for new contracting authority for the procurement of materials and facilities related to it.

Fifth—I propose the establishment of a Joint Commission on the Coinage, composed of certain members of the Congress, the Public, and the Executive Branch of the Government, to report to me later the progress made in the installation of the new coinage and to review any new technological developments and to suggest any further modifications which may be needed.

WHY THE SILVER CONTENT OF THE COINAGE MUST BE REDUCED AT THIS SESSION

These recommendations for revision of our silver coinage rest upon extensive study of the silver situation, and of alternatives to our present coinage, by both governmental and private specialists. The Treasury Department's comprehensive report, known as the *Treasury Staff Silver and Coinage Study*, is being released today as background to my recommendations. Its principal finding was that the supply of silver in the free world has become progressively incompatible with the maintenance of silver in all our subsidiary coins.

On the average, in the 5 years from 1949 through 1953, new silver production in the free world amounted to about 175 million troy ounces per year, while consumption amounted to more than 235 million ounces. There was an average deficit in those 5 postwar years of more than 60 million ounces of silver per year.

In the latest complete 5 years, 1960 through 1964, free world consumption of silver has averaged 410 million ounces annually, but new production has averaged a little less than 210 million ounces a year. The result has been an average annual deficit of about 200 million ounces. That is 3 times the average annual deficit in the 5 years from 1949 through 1953.

If no silver at all had been used for coinage there would have been a deficit in new production in free world silver during the last 5 years averaging over 40 million troy ounces, or some 1,370 tons, a year.

The gap between the production of silver and silver consumption is continuing to increase. In 1964 the silver production deficit swelled to over 300 million ounces—half again the 1963 figure. And in 1964, the use of silver in coinage, and the use of silver for the arts and industry of the free world were each—taken separately—greater than new production.

There is no dependable or likely prospect that new, economically workable sources of silver may be found that could appreciably narrow the gap between silver supply and demand. The optimistic outlook is for an increase in production of about 20 percent over the next 4 years. This would be of little help. Further, because silver is produced chiefly as a byproduct of the mining of copper, lead, and zinc, even a very large increase in the price of silver would not stimulate silver production sufficiently to change the outlook.

Short of controls that are undesirable in a peacetime free society, there is no way to diminish the bounding growth of private demand for silver for use in jewelry, silverware, photographic film, and industrial processes. The one part of the demand for silver that can be reduced is governmental demand for use in coinage.

Most free world countries no longer use silver in their coins. A few—as we now propose—continue to make limited use of it. It is true that United States coinage does not currently depend upon new silver production, because for many years we have supplied silver for our coinage out of large Treasury stocks, which still amount to 1 billion troy ounces.

But—and this is the crux of the matter—at the present pace, this stock cannot last even as much as three years. We would then be shorn of our ability to maintain the coinage, and, if there were no alternative to our present silver coinage, the nation would be faced with a chronic coin stortage. That is why definitive action is necessary at this session of the Congress.

PROTECTION OF THE COINAGE

It is necessary for the United States Government to have large stocks of silver in addition to the quantity needed for coinage.

We need these stocks because our silver coins in circulation must be protected from hoarding or destruction. Protection of the silver coinage will continue to be a necessity since we plan for it to continue to circulate alongside the new coins. Our silver coins are protected by the fact that the Government stands ready to sell silver bullion from its stocks at $1.29 a troy ounce. This keeps the price of silver, as a commodity, from rising above the face value of our coins. This, in turn, makes hoarding or melting of the silver coinage unprofitable.

It is as additional protection for the existing coinage that I am requesting standby authority to institute controls over the melting, treating, or export of United States coins.

It may be asked why we seek standby control authority since we retain a large stock of silver with which to protect our silver coins through operations in the silver market.

The answer is clear. Given the magnitudes by which demand for silver is outrunning new production, we must consider the possibility, however unlikely, that the silver stock we possess could itself require the support and protection that would be afforded by authority to forbid melting and export of our coins.

We believe our present stocks of silver to be adequate, once the large present drains from coinage are greatly reduced, to meet any foreseeable requirements for an indefinite period. However, prompt action on a new coinage will help us protect the silver coinage by freeing our silver reserves for redemption of silver certificates at $1.29 per ounce. Thus, we can assure that no incentive will be created for hoarding our present coins in anticipation of a higher price for their silver content.

There is the opposite, although in all likelihood short-run, possibility that a fall in the price of silver might result from the enactment of this legislation largely removing silver from our subsidiary coin. It is for the purpose of protecting silver producers from a precipitate drop in the price of silver resulting from the action of the Government that I am requesting authority for the Secretary of the Treasury to purchase any newly mined domestic silver offered to him, at the price of $1.25 per troy ounce.

THE SAN FRANCISCO ASSAY OFFICE

Coinage operations at the San Francisco Mint were ended in 1955. Legislation converting the Mint to the San Francisco Assay Office was passed in 1962. As part of our efforts to overcome the coin shortage of the past year, coin blanks have been cut and annealed at the San Francisco Assay Office. Present law forbids full minting there. However, we will temporarily need the facilities of this plant to move into large quantity production of the new coinage and to continue production of existing coins until enough new small money is made to make certain we have adequate supplies. Consequently, I am asking for authority to reactivate minting operations at San Francisco on a temporary basis.

A new, fully modern mint is to be built in Philadelphia. However, it cannot be completed and in operation before late 1967. It is our expectation that when the new Philadelphia Mint's capacity is added to that of the Denver Mint, our coinage requirements can be met efficiently and economically. Consequently, no more than temporary authority to mint coins in San Francisco is recommended in the draft legislation I am sending to you.

WHY COMPOSITE COINS ARE RECOMMENDED

We have no choice but to eliminate silver, for the most part, from our subsidiary coinage. The question was: What would be the best alternative? After very thorough consideration of all aspects of this highly complex problem, we have settled upon the two types of composite, or clad, coins I have already described. These are 10-cent and 25-cent pieces with cupronickel alloy faces bonded to a solid copper core, and a new half dollar with outer and inner layers of differing silver-copper alloys.

This type of coin was found to be necessary if the new coinage is to be compatible with the existing silver coinage in all the 12 million coin-operated devices in use in the United States.

The convenience of using coins in automatic merchandising and service devices is a fact that, like the coins in our pockets and in our store tills, we take for granted. But if our coinage were suddenly to be such that it would not work in coin-operated devices, the public would be subjected to very great inconvenience and serious losses would occur to business with harmful effects upon employment.

The automatic merchandising industry is a large and growing part of our national economy. Last year, $3½ billion worth of consumer items were sold through 3½ million of these machines. On more than 30 billion separate occasions a consumer made a purchase by putting a coin in a machine. In growing numbers, factories, hospitals, and other places now depend upon automatic vending for the service of goods. A million and a half people now rely upon coin-controlled vending for at least one meal a day. The use of coin-operated devices is expanding rapidly, not only in merchandise vending, but also in a number of other services.

Six million of our coin-operated devices, including nearly all vending machines, have selectors set to reject coins or imitations of coins that do not have the electrical properties of our existing silver money. Highly selective rejectors are a necessity in these machines if they are to be a low-cost source of food and other goods and services. Otherwise, fraudulent use would soon make them costly.

The sensors in these machines are set to accept or reject coins on the basis of the electrical properties of our traditional coins, which have a high proportion of silver. To be compatible in operation with our existing coinage, therefore, our new coins must duplicate the electrical properties of a coin that is 90-percent silver. No single acceptable metal or alloy does so. The composite coins, made of layers of differing metals and alloys, that I am asking the Congress to approve, are coins made to order to duplicate the electrical properties of coins with a high silver content. They are the only practical alternatives we have discovered to our present coinage.

Selectors exist that can handle coins with the widely varying electrical properties of, say, nearly pure silver and nearly pure nickel. But that is not enough. When the selectors are set to accept coins with greatly differing electrical properties, the selectivity of the mechanism declines and they will accept wrong coins and imitations. Unless the coins in use have very similar electrical properties, the coin-operated machines become subject to a high degree of fraudulent use. This would be costly to all concerned.

The future may bring selectors of a different kind able to accept coins of widely varying electrical properties while at the same time rejecting imitations and wrong coins. They are not available now. When and if they become available, our new coinage will work in them. On the other hand, if we now chose an incompatible coinage, there would be delays and interruptions lasting a year to three years in the services of these machines. This would impose heavy inconveniences upon the public and would cause business and employment losses in a large and growing industry.

In view of these considerations of public interest, we have concluded that our new coinage must without fail be able to carry out the technical merchandising functions of a modern coinage, working alongside our existing silver coinage. The new coins that I am recommending to you do this, and do it well, because they were specifically designed for the task.

The new half dollar was designed with the strong desire in mind of many Americans to retain some silver in our everyday coinage. We believe that by eliminating silver from use in the dime and the quarter, we will have enough silver to carry out market operations in protection of our existing silver coinage—and to make a half dollar of 40-percent silver content. It is clear and unmistakable that we would not have enough silver to extend this to the dime and quarter : they are heavily used, indispensable coins that we must have at all times in large quantity. We are convinced that we can include a 40-percent silver half dollar in the new coinage, but we cannot safely go beyond that. As a precaution, we intend to concentrate at first on getting out large quantities of the new quarter and dime before we embark upon quantity production of the new half dollar.

THE JOINT COMMISSION ON THE COINAGE

We believe the recommendations being made for a new coinage are sound and durable and in the best public interest. However, the installation of a new coinage is a matter so intimately affecting the life of every citizen, and so delicately related to the Nation's commerce, that it is impossible to be certain in advance that all problems have been foreseen, even by such a long and arduous process of research as has gone into the selection of the proposed new coins.

Consequently, I am including among my recommendations the proposal for a Joint Commission on the Coinage. It will be composed of the four officers of the Executive Branch most directly concerned with matters affected by the coinage—the Secretary of the Treasury, the Secretary of Commerce. the Director of the Budget Bureau, and the Director of the Mint ; of four members representing the public interest, to be appointed by the President ; of the Chairmen and ranking members of the Banking and Currency committees of the House and the Senate ; of one member each from the two Houses of the Congress, to be appointed by the Vice President and the Speaker of the House. The Commission will be appointed soon after the new coinage is issued. It will study such matters as new technological developments, the supply of various metals, and the future of the silver dollar. It will report as to the time and circumstances in which the Government should cease to maintain the price of silver. It will be directed to advise the President, the Congress, and the Secretary of the Treasury on the results of its studies.

The Coinage—Current and Prospective

I am pleased to report to the Congress substantial progress toward overcoming the coin shortage the Nation has been experiencing. Greatly increased minting has eliminated the shortage of pennies and of nickels. We are still somewhat on the short side of the demand for dimes and quarters, but this deficit is rapidly being overtaken. A severe shortage of the half dollar continues, due to the popularity of the new 50-cent pieces bearing the image of President Kennedy.

I want to emphasize that we will continue to make the existing coins while the new ones come into full production, and that we contemplate side-by-side circulation of the old and new coins for the indefinite future. There is no reason for hoarding the silver coinage we now use, because there is no reason for it to disappear.

We are gearing up for maximum production of the new coins as soon as they are authorized by the Congress. Supply of the materials for them is assured. Both copper and nickel are economical and available in North America. Their usage in coins will not add enough to overall employment of these metals to create supply or price problems.

In the first year after new coins are authorized, we expect to make 3½ billion pieces of the new subsidiary coins. That is a billion and a half more pieces than will be made of the corresponding silver coins in the current fiscal year.

In the second year after authorization of the new coinage, we expect to be able to double the first year's output of the new coins, reaching a production total of seven billion pieces.

We expect in this way to avoid any new coin shortage in the transition to production of the new coins, and within a period of less than three years to reach a point at which we could if necessary meet total coinage needs out of production of the new coins.

I am satisfied that, taking into account all of the various factors involved in this complex problem, the recommendations that I am making to you are sound and right. Your early and favorable action upon the proposed legislation will make it possible to produce and issue to the public a coinage that will be acceptable, provide the maximum convenience, and serve all the purposes—financial and technical—of modern commerce. In considering this problem the needs of the economy and the convenience of the public have been placed ahead of all other considerations. They are the factors that have resulted in my recommendations to the Congress. I urge their approval at the earliest possible date.

Lyndon B. Johnson.

The White House, *June 3, 1965.*

Exhibit 21.—Statement by Secretary of the Treasury Fowler, June 4, 1965, before the House Banking and Currency Committee, on the President's coinage and silver proposals

Mr. Chairman, I appear before you today in support of the legislation the President has recommended for a new and efficient U.S. coinage.

We are recommending a change in the coinage because there is not enough available silver to assure the continued minting of our traditional 90-percent silver coins for years in the quantities necessary to meet our rapidly increasing coinage requirements.

As much as all of us would prefer to keep our old and handsome silver coinage, there is no choice but to reduce drastically our heavy dependence upon silver for this purpose for one simple reason: the demand for silver has far outrun supply.

The only option open to us in this matter, without gravely risking the national interest in adequate and plentiful coinage, has been choice of what new material to use in the place of silver.

The new coinage the President has recommended that you authorize has all the attributes of a strong and stable coin system, and that, moreover, it is fully modern and, specifically engineered to carry out efficiently all the tasks that American merchandising of our day requires.

The new coins recommended to you will provide uninterrupted service as a medium of exchange. They can be made without the necessity of further change for a long period ahead. These coins are made of materials for which there is assured access. They can be minted without undue difficulty and at moderate cost. They can be used across the counter—and in all of the 12 million coin-operated devices in use in the United States—side by side with our existing silver coins.

There is, of course, no substitute for the appearance of silver. In one of the three new coins we are asking authority to make, the half dollar, the beauty of the "noble metal" is preserved intact, although the actual silver content is much reduced. The proposed new dime and quarter are a departure from the tradition of silver, but they are coins that have a distinctively modern appearance and that will serve us well because they can protect us from future coin shortages. The fact that they are not silver, but are composite coins made of a nickel alloy bonded to a copper core, is a change that requires getting used to. But I think the ruddy edge resulting from their copper core gives these coins a character we will come not only to accept, but to value.

The need for legislation—shrinkage of silver supplies

I think the accompanying table presents the silver supply situation as briefly as possible. I have taken it from our *Treasury Staff Study of Silver and Coinage.*

The table shows a steady worsening of our silver supplies, from a small deficiency of production in the early postwar years to a slightly bigger deficiency in the next five-year period, a much larger inadequacy in the five years from 1957–61, and to a bounding growth of the deficiency in the last two calendar years. Actual market deficits are smaller than the difference between total consumption and new production because the United States meets its coinage needs for silver out of its stocks. These, however, are being depleted at a rate which cannot be permitted to continue indefinitely.

It is notable that in 1964 each major type of usage—the use of silver by industry and the arts, and use of silver for coinage—taken separately, was greater than new supply.

This is the crux of the matter.

There is simply not enough silver appearing on the market to continue to satisfy the demand for it in the foreseeable future.

Estimated free world silver consumption and production, 1949–64

[In millions of fine troy ounces]

Calendar year	Industry and the arts	Use—Coinage demand			Total consumption	New production	Gross deficit	Deficit, excluding U.S. coinage demand
		United States	Foreign free world	Total				
1949–53 averages	153	36	48	85	238	174	64	28
1953–57 averages	190	37	36	74	264	191	73	36
1957–61 averages	216	47	51	98	314	200	114	67
1962	248	77	50	128	375	207	169	72
1963	252	112	56	167	419	214	205	93
1964	286	203	62	265	550	216	335	132

NOTE.—A troy ounce equals 480 grains, an avoirdupois pound equals 7,000 grains, a 2,000-pound ton equals 14,000,000 grains, hence, 1 billion troy ounces (480,000,000,000 grains) equals 34,285 tons.

SOURCE.—*Treasury Staff Study of Silver and Coinage,* Part III, table 1, figures rounded.

There is no dependable, or, for that matter, likely, prospect, in the opinion of experts both inside and outside the Treasury, of new economically workable sources of silver that would appreciably narrow the gap between silver supply and demand. In fact, optimistic projections envision an increase of no more than 20 percent over the next four years. Projected increases in consumption are at least equally as great. This standoff between future increases of production and consumption in a situation where deficits are already very heavy could not change the basic conclusion that use of silver in our coinage must be very sharply curtailed. Also, because silver is produced chiefly as a byproduct of the mining of copper, lead, and zinc, even a very great increase in the price of silver would not stimulate new production sufficiently to change the situation.

Most free world countries have long since ended or nearly ended the use of silver in their coinage. Except for Canada and Switzerland, those countries still using silver coins make only limited use of it, in one or two "prestige" coins, as we now propose to do with the new half dollar. As seen in the table above, in the early postwar years, the United States accounted for less than half of total free world employment of silver for coins, but at present we use more than three-quarters of all silver put into coins in the free world.

We have no choice but to make a large reduction of silver in the coinage, and no choice but to do so now. We have on hand some 1 billion ounces of silver in the Treasury stock. At current rates of mint production we are using silver for coinage at the rate of 300 million ounces a year; and for the redemption of silver certificates at 120 million ounces a year.

Even should demands upon our stock increase no more, it is clear that at present rates of use we can expect to exhaust our resources in two or three years. This gives us enough time to shift to a new coinage if we act promptly.

Basic requirement for the new coinage system

In arriving at our recommendations for new coinage alloys our overriding consideration, Mr. Chairman, was the necessity of continuing at all times to provide an adequate means of exchange and of avoiding any disruption of commerce. Experience shows all too clearly that, under modern conditions, the essential medium of exchange function is imperiled if a subsidiary coinage alloy threatens to become more valuable as a commodity than as money.

The Treasury's own staff study, and that of the Battelle Memorial Institute, establish certain other criteria which an acceptable coinage alloy should have, beyond the basic criterion of efficiency in its function as a medium of exchange. These include, the degree to which a coinage material lends itself to being minted into coins which would be durable in use; its acceptability to the public; ease and sureness of production; cost and availability of raw materials, and counterfeiting potential.

An additional criterion is a critical factor for a modern American coinage. Present day coins should perform not only as a medium of exchange, but also as technical merchandising instruments, in use in coin-operated vending and service machines.

The need for compatibility of old and new coinage

The new coins should be made compatible with the existing coinage in use in coin-operated devices, particularly, in coin-operated vending machines. This is one of the most desirable characteristics of a modern coinage, and a characteristic fully met by the President's proposal. If the new coinage could not be used in these mechanisms, the public would be subjected to great inconvenience, and trade and commerce in many sectors of distribution harassed and handicapped. If the new coins were not compatible, two alternatives would be presented, both of them undesirable from the point of view of the public at large:

(1) The vending machines would have to be shut down until new sensing and rejecting devices could be installed; or

(2) Their devices for sensing and rejecting wrong coins and slugs would have to be deliberately circumvented, exposing the machines to a high rate of fraud.

In the case of merchandise vending machines alone—that is, not including such service devices as pay telephones and coin-operated laundries—over $3½ billion worth of goods were dispensed to consumers last year, in over 30 billion separate transactions.

These vending machines are equipped with sensitive selectors, which reject wrong coins, slugs, foreign coins, and the like. Highly selective rejectors are necessary if coin machines are to be low-cost supply points for foods and for many other kinds of goods, available by night and by day, in out of the way as well as accessible places.

Approximately half of the 12 million coin-operated machines in the United States are equipped with sensors that accept or reject coins on the basis of the electrical properties of our traditional high silver content coinage. To be compatible in operation with our existing coinage, our new coins must duplicate the electrical characteristics of a coin with high silver content. The coins we are recommending to you reproduce precisely the electrical properties of coins with high silver content. Moreover, they are made of the only materials that do so, satisfactorily, among the practical alternatives. Any other course would subject the public to extensive inconvenience.

If noncompatible materials are used, there will have to be an interregnum while new selectors are developed and brought into mass production that are:

(1) capable of handling coins of high silver content together with coins that do not have the electrical properties of nearly pure silver, and

(2) at the same time capable of rejecting slugs, low value foreign coins, and coins of wrong denominations. Selectors exist that can handle coins with a wide range of electrical properties. But when they are set for a wide range, their selectivity falls, and they become subject to fraudulent use.

During the one to three years that development, manufacture, and installation of a new kind of sensor would take, the public would not be able to use the incompatible new coinage in the six million of our coin-operated devices, chiefly those vending merchandise, fitted with sensitive selectors. The choice of the coins recommended here avoids these difficulties and the attendant interferences with trade and commerce.

Outline of the recommendations

Section 1 of the proposed legislation describes the metallic content of the proposed new coinage:

A. The Minor Coinage

The penny and the five-cent piece: No change is proposed.

B. The Subsidiary Coinage

1. *The dime and the quarter:* It is proposed that silver be eliminated from the dime and quarter. Instead, they should be composite, or clad, coins, faced with an alloy of 75 percent copper and 25 percent nickel—the same cupronickel alloy used throughout the five-cent piece—bonded to a core of pure copper.

2. *The half dollar:* It is proposed that the 50-cent piece should also be a composite coin, with the silver content reduced from the present 90 percent to a new ratio of 40 percent. It would be faced with an alloy of 80 percent silver and 20 percent copper, clad on core alloy of approximately 21 percent silver and 79 percent copper.

3. *The silver dollar:* No change is proposed. Authority to make a silver dollar of the same weight and fineness (412.5 grains, 90 percent silver) made at various times since the Act of 1837, would be continued. However, we would not plan to mint any new coins of this denomination at the present time.

Section 2 provides that the new coins would be subject to the current laws as to design and inscription.

With respect to these coins, I would like to emphasize the following points, some of them already discussed:

1. It is our intention that the existing silver coinage should circulate side by side with the new coinage, indefinitely.

2. The proposed new dime and quarter would have a copper-colored edge, due to the use of a pure copper core.

3. The new coinage would meet the exacting technical requirements necessary to permit it to be used in the coin-operated devices now in use in the United States, including those fitted with rejectors set to refuse coins or imitations of coins that do not have the electrical properties of our current silver coins.

4. We expect to place the new coins in circulation sometime in 1966.

5. The new coins would be of the same size and design as present coins of the same denomination. They would be slightly lighter in weight.

Section 3 provides specific recognition of the new coins as legal tender.

Section 4 provides for continued minting of the existing coins as needed until production of the new coinage is adequate, continuing without change the standard silver dollar.

Section 5 provides for standby authority for the Secretary of the Treasury to prohibit the melting, exportation, or treating of U.S. silver coins.

Section 6 provides for sales by the Treasury of silver in excess of what is needed to back silver certificates, at a price not less than the monetary value of silver.

Section 7 would authorize the Treasury to purchase newly mined domestic silver at $1.25 per fine troy ounce.

Section 8 provides for legal authority to procure the materials and technical assistance, equipment and patents needed to make the new coinage in the required quantity.

Section 9 provides authority to continue dating the new coins as of the first year they are issued.

Section 10 would authorize the temporary use of the San Francisco Assay Office for the minting of coins, and would authorize the conversion of that facility for the refining of precious metals, if necessary, after it is no longer needed for coin production.

Sections 11–16 : An act requiring recoinage of all worn and uncurrent subsidiary silver received in the Treasury is repealed ; the minor-coinage metal fund is renamed the coinage-metal fund, and the minor-coinage profit fund is renamed the coinage-profit fund, and the amount available in the coinage-metal fund is raised from $3 million to $30 million ; expenditure of not more than $15 million is authorized for additional mint facilities to accommodate manufacturing requirements of the new materials ; the counterfeiting laws are amended to cover the new coinage ; the issuance of necessary regulations by the Secretary of the Treasury under the proposed act is authorized ; and penalties are provided for violations of regulations issued under section 5.

A separate title of the proposed legislation provides for the establishment of a Joint Commission on the Coinage after the new coinage is issued.

The Commission would be composed of the Secretary of the Treasury, the Secretary of Commerce, the Director of the Bureau of the Budget, the Director of the Mint, of four public members, not representative of interest groups, appointed by the President, of the chairmen and ranking minority members of the House and the Senate Banking and Currency committees, and of two other congressional members, one appointed by the Speaker of the House and one by the President of the Senate.

The function of the Commission would be to study the progress of the implementation of the new coinage program, new technological developments, the supply of various metals, and the future of the silver dollar. It would report as to the time and circumstances in which the Government should cease to maintain the price of silver. And it would advise the President, the Congress, and the Secretary of the Treasury on the results of its studies.

Protection of existing coinage

The continued use of coins that are 90 percent silver also requires protection of this high silver content coinage from hoarding or destruction.

There is no reason for hoarding of coins in anticipation of a coin shortage. We expect no such shortage during the period when we are installing the new coinage. We can, if necessary, step up production enough to replace completely, in less than three years, the existing silver coinage while at the same time keeping up with the normal growth of coin demand.

We can defend the existing silver coinage against the second possible danger—the threat of destruction by melting them for their silver content. To make certain that the silver coinage is not destroyed in this manner, it will be necessary for the Treasury to protect the monetary value of our silver coinage by supplying silver to the market upon demand at the present monetary price of silver of $1.29+ per troy ounce. The Treasury has been doing this since 1963 by exchanges of silver bullion against silver certificates.

The value of the silver in our existing coinage, as silver, would exceed the face value of the coins if the price were allowed to rise above a so-called melting point of these coins of $1.38 per ounce. We hold the price of $1.29+ per ounce by standing ready freely to redeem silver certificates in silver at this price. The prudent course is to maintain the price of silver at its present level.

It is as additional protection for existing silver coinage, which includes the silver dollar, that we recommend asking for standby authority to institute controls over the melting, treating, or export of U.S. coins, practices not now forbidden by law.

We believe strongly that suggestions for more extensive controls would operate against our best interests.

Sufficiency of coinage supply

As you know, we have recently experienced a shortage of coins. I am happy to say that as a result of intensive production efforts on the part of the Mint the supply of coins in circulation and in inventory in the Federal Reserve banks is improved. There is no longer a shortage of the 1-cent and 5-cent pieces. We still have a problem with dimes and quarter supply but substantial improvement has been made. The shortage of half dollars is still severe.

In view of the continuing shortages of high denomination coins and the uncertainties inevitable during the changeover period, we are gearing up for maximum production of the new coins as soon as the legislation is passed. In the first year after enactment, we expect to make at least 3½ billion of the new subsidiary coins, a billion and a half more than we will make of the silver coins in fiscal 1965. This is more than double the production in fiscal 1964 and four or five times what we would consider as a normal year's production of silver coins. In the second year after enactment we would expect to make well over seven billion of the new coins, doubling production again.

The silver dollar

The silver dollar will remain as an authorized coin of the United States, at 90-percent fineness. This is a central element in our program for holding the price of silver to its present level for the protection of our existing subsidiary silver coin. The future of the silver dollar can better be decided when the Joint Commission on the Coinage, which we have recommended, can take a look at the world's silver supply and demand situation and other relevant factors and make its recommendations. At that time, the facts can largely govern the decision on the issue of the future of the silver dollar.

Maintaining some silver in the subsidiary coinage

We have considered it desirable to maintain some silver in our subsidiary coinage. It was to this end that the new silver half dollar was designed. The new composite coin reduced the silver content of the half dollar from 90 percent to 40 percent. It nevertheless retains without readily apparent differences, the aspect and ring of a coin with high silver content, although it is slightly lighter than the present half dollar. It is to be of the same design as the present half dollar, that is, bearing the image of the late President Kennedy.

One reason for retaining some silver in our coinage is a desire to continue the 173-year-old tradition of American silver coinage. Inclusion of a 40-percent silver half dollar is as far as we can safely go to satisfy this tradition. We expect that, barring unforeseen changes in industrial demand for silver, we will have adequate silver to make this one coin in normal amounts for an indefinite period. After the new coins are in full production it should require no more than 15 million ounces a year, less than 5 percent of expected 1965 silver consumption for coins. One reason for continuing this particular coin is the fact that we could, if unforeseen difficulties developed, do without the half dollar temporarily. It can be replaced in use by two quarters.

Summary

A change in our coinage is unavoidable. We have reviewed very carefully the results of all of the studies which have been made on this subject. We are satisfied that, taking into account all of the various factors involved in this problem, our recommendations for the new coinage are sound proposals that will, if enacted, provide the United States with a dependable, technically perfect, and distinctive coinage that can be produced in whatever quantity desired. It is a coinage that, I emphasize, will perform not only across-the-counter, but will also carry out fully and without interruption its function as a technical merchandising instrument. This is absolutely necessary for the public interest. I therefore strongly urge approval of these recommendations and that they be enacted into law at the earliest possible date.

Exhibit 22.—Statement by Leland Howard, Director, Office of Domestic Gold and Silver Operations, June 8, 1965, before the House Committee on Interior and Insular Affairs, on silver policy

Mr. Chairman, I appear before you today to discuss certain phases of the silver situation. I understand that I am to tell how the silver stock of the Treasury was acquired, how it was and is used, and to give general background information on the supply and demand situation as it relates to both the industrial and monetary use of silver. As the Secretary of the Treasury is at this moment appearing before the House Banking and Currency Committee to discuss the President's coinage program, I understand I am not to present that program to this committee.

How Treasury's stock of silver was acquired

In 1933, as you know, the United States embarked upon a silver purchase program which had for its main purpose the elimination of large stocks of silver from the marketplace and the subsequent firming of price. The program was carried out through two sets of laws, one relating to the purchase of newly mined domestic silver and the other to the purchase of foreign and secondary silver.

The law relating to the purchase of foreign and secondary silver was the Silver Purchase Act of 1934. Purchases under this act were not mandatory—they were called for only when deemed "in the public interest." Over two billion one hundred million ounces were purchased under this act between 1934 and 1942. However, after 1942, no Secretary of the Treasury deemed it to be in the public interest to purchase additional foreign or secondary silver. The fact is there was very little silver available for purchase.

The proclamations and acts relating to the purchase of newly mined domestic silver made it mandatory that the Mint purchase all the newly mined silver offered to it. Under these proclamations and acts, we purchased an additional 884 million ounces of silver and, as you well know, the market price of silver was such for many years that it paid the producers to deliver all of their production to the mints.

Three billion ounces of silver, therefore, were purchased by the United States during the period 1933 to early 1959 under these purchase programs at an average price of 58.7 cents per ounce. Needless to say, the price of silver did firm, usually just under the Government buying price.

There is given below a summary of the silver receipts during the fiscal years 1934 through 1964. This table shows the sources of all silver during the period covered, whereas I have only mentioned the two large sources in the text above. Also, it should be noted that there is a duplication under the heading "Silver Bullion Ordinary," inasmuch as it contains returns of lend-lease silver which were acquired under other headings. A later table on silver issues will show the disposition of this silver under "Silver Lend-Leased to Foreign Governments."

Summary of silver receipts fiscal years 1934–64

Opening balances and receipts	Fine ounces	Value
Balances June 30, 1933:		
Silver bullion ordinary	13, 831, 051. 05	$6, 588, 389 06
Recoinage silver	13, 925, 846. 32	19, 251, 049. 27
	27, 756, 897. 37	25, 839, 438. 33
Receipts (July 1, 1933–June 30, 1964):		
Silver Purchase Act silver (act of June 19, 1934, 48 Stat. 1178)	2, 048, 490, 530. 48	1, 027, 637, 216 75
Nationalized silver (Executive Order 6814. Aug. 9, 1934)	113, 032, 915. 78	56, 528, 353. 08
Foreign debt silver (title III, act of May 12, 1933, 48 Stat. 31, 53)	22, 734, 824 35	11, 367, 412. 18
Newly mined domestic silver:		
Executive Proclamation silver (E.P. 2067 of Dec. 21, 1933, and amendments)	301, 226, 723. 50	216, 588, 371. 53
Act of July 6, 1939 (53 Stat. 998)	206, 287, 208. 67	146, 693, 123. 94
Act of July 31, 1946 (60 Stat. 750)	376, 686, 164. 80	340, 919, 995. 60
	884, 200, 096. 97	704, 201, 491. 07
Silver bullion ordinary [1]	400, 305, 969. 14	284, 245, 165. 96
Recoinage bullion from uncurrent subsidiary silver coins	62, 215, 088. 21	92, 792, 478. 39
Recoinage bullion from uncurrent silver dollars	45, 936, 330. 61	61, 818, 618. 00
Seigniorage accruing from revaluation of silver		1, 172, 867, 644. 88
Total receipts	3, 576, 915, 755. 54	3, 411, 458, 380 31
Total silver available fiscal years 1934–64	3, 604, 672, 652. 91	3, 437, 297, 818. 64

[1] Includes lend-lease silver returns.

Uses of Treasury silver

Listed below is a summary of silver issued for various purposes for fiscal years 1934 through 1964. Also listed on the table is the balance of silver on hand at the end of fiscal 1964.

Summary of silver issues and closing balances fiscal years 1934–64

Issues and closing balances	Fine ounces	Value
Issues (July 1, 1933–June 30, 1964):		
Silver processed into U.S. coins	1, 377, 338, 451. 17	$1, 115, 581, 638. 26
Silver lend-leased to foreign governments	410, 814, 344. 19	191, 713, 360. 44
Silver sold:		
Under Green Act (act of July 12, 1943, 57 Stat. 520)	167, 380, 240. 92	78, 110, 778. 17
Under Act of July 31, 1946 (60 Stat. 750)	138, 971, 143. 85	103, 749, 218. 68
Other	18, 101, 057. 50	17, 493, 771. 19
	324, 452, 442. 27	199, 353, 768. 04
Wasted in operations	661, 253. 42	363, 806. 58
Melting losses-uncurrent coin		9, 481, 701. 71
Silver used for redemption of silver certificates	48, 142, 978. 65	62, 245, 633. 00
Total issues	2, 161, 409, 469. 70	1, 578, 739, 908. 03
Balances as of June 30, 1964:		
Newly mined domestic silver-act of July 31, 1946 (60 Stat. 750)		
Silver bullion securing certificates:		
Bureau of the Mint	1, 363, 617, 352. 46	1, 763, 060, 648. 97
Other Federal agencies	64, 751, 316. 12	83, 718, 873. 72
	1, 428, 368, 668. 58	1, 846, 779, 522. 69
Silver bullion for coinage or sale at $1.29+	1, 090, 648. 14	1, 410, 130. 90
Silver bullion ordinary	13, 699, 320. 60	10, 223, 898. 49
Silver recoinage bullion from uncurrent subsidiary silver coins	102, 683. 79	141. 950. 97
Silver recoinage bullion from uncurrent silver dollars	1, 862. 10	2, 407. 56
Total balances	1, 443, 263, 183. 21	1, 858, 557, 910. 61
Total issues and balances	3, 604, 672, 652. 91	3, 437, 297, 818. 64

It should be noted that the largest use of silver has been in the production of coins; namely, 1,377 plus million ounces. The next largest issue was for lend-lease silver and, as explained above, practically all of this has been returned and appears in the table "Summary of silver receipts" under the heading "Silver bullion ordinary." Three hundred twenty-four plus million ounces have been sold for industrial use under the acts of July 12, 1943, and July 31, 1946. The act of June 4, 1963, authorized the Secretary of the Treasury to redeem silver certificates in bullion, as well as in silver dollars. The 48+ million ounces of silver represents the amount of silver acquired by the public through the exchange of silver certificates. (Because of the situation in the market price of silver, redemptions did not start until September.)

After 1933 and prior to November 28, 1961, coins were manufactured from free silver in the Treasury. By the end of November 1961, the supply of this type silver was almost depleted. In order to obtain silver to meet coinage needs, President Kennedy on November 28, 1961, directed the Treasury to retire silver certificates, thus freeing the silver back of such certificates for the manufacture of silver coins. At that time the Federal Reserve banks did not have the authority to issue Federal Reserve notes below the $5 denomination. Therefore, our supply of silver for coinage was limited to the retirement of silver certificates of $5 and above, the only certificates that could be replaced by corresponding Federal Reserve notes. The act of June 4, 1963, authorized the issuance of $1 and $2 Federal Reserve notes, thus making it possible to retire gradually all silver certificates and to free the silver as needed for coinage.

The U.S. Treasury stands ready to redeem silver certificates with silver bullion upon request at the monetary price of $1.29+ an ounce. Since the market price rose to that level in September of 1963, this has resulted in a further drain on the silver stocks.

The accompanying table shows the reduction in silver bullion by months since June 1963 through coinage allocations and certificate redemptions.

Reduction in silver bullion, by months beginning June 1963

[On basis of daily Treasury statement]

Month	Bullion released for coinage		Bullion exchanged for certificates	
	Ounces	Value	Ounces	Value
1963				
June [1]	4, 000, 000	$5, 171, 717. 17	--------------	--------------
July	5, 000, 000	6, 464, 646. 46	--------------	--------------
August	15, 000, 000	19, 393, 939. 38	--------------	--------------
September	9, 000, 000	11, 636, 363. 63	772, 481. 5	$998, 764. 00
October	10, 000, 000	12, 929, 292. 92	3, 591, 055. 6	4, 642, 981. 00
November	8, 000, 000	10, 343, 434. 34	6, 845, 056. 5	8, 850, 174. 00
December	9, 000, 000	11, 636, 363. 62	7, 764, 502. 7	10, 038, 953. 00
1964				
January	5, 000, 000	6, 464, 646. 46	3, 403, 615. 4	4, 400, 634. 00
February	15, 000, 000	19, 393, 939. 38	1, 804, 806. 4	2, 333, 487. 00
March	15, 000, 000	19, 393, 939. 38	3, 572, 474. 6	4, 618, 957. 00
April	15, 000, 000	19, 393, 939. 38	7, 281, 678. 9	9, 414, 696. 00
May	14, 000, 000	18, 101, 010. 09	3, 688, 775. 6	4, 769, 326. 00
June	11, 000, 000	14, 222, 222. 21	9, 418, 659. 7	12, 177, 661. 00
July	18, 000, 000	23, 272, 727. 26	2, 117, 453. 8	2, 737, 718. 00
August	19, 000, 000	24, 565, 656. 55	5, 740, 999. 2	7, 422, 706. 00
September	20, 000, 000	25, 858, 585. 84	21, 710, 200. 4	28, 069, 754. 00
October	22, 000, 000	28, 444, 444. 42	44, 473, 580. 5	57, 501, 195. 00
November	24, 000, 000	31, 030, 303. 01	20, 541, 383. 9	26, 558, 557. 00
December	23, 000, 000	29, 737, 373. 72	17, 518, 439. 8	22, 650, 104. 00
1965				
January	28, 000, 000	36, 202, 020. 18	11, 291, 161. 2	14, 598, 673. 00
February	23, 000, 000	29, 737, 373. 72	8, 663, 782. 4	11, 201, 658. 00
March	38, 000, 000	49, 131, 313. 11	7, 257, 219. 0	9, 383, 071. 00
April	14, 000, 000	18, 101, 010. 09	12, 375, 519. 8	16, 000, 672. 00
Totals	364, 000, 000	470, 626, 262. 32	199, 832, 846. 9	258, 369, 741. 00

[1] Public Law 88-36, passed June 4, 1963.

The following shows the balance of Treasury's silver stocks at the end of the year since 1958 and for the first four months of this year.

Date	Millions of fine ounces	Date	Millions of fine ounces
1958	2, 106. 2	1964	1, 218. 0
1959	2, 059. 9	1965:	
1960	1, 992. 2	January	1, 180. 9
1961	1, 862. 7	February	1, 152. 3
1962	1, 768. 3	March	1, 116. 7
1963	1, 584. 3	April	1, 076. 6

Industrial demand for silver

While the silver purchase program was going on, the industrial demand for silver was increasing. Silver not only continued to be used in the luxury items, but found rising new markets in the electronics and aircraft industries and other important industrial fields. At the current rates, world consumption of silver exceeds new production plus the secondary supplies coming into the market. Since 1959, the demand has been met by adding Treasury silver to these supplies either through direct sales or through the redemption of silver certificates. The coinage needs of the United States, as well as for some other countries, have been met from existing stocks and have not been a factor in the market.

In 1933, when the first Presidential Proclamation taking newly mined domestic silver off the market was issued, U.S. industrial consumption amounted to only 10.8 million ounces. During the 8-year period from 1933–40 annual average industrial consumption in the United States was 23 million ounces. In 1941, at the start of the war, it jumped to 72.4 million ounces and then averaged 116 million ounces during the war period, 1942–45. Consumption in the United States since the war has been up and down from a low of 85.5 million ounces to a high of 120 million ounces. In 1963 it was 110 million ounces and in 1964 it is estimated that the demand was about 120 million ounces.

The current situation regarding domestic production and consumption is: annual newly mined production runs around 35 million ounces and net industrial consumption amounts to about 120 million ounces. In other words, we in the United States consume industrially about three times our current production. More than 60 percent of our production in the United States comes into being as a byproduct of copper, lead, and zinc mining. The remainder comes from mines in which silver is a primary metal.

The excess over and above this domestic production must either be met by the importation of silver or from Treasury stocks. As a general rule, the United States is a net importer of silver. However, in the year just ended, with silver in rising demand in other areas, we were a net exporter. The absence of a surplus abroad, of course, added to the drain on the Treasury stocks.

Free world industrial consumption of silver (exclusive of coinage) has increased over 86 percent during the last 15 years. In 1949 it amounted to 132.5 million ounces and in 1963 it was 247.0 million ounces. Exclusive of the United States, free world industrial consumption rose from 47.4 million ounces in 1950 to the current level of about 137 million ounces in 1963.

In 1933, when the first Presidential Proclamation taking newly-mined domestic silver off the market was issued, the use of silver in coinage amounted to less than one million ounces. During the 8-year period from 1933 through 1940, the average annual consumption of silver in the U.S. coins was 16 million ounces. In 1941, at the start of the war, it jumped to 55 million ounces and an annual average of 67.5 million ounces were consumed in coinage during the war period, 1942–45. From 1945–61 the average was 38.8 million ounces. In 1962 coinage use rose to 77 million ounces and in 1963 to 111 million ounces. In 1964 we consumed a total of 203 million ounces in U.S. coinage and this year we are running at a rate of about 300 million ounces.

Meanwhile coinage consumption of silver in the rest of the free world, has decreased 13.7 percent during the past 15 years. In 1949, it amounted to 70.4 million ounces and in 1963, 60.7 million ounces.

To sum up the situation relative to the industrial and coinage uses of silver and the amount being produced, I attach a table [1] from the *Treasury Staff Study on Silver and Coinage*. It is pointed out that in 1964, the use of silver by industry and the arts, as well as the use of silver for coinage, exceeded new production.

Exhibit 23.—An act to provide for the coinage of the United States

[Public Law 89–81, 89th Congress, S. 2080, July 23, 1965]

Coinage Act
of 1965.

Be it enacted by the Senate and House of Representatives of the United States of America in Congress assembled, That this Act may be cited as the "Coinage Act of 1965."

TITLE I—AUTHORIZATION OF ADDITIONAL COINAGE

Specifications.

SEC. 101. (a) The Secretary may coin and issue pursuant to this section half dollars or 50-cent pieces, quarter dollars or 25-cent pieces, and dimes or 10-cent pieces in such quantities as he may determine to be necessary to meet the needs of the public. Any coin minted under authority of this section shall be a clad coin the weight of whose cladding is not less than 30 per centum of the weight of the entire coin, and which meets the following additional specifications:

(1) The half dollar shall have—

(A) a diameter of 1.205 inches;

(B) a cladding of an alloy of 800 parts of silver and 200 parts of copper; and

---

[1] See exhibit 21, page 308.

(C) a core of an alloy of silver and copper such that the whole coin weighs 11.5 grams and contains 4.6 grams of silver and 6.9 grams of copper.

(2) The quarter dollar shall have—

(A) a diameter of 0.955 inch;

(B) a cladding of an alloy of 75 per centum copper and 25 per centum nickel; and

(C) a core of copper such that the weight of the whole coin is 5.67 grams.

(3) The dime shall have—

(A) a diameter of 0.705 inch;

(B) a cladding of an alloy of 75 per centum copper and 25 per centum nickel; and

(C) a core of copper such that the weight of the whole coin is 2.268 grams.

(b) Half dollars, quarter dollars, and dimes may be minted from 900 fine coin silver only until such date as the Secretary of the Treasury determines that adequate supplies of the coins authorized by this Act are available, and in no event later than five years after the date of enactment of this Act.

79 STAT. 254
79 STAT. 255.

(c) No standard silver dollars may be minted during the five-year period which begins on the date of enactment of this Act.

Silver dollars, restriction. Legal tender.

SEC. 102. All coins and currencies of the United States (including Federal Reserve notes and circulating notes of Federal Reserve banks and national banking associations), regardless of when coined or issued, shall be legal tender for all debts, public and private, public charges, taxes, duties, and dues.

SEC. 103. (a) In order to acquire equipment, manufacturing facilities, patents, patent rights, technical knowledge and assistance, metallic strip, and other materials necessary to produce rapidly an adequate supply of the coins authorized by section 101 of this Act, the Secretary may enter into contracts upon such terms and conditions as he may deem appropriate and in the public interest.

Contract authority.

(b) During such period as he may deem necessary, but in no event later than five years after the date of enactment of this Act, the Secretary may exercise the authority conferred by subsection (a) of this section without regard to any other provisions of law governing procurement or public contracts.

SEC. 104. The Secretary shall purchase at a price of $1.25 per fine troy ounce any silver mined after the date of enactment of this Act from natural deposits in the United States or any place subject to the jurisdiction thereof and tendered to a United States mint or assay office within one year after the month in which the ore from which it is derived was mined.

Silver, purchase.

SEC. 105. (a) Whenever in the judgment of the Secretary such action is necessary to protect the coinage of the United States, he is authorized under such rules and regulations as he may prescribe to prohibit, curtail, or regulate the exportation, melting, or treating of any coin of the United States.

Exportation, etc., of coins.

(b) Whoever knowingly violates any order, rule, regulation, or license issued pursuant to subsection (a) of this section shall be fined not more than $10,000, or imprisoned not more than five years, or both.

Penalty.

SEC. 106. (a) There shall be forfeited to the United States any coins exported, melted, or treated in violation of any order, rule, regulation, or license issued under section 105(a), and any metal resulting from such melting or treating.

Forfeiture of coins.

(b) The powers of the Secretary and his delegates, and the judicial and other remedies available to the United States, for the enforcement of forfeitures of property subject to forfeiture pursuant to subsection (a) of this section shall be the same as

68A Stat. 869.
26 USC 7321–
7329.
those provided in part II of subchapter C of chapter 75 of the Internal Revenue Code of 1954 for the enforcement of forfeitures of property subject to forfeiture under any provision of such Code.

SEC. 107. The Secretary may issue such rules and regulations as he may deem necessary to carry out the provisions of this Act.

Definitions.
SEC. 108. For the purposes of this title—

(1) The term "Secretary" means the Secretary of the Treasury.

(2) The term "clad coin" means a coin composed of three layers of metal, the two outer layers being of identical composition and metallurgically bonded to an inner layer.

(3) The term "cladding" means the outer layers of a clad coin.

(4) The term "core" means the inner layer of a clad coin.

(5) A specification given otherwise than as a limit shall be maintained within such reasonable manufacturing tolerances as the Secretary may specify.

79 STAT. 255.
(6) Specifications given for an alloy are by weight.

79 STAT. 256.

TITLE II—AMENDMENTS TO EXISTING LAW

SEC. 201. The first sentence of section 3558 of the Revised Statutes (31 U.S.C. 283) is amended to read: "The business of San Francisco
assay office,
minting of
coins. the United States assay office in San Francisco shall be in all respects similar to that of the assay office of New York except that until the Secretary of the Treasury determines that the mints of the United States are adequate for the production of ample supplies of coins, its facilities may be used for the production of coins."

SEC. 202. Section 4 of the Act of August 20, 1963 (Public 77 Stat. 129. Law 88–102; 31 U.S.C. 294), is amended by changing "$30,000,000" to read "$45,000,000".

SEC. 203. (a) Section 3 of the Act of December 18, 1942 (56 Stat. 1065; 31 U.S.C. 317c), is amended by striking "minor" each place it appears.

Repeal.
(b) Section 9 of the Act of March 14, 1900 (31 Stat. 48; 31 U.S.C. 320), is repealed.

SEC. 204. (a) Section 3517 of the Revised Statutes (31 U.S.C. 324) is amended to read:

Inscriptions on
coins.
"SEC. 3517. Upon one side of all coins of the United States there shall be an impression emblematic of liberty, with an inscription of the word 'Liberty', and upon the reverse side shall be the figure or representation of an eagle, with the inscriptions 'United States of America' and 'E Pluribus Unum' and a designation of the value of the coin; but on the dime, 5-, and 1-cent piece, the figure of the eagle shall be omitted. The motto 'In God we trust' shall be inscribed on all coins. Any coins minted after the enactment of the Coinage Act of 1965 from 900 fine coin silver shall be inscribed with the year 1964. All other coins shall be inscribed with the year of the coinage or issuance unless the Secretary of the Treasury, in order to prevent or alleviate a shortage of coins of any denomination, directs that coins of that denomination continue to be inscribed with the last preceding year inscribed on coins of that denomination, except that coins produced under authority of sections 101(a)(1), 101(a)(2), and 101(a)(3) of the Coinage Act of 1965 shall not be dated earlier than 1965. No mint mark may be inscribed on any coins during the five-year period beginning on the date of enactment of the Coinage Act of 1965, except that coins struck at the Denver mint as authorized by law prior to such date may continue to be inscribed with that mint mark."

(b) The Act of September 3, 1964 (Public Law 88–580; 31 U.S.C. 324 note), is repealed.

Repeal.
78 Stat. 908.

SEC. 205. The first sentence of section 3526 of the Revised Statutes (31 U.S.C. 335) is amended to read: "In order to procure bullion for coinage or to carry out the purposes of section 104 of the Coinage Act of 1965, the Secretary of the Treasury many purchase silver bullion with the bullion fund."

SEC. 206. (a) Section 3528 of the Revised Statutes (31 U.S.C. 340) is amended to read:

Coinage metal fund.

"SEC. 3528. The Secretary of the Treasury may use the coinage metal fund for the purchase of metal for coinage. The gain arising from the coinage of metals purchased out of such fund into coin of a nominal value exceeding the cost of such metals shall be credited to the coinage profit fund. The coinage profit fund shall be charged with the wastage incurred in such coinage, with the cost of distributing such coins, and with such sums as shall from time to time be transferred therefrom to the general fund of the Treasury."

(b) The effect of the amendment made by subsection (a) of this section shall be to redesignate the minor coinage metal fund established under section 3528 of the Revised Statutes as the coinage metal fund, and not to authorize the creation of a new fund.

79 STAT. 256.

SEC. 207. The second sentence of section 3542 of the Revised Statutes (31 U.S.C. 355) is amended by changing ", in the case of the superintendent of melting and refining department, one-thousandth of the whole amount of gold, and one and one-half thousandths of the whole amount of silver delivered to him since the last annual settlement, and in the case of the superintendent of coining department, one-thousandth of the whole amount of silver, and one-half thousandth of the whole amount of gold that has been delivered to him by the superintendent" to read "such limitations as the Secretary shall establish."

79 STAT. 257.
Wastage allowance.

SEC. 208. Section 3550 of the Revised Statutes (31 U.S.C. 366) is repealed.

Repeal.

SEC. 209. The second sentence of section 2 of the Act of June 4, 1963 (Public Law 88–36; 31 U.S.C. 405a–1), is amended to read: "The Secretary of the Treasury is authorized to use for coinage, or to sell on such terms and conditions as he may deem appropriate, at a price not less than the monetary value of $1.292929292 per fine troy ounce, any silver of the United States in excess of that required to be held as reserves against outstanding silver certificates."

Silver excess.
77 Stat. 54.

SEC. 210. The last sentence of section 43(b)(1) of the Act of May 12, 1933 (Public Law 10, 73d Congress; 31 U.S.C. 462), is repealed.

Repeal.
48 Stat. 113.
62 Stat. 708.

SEC. 211. (a) Section 485 of title 18 of the United States Code is amended to read:

"§ 485. Coins or bars

"Whoever falsely makes, forges, or counterfeits any coin or bar in resemblance or similitude of any coin of a denomination higher than 5 cents or any gold or silver bar coined or stamped at any mint or assay office of the United States, or in resemblance or similitude of any foreign gold or silver coin current in the United States or in actual use and circulation as money within the United States; or

"Whoever passes, utters, publishes, sells, possesses, or brings into the United States any false, forged, or counterfeit coin or bar, knowing the same to be false, forged, or counterfeit, with intent to defraud any body politic or corporate, or any person, or attempts the commission of any offense described in this paragraph—

Penalty.

"Shall be fined not more than $5,000 or imprisoned not more than fifteen years, or both."

(b) The table of sections at the beginning of chapter 25 of such title is amended by striking

"485· Gold or silver coins or bars."

and inserting

"485· Coins or bars."

18 USC 331–336.

SEC. 212. (a) Chapter 17 of title 18 of the United States Code is amended by adding at the end :

"§ 337. Coins as security for loans

"Whoever lends or borrows money or credit upon the security of such coins of the United States as the Secretary of the Treasury may from time to time designate by proclamation published in the Federal Register, during any period designated in such a proclamation, shall be fined not more than $10,000 or imprisoned not more than one year, or both."

Publication in Federal Register.

(b) The table of sections at the beginning of such chapter is amended by adding at the end :

"337· Coins as security for loans."

(c) The amendments made by this section shall apply only with respect to loans made, renewed, or increased on or after the 31st day after the date of enactment of this Act.

79 STAT. 257.
79 STAT. 258.

TITLE III—JOINT COMMISSION ON THE COINAGE

Membership.

SEC. 301. The President is hereby authorized to establish a Joint Commission on the Coinage to be composed of the Secretary of the Treasury as Chairman ; the Secretary of Commerce ; the Director of the Bureau of the Budget ; the Director of the Mint ; the chairman and ranking minority member of the Senate Banking and Currency Committee, and four Members of the Senate, not members of such committee, to be appointed by the President of the Senate ; the chairman and ranking minority member of the House Banking and Currency Committee, and four members of the House of Representatives, not members of such committee, to be appointed by the Speaker ; and eight

Restriction.

public members to be appointed by the President, none of whom shall be associated or identified with or representative of any industry, group, business, or association directly interested as such in the composition, characteristics, or production of the coinage of the United States.

Vacancies.

SEC. 302. No public official or Member of Congress serving as a member of the Joint Commission shall continue to serve as such after he has ceased to hold the office by virtue of which he became a member of the Joint Commission. Any vacancy on the Joint Commission shall be filled by the choosing of a successor member in the same manner as his predecessor.

Duties.

SEC. 303. The Joint Commission shall study the progress made in the implementation of the coinage program established by this Act, and shall review from time to time such matters as the needs of the economy for coins, the standards for the coinage, technological developments in metallurgy and coin-selector devices, the availability of various metals, renewed minting of the silver dollar, the time when and circumstances under which the United States should cease to maintain the price of silver, and other considerations relevant to the maintenance of an adequate and stable coinage system. It shall from time to time, give its advice and recommendations with respect to these matters to the President, the Secretary of the Treasury, and the Congress.

Appropriation.

SEC. 304. There are authorized to be appropriated to remain available until expended, such amounts as may be necessary to carry out the purposes of this title.

Approved July 23, 1965.

Exhibit 24.—Other Treasury testimony published in hearings before congressional committees, July 1, 1964–June 30, 1965

Secretary of the Treasury Dillon

Statement on S. 797, an act to eliminate the provision of existing law that Federal Reserve banks hold gold certificates equivalent to at least 25 percent of their own deposit liabilities, published in hearings before the Committee on Banking and Currency, U.S. Senate, 89th Congress, 1st session, February 2, 1965, pages 19–24.

Public Debt Management

Exhibit 25.—Statement by Secretary of the Treasury Fowler, June 15, 1965, before the Senate Finance Committee, on the debt limit

Action is essential before the end of the current fiscal year to establish a new public debt limit adequate to accommodate our needs in the period ahead. The present temporary ceiling stands at $324 billion. On July 1, the ceiling, in the absence of congressional action, will revert to its permanent level of $285 billion, $32.4 billion below the estimated debt subject to limit at that time. Clearly, we cannot permit the credit of the United States to come under that shadow for a single day, nor doubts arise over the authority of the Treasury to finance in an orderly way the additional needs of the Federal Government that will arise later in fiscal 1966.

You will recall that the President's Budget submitted to the Congress in January of this year anticipated a deficit of $6.3 billion for fiscal 1965. As you are aware, this outlook has improved significantly since that time. Late in April the President was able to announce an expected decrease in anticipated expenditures for the fiscal year of $500 million. Meanwhile, accumulating evidence of a larger than expected flow of taxes, particularly of individual income taxes, now indicates that receipts will total at least $1.4 billion more than anticipated in January. As a result, our estimated fiscal 1965 deficit has been reduced to about $4.4 billion.

The difference between our debt ceiling needs for fiscal 1966 and the need when the Treasury appeared before this committee a year ago is primarily accounted for by this estimated fiscal 1965 deficit, for that deficit will be reflected in an approximately equivalent increase in the debt between the start of fiscal 1965 and the start of fiscal 1966.

Every year, the Treasury faces a large seasonal shortfall in revenues during the first six to eight months of a fiscal year. For instance, we typically collect less than 45 percent of our annual revenues from the end of June to the end of December. Consequently, even in years of balanced budgets, we have substantial seasonal borrowing requirements over that period, and these requirements are relatively little influenced by moderate changes in the budgetary projections for a fiscal year as a whole. The size of an anticipated surplus or deficit does, of course, determine how much of this borrowing can be purely temporary, to be paid off in the spring when revenues are seasonally flush, but it is the earlier peak seasonal needs which must be covered by the debt ceiling.

Given this recurrent seasonal pattern, it is plain that the debt ceiling must be raised not so much to take account of any prospective deficit in fiscal 1966 as a whole, but simply to take account of the fact that, as a result of the $4.4 billion deficit anticipated for the current fiscal year, we expect that we will be entering the current fiscal year with the actual debt some $4.7 billion higher than a year earlier.

I know the committee is also interested in a review of the prospects for fiscal 1966 as a whole. As you are aware, the President's January budget, in estimating fiscal year 1966 receipts at $94.4 billion, had already taken into account the $1¾ billion cut in excise taxes proposed for July 1. On the basis of recent experience, and with continued gains in economic activity, that revenue estimate, still assuming only the proposed July 1 reductions in excises, has been raised by $1.6 billion. Further allowance must now also be made for the additional cut in excise taxes of $1¾ billion on January 1, 1966, which was passed by the House of Representatives recently and upon which your committee has reported.   Enactment of that additional cut will offset an estimated $600 million of the $1.6 billion improvement in the revenue outlook.   As a result, we now estimate receipts, in fiscal 1966 at $95.4 billion, $1 billion higher than projected in the President's January budget.

I am informed by the Director of the Bureau of the Budget that, at this stage in the appropriations process, there is no sound basis for changing the expenditure estimate for fiscal 1966 in the January budget, and that the estimated spending total of $99.7 billion still represents a fair appraisal of the spending outlook.   Consequently, we now anticipate a deficit in fiscal 1966 of $4.3 billion, as compared with $5.3 billion in the President's budget.

The outlook for the public debt at midmonth and month-end dates in fiscal 1966 consistent with this budgetary outlook is shown on table I attached.   The debt levels that are shown in the last column of table I are based on the same assumptions that have been used in previous debt limit discussions.   The first assumption is that the Treasury's cash operating balance will be maintained at a constant level of $4 billion, a figure below our actual average balances in recent years.   In practice, there is, of course, a great deal of fluctuation in our actual cash balances, and at various times during the year it is feasible and desirable to achieve cash balances smaller than $4 billion.   However, that figure seems to me a necessary and prudent minimum allowance for a cash balance adequate to conduct the operations of the Treasury in an efficient manner, and it has been customary before both the House and Senate committees to use this minimum figure for advance planning.

The second assumption provides the usual $3 billion of margin for flexibility and contingencies.   This is insurance against the uncertainties that inevitably exist in projections of budgetary receipts and expenditures a year or more ahead, and also recognizes the need for financing flexibility to assure maximum efficiency in debt management operations.   For instance, Treasury obviously would prefer to refrain from new financing in an unfavorable market environment; conversely, it would like to anticipate future cash requirements by borrowing when markets are particularly favorable.   And, clearly, with receipts and expenditures subject to sharp fluctuations from day to day and week to week, it would be impractical to schedule Treasury financings so as to avoid considerable swings in the cash balance.

As table I indicates, our peak requirement, including the allowance for contingencies, is estimated at $328.9 billion at the middle of March 1966.   Consequently, a debt ceiling of $329 billion, $5 billion higher than the present temporary limit for the current fiscal year was presented to the House Ways and Means Committee as the amount that was necessary to carry the Treasury through the fiscal year 1966.   That committee suggested that this figure instead be rounded down to $328 billion, and the House has since completed action to provide a new temporary ceiling at the $328 billion figure for fiscal 1966.   I stated before the House committee that our study had been carefully done and that we believed it would be prudent to fix the ceiling at the requested figure of $329 billion.   I added that the process of shaving the assumptions could entail some measured risks.   Nevertheless, I told the House committee that I would not enter any strong objection to their then proposed action.   In consequence, I appear before you with the same data and estimates as were presented to the House committee, but with a specific request for the $328 billion ceiling as voted by the House rather than the $329 billion we had requested.

I should emphasize, in requesting your concurrence in this action, that our peak needs have not been significantly affected by the second stage of the excise tax program recommended by the President.   The estimated $600 million revenue impact of the excise tax cuts scheduled for January 1, 1966, will appear in our actual collections only with a lag of two to three months, with virtually all of the effect coming after our peak debt needs on March 15 have already passed.   In fact, substantial reduction of the debt is anticipated during the spring of 1966.

I would also like to call your attention to table II, comparing our projections of the debt subject to limitation submitted to this committee last June with actual results.   It can be seen that the actual debt in most recent months, adjusted to the assumed cash balance of $4.0 billion (column 5) fluctuated close to our earlier estimates.   While the unexpected increases in the revenue flow have permitted us to remain under our estimates by a wider margin in April and May, at the peak requirement period of mid-March the debt was only $800 million less than that which was estimated a year ago. It is, of course, this peak seasonal requirement that must be anticipated almost a year ahead. I believe the record is also clear that the $3 billion leeway implicit in the temporary ceiling of $324 billion provided for the current fiscal year has, as intended, been properly reserved as a margin for flexibility and emergencies, a margin that, fortunately, we did not need to draw upon this year.

It can also be seen that as a practical matter the operating cash balance has rarely been at or below $4 billion, and that the substantial, and not entirely predictable, monthly variations in our cash flow have occasionally resulted in considerably higher balances for brief periods. These variations, I believe, are a normal consequence of an orderly financing program designed to assure adequate balances over periods of peak cash drains, adequate flexibility in scheduling our borrowing operations, and our ability to meet the broader economic objectives of our debt management program.

It is not the intent of the Treasury to ask for any more borrowing power than is necessary and prudent. To the contrary, our firm objective is to maintain no more debt outstanding than that which is absolutely required to effectively and economically discharge the financial responsibilities of the Government.

TABLE I.—*Estimated public debt subject to limitation, fiscal year 1966*

[In billions. Based on constant minimum operating cash balance of $4.0 billion]

	Operating cash balance (excluding free gold)	Public debt subject to limitation	Allowance to provide flexibility in financing and for contingencies	Total public debt limitation required
1965				
June 30	$4.0	$310.2	$3.0	$313.2
July 15	4.0	313.1	3.0	316.1
July 31	4.0	314.3	3.0	317.3
August 15	4.0	314.7	3.0	317.7
August 31	4.0	315.7	3.0	318.7
September 15	4.0	318.8	3.0	321.8
September 30	4.0	313.1	3.0	316.1
October 15	4.0	316.2	3.0	319.2
October 31	4.0	318.7	3.0	321.7
November 15	4.0	319.7	3.0	322.7
November 30	4.0	319.6	3.0	322.6
December 15	4.0	321.3	3.0	324.3
December 31	4.0	319.6	3.0	322.6
1966				
January 15	4.0	322.8	3.0	325.8
January 31	4.0	321.5	3.0	324.5
February 15	4.0	321.6	3.0	324.6
February 28	4.0	321.9	3.0	324.9
March 15	4.0	325.9	3.0	328.9
March 31	4.0	319.5	3.0	322.5
April 15	4.0	323.0	3.0	326.0
April 30	4.0	319.0	3.0	322.0
May 15	4.0	318.3	3.0	321.3
May 31	4.0	320.1	3.0	323.1
June 15	4.0	322.8	3.0	325.8
June 30	4.0	315.2	3.0	318.2

TABLE II.—*Comparison of debt projections of June 23, 1964, with actual results*

[In billions]

Fiscal year 1965	Projections of June 23, 1964		Actual			Difference column 5 compared with column 2
	Operating cash balance (excluding free gold)	Debt subject to limitation	Operating cash balance (excluding free gold)	Debt subject to limitation	Debt subject to limitation after adjusting cash balance to $4.0 [1]	
	(1)	(2)	(3)	(4)	(5)	
1964						
June 30	$4.0	$307.9	$10.1	$312.2	$306.1	−1.8
July 15	4.0	311.0	5.9	311.2	309.3	−1.7
July 31	4.0	311.8	5.3	311.6	310.3	−1.5
August 15	4.0	313.5	6.1	313.2	311.1	−2.4
August 31	4.0	314.2	6.0	314.6	312.6	−1.6
September 15	4.0	316.9	3.8	315.7	315.9	−1.0
September 30	4.0	311.2	9.3	316.1	310.8	−.4
October 15	4.0	315.0	5.1	315.6	314.5	−.5
October 31	4.0	316.3	4.8	316.1	315.3	−1.0
November 15	4.0	318.1	4.8	317.0	316.2	−1.9
November 30	4.0	317.7	7.2	319.0	315.8	−1.9
December 15	4.0	320.5	3.3	318.7	319.4	−1.1
December 31	4.0	316.0	6.2	318.5	316.3	+.3
1965						
January 15	4.0	318.9	2.8	317.9	319.1	+.2
January 31	4.0	318.0	4.5	318.4	317.9	−.1
February 15	4.0	319.1	4.6	318.4	317.8	−1.3
February 28	4.0	318.2	6.8	320.3	317.5	−.7
March 15	4.0	321.0	4.2	320.4	320.2	−.8
March 31	4.0	315.4	8.1	318.1	314.0	−1.4
April 15	4.0	319.2	4.5	318.0	317.5	−1.7
April 30	4.0	315.6	7.9	316.9	313.0	−2.6
May 15	4.0	316.7	8.9	316.1	311.2	−5.5
May 31	4.0	317.1	9.7	319.5	313.8	−3.3
June 15	4.0	319.9				
June 30	4.0	313.9				

[1] Adjustment to $4.0 billion cash balance places data on basis comparable to estimates given on June 23 ' 1964, as shown in column (2).

Exhibit 26.—Remarks by Under Secretary of the Treasury for Monetary Affairs Roosa, November 19, 1964, before the Bankers Club of Chicago, on debt management, liquidity, and monetary stability

The title for these remarks was not selected, or at least not merely selected, because it seemed a large enough portmanteau to cover anything I might want to discuss when November 19 arrived. Nor do I have any wish to add another voice to the chorus of official and unofficial comments being heard these days on the proper present posture for monetary policy. But this title does express, perhaps more effectively than I will be able to do in talking on at greater length, a fundamental point of view on the role and usefulness of debt management:

> The design and issuance of the public debt must, of course, first be concentrated upon the effective placement in the market of obligations to replace maturing issues and to provide new money as required. But, in addition, debt management can—through the types of issues offered, and the manner and timing of offerings—be a constructive force in affecting the liquidity of the economy. That, in turn, may both exert a useful influence upon flows of funds into or out of the country and also help to maintain the monetary stability we need for balanced and continuing growth.

It has been the Treasury's aim, for several years now, to develop somewhat further these larger potentials of debt management. That is why I thought it would be useful to glance backward tonight—with special emphasis upon those dimensions of debt management that reach into our national policies affecting liquidity and monetary stability—to review what has been attempted, in an effort to learn for the future. Since my own direct association with debt management on the Treasury side has covered only the past four years, what I say will relate particularly to this period. My colleagues and I are deeply aware that we owe to our predecessors and their imaginative innovations a large part of any success we may have had in our operations, but I would not want to implicate those predecessors with responsibility for these reflections on policies of debt management.

Before turning to wider policy considerations, however, it is important to recognize the persistent and awesome pressure from the sheer passage of time that every debt manager must face. Naive as it sounds when simply stated, outstanding securities are always getting shorter, every day, and unless something is done about it the bulk of the debt could soon be in very short-term form, requiring continuous replacement. That inexorable pressure compels every debt manager to think first of housekeeping, not only for the period of his own tenure but for that of his successors. From that pressure comes, incidentally, the common bond of understanding and continuity that characterizes this aspect of work in Government, perhaps more than many other kinds of governmental activity, from one Administration to the next.

The overriding need is to keep a structure of debt that is spaced over a number of years ahead, and consists of instruments that are fully useable in and familiar to a broad and active trading market. Closely related is the clear need to keep the overall burden of interest charges upon the budget at the practicable minimum determined by a free, competitive market. Within the boundaries set by respect for those essentials, there is still considerable scope, however, for purposeful variation in offerings to further the general objectives of Government policy. There are also risks—the risks not only of unintentional error but also of attempting to do too much—risks which have at times in the past seemed so great as to persuade some that debt management should follow a straightline course without particular regard for whether the broader impact of specific financing operations helped or hindered, for example, the current objectives of the Federal Reserve and monetary policy.

Yet the simple fact that the Government debt exists, and must be managed in some way, means that the Treasury will necessarily, in any year, pass through the market 10 to 15 times as large a volume of Government securities as are represented by all Federal Reserve open market transactions in that year. Whether the Treasury wishes to or not, it is affecting the current supply of short, intermediate, or long-term issues. Subject to keeping the amounts of its offerings within the dimensions of the market's distributive capacity, and subject to keeping its terms reasonably in line with current market quotations, the Treasury can, and inescapably will, exert a strong, and at times a critical, influence upon the markets for most kinds of fixed-interest obligations, throughout the maturity range.

The challenge is to use that influence, when the imperatives of the debt structure leave a range of choice, in the manner best calculated to further the objectives of governmental economic policy as a whole, and particularly, to complement or reinforce rather than to negate the current efforts of the Federal Reserve. Under a different system of government—such as the centralized and unified direction of policy that is common in Europe, for example—such a challenge would seem to call for a blueprint of hierarchical control. Not here. For in a government of checks and balances between and among coordinate bodies, the answer can be found in communication and harmonization. That, at any rate, is the way it has seemed to me, during the brief period of my own Treasury experience, that the relationship has flourished. Nonetheless, there are certainly real risks here, too, and those who call out warnings from time to time on the need to preserve the independent integrity of the Federal Reserve are performing another essential function of our check and balance process.

Before I turn further to some of the details of our debt management experience that have seemed to me exciting during these last few years, I must first remind you, too, of the even larger frame that I meant to include in saying that we have viewed debt management as a part of overall economic policy. For the Administration and Congress have, I think, been able in the past two or three years to respond to a call that has often come from many sides, including the Federal Reserve itself, a call for bringing fiscal policy into a tacit partnership with monetary policy, for recognizing that there must be a conscious "mix" of fiscal and monetary policy, and for making clear that monetary policy should not be expected to take on alone the task of assuring the monetary and financial stability so essential to continued national prosperity and sustained balance in our international accounts.

The investment tax credit, the liberalized depreciation allowances, the massive reduction in income taxes, these were all a part of that response. And as these powerful forces were releasing their strength to help propel a major expansion in the output, employment, and incomes of the American economy, it was the agreed task of debt management, alongside the monetary policy determined by the Federal Reserve, to try to help maintain conditions in the credit and capital markets that would sustain the expansion without cumulating into an inflationary excess of aggregate demand, or a speculative spiral of securities prices and property values. At the same time, it was essential to reconcile this task of debt management with another, that of helping to nudge upward those interest rates which might be able to hold in the United States some of the volatile short-term funds that could otherwise flow out to foreign markets, aggravating our already large balance-of-payments deficit.

All of this meant that debt management was called upon to find and fill a useful place in the effort which the Government as a whole had to make to help stimulate the domestic economy, to help eliminate the balance-of-payments deficit, and to help in maintaining the conditions of monetary stability essential for both home expansion and external balance.

The place that debt management found in the effort to stimulate the economy was, very largely, though not only, protective, containing the potential for inflation that lay in the use of other, more active, stimulators. While the Government debt has continued to rise—though, to be sure, on a declining scale in recent years—as a consequence of the Government's expenditure requirements and tax policies, debt management has been able to keep the financing of the deficits in noninflationary form. Of the total increase in marketable debt of nearly $21 billion over these past four years, for example, some $20 billion is at this moment accounted for by the enlarged outstanding total of bonds of five years or more in maturity. And all this new debt, on balance, has been absorbed by nonbank investors. The total holdings of all Government securities of all maturities by the commercial banks have actually declined by about $1½ billion since the beginning of 1961.

At the same time, as the supply of longer-term Government bonds has been increased, every effort has been made to so adapt the timing and form of new issues to the current market as to exert a minimum of upward impact on longer term interest rates and to assure the continued ready availability of long-term funds for all other economic uses.

In fact, while long-term Government bonds have been issued over the past four years at several times the pace of the preceding four years, the aggregate volume of funds loaned or invested in the economy as a whole has been around one-third greater than in the preceding four years, and interest rates on mortgages, corporate bonds, and municipal bonds are still ¼ to ⅜ percent below their highs of 1961. To be sure, many other factors were at work as well in producing these results, perhaps most notably the spur to savings provided by the continuing general stability of prices. But at any rate debt management does seem to have been able to accomplish its main objective, so far as the domestic economy was concerned: to finance the growing debt in a noninflationary manner without impeding the other stimuli being given the economy by fiscal and monetary policy in the effort to promote expansion.

On the balance-of-payments side, the main problem for debt management centered in the behavior of short-term flows of funds, and the interest rates which to some extent affect them. For the Federal Reserve's continuing effort to assure a ready availability of credit, unless conditioned in some way, would mean such short-term interest rates so low as to spur an outflow of funds to other centers that would swamp out the benefits of any other gains being made toward balance in our overall external accounts. One clear way to help, along with other important methods adapted to this same need by the Federal Reserve itself, was to add to the market supply of very short-term issues, notably Treasury bills. This the Treasury has proceeded to do.

From January 1961, to the present, the supply of Treasury bills has been increased by some $15 billion, or more than one-third. This added supply has been an important factor in raising the rate on 3-month bills from 2¼ percent early in 1961 to nearly 3⅝ percent today. There have, to be sure, been intervals when neither the step by step increases that have brought about this rise, nor the effect of changes in the cost of obtaining forward cover, have been sufficient to check substantial outflows of short-term funds; but most of the time the overall deterrent effect has been clear and impressive. Certainly such flows could have been disastrously greater had not these more or less steady increases in short-term rates proved possible—during years in which we have also been in need of a continuing ample availability of funds at home for spurring domestic economic expansion.

But there are risks in adding indefinitely to the supply of Treasury bills. For these, too, represent liquidity, a form of near-money. Account had to be taken of their impact on the near-cash positions of businesses and banks, as well as the implications for debt management in the need to keep rolling over these bills in large amounts at frequent intervals. To provide at least a partial offset, the Treasury steadily reduced the supply of other short-term issues. Roughly $6½ billion of coupon issues in the under-one-year area have now disappeared; about $7½ billion has been taken out of the 1-to-5 year sector. The combined total reflects a rise of only $1 billion, on balance, in the entire maturity segment from zero years to five years. And the remainder, as already noted—roughly $20 billion of the total of about $21 billion of new marketable debt since January 1961—has all been placed in maturities beyond 5 years.

There has been another way in which debt management has been made a part of balance-of-payments policy: through the issuance of short-term bonds to foreign monetary authorities, denominated in their own currencies. With more than $1 billion of these now outstanding, and with transfers of them between other countries already having occurred, the versatility of this instrument is being demonstrated, and it may have already found a permanent place in the monetary arrangements of the future. As a possible means of absorbing foreign monetary balances that might otherwise be pressed upon us for conversion into gold, this new approach can provide direct assistance to our external monetary position, while also carrying as well as any conventional issue a corresponding amount of the debt which must, in any event, be placed with some holder somewhere.

Perhaps the most effective single technique that has been used to keep the debt well placed, as a base for continuing monetary stability in the United States, has been that of advance refunding, first introduced in 1960 by our predecessors, Secretaries Anderson and Baird. Debt extension, through this route or any other, is an omnipresent consideration because:

1. No Secretary of the Treasury can let so much debt pile up in the short-term area that he must always do his financing, literally, with his back to the wall. He needs some scope for choosing the timing, amounts, and maturities of his offerings in relation to the going market.

2. A vast array of market institutions, including a wide variety of savings intermediaries, has developed around a balanced distribution of debt instruments of short, intermediate, and long maturities. Although the proportions among these can be expected to change with changing market conditions, and changing expectations as to these conditions, there must at all times be some intermediate and some long-term issues outstanding in order to "hold a place" in the debt structure for the time when public policy calls for additions, or retirements, in one sector or another. That is, without familiarity and continuity, there will be virtually no markets in the longer sectors when the time comes for active influence to be exerted in these areas.

3. A balanced debt structure will usually assure a lower aggregate cost of debt service. It is concentration of the debt, or of current financing, in one maturity sector that risks high interest costs to the Treasury of the kind represented by the so-called Magic Fives, which we just retired last August, or their sister, the 4⅞'s, which we just retired last Monday.

4. Moreover, a significant supply must be kept in all maturity sectors in order to give the Federal Reserve a suitable market through which to exert its own desired influence. In its effort to help hold short rates at higher levels, the Federal Reserve has over the past three years and more been doing some of its buying in the intermediate or longer-term area to avoid putting downward pressure on bill yields. The additions to the market

supply of these longer issues have been useful, in helping to give the Federal Reserve an active trading market to work in.

5. The active trading markets made possible when there is a substantial supply in all maturity segments is an important medium for gauging the impact of changes in general supply and demand conditions, in a form of widely tradeable instrument free of credit risk.

6. The timing and decisiveness of Treasury action in making its own offering can also act as a catalyst for the related markets in corporate and municipal bonds. For example, the successful offering of three-quarters of a billion dollars of 21-year, 4¼ percent bonds as part of the January advance refunding at the beginning of this year seemed to give many other elements in the market a signal they were waiting for, restoring confidence to a nervous market, and actually resulting in a marked reduction of market yields. Similarly, the 10-year, 4¼ percent bond included in the regular May refunding provided a tonic to market psychology as investors took $1½ billion of the offering.

There are, reinforcing these reasons for always giving weight to the possibility of debt extension, three additional considerations that have made advance refundings particularly attractive from the Treasury's point of view:

1. The Treasury has complete initiative with respect to timing and amounts. Instead of being bound to act on a maturity date established many years earlier, the Treasury can choose when to enter the market, in the light of prevailing market conditions—accomplishing more, disturbing less.

2. Moreover, should the response be comparatively poor—either because new events intervened while the books were open, or because the design of the offering was not adequately attractive—the Treasury suffers no significant consequences. It still will have other opportunities to handle the remaining holdings of securities eligible for the advance exchange, and there will be no impact at all upon its cash position. Low response to a refunding of actually matured issues, on the other hand, raises innuendoes of "failure," and leads to a possible short-fall of cash as the Treasury pays out heavy amounts for redemptions.

3. By combining many issues in a single operation, often taking maturities scattered over a range of several years, the Treasury can reduce the total number, or the scale, or both, of its subsequent offerings. The effect can be to reduce the weight of Treasury operations in the market, particularly important in periods when the market itself is under strain as might have been anticipated through this past autumn, for example.

The role of advance refundings in the debt extension effort of recent years has been spectacular. Over the 5 years 1960–64 that advance refundings have been in use, the Treasury has issued an annual average of about $4 billion of bonds maturing in 10 years or more, compared with an average of slightly more than $1 billion per year for the 8 preceding years—the 8 years that followed the "Accord" of 1951. Or if the definition of long bonds is stretched to include 9-year maturities—which proved to be a particularly useful middle-issue in advance refunding offerings—the annual average for the past 5 years becomes more than $7 billion, while the average for the earlier years remains unchanged at about $1 billion. Another gauge of this effect is to look at the presently outstanding Treasury debt due after five years. Some $32.9 billion, or 53 percent of the current total, was issued in advance refundings. It is not often realized, when concern is expressed over loose fiscal and monetary policies in Washington, that on balance practically all of the increase in the Treasury's marketable debt since January 1961, has been financed at long-term so that it is still, despite the passage of the years since then, due in five years or more.

As a result, the long postwar decline in the average maturity of the marketable debt to a low of 4 years 2 months in September 1960, was not only ended but reversed. The average maturity is now 5 years 2 months, up about 12 months from the September 1960 low. It is worth noting, however, that by the yearend the average maturity will be practically unchanged from the end of last year, despite the issuance of $13.8 billion of Treasury bonds this year. This is eloquent evidence of the volume of new long-term financing that must be done in order to offset the impact of the passage of time on the maturity structure.

None of this is intended to imply that debt extension should be restricted to advance refundings only, any more than it has been in the past, or indeed that debt extension must be confined to offerings of long-term bonds. On the first point, for example, we achieved a modest amount of debt extension last May by selling $1.5 billion of 10-year, 4¼ percent bonds in the course of refunding a regular quarterly maturity. This operation increased the average maturity of the marketable debt by nearly one month. With regard to the second point, I would note that our continuing program to move from the old pattern of a one-year anchor issue in our quarterly refundings to an 18-month pattern has already increased the average maturity by about three-quarters of a month over what it would otherwise have been.

However, I have already continued this discussion much too long. My only excuse is that opportunities of this kind are rare, and I could not resist making the most of this one, particularly because I have suspected that I might be preaching to the converted.

I have not begun to touch on many of the other fascinating sides of debt management—the experiment in auctioning long-term bonds, the continuing role of the dealer market, the techniques for issuing Treasury bills, or the impact of cash offerings as contrasted with exchanges—to list a few.

But I have most wanted to emphasize the inherent dualism in debt management. The housekeeping is essential; proper technical placement must be assured. But there are also inherent and important other potentials. We have been gaining some added experience over the past four or five years in using these potentials to help further the broader objectives of Government economic policy. Where better than in the administration of the Government's own debt should there be concern for maintaining conditions of liquidity and credit availability that will help, as far as Government influence can, to maintain monetary stability in the United States?

Exhibit 27.—Remarks by Under Secretary of the Treasury for Monetary Affairs Deming, June 8, 1965, at the National Mortgage Banking Conference of the Mortgage Bankers Association of America, Minneapolis, Minnesota, on debt management and the long-term capital market

The basic continuing goal of debt management is to assure the capacity of the Federal Government at all times to provide the necessary cash to meet any deficit in the budget and to refinance maturing securities, and to do so in ways that will neither require inflationary money creation or disruptive influences on credit markets. Given the large size of the Federal debt in relation to the economy and to the total supply of credit market instruments, as well as its importance as a medium for portfolio adjustments by investors and for Federal Reserve operations, another related, but not identical, goal of debt management is to achieve a well distributed debt, both in terms of ownership characteristics and maturity. This entails, in particular, an amount of shorter-dated debt related to the economy's need for liquid instruments. Finally, changes in the composition of the debt over time, through its influence on the structure of interest rates, the flow of funds to other borrowers, and the liquidity of the economy, can and should contribute to the effort of economic policy as a whole to achieve non-inflationary economic growth at home and balance-of-payments equilibrium.

One continuing objective of debt management, in pursuing the broad goals, is to maintain a variety of instruments outstanding in all maturity sectors of the market, and to develop techniques that permit orderly marketing of new issues throughout the maturity spectrum, so that active trading markets and access to areas will be preserved. In the process, a key objective is to avoid a volume of shorter dated issues so large as to leave the Treasury vulnerable in its financing operations to serious marketing difficulties and sudden large increases in interest cost in periods of market strain. This, in turn, requires continuing attention to the need to offset the passage of time on the maturity structure and the development of techniques that permit the placement in the market of longer dated securities.

Efficiency in financing, in the sense of minimizing interest costs consistent with the aims described above, is a constant objective of debt management. This objective has been aided by the development of techniques that facilitate the placement of new issues with a minimum market impact, and by taking advantage of opportunities to place debt in those portions of the maturity structure where demand is relatively strong.

Against this background of basic goals and objectives, I want to talk today about the debt management operations of the Treasury Department as they affect the long-term capital markets in the United States. Actually, the net demands of the Federal Government on the markets have been, and will remain, quite moderate in relation to the demands of other borrowers, even though the overall amount of financing activity in recent years has tended to overshadow this fact.

In making that point, I don't want to minimize the kinds of problems the Treasury debt managers have had to cope with through the postwar years—problems that were reflected during much of the 1950's in a persistent shortening of the debt structure—nor the achievement of more recent years in developing ways and means of placing more of our debt in longer-term form. But it is important to keep these problems and achievements in the broader perspective of the growth of the economy and the vast size of our capital markets.

In terms of its absolute size, the Federal debt has gone up $59 billion since 1946, or by almost a quarter. But this compares with a 35-percent rise in our population, so that the debt is now nearly $200 less per capita than it was at the end of World War II. More significantly, the Federal debt has declined to less than one-quarter of total debt, reflecting the much more rapid 400-percent rise in other debt, debts of individuals, businesses, and State and local governments.

The financing of the Second World War had, of course, greatly inflated the relationship of the Federal debt to overall business activity, and we emerged from that war in 1946 with our debt equal to 116 percent of gross national product. Currently, this ratio has dropped below 50 percent, and I believe there is every prospect that, with continuing economic growth, it will continue to decline over the years ahead.

By the end of 1959, the average life of the debt had decreased from the comfortable postwar level of 7 years 11 months that existed in 1946 to a greatly reduced level of 4 years 4 months. The Treasury, during a good many of those years, had, in effect, withdrawn from the long-term market in the face of strong competing demands from other borrowers, rising interest rates and tight market conditions. And the sheer arithmetic of the passage of time works insidiously against the debt manager, year after year.

Perhaps this effect can be demonstrated most graphically by recent experience. In last month's financing operation, involving, in part, the 4¼'s of 1974, the highly successful extension of $2 billion of debt for 9 years provided something less than a one-month addition to the average life of the total marketable debt. So we are continually reminded that it is necessary to "run" to keep up with the effect of the passage of time on our debt structure, and woe betide the debt manager who fails to recognize that fact.

Since the end of 1959, a trend toward a lengthening in the average maturity of the debt has been evident. This reversal of the earlier trend was due in large part to innovations in debt management techniques begun by my distinguished fellow Twin Citian, Julian Baird, and built upon by his successor, Robert Roosa. From December 1959 to March 1965, the total amount of Federal securities outstanding increased by $27.5 billion, but nearly all of that increase was in the form of bonds maturing in more than five years. Consequently, the average life of the debt increased to 5 years 4 months. How did this vital change in direction prove possible without bringing strain on the capital market? Part of the answer lies, I believe, in the fact that the demands that were made on the capital market in order to accommodate this debt management requirement were, in the perspective of the capacity of that market, rather modest.

In order to appreciate this point, it is necessary to center attention on the public marketable issues that are held by private investors, U.S. Government investment accounts, and by the Federal Reserve System. This will eliminate from consideration the special issues held in U.S. Government investment accounts, savings bonds, other nonmarketable issues (which, in recent years, have been tailored entirely for foreign accounts), and minor amounts of guaranteed Government securities and noninterest-bearing debt. Of the $24 billion increase in the marketable debt that occurred from 1959 to the present, only a little more than $8 billion was placed in the "private" sector. Government investment accounts took about $5 billion of the added marketable issues, and the Federal Reserve banks took $11 billion.

Within the private sector, there are many classes of investors that actually hold slightly fewer governments now than in December 1959, including the important commercial banks, insurance companies, mutual savings banks, and corporations. Those whose holdings have increased are State and local governments, which have added over $5 billion; foreign and international investors, who have added $4 billion; and all other investor groups, including savings and loan associations, corporate pension funds, and dealers, whose totals have increased by $4.5 billion. The holdings of individuals are also higher by $1 billion.

This points to the fact that, in placing its added debt, the Treasury has "displaced" potential placements by other borrowers only with State and local governments, many of whom are still restricted to Government issues in any event, and probably with some corporate pension funds. And the total increase in demand in this sector of the market was certainly not much more than about $6 billion for the period observed.

Rather than competing for funds with other users, the primary accomplishment of debt management during this period was the successful restructuring of the debt within the framework of existing holdings. The principal vehicle that was used to accomplish this restructuring was the advance refunding technique. Currently, about 67 percent of outstanding 20-year and over debt was placed by this method, and the comparable percentage for the 5- to 20-year maturities is 58 percent.

The major categories of investors have been willing to accept the debt extensions that have been offered to them by the Treasury, or have been enabled to find new issues to meet their needs readily in the dealer market. Virtually all of the major investor groups have extended the average life of their portfolios since 1959.

In sheer dollar volume, the primary area of concentration of offerings in advance refundings has been in the 5- to 10-year range. This has met the desires of the commercial banks, who have wanted to extend to increase their current income; and it has proved quite acceptable to the mutual savings banks, to the savings and loan associations, and to other investors, who place considerable emphasis on liquidity requirements in their Government security portfolios. Meanwhile, life insurance companies, pension funds, and others interested in the truly long-term bonds have had repeated opportunities to exchange into such bonds, and have responded favorably to advance refunding offers in that area.

At a time of rapid growth in highly liquid savings media, this increase in the average life of the debt has had the broad advantage of forestalling any excessive buildup in liquidity for the economy as a whole. More narrowly, it has had the collateral advantage of allowing the Treasury to make less frequent trips to the market for smaller amounts of funds. Maturities of coupon issues, for example, were reduced from $40½ billion in 1959 to only $31 billion by the end of March 1965. Then, too, the advance refunding technique has allowed short-dated issues to be extended at times when the market was most receptive and, in effect, has let the market help make the decisions as to how much was to be sold in which maturity range.

I do not, of course, mean to imply that the markets are capable of absorbing indefinite amounts of longer-term debt in advance refunding operations or that there would be no problems in overly-frequent use of this technique. The extent of restructuring has to be keyed to market demand, and it has often required substantial bank and dealer underwriting in order to facilitate the ultimate placement of the securities involved. We will continue to attempt to mesh these plans with our continuing assessment of the market potential, and with recognition, too, of the continuing role and function of the dealer market in enabling investors to do their own refunding through the market. It is not our intention to strain the capital markets or to place a ceiling on prospects for price appreciation by a restructuring operation at every favorable juncture.

During the 1960's, a great deal of consideration has had to be given to the implications of our operations for the balance of payments. We have been concerned particularly about maintaining a reasonably competitive relationship between our short-term investment opportunities and alternative short-term investments in other money markets, taking account, of course, of the cost of cover.

This was a primary reason for increasing the volume of regular Treasury bills outstanding by more than $19 billion since December 1959. But, at the same time, the total of maturities due within one year has increased by only $7½ billion. This was made possible by a massive movement of the coupon bonds out of the short-term area, another change made possible by the use of the advance refunding operation.

Looking to the future, we can examine the Treasury's responsibilities in light of the perspective that has been developed. Ideally, the Treasury wants to place as much of its long-term borrowing in the hands of bona fide savers as is possible. In this connection, it is frequently pointed out that recent increments in the public debt have been accommodated without additions to the Government bond holdings of the commercial banks. The banks held $60.3 billion in December 1959, and, as of the end of March 1965, these holdings were estimated to amount to $60 billion.

It should also be pointed out that the U.S. savings bonds program is making continuing and substantial contributions in this area. During the past five and one-quarter years, Series E and H savings bonds have increased by $6 billion, while the discontinued Series F, G, J, and K bonds have declined by $4¼ billion. In this way, savings bonds, which are the only vehicle we have for directly tapping the "retail" market for savings, have made an important continuing contribution to our debt management objectives, a contribution we expect will continue, aided so greatly by the volunteer efforts of banks and businessmen in all sections of the country.

Here, I want to add a word about the financial requirements for the new fiscal year beginning in less than a month. With every prospect that the deficit for the year will be held within reasonable proportions, these requirements should be fully consistent with attainment of our basic debt management goals. Certainly, balance-of-payments considerations will require at least the same total of regular Treasury bills, and, if necessary, that total could be increased without, in my judgment, conflicting with the broader liquidity needs of the economy. At the same time, opportunities are apt to arise over the course of the year to fit additional longer-term financing into our financing pattern, consistent with the relatively modest size of our overall needs.

The financing schedule for the current fiscal year, 1965, offers a recent example of the manner in which Treasury debt operations, with an estimated deficit on the order of $4½ billion, can be fitted into the market without impeding the orderly flow of funds to other borrowers, while also making progress toward improving the debt structure. So far as cash financing was concerned, $6½ billion of marketable debt was issued in the first half of this fiscal year, with $4 billion of this accounted for by tax anticipation bills. Another $1¾ billion of tax bills were sold in January. Aside from this temporary debt, less than $4 billion of new securities were sold for cash during the course of the year, and almost half of that $4 billion merely offset normal attrition on our refunding offers. Consequently, the net addition to the marketable debt will only be about $2 billion—less than the amount absorbed by the Federal Reserve and Government investment accounts in meeting their needs. On balance, therefore, it was not necessary to call upon the market for new funds, and our financing schedule and market developments provided scope for two sizeable advance refundings to improve the debt structure.

The outlook for fiscal year 1966, in terms of our own requirements, is, if anything, for a somewhat smaller volume of cash offerings, reflecting prospects for a slight further decline in our deficit, as well as our comfortable cash balance position. And this is after having taken the fiscal 1966 impact of the pending excise tax cut into consideration.

The immediate outlook concerning the first half of fiscal 1966 is certainly not very different from the preceding year. In fact, our cash balance position would permit deferral of new borrowing well into the fiscal year. We could even, if it seems appropriate, extend to six months our period of absence from the new cash market. Later in the summer or fall, sizeable borrowing needs are certain, perhaps in an amount of $8 billion, to cover seasonal needs of this period. But, again, these needs could appropriately be met in substantial proportion by tax anticipation bills, to be retired from the seasonal surplus in March and June. The residual, more permanent, need during the period can, I believe, be handled with considerable flexibility both in timing and maturity, depending both on market developments and the broader needs of the economy, either in terms of our domestic or balance-of-payments objectives.

One can, of course, cite Government financing activities in the hundreds of billions of dollars by adding together the regular rollover of Treasury bills, normal refundings, and advance refunding takings on the scale of recent years.

But these computations do not seem to me an accurate measure of the impact of Federal finance. They divert attention from the main point that the Treasury's net demands have been, and are likely to remain, modest, when compared with any other sector of the capital market. Moreover, the financing flexibility that we have achieved—and of which I am a happy recipient of the hard-won gains of my predecessors—permits these requirements to be spread out in an orderly manner in ways that minimize any potentially disruptive impact.

In concentrating on Treasury debt management today, I do not want to leave you with any impression that I am oblivious of the current problems with which you are coping. As the yield curve has flattened, a competitive squeeze has been placed upon you, between the yield requirements of your customers and the drive to obtain the needed volume of mortgage outlets for your funds. This squeeze probably makes it more difficult to resist pressures toward a deterioration in the quality of credit in the industry.

Given the urgency of our balance-of-payments problem and the compelling need to maintain a competitive posture in the short-term area, I cannot offer any clear prospect of relief with respect to competing attractions for your customers' funds. On the other side of the coin, I think that there is ample evidence of a continuing large flow of funds available for mortgage investment, and, quite frankly, that seems to me healthy in terms of the economy as a whole. So the squeeze may well continue. And, by the same token, I believe a heavy burden of responsibility is thrust upon your own industry to cope with this situation without being tempted in the process to contribute toward a weakening in the credit structure that would create new problems in the future. In this area, there can simply be no substitute for your own vigilance.

Exhibit 28.—Remarks by Deputy Under Secretary of the Treasury for Monetary Affairs Volcker, March 9, 1965, before the North Texas Industrial Payroll Savings Bond Campaign, Dallas, Texas, on debt management and the savings bond program

I am delighted to be here today to help launch this important savings bond campaign. Those of us in the Treasury who share some of the responsibility for debt management are particularly conscious of the immense contribution the savings bond program makes to financing our Government soundly, and to the financial strength of our nation as a whole. We are also conscious of the fact that the success of this effort is directly dependent upon the willing personal support of you and other business leaders throughout the country.

We in the Treasury are especially proud of the savings bond program. No other land has achieved anything like the broad public participation in financing a Government that we, as a direct result of the savings bond program, take as a matter of course in this country. And I can think of no other Government program that has received such strong and sustained support through the years from so many volunteers—from industry, whose energetic leadership in promoting payroll savings in thousands of firms has converted tens of millions of citizens to the "savings bond habit"—from banks, which issue without charge 80 percent of all savings bonds—from the world of advertising, which annually provides millions of dollars of space and talent—and from the many others who carried the "savings bond message" into our cities and towns and schools in every part of the nation.

As a result of these efforts there is, I would venture to say, scarcely a citizen in our land who does not think of savings bonds as both a symbol and a source of national strength and of personal financial security. Yet, this program does pose one of those curious anomalies of life, for one of the main functions of this most familiar of Government programs is to support one of the most unfamiliar, and yet most essential, operations of Government: the management of our public debt.

Because the savings bond program is so important to our objective of financing the public debt in a sound and noninflationary manner, and because this relationship is so little understood, I would like to concentrate upon that aspect with you today.

One of the hard facts of life with which a debt manager has to cope is that our national debt has been rising, not, fortunately, as fast as production and incomes, nor anywhere near as fast as private debt, but nevertheless rising. From 1946-64, the increase in the total debt held by the general public was some $16 billion. But over those same 18 years, the investment in E and H bonds has grown by $18 billion. This means, of course, that the Treasury over this same period could reduce the volume of securities placed in the rest of the market by nearly $2 billion, despite an increase of $8 billion over the last four years. As a result, E and H bonds now account for 22 percent of the publicly held debt, as opposed to only 15 percent in 1946.

These figures help illustrate how important the growth in the public's holdings of savings bonds—spurred largely by efforts such as those of this group here today—has been in easing the task of debt management throughout the postwar period. And the contribution of savings bonds is no less important today. To illustrate, new sales of savings bonds have held at consistently high levels, amounting to $4.6 billion last year. That was equivalent to 40 percent of our total cash financing over the same period. These new sales exceeded the net increase in the debt placed with private investors during the year. In other words, if for some reason the savings bond program were suddenly shut off, we would have had to find a home for more than twice as much debt in other parts of the private securities market in 1964 than was in fact the case.

But these raw figures cannot themselves fully reflect the importance of the savings bond program, and the payroll savings plan effort in particular, to debt management and to the financial health and well-being of our Nation's Government. In most of its financing operations, the Treasury must in effect be a wholesaler of securities, tailoring offerings running to billions of dollars to the needs of investment institutions and businesses. There is simply no alternative. Faced with large maturities of debt on a specific day, or with large cash needs over a period of weeks, we naturally must seek out funds where they are promptly available in large amounts. And even if we could, we would not want to draw upon billions of dollars of individual savings abruptly, at the expense of disrupting the flow of savings into investment through normal channels.

But it is also important that we not overburden this "wholesale" market. The prime economic function of the savings bond program is to provide a means for the Treasury to obtain over time a fair share of the enormous "retail" market for savings generated by the great mass of individuals.

The success of this program is reflected in the widely dispersed holdings of savings bonds among our citizens at all income levels. By and large, these holdings represent the net result of gradual accumulations over the years. Thus, the Treasury has been able to tap an immense source of funds that would otherwise be extremely difficult or impossible to reach and, at the same time, to avoid an abrupt and potentially damaging impact on flows of savings through our financial institutions or to other borrowers.

In this way, the savings bond program has materially enlarged the flexibility of our entire debt management operations. This has been particularly important during the past few years, not only because we have had to finance a series of deficits, but also because debt management has been called upon to do far more than it has in the past in helping to support an orderly advance in business activity and in protecting the stability of the dollar.

Four years ago, as you know, the Nation was floundering in its fourth postwar recession. At the same time, our balance-of-payments deficits, and resulting gold outflows, had reached alarming heights. As a result, we had to boost domestic economic growth at the same time that we had to whittle down our balance-of-payments deficits. In terms of monetary and debt management policy, that meant that we had to keep open the channels of long-term credit vital to nourishing domestic economic growth, but, at the same time, we have had to keep our short-term interest rates more or less in line with those abroad in order to cut down on outflows of short-term funds abroad.

One of the ways we could help support the level of short-term rates, and thus help our balance of payments, was to issue more short-term Treasury bills. Since the end of 1960 the total volume of Treasury bills of all types outstanding has increased by some $20 billion, helping to raise the three-month bill rate from about 2¼ percent in early 1961 to just under 4 percent today.

At the same time, however, this large additional supply of bills could potentially have created another problem. Too much short-term Treasury financing could create excessive liquidity in the economy as a whole, eventually leading to inflationary pressures, and produce the kind of unbalanced debt structure that would add to future financing problems. Therefore, we have needed to offset the adverse effects of this bill financing on our total debt structure in our other financing operations. Our success in that effort can be measured by an increase in the average maturity of our marketable debt from a low of 4 years 2 months in 1960 to roughly 5 years 5 months at the end of January, the longest average maturity since the mid-1950's.

This needed restructuring of the debt was accomplished by seizing favorable opportunities in the market for longer-term financing as they appeared, and by using new techniques—such as refunding outstanding securities well in advance of their final maturity—that facilitated the sale of larger amounts of long-term bonds without disturbing the flow of funds to homebuyers, businessmen, State and local governments, and consumers. These new techniques for selling bonds were critically important at a time when it was essential that, in improving our own debt structure, we not hamper the availability of credit to other long-term borrowers, thus helping to sustain an orderly business advance.

The fact of the matter is that, since 1961, the entire increase in the marketable portion of our debt can be accounted for by securities maturing in more than five years. At the same time, commercial bank holdings of Government securities were actually slightly lower at the end of January than four years earlier. And this clear record of noninflationary finance has been accomplished without pushing rates for mortgages or municipal or corporate bonds higher.

The effective functioning of the savings bond program has been essential to these accomplishments. Without that program, we might have had to turn toward much more short-term borrowing and rely on commercial bank financing, with potentially inflationary consequences. Alternatively, we would have had to expand drastically the volume of long-term Treasury financing, with the attendant risk of diverting too many funds from other borrowers and of thus impeding our economic advance. In either event, our objective of sustained noninflationary growth would have been impaired.

Moreover, every dollar of savings bond sales make a direct contribution to our efforts to improve the maturity structure of the debt. We take pride in the fact that the average maturity of the marketable portion of the debt has been raised above five years. Savings bonds, in contrast, are held for an average period of around seven years.

Today, a sound and strong dollar is imperative for both domestic and international reasons. We need to maintain our excellent record of price stability. In this effort, a growing, vigorous savings bond program seems to me to have a more important role to play than at any time since World War II.

But in concentrating on the role of savings bonds in our debt management effort in my remarks today, I don't want to minimize the other lasting benefits of this program to the Nation as a whole and to the individual citizen who buys savings bonds. Savings bonds offer, to every American citizen, a convenient means for obtaining an absolutely safe investment, promptly convertible into cash, at an assured rate of return over a number of years. Through savings bonds, and payroll savings in particular, many of our citizens have been encouraged for the first time to develop regular savings patterns, and to help build their personal and family security.

Even beyond these individual benefits, I believe the Nation itself is strengthened in intangible ways by a program which enables all our citizens to take a direct part in financing their Government. This kind of personal participation in Government financing, in my judgment, both reflects widespread confidence in the integrity of our currency and in our financial policies, and provides our citizens with a direct stake in responsible policies in the future.

There is no more effective way to promote the sale of savings bonds than through the payroll savings plan. We have witnessed great progress in advancing payroll savings over the past several years, and today the heart of the entire program lies in purchases of Series E bonds on this basis. Some 60 percent of all E bonds are now sold through regular payroll savings plans.

Yet much still remains to be done if payroll savings plans are to make their fullest contribution to our Nation's welfare. That is why Mr. Tannery has asked you to help in this important, growing region of our country.

The Treasury stands ready to help you in every way it can. Our Savings Bonds Division will give you technical assistance, and can develop publicity and advertising. But the success of our effort, in the last analysis, rests almost entirely upon the top management of the business firms involved, upon management's personal conviction of the worth of the program and their willingness to provide the prestige and leadership necessary to bring the message to the employees of their companies. That is why your help is so vital.

You, and you alone, can keep the payroll savings plan strong and growing. In so doing, you will be contributing, and contributing directly, to the effort to keep our dollar sound—an effort essential not only to our own security and well-being, but to the security and well being of the entire free world.

Exhibit 29.—Other Treasury testimony published in hearings before congressional committees, July 1, 1964–June 30, 1965

Secretary of the Treasury Fowler

Statement on the debt limit, published in executive hearings before the Committee on Ways and Means, House of Representatives, 89th Congress, 1st session, May 25, 1965, pages 1–4.

Taxation Developments

Exhibit 30.—Message from the President to the Congress, May 17, 1965, transmitting proposed recommendations relative to excise and fuel taxes

Fourteen months ago, I signed the Revenue Act of 1964, which reduced the income taxes of the American people by $14 billion.

That action had a profound impact on the American economy:

Consumer buying rose $28 billion.

Business investment in plant and equipment rose $6½ billion.

Almost 2 million new jobs were created, and unemployment fell to the lowest level in 7 years.

Meanwhile, the stability of our prices—unmatched in the world today—held firm, and our foreign trade surplus set new records.

I am proud of the success of the 1964 tax cut. It proves that taxes do much more than raise revenue to finance Government—they also affect the health and strength of the Nation's economy.

Unwise tax policy can—

unduly restrict private purchasing power;

hold back economic growth;

stifle incentives;

distort decisions by consumers and producers;

enlarge rather than shrink budget deficits.

On the other hand, wise tax policy can—

raise the purchasing power of private citizens;

expand production and create jobs;

stimulate initiative and improve efficiency;

reduce budget deficits by expanding the tax base and increasing tax revenues.

We used tax policy last year to achieve those goals.

As a result, this month we passed a milestone in economic history: *more than 50 months of unbroken peacetime expansion.*

But we cannot stand still. We must continually adjust our tax system to assure that it makes a maximum contribution to our economic growth.

For that reason I am recommending reductions in excise taxes as well as increases in user charges.

EXCISE TAXES

I recommend an excise tax reduction of $3.5 billion in two equal stages effective July 1, 1965, and January 1, 1966.

I also recommend further reductions on January 1 of each year from 1967 through 1969 totaling $464 million.

Many of our existing excises were born of depression and war. Many were designed to restrain civilian demand in wartime and thereby free resources for military use. They need to be reexamined to assure that they do not hold back an expanding peacetime economy.

The proposed program of excise tax cuts and revisions will spur growth and move us closer to full employment by removing an unnecessary drag on consumer and business purchasing power. It will also—

lower prices to consumers;

lessen the burden of regressive taxes on low-income families;

raise business profits by expanding sales and cutting costs of tax compliance;

cut the Government's costs of tax collection and enforcement;

end an unfair burden on many businesses and workers who produce the commodities singled out for excise taxation;

free consumers from the distorting effects of these taxes on their market choices.

THE PROGRAM OF EXCISE TAX REDUCTION

In the budget for fiscal year 1966 I proposed an excise tax reduction of $1.75 billion effective July 1, 1965, and an increase in user charges of $300 million.

Our improving fiscal position, together with our developing economic situation, now makes it possible and desirable to double the recommended excise tax cut.

Responding strongly to an expanding economy, revenues for both fiscal years, 1965 and 1966, are now estimated substantially higher than our conservative January estimates:

For fiscal 1965, we now expect revenues to be $1.4 billion above the January figure of $91.2 billion.

For fiscal 1966, we now anticipate—given the tax program as proposed in January—that revenues would be about $1.6 billion above the January estimate of $94.4 billion.

We can make the recommended tax cuts and still realize total revenues well above—and a deficit well below—our earlier estimates for fiscal 1966.

Because the progress of the U.S. economy in 1965 is living up to our expectations, *the January proposal for a $1.75 billion reduction this July continues to be appropriate.*

But as we look ahead to 1966, we must be alert to the possibility that our taxes will take too much buying power out of the private economy. To foster continued strong expansion of the economy in 1966, *I am recommending an additional $1.75 billion reduction of excise taxes, effective January 1, 1966.*

The revenue impact on the fiscal 1966 budget of the additional reduction— which will affect only the last half of the fiscal year—will be about $600 million. This will leave a substantial portion of the anticipated increase in revenues above the January budget estimate to reduce the estimated budget deficit.

The reductions I am recommending will accomplish, prudently and responsibly, a major reform of the excise tax structure. We will—

eliminate most of our present excise taxes on July 1, 1965, and even more on January 1, 1966;

eliminate the tax on telephone service, in several steps, by January 1, 1969;

gradually reduce the automobile excise tax from 10 percent now to 5 percent by January 1, 1967;

leave only, in addition, the excises on alcoholic beverages, tobacco, gasoline, tires, trucks, air transportation (and a few other user-charge and special excises) which should remain a part of our tax system.

EXCISE TAX REDUCTION, DEFENSE, AND THE NATION'S ECONOMY

In proposing these reductions, I am fully aware of our present and prospective commitments for the defense of the free world. It is impossible to predict precisely what expenditures these may involve in the future. There is, however, no present indication that expenditures will increase to an extent that would make these excise tax reductions inadvisable.

Indeed, our international responsibilities require that we redouble our efforts to assure the continued healthy growth of our economy. Barring some sudden change in the present world situation, I am sure that these excise tax reductions will be a sound and profitable investment in that growth.

A careful evaluation of our labor supply and industrial capacity—and of the prospective rapid growth of both—indicates that:

The carefully timed stimulus of the excise tax cuts will help us achieve fuller use of the American economy's great and growing potential without creating pressures that might threaten our fine record of price stability.

Removal of excise taxes will, in fact, cut the prices of many items to consumers and thereby tend to ease pressures on our cost of living.

To insure that the excise tax reductions make the maximum contribution to continued price stability and balanced prosperity, *I call on American business to translate lower excise taxes promptly into lower retail prices for consumers.*

Business will share fully in the benefits of excise tax cuts through the larger sales volume they will generate. Rising volume will boost profits and create more jobs.

These advances will extend beyond the industries whose taxes are removed or reduced. Consumers and businesses will use some of their gains to enlarge their purchases of other products and services. Demand will be strengthened throughout the economy. And for products bought by businesses, the tax reductions will lower costs.

In these ways excise tax cuts, like income tax cuts, will stimulate total demand in the economy and serve to increase production and incomes by far greater amounts than the cost of the tax reduction itself.

And again, Federal revenues will grow—not shrink—as the final result of tax reduction.

Effective July 1, 1965, I recommend the following:

Retail taxes.—The complete repeal of the existing retail excise taxes on handbags and luggage, toilet articles, jewelry, and furs.

Manufacturers taxes.—The complete repeal of the manufacturers excise taxes on business machines, sporting goods (other than fishing equipment), radios, television sets, phonographs, phonograph records, musical instruments, cameras, film and other photographic equipment, refrigerators, freezers, air conditioners, electric, gas and oil appliances, fountain pens, ballpoint pens, mechanical pencils, lighters, matches, and playing cards.

Automobile tax.—A reduction of the manufacturers excise tax on passenger automobiles from 10 to 7 percent.

Miscellaneous taxes.—The complete repeal of the excise taxes on safe deposit boxes, coin-operated amusement devices, bowling alleys, and pool tables.

Refunds.—To avoid deferral of purchases, the July 1 tax reductions on automobiles and air conditioners to be made retroactive to apply to all consumer purchases after May 14, 1965. Refunds would be made to the manufacturer on presentation of evidence that the final customer had been reimbursed.

I further recommend the following later excise tax reductions:

Local and long-distance telephone service tax.—Effective January 1, 1966, a reduction from 10 to 3 percent of the tax on local and long-distance telephone service, including teletypewriter service. A further reduction of 1 percentage point, effective each January 1 through January 1, 1969, when the tax will be completely repealed.

Admissions taxes.—Effective January 1, 1966, the complete repeal of the excise taxes on admissions, including the tax on general admissions which applies to certain movies, theater performances, concerts, athletic events and racing, the tax on cabarets, and the tax on club dues.

Other manufacturers taxes.—Effective January 1, 1966, the complete repeal of the manufacturers' taxes on lubricating oil and electric light bulbs, and repeal of the tax on automobile parts and accessories except as it applies to those parts and accessories which are primarily for use only on trucks.

Automobile tax.—Effective January 1, 1966, a further reduction to 6 percent in the tax on new passenger automobiles and effective January 1, 1967, a final reduction to 5 percent. I recommend that the excise tax on new automobiles be retained as a continuing revenue source at the 5-percent rate. It is not regressive. It is an important source of Federal revenues. Its compliance and collection costs are exceptionally low.

Documentary stamp taxes.—Effective January 1, 1966, the complete repeal of the documentary stamp taxes on the issuance and transfer of stocks and bonds and on deeds of conveyance.

Other communications taxes.—Effective January 1, 1966, revision of the tax on local and long-distance telephone service so that it will no longer apply to amounts paid for private communications systems even where the private system is linked with the general telephone network. This service is almost exclusively a business cost item and competes with nontaxable business communication services. Charges for service on the general telephone network originating or terminating in the private system would be taxable until the telephone tax is completely repealed. I also recommend complete repeal of the tax on telegraph and wire and equipment service.

In the foregoing program, customer refunds are recommended for purchases after May 14 only in the case of—

air conditioners, which are unique in their seasonal purchase pattern;
automobiles, which are unique in the large dollar amount of tax per unit.

I am informed that other business groups affected by the proposed tax cuts have concluded that the advantages of possible refunds are outweighed by the cost and complexity of the paperwork they would involve.

Floor-stock refunds are appropriate for most manufacturers taxes and are so provided in the recommended program.

One further important change concerns the annual automatic reductions in the so-called Korean rates. To avoid the costly and time-consuming process of nullifying these reductions each year, *I recommend removal of the automatic reduction dates for the present excise taxes on distilled spirits, wines, beer, and cigarettes.*

The Committee on Ways and Means has already held extensive public hearings on excise tax reduction. Further, the recommended program calls for repeal of the great majority of excises, thereby minimizing the controversy and hard choices that might otherwise have delayed action. *Therefore, it is my hope and expectation that the Congress will enact these changes without undue delay.*

USER CHARGES

The reductions in excise taxes which I am recommending will contribute to greater economic efficiency and equity in our society.

Pursuit of these very same goals of efficiency and equity demands that we *increase* certain other excise taxes or impose new ones.

This special class of excise taxes is better described as "user charges." They are taxes paid by those who benefit from special services provided by the Government. These user charges serve several purposes:

They assess the costs of special services and facilities against those who reap the benefits instead of imposing unwarranted burdens on the general taxpayer.

They restrain the demands of special groups for expanded services by establishing the principle that the beneficiaries pay at least part of the costs.

In the case of transportation, they help to eliminate the economic distortions which result when competing modes of transportation rely in varying degrees on facilities or services provided by the Government.

Every President since Harry Truman has reaffirmed the principle of user charges and has proposed extension of their use.

President Eisenhower said: "Many services performed and privileges granted by the Government in the public interest also convey a special, added benefit to individuals or groups who can afford to pay for them. In some cases, the fees are substantially below the costs of providing the services. Thus, the general taxpayer is required to subsidize operations which should be self-supporting. The scope and cost of these hidden subsidies have grown considerably during the past decades. I firmly believe in the principle that Government services which give a special benefit to users should be financed by adequate charges paid by the user."

Substantial constructive action has been taken by the Congress to reaffirm and extend the principle of user charges, particularly in the field of transportation. But user charges have not been applied with an even hand. I would consider it a serious abdication of responsibility if I were to propose a substantial reduction in excise taxes without at the same time moving to correct serious inequities that exist in the field of user charges.

Users of highways come closer to reimbursing the Federal Government for its transportation investment than any other group. But inequities remain among the various classes of highway users.

The airlines and their passengers make substantial—but still insufficient— contributions toward the development and operation of the Federal airways. The airlines operate about 2,000 planes. The private, business, and pleasure aircraft which make up the general aviation sector number some 86,000. Yet general aviation, which receives a large share of the benefits of the Federal airways system, contributes very little toward the cost of the airways.

Users of the inland waterways pay nothing toward the cost either of the initial improvements or of the operation and maintenance of the waterways.

The absence of a fair system of user charges strongly affects the ability of various segments of the transportation industry to compete and obscures the inherent advantages of some modes of transportation. As a result, it unnecessarily increases the cost of transportation to the economy.

I therefore recommend new and additional transportation user charges. These proposals are designed to—

move toward the elimination of inequities among the several modes of transportation;

recover a larger part of the outlays by the Federal Government for services and facilities which mainly benefit special groups.

HIGHWAYS

New cost estimates already submitted to the Congress show that the Interstate System will cost $5.6 billion more to complete than previously estimated. The added funds are needed because of increased construction costs, additional design features, and the requirement that highway capacity be based on estimated traffic 20 years in the future rather than on the traffic anticipated by calendar year 1975. Of this cost increase, $5 billion represents the Federal share.

I recommend that Congress approve this revised cost estimate, as required by law, and authorize the additional necessary appropriations so that the Interstate System can be completed.

Existing user taxes will provide almost $2 billion of the increased costs. This leaves approximately $3 billion to be raised by extending these taxes beyond the present expiration date, or by increasing some of these taxes—or both.

In the interest of advancing this program at an orderly pace, part of this requirement should be met by a short extension of the completion date for the Interstate System and of the existing user charges. *I recommend, therefore, that the date for reduction of the taxes earmarked for the highway trust fund be extended from September 30, 1972 to February 28, 1973.*

Extending the completion date and the existing user tax program will meet most of the increased costs of the Interstate System. But unless we enact some increase in *current* revenue to the highway trust fund, a number of States will be required to cut back sharply on their construction programs.

For this reason, I recommend immediate additional user taxes on heavy trucks estimated to yield about $200 million annually until 1973.

Specifically, I recommend—

that the excise tax on highway diesel fuel be raised from 4 cents to 7 cents per gallon;

that the present truck use tax be increased from $3 to $5 per thousand pounds on trucks having a taxable gross weight of more than 26,000 pounds; and

that the tax on tread rubber, largely affecting heavy trucks, be increased from 5 cents to 10 cents per pound.

In its extensive study of highway costs and cost responsibilities—submitted to the Congress in preliminary form in 1961 and in final form this year—the Bureau of Public Roads has carefully allocated cost responsibilities among the various classes of highway users. The Bureau's studies clearly show that heavy trucks are not paying fully for the additional cost of heavier pavement and other design features needed to carry them.

The increases I am proposing will provide the added revenue required to complete the Interstate System. They will also achieve a fairer sharing of costs among the users of the highways.

I have carefully considered proposals for an increase in the limits on sizes and weights of trucks that may legally operate on the Interstate System. As I have noted, substantial *undertaxation* of heavy trucks now exists. This inequity would be further aggravated if increases in size and weight limits were to be made without imposing the additional user charges. I should not and must not approve legislation to relax these limits for vehicles on the Interstate System unless the Congress imposes these additional user charges. *I will promptly recommend that the size and weight limits on trucks using the Interstate System be raised as soon as just and appropriate user charges are enacted.*

AVIATION

In 1961 the Congress took a major step forward in the area of aviation user charges. At that time it dropped the general excise tax of 10 percent on the transportation of persons. But it retained a 5-percent tax on the transportation of persons by air to serve as a user charge. *I recommend—*

that this tax now be made permanent;

that commercial aviation bear a large share of its appropriate cost responsibilities through the enactment of a new user tax of 2 cents per gallon on jet fuels and by continuing the existing user tax of 2 cents per gallon on aviation gasoline;

that a user tax of 2 percent be levied on airfreight waybills so that shippers by air as well as air travelers will bear some part of the cost of maintaining the Federal airways.

At the present time general aviation contributes less than 4 percent of its fair share of the cost of developing and maintaining the Federal airways. To replace the present 2-cent tax on aviation gasoline used by general aviation, *I recommend a modest user charge of 4 cents per gallon on all fuels used by general aviation.* Under this proposal, general aviation would pay 9 percent of its share of total costs.

All of these taxes should be made permanent, and aviation gasoline taxes now transferred to the highway trust fund should be retained in the general fund.

Over the years the Federal Aviation Agency has provided the Congress with careful studies of the appropriate allocation of airways costs among military, commercial, and general aviation users. These studies show that even with these new user charges, the various classes of civil users will still be paying less than their full share of airways costs.

INLAND WATERWAYS

No user charge of any kind is presently in effect on the use of the inland waterways. This is unfair to the taxpayers and to competing modes of transportation. We are currently spending more than $50 million a year for operating and maintaining the inland waterways, and over $200 million a year for new investment. In view of these large and increasing public expenditures, equity requires that users of the inland waterways begin to contribute to the cost of providing their transport network. Accordingly, *I recommend a tax of 2 cents per gallon on all fuel used on the inland waterways.* The proposed tax will recover a very small fraction of the operating and maintenance costs of the waterways.

DRAFT LEGISLATION AND REVENUE IMPACT

I am transmitting herewith draft legislation to carry out my recommendations.

The attached tables provide the detailed revenue figures associated with my recommendations.

CONCLUSION

I know that the Congress and the country will join me in recognizing our good fortune in being able to declare a new fiscal dividend of nearly $4 billion in excise tax cuts out of the bounty of a prosperous and growing economy—a dividend that will help keep it prosperous and growing.

This is not our first tax cut. It will not be our last. But in consolidating our prosperity and advancing the cause of fairness and balance in our tax system, it will surely rank as one of the most important.

LYNDON B. JOHNSON.

THE WHITE HOUSE, *May 17, 1965.*

TABLE I.—*Excise tax program to be enacted in 1965 covering 1966–69*

[In millions of dollars]

	Full year revenue effect (fiscal year, 1966 level)
I. Reductions to take effect July 1, 1965:	
1. Repeal retail excises on jewelry, furs, toilet preparations, and luggage and handbags	550
2. Repeal following manufacturers taxes:	
Business machines	75
Sporting goods, except fishing equipment	25
Phonograph records	30
Musical instruments	27
Television sets	135
Radios and phonographs	90
Cameras, film, and other photographic equipment	40
Refrigerators	34
Freezers	7
Air conditioners [1]	34
Electric, gas, and oil appliances	85
Pens	8
Lighters	3
Matches	4
Playing cards	11
Subtotal	608
3. Other repeals:	
Coin-operated amusement devices	6
Bowling alleys and pool tables	7
Safe deposit boxes	7
	20
4. Rate reductions: Passenger automobiles, 3 points [1]	570
Subtotal	1,748
II. Reductions to take effect Jan. 1, 1966:	
1. Repeal taxes in admissions group:	
General admissions	55
Cabarets	47
Club dues	85
Subtotal	187
2. Communications taxes:	
Reduce general and long-distance telephone (including teletypewriter) service, 7 points	730
Expand exemption from telephone tax for private line service	39
Repeal telegraph tax	17
Repeal wire and equipment service tax	15
Subtotal	801
3. Repeal of other taxes:	
Automobile parts and accessories except certain truck parts	230
Lubricating oil	78
Electric light bulbs	45
Documentary stamps (except foreign insurance policies)	195
Subtotal	548
4. Other rate reductions: Passenger automobile tax, 1 point	190
Subtotal	1,726
Total fiscal year 1966 program	3,474
III. Reductions to take effect Jan. 1, 1967: [2]	
Reduce telephone tax, general and long distance (including teletypewriter service), 1 point	91
Reduce passenger automobile tax, 1 point	190
Subtotal	281
IV. Reductions to take effect Jan. 1, 1968 and 1969: [2] Reduce telephone tax, general and long distance (including teletypewriter service), 1 point	91

[1] Refunds as to sales after May 14, 1965.
Figures based on 1966 levels of business

TABLE II.—*Expected revenues from user charge proposals*

[In millions of dollars]

	Full year revenue, 1966 levels
Highways:	
Increase diesel fuel tax from 4 cents to 7 cents a gallon	112
Increase use tax on heavy trucks from $3 to $5 per 1,000 pounds	70
Increase tax on tread rubber from 5 cents to 10 cents a pound	24
Additional highway user charges	206
Airways:	
Transportation of persons, continue at 5 percent	140
Tax on airfreight	5
Tax fuel used in general aviation, 4 cents a gallon	13
Tax fuel used in commercial aviation, 2 cents a gallon	82
Total proposed airway user charges	240
Less existing taxes on airway users:	
Tax on transportation of persons by air	140
Tax on aviation gasoline	14
Additional airway user charges	86
Inland waterways: Fuel, 2 cents a gallon	8
Total increased revenues from user charge program	300

TABLE III.—*Excise taxes remaining after current and phased reductions*

[In millions of dollars, fiscal year 1966 levels]

	Fiscal year 1966 revenue
Group I: General taxes:	
Passenger automobiles, 5 percent	950
Certain truck parts	20
Total, general taxes	970
Group II: Alcohol and tobacco taxes:	
Alcohol	3,882
Tobacco	2,159
Total alcohol and tobacco taxes	6,041
Group III: Regulatory taxes [1]	33
Group IV: Dedicated taxes and user charges:	
Highway trust fund	[2] 3,959
Other dedicated taxes and user charges [3]	400
Total, dedicated taxes and user charges	4,359
Adjustment for unapplied collections and miscellaneous refunds	−57
Total	11,319

[1] Includes such items as narcotics, wagering, coin-operated gaming devices, white phosphorus matches manufacture and transfer of certain firearms. Also includes the manufactures tax on pistols and revolvers.
[2] After refunds.
[3] Sugar; firearms, shells, and cartridges; fishing equipment; taxes on aviation and motor boat fuel.

Exhibit 31.—Statement by Secretary of the Treasury Fowler, June 8, 1965, before the Senate Finance Committee, on H.R. 8371, the Excise Tax Reduction Act of 1965

I am pleased to be able to state the views of the Treasury Department on H.R. 8371, the Excise Tax Reduction Act of 1965.

You have the President's Message on excise tax reduction and user charge increases before you, so I will not repeat here the recommendations he has already made in that Message. You also have the report of the Ways and Means Committee on the bill.

In both the departmental and executive branch consideration and the hearings before the House Ways and Means Committee, I have voluntarily disassociated myself from any specific discussions or decisions as to how the excise tax reduction should be distributed among the various excise tax products and services and, specifically, how the passenger automobile excise tax should be handled. For that reason, I would like to confine my comments today to the general fiscal aspects of the President's recommendations and the House bill. Assistant Secretary Surrey is here with me to present the Administration's position on the differences between the President's proposed program and the bill as adopted by the House, which centers on the treatment of the passenger car excise tax. He will also present the Administration's position on the specific tax reductions proposed.

I should note that the bill before you does not deal with the recommendations for increased user taxes. The Ways and Means Committee decided to reserve the user charge recommendations for future consideration. At the same time it recognized the desirability of rapid action on the excise reductions to avoid any lengthy disturbance of the marketing of taxed products. While this procedure is understandable, I would like to emphasize that we regard user taxes as a most important part of the President's program.

Excise taxes, unlike income taxes, impose burdens on those whose income is below the level of their personal exemptions and deductions. The present excise tax reduction program will lighten the burden of regressive taxation on low- and middle-income people. A great deal of the revenue involved comes from extremely regressive taxes, which are a heavy burden on low incomes. These include the taxes on telephones, automobile parts and accessories, toilet preparations, and most of the household appliances.

The proposed reductions will simplify the tax system by greatly reducing the number of separate taxes as well as the accompanying burden on business of collecting and reporting those taxes. It will cut the Government's cost of tax collection and enforcement.

Many of the selective excises involved in this legislation are expensive to collect, and they impose heavy compliance burdens on the taxpayers. This is particularly true of the retail excises and some of the lower yield taxes, such as the tax on cabarets and safe deposit boxes.

Many of the selective excises fall on items which have nontaxed substitutes. Room air conditioners are taxed, but central air conditioning is not. Most admissions are taxed, but many are not. Some house furnishings are taxable, others not.

But an equally compelling reason for the elimination or reduction of many of these selective excises is that they are incompatible with a tax system that leaves the private economy the maximum opportunity for growth. These taxes were imposed largely in war and emergency in part to restrain production and consumption in the taxed products and services and encourage the transfer of the material and manpower resources dedicated to these products to other areas deemed more essential to the war effort. Imposed in part for this reason, it is only logical that they should be removed as a part of a normal peacetime economy. This removal of a burden on the private sector will bolster the economy in a particularly valuable way since it will strengthen the competitive forces in the marketplace, and it will entail significant price reductions, thereby contributing to wage-price stability.

The excise tax reductions recommended by the President represent the next logical step in this direction.

Reduction of our selective excise taxes increases the equity of the tax system. Many selective taxes are discriminatory and burdensome on producers, sellers, and consumers of the items subject to tax.

I believe that the Congress and the public have long felt that many of our excise taxes have no place in a permanent tax system. Thus, wherever it is appropriate to remove a particular burden on one product or another, we should strive consistent with other tax goals to provide a freely operating competitive price system, and in the President's words ". . . end an unfair burden on many businesses and workers who produce the commodities singled out for excise taxation."

The elimination or reduction of the selective excise taxes not now dedicated to particular uses such as the highway trust fund or falling into the category of sumptuary taxes such as liquor and tobacco is an important step in our continuing program of tax reform, which has included the revenue acts of 1962 and 1964 as well as the depreciation reform. We are all interested in the development of an overall tax system which is characterized by equity and simplicity and which makes a maximum contribution to economic growth.

The House bill will have substantially the same impact in fiscal years 1966 and 1967 as the President's recommendations. But in the fiscal years 1968, 1969, and 1970 the House bill will eliminate additional excise taxes in successive stages totaling nearly one billion dollars beyond the President's program.

The revenue effects of an excise tax reduction are somewhat complicated, and I would like to clarify the various figures.

When we speak of the full year gross revenue loss from repealing an excise tax, we are referring to the revenue that is collected in a full year of operation under that tax. The full year decreases in tax collections in the administrative budget under the House bill and the President's program are given in table I.

TABLE I.—*Reduction in tax collections, full-year effect, House bill and President's program*

[In billions]

	House bill		President's program	
	Separate	Cumulative	Separate	Cumulative
July 1, 1965, reduction	$1.75	$1.75	$1.75	$1.75
Jan. 1, 1966, reduction	1.68	3.43	1.73	3.48
Jan. 1, 1967, reduction	.47	3.90	.28	3.76
Jan. 1, 1968, reduction	.47	4.37	.09	3.85
Jan. 1, 1969, reduction	.47	4.84	.09	3.94

Under the House bill, the important figures here are $1.75 billion for the July 1 reduction, $1.68 billion for the January 1, 1966, reduction, and $470 million for the reduction on each January 1, 1967 to 1969. These will add eventually to a reduction of $4.8 billion in tax collections. Compared to the President's program, the principal differences occur after 1966. The reduced tax collections under the excise reduction recommendation of the President were $3.9 billion.

The committee will be particularly interested in the budget effect of these cuts. The figures in table I change in several ways as respects the gross budget effect, before feedbacks.

In the first place, the House bill provides that certain tax receipts, amounting to about $70 million, be put in the highway trust fund. This allocation to the trust fund does not reduce tax collections, but it does lower administrative budget receipts.

Second, if an excise tax is repealed effective July 1, 1965, the Federal Government will still get tax payments in July and August on taxable transactions entered into in May and June because the taxes on the transactions will be turned into the Treasury after July 1. The fiscal year loss is, of course, even less when the reduction becomes effective on January 1 in the middle of a fiscal year.

Finally, the budget effects must take into account customer refunds and floor stock refunds.

The gross fiscal year budget losses under the House bill and the President's program from the tax reduction are shown in table II.

TABLE II.—*Gross fiscal year reductions in administrative budget receipts*

[In billions]

	Fiscal year		
	1966	1967	1968
House bill:			
July 1, 1965, reduction_____	$1.63	$1.75	$1.75
Jan. 1, 1966, reduction_____	.54	1.78	1.77
Jan. 1, 1967, reduction_____	_____	.15	.49
Total_____	2.17	3.68	4.01
President's program:			
July 1, 1965, reduction_____	1.63	1.75	1.75
Jan. 1, 1966, reduction_____	.54	1.74	1.73
Jan. 1, 1967, reduction_____	_____	.09	.30
Total_____	2.17	3.58	3.78

Under the House bill the gross budget losses are (in round figures) in fiscal year 1966, $2.2 billion, in fiscal year 1967, $3.7 billion, and in fiscal year 1968, $4.0 billion.   The losses under the President's program would have been the same in fiscal year 1966, and slightly smaller in fiscal year 1967 and fiscal year 1968.

Excise tax reducton will mean that there is this much more disposable income of consumers and businesses.   As this is spent, there will be increased income taxes and more disposable income for further respending, again increasing income tax receipts.

To properly assess the excise tax reduction, we should take into account these feedbacks of increased collections under other taxes.   On this basis the expected net budget impacts of the House bill and the President's program are:

	House bill	*President's program*
	[*In billions*]	
Fiscal year 1966_____	$1.8	$1.8
Fiscal year 1967_____	2.2	2.1

In the long run the net revenue loss after feedback will be about one-half of the gross loss.

This excise tax reduction can have an important strategic effect in maintaining the upward thrust of the economy.   It is well known that a decline in the pace of our economy, leading possibly to a recession, can cause a major decline of revenues.   Federal revenues declined in the recession of 1958 and in the recession of 1960.   They did not decline during the period of the major income tax reduction in 1964–65.

Let me turn now to the specific matter of the net budget deficit.

In January of 1963 it was anticipated that the budget deficit for the fiscal year 1964 would be $12 billion.   In the end a number of circumstances, including the combination of improving economic conditions resulting from both the anticipation and enactment of the Revenue Act of 1964 and firm expenditure control, brought this figure down to $8.2 billion.

In January of this year the budget deficit for fiscal year 1965 was estimated to be $6.3 billion.   Thanks to continued expenditure control and substantial improvements in revenue collections, it was announced late in April that the deficit was likely to be $5.3 billion.   Now as a result of additional information, we anticipate that the deficit for fiscal year 1965 will be reduced to $4.4 billion.   Of this $1.9 billion reduction in the deficit below the January estimate, $500 million represents reduced expenditures, and $1.4 billion represents increased revenues.   It may be that by the end of the fiscal year the expenditure figures will show further reductions but it is too early to hazard any hard estimate.

In January the budget estimate of the deficit for fiscal year 1966 was $5.3 billion. At that time we were contemplating an excise tax reduction program of only $1.75 billion. Since then we have revised upward our estimate of revenues under the income tax by $1.6 billion. We have also recommended the enlarged excise tax reduction program which will involve for fiscal year 1966 a net budget loss after feedback of $1.8 billion. This is larger by $0.6 billion than the net budget loss that would have occurred under the original $1.75 billion program contained in the Budget Message. This additional revenue reduction of $0.6 billion combined with the expected increase in receipts of $1.6 billion still leaves a net improvement in receipts of $1.0 billion.

At this time, the Bureau of the Budget continues to expect expenditures for fiscal 1966 to be approximately the same as they were estimated to be in the January budget. There have been some increases due to increased defense operations in Vietnam, but these have been matched by economies elsewhere. The prospective improvement in the deficit figure is, then, this increase of $1.0 billion in receipts which would reduce the deficit to $4.3 billion, slightly below the $4.4 billion now anticipated for fiscal year 1965.

The question could be raised, "Would the deficit in fiscal year 1966 be lower by $1.8 billion if there were no excise tax reduction?" The answer would be "Yes" only if we ignore the strategic effect of the reduction, that is, if we ignore the particular contributions that the reduction will make to maintaining the expectation of growth, which is our basic defense against the development of recession. As I said before, deficits rise with recession but they can fall with responsible tax cuts.

For the fiscal year 1967, assuming continued economic growth at the long-term trend rate, administrative budget revenues should increase by about $5 billion. This potential gain will be slightly offset by the fact that the January 1966 excise tax cuts will be in operation for all of fiscal year 1967, compared to only half of fiscal year 1966, and some further excise tax cuts will come into effect January 1, 1967. On the other hand, we will in fiscal year 1967 be realizing more of the economic feedback of the first two stages of the program. The added revenue loss of the House bill in fiscal year 1967 over fiscal year 1966 on a net basis will be about $0.4 billion. (Under the President's program, this added revenue loss in fiscal year 1967 would have been about $0.3 billion.) Roughly, we could thus put the potential revenue gain in fiscal year 1967 at $4.6 billion.

We do not know now what expenditures in fiscal year 1967 will be, but this potential revenue gain leaves considerable room for providing such increased expenditures as might be needed by a growing population and still achieving reduction of the budgetary deficit.

On this matter of expenditures, I would like to repeat the President's statement to the Ways and Means Committee, "I would like to make clear once again my strong determination to hold expenditures to the lowest reasonable levels." As you realize, expenditure control requires hard decisions and the determination to stand behind them. I believe that the Administration has given ample evidence of this determination.

Mr. Surrey is now prepared to present the Administration's position on the specific tax reductions in the bill and the differences between the President's program and the House bill which center largely on the passenger car excise tax.

Exhibit 32.—Statement by Assistant Secretary of the Treasury Surrey, June 8, 1965, before the Senate Finance Committee, on H.R. 8371, the Excise Tax Reduction Act of 1965

H.R. 8371 can be described by saying that it repeals all of the excises except:

—those which are intended to impose part of the cost of a particular Government service in the area thereof. This category includes the highway trust fund taxes, the tax on fishing equipment and certain firearms, shells and cartridges, and the tax on air passenger travel.

—those on alcohol and tobacco, which are traditional sources of revenue. As the House Committee Report indicates, the fact that these taxes may inhibit some choices is part of the reason that we have had them.

—those which are intended to be regulatory in nature, such as the taxes on certain firearms, wagering, coin-operated gaming devices, marihuana, and opium.

The bill makes these changes in a way that is fiscally responsible through staged reductions. Where postponement of purchases in anticipation of a reduction could be a potential problem, the reduction is scheduled for the first stage, July 1, 1965. The remaining part of the reduction is scheduled for January 1, 1966 (December 31, 1965, in the case of certain admission taxes and the cabaret tax). In the case of the two taxes where very large amounts of revenue are involved, telephone service and passenger automobiles, part of the reduction is staged through 1967–69.

In two industries where the effect on sales because of the anticipated reduction on July 1 might be a serious problem, passenger automobiles and air conditioners, the bill provides customer refunds to the original announcement date, May 15. In the other situations floor stock refunds are provided where considered appropriate.

An alphabetical listing of the present excise taxes and the indicated changes under the House bill and the President's program is attached to this statement.

Let me turn now to the few instances in which the House bill differs from the President's program. The President recommended that the passenger automobile tax be reduced by half, from 10 percent to 5 percent, in reductions staged 3 percent on July 1, 1965, 1 percent on January 1, 1967, and 1 percent on January 1, 1968. The revenue obtained from a tax at a 5-percent rate is $950 million, at 1966 levels of income. This tax is efficient to collect. It is not regressive. It falls upon an item without close substitutes. Most important the revenue is large.

The House bill provides that the entire tax be phased out by January 1, 1969; 3 percent on July 1, 1965, 1 percent January 1, 1966, and 2 percent on January 1 in each year 1967, 1968, and 1969.

We believe, however, that only 5 percentage points of the automobile tax should be removed, and 5 percentage points left in effect, in accordance with the President's recommendation. This will allow future congresses to consider whether to reduce the automobile excise tax below 5 percent.

Postponing the decision with respect to this remaining 5 points of the automobile excise tax until the future is the course of fiscal prudence. In the judgment of the Administration it is unwise to enact now large tax changes to come into effect three and four years in the future. It is impossible to forecast the economic situation that far ahead. The prudent course for the Nation is to stay with the President's program.

One cannot foretell just what tax requirements for responsible fiscal policy will be in the fiscal years 1967, 1968, and 1969, depending as they do on expenditures, receipts, and the economic situation. In fact, one cannot tell just what expenditures will be forced upon us by the automobile itself. How much will we have to spend to deal with such problems as highway safety, air pollution and automobile graveyards?

The other differences in the House bill from the President's recommendation are relatively minor, and we concur in the House action.

The House bill would retain the tax on lubricating oil so far as it applies to highway users. This would be done by repealing the present tax on cutting oil and by providing refunds for use of lubricating oil in other than highway vehicles. The proceeds of this tax, $50 million, would be put in the highway trust fund.

The remaining difference in the House bill deals with the automobile parts and accessories tax so far as it applies to parts which are primarily designed for trucks. The President recommended retention of this 8-percent tax as it applies to parts which are not suitable for use in a passenger automobile. The problem here is that some large components of trucks are subject to a 10-percent tax if they are installed by a truck manufacturer on a new truck. This 10-percent tax on trucks, which is part of the highway trust fund, is not changed by this bill. If no parts tax applied, there would be a considerable incentive to install the part later as an accessory. Retaining the tax for truck parts and accessories will avoid aggravating this problem. The House bill places this truck parts tax, which amounts to about $20 million, in the highway trust fund, along with the basic tax on trucks.

Finally, I want to say a brief word about the matter of effective dates. The Ways and Means Committee went extensively into this problem, as its report indicates. It considered the potential postponements of sales and came to the same conclusions that we had reached, after the extensive discussions which trade associations and individual firms had with the Treasury and with the staff of the Joint Committee.

Two industries thought this sales postponement problem was serious. In automobiles the tax involves a large dollar amount. Postponement of a purchase until after July 1 would bring the buyer close to the new model year when he might decide to wait until fall. This could result in a significant loss of sales for the current model year and perhaps even some permanent loss of sales.

In air conditioners the problem is somewhat similar. Here, nearly 40 percent of the year's sales come in May and June. Postponement of a purchase until after July 1 would mean that part of the hot weather is gone and many potential customers would postpone the purchase until next year. In these two cases, the House considered that customer refunds were appropriate with respect to purchases between May 15 and July 1.

As to other industries, the committee noted that retroactive refunds were not provided in the last significant excise tax reduction, that of 1954, and that a retroactive date, with consumer refunds, would constitute a serious administrative burden for the industries affected. In order to provide the Internal Revenue Service with some means of verifying the refund claims, it would be necessary that they be channelled through, and consolidated by, the person who initially paid the tax. For most taxes, this would be the manufacturer. Such a procedure would involve the processing, verifying, and consolidating of thousands of small claims by a manufacturer. For manufacturers that sell many different taxed articles the burdens would be multiplied many times, and the benefit of retroactivity would be far outweighed by the burden of additional paperwork involved. Consequently, the House thought that in view of the short time between the announcement date, May 15, and the effective date of the first scheduled reduction, July 1, it would be wise to proceed in all other cases in accordance with prior practice and avoid retroactive reduction. However, as stated earlier, floor stock refunds are provided in the House bill for most of the manufacturers taxes.

The Treasury staff has been working with the staff of the Joint Committee on Internal Revenue Taxation on some technical amendments. We will be glad to discuss these matters with the committee, when it considers the bill in detail.

Excise tax program to be enacted in 1965 indicating differences between President's recommendation and H.R. 8371 [1]

	July 1, 1965	January 1, 1966	January 1967– January 1969
Admissions		Repeal	
Air conditioners	Repeal		
Automobiles:			
President's recommendation	Reduce 10% to 7%	Reduce 7% to 6%	Reduce 6% to 5% 1967.
House bill	Reduce 10% to 7%	Reduce 7% to 6%	Reduce to 4% 1967. Reduce to 2% 1968. Repeal 1969.
Automobile parts and accessories (excluding trucks parts).		Repeal	
Ball point and fountain pens, etc	Repeal		
Bowling alleys and pool tables	Repeal		
Business and store machines	Repeal		
Cabarets		Repeal	
Cameras and film, etc	Repeal		
Cigarette lighters	Repeal		
Club dues		Repeal	
Coin-operated amusement devices	Repeal		
Deeds of conveyance		Repeal	
Electric, gas, and oil appliances	Repeal		
Electric light bulbs		Repeal	
Freezers	Repeal		
Furs	Repeal		
Jewelry	Repeal		
Lubricating oil:			
President's recommendation		Repeal	
House bill		Repeal as to non-highway use. Put into highway trust fund as to highway use.	
Luggage and handbags	Repeal		
Matches	Repeal		
Musical instruments	Repeal		
Playing cards	Repeal		
Phonograph records	Repeal		
Radios and phonographs	Repeal		
Refrigerators	Repeal		
Safe deposit boxes	Repeal		
Sporting goods (except fishing)	Repeal		
Stocks and bonds—issuance		Repeal	
Stocks and bonds—transfer		Repeal	
Telegraph		Repeal	
Telephone—general and toll		Reduce 10% to 3%	Reduce to 2% 1967. Reduce to 1% 1968. Repeal 1969.
Telephone—interior communications systems		Exempt	
Television sets	Repeal		
Toilet preparations	Repeal		
Wire and equipment service		Repeal	

[1] The table does not deal with the user tax recommendations. In addition to the items in the table, the automatic reductions in present law respecting cigarettes, beer, distilled spirits, and wine are to be repealed, and the automatic reduction in the case of the general telephone tax is postponed.

Exhibit 33.—Statement by the President, June 21, 1965, at the signing of the excise tax reduction bill

Very shortly I will sign into law a bill that at midnight will lift one and three-quarters billion dollars of onerous taxes from the American economy; that next January will ease the tax burden by a further one and three-quarters billion dollars; that will pay big dividends in lower prices, in more jobs, and more sales, and in more production, not just this year, in 1965, but in 1966 and in many years to come thereafter.

So, this afternoon I want to personally congratulate the entire Congress for its very prompt and its very efficient and effective action on this measure. I asked the Congress on May 17 to reduce excise taxes. They have now completed action on that bill in exactly 32 days.

This is another shining chapter in the legislative record that a great Congress is writing a new chapter of progress in American life.

The enactment of this bill reflects the confidence of the Administration and the Congress that the benefits of excise tax reductions will be passed along to the American consumer. We can expect no less from our competitive business system.

This bill is now our third major tax action in three years.

The Revenue Act of 1962 introduced a bold new concept without precedent in American fiscal history—a 7-percent tax credit for business investment in new equipment. It laid the foundation for a sustained advance in business investment.

That uninterrupted advance has brought investment in equipment in the first quarter of 1965 to $38 billion, an increase of 52 percent in 4 years. And it is continuing. It is bringing rich rewards in the modernization of our entire industrial plant, in better products, in more efficient production, in lower costs, and, finally, in hundreds of thousands of new jobs for the working people of America.

Early last year, the Congress, in its wisdom, passed the Revenue Act of 1964. This second major tax reform simplified our income taxes, and made them fairer, and it reduced by $14 billion the taxes that American consumers and businesses owe on their 1965 incomes.

And this bill, which I am signing today, will eliminate an additional $4.7 billion of excise taxes.

The tax actions of 1962, and 1964, and 1965, taken together, are the mark of a vigorous new philosophy in our fiscal affairs.

Through the rigorous and never-ending pruning of waste, we have found the means for new programs already in education, in health, in urban and regional development, in the war on poverty, in large-scale strengthening of social efforts toward a better America, and in many new health programs.

Through a careful concern for private incentives, our tax system now better promotes growth, and efficiency, and opportunity.

And through a prudent control over total expenditures and total revenues, we have supplied consumers and businesses an expanding volume of purchasing power. The use of that growing purchasing power has carried national output to a rate that is currently running in excess of $650 billion, compared with $500 billion in the first quarter of 1961; it has raised wages and salaries by $76 billion in four years; it has raised corporate profits after taxes by $17 billion; it has reduced the unemployment rate from 7.1 percent in May 1961 to 4.6 percent in May 1965; it has created more than 5½ million new jobs in these four years.

When we cut taxes last year, there were some who felt that lower taxes could renew an expansion already old by all past standards. They were wrong.

Today that old expansion has surpassed all peacetime records for duration. In its 52d month, it displays today the youthful vigor, the healthy balance, which promises to keep it going as far into the future, as the Secretary of the Treasury said only yesterday, as we can really see.

Others feared that we were squandering the Federal revenues that were needed to reduce our deficit. And they, too, were mistaken.

Our budget has really faired better than most of us had expected.

In January 1964, we anticipated a deficit for fiscal year 1964 of $10 billion. It turned out to be $8.2 billion. In January 1965, we expected a deficit of $6.3 billion for fiscal year 1965. It now appears that it will be close to $3.8 billion.

In the 5-year period 1961 to 1966 we expect that Federal revenues will have increased more than the preceding 6 years, when there were no tax cuts at all.

We have proved that a healthy budget depends on a healthy economy. And all of us—Government officials, managers, employees, and consumers—are determined to keep our economy healthy.

A healthy economy is free of inflation. Over the past 5 years our price stability has been unmatched in the industrial world. The average level of our wholesale prices in May was only 1.7 percent higher than its average in 1958.

So, this price stability has reflected both prudent monetary and fiscal policies and the responsible actions of both labor and management.

In May, the average manufacturing worker earned $4.56 more a week than he had in May of last year. And he was also earning better pensions, and better vacations, and better insurance. Yet because the gains in his union contracts stayed, on the average, within the rise in productivity, average unit labor costs in manufacturing last month were really lower than a year earlier—or lower than they were four years earlier.

So, we are counting on management and on labor to continue to act responsibly in setting prices and wages. The Nation both expects and deserves it to act in the national interest.

And this excise tax bill will make its maximum contribution to our economic health only if businesses pass along to the consumers the full amount of the reduction in the tax. And today I urge every manufacturer, and every retailer in this country, to do just that.

I am pleased that the Congress saw fit to leave substantially unchanged my recommendations for excise tax reduction in 1965 and 1966.

The only major change the Congress made was the additional reduction in the automobile tax in later years.

I had recommended a five-point reduction in that tax, and the Congress decided to increase this to nine points.

But by postponing the additional four-point reduction, the Congress allowed time for possible modification if future developments should indicate that this should be desirable.

We in the Executive Branch will be carefully considering the possible constructive uses that might be made of the 1-percent automobile excise which the Congress decided to retain. This revenue could help to solve such related national problems as automobile safety, air pollution, highway beauty, and the disposal of discarded and abandoned automobiles.

If we should find that the need for these purposes—or the fiscal situation generally—should require retention of more than the 1-percent tax on automobiles, there will be ample time for the Congress then to consider our recommendations.

When there is again opportunity for tax revision, we hope, in particular, to provide further tax relief to those in our nation who need it most—those taxpayers who now live in the shadow of poverty.

Tax revision is a job—as all of your congressional leaders know—that is really never finished. Our tax system must be continually geared to the needs of a healthy and a growing economy.

Such an economy provides both the foundation for our national security and for a better life for all of our citizens.

So, to the members of the Senate Finance Committee, and to the members of the House Ways and Means Committee, and to the membership of the two Houses respectively, I say to you, on behalf of a grateful people, you have done your job well.

Thank you.

————————

Exhibit 34.—Statement by Secretary of the Treasury Fowler, June 30, 1965, before the Committee on Ways and Means of the House of Representatives, on H.R. 5916, a bill to reduce tax barriers to foreign investment

I am appearing before you to urge prompt and favorable action on H.R. 5916, legislation which is intended to reduce tax barriers to foreign investment in the United States. Passage of this bill will serve two important national objectives. First, it constitutes a comprehensive and integrated revision of our present system of taxing foreign individuals and foreign corporations on income derived from the United States, bringing our system of taxing foreigners into line with the rules existing generally in the other developed countries of the world. Second, the bill will make a significant contribution to our balance of payments by serving to eliminate the impediments now existing in our tax laws to foreign investment in the United States.

Background of proposals

In his Balance-of-Payments Message of July 18, 1963, President Kennedy announced he was appointing a task force to review U.S. Government and private activities which adversely affect foreign purchases of the securities of U.S. companies. The group was composed of representatives of finance, business, and Government. This task force, of which I had the privilege of serving as Chairman, studied various courses of action which could be adopted in both the private and public sectors to encourage foreign ownership of U.S. securities.

In April 1964, the task force issued its report containing 39 recommendations, which call for a broad range of actions by U.S. international business organizations and financial firms, as well as by the Federal Government, to bring about broader foreign ownership of U.S. corporate securities. Among the recommendations directed toward the Government, those dealing with the taxation of foreign individuals and foreign corporations have the most significant and immediate impact.

Issuance of the task force report prompted a broad and intensive review by the Treasury of the rules governing taxation by the United States of foreign individuals and foreign corporations. This review considered these rules not only from the standpoint of the balance of payments but also from the viewpoint of conventional tax policy considerations. As a result of this review, the Treasury Department on March 8, 1965, submitted to the Congress legislation containing not only proposals in all of the tax areas dealt with in the task force report, but also in other areas where it appeared that change was desirable to make the present system more consistent with rational tax treatment of foreign investment.

The Treasury Department agrees with the task force conclusion that many of the existing rules applicable to foreign investors in the United States are outmoded and not only serve to deter foreign investment but are inconsistent with sound tax policy. These rules were enacted many years ago and do not reflect the changes in economic conditions which have occurred over the last 15 years.

Examples of tax rules which impede foreign investment in this country are many: The present level of our estate tax—higher on foreigners than on U.S. citizens—is completely out of line with the rates generally prevailing elsewhere in the world and acts as a significant deterrent to potential foreign investors. Also, the fact that we require tax returns from foreigners merely because they make passive investments here is inconsistent with international tax practices and hinders foreign investment. These and other provisions in the Internal Revenue Code contribute to the widely-held view that investment in U.S. securities poses such serious tax problems for the ordinary foreign investor that it cannot be undertaken without the benefit of expensive tax advice. At the same time, some of these provisions are extremely difficult, if not impossible, to enforce, or are susceptible of relatively easy avoidance by the sophisticated foreign investor. Since they deter many foreign investors and are avoided by the rest, they give rise to almost no tax revenue. Enactment of all of the changes proposed in H.R. 5916 will result in a revenue loss of less than $5 million annually.

However, in proposing these changes, we have kept in mind the importance of not converting the United States into a tax haven nor of diverting funds to the United States from less-developed countries. The purpose of this bill is to remove tax barriers which have served to discourage foreigners from making investments in the United States. At the same time we recognize that no purpose will be served if the bill violates international tax standards, thereby setting off a struggle among the developed nations of the world to attract foreign investors through tax devices. To attract foreign investors, the United States must offer not "tax breaks" or "tax gimmicks": it must offer a growing and dynamic economy. We believe our record of economic growth over the last five years and our prospects for the future are sufficient to induce a substantial increase in foreign investment if our tax system does not act as a bar.

Impact of H.R. 5916 on the balance of payments

There is no way of estimating with any degree of precision the impact of the bill on foreign investment in the U.S. or the resulting benefit to our balance of payments. The factors governing securities investment are many and complex. Even in purely domestic transactions, intangibles such as habit, convenience, and past experience may be as important as yields, price-earnings ratios, and other economic indicators.

Although difficult to quantify, there is ample evidence of a sizable potential for attracting foreign investment in U.S. corporate securities, particularly stocks, by residents of the prosperous countries of continental Europe. After more than a decade of rapidly rising incomes, Europeans have to a large extent fulfilled many of their most pressing consumer needs and are accumulating savings at a high rate. Individuals in Europe are turning increasingly towards securities investment, as shown by the rising activity on European stock exchanges, the large number of new offices opening in Europe by American securities firms, and rising sales of mutual fund shares. Yet, even now, in Europe only 1 person in 30 is a shareowner, as compared to 1 in 11 in the United States.

At the end of 1964, foreigners held an estimated $12.8 billion of U.S. corporate stocks valued at market prices. In every year since 1950 except two, foreign purchases of U.S. stocks have exceeded foreign sales. In the 6 years between 1959 and 1964, net purchases by foreigners averaged $161 million. These net figures are the residual of much larger gross purchases and sales which in recent years have been on the order of $2½ billion to $3½ billion. A small percentage shift in the ratio of purchases to sales, therefore, could have had a substantial effect on the net balance of transactions.

If the amount of additional investment expected to result from H.R. 5916 were merely a function of the amount of tax saved, there would be little improvement in the balance of payments. More important than the small tax savings to foreigners, however, is the substantial effect which will result from the simplification and rationalization of our tax treatment of foreign investors. Our high estate tax on foreigners, for example, is widely considered by experts to be one of the biggest barriers to foreign investment. While the change in the estate tax proposed by H.R. 5916 would eliminate $3 million out of about $5 million of tax levied each year, existing estate tax rates almost certainly deter many foreigners from investing here at all. This is particularly so when the exemption is limited to only $2,000—any investment whatsoever will subject the estate to tax and require filing of an estate tax return, with the resulting expenses. It is not surprising under these circumstances that the small foreign investor avoids purchasing U.S. stocks because of the inconvenience of the estate tax; the big investor also avoids such purchasing but because of the size of the tax itself.

Viewed in this light, it is clear that the changes contained in H.R. 5916 should in time materially increase the volume of foreign investment in the United States. Based on the sizable potential for foreign purchases of U.S. corporate stocks which is known to exist, we expect that the legislation will eventually result in an additional capital inflow on the order of $100 million to $200 million per year, other factors remaining unchanged. Considerable time—perhaps one to two years or maybe more—will be required before foreigners can complete the adjustment of their portfolios to take advantage of H.R. 5916, but a substantial impact may be felt in the period just ahead.

Specific proposals contained in H.R. 5916

I should like to review at this time the principal substantive changes embodied in H.R. 5916.

Estate tax.—It is generally felt that our current system of taxing the U.S. estates (involving only the U.S. assets) of foreign decedents is inequitable and constitutes one of the most significant barriers in our tax laws to increasing foreign investment in U.S. corporate securities. Under present law, a foreign decedent is taxable at regular U.S. estate tax rates, ranging up to 77 percent, on U.S. property held at death. Moreover, the U.S. estates of foreign decedents are entitled to only a $2,000 exemption, compared with a $60,000 exemption available to U.S. citizen decedents, and are not entitled to the marital deduction available to U.S. citizen decedents. Thus, U.S. estate tax rates applied to nonresidents are in most cases considerably higher than those of other countries and therefore foreigners who invest in the United States suffer an estate tax burden. In addition, a foreign decedent's estate must pay heavier estate taxes on its U.S. assets than would the estate of a U.S. citizen owning the same assets.

H.R. 5916 would increase the exemption for the U.S. estates of foreign decedents from $2,000 to $30,000 and would tax such estates on the basis of a 5-10-15-percent rate schedule. With this significant increase in the exemption and sharp reduction in rates, the effective U.S. estate tax rate on foreign decedents would no longer be considerably higher than most other countries and would be more closely comparable to the rates prevailing elsewhere.

This change should have an important psychological effect on foreigners contemplating investment in U.S. securities. Where the gross U.S. estate would be less than $30,000, there would be no estate tax, and no need to file an estate tax return. In those instances where the estate is larger, the effective rate would be sharply reduced and would be comparable to the effective rate of tax of a U.S. citizen who utilizes the $60,000 exemption and the marital deduction.

Capital gains.—The present system of taxing capital gains realized by foreigners has contributed to the view that investment in the United States is something which should be approached cautiously because of the possibility of inadvertently becoming subject to tax. The Internal Revenue Code now provides for a general exemption from capital gains tax for nonresident foreigners not doing business in the United States with two exceptions. First, the foreigner's gains are subject to U.S. capital gains tax if he is physically present in the United States when the gain is realized, and second, all gains during the year are taxable if he spends 90 days or more in the United States during that year.

The physical presence restriction can be easily avoided by the experienced foreign investor if he arranges to be outside the country when the gain is realized, but is a potential trap to the foreigner who is not aware of its existence. The bill would eliminate this restriction from the general capital gains exemption.

In addition, the bill would extend the 90-day period which a foreigner may spend here without being subject to capital gains tax to 183 days. This will make the provision more consistent with international standards governing the taxation of foreigners residing in a country for a substantial period. It will also minimize the possibility that a foreigner will be taxed on capital gains realized at the beginning of a taxable year if he later spends a substantial amount of time in the United States during that year.

Graduated income tax rates.—At the present time, foreign individuals not doing business in the United States who derive more than $21,200 of investment income from U.S. sources are subject to regular U.S. income tax graduated rates on that income and are required to file returns. These requirements have produced little revenue, in part because we have eliminated graduated rate taxation of investment income in almost all of our treaties with the other industrialized countries and in part because of the ease with which this provision is avoided. Moreover, it has been indicated that graduated rate taxation and the accompanying return requirement may represent a substantial deterrent to foreign investment in the United States.

H.R. 5916 eliminates all progressive taxation of nonresident foreigners not doing business here and removes the requirement for filing returns in such cases. The liability of foreign investors deriving U.S. investment income would thus be limited to the tax withheld at the statutory 30-percent rate or a lower applicable treaty rate. The legislation would continue graduated rate taxation for foreigners who are doing business in the United States. These rules are consistent with the practices of most other industrialized countries.

Segregation of investment and business income.—Under present law, if a foreign individual is doing business in the United States he is subject to tax on all of his U.S. income, whether or not connected with his business operations, on the same basis in general as a U.S. citizen. H.R. 5916 would separate the business income of a foreign individual engaged in business here from his nonbusiness income, and would tax the nonbusiness income at the 30-percent statutory withholding rate or at the lower appropriate treaty rate. All business income would remain subject to tax at graduated rates.

With respect to foreign corporations doing business in the United States (so-called resident foreign corporations), which also have stock investments here, H.R. 5916 would likewise separate dividend income from the other income of the foreign corporation. Under the legislation, a resident foreign corporation deriving such dividend income from the United States would thus be taxable on its dividend income at the statutory 30-percent rate or at the lower applicable treaty rate. As a result, the foreign corporation would no longer receive the deduction now afforded under the Internal Revenue Code to dividends received by one corporation from another corporation.

The elimination of the dividends received deduction as respects resident foreign corporations is in part designed to end an abuse which has developed. Frequently, a foreign corporation with stock investments in the United States engages in trade or business here in some minor way and then claims the dividends received deduction on its stock investments. Such a corporation ends up paying far less than the 30-percent statutory or applicable treaty rate on its U.S. dividends, even though its position is basically the same as a corporation which is not doing business here which derives investment income from the United States. In those cases where the applicable treaty rate is 5 percent (the rate set by certain treaties where subsidiary dividends are involved), the resident foreign corporation will benefit from this proposed change.

Definition of "Engaged in trade or business."—H.R. 5916 makes clear that individuals or corporations are not engaged in trade or business in the United States—and thus subject to tax at regular graduated rates rather than the 30-percent withholding rate or lower treaty rate—because of investment activities here or because they have granted a discretionary investment power to a U.S. banker, broker, or adviser. This provision should have the effect of removing much of the uncertainty which now surrounds the question of what amounts to engaging in trade or business in the United States. Uncertainty of this type is undesirable as a matter of tax policy and has the effect of limiting foreign investment in the United States. Many foreigners are afraid of investing in U.S. stocks if they cannot give a U.S. bank or broker authority to act for them. This change will have relatively limited impact, however, since under the legislation, business income does not include dividends or gains from the sale of stock.

The bill also changes present law by giving foreign individuals and corporations an election to compute their income from real property on a net income basis at regular U.S. rates rather than at the 30-percent withholding rate or lower treaty rate on gross income. This type of treatment is common in the treaties to which the United States is a party and is designed to deal with the problem which arises from the fact that the expenses of operating real property may be high and cannot be taken into consideration if the income from real property is subject to withholding tax.

Personal holding companies and "Second dividend tax."—H.R. 5916 changes the personal holding company provisions of the Internal Revenue Code as applied to the U.S. investment income of foreign corporations and also modifies the application of the so-called second dividend tax. Under the bill, foreign corporations owned entirely by foreigners would be exempt from the personal holding company tax. This is possible because of the elimination of graduated rates as applied to foreigners which is contained elsewhere in the bill, and which makes the application of the personal holding company provision to corporations wholly-owned by foreigners no longer appropriate.

Under the bill, the second dividend tax (which is levied on dividends distributed by a foreign corporation if the corporation derives 50 percent or more of its income from the United States) would be applied only to the dividend distributions of foreign corporations doing business in the United States which have over 80-percent U.S. source income. It is desirable to retain this part of the tax to cover those cases where a resident foreign corporation has the great bulk of its business operations in the United States and to treat dividends of such a corporation as being from U.S. sources.

These changes should have the effect of eliminating application of the personal holding company tax and second dividend tax in many cases where they now apply, and which may now act as a deterrent to foreign investment.

Expatriate American citizens.—The provisions of H.R. 5916 which eliminate graduated rates for foreign individuals and substantially reduce the estate tax liability of foreign decedents may create a substantial tax incentive to U.S.

citizens who might wish to surrender their citizenship in order to take advantage of these changes in the law. While it is doubtful whether there are many who would be willing to take such a step, still the incentive would be present and might be utilized. H.R. 5916 deals with this problem by providing that an individual who had surrendered his U.S. citizenship for tax reasons within the preceding 10 years shall be subject to U.S. taxation with respect to his U.S. income and assets at the rates applicable to citizens. Such individuals will therefore not receive the benefits of this legislation but will be taxed as nonresident foreigners are at present. As I mentioned, these provisions would not apply if the expatriate American citizen can establish that the avoidance of U.S. taxes was not a principal reason for his surrender of citizenship.

Retaining treaty bargaining position.—The risk is present that by making the changes provided in H.R. 5916, the United States may be placed at a considerable disadvantage in negotiating similar concessions for Americans. In order to protect the bargaining position of the United States in international tax treaty negotiations, H.R. 5916 therefore authorizes the President, where he determines such action to be in the public interest, to reapply present law to the residents of any foreign country which he finds has not acted to provide our citizens substantially the same benefits for investment in that country as those enjoyed by its citizens on their investments in the United States as a result of this legislation. If this authority were invoked, it could be limited to those investment situations as to which U.S. citizens were not being given comparable treatment. We believe that the presence of such a provision will be a material aid in our securing appropriate provisions respecting these matters in our international tax treaties.

Conclusion

Our current system of taxing foreign investors in the United States contains elements which are inconsistent with generally accepted international tax policy principles and which, at the same time, act to discourage foreign investment in the United States. H.R. 5916 is designed to reshape our present system in order to make it a more rational vehicle for taxing foreign individuals and corporations.

The legislation is an essential element of the President's comprehensive program for dealing with our balance-of-payments problem. As such, it is one of the aspects of the President's program which is expected to have a longer term impact on our balance of payments. Foreigners will invest in this country as long as our economy remains prosperous and stable. However, it cannot be expected that the level of foreign investment will reach its full potential so long as provisions exist in our tax laws which serve to discourage foreign investment and which are not in accord with international tax standards. H.R. 5916 will eliminate or modify the provisions of present law which have complicated our system of taxing foreigners but have resulted in little revenue being realized.

Adoption of H.R. 5916 will lead to a simpler and more rational method of taxing foreigners. It will also be an important step in moving toward the elimination of our balance-of-payments deficit and the strengthening of the international position of the dollar. Because this legislation will contribute to these two vital national objectives, I urge you to support it.

Exhibit 35.—Press release, February 19, 1965, on liberalization of depreciation rules

The Treasury Department today announced three new measures liberalizing the manner in which income tax deductions for depreciation of plant and equipment can be taken to insure that business will reap the full benefit of the 1962 depreciation reform.

At the same time, the Treasury limited the ways in which such deductions can be calculated.

The combination of the new measures and the new limitations will result in increasing depreciation tax benefits during 1965 by an estimated $600 million to $800 million over what they would have been if the 1962 reform had not been modified.

The 1962 depreciation revision

The new measures modify the depreciation rules which accompanied the liberal guideline procedure initiated in 1962. Those rules were part of a thorough depreciation reform designed to foster more rapid equipment modernization.

At that time, taxpayers electing to use the guideline procedure were allowed three years as a transitional period. At the end of the three years—beginning in taxable year 1965 for most taxpayers—they would have been obliged to show that their actual equipment replacement practice is either already consistent with their depreciation deductions or clearly moving toward consistency.

The taxpayer is allowed, under the tax laws, to recover the cost of equipment by deducting it over the period he will use it, its "useful life." The 1962 depreciation guideline procedure, among other things, established guides for determining useful lives, by suggesting "guideline lives." These suggested "guideline lives" covered about 75 broad classes of industries and assets, and replaced a long list of thousands of separate suggested lives for virtually every item of equipment in use. It is usually to the advantage of a taxpayer to take as large depreciation deductions as possible as early as possible after he puts the equipment into use, thus the 1962 guideline procedure benefited taxpayers by allowing shorter useful lives.

The "reserve ratio test"

As an objective test of conformity between depreciation deductions and actual equipment replacement practice, the 1962 guideline procedure provided a "reserve ratio test."

A "reserve ratio" is the ratio of the total of depreciation deductions already taken on assets still in use (called the "depreciation reserve") to the original cost of those assets. Thus, the more of the cost that the taxpayer has already taken in deductions, the higher his reserve ratio would be. The reserve ratio test requires that the taxpayer's actual reserve ratio be compared to a standard range of reserve ratios appropriate to the useful life and the method the taxpayer is using to calculate his depreciation deductions.

The reserve ratio test is not met if the taxpayer's actual reserve ratio exceeds the upper limit of the range of standard ratios which is shown in the reserve ratio tables published in 1962. Such an excess may indicate that the taxpayer's actual equipment replacement practice does not accord with the useful life under which he has been computing his depreciation deductions. In other words, failure to meet the reserve ratio test may mean that the taxpayer has been recovering the cost of his equipment too quickly, over a period substantially shorter than its actual useful life to him. Thus, raising the upper limits of the standard range of the reserve ratio helps the taxpayer.

The purpose of the reserve ratio test was to allow taxpayers—by comparing their actual reserve ratio with an objective standard in the form of prepared tables reflecting reserve ratios appropriate to the useful lives claimed by the taxpayer under the guideline procedure for the equipment involved—to demonstrate that their choice of the useful lives, and therefore their depreciation deductions, were justified.

The new measures

Since the 1962 revision was put into effect, two problems have become apparent. The first is that a number of taxpayers will not have brought their equipment replacement practice into line with their deductions by the end of the three-year transitional period. The second is that certain ways of computing depreciation when combined with the 1962 changes can result in unjustified tax benefits.

The three new liberalizing measures are designed to meet the first problem by easing the difficulties some taxpayers otherwise would encounter under the changeover to the 1962 depreciation rules and guidelines. The limits on the ways in which depreciation deductions can be calculated are designed to meet the second problem by preventing exaggeration of tax benefits.

The three liberalizing measures include a "guideline form"—which will provide an optional substitute for the reserve ratio tables—as well as two new transitional rules.

The "guideline form"

The guideline form will allow each taxpayer to compute a reserve ratio standard tailored to his individual circumstances.

This is important because the reserve ratio tables are designed to cover the general run of taxpayers. Therefore, taxpayers who replace equipment at irregular intervals often have difficulty in meeting the test because the tables are based on the experience of the average business taxpayer. The reserve ratio tables assume an even rate of growth. For that reason, a taxpayer who purchases a large part of his equipment at one time could fail to meet the standard in the reserve ratio tables because his equipment costs are bunched and his rate of growth is uneven.

Many taxpayers who would otherwise have failed to meet the reserve ratio test will be permitted by the guideline form to meet it, because it will give them an opportunity to make proper allowance for their particular pattern of equipment acquisition. Thus, all taxpayers will have the opportunity to justify their depreciation deductions by an objective test. The form contains the same 20-percent margin of tolerance as that already built into the reserve ratio tables, so that even taxpayers who hold their asset as much as 20 percent longer than the period over which costs of the assets are deducted—usually the guideline life—will still pass the test.

Each year the taxpayer will have the option of using the guideline form or the reserve ratio tables. Even in cases where neither of these two objective tests is met, a taxpayer may still, as in the past, demonstrate the appropriateness of his depreciation practices on the basis of all the pertinent facts. The form, however, will allow more taxpayers to justify their depreciation practices simply and objectively without resorting to lengthy examinations by the Internal Revenue Service.

The new transitional rules

The 1962 revision provided two special rules for easing the transition from previous depreciation practices. The first allowed taxpayers a three-year moratorium before any test of their deductions would be required. The second allowed a subsequent period during which no test would be required as long as the taxpayer's actual practice continued to move closer to the pattern of deductions he was claiming.

Despite these liberal transition rules, studies show that a number of taxpayers who are trying to conform their practices to the 1962 revision will be unable to meet the reserve ratio test.

Therefore, two additional rules are now being adopted to ease the transition to the guidelines set forth in the 1962 revision. They are a "transitional allowance rule" and a "minimal adjustment rule." The two new rules will be applicable for a period equal to one guideline life which will begin, for calendar year taxpayers, in 1965.

The "transitional allowance rule"

The transitional allowance rule, in effect, extends the transitional period beyond three years. It raises the upper limit of the standard reserve ratio, regardless of whether the standard ratio is determined from the reserve ratio table or from the guideline form. In either case, the upper limit is stated in percentage points. The transitional allowance rule adds a certain number of percentage points to this limit. The additional number of percentage points for 1965 is 15. This number will gradually, very slowly at first, be reduced to zero over a period of years equal to a guideline life. (This transitional allowance is measured in percentage points, not percent. Thus, it will be 15 points regardless of the old upper limit figure to which it is added. It is in percentage points because the reserve ratio itself is expressed in percentage points both in the table and in the form.)

For example, if under the 1962 provisions the taxpayer found he had an upper limit of 60 percent on the reserve ratio test for 1965, he could still meet that test if his actual reserve ratio turned out to be 75 percent or less, because of the additional 15 percentage points added by the transitional allowance rule.

The "minimal adjustment rule"

The second new transitional rule, the minimal adjustment rule, is designed to help those taxpayers who cannot meet the reserve ratio test during the transitional period even with the benefit of the transitional allowance rule. This minimal adjustment rule is more liberal than the previous adjustment rule which it replaces. The old rule allowed the Internal Revenue Service to increase the life used by the taxpayer by as much as 25 percent if the taxpayer could not meet the reserve ratio test or otherwise justify the guideline life he is using to calculate deductions. (Increasing the life automatically reduces the depreciation deduction the taxpayer can claim in any single year because it spreads the total amount deductible over the longer period.)

Instead of the old 25-percent maximum, the new rule sets a new maximum adjustment of either 5 or 10 percent, depending on the extent by which the taxpayer fails to meet the reserve ratio test. Moreover, adjustments can be imposed by the Internal Revenue Service only in alternate years. In addition, if at any later time the taxpayer brings his reserve ratio within the transitional limits, he will be automatically allowed to return to the useful life he was employing before he was obliged to lengthen it under an adjustment.

The new limitations

In addition to the guideline form and the two new transitional rules, limitations are set on certain techniques used by some taxpayers in calculating depreciation. These techniques have been found to be incompatible with the guideline procedure because they exaggerate the benefits of the 1962 revision and they become particularly inappropriate in the transitional period when liberal transitional rules are in force.

In order to prevent use of such techniques with the guideline procedure taxpayers will not be allowed to use the guideline procedure (beginning in general with the fourth taxable year to which the guideline procedure is applicable, which would be 1965 for calendar year taxpayers) if they use the straight-line method or the sum of the years digits method—unless the cost of current acquisitions is recorded in year's acquisition accounts or in item accounts. Accounts depreciated under the declining balance method will not be affected.

The effect of the new measures

Without the new liberalization, an estimated 60 percent of larger firms using the guidelines would have failed the reserve ratio test in 1965. Failures under the test would have reduced the total tax benefits in 1965 resulting from the 1962 revision, estimated at $1.8 billion, by some $700 million to $900 million.

The three liberalizing measures will allow the great bulk of the firms which would have failed the test in 1965 to meet it. These measures, even taking account of the limitations, will allow such firms some $600 million to $800 million of the benefits which otherwise they would not have been eligible to receive.

At the request of the Treasury, the National Industrial Conference Board (NICB) last September made a survey of the depreciation practices of several hundred large firms, chiefly those with assets of $10 million or more. Of the firms surveyed, about 60 percent were found to be using the guideline procedure established in 1962. Since the survey, a number of taxpayers have elected to switch to the guideline procedure, and more are expected to do so. Of these guideline users, about 15 percent would have met the reserve ratio test automatically. About 25 percent more of these guideline users would have been enabled to meet the test with the help of the transitional rule provided in the 1962 revision. Thus some 60 percent of guideline users in the survey would have found themselves unable to meet the test in 1965. Based on NICB data for larger firms, with the application of the new liberalizing changes, some 95 percent of all adopters will be able to meet it with the help of the new guideline form or transitional allowance rule or both. That will leave only about 5 percent of all guideline users unable to meet the liberalized test in 1965.

The Treasury did not rely solely on the NICB Survey in making its decision. Detailed information on guideline adoption was obtained by analyzing studies by the Internal Revenue Service and by the Commerce Department. In addition, information on the number of firms which would have failed the reserve ratio test in 1965 under the 1962 procedure was drawn from a broad range of larger companies, as well as industry groups. The information obtained covered electric and gas utilities, railroads, and other industries. The information obtained from these varied sources confirmed the high percentage of firms using the 1962 guidelines which would fail to meet the reserve ratio test in 1965 unless action was taken to liberalize the guideline procedure.

Separate values for each of the three liberalizing measures cannot be estimated accurately because the measures will be used in combination. However, if the transitional allowance rule were adopted by itself, it probably would allows taxpayers about three-fourths of the $700 million to $900 million in benefits which they would otherwise lose in 1965 through failure to meet the reserve ratio test. Of the remaining benefit to taxpayers by adding the guideline form and the minimal adjustment rule, probably the bulk of the additional benefit is provided by the new guideline form.

The technical details of the three liberalizing procedures and the new limitation will be published soon by the Internal Revenue Service and will be effective for most taxpayers for the taxable year 1965. These changes are in accordance with the Treasury policy, announced in 1962, of keeping its tax treatment of depreciation as up-to-date as possible.

That policy was stated in the 1962 revision as follows:

"The experience under the new guideline lives, industry and asset classifications and administrative procedures will be watched carefully with a view to possible corrections and improvements. Periodic reexamination and revision will be essential to maintain tax depreciation treatment which is in keeping with modern industrial practices."

Depreciation policy

Proper depreciation policy requires that equipment replacement practice be consistent with depreciation deductions, so that deductions for business expenditures reasonably reflect actual costs.

The reserve ratio test provides an objective test of the reasonableness of taxpayer depreciation deductions. The new measures make the reserve ratio test useful to almost all present and future users of the 1962 guideline procedures. Moreover, they give taxpayers substantially more time to adjust their actual depreciation practices by making the reserve ratio test easier to meet during the transitional period.

Thus, all but a few guideline users will be able to take full advantage of the 1962 depreciation liberalizations and to validate their deductions without being obliged to undergo lengthy and detailed examination of their entire depreciation practice by the Internal Revenue Service.

Exhibit 36.—Statement by Secretary of the Treasury Dillon, July 21, 1964, before Subcommittee No. 1 of the Select Committee on Small Business of the House of Representatives, on tax-exempt foundations

Mr. Chairman, I appreciate your invitation to testify before this subcommittee on the important question of tax-exempt charitable foundations. As you know, these foundations play a very significant role in American life. Their effect is felt in all aspects of education, charity, science, medicine, the literary arts, and religion. Each year substantial sums are contributed to foundations, and the foundations, in turn, make substantial, annual disbursements on which many people and institutions are vitally dependent.

Because of the importance which we as a nation attach to private philanthropy, we have promoted it by generous provisions for tax exemption. This privilege applies to activities of foundations as well as to the tax deductions which are available to contributors to foundations. Because of this privilege it is healthy, indeed necessary, that the Congress and the Administration periodically reexamine those areas where tax exemption and tax deductions are provided. It is important to make sure that no one is abusing the privilege of tax exemption, and to put an end to such abuses as may be found. For example, study is necessary to determine whether any foundations have been the subject of a misuse which affords unintended or undesirable tax benefits to contributors and others;

whether situations exist where the interests of the intended beneficiaries of charitable bounty have been unduly slighted in deference to the financial interests of foundation contributors or those in control of foundations; whether some investment policies of certain foundations may have been geared more to the interests of controlling private properties than to the interests of charity; whether charity has received less than a full dollar of value for every dollar of tax deduction and tax exemption; and whether any foundations have engaged in business activities to the detriment of their primary charitable concern, to the advantage of their contributors and managers, or to the disadvantage of competing private business operating without tax exemption.

Both the Congress and the Treasury have studied these problem areas in the past. A major study resulted in important legislation in 1950 when opportunities for self-dealing were restricted and the unrelated business income of tax-exempt foundations was subjected to income tax. The Revenue Act of 1964 further restricted the opportunities for self-dealing in the case of foundations seeking to qualify for unlimited charitable contributions, and those organizations are now required to make substantial disbursements of their income and contributed assets.

It is now 14 years since the major revisions of 1950 were adopted, and it is time to see whether the legislation of that period was adequate to the task of remedying the abuses it was designed to eliminate; whether the legislation needs strengthening, either from a policy or administrative point of view; and whether other abuses have developed since 1950 which require correction by legislative or administrative action.

Both the Senate Finance Committee and the House Ways and Means Committee have requested that the Treasury Department prepare a report on this subject, and your subcommittee has, of course, already issued reports calling attention to a number of possible problem areas. The Treasury began its current study of foundation problems in 1961. In its early stages the study proceeded with limitations imposed by the priorities given to the Revenue Act of 1962 and the Revenue Act of 1964. However, the study will be completed and our report submitted by the end of this year.

In conjunction with the Treasury's study, in 1963 I appointed an Informal Advisory Committee on Foundations composed of reputable and responsible individuals who are associated with foundations on a full-time, professional basis, lawyers and accountants who have worked in the foundation area in their private practices, and a law professor who has been a scholarly observer of foundations and has written on the subject. The Committee has met on five occasions with Assistant Secretary Surrey, the Tax Legislative Counsel, and others from the Treasury and Internal Revenue Service. The purpose of these meetings was to canvass the views of knowledgeable people on the practices of taxpayers with respect to foundations, on the management, investment, and disbursement practices of foundations, and on various alleged abuses and proposed remedies which have been discussed in this subcommittee's reports and elsewhere. The Treasury found these meetings valuable as a source of informed opinion, but our ultimate conclusions and recommendations will be based on all aspects of our studies and from evidence drawn from varied sources, including, of course, field studies by the Internal Revenue Service and data provided by this subcommittee.

This subcommittee's reports contain statistics gleaned from a study of several hundred foundations, including their asset values, receipts, accumulations, and disbursements. The Treasury study will benefit from that information and from updated statistical data based upon an extensive survey of the information returns which foundations have filed on Form 990-A for the year 1962. It will also benefit from the responses to a questionnaire which we are sending to a number of foundations requesting additional statistics and information not available from existing sources. I would like at this point to submit for the record a copy of this questionnaire. Information provided by the Foundation Directory (published by the Russell Sage Foundation) is also being studied. Thus, to the extent available, concrete facts and figures will provide the background material for the Treasury's ultimate conclusions and recommendations.

Although policy considerations will be fundamental to the Treasury's ultimate recommendations, and to the Congress' ultimate judgments, each policy question carries with it technical aspects which are important to the overall statutory scheme, to equity and administrative practicability. Treasury lawyers intend to study these technical matters in conjunction with the staff of the Joint Committee on Internal Revenue Taxation so that the ultimate report will place each conclusion and recommendation in proper perspective, indicating its linkage with related provisions of law and other relevant considerations.

As part of the Treasury's general interest in the foundation area, and as Mr. Caplin will tell you in greater detail, the Internal Revenue Service has, in the last three years, stepped up its program for auditing exempt organization returns. Whereas only approximately 2,000 exempt organization returns per year had been audited before, about 10,000 exempt organization returns were examined in fiscal year 1964. This should bring about more widespread and fuller compliance with existing provisions of law. It will also help us to form judgments as to which abuses can be corrected by the vigorous enforcement of existing law and which require new legislation. In order to provide more meaningful information and to bring to light areas of possible concern, the information return required of foundations was modified recently and is undergoing continued reevaluation.

The scope of existing law is also being determined in litigation. Appropriate cases are being diligently litigated by the Office of the Chief Counsel of the Internal Revenue Service and by the Tax Division of the Justice Department. Court decisions are helping to mark off those areas where vigorous enforcement of existing law will carry out the congressional objectives from those where new action by the Congress may be necessary. Such litigation tests some of the judgments made in 1950 in light of the years of experience which have passed since then. A vigorous litigation policy is a continuous necessity if the effects of legislation are to be reviewed on an empirical basis. This Administration has pursued such a policy where warranted.

Both the administrative and litigation experience since 1950 will shed light on the propriety of the sanctions which the law now provides in cases of abuse and outright violation of law. The study will examine whether, in some cases, sanctions are inadequate or misdirected, and whether in other cases sanctions are so stringent and automatic that courts may be reluctant to hold them applicable.

Conclusion

Privately administered philanthropy has a vital, affirmative contribution to make to a dynamic, democratic society like ours. Ours is a pluralistic society composed of people and groups with diverse, competing interests and ideas; it is dependent on a free marketplace for these ideas and for qualified people to experiment with them. Foundations directed by private individuals, not by Government, have made great contributions in education, in science, in medicine, in fostering an environment for the creation of ideas, for their debate, and for experiment and innovation. Government has contributed to this healthy environment in many ways, not the least of which is by providing tax benefits. This is a cost which the Congress has always considered worth incurring. It is essential, however, that the cost be a measured one—that abuses and inequitable tax advantages claimed under the shelter of provisions of law designed to aid philanthropy be ferreted out and eliminated. The 1950 amendments were expected to eliminate abuses and undesirable private benefit cases such as those involving self-dealing between a contributor and the foundation which he controls. To the extent that they may not have proved fully effective, they must be strengthened. The study now under way will explore this type of problem along with others. It is our hope that we will be able to devise recommendations which will eliminate abuses and make for efficient, even-handed administration— this without detracting from the policy and provisions of law which encourage society's realization of the true values of modern philanthropy.

The Treasury's study is proceeding with care and impartiality. Until it is concluded and our report is submitted to the competent legislative committees, it would be neither desirable nor proper for me to discuss in any detail particular issues or recommendations which may be under consideration. You may be sure, however, that all available data and views, including those set forth in this subcommittee's reports, are being given our utmost attention.

Exhibit 37.—Introduction and summary of U.S. Treasury Department report on private foundations, February 2, 1965

Introduction

Because of the importance which this Nation attaches to private philanthropy, the Federal Government has long made generous provision for tax exemptions of charitable[1] organizations and tax deductions for the contributors to such organizations. Since the Federal tax laws in this way encourage and, in substantial measure, finance private charity, it is altogether proper, indeed, it is imperative, for Congress and the Treasury Department periodically to reexamine the character of these laws and their impact upon the persons to which they apply to insure that they do, in fact, promote the values associated with philanthropy and that they do not afford scope for abuse or unwarranted private advantage.

This report responds to requests by the Committee on Finance of the U.S. Senate and the Committee on Ways and Means of the House of Representatives that the Treasury Department examine the activities of private foundations for tax abuses and report its conclusions and recommendations. Both the Congress and the Treasury Department have investigated these problem areas in the past. A major study resulted in important legislation in 1950, when opportunities for self-dealing and the accumulation of income were restricted and, in addition, the income of feeder organizations and the unrelated business income of certain classes of organizations were subjected to tax. The Revenue Act of 1964 imposed further restrictions on foundations seeking to qualify as recipients of unlimited charitable contributions. However, the major revisions of 1950 have not been comprehensively reviewed since their enactment. In its present study, the Treasury Department has sought to determine whether existing legislation has eliminated the abuses with which it was designed to cope, and whether additional abuses have developed which require correction by legislative action.

In keeping with the congressional requests which prompted it, the scope of this report is limited to private foundations. The discussion of problems and proposed solutions, thus, is confined to that context. The restriction of the report to private foundations does not indicate any judgment upon whether or not similar or other types of problems may exist among other classes of exempt organizations. For purposes of this report, the term "private foundation" designates:

(1) Organizations of the type granted tax exemption by section 501(c)(3) (that is, generally, corporations or trusts formed and operated for religious, charitable, scientific, literary, or educational purposes, or for testing for public safety or the prevention of cruelty to children or animals), with the exception of—

(a) Organizations which normally receive a substantial part of their support from the general public or governmental bodies;[2]

(b) Churches or conventions or associations of churches;

(c) Educational organizations with regular faculties, curriculums, and student bodies;[3] and

(d) Organizations whose purpose is testing for public safety;[4] and

(2) Nonexempt trusts empowered by their governing instruments to pay or permanently to set aside amounts for certain charitable purposes.

In carrying forward its study, the Treasury Department has conducted an extensive examination of the characteristics and activities of private foundations. It has investigated and evaluated the experience of the Internal Revenue Service and the Department of Justice in the administration of the laws governing the taxation of foundations, their contributors, and related parties. It's study has drawn upon pertinent information assembled in investigations conducted by other

---

[1] The terms "charity" and "charitable" are used in their generic sense in this report, including all philanthropic activities upon which the relevant portion of the Internal Revenue Code of 1954 (sec. 501(c)(3)) confers exemption. Unless otherwise indicated, all statutory references are to the Internal Revenue Code of 1954, as amended.

[2] Described in sec. 503(b)(3).

[3] Described in sec. 503(b)(2).

[4] While organizations within this minor category are exempt from tax, contributions to them are not deductible; and they would therefore appear to be more closely analogous to business leagues, social welfare organizations, and similar exempt groups than to foundations.

groups.[1] It has conducted a special canvass of approximately 1,300 selected foundations. From these and other sources, it has compiled and tabulated a variety of classes of relevant statistical data. It has discussed the area with an Informal Advisory Committee on Foundations appointed by Secretary Dillon.[2] It has, further, considered a broad range of proposals for reform, extending from remedies narrowly tailored to end specific abuses to sweeping recommendations for the elimination or restriction of tax exemptions and deductions for certain classes of foundations.

The Department's investigation has revealed that the preponderant number of private foundations perform their functions without tax abuse. However, its study has also produced evidence of serious faults among a minority of such organizations. Six major classes of problems exist; other problems are also present. While the Internal Revenue Service has taken vigorous action in recent years to improve its administration of the existing laws which govern foundations and their contributors,[3] additional legislative measures appear necessary to resolve these problems.

This report seeks first to place private foundations in general perspective, by considering the values associated with philanthropy and the part played by private foundations in realizing those values. Against this background, it explores the major problems in detail and presents possible solutions.[4] In a separate part it describes additional problems of less general significance and recommends approaches to deal with them.[5] Appendixes present tables of relevant statistics and other information.

Summary of Report

I. An Appraisal of Private Foundations

While private foundations have generally been accorded the same favorable tax treatment granted other philanthropic organizations—exemption from tax and the privilege of receiving donations deductible by the donors—previous legislation has placed several special restrictions upon them. To determine whether additional restrictions are necessary, one must first inquire into the character of the contribution which private foundations make to private philanthropy and the validity of the general criticisms which have been leveled at them.

A. PHILANTHROPIC VALUES AND PRIVATE FOUNDATIONS

Private philanthropy plays a special and vital role in our society. Beyond providing for areas into which Government cannot or should not advance (such as religion), private philanthropic organizations can be uniquely qualified to initiate thought and action, experiment with new and untried ventures, dissent from prevailing attitudes, and act quickly and flexibly.

---

[1] E.g., Subcommittee No. 1, Select Committee on Small Business of the House of Representatives, whose chairman is Representative Wright Patman. The reports of the investigations of this subcommittee, entitled "Tax-Exempt Foundations and Charitable Trusts: Their Impact on Our Economy," have been published in three installments (dated, respectively, Dec. 31, 1962, Oct. 16, 1963, and Mar. 20, 1964) and are hereinafter referred to as the "Patman Reports." A transcript of hearings held by the group in 1964 has been published recently. See "Tax-Exempt Foundations: Their Impact on Small Business," hearings before subcommittee No. 1 on Foundations, 88th Cong., 2d sess., 1964.

[2] This Committee met with Treasury officials on several occasions, and was a valuable source of informed opinion; but the conclusions and recommendations of this report are those of the Treasury Department, and are, of course, based on facts and views drawn from many additional sources.

[3] Appendix B, which may be found in the complete Treasury Department report on private foundations, summarizes the administrative improvements which have been effected by the Internal Revenue Service.

[4] The report does not deal with the problem of distinguishing between permissible educational activities of foundations and dissemination of propaganda. The distinction is drawn by existing law. The Internal Revenue Service has been investigating situations of questionable operations and taking the action appropriate under presently applicable rules. This program will continue.

[5] The provisions designed to insure compliance with existing law will have to be reexamined to determine their adequacy to the task of securing compliance with the rules proposed in this report. The fundamental objective of such provisions should be to make certain that funds which have been committed to charity and for which tax benefits have been granted will in fact be devoted to charitable ends. Also, effective enforcement of the rules recommended here will require the filing of information returns by the organizations to which the rules apply. Since certain private foundations are not now required to file such returns, suitable revisions will have to be made in the relevant provisions of existing law.

Private foundations have an important part in this work. Available even to those of relatively restricted means, they enable individuals or small groups to establish new charitable endeavors and to express their own bents, concerns, and experience. In doing so, they enrich the pluralism of our social order. Equally important, because their funds are frequently free of commitment to specific operating programs, they can shift the focus of their interest and their financial support from one charitable area to another. They can, hence, constitute a powerful instrument for evolution, growth, and improvement in the shape and direction of charity.

B. EVALUATION OF GENERAL CRITICISMS OF PRIVATE FOUNDATIONS

Three broad criticisms have been directed at private foundations. It has been contended that the interposition of the foundation between the donor and active charitable pursuits entails undue delay in the transmission of the benefits which society should derive from charitable contributions; that foundations are becoming a disproportionately large segment of our national economy; and that foundations represent dangerous concentrations of economic and social power. Upon the basis of these contentions, some persons have argued that a time limit should be imposed on the lives of all foundations. Analysis of these criticisms, however, demonstrates that the first appears to be susceptible of solution by a measure of specific design and limited scope, the second lacks factual basis, and the third is, for the present, being amply met by foundations themselves. As a consequence, the Treasury Department has concluded that prompt and effective action to end the specific abuses extant among foundations is preferable to a general limitation upon foundation lives.

II. MAJOR PROBLEMS

The Treasury Department's study of private foundations has revealed the existence of six categories of major problems.

A. SELF-DEALING

Some donors who create or make substantial contributions to a private foundation have engaged in other transactions with the foundation. Property may be rented to or from it; assets may be sold to it or purchased from it; money may be borrowed from it or loaned to it. These transactions are rarely necessary to the discharge of the foundation's charitable objectives; and they give rise to very real danger of diversion of foundation assets to private advantage.

Cognizant of this danger, the House of Representatives in 1950 approved a bill which would have imposed absolute prohibitions upon most financial intercourse between foundations and donors or related parties, and which would have severely restricted other such dealings. However, the measure finally adopted, which has been carried without material change into present law, prohibits only loans which do not bear a "reasonable" rate of interest and do not have "adequate" security, "substantial" purchases of property for more than "adequate" consideration, "substantial" sales of property for less than "adequate" consideration, and certain other transactions.

Fourteen years of experience have demonstrated that the imprecision of this statute makes the law difficult and expensive to administer, hard to enforce in litigation, and otherwise insufficient to prevent abuses. Whatever minor advantages charity may occasionally derive from the opportunity for free dealings between foundations and donors are too slight to overcome the weight of these considerations. Consequently, the report recommends legislative rules patterned on the total prohibitions of the 1950 House bill. The effect of this recommendation would, generally, be to prevent private foundations from dealing with any substantial contributor, any officer, director, or trustee of the foundation, or any party related to them, except to pay reasonable compensation for necessary services and to make incidental purchases of supplies.

B. DELAY IN BENEFIT TO CHARITY

The tax laws grant current deductions for charitable contributions upon the assumption that the funds will benefit the public welfare. This aim can be thwarted when the benefits are too long delayed. Typically, contributions to a foundation are retained as capital, rather than distributed. While this procedure is justified by the advantages which private foundations can bring to our society, in few situations is there justification for the retention of income (except long-term capital gains) by foundations over extended periods. Similarly, the purposes of charity are not well served when a foundation's charitable disbursements are restricted by the investment of its funds in assets which produce little or no current income.

Taking note of the disadvantages to charity of permitting unrestricted accumulations of income, Congress in 1950 enacted the predecessor of section 504 of the present Internal Revenue Code, which denies an organization's exemption for any year in which its income accumulations are (a) "unreasonable" in amount or duration for accomplishing its exempt purposes, (b) used to a "substantial" degree for other purposes, or (c) invested in a way which "jeopardizes" the achievement of its charitable objectives.[1] The indefiniteness of the section's standards, however, has rendered this provision difficult to apply and even more difficult to enforce. Two changes in the law are needed for private foundations which do not carry on substantial active charitable endeavors of their own.

First, such private foundations should be required to devote all of their net income[2] to active charitable operations (whether conducted by themselves or by other charitable organizations) on a reasonably current basis. To afford flexibility, the requirement should be tempered by a 5-year carryforward provision and a rule permitting accumulation for a specified reasonable period if their purpose is clearly designated in advance and accumulation by the foundation is necessary to that purpose.

Second, in the case of nonoperating private foundations which minimize their regular income by concentrating their investments in low yielding assets, an "income equivalent" formula should be provided to place them on a parity with foundations having more diversified portfolios. This result can be accomplished by requiring that they disburse an amount equal either to actual foundation net income[2] or to a fixed percentage of foundation asset value, whichever is greater.

C. FOUNDATION INVOLVEMENT IN BUSINESS

Many private foundations have become deeply involved in the active conduct of business enterprises. Ordinarily, the involvement takes the form of ownership of a controlling interest in one or more corporations which operate businesses; occasionally, a foundation owns and operates a business directly. Interests which do not constitute control may nonetheless be of sufficient magnitude to produce involvement in the affairs of the business.

Serious difficulties result from foundation commitment to business endeavors. Regular business enterprises may suffer serious competitive disadvantage. Moreover, opportunities and temptations for subtle and varied forms of self-dealing—difficult to detect and impossible completely to proscribe—proliferate. Foundation management may be drawn from concern with charitable activities to time-consuming concentration on the affairs and problems of the commercial enterprise.

For these reasons, the report proposes the imposition of an absolute limit upon the participation of private foundations in active business, whether presently owned or subsequently acquired. This recommendation would prohibit a foundation from owning, either directly or through stock holdings, 20 percent or more of a business unrelated to the charitable activities of the foundation (within the meaning of sec. 513). Foundations would be granted a prescribed reasonable period, subject to extension, in which to reduce their present or subsequently acquired business interests below the specified maximum limit.

D. FAMILY USE OF FOUNDATIONS TO CONTROL CORPORATE AND OTHER PROPERTY

Donors have frequently transferred to private foundations stock of corporations over which the donor maintains control. The resulting relationships among the foundation, corporation, and donor have serious undesirable consequences

---

[1] Section 681 imposes similar restrictions upon nonexempt trusts which, under section 642(c), claim charitable deductions in excess of the ordinary percentage limitations on individuals' deductible contributions.
[2] Except long-term capital gains.

which require correction. Similar problems arise when a donor contributes an interest in an unincorporated business, or an undivided interest in property, in which he or related parties continue to have substantial rights. In all of these situations, there is substantial likelihood that private interests will be preferred at the expense of charity. Indeed, each of the three major abuses discussed thus far may be presented in acute form here. The problems here are sufficiently intensified, complex, and possessed of novel ramifications to require a special remedy.

To provide such a remedy, the Treasury Department recommends the adoption of legislation which, for gifts made in the future, would recognize that the transfer of an interest in a family corporation or other controlled property lacks the finality which should characterize a deductible charitable contribution. Under this recommendation, where the donor and related parties maintain control of a business or other property after the contribution of an interest in it to a private foundation, no income tax deduction would be permitted for the gift until (a) the foundation disposes of the contributed asset, (b) the foundation devotes the property to active charitable operations, or (c) donor control over the business or property terminates. Correlatively, the recommended legislation would treat transfers of such interests, made at or before death, as incomplete for all estate tax purposes unless one of the three qualifying events occurs within a specified period (subject to limited extension) after the donor's death. For the purposes of this rule, control would be presumed to exist if the donor and related parties own 20 percent of the voting power of a corporation or a 20-percent interest in an unincorporated business or other property. This presumption could be rebutted by a showing that a particular interest does not constitute control. In determining whether or not the donor and related parties possess control, interests held by the foundation would be attributed to them until all of their own rights in the business or other underlying property cease.

The Treasury Department has given careful consideration to a modification of this proposal which would postpone the donor's deduction only where, after the contribution, he and related parties control the business or other underlying property and, in addition, exercise substantial influence upon the foundation to which the contribution was made. Such a rule would permit an immediate deduction to a donor who transfers controlled property to a foundation over which he does not have substantial influence. Analysis of this modification indicates that it possesses both advantages and disadvantages. Congressional evaluation of the matter, hence, will require careful balancing of the two.

E. FINANCIAL TRANSACTIONS UNRELATED TO CHARITABLE FUNCTIONS

Private foundations necessarily engage in many financial transactions connected with the investment of their funds. Experience has, however, indicated that unrestricted foundation participation in three classes of financial activities which are not essential to charitable operations or investment programs can produce seriously unfortunate results.

Some foundations have borrowed heavily to acquire productive assets. In doing so, they have often permitted diversions of a portion of the benefit of their tax exemptions to private parties, and they have been able to swell their holdings markedly without dependence upon contributors. Certain foundations have made loans whose fundamental motivation was the creation of unwarranted private advantage. The borrowers, however, were beyond the scope of reasonable and administrable prohibitions on foundation self-dealing, and the benefits accruing to the foundation's managers or donors were sufficiently nebulous and removed from the loan transactions themselves to be difficult to discover, identify, and prove. Some foundations have participated in active trading of securities or speculative practices.

The Treasury Department recommends special rules to deal with each of these three classes of unrelated financial transactions. First it proposes that all borrowing by private foundations for investment purposes be prohibited.[1] Second, it recommends that foundation loans be confined to categories which are clearly necessary, safe, and appropriate for charitable fiduciaries. Third, it proposes that foundations be prohibited from trading activities and speculative practices.

---

[1] This recommendation would not prevent foundations from borrowing money to carry on their exempt functions.

F. BROADENING OF FOUNDATION MANAGEMENT

Present law imposes no limit upon the period of time during which a donor or his family may exercise substantial influence upon the affairs of a private foundation. While close donor involvement with a foundation during its early years can provide unique direction for the foundation's activities and infuse spirit and enthusiasm into its charitable endeavors, these effects tend to diminish with the passage of time, and are likely to disappear altogether with the donor's death. On the other hand, influence by a donor or his family presents opportunities for private advantage and public detriment which are too subtle and refined for specific prohibitions to prevent; it provides no assurance that the foundation will receive objective evaluation by private parties who can terminate the organization if, after a reasonable period of time, it has not proved itself; and it permits the development of narrowness of view and inflexibility in foundation management. Consequently, the Treasury Department recommends an approach which would broaden the base of foundation management after the first 25 years of the foundation's life. Under this proposal, the donor and related parties would not be permitted to constitute more than 25 percent of the foundation's governing body after the expiration of the prescribed period of time. Foundations which have now been in existence for 25 years would be permitted to continue subject to substantial donor influence for a period of from 5 to 10 years from the present time.

III. Additional Problems

Review of the practice of private foundations and their contributors discloses the existence of several problems which have less general significance than those discussed in Part II of the report. Part III of the report draws the following conclusions about these problems:

A. Gifts to private foundations of certain classes of unproductive property should not be deductible until the foundation sells the property, makes it productive, applies it to a charitable activity, or transmits it to a charitable organization other than a private foundation.

B. Charitable deductions for the contribution to private foundations of section 306 stock (generally, preferred stock of a corporation whose common stock is owned by the donor) and other assets should be reduced by the amount of the ordinary income which the donor would have realized if he had sold them.

C. Reforms of a technical nature should be made in certain estate tax provisions which govern tax incidents of contributions to private foundations.

D. A sanction less severe than the criminal penalty of existing law should apply for the failure to file a return required of a private foundation.

*   *   *   *   *   *   *

These Treasury Department proposals are based upon a recognition that private foundations can and do make a major contribution to our society. The proposals have been carefully devised to eliminate subordination of charitable interests to personal interests, to stimulate the flow of foundation funds to active, useful programs, and to focus the energies of foundation fiduciaries upon their philanthropic functions. The recommendations seek not only to end diversions, distractions, and abuses, but to stimulate and foster the active pursuit of charitable ends which the tax laws seek to encourage. Any restraints which the proposals may impose on the flow of funds to private foundations will be far outweighed by the benefits which will accrue to charity from the removal of abuses and from the elimination of the shadow which the existence of abuse now casts upon the private foundation area.

Exhibit 38.—Other Treasury testimony published in hearings before congressional committees, July 1, 1964–June 30, 1965

Secretary of the Treasury Dillon

Statement on the tax treatment of the distribution of General Motors common stock by the Christiana Securities Company, published in hearings before the Senate Finance Committee, 89th Congress, 1st session, March 17, 1965, pages 13–17.

International Financial and Monetary Developments

Exhibit 39.—Excerpts from remarks by Secretary of the Treasury Dillon, February 17, 1965, before the Government-Industrial Conference of the National Industrial Conference Board

The economic weather in that February of four years ago, when you last held a Government-Industry conference, was a far cry from the balmy economic climate we enjoy today. We were then in the trough of a recession, and our economic problems were legion. I will not review all the immense advances we have since made, for you are thoroughly familiar with them. Instead, I would like to talk briefly about one area in which, while we have made material progress, we must now move ahead even more quickly and decisively—our balance of payments.

Last week, as you know, President Johnson sent to the Congress a special Message, in which he reasserted in unmistakable terms our determination to end our balance-of-payments deficit, assessed the progress we have already made and the problems that confront us, and proposed additional measures to speed us on our way toward balance.

We need these new measures, as the President has made emphatically clear, not because our advances have been illusory or temporary or slight, for they have been sound and strong and lasting. We need these new measures because, solid as our progress has been, we need more of it now, not tomorrow.

When a new Administration took office four years ago, the United States had just experienced its third successive year of large payments deficits. On the basis of regular transactions, these deficits had averaged almost $4 billion a year from 1958–60, and had touched off an increasing loss of confidence in the dollar. They brought with them, as well, an accelerating outflow of gold amounting to more than $5 billion in the same three-year period, an outflow that reached a climax in the fall of 1960, when speculators pushed the price of gold in London up to $40 an ounce.

There were those who believed then—as there are those who believe now—that we could not simultaneously advance our economic growth at home and move toward balance in our international accounts. The only sure way, they insisted, to restore balance to our international payments was to clamp down severely on credit at home, despite the harm that would visit upon an already ailing economy. To promote economic expansion at home—and adopt credit policies to nourish that expansion—would, they warned, invite a rising tide of imports which would inevitably aggravate our payments deficits.

That view might well have been correct if our situation had been the classic one in which domestic inflation and over-consumption foster deficits in a nation's international accounts. But our situation was entirely different, for our balance-of-payments deficts existed side-by-side with excessive unemployment, under-utilized manufacturing capacity, and stable price levels. We had, therefore, to seek greater economic growth at home, and to seek it in a way that would advance, rather than retard, the reduction of our payments deficit.

We were convinced—and events have more than upheld our conviction—that the way to enduring progress in our balance of payments was through sound and strong economic growth, accompanied by basic price stability. For only in such a domestic climate could we achieve the gains in productivity essential to improving our international competitive position. And only a flourishing domestic economy would prove attractive to both foreign and domestic private investment.

Obviously, however, we could not rely on domestic expansion alone, for although it held the long-range answer to our payments problem, it could not solve the problem immediately before us. It was imperative that, as we moved toward balance over the long run, we also make prompt and substantial reductions in our payments deficit. It is in this area that our performance has been disappointing and must be improved.

Even though much more remains to be done, there has been much solid progress during the past four years. We set in motion a broad array of special measures designed to attack directly every major area of weakness in our international accounts. We adapted our monetary policy to the dual needs of external balance and domestic growth—raising short-term interest rates by nearly 1¾ percent, a 75 percent increase—to keep them reasonably on a par with those abroad. And this policy is being continued. At the same time ample amounts of long-term credit were made available for domestic growth. We took vigorous steps to encourage exports, instituting an entirely new system of export credit guarantees. We drastically reduced the adverse payments impact of Government outlays overseas. We eliminated the attraction of foreign tax havens for our private capital, and we reduced the special exemptions given tourists to make duty free purchases abroad.

Over the past four years, our commercial exports—excluding those financed by the Government—have grown by more than one-fourth, boosting our commercial trade surplus to a new high of $3.7 billion: $900 million more than in 1960 and $1.5 billion more than in 1963. By a drastic policy of tying foreign aid expenditures to U.S. goods and services, we have saved almost $500 million. We have cut military outlays abroad by more than $200 million—despite sharply rising prices in the countries where our forces are stationed—and we have increased military sales abroad through the Defense Department by another $450 million. In addition, our earnings from past private investments abroad have gone up by nearly $1.9 billion.

Together, these gains add up to about $3.9 billion worth of solid improvement in our underlying balance-of-payments position, enough, all else aside, to have brought our payments into actual balance last year. Our problems today arise from the fact that the full force of these gains has, thus far, been largely neutralized by a $2.5 billion boost in private capital outflows since 1960, $2 billion of which happened last year.

The interest equalization tax proved highly successful by holding purchases of foreign securities last year to the 1960 level, $400 million less than during 1963. But, the expansion of long-term bank loans abroad last year amounted to over $900 million, $800 million above 1960 and $400 million above 1963. Short-term capital outflows in the form of bank credits and corporate funds rose to $2.2 billion, more than $800 million higher than the 1960 level, and $1.4 billion higher than the 1963 level despite the fact that our money market rates remained generally in line with those abroad. And direct investment abroad by American companies, for the most part in Canada and Europe, exceeded the 1960 rate by almost $500 million and the 1963 rate by about $250 million. A rise of $300 million in other long-term capital outflows makes up the total $2.5 billion increase.

Alongside these swelling capital outflows, American travel and tourist spending abroad last year was $600 million higher than in 1960: three times the corresponding rise in foreign travel outlays in this country. Our travel deficit grew by $400 million and last year stood at $1.7 billion.

As a result of all these factors, we had a balance-of-payments deficit last year—in terms of regular transactions—of $3 billion, an improvement of only $900 million over 1960. To be sure, half of last year's $3 billion deficit occurred in the fourth quarter alone, and some of the deterioration in the fourth quarter resulted from temporary factors. But when all this is said, there is no gainsaying the fact that our deficit is still far too large, that we cannot continue to sustain such deficits, and that the data for the fourth quarter reveal weaknesses in our payments posture that must be remedied without delay. We must act, and act now, when we can do so from a position of strength.

And let no one doubt the strength of the dollar today in all markets of the world, a strength supported by hard facts. For while we have suffered gold losses, we have curtailed these losses in recent years. We still hold 35 percent of the entire free world monetary stock of gold. Leaving aside the $22 billion of U.S. Government claims on foreigners, our private investments abroad by themselves exceed the total of all foreign investment plus all foreign dollar holdings both public and private by more than $15 billion. And that margin has been widening every year. Our international balance sheet grows stronger year by year. And our ability to compete in world markets remains beyond question, our commercial trade surplus is far and away the world's largest. Last year it was more than twice the size of West Germany's, the next largest.

Backed by such solid elements of strength, we need have no fears for the security of the dollar, as long as we demonstrate by our deeds that we are determined to bring our balance-of-payments deficit to an end. We must end the growth of our short-term international liabilities. It is no longer good enough merely to offset the growth of these liabilities by an even larger growth of long-term assets. When we talk of substantial improvement in 1965, I want to make it amply clear that we are not thinking of a few hundred million dollars. Even a full billion dollar improvement would not meet our needs. We can and must do considerably more.

It is for that reason that President Johnson proposed last week a 10-point program to reinforce the measures already underway. Most of you, I am sure, are by now familiar with the President's proposals. They feature a massive, many-sided attack by all sectors of the American economy upon the swelling capital outflows that, more than any other single factor, have inflated our recent international deficits. They call upon the American businessman, upon the American banker, and upon all Americans to join in a truly national effort to stem the outpouring of dollars abroad.

The President has asked Congress to extend for two years the interest equalization tax on purchases by Americans of foreign securities, a tax scheduled to expire at the end of this year. That tax has proven a highly effective rein upon such purchases since legislation was submitted to Congress in July of 1963. Moreover, it has shown itself a strong catalyst to the growth of European capital markets, which are essential for the adequate financing of economic growth in the free world in the years that lie ahead.

But it is now clear that outflows stemmed by the interest equalization tax have all too frequently found other channels abroad. Last year, for example, American bank loans with maturities of over one year to foreign borrowers in developed countries rose by more than $650 million, in contrast to a peak annual increase of $122 million for the years before the interest equalization tax was proposed.

A careful analysis of these outflows shows that a large and growing portion of recent loans are definite substitutes for new security issues. It is significant, also, that of the new term loan commitments to industrial countries last year, only 15 percent financed U.S. exports, while 28 percent went for plant expansion.

Thus the President, under authority granted by the interest equalization tax law, has issued an Executive Order, effective last Thursday, February 11, imposing the tax on bank loans to foreigners with maturities of one year or more, with exemptions for borrowers in developing countries. I should make clear that the current exemption under the interest equalization tax law will continue to be granted to all export-connected loans of banks, thus assuring the banks' ability to support the efforts of American business to compete more effectively abroad.

But the heart of the new program lies not in new legislation, but rather in the President's action to enlist the voluntary but active cooperation of the business and banking community with the Government in cutting back sharply on the increasing outflow of dollars abroad. It is to this cooperative effort that we look for the greatest savings. We are convinced that American business will rise to the challenge. Failure is unthinkable.

The Government, will intensify its already effective efforts to stanch the dollar drain from our economic aid and military commitments abroad. At least $200 million of additional savings are in sight in this area.

And, finally, the President has set forth several other important measures to heighten the effectiveness of our export expansion program, to encourage foreign investment in U.S. securities, to foster greater foreign travel in this country, and to cut the outflow of our tourist and travel dollars abroad.

What distinguishes all these measures—and the President's message—is the degree to which their success depends upon the voluntary cooperation and support of American business and the American public. The President has set forth, for all to understand, the challenge that confronts us, and he has set forth the steps that we must take to meet that challenge. He has issued a call to arms to all Americans, and upon their response rests the solution to a stubborn, difficult, and important problem.

—

Exhibit 40.—Statement by Secretary of the Treasury Dillon, March 9, 1965, before the Subcommittee on International Finance of the Senate Banking and Currency Committee

At the outset of these hearings, it may be useful if I review in a general way the problems that we have faced and the policies that we have followed in dealing with the balance-of-payments deficit, before describing briefly the Administration's new program. Other witnesses will be commenting in greater detail upon those aspects of the President's 10-point program for which they have specific responsibility. For my own part, I will aim at an overall view of the progress that we have made to date and the tasks that still lie ahead of us.

Certainly, there is a clear need to achieve prompt and decisive reductions in our balance-of-payments deficit. That deficit has been with us for too long and it remains far too large. International trade today rests on the foundation of a sound dollar which is essential to the continued growth and stability of the entire free world. And the maintenance of a sound dollar now demands a quick end to our payments deficit.

Last year, a swelling tide of private capital outflows joined with other, more special, factors in carrying our deficit on regular transactions to a fourth-quarter annual rate of $5.8 billion. Because of the very real progress we had been making in most areas of our accounts, the deficit on regular transactions for the full year 1964 was held to about $3 billion, the smallest deficit on a comparable basis since 1957. But that is not nearly good enough. We must fully implement President Johnson's 10-point program to assure the rapid and substantial improvement that is required.

Basic approach to the balance-of-payments problem

Our underlying approach to the payments deficit has been, from the start, to seek a solution within the framework of a more vigorous domestic economy, operating closer to its full potential and offering improved incentives for investment. Our international competitive position had deteriorated by the late 1950's because of an inadequate rate of new cost-cutting investment coupled with an upward trend in certain key prices that had persisted throughout the decade. Moreover, the slow growth of our economy was enhancing the relative attractiveness of foreign investment. As a result, the years 1958–60 saw three successive balance-of-payments deficits that, on the basis of regular transactions, averaged close to $3.9 billion annually.

These large payments deficits certainly could not be attributed to an overstrained economy. In early 1961, we were faced with excessive unemployment, underutilized manufacturing capacity, and a very low rate of economic growth, all of which had to be corrected. We could not seek a deflationary solution to our balance-of-payments problem by clamping down tightly on money and credit. Quite the opposite, it was essential to spur more rapid growth at home, while finding the solution to our external problems in the rising productivity and improved climate for domestic investment that this growth would bring. This was a new and unique kind of balance-of-payments problem. Because the standard remedies were inapplicable, a new course had to be charted.

To achieve more rapid economic growth within a framework of stable costs and prices, basic reliance was placed upon tax reduction and investment incentives. Similar results might, in theory, have been sought through a very active use of monetary policy. But, an extremely easy monetary policy would only have worsened the problem of capital outflows, and so was necessarily ruled out, in spite of the slack in our domestic economy.

Our overall financial effort—in both the monetary and debt management areas—has continually aimed at maintaining our short-term interest rates in reasonable alignment with key rates in foreign money markets. At the same time, growing prosperity has added to the large flows of savings moving into our capital markets, and the long-term interest rates important for domestic investment and residential construction have remained stable or even declined.

We felt, and continue to feel, that a more productive domestic economy is an essential element in any long-range solution to our payments problem. However, in early 1961, it was imperative to seek immediate and substantial reductions in the payments deficit, because the longer run correctives could not be expected to yield their benefits at once. Therefore, we undertook a broad array of special measures designed to attack directly the major areas of weakness in our international accounts.

A series of 14 tables, showing our progress since 1960 and illustrating various other aspects of our balance of payments, is attached as Annex I of this statement.[1]

Special measures to achieve payments gains

We took vigorous steps to encourage exports, including both an entirely new system of export credit guarantees and vastly improved Government information and promotion services for exporters. We drastically reduced the adverse payments impact of Government outlays overseas. We eliminated the attraction of foreign tax havens for our private capital, and, in mid-1963, we proposed the interest equalization tax which increased the cost to other industrialized countries of raising funds in our markets through the sale of securities.

All of these measures have demonstrated their effectiveness. Since 1960, our commercial exports have grown by more than one-fourth. While special factors have helped, much of the improvement is attributable to our very impressive record of cost-price stability while foreign costs and prices were steadily rising. In 1964 alone, our commercial exports increased by $3.0 billion, or 15 percent. This was enough to more than offset the increase in imports which naturally accompanied our expanding economy. It gave us a commercial trade surplus in 1964, omitting all Government financed transactions, of $3.7 billion; over $900 million more than in 1960 and $1.4 billion more than in 1963.

In our aid program, we have adopted a rigorous policy of tying our assistance, and over 85 percent of new AID commitments are now tied to U.S. goods and services. As a result of this policy, the adverse effect of AID expenditures on the balance of payments has been cut in half since 1960. In 1960, out of gross expenditures of $1.7 billion under the Foreign Assistance Act, over $1 billion resulted in dollar payments abroad; in 1964, out of gross expenditures of $2 billion, dollar payments abroad were down to about $500 million.

The cost of maintaining our military posture abroad of course involves a major drain in our balance of payments. The task both Presidents Kennedy and Johnson set was to get this drain down to an irreducible minimum. Three principal methods have been used to do this: streamlining and adjusting overseas operations with savings in both military and civilian manpower, returning procurement to the United States, and making offsetting sales of U.S. military equipment.

By streamlining operations and cutting procurement, the Department of Defense expects to come close to achieving President Kennedy's objective, set in July of 1963, of trimming gross defense expenditures abroad by $300 million between 1962 and 1965. This will be the case even though sharply rising prices abroad have canceled out a goodly portion of the savings that have been effected. Because of savings in the overseas procurement of uranium, overall defense expenditures in 1964 were nearly $250 million lower than in 1960 and should go lower still this year as a result of economies already effected.

It is in the third area of action, military sales to other countries, where the most impressive results in dollar terms have been achieved. Beginning in 1961, with the views of Congress very much in mind, military assistance programs were increasingly shifted from grant aid to sales, and financed at market interest rates instead of zero percent. The Departments of Treasury and Defense undertook a major effort to maximize sales of U.S. military equipment. As a result, the export efforts of the American defense industry have been greatly strengthened. Our Export-Import Bank has cooperated in this new field; private banks are becoming interested; and, last year, the Congress wisely authorized the Department of Defense to issue guarantees under which many additional nations are able to finance military purchases in the United States.

The results of this program have been striking. Cash receipts from sales of military equipment rose from approximately $300 million in 1960 to over $1 billion during each of the years 1962, 1963, and 1964. An outstanding example of cooperation by an allied government is the agreement of the Federal Republic of Germany to buy military equipment from the United States in amounts equivalent to U.S. military dollar expenditures in Germany affecting the balance of payments. Recent examples of major military sales are the arrangements with

---

[1] Omitted from this exhibit; for document reference see note at end of this statement.

the United Kingdom and Australia for purchases of U.S. military equipment totaling about $1 billion.

The net effect of these various programs has been to reduce our actual net defense dollar outlays abroad from over $2.7 billion in 1960 to a little over $1.6 billion in 1964, a most gratifying result. The outstanding success of this effort has not been fully appreciated, since, on a regular transactions basis as shown in our official balance-of-payments statistics, the 1964 figure for net defense expenditures was just over $2 billion. This difference between the actual results of our efforts in the defense area and our official statistics arises for two reasons. First, because military sales are recorded in our balance of payments on a delivery basis with no credit for progress payments actually received ; and, second, because such of our sales of military equipment as pass through commercial channels are included in our commercial export figures rather than in the military accounts.

Progress since 1960 and the capital outflow problem

The extent of our overall progress and the problems we still face can be highlighted by comparing last year's balance-of-payments results with those of 1960, as shown in Table 4 of Annex I.[1] Last year our commercial trade balance had improved $900 million relative to 1960 and cuts in Government overseas dollar expenditures, military and nonmilitary, of $1.1 billion had been achieved. Along with an increase of $1.5 billion in our net receipts of private investment income, the full improvement relative to 1960 added up to a massive $3.5 billion.

This would have been enough, all else aside, to have brought our payments close to balance last year. But, over the same period of time, the outflow of private capital rose by $2.3 billion, with $1.9 billion of this increase occurring in 1964 alone, when the total outflow of U.S. private capital soared to well over $6 billion.

This marked a return to private capital outflows matching the scale of the second quarter of 1963, when the outpouring of funds was particularly heavy in the long-term portfolio capital area. Therefore, the interest equalization tax was proposed in mid-July of 1963 with highly successful results. In 1964, net sales of foreign securities to Americans were less than $700 million, one-third the rate in the six months prior to the interest equalization tax and virtually the same as the outflow four years ago.

But, in areas uncovered by the interest equalization tax, capital outflows in 1964 were inordinately large. The expansion of long-term bank loans last year amounted to more than $900 million, almost $800 million above 1960 and about $300 million above 1963. At the same time, short-term bank credits rose by $1.5 billion in 1964, $500 million more than in 1960, and $750 million more than in 1963. In 1964, other short-term capital outflows, much of which represent temporary investment of corporate funds, were $200 million more than in 1960 and $500 million above 1963, despite our relatively successful efforts to keep our domestic money market rates in line with those abroad.

Direct investment abroad by American companies—for the most part in Canada and Europe—rose to $2.2 billion and exceeded the 1960 rate by more than $500 million and the 1963 rate by more than $300 million. A rise of about $300 million in other long-term capital outflows over the level of 1960 accounts for the remainder of the increase of $2.3 billion that has done so much to thwart our efforts to achieve balance.

There have been many signs of a further step-up in the already rapid pace of U.S. corporate investment in Europe. In the past four years, it is reported that there have been 2,500 new ventures in Europe by U.S. firms. Increasingly large sums have been spent as U.S. firms have bought into existing European enterprises. There is no question that U.S. investment in Europe is highly desirable, and we welcome a return flow of European investment here. But, the question necessarily arises as to how rapid a pace of new foreign investment we can afford at a time when our overall payments gap is so large.

Alongside these swelling capital outflows, American travel and tourist spending abroad last year was about $600 million higher than in 1960, 2½ times the corresponding rise in foreign travel outlays in this country. Thus, our travel deficit has grown by $350 million since 1960 and last year stood at over $1.6 billion.

---

[1] Omitted from this exhibit ; for document reference see note at end of this statement.

As a result of all these factors, our balance-of-payments deficit last year—in terms of regular transactions—was $3 billion, an improvement of only $900 million over 1960. We must do much better.

Deficits and foreign dollar holdings

We fully recognize that the private capital outflows that today are preventing the achievement of balance will eventually come back to us in the form of dividends, interest, and loan repayments. But the need is to bring our accounts into balance now, not at some indeterminate time in the distant future. To insure success, all areas of our payments must make their contribution. Consequently, to complement our success in improving other areas of our payments, we must now hold our outflows of private capital to levels that are consistent with the early achievement of equilibrium. Clearly, capital outflows surged well beyond those levels last year.

But while we must moderate our private capital outflow in view of the paramount national interest in achieving early equilibrium in our international payments, we must not forget that these outflows acquire valuable assets. Our net international creditor position is extremely large. Leaving aside all U.S. Government claims on foreigners, our private investments abroad, by themselves, exceed the total of foreign investment in the United States plus all other liabilities to foreigners by some $18 billion, and this figure is growing larger every year. This strong financial position is buttressed by our impressive ability to compete in world markets. Our commercial trade surplus is far and away the world's largest. Last year it was more than twice the size of West Germany's, the next largest.

Building on these solid elements of strength, there is ample justification for confidence in the future of the dollar. But the time has come when we must bring our balance-of-payments deficit to an early end and curtail the constant buildup of short-term liquid liabilities to foreigners. Of our total liabilities, the International Monetary Fund holds approximately $3 billion received in connection with the U.S. subscription to that institution, and these dollars do not of course represent a claim on our gold stock. Omitting the IMF holdings, foreign dollar holdings now amount to about $28 billion, roughly half of which is held by foreign governments and central banks and thus represents a direct claim upon our gold stock; the other half is held by private foreign banks, businesses, individuals, and nonmonetary international institutions.

Indeed, more than half of last year's $3.0 billion deficit was financed by an increase in private holdings of dollars, acquired voluntarily for commercial and other purposes. But, as our balance-of-payments deficit is now calculated, it makes no difference whether the increase in liquid dollar claims is held by foreign official institutions or by private holders and nonmonetary international institutions. If private dollar holdings were not counted as part of the balance-of-payments deficit but rather as a capital inflow—a method which parallels the course followed by other major countries—our balance of payments last year would have shown a deficit of only $1.3 billion, a $1 billion improvement over the 1963 deficit calculated on the same basis, as shown in Table 14 of Annex I.[1]

But, whatever way we calculate our deficit, further action is clearly required to speed up our progress toward equilibrium. Only by demonstrating that we are moving decisively in this direction can we insure that foreigners will continue to be willing to hold their large dollar balances.

In addition, we can and should encourage the continued investment of foreign officials funds in this country by extending the exemption from regulatory ceilings of the interest rates that our commercial banks can pay on time deposits of foreign governments and monetary authorities and certain international institutions. This exemption, originally enacted in October 1962, has proved its value in reducing calls on our gold stock. As matters stand, our banks have no authority to pay higher rates beyond next October. I urge approval of legislation to continue this exemption when, in due course, the matter is considered by your committee.

President Johnson's 10-point program

The pressing need at this time is to proceed promptly with the elimination of our deficit. Therefore, the President has called upon the American business-

---

[1] Omitted from this exhibit; for document reference see note at end of this statement.

man, upon the American banker, and indeed upon all Americans to join in a truly national effort to stem the outpouring of dollars abroad.

The President's program calls for a redoubling of our efforts to cut Government expenditures abroad and to expand exports. To narrow the tourist deficit, legislation is being requested to further limit the duty exemption for American tourists. Americans, as well as foreigners, are being encouraged to travel more in this country. In order to draw more investment from abroad, the President has requested new tax legislation to remove barriers to foreign investment in U.S. corporate securities.

The President has imposed the interest equalization tax on bank loans of one year or more under the authority of the Gore Amendment and is requesting legislation to extend the interest equalization tax through 1967, and to broaden its coverage to nonbank credit of one- to three-year maturity.

But the most significant element of the new program is not new legislation, important as that is, but rather the President's action to enlist the voluntary but vigorous cooperation of the business and banking community in cutting back sharply on the increasing outflow of dollars abroad. It is to this cooperative effort that we look for the greatest savings and the quickest results.

A week after the President's Balance-of-Payments Message was sent to the Congress, the President, together with Secretary Connor, Chairman Martin, and I, described our balance-of-payments situation to a group of distinguished business and financial leaders and outlined the nature of this voluntary program. I am sure they will respond to the challenge quickly and effectively.

The banks are being asked to hold their 1965 increase in foreign credits outstanding to 5 percent of the end-of-1964 level. A set of 14 guidelines, developed by the Board of Governors of the Federal Reserve System and published yesterday, sets forth procedures for implementing this program. These guidelines are designed so as to assure that needs for export credits and loans to less-developed countries will be met. This means that, over the coming months, bank loans to Western Europe will have to be reduced substantially. Within these general guidelines, it has been left up to each bank to decide how to direct its own activities.

Concrete evidence of the prompt cooperation of the banks is revealed in the data we received on their new commitments for loans of one year or more. These commitments to borrowers in developed countries totaled over $1.0 billion in the full year 1964. And, this year, in the period prior to the President's Message on February 10, commitments to developed countries amounted to about $500 million, of which some $180 million was for advance extensions of loans beyond their original 1966–67 maturity dates. But since February 10, reports of new loan commitments to borrowers from the developed countries have been negligible in amount, well under $5 million.

A somewhat similar approach is being followed in the case of the foreign lending and investing activity of nonbank financial institutions. However, in the case of these institutions, there are no guidelines for securities with final maturities of over five years, since that area is effectively covered by the interest equalization tax and by separate agreements governing the access of Canada and Japan to our capital markets.

Industrial corporations are also being asked to improve their individual balance-of-payments accounts. This means that companies whose earnings from abroad in the form of exports, dividends, royalties, fees, etc., have exceeded their capital outflows from the United States should strive to increase this surplus. Companies which had a deficit on these items should strive to reduce that deficit or turn it into a surplus. The prospects for the success of the President's program in the corporate area have been greatly enhanced by evidence that the Nation's top corporate executives are willingly assuming personal responsibility for their own company programs. In the corporate, as well as the financial areas of the President's program, there is to be no change in our overall policy of encouraging investment in the less-developed countries. A personal letter detailing what is expected will be sent later this week by the Secretary of Commerce to the heads of about 500 corporations, including all which are active abroad.

It would, however, be a mistake to expect the full impact of the program of voluntary restraint to be registered overnight. Data are still far too fragmentary to reveal whether or not the deficit for the first quarter will fall back to the levels characteristic of the first three quarters of last year. The information currently available to us, limited and incomplete as it is, suggests appreciable improvement over the fourth-quarter results and provides no basis whatsoever for the occasional rumors of a vastly enlarged first-quarter deficit.

The impact of the new program can also be seen in the current increase in Eurodollar rates, which indicates a decline in the supply of dollars in that market. Finally, the dollar has begun to strengthen significantly in the world's foreign exchange markets. All in all, it appears that we are off to a good start.

Since the President's new balance-of-payments program was not developed until mid-February, the complete first-quarter results, which will not be known until May, are likely to include some crosscurrents, with the favorable results of the new program only incompletely reflected in the overall total. But certainly by the second, and more fully by the third quarter of this year, we should be reaping very substantial dividends from the measures contained in the President's program.

What distinguishes all those measures, and the President's Message, itself, is the degree to which their success will draw upon the voluntary cooperation and support of American business and the American public. The President has set forth, for all to understand, the challenge that confronts us. Upon the response to this challenge rests the solution to a stubborn and difficult problem. I am confident that challenge will be met.

NOTE.—The annexes omitted from this exhibit are published in hearings before a subcommittee of the Committee on Banking and Currency, U. S. Senate, 89th Congress, 1st session, on the continuing deficits in our balance of payments and the resulting outflow of gold, Part 1, March 9, 1965, pages 14–39.

Exhibit 41.—Remarks by Under Secretary of the Treasury for Monetary Affairs Roosa, September 28, 1964, before the sixth annual meeting of the National Association of Business Economists, on the meaning of international financial cooperation

You have undoubtedly heard much in recent years about international financial cooperation. But you must also be wondering, from the newspaper accounts of the past two weeks, what happened to cooperation in Tokyo. To compound the confusion, I can assure you that the accounts were entirely accurate. Yet the answer I would give to that question, paradoxical as it may seem, is that this Tokyo experience has been one of the most striking evidences that has yet appeared of the strength and reliability of the international financial cooperation which now exists.

The differences expressed in Tokyo were not the unfortunate or accidental results of any failures of communication or of understanding. They were not the expression of suspicions or ambitions by one country or another. They were instead an open invitation to every interested person everywhere to begin to participate more fully, alongside the representatives of the various governments, in a fundamental analysis of some of the issues which have arisen as those governments have attempted, thus far behind closed doors, to survey the possible longrun course of the international monetary system.

The Minister or the Governor or the Chancellor or the Secretary who urged consideration of one possible line of thought or another at Tokyo did so knowing that there would be no impairment of the effective current functioning of the monetary system because one or another of them ventured to raise questions about the shape that system might take, or be moving toward, some years in the future. Each fully understood the profound concern of the other. Each recognized that the quality of any decisions that might be necessary in the future would be improved if there could be wider consideration of these various approaches inside and among all of the countries participating in the International Monetary Fund.

Each also knew that a thorough analysis of the current functioning of the system had just been completed by the International Monetary Fund, looking at the world as a whole, and by the so-called Group of Ten, looking at some of the additional special problems centering in the more industrialized countries. Each knew that, despite a number of genuine present needs for specific measures of improvement, there had been a unanimous finding that the basic structure of the system is sound, and its performance both healthy and flourishing. Moreover, every one of the principal actors on the Tokyo stage knew there was firm agreement that any unexpected crisis which might threaten to impair the smooth and sustained functioning of the international monetary system could and would be met and overcome by utilizing facilities which were fully developed, tested, and agreed upon.

There was no danger now of any speculative unrest because Ministers revealed, with an invitation to public debate, the differences they had discovered in their private discussions. This is what I mean, then, when I say that the open discussion of important differences in monetary analysis and in possible prescriptions for the future, as this occurred in Tokyo, was in fact a reassuring demonstration of the solid strength on which our arrangements for international financial cooperation are now based.

I will not try today to restate, nor to elaborate upon, the differences in diagnosis that were brought forth in Tokyo. I would like to take a brief look, with you, at the nature and meaning of the kind of international cooperation we have been evolving in the financial area. To do that leads, initially, to a look at some of the developments that have brought about this new emphasis upon international financial cooperation. Then, after some further explanation of what the cooperation actually consists of, perhaps I can make a little clearer the reasons why the debate which has now been initiated fits so well into the current phase in the evolution of that cooperation. Or, to put all this another way, if I may use the rather terrifying jargon of internationally negotiated language, I want to make a few comments, first, about "multilateral and bilateral credit facilities," then second, about "multilateral surveillance," and third, about the possible place of additional methods for the "creation of owned reserves."

Fortunately, I have to make some other speeches on these matters over the next few weeks, so I will save a few thousand words for those efforts and will not actually try to keep you here until sundown, as perhaps you might apprehensively have suspected from this outline.

I.

The impetus to increased use of the International Monetary Fund, and to increasingly active bilateral operations among those leading countries whose performance can have wide repercussions upon the trade and payments of the world as a whole, came with currency convertibility at the end of 1958. The entire drive of the postwar period, through the successive miracles of reconstruction and renewed development, was toward a world of greater freedom for trade and payments among nations. The unprecedented flourishing of prosperity during these two postwar decades testifies that the decision to move in this direction has been sound and that the potential to be realized by freeing the forces of the marketplace is enormous. But the problem has been, as new strands created by the international division of labor wove increasingly complex patterns of economic relations among countries, to find and accept workable standards for normative behavior. A lunge toward full freedom meant chaos or anarchy. Yet the drive toward it had to be kept in motion. Quite understandably, it was to money—or, more broadly, to liquidity arrangements—the common denominator of economic affairs, that the world turned for some of its needed answers.

The world had already, at Bretton Woods in 1944, discarded the discredited concept of an automatic gold standard. In creating, and adhering to, the International Monetary Fund, the countries of a free trading world were declaring that international economic relations could no longer, in realistic practice, be guided by simple adherence to a system of rather rigid rules. No one was willing to repeat the turbulent history of the post World War I period, when that kind of system, trying to function within a modern environment, brought the gold standard crisis of the early 1930's, the shattering depression which followed, "beggar-my-neighbor" trade policies, and eventually open economic warfare. Instead, the need after World War II was for a system of guidelines and facilities, flexibly utilized under a rule of reason. In the monetary field, that need was to be met by the International Monetary Fund.

The Fund introduced for the first time, on an organized and fully multilateral basis, the principle of reliance upon credit facilities to supplement the use of gold and the dollars, sterling or francs that had become imbedded in the "owned reserves" of various countries. In the IMF system, provided that a given country's reserves came under pressure because of unusual seasonal developments, or because its cyclical phasing differed from that of many other countries with whom it had extensive trade or because its own growth pace had imposed strains that would require some time to relieve, the Fund could furnish credit for a period of three to five years in order to help bridge over the needed adjustments. As a country's drawings became larger, in relation to its size as reflected in Fund quotas, the degree of scrutiny and advice from the Fund would be intensified, and interest charges would rise. This could provide the needed measure of discipline as a substitute for the grotesque and grueling "contraction into balance" that the old gold standard, or presumably and purely automatic arrangement, would impose in today's world.

The questions for the further future, once the Fund began to meet the tests of widespread convertibility, were whether its own resources were adequate, whether facilities for the use of such resources on a fully multilateral basis could be suitably adapted to the full range of differences in relations among individual countries that might emerge, and whether the Fund itself or any possible supplementary arrangements could preserve the element of discipline which must still be retained if the new resources were to be kept revolving from one use to another and not drained permanently into the continuing deficits of particular countries which proved unable or unwilling to keep their external accounts, over time, in balance.

What soon became compellingly clear, once most of the leading countries were convertible (at least on current account), was that money was now much easier and freer to move than goods or people or fixed capital. Whenever differences might then develop among countries, in the pace, or even in the composition, of their continuing advance, or in their capacity and readiness for trade, the compensating action could ordinarily be expected to occur first through the movements of short-term funds. And since the underlying causes of such movements at the time were often difficult to discern and slow to appear, there was a ready propensity for a movement of funds in any direction, once started, to become cumulative. Moreover, the mere existence of free and open markets in foreign exchange required the presence of private speculators, performing their accustomed role in a free and flexible market, so that sensitive market facilities for the transmission of capital flows quite naturally and indeed necessarily developed.

In these circumstances, it was appropriate, in 1961, to question whether not only the facilities, but even more importantly, some of the "rules of the game" provided by the International Monetary Fund were fully adequate to the new conditions. The answer then found was that a number of the leading industrial countries, whose currencies had become (or were about to become) convertible, would have to accept an increasing degree of special responsibility. They would among themselves have to assure the adequacy of resources available to the International Monetary Fund in the event that others among them encountered heavy need to draw on the Fund, most notably the United States. That is why the so-called Group of Ten was established to provide, within the framework of the Fund, the General Arrangements to Borrow, making up to $6 billion equivalent in additional resources available to meet the needs of these countries, in the large magnitudes that such needs might reach, without impairing the capacity of the Fund to meet at the same time the current needs of any of its other members.

It followed from this recognition of common interest and special responsibility that the individual countries should attempt, as possibilities appeared, to develop additional arrangements for meeting and financing payments flows among themselves, in an effort to reduce somewhat the direct burden that might have to be carried, in the event of more lasting needs, through the Fund. With the United States, throughout this period of convertibility, having moved into substantial deficit, it had perhaps the broadest opportunities for the development of new and flexible bilateral payments arrangements, in conjunction with other interested countries. The U.S. effort centered, quite properly, on the handling of those aspects of its requirements that might be comparatively short lived or reversible. At the same time, as situations occurred in which these bilateral facilities could suitably be introduced, attention was also given to the possibility that these same arrangements might be used by other countries to meet heavy or unusual needs of their own. And indeed, over the past three or more years, the actual magnitude of the use of the new bilateral facilities has been greater for meeting the unusual needs of other countries participating in these arrangements than it has been for the United States itself.

Paralleling the increase in reliance upon the IMF as the source of multilateral credit facilities, and as the working center of the international monetary system, and accompanying the more recent elaboration of bilateral credit facilities, there have been the continued large balance-of-payments deficits of the United States. While these deficits have poured billions of dollars into the outright, or owned, reserves of many countries, there must be no doubt that the phase of large U.S. dollar deficits is nearing its end. That is a principal reason why the present phase in the evolutionary progress of the monetary system calls for increasing reliance upon credit rather than upon owned reserves, and upon cooperation rather than upon unilateral action by us or any country.

As Secretary Dillon so forcefully emphasized at Tokyo, this is now the time to make greater use of the whole range of credit facilities, multilateral and bilateral, that form such an important part of the liquidity spectrum, while digesting and redistributing the large volume of owned reserves that has already been created. If that pattern is followed, as seems widely expected at least for the next few years, then it is indeed necessary, in our interest and that of the Group of Ten and of the IMF as a whole, that all countries understand and use, as appropriate, the facilities which those of us who were "Deputies of the Ten" have felicitously titled "multilateral surveillance."

II.

It was not altogether clear at first that a continuing role would be found for bilateral financial arrangements in the form of swaps, or forward operations, or the acquisition of foreign currencies on open account by the United States itself, or by other countries, or for the issuance by the United States of bonds denominated in other currencies. But enough had been accomplished with these facilities by the autumn of 1963 to raise a question as to the need for finding some way of keeping such bilateral arrangements subject to a general review and appraisal by the other countries which were most directly affected by them, and which were most likely to be involved in them because of the strength and wide-spread use of their own currencies.

Such appraisal had, in various informal ways, already begun to evolve at the monthly meetings of the Bank for International Settlements attended by the various central bank governors and their principal associates. A parallel opportunity had been found within the OECD through the establishment of a limited membership group known as Working Party 3, in which responsible representatives of most of these same governments and central bank representatives could participate in a full review of their balance-of-payments positions, the interactions between these and domestic economic policies, the progress being made toward equilibrium, and the methods being used by each to finance its external deficit, or carry its surplus. In addition, the creation of the General Arrangements to Borrow had itself prompted meetings two or three times a year among the Finance Ministers and Central Bank Governors of the 10 countries to assure that the evolving situation was kept in view by all of them in order that they would be ready and able to act promptly in the event of need.

It was out of the combined results of these frequent contacts, and the unprecedented opportunities they gave responsible officials to know more about current developments affecting the economic policies and foreign economic position of each other, at first hand, that programs of special action have evolved for providing a tight ring of defenses around all the world's leading currencies. These made possible the almost instantaneous activation of resources to meet and withstand the series of potential speculative crises that have occurred over the past several years, including the Canadian dollar crisis in mid-1962, the threatened crisis at the time of the Cuban confrontation in October 1962, the shock of the President's assassination in November 1963, and the possibility of imminent crisis in the Italian foreign exchange market in March 1964. Over most of this period, since late in 1961, a number of the same countries have also been able to carry out joint operations in the London gold market, discouraging harmful speculation and encouraging a maximum flow of newly produced gold into official reserves rather than into speculative private hoards.

These are the concrete, creditable, and conspicuous results of the cooperation. But the needs to be met by the world's monetary system are not only those calling for protection against crisis, as important as such protection is. There are also regular needs for provision of the means of payment used in carrying on the daily transactions of a growing and diversifying world. And the potential for international financial cooperation extends beyond the averting of calamity to the helpful improvement of facilities for settling the net differences among nations that result from the conglomerate of their everyday trade and payments.

To generalize broadly, most of the direct uses thus far made by other countries of the new bilateral facilities have been to forestall crisis; most of the uses thus far made by the United States have been to smooth out the patterns of balance-of-payments settlements, both between ourselves and other countries and among other leading countries which make their settlements in dollars. Bilateral credit facilities can now be used, in the ordinary course (and distinct from crisis situations), as temporary supplements to the settlements which nations make by using, or by adding to, their own reserves of gold and foreign exchange. Bilateral credit facilities can also be used to reduce in some measure the recourse which countries have to make to the International Monetary Fund, in calling upon multilateral credit facilities to help settle balance-of-payments accounts.

Before we jump to the conclusion that we have discovered the Aladdin's lamp of liquidity, however, we had best remember that credit of any kind, however extended, is in fact a claim upon the real resources of whomever extends the credit. That is why it is impractical to expect that there can ever, on any massive scale, be "fully automatic" credit facilities on which countries in balance-of-payments deficit may freely draw. The ultimate decision as to whether or not additional credit can safely and usefully be extended must remain with the creditor himself.

That fact, and the rapid recent increase in the use of bilateral facilities, has made all of us aware of the need for a critical evaluation, of the kind just conducted by both the Fund and the Ten. We had to determine whether, and if so, how, to regularize and carry forward what has been so successfully achieved, ad hoc, in these few recent years. That is why the United States has, from the beginning, been scrupulous in publishing, as soon after each event as prudence would permit, the full record of its operations. That is where, now, "multilateral surveillance" comes in.

Multilateral surveillance is essentially a means for improving the information available concerning the credit extended and the debt contracted by the leading industrial countries in the course of carrying their surpluses or financing their deficits. Quite obviously, the volume of trade and capital transactions of the countries in the Group of Ten, now happily joined for this purpose by Switzerland (which is not a member of the International Monetary Fund), can, if they move seriously out of alignment, have grave repercussions on the functioning of the world economy as a whole. Detailed, confidential and systematic exchanges among these countries are clearly essential. In effect, what the Ten (or eleven) countries are now providing through their arrangements for multilateral surveillance is a sort of international credit interchange bureau.

To assure efficient and informed processing of this information the Ministers and Governors of the Ten have called upon the management of the Bank for International Settlements, which has agreed to perform these services. To assure full access, in suitably confidential form, to the management of the International Fund, representatives of the Fund have participated in all stages of the development of these new arrangements, and senior officials of the Fund, including where appropriate the Managing Director himself, will participate in any review and appraisal of the information being gathered.

Discussions based on this information will occur, as they have informally for a number of years, among the Central Bank Governors and their associates attending the monthly meetings of the BIS in Basle. Critical analysis by representatives of the various governments will occur as the new and regularized flow of information is made available to Working Party 3 of the OECD, on which, for example, I represent the United States, accompanied ordinarily by a senior spokesman for the Department of State, the Council of Economic Advisers, and, of course, the Federal Reserve System.

I was asked at a press briefing a few weeks ago, when the Group of Ten statement [1] of August 10 was published, whether multilateral surveillance meant that the countries involved would be giving us more advice than in the past. My reply then, and I think it is still fully applicable, was: "It would be hard to say that either they or we could give or get more advice than we have had in the last few months. This only means that, as the advice is being exchanged, the information base on which it rests is a little more assured and a little more current." And indeed it is in keeping each other more systematically informed concerning the flows that are taking place, as well as concerning the compensating action which one country or another initiates, that the procedures under "multilateral surveillance" will make their major contribution.

As you well know, a great variety of private capital movements, in addition to movements of official funds, are constantly exerting an impact both upon official reserves and upon commercial balances in the major countries. Some of these capital flows are equilibrating in nature, some are disequilibrating, some are seasonal, some are speculative. Current approximations as to the basic balance-of-payments implications for the various countries can be reached much more rapidly, and we in the United States can reach our own conclusions as to what they mean for us and the position of the dollar with much greater assurance, if we can have promptly available the best results that the responsible authorities

---

[1] See 1964 annual report, exhibit 49.

of each country can produce, in attempting to distinguish between those movements of their own funds which represent true settlements of current transactions, those which represent long-term investment, and those which may be speculative or capricious.

Multilateral surveillance involves the creation of no new institution, but rather the strengthening of activity already underway, and the establishment of facilities for expediting and standardizing the flow of information among the Group of Ten (or eleven) countries. It does not, indeed could not, require multilateral approval of particular transactions. It will not occasion delay in any foreign exchange transactions or the activation of swap arrangements. For it is the speed and flexibility with which these facilities have been used that have given international monetary cooperation its remarkable record of recent achievement.

It will be possible, as a result of the newly improved procedures, however, for any of the countries to take better stock of the financial factors affecting its own position as a basis for determining its own individual course of action, not merely in extending credits or arranging to obtain them, but more importantly in formulating its own national economic policies with a view to furthering its own adjustment toward balance-of-payments equilibrium. And this orderly exchange of information will, as Secretary Dillon said at Tokyo, avoid any risk that a participating country "might drift into heavy and continuous reliance upon such essentially short-term credit facilities, delaying too long the necessary corrective action that should be taken to adjust its balance of payments."

III.

It was not multilateral surveillance that occasioned the differences at Tokyo. Those differences related to steps that might be taken at some time further on in the future, not in connection with the use of credit facilities, but in finding new ways to create actual, or owned, reserves. I have promised you a word of explanation as to why the expression of these differences came so fittingly at the current phase in the evolution of the international monetary system, when we are not in fact concerned by any shortage of owned reserves on a global basis but are instead pressing to improve the distribution of existing primary reserves, through the Fund and bilaterally.

The answer, bluntly abbreviated, is that the various approaches now being utilized for the elaboration of credit facilities can, if we watch them closely, furnish important evidence bearing upon the other kind of choice that may have to be made in later years. Let me illustrate by briefly characterizing two of the more prominent positions expressed as to the future creation of owned reserves.

The United States, without pegging itself to an absolute commitment, would genuinely prefer that any further additions to the world's arrangements for creating owned reserves be established within the International Monetary Fund. We would, at least in our present thinking, like to see any such development, if it occurs, evolve out of practices with which countries are already familiar in the Fund. We would hope it could represent, step by step, comparatively modest changes toward what might, of course, in time prove to be a major change in the composition of the world's monetary reserves.

By contrast, the French and some other countries believe that it will eventually be necessary to make a clean start, in deliberately displacing or replacing what we have, by consciously and explicitly creating something that is truly new. Their suggestion for the establishment of a composite reserve unit would involve a contribution by several of the leading industrial countries, putting agreed amounts of their own currencies into a common pool. Shifts among the participating countries in their claims on this pool would then be linked by a fixed ratio to gold transfers among these same countries. The ratio would naturally be changed as the participating countries altered the volume of composite reserve units. This is the heart of the French suggestion. Details might be spelled out in many ways, just as there are many variants for possible creation of owned reserves through the International Monetary Fund. No one, so far as I know, has an unalterable position on any of these matters. But we have taken clear initial positions in order to make certain that the relevant issues will in fact be thoroughly debated and analyzed as logically and fully as major decisions of this significance deserve.

I am sure you already see, with me, the very interesting parallels between this debate over the future creation of owned reserves and the pattern of experimentation that is now being followed as we proceed in the current phase toward elaboration of credit facilities. For we have today, as the principal source of credit facilities and the major guardian of the financial conscience of the world, the Interntional Monetary Fund. But we have also found, as time went on, that there was some place for purely supplemental arrangements among countries whose special needs might be adapted to special techniques, while yet adhering consistently to the Fund itself. And we are now initiating additional arrangements for improving our performance with respect to those aspects of credit facilities that are centered in the Group of Ten.

None of us has as yet surrendered any sovereignty to the Group of Ten. None of us is bound to accept advice from the Group of Ten. Each of us is free to withhold or to grant credits in forms that come under multilateral surveillance. But we are gaining, every month and year, more experience in working together to meet some of the special problems that are, at least in a relative sense, unique among countries of the size and characteristics included in the Ten. How better then could we be poised for a testing, in practical and operational terms, of the various kinds of considerations that are certain to arise in the studies of reserve asset creation?

The monetary authorities, and those interested in monetary affairs, in all countries are in a fortunate position. Our studies are going forward, *pari passu*, with the testing of some of the important premises on which a choice, among the various results of the studies, may ultimately depend. It is an exciting, in some ways an unprecedented, opportunity for rational progress in organizing international economic relations. It is one in which, I know, every economist will want to participate. The debate is on; I hope you will all join in.

Exhibit 42.—Remarks by Under Secretary of the Treasury for Monetary Affairs Roosa, October 14, 1964, at the conference on "International Financing—1964" of the National Industrial Conference Board, Inc., on the future of the international monetary system

I.

Following the recent annual meetings of the Bank and Fund in Japan, some of my colleagues were able to visit Kyoto, the ancient capital of our host country, for a little longer than I. They came back particularly fascinated with a rock garden they had seen there, created more than 450 years ago by an artist who fused aesthetic experience with a striking reflection of the philosophy of his Zen-Buddhist religion. For he created a garden consisting solely of 15 rocks, of widely varying shape, located in a rectangular bed of fine stones. He so placed the 15 rocks that the viewer can never see more than 14 of them, no matter from what angle he approaches the garden. Anyone viewing the garden, I am told, always has a sense or awareness of something more than meets the eye.

Without that artistry, many of us have had a similar experience in the course of the past year's study of the international monetary system, on which the Tokyo meetings were so largely concentrated. For not only the reports published in August by the International Monetary Fund and by the Group of Ten,[1] but also virtually every address or comment at the meetings, reflected an awareness, not often explicit, of something else, essential to the whole, which most of us now consider as certain and secure as the 15th stone of the garden at the Ryoanji shrine. It went without saying at Tokyo that the price of gold, having been fixed for three decades at $35 per ounce, is now taken as the cornerstone of the international monetary system.

The world has long since, to be sure, left behind the simplicity and the rigidity of the older "pure" gold standard. But men everywhere continue to acknowledge, or to sense, the need for a fixed reference point to which all other currencies and measures of value can be related. After a succession of disastrous experiences related to changes in the gold price itself, the world has since 1934 come to accept the limiting constraint of a fixed price of gold, while building upon that base an expanding structure of money and credit to support the almost

---

[1] See 1964 annual report, exhibit 49.

incredible growth that the world has since experienced, both in physical production and in population.

While the process of economizing on the use of gold has certainly also involved some slippage, as many world prices have moved upward, the readiness and ability of the United States to maintain the convertibility of its dollar for gold at the fixed maximum price has remained as a firm anchor, to which one currency after another has been tied (through convertibility with the dollar) as countries have sought to exert meaningful and general control over their own price developments in the quest for monetary stability.

II.

Needed expansion in the liquidity that has been available for the world at large, since World War II, has come in three ways. (1) Gold supplies have themselves increased, but even more importantly, gold holdings have been massively redistributed from the United States to other countries. (2) Dollars, and to some extent sterling, and for some areas the French franc, have provided reserves that many countries could hold alongside gold, or as a substitute for gold, in their central monetary institutions, reserves which both supported the necessary internal expansion of money and credit and also provided the means of payment for settling the net balance of accounts between each country and the world outside. (3) As a further supplement to gold and reserve currencies, the International Monetary Fund since World War II has been providing a form of multilateral credit facility, through which additional use could be made of the existing supplies of gold, or reserve currencies, or even of other convertible currencies as these gained in strength and acceptability.

Viewed against the pace of monetary advance over the past century, the range and flexibility of the additional liquidity made available since World War II has been remarkable. But within the past four or five years still another phase has been reached in this monetary evolution. Spurred by the existence of large and continuing deficits in the U.S. balance of payments, but by no means necessarily related to the existence or continuance of such deficits, an impressive new array of bilateral credit facilities has also been developed. Through these credit facilities, countries whose currencies have reached a stage of worldwide usability have joined with the United States, in effect, to make still more intensive use of the existing supplies of international monetary reserves. They have, if I may make a loose analogy to the nomenclature of Irving Fisher's old equation, added to the M' and the V' of the world's monetary system.

In a moment, I want to turn with you to the statistical tables included in the *Ministerial Statement* that has been distributed to each of you, in order to note more systematically the way in which this array of gold, reserve currencies, multilateral credit facilities, and bilateral credit facilities has now developed. But all of that will only serve as an introduction for the special attention I would like to draw, today, toward what may become a still further stage in the evolution of the international monetary system—that in which, supplementing all we now have, there may by international agreement be further arrangements introduced for creating additional primary reserves. This would mean the introduction of some additional form of internationally acceptable reserve asset which countries could hold alongside the gold, or the dollars, or other foreign exchange or other claims which now meet the "owned reserve" part of global liquidity requirements.

Not because the need for added creation of reserve assets is actually upon us, but because any deliberate innovation in the monetary field must be carefully studied well in advance, both the International Monetary Fund and the associated Group of Ten (that is, 10 of the leading industrialized countries with the participation of Switzerland) are looking more closely at this question. Pushing beyond their studies of the past year, which appraised the present functioning of the international monetary system, they intend now to analyze the potentialities for the actual creation of additional owned reserves, whenever such need may arise in the future. If anything ever comes of all this, it will be the closest approach to successful alchemy that the world has yet attempted. The implication of any decisively new arrangements could be far-reaching for the functioning of every money-using economy, but particularly for the free world. That is why this is no matter for swift, or precipitate, or sentimentalized decision. It requires long and careful study, to be followed by extensive and extended negotiation. No one need apologize for taking time for appraisal where the money that men believe in, and rely upon, is involved.

III.

It is not only useful in evaluating what we now have, but also in sorting out some of the possible lines on which actual reserve creation might proceed in the future, to step aside for a moment to look at the tables to which I have just referred from the *Ministerial Statement*.[1] Tables I and II are condensed summaries, the first showing overall changes in international liquidity for the decade which ended at the close of 1963; the second shows the changes over the four years ending on the same date, the period when most of the bilateral credit facilities were introduced. Tables III and IV cover the same two spans of time, but show much more detailed breakdowns among groupings of countries. While I would like to commend these tabulations to much wider attention and deeper study than any of us have yet been able to give them, I can today only highlight the analysis that these data suggest by referring to the column headings which are, of course, the same across the top of each of the four tables.

As you see, the liquidity available in the world today is fairly easily divided between reserves, which are owned outright and are readily usable by the holder, and "credit facilities," which in effect provide ways for some countries to lend existing reserves to other countries, directly or through an international institution, in order to meet particular needs for monetary reserves. The reserves themselves, as shown by the column headings, include not only the traditional forms of holdings in gold and foreign exchange with which most of us have long been familiar, but they also include other forms that are becoming increasingly important. Some countries, for example, already consider their so-called gold tranche claims on the Fund (column 4) as a part of their foreign exchange reserves. However, treated statistically, these drawing rights are clearly close alternatives to gold or outright holdings of foreign exchange.

The gold tranche consists, of course, not only of the drawing rights acquired by countries when they pay gold into the Fund as a part of their quota subscriptions, but it also includes those drawing rights acquired by a country when its own currency has been made available by the Fund to some other country in need of credit. This latter type of asset, known colloquially as the "super gold tranche," is usable, like the gold tranche itself, virtually on demand by the country whose currency has previously been paid out by the Fund. Moreover, unlike a drawing in the regular gold tranche, such a drawing in the super gold tranche need not be repaid. What this means is that whenever German marks or Dutch guilders or French francs, for example, are drawn by some country from the Fund—and the drawing is not offset through repayment of the same currencies by some other country discharging an earlier debt to the Fund—then Germany or the Netherlands or France has, in effect, added to its own reserves. It has acquired a super gold tranche equal to the net amount of its own currency drawn from the Fund.

It is not only through the Monetary Fund, however, that our existing arrangements for credit facilities are already capable of providing countries with a usable reserve asset. For the bilateral facilities developed more recently may create similar kinds of claims. Column 5 refers to special bonds that the United States, as a reserve currency country, has sold to ready buyers among the monetary authorities abroad. These bonds, while initially denominated in Italian lire, for example, and purchased by the Italian monetary authorities from the United States, can in case of need be virtually transferred to, say, the German Bundesbank, being reissued in that event in German marks. Transfers of exactly this kind occurred last spring, when the Italian authorities were able to use these assets, acquired in an earlier period of Italian surplus, to help finance a deficit in their accounts that was running strongly in the direction of Germany.

A somewhat similar effect is obtained through the reserves noted in column 6. For when the United States draws on a swap line, previously arranged with Switzerland, for example, the Swiss National Bank obtains a corresponding

---

[1] The tables referred to were reproduced in the 1964 annual report, pages 357–64.

claim on our own Federal Reserve. At the least, the Swiss National Bank can be certain that it will come into additional funds when the United States pays off the swap on maturity and, for that reason, could carry its claim for future reversal of the swap as a sort of reserve asset. But the usability of the claim is even greater than that. If for any reason Switzerland should want to use some part of these dollar swap claims, it can draw at will, though of course after mutual consultation, against the balances set up to its credit at the moment the Federal Reserve initially activated its own drawing of Swiss francs under the swap arrangement.

This quick attempt to summarize the concepts lying behind these columns of figures may be more confusing than clarifying, but the essential point comes out if you glance with me at the bottom row in Table I. What this shows is that little more than one-fifth of the total growth in world liquidity during the decade from 1953–63 was provided by net increases in the monetary holdings of gold, although, as I have already mentioned, a significant redistribution of those holdings did also occur. A substantially larger part of total reserves, and of liquidity, came from added holdings of foreign exchange, which over this decade consisted almost entirely of dollars. But gold and foreign exchange together (column 3) still only accounted for but slightly more than one-half of the total growth in liquidity shown in column 19. Actually, the other forms of additions to reserves, mainly reflecting the fact that IMF quotas were increased about midway in this decade, provided more than $3 billion of the total change in reserves, representing roughly half as much as the growth of gold itself as a component of total reserves.

Some $10 billion, or a little more than one-third of the total growth in liquidity, came however, from credit facilities that were superimposed upon the supply of actual reserves. These credit facilities divide logically into two kinds, those which have been fully negotiated and are available, at least for short-term use, virtually on call, and the others which would be available only on the basis of some further negotiation, although all necessary legal authorization on the part of any countries concerned would have been completed. On a rough basis, assured arrangements, mainly in the form of agreed swaps that were not actually in use at the end of 1963, accounted for about one-third of the increase in liquidity brought about through credit facilities, and credits potentially available through the International Monetary Fund, although still subject to some negotiation if and when need might arise, accounted for about two-thirds of the increase in credit facilities.

It is against the background of this pattern of evolution in the development both of reserves and of credit facilities over the past decade that we must orient our thinking in looking ahead toward the next decade and beyond. The decisions taken in Tokyo give assurance that another major advance in the supply of credit facilities will be formally approved sometime next year, as increases aggregating $4 billion to $5 billion are established in the quotas of member countries in the Fund. Alongside this development, the arrangements agreed upon by the Group of Ten, as summarized in the *Ministerial Statement*,[1] assure the further elaboration and use of bilateral credit facilities. These, joined with whatever modest further gains may occur in holdings of gold, or of foreign exchange, assure a reasonable adequacy in the global supply of liquidity, and in the access to liquidity, over the next few years.

What the Fund and various governments will be studying, however, and what we want to encourage in the financial, business, and academic communities, is consideration of the methods that might be appropriate, if we reach a stage in which purposive further additions are to be made in owned reserves; additions that would be reflected in column 9 of our various tables, whether or not they were specifically identified with the items embraced in any of the preceding columns as we now know them.

IV.

The creation of a new reserve asset depends ultimately upon the readiness of the monetary authorities of various countries to accept a claim of some sort upon other countries as a suitable addition to their own reserves. Much of the

---

[1] See 1964 annual report, exhibit 49.

reserve asset creation thus far has rested upon the readiness of all, or at any rate most, countries to accept direct claims upon the reserve currency countries. Part, too, as we have seen in reviewing the tables, has arisen from the readiness of Fund members to accept claims upon the Fund.

There are not at present any other individual countries who are willing to accept the obligations and the exposure implied by serving alone as a reserve currency country. Nor is there any limited group of countries now prepared to act together to function in a manner comparable to the role fulfilled by the present reserve currencies. This means, so long as these national attitudes continue, that any different form of reserve asset creation in the future will probably have to occur through some kind of an international institution.

There are broadly three ways in which this further evolution, if it is to come about, might occur. One would be for a group of the leading industrialized countries to join together to form a collective or composite reserve unit. Various approaches of this kind have been suggested during the course of the Group of Ten discussions, most of them looking to the Bank for International Settlements to serve as the international institution at the center, in a manner somewhat comparable to the role it performed for the European Payments Union that evolved under the Marshall Plan. A second approach would rely instead upon the International Monetary Fund, permitting strong currency countries to deposit some amount of their currencies with the Fund, while the Fund in turn would put these into active circulation by making investments for its own account, for example, through purchasing bonds of the International Bank. A third approach, also centered upon the IMF, would give more explicit recognition as international reserve assets to the gold tranche and super gold tranche claims to which I have already referred in describing the tables.

Perhaps now we can glance somewhat more closely at each of the three approaches, recognizing that there are many variants of each and that adequate examination will require months and years, rather than a few minutes.

Composite or Collective Reserve Unit

The proponents of this approach regard it as a convenient form for, in effect, multilateralizing and making permanent some part of the money creation potential that is inherent in swap arrangements. Working through the BIS as a central clearing house, participating countries could deposit agreed amounts of their own currencies in a common pool and receive initially an equal amount of claims on the common pool. Or, conceivably, countries could deposit some part of their own existing holdings of gold with the BIS and receive claims on the resulting pool. In effect, each would be making entries on the books of its own monetary authority quite similar to those it makes in the case of any activated swap. In this case, it would give up some of its own currency and receive, instead of a specific claim on another currency, a generalized claim on all currencies being deposited in the pool.

Each of the countries participating in the pool would then presumably undertake, when in surplus, to accept such claims in settlement of its net balance-of-payments gains vis-a-vis the other participating countries, or to pay out such claims when in deficit. The actual procedures for settlement, and the equally important procedures for determining the amount of such pooled claims to be created, could, according to the proponents of this approach, be resolved in various ways. But when one attempts to begin to transcribe this appealingly simple concept into specific procedures, several serious problems begin to appear.

First, of course, there is the necessity of deciding which countries may be included in a select group of this kind. That also means determining, and agreeing upon, the criteria which would permit the addition of other countries, or require the exclusion of some, at a later time. Perhaps even more troublesome, doubts begin to arise concerning each other's internal policies, if countries are to be mutually dependent upon each other for the creation of an important part of their own primary reserves. Some may see a mutual interest in determining the relationship that should prevail between each country's holdings of reserves in the common pool and its own creation of internal credit. Perhaps such questions can be resolved without an impairment of sovereignty that would exceed realistic possibilities, but, even then, it seems already agreed, some aspects of the decision-making process would very likely have to depend upon a unanimous vote of the participating countries. There would, for example, probably have to be unanimous agreement on the total amount of Collective Reserve Units (CRU's) to be created and upon the shares that each country would have in the initial total of created assets. Similar agreement as to total and shares would appear to be needed whenever any subsequent increases might occur.

A second requirement that has been considered essential by many proponents is that, once issued, the holdings of the composite reserve unit should have a fixed relationship to the gold holdings of each of the participants. To be sure, a transition period would be contemplated, pending some further substantial redistribution of gold holdings among the participating countries. But from the very beginning, the transfers related to net current settlements among the participants would be made, so it is proposed, by payment or receipt of CRU's and gold in a fixed ratio. The ratio would be determined by the proportion which the total gold holdings of all participating countries would bear to the total of CRU's in existence.

If the CRU were to have been created at the end of 1963, for example, by the Group of Ten countries plus Switzerland, their combined gold holdings, as shown in column 1 of table I, were approaching $35 billion. If the group decided to begin by creating $1 billion equivalent of CRU's, then all net settlements among members of the group would proceed on the basis of $35 of gold and $1 of CRU claims. The United States in these circumstances would have to make net payments to any of the other countries, in this ratio, not only as a result of the direct balance-of-payments relations between the United States and that country, but also reflecting the net use of dollars by all other countries in the world, as they employed their dollar holdings to settle balances which they owed to any of the other members of the group.

A third requirement, implied by what I have already said, is that the actual use of the CRU's would be necessarily limited to members of the participating group. There would thus be no assurance that the aggregate of liquidity available to all other countries would remain adequate, merely because certain large countries at the center of the system were assuring an adequate volume of reserves for themselves. Nor could it be certain, given the apparent dependence upon a unanimity rule, that even the supply of CRU's would be increased adequately over time.

In effect, the present system which operates through a series of checks and balances, as countries acquire more of a particular kind of reserve asset than they might wish to hold, would be replaced by one clearly dependent upon a specified voting arrangement. There would be both the logic and the rigidity of clear-cut, voted decisions. One serious question is whether a monetary system, dependent both upon usage and upon confidence, and serving variable needs which have always in the past required the element of flexibility inherent in the relationship between money creation and credit extension, can be reduced entirely to a voting system, even if one could be devised without a unanimity requirement.

The countries that see a need for global constriction of reserves should be able to exert a clear influence upon the result, but one may question whether they individually or as a group should be able to exercise a full veto upon the views and needs of the countries which see scope for expansion. There might instead be a serious risk that countries in balance-of-payments surplus should, when their surpluses have continued long or become large, rely mainly upon their power to limit the world's money supply in order to try to achieve balance, rather than fully reexamining their potential for additional imports, for example, or for making capital exports. In such circumstances, any other advancing countries might suffer severe constraint or hardship, perhaps unnecessarily. There is, therefore, inherent in reliance upon a single definitive scheme, such as the CRU, the risk of placing too much dependence for the future upon precise control over the international money supply, a risk that most countries have long since learned to avoid in handling their own domestic affairs. At home, most countries instead attempt now to influence the entire spectrum of internal liquidity, and rely in fact upon the self-enforcing restraints of the credit-granting process.

I mention these risks frankly, and argumentatively, because that is the way to full and fruitful examination. I do not wish to imply that I, or anyone in the U.S. Government, considers the case for the CRU closed. I do think the necessary evaluation would be less than complete if questions of this kind could not be resolved before any future step toward a CRU were seriously considered.

Deposits and investments through the International Monetary Fund

One possible way around some of the difficulties just mentioned would be to establish a much looser arrangement, through which individual strong countries whose currencies are used by the Fund—subject to general conditions agreed upon by all members of the International Monetary Fund—could help further to satisfy the liquidity requirements of the international community. This might be for particular countries to make voluntary deposits of their own currency with the Fund (or alternatively, the Fund itself might borrow from such countries in their own currencies). Such deposits would be above the amounts of their currency required for their own quotas. The country could be given drawing rights comparable to those of the super gold tranche as "consideration" for the deposit, in accordance with the conditions agreed upon.

The additional resources thus obtained might, of course, be held by the Fund for use in meeting regular drawing requests. If this method should not prove sufficient to assure adequate liquidity for the rest of the world, at least in the form of owned reserves, the Fund might use these deposits of currencies, according to some agreed criteria, for making investments. The investments might flow to the assistance of many of the less-developed countries if the Fund were to purchase obligations, say, of the IBRD, which might perhaps in turn make some of its resources available to the International Development Association. Or another possibility, subject to a greater degree both of credit risk and of difficulty in allocation among countries, would be for the Fund to invest directly in the securities of certain countries, possibly countries with well-established securities markets.

There are, to be sure, serious risks on both sides of this suggestion, that is, both in terms of the deposit or similar borrowing arrangements and in terms of the investment possibilities. Agreement on criteria, and the necessity for periodic review and revision of the criteria, might also become an exercise in futility, leading to a stalemate or contraction in the supply of actually available liquid resources. Moreover, on the depositing side, great care would be needed to avoid making the deposits so attractive as to discourage efforts of surplus countries to bring their international accounts into balance or to deter member countries from accepting actual quota increases of an appropriate amount, such as the occasion of the regularly scheduled quinquennial Fund quota reviews. On the investment side, questions would certainly be raised as to the liquidity of the Fund itself, if it added potential short-term obligations, available virtually on call, while acquiring what might prove to be relatively illiquid investments of longer term. Moreover, such investments are likely to involve a greater loss potential, and there would have to be an adequate provision for this problem, if its new ventures were not to undermine the prestige it has thus far attained as the responsible and reliable center of the world's monetary system.

These are only a few of the risks. I have not even begun to mention the difficulties that would be encountered in establishing criteria. Nonetheless, I would no more wish to imply that these approaches should be dismissed than I would wish to suggest that the CRU no longer deserves careful attention and examination.

Creating reserves through existing Fund facilities

Whether or not either of the two preceding approaches proved practicable at some stage in the future, it is probably fair to say that any approach through the Monetary Fund is less likely than an entirely separate new entity to cause a divisive fragmentation among the monetary authorities of the various countries of the world. Action through the Fund is probably also much more likely to build upon, rather than to supplant, the existing currency and credit facilities in use in the international monetary system of today. That is an important consideration pointing toward a third, and more modest, possibility for introducing an additional element of reserve asset creation into the system. For this third possibility would build entirely on existing arrangements with a minimum of change and a maximum of continued reliance for settlement among countries through transactions in the actual currencies used in foreign exchange trading among the nationals of these countries. This third approach would simply be to make explicit a fuller reliance upon gold tranche rights as an actual part of the owned reserves of member countries of the Fund.

As I attempted to explain when we were looking at the tables, the so-called super gold tranche is already the result of a form of reserve asset creation, though we have all become familiar with its operation without many of us appreciating that reserve assets were actually being created. The monetary authorities of the United States, to be sure, have realized for some time that they had acquired $1.3 billion of a "hidden reserve" when other countries in the earlier postwar years drew that amount of dollars on balance from the Fund. And up through 1962, as we encountered heavy deficits, we financed a significant part of them through the use of that $1.3 billion as other countries made repayments to the Fund in dollars which might otherwise have remained outstanding as added liquid claims upon us, or perhaps have been used by receiving central banks to exercise their rightful claim to purchase gold from our monetary stocks.

Italy experienced the same usefulness of the super gold tranche when, as a part of its balance-of-payments financing earlier this year, a substantial part of the amount it drew from the Fund did not have to be repaid. For Italy's super gold tranche claim represented merely a taking back, for its own use, of resources that had already been put into the Fund when, in earlier years, other countries made drawings of lire from the Fund.

What may develop, then, over the years as more of the countries with usable currencies acquire larger quotas in the Fund, is that more of such countries, more of the time, will hold super gold tranche drawing rights in the Fund. These will represent additional highly liquid and fully transferable primary reserve assets from the point of view of the originating country. To those countries which have drawn these currencies from the Fund, they will represent foreign exchange holdings acquired on a borrowed basis, for use in meeting some of the swings in their balance-of-payments requirements for which liquidity of some kind had to be obtained. For this kind of expansion in reserve assets, nothing is needed save additional reliance upon the Fund and a relatively steady increase in the quotas of countries whose currencies can be used in Fund drawings.

But there is another way in which gold tranche claims can also be increased. It would be relatively simple, whenever the time seemed appropriate, to permit countries to pay all or a part of their gold subscriptions, in connection with a quota increase, through giving the Fund a callable claim on gold. Such a Fund claim on callable gold, corresponding to the customary business practice of subscribing capital that is not fully paid in, could be exercised by the Fund in accordance with agreed voting procedures. The right of making payment in whole or in part through gold certificates could be granted to countries according to agreed criteria of reasonable acceptability.

But before I get carried away with this particular version of the money-creating process, it is important to note that this, as any other form of money creation, can be possible only if it proceeds under arrangements and policies that will sustain confidence in the bank itself and in the currency which it issues: in this case the Monetary Fund and claims upon it. There are obvious and dangerous risks that would have to be provided against in the instituting of any arrangement of this kind. Agreed standards of eligibility for making payment in this form, and procedures for determining the Fund's need for calling up the gold, could become the subject of extensive and difficult negotiation. But, of course, there are risks of the same type in any effort to introduce a new method, beyond those methods with which the financial community is already fully familiar, for adding to the supply of created reserves that serves the international monetary system. The fundamental decision that will have to be taken, when the time is reached for actual consideration of such possibilities, is whether the gain, from following any of these possible lines, is worth the risk.

I have not today tried to face this final question. I am convinced that the students and the practitioners of international monetary finance will be greatly benefited by a thorough and extensive international debate on the pros and cons of proposals of the kind I have so briefly outlined today. Whether then to follow any variant of any of these approaches, and if so, when, can be best debated after much more progress has been made in sorting out the issues inherent in the various approaches themselves.

Exhibit 43.—Remarks by Under Secretary of the Treasury for Monetary Affairs Deming, April 29, 1965, at the Ohio State University, in connection with "Distinguished Lectures in Monetary Policy"

Fifteen days ago, the Prime Minister of Great Britain, Mr. Harold Wilson, devoted a section of his major public speech in New York to consideration of international liquidity. He took the view that the world should push forward promptly in comprehensive planning to avoid a liquidity squeeze which might result from the disappearance of the U.S. balance-of-payments deficit.

Some weeks ago, President de Gaulle suggested that the world should return to a gold standard system, and Mr. Jacques Rueff, a well-known French economist, has recently proposed the same course of action, with the additional suggestion that the price of gold be doubled in order that reversion to a gold standard system might take place without drastic deflationary consequences for the world economy.

The President of the German Bundesbank, Karl Blessing, recently endorsed the present international monetary system but suggested the possible desirability of standardizing the composition of national reserves by agreeing on an appropriate ratio between holdings of gold and reserve currencies.

Former Secretary of the Treasury Douglas Dillon in his last press conference suggested that one of the major questions with which his successor would have to wrestle would be that of the future adequacy of world liquidity. Secretary Fowler has agreed "that the greatest challenge in this area is to work out a steadily improving international monetary system so as to facilitate a continuing expansion of trade and economic development in the free world."

The U.S. position with respect to the liquidity issue has been made very clear by President Johnson, who said in his Message to Congress on the Balance of Payments:

"The measures I have proposed in this message will hasten our progress toward international balance without damage to our security abroad or our prosperity at home. But our international monetary responsibilities will not end with our deficit. Healthy growth of the free world economy requires orderly but continuing expansion of the world's monetary reserves.

"During the past decade, our deficits have helped meet that need. The flow of deficit dollars into foreign central banks has made up about half of the increase in free world reserves. As we eliminate that flow, a shortage of reserves could emerge. We need to continue our work on the development of supplementary sources of reserves to head off that threat.

"We must press forward with our studies and beyond, to action—evolving arrangements which will continue to meet the needs of a fast growing world economy. Unless we make timely progress, international monetary difficulties will exercise a stubborn and increasingly frustrating drag on our policies for prosperity and progress at home and throughout the world."

Today I would like to discuss with you just what it is that all of these distinguished people are talking about and why there is this general and widespread interest in international liquidity.

We might start with a very simple statement as to the purpose of international reserves. Their primary purpose is to permit a country to ride through any balance-of-payments deficit while making an orderly adjustment of its international and domestic policies to restore balance-of-payments equilibrium. In this, the purpose of international reserves is very similar to the purpose of individuals and businesses in setting aside and holding liquid assets for an emergency. A complication with which I shall not deal today is that international reserves in many countries play an additional role as partial determinants of the domestic money supply.

International reserves, of course, are not held in the same form as the reserves of a private business. The traditional reserves of nations are gold and reserve currencies. A reserve currency, if you will excuse the tautology, is a currency which, by general agreement, nations are prepared to hold in their reserves. The dollar is today the major reserve currency. The pound sterling is held rather widely, particularly by sterling area countries, and the French franc is regarded as a reserve currency in some parts of Africa. Each nation makes its own decision as to what it will regard as a reserve currency. It bases its decision on the extent to which that currency can be widely used in international transactions, the confidence it has in the stability of that currency in terms of gold and in terms of goods, and the ease with which it may invest and disinvest both its working balances and additional holdings of the currency in question.

The status of the dollar as a reserve currency developed over the years, particularly since the Second World War, from the voluntary decision of many countries that this was the currency which best met their needs as a reserve asset. The reserve currency status of the dollar is greatly buttressed by the fact that the United States is the only country which stands ready to deliver gold at the fixed price of $35 an ounce to foreign monetary authorities upon request.

But international liquidity has broader dimensions than gold and reserve currencies. When representatives of the Group of Ten leading industrial countries began a couple of years ago to study what has come to be called the "liquidity problem," they placed emphasis upon a broad liquidity spectrum which shaded from owned reserves through certain credit availabilities.

It was agreed that the first additional asset to be included in the broader liquidity concept should be the "gold tranche" position of member countries in the International Monetary Fund. The International Monetary Fund has 102 member countries, and each of these has a borrowing quota for which it has paid one-quarter in gold and three-quarters in its own national currency. As a result, one-quarter of its drawing or borrowing rights in the Fund are referred to as its "gold tranche" rights. Any member country is entitled to borrow from the Fund, virtually without question, any currency it may need up to the amount of its gold tranche position. There is general agreement, accordingly, that the aggregate of gold tranche positions in the Fund, amounting to approximately $4 billion, should appropriately be considered an element in international liquidity. I might mention parenthetically that such gold tranche positions will be increased to $5 billion when the 25-percent increase in Fund quotas now under way has been completed.

There are other forms of international credit about as liquid as gold tranche positions in the Fund. In the last four or five years, a network of short-term credit facilities has been created among monetary authorities and central banks of the highly industralized countries. These are generally referred to as "swap" lines. They consist of agreements that the authorities of one country will make its currency available to its swap partners up to agreed amounts, usually for an initial period of 90 days. If, for example, Italy should find itself in need of dollar currency, it could deposit lire to the account of the Federal Reserve System and the Federal Reserve System would deposit an equivalent sum in dollars to the credit of the Italian authorities. These agreements represent a highly liquid asset for the countries concerned. Swap lines can be activated on only a few hours' notice, and many of them have been so activated throughout the network in many directions in recent years. The total of swap agreements at the present time throughout the network amounts to more than $2½ billion.

Another substantial element in international liquidity is represented by special Government bonds which the United States has issued to certain of its creditors in recent years to help finance the U.S. balance-of-payments deficit. These may be denominated in the currency of the holder and are convertible at short notice by the holders into cash. Foreign currency bonds now outstanding amount to $1.1 billion. Foreign monetary authorities holding these bonds regard them either as part of their reserve assets or as an asset similar to reserves.

In considering international liquidity, it is also appropriate to take into account the availability of credit from the International Monetary Fund beyond the gold tranche positions. As I have said, one-quarter of a country's quota represents its gold tranche; three-quarters represents its drawing rights beyond the gold tranche. These borrowing rights are not so automatic as gold tranche drawing rights and, hence, not so highly liquid. Consequently, they are not generally regarded as reserves. However, they are available in accordance with well understood standards and have been widely used for many years. They represent an important element in total international liquidity.

The report[1] of the Deputies of the Group of Ten, released in August of last year, following their study, brought out several interesting points relative to the growth of international liquidity, as the report defined it, during the 10 years from 1954–63. As noted, they dealt with international liquidity as being a spectrum divided into two broad categories: "reserves" and "credit facilities."

---

[1] See 1964 annual report, exhibit 49.

The dividing line between these two closely related classifications was fixed in this manner. Credit availabilities that had not been utilized were, broadly speaking, treated as credit facilities, and these might be available to potential deficit countries in the future, subject to individual credit arrangements. Reserve assets represented the claims of creditor countries that had been established by the extensions of credit to others in the past on their part, through the International Monetary Fund or directly, and that could readily be mobilized for their own use in case they, in their turn, needed foreign exchange resources. This latter category included also the gold tranche claims on the Fund acquired by past subscriptions of gold to the IMF.

During the 10-year period, the reserves of all the countries in the free world rose about $17 billion or nearly a third. Gold accounted for nearly $6 billion. Foreign exchange, principally in the form of dollars and sterling, rose nearly $8 billion, and $3 billion was contributed by increased claims on the Fund and by the use of bilateral credit facilities.

You will note that only about a third of the total addition to reserves, defined broadly to include the reserve assets noted, was provided by gold. At the end of 1963, countries held in their reserves about $40 billion in gold or about 57 percent of the total reserves of $70 billion. Twenty-five billion dollars was held in the form of foreign exchange, one-half in sterling, and one-half in dollars. These foreign exchange holdings were official reserves and take no account of some $15 billion in liquid assets held by nonofficial private entities, almost entirely as claims in dollars or sterling.

Apart from the global picture, it is useful to pause a moment to look at the regional aspects of this growth in reserves. During the 10-year period, the 8 major nonreserve currency countries of the Group of Ten and Switzerland acquired $18½ billion of reserve assets, or $1½ billion more than the world as a whole. This group of countries includes the major part of a persistent surplus area in continental Europe, which has had an unexampled prosperity and an unprecedentedly strong balance-of-payments position. Moreover, this group of countries acquired nearly $11 billion in gold, nearly twice the total of new gold supplies available for monetary use in the world as a whole. They were able to do so through a substantial redistribution of the gold reserves of the United States.

This was the pattern of the 10 years prior to the study undertaken by the Group of Ten in 1964. Against this pattern, the Ministers and Governors concluded that, "For the international monetary system as a whole, supplies of gold and reserve currencies are fully adequate for the present and are likely to be for the immediate future. These reserves are supplemented by a broad range of credit facilities. The continuing growth of world trade and payments is likely to entail a need for larger international liquidity. This need may be met by an expansion of credit facilities and, in the longer run, may possibly call for some new form of reserve asset."

The Ministers and Governors of the Group of Ten then took several decisions looking toward the future of the monetary system. They undertook a thorough study of the measures and instruments best suited for avoiding and correcting large and persistent international imbalances, compatibly with the pursuit of essential internal objectives. They recommended a procedure for "multilateral surveillance" of the ways and means of financing balance-of-payments disequilibria. Looking further into the future, since there was a possibility that the supply of gold and foreign exchange reserves may prove to be inadequate for the overall reserve needs of the world economy, they authorized a study group to examine various proposals regarding the creation of reserve assets either through the IMF or otherwise. Finally, they agreed that they would support a moderate general increase in quotas of the IMF.

It might be asked why there was so much concern regarding the future of international liquidity when reserves had increased so rapidly in the previous 10 years. The eight members of the Group of Ten and Switzerland nearly tripled their reserves during the 10-year period, 1954–63. In fact, some of these countries consider that the growth in their reserves has been excessive and been a contributing factor to inflationary pressures on the European Continent. Thus, they are particularly concerned that the growth in reserves not be excessive in the future, as a result of continuing deficits in the U.S. balance of payments.

At the same time, they join with the United States in recognizing that there may be conditions in the future, given the remarkably vigorous expansion of world trade and investment, when annual supplies of new monetary gold would alone be insufficient to provide an adequate secular growth in reserves. You will recall that new gold supplied only about one-third of the 10-year growth in reserve assets.

The United States also looks forward to a changing situation; it is not in our interest to continue substantial balance-of-payments deficits, to pay out increasing amounts of dollars to the rest of the world, and then to be faced with financing a substantial part of that deficit in gold because other countries no longer wish to accumulate important amounts of dollars in their reserves. There is certainly no fixed or absolute level or ratio of our short-term dollar liabilities to our gold reserves. But officially held dollar claims of a liquid character are now just about equal to our gold reserves. They have been rising for about 15 years, and rising quite sharply since 1958. It is quite essential that we bring this long series of balance-of-payments deficits to a halt. In doing so, we will also stop the process of providing gold and dollar reserves to the rest of the world.

When this happens, there may then be a question as to how to provide supplementary reserves in some form, to add to gold and the existing holdings of dollars and sterling exchange. It is, in my view, unrealistic to assume that the world can or should attempt to do away with these existing foreign exchange holdings. The gold exchange standard in itself is a useful and meritorious instrument. But at the same time, we must exercise moderation in its use, and realize that it has been overstrained by the size and persistence of U.S. deficits, and the resulting supply of dollars.

It is no secret that some European countries feel that the long continued deficit of the United States has been at best made possible and at worst encouraged and stimulated by the ability of the United States to finance a very substantial portion of its deficit during the past seven years by paying out dollars that have been added to foreign reserves. If the U.S. deficit had been settled entirely in gold, they assert, the United States would have taken earlier and more rigorous steps to bring its payments into equilibrium.

Accordingly, some of these countries are prepared to argue that the international monetary system at the present time is experiencing a surplus of liquidity, not a shortage. This is perhaps the basis for the suggestion of General de Gaulle that the world should return to a gold standard system. A return to a gold standard would imply a sharp curtailment of world reserves and world liquidity and would carry the threat of worldwide deflation. I need not, for this audience, spell out the detailed mechanism by which this would come about. I mentioned Jacques Rueff, who recently expressed his support for a return to the gold standard in public statements in the United States. Recognizing that this alone would create dangerous deflationary pressures, he couples his proposal with the suggestion that the price of gold be doubled and that the United States then pay off its liquid liabilities to foreign central banks in gold at the new price. That would mean redeeming some $14.5 billion of dollar reserves of foreign official holders at a rate of $70 for an ounce of gold rather than the existing $35 per ounce. The United States would be left at the end of the operation with gold reserves near the present level, according to the new valuation, and would have wiped out its official liabilities to foreign monetary authorities.

Such a proposal is thoroughly unacceptable to the United States. It combines the proposal that the world once again accept automatic regulation of its money supply according to the vagaries of world gold production with the proposal that the implied and stated commitments of the gold exchange standard be repudiated to the advantage of a few and the disadvantage of many. It is easy to see how it might be appealing to the major gold-producing countries, including the Union of South Africa and the U.S.S.R., and to some countries holding a high proportion of their reserves in gold. It would, of course, be discriminatory against countries which have kept a substantial fraction of their reserves in the form of reserve currencies. Our commitment to maintain the fixed parity of $35 an ounce between gold and dollars is basic to the stability of the world monetary system. President Johnson has reiterated our unchanging determination to maintain this parity.

We share fully, however, the European view that our balance-of-payments deficit should be promptly corrected. We do not believe that the existence of the present monetary system has weakened our resolve to eliminate our balance-of-payments deficit. We have, however, insisted that the deficit be eliminated by measures which would have a minimum impact both on the rate of economic growth in our own country and on the continued economic prosperity of the rest of the free world. We have ruled out measures which would have denied our responsibilities in defense of the free world or in the economic development of less-developed countries, and we have done so in the interest of free men everywhere. Our deep reluctance to adopt more restrictive monetary or fiscal policies at home has derived from the unshakable conviction that a strong and growing economy in the United States is a prerequisite both to lasting correction of our balance-of-payments difficulties and to continued prosperity in the Western World.

I shall not digress at any length to review the extent to which our balance-of-payments position has, in fact, been strengthened in recent years. The splendid record of price stability which we have maintained through 50 months of steady economic growth has established for us a strong competitive position in world trade and our trade balance is highly favorable. We have reduced the balance-of-payments impact of our military and foreign aid operations without retreating from our commitments in these areas. More recently, measures have been taken to dampen the outflow of capital from the United States by means of the voluntary cooperation of the banking system and the business community. The United States will, however, continue to be an important source of productive capital.

Before I resume commenting briefly on what I think will be the principal issues to be decided as we cooperate in working out arrangements to assure that adequate world liquidity will be maintained when our deficit has been corrected, I should acknowledge that there is a school of thought—and one which appears to be quite strong in academic circles—that believes in solving the liquidity problem not by increasing liquidity but by reducing the need for liquidity. Members of that school are the advocates of floating exchange rates. They hold that fixed exchange rates alone create the need for large reserves. More importantly, perhaps, they feel that fixed exchange rates constitute a restraining influence preventing individual countries from following domestic policies which might be deemed appropriate for domestic aims. If exchange rates were free to move up and down in the market, a balance-of-payments deficit would be reflected in a cheapening of the country's currency rather than in a loss of reserves. The cheapening of the currency, in turn, the argument runs, would bring about adjustments in the trade pattern, lower imports and higher exports, among other changes, which would restore balance-of-payments equilibrium. No country would need to hold large reserves and each country could choose its internal monetary and fiscal policies according to its own system of priorities and without regard for balance-of-payments effects.

I am not going to try to argue the case for or against floating rates. I would admit, as any student of economics will admit, that the theoretical arguments for floating exchange rates can be presented with great precision and appeal. Operation of the system in a world of imperfect knowledge, imperfect governmental and monetary institutions, and conflicting national ambitions and policies would be something else again. I will merely express the opinion, which is shared by an overwhelming majority of commercial and financial interests, that such a system, in practice, would prove extremely disruptive to world trade and financial transactions. The Ministers and Governors of the Group of Ten have ruled out consideration of any such system and the International Monetary Fund has operated for nearly 20 years in defense of a regime of generally fixed exchange rates, with individual exchange rate adjustments regarded as appropriate from time to time when individual countries have fallen into a position of fundamental disequilibrium.

As we consider possible methods for assuring adequate liquidity in the future, the next question is whether some new type of asset should be created or whether liquidity needs can be met by further development and refinement of existing credit mechanisms.

On the credit side, agreement has already been reached, in principle, on a 25-percent increase in International Monetary Fund quotas. I say "in principle" because, while more than 80 percent of the membership favored the increase, each member must now determine for itself, in accordance with its own legislative procedures, whether it will accept its appropriate share of such increase. The U.S. Administration is seeking congressional approval for an increase of $1,035 million in the U.S. quota. The House of Representatives voted favorably on this bill on Tuesday of this week. We are confident that the total of aggregate quotas in the Fund will be increased from about $16 billion to about $21 billion when this operation has been completed. That will provide an appreciable addition for international liquidity in the form of credit facilities.

The most intriguing aspect of the liquidity question, however, doubtless lies in efforts to devise a new type of reserve asset. I mentioned that the Deputies of the Group of Ten, in their Report to Ministers, announced that they had established a "Study Group on the Creation of Reserve Assets" to study the problem which its name implies. The Group is meeting periodically. It is expected to present to the Deputies some time this summer a study which will "assemble the elements necessary for evaluation of the various proposals" which have been put forward.

I cannot speak in detail about the work of this Group. But its terms of reference are public information. The Deputies to the Group of Ten spoke of two types of proposals: "One, the introduction, through an agreement among the member countries of the Group, of a new reserve asset which would be created according to appraised overall needs for reserves; and the other based on the acceptance of gold tranche or similar claims on the (International Monetary) Fund as a form of international asset, the volume of which would, if necessary, be enlarged to meet an agreed need."

Proposals of the first type vary substantially in detail. Essentially, however, these schemes provide that a limited group of countries, by depositing their own currencies or gold, establish a central pool of monetary resources which would provide the backing for a new reserve unit. Members would receive in exchange for their respective subscriptions an equal value of reserve units. These would represent proportionate claims upon the aggregate pool of resources and these claims or units would be transferable among the members in settlement of surpluses or deficits. The reserve unit itself would be held or used much as gold is now held in reserves or used in international settlements. By agreement among the members: it would assume the nature of gold; it would be held as reserves; its value would be fixed in terms of gold; and, its acceptance by any member would be automatic according to stipulated conditions.

For example, some proposals would call for creation of a limited amount of reserve units and for the use of these units in fixed proportion with gold in making all settlements among members. The economic effect would be little different from the gold standard itself. It would operate like the gold standard with some reserve units added. Like a return to the gold standard, itself, it could call into question the continuing usefulness of reserve currency holdings and would probably encourage the conversion of some holdings into gold. To the extent such conversions should occur, the world would face a decline in total world liquidity, rather than an increase.

A second important condition would be that dealing with the manner in which decisions would be made for increasing or, if necessary, decreasing the amount of units in existence. To oversimplify, it would be in the apparent interest of creditor countries to resist—and of debtor countries to favor—the creation of additional units. If new issues were to be subject to a unanimous agreement, which is to say if any country could veto an expansion or a contraction, it would hardly be accurate to say that decisions regarding the adequacy of international liquidity had been placed under international control in any meaningful way.

The importance of the conditions which might govern creation of new assets would be no less if new reserve assets should be created in the International Monetary Fund. Proposals of this type call for creation of claims on the Fund that can be drawn upon at will to meet balance-of-payments deficits. For example, automatic drawing rights could be accorded against some part of the existing credit tranches in the Fund. Another proposal, is that the Fund might be authorized to invest some of its holdings of currencies in member countries, thereby providing those countries with assets usable internationally.

Again, a number of questions would have to be considered. Would operation of the normal weighted voting procedures in the Fund serve the interests of creditor and debtor countries equitably? Should reserve assets be created for all countries or for only those countries that might be expected to be in both surplus and deficit over a period of years?

However additional reserves are created, their use implies a credit operation. The original creation could take the form for each participating country of an equal increase in its liabilities and in its assets, the latter becoming, by terms of the agreement, an international reserve asset. There would be no real economic impact at this stage. But as soon as the newly-created asset or unit began to be used, those surplus countries which accumulated the unit would be extending credit to the deficit countries. And the extension of credit from one country to another reflects the transfer of real assets. The surplus country foregoes present consumption in exchange for higher reserves, or for future potential consumption. A creditor country has, of course, considerable freedom of action in controlling the credit it will extend. There are many acceptable ways in which a balance-of-payments surplus can be reduced. Study of the adjustment process to determine appropriate policies to be followed—both by deficit countries to correct their deficits and by surplus countries to reduce their surpluses—is another area to which the Group of Ten is giving attention.

With respect to the deficit countries, no country can expect to receive unlimited automatic credit from its trading partners. The search for assurance that adequate international liquidity will be maintained in the future will not in any sense be a search for automatic credit for persistent debtors.

I have mentioned a few of the issues connected with the liquidity discussions without giving any clear indication of what the answers should be. The answers must await continued hard study and, at an appropriate stage, perhaps hard negotiations. I will advance only three questions for your consideration at this time.

First, how can we make certain that any new scheme will be entirely compatible with the evolution of the existing system? This will require that nations should not be penalized, nor benefited, as a result of the composition of their reserves, when and if some new liquidity asset is developed.

Secondly, how can we assure that any new system will increase and not reduce world liquidity? World liquidity would be reduced to the extent that existing reserve currency holdings are converted into gold. What, then, should be our attitude toward proposals which might stimulate such conversion or cast doubt upon the stability or the convertibility of existing reserve currency holdings?

Thirdly, how can we make sure that any new system will maintain machinery for giving appropriate weight to the views of both creditor and debtor countries? Should it be subject to the arbitrary control of either, or to the veto of a single country?

These are three broad questions, among many, that will need to be kept in mind as we proceed to examine most carefully the various ideas that have been or may be suggested. We are conscious that the creation of any new type of reserve asset by international agreement would be a step of profound significance. We must be sure that it is a step in the right direction. The mechanism of the international monetary system is an intricate and complicated mechanism, the successful functioning of which is of worldwide concern. We must make certain that any adjustments made in that mechanism will be the best that experience and intelligence and concern for the welfare of all nations can devise.

Exhibit 44.—Excerpts from remarks by Under Secretary of the Treasury for Monetary Affairs Deming, May 18, 1965, at the forty-third annual meeting of the Bankers Association for Foreign Trade, on the U.S. balance of payments— problem and program

The U.S. balance of international payments, except for one year, has been in deficit since 1949. In terms of the "balance on regular transactions" which we currently use in our official payments statistics, and which I use throughout this talk, the cumulative deficit was almost $35 billion.

We had 7 consecutive years of deficit from 1950–56, one year of surplus in 1957, and then 7 more consecutive years of deficit. What I hope to demonstrate in this talk is that the first 7 years of deficit constituted no great problem but that the deficits of the last 7 years have been a major problem and that the form of the problem and its seriousness has shifted appreciably during that period. I also hope to show you that the corrective program has shifted in keeping with the shifts in form and scope of the problem and that there is good prospect that we are on the way to a solution of it.

To help accomplish my purpose, I first want to sketch briefly the history of the U.S. payments position during the entire post-World War II period. This, I hope, will give the picture both perspective and dimension.

In the first four postwar years, 1946–49, our payments balance registered fairly large surpluses, totaling about $7 billion and averaging about $1¾ billion per year. In the light of the acute reconstruction needs and the badly depleted gold and foreign exchange reserves of the war-torn countries, both of which were only partially ameliorated by the very substantial economic assistance we were extending to these countries, U.S. surpluses of this size represented a relatively severe strain on the payments and reserve positions of our trading partners. More than half of our $7 billion cumulative payments surplus for those years was settled in gold, and, during the period, our gold stock rose by $4.5 billion and amounted, at the close of 1949, to $24.6 billion.

Beginning in 1950 and for a 7-year period through 1956, we ran deficits at a rate averaging $1.5 billion per year. Compared with our cumulative deficit of $10.7 billion for the period, the decline in our gold stock was relatively small, only $2.5 billion.

These U.S. payments deficits and gold losses were considered both moderate in size and not a cause for concern because of the general circumstances of the world's international payments situation during that period. Most other countries' gold and foreign exchange reserves, as I have said, had been badly depleted. What was perhaps the most important difference from our present day situation, virtually all of those countries wanted to have earning assets in their reserves and, thus, could be regarded as more than willing holders of such dollars as might accrue to them from our payments deficits. During that 7-year period, foreign dollar holdings virtually doubled to over $16 billion.

The year of the Suez crisis, 1957, brought a small surplus again in our foreign payments, our first and only such surplus since 1949. The amount was $500 million, and it was accompanied by a gold gain of $800 million. This brought our gold stock, at the close of the year, to $22.9 billion, which represented a net decline of only $1.8 billion from the earlier peak and was almost $3 billion more than we had as of the close of World War II.

In 1958, we resumed our international payments deficit position but with profound change in both scope and circumstance. The annual deficits in the three years, 1958–60, were not only much larger than had been the case in the early 1950's but they presented a new and difficult financing problem. Over these 3 years, the cumulative deficit was $11.6 billion, or almost $3.9 billion average per year, and our gold loss totaled more than $5 billion.

The major industrial countries of the world, particularly those in Western Europe, by 1958 had made great gains in general economic and financial strength, due in substantial measure to our economic aid. They had largely reached the stage of currency convertibility and, by their own standards, had reasonably adequate levels of official dollar reserves. Thus, they wanted, and took, more gold to finance their surpluses.

But not only had Western Europe grown relatively stronger in economic terms, the inflationary pressures of the early 1950's had weakened the U.S. competitive position somewhat so that our commercial trade and service balance had deteriorated at the same time that our governmental expenses overseas were rising and overseas investment opportunities were increasing in attractiveness. Thus the U.S. deficit was not only larger but more menacing just as our financing possibilities seemed to become more limited.

With the appearance of these large deficits and gold losses in 1958 and 1959, it became widely recognized that this new and disturbing situation could not be allowed to continue long. But it was also recognized that, despite some deterioration in our international competitive position from a cost standpoint, we did not face a classic type of payment deficit characterized by domestic inflation and overfull employment, with accelerating demands for imports and dwindling exports. Rather we had rising unemployment, underutilization of capacity and, from 1958 on, stable to declining production costs and prices. And while our surpluses on goods and services exports were not large enough to balance our heavy governmental and growing private investment outlays abroad, there continued to be surpluses.

Thus it was decided that the solution to our problem must be sought within a framework of a vigorous and growing domestic economy with stable costs and prices. A broad program was developed and launched in early 1961. It laid emphasis on tax incentives and ample credit to encourage growth and improve productivity through increased domestic investment. Monetary policy, while designed to be broadly stimulative, also aimed at keeping our short-term interest rates generally competitive with those abroad and, in this effort, was aided by Treasury debt management policy.

In addition to this broad policy approach, a number of other actions were undertaken. A vigorous program of export encouragement got under way with a new system of export credit guaranties and a major strengthening and broadening of Government information and promotion services for exporters. Strong actions were taken to achieve reductions in the foreign exchange costs of Government outlays overseas, and some steps were taken in the Revenue Act of 1962 to reduce the attractiveness of foreign tax havens for U.S. private capital.

The program was eminently successful in the areas affected. Thus, in 1964, as compared with 1960, our commercial trade surplus showed a net gain, despite a $3.9 billion increase in the imports required by our growing domestic economy, of $900 million, and reached a record figure in 1964 of $3.7 billion. Our trade gain during 1964 alone was most impressive, with gross commercial exports rising by $3.1 billion, or 16 percent, while the increase in our imports remained moderate in relation to our growing GNP.

We also achieved, between 1960 and 1964, a net improvement of more than $1 billion in our military expenditures and Government grant and capital payments abroad. By tying more and more of our foreign aid, with over 85 percent of new AID commitments now being limited to the purchase of U.S. goods and services, we halved the net drain from this factor, from $1 billion in 1960 to less than $500 million last year. By streamlining operations and cutting procurement from foreign sources, our gross defense expenditures abroad were reduced by $250 million over this period, despite rising cost levels in the areas where most of our forces were stationed overseas. In addition, we made offsetting sales of U.S. military equipment to Allied Foreign Governments, raising our receipts from this source from $300 million in 1960 to more than $1 billion in each of the years 1962–64.

The gains made in these two major areas directly affected by our balance-of-payments program were supplemented, moreover, by the very rapid further growth in total income receipts from U.S. private investments abroad, which, over the course of these 4 years, added a further $1.5 billion annually to our total payments receipts.

These 3 areas of major gains, taken together, added up to a $3.6 billion gross improvement in this portion of our international transactions, a remarkable and impressive achievement, which, other things being equal, would have been virtually enough to eliminate our balance-of-payments deficit.

But other things were not equal. In 1964, the deficit was $3.1 billion. During the four years, 1960–64, the deficits totaled $13.0 billion, or $3.2 billion average per year. So the impressive improvements noted led to a relatively modest net gain. And while our gold losses during the four years were less than half those of the preceding three years, mainly because of new and imaginative financing methods, they totaled $2.3 billion. At the close of 1964, our gold stock was about $15.5 billion.

The failure to gain more ground was due primarily to two factors: private capital outflow and tourist expenditures.

Despite impressive percentage gains in our earnings last year from foreign tourists, our net tourist deficit showed an increase of $300 million over the four-year period, amounting in 1964 to $1.6 billion.

Very much larger than this, and obviously the major factor in the worsening of our payments position which developed between the very encouraging first quarter and the final quarter of last year, was the swelling outflow of nearly all types of private capital investment. Our total outflow of private capital during 1964 amounted to almost $6.5 billion, up almost $2.2 billion from the preceding year and $2.6 billion higher than the 1960 level.

Private capital outflow began to grow in the late 1950's and short-term outflow was particularly heavy in 1960. Such outflows, of course, generate earnings, and I also noted the rise in investment income during the period 1960–64. But the relatively rapid rise in capital outflows in early 1963 gave cause for concern and led to the mid-1963 program of additional monetary policy action to keep short rates more competitive and to the introduction of interest equalization tax legislation designed to hold down the rapid expansion of foreign securities marketing in this country.

The $6.5 billion capital outflow in 1964 breaks down as follows. Direct investment abroad totaled $2.4 billion, or $700 million more than in 1960 and $500 million more than in 1963. This figure does not include investment of retained earnings abroad. We do not have the data for 1964, but for 1963 such reinvestment totaled $1.6 billion.

Long- and short-term bank credit outstanding increased during 1964 by $2.5 billion, a very sharp gain. The rise in short-term credits alone was $1.5 billion, or more than $500 million greater than in 1960, while the gain in long-term credits was more than $900 million, 6 times that for 1960. While much of the short-term finance provided support for American exports, very little of the long-term finance, only 15 percent, was for that purpose. Most of it represented financing of foreign business enterprises in various countries, and much of it seems to have been a substitute for capital market borrowing which was inhibited by the interest equalization tax. Foreign securities purchases by Americans were less than $700 million in 1964, about equal to their 1960 level and only one-third as large as the annual rate prevailing in the first half of 1963.

Finally, outflows of nonbank short-term capital, much but not all of which represented temporary placements of U.S. corporate liquid funds abroad, were almost $600 million in 1964, or $200 million more than in 1960. Other long-term capital outflow totaled more than $300 million in 1964, up very much from 1960, but the bulk of this represented a special transaction to finance the British Columbia hydroelectric project.

So here you have the setting for the President's Balance-of-Payments Message of February 10, 1965. Let me restate it in brief summary form.

The success of the program begun in 1961 had led to gross improvement of $3.6 billion, resulting mainly from bigger net exports, rising investment income, and savings on Government expenditures abroad. The economy had grown significantly with stable costs and prices. Monetary policy, aided by debt management policy, had kept our short rates reasonably competitive and had moderated short-term outflows responsive to interest rate differentials. The interest equalization tax legislation had cut back sales of foreign securities to Americans from the extraordinary levels of early 1963. But the overall outflow of capital was very heavy and, coupled with rising net expense on tourist account, had far more than offset such gains as had occurred in other areas. Thus the problem had shifted again and the new program was designed to deal with that shift.

This program included a variety of measures strengthening and rounding out various aspects of the broad effort we had been making to improve the various segments of the balance of payments since early 1961. Strong additional measures to achieve further cuts in the balance-of-payments cost of Government expenditures abroad were requested, along with continuing and intensified efforts to expand our exports. The President also requested a program aimed at increasing travel in the United States, by both foreigners and Americans, and asked for legislation to reduce further the duty-free allowance for American tourists returning from abroad. This measure, we believe, should help directly to reduce somewhat the total amount which American tourists would spend abroad during the next two years, while also serving to remind all travelers and citizens that such expenditures are a significant element in the balance-of-payments situation we are dealing with. He also asked for legislation, as recommended by a special task force which had been appointed by President Kennedy, to give added encouragement to private investments by foreigners in the United States by removing unnecessary tax barriers or discouragements to such investment.

In addition to this reinforcement of earlier programs, it was necessary to bring about a prompt and substantial cutback in the very large outflow of private lending and investment abroad. The President's Message therefore included a series of new and much more comprehensive measures.

First, under authority provided to him in the interest equalization tax law, he announced the immediate application of that tax to bank lending of one year or more maturity. He also requested that the Congress extend the life of the tax by a further two years, from the end of 1965 to the end of 1967, and broaden its coverage to include nonbank lending in the one- to three-year maturity area.

Secondly, and most important of all, the President also called for a broad program of voluntary restraint by banks and business firms, applicable to all types of capital outflows.

This program of voluntary restraint is, as you know, being implemented on the basis of rather specific guidelines circulated by the Federal Reserve System and the Secretary of Commerce, respectively, to the banks and other financial institutions and business corporations which are involved. The guidelines for banks call for a limitation of total outstanding loans to foreigners at the end of this year to a level not more than 5 percent above the end of December 1964 level and provide that, within these ceilings, priority should be given to export financing and to credits to less-developed countries and to avoid restrictive policies that would place an undue burden on Canada, Japan, and the United Kingdom.

In the development and implementation of these guidelines, special pains have been taken to avoid an adverse impact on the continued availability of adequate bank financing for U.S. exports. Such financing of exports is, after all, one of the most important ways in which banks can contribute to our overall balance-of-payments program. Our ultimate success in achieving the kind of long-run balance we are seeking in our international payments will, in the end, depend very heavily on the adequacy of the continuing growth we can attain in our exports.

The guidelines for business corporations under this program call for each firm, using 1964 as a reference point, establishing for itself a quantitative target for substantial improvement in the balance-of-payments impact of its foreign transactions during the current year.

We are aware that recent large outflows of such capital are, in one sense, both a result and a demonstration of the great and growing general strength of our economy: its ability to generate a large flow of savings, the capacity and flexibility and efficiency of our financial institutions and other mechanisms for directing investable funds to available investment opportunities, and the general competitive drive and effectiveness of our financial firms and business corporations.

The basic point which we have to face up to, however, is that recent heavy outflows of private capital, portfolio outflows, long- and short-term bank lending, direct investments, and liquid deposits abroad by business firms, have together put a very heavy strain on our international liquidity position and must, for the time being, be substantially curtailed. Despite the long-term benefits which we reap from such capital outflows over the years ahead, we simply cannot afford, as a short-term matter, to let these outflows get so far out of line, relative both to inflows of foreign investment funds into our own economy and to the overall level of international earnings from exports and other foreign transactions. It is essential that we bring our total foreign payments accounts into balance, not sometime in the indefinite future, but soon. To achieve this, it is necessary that all sectors of our economy cooperate in this overall effort.

Exhibit 45.—Excerpts from remarks by Under Secretary of the Treasury for Monetary Affairs Deming, June 22, 1965, at the annual convention of the Washington State Bankers Association, on international banking in relation to the balance of payments and international liquidity

Private capital movements and the U.S. balance of payments

I do not intend to review the policies applied in 1961 and 1962 to correct our balance of payments and at the same time revitalize the domestic economy. We did achieve substantial progress in 1961–64 in enlarging our commercial export surplus, despite a rising total of imports, and in reducing the balance-of-payments impact of our military and aid programs. With a steady increase in our services income, our deficit would have been largely eliminated if the capital accounts had remained constant.

But this was not the case. The outflow of private U.S. capital in all forms had already jumped sharply in 1956 from the moderate levels of 1950–55, and ranged between $2½ billion and $4 billion in the years 1956–60. In 1964 it reached almost $6½ billion, with a very decided surge in the latter part of the year. Between 1960 and 1964 U.S. security and credit transactions grew from $2.2 billion to $4.1 billion. In July 1963, the interest equalization tax had been announced when the early manifestations of these latest capital demands on our markets appeared, particularly in the form of potential placements by other industrial countries in our capital market. The further dramatic evidence of the volatile capital accounts in 1964 led President Johnson to propose on February 10, 1965, a comprehensive program calling for the cooperation of the business and financial communities in reducing this drain on the balance of payments.

The response of businessmen and bankers has been most impressive. While the limited data yet available are difficult to evaluate because of special factors, they suggest that this cooperation, upon which the program depends, has begun to have a significant effect. The deficit on regular transactions for the first quarter was reduced to about half the magnitude of the very large figures in the final quarter of 1964. Such indications as we have since the end of March have continued to be even more favorable. But I cannot overemphasize that we need to establish a record of clear and sustained equilibrium, to demonstrate our full recovery from the long continued malady of deficits. We cannot, therefore, contemplate any early relaxation of our efforts.

The U.S. position as international banker

We have all heard much about the U.S. role as an international banker and about our tendency to pile up long-term investments while accumulating short-term liabilities. We have large and competitive money and capital markets, as compared with the narrower and less competitive markets in the other industrial countries. There has been increasing desire for capital investment abroad, arising from the long-continued European prosperity, the Common Market preferences, and the rapidly growing European demand for many products in which American corporations have traditionally been interested. While these latter are factors that are particularly significant in the area of direct investment, they also may account for some movement of banking funds to supply the needs of some U.S. subsidiaries abroad. Finally, there is the differential between interest rates here and abroad, particularly at longer term.

Let us recall briefly the general structure of our international investment position. We do not yet have detailed figures for 1964, but at the close of 1963, private long-term investments abroad were valued at $58 billion, of which $40.6 billion was direct investments, and $17.6 billion represented other types of long-term assets. Foreign long-term investments in the United States amounted to nearly $23 billion, leaving a net balance in our favor on private long-term investment account of about $35 billion. Note that this does not count any of our governmental claims on foreign countries.

At short term, however, the position was rather different. Foreign short-term claims on the United States, both private and official, amounted to $28.7 billion at the end of 1963. This figure includes about $3 billion that are not considered liquid financial liabilities. Nearly half of the total amount was officially held. Against this, the United States then held $15.6 billion in gold, and other reserve-type assets of $1.2 billion. In addition, our privately held short-term claims on foreigners were about $8 billion.

Moving from the cross section to the changing pattern over time, our net position on private long-term capital account had improved from $27 billion to $35 billion, from 1960 to 1963, while our net official and private position on short-term account (including gold), worsened by $5 billion.

The major channels through which these capital funds have recently been flowing out, apart from Canadian security issues in New York, are the direct lending operations of the banking system, or the placement of funds with foreign banks, or with foreign branches of American banks, by nonbanking entities. While some of the proceeds in the form of dollars were added to the rising total of foreign private dollar holdings, foreign official dollar balances were built up as well.

While our private investments abroad, both short- and long-term, are presumably sound and profitable ones in the sense of income-earning assets, they have clearly tended to exceed the net surplus on other accounts. This adds to our liquid liabilities to foreigners, and these liabilities, in turn, may be converted into gold.

Thus, while our balance-of-payments program has consistently aimed at improving both our current accounts and our governmental accounts, increasing attention has had to be devoted since July 1963 to the large flow of capital abroad, particularly to other industrial countries.

Through the interest equalization tax, we have sought to provide a market-type regulator. We have hoped in this way to strengthen the incentive to other industrial countries to utilize their savings more effectively to meet the demands that would otherwise come to the United States. More recently, in the wake of the very sharp deterioration in our capital accounts and in the balance of payments, generally, during the period since July 1964, we have adopted the voluntary credit restraint program on February 10. This program, too, is increasing the awareness of other advanced countries that they should readjust their financing patterns so as to obtain capital resources out of their own savings.

As noted, the tendency to seek U.S. funds may be in part due to the generally high cost of borrowing in foreign countries.

But there are other reasons why some types of borrowers are attracted to the U.S. market. These include the narrowness and high cost of security issue markets in Europe, the favored position of governmental borrowing entities and nationalized industries to some capital markets abroad, the channeling of savings of the public through savings banks and mortgage banks into government securities or mortgages, and the tendency in many countries of the large banks to maintain a relatively rigid pattern of lending policies.

Efforts are being made to explore these and other structural problems in the European financial system, in the hope of developing more efficient and more competitive capital markets that can meet the types of demands that now fall so heavily upon the United States. Indeed, as strong surplus and creditor countries, many continental European countries would normally be expected to be net sources of capital to the rest of the world. But instead of becoming capital exporters, they have continued to import capital from the United States, and have, in effect, banked the proceeds with their central banks in the form of reserves.

Particularly in Europe, it is frequently suggested that the way to restrain the tendency for capital to flow out of the United States would be to bring about a higher level of long-term interest rates in the United States. But a moment's reflection will indicate the difficulties of applying such a prescription to the situation in which we find ourselves. One very large economic entity, the industrial nations of continental Europe, has a historically high level of interest rates that has prevailed during a period of generally full or overfull employment and inflationary pressures on prices and wages. The entire structure of the capital values in these countries has for a long time been geared to a plateau of rates substantially higher than that in our own economy. This European rate structure seems likely to come down slowly, if at all, as inflationary pressures subside.

On the other hand, long-term interest rates in the United States are also at high levels in terms of our own background and history. There are several reasons for doubting that a simple prescription of higher long-term interest rates in the United States is an effective answer. The spread between long-term rates here and in most of Europe is so wide that the possibility of any substantial narrowing of the differential by U.S. action is open to considerable question from a purely technical standpoint, because of the massive volume of savings in the United States. Second, as noted, present levels are not low historically, and a significantly higher level of rates might well do harm to the domestic economy. Thirdly, as noted, the European rates not only are influenced by the pressure of demands from borrowers on savings, but also probably reflect the general tendency for prices to rise, thus reducing considerably the real rate of interest, in terms of purchasing power over goods.

It should be noted that, even today, foreign placements are small in relation to our annual gross private domestic investment of $73 billion, or with respect even to our personal savings of $35 billion a year. Moreover, the capital drawn from the United States represents a small percentage of the total savings and investment in Europe.

All in all, leaving aside direct investment, some $4 billion of U.S. capital moved out last year. About half went to Canada and Japan, less than a quarter directly to Western Europe, and the remainder to Latin America, Asia, and other regions. The reductions we anticipate from the programs now in effect, particularly when the impact is directed toward the other industrial countries, should form a relatively small part of the total investment financed in those countries. In the major countries of Western Europe alone annual investment in all forms probably equals that in the United States. Hence the relationship of this correction of our deficit to world business activity is marginal, and should not be overstressed.

As the world moves farther away from the restrictions and restraints of the earlier postwar period, the stream of financial capital moving between these two great industrial complexes in Europe and the United States might tend to widen. At the same time, the United States cannot reasonably be expected to continue to supply capital as an international banker if its reserve position is steadily reduced by a continuing deficit. This may well present a challenge to Europe and the United States to find an appropriate set of policies to meet on a continuing basis the capital flows problem. European countries, it is true, made some progress in 1964 in enlarging their capital markets, and in accommodating the needs of some foreign borrowers, particularly Japan; some countries have applied special disincentives to the attraction of foreign capital into their monetary reserves. But there remains the need to reduce European capital imports and to stimulate larger foreign investments, without a corresponding increase in its current account position.

Capital flows and European reserves

A reduction in the flow of financial capital from the United States and an associated shrinkage of the U.S. deficit could have a considerable effect on international liquidity. Without a U.S. deficit, the increase in world reserves would be limited essentially to the amount of new gold production flowing into monetary channels, that is, to about $500 million to $700 million per year. Since a number of countries on the continent of Europe have become accustomed to much larger aggregate increases in their reserves year by year, some adjustments could be expected. While the authorities in some of these countries might look with favor upon a position of U.S. equilibrium and somewhat slower growth in their reserves, there are voices here and abroad that express concern about the effect upon these economies of a considerable and rapid tapering off of these customary reserve increases. They would fear that domestic credit might tighten too sharply, and that this might place an additional brake on expansion, already slowing down in several continental countries, and that this could affect the level of activity in the outside world.

It is certainly true that some adjustments will need to be made in these countries, for any change in capital flows to the outside world will have its economic effect, through our overall balance-of-payments position. But there are several qualifications to bear in mind. One is that these countries have for some time been facing heavy pressures on savings, on prices, and on labor supplies. Under such conditions it should be possible for these countries to absorb without adverse results a considerable part of the impact of a smaller volume of foreign receipts. Secondly, as noted, the amount of these receipts is small in relation to total investment and savings of the European economies. Thirdly, the movement of reserves frequently seems to be the dependent variable in the equation. Especially in recent years, persistent reserve increases seem in some cases not to have been the result of policies directed specifically toward the external accounts, but rather a byproduct of action taken to dampen domestic inflationary pressures.

Actually the growth in liquidity in the past 10 years has been concentrated largely in the surplus industrial countries. When we look at the position of international reserves and their recent growth, we are struck at once by the really phenomenal enlargement of reserves in the industrial countries, excluding the United States and the United Kingdom. From the end of 1953 to the end of 1964, the gold and foreign exchange reserves of 8 leading industrial countries in the Group of Ten and Switzerland rose from $10.6 billion to $27.6 billion, or by $17 billion. This amounted to nearly tripling their total reserves.

Moreover, during this period, while these countries increased their reserves in gold and foreign exchange, the rest of the world lost about $3 billion of reserves in this form.

It is especially worthy of note that the demand of these countries for gold to add to their reserves, at $12 billion, was about twice the availability of new monetary gold supplies for the world as a whole. This was made possible only by large-scale transfers of gold to them from U.S. reserves.

I do not attempt today more than to sketch out some of the relationships between international capital flows and our balance-of-payments and liquidity problems. As and when our balance of payments shows continuing strength, some of the uncertainties that have to date surrounded the liquidity problem should begin to clear. We can then see what we face, once the all-embracing screen of the massive U.S. deficit has been lifted and moved aside. The essential questions that will have to be answered are: What will be the reserve needs of the world? How much will the major industrial countries require in the form of gold? And, what will they be willing to take into their reserves in addition to gold?

There are a number of technical possibilities for creating additional reserve assets to meet these or other situations in the future. They involve essentially an agreement or understanding among monetary authorities to treat a particular type of credit claim, either on another country or on an institution, as a monetary-reserve asset.

One method, frequently mentioned, is the further extension of the technique of reciprocal acquisition of currencies, as in the short-term swaps of the Federal Reserve, but for a long term. Each country then regards its claim on the other partner as a reserve asset. The countries could also issue special securities to each other, with appropriate provisions as to maturity, interest rates, and exchange protection.

Another approach would be a further evolution of the present reserve claims on the International Monetary Fund. These claims are drawing rights that countries have obtained, and can use virtually at will, as a result either of having paid gold subscriptions to the Fund, or from the use of their currencies by the Fund to extend credits to other countries. The Managing Director of the Fund, Mr. Schweitzer, has recently indicated how this might be done, either by increasing the present readily available drawing rights or by creating special claims on the Fund to be used as reserve assets.

Other suggestions have been made involving more restrictive procedures, both as to participation and governing rules. I do not propose to comment in any detail on any of these approaches. However, I would like to underline some of the characteristics of any approach which seem to me especially significant. First, additional or new reserve assets should be accepted as such by the major industrial countries. Secondly, they should be held as reserve assets without directly or indirectly leading to a reduction in reserve currencies or other supplements to gold reserves. That is, they should not accentuate demands on gold. Thirdly, the method of providing additional reserves should be in general evolutionary, in the sense of general public acceptance with a minimal disturbance of financial and exchange markets and with especial care to avoid encouragement to gold hoarding and gold speculation. Fourth, a balance would have to be achieved between the fears of some that creation of international reserves becomes too easy, with a general overexpansionary effect on world supplies of money and credit, and those who fear that international decisions would be too cumbersome and too restrictive. There are, of course, many other questions that might divide proponents of this or that technique, or appeal to particular countries, including the always important questions of who participates in the benefits and responsibilities of reserve creation, and how they are shared.

Reserve assets, once created, in a satisfactory way or ways, could be shifted from country to country and earned or borrowed in ways similar to gold, reserve currencies, or existing claims in the Fund. That is, they could make possible the simultaneous existence of surpluses among the major countries, including the United States, in excess of new monetary gold supplies, and without redistribution of existing gold reserves or cancellation of other reserve assets. They would then be true supplements to existing reserves.

A concensus may not emerge easily or quickly. For the world has to date relied essentially on gold and reserve currencies, and the public everywhere tends to be cautious and pragmatic in monetary matters. Money is peculiarly sensitive to public acceptance and public confidence.

We shall not find answers to these questions overnight. Indeed, the answers can probably evolve only as they are shaped and molded by the actual course of monetary history in the making. What we must insure is that the monetary authorities of the world have a common awareness of the type of problem which may arise as dollars become more scarce and have a common objective of shaping the evolving international monetary system in a cooperative way to the benefit of the sound economic aspirations of developed and developing nations alike.

Exhibit 46.—Remarks by Assistant Secretary of the Treasury for International Affairs Trued, May 18, 1965, before the Financial Analysts Federation 18th annual convention, on the interest equalization tax

The invitation to be with you today and to discuss the interest equalization tax provides a welcome opportunity. Two years ago, almost precisely at this time, we were developing this tax proposal. Faced with a flow of U.S. investment into foreign securities that threatened to swamp our balance of payments with an intolerable deficit and the dollar along with it, we were carefully assessing the various possibilities for curtailing this flow.

I should like to revert later in this talk to a brief consideration as to why we chose the tax as the particular method to deal with this problem in our balance of payments. Let me note at the outset simply that two years' experience provides a timely occasion to review the performance of the interest equalization tax in terms of markets and prices, as well as in terms of our current, more pervasive efforts to deal with our payments deficit. It is particularly timely moreover because we have now asked the Congress to extend this tax for a further two-year period to expire December 31, 1967.

It is perhaps useful, before discussing the interest equalization tax in the context of our present program, to discuss the market impact of the interest equalization tax and evaluate it in terms of the incentives which we felt it offered, over time, in assisting us toward bringing about a generation of forces working toward international adjustment in the balance-of-payments positions of the various countries, surplus and deficit alike.

When we asked the Congress in July 1963 to adopt the interest equalization tax, the measure was conceived as a limited response to a situation that was threatening to nullify the improvement we had been making in other than the capital sector of our balance of payments. New foreign issues in our market, on an annual rate basis, doubled between 1961 and 1962, then redoubled between 1962 and the first six months of 1963. There were without doubt, some unusually heavy although temporary concentrations of certain issues during this latter period. But it was quite clear that the accelerated outflow of portfolio capital would continue, and that would have pushed our balance-of-payments deficits to new heights unless, as seemed unlikely, other capital flows simultaneously declined or movements of a compensating nature occurred elsewhere in our balance-of-payments position.

To deal with the situation by forcing long-term interest rate levels in the United States fully into line with those abroad would have been totally unacceptable in the light of our unemployment and unutilized plant capacity, even if it were a practical possibility. Domestically, we simply did not—and this has been confirmed by experience since then—need either higher interest rates or tighter credit. And, I might add parenthetically, there is no evidence now that these are needed.

The solution of a major upward readjustment in long-term rates therefore was not feasible. Indeed, untimely action toward domestic restraint, by threatening to stifle economic expansion and growth, could have in fact impeded the continued development of international financial cooperation and a stronger international payments system. Sound developments in these areas can only be assured with an American economy that performs without waste of human or natural resources.

There were, in our view, serious doubts that the major alternative for dealing with this problem—the establishment of a Capital Issues Committee—would in fact provide a sound approach. Speculation at home and abroad as to the scope of the Committee's activities, particularly during its formative period, would in all likelihood have stimulated more capital flight than the Committee's actions could possibly have deterred. Moreover, a Capital Issues Committee could not have dealt with the problem of curtailing outflows owing to investments by Americans in outstanding foreign securities, outflows which on occasion had involved quite substantial amounts in the U.S. balance of payments. In addition to these very practical considerations, there is finally the important consideration of seeking to establish a ground rule which is as nondiscriminatory as possible and is little subject to arbitrary administration. It, therefore, seemed far better to let the individual investor decide about transactions in foreign securities in the light of a nondiscriminatory and clearly identified tax rather than having a Committee or person continually deciding which new foreign issues individually, was to be allowed into the U.S. market.

To some it may seem that the administration of the tax involves arbitrary decisions regarding exemptions and other matters perhaps little different from those that would face a Capital Issues Committee. But I submit there is a fundamental difference. Under the interest equalization tax, the Administration explained to the Congress at the beginning the nature of its operating guidelines and these by and large avoided discrimination among individual foreign issues. A Capital Issues Committee would inject the Government into a decisive role with regard to acceptance or rejection of individual foreign issues, a state of affairs which could well create market speculation as to decisions on particular issues and thus unhealthy influence over both the market and the issuer.

We also wanted to avoid any measure that would create doubts about the continued usefulness of the dollar as the major international currency. The outflow of capital was not a sign of basic weakness in our economy. It stemmed from the combination of two factors: a large and rising volume of domestic savings, efficiently channeled into whatever investments at home or abroad seemed to offer the highest yields; and a persistent demand for private long-term investment funds from borrowers in other developed countries.

Many of these borrowers wanted local currency funds, not foreign exchange in the form of dollars. To some extent the United States played the role of a financial intermediary, particularly between continental Western European savers and borrowers. The former have a penchant for keeping their savings in rather liquid forms; while the latter wanted long-term funds. Local banking systems to some degree performed the role of intermediaries between savers and borrowers; but various legal and institutional factors limited this role.

The United States, therefore, helped as an intermediary by providing substantial amounts of long as well as short-term dollars to Western European borrowers who converted them into the required local currencies at their banks. The latter, as a result, accumulated dollars which they hold with varying degrees of firmness depending on the usefulness of more dollar holdings to them in their own particular situations. We did not want to adopt any measure that would reduce that usefulness.

I mention some of this background thinking in order to provide a basis for appraising the effectiveness of the interest equalization tax. It was designed to help reduce our balance-of-payments deficit by reducing a particular form of capital outflow to particular areas with a minimum of interference with investors' choices and without undesirable side effects on the international usefulness of the dollar. That it has accomplished this major purpose to date is quite evident.

What have been the results since the interest equalization tax was proposed by the President to be effective July 19, 1963? Since then, new foreign security issues taken by foreigners have averaged a quarterly rate less than one-half the rate of the three quarters prior to the announcement. While part of this decline was due to uncertainties about the passage by Congress of the tax, the interesting point is that since passage of the bill in September there has been no upsurge in issues floated in the United States by advanced countries other than Canada. The amount of such issues purchased by U.S. residents has remained insignificant.

On the other hand, the interest equalization tax has been a powerful stimulus to development of the European capital market as Japanese and European borrowers have turned to it to meet their needs. New foreign bond issues in Europe in 1964 reached $1 billion, almost double the 1963 figure. Significantly, issues denominated in dollars which were about $100 million in 1963 rose to over half a billion dollars in 1964 attesting to the broad acceptance of the dollar as a standard of value in the long-term international capital market.

These dollar issues served as a vehicle for the development of new underwriting and marketing techniques which might not otherwise have been forthcoming. I am particularly pleased that U.S. underwriters have played an important role in this development. In addition, with London frequently serving as the base, underwriters from other countries have also handled these issues, placing them with a variety of buyers in markets abroad.

The European market naturally enough primarily took issues of European borrowers. These amount to 60 percent of the 1964 total. However, Japan accounted for 24 percent of the total issues, $200 million, making it the largest single borrower, and Japanese issues in European markets in previous years had been very small. Denmark and Norway, two other countries which had previously sold substantial amounts in the United States, also raised large sums in Europe last year.

To sum up, there has been noteworthy and favorable reaction to the incentives which the interest equalization tax offered. To potential borrowers, there was encouragement to seek funds in other markets; these borrowers have done just that. On the supply side of the market, attention was riveted on the lack of depth and broadness in markets which limited their ability to satisfy either domestic or external demand. A number of studies continue in this area by the Common Market countries, in the Organization for Economic Cooperation and Development (OECD) and elsewhere. Finally, the marketers of issues responded by seeking new sources of supply and a greater internationalization of the capital markets.

Now for a brief note on new issues which are not subject to the tax. As regards Canada, and the special exemption applied to its new issues, borrowers held back to some extent from the U.S. market until after enactment of the tax and confirmation of its proposed exemption. A very large amount, $383 million, of Canadian new issues hit our market in the fourth quarter of 1964, then fell off to about $150 million in the following quarter. Less-developed countries and international institutions, also exempt from the interest equalization tax, substantially increased their issues in 1964. In part this was due to the reentry of Mexico into the bond market on a sizable scale and to borrowings of the Inter-American Development Bank. This year also the International Bank for Reconstruction and Development, after an absence of three years from our market, floated a large issue, of which $160 million was placed with American investors.

But attention simply to new issues is misleading. The interest equalization tax also applies to trade in outstanding issues.

Prior to the announcement of the interest equalization tax there had been several years of net purchases by Americans of such issues. Purchases of outstanding foreign bonds which had been sizable in the first half of 1963 almost ceased in the second half of 1963 and have not resumed to date. U.S. purchases of foreign stocks which had already fallen off in the months preceding announcement of the tax changed to large net sales in the second half and these have continued to date.

The combination of these changes was that net U.S. transactions in outstanding foreign securities by Americans shifted from purchases of about $250 million for the seven quarters prior to the interest equalization tax to sales of $340 million for the seven subsequent quarters. In balance-of-payments terms, this represents a reversal of nearly $600 million.

While the change in net transactions in outstanding foreign securities has been favorable for the U.S. balance of payments since mid-1963, it is important to consider, from the viewpoint of effectiveness of the interest equalization tax, whether this has happened at a relatively high or at a greatly reduced level of gross transactions. If gross purchases of outstanding foreign securities from foreigners by Americans have not been restricted substantially by the tax, the net movement could again become troublesome for the U.S. balance of payments whenever foreign gross purchases of outstanding foreign securities from Americans fell off.

Available data do not reveal the volume of gross purchases directly. A major indicator, however, suggests that they have fallen off substantially since the first half of 1963. This indicator is the relatively small volume of purchases reported to Internal Revenue Service for purposes of the tax. Based on the amount of tax collected in the first quarter of this year, it would appear that gross purchases of taxable foreign securities from foreigners have been quite small.

I do not mean in any way to suggest that the interest equalization tax has been the only factor leading to the apparent reduction in gross purchases of foreign securities from foreigners by Americans. The domestic business climate and the course of U.S. security prices may have had as much or more effect. This becomes apparent in considering why the tax has not opened up a substantial price margin between the prices of American-held foreign securities and foreign-held foreign securities. In the case of bonds traded on the New York Stock Exchange, there has been little or no premium. In the case of stocks, premiums have been more variable but generally have been much lower than 10 percent.

Before congressional approval of the tax last September, temporary uncertainties may have accounted in part for this situation. But certainly in the period since last September one must conclude that, in general, there has been such a weak American demand for many foreign securities that, as a group, Americans have been willing to unload many of these securities at close to current foreign prices even at times when foreign demand for them has been heavy. The reason for this situation, as noted above, undoubtedly lies in part in the vigorous expansion of our own securities market, as compared to declines in major stock markets abroad, at least until quite recently.

There have, of course, been some individual foreign stocks which have attracted strong United States, as well as foreign, demand, and the premiums on these have become substantial at times. But American demand for many foreign stocks has remained weak despite the steady attrition in the tax-free American-held supply over the last year and a half.

Balance-of-payments effect

The interest equalization tax has been criticized as not having helped the balance of payments, however much it has reduced purchases by Americans of securities of other industrialized countries. I began by saying that the interest equalization tax was a limited measure. It was realized, of course, that foreign borrowers might be induced to seek U.S. funds through other channels than the U.S. capital market after the tax had been announced. But it was believed that there was a limit to the extent of such substitution and that the tax would at least reduce one form of capital outflow which had been rising at an alarming rate.

There is no doubt that the rise in long-term bank loans during 1964 and early 1965 reflected to some degree an effort to escape from the tax on securities. There is no way of demonstrating with certainty what that degree was; but, whatever it was, the rising volume of bank loans to foreigners in 1964 made one thing clear. We could not prudently assume that the operation of European security markets in the near future would reduce sufficiently the pressure of foreign demand for U.S. capital. Long-term interest rates in Europe which generally rose during 1964, substantially in some cases, have continued to rise this year despite the fact that European interest rate levels are high by historical standards. Indeed U.S. rates are on the high side by any historical standard. Continuation of this movement could increase the relative attractiveness of the U.S. capital market to foreign borrowers despite the tax. Hence it appeared desirable to supplement the interest equalization tax by a direct appeal to the American financial and business community to cooperate voluntarily in restraining capital outflows of all types to other advanced countries.

The tax itself, of course, acted as a voluntary as well as a market restraint on the sale of new foreign security issues to American investors. I think this is one of the reasons why, after uncertainties about the nature of the tax were resolved by its passage, the American financial community did not resume any substantial marketing of new issues of other advanced countries (excluding Canada), but the growing pressure to market foreign issues in this country as the long-term interest differential widened would eventually, if continued, have reduced the effectiveness of the tax. It therefore seemed desirable, in establishing the voluntary control program, to apply it not only to forms of capital outflow previously untaxed, but also an added dissuader, to those that were taxed.

The Administration has asked for the extension of the tax for an additional two years, that is, up to the end of 1967 and has asked for its application generally to loans of one year or more maturity. With the passage of such legislation the Administration will have, broadly speaking, a double-edged restraint on all forms of investment abroad, except direct investment and loans of under one year, to which only the voluntary restraint program applies. These exceptions were based to a considerable extent on administrative difficulties as well as the closer involvement of these forms of investment with U.S. exports.

It seems apparent, therefore, that the interest equalization tax remains a major deterrent in the area it affects. With congressional approval, the tax will be broadened to apply also to the one- to three-year lending of nonbank financial institutions, following the application of the Gore Amendment imposing the tax on bank loans of one year or longer.   However, the primary influence on bank lending is the guidelines issued by the Federal Reserve System which deal with curbing flows by limiting availability.   In the longer term area in which foreign issues are most likely to fall and for those investors which historically have been most interested in purchasing such securities, we continue to rely on the interest equalization tax.

It seems quite clear that heavy capital demands will characterize the free world for years and years to come.   At the same time, there may be a question as to how much of this demand the United States can meet and cover with a surplus in our current account.   If actual developments over time do show a need for some dampener on U.S. supplies of capital to the free world, the question as to the technique to be used will again be raised.   This is a highly "iffy" question.   However, in theoretical terms, I would submit that there is much to be said for the tax method, if indeed our objective remains one of interfering as little as possible in the operations of free markets.   The tax method does remain a nondiscriminatory allocator by the cost method and it provides the incentives for correctives permitting its eventual elimination.   I would think that these are not inconsiderable benefits to be lightly discarded.

It is always difficult to predict with any degree of accuracy the future state of our balance of payments or the year-to-year developments that might take place.   There are, however, some significant factors to be noted.   There are changes in the depth and quality of markets abroad taking place, slowly to be sure but nonetheless important.   Most importantly, there is in our balance-of-payments situation deep underlying strength.   There are favorable trends in our Government expenditures overseas as they affect the balance of payments; there is the fundamental encouragement growing out of the price stability characterizing our domestic economy and the increasing general competitiveness of the United States in world markets, key factors to the maintenance and strengthening of our trade position; there is also the growing amount of earnings arising from U.S. investments abroad over past decades which should sharply improve our balance-of-payments position in the years ahead.   How strong these forces will be and how quickly their strengthening will appear will have much to do with the timing of the day when we can begin to thaw out the restraints employed to bring, over the shorter term, a sharply improved balance-of-payments position.

Some may wonder whether this disappearance will be hastened by the achievement of a reinforced international payments system.   We are certainly going to continue to search for ways in which the international payments system can be further reinforced.   But this task should not be misinterpreted as one of finding a system which will permit any and all nations at their discretion to be perpetually in deficit.   It seems highly doubtful indeed that the countries of the free world will be willing to accept a situation in which the United States, for example, would run, in a future as in the past period of 15 years, deficits totaling $35 billion settled only 25 percent in gold.   Rather the search is one of exploring all means by which the system can be adapted, modified, and built upon to reinsure a system in which countries can avoid severe shocks either to their domestic economy or to other countries in correcting balance-of-payments positions.   In whatever system emerges, I am confident that the dollar will play a key role both as a trading and reserve currency.

Exhibit 47.—Remarks by Deputy Under Secretary of the Treasury for Monetary Affairs Volcker, June 8, 1965, before the Forecasting Conference of the Chicago Chapter of the American Statistical Association, on critical factors in the balance-of-payments problem

I do not need tonight, before this expert audience, to review in detail our balance-of-payments performance.   The overall results of recent years are familiar to all of us, and I will not belabor the basic point that our deficits have been both too large and too prolonged.

These deficits have persisted despite the many elements of underlying strength in our position: our enormous potential to produce, and in particular to produce efficiently the kinds of new and complex equipment in growing demand in world markets; the productivity of our agriculture in a world of rapidly rising population and heavy pressure on resources; our steadily growing world creditor position, and the rising returns our foreign investments will yield us in the years ahead; and, not least, I would also add the progress we have been making, in business and Government alike, in learning to develop policies that support our objective of reasonably steady growth in employment, output, and income at home without inflationary excesses.

These are some of the factors, in addition to our still large gold stock, that have made, and continue to make, the dollar the premier currency in the world. But these elements of long-term strength can in no way substitute for effective action to close promptly the imbalance in our payments, not just for a few months or a year, but without relapse into the chronic deficits of recent years.

One of the first lessons that is drilled into an economist is that a dollar earned in the future cannot be equated with a dollar earned today. That basic lesson applies with special force to the balance of payments. Whatever our future prospects, failure to take whatever action is required to protect the dollar today would strike at the vital underpinnings of the international financial system. The result would be to impair the hard won gains in trade and freer payments during the postwar period, and to undermine both our own prosperity and that of our trading partners. Moreover, the issues are not narrowly economic. It is plain that a strong dollar is an essential part of our ability to discharge effectively our farflung military, diplomatic, and foreign policy objectives.

This overriding need to protect the dollar is the essential setting for the balance-of-payments program set forth by President Johnson in February, a program that commits us to early elimination of our balance-of-payments deficit as a matter of high national priority.

I do not mean tonight to debate the particulars of that program. As you know, it includes a variety of measures to strengthen and reinforce our earlier efforts in a number of directions. But we all recognize that the key new element was the call to the, business and financial communities for cooperation, even at the expense of some short-run profit opportunities, in reducing the swelling outflow of private capital that was threatening to undercut our entire balance-of-payments position. These are not the kind of measures that we want to, or even could, live with forever. But, after years of sustained deficit, it is clear that extraordinary measures are essential, and that they must be made to work.

Recognition of that simple fact is implicit, I think, in the willing and gratifying response of businessmen and bankers to the program. The fragmentary data at hand suggest that over the three months since the program was announced our international accounts have returned to balance, and possibly to a surplus, a sharp contrast to the very large deficits in the fourth quarter of 1964 and the early weeks of this year. That turnabout was clearly importantly influenced by the end of the dock strike in February, and by other temporary factors, and it is far too soon to try to isolate and evaluate the particular contribution of the new program. But there are signs that, amid the other crosscurrents at work, the special efforts of the banks and businesses are beginning to have an effect.

It would, however, be a great mistake to conclude, on the basis of these early results, that the problem is already solved, or that we can look forward to any early relaxation of our efforts. In fact, the first few months were bound to be the easiest. It is very useful, for instance, to achieve some reflow of liquid funds originally placed abroad simply for the purpose of achieving a slightly higher interest return, and such reflows appear to have been one source of balance-of-payments improvement in recent months. But that source of improvement is, by its nature, a limited "one-shot" affair, and cannot substitute for hard and continuing efforts to achieve increased exports, to maximize the financing of foreign investment projects with foreign funds, and to reassess or defer marginal investment projects. Similarly, it is one thing for the banks to cut back for a few months the extraordinary bulge in foreign lending that developed in 1964 and during the earlier weeks of this year, as they appear to be doing, and another thing to observe the Federal Reserve guidelines, and the priorities within those guidelines, over time as customer demands build up. But, I see no basis for optimism that the special disciplines of the cooperative program can be relaxed in any way until our ability to maintain a balance over a sustained period has been fully demonstrated and proved.

In asserting this, however, I also recognize that full success in our effort to restore equilibrium cannot be claimed until we can finally phase out these voluntary restraints, and achieve equilibrium under conditions more consistent with normal market incentives and processes. So, it is a fair question to ask whether there are forces and programs at work, alongside the voluntary effort, that give promise of continued progress toward lasting equilibrium in our international accounts.

Without pretending a full analysis of that question tonight, I would like to touch upon developments in several of the critical areas that seem to me to bear directly upon the issue.

First of all, as you know, heartening evidence of an improvement in our trade position is already evident. The U.S. commercial trade surplus, excluding all Government financed shipments, reached a new peak of $3.7 billion last year, an improvement of $900 million since 1960, just before our balance-of-payments effort got underway in earnest. This performance is all the more noteworthy for the fact that it took place during a period of continuing expansion in the American economy, an expansion that has generated an increase of over 25 percent in our import bill since 1960.

To be sure, some nonrecurring factors helped our 1964 performance, and we cannot blithely count on so favorable results this year. But, I believe evidence is accumulating that a number of our industries have begun to benefit from the invigorating effects of increased competitiveness in world markets and that our efforts to step-up export promotion and improve export credit facilities are beginning to pay dividends.

The key to progress in this area has been and must remain, price stability. In contrast to the noticeable inflationary pressures and rising costs in nearly all other industrialized countries, our own expansion, despite some lapses in particular cases, has so far been notable for stability in our unit labor costs and the flatness of our industrial prices. Our wholesale prices, for instance, average only about 1 percent higher than in 1960, while the increases in France, Germany, the U.K., Italy, and Austria, to take a few leading European examples, have ranged from 8 percent to 15 percent. The contrast in consumer prices is at least as great, with European increases generally ranging from 12 percent to 24 percent, contrasting with about 5 percent in the United States.

I am aware that changes of this kind in internal price structures are not translated uniformly into export prices, and that the impact of rising average costs on international competitive positions and flows of trade is typically delayed. I am also aware that our relative price position in export markets deteriorated during the 1950's, so we have had ground to make up, and that, in the broader interests of orderly growth in the free world, we cannot expect or desire that our competitors in world markets live with inflation. But, with all the qualifications, recent trends seem to me to provide encouraging evidence that, in a context of vigorously expanding world markets, and with responsible policies at home alert to counter price pressures as they appear, our large export surplus can be maintained and even increased in the years ahead.

Side by side with the gradual recovery in our international competitive position, our current account has also benefited from a swelling flow of interest and dividends from abroad. This flow reached nearly $4 billion in 1964 alone, an increase of $1.6 billion over 1960. And further increases in these returns will eventually follow from the continuing heavy outflows of investment in recent years, as well as from further gains in business activity abroad.

It has, of course, been precisely in this area of capital outflows that our recent problems have been centered. The United States has been, and clearly should remain, a sizable capital exporter, both in our own interests and those of a world in critical need of capital for development. But the total of our capital outflow in 1964—reaching $6½ billion, or more than $2½ billion more than the already large figure of 1960—was clearly placing an intolerable burden on our balance of payments.

In examining the disequilibrium in international payments in recent years, and in speculating on their future shape, this outflow of American capital—and in particular the flow of American capital from the United States to Western Europe—assumes special importance. In 1964 the flow to Europe, as we record it in our statistics, totaled about $2.1 billion, equivalent to two-thirds of our entire deficit on regular transactions and about equal to the whole of the net increase in European monetary reserves. Viewed in the broader context of the basic capital needs of the world economy, as well as an immediate source of disequilibrium in world payments, it is incongruous, to say the least, that so much of our capital outflow should be diverted to the second richest area of the world, an area that should be fully capable of generating its own surplus of savings in helping to meet the urgent needs of the developing countries.

Are there forces in motion that promise, in this area, too, to restore an equilibrium, forces that will permit in time a relaxation of the special measures undertaken in February? Will the voluntary program itself help pave the way by forcing market adjustments that will themselves ease the task?

I would argue without pretending to foresee the future in detail or to deal with all the uncertainties, that there are some hopeful auguries, as well as continuing problems. For instance, partly responding to the incentives implicit in the interest equalization tax, Europe has already demonstrated its ability to absorb a much larger volume of new foreign bond issues, with the total in 1964 reaching nearly a billion dollars, almost double the previous record. And this burst of activity was accompanied by some useful experimentation with new institutional arrangements to broaden the market, including notably the widespread use of the dollar as, in effect, a common unit of account.

Against this encouraging development must be set the fact that, as the European markets absorbed this larger volume of foreign financing in 1964, long-term interest rates rose, and in some cases sharply. For instance, in the German market, where the largest portion of the foreign issues was placed, long-term rates have now reached 7 percent or more, in contrast to 6 percent 18 months ago. Increases of one-half percent or more in other countries were common. And, as the pressures on the European markets increased, foreign demands for capital tended to seep back into the American market through bank loans or other channels.

In the Euro-dollar market, to take the other end of the maturity spectrum, rates have moved up appreciably since February. So in that case, too, restraint by the United States may have had the effect, at least in the short run, of somewhat increasing interest rate differentials.

In part, these developments seem to me a symptom of underdeveloped capital markets in Europe, the full consequences of which the Europeans have escaped in the past by ready access to our own markets as a source of marginal capital. But more broadly, it is also a reflection of the fact that the European economies, by and large, have been running full tilt, with inflationary pressures of a kind that their monetary authorities would like to brake, and have been braking, through monetary policy. And beneath the surface is the implication of a high rate of return on capital investment in Europe, and in the end funds tend to flow where the profit outlook is best.

The extent to which the Europeans carry through in improving their own capital markets remains to be seen. Certainly, until European markets achieve the greater degree of cohesion, flexibility, and efficiency necessary if they are to provide at rates within a normal range, the large blocks of capital essential for their own growth, and for meeting a portion of the needs of other countries, the threat of recurring disequilibrating capital flows will remain. There are hopeful signs of progress, but also many obstacles to the kind of relaxation of restraints and restrictions in foreign markets, government or private, that circumstances would seem to warrant.

Meanwhile, the interest equalization tax, by raising in a nondiscriminatory way, the interest cost for borrowers in developed countries entering our market, is designed to afford protection against this kind of structural disequilibrium in world capital markets. We have asked that that tax be extended through 1967. A tax of this kind, operating through price and cost incentives in ways consistent with normal market forces, seems to me a tool well adapted to meeting this particular kind of problem.

Beyond the question of structural market differences, there is little doubt that we have made progress toward closing the gap which had so clearly developed during the 1950's in basic rates of return and profitability on investment between the United States and Europe. Let me review just a few figures bearing on the issue.

Corporate profits in the United States from 1957–60 averaged $21.9 billion after taxes, and the ratio to GNP had declined to 4.7 percent, a fact reflected in the widespread concern expressed over a "profits squeeze." By the first quarter of this year, however, aftertax profits were running two-thirds higher at $36.5 billion, and had returned to 5.6 percent of GNP, despite the effects of more liberal depreciation guidelines in encouraging corporations to increase depreciation allowances at the expense of reported profits. Looking at manufacturing industries alone, aftertax profit margins on sales rose from 4.5 percent in the 1957–60 period to 5.4 percent in the final quarter of 1964, a gain of 20 percent. And even more directly relevant to investment decisions, the rate of return on equity in manufacturing industries has climbed over the same period from 9.8 percent to 12.4 percent.

Clearly, this improved climate for investment in the United States has not, in itself, so far prevented a rising capital outflow—or encouraged an equivalent rise in foreign investment here—amid all the other factors bearing upon these investment decisions. But there are signs that the extraordinary investment and profit opportunities in Europe that developed out of its rapid growth and the development of the Common Market in the late 1950's and early 1960's are gradually being exhausted. And it does seem to me that, slowly but surely, this kind of narrowing of the gap in investment prospects cannot fail to exert a favorable effect in bringing a more balanced flow of funds internationally, as long-range investment programs are established and formulated not on the basis of conditions that existed a few years ago, but on the basis of today's facts and the brighter prospects for the home market.

This is an area in which our domestic needs coincide directly with the requirements of international equilibrium. As you know, our fiscal policies have been fundamentally reoriented in recent years to help sustain our busines expansion and improve our profit potential. The results, in terms of our domestic economy, are plain, and I am confident the improved domestic investment climate should help us internationally as well. Moreover, we have proposed measures to encourage foreigners themselves to share in these benefits by removing features of our tax structure that discourage foreign investment here out of all proportion to the revenues generated.

In summary, as we look ahead, in the investment area as in the current account, there are some encouraging signs that basic forces are at work toward equilibrium. Many problems remain and no precise timetable can be specified. But the opportunities are clear, if we have the will and wisdom to seize them.

The nature of the challenge is clear. For example, past experience indicates that the task of maintaining price stability can be even more difficult as levels of unemployment decline. Good as our past performance has been in this respect, Government, business, and labor must continue to face up to their own responsibilities in protecting and extending that record against any new threats on the horizon. We must be equally alert to the dangers of recession or stagnation that could only impair investment prospects at home and increase incentives to the outflow of funds, while undermining our prospects for continuing growth in productivity and maintaining our lead in technology. At the same time, as our accounts begin to respond to the voluntary program, we must not be under any illusion that we can delay or weaken measures, large or small, to reduce the outflow of Government dollars abroad, to spur our exports, and to encourage tourism in the United States.

The other side of the coin seems to me equally clear. There is no room for relaxation of the voluntary program in a presumption that the long-range factors and other measures upon which I have concentrated tonight will predictably and promptly restore equilibrium, no matter how favorable they may appear to be. The time has come when we must end our deficits, and end them decisively. We cannot escape into the long run, nor can we procrastinate in the idle hope that some alchemy in the form of a new international monetary system will ease the task.

I am confident that, with the continued willing cooperation of the business and financial communities, we will succeed in our effort. Anything less will fall short of our needs.

Exhibit 48.—Treasury and Federal Reserve foreign exchange operations, March–August 1964

This fifth joint interim report reflects the Treasury-Federal Reserve policy of making available additional information on foreign exchange operations from time to time. The Federal Reserve Bank of New York acts as agent for both the Treasury and the Federal Open Market Committee of the Federal Reserve System in the conduct of foreign exchange operations.

This report was prepared by Charles A. Coombs, Vice President in charge of the Foreign Department of the Federal Reserve Bank of New York, and Special Manager, System Open Market Account.[1]

During the 6-month period March–August 1964, international credit facilities, both bilateral and multilateral, were again frequently called upon to cushion the impact upon gold and foreign exchange reserves of payments imbalances among the major trading nations. Official operations in the forward markets helped to smooth temporary swings during the period, while the gold pool arrangements continued to operate effectively. Transfers of gold among the central banks also fulfilled their customary role of helping to settle payments imbalances, but the volume of such official gold transfers declined still further. The decline reflected both a tendency toward narrowing of payments imbalances as well as economies in the use of gold made possible by the development of international credit facilities.

At the short-term end of the credit spectrum, the Federal Reserve swap network had been broadened by late 1963 to include 12 foreign official institutions, involving reciprocal credit lines totaling $2,050 million. During the period under review the short-term credit needs of the various central banks concerned were readily accommodated under the existing swap lines and other central bank credit facilities. From March through late August, drawings by the Federal Reserve and by three foreign central banks amounted to $262 million.

From the inception of the swap network in March 1962 through late August 1964, total central bank drawings amounted to $1,870 million. Of this amount $1,753 million, or 94 percent, was repaid, generally within 6 months. The Federal Reserve shifted from a peak net debtor position of $342 million on December 13, 1963, to a net creditor position of $44.5 million in late August 1964. Drawings on the Federal Reserve swap network outstanding in late August included $80 million by the Bank of Japan, partially offset by Federal Reserve use of $28 million drawn on the Netherlands Bank and $7.5 million on the National Bank of Belgium.

TABLE I.—*Federal Reserve reciprocal currency agreements, Aug. 31, 1964*

Other party to agreement	Amount of facility (in millions of dollars)	Term (months)
Bank of France	100	3
Bank of England	500	12
Netherlands Bank	100	3
National Bank of Belgium	50	6
Bank of Canada	250	12
Bank for International Settlements	150	6
Swiss National Bank	150	6
German Federal Bank	250	6
Bank of Italy	250	6
Austrian National Bank	50	12
Bank of Sweden	50	12
Bank of Japan	150	12
Total for all banks	2,050	

The Federal Reserve and U.S. Treasury in cooperation with foreign central banks, also conducted short-term forward operations in sterling, German marks, Swiss francs, and Canadian dollars, in order to restrain short-term money flows

---

[1] For previous reports on Treasury and Federal Reserve foreign exchange operations, see 1962 annual report, pp. 469–80; 1963 annual report, pp. 386–93; and 1964 annual report, pp. 322–39.

arising either from speculation or interest arbitrage. Over the period the Treasury reduced its commitments in the forward markets from $248 million to $82.5 million, all in 'Swiss francs, on August 31, while the Federal Reserve position on market transactions was in balance on the latter date. The central banks of Germany, Canada, Switzerland, and Italy also operated from time to time in the forward markets, and in each case achieved the desired effect on the flow of funds.

As noted in the report of the Deputies of the Group of Ten, "These demonstrations of close central bank cooperation are themselves an effective deterrent to speculative movements. Their informality, speed, and flexibility make them especially suitable as a first line—and short-term—defense against sudden balance of payments pressures. Over the past several years, they have mobilized massive resources in a short time to-combat and limit speculative and crisis situations. Their success has greatly reduced the threat to official reserves from disequilibrating movements of private short-term capital." [1]

TABLE II.—*Operations under Federal Reserve reciproca currency agreements, 1962–64*

[In millions of dollars]

Bank	1962				1963				1964		Total
	I	II	III	IV	I	II	III	IV	I	II	
Bank of France											
Drawings	50.0	------	------	------	------	------	12.5	9.0	------	------	71.5
Repayments	------	------	50.0	------	------	------	------	12.5	9.0	------	71.5
Bank of England											
Drawings	------	50.0	------	------	25.0	[1]25.0	------	10.0	------	[1]15.0	125.0
Repayments	------	------	50.0	------	------	25.0	[1]25.0	10.0	------	------	110.0
Netherlands Bank											
Drawings	------	10.0	40.0	10.0	------	50.0	40.0	60.0	------	------	210.0
Repayments	------	------	50.0	------	10.0	------	------	50.0	55.0	25.0	210.0
National Bank of Belgium [2]											
Drawings	------	------	10.5	20.0	30.0	15.0	10.0	15.0	------	------	100.5
Repayments	------	------	10.5	5.0	32.5	17.5	5.0	15.0	15.0	------	100.5
Bank of Canada											
Drawings	------	------	[1]250.0	------	------	------	------	20.0	------	------	270.0
Repayments	------	------	------	[1]250.0	------	------	------	20.0	------	------	270.0
Bank for International Settlements											
Drawings	------	------	60.0	20.0	------	------	50.0	100.0	------	------	230.0
Repayments	------	------	10.0	15.0	9.5	45.5	------	5.0	15.0	130.0	230.0
Swiss National Bank											
Drawings	------	------	50.0	------	------	------	------	80.0	------	25.0	155.0
Repayments	------	------	------	------	------	50.0	------	5.0	------	100.0	155.0
German Federal Bank											
Drawings	------	------	------	------	------	150.0	------	136.0	55.0	------	341.0
Repayments	------	------	------	------	------	------	113.0	113.0	115.0	------	341.0
Bank of Italy											
Drawings	------	------	------	50.0	------	------	------	[1]50.0	[1]100.0	------	200.0
Repayments	------	------	------	------	50.0	------	------	------	------	[1]150.0	200.0
Austrian National Bank											
Drawings	------	------	------	50.0	------	------	------	------	------	------	50.0
Repayments	------	------	------	------	50.0	------	------	------	------	------	50.0
Bank of Japan											
Drawings	------	------	------	------	------	------	------	------	------	[1]50.0	50.0
Repayments	------	------	------	------	------	------	------	------	------	------	
Total for all banks											
Drawings	50.0	310.0	160.5	150.0	55.0	240.0	112.5	480.0	155.0	90.0	1,803.0
Repayments	------	------	170.5	270.0	152.0	138.0	193.0	200.5	209.0	405.0	1,738.0

[1] Drawings and repayments made by foreign central bank.
[2] Data represent disbursements and repurchases under the $50 million arrangement, which has remained fully drawn since its inception. A total of $45 million disbursements were initiated by the National Bank of Belgium.

In the medium-term segment of the international credit spectrum, the U.S. Treasury issued an additional $474 million of bonds in the foreign currency series, while redeeming $200 million for a net addition of $274 million equiva-

[1] *Ministerial Statement of The Group of Ten and Annex Prepared by Deputies*, Aug. 10, 1964, published in 1964 annual report, pp. 343–365.

lent. The total of foreign currency securities outstanding on August 31 amounted to $1,035 million, distributed as shown in table III.

Of the $474 million of foreign currency bonds issued during the period under review, $70 million were employed to fund indebtedness previously incurred by the Federal Reserve by drawings upon the swap network. Of total Federal Reserve repayments of swap drawings since the inception of the network, $120 million, or roughly 9 percent, have been so financed.

TABLE III.—*U.S. Treasury securities denominated in foreign currencies, Aug. 31, 1964*

[In millions]

Issued to	Amount in foreign currency		U.S. dollar equivalent
Austrian National Bank	Sch.	1,300	$50.3
National Bank of Belgium	B F	1,500	30.1
German Federal Bank	DM	2,500	628.2
Swiss National Bank	S F	1,112	[1] 257.3
Bank for International Settlements	S F	300	69.5
Total			1,035.4

[1] Includes a $30 million equivalent, 1-year certificate of indebtedness.

Also in the medium-term credit area, the United States drew $250 million of foreign currencies during the first 8 months of the year under a $500 million standby agreement with the International Monetary Fund (renewed for another year in July 1964) in order to facilitate repayments to the Fund by other member countries. In other sizable Fund transactions, the Bank of Italy in March drew a total of $225 million. Also in March Japan was granted standby facilities in the amount of $305 million. In August the United Kingdom renewed its standby arrangement of $1,000 million with the Fund.

Liquid resources for cushioning payments imbalances have thus continued to be flexibly provided through the international credit machinery. As noted in the report of the Deputies of the Group of Ten, "A country's liquidity is no longer measured solely by the level of its reserves in the form of gold and reserve currency balances (primary reserves). There is now a variety of ways in which monetary authories can, at need, replenish their balances of the currencies used for operations. Primary reserves are thus supplemented by a broad spectrum of other resources and facilities. At one end of this range come 'other reserves' of only slightly less liquidity but of unquestioned availability; at the other end of the range are negotiated credits, including those which will only be available when an international institution is satisfied that the borrower will employ effective adjustment processes to correct his deficit."

Sterling

In early February sterling came under some speculative selling pressure. The main factors involved seemed to be uncertainties generated by expectations of a general election in the spring, by publication of January trade data showing an unusually large trade deficit, and by market rumors of a revaluation of the German mark. These speculative pressures were resisted by Bank of England intervention in the exchange markets and, in a minor way, by Federal Reserve purchases of sterling in New York.

On February 27 the Bank of England raised its discount rate from 4 percent to 5 percent. This decisive action produced an immediate strengthening of market confidence in sterling and the sterling rate recovered sharply. Following the increase in the discount rate, the British Treasury bill rate rose to a level about 0.60 percent per annum over the U.S. bill rate, but the forward discount on sterling promptly widened, and the covered arbitrage margin on Treasury bills settled at about zero. Almost simultaneously with the British discount rate increase, the Federal Reserve and U.S. Treasury joined forces with the German Federal Bank in both spot and forward operations in German marks. As detailed elsewhere in this report, these operations seemed to achieve their objective of dispelling market rumors of a possible change in the mark parity, and thereby also helped to relieve the pressure on sterling that had been coming from this source.

In early April sterling strengthened further following the announcement that the British general elections would not be held until October. Immediately thereafter commercial interests that had previously postponed their purchases bought sterling to cover their near-term requirements, and the spot rate for the pound sterling rose to $2.8002 by the end of the month. Demand from this source, together with the continued strength of the payments positions of the overseas sterling area, bolstered during April and most of May.

In the last few days of May, however, sterling once again came under pressure as the covering of commitments was completed and as very tight conditions in several continental money markets, as well as in the Euro-dollar market, drew funds from London. Moreover, toward the end of June the usual midyear "window dressing" by continental banks put additional temporary pressure on sterling. To temper the impact of these movements of funds on official reserves, the Bank of England on June 30 drew $15 million against its $500 million swap line with the Federal Reserve. The drawing was repaid on July 13. Also in June, the Federal Reserve Bank of New York purchased for U.S. Treasury account approximately $6 million in sterling.

As the credit squeeze in continental European money market centers continued into July, sterling was subject to recurrent selling pressure and the spot rate on sterling moved downward with a minimum of official support to a low for the month of $2.7874 on July 20. In a market aware of British Government determination to defend the sterling parity with the ready support, if needed, of the IMF standby arrangement, the Federal Reserve swap line, and credit facilities at other central banks, the decline of the spot rate was taken in stride with no speculative reaction developing. Moreover, as the spot rate declined, the technical position of sterling was correspondingly improved by the increasing risk of a rebound of the spot rate and consequent loss to those with short positions in sterling. Again reflecting the underlying strength of market confidence in the sterling parity, the discount on forward sterling also tended to narrow as the spot rate declined.

The strength of the forward sterling rate, while gratifying to all concerned, nevertheless created certain complications. As the discount on forward sterling tightened, the covered interest arbitage differential favoring London on Treasury bills became correspondingly more attractive and by July 13 had reached the level of 0.44 percent per annum. To forestall private covered outflows in response to this arbitrage inducement, the Federal Reserve with the agreement of the British authorities intervened in the market to widen out the discount on forward sterling and thereby reduce the arbitrage differential. This intervention, amounting to a total of $28 million equivalent during a 5-day period, was accomplished by swap transactions in the New York market, with the Federal Reserve Bank of New York, for System account, buying sterling spot and selling sterling forward against U.S. dollars. At the same time, on July 20, the Treasury announced that it was offering an additional $1 billion of Treasury bills to help strengthen U.S. bill rates. By July 23 the arbitrage margin on Treasury bills in favor of London had been reduced to 0.32 percent per annum, and intervention was discontinued.

In mid-August sterling once again came under pressure in the spot market as continental holders apparently shifted funds from sterling into the Euro-dollar market. Spot sterling reached a low in New York of $2.7839 on August 27, but the forward rate stayed relatively firm as market confidence in the sterling parity remained undisturbed.

On March 31 the Federal Reserve sold to the U.S. Treasury $10 million equivalent of sterling, which was used by the Treasury, together with $5 million equivalent of its own sterling holdings, to acquire $15 million equivalent of Swiss francs through a sterling–Swiss franc swap with the Bank for International Settlements. Federal Reserve and Treasury swaps of this nature—involving the exchange of one foreign currency for another—have now included five European currencies and amounted to a total of $115 million equivalent. Of this total, $51 million equivalent remained outstanding at the end of August—$13 million equivalent for System account and $38 million equivalent for Treasury account—all involving the purchase of Swiss francs against sterling.

German marks

During 1963, there was almost continuous upward pressure on the German mark. The pressure reflected mainly a substantial increase in the German foreign trade surplus, large inflows of long-term capital, and occasional inflows of short-term funds in response to tight money market conditions or hedging operations. Although the Federal Reserve frequently drew upon its $250 million swap line with the German Federal Bank in order to cushion these pressures, all drawings effected during 1963 had been repaid by January 9, 1964, through operations summarized in the preceding report in this series.

In late January and February 1964, buying pressure on the mark resumed in even greater force, with indications of speculative overtones developing. To counter these pressures, the German Federal Bank intervened strongly in Frankfurt—buying dollars at rates just below the ceiling on the mark. In addition, the Federal Reserve made sizable new drawings on the swap line to support market intervention in New York and to absorb dollars taken in by the German Federal Bank. During the first half of March, Federal Reserve drawings totaled $55 million equivalent.

These operations in the spot market were reinforced by a resumption—for the first time since 1961—of joint operations by the U.S. Treasury and the German Federal Bank in the forward market in an effort to dispel rumors of a prospective change in the mark parity. Sales of 3-month forward marks amounted to approximately $21 million equivalent between the end of February and the middle of March at rates ranging between 0.96 percent and 0.75 percent per annum premium on the mark. All of these contracts were liquidated without difficulty at maturity.

On March 23 an important turning point occurred as the German Government announced its intention to propose to Parliament the imposition of a 25 percent withholding tax on the interest income of nonresidents. This action not only checked the long-term capital inflow, but actually induced liquidation of a considerable volume of foreign investments in German fixed-interest securities. Earlier, on March 10, the German Federal Bank had already taken steps to encourage an outflow of German funds into dollar investments by providing dollars on a swap basis—selling dollars spot and repurchasing them 90 to 180 days forward—to German commercial banks for purchases of U.S. Treasury bills at a preferential discount of 0.50 percent per annum on the forward dollar. This compared with a market discount at the time of more than 0.75 percent per annum. By April 15 the total of such dollar investment swaps outstanding had risen to $186 million. As a consequence of the outflows on both short- and long-term capital account, the exchange market moved into a much closer balance that continued to prevail during April and May.

In these circumstances, the Federal Reserve Bank of New York was able in late March to acquire for System account $20 million equivalent of marks and thereby to reduce its swap drawings from $55 million to $35 million equivalent. This remaining drawing was liquidated on March 31 by purchase from the Bank of Italy of $35 million of marks originating in an Italian drawing of marks from the IMF. On the same date, the U.S. Treasury acquired $45 million equivalent of marks from the same source. The Treasury subsequently employed the bulk of these mark funds to absorb dollars taken in by the German Federal Bank.

These exchange transactions illustrate how the United States, because of the reserve-currency role of the dollar, now responds to the ebb and flow of the payments balances of foreign countries. During the winter months of 1963–64 the large surplus in the German balance of payments was accompanied by a very large deficit in Italian payments. This imbalance within the Common Market brought about a simultaneous weakening of the lira and a strengthening of the mark against the dollar, the currency in which both the Bank of Italy and the German Federal Bank customarily settle their international accounts. These exchange market pressures were intensified by widespread rumors of a revaluation of the mark and a devaluation of the lira.

As a short-run defensive measure, recourse to central bank credit, in the form of Bank of Italy drawings of dollars from the Federal Reserve and Federal Reserve drawings of marks from the German Federal Bank, served to temper these potentially disturbing market pressures with benefit for all concerned. Consequently when the Italian Government had recourse to the IMF, it was entirely appropriate for the Federal Reserve and the U.S. Treasury, which had operated to cushion the immediate impact of both the Italian deficit and the German surplus, to liquidate their mark commitments by acquiring marks drawn by Italy from the IMF.

A second aspect of U.S. involvement in the German-Italian payments imbalance was the repayment by the U.S. Treasury of $200 million of lira bonds issued to the Bank of Italy in 1962 and the issuance to the German Federal Bank of $200 million equivalent of mark bonds. In effect, medium-term foreign currency bonds, previously acquired by the Bank of Italy in partial settlement of the surplus in its balance of payments, were transformed, as had been originally understood, into a usable reserve asset as Italy shifted from a creditor to a debtor position. The lira bonds were redeemed and, in practice, transferred to the German Federal Bank, becoming an attractive investment medium denominated in German marks in which Germany could hold a part of its balance of payments surplus.

The rationale of this operation had been foreshadowed in a joint central bank report published in August 1963, which suggested : [1]

"Even after the United States has regained equilibrium in its payments accounts, certain countries will from time to time move into a strong creditor position which will, in turn, expose the United States, as banker for the international financial system, to the risk of net drains upon its gold stock. We have previously suggested that informal understandings should be sought whereby the creditor countries might attempt, either through greater flexibility in their gold policy or through more extensive use of forward exchange and related operations, to avoid causing a net drain upon the U.S. gold stock. To round out such a system of minimizing net losses of gold by the United States as a result of pronounced surplus and deficit positions in other countries, the United States might also find it useful on occasion to provide the creditor country with an investment outlet for its surplus in the form of special bonds denominated in the creditor's currency."

Still a third aspect of the pivotal role of the United States in the international financial mechanism was a sale of $200 million of gold by the Bank of Italy to the U.S. Treasury in order to replenish the dollar reserves of the Bank of Italy. The Treasury immediately resold this gold to the German Federal Bank in recognition of the fact that the Italian deficit and German surplus were, to a considerable extent, opposite sides of the same coin.

No further operations in German marks for either Federal Reserve or Treasury account occurred until early June when a brief revival of speculation concerning a mark revaluation was met by sales on the New York market of $5 million of marks for Federal Reserve account and $6 million for U.S. Treasury account. The German Federal Bank simultaneously supported the dollar with sizable operations in Frankfurt, and on June 3 the Treasury employed $40 million equivalent of mark balances acquired at the time of the Italian drawing on the IMF to absorb dollars taken in by the German Federal Bank. Buying pressure on the mark was further intensified in mid-June by commercial bank window-dressing operations, and $150 million of the resultant inflow to the German Federal Bank was absorbed by an additional Treasury issue of mark-denominated bonds. This latest issue raised the total of such mark bonds outstanding to $628 million equivalent.

On July 9 the German Federal Bank announced an increase in commercial bank reserve requirements effective August 1. The mark again was subject to upward pressure and the U.S. Treasury sold a total of $4 million equivalent of marks in New York on July 9 and 10. To counter possible repatriation of short-term bank funds, the German Federal Bank on July 13 reduced the investment swap discount on forward dollars from 0.50 to 0.25 percent per annum. The demand for marks then eased, and no further operations were undertaken by either the Federal Reserve or U.S. Treasury through the end of August.

Italian lira

The Italian lira came under increasingly heavy selling pressure during the winter of 1963-64 as a result of a widening payments deficit on current account, sizable capital outflows, and repayments of foreign indebtedness by the Italian commercial banks. To deal with the situation, the Italian authorities initiated various corrective policy measures, which were expected to take effect over a

---

[1] "Conversations on International Finance," by C. A. Coombs, M. Iklé (Banque Nationale Suisse), E. Ranalli (Banca d' Italia), and J. Tungeler (Deutsche Bundesbank), *Monthly Review*, Federal Reserve Bank of New York, August 1963, pp. 114-21.

period of months. Meanwhile, as heavy drains upon the Bank of Italy's reserves continued, the need for short-term credit and other assistance became clear.

Under the $250 million swap line with the Federal Reserve, the Bank of Italy made three successive drawings of $50 million each in October 1963, January 1964, and March 1964. Acquisition of lire by the U.S. authorities for eventual repayment of $200 million equivalent of lira bonds issued to the Bank of Italy in 1962 also helped the Bank of Italy to replenish its liquid reserves. In anticipation of such repayments, the U.S. Treasury had purchased $67 million equivalent of lire from the Bank of Italy in the early fall of 1963. Of this total, $17 million was temporarily employed in a swap against Swiss francs with the BIS.

This program of advance acquisition of lire to meet prospective maturities of lira bonds was carried further by Federal Reserve purchases of $50 million equivalent of lire in December 1963, another $50 million in January 1964, and a final purchase of $33 million in March. These lire were simultaneously sold forward to the U.S. Treasury, which redeemed one $50 million lira bond at its first maturity on March 9, and on April 1 prepaid the remaining $150 million of lira bonds outstanding. These Federal Reserve and Treasury operations, totaling $350 million, cushioned the decline in the Bank of Italy's reserves and thereby helped restrain speculative pressure.

During the week of March 9 to 14, 1964, an Italian delegation, headed by Governor Carli of the Bank of Italy, visited Washington to discuss with the World Bank and the International Monetary Fund various possible sources of financing for Italy's longer-term investment requirements and its expected further balance-of-payments deficits. In the midst of these discussions the lira was suddenly struck by a burst of speculation, which brought heavy pressure not only on the spot rate but also on the forward rate, which for a 3-month maturity moved to a discount of 7 percent per annum. In this dangerous situation, an immediate and massive reinforcement of the Italian reserve position was clearly called for, and within 48 hours the Italian authorities were able to announce that approximately $1 billion of external assistance was at their disposal. This credit package included: (1) a $100 million swap arrangement with the U.S. Treasury (in addition to the partly drawn swap facility with the Federal Reserve System), (2) a $200 million standby credit from the Export-Import Bank, (3) $250 million in credits of up to 3 years from the U.S. Commodity Credit Corporation, and (4) short-term credit facilities of $250 million from the Bank of England and the German Federal Bank. Had time permitted, other foreign official sources of short-term credit could readily have been tapped.

Announcement of this credit package immediately broke the speculative wave. As market confidence in the lira revived, the Bank of Italy temporarily withdrew its support from the spot market and allowed the lira to decline to a level close to par, where it settled in relatively orderly and balanced trading. At the same time, the discount on the 3-month forward lira narrowed from 7 percent to 3 percent, further reflecting the improvement in market confidence.

At the end of March the Italian Government made a drawing of $225 million on the IMF in various currencies. Of this total, $80 million equivalent of German marks were immediately sold to the Federal Reserve and the U.S. Treasury, and $20 million equivalent of guilders to the Federal Reserve. These transactions enabled the Federal Reserve to settle outstanding commitments in the respective currencies and provided marks to the Treasury to meet possible future operational needs. In June, against the background of substantial earlier movements of funds from Italy to Switzerland, the Bank of Italy negotiated a $100 million equivalent lira–Swiss franc swap with the Swiss National Bank. In this instance, too, the entire Swiss franc proceeds were sold by the Bank of Italy to the Federal Reserve for dollars. (The System then employed these Swiss francs to liquidate outstanding Swiss franc indebtedness to the Swiss National Bank.)

With its dollar reserve position reinforced not only by bilateral credits and the Fund drawing, but also by net accruals of dollars in the exchange market, the Bank of Italy proceeded to repay during the second quarter of the year all of its previous drawings of $150 million on the Federal Reserve as well as the short-term credit drawn under the facility provided by the German Federal Bank. In addition, about one-third of the $100 million credit from the Swiss National Bank had also been repaid by the end of August. (No drawings had been made under the credit facilities made available by the U.S. Treasury or the Bank of England. Nor has there as yet been any utilization of the credits made available by the Commodity Credit Corporation or the Export-Import Bank, although use of these credits is expected to begin shortly.)

One of the most satisfactory aspects of this display of international cooperation in beating back a speculative attack on the Italian lira was that the provision of massive credit assistance to Italy more or less coincided with a turning point in the Italian economic and financial scene. During the first quarter of 1964, the Italian balance of payments had registered a deficit of $436 million. This turned into a surplus of $226 million in the second quarter as the corrective policy measures previously initiated by the Italian authorities began to take effect and as a reversal in the leads and lags brought about the covering of short positions in lire. In early July a governmental crisis generated a temporary speculative flurry, but forceful operations in the forward market by the Bank of Italy through the agency of the Federal Reserve Bank of New York provided reassurance, and the speculation quickly subsided. Indeed, Italy gained reserves during the summer and on September 1 repaid $65 million of its $225 million IMF drawing. This repayment reduced the Fund's holdings of lire to 75 percent of the Italian quota. Thus, Italy's obligation to the Fund has been completely liquidated.

As reported in previous articles in this series, the U.S. Treasury in January 1962 had undertaken to share with the Bank of Italy contracts to purchase forward dollars that that institution had entered into with Italian commercial banks in order to encourage a reexport of dollars during the period of heavy balance-of-payments surpluses. The initial value of the contracts taken over by the U.S. Treasury in January 1962 amounted to $200 million. Total U.S. commitments to supply forward lire rose to a peak of $500 million in August of that year, and thereafter—with some fluctuations—generally declined as Italian commercial banks reduced their dollar holdings. The last of the contracts were reacquired by the Italian authorities in March of this year, thus fully liquidating the Treasury's forward lira commitments.

Swiss franc

Very heavy inflows of short-term funds into Switzerland at the end of 1963 reflected the usual window-dressing operations by Swiss commercial banks. To absorb part of the resultant accumulation of dollars on the books of the Swiss National Bank, the Federal Reserve increased its swap drawings in Swiss francs on the BIS from $95 million to $145 million equivalent and on the Swiss National Bank from $55 million to $75 million, for a combined total of $220 million. Prior to this yearend bulge, outstanding drawings during most of the last quarter ranged around $150 million. During the autumn, the Treasury had also entered into forward transactions in Swiss francs of nearly $150 million equivalent.

Some easing of the Swiss franc developed after the yearend, but continuing inflows of capital during the first quarter limited the usual seasonal weakening. Moreover, interest rates in Switzerland had risen rapidly from the fall of 1963 through the first quarter of 1964. The rate paid by Swiss banks on 3-month time deposits, which had ranged from about 2.65 percent to 3 percent during most of 1963, moved up to 3.25 percent in March, while Euro–Swiss franc deposit rates, which closely reflect credit conditions in Switzerland, advanced one-half of a percentage point to 3.62 percent during the first quarter. Consequently, opportunities for the Federal Reserve to acquire Swiss francs for settlement of its outstanding Swiss franc indebtedness developed more slowly than expected, and by mid-April it had paid off only $45 million equivalent of its drawings on the BIS.

In April a severe tightening of the Swiss credit market pushed interest rates up further and drove the Swiss franc to the ceiling once more, and the Swiss National Bank was forced to take in a sizable amount of dollars at that level. Part of this inflow was absorbed when the Federal Reserve made a new drawing of $25 million equivalent on its swap line with the Swiss National Bank, thus putting the Federal Reserve debt in Swiss francs back to $200 million.

In order to curb inflationary pressures in the Swiss economy, the Swiss Government in March had placed restrictions on construction activity and had authorized the Swiss National Bank to introduce measures limiting credit expansion by banks and discouraging the inflow of foreign funds. Similar arrangements between the central bank and the banks had been in effect for several years on a voluntary basis. The gentlemen's agreements concerning restrictions on domestic credit growth took on legal force in May 1964. In an effort to halt the heavy inflow of foreign capital and the rise in dollar holdings of the Swiss National Bank, restraints on the inflow of funds from abroad were implemented at the end of March. All Swiss banking institutions were forbidden to pay interest on foreign deposits received after January 1, 1964, and were required to invest in foreign currency assets or to deposit with the Swiss National Bank any increase since January 1, 1964, in their net Swiss franc liabilities to foreigners.

While these measures were successful in halting further inflows of foreign funds, they did not of course prevent the repatriation by Swiss banks of funds already held abroad. Since the credit squeeze in Switzerland was continuing, there seemed little likelihood of any reversal of the previous inflow of funds. As a result, following the Federal Reserve swap drawing in April, the Swiss and U.S. authorities agreed on a combination of special measures to liquidate all of the Federal Reserve swap drawings and reduce the Treasury's outstanding forward contracts.

The first step was taken in May, when the U.S. Treasury issued to the BIS a $70 million Swiss franc bond. To acquire the Swiss francs, the BIS had issued 3-month promissory notes to the Swiss banks. The Swiss franc proceeds of this bond issue were then sold to the Federal Reserve, which immediately repaid an equivalent amount of its Swiss franc debt to the BIS. The second step came in June when, as previously noted, the Bank of Italy entered into a $100 million lira–Swiss franc swap agreement with the Swiss National Bank. The Bank of Italy sold the Swiss francs it acquired to the Federal Reserve, which retired the remainder of its Swiss franc debt to the Swiss National Bank. At the end of June the Federal Reserve paid off the remaining $30 million of its swap drawings on the BIS with francs obtained in conjunction with a sale of gold to the Swiss National Bank by the Treasury. The Federal Reserve swap arrangements with the BIS and the Swiss National Bank thus reverted to a standby basis.

Meanwhile, interest rates in Switzerland had risen still further as the heavy demands imposed on the Swiss money and capital markets by the continuing high level of economic activity further squeezed the liquidity position of Swiss banks and firms. The interest rate on 3-month deposits reached 3.50 percent in June, an increase of about 0.75 percent over the previous year, while the average yield on Government bonds moved up to 4.05 percent, as compared with 3.15 percent a year earlier. To relieve the squeeze on their liquidity positions and to satisfy midyear window-dressing purposes, the Swiss commercial banks made further sizable repatriations of funds during June.

These commercial bank operations caused the Swiss National Bank once again to take in a sizable amount of dollars. In July the unwinding of some window-dressing operations and an easing of the Swiss money market brought about only a partial reversal of the previous inflows. In these circumstances, the U.S. Treasury issued to the Swiss National Bank on August 4 an additional Swiss franc bond in the amount of $52 million equivalent and used the proceeds to absorb an equivalent amount of dollars on the books of the Swiss National Bank. At the same time the Swiss National Bank placed with the Swiss commercial banks an equivalent amount of "sterilization rescriptions" (a form of short-term paper issued by the Swiss Confederation) to reduce excess domestic liquidity.

As noted above, the U.S. Treasury in the latter half of 1963 had sold in the market nearly $150 million equivalent of 3-month forward Swiss francs to encourage outward investment flows by Swiss commercial banks. By the end of the year the Treasury's forward commitments had been reduced to $121 million. Additional sales of $9 million equivalent occurred in January, and the outstanding contracts were rolled over at maturity until May 1964, when $9 million equivalent was paid off. An additional $19 million was liquidated in June, and in August, at U.S. Treasury initiative, a further $19 million was paid off at maturity. This left a total of $83 million still outstanding. In addition, there were outstanding $38 million equivalent in U.S. Treasury–Swiss franc liabilities arising from swaps of sterling for Swiss francs with the BIS. During this period a $17 million swap of lire for Swiss francs was liquidated, and a $15 million sterling–Swiss franc swap was substituted.

Taking the Federal Reserve swap drawings and Treasury forward commitments together, temporary financing had reached a maximum of nearly $350 million at the end of 1963. By the end of August, 1964, the swap drawings had been entirely paid off and, as indicated above, Treasury forward commitments in the market had been reduced to $83 million. A good part of this reduction in short-term Swiss franc commitments, however, was achieved through the issuance of $122 million equivalent of Swiss franc bonds, the sale of $30 million in gold to the Swiss National Bank, and purchases of Swiss francs from the Swiss National Bank, thereby increasing that Bank's dollar holdings.

Netherlands guilder

The Netherland guilder declined during the first 2 months of 1964 as the Dutch trade position began to weaken, and toward the end of March the Federal Reserve Bank of New York was able to purchase for System account $5 million equivalent of guilders from the Netherlands Bank. At about the same time, the System acquired $20.1 million equivalent of guilders from the Bank of Italy, which had taken guilders as part of its drawing on the IMF. With these guilder funds, the Federal Reserve on April 2 paid off at maturity its outstanding $25 million equivalent swap drawing from the Netherlands Bank, thus placing the entire $100 million swap arrangement on a standby basis.

During most of the second quarter the guilder continued to decline as the Dutch trade deficit increased. In early June the Netherlands Bank raised its discount rate by one-half of a percentage point to 4½ percent. The money market then began to tighten, and in July Dutch commercial banks repatriated funds, causing a strengthening of the spot guilder. The Netherlands Bank took in dollars in moderating the rise in the rate, and during the first week in August the Federal Reserve drew $20 million equivalent of guilders under the swap line and immediately used the guilders to absorb some of the Netherlands Bank's dollar accruals.

On August 10 the Federal Reserve drew another $10 million equivalent of guilders in anticipation of possible market operations. Subsequently it sold $8 million equivalent to the Netherlands Bank to mop up additional dollars held by that Bank.

Japanese yen

During most of the first half of 1964 the Japanese yen remained at or close to its floor, as a continuing increase in Japan's deficit on current account was covered only in part by long- and short-term capital inflows. The Japanese authorities had initiated a series of restraint measures beginning in October 1963, and in March of this year the Bank of Japan raised its discount rate from 5.84 percent to 6.57 percent. In order to avoid further deterioration in its reserve position until the restraint measures should bring about the desired effect, as well as to support confidence in the yen in connection with the acceptance by Japan on April 1 of Article VIII status under the IMF Articles of Agreement, the Bank of Japan on April 30 drew $50 million under the $150 million swap arrangement with the Federal Reserve—the first use of this facility since its inception in October 1963. The pressure on reserves continued over the summer months, and on July 30 the Bank of Japan renewed the $50 million drawing for another 3 months and on July 31 drew an additional $30 million under the swap arrangement. In August, however, Japanese reserves registered an increase.

Canadian dollars

The spot market for Canadian dollars was relatively quiet through the first half of 1964, but there was considerable activity in the forward market as a result of grain sales to the Soviet Union. These sales generated heavy demands on the part of grain dealers for Canadian dollars against U.S. dollars for future delivery. (The contracts with the U.S.S.R. called for payment in U.S. dollars, whereas the grain companies had to purchase the wheat from the Canadian Wheat Board with Canadian dollars.) After meeting the grain dealers' demand—and after covering these forward sales to some extent through spot purchases—commercial banks attempted to balance their positions by engaging in swap transactions, selling Canadian dollars spot against forward purchases timed to meet likely calls on their forward commitments to the grain dealers. Consequently, the forward Canadian dollar advanced to a premium while the spot rate tended to decline.

In order to offset some of these pressures, the Bank of Canada sold U.S. dollars spot and purchased them forward, thus providing some counterpart to the commercial banks' swap needs. Despite such operations on a substantial scale by the Bank of Canada, the forward Canadian dollar remained at a premium, and the incentive to move funds from the United States to Canada on a covered basis as measured by the differential on 3-month Treasury bills rose to about 0.34 percent in the latter part of March. The situation became a source of concern to the U.S. authorities when it became evident that funds actually had been moving to Canada in some size, and with the agreement of the Canadian authorities, the Federal Reserve began in late March to sell Canadian dollars forward against spot purchases. As it turned out, the pressures on the forward Canadian dollar temporarily subsided, and Federal Reserve swaps in the market amounted to only $2 million. The matching of forward exchange commitments with shipment deliveries in connection with the very large grain sales continued to dominate the forward market in Canadian dollars through the end of June. Although the 3-month forward Canadian dollar widened to a premium of well over one-quarter of 1 percent per annum, the covered differential in favor of Canada held below 0.40 percent as Canadian short-term interest rates declined, and no further operations by the U.S. authorities were necessary.

By the end of July, Canadian grain shipments to the Soviet Union had been fairly well completed and pressures on the forward market consequently eased. Then during August a series of developments actually reversed the pressures in the Canadian dollar market. There was some buying of spot Canadian dollars by continental interests at the time of the Vietnam crisis, and as the spot rate rose in a thin market, Canadian exporters proceeded to sell out U.S. dollar balances. In addition, there were new grain purchases by several Eastern European countries, the effect of which was felt mainly in the spot market. At about the same time, there was a tightening of the Canadian money market and a flow of funds into Canada from the United States. The incentive for interest arbitrage flows was soon eliminated, however, by a sharp rise in the spot Canadian dollar rate and a decline in the forward rate. At the close of the period, the market was in balance.

Other currencies

Throughout most of the second quarter the Belgian franc moved narrowly in a market that was essentially in balance, and there was no occasion for either the Federal Reserve or the National Bank of Belgium to employ the swap balances held under the fully drawn swap arrangement. Early in July, however, the Belgian franc strengthened following the announcement of new measures designed to curb the growth of credit in Belgium. On July 3 the Belgian National Bank raised its discount rate by one-half a percentage point to 4¾ percent and announced that effective August 17 it would impose a cash reserve requirement against commercial bank deposits for the first time. Early in August the Federal Reserve used $7.5 million equivalent of Belgian francs drawn under the swap to absorb dollars on the books of the Belgian National Bank.

The French franc held firmly at its ceiling throughout most of the period, as the French balance of payments continued in surplus, and there were no Federal Reserve or Treasury operations in the market. As indicated in the following section, however, the Treasury did effect certain sales of French francs to various countries for repayments to the IMF. These repayments were spread out over a period of several months. Since the Treasury did not wish to leave sizable franc balances uninvested, a swap arrangement was entered into with the Bank of France, with provision for gradual reductions of the swap as the francs were required.

There were no Federal Reserve or Treasury operations in Swedish kronor or Austrian schillings during the March–August period.

IMF Drawing

In addition to the exchange operations discussed above, since the beginning of the year, the U.S. Treasury has sold foreign currencies to 16 different countries—including Canada, India, and a number of Latin American nations—for use in making repurchases from the IMF. (With the Fund's holdings of dollars now in excess of the dollar portion of the U.S. subscription, the Fund cannot at this time accept further dollars in repayment.) The U.S. Treasury acquired the foreign currencies sold, predominantly German marks and French francs, through two drawings on the IMF, on February 13 and June 1, in the amount of $125 million equivalent each under the $500 million standby agreement with the Fund announced by President Kennedy in July 1963. Of this $250 million equivalent drawn by the United States, the bulk had been utilized by the middle of August.

Pending disbursement of remaining balances from the second drawing, the marks were invested by the Treasury in German Treasury bills, and the French francs were returned to the Bank of France by means of the dollar–French franc swap mentioned above. On July 23, the original standby expired, and the Treasury announced that it had made a further standby arrangement with the IMF for another year, restoring the amount available to $500 million.

The first drawing under the new standby arrangement was made on September 1, when the United States drew $50 million in five European currencies. This drawing was occasioned by Italy's repayment to the Fund of $65 million.

Gold Market and U.S. Gold Transactions

Throughout the first 8 months of 1964 the London gold market was generally stable with prices seldom in excess of $35.09. There were brief periods when political uncertainties generated some speculative buying. In January, for example, private demand for gold picked up in large part because of unsettled conditions in Cyprus and Vietnam. Early in March these pressures were reinforced by buying from Italy, and gold fixing prices advanced to a high of $35.0986. The pressures quickly abated, however, and in the latter part of March, when the Soviet Union again appeared in the market as a seller of gold in connection with renewed grain purchases from the West, the price receded to $35.0586. Although the Soviet Union had withdrawn from the market by the end of April, market supply generally continued to exceed demand. Early in August the military flare-up in Vietnam and Cyprus again touched off a brief surge of speculative buying, but these tensions also faded quickly.

TABLE IV.—*U.S. net monetary gold transactions with foreign countries and international institutions, January–June 1964*

[In millions of dollars at $35 per fine troy ounce.   U.S. net sales (−); net purchases (+)]

Country	First quarter	Second quarter
Austria	−32. 1	−23. 2
Brazil	−1. 0	+28. 1
France	−101. 3	−101. 3
Germany	−200. 0	
Italy	+200. 0	
Switzerland		−30. 0
Turkey	−1. 2	+15. 0
United Kingdom	+109. 3	+220. 9
All other	−1. 2	−14. 5
Total	−27. 5	+95. 0

During the first half of the year, the United States continued to acquire sizable amounts of gold through the operation of the London gold pool. Such acquisitions are included in net gold purchases from the United Kingdom as shown in table IV, though the gold pool component in this figure will vary from one period to the next. Also shown in the table is the triangular gold transaction mentioned earlier, in which $200 million of gold sold to the United States by the Bank of Italy was immediately resold to the German Federal Bank. France, which had a continuing surplus in its balance of payments, remained the largest purchaser of gold from the United States. During the first half of the year French reserves rose some $280 million. On balance, after taking account of sales to domestic users of about $40 million, total U.S. gold holdings—including Stabilization Fund holdings along with the Treasury gold stock—increased by $27 million during the first 6 months of the year.

Exhibit 49.—Treasury and Federal Reserve foreign exchange operations,
September 1964–February 1965

*This sixth joint interim report reflects the Treasury-Federal Reserve policy of
making available additional information on foreign exchange operations from
time to time.[1]*

*This report was prepared by Charles A. Coombs, Vice President in charge of the
Foreign Department of the Federal Reserve Bank of New York, and Special
Manager, System Open Market Account.*

As noted in the previous report covering the period March–August 1964, the
Federal Reserve had completely liquidated its outstanding swap drawings by
the end of June, while drawings made by other central banks amounted to no
more than $65 million. Such diminished use of international credit facilities
reflected a reduced deficit in the U.S. balance of payments and a general narrowing of payments imbalances throughout the world.

This general movement toward international payments equilibrium suffered a
setback during the second half of 1964, however, mainly owing to the eruption of
the sterling crisis, heavy outflows of U.S. bank credit and long-term investment,
and the continuation and even further tightening of the credit squeeze in continental European markets. The risk of sudden, heavy strains upon the gold
exchange system had been well anticipated by the central banks and treasuries of
the major industrial countries, but the severity of the pressures developing in
late 1964 required a further reinforcement of intergovernmental defenses against
currency speculation.

During the reporting period September 1964–February 1965, the Federal
Reserve swap network was strengthened by increases in the swap arrangement
with the National Bank of Belgium from $50 million to $100 million and in the
arrangement with the Bank of England from $500 million to $750 million. The
swap network now covers reciprocal credit lines totaling $2,350 million, as shown
in table I.

The short-term credits extended to the Bank of England by the central banks of
Europe, Canada, and Japan in November 1964 provided further impressive evidence of the solidarity of central bank defenses when confronted with a currency
crisis. Also during the period, the authority of the International Monetary Fund
to borrow from its member countries was invoked for the first time, and much
progress was made toward the scheduled 25 percent increase in IMF quotas
during 1965. This process of challenge and timely response will no doubt continue to guide the further evolution of the international financial system.

The sterling emergency necessitated sizable drawings by the Bank of England
upon the Federal Reserve, which more or less concurrently drew heavily upon its
swap lines with the continental European central banks in order to cushion the
impact of heavy dollar inflows arising from both the British and U.S. deficits.
Bank of England drawings on the Federal Reserve swap line rose to a peak of
$700 million on November 27 but have subsequently been greatly reduced.

To absorb part of the dollar flows to the continental European central banks,
the Federal Reserve made drawings upon the swap lines with the central banks
of Switzerland, Germany, Belgium, the Netherlands, and Italy and with the Bank
for International Settlements. Of these drawings, $380 million remained out-
standing as of the end of February 1965. Further assisting the financing of both
British and U.S. payments imbalances, the central banks and governments of
other countries provided short- and medium-term financing through accumulations of dollars, extension of credits to the United Kingdom, purchases of U.S.
Treasury foreign currency securities, and provision of credit through the IMF.

In addition to central bank swap operations, both the Treasury and Federal
Reserve also engaged in forward operations in Netherlands guilders and Swiss
francs in order to calm market fears and encourage an outward flow of short-
term funds from Amsterdam and Zurich. The Swiss National Bank took steps
to help cushion the effects of anticipated yearend pressures on the Swiss franc.
The German Federal Bank also made available swap facilities to German commercial banks for investments in U.S. Treasury bills in order to reduce or offset
temporary pressures on the exchange market resulting from short-term capital
flows. Similarly, extensive use of forward operations was made by the Bank

---

[1] See also exhibit 48.

of England in December 1964 to reassure the market and relieve pressure on the spot rate.

The foreign currency bonds issued by the U.S. Treasury rose from a total of $1,035 million outstanding as of the end of August 1964 to $1,137 million as of early March 1965 (see table II). Additional issues of $50 million were made to the German Federal Bank and $50 million to the Austrian National Bank to absorb surplus dollars on the books of these central banks.

While these central bank and intergovernmental credit operations provided partial and temporary financing of the payments imbalances developing during the period, gold continued to play its traditional role. During the third and fourth quarters of 1964, sales of gold by the U.S. Treasury amounted to $442 million, against gold purchases of $338 million.

The international financial system was thus confronted with a major challenge in late 1964 that was successfully countered. The unprecedented mobilization of $4 billion of international liquidity in defense of sterling was a striking illustration of the strength and flexibility of the central bank and IMF defenses against currency crises. Perhaps even more remarkable is the fact that the international defense of sterling was accomplished in the face of a serious deterioration in the balance of payments of the other major reserve currency center, the United States.

Such a rallying of governmental and central bank support for the present system depended, however, upon one basic assumption: that both the British and the U.S. Governments would quickly put in motion forceful corrective programs to eliminate their payments deficits. These corrective programs are now under way and, if pursued with determination, will soon relieve the international financial mechanism of the enormous pressures generated by simultaneous deficits in the two major reserve currency countries. Under such conditions, the gold exchange standard, adapting as it has in the past to changing world conditions, can efficiently facilitate a continuing growth of world trade and payments.

The successful response to the challenge of the sterling crisis has unfortunately been marred by the widespread and exaggerated publicity given to the French Government's call for a return to the gold standard and for the elimination of dollars and sterling from official reserves. This approach has found no support among central banks and treasuries of other countries. The main effect has been to stir up some previously dormant private speculation in the London gold market to the detriment of official acquisitions of newly mined gold.

Sterling

Early in 1964 sterling showed weakening tendencies as a result of the deteriorating trade position of the United Kingdom, and various uncertainties connected with the general election to be called sometime during the year. A timely increase of the Bank of England discount rate from 4 percent to 5 percent in late February temporarily relieved market pressures, while delay of the general election until October induced some short covering by commercial interests.

Late in May, however, tight conditions in several continental money markets exerted new pressure on sterling. These pressures became strong toward the end of June because of heavier-than-usual midyear window-dressing by continental banks. To temper the impact of these movements of funds on official reserves, the Bank of England on June 30 drew $15 million against its $500 million swap line with the Federal Reserve; it repaid the drawing on July 13.

As the credit squeeze in the continental money market centers extended into July, moderate selling of sterling continued, and the spot rate moved downward with a minimum of official support to a low for the month of $2.7874 on July 20. The decline in the spot rate was taken in stride by the market without any speculative reaction developing. Indeed, market confidence in the sterling parity at that time was such that the discount on forward sterling tended to narrow as the spot rate declined.

As the discount on forward sterling was reduced, the covered interest-arbitrage differential on Treasury bills in favor of London became correspondingly more attractive and by July 13 had reached 0.44 percent per annum. To forestall private covered outflows in response to this arbitrage inducement, the Federal Reserve, with the agreement of the Bank of England, intervened in the market to reduce the arbitrage differential. This intervention, amounting to a total of $54 million equivalent in mid-July and again in late August, was accomplished by swap transactions in the New York market, with the Federal Reserve buying sterling spot and selling sterling forward against U.S. dollars. These operations had the dual effect of protecting the dollar against short-term flows of funds from New York to London while at the same time lending useful support to the spot rate on sterling.

In September, sterling came under increased pressure, owing mainly to increasingly widespread recognition of the mounting balance-of-payments deficit of the United Kingdom, which became further aggravated by the usual seasonal weakness during the autumn and early winter months. Uncertainties connected with the general election called for October 15 further unsettled the sterling exchange market, and the problem of maintaining confidence in sterling seemed likely to become increasingly difficult.

In anticipation of reserve losses, the Bank of England in mid-September made timely arrangements to supplement the $500 million swap line with the Federal Reserve by another $500 million of short-term credit facilities with other central banks in Europe and with the Bank of Canada. This reinforcement of the British reserve position cushioned the impact of recurrent, and increasingly forceful, waves of selling during September and October. Net drawings by the Bank of England on the Federal Reserve swap line and on short-term facilities provided by other central banks rose to $415 million by the end of October.

The new Labor Government elected on October 15 was thus immediately confronted with a grave balance-of-payments situation. The announcement on October 26 of emergency surcharges of 15 percent on a wide range of imports brought only brief relief as critical reactions appeared among Britain's trading partners worldwide, more particularly the European Free Trade Association (EFTA) group.

In a formal budget presented to parliament on November 11, the Government proposed certain new welfare benefits, to be financed by tax increases, and announced that it intended to introduce a capital gains tax and to substitute a new corporation tax for the existing application of the income tax to corporations. These proposals created uncertainty in business circles, in part because the immediate deflationary influence of the increased tax on fuel and of the import surcharge was to some extent obscured by the other measures. These uncertainties in domestic financial markets were in turn communicated to the exchange market.

During this period the exchange market began to anticipate action on the discount rate on each successive Thursday, and thus a pattern developed of a strengthening of sterling prior to Thursday of each week, followed by a major selling wave on Friday as the discount rate remained unchanged. When the bank rate remained unchanged on Thursday, November 19, reserve losses by the Bank of England on the following day reached such proportions that action could no longer be postponed. On Monday, November 23, the Bank of England raised its discount rate from 5 percent to 7 percent.

Perversely enough, market reaction to such forceful use of monetary policy by the Labor Government quickly degenerated into fears that the threat to sterling must have reached a truly crisis stage. Whether these reactions might have been averted by earlier discount rate action, more particularly on the usual Thursday date for discount rate announcements, may be debated for some time to come.

In any event, the market seized on rumors that the $1 billion of short-term central bank credits at the disposal of the Bank of England in September had now been exhausted; that the $1 billion standby credit from the IMF secured by the British Government in August had accordingly been fully committed to repayment of such central bank credits; and, hence, that the United Kingdom would have to fall back in defense of sterling upon its reserves of roughly $2 billion. (The still substantial unused drawing rights on the IMF would have required longer to mobilize than events at that time allowed.)

This situation assumed increasingly grave significance on the London afternoon, and the New York morning, of November 24 when a virtual avalanche of selling developed. If sterling were to be rescued, it was clear that a major package of international credit assistance would be required. On the afternoon of the 24th, the Federal Open Market Committee, meeting through a telephone conference, committed itself to an increase in the Federal Reserve–Bank of England swap line from $500 million to $750 million if credit assistance on a roughly corresponding scale could be secured from other central banks. That evening the Export-Import Bank gave assurance of a $250 million standby facility. Beginning early on the morning of November 25, the Bank of England, the Federal Reserve Bank of New York, and the central banks of other major countries were in almost continuous telephone communication. At 2 p.m., New York time, it was announced that a $3 billion credit package provided by 11 countries and the BIS was at the disposal of the Bank of England.

As a result of the heavy reserve losses, not only were the $500 million Federal Reserve swap and the additional $500 million of other central bank credit facilities made available to the Bank of England in September fully exhausted, but also immediate drawings of $200 million on the new credit facilities were required. From the end-of-October figure of $415 million, recourse by the Bank of England to central bank credit facilities thus rose by $785 million during November to a total of $1.2 billion. Of this total, the Federal Reserve share was $675 million.

In early December the British Government drew the full amount of its $1 billion standby facility with the IMF and so repaid an equivalent amount of the central bank credits outstanding, including $500 million of the Federal Reserve credit. At the same time Switzerland, which, although not a member of the IMF, is associated with the General Arrangements to Borrow, provided the United Kingdom with a 3-year credit of $80 million; $50 million of the Swiss credit was used to repay an earlier loan from Switzerland, outstanding from the sterling crisis of 1961.

With its exchange reserves thus heavily reinforced, the British Government could face with confidence further temporary pressures on sterling during December. Selling was particularly heavy just prior to the long Christmas weekend, and during the month the Bank of England increased its use of short-term central bank credit facilities from the $200 million outstanding early in December to $525 million at the yearend. Of this $325 million increase, $25 million was secured by an increased use of the Federal Reserve swap line, raising the total outstanding from $175 million to $200 million, while $300 million was drawn from other central banks.

Beginning in late November heavy selling of sterling appeared in the forward market, mainly by commercial interests insuring their future exchange transactions. This selling threatened to move the forward sterling rate to an excessive discount and hence intensify sales of sterling in the spot market. Accordingly, the Bank of England gave firm support to the forward rate. This support not only served to lessen the drain on reserves from spot transactions at the time, but more generally helped to buttress confidence in sterling by providing official reassurance that the sterling parity would be maintained. The operation was comparable to the determined stand taken in the forward market by other central banks in recent years, and it promised to achieve the same useful results.

After the turn of the year, both the spot and forward markets for sterling returned to a more balanced position. Since then, sterling has shown an increasingly buoyant trend. On February 10 it was announced that those of the central bank credit facilities made available last November which were shortly due to expire would be replaced by new facilities, available to the end of May, thus reconstituting the entire $3 billion credit package By the end of February the Bank of England was able to start repaying its debts.

In addition to direct swap transactions with the Bank of England, the Federal Reserve Bank of New York also moved into the market at various times during the autumn months to purchase sterling for both System and Treasury account. These acquisitions were made on both an outright and a swap basis; the particular technique used was determined by market conditions at the time, in consultation with the Bank of England.

Swiss franc

At the beginning of 1964, Federal Reserve swap drawings of Swiss francs under the swap lines of $150 million equivalent with both the Swiss National Bank and the BIS amounted to $220 million equivalent. By the end of June, these drawings had been completely liquidated through gold sales of $30 million to the Swiss National Bank, purchase from the Bank of Italy of the Swiss franc proceeds of a $100 million equivalent lira-Swiss franc swap, issuance by the U.S. Treasury of a $70 million equivalent Swiss franc bond to the BIS, and purchases of Swiss francs from the Swiss National Bank. U.S. Treasury market commitments in forward Swiss francs were reduced during the course of the year from $121 million to $51.5 million. At the outset of 1964, the U.S. Treasury and the Federal Reserve also had outstanding a combined total of $53 million in swaps of third currencies into Swiss francs. These contracts had been reduced to $15 million by the end of February 1965.

Despite the progress thus made in liquidating Treasury and Federal Reserve commitments in Swiss francs incurred in late 1963, new problems arose when sizable short-term funds—mainly repatriated Swiss assets—again flowed into Switzerland, both at midyear and particularly toward the close of the year as the pound sterling came under pressure.

During the spring of 1964, interest rates in Switzerland continued to rise as the heavy demands imposed on the Swiss money and capital markets by the continuing high level of economic activity further squeezed the liquidity position of Swiss banks and firms. The interest rate on 3-month deposits reached 3.50 percent in June, an increase of about 0.75 percent per annum over the previous year, while the average yield on government bonds moved up to 4.05 percent, compared with 3.15 percent a year earlier. To relieve the squeeze on their liquidity positions, and to satisfy midyear window-dressing needs, the Swiss commercial banks made sizable repatriations of funds during June.

These commercial bank operations caused the Swiss National Bank once again to take in substantial amounts of dollars. In July the reversing of some window-dressing operations and an easing of the Swiss money market brought about only a partial reversal of the previous inflows. In these circumstances the U.S. Treasury issued to the Swiss National Bank on August 4 an additional Swiss franc bond in the amount of $52 million equivalent and used the proceeds to absorb an equivalent amount of dollars on the books of the Swiss National Bank. (This issue brought the outstanding amount of U.S. Treasury securities denominated in Swiss francs to $327 million equivalent.)

Generally easier conditions prevailed in the market for Swiss francs from mid-August to mid-October, and the Swiss franc declined from its ceiling for a while, only to firm again in late October as the Swiss money market tightened. Then in the early part of November, funds began to move into Switzerland in quantity, some directly out of sterling, some through the Euro-currency markets in response to the general uneasiness that pervaded the exchanges. Throughout the rest of the year, sizable increases occurred in the dollar holdings of the Swiss National Bank.

To absorb part of this intake of dollars, the Federal Reserve reactivated its $150 million swap with the BIS in early December by drawing $100 million of Swiss francs, which was simultaneously employed to purchase dollars from the Swiss National Bank. A further Swiss franc drawing of $60 million equivalent on the Swiss National Bank was made on January 19 for the same purpose. In addition, to calm the market and to encourage Swiss banks to invest abroad dollars that they might otherwise have sold to the Swiss National Bank, the Federal Reserve began in December to sell Swiss francs forward to the market through the Swiss National Bank. By January 8, 1965, such forward sales reached a peak of $32.5 million equivalent. Most of these contracts had been paid off by the end of February through spot purchases of Swiss francs. (The Swiss franc began to ease shortly after the yearend as Swiss banks, finding themselves liquid, started to place funds abroad.) During the second half of 1964 the dollar acquisitions of the Swiss National Bank were further reduced by purchases of $51 million of gold from the U.S. Treasury.

Netherlands guilder

At the beginning of 1964 Federal Reserve commitments in guilders amounted to $80 million equivalent, all in the form of outstanding swap drawings. These were fully repaid by early April, as earlier inflows of funds into the Netherlands were reversed.

In May the Netherlands money market began to tighten, and in early June the Netherlands Bank raised its discount rate from 4 percent to 4½ percent. In July Netherlands commercial banks began to repatriate funds in substantial amounts. Moreover, the Netherlands balance of payments strengthened, owing to a better trade balance and an inflow of long-term capital. By November the intensified pressures on sterling and the ensuing movement of some funds out of sterling and into guilders helped push the guilder to its ceiling.

Meanwhile, the Netherlands Bank had been taking in dollars in an effort to moderate the rise in the guilder rate. During the first week of August the Federal Reserve drew $20 million equivalent of guilders under the swap line and immediately used the guilders to absorb some of the Netherlands Bank's accruals of dollars. Further Federal Reserve drawings and sales of guilders followed in rapid sequence, and by mid-October the $100 million swap facility had been fully drawn. Additional dollars were purchased by the Federal Reserve and the U.S. Treasury from the Netherlands Bank in September and December with guilders acquired through 3-month swaps of sterling for guilders with the BIS, for a total of $50 million equivalent. As intensified buying pressures on the guilder developed in late December, a temporary swap arrangement for $35 million between the Netherlands Bank and the U.S. Treasury was agreed upon and fully employed.

In mid-December recourse was also had to forward operations in Netherlands guilders for both Federal Reserve and Treasury account in order to provide reassurance to the market and induce covered capital outflows from the Netherlands. These operations, together with Netherlands provision of dollar credits to the Bank of England and purchases of gold from the U.S. Treasury, reduced the dollar holdings of the Netherlands Bank sufficiently to permit complete liquidation of the Treasury-Netherlands Bank $35 million swap by early January and repayment of $30 million of the Federal Reserve swap drawings in early February. As of the end of February, Federal Reserve drawings upon the swap line with the Netherlands Bank had thus been reduced to $70 million equivalent. During the second half of 1964, gold puchases by the Netherlands Bank from the U.S. Treasury amounted to $60 million.

German mark

During 1963 and early 1964, there had been almost continuous upward pressure on the German mark. This pressure reflected a substantial increase in the German foreign trade surplus, large inflows of long-term capital, and occasional inflows of short-term funds in response to tight money market conditions or hedging operations. To ease the strain, the German Federal Bank, the Federal Reserve, and the U.S. Treasury jointly conducted various spot and forward exchange operations, as outlined in previous reports in this series.

On March 23, 1964, an important turning point occurred as the German Government announced its intention to propose to parliament the imposition of a 25 percent withholding tax on income from German fixed-interest securities held by nonresidents. This action not only checked the long-term capital inflow, but also actually induced liquidation of a considerable volume of foreign investments in fixed-interest securities. Earlier surpluses on trade account also diminished as the year progressed, and this helped to restore a stable equilibrium in the exchange markets.

The effect on the exchange market of these basic shifts in the German balance of payments was reinforced by a number of technical measures initiated by the German authorities to reduce temporary pressures on the exchange market resulting from short-term capital flows. The special swap facilities made available by the German Federal Bank to German commercial banks for investments in U.S. Treasury bills were used flexibly throughout the second half of the year, with maturities providing the banks with liquidity at the yearend. In addition, under a special temporary arrangement in December, German commercial banks were permitted to borrow against collateral from the central bank at an effective cost lower than the posted rate.

Nevertheless, the sterling crisis led to some inflow of funds to Germany in late December. Consequently, the Federal Reserve reactivated its $250 million swap facility with the German Federal Bank by drawing $50 million equivalent of marks in order to absorb $50 million of German dollar reserves. This drawing was reversed in late January 1965, as short-term outflows from Germany combined with German military purchases in the United States enabled the Federal Reserve to acquire $50 million of marks from the German Federal Bank. Another small drawing of $15 million equivalent was made by the Federal Reserve on February 4 to help control any speculative tendencies resulting from President de Gaulle's press conference on the same date.

During the 6-month period through February, the U.S. Treasury issued to the German Federal Bank in October 1964 a $50 million equivalent mark-denominated bond. This latest issue raised the total of such mark bonds outstanding to $679 million equivalent. The mark proceeds of this bond, together with $7 million of Treasury mark balances remaining from U.S. drawings of marks from the IMF, were sold to Canada to enable that country to make an IMF repayment. Subsequently, in early December when the U.S. Treasury drew $125 million equivalent of marks from the IMF, it used $50 million equivalent to purchase excess dollars from the German Federal Bank, in effect compensating for the fact that marks derived from the earlier bond issue had been used in conjunction with Canada's repayment to the IMF.

Italian lira

Italy's balance-of-payments deficit had assumed major proportions in the fall of 1963, and the Federal Reserve and U.S. Treasury joined forces with the Bank of Italy in defense of the lira. As outlined in the previous report, Federal Reserve and Treasury operations in the autumn of 1963 and the first quarter of 1964 cushioned the decline in the Bank of Italy's reserves to the extent of some $350 million and thereby helped to restrain speculative pressures against the lira.

During the week of March 9 through March 14, 1964, an Italian delegation headed by Governor Carli of the Bank of Italy visited Washington to discuss with the World Bank and the IMF various possible sources of financing for Italy's longer-term investment requirements and its expected further balance-of-payments deficits. In the midst of these discussions, the lira was suddenly struck by a burst of speculation. This brought heavy pressures not only on the spot rate but also on the forward rate, which for a 3-month maturity moved to a discount of 7 percent per annum. In this dangerous situation, an immediate and massive reinforcement of the Italian reserve position was clearly called for. Within 48 hours the Italian authorities were able to announce that they had arranged for approximately $1 billion of external assistance provided by the United States, the Bank of England, and the German Federal Bank.

One of the most satisfactory aspects of this display of international cooperation in beating back a speculative attack on the Italian lira was that the provision of massive credit assistance to Italy more or less coincided with a turning point in the Italian economic and financial scene. During the first quarter of 1964 the Italian balance of payments had registered a deficit of $436 million. A surplus of $226 million was recorded in the second quarter, as corrective policy measures initiated by the Italian authorities began to take effect and as a reversal in the leads and lags in payments brought about the covering of short positions in lira. In early July, a governmental crisis generated a temporary speculative flurry, but operations in force in the forward market by the Bank of Italy through the agency of the Federal Reserve Bank of New York provided reassurance and the speculation quickly subsided.

Italy continued to run a payments surplus during the third and fourth quarters of 1964, and by the yearend Italian official reserves, which had dipped $233 million during the first quarter, were $389 million higher than at the outset of 1964. The reappearance of political uncertainties in the late summer triggered some selling of forward lira, and discounts for 3-month maturities tended to widen at times to 4 percent per annum. In such instances, the Federal Reserve Bank of New York again intervened for account of the Bank of Italy to support the forward lira in the New York market and thus helped to relieve market uncertainties. By early October the discount on the 3-month forward lira had narrowed to less than 1 percent per annum.

Continuing heavy flows of dollars to Italy in the closing months of 1964 and early 1965 may have partially reflected the sterling crisis. To absorb part of these dollar inflows, the Federal Reserve on January 22 reactivated its $250 million swap arrangement with the Bank of Italy by drawing $50 million equivalent of lire.

Canadian dollar

The spot market for Canadian dollars was relatively quiet through the first half of 1964, but there was considerable activity in the forward market as a result of grain sales to the Soviet Union beginning in the previous autumn. These sales generated heavy demands on the part of grain dealers for Canadian dollars for future delivery against U.S. dollars. In order to offset some of these pressures, the Bank of Canada sold U.S. dollars spot and purchased them forward, thus providing some counterpart to the commercial banks' swap needs, while the Federal Reserve also intervened on a small scale. By the end of July, Canadian grain shipments to the Soviet Union had been fairly well completed, and pressures on the forward market eased.

In August, heightening tensions in Vietnam generated some buying of spot Canadian dollars by continental interests, and as the spot rate rose in a thin market, Canadian exporters began to sell out U.S. dollar balances. New grain purchases by several eastern European countries exerted further upward pressure on the spot rate. At about the same time there was a tightening of the Canadian money market, which induced a temporary flow of short-term funds into Canada from the United States on a covered basis.

Substantial Canadian long-term borrowings in the U.S. market, the sterling crisis, and fiscal yearend positioning by Canadian banks in October and November pushed the spot rate for the Canadian dollar to its effective ceiling by November. As the Canadian dollar strengthened, the Bank of Canada intervened to moderate the rise in the rate, with the result that Canadian reserves increased by $210 million during the August–November period despite repayments of $107 million to the IMF in September and October. By December the market had returned to a more balanced position.

In early February the Canadian dollar softened, as press discussion of prospective U.S. balance-of-payments measures led to some apprehension in the markets that Canada might be unfavorably affected. The U.S. balance-of-payments program, announced on February 10, made it clear that there was no U.S. intention to deprive the Canadian economy of essential inflows of capital. Nevertheless, the Canadian dollar weakened somewhat further in the second half of the month, reportedly reflecting Canadian commercial buying of U.S. dollars and unfavorable seasonal factors.

Belgian franc

Early in July 1964 the Belgian franc strengthened, following the announcement of new measures designed to curb the growth of credit in Belgium. On July 3 the National Bank of Belgium raised its discount rate by one-half a percentage point to 4¾ percent and announced that, effective August 17, it would impose a cash reserve requirement against commercial bank deposits for the first time. Tighter money market conditions developed and—in conjunction with long-term investment in Belgium, an improved trade balance beginning in the third quarter and the sterling crisis later in the year—contributed to substantial dollar inflows into Belgium.

Early in August the Federal Reserve used $7.5 million equivalent of Belgian francs drawn under the $50 million swap arrangement to absorb dollars on the books of the National Bank of Belgium. By mid-October the entire $50 million equivalent of franc balances had been so utilized. Effective October 22 the Federal Reserve and the National Bank of Belgium expanded the existing $50 million swap facility with an additional $50 million arrangement to be available on a standby basis. As dollars continued to flow into Belgium, the Federal Reserve made further drawings on this additional swap and by the end of November had used the full amount.

The Federal Reserve was able to reduce its swap commitments to Belgium to $25 million equivalent in early December, when the National Bank of Belgium purchased $75 million from the Federal Reserve to make special outpayments. On December 30, however, the Federal Reserve again drew $20 million equivalent of francs in order to absorb further inflows of dollars into Belgium, and further utilization of $40 million equivalent under the swap arrangement became necessary in January and February 1965. As of the end of February, total Federal Reserve use of the $100 million swap arrangement with the National Bank of Belgium amounted to $85 million equivalent. Meanwhile, during the second half of 1964, the National Bank of Belgium had purchased $40 million of gold from the United States.

Japanese yen

On April 30 the Bank of Japan drew $50 million under the $150 million swap arrangement with the Federal Reserve in order to cushion a decline in Japanese reserves. This drawing was renewed on July 30, as reserve pressures continued, and a further drawing of $30 million was made on July 31. In August, however, domestic restraint measures began to take effect : import demand diminished and, with a continued growth in exports, the trade balance improved considerably. With this improvement in Japan's balance-of-payments and reserve position, the Bank of Japan began repaying its swap obligations at the end of September, and by early November it had liquidated them in full.

Austrian schilling

There were no System operations in Austrian schillings during the period. Although the Austrian balance of payments registered a considerable deficit in the last quarter of 1964, the figures for 1964 as a whole continued to show a surplus. Therefore, on February 23 and March 3, 1965, the Treasury issued to the Austrian National Bank two $25 million equivalent 18-month bonds denominated in Austrian schillings, using the proceeds to absorb some of that bank's dollar holdings. These issues brought the outstanding total of U.S. Treasury bonds denominated in Austrian schillings to $100 million equivalent.

Swedish krona and French franc

There were no Federal Reserve or Treasury operations in Swedish kronor or French francs during the period under review.

U.S. Drawing on the International Monetary Fund

Over the course of several years before 1964, foreign countries had been repaying more dollars to the IMF than the IMF had been paying out in new drawings. As a result, the IMF's dollar holdings rose to a point where they equaled the amount that the United States has paid into the IMF as part of its quota. At this point the IMF, under its rules, could no longer accept dollars in repurchase, and countries having repurchase obligations could make repayments only with gold or with other eligible convertible currencies.

So as to be able to sell such currencies to countries having repurchase obligations, the U.S. Treasury on February 13 and June 1, 1964, made two drawings on the IMF, predominantly in German marks and French francs, in the amount of $125 million equivalent each under the $500 million standby agreement with the IMF announced by President Kennedy in July 1963. By September 1, the bulk of these currencies had been sold to various countries effecting repayments to the IMF.

On July 23, 1964, the original standby arrangement expired, and the Treasury announced that it had made a further standby arrangement with the IMF for another year. This restored the amount available to $500 million. The first drawing under the new standby arrangement was made on September 1, when the United States drew $50 million in five European currencies. Unlike the first two drawings under the original arrangement, which were used to cover a number of transactions that took place during ensuing weeks, this drawing was occasioned by Italy's repurchase of $65 million equivalent of lire from the IMF. Again, on September 30, the U.S. Treasury drew equal amounts of Dutch guilders and German marks totaling $100 million equivalent, half of which was immediately sold to Canada in connection with a repayment to the IMF. The remaining balances were disbursed in subsequent weeks. On December 7 a third drawing of $125 million equivalent was made, this time solely in German marks.

Since this program was initiated, the U.S. Treasury has drawn $525 million equivalent of seven continental European currencies, of which some $15 million equivalent remained undisbursed as of the end of February 1965. The effect of these drawings on the U.S. position in the IMF has been offset to a considerable extent, however, by drawings of dollars by other countries. The largest single dollar drawing was $200 million, under the $1 billion equivalent multicurrency drawing in December by the United Kingdom. As a result the U.S. repayment obligation to the IMF as of the end of February 1965 had been reduced to $256 million.

The Gold Market and U.S. Gold Transactions

Throughout the first 8 months of 1964 the London gold market was generally stable, with the gold-fixing price ranging between $35.06 and $35.10. With the improvement in the U.S. balance of payments, and consequent strengthening of confidence in the dollar, speculative demand for gold receded, and as new production increased, the gold pool regularly absorbed surpluses of output reaching the market. The pool took in further sizable amounts of gold from Russian sales, which were heavily concentrated over a few weeks' span in late March and early April.

Over the closing months of 1964, various political and financial disturbances tended to rekindle speculative buying of gold. International tensions arising out of the Vietnam conflict continued to generate market apprehension. But renewed speculation in the gold market was also attributable to the increasing pressures on sterling during the latter part of the year.

In addition, the sharp deterioration in the U.S. balance of payments during the closing months of 1964 contributed to market uncertainties, especially after the turn of the year. In February, various pronouncements emanating from Paris further stimulated speculative buying of gold by private interests. Both the United Kingdom and the United States have now taken forceful action to deal with their balance-of-payments deficits, and if these corrective programs are vigorously pursued, speculative pressures in the gold market may be expected to subside.

The Bank of England, on behalf of the gold pool, continued to exert a stabilizing influence on the market and to moderate price movements. Although private demand for gold increased during the closing months of 1964, over the year as a whole the pool once again acquired and distributed to its members more than $600 million.

During the fourth quarter of 1964, continental central banks took in sizable amounts of dollars, and several sold part of their acquisitions to the U.S. Treasury for gold. These conversions, as well as the continued French purchases of gold each month, more than offset U.S. acquisitions from other sources. As a result, the United States became a net seller of gold in its international monetary transactions after having been a net purchaser earlier in the year (see table III). For 1964 as a whole, taking into account sales of about $89 million to domestic users, total U.S. gold holdings—including Stabilization Fund holdings as well as the Treasury gold stock—declined by $125 million. During the first two months of 1965, the Treasury gold stock declined by an additional $450 million.

TABLE I.—*Federal Reserve reciprocal currency agreements, Mar. 1, 1965*

Other party to agreement	Amount of facility (in millions of dollars)	Term (months)
Bank of France	100	3
Bank of England	750	12
Netherlands Bank	100	3
National Bank of Belgium	100	12
Bank of Canada	250	12
Bank for International Settlements	150	6
Swiss National Bank	150	6
German Federal Bank	250	6
Bank of Italy	250	12
Austrian National Bank	50	12
Bank of Sweden	50	12
Bank of Japan	150	12
Total for all banks	2,350	

TABLE II.—*U.S. Treasury securities denominated in foreign currencies, Mar. 3, 1965*

[In millions]

Issued to	Amount in foreign currency		U.S. dollar equivalent
Austrian National Bank	Sch.	2,600	$100.6
National Bank of Belgium	BF	1,500	30.1
German Federal Bank	DM	2,700	679.0
Swiss National Bank	SF	1,112	257.5
Bank for International Settlements	SF	300	69.5
Total			1,136.7

TABLE III.—*U.S. net monetary gold transactions with foreign countries and international institutions, July–December 1964*

[In millions of dollars at $35 per fine troy ounce.   U.S. net sales (−); net purchases (+)]

Country	Third quarter	Fourth quarter
Austria		
Belgium		−40.1
Brazil	−1.1	+28.2
France	−101.4	−101.4
Germany	−25.0	
Italy		
Netherlands		−60.0
Spain		−30.0
Switzerland		−51.0
Turkey		−12.5
United Kingdom	+162.5	+125.0
All other	+6.0	−2.8
Total	+41.0	−144.6

Exhibit 50.—Press Release, July 23, 1964, announcing renewal of standby arrangement with the International Monetary Fund

Secretary of the Treasury Douglas Dillon announced today that the United States has renewed its standby arrangement with the International Monetary Fund to run for another year.   The standby will again be in an amount of $500 million.

One-half of the $500 million available under last year's standby arrangement was drawn by the United States in two amounts of $125 million each in February and May of this year.   The new standby restores the amount available for further drawings to $500 million.

It is expected that the proceeds of U.S. drawings will be used principally for the same purposes as the drawings under the previous standby.   These drawings enable other members to continue in effect to use their holdings of dollars to make repayments to the IMF.   The new standby arrangement is expected to be sufficient to cover presently foreseeable needs over the coming year.

Exhibit 51.—Press Release, July 30, 1964, announcing Treasury rescheduling of Brazilian obligations

Secretary of the Treasury Douglas Dillon and the Ambassador of Brazil, Juracy Magalhaes, today signed an amendment to the exchange agreement of May 1961 between the Treasury, the Government of Brazil, and the Banco do Brasil.

The amendment signed today provides for a postponement of $25.3 million in principal repayments due to the Treasury, under the terms of the agreement, in the remainder of 1964.   Repayment will be effected by Brazil in monthly installments, beginning in January 1965 and with full repayment completed in December 1966.

The rescheduling of Brazil's obligations to the Treasury supplements the multilateral rescheduling and refinancing of certain debt obligations agreed between Brazil and nine "Hague Club" countries, including the United States, as announced in Paris on July 1.

Exhibit 52.—Press Release, August 10, 1964, on U.S. program of assistance for the Dominican Republic

The United States today announced that it is concluding a $10,250,000 program of assistance for the Dominican Republic.   This includes a $6,250,000 exchange agreement with the U.S. Treasury and a $4,000,000 loan from the Agency for International Development.

The assistance is being made in support of the financial stabilization program being undertaken by the Dominican Government to provide a sound foundation for economic and social development of the country.

In additon, the Embassy and the Dominican Government are currently reviewing various projects which will further the program of the Dominican Government to achieve for the Dominican people, under the Alliance for Progress, the long-range goals of the Charter of Punta del Este.

Among projects under study are those aimed at increased and more varied agricultural production; accelerated agrarian settlement; broadened and improved educational opportunities for the people at large; promotion of private industry, particularly in the processing and distribution of agricultural products; and expansion of the road network to open up new areas for production.

Other projects compatible with short-term measures called for by the stabilization program of the Dominican Government are being studied. These projects will be implemented as the studies are completed and in coordination with the stabilization effort. At the same time, U.S. technical assistance is being increased to complement current and future development programs in the Dominican Republic.

The stabilization effort will be reflected principally in greater austerity affecting virtually all the Dominican people. As such internal sacrifices pave the way for achieving new financial stability, United States and other external funds can help support Dominican investment for development. That investment will in the long-run form the basis of sound economic growth and steady improvement in the standard of living and well being of all Dominicans.

The U.S. agreements with the Dominican Republic supplement the resources available to the Dominican Republic under a $25 million standby arrangement announced by the International Monetary Fund on August 5, 1964.

The exchange agreement with the U.S. Treasury is effective for a one-year period. It, like the AID loan, is designed to assist the Dominican Republic in its efforts to promote economic stability and freedom in its trade and exchange system and to restore full convertibility of the peso.

Exhibit 53.—Press Release, September 1, 1964, announcing the third U.S. drawing from the International Monetary Fund

Secretary of the Treasury Douglas Dillon today announced a third drawing of foreign currencies by the U.S. from the International Monetary Fund.

The drawing is for $50 million, and is the first under the new standby arrangement of $500 million announced on July 23, 1964. It brings total drawings to $300 million. Two drawings of $125 million each were made on February 13 and June 1 of this year.

As in the case of the previous drawings, the new currencies obtained by the U.S. will be sold for dollars to other Fund members for their use in making repayments to the Fund.

This drawing was occasioned by Italy's repayment of $65 million to the IMF, fully restoring that country's quota position. The Italian repayment reflects the improved financial position of that country since March 13 when credits totaling $1 billion were made available to Italy by the United States and others in addition to the $225 million Italian Fund drawing at the end of March.

The current U.S. drawing includes, for the first time, the currencies of Austria, Belgium, the Netherlands, and Sweden in addition to German marks which had also been included in the earlier drawings.

After meeting Italian requirements, a balance will remain from the proceeds of this drawing sufficient to cover other presently scheduled repayments to the Fund over the next several weeks.

Exhibit 54.—Press Release, September 30, 1964, announcing the fourth U.S. drawing from the International Monetary Fund

Secretary of the Treasury Douglas Dillon today announced a fourth drawing of foreign currencies by the United States from the International Monetary Fund.

The drawing is for $100 million in the currencies of Germany and the Netherlands. Total drawings, the first of which was made on February 13 of this year, now amount to $400 million.

As in the case of the previous drawings, the currencies will be sold for dollars to other Fund members for their use in making repayments to the Fund, including a current $50 million repayment by Canada.

Exhibit 55.—Press Release, November 25, 1964, on assistance to the United Kingdom

The Federal Reserve System and the U.S. Treasury today issued the following statement:

"The United Kingdom and 11 other countries today made arrangements providing $3 billion to back up Britain's determination to defend the pound sterling.

"Today's funds are in addition to the $1 billion drawing the United Kingdom will obtain from the International Monetary Fund at the end of this month under an existing standby.

"Austria, Belgium, Canada, France, Germany, Italy, Japan, the Netherlands, Sweden, Switzerland, and the United States, together with the Bank for International Settlements, moved quickly to mobilize a massive counter-attack on speculative selling of the pound.

"The IMF drawing, which can have a maturity of up to three years, will enable the British to pay off all outstanding short-term credits from central banks including the Federal Reserve.

"The currency swap arrangement with the Federal Reserve System has been raised by $250 million to $750 million and a $250 million credit has been made available by the U.S. Export-Import Bank. (These amounts are included in the total package of $3 billion.)"

Exhibit 56.—Press Release, December 7, 1964, announcing a U.S. drawing in German marks from the International Monetary Fund

Secretary of the Treasury Douglas Dillon today announced a drawing by the United States on the International Monetary Fund. The drawing in the amount of $125 million is the fifth made by the United States and is in German marks.

Total drawings in 1964 now amount to the equivalent of $525 million in various foreign currencies. A sizable part of these drawings has been offset, however, by the drawings of U.S. dollars by other countries during the period. When other countries draw dollars from the Fund it restores the U.S. position and in effect amounts to repayment by the United States. As a result the net reduction in U.S. drawing rights on the Fund has been only about $265 million.

The currency drawn is expected to be used, as in the past, for sale for dollars to other Fund members for their use in making repayments to the Fund.

Exhibit 57.—Press Release, December 16, 1964, containing the text of a communique on the Ministerial Meeting of the Group of Ten

Following is the text of a communique released yesterday in Paris by the French Finance Ministry on Ministerial Meeting of the Group of Ten:

"1. The representatives of the 10 countries participating in the General Arrangements to Borrow (GAB) met at the Ministry of Finance in Paris on December 15th 1964. Mr. Emilio Colombo, the present Chairman, who was unable to attend, asked M. Valéry Giscard d'Estaing to preside in his place. The Managing Director of the IMF attended the meeting as did the Secretary General of the OECD and the General Manager of the BIS. An observer from the Swiss National Bank was also present.

"2. The Ministers and Governors examined the issues raised by the forthcoming general increase in IMF quotas and especially the problems related to gold payments of 25 percent in connection with the quota increase. They had a full exchange of views looking towards the continuation of the discussion in the IMF.

"3· They heard a report on the activity of the study group on the creation of reserve assets and decided that this group should make its report to the deputies by next June so as to enable the Ministers and Governors to take up the subject at their next meeting in September 1965.

"4· The representatives of the Ten reviewed the recent evolution of the international monetary situation. They took note of the satisfactory working of the GAB on the occasion of its first activation.

"5· The Ministers and Governors had a preliminary exchange of views on the renewal of the GAB about which a decision has to be taken before October 1965."

Exhibit 58.—Press Release, February 4, 1965, announcing the signing of an exchange agreement by the United States and Chile

Secretary of the Treasury Douglas Dillon and the Ambassador of Chile, Sergio Gutierrez, today signed a $16,120,000 exchange agreement between the United States and the Government and Central Bank of Chile.

The agreement, which is effective for a one-year period, replaces one for $15 million signed in March 1964. Under the exchange agreement, Chile may request the U.S. Exchange Stabilization Fund to purchase Chilean escudos. Any escudos acquired by the U.S. Treasury would subsequently be repurchased by Chile with dollars.

The agreement will assist Chile in maintaining orderly conditions in the foreign exchange markets as part of its program of economic stabilization and growth, and is designed to supplement the resources available under the $36 million standby arrangement announced by the International Monetary Fund on January 6, 1965.

Exhibit 59.—Press Release, February 4, 1965, on President de Gaulle's statement on the gold standard

The Treasury today released the following statement:

"President de Gaulle has recommended that the gold exchange standard, based on the use of dollars freely convertible into gold at $35.00 an ounce, and which has served the world well for 30 years be abandoned. He has proposed that instead we retreat to the full gold standard which collapsed in 1931 and which proved incapable of financing the huge increase of world trade that has marked the twentieth century.

"Studies of possible ways to improve the world monetary system have been underway for the past 18 months in the International Monetary Fund and in the Group of Ten countries making up the GAB. The new French proposal will presumably be introduced in these forums where a number of other proposals have been under study for some time. However, a move toward the restoration of the so-called gold standard, with all its rigidities and sharp deflationary consequences, would be quite contrary to the main stream of thinking among the governments participating in these studies.

"In no event would any solution be acceptable that involved a change in the fixed $35.00 price of gold. It is also essential that any changes in the system ensure that adequate international credit will continue to be available to finance the swings in trade typical of a growing world economy."

Exhibit 60.—Press Release, February 10, 1965, on Treasury actions following the President's Balance-of-Payments Message

Treasury Secretary Douglas Dillon today announced that he has put regulations into effect to carry out President Johnson's Executive Order applying the interest equalization tax to U.S. bank loans to foreigners.

This and other steps within the Treasury's area of responsibility were outlined by the Secretary following the President's Balance-of-Payments Message sent to Congress earlier today.

Secretary Dillon said that the Treasury is sending to the Congress a bill extending the present interest equalization tax on foreign securities sold in this country for another two years and expanding its scope to cover one to three year loans.

Commenting on this and other actions asked for by the President, Secretary Dillon said:

"The voluntary cooperation and support of the President's entire program by American business and the general public is essential to its success. The measures taken today will complement, but not substitute for, these voluntary efforts."

As announced in the Balance-of-Payments Message, the President has exercised his power to extend the interest equalization tax to commercial bank loans to developed countries with a period to maturity of one year or more. The Executive Order and Treasury Regulations implementing it have been filed with the *Federal Register* and will become effective tomorrow, February 11, 1965.

Under the law, export-connected loans of banks are exempted from the tax, assuring the ability of banks to support the efforts of American business to compete more effectively abroad. Also exempted are loans repayable in foreign currencies by foreign branches of U.S. banks and direct investments in foreign subsidiary banks. These exemptions are designed to permit foreign offices of U.S. banks flexibility in conducting their normal operations in the countries where they are located. The President's order also made clear that the existing exemption for new Canadian issues would not apply to bank loans.

As provided by the law, the President issued the order extending the tax after concluding that commercial bank loans to foreigners had materially impaired the effectiveness of the interest equalization tax by replacing other types of acquisitions which were subject to the tax.

Application of the tax to all credits to Japan with a period of maturity of one year or more would, in the opinion of the President, have such consequences for that country as to threaten to imperil the stability of the international monetary system. Consequently, the President has stated that he will exempt from tax this year up to $100 million of borrowings by, or guaranteed by, the Government of Japan which would otherwise be subject to the tax.

In requesting Congress to extend the interest equalization tax for two years (to expire on December 31, 1967) the President also asked that its scope be extended so as to subject to tax those acquisitions by all U.S. persons of foreign debt obligations with a period to maturity of one year or more. Existing exemptions, including those for export credit, direct investment, and loans to less-developed countries, will continue to apply.

In order to be certain that the proposed amendments to the interest equalization tax do not serve as an inducement to accelerate acquisitions of foreign debt obligations, the President requested Congress to make these amendments effective tomorrow, February 11, 1965. However, these amendments would not be effective with respect to acquisitions made pursuant to firm commitments in effect as of February 10, 1965.

A bill incorporating the proposed amendments to the interest equalization tax is being submitted by Secretary Dillon to Congress.

As indicated by the President in his message, the Treasury will shortly submit to Congress a bill embodying specific proposals to improve the tax treatment of foreign investment in U.S. corporate securities, generally along the lines recommended by a special task force appointed by President Kennedy.

Secretary Dillon also noted that the Department of Justice will shortly propose legislation to the Congress that would provide assurance that voluntary efforts, and any voluntary agreements, undertaken by financial institutions as part of the President's program will not be subject to antitrust action.

Exhibit 61.—Press Release, February 23, 1965, announcing signing of a new exchange agreement between the United States and Brazil

Secretary of the Treasury Douglas Dillon and the Ambassador of Brazil, Juracy Magalhaes, today signed a $53,660,000 exchange agreement between the United States, the Government of Brazil, and the Bank of Brazil.

Under the agreement, which is effective for a one-year period, Brazil may request the U.S. Exchange Stabilization Fund to purchase Brazilian cruzeiros in amounts not exceeding the value of the agreement. Any cruzeiros so acquired by the U.S. Treasury would subsequently be repurchased by Brazil with dollars.

The agreement will assist Brazil in maintaining orderly conditions in her foreign exchange markets as part of her program of economic stabilization and growth, and is designed to supplement the resources available under the $125 million standby arrangement announced by the International Monetary Fund on January 13, 1965.

The agreement signed today implements the Treasury portion of various U.S. Government economic and financial programs in Brazil in 1965, estimated to total more than $450 million, which were announced December 14, 1964, on the occasion of the signing of a $150 million program loan of the Agency for International Development.

Exhibit 62.—Press Release, March 22, 1965, announcing the first U.S. drawing in 1965 from the International Monetary Fund

Secretary of the Treasury Douglas Dillon today announced a drawing by the United States on the International Monetary Fund. The drawing in the amount of $75 million is the first made this year by the United States and is in equal amounts of German marks, Canadian dollars, and Italian lire.

Total drawings, since their inception in February 1964, now amount to the equivalent of $600 million in various foreign currencies. A sizable part of these drawings has been offset, however, by the drawings of U.S. dollars by other countries during the period. When other countries draw dollars from the Fund it restores the U.S. position and in effect amounts to repayment by the United States. As a result, the net reduction in U.S. drawing rights on the Fund has been about $330 million.

The currency drawn is expected to be used, as in the past, for sale for dollars to other Fund members for their use in making repayments to the Fund over the next several months.

Exhibit 63.—Press Release, April 6, 1965, announcing that the Bahamas, Bermuda, Ireland, Kuwait, and Portugal are to be made subject to interest equalization tax

The President today notified the Congress that on or shortly after May 6, 1965, he intends to issue an Executive Order terminating the "less developed" designation of the Bahamas, Bermuda, Ireland, Kuwait, and Portugal for purposes of the interest equalization tax.

The President's action will have the effect of applying the interest equalization tax to purchases by U.S. citizens from foreigners of stock and debt obligations originating from the three countries and the Bahamas and Bermuda which are currently exempt from the tax. All such purchases made after the date of the Executive Order will be subject to the tax, except those for which firm written commitments existed prior to today.

The interest equalization tax has been applied to the acquisitions of various foreign securities by U.S. citizens since July 18, 1963. The tax is designed to help curb the outflow of capital from the United States, which has been a major factor contributing to this country's adverse balance-of-payments position. The tax does not apply to stock and debt obligations issued by countries which, for the purpose of this tax, are determined to be "less-developed countries," and by certain corporations and residents of such countries.

The interest equalization tax law authorizes the President to expand the list of countries considered not to be "less developed," so that the application of the tax can be adjusted to reflect economic development in different parts of the world. When such changes are to be made, however, Congress must be given 30 days advance notice.

In connection with the intensified balance-of-payments program announced by President Johnson on February 10, 1965, the Administration has reviewed the list of "less-developed countries" currently exempt from the tax. The review showed that each of the five areas to be covered by the new Executive Order has progressed to the point where its borrowers should not be in a privileged position in the acquisition of capital in the United States. Each is experiencing satisfactory domestic economic growth, and each has relatively large international resources to draw upon if it requires additional resources. Kuwait has become a net exporter of capital. The other four, in addition to their own domestic capital resources, have access to the capital markets of Europe.

Exhibit 64.—Press Release, May 20, 1965, announcing that U.S. citizens may buy Indian rupees owned by the U.S. Government

The Department of State and the Treasury Department announced today that the American Embassy at New Delhi and the American Consulates at Madras, Calcutta, and Bombay, India, have been authorized to sell to American citizens Indian rupees received by the United States from the sale of surplus agricultural commodities.

To ensure that maximum use of U.S.-owned foreign currencies is made for the benefit of the U.S. balance of payments, the President recently ordered a Government-wide reexamination of foreign currency utilization. In support of this effort, American tourists are encouraged to purchase their local currency needs from U.S. sources in countries where such sales are authorized. By buying their local currency needs at the respective embassies or consulates in these countries American citizens are in effect keeping their dollars "at home" and are assisting the U.S. balance of payments.

The initiation of Indian rupees sales to American citizens in India brings to three the number of countries where such sales of local currency, held in amounts excessive to the needs of the U.S. Government, are now in effect. The United States has been selling Israeli and Egyptian pounds to U.S. citizens in those two countries for some time.

The action announced today was taken in accordance with a provision of an amendment signed on December 31, 1964, to the Food for Peace Agreement of September 30, 1964, with India.

American tourists and businessmen, upon presentation of their passports for identification, can obtain Indian rupees at the official rate of exchange at the Embassy or Consulates in exchange for U.S. currency, personal checks drawn on a bank in the United States, or U.S. travelers checks.

In most of the countries throughout the world, the U.S. Government holds foreign currencies only as working balances. This area includes all of Western Europe, Latin America, Africa, with the exception of Guinea, and the Far East, except for Burma, India, and Pakistan. In these nations, the Government-owned balances of foreign currency are inadequate or barely adequate to cover official requirements and supplemental purchases are made with dollars. There is, therefore, no balance-of-payments benefit to be gained by sales to private persons.

As additional sales for foreign currencies are made, as repayments under previous agreements are received and as U.S. official requirements change, arrangements will be negotiated where possible and procedures established for sales to private U.S. citizens.

Exhibit 65.—Press Release, June 16, 1965, announcing the intention of France to make a further prepayment on its debt to the United States

The Government of France today announced its intention to make in the near future a further prepayment in the amount of $178.6 million of principal outstanding on debts owed to the United States.

The prepayment will be applied to the Export-Import Bank Lend-Lease Termination Loan contracted in the early postwar years of French reconstruction and completes repayment of that loan. Previous prepayments on this and other debts to the United States in 1962 and 1963 amounted to approximately

$630 million. The prepayment announced today, along with regularly scheduled midyear payments on other debts, will reduce the principal remaining on the French Government's post World War II debt to the United States to slightly under $400 million.

The U.S. Treasury welcomes the prepayment announced today by the Government of France.

Exhibit 66.—Statement on discussions held June 29, 1965, by Chancellor of the Exchequer James Callaghan of Great Britain and Secretary of the Treasury Henry H. Fowler at the U.S. Treasury

British Chancellor of the Exchequer James Callaghan and Secretary of the Treasury Henry H. Fowler agreed in their talks at the U.S. Treasury that in present circumstances the primary contribution of both the United Kingdom and the United States to international financial stability and the improvement in the international monetary system is to achieve and sustain a broad equilibrium in their international balance of payments.

Secretary Fowler noted that the voluntary effort by American bankers and businessmen to reduce their net dollar outlays abroad, undertaken earlier this year at the President's request, is having an encouraging effect. Provisional indications are that this, and the wide range of other efforts being made to end the U.S. payments deficit, resulted in surpluses during March, April, and probably in May. However, the United States plans no relaxation of its efforts. The country is now entering the period of the year when tourist expenditures increase dollar payments to foreigners markedly. Imports are rising with continued internal expansion and there are increased dollar outlays in South Vietnam and in the Dominican Republic. The accumulation of dollars in reserve holdings abroad in past years is the cause of large continued gold outflows, such as those of the current year.

The Chancellor of the Exchequer and Secretary Fowler agreed that the prospects for an early and sustained equilibrium in the U.S. balance of payments resulting from the efforts of the last four years were good, and that there should be no relaxation in the execution of President Johnson's program of February 10, 1965.

The Chancellor said that a substantial improvement had taken place in the British balance of payments during the first quarter of 1965. He expected a big reduction in the deficit on current and long-term capital account for 1965 as a whole. The measures which the British Government had taken in the fields of fiscal policy, credit control, the stimulation of industrial efficiency, incomes policy, and economic planning were beginning to work through the economy; and he reiterated his aim of balancing Britain's overseas payments in the second half of 1966.

In discussing the interaction of the balance-of-payments programs of the two countries, the Chancellor drew attention to the effect on the British position of the measures which the United States had undertaken to correct its balance of payments. In this connection, Secretary Fowler emphasized that the guidelines for the voluntary restraint program take account of the United Kingdom payments problem. The United States pointed out that the British Government's program described by Chancellor Callaghan to the British Parliament on the 12th April, for continuing to raise gradually the proportion of the United Kingdom Government's holdings of nonsterling securities in a liquid form, and their use to reinforce the reserves, would involve an adverse impact on the U.S. balance of payments. Secretary Fowler recognized the need for this British program; and the Chancellor reiterated earlier assurances that the British authorities would continue to cooperate by managing the portfolio in such a way as to minimize the impact of the operations on the U.S. balance of payments and avoid any significant impact on the U.S. security markets. He added that these operations had now been carried to a point where the portfolio could be used to reinforce the United Kingdom reserves at short notice.

With respect to the problem of international liquidity, it was felt that a number of countries will require time to consider their attitudes in the light of changing developments in international payments, and with the benefit of technical studies now being completed in the Group of Ten. In this connection, the Chancellor referred to the discussions which he had held with M. Giscard d'Estaing, the French Minister of Finance; and Secretary Fowler indicated that he hoped to have talks with the Finance Ministers of other major countries in the latter part of the year on the subject of international liquidity.

These talks would explore the various possibilities with a view toward any reinforcement that would help to assure a payments system fully responsive to the continued growth of international trade.

The British and American ministers were agreed that any such reinforcement must await the development, out of the present divergent opinions, of an international consensus on this subject; but that constant and persistent efforts should be pressed at the Ministerial level, both during and after the meetings of the World Bank and International Monetary Fund. In this connection the Chancellor stressed the importance of the needs of the developing countries.

The Ministers agreed that the two reserve currencies would continue to play an essential part in the financing of international trade and as a medium in which to hold reserves. They recognized that the interests of the two currencies were closely bound up with one another. This identity of interest had already been recognized in the measures of financial cooperation taken by the two countries, which should be maintained and intensified.

In addition to the Chancellor and the Secretary, participants in the Treasury discussion included:

Sir Patrick Dean, British Ambassador to the United States; Sir William Armstrong, Joint Permanent Secretary of the British Treasury; Sir Denis Rickett, Second Secretary of the British Treasury, Mr. Robert Neild, Economic Adviser to the British Treasury, Mr. M. H. Parsons, Executive Director, Bank of England and Mr. John Stevens, Economic Minister in the British Embassy, Washington.

Mr. Joseph W. Barr, Under Secretary of the U.S. Treasury; Mr. Frederick L. Deming, Under Secretary of the Treasury for Monetary Affairs; Mr. Merlyn N. Trued, Assistant Secretary of the Treasury for International Affairs, and Mr. Stanley S. Surrey, Assistant Secretary of the Treasury for Tax Policy.

Exhibit 67.—Press Release, July 1, 1965, announcing the consent of the United States to an increase in its quota in the International Monetary Fund

Secretary of the Treasury Henry H. Fowler, as U.S. Governor of the International Monetary Fund, has informed the Fund of U.S. consent to an increase of $1,035 million in the U.S. quota.

Secretary Fowler's action followed President Johnson's signing yesterday of appropriations legislation which implemented earlier congressional authorization for the increase.

The increase in the U.S. quota will be paid 25 percent or $258.75 million in gold, and 75 percent or $776.25 million through a letter of credit. The action is in accordance with the Resolution of the International Monetary Fund Board of Governors providing for the increase in members' quotas. In return for its gold payment the United States will receive an equally valuable reserve asset in the form of virtually automatic "gold tranche" drawing rights on the Fund. No expenditures under the letter of credit will be required for the foreseeable future. Accordingly, the quota increase payment will have no effect upon the U.S. international reserve position, or upon its balance-of-payments position.

The increase in the U.S. quota is part of a general expansion of all members' quotas by 25 percent, plus larger increases for 16 countries. Secretary Fowler said that the action of the U.S. Government demonstrates the importance which it places on ensuring that adequate resources shall be available to the Fund so that it can continue to play a vital role in the international monetary system.

Exhibit 68.—Other Treasury testimony published in hearings before congressional committees, July 1, 1964–June 30, 1965

Secretary of the Treasury Dillon

Statement in support of H.R. 12010, published in hearings before the Subcommittee on International Finance of the Committee on Banking and Currency, House of Representatives, 88th Congress, 2d Session, on H.R. 12010, a bill to amend the Inter-American Development Bank Act to authorize the United

States to participate in an increase in the resources of the Fund for Special Operations of the Inter-American Development Bank, August 11, 1964, pages 2–9.

Statement in support of H.R. 45, published in hearings before the Committee on Banking and Currency, House of Representatives, 89th Congress, 1st Session, on H.R. 45, a bill to amend the Inter-American Development Bank Act to authorize the United States to participate in the resources of the Fund for Special Operations of the Inter-American Development Bank, February 3, 1965, pages 3–13.

Statement in support of S. 805, published in hearings before the Committee on Foreign Relations, U.S. Senate, 89th Congress, 1st Session, on S. 805, a bill to amend the Inter-American Development Bank Act to authorize the United States to participate in an increase in the resources of the Fund for Special Operations of the Inter-American Development Bank, February 5, 1965, pages 2–68.

Statement in support of H.R. 6497, published in hearings before the Committee on Banking and Currency, House of Representatives, 89th Congress, 1st Session, on H.R. 6497, a bill to amend the Bretton Woods Agreements Act to authorize an increase in the International Monetary Fund quota of the United States, March 23, 1965, pages 44–53.

Secretary of the Treasury Fowler

Statement in support of H.R. 7368, published in hearings before the Committee on Ways and Means, House of Representatives, 89th Congress, 1st Session, on H.R. 7368, a bill to amend the tariff schedules of the United States to reduce until January 1, 1968, the exemption from duty enjoyed by returning residents to $50 fair retail value, May 3, 1965, pages 19–23.

Statement in support of H.R. 6497, published in hearings before the Committee on Foreign Relations, U.S. Senate, 89th Congress, 1st Session, on H.R. 6497, a bill to amend the Bretton Woods Agreements Act to authorize an increase in the U.S. quota in the International Monetary Fund, May 6, 1965, pages 2–25.

Statement in opposition to H.R. 8147, published in hearings before the Committee on Finance, U.S. Senate, 89th Congress, 1st Session, on H.R. 8147, a bill relating to certain customs exemptions for returning residents, June 24, 1965, pages 2–8.

Under Secretary of the Treasury for Monetary Affairs Deming

Statement in support of H.R. 5280, published in hearings before the Antitrust Subcommittee of the Committee on the Judiciary, House of Representatives, 89th Congress, 1st Session, on H.R. 5280, a bill to provide for exemptions from the antitrust laws to assist in safeguarding the balance-of-payments position of the United States, March 3, 1965, pages 4–8.

Statement in support of an appropriation to increase the U.S. quota to the International Monetary Fund, published in hearings before the Committee on Appropriations, U.S. Senate, 89th Congress, 1st Session, on H.R. 7060, a bill for various appropriations, June 3, 1965, pages 2–14.

Assistant Secretary of the Treasury Trued

Statement in connection with improving the U.S. balance of payments by reducing the deficit on tourist account, published in hearings before the Special Subcommittee on Tourism of the Committee on Banking and Currency, House of Representatives, 88th Congress, 2d Session, on international travel in relation to the balance-of-payments deficit, November 30, 1964, pages 4–6.

Statement before the Committee on Foreign Relations, U.S. Senate, in support of S. 1742, a bill containing three separate proposals relating to the International Bank for Reconstruction and Development and the International Finance Corporation, published in Appendix to Calendar No. 360, Report No. 372, U.S. Senate, 89th Congress, 1st Session, June 7, 1965, pages 8–11.

Statement in support of S. 1760, a bill authorizing the Secretary of the Treasury to conclude the settlement of a debt arising from a U.S. loan to Greece in 1929, published in Appendix B of Calendar No. 351, Report No. 362, U.S. Senate, 89th Congress, 1st Session, June 7, 1965, pages 8–10.

Organization and Procedure

Exhibit 69.—Secretaries, Under Secretaries, General Counsels, Assistant Secretaries, and Deputy Under Secretaries for Monetary Affairs serving in the Treasury Department from September 11, 1789, to January 20, 1965, and the Presidents under whom they served

| Term of service | | Official | Served under— | |
From—	To—		Secretary of the Treasury	President
		Secretaries of the Treasury		
Sept. 11, 1789	Jan. 31, 1795	Alexander Hamilton, New York		Washington.
Feb. 3, 1795	Dec. 31, 1800	Oliver Wolcott, Connecticut		Washington, Adams.
Jan. 1, 1801	May 13, 1801	Samuel Dexter, Massachusetts		Adams, Jefferson.
May 14, 1801	Feb. 9, 1814	Albert Gallatin, Pennsylvania [1]		f n, Madison.
Feb. 9, 1814	Oct. 5, 1814	Ge W. Campbell, Tennessee		Madison.
Oct. 6, 1814	Oct. 21, 1816	Alexander J. Dallas, Pennsylvania		Madison.
Oct. 22, 1816	Mar. 6, 1825	Wm. H. Crawford, ia		n, Monroe.
Mar. 7, 1825	Mar. 5, 1829	Richard Rush, Pennsylvania [2]		Adams, J. Q.
Mar. 6, 1829	June 20, 1831	Samuel D. Ingham, Pennsylvania [3]		n.
Aug. 8, 1831	May 28, 1833	Louis McLane, Delaware		Jackson.
May 29, 1833	Sept. 22, 1833	Wm. J. Duane, Pennsylvania		Jackson.
Sept. 23, 1833	June 25, 1834	Roger B. Taney, Maryland		Jackson.
July 1, 1834	Mar. 3, 1841	Levi Woodbury, New Hampshire		Jackson, Van Buren.
Mar. 6, 1841	Sept. 11, 1841	as Ewing, Ohio		Harrison, Tyler.
Sept. 13, 1841	Mar. 1, 1843	er Forward, Pennsylvania		Tyler.
Mar. 8, 1843	May 2, 1844	John C. Spencer, New York [4]		Tyler.
July 4, 1844	Mar. 7, 1845	Geo. M. o, Kentucky		Tyler, Polk.
Mar. 8, 1845	Mar. 5, 1849	Robt. J. Walker, Mississippi		Polk.
Mar. 8, 1849	July 22, 1850	W. M. Meredith, Pennsylvania		Taylor, Fillmore.
July 23, 1850	Mar. 6, 1853	Thos. Corwin, o		Fillmore.
Mar. 7, 1853	Mar. 6, 1857	es Guthrie, Kentucky		e.
Mar. 7, 1857	Dec. 8, 1860	Howell b, Georgia		Buchanan.
Dec. 12, 1860	Jan. 14, 1861	Philip F. Thomas, Maryland		Buchanan.

Footnotes at end of table.

Exhibit 69.—Secretaries, Under Secretaries, General Counsels, Assistant Secretaries, and Deputy Under Secretaries for Monetary Affairs serving in the Treasury Department from September 11, 1789, to January 20, 1965, and the Presidents under whom they served—Continued

Term of service		Official	Served under—	
From—	To—		Secretary of the Treasury	President
		Secretaries of the Treasury—Continued		
Jan. 15, 1861	Mar. 6, 1861	John A. Dix, New York		Buchanan.
Mar. 7, 1861	June 30, 1864	Salmon P. Chase, Ohio		Lincoln.
July 5, 1864	Mar. 3, 1865	W. P. Fessenden, Maine		Do.
Mar. 9, 1865	Mar. 3, 1869	Hugh McCulloch, Indiana [5]		Lincoln, Johnson.
Mar. 12, 1869	Mar. 16, 1873	Geo. S. Boutwell, Massachusetts		Grant.
Mar. 17, 1873	June 3, 1874	W. A. Richardson, Mass.		Grant.
June 4, 1874	June 20, 1876	Benj. H. Bristow, Kentucky		Grant.
July 7, 1876	Mar. 9, 1877	Lot M. Morrill, Maine		Grant, Hayes.
Mar. 10, 1877	Mar. 3, 1881	John Sherman, Ohio		Hayes.
Mar. 8, 1881	Nov. 13, 1881	Wm. Windom, Minn.[6]		Garfield, Arthur.
Nov. 14, 1881	Sept. 4, 1884	Chas. J. Folger, New York		Arthur.
Sept. 25, 1884	Oct. 30, 1884	Walter Q. Gresham, Indiana [5]		Arthur.
Oct. 31, 1884	Mar. 7, 1885	Hugh McCulloch, Indiana [5]		Arthur, Cleveland.
Mar. 8, 1885	Mar. 31, 1887	Daniel Manning, New York		Cleveland.
Apr. 1, 1887	Mar. 6, 1889	Chas. S. Fairchild, New York [6]		Cleveland, Harrison.
Feb. 25, 1891	Mar. 6, 1893	Chas. Foster, Ohio		Harrison.
Mar. 7, 1893	Mar. 5, 1897	John G. Carlisle, Kentucky		Harrison, Cleveland.
Mar. 6, 1897	Jan. 31, 1902	Lyman J. Gage, Illinois		Cleveland, McKinley.
Feb. 1, 1902	Mar. 7, 1907	L. M. Shaw, Iowa		McKinley, Roosevelt.
Mar. 4, 1907	Mar. 3, 1909	George B. Cortelyou, New York		Roosevelt.
Mar. 8, 1909	Mar. 5, 1913	Franklin MacVeagh, Illinois		Roosevelt.
Mar. 6, 1913	Dec. 15, 1918	W. G. McAdoo, New York		Taft.
Dec. 16, 1918	Feb. 1, 1920	Carter Glass, Virginia		Wilson.
				Wilson.

Feb. 2, 1920	Mar. 3, 1921	David F. Houston, Missouri		
Mar. 4, 1921	Feb. 12, 1932	Andrew W. Mellon, Pennsylvania		Harding, Coolidge, ...
Feb. 13, 1932	Mar. 3, 1933	Ogden L. Mills, New York		Hoover.
Mar. 4, 1933	Dec. 31, 1933	William H. ..., New York		Roosevelt.
Jan. 1, 1934	July 22, 1945	Henry Morgenthau, Jr., New York		...t, Truman.
July 23, 1945	June 23, 1946	Fred M. ..., Kentucky		Truman.
June 25, 1946	Jan. 20, 1953	John W. Snyder, ...		...
Jan. 21, 1953	July 28, 1957	George M. Humphrey, Ohio		Eisenhower.
July 29, 1957	Jan. 20, 1961	...rt B. ..., ...nn.		Eisenhower.
Jan. 21, 1961		Douglas Dillon, New ...		Kennedy, ...dn.

Under Secretaries [7]

July 1, 1921	Nov. 17, 1923	S. Parker Gi..., Jr., New Jersey	Mellon	Harding, Coolidge.
Nov. 20, 1923	Feb. 1, 1927	Garrard B. ..., I...	...on	Coolidge.
Mar. 4, 1927	Feb. 12, 1932	Ogden L. Mills, New York [8]	Mellon	...dge, Hoover.
Feb. 13, 1932	May 15, 1933	Arthur A. Ballantine, New York	Mills, Woodin	Hoover, Roosevelt.
May 19, 1933	Nov. 16, 1933	Dean G. Acheson, Maryland	Woodin	Roosevelt.
Nov. 17, 1933	Dec. 31, 1933	...ry Morgenthau, Jr., New York [9]	...in	Roosevelt.
Jan. 1, 1934	Feb. 15, 1936	...as Jefferson Coolidge, Massachusetts	Morgenthau	Roosevelt.
May 2, 1934	Sept. 15, 1938	...well Magill, New ...	...au	Roosevelt.
Jan. 29, 1937	Dec. 31, 1939	John W. Hanes, North ...	Morgenthau	Roosevelt.
Nov. 1, 1938	Dec. 31, 1945	Daniel W. Bell, Illinois	...u, Vinson	Roosevelt, Truman.
Jan. 18, 1940	Jan. 14, 1946	O. Max Gardner, North Carolina	Vinson, Snyder	Truman.
Mar. 4, 1946	July 14, 1948	A. L. M. Wiggins, South Carolina	Snyder	...
Jan. 23, 1947	Jan. 20, 1953	Edward H. Foley, New York	Snyder	...
July 15, 1948	July 31, 1955	Marion B. Folsom, New York	Humphrey	Eisenhower.
Jan. 28, 1953	Jan. 31, 1956	H. ... ...an Rose, Ohio	...pey	Eisenhower.
Aug. 3, 1955	Jan. 20, 1961	Fred C. Scribner, Jr., ...	Anderson	Eisenhower.
Aug. 9, 957	Apr. 10, 1964	...ry H. Fowler, Virginia	Dillon	Kennedy, Johnson.
Feb. 3, 1961				

Under Secretaries for Monetary Affairs [10]

Aug. 3, 1954	Sept. 25, 1957	W. Randolph Burgess, Maryland	Humphrey, Anderson	Eisenhower.
Sept. 30, 1957	Jan. 20, 1961	Julian B. Baird, Minnesota	Anderson	Eisenhower.
Jan. 31, 1961	Dec. 31, 1964	Robert V. Roosa, New York	Dillon	Kennedy, Johnson.

Footnotes at end of table.

Exhibit 69— Secretaries, Under Secretaries, General Counsels, Assistant Secretaries, and Deputy Under Secretaries for Monetary Affairs serving in the Treasury Department from September 11, 1789, to January 20, 1965, and the Presidents under whom they served—Continued

Term of service		Official	Served under—	
From—	To—		Secretary of the Treasury	President
		General Counsels [11]		
June 20, 1934	Jan. 11, 1939	Herman Oliphant, Maryland	Morgenthau	Roosevelt.
May 19, 1939	July 24, 1942	Edward H. Foley, Jr., New York [12]	Morgenthau	Roosevelt.
Aug. 7, 1942	Mar. 22, 1944	Randolph E. Paul, New York	Morgenthau	Roosevelt.
May 10, 1944	Aug. 11, 1947	Joseph J. O'Connell, Jr., New York	Morgenthau, Vinson, Snyder.	Roosevelt, Truman.
June 10, 1948	Jan. 20, 1953	Thomas J. Lynch, Ohio	Snyder	Truman.
Jan. 30, 1953	Sept. 1, 1954	Elbert P. Tuttle, Georgia	Humphrey	Eisenhower.
Jan. 26, 1955	Aug. 2, 1955	David W. Kendall, Michigan [13]	Humphrey	Eisenhower.
Sept. 22, 1955	Apr. 17, 1957	Fred C. Scribner, Jr., Maine [14]	Humphrey	Eisenhower.
Jan. 28, 1958	Oct. 17, 1959	Nelson P. Rose, Ohio	Humphrey	Eisenhower.
Oct. 2, 1959	Jan. 20, 1961	David A. Lindsay, New York	Anderson	Eisenhower.
Apr. 5, 1961	Oct. 6, 1962	Robert H. Knight, Virginia	Dillon	Kennedy.
Nov. 16, 1962		G. d'Andelot Belin, Massachusetts	Dillon	Kennedy, Johnson.
		Assistant Secretaries [15]		
Mar. 12, 1849	Oct. 9, 1849	Charles B. Penrose, Pennsylvania	Meredith	Taylor.
Oct. 10, 1849	Nov. 15, 1850	Allen A. Hall, Pennsylvania	Meredith, Corwin	Taylor, Fillmore.
Nov. 16, 1850	Mar. 13, 1853	William L. Hodge, Tennessee	Corwin,	Fillmore, Pierce.
Mar. 14, 1853	Mar. 12, 1857	Peter G. Washington, District of Columbia	Guthrie, Co.	Pierce, Buchanan.
Mar. 13, 1857	Jan. 16, 1861	Philip Clayton, Georgia	Co., Thomas, Dix	Buchanan.
Mar. 13, 1861	July 11, 1865	George Harrington, District of Columbia [16]	Chase, Fessenden, McCulloch.	Lincoln, Johnson.
Mar. 18, 1864	June 15, 1865	Maunsell B. Field, New York	...e, Fessenden, McCulloch.	Lincoln, Johnson.

		Name		President
d 5, 85	Nv. 30, 87	William E. Chandler, New Hampshire	Fessenden, M	
Jy 1, 85	My 4, 85	John F. Hartley, Maine	Richardson, Bristow.	
Dec. 2, 87	Jy 31, 88	Edmund Cooper, Tennessee	Boutwell	Grant.
Mar. 20 1869	Mar. 17, 1873	William A. Richardson, Massachusetts	Richardson,	Grant.
A , 83	June 3, 84	Frederick A. Sawyer, South Carolina	, Morrill,	
Jy 1, 84		Charles F. Conant, New Hampshire	Sherman.	
A 4 85	he 30, 86	Curtis F. Burnam, Kentucky	Morrill, Sherman,	
Ag. 1 26	9, 1885	Henry F. French, Massachusetts	, Folger, Mg.	
Apr. 3, 1877	Dec. 8, 1877	Richard C. McCormick, Arizona	n	
Dec. 9, 1877	Mar. 31, 1880	John B. Hawley, Illinois	Sherman, Windom,	eld,
Apr. 0, 1880	Dec. 3, 1881	J. Kendrick Upton, New Hampshire	Folger.	
b. 28, 1882	b. 16, 1884	John C. New, Indiana	Folger, Gresham,	, Cleveland.
r 7, 1884	Nov. 0, 1885	Charles E. Coon, New York	lloch, Manning.	
Mar. 14, 85	r. 1, 87	Charles S. Fairchild, New York [17]	Mg	Cleveland.
Nv. 0, 85	une 0, 86	William E. Smith, New York	Manning,	Cleveland.
Jy 2, 86	Mar. 12, 1889	Hugh S. Thompson, South Carolina	, Fairchild,	Cleveland, Harrison.
r. 6, 87	Mar. 11, 89	Isaac N. Maynard, New York	r,	Cleveland, Harrison.
r. 1, 89	Jy 0 90	George H. Tichner, Illinois	Wm	Harrison.
Jy 22, 90	Oct. , 90	George T. Batchelder, New York [18]	h	Harrison.
Jy 3 90	c. 1, 92 June 0, 83	A. B. Nettleton, Minnesota	W,	Harrison.
		Oliver L. Spaulding, Michigan	M, os t, Gr-	Harrison, Cleveland.
r. 27, 81	31	Lorenzo Crounse, Nebraska	Be	Harrison.
Nov. 2, 82	a	John H. Gear, Iowa	r-	Harrison.
Dec. 2, 82	r. 3,	Genio M. Lambertson, Nebraska		Harrison, Cleveland.
r. 2, 83	r. 7, 97	Charles S. Hamlin, Massachusetts	ge	Cleveland, McKinley.
r. 13, 83	Mar. 31, 197	William E. Curtis, New York	Carlisle, Gage	Cleveland, McKinley.

ts at ed of table.

Exhibit 69.— Secretaries, Under Secretaries, General Counsels, Assistant Secretaries, and Deputy Under Secretaries for Monetary Affairs serving in the Treasury Department from September 11, 1789, to January 20, 1965, and the Presidents under whom they served—Continued

| Term of service | | Official | Served under— | |
From—	To—		Secretary of the Treasury	President
		Assistant Secretaries [15]—Continued		
July 1, 1893	Jy 4, 1897	Scott Wike, Illinois	Carlisle, Gage	Cleveland, McKinley.
7, 1897	Mr. 10, 1899	W illm B. , Ħ, New Jersey	Gage	McKinley.
Ar. 7, 1897	Mar. 4, 1903	Igr L. Spaulding, Michigan	Gage, Shaw	McKinley, Roosevelt.
June 1, 1897	Mar. 5, 01	Frank A. (Ħ, rĦis	Gage	McKinley.
Mar. 13, 1899	Ħe 3, 1906	Horace A. Taylor, Wisconsin	Gage, Shaw	McKinley, Roosevelt.
Ħr. 6, 01	Ħr. 15, 1903	Milton E. Ailes, Ko-	Gage, Shaw	McKinley, Roosevelt.
Mr. 5, 1903	Mar. 5, 1905	Robert B. Armstrong, Iowa	Shaw	Roosevelt.
My 27, 1903	Ħn. 21, 07	Charles H. Keep, New York	Shaw, Ctelyou, MacVeagh.	Roosevelt.
Ħr. 6, 1905	Ħv. 1, 09	J mes B. Reynolds, Massachusetts	Shaw, Ctelyou, MacVeagh.	Roosevelt, Taft.
Jy 1, 1906	Mr. 15, 1908	John H. Edwards, Ohio	Shaw, Cortelyou	Roosevelt.
Ħn. 22, 1907	Feb. 8, 07	Arthur F. Statter, Oregon	Shaw	Roosevelt.
Ħr. 3, 1907	Mar. 6, 0	Beekman Winthrop, New York	Ħn	Roosevelt.
Mr. Ħ, 1908	Ħr. 0, 09	Louis A. Coolidge, Massachusetts	Cortelyou, MacVeagh.	Roosevelt, Taft.
Ħr. 5, 09	June 8, 1910	Charles D. Norton, Il lnois	MacVeagh	Taft.
Apr. 19, 1909	Ħr. 3, 1911	Charles D. Hilles, New Ħ	MacVeagh	Taft.
Ħr. 7, 1909	Jy 31, 1913	James F. Curtis, Massachusetts	Ħac Veagh, McAdoo.	Taft, Wilson.
Ħe 8, 90	Jy 3, 1912	A. Piatt Andrews, Massachusetts	MacVeagh	Taft.
Ħr. 4, 91	Mar. 3, 1913	Rogert O. Bailey,	MacVeagh	Ħ.
Jy 20, 1912	Sept. 30, 1913	Ħan P. Adm, Vermont	MacVeagh, McAdoo.	Taft, Wilson.
Mar. 24, 1913	Feb. 2, 94	John Skelton Ħs, Virginia	M	Wilson.
Ag. 1, 1913	Ag. 9, 94	C Ħles S. Hamlin, Massachusetts	M	Wilson.
Ħ 1, 1913	Sept. 30, 97	Byron R. Nwton, New York	McAdoo	Wilson.

Name		President
William P. Malburn, Colorado	Mo.	Wn.
Andrew J. Peters, Massachusetts	Mo.	Wn.
Oscar T. Crosby, Virginia	Mo.	Wn.
Leo S. Rowe, Pennsylvania	Mo., Glass	Wn., Harding.
James H. Moyle, Utah	Houston, Mellon.	
Russell C. Leffingwell, New York [19]		San.
Thomas B. Love, Texas		Wn., Harding.
Albert Rathbone, New York	Glass,	Wn.
Jouett Shouse, Kansas	G., Houston	Wn.
... H. Davis, ...	G., Houston	Wn., Harding.
... Kelley, New York	Houston,	
S. ..., Jr., New Jersey [20]	Houston,	Wn.,
Ewing ...	Houston,	Wn., Coolidge.
Eliot Wadsworth, ...	Mellon.	Harding.
... Clifford, ...	Mellon.	Harding.
Elmer Dover, Washington	Mellon.	Harding, Coolidge.
McKenzie Moss, Kentucky		Coolidge.
Garrard B. ..., Illinois [21]	Mellon.	Coolidge.
... S. Dewey, ...	Mellon.	Coolidge, Hoover.
Carl T. Schuneman, Minnesota	Mellon.	Hoover.
Seymour Lowman, New York		
Ferry K. Heath, ...	Mellon.	Hoover.
...r Ewing Hope, New ...		Hoover.
Arthur A. Ballantine, New York [2]		Hoover.
... H. Douglas, Jr., ...	Mills.	Hoover.
Lawrence W. Robert, Jr., ...		Roosevelt.
... Hewes, ...		Roosevelt.
... C. Taylor, Illinois [23]		Roosevelt.
... W. H..., North		Roosevelt.
Herbert E. G..., New York	..., Vinson	...velt, Truman.

F notes at end of table.

Exhibit 69.—Secretaries, Under Secretaries, General Counsels, Assistant Secretaries, and Deputy Under Secretaries for Monetary Affairs serving in the Treasury Department from September 11, 1789, to January 20, 1965, and the Presidents under whom they served—Continued

Term of service		Official	Served under—	
From—	To—		Secretary of the Treasury	President
		Assistant Secretaries [15]—Continued		
Jan. 18, 1940	Nov. 30, 1944	John L. Sullivan, New Hampshire	Morgenthau	Roosevelt.
Jan. 24, 1945	May 1, 1946	Harry D. ...	...	Roosevelt, Truman.
Apr. 15, 1946	July 14, 1948	Edward H. ..., New York [12]	Vinson, ...	Truman.
July 16, 1948	Jan. 20, 1953	John S. ...	Snyder	Truman.
Feb. 8, 1949	Mar. 31, 1951	William ..., Ga.	Snyder	...
Jan. 24, 1952	Feb. 28, 1957	Andrew N. Overby, District of Co...	Snyder, Humphrey	Truman, Eisenhower.
Jan. 28, 1953	Aug. 2, 1955	H. ..., Ohio [24]	Humphrey	Eisenhower.
Sept. 20, 1954	Jan. 20, 1961	... B. Robbins, ... [25]	Humphrey	Eisenhower.
Aug. 3, 1955	Dec. 15, 1957	David W. ..., Mi...	Humphrey	...
Pt. 18, 1957	Aug. 8, 1957	Fred C. ..., Jr., ...	Humphrey	...
Dec. 4, 1957	Dec. 15, 1958	... B. Coughran, ..., [14]	...	...Eisenhower.
Dec. 16, 1957	Dec. 19, 1961	A. Gilmore Fluss, ...	Anderson, Dillon	..., Kennedy.
Dec. 17, 1958	Dec. 18, 1960	T. ... Upton, Pennsylvania	...	Eisenhower.
Dec. 20, 1960	Jan. 20, 1961	John M. Leddy, Virginia	Anderson	...
Apr. 5, 1961	Oct. 31, 1962	Stanley S. Surrey	Dillon	Kennedy.
Apr. 24, 1961		... A. Reed, New ...	Dillon	Kennedy, ...
Dec. 20, 1961		John C. ..., New ...	Dillon	Kennedy, ...
Dec. 8, 1962	Oct. 15, 1964	Robert A. Wallace, Ill... [26]	Dillon	Kennedy, ...
Sept. 18, 1963			Dillon	Kennedy, ...
		Deputy Under Secretaries for Monetary Affairs		
Dec. 21, 1961	Nov. 28, 1963	J. Dewey Daane, District of Columbia	Dillon	Kennedy, Johnson.
Dec. 3, 1963		Paul A. Volcker, New Jersey	Dillon	Johnson.

Fiscal Assistant Secretaries [27]

Mar. 6, 1945	June 17, 1955	Edward F. Bartelt, Illinois	Morgenthau, Vinson, Snyder, Humphrey, Anderson, Dillon.	Roosevelt, Truman, Eisenhower, Kennedy, Johnson.
June 9, 1955	Mar. 31, 1962	William T. Heffelfinger, District of Columbia	Snyder, Humphrey, Anderson, Dillon.	Eisenhower, Kennedy.
June 5, 1962		John K. Carlock, Arizona	Dillon.	Eisenhower, Kennedy, Johnson.

Assistant Secretaries for Administration [28]

Aug. 2, 1950	Aug. 31, 1959	William W. Parsons, California	Snyder, Humphrey, Anderson.	Truman, Eisenhower.
Sept. 14, 1959		A. E. Weatherbee, Maine	Anderson, Dillon.	Eisenhower, Kennedy, Johnson.

[2] ... Mar. 5, 85, ... Mar. 7, 85, ... Secretary of the Navy), ...

[3] ... July 31, 85.

[4] ... as Secretary ... May 2, 85; ... July 3, 1844; ...

[5] ... was Secretary ... Mar. 9, 85, to Mar. 3, ...

[6] ... Mar. 7, 85. ... Mar. 8, 81, to Nov. 13, 1 81, an ... from ...

[7] ... De 16, 1921; ...

[8] Became Secretary ... Feb. 13, 82.

[9] ... by act of July 22, 1954; appointed by the President.

[10] ... by act of May 0, 1934 (5 U.S.C. 248a); appointed by the President.

[11] ... Secretary Apr. 15, 1946, and Under Secretary July 15, 1948.

[13] ... Secretary ... A. 3, 195.

[14] Became ... Apr. 8, 97. ... by ... at of Mar. 3, 1849; ... subject to ...

[15] ... 1857, ... Act of ...

[16] Act of Mar. 14, 18, ... or an ...

[17] Became ... Apr. 1, 87.

[18] Act of July 11, 19, ... or ...

[19] Act of Oct. 6, 19, ... of war ...

[20] Became Under ... July 1, 191.

[21] Became Under Secretary Nov. 0, 93.

[22] ... Became Under Secretary Feb. 13, 1932.

[23] Became Under ... Nov. 1, 98.

[24] ... Under ... A. 3, 85.

[25] Act of July 22, 94, ... for an additi...

[26] Act of July 8, 19, ... for a ...

[27] ... by Reorganization Plan No. 26, of 90. Title ... Secretary ...

Exhibit 70.—Treasury Department orders relating to organization and procedure

No. 150–62, OCTOBER 26, 1964.—DELEGATION TO COMMISSIONER OF INTERNAL REVE-
NUE OF CERTAIN FUNCTIONS RELATING TO EXTENSION OF TIME

By virtue of and pursuant to the authority vested in me by Reorganization
Plan No. 26 of 1950, there are hereby transferred to the Commissioner of Internal
Revenue the functions of the Secretary of the Treasury—
    (1) Under section 6081 of the Internal Revenue Code of 1954 with respect
to the granting of extensions of time for filing any return, declaration,
statement, or other document required by chapter 41 of such Code as added
by the Interest Equalization Tax Act (78 Stat. 809) ; and
    (2) Under section 6161 of such Code with respect to granting extensions
of time to pay the tax shown, or required to be shown, on any return or
declaration required under such chapter 41 of such Code.
The functions herein transferred to the Commissioner may be exercised by any
officer or employee of the Internal Revenue Service who is so authorized by the
Commissioner, under such rules as may be prescribed by him.

DOUGLAS DILLON,
Secretary of the Treasury.

No. 150–63, OCTOBER 23, 1964.—REALIGNMENT OF BOUNDARIES OF THE ALBANY AND
BUFFALO INTERNAL REVENUE DISTRICTS

By virtue of the authority vested in me as Secretary of the Treasury by
Reorganization Plan No. 26 of 1950, Reorganization Plan No. 1 of 1952, section
7621 of the Internal Revenue Code of 1954, as amended, and Executive Order
10289, approved September 17, 1951, made applicable to the Internal Revenue
Code of 1954 by Executive Order 10574, approved November 5, 1954, it is hereby
ordered :
    1. Albany District.   The Internal Revenue District, Albany, shall include the
counties of Albany, Clinton, Columbia, Dutchess, Essex, Franklin, Fulton, Greene,
Hamilton, Montgomery, Orange, Putnam, Rensselaer, Saratoga, Schenectady,
Schoharie, St. Lawrence, Sullivan, Ulster, Warren, and Washington, within the
State of New York.
    2. Buffalo District.   The Internal Revenue District, Buffalo, shall include the
counties of Allegany, Broome, Cattaraugus, Cayuga, Chautauqua, Chemung, Che-
nango, Courtland, Delaware, Erie, Genesee, Harkimer, Jefferson, Lewis, Living-
ston, Madison, Monroe, Niagara, Oneida, Onondaga, Ontario, Orleans, Oswego,
Otsego, Schuyler, Seneca, Steuben, Tioga, Tompkins, Wayne, Wyoming, and Yates,
within the State of New York.
    3. Effective date and implementation.   The provisions of sections 1 and 2 of
this order shall be effective January 1, 1965.   Effective immediately, the Commissioner of Internal Revenue is authorized to effect, at appropriate times and
in an orderly manner, such transfers of functions, personnel, positions, equipment, and funds as may be necessary to implement the provisions of this order.
    4. Treasury Department Order No. 150–58, dated May 17, 1963, is amended
with respect to the boundaries of the Albany and Buffalo Internal Revenue
Districts.

DOUGLAS DILLON,
Secretary of the Treasury.

GENERAL COUNSEL ORDER NO. 34, DECEMBER 23, 1964.—RESTATEMENT OF FUNCTIONS
OF THE CHIEF COUNSEL FOR THE INTERNAL REVENUE SERVICE

By virtue of the authority vested in me as General Counsel for the Department
of the Treasury by section 7801 of the Internal Revenue Code of 1954, as amended,
and by Treasury Department Order No. 190 (Rev. 2) dated October 23, 1963,
and as set forth below, I hereby delegate the following authority to the Chief
Counsel for the Internal Revenue Service, subject to my review as occasion
may require :
    1. The Chief Counsel shall be the legal advisor to the Commissioner of In-
ternal Revenue and his officers and employees.   In performing his assigned func-

tions, the Chief Counsel shall consult with and assist the Commissioner of Internal Revenue with a view to furthering the policies and programs of the Treasury Department and the Internal Revenue Service. Also, where appropriate, the Chief Counsel will furnish assistance to the Office of the Secretary. It is understood that any legal matter involving Treasury policy about which the Commissioner disagrees with the advice given him by the Chief Counsel will be submitted by the Commissioner to the Secretary or the Under Secretary for resolution.

2. To furnish legal opinions, and to assist the Commissioner in the preparation and review of rulings, closing agreements, memorandums of technical advice, and revenue rulings and procedures, and other proposed publications or releases, with respect to laws affecting the Internal Revenue Service.

3. To prepare, review, or assist in the preparation of proposed legislation, treaties, regulations, and executive orders relating to laws affecting the Internal Revenue Service.

4. To represent the Commissioner of Internal Revenue in cases pending in the Tax Court of the United States as prescribed in section 7452 of the Internal Revenue Code of 1954, and in such cases to exercise the function of decision whether and in what manner to defend, or to prosecute a claim, or to settle, or to abandon a claim or defense therein, subject to Chief Counsel Order 1958–5 (Commissioner Delegation Order No. 60) ; to acknowledge in the name of the Commissioner the receipt of Tax Court subpoenas served upon the Commissioner of Internal Revenue; to determine whether, and the extent to which, officers and employees of the Internal Revenue Service shall be permitted to disclose Internal Revenue records and information in response to a subpoena or other order of the Tax Court; to determine whether to acquiesce in the decisions of said Court; to file petitions for review of Tax Court decisions ; and to enter into written stipulations of venue for review of Tax Court decisions by a U.S. Court of Appeals.

5. To determine what civil actions should be brought in the courts under the laws affecting the Internal Revenue Service and to prepare recommendations to the Department of Justice for the commencement of such actions and to authorize or sanction commencement of such actions.

6. To determine whether referred income and wagering tax cases should be prosecuted in the criminal courts, to make appropriate recommendations to the Department of Justice in the prosecution of such cases and to make a like determination and recommendation on any other case referred to the Chief Counsel by the Commissioner of Internal Revenue.

7. To determine how actions brought in the courts against the United States or officers or employees thereof should be conducted and to make recommendations to the Department of Justice with respect thereto. .

8. To determine which court decisions should be appealed or further reviewed and to make recommendations to the Department of Justice with respect thereto.

9. To cooperate with and, at the request of the Department of Justice or of U.S. attorneys, to assist in conducting litigation in the courts, both civil and criminal, and in preparing briefs and arguments with respect thereto.

10. To accept or reject, in my name, railroad reorganization plans, corporate reorganization plans, and real property arrangements (sections 77(e), 199, and 455 of the Bankruptcy Act), in cases wherein the claims of the United States consist solely of Internal Revenue taxes.

11. To review all cases within the provisions of section 6405 of the Internal Revenue Code of 1954 and to prepare and sign the reports required by that section to be submitted to the Joint Committee on Internal Revenue Taxation.

12. To perform the functions prescribed for the General Counsel by section 7122 of the Internal Revenue Code of 1954 and by section 3469 of the Revised Statutes (31 U.S.C. 194), with respect to compromise matters arising in the administration of the Internal Revenue laws.

13. To supervise and evaluate the work of all officers and employees in the Office of the Chief Counsel, and to take the necessary action in all personnel matters pertaining thereto, including those for the appointment, classification, promotion, demotion, reassignment, transfer, or separation of such officers and employees, with the exceptions of appointments of attorneys and of promotions, transfers, reassignments, and separations of attorneys above GS-11.

14. To be responsible to me for the establishment and maintenance of appropriate standards of practice and for the professional competence, recruitment, and evaluation of the work of the employees of his office.

15. Subject to my approval, to designate the titles and duties of officers and employees in the Office of the Chief Counsel, and to establish in the Office such divisions and subdivisions as he may deem advisable.

16. To redelegate any of the authority delegated in this Order to any officer or employee in the Office of the Chief Counsel, and to authorize further redelegation of such authority.

This order supersedes the Order Delegating Authority of September 21, 1937, and amendments thereto, together with General Counsel Order dated May 8, 1952, which are hereby revoked. This order also supersedes the provisions of paragraph 2 of General Counsel Order No. 7 dated March 8, 1954. Chief Counsel's Order 1958–5 (Commissioner's Delegation Order No. 60) shall remain in effect. All other delegation orders are hereby modified to conform with the provisions of this order.

G. D'ANDELOT BELIN,
General Counsel.

_____

No. 150–64, DECEMBER 29, 1964.—APPROVAL OF GENERAL COUNSEL ORDER No. 34 AND REVOCATION OF PARAGRAPHS 2, 3, AND 4 OF TREASURY DEPARTMENT ORDER No. 150–37 OF MARCH 17, 1955

General Counsel Order No. 34, issued today with my approval, constitutes a restatement of all powers delegated to the Chief Counsel for the Internal Revenue Service, including matters covered by paragraphs 2, 3, and 4 of Treasury Department Order No. 150–37, issued March 17, 1955.

Accordingly, paragraphs 2, 3, and 4 of Treasury Department Order No. 150–37 are hereby revoked.

DOUGLAS DILLON,
Secretary of the Treasury.

_____

No. 150–65, JANUARY 4, 1965.—CONSOLIDATION OF NEW YORK AND NORTHEAST INTERNAL REVENUE REGIONS

By virtue of the authority vested in me as Secretary of the Treasury by Reorganization Plan No. 26 of 1950, Reorganization Plan No. 1 of 1952, section 7621 of the Internal Revenue Code of 1954, as amended, and Executive Order 10289, approved September 17, 1951, made applicable to the Internal Revenue Code of 1954 by Executive Order 10574, approved November 5, 1954, it is hereby ordered:

1. Abolition of office of Regional Commissioner. The office of Regional Commissioner of Internal Revenue, Northeast Region, is abolished.

2. Redesignation and realignment of New York Internal Revenue Region. The designation of the New York Internal Revenue Region is changed to the North-Atlantic Region, and its territory is extended to include the States of Connecticut, Maine, Massachusetts, New Hampshire, New York, Rhode Island, and Vermont. The headquarters office shall be in New York, New York.

3. Effective date. The provisions of this order shall be effective immediately. The Commissioner of Internal Revenue is authorized to effect, at appropriate times and in an orderly manner, such transfers of functions, personnel, positions, equipment, and funds as may be necessary to implement the provisions of this order.

4. Effect on other documents. Treasury Department Orders 150–58, dated May 17, 1963, and 150–59, dated February 11, 1964, are amended to the extent that they are in conflict with the provisions of this order.

DOUGLAS DILLON,
Secretary of the Treasury.

_____

No. 160–3, JULY 17, 1964.—CRYPTOGRAPHIC SECURITY PROGRAM OF THE TREASURY DEPARTMENT

1. Authority

Cryptographic security regulations are issued under the authority of sections 4(e), 6(d) and 13(b) of Executive Order 10501, as amended. The delegations herein are made pursuant to Reorganization Plan 26 of 1950 (3 CFR, 1950 Supp., ch. III).

2. Supplements to this Order

The Cryptographic Security Program of the Treasury Department is supplemented by KAG-1C/TSEC, and KAG-8C/TSEC, which were published by the Department of Defense, National Security Agency, Washington 25, D.C.

3. Responsibility of Cryptographic Regulations and Procedures

The Director, Office of Security, or his designee shall be responsible for the enforcement and development of regulations and procedures for the control of cryptographic security to be observed in the Treasury Department.

4. Cryptographic Security Officer

The Director, Office of Security, or his designee shall be the Cryptographic Security Officer. The Cryptographic Security Officer or his designee shall be responsible for the safeguarding of and accounting for cryptographic material within the Treasury Department. Also refer to KAG-1C/TSEC, paragraph 2002, for additional responsibilities.

5. Individual Responsibility

Each individual having access to cryptographic information or material is responsible for knowing and complying with the cryptographic security regulations in this Order and in KAG-1C/TSEC and KAG-8C/TSEC. Each individual who uses a cryptographic system is responsible for knowing and complying with all instructions concerning the operation of the system. These individuals are also responsible for any cryptographic information or material that may come into their possession at any time.

6. Eligibility for Authorization for Access to Classified Cryptographic Information or Material

Those individuals within the Treasury Department whose official duties require access to classified cryptographic information or material must possess a valid TOP SECRET security clearance issued by the Director, Office of Security, prior to the granting of a formal authorization for access to classified cryptographic information. These individuals;

    (a) Shall be of excellent character and discretion, and of unquestioned loyalty to the United States. There shall be no exception to this requirement.

    (b) Shall be a U.S. citizen, preferably by birth. If he is a naturalized citizen, final papers must have been held for a ten year period. The members of his immediate family should also be U.S. citizens.

    (c) Shall be a person, no member of whose immediate family nor any person to whom he may reasonably be considered to be bound by ties of affection, kinship, or obligation shall be of dubious loyalty to the United States nor a resident of a foreign country having basic or critical national interests opposed to those of the United States, and

    (d) Shall be required to read and comprehend the provisions of Title 18, U.S.C., sections 793, 794 and 798; Executive Order 10501, as amended; and effective Treasury Department regulations prior to the granting of a formal authorization for access to classified cryptographic information.

A. E. WEATHERBEE,
Administrative Assistant Secretary.

No. 165, REVISED—AMENDMENT 6, SEPTEMBER 23, 1964.—AMENDMENT OF DELEGATION RELATING TO DECISIONS WITH RESPECT TO CLAIMS, FINES, PENALTIES, AND FORFEITURES

By virtue of the authority vested in the Secretary of the Treasury by Reorganization Plan No. 26 of 1950 (3 CFR, 1949–1953 Comp. p. 1017) and pursuant to authorization given to me by Treasury Department Order No. 190, Revision 2 (28 F.R. 11570), it is hereby ordered that subparagraph (h) of paragraph 1 of Treasury Department Order No. 165, Revised, dated November 2, 1954 (T.D. 53654; 19 F.R. 7241), as amended, is further amended by deleting:

    (h) No decision with respect to any claim (including claim for liquidated damages), fine, or penalty (including forfeiture) in excess of $20,000 shall be made without the approval of the Secretary of the Treasury, except that such approval shall not be required with respect to any claim (including claim for liquidated damages), fine, or penalty (including forfeiture) incurred or arising under:

and substituting in lieu thereof the following:

(h) Any decision with respect to any claim (including claim for liquidated damages), fine, or penalty (including forfeiture) in excess of $100,000 shall be made by the Secretary of the Treasury, except decisions with respect to claims (including claims for liquidated damages), fines, or penalties (including forfeitures) incurred or arising under:

JAMES A. REED,
Assistant Secretary of the Treasury.

No. 165–15, SEPTEMBER 18, 1964.—ESTABLISHMENT OF NEW OFFICES AND REDESIGNATION OF EXISTING OFFICES IN THE BUREAU OF CUSTOMS

By virtue of the authority vested in me as Secretary of the Treasury, there are hereby established in the Bureau of Customs new offices designated as follows:

Office of Regulations and Rulings
Office of Operations
Office of Administration
Office of Investigations

There is also established a Division of Collectors' Operations.

To the extent that the Commissioner of Customs determines feasible, the functions of the present Divisions of the Bureau of Customs are assigned as follows:

Divisions of Classification and Drawback; Entry, Value and Penalties; and Marine Administration to the Office of Regulations and Rulings.

Divisions of Appraisement Administration; Technical Services; and Collectors' Operations to the Office of Operations.

Division of Management and Controls to the Office of Administration.

Division of Investigations and Enforcement to the Office of Investigations.

The Divisions of Management and Controls and Investigations and Enforcement are abolished on the establishment of the new offices.

Nothing in this Order is to be interpreted to preclude the Commissioner of Customs from assigning to any of the appropriate offices any of the functions or activities of any division which he determines is necessary or desirable.

Each of the above offices and divisions will be headed by a Deputy Commissioner of Customs.

This Order shall become effective on October 1, 1964.

DOUGLAS DILLON,
Secretary of the Treasury.

No. 167–62, AUGUST 5, 1964.—DELEGATION TO THE COMMANDANT, U.S. COAST GUARD, OF FUNCTIONS RELATING TO MILITARY PAY ENTITLEMENTS

By virtue of the authority vested in the Secretary of the Treasury by Reorganization Plan No. 26 of 1950 and 14 U.S.C. 631 and pursuant to the powers delegated to me in Treasury Department Order No. 190 (Revision No. 2), the Commandant, U.S. Coast Guard is hereby authorized to prescribe regulations under Executive Order No. 11157, dated 22 June 1964, governing the following military pay entitlements:

a. Incentive pay for hazardous duty.
b. Special pay for sea duty and duty at certain places.
c. Basic allowances for subsistence.
d. Basic allowances for quarters.

Such regulations shall conform with those of the other military Services to the fullest extent practicable.

Sections 1, 3, 5, and 6 of Treasury Department Order No. 167–30, which previously delegated authority in the areas covered by a, b, c, and d above, are hereby revoked.

JAMES A. REED,
Assistant Secretary of the Treasury.

No. 167–63, November 19, 1964.—Delegation to the Commandant, U.S. Coast Guard, of Functions Relating to Retention of Reserve Officers in an Active Status

By virtue of the authority vested in the Secretary of the Treasury by Reorganization Plan No. 26 of 1950 and 14 U.S.C. 631 and pursuant to the powers delegated to me by Treasury Department Order No. 190 (Revision No. 2), and Treasury Department Order No. 191 (Revision 3), there are transferred to the Commandant, U.S. Coast Guard, the functions of the Secretary under 14 U.S.C. 787a, pertaining to the convening of boards to select and recommend Reserve officers for retention in an active status.

The Commandant may provide for performance by subordinates in the Coast Guard of the functions delegated herein.

James A. Reed,
Assistant Secretary of the Treasury.

No. 167–64, December 7, 1964.—Delegation to the Commandant, U.S. Coast Guard, of Functions Concerning the Exemption of Certain Coast Guard Vessels from Lighting Requirements Prescribed by the International Regulations for Preventing Collisions at Sea

By virtue of the authority vested in the Secretary of the Treasury by Reorganization Plan No. 26 of 1950 and 14 U.S.C. 631, and pursuant to the authority delegated to me by Treasury Department Order No. 190 (Revision 2), there are transferred to the Commandant, U.S. Coast Guard, the functions of the Secretary of the Treasury contained in 33 U.S.C. 1052, concerning the exemption of specially constructed Coast Guard vessels from the lighting requirements prescribed by the International Regulations for Preventing Collisions at Sea.

The Commandant may provide for the performance by subordinates in the Coast Guard of any function herein delegated.

James A. Reed,
Assistant Secretary of the Treasury.

No. 167–65, February 26, 1965.—Delegation of Functions to Coast Guard Board of Contract Appeals

The regulations which created the newly constituted Coast Guard Board of Contract Appeals and which were published in the *Federal Register* on December 24, 1964 (29 F.R. 18368) vest in that Board (hereinafter referred to as the "New Board") the authority to take final action in contract dispute appeal cases which it considers.

Before the establishment of the New Board, Coast Guard Boards of Contract Appeals (hereinafter referred to as the "Old Board(s)") operated under regulations which provided that the Secretary of the Treasury, or his designated representative, would review and accept, reject, or modify and thus take final action on the Recommendations and Findings of the Old Boards in contract appeals disputes.

It has now been determined that the New Board shall assume the full functions of the Secretary of the Treasury to review, accept, reject, or modify and thus take final action on the Recommendations and Findings of the Old Boards in any case in which the Recommendations and Findings of an Old Board have not as yet been reviewed, accepted, rejected or modified by the Secretary or his delegate.

Pursuant to the authority of 40 U.S.C. 486(c), and by virtue of the authority delegated to me by Treasury Department Order No. 190 (Revision 2) the Coast Guard Board of Contract Appeals (the New Board) is hereby authorized to take final action in all Coast Guard contract appeals now pending regardless of the date on which any such appeal was filed.

James A. Reed,
Assistant Secretary of the Treasury.

No. 186 (REVOCATION), AUGUST 12, 1964.—ABOLISHMENT OF COMMITTEE
ON INVESTMENT POLICIES FOR TRUST FUNDS

The Committee on Investment Policies for Trust Funds established by
Treasury Department Order No. 186 on July 7, 1958, is hereby abolished.

DOUGLAS DILLON,
Secretary of the Treasury.

No. 202, OCTOBER 14, 1964.—ESTABLISHMENT OF OFFICE OF ASSISTANT SECRETARY
FOR INTERNATIONAL AFFAIRS

1. The Office of Balance of Payments, Office of Financial Policy Coordination,
Office of International Economic Activities, Office of Industrial Nations, Office
of Developing Nations and Office of Latin America established as constituent
units of the Office of International Affairs by Treasury Department Order No.
198, dated October 15, 1962, are hereby transferred to the Office of the Assistant
Secretary for International Affairs. In addition, there is hereby established
within the Office of the Assistant Secretary for International Affairs, the Office
of International Gold and Foreign Exchange Operations, and the Office of
Administration.

The organizational titles of the Office of Financial Policy Coordination and the
Office of Balance of Payments are hereby changed to:

Office of International Financial Policy Coordination and Operations; and
Office of Balance of Payments Programs, Operations and Statistics,
respectively.

The responsibilities and scope of activities of these Offices shall be as described
in appendices 1–8[1] of this Order. Directors of these Offices shall be designated
by the Assistant Secretary for International Affairs with the concurrence of the
Secretary of the Treasury.

2. There are hereby established two positions of Deputy to the Assistant
Secretary for International Affairs. The titles of these positions will be:

Deputy to the Assistant Secretary, for International Monetary Affairs
Deputy to the Assistant Secretary, for International Financial and Economic
Affairs.

Incumbents of these positions will be the senior career officials of the Treasury
Department having responsibility for advising and assisting the Secretary of the
Treasury and other senior Departmental officials in the formulation and execution of policies and programs relating to the responsibilities of the Treasury
Department in the international economic, financial and monetary fields. They
will be designated by the Secretary of the Treasury and will report to him
through the Assistant Secretary for International Affairs.

3. The Assistant Secretary for International Affairs shall maintain such
Treasury representatives abroad as may be required to assist in the discharge
of the overall responsibilities of his Office.

4. Each Director of an Office established in paragraph 1 shall be responsible,
within the overall policies and procedures of the Assistant Secretary for International Affairs, for the effective functioning of his Office and of any Treasury
representatives stationed in assigned countries. To do so, he will be required,
among other things, to:

(a) Plan and manage the activities of his Office to meet its objectives and be
responsive to the needs of the Treasury;

(b) Originate ideas and initiate necessary research and work projects;

(c) Maintain effective and reliable communications and cooperation with the
other Offices reporting to the Assistant Secretary for International Affairs and
with other senior policy officials;

(d) Provide for the greatest effectiveness of his staff through careful selection, professional development and advancement of individuals, and maintenance
of a high level of morale and of professional approach to assigned tasks;

(e) Provide for the greatest effectiveness of Treasury representatives abroad
by: maintaining direct contact, furnishing information and guidance regarding

---

[1] Omitted from this exhibit; appendices are available in the Office of the Assistant Secretary for Administration.

Treasury policy and requirements; obtaining information, assistance and advice as appropriate; and initiating personnel and administrative recommendations.

5. All present functions, duties, and personnel of the Office of International Affairs shall be transferred to the Office of the Assistant Secretary for International Affairs and Treasury Department Order No. 198, dated October 15, 1962, is hereby cancelled.

DOUGLAS DILLON,
Secretary of the Treasury.

No. 204, APRIL 22, 1965.—DELEGATION OF AUTHORITY RELATING TO RENTS FOR QUARTERS AND CHARGES FOR RELATED FACILITIES FURNISHED TO EMPLOYEES

By virtue of the authority vested in the Secretary of the Treasury by Reorganization Plan No. 26 of 1950, and pursuant to the authorization given to me by Treasury Department Order No. 190 (Revision No. 2), Heads of Bureaus of the Treasury Department are hereby authorized to set and administer rents for quarters and charges for related facilities supplied to employees and others, and to formalize and record the regulations and procedures therefor, in accordance with the methods set forth in Bureau of the Budget Circular No. A–45 Revised, October 31, 1964.

This authorization is retroactive to include all policies and procedures established by the Bureaus under the last revision of the Circular.

Administrative Circular No. 121, dated December 9, 1964, regarding the submission of Bureau regulations and procedures to the Bureau of the Budget through the Office of the Director of Administrative Services, shall remain in effect until changed by the appropriate authority.

A. E. WEATHERBEE,
Assistant Secretary for Administration.

Advisory Committees

EXHIBIT 71.—Advisory committees utilized by the Treasury Department under Executive Order 11007

During the fiscal year 1965, the Secretary of the Treasury found the formation or use by the Department of the following advisory committees to be in the public interest in accordance with the requirements of Executive Order 11007, dated February 26, 1962. The information concerning these committees is being published in the annual report in compliance with section 10 of the order.

Office of the Secretary

DEBT MANAGEMENT COMMITTEES

The Treasury Department, in connection with debt management duties, uses in an advisory capacity the services of a number of committees representing organizations which form a cross section of the American financial community. The committees meet periodically, at the invitation of the Treasury, to discuss and advise upon current and future Federal financings. The Treasury finds discussions with these advisory groups to be of great value, primarily in assessing the general market sentiment prior to a major refinancing of maturing obligations. Their recommendations are carefully considered by Treasury officials and serve as a part of the background environment for the final financing decisions. These committees are as follows:

> American Bankers Association, Government Borrowing Committee
> Investment Bankers Association of America, Governmental Securities Committee
> National Association of Mutual Savings Banks, Committee on Government Securities and the Public Debt
> Life Insurance Association of America and American Life Convention, Joint Economic Policy Committee

U.S. Savings and Loan League, National League of Insured Savings Associations, Advisory Committee on Government Securities

Independent Bankers Association, Government Fiscal Policy Committee

Four meetings were held with the Government Borrowing Committee of the American Bankers Association in fiscal 1965, on July 23–24, October 25 and 28, January 26–27, and April 27–28.

Membership of the Committee was as follows:

David M. Kennedy (Chairman)	Chairman, Continental Illinois National Bank and Trust Company of Chicago, Chicago, Ill.
Henry C. Alexander	Chairman, Morgan Guaranty Trust Company of New York, New York, N.Y.
Julian B. Baird	Advisory Director, The First National Bank of St. Paul, St. Paul, Minn.
George Champion	Chairman, The Chase Manhattan Bank, New York, N.Y.
Kenton R. Cravens	Chairman and Chief Executive Officer, Mercantile Trust Company, St. Louis, Mo.
Robert V. Fleming	Advisory Chairman of the Board, The Riggs National Bank of Washington, D.C., Washington, D.C.
Sam M. Fleming	President, Third National Bank, Nashville, Tenn.
Charles J. Gable, Jr.	Senior Vice President, The First Pennsylvania Banking and Trust Company, Philadelphia, Pa.
William F. Kelley	President, The First Pennsylvania Banking and Trust Company, Philadelphia, Pa.
M. Monroe Kimbrel	Chairman, First National Bank, Thomson, Ga.
Frank L. King	Chairman, United California Bank, Los Angeles, Calif.
S. J. Kryzsko	President, Winona National and Savings Bank, Winona, Minn.
Frederick G. Larkin, Jr.	President, Security First National Bank, Los Angeles, Calif.
John J. Larkin	Vice President, First National City Bank, New York, N.Y.
Homer J. Livingston	Chairman, The First National Bank of Chicago, Chicago, Ill.
John A. Mayer	President and Chief Executive Officer, Mellon National Bank and Trust Company, Pittsburgh, Pa.
George A. Murphy	Chairman, Irving Trust Company, New York, N.Y.
Reno Odlin	Chairman, The Puget Sound National Bank, Tacoma, Wash.
F. Raymond Peterson	Chairman, First National Bank of Passaic County, Paterson, N.J.
R. A. Peterson	President, Bank of America N.T. & S.A., San Francisco, Calif.
James D. Robinson, Jr.	Chairman, The First National Bank of Atlanta, Atlanta, Ga.
James S. Rockefeller	Chairman, First National City Bank, New York, N.Y.
Robert G. Rouse	Partner, Laidlaw and Co., New York, N.Y.
Dietrich Schmitz	Chairman, Washington Mutual Savings Bank, Seattle, Wash.
Norfleet Turner	Chairman, The First National Bank of Memphis, Memphis, Tenn.
Joseph C. Welman	President, Bank of Kennett, Kennett, Mo.
Paul I. Wren	President, Old Colony Trust Company, Boston, Mass.
Charls E. Walker	Executive Vice President and Executive Manager, The American Bankers Association, New York, N.Y.

William T. Heffelfinger	Federal Administrative Adviser, The American Bankers Association, Washington, D.C.
Leslie C. Peacock	Associate Secretary, Deputy Manager, The American Bankers Association, New York, N.Y.

Four meetings were held with the Governmental Securities Committee of the Investment Bankers Association in fiscal year 1965, on July 23–24, October 27–28, January 26–27, and April 27–28.

Membership of the Committee was as follows:

Robert B. Blyth (Chairman)	First Vice President, The National City Bank, Cleveland, Ohio.
Robert H. Bethke	Vice President, Discount Corp. of New York, New York, N.Y.
Loring T. Briggs	Vice President, Blyth and Co., Inc., New York, N.Y.
Alan K. Browne	Vice President, Bank of America, N.T. & S.A., San Francisco, Calif.
F. Newell Childs	President, C. F. Childs and Co., Inc., Chicago, Ill.
Carl F. Cooke	Vice President, First Boston Corporation, New York, N.Y.
James. A. Cranford	Executive Vice President, The Atlantic National Bank, Jacksonville, Fla.
G. Lamar Crittenden	Vice President, The First National Bank, Boston, Mass.
Stewart A. Dunn	Vice President, Merrill, Lynch, Pierce, Fenner & Smith, Inc., New York, N.Y.
Lester H. Empey	Senior Vice President, Wells Fargo Bank American Trust Company, San Francisco, Calif.
Alfred H. Hauser	Senior Vice President, Chemical Bank New York Trust Company, New York, N.Y.
Hardin H. Hawes	Senior Vice President, Harris Trust and Savings Bank, Chicago, Ill.
Alger J. Jacobs	Senior Vice President, Crocker-Citizens National Bank, San Francisco, Calif.
Ralph E. Leach	Senior Vice President and Treasurer, Morgan Guaranty Trust Company, New York, N.Y.
Eugene S. Lee	Senior Vice President, Valley National Bank of Arizona, Phoenix, Ariz.
Edward D. McGrew	Vice President, The Northern Trust Company, Chicago, Ill.
John H. Perkins	Vice President, Continental Illinois National Bank and Trust Company, Chicago, Ill.
William W. Pevear	Vice President, Irving Trust Company, New York, N.Y.
Delmont K. Pfeffer (Chairman)	Senior Vice President, The First National City Bank of New York, New York, N.Y.
L. Sumner Pruyne	Senior Vice President, The First National Bank of Boston, Boston, Mass.
Robert B. Rivel	Vice President, The Chase Manhattan Bank, New York, N.Y.
Arthur W. Schlichting	Vice President, Bankers Trust Company, New York, N.Y.
Charles H. Schmidt	Vice President, National Bank of Detroit, Detroit, Mich.
Girard L. Spencer	Partner, Salomon Brothers and Hutzler, New York, N.Y.
Franklin Stockbridge	Vice President, Security First National Bank, Los Angeles, Calif.
Paul E. Uhl	Vice President, United California Bank, Los Angeles, Calif.

William J. Wallace
Vice President, Mellon National Bank and Trust Company, Pittsburgh, Pa.

C. Richard Youngdahl
President, Aubrey G. Lanston and Company, Inc., New York, N.Y.

One meeting was held with the Committee on Government Securities and the Public Debt of the National Association of Mutual Savings Banks in fiscal 1965, on May 20.
Membership of the Committee was as follows:

John W. Kress (Chairman)
President, The Howard Savings Institution, Newark, N.J.

Herman J. Arnott
President, The Farmers and Mechanics Savings Bank, Minneapolis, Minn.

Morris D. Crawford, Jr.
President, The Bowery Savings Bank, New York, N.Y.

William H. Harder
President, Buffalo Savings Bank, Buffalo, N.Y.

Maynard L. Harris
Chairman of the Board, Suffolk Franklin Savings Bank, Boston, Mass.

G. Churchill Francis
Executive Vice President, The Boston Five Cents Savings Bank, Boston, Mass.

Theodore W. Lowen
President, Savings Bank Trust Co., New York, N.Y.

Alfred C. Middlebrook
Senior Vice President, East River Savings Bank, New York, N.Y.

Robert M. Morgan
President, Boston Five Cents Savings Bank, Boston, Mass.

Barrett C. Nichols
Executive Vice President, Maine Savings Bank, Portland, Maine.

Frederick P. Smith
President, Burlington Savings Bank, Burlington, Vt.

Howard B. Smith
President, The Middletown Savings Bank, Middletown, Conn.

Dr. Grover W. Ensley
Executive Vice President, National Association of Mutual Savings Banks, New York, N.Y.

Saul B. Klaman
Staff Member, NAMSB
Director of Research, NAMSB

Robert R. Poston
Director-Counsel, Washington Office, NAMSB, Washington, D.C.

One meeting was held with the Joint Economic Policy Committee of the Life Insurance Association of America and the American Life Convention in fiscal 1965, on May 17.
Membership of the Committee was as follows:

Richard K. Paynter, Jr. (Chairman)
Chairman, New York Life Ins. Co., New York, N.Y.

G. D. Brooks
President, The National Life and Accident Ins. Co., Nashville, Tenn.

E. F. Bucknell
President, Bankers Life Co., Des Moines, Iowa.

T. S. Burnett
Chairman, Pacific Mutual Life Ins. Co., Los Angeles, Calif.

George T. Conklin, Jr.
Senior Vice President, The Guardian Life Insurance Company of America, New York, N.Y.

George B. Cook
President, Bankers Life Insurance Company of Nebraska, Lincoln, Nebr.

Byron K. Elliott
President and Chairman, John Hancock Mutual Life Ins. Co., Boston, Mass.

Gilbert W. Fitzhugh
President, Metropolitan Life Ins. Co., New York, N.Y.

Frank J. Hoenemeyer, Jr.
Senior Vice President, The Prudential Insurance Co., Newark, N.J.

Roger Hull
President, The Mutual Life Insurance Co., New York, N.Y.

Charles E. Phillips
President, Equitable Life Insurance Company, Washington, D.C.

G. Frank Purvis, Jr.	President, Pan-American Life Insurance Co., Washington, D.C.
Howard C. Reeder	Co-Chairman, Continental Assurance Co., Chicago, Ill.
Olcott D. Smith	Chairman, Aetna Life Ins. Co., Hartford, Conn.
Charles A. Taylor	President, The Life Insurance Co. of Virginia, Richmond, Va.

Staff Members of the Associations

American Life Convention:

Arthur Fefferman, Director of Economic Analysis, Washington, D.C.

Glendon E. Johnson, Vice President and General Counsel, Washington, D.C.

Life Insurance Association of America:

Eugene M. Thoré, President, Washington, D.C.

James J. O'Leary, Vice President and Director of Economic Research, New York, N.Y.

Kenneth L. Kimble, Vice President and General Counsel, Washington, D.C.

Ralph J. McNair, Vice President, Washington, D.C.

A meeting was held with the Advisory Committee on Government Securities of the Savings and Loan Business in fiscal 1965, on May 26.

Membership of the Committee was as follows:

Junius F. Baxter	Executive Vice President, Western Federal Savings and Loan Association, Denver, Colo.
James E. Bent	President, Hartford Federal Savings and Loan Association, Hartford, Conn.
Frederick Bjorklund	President, Minnesota Federal Savings and Loan Association, St. Paul, Minn.
Lacy Boggess	President, Mutual Savings and Loan Association, Fort Worth, Tex.
C. L. Clements (Chairman)	Chairman, Chase Federal Savings and Loan Association, Miami Beach, Fla.
Carl Distelhorst	Director, Winter Park Federal Savings and Loan Association, Winter Park, Fla.
W. O. DuVall	President, Atlanta Federal Savings and Loan Association, Atlanta, Ga.
E. Stanley Enlund	President, First Federal Savings and Loan Association, Chicago, Ill.
Richard G. Gilbert	President, The Citizens Savings Association, Canton, Ohio.
L. W. Grant	Chairman, Home Federal Savings and Loan Association, Tulsa, Okla.
Roy M. Marr	Chairman, Leader Federal Savings and Loan Association, Memphis, Tenn.
Allen G. Pflugradt	President, First Federal Savings and Loan Association, Milwaukee, Wis.
John W. Stadtler	President, National Permanent Savings and Loan Association, Washington, D.C.
A. D. Theobald	President, First Federal Savings and Loan Association, Peoria, Ill.
Gerrit Vander Ende	President, Pacific First Federal Savings and Loan Association, Tacoma, Wash.
W. C. Warman	Staff Vice President, U.S. Savings and Loan League, Chicago, Ill.
William J. Kerwin	Assistant Managing Director, National League of Insured Savings Associations, Washington, D.C.
James A. Hollensteiner	Staff Vice President, U.S. Savings and Loan League, Chicago, Ill.

A meeting was held with the Government Fiscal Policy Committee of the Independent Bankers Association on May 19, 1965.

Membership of the Committee was as follows:

Milton J. Hayes (Chairman)	Vice President, American National Bank & Trust Co., Chicago, Ill.
Theo. W. Sette	President, State Bank of Burleigh County, Bismarck, N. Dak.
Stanley Barber	President, Wellman Savings Bank, Wellman, Iowa.
Joseph V. Johnson	Chairman, Johnson County Bank, Tecumseh, Nebr.
O. K. Johnson	President, Whitefish Bay State Bank, Milwaukee, Wis.
O. M. Jorgenson	Chairman, Security Trust and Savings Bank, Billings, Mont.
S. E. Babington	President, Brookhaven Bank and Trust Co., Brookhaven, Miss.
W. W. Marshall, Jr.	Executive Vice President, Commercial National Bank and Trust Co., Grand Island, Nebr.
Ralph L. Zaun	Executive Vice President, Grafton State Bank, Grafton, Wis.
Gene Moore	Secretary, Independent Bankers Association, Sauk Centre, Minn.
C. Herschell Schooley	Washington Office, Independent Bankers Association, Washington, D.C.

Commissioner of Customs

JOINT CUSTOMS/AIRLINE WORKING GROUP ON AIR CARGO

This Group was established by memorandum dated May 8, 1964, from the Secretary of the Treasury to the Commissioner of Customs.

The functions of the Group are to review industry procedures for handling air cargo, and related customs procedures for the assessment and collection of duties and taxes on imported merchandise, to determine if these procedures can be integrated into a system which will provide clearance with a minimum of delay and provide adequate controls for customs purposes.

The members of the Group, which met in fiscal year 1965 on July 15, November 10, December 9–10, and April 22, were as follows:

G. R. Dickerson, Chairman	Assistant Deputy Commissioner, Bureau of Customs, Treasury Department, Washington, D.C.
W. P. Jones	Assistant Deputy Commissioner, Bureau of Customs, Treasury Department, Washington, D.C. (died April 21, 1965)
G. H. Heidbreder	Operations Officer (Air), Bureau of Customs, Treasury Department, Washington, D.C.
D. D. Kast	Legal Assistant, Bureau of Customs, Treasury Department, Washington, D.C.
N. J. Marsh	Liaison Officer, Bureau of Customs, Treasury Department, Washington, D.C. (vice W. P. Jones, deceased)
J. R. Gorson	Manager—Facilitation, Air Transport Association, Washington, D.C.
S. W. McMillion	Manager—Traffic, Agreements and Procedures, United Air Lines, Chicago, Ill.
L. M. Rogers	Director, Traffic Administration, American Airlines, New York, N.Y.
J. L. Sheppard	Manager—Facilitation, Pan American World Airways, New York, N.Y.

Commissioner of Internal Revenue

ADVISORY GROUP TO THE COMMISSIONER OF INTERNAL REVENUE

This Group was established by the Commissioner of Internal Revenue on June 17, 1959.

This Committee, which represents professional and other private groups concerned with Federal taxation, provides constructive criticism of Internal Revenue policies and procedures and suggests ways in which the Service can improve its operations.

The Advisory Group appointed in March 1964 and shown in the 1964 annual report, page 382, met on October 1–2, 1964, and December 17–18, 1964.

In keeping with the practice of periodically changing the membership, the Commissioner appointed a new Advisory Group in April 1965, which met twice during fiscal 1965 on April 29–30, and June 14–15, 1965. The members of the new Group are as follows:

Nina Miglionico	Attorney, Birmingham, Ala.
Raphael Sherfy	Turner, Major, Markham and Sherfy, Washington, D.C.
Sam G. Winstead	Jackson, Walker, Winstead, Cantwell & Miller, Dallas, Tex.
Andrew B. Young	Stradler, Ronon, Stevens & Young, Philadelphia, Pa.
Hilbert P. Zarky	Mitchell, Silberberg & Knupp, Los Angeles, Calif.
Mortimer M. Caplin	Caplin, Battle & Harris, Washington, D.C.
Richard H. Austin	Richard H. Austin & Co., Detroit, Mich.
Robert E. Witschey	Witschey, Harman and White, Charleston, W. Va.
Peter Yosinoff	Public Accountant, Providence, R. I.
Bruce Greenfield	Bankers Securities Corporation, Wyncote, Pa.
Ream V. Miller	Shell Oil Co., New York, N.Y.
Nathaniel Goldfinger	AFL–CIO, Washington, D.C.
Vance N. Kirby	Northwestern University Law School, Chicago, Ill.

TREASURY-INTERNAL REVENUE SERVICE COMMITTEE ON STATISTICS

The Commissioner of Internal Revenue established this Committee on March 30, 1962. It was reconstituted in July 1963.

The Committee is expected to make suggestions concerning appropriate statistical and economic information to be obtained from income tax returns.

The Committee consists of economists and statisticians, representing private associations and universities, and Government representatives.

Meetings of this Committee were held in fiscal 1965 on October 5, 1964, and May 6, 1965.

Membership in the fiscal year 1965 was as follows:

William H. Smith, Chairman	Assistant Commissioner (Planning and Research), Internal Revenue Service, Washington, D.C.
Vito Natrella, Executive Secretary	Director, Statistics Division, Internal Revenue Service, Washington, D.C.
Harvey E. Brazer	University of Michigan, Ann Arbor, Mich.
Warren N. Cordell	Vice President, A. C. Nielsen Company, Chicago, Ill.
W. R. Currie	Chief Financial Economist, Department of Finance, State of California, Sacramento, Calif.
Sidney Glaser (Alternate)	Assistant to the Director, Division of Taxation, Trenton, N.J.
Robert Eisner	Northwestern University, Evanston, Ill.
Irwin Friend	Wharton School of Finance and Commerce, University of Pennsylvania, Philadelphia, Pa.
George Jaszi	Director, Office of Business Economics, Department of Commerce, Washington, D.C.
James W. Knowles	Joint Economic Committee, Washington, D.C.
Alan P. Murray (Alternate)	Joint Committee on Internal Revenue Taxation, Washington, D.C.
Raymond Nassimbene	Office of Statistical Standards, Bureau of the Budget, Washington, D.C.
Alice M. Rivlin	The Brookings Institution, Washington, D.C.
J. A. Stockfisch	Deputy Assistant Secretary, Treasury Department, Washington, D.C.
Gabriel G. Rudney (Alternate)	Chief, Personal Taxation Staff, Office of Tax Analysis, Treasury Department, Washington, D.C.
James H. Symons	Joint Committee on Internal Revenue Taxation, Washington, D.C.

Norman B. Ture — Director of Tax Studies, National Bureau of Economic Research, Washington, D.C.

U.S. Coast Guard

CHEMICAL TRANSPORTATION ADVISORY PANEL

This Panel, established on May 4, 1949, acts as an advisory body on matters concerned with the bulk transportation of chemicals or hazardous cargo. Such expert advice from industry is mandatory to keep current and effective the dangerous cargo, tank vessel, cargo, and other associated regulations promulgated and enforced by the Coast Guard.

Membership of the Panel, which met in fiscal 1965 on December 15 and 16, 1964, follows:

Oliver E. Beutel, Chairman	Manager, Distribution and Traffic, The Dow Chemical Company, Midland, Mich.
G. H. Mayhood, Secretary	Transportation Engineer, Manufacturing Chemists' Association, Inc., Washington, D.C.
Commander Eric Grundy, USCG, Liaison Officer	Chief, Chemical Engineering Branch, Merchant Marine Technical Division, USCG Headquarters, Washington, D.C.
George R. Benz	Consultant, Engineering Department, Phillips Petroleum Company, Bartlesville, Okla.
G. W. Feldman	Senior Distribution Engineer, Development Division, Traffic Department, E. I. du Pont de Nemours and Co., Wilmington, Del.
Captain G. C. Steinman, USCG (Ret.)	Vice President, Breit Engineering, Inc., New Orleans, La.
J. R. Black	Manager, Marine Services, Olin Mathieson Chemical Corp., New York, N.Y.
J. C. Clarke	Vice President, Marine Transport Lines, Inc., New York, N.Y.
R. W. Krieger	President, Jeffersonville Boat and Machine Co., Jeffersonville, Ind.
T. J. Lengyel	Assistant Manager, Marine Department, Shell Oil Co., New York, N.Y.
R. B. Mitchell	Chemical Carriers, Inc., New York, N.Y.
T. W. Rodes	Plant Superintendent, Union Carbide Chemical Co., Carteret, N.J.
George P. Jacobson	Assistant Manager, Marine Transportation, Allied Chemical Corp., New York, N.Y.
Albert N. Narter	Principal Surveyor, American Bureau of Shipping, New York, N.Y.
R. T. Williams	Project Engineer, Marine Division, Humble Oil and Refining Co., Houston, Tex.
James E. Weaver	Manager of Transportation, Pittsburgh Plate Glass Co., Pittsburgh, Pa.
R. J. Wheeler	Manager, Marine Transportation, Phillips Petroleum Co., Bartlesville, Okla.

Ex Officio Members:

M. F. Crass, Jr.	Secretary-Treasurer, Manufacturing Chemists' Association, Inc., Washington, D.C.
F. R. Fetherston	Secretary-Treasurer, Compressed Gas Association, Inc., New York, N.Y.
B. H. Lord, Jr.	Director, Division of Transportation, American Petroleum Institute, Washington, D.C.
Robert L. Mitchell, Jr.	Secretary-Treasurer, The Chlorine Institute, Inc., New York, N.Y.

MOTORBOAT AND YACHT ADVISORY PANEL

This Panel, established on December 24, 1946, advises on problems relating to the safe operation of small craft of both commercial and recreational types. The Panel, consisting of the members listed below, met on February 8, 1965, in New York City.

Mr. Joseph E. Choate, Chairman	National Assn. of Engine & Boat Mfrs., New York, N.Y.

Mr. William J. Bailey	Wilcox-Crittenden Division, North & Judd Manufacturing Co., Middistown, Conn.
Mr. N. C. Barnard	Chairman, General Safety Committee, U.S. Power Squadrons, Westfield, N.J.
Mr. R. C. Bolling	The Palmer Engine Co., River Road, Cos Cob, Conn.
Mr. W. Melvin Crook	Associate Editor, *Yachting*, New York, N.Y.
Mr. Fred L. Hewitt, Jr.	President, Century Boat Co., New York, N.Y.
Mr. Ralph Ianuzzi	H. A. Bruno & Associates, New York 20, N.Y.
Mr. William Edgar John	Wm. Edgar John & Associates, Inc., Rye, N.Y.
Mr. Charles Jones	The Boating Industry, New York, N.Y.
Mr. William P. Kennedy, Sr.	Kennedy Marine Engine Co., Biloxi, Miss.
Mr. John G. Kingden	American Boat & Yacht Council, New York, N.Y.
Mr. Emil A. Kratovil	Wm. H. McGee & Co., Inc., New York, N.Y.
Mr. Howard F. Larson	Vice President, Outboard Marine Corp., Milwaukee, Wis.
Mr. David P. Levy	Equitable Equipment Co., Inc., New Orleans, La.
Mr. Fred B. Lifton	Executive Director, Outboard Boating Club of America, Chicago, Ill.
Mr. A. W. MacKerar	Vice-President, Chris-Craft Corp., Pompano Beach, Fla.
Mr. Everett B. Morris	Author and Correspondent, Boating Publication, Port Washington, Long Island, N.Y.
Mr. Cooper Schieffelin	Penn Yan Boats, New York, N.Y.
Mr. Robert A. Southworth	Mobil Oil Company, New York, N.Y.
Mr. Olin J. Stephens	Sparkman & Stephens, Inc., New York, N.Y.
Capt. John E. Suydam	President, National Party Boat Owners Alliance, Inc., Lindenhurst, Long Island, N.Y.
Mr. E. S. Terwilligar	Executive Vice President, Yacht Safety Bureau, Inc., Westwood, N.J.
Mr. Leon E. Travis	President, National Association of Engine and Boat Manufacturers, New York, N.Y.
Mr. William F. Warm	Marine Office of America, Manager, Engineering Department, New York, N.Y.
Mr. Bliss Woodward	Past National Commodore, USCG Auxiliary, Mamaroneck, N.Y.

NATIONAL OFFSHORE OPERATIONS PANEL

This Panel was established on December 15, 1959, to advise the U.S. Coast Guard on matters related to the highly specialized construction and operation of geophysical survey vessels, drilling platforms, and associated vessels and barges.

Members of the Panel, which met in fiscal 1965 on August 5 and 6, were as follows:

R. T. Sessums, Chairman	Vice President, Freeport Sulphur Co., New Orleans, La.
H. E. Denzler, Jr., Secretary	Assistant to General Superintendent, Transportation, The California Co., New Orleans, La.
E. E. Clark	Area Superintendent, Phillips Petroleum Co., Santa Barbara, Calif.
O. L. Furse	Regional Production Manager, Southeast Esso Region, New Orleans, La.
W. H. LeGrand	District Production Manager, Gulf Oil Corp., New Orleans, La.
J. C. Craig(*)	General Superintendent, Continental Oil Co., Houston, Tex.
R. N. Crews	Vice President, J. Ray McDermott and Co., Inc., New Orleans, La.
J. T. Crooker	Manager, Producing Department, Standard Oil Co. of California, Western Operations, Inc., La Habra, Calif.
James W. Greely	Kerr-McGee Oil Industries, Inc., Oklahoma City, Okla.
W. H. Henderson	President, Gulf Offshore Marine Service Association, New Orleans, La.

Donald S. Hare	Manager of Offshore Operations, Pauley Petroleum Inc., Los Angeles, Calif.
W. M. House	Division Manager, Signal Oil and Gas Co., Los Angeles, Calif.
M. E. Lundfelt	Assistant General Manager, Marine Department, Texaco, Inc., New York, N.Y.
J. W. Pittman	Manager Production Department, Shell Oil Co., New Orleans, La.
R. O. Pollard	Manager, Production Department, Richfield Oil Co., Long Beach, Calif.
G. S. Young, Jr.	Producing Superintendent, Mobil Oil Co., Lafayette, La.
(*) Succeeded by:	
M. S. Kendrick	Regional Manager, Continental Oil Co., Houston, Tex.

OIL POLLUTION PANEL

The Oil Pollution Panel, established on August 3, 1954, acts as an advisory body on pollution problems and obtains views as to means of eliminating the oil pollution of the seas and seacoast. All members are directly connected with the operation of commercial vessels.

The members of the Panel, who met in fiscal 1965 on September 10, December 9, and June 23, were:

Mr. F. C. Grant, Chairman	General Operating Manager, United States Lines Co., New York, N.Y.
Capt. A. H. Stephens, Vice Chairman	Manager, Operations, California Shipping Co., San Francisco, Calif.
Capt. Herbert S. Brewster, Vice Chairman	Director of Operations, Marine Department, Gulf Oil Corp., New York, N.Y.
Capt. Richard J. Anderson	Assistant Vice President, Operations, Prudential Lines, Inc., New York, N.Y.
Mr. A. Bacols	Marine Superintendent, Isthmian Lines Inc., New York, N.Y.
Capt. Gordon F. Beal	Marine Superintendent, United Fruit Co., New York, N.Y.
Capt. S. Blackledge	Vice President, American Export and Isbrandtsen Lines, New York, N.Y.
Capt. M. Breece	Manager, Port of New York Office, Marine Division, Humble Oil and Refining Co., Bayonne, N.J.
Mr. William Dignes	Port Engineer, Farrell Lines, Inc., New York, N.Y.
Capt. T. Fender	Marine Superintendent, Inland Waterways Operations, Socony Mobil Oil Co., Inc., New York, N.Y.
Capt. George Larimer	Port Captain, Sun Oil Co., Marcus Hook, Pa.
Mr. B. H. Lord, Jr., Secretary	Director, Division of Transportation, American Petroleum Institute, Washington, D.C.
Mr. H. F. Munroe	American President Lines, San Francisco, Calif.
Capt. Walter D. Nunley	Texaco Inc., New York, N.Y.
Capt. Ben M. Perkins	Port Captain, States Steamship Co., San Francisco, Calif.
Capt. C. D. Phillips	Manager of Operations, Ocean Tanker Department, The American Oil Co., New York, N.Y.
Capt. Norman Short	Assistant Director of Engineering, Grace Line, Inc., New York, N.Y.
Capt. Corben C. Shute, USN (Ret.)	Superintendent, Operating Section, Marine Division, Atlantic Refining Co., Philadelphia, Pa.
Capt C. C. Williams	Manager, Operating Department, Keystone Shipping Co., Philadelphia, Pa.

PORT ADVISORY COUNCILS

Port Advisory Councils provide a forum for discussion and interpretation of Coast Guard policies and directives, thereby furthering cooperation. The Councils, representing the various port interests, also furnish advice and information to Coast Guard authorities. Three of these councils held meetings during fiscal 1965. The lists of members and dates of meetings for these advisory groups, New Orleans, La., Corpus Christi, Tex., and Houston, Tex., follow.

PORT ADVISORY COUNCIL, NEW ORLEANS, LOUISIANA

This advisory council, founded in 1960, met on May 6, 1965. Its membership follows:

Forsee "Jack" Estes, Chairman	P.O. Box 23134, Point Landing, Inc., New Orleans, La.
W. S. Smith, Co-Chairman	524 Hibernis Bldg., T. Smith & Son, Inc., New Orleans, La.
Capt. E. B. Hendrix, 2d Co-Chairman	Lykes Bros. Steamship Co., P.O. Box 50998, New Orleans, La.
Capt. Harold Land, USCG, Secretary	Captain of the Port, USCG, 1201 Lakeshore Drive, New Orleans, La.
Capt. C. L. Spicer	P.O. Box 50250, Delta Steamship Co., New Orleans, La.
Capt. T. L. Lewis	Deputy Port Director, Board of Commissioners, P.O. Box 60046, New Orleans, La.
Henry R. Rauber	Safety Officer, Board of Commissioners, Port of New Orleans, P.O. Box 60046, New Orleans, La.
Harry J. Rome	Superintendent of Docks, Board of Commissioners, Port of New Orleans, P.O. Box 60046, New Orleans, La.
Capt. R. T. McKenzie, USCG	Marine Inspection Office, USCG, Room 310, Custom House, New Orleans, La.
A. J. Heyd	Superintendent, New Orleans Fire Department, 317 Decatur Street, New Orleans, La.
E. J. O'Brien	Asst. Superintendent, New Orleans Fire Department, 317 Decatur Street, New Orleans, La.
G. D. Summers	Deputy Superintendent, New Orleans Fire Department, 317 Decatur Street, New Orleans, La.
Otis M. Jernigan	Army Engineer District, New Orleans, Corps of Engineers, P.O. Box 60267, New Orleans, La.
Capt. R. E. McNeeley	Crescent River Pilots Assn., 1417 Whitney Bldg., New Orleans, La.
Capt. S. K. Sprada	N. O.–Baton Rouge Pilots Assn., Room 304, Cigali Bldg., New Orleans, La.
Sam Giallaoza	Vice President, N. O. Steamship Assn., 219 Carondelet Street, New Orleans, La.
McVey F. Ward	American Waterways, Operators, Inc., 435 Whitney Bldg., New Orleans, La.
H. E. Denzler, Jr.	Production Engineer, The California Co., California Bldg., New Orleans, La.
B. C. Weaver	Bureau of Explosives, 909 Walker Street, New Orleans, La.
Maj. Gen. Raymond Bufft	Bureau of Customs, Room 233, Custom House, New Orleans, La.
Claude E. Blancq, Jr.	Bureau of Customs, Room 200, Custom House, New Orleans, La.
H. L. LeBlanc	Bureau of Customs, Room 229, Custom House, New Orleans, La.
Capt. Henry B. Dunlap	La. Civil Defense Agency, Bldg. 309A, Area B, Jackson Barracks, New Orleans, La.
Louis C. LaCour	U.S. Attorney, 400 Royal Street, New Orleans, La.

Professor A. Lee Dunlap	Chairman, Fire Prevention, 935 Pine Street, New Orleans, La.
David Fontaine, Jr.	Fire Prevention Bureau, Room 7W11, City Hall, New Orleans, La.

PORT ADVISORY COUNCIL, CORPUS CHRISTI, TEXAS

Established in March 1960, this advisory group, consisting of the following members, holds regular monthly meetings.

Duane Orr, Chairman	Navigation District Engineer, P.O. Box 1541, Corpus Christi, Tex.
Capt. Herbert Weeks	Texas Highway Patrol, P.O. Box 5277, Corpus Christi, Tex.
John Mitchell	Sheriff, P.O. Box 1940, Corpus Christi, Tex.
Col. Earl Dunn	Director, Civil Defense, City Hall, P.O. Box 1622, Corpus Christi, Tex.
Reuben Traynham	Deputy Collector, U.S. Customs, P.O. Box 1027, Corpus Christi, Tex.
Cdr. W. M. Flenniken, USN	Security Officer, c/o U.S. Naval Air Station, Corpus Christi, Tex.
Jack Graham	Public Works, P.O. Box 1622, Corpus Christi, Tex.
C. R. Kuss	Central Power & Light Co., 120 N. Shoreline, Corpus Christi, Tex.
Ray Grandy	Patrolman, National Maritime Union, 2907 N. Shoreline, Corpus Christi, Tex.
H. E. Ammerman	Mgr. Corpus Christi Refinery Terminal Fire Company, P.O. Box 4162, Corpus Christi, Tex.
Cdr. W. A. Mayberry, USCG	101 Federal Building, Corpus Christi, Tex.
R. T. Runyan	Chief of Police, P.O. Box 150, Corpus Christi, Tex.
John Carlisle	Fire Chief, 1401 Morgan Street, Corpus Christi, Tex.

PORT ADVISORY COUNCIL, HOUSTON, TEXAS

This advisory council, organized on March 26, 1959, held meetings on September 3 and November 5, 1964, and on January 14, April 1, and May 13, 1965. Its membership follows:

Mr. B. H. Moore	Airfilter, Inc, 915 World Trade Bldg., Houston, Tex.
Capt. R. L. Wynne	American Institute of Marine Underwriters, RM7, Cotton Exch. Bldg., Houston, Tex.
Mr. H. Anderson, Sr.	Anderson Petroleum Transport Co., P.O. Box 12513, Houston, Tex.
Mr. Robert A. Feltner	Attorney at Law, 914 World Trade Bldg., Houston, Tex.
Mr. J. E. Ross	Attorney at Law, 1817 Chamber of Commerce Bldg., Houston, Tex.
Mr. F. V. Thompson	Biehl Steamship Co., World Trade Bldg., Houston, Tex.
Mr. F. Van Heuten	Biehl Steamship Co., World Trade Bldg., Houston, Tex.
Mr. R. F. Mercer	Bloomfield Steamship Co., Cotton Exch. Bldg., Houston, Tex.
Mr. C. M. Pogue	Bloomfield Steamship Co., P.O. Box 1450, Houston, Tex.
Mr. J. L. Henderson	Champion Paper Co., P.O. Box 872, Pasadena, Tex.
Mr. R. C. Bredehoeft	City of Houston, 1020 Bagby, Houston, Tex.
Mr. W. O. Hunter	City of Houston, 1020 Bagby, Houston, Tex.
Mr. H. E. Short	City of Houston, 61 Reisner, Houston, Tex.
Mr. R. J. Edwards	Coast Guard Auxiliary, P.O. Box 66689, Houston, Tex.
CDR·J. E. Fleming	Coast Guard Houston Station, P.O. Box 446, Galena Park, Tex.
Capt. G. W. Walker	U.S. Coast Guard Marine Inspection Office, 7300 Wingate, Houston, Tex.

CDR W. T. Smith	U.S. Coast Guard, (Ret.), 6663 Fairfield Dr., Houston, Tex.
Mr. J. H. Colby	Diamond Alkali, P.O. Box 686, Pasadena, Tex.
Mr. H. Cunningham	Ethyl Corp., P.O. Box 472, Pasadena, Tex.
Mr. J. E. Mills	Fire Prevention and Engineering Bureau, Suite 204, 2903 Richmond, Houston, Tex.
Mr. B. Alford	General American Tank Storage Co., P. O. Box 486, Galena Park, Tex.
Mr. A. V. Rifmer	General American Tank Storage Co., Galena Park, Tex.
Mr. R. G. Esterlein	G. & H. Towing, P.O. Box 5336, Houston, Tex.
Mr. David Wilson	G & H Towing, 509 Texas Bldg., Galveston, Tex.
Mr. R. S. Reid	Hansen & Tidemann, Inc., 1312 Texas Ave., Houston, Tex.
Mr. H. V. Conroy	Harris County Defense and Disaster Relief, 413 Civil Courts Bldg., Houston, Tex.
Mr. J. M. Rodden	Harris County Defense and Disaster Relief, 413 Civil Courts Bldg., Houston, Tex.
Mr. Vernon Bailey	Harris County Navigation District, P.O. Box 2562, Houston, Tex.
Mr. C. E. Bullock	Harris County Navigation District, P.O. Box 2562, Houston, Tex.
Mr. C. L. Shuptrine	Harris County Navigation District, P.O. Box 2562, Houston, Tex.
Mr. J. P. Turner	Harris County Navigation District, P.O. Box 2562, Houston, Tex.
Mr. V. D. Williams	Harris County Navigation District, P.O. Box 2562, Houston, Tex.
Capt. Bob Leonard	Harris County Sheriffs Department, 300 Fannin, Houston, Tex.
Mr. W. R. Jameson	Hess Terminals, P.O. Box 52, Galena Park, Tex.
Mr. B. K. Parker, Jr.	Houston Barge Lines, Inc., P.O. Box 26617, Houston, Tex.
Mrs. E. Lancaster	Houston Maritime Association, 510 Cotton Exch. Bldg., Houston, Tex.
Capt. T. H. Bratcher	Houston Pilots, 510 East Harris, Pasadena, Tex.
Capt. L. R. Murray, Jr.	Houston Pilots, 6302 Gulf Freeway, Houston, Tex.
Mr. L. J. Fentiman	Humble Oil and Refining Co., 508 Whiting, Baytown, Tex.
Mr. F. L. Hooper	Humble Oil and Refining Co., P.O. Box 1512, Houston, Tex.
Mr. T. J. McTaggart	Humble Oil and Refining Co., P.O. Box 1512, Houston, Tex.
Mr. R. F. Stap	Humble Oil and Refining Co., P.O. Box 1512, Houston, Tex.
Mr. H. C. Board	International Longshoremen's Association, 7524 Avenue N, Houston, Tex.
Mr. W. G. Wells	International Longshoremen's Association, 7811 Harrisburg, Houston, Tex.
Capt. K. H. Eitzen	Keystone Shipping Co., 2407 Sieber, Houston, Tex.
Mr. J. H. Branard	Long Reach Docks, P.O. Box 2588, Houston, Tex.
Capt. J. E. Baker	Lykes Brothers Steamship Co., P.O. Box 1243, Houston, Tex.
Mr. A. W. Lott	Lykes Brothers Steamship Co., P.O. Box 1243, Houston, Tex.
Mr. Lee Throgmorton	Lykes Brothers Steamship Co., P.O. Box 1243, Houston, Tex.
Mr. H. Heard	Manchester Terminal Corp., P.O. Box 52278, Houston, Tex.
Mr. H. C. Hix	Manchester Terminal Corp., P.O. Box 52278, Houston, Tex.
Mr. L. L. Beal	Marine Office of America, 811 Westheimer Houston, Tex.

Mr. Hardin Ellis	Marine Office of America, 811 Westheimer, Houston, Tex.
Mr. V. P. Piana	Phillips Petroleum Co., P.O. Box 792, Pasadena Tex.
Mr. W. D. Farnsworth	National Cargo Bureau, 903 World Trade Bldg., Houston, Tex.
Mr. T. J. Bryant	Port Houston Shipyards, Inc., P.O. Box 2065, Houston, Tex.
Mr. Russel Brierly	Rutherford & Brierly Marine Surveyors, 8102 DeLeon, Houston, Tex.
Mr. H. C. Blaylock	Shell Oil Co., P.O. Box 100, Deer Park, Tex.
Mr. L. Grossheim	Shell Oil Co., P.O. Box 100, Deer Park, Tex.
Mr. R. K. Perkins	Signal Oil Co., P.O. Box 5008, Houston, Tex.
Capt. C. Rykiel	Sinclair Refining Co., P.O. Box 2451, Houston, Tex.
Mr. Ray Garrigus	Tenneco Oil Co., P.O. Box 2511, Houston, Tex.
Mr. John Byrnes	Tenneco Oil Co., P.O. Box 2511, Houston, Tex.
Mr. P. E. Kuntz	Texas Transport and Terminal Co., Inc., 711 Fannin, Houston, Tex.
Mr. O. D. Nesmith	United States Army Engineers, P.O. Box 1229, Galveston, Tex.
Col. J. E. Unverferth	United States Army Engineers, P.O. Box 1229, Galveston, Tex.
Mr. E. G. White	U.S. Department of Labor, 515 Rusk, Houston, Tex.
Mr. W. H. McNeil	U.S. Gypsum Co., P.O. Box 25, Galena Park, Tex.
Mr. J. F. Kanapaux	U.S. Salvage Association, 3400 Montrose, Houston, Tex.
Mr. F. T. Fendley, Jr.	W. D. Haden Company, P.O. Box 5217, Houston, Tex.
Mr. William Robb	Young & Co., 1402 70th Street, Houston, Tex.

RULES OF THE ROAD COORDINATING PANEL

This panel, established on December 14, 1960, assures that the positions of the maritime industry concerning proposals affecting the Rules of the Road are made known to the Coast Guard. The membership of this Panel, which met on May 26 and 27, 1965, follows:

Rear Commander Norris C. Barnard	General Safety Committee, United States Power Squadrons, Westfield, N.J.
Captain Charles A. Blocher	Admiralty Division, Office of the Judge Advocate General, Navy Department, Washington, D.C.
Mr. Braxton B. Carr	President, American Waterways Operators, Inc., Washington, D.C.
Mr. Ralph E. Casey	President, American Merchant Marine Institute, New York, N.Y.
Mr. Joseph E. Choate	National Association of Engine & Boat Mfrs., New York, N.Y. Also, Chairman, Motorboat & Yacht Advisory Panel.
Captain Ernest A. Clothier	President, American Pilots' Association, Washington, D.C.
Mr. Ralph B. Dewey	President, Pacific American Steamship Assn., San Francisco, Calif.
Mr. W. Mahlon Dickerson	Browne, Hyde & Dickerson, New York, N.Y.
Mr. Nicholas J. Healy, III, Chairman	President—Maritime Law Association, New York, N.Y.
Vice Admiral James A. Hirshfield	President, Lake Carriers' Association, Cleveland, Ohio.
Mr. H. K. Rigg	Chairman, National Assn. of Boating Magazines, c/o Skipper Magazine, Annapolis, Md.
Mr. Lloyd W. Sheldon	President, International Organization of Masters, Mates and Pilots, New York, N.Y.

SHIP STRUCTURE COMMITTEE

This Committee was established by memorandum dated July 26, 1946, from the Secretary of the Treasury to the Commandant of the U.S. Coast Guard.

The functions of the Committee are to conduct a research program to improve the hull structures of ships and to integrate and interpret the results to all member agencies. This information is then distributed to all persons interested in the building and operating of ships.

Members of the Committee, which met in fiscal 1965 on December 1 and April 22, were as follows:

Rear Admiral John B. Oren, USCG, Chairman — Chief, Office of Engineering, USCG Headquarters, Washington, D.C.

Rear Admiral J. A. Brown, USN — Assistant Chief, Bureau for Design, Shipbuilding, and Fleet Maintenance, Bureau of Ships, Navy Department, Washington, D.C.

Captain P. E. Shetenhelm, USN — Maintenance and Repair Officer, MSTS, Navy Department, Washington, D.C.

E. M. MacCutcheon — Chief, Office of Research and Development, Maritime Administration, Department of Commerce, Washington, D.C.

D. B. Bannerman, Jr. — Vice President, American Bureau of Shipping, New York, N.Y.

Lt. Comdr. Richard Nielsen, Jr. — Technical Staff, Office of Engineering, USCG Headquarters, Washington, D.C.

U.S. LOAD LINES COMMITTEE

The U.S. Load Lines Committee, established on August 20, 1958, is assisting in the preparation of the U.S. position on load line matters for an international conference on revisions to the International Load Line Convention, 1930. The Committee, appointed by the Commandant, consists of members nominated by groups from the shipping industry as well as representation from allied Government agencies. This advisory group, made up of the members listed below, met in fiscal 1965 on April 14.

David B. Bannerman, Jr., Chairman — Vice President-Technical, American Bureau of Shipping, New York, N.Y.

Lt. Comdr. John G. Beebe-Center, Jr., USCG, Administrative Secretary — Merchant Marine Technical Branch, Third Coast Guard District, New York, N.Y.

Captain David Baer — Association of American Ship Owners, Assistant Vice President, Maritime Overseas Corp., New York, N.Y.

William A. Baker — Shipbuilders Council of America, 10 Rice Street, Hingham, Mass.

Captain R. L. Bigler — Pacific American Tankship Association, Operations Manager, California Shipping Co., Perth Amboy, N.J.

A. F. Cooperman — U.S. Weather Bureau, Office of Climatology, Washington, D.C.

D. A. Groh — Lake Carriers' Association, Interlake Steamship Co., Cleveland, Ohio

Ralston Hayden — American Bureau of Shipping, New York, N.Y.

C. E. Hoch — Military Sea Transportation Service, Deputy Head, Maintenance and Repair Office, Department of the Navy, Washington, D.C.

D. L. Butts — American Merchant Marine Institute, Naval Architect, Marine Department, Texaco, Inc., New York, N.Y.

C. R. Jones — Pacific American Steamship Association, Assistant Operations Manager, Weyerhauser Steamship Co., New York, N.Y.

Hubert Kempel — Military Sea Transportation Service, Head, Technical Branch, Department of the Navy, Washington, D.C.

Willey E. Magee — U.S. Coast Guard, Chief, Hull Scientific Branch, USCG Headquarters, Washington, D.C.

R. V. McIntyre	Bureau of Customs, Deputy Commissioner, Division of Marine Administration, Treasury Department, Washington, D.C.
H. C. Moore	Vice President, Moran Towing and Transportation Co., New York, N.Y.
B. A. Lord	American Petroleum Institute, Director, Division of Transportation, Washington, D.C.
J. B. Robertson, Jr.	U.S. Coast Guard, Technical Assistant to Chief, MMT Division, USCG Headquarters, Washington, D.C.
V. L. Russo	Maritime Administration, Deputy Chief, Office of Ship Construction, Department of Commerce, Washington, D.C.
H. J. Saalwachter	American Merchant Marine Institute, Assistant Manager, Naval Architecture, Ore Navigation Corp., New York, N.Y.
C. S. Smith	Lake Carriers' Association, Shenango Furnace Co., Cleveland, Ohio
J. L. Stevens	Shipbuilders Council of America, Chief, Hull Technical Department, Newport News S/B and D/D Co., Newport News, Va.
E. V. Lewis	Webb Institute of Naval Architecture, Glen Cove, Long Island, N.Y.
Captain A. H. McComb, Jr., USCG	Chief, International Maritime Safety Coordinating Staff, USCG Headquarters, Washington, D.C.
Captain B. D. Shoemaker, Jr., USCG	Assistant Chief, Office of Merchant Marine Safety, USCG Headquarters, Washington. D.C.
J. R. Lindgren	American Institute of Marine Underwriters, U.S. Salvage Association, Inc., New York, N.Y.
Edwin L. Stewart	Society of Naval Architects and Marine Engineers, Scarsdale, N.Y.
H. S. Townsend	U.S. Salvage Association, Inc., New York, N.Y.
W. G. Watt	U.S. Naval Oceanographic Office, Director, Maritime Safety Division, Suitland, Md.
Captain H. J. Parker	National Cargo Bureau, Chief Surveyor, New York, N.Y.
M. F. York	American Institute of Marine Underwriters, President, Atlantic Mutual Insurance Co., New York, N.Y.

WESTERN RIVERS PANEL

The Western Rivers Panel, formed on March 12, 1943, advises on the various aspects of shipping on the western rivers system. The increase in bulk cargo shipments by barge and the technological advances in this method of transportation require the continued advice of this panel to ensure safety of life and property on the inland waterways.

The panel, consisting of the members listed below, met on August 19, 1964.

Braxton B. Carr, Chairman	The American Waterways Operators, Inc., Washington, D.C.
Harry W. Anderson	President, Anderson Petroleum Transportation Co., Houston, Tex.
Munger T. Ball	Chairman of the Board, Sabine Towing and Transportation Co., Inc., Port Arthur, Tex.
J. Clarke Berry	Vice President, Canal Barge Co., Inc., New Orleans, La.
Jesse E. Brent	President, Brent Towing Co., Inc., Greenville. Miss.
Ruel E. Bridges	Consultant and Chairman of the Management Committee, Ingram Barge Co., New Orleans, La.
W. A. Creelman	Vice President of Operations, National Marine Service, Inc., Hartford, Ill.
B. O. Caplener	Marine Superintendent, Federal Barge Lines, Inc., St. Louis, Mo.

Captain John L. Cathey	Vice President-Operations, Crounse Corp., Paducah, Ky.
Gale H. Chapman	Vice President, Upper Mississippi Towing Corp., Minneapolis, Minn.
Bailey T. DeBardeleben	Coyle Lines Inc., New Orleans, La.
W. B. Foute	Vice President, Mid-South Towing Co., St. Louis, Mo.
Robert L. Gray	Manager, River Operations, Ashland Oil and Refining Co., Inc., Ashland, Ky.
Robert H. Hertzberg	Marine Superintendent, Cargo Carriers, Inc., Minneapolis, Minn.
Gresham Hougland	Vice President, Hougland Barge Line, Inc., Paducah, Ky.
Captain Robert B. McCulloch	Port Captain, The Ohio River Co., Huntington, W. Va.
W. L. McElroy	Vice President, Warrior and Gulf Navigation Co., Chickasaw, Ala.
D. L. Mechling	A.IL. Mechling Barge Lines, Inc., New Orleans, a.
William K. Nestor	Vice President-Operations, Arrow Transportation Co., Sheffield, Ala.
Alvan D. Osbourne	Vice President-Operations, Union Barge Line Corp., Pittsburgh, Pa.
Bert C. Puncey, Jr.	Anoka Boat and Towing Co., Inc., Hughes, Ark.
C. W. Rushing	Manager, Missouri Barge Line Co., Cape Girardeau, Mo.
Frank P. Silliman	President, Hillman Transportation Co., Pittsburgh, Pa.
Arnold Sobel	Vice President. Material Service Division, General Dynamics Corp., Chicago, Ill.
M. F. Spellacy	Manager, Marine Division, Inland Waterways Department, Humble Oil and Refining Co., Houston, Tex.
Captain Roy Streckfus	President, Streckfus Steamers, Inc., St. Louis, Mo.
J. W. Weaver	Standard Oil Co. (Kentucky), Louisville, Ky.
Captain Jack D. Wofford	American Commercial Barge Line Co., Jeffersonville, Ind.

TABLES

NOTE.—Details of figures may not add to totals because of rounding.

Bases of Tables

The figures in this report are shown on the basis of: (a) The *Daily Statement of the United States Treasury;* (b) the *Monthly Statement of Receipts and Expenditures of the United States Government;* (c) warrants issued; (d) public debt accounts; and (e) administrative accounts and reports. Where no basis is indicated, the figures are derived from administrative reports prepared according to various specifications. Where more than one basis is used in a single table covering a period of years, the date of the change in basis is stated. The term "security," wherever used in the various tables, means any obligation issued pursuant to law for valuable consideration and includes bonds, notes, certificates of indebtedness, debentures, and other evidences of indebtedness.

Following are general explanations of the various bases. For background on the first two bases (the daily and monthly statements) see exhibits 69, 70, and 71 in the 1954 annual report; and for the third (warrants issued) see 1962 annual report, page 502.

Daily Statement of the United States Treasury

The daily Treasury statement was the basis for receipts, expenditures, and the resulting surplus or deficit shown in this report for the fiscal years 1916–52, and from 1916 to present it has been the basis for much of the public debt data and all of the figures on the account of the Treasurer of the United States. Since 1916 the daily statement has been based on bank transcripts (summarizing charges for checks paid and credits for deposits on the books of the banks) cleared and processed through the accounts of the Treasurer's office in Washington. Telegraphic reports are used to provide more timely data for certain major types of information pending receipt of the bank transcripts. For the fiscal years 1946–52, expenditures for agencies using the facilities of the Treasury Department's Division of Disbursement were shown on the basis of reports of checks issued. Total expenditures, however, as well as expenditures for the military departments and other agencies using their own disbursing facilities, were on the basis of bank transcripts cleared.

During the time it served as the basis for the budget results, the daily statement covered certain transactions processed through commercial bank accounts held in the name of Government officers other than the Treasurer of the United States, and included intragovernmental and other noncash transactions. The present daily Treasury statement reports the status of the Treasurer's account and summarizes the various transactions representing deposits and withdrawals in that account, excluding noncash transactions (with minor exceptions) and transactions involving cash held outside the Treasurer's account. Only a limited number of deposit and withdrawal classifications are shown. These data do not purport to represent budget results.

Monthly Statement of Receipts and Expenditures of the United States Government

Beginning with the figures for the fiscal year 1953, this monthly statement replaced the daily statement as the primary source of administrative budget results (surplus or deficit) and other receipt and expenditure data classified by type of account. This statement shows all receipts and expenditures of the Government including those made from cash accounts held outside the Treasurer's account. The information in the monthly statement is based on the central accounts relating to cash operations (see "Description of Accounts Relating to Cash Operations," below).

Warrants issued

Receipt and expenditure data shown for fiscal years before 1916 were taken from reports based on warrants issued.

For receipts, covering warrants were prepared from certificates of deposit mailed to the Treasury, principally by Government depositaries, showing deposits received. The figures thus compiled were on a "warrants-issued" basis. Since these certificates did not reach the Treasury simultaneously, all receipts for a fiscal year could not be covered into the Treasury by warrant of the Secretary immediately upon the close of the fiscal year. Therefore, certain certificates of deposit representing amounts deposited during one fiscal year were reported as the next year's receipts.

Reports of expenditures were based on the amount of accountable and settlement warrants issued and charged to appropriation accounts. Since accountable warrants covered advances to disbursing officers, rather than actual payments, reported expenditures necessarily included the changes in balances of funds remaining unexpended to the credit of disbursing officers at the close of the fiscal year.

Public debt accounts

The figures reported on this basis represent transactions which have been audited by the Bureau of the Public Debt. It is sometimes several months after a financing operation before all the transactions have been reported and audited. Therefore, the public debt figures on this basis differ from those reported in the daily Treasury statement since the latter consist of transactions cleared through the Treasurer's account during the reporting period (see explanation under "Daily Statement of the United States Treasury," above). A reconciliation of figures on the two bases is given in table 35.

Administrative accounts and reports

Certain tables in this report are developed from the accounts, records, and reports of the administrative agencies concerned, which may be on various bases. These tables include internal revenue collections, customs statistics, foreign currency transactions in the accounts of the Secretary of the Treasury, and balance sheets, statements of income and expense, and source and application of funds of public enterprise funds.

Description of Accounts Relating to Cash Operations

The classes of accounts maintained in connection with the cash operations of the Federal Government, exclusive of public debt operations, include: (1) The accounts of fiscal officers or agents, collectively, who receive money for deposit in the U.S. Treasury or for other authorized disposition or who make disbursements by drawing checks on the Treasurer of the United States or by effecting payments in some other manner; (2) the accounts of administrative agencies which classify receipt and expenditure (disbursement) transactions according to the individual receipt, appropriation, or fund account; and (3) the accounts of the Treasurer of the United States whose office, generally speaking, is responsible for the receipt and custody of money deposited by fiscal officers or agents, for the payment of checks drawn on the Treasurer, and the payment of public debt securities redeemed. A set of central accounts is maintained in the Treasury Department for the purpose of consolidating financial data reported periodically from these three sources in order to present the results of cash operations in central financial reports on a unified basis for the Government as a whole, and as a means of internal control.

The central accounts relating to cash operations disclose monthly and fiscal year information on: (1) The Government's receipts by principal sources, and its expenditures according to the different appropriations and other funds involved; and (2) the cash transactions, classified by types, together with certain directly related assets and liabilities which underlie such receipts and expenditures. The accounting for receipts is substantially on the basis of collections (i.e. as of the time cash receipts are placed under accounting control), and that for expenditures is substantially on the basis of checks issued (and cash payments made) except that since June 1955 interest on the public debt has been on an accrual basis. The structure of the accounts provides for a reconciliation, on a firm accounting basis, between the published reports of receipts and expenditures for the Government as a whole and changes in the Treasurer's cash balance by means of such factors as checks outstanding, deposits in transit, and cash held outside the Treasury. Within the central accounts, receipt and expenditure accounts are classified as described in the following paragraphs.

Administrative budget accounts

General fund accounts.—General fund receipt accounts are credited with all receipts which are not earmarked by law for a specific purpose. General fund receipts consist principally of internal revenue collections, which include income taxes, excise taxes, estate, gift, and employment taxes. The remainder consist of customs duties and a large number of miscellaneous receipts, including fees for permits and licenses; fines, penalties, and forfeitures; interest and dividends; rentals; royalties; sale of Government property; and seigniorage. General fund expenditure accounts are established to record amounts appropriated by the Congress to be expended for the general support of the Government.

Special fund accounts.—Special fund accounts are credited with receipts from specific sources which are earmarked by law for a specific purpose, but which are not generated from a cycle of operations.

Revolving fund accounts.—These are funds authorized by specific provisions of law to finance a continuing cycle of operations in which expenditures generate receipts, and the receipts are available for expenditure without further action by Congress. They are classified as (a) public enterprise funds where receipts come primarily from sources outside the Government and (b) intragovernmental funds where receipts come primarily from other appropriations or funds. Treasury reports generally show the net effect of operations (excess of disbursements or collections and reimbursements for the period) on the administrative budget surplus or deficit.

Management fund accounts (including consolidated working funds).—These are working fund accounts authorized by law to facilitate accounting for and administration of intragovernmental activities (other than a continuing cycle of operations) which are financed by two or more appropriations.

Other accounts

Trust fund accounts.—These are accounts maintained to record the receipt and expenditure of moneys held in trust by the Government for use in carrying out specific purposes or programs in accordance with the terms of a trust agreement or statute. The receipts of many trust funds, especially the major ones, to the extent not needed for current payments, are invested in public debt securities and other Government agency securities. Generally, trust fund accounts consist of separate receipt and expenditure accounts, but when the trust corpus is established to perform a business-type operation, the fund entity is called a "trust revolving fund" and a combined receipt and expenditure account is used.

Deposit fund accounts.—Deposit funds are combined receipt and expenditure accounts established to account for receipts that are either (a) held in suspense temporarily and later refunded or paid into some other fund of the Government upon administrative or legal determination as to the proper disposition thereof, or (b) held by the Government as banker or agent for others and paid out at the direction of the depositor.

Summary of

TABLE 1.—*Summary of fiscal operations*,

[On basis of daily Treasury statements through 1952; thereafter on basis of "Monthly Statement

Fiscal year or month	Administrative budget receipts and expenditures			Trust and other transactions, net receipts, or expenditures (−) [4]	Clearing account [5]	Public debt, net increase, or decrease (−) [1]
	Net receipts [2]	Expenditures [3]	Surplus, or deficit (−)			
1940	$5,137,249,771	$9,055,268,931	−$3,918,019,161	$442,538,143		$2,527,998,627
1941	7,095,676,052	13,254,948,411	−6,159,272,358	907,790,781		5,993,912,498
1942	12,546,618,755	34,036,861,487	−21,490,242,732	−1,612,785,695		23,461,001,581
1943	21,947,283,157	79,367,713,522	−57,420,430,365	−337,796,138		64,273,645,214
1944	43,562,609,460	94,986,002,002	−51,423,392,541	−2,221,918,654		64,307,296,891
1945	44,362,020,944	98,302,937,069	−53,940,916,126	791,293,666		57,678,800,189
1946	39,649,870,986	60,326,041,595	−20,676,170,609	−523,587,210		10,739,911,763
1947	39,677,167,024	38,923,379,364	753,787,660	−1,102,524,942	$554,706,981	−11,135,716,065
1948 [7]	41,374,701,989	32,955,232,145	8,419,469,844	−294,342,662	−507,106,039	−5,994,136,596
1949 [7]	37,662,972,939	39,474,412,987	−1,811,440,048	−494,733,365	366,441,900	478,113,347
1950	36,421,934,577	39,544,036,935	−3,122,102,357	99,137,360	482,656,886	4,586,992,491
1951	47,480,067,075	43,970,284,450	3,509,782,624	679,223,478	−214,140,135	−2,135,375,536
1952	61,286,560,916	65,303,201,294	−4,016,640,378	147,077,201	−401,389,312	3,883,201,970
1953	64,670,584,424	74,119,797,882	−9,449,213,457	434,671,979	−249,920,729	6,965,882,853
1954	64,420,034,061	67,537,000,317	−3,116,966,256	327,762,083	−303,126,484	5,188,537,469
1955	60,208,508,692	64,388,737,614	−4,180,228,921	231,296,942	283,518,269	3,114,623,694
1956	67,849,951,339	66,224,397,935	1,625,553,403	−193,580,583	521,955,153	−1,623,409,153
1957	70,561,886,113	68,966,314,562	1,595,571,550	194,731,536	−522,892,840	−2,223,641,752
1958	68,549,720,044	71,369,174,086	−2,819,454,041	632,513,036	530,045,771	5,816,045,849
1959	67,915,348,624	80,342,335,375	−12,426,986,751	−328,663,331	−5,750,464	8,362,689,332
1960	77,763,460,221	76,539,412,799	1,224,047,422	−49,526,275	−145,025,682	1,624,853,770
1961	77,659,424,906	81,515,167,454	−3,855,742,548	−602,403,079	507,346,821	2,640,177,762
1962	81,409,092,073	87,786,766,581	−6,377,674,508	435,641,579	448,422,413	9,229,884,111
1963	86,376,210,348	92,641,797,059	−6,265,586,711	96,541,467	196,017,584	7,658,810,276
1964	89,458,664,072	97,684,374,795	−8,225,710,723	550,608,332	741,391,176	5,853,266,261
1965	93,071,796,892	96,506,904,210	−3,435,107,319	426,395,153	−977,754,134	5,560,999,726
1964—July	3,486,850,788	7,409,814,216	−3,922,963,428	−40,431,567	−392,913,531	−529,853,048
Aug	6,653,126,843	8,082,658,540	−1,429,531,698	65,622,319	−902,575,244	2,906,152,686
Sept	10,071,897,921	8,449,691,325	1,622,206,597	−129,945,464	387,461,160	1,520,315,360
Oct	3,398,194,410	8,328,598,594	−4,930,404,184	365,593,506	41,350,926	25,679,775
Nov	7,036,605,028	7,051,330,313	−14,725,284	171,302,629	−595,278,204	2,851,096,281
Dec	8,856,423,523	8,770,331,865	86,091,658	−188,192,878	−160,851,769	−545,817,594
1965—Jan	5,642,184,681	7,675,623,231	−2,033,438,550	64,487,372	376,815,299	42,265,130
Feb	7,517,643,441	7,146,047,051	371,596,390	193,493,516	−268,106,316	1,899,792,785
Mar	11,188,337,522	8,139,187,691	3,049,149,831	146,105,285	279,457,457	−2,186,012,144
Apr	8,548,884,214	8,268,417,023	280,467,191	972,215,921	−7,510,759	−1,139,874,131
May	7,267,581,177	8,115,642,874	−848,061,698	−576,990,252	243,649,033	2,660,934,888
June	13,404,067,344	9,069,561,488	4,334,505,856	−616,865,234	20,747,814	−1,943,680,262

[1] Public debt includes debt incurred to finance expenditures of wholly owned Government corporations and other business-type activities in exchange for which securities of the corporations and activities were issued to the Treasury. (See table 110.)

[2] Total receipts less refunds of receipts and less transfers of tax receipts to certain major trust accounts (as shown in table 3). Excludes certain interfund transactions (also excluded from expenditures). See footnote 3.

[3] Expenditures are net after allowance for reimbursements to appropriations, receipts of revolving fund accounts, and receipts credited to disbursing accounts of corporations and agencies having authority to use collections without formal covering into the Treasury. The figures include transfers to trust accounts. Beginning with 1951, the net investments by wholly owned Government corporations and agencies in public debt securities are excluded from budget expenditures and included in trust and other transactions. The expenditure figures also exclude public debt retirements chargeable to the sinking fund, etc., under special provisions of law. Effective July 1, 1948, payments to the Treasury, principally by wholly owned Government corporations, for retirement of capital stock and disposition of earnings are excluded from both receipts and expenditures. Prior year adjustments of such payments are shown in the 1958 annual report, p. 396, table 2, footnote 3. Certain interfund transactions are excluded, as from net receipts. For interfund transactions excluded from both net budget receipts and expenditures, see 1961 annual report pp. 450–457, and table 8, this report.

Fiscal Operations

fiscal years 1940–65 and monthly 1965

of Receipts and Expenditures of the United States Government," see "Bases of Tables"]

Balance in account of the Treasurer of the United States, net increase, or decrease (−)	Balance in account of the Treasurer of the United States	Amount, end of period			
		Debt outstanding [1]			
		Public debt	Guaranteed securities held outside the Treasury	Total	Subject to limitation [6]
−$947,482,391	$1,890,743,141	$42,967,531,038	$5,529,070,655	$48,496,601,693	$43,219,123,375
742,430,921	2,633,174,062	48,961,443,536	6,370,252,580	55,331,696,116	49,493,588,731
357,973,154	2,991,147,216	72,422,445,116	4,563,259,630	76,990,704,746	74,154,457,607
6,515,418,710	9,506,565,926	136,696,090,330	4,099,943,046	140,796,033,376	140,469,083,742
10,661,985,696	20,168,551,622	201,003,387,221	1,623,069,301	202,626,456,522	208,077,255,051
4,529,177,729	24,697,729,352	258,682,187,410	433,158,392	259,115,345,802	268,670,763,468
−10,459,846,056	14,237,883,295	269,422,099,173	476,384,859	269,898,484,033	268,932,355,302
−10,929,746,366	3,308,136,929	258,286,383,109	89,520,185	258,375,903,294	257,491,416,060
1,623,884,548	4,932,021,477	252,292,246,513	73,460,818	252,365,707,331	251,541,571,385
−1,461,618,165	3,470,403,312	252,770,359,860	27,275,408	252,797,635,268	252,027,712,585
2,046,684,380	5,517,087,692	257,357,352,351	19,503,034	257,376,855,385	256,652,133,429
1,839,490,432	7,356,578,123	255,221,976,815	29,227,169	255,251,203,984	254,566,629,670
−387,750,519	6,968,827,604	259,105,178,785	45,565,346	259,150,744,131	258,506,598,138
−2,298,579,356	4,670,248,248	266,071,061,639	52,072,761	266,123,134,400	265,521,736,381
2,096,206,813	6,766,455,061	271,259,599,108	81,441,386	271,341,040,494	270,790,304,616
−550,790,014	[8] 6,215,665,047	274,374,222,802	44,142,961	274,418,365,763	273,914,849,696
330,518,820	6,546,183,868	272,750,813,649	73,888,475	272,824,702,124	272,361,216,449
−956,231,505	5,589,952,362	270,527,171,896	107,137,950	270,634,309,846	270,188,322,086
4,159,150,615	9,749,102,977	276,343,217,745	101,220,600	276,444,438,345	276,013,439,621
−4,398,711,214	5,350,391,763	284,705,907,078	111,019,150	284,816,926,228	284,398,474,090
2,654,349,235	8,004,740,998	286,330,760,848	139,841,775	286,470,602,623	286,064,964,324
−1,310,621,045	6,694,119,954	288,970,938,610	240,215,450	289,211,154,060	288,861,862,530
3,736,273,595	10,430,393,549	298,200,822,721	444,218,925	298,645,041,646	298,211,767,263
1,685,782,615	12,116,176,163	305,859,632,996	606,610,375	306,466,243,371	306,098,500,044
−1,080,444,954	11,035,731,209	311,712,899,257	812,991,925	312,525,891,182	312,164,173,634
1,574,533,426	12,610,264,635	317,273,898,984	590,326,050	317,864,225,034	317,580,860,048
−4,886,161,573	6,149,569,636	311,183,046,210	821,353,850	312,004,400,060	311,643,279,465
639,668,063	6,789,237,698	314,089,198,896	848,445,000	314,937,643,896	314,577,118,825
3,400,037,652	10,189,275,351	315,609,514,256	886,190,100	316,495,704,356	316,135,305,259
−4,497,779,976	5,691,495,375	315,635,194,031	820,607,275	316,455,801,306	316,096,009,074
2,412,395,422	8,103,890,796	318,486,290,312	833,751,225	319,320,041,537	319,033,635,813
−808,770,583	7,295,120,213	317,940,472,718	809,241,900	318,749,714,618	318,463,813,849
−1,549,870,749	5,745,249,484	317,982,737,848	663,595,875	318,646,333,723	318,360,718,063
2,196,776,375	7,942,025,839	319,882,530,633	692,713,100	320,575,243,733	320,289,909,169
1,288,700,430	9,230,726,269	317,696,518,489	719,240,050	318,415,758,539	318,130,965,177
105,298,222	9,336,024,490	316,556,644,358	656,740,650	317,213,385,008	316,929,270,040
1,479,531,971	10,815,556,461	319,217,579,245	605,852,725	319,823,431,970	319,539,694,826
1,794,708,174	12,610,264,635	317,273,898,984	590,326,050	317,864,225,034	317,580,860,048

[4] Consists of transactions of trust and deposit fund accounts, net investments by Government agencies in public debt securities, and net redemptions or sales of securities of Government agencies in the market. (See tables 5–7.) Investments by wholly owned Government corporations in public debt securities are included in budget expenditures before 1951.

[5] For checks outstanding and telegraphic reports from Federal Reserve banks; public debt interest accrued and unpaid beginning with June and the fiscal year 1955 (previously included from November 1949 as interest checks and coupons outstanding); also deposits in transit and changes in cash held outside the Treasury and in certain other accounts beginning with the fiscal year 1954. For 1955, includes adjustment of −$207,183,858 for effect on balance in Treasurer's account of Post Office disbursing accounts reclassified in November 1954.

[6] A summary of legislation on debt limitation under the Second Liberty Bond Act, as amended, from Sept. 24, 1917, through June 30, 1965, is shown in table 40. Guaranteed securities held outside the Treasury are included in the limitation beginning Apr. 3, 1945. In computing statutory debt limitation, savings bonds are carried at maturity value from their origin in 1935 until June 26, 1946; from that date, as in the public debt outstanding, they are carried at current redemption value.

[7] Excludes transfer of $3,000,000,000 in 1948 and includes transfer of a like amount in 1949 to the Foreign Economic Cooperation Trust Fund. (See table 2, footnote 9.)

[8] Includes adjustment of −$207,183,858 for reclassification in November 1954 of Post Office Department and postmasters' disbursing accounts (formerly treated as liability accounts of the Treasurer of the United States) to net expenditures on the basis of cash receipts and expenditures as reported by the Post Office Department.

Receipts and

TABLE 2.—*Receipts and expenditures,*

On basis of warrants issued from 1789 to 1915 and on basis of daily Treasury statements for 1916 through of the United States Government." General, special, emergency, and trust accounts combined from see "Bases of Tables"]

Year [1]	Receipts					
	Customs (including tonnage tax)	Internal revenue		Other receipts [2]	Total receipts [3]	Net receipts
		Income and profits taxes	Other			
1789–91	$4,399,473			$19,440	$4,418,913	
1792	3,443,071		$208,943	17,946	3,669,960	
1793	4,255,307		337,706	59,910	4,652,923	
1794	4,801,065		274,090	356,750	5,431,905	
1795	5,588,461		337,755	188,318	6,114,534	
1796	6,567,988		475,290	1,334,252	8,377,530	
1797	7,549,650		575,491	563,640	8,688,781	
1798	7,106,062		644,358	150,076	7,900,496	
1799	6,610,449		779,136	157,228	7,546,813	
1800	9,080,933		809,396	958,420	10,848,749	
1801	10,750,779		1,048,033	1,136,519	12,935,331	
1802	12,438,236		621,899	1,935,659	14,995,794	
1803	10,479,418		215,180	369,500	11,064,098	
1804	11,098,565		50,941	676,801	11,826,307	
1805	12,936,487		21,747	602,459	13,560,693	
1806	14,667,698		20,101	872,132	15,559,931	
1807	15,845,522		13,051	539,446	16,398,019	
1808	16,363,551		8,211	688,900	17,060,662	
1809	7,296,021		4,044	473,408	7,773,473	
1810	8,583,309		7,431	793,475	9,384,215	
1811	13,313,223		2,296	1,108,010	14,423,529	
1812	8,958,778		4,903	837,452	9,801,133	
1813	13,224,623		4,755	1,111,032	14,340,410	
1814	5,998,772		1,662,985	3,519,868	11,181,625	
1815	7,282,942		4,678,059	3,768,023	15,729,024	
1816	36,306,875		5,124,708	6,246,088	47,677,671	
1817	26,283,348		2,678,101	4,137,601	33,099,050	
1818	17,176,385		955,270	3,453,516	21,585,171	
1819	20,283,609		229,594	4,090,172	24,603,375	
1820	15,005,612		106,261	2,768,797	17,880,670	
1821	13,004,447		69,028	1,499,905	14,573,380	
1822	17,589,762		67,666	2,575,000	20,232,428	
1823	19,088,433		34,242	1,417,991	20,540,666	
1824	17,878,326		34,663	1,468,224	19,381,213	
1825	20,098,713		25,771	1,716,374	21,840,858	
1826	23,341,332		21,590	1,897,512	25,260,434	
1827	19,712,283		19,886	3,234,195	22,966,364	
1828	23,205,524		17,452	1,540,654	24,763,630	
1829	22,681,966		14,503	2,131,158	24,827,627	
1830	21,922,391		12,161	2,909,564	24,844,116	
1831	24,224,442		6,934	4,295,445	28,526,821	
1832	28,465,237		11,631	3,388,693	31,865,561	
1833	29,032,509		2,759	4,913,159	33,948,427	
1834	16,214,957		4,196	5,572,783	21,791,936	
1835	19,391,311		10,459	16,028,317	35,430,087	
1836	23,409,941		370	27,416,485	50,826,796	
1837	11,169,290		5,494	13,779,369	24,954,153	
1838	16,158,800		2,467	10,141,295	26,302,562	
1839	23,137,925		2,553	8,342,271	31,482,749	
1840	13,499,502		1,682	5,978,931	19,480,115	
1841	14,487,217		3,261	2,369,682	16,860,160	
1842	18,187,909		495	1,787,794	19,976,198	
1843 [4]	7,046,844		103	1,255,755	8,302,702	
1844	26,183,571		1,777	3,136,026	29,321,374	
1845	27,528,113		3,517	2,438,476	29,970,106	
1846	26,712,668		2,897	2,984,402	29,699,967	
1847	23,747,865		375	2,747,529	26,495,769	
1848	31,757,071		375	3,978,333	35,735,779	
1849	28,346,739			2,861,404	31,208,143	
1850	39,668,686			3,934,753	43,603,439	
1851	49,017,568			3,541,736	52,559,304	
1852	47,339,327			2,507,489	49,846,816	
1853	58,931,866			2,655,188	61,587,054	
1854	64,224,190			9,576,151	73,800,341	
1855	53,025,781			12,324,781	65,350,575	
1856	64,022,863			10,033,836	74,056,699	

Footnotes at end of table.

Expenditures

fiscal years 1789–1965

1952. Beginning with fiscal year 1953 on basis of the "Monthly Statement of Receipts and Expenditures 1789 through 1930. Trust accounts excluded for 1931 and subsequent years. For explanation of accounts

		Expenditures			
Department of the Army (formerly War Department) [4]	Department of the Navy [4]	Interest on the public debt	Other [3][5]	Total expenditures [3]	Surplus, or deficit (−) [5]
$632, 804	$570	$2, 349, 437	$1, 286, 216	$4, 269, 027	$149, 886
1, 100, 702	53	3, 201, 628	777, 149	5, 079, 532	−1, 409, 572
1, 130, 249	-------------	2, 772, 242	579, 822	4, 482, 313	170, 610
2, 639, 098	61, 409	3, 490, 293	800, 039	6, 990, 839	−1, 558, 934
2, 480, 910	410, 562	3, 189, 151	1, 459, 186	7, 539, 809	−1, 425, 275
1, 260, 264	274, 784	3, 195, 055	996, 883	5, 726, 986	2, 650, 544
1, 039, 403	382, 632	3, 300, 043	1, 411, 556	6, 133, 634	2, 555, 147
2, 009, 522	1, 381, 348	3, 053, 281	1, 232, 353	7, 676, 504	223, 992
2, 466, 947	2, 858, 082	3, 186, 288	1, 155, 138	9, 666, 455	−2, 119, 642
2, 560, 879	3, 448, 716	3, 374, 705	1, 401, 775	10, 786, 075	62, 674
1, 672, 944	2, 111, 424	4, 412, 913	1, 197, 301	9, 394, 582	3, 540, 749
1, 179, 148	915, 502	4, 125, 039	1, 642, 369	7, 862, 118	7, 133, 676
822, 056	1, 215, 231	3, 848, 828	1, 965, 538	7, 851, 653	3, 212, 445
875, 424	1, 189, 833	4, 266, 583	2, 387, 602	8, 719, 442	3, 106, 865
712, 781	1, 597, 500	4, 148, 999	4, 046, 954	10, 506, 234	3, 054, 459
1, 224, 355	1, 649, 641	3, 723, 408	3, 206, 213	9, 803, 617	5, 756, 314
1, 288, 686	1, 722, 064	3, 369, 578	1, 973, 823	8, 354, 151	8, 043, 868
2, 900, 834	1, 884, 068	3, 428, 153	1, 719, 437	9, 932, 492	7, 128, 170
3, 345, 772	2, 427, 759	2, 866, 075	1, 641, 142	10, 280, 748	−2, 507, 275
2, 294, 324	1, 654, 244	2, 845, 428	1, 362, 514	8, 156, 510	1, 227, 705
2, 032, 828	1, 965, 566	2, 465, 733	1, 594, 210	8, 058, 337	6, 365, 192
11, 817, 798	3, 959, 365	2, 451, 273	2, 052, 335	20, 280, 771	−10, 479, 638
19, 652, 013	6, 446, 600	3, 599, 455	1, 983, 784	31, 681, 852	−17, 341, 442
20, 350, 807	7, 311, 291	4, 593, 239	2, 465, 589	34, 720, 926	−23, 539, 301
14, 794, 294	8, 660, 000	5, 754, 569	3, 499, 276	32, 708, 139	−16, 979, 115
16, 012, 097	3, 908, 278	7, 213, 259	3, 453, 057	30, 586, 691	17, 090, 980
8, 004, 237	3, 314, 598	6, 389, 210	4, 135, 775	21, 843, 820	11, 255, 230
5, 622, 715	2, 953, 695	6, 016, 447	5, 232, 264	19, 825, 121	1, 760, 050
6, 506, 300	3, 847, 640	5, 163, 538	5, 946, 332	21, 463, 810	3, 139, 565
2, 630, 392	4, 387, 990	5, 126, 097	6, 116, 148	18, 260, 627	−379, 957
4, 461, 292	3, 319, 243	5, 087, 274	2, 942, 944	15, 810, 753	−1, 237, 373
3, 111, 981	2, 224, 459	5, 172, 578	4, 491, 202	15, 000, 220	5, 232, 208
3, 096, 924	2, 503, 766	4, 922, 685	4, 183, 465	14, 706, 840	5, 833, 826
3, 340, 940	2, 904, 582	4, 996, 562	9, 084, 624	20, 326, 708	−945, 495
3, 659, 914	3, 049, 084	4, 366, 769	4, 781, 462	15, 857, 229	5, 983, 629
3, 943, 194	4, 218, 902	3, 973, 481	4, 900, 220	17, 035, 797	8, 224, 637
3, 938, 978	4, 263, 877	3, 486, 072	4, 450, 241	16, 139, 168	6, 827, 196
4, 145, 545	3, 918, 786	3, 098, 801	5, 231, 711	16, 394, 843	8, 368, 787
4, 724, 291	3, 308, 745	2, 542, 843	4, 627, 454	15, 203, 333	9, 624, 294
4, 767, 129	3, 239, 429	1, 913, 533	5, 222, 975	15, 143, 066	9, 701, 050
4, 841, 836	3, 856, 183	1, 383, 583	5, 166, 049	15, 247, 651	13, 279, 170
5, 446, 035	3, 956, 370	772, 562	7, 113, 983	17, 288, 950	14, 576, 611
6, 704, 019	3, 901, 357	303, 797	12, 108, 379	23, 017, 552	10, 930, 875
5, 696, 189	3, 956, 260	202, 153	8, 772, 967	18, 627, 569	3, 164, 367
5, 759, 157	3, 864, 939	57, 863	7, 890, 854	17, 572, 813	17, 857, 274
12, 169, 227	5, 807, 718	--------------	12, 891, 219	30, 868, 164	19, 958, 632
13, 682, 734	6, 646, 915	--------------	16, 913, 847	37, 243, 496	−12, 289, 343
12, 897, 224	6, 131, 596	14, 997	14, 821, 242	33, 865, 059	−7, 562, 497
8, 916, 996	6, 182, 294	399, 834	11, 400, 004	26, 899, 128	4, 583, 621
7, 097, 070	6, 113, 897	174, 598	10, 932, 014	24, 317, 579	−4, 837, 464
8, 805, 565	6, 001, 077	284, 978	11, 474, 253	26, 565, 873	−9, 705, 713
6, 611, 887	8, 397, 243	773, 550	9, 423, 081	25, 205, 761	−5, 229, 563
2, 957, 300	3, 727, 711	523, 595	4, 649, 469	11, 858, 075	−3, 555, 373
5, 179, 220	6, 498, 199	1, 833, 867	8, 826, 285	22, 337, 571	6, 983, 803
5, 752, 644	6, 297, 245	1, 040, 032	9, 847, 487	22, 937, 408	7, 032, 698
10, 792, 867	6, 454, 947	842, 723	9, 676, 388	27, 766, 925	1, 933, 042
38, 305, 520	7, 900, 636	1, 119, 215	0, 066, 041	57, 281, 412	−30, 785, 643
25, 501, 963	9, 408, 476	2, 390, 825	8, 075, 962	45, 377, 226	−9, 641, 447
14, 852, 966	9, 786, 706	3, 565, 578	16, 846, 407	45, 051, 657	−13, 843, 514
9, 400, 239	7, 904, 709	3, 782, 331	18, 456, 213	39, 543, 492	4, 059, 947
11, 811, 793	9, 005, 931	3, 696, 721	23, 194, 572	47, 709, 017	4, 850, 287
8, 225, 247	8, 952, 801	4, 000, 298	23, 016, 573	44, 194, 919	5, 651, 897
9, 947, 291	10, 918, 781	3, 665, 833	23, 652, 206	48, 184, 111	13, 402, 943
11, 733, 629	10, 798, 586	3, 071, 017	32, 441, 630	58, 044, 862	15, 755, 479
14, 773, 826	13, 312, 024	2, 314, 375	29, 342, 443	59, 742, 668	5, 607, 907
16, 948, 197	14, 091, 781	1, 953, 822	36, 577, 226	69, 571, 026	4, 485, 672

TABLE 2.—*Receipts and expenditures,*

Year [1]	Customs (including tonnage tax)	Internal revenue Income and profits taxes	Other	Other receipts [2]	Total receipts [3]	Net receipts
1857	$63,875,905			$5,089,408	$68,965,313	
1858	41,789,621			4,865,745	46,655,366	
1859	49,565,824			3,920,641	53,486,465	
1860	53,187,512			2,877,096	56,064,608	
1861	39,582,126			1,927,805	41,509,931	
1862	49,056,398			2,931,058	51,987,456	
1863	69,059,642	$2,741,858	$34,898,930	5,996,861	112,697,291	
1864	102,316,153	20,294,732	89,446,402	52,569,484	264,626,771	
1865	84,928,261	60,979,329	148,484,886	39,322,129	333,714,605	
1866	179,046,652	72,982,159	236,244,654	69,759,155	558,032,620	
1867	176,417,811	66,014,429	200,013,108	48,188,662	490,634,010	
1868	164,464,600	41,455,598	149,631,991	50,085,894	405,638,083	
1869	180,048,427	34,791,856	123,564,605	32,538,859	370,943,747	
1870	194,538,374	37,775,874	147,123,882	31,817,347	411,255,477	
1871	206,270,408	19,162,651	123,935,503	33,955,383	383,323,945	
1872	216,370,287	14,436,862	116,205,316	27,094,403	374,106,868	
1873	188,089,523	5,062,312	108,667,002	31,919,368	333,738,205	
1874	163,103,834	139,472	102,270,313	39,465,137	304,978,756	
1875	157,167,722	233	110,007,261	20,824,835	288,000,051	
1876	148,071,985	588	116,700,144	29,323,148	294,095,865	
1877	130,956,493	98	118,630,310	31,819,518	281,406,419	
1878	130,170,680		110,581,625	17,011,574	257,763,879	
1879	137,250,048		113,561,611	23,015,526	273,827,185	
1880	186,522,064		124,009,374	22,995,173	333,526,611	
1881	198,159,676	3,022	135,261,364	27,358,231	360,782,293	
1882	220,410,730		146,497,596	36,616,924	403,525,250	
1883	214,706,497		144,720,369	38,860,716	398,287,582	
1884	195,067,490	55,628	121,530,445	31,866,307	348,519,870	
1885	181,471,939		112,498,726	29,720,041	323,690,706	
1886	192,905,023		116,805,936	26,728,767	336,439,726	
1887	217,286,893		118,823,391	35,292,993	371,403,277	
1888	219,091,174		124,296,872	35,878,029	379,266,075	
1889	223,832,742		130,881,514	32,335,803	387,050,059	
1890	229,668,585		142,606,706	30,805,693	403,080,984	
1891	219,522,205		145,686,250	27,403,992	392,612,447	
1892	177,452,964		153,971,072	23,513,748	354,937,784	
1893	203,355,017		161,027,624	21,436,988	385,819,629	
1894	131,818,531		147,111,233	27,425,552	306,355,316	
1895	152,158,617	77,131	143,344,541	29,149,130	324,729,419	
1896	160,021,752		146,762,865	31,357,830	338,142,447	
1897	176,554,127		146,688,574	24,479,004	347,721,705	
1898	149,575,062		170,900,642	84,845,631	405,321,335	
1899	206,128,482		273,437,162	36,394,977	515,960,621	
1900	233,164,871		295,327,927	38,748,054	567,240,852	
1901	238,585,456		307,180,664	41,919,218	587,685,338	
1902	254,444,708		271,880,122	36,153,403	562,478,233	
1903	284,479,582		230,810,124	46,591,016	561,880,722	
1904	261,274,565		232,904,119	46,908,401	541,087,085	
1905	261,798,857		234,095,741	48,380,087	544,274,685	
1906	300,251,878		249,150,213	45,582,355	594,984,446	
1907	332,233,363		269,666,773	63,960,250	665,860,386	
1908	286,113,130		251,711,127	64,037,650	601,861,907	
1909	300,711,934		246,212,644	57,395,920	604,320,498	
1910	333,683,445	20,951,781	268,981,738	51,894,751	675,511,715	
1911	314,497,071	33,516,977	289,012,224	64,806,639	701,832,911	
1912	311,321,672	28,583,304	293,028,896	59,675,332	692,609,204	
1913	318,891,396	35,006,300	309,410,666	60,802,868	724,111,230	
1914	292,320,014	71,381,275	308,659,733	62,312,145	734,673,167	
1915	209,786,672	80,201,759	335,467,887	72,454,509	697,910,827	
1916	213,185,846	124,937,253	387,764,776	56,646,673	782,534,548	
1917	225,962,393	359,681,228	449,684,980	88,996,194	1,124,324,795	
1918	179,998,385	2,314,006,292	872,028,020	298,550,168	3,664,582,865	
1919	184,457,867	3,018,783,687	1,296,501,292	652,814,290	5,152,257,136	
1920	322,902,650	3,944,949,288	1,460,082,287	966,631,164	6,694,565,389	
1921	308,564,391	3,206,046,158	1,390,379,823	719,942,589	5,624,932,961	
1922	356,443,387	2,068,128,193	1,145,125,064	539,407,507	4,109,104,151	
1923	561,928,867	1,678,607,428	945,865,333	820,733,853	4,007,135,481	
1924	545,637,504	1,842,144,418	953,012,618	671,250,162	4,012,044,702	

Footnotes at end of table.

fiscal years 1789–1965—Continued

		Expenditures			Surplus, or deficit (−)[5]
Department of the Army (formerly War Department)[4]	Department of the Navy[4]	Interest on the public debt	Other[2][5]	Total expenditures[3]	
$19,261,774	$12,747,977	$1,678,265	$34,107,692	$67,795,708	$1,169,605
25,485,383	13,984,551	1,567,056	33,148,280	74,185,270	−27,529,904
23,243,823	14,642,990	2,638,464	28,545,700	69,070,977	−15,584,512
16,409,767	11,514,965	3,177,315	32,028,551	63,130,598	−7,065,990
22,981,150	12,420,888	4,000,174	27,144,433	66,546,645	−25,036,714
394,368,407	42,668,277	13,190,325	24,534,810	474,761,819	−422,774,363
599,298,601	63,221,964	24,729,847	27,490,313	714,740,725	−602,043,434
690,791,843	85,725,995	53,685,422	35,119,382	865,322,642	−600,695,871
1,031,323,361	122,612,945	77,397,712	66,221,206	1,297,555,224	−963,840,619
284,449,702	43,324,118	133,067,742	59,967,855	520,809,417	37,223,203
95,224,415	31,034,011	143,781,592	87,502,657	357,542,675	133,091,335
123,246,648	25,775,503	140,424,046	87,894,088	377,340,285	28,297,798
78,501,991	20,000,758	130,694,243	93,668,286	322,865,278	48,078,469
57,655,676	21,780,230	129,235,498	100,982,157	309,653,561	101,601,916
35,799,992	19,431,027	125,576,566	111,369,603	292,177,188	91,146,757
35,372,157	21,249,810	117,357,840	103,538,156	277,517,963	96,588,905
46,323,138	23,526,257	104,750,688	115,745,162	290,345,245	43,392,960
42,313,927	30,932,587	107,119,815	122,267,544	302,633,873	2,344,883
41,120,646	21,497,626	103,093,545	108,911,576	274,623,393	13,376,658
38,070,889	18,963,310	100,243,271	107,823,615	265,101,085	28,994,780
37,082,736	14,959,935	97,124,512	92,167,292	241,334,475	40,071,944
32,154,148	17,365,301	102,500,875	84,944,003	236,964,327	20,799,552
40,425,661	15,125,127	105,327,949	106,069,147	266,947,884	6,879,301
38,116,916	13,536,985	95,757,575	120,231,482	267,642,958	65,883,653
40,466,461	15,686,672	82,508,741	122,051,014	260,712,888	100,069,405
43,570,494	15,032,046	71,077,207	128,301,693	257,981,440	145,543,810
48,911,383	15,283,437	59,160,131	142,053,187	265,408,138	132,879,444
39,429,603	17,292,601	54,578,379	132,825,661	244,126,244	104,393,626
42,670,578	16,021,080	51,386,256	150,149,021	260,226,935	63,463,771
34,324,153	13,907,888	50,580,146	143,670,952	242,483,139	93,956,587
38,561,026	15,141,127	47,741,577	166,488,451	267,932,181	103,471,096
38,522,436	16,926,438	44,715,007	167,760,920	267,924,801	111,341,274
44,435,271	21,378,809	41,001,484	192,473,414	299,288,978	87,761,081
44,582,838	22,006,206	36,099,284	215,352,383	318,040,711	85,040,273
48,720,065	26,113,896	37,547,135	253,392,808	365,773,904	26,838,543
46,895,456	29,174,139	23,378,116	245,575,620	345,023,331	9,914,453
49,641,773	30,136,084	27,264,392	276,435,704	383,477,953	2,341,676
54,567,930	31,701,294	27,841,406	253,414,651	367,525,281	−61,169,965
51,804,759	28,797,796	30,978,030	244,614,713	356,195,298	−31,465,879
50,830,921	27,147,732	35,385,029	238,815,764	352,179,446	−14,036,999
48,950,268	34,561,546	37,791,110	244,471,235	365,774,159	−18,052,454
91,992,000	58,823,985	37,585,056	254,967,542	443,368,583	−38,047,248
229,841,254	63,942,104	39,896,925	271,391,896	605,072,179	−89,111,558
134,774,768	55,953,078	40,160,333	289,972,668	520,860,847	46,380,005
144,615,697	60,506,978	32,342,979	287,151,271	524,616,925	63,068,413
112,272,216	67,803,128	29,108,045	276,050,860	485,234,249	77,243,984
118,629,505	82,618,034	28,556,349	287,202,239	517,006,127	44,874,595
165,199,911	102,956,102	24,646,490	290,857,397	583,659,900	−42,572,815
126,093,894	117,550,308	24,590,944	299,043,768	567,278,914	−23,004,229
137,326,066	110,474,264	24,308,576	298,093,372	570,202,278	24,782,168
149,775,084	97,128,469	24,481,158	307,744,131	579,128,842	86,731,544
175,840,453	118,037,097	21,426,138	343,892,632	659,196,320	−57,334,413
192,486,904	115,546,011	21,803,836	363,907,134	693,743,885	−89,423,387
189,823,379	123,173,717	21,342,979	359,276,990	603,617,065	−18,105,350
197,199,491	119,937,644	21,311,334	352,753,043	691,201,512	10,631,399
184,122,793	135,591,956	22,616,300	347,550,285	689,881,334	2,727,870
202,128,711	133,262,862	22,899,108	366,221,282	724,511,963	−400,733
208,349,746	139,682,186	22,863,957	364,185,542	735,081,431	−408,264
202,160,134	141,835,654	22,902,897	393,688,117	760,586,802	−62,675,975
183,176,439	153,853,567	22,900,869	374,125,327	734,056,202	48,478,346
377,940,870	239,632,757	24,742,702	1,335,365,422	1,977,681,751	−853,356,956
4,869,955,286	1,278,840,487	189,743,277	6,358,163,421	12,696,702,471	−9,032,119,606
9,009,075,789	2,002,310,785	619,215,569	6,884,277,812	18,514,879,955	−13,362,622,819
1,621,953,095	736,021,456	1,020,251,622	3,025,117,668	6,403,343,841	291,221,548
1,118,076,423	650,373,836	999,144,731	2,348,332,700	5,115,927,690	509,005,271
457,756,139	476,775,194	991,000,759	1,447,075,808	3,372,607,900	736,496,251
397,050,596	333,201,362	1,055,923,690	1,508,451,881	3,294,627,529	712,507,952
357,016,878	332,249,137	940,602,913	1,418,809,037	3,048,677,965	963,366,737

TABLE 2.—Receipts and expenditures, fiscal years 1789–1965—Continued

Year [1]	Customs [4]	Internal revenue		Other receipts [2]	Total receipts by major sources [3]	Refunds and transfers [7]	Receipts, less refunds and transfers	Interfund transactions [8] (deduct)	Net receipts
		Income and profits taxes	Other						
1925	$547,561,226	$1,760,537,824	$825,638,068	$643,411,567	$3,780,148,685		$3,780,148,685		$3,780,148,685
1926	579,430,093	1,982,040,088	855,599,289	545,686,220	3,962,755,690		3,962,755,690		3,962,755,690
1927	605,499,983	2,224,992,800	644,421,542	654,480,116	4,129,394,441		4,129,394,441		4,129,394,441
1928	568,986,188	2,173,952,557	621,015,666	678,390,745	4,042,348,156		4,042,348,156		4,042,348,156
1929	602,262,786	2,330,711,823	607,307,649	492,968,067	4,033,250,225		4,033,250,225		4,033,250,225
1930	587,000,903	2,410,986,978	623,308,036	551,645,785	4,177,941,702	$74,081,709	4,177,941,702		4,177,941,702
1931	378,354,006	1,860,394,295	569,395,721	381,503,611	3,189,638,632	--------	3,115,556,923		3,115,556,923
1932	327,754,969	1,057,335,853	503,670,481	116,964,134	2,006,725,437	81,812,320	1,923,913,117	$21,294	1,923,891,824
1933	250,750,251	746,206,445	858,217,512	224,522,534	2,079,696,742	83,483,799	2,021,212,943	24,369,110	1,996,843,833
1934	313,434,302	817,961,481	1,822,642,347	161,515,919	3,115,554,050	51,286,138	3,064,267,912	49,298,113	3,014,969,799
1935	313,353,034	1,099,118,638	2,178,571,390	179,424,141	3,800,467,202	70,553,357	3,729,913,845	23,958,245	3,705,955,600
1936	386,811,594	1,426,575,494	2,086,276,174	216,283,413	4,115,986,615	47,019,926	4,068,936,689	71,877,714	3,997,058,975
1937	486,335,599	2,163,413,817	2,433,726,286	210,093,535	5,293,590,237	314,980,542	4,978,600,695	22,988,139	4,955,612,556
1938	359,187,249	2,640,284,711	3,034,033,728	208,155,541	6,241,661,227	626,440,065	5,615,221,162	27,209,289	5,588,011,873
1939	318,837,311	2,188,757,289	2,972,463,558	187,765,468	5,667,823,626	671,524,096	4,996,299,530	17,233,572	4,979,065,958
1940	348,590,636	2,125,324,635	3,177,809,353	241,643,315	5,893,367,939	749,354,895	5,144,013,044	6,763,273	5,137,249,771
1941	391,870,013	3,460,637,849	3,892,037,133	242,066,545	7,995,611,580	892,680,197	7,102,931,383	7,255,331	7,095,676,052
1942	388,945,427	7,960,464,973	5,032,652,915	294,614,145	13,676,680,460	1,121,244,376	12,555,436,084	8,817,329	12,546,618,755
1943	324,290,777	16,083,668,781	6,050,300,218	934,062,619	23,402,322,396	1,416,621,609	21,986,700,787	39,417,630	21,947,283,157
1944	431,252,168	34,654,861,852	7,030,135,473	3,324,809,903	45,441,049,402	1,805,734,046	43,635,315,356	72,705,896	43,562,609,460
1945	354,775,542	35,173,061,373	8,728,950,555	3,493,528,991	47,750,306,371	3,275,002,706	44,475,303,665	113,282,721	44,362,020,944
1946	435,475,072	30,884,796,016	9,425,337,282	3,492,326,920	53,238,135,290	4,466,731,580	39,771,403,710	121,532,724	39,649,870,986
1947	494,078,260	29,305,568,454	10,073,840,241	4,634,701,652	44,508,189,607	4,722,007,571	39,786,181,036	109,014,012	39,677,167,024
1948 [5]	421,723,028	31,170,968,403	10,682,516,849	3,823,599,033	46,098,807,314	4,610,628,472	41,488,178,842	113,476,853	41,374,701,989
1949 [5]	384,454,796	29,432,283,759	10,825,001,116	2,081,735,850	42,773,505,520	5,077,956,071	37,695,549,449	32,576,510	37,662,972,939
1950	422,650,329	28,262,671,097	11,185,936,012	1,439,370,414	41,310,627,852	4,815,727,015	36,494,900,837	72,966,260	36,421,934,677
1951	624,008,052	37,752,553,688	13,353,541,306	1,638,566,845	53,368,671,892	5,801,058,409	47,567,613,484	87,546,409	47,480,067,075
1952	550,696,379	51,346,525,736	14,283,388,522	1,813,778,921	67,999,369,558	6,608,425,006	61,390,944,552	104,383,636	61,296,560,916
1953	613,419,582	54,362,967,793	15,808,006,063	1,864,741,185	72,649,134,647	7,824,090,621	64,825,044,026	154,459,602	64,670,584,424
1954	562,020,618	53,905,570,964	16,394,080,537	2,311,263,612	73,172,935,738	8,517,548,748	64,655,386,989	235,352,928	64,420,034,061

Year [1]	Department of the Army (formerly War Department) [4]	Department of the Navy [4]	Department of the Air Force [4]	Interest on the public debt	Other [1][2]	Total expenditures by major purposes [3][5]	Interfund transactions (deduct) [6]	Total expenditures [4][5]	Surplus, or deficit (−) [5]
				Expenditures					
1925	$370,980,708	$346,142,001		$881,806,662	$1,464,175,961	$3,063,105,332		$3,063,105,332	$717,043,353
1926	364,089,945	312,743,410		831,937,700	1,588,840,768	3,097,611,823		3,097,611,823	865,143,867
1927	369,114,122	318,909,096		787,019,578	1,498,986,878	2,974,029,674		2,974,029,674	1,155,364,766
1928	400,989,683	331,335,492		731,764,476	1,639,175,204	3,103,264,855		3,103,264,855	939,083,301
1929	425,947,194	364,561,544		678,330,400	1,830,020,348	3,298,859,486		3,298,859,486	734,390,739
1930	464,853,515	374,165,639		659,347,613	1,941,902,117	3,440,268,884		3,440,268,884	737,672,818
1931	486,141,754	353,768,185		611,559,704	2,125,964,360	3,577,434,003		3,577,434,003	−461,877,080
1932	476,305,311	357,517,834		599,276,631	3,226,103,049	4,659,202,825	$21,294	4,659,181,532	−2,735,289,708
1933	434,620,860	349,372,794		689,365,106	3,149,506,267	4,622,865,028	24,369,110	4,598,495,918	−2,601,652,085
1934	408,586,783	296,927,450		756,617,127	5,231,768,454	6,693,899,854	49,298,113	6,644,601,741	−3,029,631,943
1935	487,995,220	436,265,532		820,926,353	4,775,778,841	6,520,965,945	23,958,245	6,497,007,700	−2,791,052,100
1936	618,687,184	528,882,143		749,396,802	6,596,619,790	8,493,485,919	71,877,714	8,421,608,205	−4,424,649,230
1937	628,104,285	556,674,066		866,384,331	5,704,858,728	7,756,021,409	22,988,139	7,733,033,270	−2,777,420,714
1938	644,263,842	596,129,739		926,280,714	4,625,163,465	6,791,837,760	27,209,289	6,764,628,471	−1,176,616,598
1939	695,256,481	672,722,327		940,539,764	6,549,938,998	8,858,457,570	17,233,572	8,841,223,998	−3,862,158,040
1940	907,160,151	891,484,523		1,040,935,697	6,222,451,833	9,062,032,204	6,763,273	9,055,268,931	−3,918,019,161
1941	3,938,943,048	2,313,057,956		1,110,692,812	5,899,509,926	13,262,203,742	7,265,331	13,254,948,411	−6,159,272,358
1942	14,325,508,098	8,579,588,976		1,260,085,336	9,880,496,406	34,045,678,816	8,817,329	34,036,861,487	−21,490,242,732
1943	42,625,562,523	20,888,349,026		1,808,160,396	14,185,059,207	79,407,131,152	39,417,630	79,367,713,522	−57,420,430,365
1944	49,438,330,158	26,537,633,877		2,608,979,806	16,473,764,057	95,058,707,898	72,705,896	94,986,002,002	−51,423,392,541
1945	50,490,101,935	30,047,152,135		3,616,686,048	14,262,279,670	98,416,219,790	113,282,721	98,302,937,069	−53,940,916,126
1946	27,986,769,041	15,164,412,379		4,721,957,683	12,574,435,216	60,447,574,319	121,532,724	60,326,041,595	−20,676,170,609
1947	9,172,138,869	5,597,203,036		4,957,922,494	19,305,128,987	39,032,393,376	109,014,012	38,923,379,364	753,787,660
1948 [9]	7,698,546,403	4,284,619,125	$1,690,460,724	5,211,101,865	15,874,431,605	33,068,708,998	113,476,853	32,955,232,145	8,419,469,844
1949 [9]	7,862,397,097	4,434,705,920		5,339,396,336	20,180,029,420	39,506,989,497	32,576,510	39,474,412,987	−1,811,440,048
1950	5,789,467,599	4,129,545,653	3,520,632,580	5,749,913,064	20,427,444,299	39,617,003,195	72,966,260	39,544,036,935	−3,122,102,357
1951 [10]	8,635,938,754	5,862,548,845	6,358,603,828	5,612,654,812	17,688,084,620	44,057,830,859	87,546,409	43,970,284,450	3,509,782,624
1952	17,452,710,349	10,231,264,765	12,851,619,343	5,859,263,437	19,012,727,036	65,407,684,930	104,383,636	65,303,301,294	−4,016,640,378
1953	17,054,333,370	11,874,830,152	15,085,227,952	6,503,580,030	23,756,285,980	74,274,257,484	154,459,602	74,119,797,882	−9,449,213,457
1954	13,515,388,452	11,292,803,940	15,668,473,393	6,382,485,640	20,913,201,820	67,772,353,245	235,352,928	67,537,000,317	−3,116,966,256

Footnotes on following pages.

TABLE 2.—*Receipts and expenditures, fiscal years 1789–1965*—Continued

Year [1]	Receipts								Net receipts
	Customs [6]	Internal revenue		Other receipts [2]	Total receipts by major sources [3]	Refunds and transfers [7]	Receipts, less refunds and transfers	Interfund transactions [8] (deduct)	
		Income and profits taxes	Other						
1955	$606,396,634	$49,914,825,888	$16,373,865,694	$2,559,107,420	$69,454,195,640	$9,064,451,745	$60,389,743,895	$181,235,203	$60,208,508,692
1956	704,897,516	56,632,598,140	18,476,485,054	3,006,445,461	78,820,426,174	10,655,096,592	68,165,329,582	315,378,243	67,849,951,339
1957	754,461,446	60,560,424,638	19,611,546,168	2,748,872,386	83,675,304,639	12,646,654,662	71,028,649,978	466,763,865	70,561,886,113
1958	799,504,808	59,101,874,167	20,876,602,316	3,195,519,017	83,973,500,309	14,856,782,998	69,116,717,311	566,997,267	68,549,720,044
1959	948,412,215	58,826,253,507	20,971,719,301	3,157,881,036	83,904,266,060	15,634,013,346	68,270,252,715	354,904,091	67,915,348,624
1960	1,123,037,579	67,125,125,683	24,649,677,141	4,064,357,669	96,962,198,071	18,504,765,198	78,457,432,873	693,972,652	77,763,460,221
1961	1,007,755,214	67,917,940,793	26,483,145,605	4,082,499,734	99,491,341,346	21,177,963,732	78,313,377,614	653,952,709	77,659,424,906
1962	1,171,205,974	71,945,304,905	27,495,534,340	3,205,528,779	103,817,573,998	21,775,825,509	82,041,748,489	632,656,417	81,409,092,073
1963	1,240,537,884	75,323,714,353	30,601,680,928	4,435,613,440	111,601,546,606	24,711,939,419	86,889,607,187	513,396,839	86,376,210,348
1964	1,284,176,379	78,891,217,620	33,369,039,495	4,077,121,266	117,621,554,760	27,499,269,069	90,122,285,691	663,621,619	89,458,664,072
1965	1,477,548,820	79,792,016,279	34,642,617,442	4,622,351,942	120,534,534,483	26,592,872,291	93,941,662,193	869,865,301	93,071,796,892

[1] [illegible] 1789 to 1842 the [illegible] ended Dec. 31; from 1844 to date, on June 30. Figures for 1843 are for a half year, Jan. 1 to June 30.

[2] For postal [illegible], see table 26.

[3] [illegible] Jan. 3, 19[illegible], [illegible] by the [illegible] over- [illegible] as [illegible] as [illegible]. Also, [illegible] July 1, 19[illegible], [illegible] to the [illegible] of capital [illegible] both [illegible] surplus or deficit. Prior year [illegible] with [illegible], have been [illegible] table 3. [illegible] for [illegible] 1931 [illegible], see 1938 [illegible], p. 36, table 3.

[4] [illegible] all [illegible] of the Departments of the [illegible] (including [illegible]), the [illegible] 1949 the Air Force, [illegible] of War and Navy at [illegible] 1915. Department of the [illegible] those of the Department of the Air Force [illegible] Sept. 18, 1947) [illegible] 1949. Beginning with [illegible] of the Department of Defense [illegible] under "Other." [illegible]."

[5] [illegible] of including [illegible] 1948. Such [illegible] in [illegible] the "Surplus or deficit" [illegible] into account [illegible]. [illegible] 46 [illegible] of [illegible] debt [illegible]

Year[1]	Expenditures								Surplus, or deficit (−)[4]
	Department of the Army (formerly War Department)[4]	Department of the Navy[4]	Department of the Air Force[4]	Interest on the public debt	Other[2][4]	Total expenditures by major purposes[3][4]	Interfund transactions (deduct)[5]	Total expenditures[2][4]	
1955	$9,450,383,082	$9,731,611,019	$16,405,038,348	$6,370,361,774	$22,612,578,594	$64,569,972,817	$181,235,203	$64,388,737,614	−$4,180,228,921
1956	9,274,300,874	9,743,715,334	16,749,647,622	6,786,598,862	23,985,513,498	66,539,776,178	315,378,243	66,224,397,935	1,625,553,403
1957	9,704,788,331	10,397,223,998	18,360,926,051	7,244,193,486	23,725,946,561	69,433,078,427	466,763,865	68,966,314,562	1,595,671,650
1958	9,775,877,444	10,913,287,404	18,436,830,585	7,606,774,062	25,203,401,856	71,935,171,353	566,997,267	71,369,174,086	−2,819,44,61
1959	10,284,059,445	11,720,053,749	19,083,326,404	7,592,769,102	32,017,030,764	80,697,239,466	354,904,091	80,342,335,375	−12,426,986,751
1960	10,283,993,401	11,642,486,702	19,065,244,298	9,179,588,857	27,052,072,193	77,233,385,451	693,972,652	76,539,412,799	1,224,047,422
1961	11,102,620,707	12,214,297,075	19,777,722,554	8,957,241,615	30,117,238,211	82,169,120,163	653,952,709	81,515,167,454	−3,855,742,648
1962	12,425,939,098	13,280,183,267	20,839,825,719	9,119,759,908	32,773,715,105	88,419,422,997	632,656,417	87,786,766,581	−6,377,674,508
1963	12,782,038,071	14,092,991,160	20,822,869,577	9,895,303,949	35,561,991,141	93,155,193,898	513,396,839	92,641,797,059	−6,265,586,711
1964	13,406,914,629	14,652,424,948	20,749,576,521	10,665,858,127	38,873,222,190	98,347,996,414	663,621,619	97,684,374,795	−8,225,710,723
1965	13,040,706,276	13,553,468,854	18,471,150,005	11,346,454,580	40,964,989,796	97,376,769,511	809,865,301	96,506,904,210	−3,435,107,319

Economic Cooperation trust fund are treated as budget expenditures in this table. If effect is given to sec. 114(f) of the Economic Cooperation Act of 1948, the budget results for the fiscal years 1948 and 1949 would be as follows:

	Fiscal year 1948	Fiscal year 1949
Budget receipts	$41,374,701,989	$37,662,972,939
Budget expenditures	35,955,232,145	36,474,412,987
Budget surplus	5,419,469,844	1,188,559,952

[10] Beginning with fiscal 1951, investments of wholly owned Government corporations in public debt securities are excluded from budget expenditures and included in "Trust account and other transactions." See tables 6 and 16

TABLE 3.—*Refunds of receipts and transfers*

[On basis of daily Treasury statements through 1952; thereafter on basis of "Monthly Statement of

Fiscal year	Refunds of receipts [1] [2]				
	Internal revenue applicable to— [3]		Customs	Other	Total refunds of receipts
	Budget accounts	Trust accounts			
1931	$52, 561, 657		$21, 369, 007	$151, 045	$74, 081, 709
1932	64, 528, 539		17, 202, 969	80, 813	81, 812, 320
1933	45, 814, 734		12, 576, 842	92, 224	58, 483, 799
1934	37, 195, 935		14, 046, 350	43, 853	51, 286, 138
1935	49, 747, 858		20, 715, 688	89, 811	70, 553, 357
1936	32, 914, 628		14, 085, 195	20, 103	47, 019, 926
1937	33, 405, 891		16, 549, 408	34, 242	49, 989, 542
1938	76, 842, 701		16, 156, 340	38, 437	93, 037, 478
1939	44, 684, 686		16, 678, 803	63, 194	61, 426, 683
1940	61, 154, 655		17, 500, 945	49, 295	78, 704, 894
1941	52, 802, 242		27, 331, 472	55, 755	80, 189, 469
1942	65, 192, 248		19, 495, 861	87, 429	84, 775, 537
1943	53, 834, 008		16, 404, 512	86, 888	70, 325, 408
1944	242, 856, 877		14, 200, 774	196, 617	257, 254, 269
1945	1, 664, 545, 567		13, 843, 208	389, 150	1, 678, 777, 924
1946	2, 957, 114, 348		11, 224, 891	4, 688, 639	2, 973, 027, 879
1947	2, 982, 487, 490		17, 480, 263	6, 122, 643	3, 006, 090, 396
1948	2, 250, 391, 383		19, 050, 115	2, 433, 279	2, 271, 874, 777
1949	2, 817, 005, 313		17, 173, 186	3, 363, 506	2, 837, 542, 006
1950	2, 135, 455, 950		16, 091, 134	7, 959, 405	2, 159, 506, 489
1951	2, 082, 431, 536		15, 324, 391	8, 774, 689	2, 106, 530, 616
1952	2, 275, 188, 203		17, 520, 381	9, 497, 810	2, 302, 206, 394
1953	3, 094, 798, 198	$33, 000, 000	16, 949, 065	6, 091, 123	3, 150, 838, 386
1954	3, 345, 495, 593	40, 500, 000	20, 481, 971	11, 259, 809	3, 417, 737, 374
1955	3, 399, 978, 359	51, 000, 000	21, 619, 848	4, 389, 417	3, 476, 987, 625
1956	3, 652, 611, 883	66, 000, 000	23, 176, 262	8, 241, 988	3, 750, 030, 132
1957	3, 894, 119, 614	58, 206, 830	19, 907, 757	3, 315, 117	3, 975, 549, 317
1958	4, 412, 603, 597	165, 378, 009	17, 837, 948	2, 191, 001	4, 598, 010, 555
1959	4, 907, 159, 180	180, 329, 743	23, 220, 638	3, 043, 107	5, 113, 752, 669
1960	5, 024, 470, 807	192, 662, 543	18, 483, 391	1, 897, 066	5, 237, 513, 807
1961	5, 724, 571, 444	223, 737, 682	25, 439, 532	2, 260, 573	5, 976, 009, 231
1962	5, 957, 115, 953	278, 008, 196	29, 319, 402	1, 225, 761	6, 265, 669, 311
1963	6, 266, 560, 113	· 268, 950, 960	35, 174, 904	700, 987	6, 571, 386, 963
1964	6, 817, 461, 650	297, 114, 145	32, 313, 299	1, 196, 525	7, 148, 085, 619
1965	5, 668, 191, 495	322, 985, 824	35, 205, 161	3, 161, 988	6, 029, 544, 469

[1] Refunds of principal only; interest is included in expenditures.
[2] Internal revenue refunds by States for fiscal 1965 are shown in table 22.
[3] Beginning fiscal 1953, the principal amounts for refunds of employment taxes and certain excise taxes

to trust funds, fiscal years 1931–65

Receipts and Expenditures of the United States Government," see "Bases of Tables"]

| | Transfers to trust funds [3][4] | | | | | | Total refunds and transfers |
Federal old-age and survivors insurance trust fund	Federal disability insurance trust fund	Highway trust fund	Railroad retirement account	Unemployment trust fund	Total transfers to trust accounts	Total refunds and transfers
						$74,081,709
						81,812,320
						58,483,799
						51,286,138
						70,553,357
						47,019,926
$265,000,000					$265,000,000	314,989,542
387,000,000			$146,402,587		533,402,587	626,440,065
503,000,000			107,097,413		610,097,413	671,524,096
550,000,000			120,650,000		670,650,000	749,354,895
688,140,728			124,350,000		812,490,728	892,680,197
895,618,839			140,850,000		1,036,468,839	1,121,244,376
1,130,495,201			214,801,000		1,345,296,201	1,415,621,609
1,292,122,434			256,357,343		1,548,479,777	1,805,734,046
1,309,919,400			286,305,382		1,596,224,782	3,275,002,706
1,238,218,447			255,485,254		1,493,703,701	4,466,731,580
1,459,491,921			256,425,254		1,715,917,175	4,722,007,571
1,616,162,044			722,591,651		2,338,753,695	4,610,628,472
1,690,295,705			550,118,361		2,240,414,065	5,077,956,071
2,106,387,806			549,832,720		2,656,220,526	4,815,727,015
3,119,536,744			574,991,049		3,694,527,792	5,801,058,408
3,568,556,584			737,662,028		4,306,218,612	6,608,425,006
4,053,293,392			619,958,843		4,673,252,235	7,824,090,622
4,496,769,800			603,041,575		5,099,811,375	8,517,548,749
4,988,572,594			598,891,526		5,587,464,120	9,064,451,745
6,270,804,603			634,261,857		6,905,066,460	10,655,096,592
6,243,000,673	$333,276,575	$1,478,908,221	615,919,876		8,671,105,345	12,646,654,662
6,794,896,660	862,861,610	2,026,115,202	574,898,971		10,258,772,443	14,856,782,998
7,083,993,756	836,931,036	2,074,116,121	525,219,764		10,520,260,677	15,634,013,346
9,192,428,378	928,931,781	2,539,026,576	606,864,657		13,267,251,392	18,504,765,198
10,537,230,762	953,312,408	2,797,537,781	570,712,994	$343,160,557	15,201,954,501	21,177,963,732
10,600,021,548	944,542,132	2,948,690,128	564,264,483	452,637,906	15,510,156,198	21,775,825,509
12,351,191,003	993,762,625	3,278,697,756	571,534,041	945,367,031	18,140,552,456	24,711,939,419
14,335,126,928	1,056,855,735	3,519,156,643	593,476,801	846,567,343	20,351,183,450	27,499,269,069
14,572,359,321	1,082,023,273	3,658,509,171	635,545,447	614,890,010	20,563,327,822	26,592,872,291

(highway) are excluded from the transfers and are included with refunds of internal revenue receipts, applicable to trust accounts.

4 Tax receipts transferred and appropriated to the respective trust accounts. Details of these trust funds may be found in the table for each fund, beginning with table 67 of this annual report.

Table 4.—*Administrative budget receipts and expenditures, fiscal years 1963, 1964, and 1965*

[In thousands of dollars.   On basis of "Monthly Statement of Receipts and Expenditures of the United States Government," see "Bases of Tables"]

Receipts [1]	1963 [2]	1964 [2]	1965
Internal revenue:			
Individual income taxes:			
Withheld [3]_____	38,718,702	[2] 39,258,881	[4] 36,840,394
Other [3]_____	14,268,878	[2] 15,331,473	[4] 16,820,288
Total individual income taxes_____	52,987,581	54,590,354	53,660,683
Corporation income taxes_____	22,336,134	24,300,863	26,131,334
Excise taxes_____	13,409,737	13,950,232	14,792,779
Employment taxes:			
Federal Insurance Contributions Act and Self-Employment Contributions Act [3]_____	13,484,379	15,557,783	[4] 15,846,073
Railroad Retirement Tax Act_____	571,644	593,864	635,734
Federal Unemployment Tax Act_____	948,464	850,858	622,499
Total employment taxes_____	15,004,486	17,002,504	17,104,306
Estate and gift taxes_____	2,187,457	2,416,303	2,745,532
Total internal revenue_____	105,925,395	112,260,257	114,434,634
Customs duties_____	1,240,538	1,284,176	1,477,549
Miscellaneous receipts:			
Interest_____	764,782	954,625	1,077,419
Dividends and other earnings_____	859,655	983,911	1,392,918
Realization upon loans and investments_____	1,075,692	752,312	496,249
Recoveries and refunds_____	199,656	129,711	131,852
Royalties_____	123,909	130,560	132,059
Sales of Government property and products_____	633,426	740,516	858,760
Seigniorage_____	44,896	68,745	116,997
Other_____	733,597	316,741	416,097
Total miscellaneous receipts_____	4,435,613	4,077,121	4,622,352
Gross receipts_____	111,601,547	117,621,555	120,534,534
Deduct:			
Refunds of receipts: [5]			
Internal revenue:			
Applicable to budget accounts:			
Individual income taxes_____	5,399,835	5,893,412	4,869,011
Corporation income taxes_____	757,234	808,341	670,389
Excise taxes_____	89,300	93,004	99,423
Estate and gift taxes_____	20,192	22,704	29,369
Applicable to trust accounts:			
Federal old-age and survivors insurance trust fund_____	127,850	152,470	178,626
Federal disability insurance trust fund_____	11,575	13,330	13,064
Highway trust fund_____	126,319	126,637	123,498
Railroad retirement account_____	109	387	189
Unemployment trust fund_____	3,097	4,291	7,609
Subtotal internal revenue refunds_____	6,535,511	7,114,576	5,991,177
Customs_____	35,175	32,313	35,205
Other_____	701	1,197	3,162
Total refunds of receipts_____	6,571,387	7,148,086	6,029,544
Transfers to trust accounts: [6]			
Federal old-age and survivors insurance trust fund [3]___	12,351,191	14,335,127	[4] 14,572,359
Federal disability insurance trust fund [3]_____	993,763	1,056,856	[4] 1,082,023
Highway trust fund_____	3,278,698	3,519,157	3,658,509
Railroad retirement account_____	571,534	593,477	635,545
Unemployment trust fund_____	945,367	846,567	614,891
Total transfers to trust accounts_____	18,140,552	20,351,183	20,563,328

Footnotes at end of table.

TABLE 4.—*Administrative budget receipts and expenditures, fiscal years 1963, 1964, and 1965*—Continued

[In thousands of dollars]

Receipts [1] and expenditures	1963 [2]	1964 [2]	1965
Deduct—Continued			
Interfund transactions:			
Interest on loans to Government-owned enterprises___	499,383	648,044	852,289
Reimbursements_____	13,623	15,108	17,155
Fees and other charges_____	390	469	421
Total interfund transactions [7]_____	513,397	663,622	869,865
Total deductions_____	25,225,336	28,162,891	27,462,738
Net administrative budget receipts_____	86,376,210	89,458,664	93,071,797
EXPENDITURES [8]			
Legislative branch:			
Senate_____	29,310	29,921	34,194
House of Representatives_____	52,983	55,647	63,693
Architect of the Capitol_____	33,516	23,150	25,459
Botanic Garden_____	459	516	532
Library of Congress_____	18,264	21,197	23,848
Government Printing Office:			
General fund appropriations_____	19,613	22,125	23,842
Revolving fund (net)_____	−6,939	−1,044	−6,388
Total legislative branch_____	147,205	151,512	165,180
The judiciary:			
Supreme Court of the United States_____	2,012	2,108	2,491
Court of Customs and Patent Appeals_____	363	389	414
Customs Court_____	903	917	1,053
Court of Claims_____	1,026	1,107	1,244
Courts of appeals, district courts, and other judicial services_____	57,243	60,606	68,853
Total the judiciary_____	61,546	65,127	74,056
Executive Office of the President:			
Compensation of the President_____	150	150	150
The White House Office_____	2,502	2,705	2,872
Special projects_____	1,039	1,212	1,090
Executive mansion and grounds_____	660	662	686
Bureau of the Budget_____	5,825	6,636	7,089
Council of Economic Advisers_____	675	613	655
National Aeronautics and Space Council_____	394	419	459
National Council on the Arts_____	_____	_____	25
National Security Council_____	485	515	608
Office of Emergency Planning:			
Civil defense and defense mobilization functions of Federal agencies_____	4,792	3,789	3,915
Other_____	6,150	5,137	5,152
Office of Science and Technology_____	464	823	930
Special representative for trade negotiations_____	_____	400	562
Miscellaneous_____	−22	−156	−151
Total Executive Office of the President_____	23,113	22,904	24,043
Funds appropriated to the President:			
Disaster relief_____	30,803	21,191	43,461
Emergency fund for the President_____	389	509	940
Expansion of defense production (net)_____	−57,069	90,883	59,553
Expenses of management improvement_____	127	181	335
Peace Corps_____	42,259	60,397	78,573
International financial institutions:			
Investment in Inter-American Development Bank___	60,000	50,000	_____
Subscription to the International Development Association_____	61,656	61,656	61,656
Increase in quota in the International Monetary Fund_	_____	_____	258,750
Public works acceleration_____	62,460	331,820	321,625
Alaska programs_____	3,110	19,430	522
Other_____	671	673	636
Office of Economic Opportunity:			
Economic Opportunity Program_____	_____	_____	194,076
Public enterprise funds (net)_____	_____	_____	17,158

Footnotes at end of table.

TABLE 4.—*Administrative budget receipts and expenditures, fiscal years 1963, 1964, and 1965*—Continued

[In thousands of dollars]

Expenditures [8]	1963 [2]	1964 [2]	1965
Funds appropriated to the President—Continued			
Mutual defense and development:			
Military assistance:			
Office of Secretary of Defense:			
Repayment of credit sales [9]	−46, 402	−48, 154	−41, 069
Other	123, 984	85, 783	52, 810
Department of the Army	806, 322	620, 935	581, 037
Department of the Navy	198, 314	202, 365	196, 235
Department of the Air Force	630, 051	612, 610	434, 871
Agency for International Development	570	2, 576	1, 538
All other agencies	7, 915	9, 162	3, 158
Total military assistance	1, 720, 755	1, 485, 277	1, 228, 579
Economic assistance:			
Technical cooperation and development grants:			
General	244, 877	226, 305	226, 987
Alliance for Progress	94, 942	94, 430	97, 703
Social progress fund, Inter-American Development Bank	49, 000	65, 000	67, 016
Supporting assistance	493, 692	370, 969	387, 251
International organizations and programs	93, 568	178, 890	99, 711
Contingencies	137, 186	121, 804	150, 807
Other	56, 539	63, 600	63, 418
Public enterprise funds (net):			
Alliance for Progress, development loans	190, 595	112, 580	201, 818
Development loan funds	685, 622	768, 045	754, 468
Foreign investment guarantee fund	−2, 931	−4, 831	−7, 778
Total economic assistance	2, 043, 092	1, 996, 793	2, 041, 400
Total mutual defense and development	3, 763, 846	3, 482, 071	3, 269, 979
Total funds appropriated to the President	3, 968, 252	4, 118, 812	4, 307, 263
Agriculture Department:			
Agricultural Research Service:			
Intragovernmental funds (net)	137	−14	−67
Other	175, 618	191, 833	209, 933
Cooperative State research service	37, 992	41, 614	46, 867
Extension Service	74, 545	79, 402	84, 732
Farmer Cooperative Service	654	1, 213	1, 119
Soil Conservation Service:			
Conservation operations	92, 997	96, 214	105, 471
Flood prevention, watershed protection, and other	79, 608	85, 158	91, 324
Great Plains conservation program	9, 746	11, 882	12, 493
Economic Research Service	9, 742	10, 016	10, 138
Statistical Reporting Service	10, 019	11, 184	11, 587
Consumer and Marketing Service:			
Marketing services	40, 615	43, 540	39, 991
Payments to States and possessions	1, 425	1, 500	1, 500
Special milk program	95, 370	97, 484	86, 609
School lunch program	169, 596	180, 664	178, 580
Food stamp program			34, 395
Removal of surplus agricultural commodities	131, 784	270, 059	272, 932
Intragovernmental funds (net)	−5	−92	103
Other	773	835	847
Total Consumer and Marketing Service	439, 556	593, 990	614, 957
Foreign Agricultural Service	16, 562	19, 935	18, 482
Commodity Exchange Authority	1, 048	1, 117	1, 144
Agricultural Stabilization and Conservation Service:			
Expenses, Agricultural Stabilization and Conservation Service	r 88, 561	116, 845	107, 886
Sugar act program	76, 929	87, 071	92, 108
Agricultural conservation program	210, 788	213, 563	216, 139
Appalachian region conservation program			215
Cropland conversion program	3, 996	7, 097	9, 667
Emergency conservation measures	2, 701	3, 393	10, 008
Soil bank program	305, 378	289, 933	193, 698
Indemnity payments to dairy farmers			261
Intragovernmental funds (net)	11, 010	−109	

Footnotes at end of table.

TABLE 4.—*Administrative budget receipts and expenditures, fiscal years 1963, 1964, and 1965*—Continued

[In thousands of dollars]

Expenditures [8]	1963 [2]	1964 [2]	1965
Agriculture Department—Continued			
Commodity Credit Corporation:			
Foreign assistance and special export programs	2,091,022	1,889,044	2,492,151
Public enterprise funds (net):			
Price support and related programs [10]	3,115,735	r 3,174,896	2,645,754
Special activities [11]	−68,672	r 36,390	−740,268
Total Commodity Credit Corporation	5,138,085	5,100,330	4,397,638
Federal Crop Insurance Corporation:			
Administrative expenses	6,794	7,134	7,518
Federal Crop Insurance Corporation fund (net)	7,713	−819	903
Rural Electrification Administration:			
Loans	331,656	330,194	380,582
Salaries and expenses	10,396	11,354	11,832
Farmers Home Administration:			
Rural housing grants and loans	184,204	130,578	134,656
Rural renewal		143	946
Salaries and expenses	35,690	39,127	41,333
Public enterprise funds (net):			
Direct loan account	55,012	56,129	67,971
Emergency credit revolving fund	7,384	−9,138	30,257
Agricultural credit insurance fund	13,549	42,461	9,000
Rural housing for the elderly, revolving fund		100	1,008
Total Farmers Home Administration	295,838	259,400	285,171
Rural Community Development Service	−156	187	274
Office of the Inspector General			9,703
Office of General Counsel	3,774	4,032	3,965
Office of Information	1,577	1,644	1,698
Centennial observance of Agriculture	59		
National Agricultural Library	1,154	1,460	1,627
Office of Management Services			2,401
General administration:			
Intragovernmental funds (net)	241	−330	41
Other	3,424	3,902	3,487
Forest Service:			
Intragovernmental funds (net)	256	−1,183	−1,671
Other	286,861	318,223	354,721
Total Agriculture Department	7,735,260	7,896,864	7,298,052
Commerce Department:			
General administration:			
Public enterprise funds (net)	−13	−18	−7
Other	7,669	15,518	6,655
Economic development:			
Area Redevelopment Administration:			
Public enterprise funds (net)	−495	−2,389	−4,594
Other	39,460	71,600	80,596
Office of Appalachian Assistance			(*)
Community Relations Service			493
Office of Business Economics	1,848	1,908	2,312
Bureau of the Census	19,393	30,274	37,797
Business and Defense Services Administration	r 3,996	r 5,071	4,830
Office of Field Services	3,388	3,637	4,110
International activities	10,026	12,002	14,257
U.S. Travel Service	2,902	2,561	2,432
Total economic development	80,518	124,665	142,233
Science and technology:			
Coast and Geodetic Survey	25,077	33,496	33,758
Patent Office	26,504	27,277	30,652
National Bureau of Standards:			
Intragovernmental funds (net)	−3,513	−2,391	7,022
Other	r 46,020	r 51,065	56,768

Footnotes at end of table.

TABLE 4.—*Administrative budget receipts and expenditures, fiscal years 1963, 1964, and 1965*—Continued

[In thousands of dollars

Expenditures [8]	1963 [2]	1964 [2]	1965
Commerce Department—Continued			
Science and technology—Continued			
Weather Bureau	85, 294	89, 400	100, 585
Total science and technology	179, 382	198, 847	229, 385
Transportation:			
Inland Waterways Corporation (net)	−825	−800	
Maritime Administration:			
Public enterprise funds (net)	9, 131	5, 150	−2, 365
Operating-differential subsidies	220, 677	203, 037	213, 334
Other	134, 989	98, 662	125, 759
Bureau of Public Roads [12]	44, 121	40, 359	42, 307
Transportation research	1	922	1, 096
Total transportation	408, 094	347, 332	380, 131
Total Commerce Department	675, 650	686, 344	758, 397
Defense Department:			
Military:			
Military personnel:			
Department of the Army	4, 302, 548	4, 602, 457	4, 696, 875
Department of the Navy	3, 485, 621	3, 833, 389	4, 020, 657
Department of the Air Force	4, 196, 666	4, 549, 838	4, 669, 092
Defense agencies	1, 014, 673	1, 209, 447	1, 384, 286
Total military personnel	12, 999, 509	14, 195, 131	14, 770, 910
Operation and maintenance:			
Department of the Army	3, 757, 264	3, 637, 623	3, 681, 146
Department of the Navy	3, 058, 088	3, 071, 007	3, 369, 994
Department of the Air Force	4, 682, 113	4, 718, 975	4, 771, 019
Defense agencies	351, 169	504, 435	526, 558
Total operation and maintenance	11, 848, 634	11, 932, 040	12, 348, 718
Procurement:			
Department of the Army	2, 370, 713	2, 314, 565	1, 764, 065
Department of the Navy	6, 580, 951	6, 042, 190	4, 932, 523
Department of the Air Force	7, 698, 028	6, 959, 249	5, 100, 536
Defense agencies	6, 774	34, 822	42, 216
Subtotal	16, 656, 466	15, 350, 826	11, 839, 339
Classification adjustment [13]	−339, 100		
Total procurement	16, 317, 366	15, 350, 826	11, 839, 339
Research, development, test, and evaluation:			
Department of the Army	1, 354, 425	1, 338, 005	1, 344, 396
Department of the Navy	1, 429, 341	1, 577, 846	1, 293, 639
Department of the Air Force	3, 300, 374	3, 721, 620	3, 145, 756
Defense agencies	291, 424	383, 977	452, 425
Subtotal	6, 375, 564	7, 021, 448	6, 236, 216
Classification adjustment [13]	339, 100		
Total research, development, test, and evaluation	6, 714, 664	7, 021, 448	6, 236, 216
Military construction:			
Department of the Army	178, 352	232, 523	216, 272
Department of the Navy	195, 784	190, 275	251, 900
Department of the Air Force	741, 984	554, 361	507, 066
Defense agencies	27, 468	49, 134	31, 669
Total military construction	1, 143, 588	1, 026, 292	1, 006, 908

Footnotes at end of table.

TABLE 4.—*Administrative budget receipts and expenditures, fiscal years 1963, 1964, and 1965*—Continued

[In thousands of dollars]

Expenditures [8]	1963 [2]	1964 [2]	1965
Defense Department—Continued			
Military—Continued			
Family housing:			
Department of the Army	155,499	204,015	206,538
Department of the Navy	87,843	132,386	154,592
Department of the Air Force	181,291	240,903	255,106
Defense agencies	2,026	2,215	2,418
Total family housing	426,658	579,519	618,653
Civil defense	202,614	106,825	92,726
Revolving and management funds (net):			
Public enterprise funds:			
Department of the Army:			
Defense production guarantees	−72	−37	−37
Department of the Navy:			
Defense production guarantees	−696	1,095	−1,236
Other	−24	42	−14
Department of the Air Force, defense production guarantees	4,436	2,672	−1,211
Defense agencies, defense production guarantees		−1	(*)
Civil defense procurement fund	−41	(*)	−8
Intragovernmental funds:			
Department of the Army	−464,729	−75,244	−102,360
Department of the Navy	−743,917	−195,808	−468,589
Department of the Air Force	17,949	1,933	23,753
Defense agencies	−213,519	−187,136	−190,900
Total revolving and management funds	−1,400,613	−452,483	−740,601
Total military	48,252,421	49,759,598	46,172,869
Civil:			
Army:			
Corps of Engineers:			
Rivers and harbors and flood control	1,069,380	1,091,869	1,177,364
Intragovernmental funds (net)	2,543	839	−8,392
The Panama Canal:			
Canal Zone Government	26,720	30,806	32,986
Panama Canal Company:			
Public enterprise funds (net)	8,364	2,074	3,100
Thatcher Ferry Bridge	1,716	−311	327
Total the Panama Canal	36,801	32,569	36,412
Other	19,314	27,730	28,426
Navy, wildlife conservation, etc		2	3
Air Force, wildlife conservation, etc	28	25	34
Total civil	1,128,066	1,153,035	1,233,847
Total Defense Department	49,380,487	50,912,634	47,406,716
Health, Education, and Welfare Department:			
Food and Drug Administration:			
Public enterprise fund (net)		−111	−199
Other	29,227	38,386	40,848
Office of Education:			
Payments to school districts	276,869	283,688	311,413
Assistance for school construction	66,242	50,601	41,846
Defense educational activities	198,336	239,576	270,284
Other	82,258	86,023	218,332
Vocational Rehabilitation Administration	97,594	119,908	137,313
Public Health Service:			
Community health:			
Hospital construction activities	189,117	194,482	203,518
Other	80,616	ͬ119,259	159,173

Footnotes at end of table.

TABLE 4.—*Administrative budget receipts and expenditures, fiscal years 1963, 1964, and 1965*—Continued

[In thousands of dollars]

Expenditures [8]	1963 [2]	1964 [3]	1965
Health, Education, and Welfare Department—Continued			
Public Health Service—Continued			
Environmental health	111, 537	141, 426	152, 963
Medical services	118, 799	124, 683	132, 773
National Institutes of Health	723, 596	909, 601	779, 787
Operation of commissaries, narcotic hospitals (net)	3	−3	7
Emergency health activities	19, 998	20, 080	12, 631
Other	10, 939	[r] 36, 091	12, 211
Total Public Health Service	1, 254, 604	1, 545, 619	1, 453, 063
Saint Elizabeths Hospital	7, 490	9, 348	9, 959
Social Security Administration:			
Operating fund, Bureau of Federal Credit Unions (net)	−132	116	−175
Other	32	5	78
Welfare Administration:			
Grants to States for public assistance	2, 729, 582	2, 944, 052	3, 059, 498
Grants for maternal and child welfare	76, 058	89, 355	109, 796
Other	65, 862	61, 437	55, 342
Special institutions:			
American Printing House for the Blind	719	775	865
Freedmen's Hospital	3, 740	4, 174	3, 929
Gallaudet College	1, 983	2, 354	4, 355
Howard University	11, 127	12, 088	11, 618
General administration and other:			
Intragovernmental funds (net)	49	−81	−337
Other	7, 700	10, 419	12, 334
Total Health, Education, and Welfare Department	4, 909, 340	5, 497, 732	5, 740, 161
Interior Department:			
Public land management:			
Bureau of Land Management	113, 568	118, 599	131, 345
Bureau of Indian Affairs:			
Public enterprise funds (net):			
Revolving fund for loans	4, 861	5, 094	179
Other	2	−2	−1
Other	191, 330	199, 123	234, 483
National Park Service	110, 543	127, 830	130, 296
Bureau of Outdoor Recreation	969	1, 900	3, 827
Office of Territories:			
Public enterprise funds (net)	23	−103	280
Other	31, 034	40, 245	24, 946
The Alaska Railroad (net)	−942	1, 809	15, 025
Mineral resources:			
Geological Survey	[r] 57, 982	[r] 61, 077	68, 209
Bureau of Mines:			
Public enterprise funds (net)	−9, 508	9, 794	20, 425
Other	37, 366	38, 854	40, 962
Office of Coal Research	1, 470	2, 627	3, 822
Office of Minerals Exploration	[r] 569	[r] 538	627
Office of Oil and Gas	556	613	686
Fish and Wildlife Service:			
Office of Commissioner of Fish and Wildlife	376	380	443
Bureau of Commercial Fisheries:			
Public enterprise funds (net)	−1, 402	−537	391
Other	27, 166	32, 725	37, 778
Bureau of Sports Fisheries and Wildlife	65, 791	70, 229	79, 498
Water and power development:			
Bureau of Reclamation:			
Public enterprise funds (net):			
Continuing fund for emergency expenses, Fort Peck project, Montana	−996	−896	−2, 332
Upper Colorado River Basin fund	106, 529	95, 123	60, 312
Other	238, 644	245, 156	269, 966
Total Bureau of Reclamation	344, 177	339, 383	327, 947
Bonneville Power Administration	29, 970	44, 991	54, 895
Southeastern Power Administration	457	758	644
Southwestern Power Administration	6, 216	10, 303	7, 776
Office of Saline Water	8, 674	9, 494	11, 468

Footnotes at end of table.

TABLE 4.—*Administrative budget receipts and expenditures, fiscal years 1963, 1964, and 1965*—Continued

[In thousands of dollars]

Expenditures [8]	1963 [2]	1964 [2]	1965
Interior Department—Continued			
Secretarial offices:			
Office of the Solicitor	3,677	3,902	4,374
Office of the Secretary	3,322	3,831	4,206
Office of Water Resources Research			2,296
Virgin Islands Corporation (net)	554	326	−2,074
Total Interior Department	1,028,800	1,123,784	1,204,753
Justice Department:			
Legal activities and general administration	58,083	60,893	64,830
Federal Bureau of Investigation	135,527	143,024	159,507
Immigration and Naturalization Service	66,323	67,101	72,207
Federal Prison System:			
Federal Prison Industries, Inc. (net)	−3,121	−4,610	−1,439
Other	60,222	61,586	63,053
Total Justice Department	317,035	327,994	358,158
Labor Department:			
Bureau of Labor Statistics	15,825	17,870	18,161
Bureau of International Labor Affairs	791	938	722
Manpower Administration:			
Public enterprise funds (net):			
Advances to employment security administration account, unemployment trust fund	−85,248	−7,435	−2,226
Farm labor supply revolving fund	−1,226	−1,200	−358
Manpower development and training activities	51,824	109,970	230,041
Bureau of Apprenticeship and Training	5,291	5,647	5,547
Payment to the Federal extended compensation account	2,392	−19,358	
Unemployment compensation for Federal employees and ex-servicemen	152,859	152,514	122,398
Other	9,998	9,250	7,870
Total Manpower Administration	135,889	249,389	363,272
Labor-management relations:			
Bureau of Veterans' Reemployment Rights	653	756	813
Labor-Management Services Administration	5,929	7,239	7,223
Wage and labor standards:			
Bureau of Labor Standards	4,156	3,709	3,601
Women's Bureau	914	802	773
Wage and Hour Division	17,789	19,926	20,295
Bureau of Employees' Compensation:			
Employees' compensation claims and expenses	65,263	58,812	52,658
Other	3,894	4,369	4,432
Office of the Solicitor	4,306	4,616	4,851
Office of the Secretary	1,870	1,989	2,728
Total Labor Department	257,279	370,415	479,529
Post Office Department:			
Public enterprise fund (net)—postal fund	770,335	577,699	804,542
State Department:			
Administration of foreign affairs:			
Salaries and expenses	151,915	148,852	[14] 175,024
Acquisition, operation, and maintenance of buildings abroad	13,427	15,690	26,196
Intragovernmental funds (net)	−1,450	356	854
Other	2,957	3,272	3,631
Total administration of foreign affairs	166,849	168,170	205,705
International organizations and conferences:			
Contributions to international organizations	94,554	99,503	86,790
Loans to the United Nations	72,070	4,193	
Other	4,231	4,931	5,852

Footnotes at end of table.

TABLE 4.—*Administrative budget receipts and expenditures, fiscal years 1963, 1964, and 1965*—Continued

[In thousands of dollars]

Expenditures [6]	1963 [2]	1964 [2]	1965
State Department—Continued			
International commissions	15,999	12,556	16,489
Educational exchange	45,580	45,956	58,358
Other	9,211	11,817	9,800
Total State Department	408,493	347,126	382,993
Treasury Department:			
Office of the Secretary:			
Public enterprise funds (net):			
Reconstruction Finance Corporation liquidation fund	−3,127	−2,436	19
Federal Farm Mortgage Corporation liquidation fund	−533	−410	−277
Civil defense program fund	−135	−59	−28
Intragovernmental funds (net)	−1	1	1
Other	4,625	5,283	5,812
Bureau of Accounts:			
Interest on uninvested funds	10,917	10,719	11,752
Claims, judgments, and relief acts	26,248	31,896	74,424
Government losses in shipment fund (net)	536	339	44
Salaries and expenses	31,935	31,853	32,115
Other	(*)	(*)	1
Bureau of Customs:			
Intragovernmental funds (net)			−1
Other	67,268	74,621	77,953
Bureau of Engraving and Printing:			
Intragovernmental funds (net)	−2,272	253	906
Other	43	148	272
Bureau of the Mint	7,534	9,164	15,346
Bureau of Narcotics	4,659	5,389	5,458
Bureau of the Public Debt	48,787	48,545	49,651
U.S. Coast Guard:			
Intragovernmental funds (net)	−2,195	−1,630	−172
Other	298,777	351,436	386,665
Internal Revenue Service:			
Interest on refunds of taxes	73,857	88,409	77,237
Payments to Puerto Rico for taxes collected	44,780	44,962	42,941
Other	497,273	560,196	586,627
Office of the Treasurer:			
Check forgery insurance fund (net)	−2	20	2
Other	16,111	13,657	6,342
U.S. Secret Service	7,540	9,134	10,462
Interest on the public debt: [16]			
Public issues	8,604,272	9,280,107	9,803,834
Special issues	1,291,032	1,385,751	1,542,620
Total interest on the public debt	9,895,304	10,665,858	11,346,455
Total Treasury Department	11,027,931	11,947,349	12,730,006
Atomic Energy Commission	2,757,876	2,764,565	2,624,996
Federal Aviation Agency:			
Grants-in-aid for airports	51,493	65,248	70,598
Other	674,817	685,302	724,015
Total Federal Aviation Agency	726,311	750,550	794,613
General Services Administration:			
Real property activities:			
Construction, public buildings projects	91,779	160,818	136,033
Repair and improvement of public buildings	62,502	73,365	82,730
Intragovernmental funds (net)	5,707	−21,162	12,531
Other	232,420	260,128	274,601
Personal property activities:			
Intragovernmental funds (net)	−17,895	28,313	13,356
Other	40,091	46,610	53,426
Utilization and disposal activities	9,699	9,585	9,713
Records activities	14,389	14,546	16,011
Transportation and communications activities	4,652	4,230	7,382

Footnotes at end of table.

TABLE 4.—*Administrative budget receipts and expenditures, fiscal years 1963, 1964, and 1965*—Continued

[In thousands of dollars]

Expenditures [8]	1963 [2]	1964 [2]	1965
General Services Administration—Continued			
Defense materials activities:			
Public enterprise funds (net)			3
Intragovernmental funds (net)	−859	−114	68
Strategic and critical materials	22,671	15,957	16,284
General activities:			
Public enterprise funds (net)	−168	−582	−218
Intragovernmental funds (net)	−700	−729	−230
Other	1,609	1,746	1,985
Total General Services Administration	465,896	592,711	623,676
Housing and Home Finance Agency:			
Office of the Administrator:			
Public enterprise funds (net):			
College housing loans	283,574	219,334	220,744
Liquidating programs	−2,014	−1,799	−985
Urban renewal fund	173,208	235,012	324,352
Rehabilitation loan fund		195	180
Urban mass transportation			11,068
Other	53,608	79,919	87,508
Open-space land grants	265	5,130	6,212
Other	27,180	ʳ31,214	34,486
Total Office of the Administrator	535,821	569,006	683,563
Federal National Mortgage Association (net):			
Loans for secondary market operations		4,460	−4,460
Purchase of preferred stock		−70,820	−38,000
Management and liquidating functions fund	−162,265	−138,359	−105,412
Special assistance functions fund	−277,044	−141,925	−375,849
Government mortgage liquidation fund			[16] −24,927
Total Federal National Mortgage Association	−439,309	−346,644	−548,648
Federal Housing Administration (net)	134,951	−43,442	−115,350
Public Housing Administration (net)	178,867	149,207	230,116
Total Housing and Home Finance Agency	410,330	328,127	249,681
National Aeronautics and Space Administration	2,552,347	4,170,997	5,092,904
Veterans' Administration:			
Compensation, pensions, and benefit programs	4,001,326	4,057,282	4,180,995
Public enterprise funds (net):			
Direct loans to veterans and reserves	−86,187	−32,303	−129,834
Loan guaranty revolving fund	−22,922	76,498	38,301
Other	−20,676	−16,820	−29,095
Other	1,301,282	1,393,444	1,427,577
Total Veterans' Administration	5,172,823	5,478,101	5,487,944
Other independent agencies:			
Advisory Commission on Intergovernmental Relations	412	366	422
Alaska International Rail and Highway Commission	−1		
Alaska Temporary Claims Commission			5
American Battle Monuments Commission	1,826	1,786	1,952
Central Intelligence Agency—construction	1,722	285	354
Civil Aeronautics Board:			
Payments to air carriers	81,857	84,122	80,423
Other	9,374	10,023	11,205
Civil Service Commission:			
Payment to civil service retirement and disability fund	30,000	62,000	65,000
Government payment for annuitants, employees health benefits fund	6,789	9,500	12,210
Government contribution, retired employees health benefits fund	13,200	14,800	14,800
Other	23,694	25,118	25,102
Total Civil Service Commission	73,683	111,418	117,112
Commission of Fine Arts	82	87	95
Commission on Civil Rights	1,046	817	1,151
Commission on International Rules of Judicial Procedure	3	7	(*)
Equal Employment Opportunity Commission			29
Export-Import Bank of Washington (net)	−391,550	−701,784	−357,231

Footnotes at end of table.

TABLE 4.—*Administrative budget receipts and expenditures, fiscal years 1963, 1964, and 1965*—Continued

[In thousands of dollars]

Expenditures [8]	1963 [2]	1964 [2]	1965
Other independent agencies—Continued			
Farm Credit Administration (net):			
Short-term credit investment fund	13, 310	5, 490	3, 375
Banks for cooperatives investment fund	−11, 980	−13, 926	−20, 287
Revolving fund for administrative expenses	2, 567	−161	99
Total Farm Credit Administration	3, 898	−8, 598	−16, 813
Federal Coal Mine Safety Board of Review	59	64	66
Federal Communications Commission	14, 088	16, 717	16, 747
Federal Home Loan Bank Board (net):			
Federal Savings and Loan Insurance Corp. fund	−263, 543	−248, 096	−204, 698
Other	−118	−322	134
Federal Maritime Commission	2, 142	2, 611	2, 857
Federal Mediation and Conciliation Service	5, 052	5, 702	6, 284
Federal Power Commission	10, 712	12, 324	13, 116
Federal Development Planning Committees for Alaska		−30	87
Federal Trade Commission	11, 515	12, 118	13, 662
Foreign Claims Settlement Commission	804	8, 924	35, 047
General Accounting Office	42, 294	45, 116	44, 948
Historical and memorial commissions	100	123	135
Indian Claims Commission	269	294	303
Interstate Commerce Commission	23, 519	24, 378	26, 491
National Capital Housing Authority	40	43	39
National Capital Planning Commission	1, 882	735	3, 538
National Capital Transportation Agency	2, 323	982	617
National Commission on Food Marketing			408
National Commission on Technology, Automation, and Economic Progress			134
National Labor Relations Board	20, 945	22, 049	25, 221
National Mediation Board	1, 812	1, 939	1, 892
National Science Foundation	206, 372	310, 072	308, 892
Outdoor Recreation Resources Review Commission	88	(*)	
Participation in Interstate Federal Commissions:			
Appalachian Regional Commission			40
Delaware River Basin Commission	130	153	131
Interstate Commission on the Potomac River Basin	5	5	5
President's Advisory Committee on Labor-Management Policy	120	113	106
Railroad Retirement Board	−601		
Railroad Retirement Board—Military service credits			13, 834
Renegotiation Board	2, 325	2, 509	2, 650
St. Lawrence Seaway Development Corp. (net)	1, 437	154	905
Securities and Exchange Commission	13, 207	14, 337	15, 276
Selective Service System	34, 489	40, 936	43, 211
Small Business Administration:			
Public enterprise fund (net)	137, 408	124, 316	236, 221
Salaries and expenses	4, 850	8, 591	6, 658
Other	150	25	43
Total Small Business Administration	142, 407	132, 933	242, 922
Smithsonian Institution	20, 204	21, 791	27, 986
Subversive Activities Control Board	338	348	409
Tariff Commission	2, 767	2, 932	3, 271
Tax Court of the United States	1, 770	1, 928	2, 087
Tennessee Valley Authority (net)	53, 449	59, 291	47, 937
U.S. Arms Control and Disarmament Agency	2, 333	6, 195	7, 302
U.S. Information Agency:			
Informational media guaranties fund (net)	1, 850	940	873
Salaries and expenses	131, 564	140, 620	150, 168
Construction of radio facilities	14, 756	12, 157	6, 639
Other	7, 294	7, 392	7, 434
Total U.S. Information Agency	155, 463	161, 109	165, 114
U.S.-Puerto Rico Commission on the status of Puerto Rico			44
U.S. study commissions	775	170	(*)
Total other independent agencies	293, 322	159, 177	707, 854

Footnotes at end of table.

TABLE 4.—*Administrative budget receipts and expenditures, fiscal years 1963, 1964, and 1965*—Continued

[In thousands of dollars]

Expenditures [8]	1963 [2]	1964 [2]	1965
District of Columbia:			
Federal payment to District of Columbia	33, 199	40, 368	40, 720
Advances for general expenses (repayable)	7, 000	7, 000	9, 000
Loans to District of Columbia for capital outlay	24, 950	9, 450	10, 700
Loans to District of Columbia (stadium fund)	416	656	832
Interfund transactions (−) [7]	−513, 397	−663, 622	−869, 865
Net administrative budget expenditures	92, 641, 797	97, 684, 375	96, 506, 904
Administrative budget surplus, or deficit (−)	−6, 265, 587	−8, 225, 711	−3, 435, 107

r Revised.
* Less than $500.
[1] Internal revenue and customs receipts are stated on a collection basis. Other receipts are reported on a deposits confirmed basis. See "Bases of Tables," annual report 1962, p. 502.
[2] Certain figures for the fiscal years 1963 and 1964 have been adjusted to correspond to classifications for fiscal 1965.
[3] Distribution between income taxes and employment taxes is made in accordance with provisions of section 201 of the Social Security Act, as amended, for transfer to the Federal old-age and survivors and Federal disability insurance trust funds (42 U.S.C. 401(a)).
[4] Includes adjustments of prior estimates as follows: Income taxes withheld, $99,145,461; income taxes—other, $75,781,944; transfers to Federal old-age and survivors insurance trust fund, −$169,015,179; and transfers to Federal disability insurance trust fund, −$5,912,226.
[5] Amounts of refunds of principal of overpaid taxes formerly reported net of reimbursements from trust fund accounts are reported herein on a gross basis. These reimbursements to the Internal Revenue Service for refunds are included and netted with amounts of transfers to the respective trust fund accounts.
[6] The principal amount of refunds of employment taxes and excise (highway) taxes are excluded from the transfers and are included in refunds of internal revenue receipts applicable to trust accounts.
[7] Mainly interest payments by Government corporations and agencies that borrow from the Treasury. For details of these interfund transactions, fiscal years 1962-65, see table 8. These interfund transactions deducted from budget receipts and expenditures do not include payments to the Treasury by wholly owned Government corporations for retirement of their capital stock and for disposition of earnings. Those capital transfers have been excluded from budget receipts and expenditures since July 1, 1948.
[8] Expenditures are stated on the basis of checks issued (except interest on the public debt) and certain cash payments. See "Bases of Tables."
[9] Net cash transactions under provisions of the act of Sept. 4, 1961 (22 U.S.C. 2316).
[10] Residual of gross receipts and expenditures after reduction for certain costs which are included in amounts shown for special activities financed by Commodity Credit Corporation.
[11] Includes certain amounts transferred from price support operations for which expenditures may have been made in prior years, in addition to adjustments representing recoveries received from other programs.
[12] Most Bureau of Public Roads expenditures are made from the highway trust fund and do not appear in this table.
[13] Estimated adjustments to reclassify expenditures for comparability with the 1964 budget appropriation structure. These adjustments are between the major categories of expenditures and do not affect the total expenditures for military functions. Amounts shown for the respective departments represent the expenditures as recorded in accounts of the departments and do not include any adjustments for comparability.
[14] Gives effect to reimbursements collected for administrative support furnished to other agencies amounting to $87,445,411.
[15] Expenditures are stated on an accrual basis.
[16] The proceeds from sale of participation certificates amounting to $299,262,000 were credited to this fund and paid over to Veterans' Administration and to the Special Assistance Functions fund, FNMA.

TABLE 5.—*Trust receipts and expenditures, fiscal years 1963, 1964, and 1965*

[In thousands of dollars.   On basis of "Monthly Statement of Receipts and Expenditures of the United States Government," see "Bases of Tables"]

Receipts	1963 [1]	1964 [1]	1965
Legislative Branch:			
Payments from general fund	179	180	180
Other	1, 451	1, 831	1, 463
The judiciary:			
Judicial survivors annuity fund:			
Contributions	595	645	790
Interest on investments	63	76	90
Funds appropriated to the President:			
Mutual defense and development:			
Military assistance advances	949, 789	719, 701	824, 431
Economic assistance	3, 624	769	1, 584
Other	128	164	231
Agriculture Department	51, 035	55, 711	57, 948
Commerce Department:			
Highway trust fund: [2]			
Transfers from general fund receipts	3, 405, 017	3, 645, 793	3, 782, 008
Less refunds of taxes	−126, 319	−126, 637	−123, 498
Interest on investments	14, 268	20, 361	11, 035
Total highway trust fund	3, 292, 966	3, 539, 518	3, 669, 544
Other	28, 499	33, 052	10, 317
Defense Department:			
Military	5, 549	5, 178	5, 745
Civil:			
Payments from general fund	2, 957	3, 057	3, 136
Other	34, 689	42, 940	25, 965
Health, Education, and Welfare Department:			
Federal old-age and survivors insurance trust fund: [3]			
Transfers from general fund receipts:			
Appropriated	12, 466, 041	14, 488, 597	14, 777, 985
Unappropriated	13, 000	−1, 000	−27, 000
Less refunds of taxes	−127, 850	−152, 470	−178, 626
Deposits by States	989, 571	1, 166, 599	1, 257, 853
Interest and profits on investments	512, 408	539, 044	583, 125
Other	2, 490	2, 604	3, 190
Total Federal old-age and survivors insurance trust fund	13, 855, 660	16, 043, 374	16, 416, 527
Federal disability insurance trust fund: [4]			
Transfers from general fund receipts:			
Appropriated	1, 006, 338	1, 070, 186	1, 095, 088
Unappropriated	−1, 000		
Less refunds of taxes	−11, 575	−13, 330	−13, 064
Deposits by States	81, 858	86, 305	93, 221
Interest and profits on investments	69, 635	67, 660	65, 247
Other			17
Total Federal disability insurance trust fund	1, 145, 256	1, 210, 821	1, 240, 508
Other	541	867	338
Interior Department:			
Indian tribal funds	46, 504	70, 253	58, 591
Payments from general fund	22, 654	23, 468	65, 843
Other	11, 455	10, 835	12, 870
Labor Department:			
Unemployment trust fund: [5]			
Employment security administration account:			
Transfers (Federal unemployment taxes):			
Appropriated	948, 339	854, 306	622, 038
Unappropriated	126	−3, 448	461
Less refunds of taxes	−3, 097	−4, 291	−7, 609
Advances from general (revolving) fund	173, 500	239, 705	194, 968
Less return of advances to the general fund	−255, 412	−244, 205	−194, 968
State accounts—deposits by States	3, 008, 934	3, 042, 408	3, 051, 539
Federal unemployment account—Less transfer of receipts to Labor			(*)
Railroad unemployment insurance account:			
Deposits by Railroad Retirement Board	149, 798	144, 087	142, 781
Advances from railroad retirement account	37, 699	35, 187	58, 230
Advances from general fund			
Less return of advances to the general fund	−601		

Footnotes at end of table.

TABLE 5.—*Trust receipts and expenditures, fiscal years 1963, 1964, and 1965*—Con.

[In thousands of dollars]

Receipts	1963 [1]	1964 [1]	1965
Labor Department—Continued			
Unemployment trust fund [5]—Continued			
Railroad unemployment insurance administration fund:			
Deposits by Railroad Retirement Board	7,884	11,970	9,520
Federal extended compensation account:			
Advances from general fund	2,392	ʳ1	
Interest and profits on investments	191,107	212,608	255,265
Total unemployment trust fund	4,260,668	4,288,328	4,132,225
Other	39	89	130
State Department:			
Foreign service retirement and disability fund:			
Deductions from salaries and other receipts	3,298	3,440	3,878
Employing agency contributions	3,136	3,308	3,687
Receipts from civil service retirement and disability fund	336	385	796
Interest on investments	1,461	1,507	1,577
Other	110	338	1,258
Treasury Department	16,454	26,054	24,235
Atomic Energy Commission	274	629	1,230
Federal Aviation Agency	4		
General Services Administration	2,001	283	2,244
National Aeronautics and Space Administration	1	201	541
Veterans' Administration:			
Government life insurance fund:			
Premiums and other receipts	16,926	15,805	14,733
Payments from general fund	−240	−143	−119
Interest on investments	35,114	34,464	33,762
National service life insurance fund:			
Premiums and other receipts	476,733	478,300	472,984
Payments from general fund	5,993	5,969	7,029
Interest on investments	175,023	176,471	182,145
Other	1,889	1,870	1,811
Total Veterans' Administration	711,438	712,737	712,344
Other independent agencies:			
Civil Service Commission:			
Civil Service retirement and disability fund:			
Deductions from employees' salaries, etc	920,753	979,886	1,050,416
Payments from other funds:			
Employing agency contributions	920,853	979,941	1,050,356
Federal contribution	30,000	62,000	65,000
Voluntary contributions, donations, etc	13,191	14,592	16,430
Interest and profits on investments	362,259	419,838	482,171
Total Civil Service Commission	2,247,055	2,456,257	2,664,373
Railroad Retirement Board:			
Railroad retirement account:			
Transfers (Railroad Retirement Act taxes):			
Appropriated	559,049	608,970	630,430
Unappropriated	12,486	−15,493	5,116
Fines and penalties		(*)	
Interest and profits on investments	105,214	130,128	143,134
Interest on advances to railroad unemployment insurance account	8,946	9,508	12,167
Repayment of advances to railroad unemployment insurance account		37,454	77,935
Payment from Federal old-age and survivors and Federal disability insurance trust funds	442,132	421,775	459,253
Other			13,834
Total Railroad Retirement Board	1,127,826	1,192,341	1,341,868
Other	24,325	48,098	9,824
District of Columbia:			
Revenues from taxes, etc	253,836	272,163	287,263
Payments from general fund:			
Federal contribution	33,199	40,368	40,720
Advances for general expenses	10,000	33,000	50,000
Less return of advances to general fund	−3,000	−26,000	−41,000
Loans for capital outlay	24,950	9,450	10,700
Other loans and grants	22,380	26,606	41,705

Footnotes at end of table.

TABLE 5.—*Trust receipts and expenditures, fiscal years 1963, 1964, and 1965*—Con.

[In thousands of dollars]

Receipts and expenditures	1963 [1]	1964 [1]	1965
Interfund transactions (−):			
Payments to employees' retirement fund receipts	−13, 320	−14, 563	−16, 340
Payments between funds:			
FOASI trust fund to railroad retirement account	−422, 523	−402, 636	−435, 638
Unemployment trust fund from railroad retirement account	−37, 699	−35, 187	−58, 230
Other	−31, 305	−68, 994	−128, 230
Total interfund transactions (−)[5]	−504, 847	−521, 379	−638, 438
Net trust receipts	27, 688, 538	30, 330, 646	31, 047, 259
EXPENDITURES			
Legislative Branch	1, 723	1, 644	1, 897
The judiciary-judicial survivors annuity fund	416	490	488
Funds appropriated to the President:			
Mutual defense and development:			
Military assistance advances	673, 736	480, 751	744, 553
Economic assistance	1, 015	2, 024	2, 172
Other	70	152	139
Agriculture Department:			
Trust enterprise funds (net)	−518	717	−1, 083
Other	45, 776	50, 854	53, 108
Commerce Department:			
Highway trust fund-Federal-aid highways	3, 016, 701	3, 645, 013	4, 026, 117
Other	26, 141	25, 303	20, 962
Defense Department:			
Military	5, 116	5, 149	5, 439
Civil:			
Trust enterprise funds (net)	10	6	−2
Other	29, 162	44, 142	31, 387
Health, Education, and Welfare Department:			
Federal old-age and survivors insurance trust fund:			
Administrative expenses—Bureau of Old-Age and Survivors Insurance	275, 423	312, 382	322, 788
Reimbursement of administrative expenses from Federal disability insurance trust fund	−62, 935	−63, 850	−75, 111
Payments to general fund—administrative expenses	48, 458	51, 714	52, 378
Payments to Railroad Retirement Board	422, 523	402, 636	435, 638
Benefit payments	13, 844, 584	14, 579, 166	15, 225, 894
Construction	1, 657	2, 558	305
Total Federal old-age and survivors insurance trust fund	14, 529, 710	15, 284, 607	15, 961, 893
Federal disability insurance trust fund:			
Administrative expenses—reimbursement to Federal old-age and survivors insurance trust fund	65, 349	66, 358	78, 223
Payments to general fund—administrative expenses	3, 577	3, 841	3, 768
Benefit payments	1, 170, 678	1, 251, 207	1, 392, 190
Payment to Railroad Retirement Board	19, 609	19, 139	23, 615
Total Federal disability insurance trust fund	1, 259, 214	1, 340, 545	1, 497, 796
Other	549	833	562
Interior Department:			
Indian tribal funds	66, 871	66, 093	74, 015
Other	12, 067	10, 882	11, 250
Justice Department (net):			
Alien property activities	31, 689	52, 783	−168, 758
Federal Prison System commissary funds	18	11	27
Labor Department:			
Unemployment trust fund: [5]			
Employment security administration account:			
Salaries and expenses, Bureau of Employment Security	11, 552	12, 829	13, 357
Grants to States for unemployment compensation and employment service administration	336, 420	412, 707	399, 396
Payments to general fund:			
Reimbursements and recoveries	5, 604	54, 594	112, 018
Interest on refunds of taxes	73	93	172
Payment of interest on advances from general (revolving) fund	3, 337	2, 935	2, 226

Footnotes at end of table.

TABLE 5.—*Trust receipts and expenditures, fiscal years 1963, 1964, and 1965*—Con.

[In thousands of dollars]

Expenditures	1963 [1]	1964 [1]	1965
Labor Department—Continued			
Unemployment trust fund [1]—Continued			
Railroad unemployment insurance account:			
Benefit payments	166, 744	133, 912	115, 243
Temporary extended unemployment benefits	94		
Repayment of advances to railroad retirement account		37, 454	77, 935
Payment of interest on advances from railroad retirement account	8, 946	9, 508	12, 167
Repayment of advances from general fund	9, 853	7, 090	
Railroad unemployment insurance administration fund:			
Administrative expenses	8, 840	9, 070	7, 861
State accounts:			
Withdrawals by States	2, 812, 637	2, 703, 275	2, 389, 612
Reimbursements from Federal extended compensation account	−2, 392	−1	
Federal extended compensation account:			
Temporary extended unemployment compensation payments	−14, 967	−2, 305	−1
Reimbursements to State accounts	2, 392	1	
Repayment of advances from general fund	466, 327	325, 402	−1
Total unemployment trust fund	3, 815, 459	3, 706, 564	3, 129, 985
Other	166	126	234
State Department:			
Foreign service retirement and disability fund	7, 085	7, 486	8, 307
Other	193	300	1, 243
Treasury Department	22, 677	18, 492	22, 959
Atomic Energy Commission	125	638	942
Federal Aviation Agency	19	36	
General Services Administration:			
Trust enterprise funds (net)	4	−19	−4
Other	2, 169	383	214
Housing and Home Finance Agency:			
Federal National Mortgage Association (net):			
Loans for secondary market operations and purchase of preferred stock		66, 360	42, 460
Other secondary market operations	−730, 222	−103, 752	49, 008
National Aeronautics and Space Administration		98	50
Veterans' Administration:			
Government life insurance fund-benefits, refunds, and dividends	79, 131	72, 204	70, 528
National service life insurance fund-benefits, refunds, and dividends	747, 095	585, 267	544, 996
Other	1, 660	1, 655	1, 514
Other independent agencies:			
Civil Service Commission:			
Civil service retirement and disability fund	1, 175, 887	1, 318, 296	1, 438, 147
Employees health benefits fund (net)	−12, 326	−14, 562	−9, 278
Employees' life insurance fund (net)	−32, 239	−49, 383	−26, 361
Retired employees health benefits fund (net)	−143	−115	−783
Total Civil Service Commission	1, 131, 179	1, 254, 236	1, 401, 726
National Capital Housing Authority (net)	−2, 437	−436	588
Railroad Retirement Board:			
Railroad retirement account:			
Administrative expenses	9, 833	11, 021	10, 342
Benefit payments, etc	1, 064, 001	1, 092, 451	1, 116, 370
Advances to railroad unemployment insurance account	37, 699	35, 187	58, 230
Interest on refunds of taxes	1	(*)	9
Total Railroad Retirement Board	1, 111, 533	1, 138, 659	1, 184, 951
Other:			
Trust enterprise funds (net)	10	43	−116
Other	289	652	377
District of Columbia	333, 546	355, 247	384, 522

Footnotes at end of table.

TABLE 5.—*Trust receipts and expenditures, fiscal years 1963, 1964, and 1965*—Con.

[In thousands of dollars]

Expenditures	1963 [1]	1964 [1]	1965
Deposit fund accounts:			
Food stamps issued (receipts):			
Payments from general fund	−18, 640	−28, 646	−32, 505
Receipts from sales	−31, 051	−44, 996	−52, 844
Food stamps redeemed (expenditures)	48, 602	73, 663	83, 774
Other deposit funds (net)	146, 756	−566, 999	−208, 031
Subtotal trust and deposit fund expenditures	26, 364, 812	27, 549, 262	28, 896, 842
Government-sponsored enterprises (net):			
Farm Credit Administration:			
Banks for cooperatives	29, 289	37, 092	189, 231
Federal intermediate credit banks	276, 889	182, 203	149, 032
Federal land banks	176, 418	248, 401	561, 021
Federal Home Loan Bank Board:			
Home loan banks	363, 215	1, 571, 914	659, 661
Federal Deposit Insurance Corporation	−160, 546	−182, 866	−179, 957
Total Government-sponsored enterprises	685, 265	1, 856, 744	1, 378, 989
Interfund transactions (−)[6]	−504, 847	−521, 379	−638, 438
Net trust expenditures	26, 545, 231	28, 884, 626	29, 637, 393
Excess of trust receipts, or expenditures (−)	1, 143, 307	1, 446, 019	1, 409, 866

r Revised.
*Less than $500.
[1] Certain figures for the fiscal years 1963 and 1964 have been adjusted to correspond to classifications for fiscal 1965.
[2] Details of this trust fund may be found in table 75.
[3] Details of this trust fund may be found in table 73.
[4] Details of this trust fund may be found in table 72.
[5] Details of this trust fund may be found in table 82.
[6] Mainly financial interchanges between trust funds resulting in receipts and expenditures. For details of these interfund transactions for the fiscal years 1962–65, see table 9.

TABLE 6.—*Investments in public debt and agency securities (net), fiscal years 1963, 1964, and 1965*

[In thousands of dollars. On basis of "Monthly Statement of Receipts and Expenditures of the United States Government," see "Bases of Tables"]

Investing agency	1963 [1]	1964 [1]	1965
Public enterprise funds:			
Commerce Department:			
Federal ship mortgage insurance fund	3, 543	−2, 785	
War risk insurance revolving fund	3, 153	212	96
Federal National Mortgage Association:			
Public debt securities:			
Government mortgage liquidation fund			5, 794
Guaranteed securities (FHA debentures):			
Management and liquidating functions	−4, 891	−55, 675	−21, 706
Special assistance functions fund	−22, 445	−8, 051	−961
Not guaranteed securities:			
Government mortgage liquidation fund			19, 115
Federal Housing Administration:			
Public debt securities	−4, 965	62, 309	−195, 060
Guaranteed securities (FHA debentures)	41, 322	76, 053	1, 694
Public Housing Administration		24, 500	−17, 000
Federal Savings and Loan Insurance Corporation	268, 594	244, 000	207, 528
Tennessee Valley Authority	−10, 000		
Other:			
Housing and Home Finance Administrator (FHA debentures)	−4		
Veterans' Administration	12, 632	22, 585	28, 566
Total public enterprise funds	286, 938	363, 147	28, 066
Trust accounts, etc.:			
Judicial survivors annuity fund	241	225	430
Highway trust fund	241, 808	−68, 715	−343, 634
Foreign service retirement and disability fund	1, 181	1, 023	1, 530
Federal disability insurance trust fund [2]	−128, 894	−138, 735	−262, 943
Federal old-age and survivors insurance trust fund [2]	−821, 476	691, 679	460, 855
Unemployment trust fund [2]	456, 478	573, 223	966, 764
Federal National Mortgage Association:			
Secondary market operations:			
Public debt securities	91, 500	−91, 500	
Guaranteed securities (FHA debentures)	−15, 423	−18, 264	1, 006
Not guaranteed securities	59, 570	−59, 570	
Veterans' life insurance funds:			
Government life insurance fund:			
Public debt securities	−24, 807	−47, 162	−22, 386
Not guaranteed securities		25, 000	
National service life insurance fund	−89, 614	69, 077	125, 765
Civil Service Commission:			
Civil service retirement and disability fund	1, 073, 961	1, 124, 529	1, 212, 396
Employees health benefits fund	14, 426	15, 103	8, 920
Employees' life insurance fund	55, 836	49, 503	26, 614
Retired employees health benefits fund	−1, 531		1, 225
Railroad retirement account	501	68, 963	149, 281
Government-sponsored enterprises (net):			
Farm Credit Administration:			
Banks for cooperatives	51	1, 408	−91
Federal intermediate credit banks	781	−53	−1, 728
Federal land banks	−1, 933	−79	−2, 106
Federal Home Loan Bank Board:			
Home loan banks	611, 935	−140, 744	−103, 846
Federal Deposit Insurance Corporation	160, 546	182, 866	179, 957
Other [3]	96, 703	174, 299	−70, 546
Total trust accounts, etc	1, 781, 840	2, 412, 077	2, 327, 464
Net investments, or sales (−)	2, 068, 778	2, 775, 224	2, 355, 530

[1] Certain figures for the fiscal years 1963 and 1964 as published in previous annual reports have been adjusted to correspond to classifications for the fiscal year 1965.
[2] Takes into account accrued interest, discount, or premium on securities purchased, and net amortization or repayments.
[3] Includes Exchange Stabilization Fund.

TABLE 7.—*Sales and redemptions of Government agency securities in market (net), fiscal years 1963, 1964, and 1965*

[In thousand of dollars. On basis of "Monthly Statement of Receipts and Expenditures of the United States Government," see "Bases of Tables"]

Issuing agency	1963 [1]	1964 [1]	1965
Public enterprise funds:			
Guaranteed by the United States:			
Federal Farm Mortgage Corporation in liquidation_____	9	17	12
Federal Housing Administration:			
Issues (net) to Government agencies_____	r 1,442	5,937	19,967
Issues (net) to the public_____	−163,854	−212,350	202,718
Homes Owners' Loan Corporation_____	12	14	8
Not guaranteed by the United States:			
Federal National Mortgage Association (management and liquidating functions)_____	5		
Home Owners' Loan Corporation_____	1	(*)	(*)
Tennessee Valley Authority_____		−35,000	−45,000
Trust enterprise funds:			
Not guaranteed by the United States:			
Federal National Mortgage Association (secondary market operations)_____	597,018	261,710	−98,592
Government-sponsored enterprises (net):			
Not guaranteed by the United States:			
Farm Credit Administration:			
Banks for cooperatives_____	−29,340	−38,500	−189,140
Federal intermediate credit banks_____	−277,670	−182,150	−147,305
Federal land banks_____	−174,486	−248,322	−558,915
Federal Home Loan Bank Board:			
Home loan banks_____	−975,150	−1,431,170	−555,815
Net redemptions, or sales (−)_____	−1,022,013	−1,879,813	−1,372,060

r Revised.
*Less than $500.
[1] Certain figures for fiscal years 1963 and 1964 as published in previous annual reports have been adjusted to correspond to classifications for fiscal year 1965.

TABLE 8.—*Interfund transactions excluded from both net budget receipts and budget expenditures, fiscal years 1962–65*

[In thousands of dollars]

Interest and other payments	Fiscal Year			
	1962	1963	1964	1965
Interest paid Treasury by revolving funds: [1]				
Funds appropriated to the President, expansion of defense production [2]	7,860	6,328	154,294	124,948
Department of Agriculture:				
Commodity Credit Corporation	329,584	186,384	199,169	458,861
Farmers Home Administration:				
Agricultural credit insurance fund	923	998	2,296	2,763
Direct loan account	9,000	10,706	12,019	13,805
Economic opportunity loan fund				124
Department of Commerce, Federal ship mortgage insurance fund	9		263	353
Department of Defense—civil, Panama Canal Company fund	9,364	10,006	10,894	11,336
Department of Health, Education, and Welfare, Bureau of Federal Credit Unions				
Department of the Interior:				
Colorado River Dam fund, Boulder Canyon project	3,081	3,030	2,946	2,857
Upper Colorado River storage project				752
Virgin Islands Corporation	346	364	403	406
Treasury Department, Civil defense program fund	19	13	8	4
Housing and Home Finance Agency:				
Office of the Administrator:				
College housing loans	25,314	32,502	41,394	48,968
Urban renewal fund	3,227	4,944	5,344	5,895
Public facility loans	2,006	2,709	3,540	4,903
Federal National Mortgage Association	114,096	118,279	99,410	86,872
Public Housing Administration	1,128	1,441	2,099	187
Veterans' Administration, direct loans to veterans and reserves	40,050	47,474	48,795	36,324
Export-Import Bank [2]	56,757	51,134	34,381	15,139
St. Lawrence Seaway Development Corporation	2,165	2,200	2,952	4,000
Small Business Administration	14,249	20,149	26,521	30,740
Tennessee Valley Authority		148	695	2,396
U.S. Information Agency, informational media guaranties fund	610	571	622	656
Total interest payments	619,789	499,383	648,044	852,289
Other payments:				
Department of Defense, civil:				
Reimbursements:				
Panama Canal Company:				
Net cost of Canal Zone Government [4]	11,829	13,193	14,678	16,725
Part of treaty payment to Panama for use of Canal Zone	410	430	430	430
Fees and other charges	628	390	469	421
Total other payments	12,868	14,014	15,577	17,576
Total interfund transactions	632,656	513,397	663,622	869,865

[1] On loans and other interest-bearing U.S. investments.
[2] By various agencies for programs under the Defense Production Act.
[3] Excludes transactions under Defense Production Act.
[4] Less tolls paid for U.S. Government vessels.
NOTE.—For figures from 1932–61, see annual report for 1961, pp. 450–456.

TABLE 9.—*Interfund transactions excluded from both net trust account receipts and net trust account expenditures, fiscal years 1962–65*

[In thousands of dollars]

Trust fund	1962	1963	1964	1965
Federal old-age and survivors insurance trust fund [1]	360,788	422,523	402,636	435,638
Federal disability insurance trust fund [1][2]	13,235	22,023	21,647	26,727
Railroad retirement account [1][3]	101,470	37,699	35,187	58,230
Unemployment trust fund [3][4]	37,215	8,946	46,962	90,102
Federal employees' retirement funds [5]	2,836	336	385	796
District of Columbia [6]	12,254	13,320	14,563	17,445
Alien property activities [7]	----------	----------	----------	9,500
Total	527,797	504,847	521,379	638,438

[1] Payments are made between the railroad retirement account and the Federal old-age and survivors insurance and Federal disability insurance trust funds so as to place those funds in the position in which they would have been if railroad employment after 1936 had been included under social security coverage.

[2] Includes interest on amounts reimbursed to the Federal old-age and survivors insurance trust fund for administrative expenses.

[3] Includes temporary advances to the railroad unemployment insurance account in the unemployment trust fund when the balance in the account is insufficient to meet payments of benefits and refunds due or to become due.

[4] Repayment of advances with interest to the railroad retirement account.

[5] Transfers from the civil service retirement and disability fund to the foreign service retirement and disability fund.

[6] Contributions and transfers of deductions from employees' salaries to the civil service retirement and disability fund; and advances to National Park Service for fiscal 1965.

[7] Payment to Foreign Claims Settlement Commission.

TABLE 10.—*Public enterprise (revolving) funds, receipts and expenditures for fiscal year 1965 and net for 1964 and 1965*

[In thousands of dollars. On basis of "Monthly Statement of Receipts and Expenditures of the United States Government," see "Bases of Tables"]

Classification	Fiscal year 1965			Fiscal year 1964
	Receipts	Expenditures	Net receipts (−), or expenditures	Net receipts (−), or expenditures
Funds appropriated to the President:				
Expansion of defense production	67,702	127,255	59,553	90,883
Office of Economic Opportunity	135	17,293	17,158	
Mutual defense and development—economic assistance:				
Alliance for Progress, development loans	61,531	263,349	201,818	112,580
Development loan funds	51,813	806,280	754,468	768,045
Foreign investment guarantee fund	7,790	12	−7,778	−4,831
Total funds appropriated to the President	188,972	1,214,190	1,025,218	966,678
Agriculture Department:				
Commodity Credit Corporation:				
Price support and related programs [1]	3,238,552	5,884,307	2,645,754	3,174,896
Special activities [1]	274,887	−465,380	−740,268	36,390
Federal Crop Insurance Corporation	27,939	28,842	903	−819
Farmers Home Administration:				
Direct loan account	327,584	395,556	67,971	56,129
Other	285,054	325,319	40,265	33,423
Total Agriculture Department	4,154,018	6,168,644	2,014,627	3,300,019
Commerce Department:				
Area Redevelopment Administration	4,740	146	−4,594	−2,389
Maritime Administration	9,446	7,080	−2,365	5,150
Other	16	9	−7	−817
Total Commerce Department	14,201	7,235	−6,966	1,945
Defense Department:				
Military:				
Defense production guarantees	15,016	12,533	−2,484	3,729
Other	708	687	−21	42
Civil–Panama Canal Company	131,609	134,709	3,100	2,074
Total Defense Department	147,334	147,929	595	5,846
Health, Education, and Welfare Department	7,658	7,290	−368	3
Interior Department:				
Bureau of Indian Affairs	2,261	2,439	178	5,093
Bureau of Mines	24,482	44,906	20,425	9,794
Bureau of Reclamation	13,902	71,882	57,980	94,227
Other	26,629	40,251	13,622	1,495
Total Interior Department	67,273	159,479	92,205	110,609
Labor Department:				
Advances to employment security administration account, unemployment trust fund	197,194	194,968	−2,226	−7,435
Farm labor supply revolving fund	1,687	1,329	−358	−1,200
Total Labor Department	198,881	196,298	−2,583	−8,635
Post Office Department, postal fund	4,662,663	5,467,205	804,542	577,699
Treasury Department:				
Office of the Secretary	323	37	−286	−2,905
Bureau of Accounts, Government losses in shipment fund	(*)	44	44	339
Office of the Treasurer, check forgery insurance fund	673	675	2	20
Total Treasury Department	997	757	−240	−2,546
General Services Administration	233	17	−215	−582

Footnotes at end of table.

TABLE 10.—*Public enterprise (revolving) funds, receipts and expenditures for fiscal year 1965 and net for 1964 and 1965*—Continued

[In thousands of dollars]

Classification	Fiscal year 1965			Fiscal year 1964
	Receipts	Expenditures	Net receipts (−), or expenditures	Net receipts (−), or expenditures
Housing and Home Finance Agency:				
Office of the Administrator:				
College housing loans	99, 030	319, 773	220, 744	219, 334
Liquidating programs	1, 265	279	−985	−1, 799
Urban renewal fund	191, 686	516, 037	324, 352	235, 012
Rehabilitation loan fund		180	180	
Urban mass transportation	310	11, 378	11, 068	195
Other	30, 037	117, 544	87, 508	79, 919
Federal National Mortgage Association:				
Loans for secondary market operations	566, 820	562, 360	−4, 460	4, 460
Purchase of preferred stock	38, 000		−38, 000	−70, 820
Management and liquidating functions fund	284, 577	179, 165	−105, 412	−138, 359
Special assistance functions fund	574, 660	198, 811	−375, 849	−141, 925
Government mortgage liquidation fund	47, 171	22, 244	[3] −24, 927	
Federal Housing Administration	953, 126	837, 775	−115, 350	−43, 442
Public Housing Administration	175, 910	406, 026	230, 116	149, 207
Total Housing and Home Finance Agency	2, 962, 591	3, 171, 575	208, 984	[r] 291, 782
Veterans' Administration:				
Direct loans to veterans and reserves	341, 378	211, 544	−129, 834	−32, 303
Loan guaranty revolving fund	362, 096	400, 397	38, 301	76, 498
Other	97, 945	68, 850	−29, 095	−16, 820
Total Veterans' Administration	801, 418	680, 790	−120, 628	27, 375
Other independent agencies:				
Export-Import Bank of Washington	1, 083, 926	726, 695	−357, 231	−701, 784
Farm Credit Administration	23, 123	6, 309	−16, 813	−8, 598
Federal Home Loan Bank Board	342, 459	137, 894	−204, 565	−248, 419
Saint Lawrence Seaway Development Corp	5, 761	6, 665	905	154
Small Business Administration	288, 676	524, 896	236, 221	124, 316
Tennessee Valley Authority	321, 578	369, 515	47, 937	59, 291
United States Information Agency	2, 734	3, 607	873	940
Total other independent agencies	2, 068, 256	1, 775, 582	−292, 674	−774, 098
Total public enterprise funds	15, 274, 494	18, 996, 991	3, 722, 497	[r] 4, 496, 095

[r] Revised.   *Less than $500.

[1] Residual of gross receipts and expenditures after reduction for certain costs which are included in amounts shown for special activities.

[2] Includes certain costs transferred from price support operations for which expenditures may have been made in prior years, in addition to adjustments representing recoveries received from other programs.

[3] The proceeds from sale of participation certificates amounting to $299,262,000.00 were credited to this fund and paid to the Veterans' Administration and to the Special Assistance Functions fund, FNMA.

NOTE.—This table supplies receipt and expenditure data for public enterprise funds included in table 4 on a net basis.

TABLE 11.—*Trust enterprise (revolving) funds, receipts and expenditures for fiscal year 1965 and net for 1964 and 1965*

[In thousands of dollars. On basis of "Monthly Statement of Receipts and Expenditures of the United States Government," see "Bases of Tables"]

Classification	Fiscal year 1965			Fiscal year 1964
	Receipts	Expenditures	Net receipts (−), or expenditures	Net receipts (−), or expenditures
Agriculture Department:				
Farmers Home Administration	8, 513	7, 431	−1, 083	717
Defense Department—Civil:				
U.S. Soldiers' Home	136	134	−2	6
Justice Department:				
Alien property activities	331, 112	162, 354	−168, 758	52, 783
Federal Prison System, commissary funds	2, 472	2, 499	27	11
General Services Administration:				
Records activities: National Archives trust fund	574	570	−4	−19
Housing and Home Finance Agency:				
Federal National Mortgage Association:				
Loans for secondary market operations and purchase of preferred stock	562, 360	604, 820	42, 460	66, 360
Other secondary market operations	367, 814	416, 823	49, 008	−103, 752
Other independent agencies:				
Civil Service Commission:				
Employees health benefits fund	464, 222	454, 944	−9, 278	−14, 562
Employees' life insurance fund	181, 889	155, 528	−26, 361	−49, 383
Retired employees health benefits fund	27, 872	27, 090	−783	−115
National Capital Housing Authority	10, 409	10, 997	588	−436
Federal Communications Commission	401	285	−116	43
Total trust enterprise funds	1, 957, 774	1, 843, 474	−114, 300	−48, 346

NOTE.—This table supplies receipt and expenditure data for trust enterprise funds included in table 5 on a net basis.

TABLE 12.—Administrative budget receipts and expenditures monthly and total for fiscal year 1965

[In millions of dollars.   On basis of "Monthly Statement of Receipts and Expenditures of the United States Government," see "Bases of Tables"]

Receipts and expenditures	July	August	September	October	November	December	January	February	March	April	May	June	Total 1965
RECEIPTS													
Internal Revenue:													
Individual income taxes withheld	1,172	4,809	2,669	1,158	4,956	2,969	1,181	5,302	3,207	1,091	5,371	2,956	36,840
Individual income taxes—other	377	159	2,255	264	112	430	2,506	872	928	5,852	696	2,369	16,820
Corporation income taxes	646	419	3,950	572	449	3,953	607	473	6,759	1,187	520	6,597	26,131
Excise taxes	1,234	1,284	1,203	1,176	1,244	1,257	1,045	1,214	1,303	1,150	1,325	1,357	14,793
Employment taxes	624	2,338	1,148	479	1,491	1,779	399	2,810	1,459	1,311	2,861	1,406	17,104
Estate and gift taxes	219	219	166	205	168	192	183	213	308	370	283	218	2,746
Customs	120	112	122	126	124	76	76	106	155	139	128	145	1,478
Miscellaneous receipts	739	323	252	294	429	330	332	338	398	322	398	477	4,622
Gross receipts	5,131	9,662	11,766	4,275	8,972	10,025	6,329	11,329	14,517	11,423	11,582	15,525	120,535
Deduct:													
Refunds of receipts:													
Applicable to budget accounts	215	206	215	90	100	90	-85	620	1,582	1,284	1,066	323	5,707
Applicable to trust accounts	4	(*)	1	85	(*)	(*)	192	33	(*)	2	5	1	323
Transfers to trust accounts	948	2,718	1,472	691	1,827	1,059	502	3,118	1,745	1,580	3,152	1,752	20,563
Interfund transactions	477	84	6	10	9	19	77	40	8	8	92	45	870
Total deductions	1,644	3,009	1,694	877	1,935	1,168	687	3,811	3,328	2,874	4,315	2,121	27,463
Net receipts	3,487	6,653	10,072	3,398	7,037	8,856	5,642	7,518	11,188	8,549	7,268	13,404	93,072
EXPENDITURES													
Legislative branch	11	12	19	13	12	9	14	11	14	16	20	16	165
The Judiciary	5	6	5	7	5	7	5	5	6	9	6	6	74
Executive Office of the President	2	2	2	2	2	2	2	2	2	2	3	2	24
Funds appropriated to the President:													
Mutual defense and development:													
Military assistance	26	32	69	49	67	70	79	69	105	82	197	382	1,229
Economic assistance	129	237	131	156	171	181	199	118	152	191	153	223	2,041
Other	40	60	47	48	88	42	30	48	42	39	145	408	1,037
Agriculture Department:													
Commodity Credit Corp	839	686	370	483	50	323	-127	36	105	11	-71	-801	1,905
Foreign assistance and special export programs	229	73	145	162	165	138	187	149	193	226	179	875	2,492
Other	91	220	173	225	331	283	394	138	226	240	200	242	2,900
Commerce Department		54	42	87	49	51	73	73	45	69	49	77	758

Defense Department:												
Military:												
Department of the Army	721	932	1,034	961	1,008	1,042	951	894	989	982	954	1,339	11,807
Department of the Navy	907	891	1,068	1,207	1,057	1,213	1,099	1,095	1,216	1,273	1,130	1,396	13,553
Department of the Air Force	1,372	1,392	1,557	1,597	1,449	1,698	1,435	1,353	1,743	1,578	1,531	1,767	18,471
Defense agencies	168	171	181	181	178	223	169	198	187	204	187	201	2,249
Undistributed stock fund transactions	62	117	59	−21	20	−13	30	26	38	19	39	−377	....
Civil defense	8	9	8	10	14	12	7	7	8	7	7	−4	93
Total military	3,238	3,512	3,907	3,936	3,726	4,174	3,691	3,574	4,183	4,063	3,848	4,322	46,173
Health, Education, and Welfare Department	92	104	120	122	107	111	77	79	89	102	95	137	1,234
Interior Department	457	468	493	482	417	509	495	482	314	541	547	535	5,740
Justice Department	115	112	137	114	91	108	78	85	99	80	88	97	1,205
Labor Department	36	28	27	29	38	38	29	26	29	30	27	31	358
Post Office Department	70	74	73	40	53	67	80	−156	52	28	53	46	480
State Department	32	73	95	74	23	31	82	102	44	33	86	129	805
Treasury Department:	59	33	45	42	34	33	35	31	22	−3	19	33	383
Interest on the public debt	957	913	927	923	917	955	966	933	961	948	955	989	11,346
Interest on refunds, etc.	7	10	9	9	6	8	7	9	5	9	5	6	89
Other	99	91	87	141	95	116	100	97	98	111	129	131	1,295
Atomic Energy Commission	261	228	225	238	207	230	213	191	219	199	184	230	2,625
Federal Aviation Agency	67	66	66	65	81	77	61	56	59	61	63	74	795
General Services Administration	49	63	46	42	39	57	71	42	63	50	48	53	624
Housing and Home Finance Agency:													
Federal National Mortgage Assoc.	−14	−39	102	−159	−188	75	−107	−42	−37	−73	−39	−28	−549
Other	114	78	59	24	51	99	86	56	75	51	73	33	798
National Aeronautics and Space Administration	334	385	386	387	406	435	407	423	461	529	433	507	5,093
Veterans' Administration	441	478	487	466	364	494	448	477	458	450	449	474	5,488
Other agencies:													
Export-Import Bank of Washington	−29	−29	−19	34	−422	−39	−27	3	−14	55	167	−35	−357
Small Business Administration	15	61	24	20	27	30	17	12	11	3	10	12	243
Other	4	7	8	9	4	4	2	(*)	−3	−1	3	12	48
Tennessee Valley Authority	88	57	154	67	54	69	68	59	62	141	63	−109	774
District of Columbia	23	8	−6	(*)	1	1	16	....	1	−11	24	3	61
Interfund transactions (−)[4]	−477	−84	−6	−10	−9	−19	−77	−40	−2	−8	−92	−45	−870
Net expenditures	7,410	8,083	8,450	8,329	7,051	8,770	7,676	7,146	8,139	8,268	8,116	9,070	96,507
Surplus, or deficit (−)	−3,923	−1,430	1,622	−4,930	−15	86	−2,033	372	3,049	280	−848	4,335	−3,435

*Less than $500,000.
[1] Interest on refunds is included in Expenditures: Treasury Department.
[2] Mainly internal revenue income, excise, and estate and gift taxes; and customs collections.
[3] Employment taxes and highway excise taxes.
[4] Mainly interest payments by Government corporations and agencies that borrow from the Treasury. For details of these transactions for fiscal years, 1962-65, see table 8. These interfund transactions do not include payments to the Treasury by wholly owned Government corporations for retirement of their capital stock and for disposition of earnings.

TABLE 13.—*Trust receipts and expenditures monthly and total for fiscal year 1965*

[In millions of dollars. On basis of "Monthly Statement of Receipts and Expenditures of the United States Government," see "Bases of Tables"]

Receipts and expenditures	July	August	September	October	November	December	January	February	March	April	May	June	Total 1965
RECEIPTS													
Highway trust fund	326	383	326	214	337	281	296	308	287	271	293	348	3,670
Federal old-age and survivors insurance trust fund	568	2,493	1,028	455	1,591	894	99	2,312	1,296	1,219	2,997	1,466	16,417
Federal disability insurance trust fund	42	176	79	35	122	78	8	155	105	97	222	122	1,241
Unemployment trust fund	273	740	95	148	468	180	214	622	87	242	901	161	4,132
Veterans' life insurance funds	49	39	42	41	37	44	46	35	46	41	38	251	711
Civil service retirement and disability fund	190	170	246	174	171	190	183	162	194	193	172	617	2,664
Railroad retirement account	16	95	92	13	88	76	15	100	81	19	102	644	1,342
District of Columbia	38	26	34	57	21	17	35	22	41	27	48	24	389
All other	33	58	73	96	100	232	133	41	63	103	118	71	1,121
Interfund transactions (−)¹	−4	−8	−22	−10	−9	−26	−21	−11	−25	−11	−6	−485	−638
Net trust receipts	1,532	4,171	1,994	1,224	2,028	1,966	1,007	3,746	2,175	2,201	4,885	3,219	31,047
EXPENDITURES													
Highway trust fund	405	426	441	436	400	383	269	216	252	211	229	358	4,026
Federal old-age and survivors insurance trust fund	1,270	1,275	1,286	1,282	1,275	1,230	1,290	1,308	1,320	1,322	1,323	1,779	15,962
Federal disability insurance trust fund	110	110	112	111	112	193	116	122	116	122	122	150	1,498
Unemployment trust fund	235	217	210	165	251	280	308	296	429	279	212	248	3,130
Veterans' life insurance funds	43	37	36	37	33	34	208	39	42	37	35	34	616
Civil service retirement and disability fund	116	117	117	119	117	118	118	118	124	124	124	126	1,438
Railroad retirement account	96	100	93	100	101	93	104	103	95	104	100	95	1,185
District of Columbia	37	31	22	36	29	37	31	28	31	32	31	40	385
(net)	246	188	11	−33	−165	346	−256	−90	−38	626	58	486	1,379
Deposit funds (net)	74	18	−247	−201	−8	−95	−148	−24	−75	−112	10	599	−210
All other (net)	85	92	−93	−243	56	−29	177	77	−208	214	85	169	868
Interfund transactions (−)¹	−4	−8	−22	−10	−9	−26	−21	−11	−25	−11	−6	−485	−638
Net trust expenditures	2,713	2,602	1,966	2,286	2,191	2,565	2,197	2,183	2,064	2,949	2,323	3,599	29,637
Excess of trust receipts, or expenditures (−)	−1,181	1,570	28	−1,062	737	−599	−1,191	1,563	110	−748	2,562	−380	1,410
Net investments in, or sales (−), of public debt and agency securities	−1,205	1,882	49	−1,360	691	−550	−1,537	1,353	292	−1,471	3,597	615	2,356
Net redemptions, or sales (−), of Government agency securities in the market	64	−378	108	−67	−125	139	282	16	−327	−249	−458	−378	−1,372

¹ Mainly financial interchanges between trust funds resulting in receipts and expenditures. For details of these interfund transactions for fiscal years 1962–65, see table 9.

TABLE 14.—*Trust receipts by sources and expenditures by major functions, fiscal years 1957–65*

[In millions of dollars. On basis of 1967 Budget document]

Receipts and expenditures	1957	1958	1959	1960	1961	1962	1963	1964	1965
RECEIPTS									
Employment	7,250	8,308	8,530	10,817	12,502	12,708	15,004	17,003	17,004
Less	-58	-75	-83	-89	-98	-147	-143	-170	-199
Unemployment	1,542	1,501	1,701	2,167	2,398	2,729	3,009	3,042	3,052
Excise	1,479	2,116	2,171	2,642	2,923	3,080	3,405	3,646	3,682
Less	(*)	-90	-97	-103	-126	-131	-126	-127	-123
	1,175	1,252	1,507	1,504	1,740	1,756	1,878	2,029	73
Trust ufd investments	1,318	1,342	1,315	1,327	1,404	1,423	1,467	1,602	1,758
Uninvested trust fds	6	8	9	10	10	10	11	11	12
life ins	28	27	24	22	20	18	17	16	15
life	425	459	453	460	484	483	477	478	473
Miscellaneous	1,146	1,317	1,375	2,494	2,840	2,889	3,195	3,322	3,639
Subtotal trust receipts	14,311	16,164	16,904	21,250	24,097	24,818	28,193	30,852	31,686
Interfund transactions (−)	-10	-11	-135	-908	-515	-528	-505	-521	-638
Net trust receipts	14,301	16,153	16,769	20,342	23,583	24,290	27,689	30,331	31,047
EXPENDITURES									
	93	344	229	256	196	366	679	487	751
	13	1	21	48	13	15	44	62	-160
	426	357	645	458	416	398	507	(*)	(*)
	85	101	94	116	183	112	122	496	97
Natural	866	1,401	2,493	2,831	2,505	2,662	2,877	137	34
Housing	1,044	1,295	1,263	1,439	-273	1,524	-36	3,482	3,84
Health, labor, nd welfare	9,585	12,775	14,306	16,358	19,236	20,382	21,855	1,889	1,36
	1	1	1	1	1	1	2	22,733	23,2
government	608	671	651	673	811	733	835	2	2
Deposit	8	10	10	17	16	20	19	666	624
	217	-29	-60	-78	203	-644	146	18	21
								-567	-210
Subtotal	12,947	15,335	19,655	22,120	23,308	25,669	27,050	29,406	30,276
Interfund transactions (−)	-10	-11	-135	-908	-515	-528	-505	-521	-638
Net trust expenditures	12,938	15,325	19,521	21,212	22,793	25,141	26,545	28,885	29,637
Excess of trust receipts, or expenditures (−)	1,363	829	-2,751	-870	790	-851	1,143	1,446	40

*Less than $500,000.

TABLE 15.—Administrative budget receipts by sources and expenditures by major functions, fiscal years 1957–65

[In millions of dollars. Expenditures classified on basis of 1967 Budget document]

Receipts and expenditures	1957	1958	1959	1960	1961	1962	1963	1964	1965
RECEIPTS									
Individual income taxes	39,030	38,569	40,735	44,946	46,153	50,650	52,988	54,590	53,661
Corporation income taxes	21,531	20,533	18,092	22,179	21,765	21,296	22,336	24,301	26,131
Excise taxes	10,638	10,814	10,760	11,865	12,064	12,752	13,410	13,950	14,793
Employment taxes	7,581	8,644	8,854	11,159	12,502	12,708	15,004	17,003	17,104
Estate and gift taxes	1,378	1,411	1,353	1,626	1,916	2,035	2,187	2,416	2,746
Internal revenue taxes not otherwise classified	15	7	5						
Total internal revenue	80,172	79,978	79,798	91,775	94,401	99,441	105,925	112,260	114,435
Customs	754	800	948	1,123	1,008	1,171	1,241	1,284	1,478
Miscellaneous receipts	2,749	3,196	3,158	4,064	4,082	3,206	4,436	4,077	4,622
Total receipts by major sources	83,675	83,974	83,904	96,962	99,491	103,818	111,602	117,622	120,535
Deductions:									
Refunds of receipts (excluding interest): [1]									
Internal revenue applicable to:									
Budget accounts	3,894	4,413	4,907	5,024	5,725	5,957	6,257	6,817	5,668
Trust accounts	58	165	180	193	224	278	35	297	323
Customs	20	18	23	18	25	29	269	32	35
Other	3	2	3	2	2	1	1	1	3
Total refunds of receipts	3,976	4,598	5,114	5,238	5,976	6,266	6,571	7,148	6,030
Transfers to trust accounts: [1]									
Federal old-age and survivors insurance trust fund	6,243	6,795	7,084	9,192	10,537	10,600	12,351	14,335	14,572
Federal disability insurance trust fund	333	863	837	929	953	945	994	1,057	1,082
Highway trust fund	1,479	2,026	2,074	2,539	2,798	2,949	3,279	3,619	3,659
Railroad retirement account	616	575	525	607	571	564	572	593	636
Unemployment trust fund					343	453	945	847	615
Total transfers to trust accounts	8,671	10,259	10,520	13,267	15,202	15,510	18,141	20,351	20,563
Total deductions	12,647	14,857	15,634	18,505	21,178	21,776	24,712	27,499	26,593
Subtotal receipts	71,029	69,117	68,270	78,457	78,313	82,042	86,890	90,122	93,942
Deductions:									
Interfund transactions (included in both receipts and expenditures) [2]	467	567	355	694	654	633	513	664	870
Net administrative budget receipts	70,562	68,550	67,915	77,763	77,659	81,409	86,376	89,459	93,072
EXPENDITURES [3]									
National defense:									
Department of Defense—military:									
Military personnel	11,409	11,611	11,801	11,738	12,085	13,032	13,000	14,195	14,71
Operation and maintenance	9,457	9,761	10,378	10,223	10,611	11,594	11,874	11,932	2,89
Procurement	13,488	14,083	14,409	13,334	13,095	14,532	16,632	15,351	11,839
Research, development, test, and evaluation	2,406	2,594	2,866	4,710	6,131	6,319	6,376	7,021	86
Military construction	1,968	1,753	1,948	1,626	1,605	1,347	1,144	1,026	1,07
Family housing							427	560	69

Ci vil								
Revolving ad	93	107	203	90				
	-741	-452	-1,401	-99	-300	-416	-179	-643	-323
Ttl Department of Defense—military	46,173	49,760	48,252	46,815	43,227	41,215	41,223	39,071	38,436
May	1,229	1,485	1,721	1,390	1,449	1,609	2,340	2,187	2,352
the energy	2,625	2,765	2,788	2,806	2,713	2,623	2,541	2,268	1,990
Defense-related	136	172	24	92	104	244	379	709	590
Ttl	50,163	54,181	52,755	51,103	47,494	45,691	46,483	44,234	43,368
al its ad	346	297	346	249	216	217	237	173	157
t of foreign	2,04	1,479	1,826	2,130	1,927	1,381	3,305	1,788	1,559
aid ... nd	223	207	201	197	158	137	139	149	133
Foreign t ae	1,641	1,704	1,779	1,726	1,653	1,327	1,120	1,195	1,463
Food dr								
Ttl firs and the	4,304	3,687	4,151	4,301	3,954	3,064	4,802	3,305	3,311
Space research and technology:								
Manned space flight	3,538	2,768	1,516	565	279	113	11		
Scientific investigations in space	662	641	483	359	232	125	25		
Meteorology and other space applications	89	112	92	61	17	8	1		
Other research, technology, and supporting operations	804	650	460	272	217	154	109		
Total space research and technology	5,093	4,171	2,552	1,257	744	401	145	89	76
Agriculture and agricultural resources:								
Farm income stabilization	3,438	4,144	3,954	3,093	2,345	2,370	4,275	2,211	2,092
Financing farming and rural housing	268	251	300	234	349	289	311	269	248
Financing rural electrification and rural telephones	392	342	342	303	301	330	315	297	267
Agricultural land and water resources	341	324	324	367	347	324	341	289	353
Research and other agricultural services	457	414	391	341	324	293	291	255	227
Total agriculture and agricultural resources	4,898	5,475	5,311	4,338	3,667	3,606	5,533	3,320	3,186
Natural resources:								
Land and water resources	1,922	1,832	1,779	1,623	1,444	1,279	1,219	1,165	947
Forest resources	374	332	303	280	331	220	201	174	163
Mineral resources	105	91	71	68	61	65	71	59	62
Fish and wildlife resources	120	105	94	81	73	68	68	60	51
Recreational resources	134	130	112	94	91	74	85	44	59
General resource surveys and administration	94	73	73	60	55	51	61		38
Total natural resources	2,750	2,563	2,431	2,206	2,056	1,757	1,705	1,570	1,320
Commerce and transportation:								
Aviation	875	835	808	781	716	508	494	315	219
Water transportation	728	658	672	654	569	508	436	392	365
Highways	39	39	41	33	36	38	30	31	40
Postal service	805	578	770	797	914	525	774	674	518
Advancement of business	557	401	366	427	271	265	234	170	119
Area and regional development [4]	398	401	101	7	67	59	68	(*)	45
Regulation of business	98	91	84	74				49	
Total commerce and transportation	3,499	3,002	2,843	2,774	2,573	1,963	2,025	1,632	1,305

Footnotes at end of table.

Table 15.—*Administrative budget receipts by sources and expenditures by major functions, fiscal years 1957-65*—Continued

[In millions of dollars]

Expenditures	1957	1958	1959	1960	1961	1962	1963	1964	1965
EXPENDITURES[1]—Continued									
Housing and community development:									
Aids to private housing	-254	-126	732	-172	-44	-149	-537	-595	-818
Public housing programs	60	51	97	134	150	163	178	149	230
Urban renewal and community facilities	49	78	108	130	162	261	222	306	420
National Capital region	27	26	33	30	51	74	70	59	64
Total housing and community development	-118	30	970	122	320	349	-67	-80	-104
Health, labor, and welfare:									
Health services and research[3]	461	540	700	815	961	1,233	1,511	1,878	1,882
Labor and manpower	397	488	924	510	809	591	224	345	464
Public assistance[4]	1,558	1,797	1,969	2,061	2,147	2,331	2,631	2,786	2,827
Economic opportunity program									211
Other welfare services	216	234	284	304	327	382	423	466	513
Total health, labor, and welfare	2,632	3,059	3,877	3,680	4,244	4,638	4,789	5,475	5,898
Education:									
Assistance for elementary and secondary education	174	189	259	327	332	337	392	404	418
Assistance for higher education	110	178	225	261	286	350	428	383	413
Assistance to science education and basic research	46	50	106	120	143	183	206	310	309
Other aids to education	108	124	141	156	181	207	219	241	405
Total education	437	541	732	866	943	1,076	1,244	1,339	1,544
Veterans' benefits and services:									
Veterans' service-connected compensation	1,876	2,024	2,071	2,049	2,034	2,017	2,116	2,158	2,176
Veterans' nonservice-connected pensions	950	1,037	1,152	1,265	1,532	1,635	1,698	1,743	1,864
Veterans' readjustment benefits	977	1,025	864	725	559	388	-13	113	-50
Veterans' hospitals and medical care	801	856	921	961	1,030	1,094	1,145	1,229	1,270
Other veterans' benefits and services	266	242	280	266	259	279	240	249	235
Total veterans' benefits and services	4,870	5,184	5,287	5,266	5,414	5,403	5,186	5,492	5,495
Interest:									
Interest on the public debt	7,244	7,607	7,593	9,180	8,957	9,120	9,895	10,666	11,346
Interest on refunds of receipts	57	74	69	76	83	68	74	88	77
Interest on uninvested funds	6	8		10	10	10	11	11	12
Total interest	7,307	7,689	7,671	9,266	9,050	9,198	9,980	10,765	11,435

General government:									
Legislative functions	90	89	102	109	118	135	131	126	142
Judicial functions	40	44	47	49	52	57	63	66	76
Executive direction and management	12	19	21	20	22	22	21	22	23
Central fiscal operations	476	502	566	558	607	653	715	791	825
General property and records management	201	245	295	372	372	419	444	576	606
Central personnel management	602	84	95	84	140	153	142	174	174
Protective services and alien control	219	233	255	263	299	300	323	335	366
Other general government	100	69	86	88	109	138	139	189	190
Total general government	1,738	1,284	1,466	1,512	1,709	1,875	1,979	2,280	2,402
Total expenditures by major functions	69,433	71,936	80,697	77,233	82,169	88,419	93,155	98,348	97,377
Deductions:									
Interfund transactions (included in both receipts and expenditures)²	467	567	355	694	664	633	513	664	80
Net administrative budget expenditures	68,966	71,369	80,342	76,539	81,515	87,787	92,642	97,684	96,67
Administrative budget surplus, or deficit (−)	1,596	−2,819	−12,427	1,224	−3,856	−6,378	−6,266	−8,226	−3,85

*Less than $500,000.

¹ Amounts representing refunds of principal for overpaid taxes formerly reported net of reimbursements from trust fund accounts are shown herein on a gross basis. These reimbursements to the Internal Revenue Service for refunds are included and netted with amounts for transfers to the respective trust fund accounts.

² For details of these transactions for fiscal years 1962-65, see table 8.

³ Expenditures are net of receipts of public enterprise funds.

⁴ Beginning with 1963 includes the temporary public works acceleration program which supplements expenditures in various other categories.

⁵ Beginning with 1961, the portion of the appropriation for "Public assistance" which finances medical and hospital care for the aged has been reclassified from "Public assistance" to "Health services and research."

TABLE 16.—Trust and other transactions by major classifications, fiscal years 1955–65

[In millions of dollars. On basis of the "Monthly Statement of Receipts and Expenditures of the United States Government," see "Bases of Tables"]

Classification	1955	1956	1957	1958	1959	1960	1961	1962	1963	1964	1965
TRUST ACCOUNTS, ETC.											
RECEIPTS											
Federal old-age and survivors insurance trust fund	5,586	7,003	7,159	7,900	8,182	10,439	11,910	12,141	13,984	16,196	16,595
Less refunds	-51	-66	-58	-75	-74	-79	-86	-130	-128	-152	-179
Federal disability insurance trust fund			339	943	938	1,071	1,093	1,104	1,157	1,224	1,254
Less refunds					-10	-10	-10	-12	-12	-13	-13
Railroad retirement account	700	739	723	695	758	1,403	1,051	1,081	1,128	1,192	1,342
Unemployment trust fund	1,425	1,728	1,912	1,855	1,997	2,703	4,055	4,276	4,519	4,537	4,335
Refunds of ...								-2	-5	-4	-8
Return of advances to ...						-359	-250	-285	-255	-244	-195
National service life insurance fund	590	649	608	640	634	643	668	664	658	661	662
Government life insurance fund	78	73	69	67	63	61	58	54	52	50	48
Federal employees' retirement funds	708	1,025	1,397	1,458	1,741	1,766	2,033	2,086	2,255	2,465	2,674
Highway trust fund			1,482	2,134	2,185	3,003	2,985	3,087	3,419	3,666	3,793
Less: Return of advances to ...				-90	-97	-103	-126	-131	-126	-127	-123
Less: ...							-60				
Other trust funds and accounts [2]	449	467	631	638	585	711	778	890	1,546	1,402	1,500
Less certain ... [3]	-16	-12	-10	-11	-135	-908	-515	-528	-505	-521	-638
Net receipts [4]	9,470	11,607	14,301	16,153	16,769	20,342	23,583	24,290	27,689	30,331	31,047
EXPENDITURES											
Federal old-age and survivors insurance trust fund [1]	4,436	5,485	6,665	8,041	9,380	11,073	11,752	13,270	14,530	15,285	15,962
Federal disability insurance trust fund		1	1	181	361	561	746	1,089	1,259	1,341	1,498
Railroad retirement account	585	611	682	730	778	1,136	1,124	1,135	1,112	1,139	1,185
Unemployment trust fund	1,965	1,393	1,644	3,148	3,054	2,736	4,734	3,906	3,815	3,707	3,130
National service life insurance fund	538	512	515	544	562	582	707	626	747	585	545
Government life insurance fund	84	87	86	120	80	83	94	96	79	72	71
Federal employees' retirement funds [1]	430	507	591	699	792	896	955	1,063	1,183	1,336	1,446
Highway trust fund			966	1,512	2,613	2,945	2,620	2,784	3,017	3,645	4,026
Federal National Mortgage Association	-84	112	971	105	134	988	-89	317	-730	-37	91
Other trust funds and accounts [3]	483	425	565	915	672	711	698	835	1,208	1,055	1,152
Deposit fund accounts (net)	56	168	216	-31	-61	-75	205	-544	146	-557	-210
Government-sponsored enterprises (net):											
Farm Credit Administration:											
Banks for cooperatives	(*)	23	44	21	86	46	49	50	29	37	189
Federal intermediate credit banks	53	241	230	95	236	142	122	129	277	182	149
Federal land banks					241	249	225	195	176	248	561
Federal Home Loan Bank Board:											
Home loan banks	144	164	-124	-628	854	182	-487	872	363	1,572	660
Federal Deposit Insurance Corporation	-98	-104	-104	-115	-124	-134	-148	-154	-161	-183	-180
Total Government-sponsored enterprises	99	324	46	-627	1,292	484	-239	1,092	685	1,857	1,379

Less certain trust expenditures which are also receipts [3]	−16	−12	−10	−11	−135	−908	−515	−528	−505	−521	−638
Net expenditures [4]	8,577	9,611	12,938	15,325	19,621	21,212	22,793	25,141	26,545	28,885	29,637
Excess of receipts, or expenditures (−)	892	1,996	1,363	829	−2,751	−870	790	−851	1,143	1,446	1,410

INVESTMENTS OF GOVERNMENT AGENCIES IN PUBLIC DEBT AND AGENCY SECURITIES (NET) [7]

Employees' life ... trust fd	1,241	1,463	5	36	58	48	47	51	56	50	27
Federal old age ... res ... trust fd			220	−499	−1,290	−726	−225	−1,089	−821	692	461
Federal disability	141	121	325	729	552	494	−285	21	−129	−139	−263
Railroad	−645	238	36	−33	−35	264	−78	−63	1	69	149
Unemployment trust fd	73	135	274	−1,255	−1,011	−41	−952	72	456	573	967
... service life insurance fd	−1	−16	89	95	76	62	−44	44	−90	69	126
... life ... fds	314	648	−16	−56	−17	−21	−35	44	−25	−22	−22
Federal ... fds [1]			803	671	958	871	1,063	1,034	1,075	1,126	1,214
Highway ... fd	14	77	404	418	−303	−428	233	202	242	−60	−344
Other trust ... fds [2]	126	101	122	−69	−60	−2	−20	42	245	20	−59
Public ... fds	170	548	39	460	−70	239	434	30	771	43	72
Net investments, or sales (−)	1,532	3,235	2,339	597	−1,130	925	855	493	2,069	2,775	2,356

SALES AND REDEMPTIONS OF GOVERNMENT AGENCY SECURITIES IN THE MARKET (NET)

Guaranteed: Public enterprise funds	37	−30	−33	6	−10	(*)	−81	−204	−162	−206	223
Trust enterprise funds						−28	−19				
Not guaranteed: Public enterprise funds	−639	−44	136	−233	6	(*)	747	−95	(*)	−35	−45
Trust enterprise funds		−100	−1,188	−340	−67	994	86	−359	597	262	−99
Government-sponsored enterprises	−269	−872	−86	167	−1,222	−723	−195	−1,122	−1,457	−1,900	−1,451
Net redemptions, or sales (−)	−871	−1,046	−1,171	−400	−1,293	−1,746	537	−1,780	−1,022	−1,880	−1,372

* Less than $500,000.

TABLE 17.—Receipts from and payments to the public, fiscal years 1955-65

[In millions of dollars. On basis of the "Monthly Statement of Receipts and Expenditures of the United States Government"]

PART I—SUMMARY OF FEDERAL GOVERNMENT CASH TRANSACTIONS WITH THE PUBLIC

Classification	1955	1956	1957	1958	1959	1960	1961	1962	1963	1964	1965
Federal receipts from the public:											
Administrative budget receipts (net)[1]	60,209	67,850	70,562	68,550	67,915	77,763	77,659	81,409	86,376	89,459	93,072
Trust and other receipts (net)[1]	9,470	11,607	14,301	16,153	16,769	20,342	23,583	24,290	27,689	30,331	31,047
Intragovernmental and other noncash transactions (see receipt adjustments Part II)	-1,843	-2,370	-2,758	-2,811	-3,025	-3,027	-4,001	-3,834	-4,325	-4,259	-4,420
Total Federal receipts from the public	67,836	77,087	82,105	81,892	81,660	95,078	97,242	101,865	109,739	115,530	119,699
Federal payments to the public:											
Administrative budget expenditures (net)[1]	64,389	66,224	68,966	71,369	80,342	76,539	81,515	87,787	92,642	97,684	96,507
Trust fund and other expenditures (net)[1]	8,577	9,611	12,938	15,325	19,521	21,212	22,793	25,141	26,545	28,885	29,637
Intragovernmental and other noncash transactions (see payment adjustments Part II)	-2,429	-3,290	-1,899	-3,222	-5,111	-3,423	-4,766	-5,266	-5,436	-6,237	-3,749
Total Federal payments to the public	70,537	72,546	80,006	83,472	94,752	94,328	99,542	107,662	113,751	120,332	122,395
Excess of cash receipts from, or payments to (-) the public.	-2,702	4,541	2,099	-1,580	-13,092	750	-2,300	-5,797	-4,012	-4,802	-2,696
Cash borrowing from the public, or repayment (-):											
Public debt increase, or decrease (-).	3,115	-1,623	-2,224	5,816	8,363	1,625	2,640	9,230	7,659	5,853	5,561
Net sales of Government agency securities in market (net)	871	1,046	1,171	400	1,293	1,746	-537	1,780	1,022	1,880	1,372
Net investment (-) in public debt and agency securities.	-1,532	-3,235	-2,339	-597	1,130	-925	-855	-493	-2,009	-2,775	-2,356
Other noncash transactions (see borrowing adjustments, Part II).	-644	-623	292	200	-2,160	-597	-536	-923	-1,033	-1,099	-250
Total net cash borrowing from the public, or repayment (-).	1,809	-4,436	-3,100	5,820	8,626	1,848	712	9,594	5,579	3,859	4,328
Seigniorage[3]	29	23	49	59	44	53	55	58	45	69	117
Total cash transactions with the public.	-863	128	-952	4,299	-4,422	2,651	-1,533	3,854	1,611	-874	1,749
Cash balances—net increase, or decrease (-):											
Treasurer's account	-551	331	-956	4,159	-4,399	2,654	-1,311	3,736	1,686	-1,080	1,575
Cash held outside Treasury	-312	-202	5	140	-23	-4	-222	118	-74	206	174
Total changes in the cash balances	-863	128	-952	4,299	-4,422	2,651	-1,533	3,854	1,611	-874	1,749

[Showing details of amounts included as adjustments in Part I]

Classification	1955	1956	1957	1958	1959	1960	1961	1962	1963	1964	1965
Adjustments applicable to receipts:											
Intragovernmental transactions:											
Interest on trust fund investments	1,173	1,207	1,318	1,342	1,315	1,327	1,404	1,423	1,467	1,603	1,759
Civil service retirement—payroll deductions for employees [4]	436	571	641	660	744	744	838	845	914	973	1,042
Civil service retirement—employers' share [4]	30	233	525	579	744	744	838	845	914	973	1,042
Other	175	335	224	170	178	159	866	663	986	612	459
Subtotal	1,814	2,346	2,709	2,751	2,980	2,975	3,945	3,776	4,281	4,190	4,303
Excess profits tax refund bonds [5]	(*)	(*)	(*)	(*)	(*)	(*)	(*)	(*)	(*)	(*)	(*)
Seigniorage [3]	29	23	49	59	44	53	55	58	45	60	117
Total receipt adjustments	1,843	2,370	2,758	2,811	3,025	3,027	4,001	3,834	4,326	4,259	4,420
Adjustments applicable to payments (see detail under receipt adjustments):											
Intragovernmental transactions	1,814	2,346	2,709	2,751	2,980	2,975	3,945	3,776	4,281	4,190	4,303
Applicable also to net borrowings:											
Savings and retirement plan bonds increment [6]	463	393	336	385	383	136	430	496	577	611	571
Discount on securities	33	62	52	−131	418	205	−209	145	119	268	144
International Monetary Fund notes	156	175	−674	−450	1,361	259	258	171	255	117	−472
Other special security issues [7]	−8	−7	−6	−4	−2	−2	56	111	83	103	6
Subtotal	644	623	−292	−200	2,160	597	536	923	1,033	1,099	250
Accrued interest on public debt [8]	26	82	39	93	76	132	6	18	186	38	110
Checks outstanding and other accounts [9]	−55	238	−557	576	−105	−281	279	548	−64	910	−913
Total payment adjustments	2,429	3,290	1,899	3,222	5,111	3,423	4,766	5,266	5,436	6,237	3,749
Adjustments applicable to net borrowings:											
Debt issuance representing:											
Receipts—excess profits tax refund bonds [5]	(*)	(*)	(*)	(*)	(*)	(*)	(*)	(*)	(*)	(*)	(*)
Payments (see detail under payment adjustments)	644	623	−292	−200	2,160	597	536	923	1,033	1,099	250
Total borrowing adjustments (net)	644	623	−292	−200	2,160	597	536	923	1,033	1,099	250

* Less than $500,000.
1 For details see table 12.
2 For details see table 13.
3 Includes the increment resulting from reduction in the weight of the gold dollar; excluded from receipts from the public but included in cash deposits in the Treasurer's account.
4 Beginning with fiscal 1958 excludes District of Columbia.
5 Treated as noncash refund deductions from receipts when issued and as cash refund deductions when redeemed.
6 Accrued interest on bonds, i.e., the difference between the purchase price and the current redemption value less interest paid on bonds redeemed.

7 Includes adjustments for payments of adjusted service bonds and Armed Forces leave bonds; the net issue or redemption of special notes to the International Development Association and the Inter-American Development Bank; and special bonds to U.N. funds.
8 Net increase or decrease of public debt interest due and accrued beginning June 30, 1955, effective date of the change in accounting and reporting from a due and payable basis to an accrual basis.
9 Checks outstanding less deposits in transit, and changes in other accounts; net increase, or decrease (−). (See also footnote 6.)

TABLE 18.—*Administrative budget receipts and expenditures based on existing and proposed legislation, actual for the fiscal year 1965 and estimated for 1966 and 1967*

[In millions of dollars.   On basis of 1967 Budget document]

Source	1965 actual	1966 estimate	1967 estimate
ADMINISTRATIVE BUDGET RECEIPTS			
Internal revenue:			
Individual income taxes:			
Withheld	36,840	40,800	46,440
Other	16,820	16,300	16,100
Total individual income taxes	53,661	57,100	62,540
Corporation income taxes	26,131	30,400	35,100
Excise taxes:			
Alcohol taxes:			
Distilled spirits	2,701	2,720	2,840
Beer	915	890	915
Rectification tax	25	24	25
Wines	110	111	117
Special taxes in connection with liquor occupations	22	23	24
Total alcohol taxes	3,773	3,768	3,921
Tobacco taxes:			
Cigarettes (small)	2,070	2,055	2,065
Manufactured tobacco (chewing, smoking, and snuff) [1]	17	9	
Cigars (large)	61	59	60
Cigarette papers and tubes	1	1	1
All other	1	1	1
Total tobacco taxes	2,149	2,125	2,127
Documents, other instruments, and playing cards taxes:			
Issues of securities, stock, and bond transfers [1]	} 178	110	50
Deeds of conveyance and foreign insurance policies			
Playing cards [2]	8		
Total taxes on documents, other instruments, and playing cards	186	110	50
Manufacturers excise taxes:			
Gasoline	2,687	2,795	2,932
Lubricating oils used in highway vehicles [3]	} 76	78	77
Lubricating oils not used in highway vehicles [1]			
Passengers automobiles [4]	1,888	1,460	1,330
Automobile trucks, buses, and trailers	425	452	442
Parts and accessories for automobiles [1]	} 253	137	20
Parts and accessories for trucks [3]			
Tires, inner tubes, and tread rubber	440	472	488
Electric, gas, and oil appliances [2]	81	11	
Electric light bulbs [1]	43	30	
Radio and television receiving sets, phonographs, phonograph records, and musical instruments [2]	274	30	
Mechanical refrigerators, quick-freeze units, and self-contained air-conditioning units [2]	76	16	
Business and store machines [2]	74	11	
Photographic equipment [2]	35	7	
Matches [2]	4	1	
Sporting goods [2]	21	3	
Fishing rods, creels, etc	7	7	7
Firearms, shells, and cartridges	20	24	25
Pistols and revolvers	2	3	3
Fountain and ballpoint pens, mechanical pencils [2]	9	2	
Total manufacturers excise taxes	6,418	5,539	5,324
Retailers excise taxes:			
Jewelry [2]	205	39	
Furs [2]	31	3	
Toilet preparations [2]	196	31	
Luggage, handbags, wallets, etc. [2]	81	19	
Total retailers excise taxes	513	92	

Footnotes at end of table.

TABLE 18.—*Administrative budget receipts and expenditures based on existing and proposed legislation, actual for the fiscal year 1965 and estimated for 1966 and 1967*—Continued

[In millions of dollars]

Source	1965 actual	1966 estimate	1967 estimate
ADMINISTRATIVE BUDGET RECEIPTS—Continued			
Internal revenue—Continued			
Excise taxes—Continued			
Miscellaneous excise taxes:			
General and toll telephone and teletypewriter service [6]	} 1,079	940	1,090
Other communications services [1]			
Transportation of persons by air	126	154	197
Transportation of freight by air			6
Fuel used on inland waterways			7
Jet fuel			3
Diesel fuel used on highways	152	165	178
Use tax on certain vehicles	102	101	102
Admissions, exclusive of carbarets, roof gardens, etc.[6]	52	41	
Cabarets, roof gardens, etc.[6]	44	31	
Wagering taxes, including occupational taxes	7	7	7
Club dues and initiation fees [1]	80	35	
Leases of safe deposit boxes [2]	7	2	
Sugar tax	97	100	101
Coin-operated amusement devices [2]	4		
Coin-operated gaming devices	15	17	18
Bowling alleys and billiard and pool tables [2]	5		
Interest equalization tax	15	12	12
All other miscellaneous excise taxes	2	2	25
Total miscellaneous excise taxes	1,786	1,607	1,746
Undistributed depositary receipts and unapplied collections	−32	15	
Total excise taxes before proposed increase in highway taxes	14,793	13,256	13,168
Effect of proposed legislation		60	389
Total excise taxes including effect of proposed increase in highway taxes	14,793	13,256	13,557
Employment taxes:			
Federal Insurance Contributions Act and Self-Employment Contributions Act	15,846	17,832	23,267
Railroad Retirement Tax Act	636	683	772
Federal Unemployment Tax Act	622	544	544
Total employment taxes	17,104	19,059	24,583
Estate and gift taxes	2,746	2,957	3,331
Total internal revenue	114,435	122,772	139,111
Customs	1,478	1,690	1,880
Miscellaneous receipts:			
Miscellaneous taxes	6	6	6
Seigniorage	117	901	1,568
Bullion charges	1	1	1
Fees for permits and licenses	83	101	123
Fines, penalties, forfeitures	87	14	15
Gifts and contributions	2	1	1
Interest	1,077	831	968
Dividends and other earnings	1,393	1,725	1,820
Rents	109	222	408
Royalties	132	146	204
Sales of products	427	373	396
Fees and other charges for services and special benefits	128	151	163
Sale of Government property	431	1,009	1,058
Realization upon loans and investments	496	185	194
Recoveries and refunds	132	126	127
Total miscellaneous receipts	4,622	5,794	7,050
Gross receipts	120,535	130,256	148,041

Footnotes at end of table.

TABLE 18.—*Administrative budget receipts and expenditures based on existing and proposed legislation, actual for the fiscal year 1965 and estimated for 1966 and 1967—*
Continued

[In millions of dollars]

Source	1965 actual	1966 estimate	1967 estimate
ADMINISTRATIVE BUDGET RECEIPTS—Continued			
Deduct:			
Transfers to:			
Federal old-age and survivors insurance trust fund	14,572	15,486	18,932
Federal disability insurance trust fund	1,082	1,345	1,886
Federal hospital insurance trust fund		766	2,210
Railroad retirement account	636	683	772
Unemployment trust fund	615	540	540
Highway trust fund	3,659	3,859	4,378
Refunds of receipts:			
Internal revenue:			
Individual income taxes	4,869	5,700	6,300
Corporation income taxes	670	700	700
Excise taxes	223	228	300
Employment taxes	199	239	243
Estate and gift taxes	29	25	30
Total internal revenue	5,991	6,892	7,573
Customs	35	35	35
Miscellaneous receipts	3	3	3
Total refunds of receipts	6,030	6,930	7,611
Deduct: Interfund transactions (included in both receipts and expenditures)	870	647	712
Net administrative budget receipts	93,072	100,000	111,000
NET ADMINISTRATIVE BUDGET EXPENDITURES			
Legislative branch	165	191	205
The judiciary	74	82	91
Executive Office of the President	24	29	31
Funds appropriated to the President	4,307	4,868	5,028
Agriculture Department	7,298	6,889	5,798
Commerce Department	758	808	923
Defense Department:			
Military	46,173	52,925	57,150
Civil	1,234	1,314	1,369
Health, Education, and Welfare Department	5,740	7,662	10,191
Housing and Urban Development Department [7]	250	436	−414
Interior Department	1,205	1,242	1,322
Justice Department	358	384	405
Labor Department	480	522	522
Post Office Department	805	878	755
State Department	383	407	405
Treasury Department	12,730	13,429	14,247
Atomic Energy Commission	2,625	2,390	2,300
Federal Aviation Agency	795	800	840
General Services Administration	624	600	635
National Aeronautics and Space Administration	5,093	5,600	5,300
Veterans' Administration	5,488	5,177	5,718
Other independent agencies	708	301	275
District of Columbia	61	65	111
Allowances, undistributed		75	350
Subtotal administrative budget expenditures	97,377	107,075	113,559
Deduct: Interfund transactions (included in both receipts and expenditures)	870	647	712
Net administrative budget expenditures	96,507	106,428	112,847
Administrative budget surplus, or deficit (−)	−3,435	−6,428	−1,847

[1] Repealed as of Jan. 1, 1966.
[2] Repealed as of June 22, 1965; consumer refunds on sales of air conditioners after May 14, 1965.
[3] Transferred to highway trust fund as of Jan. 1, 1966.
[4] Tax reduced from 10 percent to 7 percent on June 22, 1965; with consumer refunds on sales after May 14, 1965; reduction to 6 percent as of Jan. 1, 1966; proposed increase to 7 percent as of Mar. 15, 1966.
[5] Tax reduced from 10 percent to 3 percent as of Jan. 1, 1966; proposed return to 10 percent as of Apr. 1, 1966.
[6] Repealed as of noon, Dec. 31, 1965.
[7] Functions of Housing and Home Finance Agency transferred to this Department pursuant to P.L. 89-174, Sept. 9, 1965.

TABLE 19.—*Trust and other transactions, actual for the fiscal year 1965 and estimated for 1966 and 1967*

[In millions of dollars. On basis of 1967 Budget document]

Source	1965 actual	1966 estimate	1967 estimate
TRUST ACCOUNTS, ETC.			
RECEIPTS			
Federal old-age and survivors insurance trust fund:			
Employment taxes	14,751	15,705	19,155
Less: Refunds of taxes	−179	−219	−223
Deposits by States	1,258	1,378	1,511
Interest on investments	583	556	590
Federal payment for military service credits		78	78
Other	3	4	2
Federal disability insurance trust fund:			
Employment taxes	1,095	1,361	1,902
Less: Refunds of taxes	−13	−16	−16
Deposits by States	93	114	151
Interest on investments	65	57	57
Federal payment for military service credits		16	16
Other	(*)	(*)	(*)
Federal hospital insurance trust fund:			
Transfers from general fund		766	2,210
Deposits by States		45	171
Interest payments by Railroad Retirement Board			16
Interest and profits on investments		9	40
Federal payment for military service credits		11	11
Federal payment for transitional coverage		26	283
Federal supplementary medical insurance trust fund:			
Premiums deposited by States and Social Security Administration			550
Repayable advances from general fund			550
Interest and profits on investments			4
Unemployment trust fund:			
Deposits by States	3,052	2,900	2,900
Federal unemployment taxes	622	544	544
Less: Refunds of taxes	−8	−4	−4
Railroad unemployment insurance account:			
Deposits by Railroad Retirement Board	143	145	145
Other receipts	68	59	59
Interest on investments	255	268	280
Railroad retirement accounts:			
Employment taxes	636	683	772
Interests and profits on investments	143	148	154
Payment from FOASI trust fund	436	445	520
Payment from Federal disability insurance trust fund	24	25	27
Repayment of advances and interest on loans to railroad unemployment insurance account	90	95	94
Payment for military service credits and other	14	17	17
Federal employees' retirement funds:			
Deductions from employees' salaries	1,054	1,077	1,085
Payment from other funds:			
Employing agency contributions	1,054	1,077	1,085
Federal contributions	65	67	73
Voluntary contributions, donations, etc	16	16	16
Interest and profits on investments	484	541	601
Highway trust fund:			
Excise taxes	3,782	3,987	4,578
Less: Refunds of taxes	−123	−128	−200
Interest on investments	11	5	3
Veterans' life insurance fund:			
Premiums and other receipts	488	490	490
Payments from general and special funds	7	7	6
Interest on investments	216	224	226
Foreign assistance–military	824	860	1,004
Indian tribal funds	124	104	103
District of Columbia	389	420	493
All other trust funds	162	371	243
Subtotal	31,686	34,334	42,374
Less: Interfund transactions [1]	−638	−795	−767
Net receipts	31,047	33,539	41,608
EXPENDITURES			
Federal old-age and survivors insurance trust fund:			
Benefit payments	15,226	18,125	19,064
Administrative expenses and construction	300	278	293
Payment to Railroad Retirement Board	436	445	520

Footnotes at end of table.

TABLE 19.—*Trust and other transactions, actual for the fiscal year 1965 and estimated for 1966 and 1967*—Continued

[In millions of dollars]

Source	1965 actual	1966 estimate	1967 estimate
TRUST ACCOUNTS, ETC.—Continued			
EXPENDITURES—Continued			
Federal disability insurance trust fund:			
Benefit payments	1,392	1,715	1,782
Administrative expenses-reimbursement to Federal old-age and survivors insurance trust fund	78	90	
Payment to railroad retirement account	24	25	27
Proposed increase in benefit payments and administrative expenses	4	104	117
Other		6	16
Federal hospital insurance trust fund:			
Administrative expenses		53	87
Benefit payments			2,338
Other		(*)	1
Federal supplementary medical insurance trust fund:			
Administrative expenses-reimbursement to Federal old-age and survivors insurance trust fund			47
Payment to general fund-administrative expenses			86
Benefit payments			765
Other			1
Unemployment trust fund:			
Withdrawals by States	2,390	2,182	2,203
Grants to States for unemployment compensation and employment service administration	399	458	509
Railroad unemployment benefit payments	115	102	102
Temporary extended unemployment compensation:			
Benefits	−1		
Repayment of general fund advances	−1		
Temporary unemployment compensation (1958 act)-repayment of advances to Treasury	106	21	2
Interest payments [2]	15	14	15
Administrative expenses	27	30	34
Repayment of advances to railroad retirement account	78	83	83
Railroad retirement account:			
Benefit payments	1,116	1,176	1,195
Administrative expenses	10	12	11
Advances to railroad unemployment insurance account	58	52	52
Interest on refund of taxes	(*)		
Payment to Federal hospital insurance trust fund			16
Federal employees' funds:			
Retirement funds	1,446	1,624	1,802
Employees health benefits fund (net)	−9	9	−8
Employees' life insurance fund (net)	−26	−15	−50
Retired employees health benefits fund (net)	−1	(*)	1
Highway trust fund:			
Federal-aid highways	4,025	3,970	3,970
Improvement of the Pentagon road network	1	(*)	
Forest highways			33
Highway beautification			68
Public lands highways			9
Veterans' life insurance funds	616	543	672
Federal National Mortgage Association trust fund (net)	91	1,400	500
Foreign assistance—military	745	867	891
Indian tribal funds	74	70	59
District of Columbia funds	385	446	489
Deposit funds and all other trust funds	−224	206	280
Government-sponsored enterprises (net)	1,379	493	569
Subtotal	30,276	34,581	38,649
Less: Interfund transactions [1]	−638	−795	−767
Net expenditures	29,637	33,786	37,882
Excess of receipts (−), or expenditures	−1,410	247	−3,726

Footnotes at end of table.

TABLE 19.— *Trust and other transactions, actual for the fiscal year 1965 and estimated for 1966 and 1967*—Continued

[In millions of dollars]

Source	1965 actual	1966 estimate	1967 estimate
INVESTMENTS OF GOVERNMENT AGENCIES IN PUBLIC DEBT AND AGENCY SECURITIES (NET)			
Federal disability insurance trust fund	−263	−432	164
Federal old-age and survivors insurance trust fund	461	−1,443	1,200
Federal employees' funds	1,251	1,156	1,106
Railroad retirement account	149	174	307
Unemployment trust fund	967	1,003	976
Veterans' life insurance funds	103	179	51
Highway trust fund	−344	−105	−90
Federal National Mortgage Association trust fund	1	−6	
District of Columbia municipal Government funds	−2	−2	−1
Other trust accounts	−68	819	474
Public enterprise funds	28	273	434
Government-sponsored enterprises	72	322	323
Net investments, or sales (−)	2,355	1,936	4,944
SALES AND REDEMPTIONS OF GOVERNMENT AGENCY SECURITIES IN THE MARKET (NET)			
Federal National Mortgage Association: Secondary market operations	−99	−1,387	−500
Federal Housing Administration	223	192	154
Tennessee Valley Authority	−45	−70	−100
Government-sponsored enterprises	−1,451	−814	−892
Other	(*)	(*)	(*)
Net redemptions, or sales (−)	−1,372	−2,079	−1,338

*Less than $500,000.
1 For details of transactions for the fiscal year 1965, see table 9.
2 Payment of interest on advances from general fund and railroad retirement account and interest on refund of taxes.

TABLE 20.—*Effect of financial operations on the public debt, actual for the fiscal year 1965 and estimated for 1966 and 1967*

[In millions of dollars. On basis of 1967 Budget document]

Source	1965 actual	1966 estimate	1967 estimate
Administrative budget receipts and expenditures:			
Net receipts	93,072	100,000	111,000
Net expenditures	96,507	106,428	112,847
Administrative budget deficit	3,435	6,428	1,847
Trust fund receipts and expenditures:			
Net receipts	31,047	33,539	41,608
Net expenditures	29,637	33,786	37,882
Excess of expenditures, or receipts (−)	−1,410	247	−3,726
Excess of investments in, or sales (−) of public debt and agency securities	2,355	1,936	4,944
Excess of sales (−), or redemptions of Government agency securities in market (net)	−1,372	−2,079	−1,338
Increase (−), or decrease in checks outstanding, deposits in transit (net), etc	804	−107	108
Changes in cash balances:			
Treasurer's account 1	1,575	−3,910	
Held outside Treasury	174	−186	
Net increase, or decrease ( )	1,749	−4,096	
Increase in public debt	5,561	2,328	1,835
Gross debt beginning of period	311,713	317,274	319,602
Gross debt end of period	317,274	319,602	321,436
Guaranteed securities of Government agencies, not owned by Treasury	590	398	244
Total public debt and guaranteed securities	317,864	320,000	321,680
Less debt not subject to statutory limitation	283	200	175
Total debt subject to statutory limitation	317,581	319,800	321,505

1 The balance in the Treasurer's account at the end of each year is as follows: $12,610 million for 1965;

Table 21.—Internal revenue collections by tax sources, fiscal years 1936–65 [1]

[In thousands of dollars. As reported by Internal Revenue Service, see "Bases of Tables" and Note]

| Fiscal year | Income and profits taxes | | | | | Employment taxes | | | | Capital stock tax [4] | Estate tax | Gift tax |
| | Individual income taxes [2] | | | Corporation income and profits taxes [3] | Total income and profits taxes [1] | Old-age and disability insurance taxes [2] | Unemployment insurance taxes | Railroad retirement tax | Total employment taxes [2] | | | |
	Withheld by employers	Other	Total individual income taxes [2]									
1936		674,416	674,416	753,032	1,427,448			48	48	94,943	218,781	160,059
1937		1,091,741	1,091,741	1,088,101	2,179,842	207,339	58,119	287	265,745	137,499	281,636	23,912
1938		1,286,312	1,286,312	1,342,718	2,629,030	502,918	90,267	149,476	742,660	139,349	382,175	34,699
1939		1,028,834	1,028,834	1,156,281	2,185,114	529,836	101,167	104,427	740,429	127,203	332,280	28,436
1940		982,017	982,017	1,147,592	2,129,609	605,350	106,123	122,048	833,521	132,739	330,886	29,185
1941		1,417,655	1,417,655	2,053,469	3,471,124	687,328	100,658	137,871	925,856	166,653	355,194	51,864
1942		3,262,800	3,262,800	4,744,083	8,006,884	895,336	119,617	170,409	1,185,362	281,900	340,323	92,217
1943	686,015	6,943,917	6,629,932	9,668,956	16,298,888	1,131,546	156,008	211,151	1,498,705	328,795	414,631	32,965
1944	7,823,435	10,437,570	18,261,005	14,766,796	33,027,802	1,290,025	183,337	265,011	1,738,372	380,702	473,466	37,745
1945	10,264,219	8,770,094	19,034,313	16,027,213	35,061,526	1,307,931	186,489	284,758	1,779,177	371,999	596,137	46,918
1946	9,857,589	8,846,947	18,704,536	12,553,602	31,258,138	1,237,825	178,745	284,258	1,700,828	352,121	629,601	47,232
1947	9,842,282	9,501,015	19,343,297	9,676,459	29,019,756	1,458,934	185,876	379,555	2,024,365	1,597	708,794	70,497
1948	11,533,577	9,464,204	20,997,781	10,174,410	31,172,191	1,612,721	208,508	560,113	2,381,342	1,723	822,380	76,965
1949	10,055,502	7,996,320	18,051,822	11,553,669	29,605,491	1,687,151	226,228	562,734	2,476,113	6,138	735,781	60,757
1950	9,888,976	7,264,332	17,153,308	10,854,351	28,007,659	1,873,401	223,135	548,038	2,644,575	266	657,441	91,207
1951	13,089,770	9,907,539	22,997,308	14,387,569	37,384,878	2,810,749	236,952	579,778	3,627,480	(⁵)	638,523	48,785
1952	17,929,047	11,345,060	29,274,107	21,466,910	50,741,017	3,584,025	259,616	630,622	4,464,264	(⁵)	750,591	82,556
1953	21,132,275	11,403,942	32,536,217	21,594,515	54,130,732	3,816,252	273,182	628,969	4,718,403	(⁵)	784,590	106,694
1954	22,077,113	10,736,578	32,813,691	21,546,322	54,360,014	4,218,520	283,882	605,221	5,107,623	(⁵)	848,492	71,778
1955	21,253,625	10,396,480	31,650,106	18,264,720	49,914,826	5,333,573	279,986	600,106	6,219,665	(⁵)	863,344	87,775
1956	24,015,676	11,321,966	35,337,642	21,298,522	56,636,164	6,336,805	324,656	634,323	7,295,784	(⁵)	1,053,867	117,370
1957	26,727,543	12,302,229	39,029,772	21,530,653	60,560,425	6,634,467	330,034	616,020	7,580,522	(⁵)	1,253,071	124,928
1958	27,040,911	11,733,369	38,568,559	20,533,316	59,101,874	7,733,223	324,020	575,252	8,644,386	(⁵)	1,277,052	133,873
1959	29,001,375	11,627,643	40,734,744	18,091,509	58,826,254	8,004,355	335,880	625,369	8,853,744	(⁵)	1,235,823	117,160
1960	31,674,588	13,271,124	44,945,711	22,179,414	67,125,126	10,210,550	341,108	606,931	11,158,589	(⁵)	1,439,259	187,089
1961	32,977,654	13,175,346	46,153,001	21,764,940	67,917,941	11,586,283	345,356	570,812	12,502,451	(⁵)	1,745,480	170,912
1962	36,246,109	14,403,485	50,649,594	21,295,711	71,945,305	11,686,231	457,629	571,644	12,708,171	(⁵)	1,796,227	238,960
1963	38,718,702	14,298,878	52,987,581	22,336,134	75,323,714	13,484,379	948,464	564,311	15,004,486	(⁵)	1,971,614	215,843
1964	39,258,881	15,331,473	54,590,354	24,300,863	78,891,218	15,557,783	850,858	593,864	17,002,504	(⁵)	2,110,992	305,312
1965	36,840,394	16,820,288	53,660,683	26,131,334	79,792,016	15,846,073	622,499	635,734	17,104,206	(⁵)	2,454,332	291,201

| | Excise taxes | | | | | | | | | Documents, other instruments, and playing cards [7] |
| Fiscal year | Alcohol taxes [5] | | | | | Tobacco taxes [5] | | | | |
	Distilled spirits [6]	Beer [6]	Wines	Other, including occupational taxes	Total alcohol taxes	Cigarettes	Cigars	Other	Total tobacco taxes, etc.	
1936	222,431	244,581	8,908	29,494	505,464	425,505	12,361	63,299	501,166	68,990
1937	274,049	277,455	5,991	36,750	594,245	476,046	13,392	62,816	552,254	69,919
1938	260,066	269,348	5,892	32,673	567,979	493,454	12,882	61,846	568,182	46,233
1939	283,575	259,704	6,395	38,126	587,800	504,056	12,913	63,190	580,159	41,083
1940	317,732	264,579	8,060	33,882	624,253	533,059	12,995	62,464	608,518	38,681
1941	428,642	316,741	11,423	63,250	820,056	616,757	13,514	67,805	698,077	39,057
1942	574,598	366,161	23,986	83,772	1,048,517	704,949	14,482	61,551	780,982	41,702
1943	781,873	455,634	33,663	152,476	1,423,646	835,250	23,172	65,425	923,857	45,155
1944	899,437	559,152	34,095	126,091	1,618,775	904,046	30,259	54,178	988,483	50,800
1945	1,484,306	638,682	47,391	139,487	2,309,866	830,753	36,678	58,714	932,145	65,528
1946	1,746,580	650,824	60,844	67,917	2,526,165	1,072,971	41,454	51,094	1,165,519	87,676
1947	1,685,369	661,418	57,196	70,779	2,474,762	1,145,268	48,354	44,146	1,237,768	79,978
1948	1,436,233	697,097	60,962	61,035	2,255,327	1,208,204	46,752	45,325	1,300,290	79,466
1949	1,397,954	636,363	65,782	60,504	2,210,607	1,232,735	45,590	43,550	1,321,875	72,828
1950	1,421,900	667,411	72,601	57,291	2,219,202	1,242,851	42,170	43,443	1,328,464	84,648
1951	1,746,834	665,009	67,254	67,711	2,546,808	1,293,973	44,275	42,148	1,380,396	93,107
1952	1,589,730	727,604	72,374	159,412	2,549,120	1,474,072	44,810	46,281	1,665,162	84,995
1953	1,846,727	762,983	80,535	90,681	2,780,925	1,586,782	46,326	21,803	1,654,911	90,319
1954	1,873,630	769,774	78,678	60,928	2,783,012	1,513,740	45,618	20,871	1,580,229	90,000
1955	1,870,599	737,233	81,824	53,183	2,742,840	1,504,197	46,246	20,770	1,571,213	112,049
1956	2,023,334	785,441	86,580	45,219	2,920,574	1,549,045	45,040	19,412	1,613,497	114,927
1957	2,080,104	760,520	87,428	45,143	2,973,195	1,610,908	44,858	18,283	1,674,050	107,546
1958	2,054,184	757,597	90,303	44,377	2,946,461	1,666,208	47,247	18,566	1,734,021	109,452
1959	2,098,496	767,205	90,918	45,477	3,002,096	1,738,050	51,101	17,665	1,806,816	133,817
1960	2,255,761	796,233	98,850	42,870	3,193,714	1,863,562	50,117	17,825	1,931,504	139,231
1961	2,276,543	795,427	96,073	44,757	3,212,801	1,923,540	49,604	17,974	1,991,117	149,350
1962	2,386,437	813,482	98,033	43,281	3,341,282	1,956,127	49,728	19,483	2,025,736	159,319
1963	2,467,521	825,412	101,871	46,853	3,441,656	2,010,524	50,232	18,481	2,079,237	159,069
1964	2,535,596	r 887,560	107,779	r 46,564	3,577,499	1,976,675	56,309	19,561	2,052,545	171,614
1965	2,700,976	915,345	110,153	46,165	3,772,638	2,069,695	60,923	17,976	2,148,594	186,289

Footnotes at end of table.

TABLE 21.—Internal revenue collections by tax sources, fiscal years 1936–65 ¹—Continued

[In thousands of dollars]

Fiscal year		Excise taxes—Continued											
		Manufacturers excise taxes ⁸											
	Gasoline	Lubricating oils	Passenger automobiles and motorcycles ⁹	Automobile trucks and busses	Parts and accessories for automobiles	Tires, tubes, and tread rubber	Business and store machines ¹⁰	Refrigerators, freezers, air-conditioners, etc. ¹¹	Radio and television receiving sets and phonographs, parts ¹⁰	Electric, gas, and oil appliances ¹⁰	Electrical energy	All other ¹³	Total manufacturers excise taxes
1936	177,340	27,103	48,201	7,000	7,110	32,208		7,939	5,075		33,575	37,165	382,716
1937	196,533	31,463	65,265	9,031	10,086	40,819		9,913	6,754		35,975	44,744	450,581
1938	203,648	31,565	43,365	6,697	7,989	31,567		8,829	5,849		38,455	39,188	417,152
1939	207,019	30,497	42,723	6,008	7,935	34,819		6,958	4,834		39,859	16,323	396,975
1940	226,187	31,233	59,351	7,866	10,630	41,555		9,954	6,080		42,339	11,957	447,152
1941	343,021	38,221	81,403	10,747	13,084	51,054		13,279	6,935		47,021	12,609	617,373
1942	369,587	46,432	77,172	18,361	28,088	64,811	6,972	16,246	19,144	17,702	49,978	57,406	771,898
1943	288,786	43,318	1,424	4,230	20,478	18,345	6,461	5,966	5,561	6,913	48,705	54,559	504,746
1944	271,217	52,473	1,222	3,247	31,551	40,334	3,760	2,406	3,402	5,027	51,239	37,884	503,462
1945	405,563	92,865	2,558	20,847	49,440	75,257	10,120	1,637	4,753	12,060	57,004	50,406	782,611
1946	405,695	74,602	25,893	37,144	68,871	118,092	15,792	9,229	13,385	25,492	69,112	69,365	922,671
1947	433,676	82,015	204,680	62,099	99,932	174,927	25,183	37,352	63,856	65,608	63,014	113,052	1,423,395
1948	478,638	80,887	270,958	91,963	122,951	159,284	32,797	58,473	67,267	87,858	69,701	128,548	1,649,234
1949	503,647	81,760	332,812	136,797	120,138	151,795	33,344	77,833	49,160	80,935	79,347	124,860	1,771,533
1950	534,270	70,072	452,066	123,630	88,733	151,795	30,012	64,316	42,085	80,406	85,704	112,966	1,836,653
1951	588,647	77,639	653,363	121,285	119,475	198,383	44,491	96,319	128,187	121,996	93,184	140,706	2,383,677
1952	734,715	73,746	578,149	147,445	164,135	161,228	48,515	57,970	118,244	89,544	63,094	124,059	2,345,943
1953	890,679	73,321	785,716	210,032	177,924	180,047	50,259	87,424	159,383	113,390	(¹²)	134,613	2,862,788
1954	836,893	68,029	867,482	149,914	134,759	152,567	48,992	78,059	135,535	97,415	(¹²)	122,488	2,689,133
1955	954,678	69,818	1,047,813	134,805	136,709	164,316	57,281	38,004	136,849	50,569	(¹²)	93,883	2,885,016
1956	1,030,397	74,884	1,376,372	189,434	145,797	177,872	70,146	49,078	161,098	71,064	(¹²)	110,171	3,456,013
1957	1,458,217	73,601	1,144,233	199,298	157,291	251,454	83,175	46,894	149,192	75,196	(¹²)	123,374	3,761,925
1958	1,636,629	69,996	1,170,003	206,104	166,720	259,820	90,658	39,379	146,422	61,400	(¹²)	127,004	3,974,135
1959	1,700,253	73,685	1,039,272	215,279	168,234	278,911	93,894	40,593	152,566	62,373	(¹²)	135,728	3,958,789
1960	2,015,863	81,679	1,331,292	271,638	189,476	304,466	99,370	50,034	169,451	64,276	(¹²)	152,285	4,735,129
1961	2,370,303	74,296	1,228,629	236,659	188,819	279,572	98,305	55,926	148,989	64,683	(¹²)	150,628	4,806,902
1962	2,412,714	73,012	1,300,440	257,200	198,077	361,662	81,719	54,638	173,024	66,435	(¹²)	154,129	5,132,949
1963	2,497,316	74,410	1,559,510	303,144	224,507	398,860	81,845	61,498	184,220	68,171	(¹²)	163,827	5,610,309
1964	2,618,370	76,316	1,745,969	359,945	228,762	411,483	74,867	62,799	191,595	67,576	(¹²)	178,861	6,020,543
1965	2,687,135	76,095	1,887,691	425,361	252,874	440,467	74,426	75,987	221,769	80,983	(¹²)	195,536	6,418,145

Excise taxes—Continued

Retailers excise taxes[10] — Jewelry, Furs, Toilet preparations, Luggage handbags wallets, Total retailers excise taxes.
Miscellaneous excise taxes — Toll telephone telegraph radio and cable services, General telephone service, Transportation of persons[14], Transportation of property (including coal), Admissions (General admissions, Cabarets).

Fiscal year	Jewelry	Furs	Toilet preparations	Luggage, handbags, wallets	Total retailers excise taxes	Toll telephone, telegraph, radio, and cable services	General telephone service	Transportation of persons[14]	Transportation of property (including coal)	General admissions	Cabarets
1936						21,098				15,773	1,339
1937						24,570				18,185	1,555
1938						23,977				19,284	1,517
1939						24,094				18,029	1,442
1940						26,368				20,265	1,623
1941						27,331				68,620	2,343
1942	41,501	19,744	18,922		80,167	48,231	26,791	21,379		107,633	7,400
1943	88,306	44,223	32,677		165,266	91,174	66,987	87,132	82,556	138,054	16,397
1944	113,373	58,726	44,790	8,343	225,232	141,275	90,199	153,683	221,488	178,563	26,726
1945	184,220	79,418	86,615	73,851	424,105	208,018	133,569	234,182	215,088	300,589	56,877
1946	223,342	91,706	95,574	81,423	492,046	234,393	145,689	226,730	220,121	343,591	72,877
1947	236,615	97,481	95,542	84,588	514,227	252,746	164,944	244,903	275,701	392,873	63,330
1948	217,899	79,539	91,832	80,632	469,923	275,255	193,521	246,323	317,203	385,101	53,857
1949	210,688	61,946	93,999	82,607	449,211	311,380	224,581	251,359	337,030	385,844	48,857
1950	190,820	45,781	94,995	77,532	409,128	312,339	247,581	228,738	321,193	371,244	41,853
1951	210,239	57,604	106,339	82,831	457,013	354,660	290,320	237,617	381,342	346,492	42,646
1952	220,339	51,436	112,892	90,799	475,406	395,434	310,337	275,174	388,389	330,816	45,489
1953	234,659	49,923	115,676	95,750	496,009	417,940	357,933	287,408	419,604	312,831	46,691
1954	209,256	39,036	110,149	79,891	417,940	412,508	359,473	247,415	395,554	271,952	38,312
1955	142,306	27,053	71,829	50,896	292,145	230,251	290,198	200,465	398,039	106,086	39,271
1956	152,340	28,261	83,776	57,519	321,896	241,543	315,690	214,903	430,679	104,018	42,255
1957	156,604	29,494	92,868	57,116	336,081	266,186	347,024	222,158	467,978	75,847	43,241
1958	156,134	28,644	98,158	58,785	341,621	279,375	370,810	225,809	462,989	54,683	42,919
1959	156,382	29,909	107,968	61,468	355,728	292,412	398,023	227,044	143,260	49,977	45,117
1960	165,699	30,207	120,211	62,573	378,690	312,055	426,242	255,459	[15] 3,140	34,494	49,605
1961	168,498	29,226	131,743	68,182	397,649	343,894	483,408	264,262	1,306	36,679	33,603
1962	176,023	31,163	144,894	69,384	421,163	350,566	492,912	262,760	568	39,169	35,606
1963	181,902	29,287	158,351	74,019	443,558	364,618	515,987	233,928	451	42,789	39,794
1964	189,437	30,016	176,857	78,704	475,013	379,608	530,558	106,062	277	47,053	41,026
1965	204,572	31,390	195,833	81,386	513,181	468,057	620,880	125,890	215	51,968	43,623

Footnotes at end of table.

TABLE 21.—Internal revenue collections by tax sources, fiscal years 1936-65 [1]—Continued

[In thousands of dollars]

Fiscal year	Excise taxes—Continued — Miscellaneous excise taxes—Continued							Total excise taxes	Taxes not otherwise classified	Grand total
	Club dues and initiation fees	Sugar	Diesel and special motor fuels [14]	Use tax on highway motor vehicles weighing over 26,000 lbs. [16]	All other [17]	Total miscellaneous excise taxes	Unclassified excise taxes [18]			
1936	6,091				44,656	88,957		1,547,293	[19] 71,637	3,520,208
1937	6,288				46,964	97,561		1,764,561		4,653,195
1938	6,551	30,569			49,410	131,307		1,730,853		5,658,765
1939	6,217	65,414			46,900	182,066		1,768,113		5,181,574
1940	6,335	68,145			43,171	165,907		1,884,512		5,340,452
1941	6,583	74,835			45,143	224,855		2,399,417		7,370,108
1942	6,792	68,230			131,461	417,916		3,141,183		13,047,869
1943	6,520	53,552			192,400	734,831		3,797,503		22,371,386
1944	9,182	68,789			193,017	1,076,921		4,463,674		40,121,760
1945	14,160	73,294			188,700	1,430,476		5,944,630		43,800,388
1946	18,899	56,732			172,249	1,490,101		6,684,178		40,672,097
1947	23,299	59,152			75,176	1,551,245		7,283,376		39,108,386
1948	25,499	71,247			88,035	1,655,711		7,409,941		41,864,542
1949	27,790	76,174			89,799	1,752,792		7,578,846		40,463,125
1950	28,740	71,188			98,732	1,720,908		7,598,405		38,957,132
1951	30,120	80,192			79,210	1,842,598		8,703,599		50,445,686
1952	33,592	78,473	7,138		82,430	1,947,472		8,971,158		65,009,586
1953	36,829	78,130	15,091		88,708	2,061,164		9,946,116		69,686,535
1954	31,978	74,477	17,969		86,889	1,936,527		9,517,233	[20] 7,352	69,919,991
1955	41,963	78,512	22,892		85,156	1,492,633	114,687	9,210,882	[20] 5,269	66,288,692
1956	47,171	82,894	24,464		84,981	1,608,497	-31,206	10,004,195	[20] 15,432	75,112,649
1957	54,236	86,091	39,454	27,163	89,132	1,718,509	66,237	10,637,544	[20] 7,024	80,171,971
1958	60,338	85,911	46,661	33,117	79,316	1,741,327	-32,749	10,814,268	[20] 5,444	79,978,476
1959	64,813	86,378	52,228	32,532	43,879	1,435,953	66,351	10,759,549		9,977,973
1960	67,187	89,856	71,869	38,333	38,688	1,386,829	99,644	11,864,741		91,774,803
1961	64,357	91,818	88,556	45,575	43,767	1,497,526	-80,943	12,064,302		94,401,086
1962	69,452	96,636	105,178	79,761	37,651	1,570,258	101,468	12,752,176		99,440,839
1963	71,097	99,903	113,012	99,481	38,596	1,619,656	66,251	13,409,737		105,925,395
1964	75,120	95,411	128,079	100,199	43,206	1,546,631	106,387	13,950,232		112,260,257
1965	79,671	97,109	152,188	102,038	54,412	1,786,051	-32,119	14,792,779		114,434,634

TABLE 22.—*Internal revenue collections and refunds by States, fiscal year 1965*

[In thousands of dollars.   On basis of Internal Revenue Service reports]

States, etc.	Individual income and employment taxes	Corpora- tion income taxes	Excise taxes	Estate and gift taxes	Total collections	Refunds of taxes
Alabama	565,754	133,924	22,760	18,183	740,620	63,825
Alaska	74,858	5,797	2,582	243	83,480	12,290
Arizona	336,311	40,725	9,128	40,977	427,140	51,729
Arkansas	272,556	46,568	23,330	10,544	352,998	35,780
California	7,423,957	1,644,593	1,028,126	346,565	10,443,242	832,606
Colorado	1,051,734	133,456	121,683	16,031	1,322,904	69,111
Connecticut	1,238,137	401,763	173,207	90,232	1,903,340	95,368
Delaware	442,830	565,055	4,162	79,537	1,091,584	17,055
Florida	1,364,656	306,978	105,462	98,338	1,875,434	149,659
Georgia	976,643	310,362	166,278	25,048	1,478,331	97,764
Hawaii	219,717	53,039	11,435	5,972	290,164	27,439
Idaho	163,267	39,646	5,507	5,721	214,141	21,885
Illinois	5,338,608	2,154,166	1,074,168	158,052	8,725,054	370,477
Indiana	1,699,427	431,902	379,515	34,356	2,545,200	135,473
Iowa	630,117	176,882	33,067	21,833	861,899	74,242
Kansas	540,169	132,496	24,629	20,210	717,503	62,205
Kentucky	556,636	195,873	1,141,530	27,873	1,921,912	66,296
Louisiana	703,549	184,165	64,629	22,522	974,866	75,994
Maine	196,858	43,911	6,841	14,910	262,519	27,857
Maryland [1]	2,012,381	323,064	305,325	71,602	2,712,372	143,460
Massachusetts	2,107,775	687,092	223,587	96,879	3,115,332	183,660
Michigan	3,637,600	2,970,632	2,514,886	72,559	9,195,677	247,302
Minnesota	1,198,203	428,983	122,427	33,282	1,782,894	113,915
Mississippi	267,675	44,398	13,294	10,850	336,217	34,472
Missouri	1,675,549	629,148	301,710	55,051	2,661,458	147,417
Montana	142,017	28,793	4,616	4,763	180,188	19,492
Nebraska	444,120	108,487	52,549	13,500	618,657	39,744
Nevada	165,887	35,061	13,818	6,210	220,977	20,225
New Hampshire	178,945	37,663	4,199	7,269	228,077	21,803
New Jersey	2,437,397	862,522	368,881	98,169	3,766,970	224,262
New Mexico	196,518	24,598	9,738	6,564	237,417	27,264
New York	10,343,416	6,774,262	1,642,947	516,704	19,277,329	705,565
North Carolina	969,824	535,109	1,305,588	32,430	2,842,950	93,665
North Dakota	109,272	10,747	4,559	2,439	127,017	16,515
Ohio	4,240,605	1,696,028	775,466	110,999	6,823,098	319,781
Oklahoma	581,317	163,948	253,878	22,819	1,021,963	64,305
Oregon	585,529	126,611	28,370	26,016	766,526	58,682
Pennsylvania	4,587,622	1,300,195	828,591	168,474	6,884,882	328,218
Rhode Island	328,976	92,285	23,513	28,907	473,681	28,220
South Carolina	387,224	108,778	19,865	15,775	531,643	46,989
South Dakota	114,788	17,950	6,825	3,123	142,686	17,177
Tennessee	770,756	199,128	60,337	25,019	1,055,239	74,104
Texas	2,705,318	786,916	710,940	131,503	4,334,678	268,047
Utah	232,155	52,264	18,382	3,947	306,748	33,426
Vermont	86,297	16,495	4,615	4,136	111,543	10,133
Virginia	998,597	273,203	432,964	38,227	1,742,990	102,308
Washington	960,765	211,339	107,680	27,222	1,307,006	104,531
West Virginia	300,697	61,187	18,633	14,104	394,621	37,090
Wisconsin	1,266,341	463,239	212,089	40,646	1,982,315	124,849
Wyoming	76,466	7,424	10,929	2,970	97,790	10,501
International [2]	289,411	52,484	48,746	16,224	406,864	35,510
Undistributed:						
Depositary receipts [3]	2,580,293	----------	−55,210	----------	2,525,083	----------
Transferred to Government of Guam	−4,055	----------		----------	−4,055	----------
Withheld taxes of Federal employees [4]	−6,536	----------	----------	----------	−6,536	----------
Unclassified	----------	----------	----------	----------	----------	1,489
Total	[5] 70,764,989	26,131,334	[6] 14,792,779	2,745,532	114,434,634	[7] 5,991,177

Footnotes on next page.

Footnotes to table 22

[1] Includes the District of Columbia.
[2] Collections from and refunds to U.S. taxpayers in Puerto Rico, Canal Zone, etc., and in foreign countries.
[3] Consists of all those issued during the fiscal year minus those received with tax returns which are included in the State totals.
[4] Net transactions in the clearing account on the central books of the Treasury for withheld income taxes from salaries of Federal employees.
[5] Includes $16.9 billion transferred to the Federal old-age and survivors insurance trust fund, the Federal disability insurance trust fund, the railroad retirement account, and the unemployment trust fund.
[6] Includes $3.7 billion gasoline and certain other highway user levies transferred to the highway trust fund for highway construction in the States, in accordance with the Highway Revenue Act of 1956, as amended (23 U.S.C. 120 note). Also includes internal revenue collections made by Customs.
[7] Inclusive of the reimbursement of $323 million to the general fund from the Federal old-age and survivors insurance trust fund, the Federal disability insurance trust fund, the highway trust fund, and the Federal Unemployment Tax Act (42 U.S.C. 1101(b)(3)) which is the estimated aggregate of refunds due on taxes collected and transferred.

NOTE.—Receipts in the various States do not indicate the Federal taxes paid by taxpayers in each, since in many instances, taxes are collected in one State from residents of another State. For example, withholding taxes reported by employers located near State lines may include substantial amounts withheld from salaries of employees who reside in neighboring States. Likewise, payments of refunds within a State may not be applicable to the collections within that State, since refunds are payable in the State of residence or principal place of business of the taxpayer which may not be the point at which collections are made.

Collections in full detail by tax source and region are shown in the *Annual Report of the Commissioner of Internal Revenue* and in lesser detail in the *Combined Statement of Receipts, Expenditures and Balances of the United States Government.*

TABLE 23.—*Deposits by the Federal Reserve banks representing interest charges on Federal Reserve notes, fiscal years 1947–65* [1]

Federal Reserve banks	1947–62	1963	1964	1965	Cumulative through 1965
Boston	$354,748,189.13	$38,901,283.76	$45,569,975.47	$67,883,240.59	$507,102,688.95
New York	1,621,943,543.84	216,680,578.14	251,545,129.94	354,317,201.70	2,444,486,453.62
Philadelphia	393,997,888.24	46,988,497.86	51,235,869.29	74,907,236.98	567,129,492.37
Cleveland	551,732,832.31	68,778,971.52	79,608,803.67	113,661,624.75	813,782,232.25
Richmond	399,406,894.38	53,324,241.72	62,318,919.41	89,242,724.65	604,292,780.16
Atlanta	320,629,547.77	39,412,461.36	47,558,768.86	70,172,287.20	477,773,065.19
Chicago	1,110,659,192.97	146,169,908.00	163,061,035.08	231,749,555.70	1,651,639,691.75
St. Louis	266,283,943.80	31,823,672.41	34,848,808.20	48,676,706.80	381,633,131.21
Minneapolis	147,154,669.74	14,250,491.80	15,420,548.72	25,285,916.53	202,111,626.79
Kansas City	271,240,522.76	33,045,730.25	35,151,829.02	51,198,738.46	390,636,820.49
Dallas	229,267,193.81	30,648,878.58	33,093,813.70	55,148,759.71	348,158,645.80
San Francisco	658,414,880.40	108,461,062.33	127,098,021.21	189,799,248.84	1,083,773,212.78
Total	6,325,479,299.15	828,485,777.73	946,511,522.57	1,372,043,241.91	9,472,519,841.36

[1] Pursuant to section 16 of the Federal Reserve Act, as amended (12 U.S.C. 414). Through 1959 consists of approximately 90 percent of earnings of the Federal Reserve banks after payment of necessary expenses and statutory dividends, and after provisions for restoring the surplus of each bank to 100 percent of subscribed capital where it fell below that amount. Beginning in 1960, pursuant to a decision by the Board of Governors of the Federal Reserve System, consists of all net earnings after dividends and after provisions for building up surplus to 100 percent of subscribed capital at those banks where surplus is below that amount and also of the amounts by which surplus at the other banks exceeds subscribed capital.

TABLE 24.—*Customs collections and payments by districts, fiscal year 1965*

District	Collections				Payments			Cost to collect $100
	Duties and miscellaneous customs collections	Internal Revenue Service	Collections for others	Total	Refunds		Expenses (net obligations)	
					Excessive duties and similar refunds	Drawback		
Alaska	$437,401	$108,905		$546,306	$7,771		$306,037	$56.02
Arizona	8,885,221	9,900		8,895,121	346,467		652,208	7.33
Buffalo	23,867,547	2,344,052	$19	26,211,618	223,859	$103,781	2,033,083	7.76
Chicago	53,181,426	37,276,958	58	90,458,442	599,243	145,953	2,366,283	2.62
Colorado	1,083,620	2,029,141		3,112,761	9,649	127	121,355	3.90
Connecticut	6,085,455	8,092,729		14,178,184	80,164	66,987	250,424	1.77
Dakota	4,883,184	40,234		4,923,418	29,710	1,341	738,909	15.01
Duluth and Superior	6,585,811	46,570		6,632,381	19,261	2,052	465,229	7.01
El Paso	5,128,956	9,225		5,138,181	124,157	131	957,138	18.63
Florida	27,891,128	17,570,641	105	45,461,874	338,884	1,655,992	3,549,657	7.81
Galveston	27,119,632	11,243,931	2,379	38,365,942	525,511	86,782	2,725,363	7.10
Georgia	8,543,568	1,827,826	214	10,371,608	213,263	52,803	417,064	4.02
Hawaii	7,782,638	2,005,526	22	9,788,186	120,565	3,584	1,046,990	10.70
Indiana	1,552,815	5,362,490		6,915,305	9,588	192,318	141,069	2.04
Kentucky	3,457,897	13,026,709		16,484,606	5,375	118,202	101,330	.61
Laredo	15,205,534	44,857	2,375	15,252,766	371,499	51,145	1,966,112	12.89
Los Angeles	108,347,892	36,589,101	256	144,937,249	1,221,054	972,509	4,559,876	3.15
Maine and New Hampshire	4,488,886	20,435		4,509,321	64,934	981	1,301,799	28.87
Maryland	36,633,400	21,737,235	293	58,370,928	515,292	160,527	2,016,866	3.46
Massachusetts	73,100,616	20,653,367	345	93,754,328	789,039	70,267	3,156,251	3.37
Michigan	58,329,751	97,741,802	198	156,071,751	688,311	2,472,836	2,635,306	1.69
Minnesota	2,974,598	3,954,432		6,929,030	41,969	12,154	316,326	4.57
Mobile	5,410,948	1,207,846	541	6,619,335	32,450	5,064	305,525	4.62
Montana and Idaho	3,381,190	2,717		3,383,907	15,320	7	406,113	12.00
New Mexico	113,994	274		114,268			55,278	48.88
New Orleans	35,121,555	7,500,117	1,251	42,622,923	506,615	734,169	2,164,416	5.08
New York	643,624,260	145,020,062	575	788,644,897	7,274,460	6,145,241	26,169,646	3.32
North Carolina	17,223,343	1,107,103		18,330,446	80,652	167,377	292,996	1.60
Ohio	16,168,324	17,281,605		33,449,929	133,931	298,693	917,331	2.74
Oregon	14,679,520	1,488,175	87	16,167,782	158,793	24,166	572,314	3.54
Philadelphia	77,271,115	21,982,080	386	99,253,581	611,796	1,696,673	2,486,411	2.51
Pittsburgh	3,015,166	9,202,566		12,217,732	70,146	58,119	186,651	1.53
Rhode Island	4,312,834	1,721,497		6,034,331	40,291	9,520	201,543	3.34
Rochester	7,058,872	3,448,884		10,507,756	15,142	975,187	277,798	2.64
Sabine	1,508,041	27,210	1,566	1,536,817	7,784		179,329	11.67
St. Lawrence	18,688,965	27,261,319		45,950,284	146,930	41,826	1,493,519	3.25
St. Louis	9,298,521	7,218,384		16,516,905	70,995	5,725	364,587	2.21
San Diego	7,024,198	231,532	75	7,255,805	38,382		1,149,360	15.84
San Francisco	56,262,210	24,801,963	326	81,064,499	1,382,181	420,406	2,632,000	3.25
South Carolina	20,239,841	778,042		21,017,883	166,658		362,551	1.72
Tennessee	1,736,682	1,209,794		2,946,476	27,316	9,850	130,609	4.43
Vermont	5,247,453	2,629,674		7,877,127	48,689	721	1,429,362	18.15
Virginia	25,583,694	1,376,343	261	26,960,298	164,908	20,224	916,721	3.40
Washington	23,581,952	14,908,279	292	38,490,523	220,742	35,382	2,093,044	5.44
Wisconsin	4,365,136	2,550,314		6,915,450	58,072	766,554	288,931	4.18
Puerto Rico [1]	260,733	53,111	30	313,874	1,246			
Items not assigned to districts	41,392			41,392	721		[2] 5,389,202	
Total	1,486,786,915	[3] 574,744,957	11,654	2,061,543,526	17,619,785	17,585,376	82,289,912	3.99

[1] Does not include collections of $21,716,581 deposited to the trust fund: Refunds, transfers, and expenses of operations, Puerto Rico, Bureau of Customs.
[2] Washington headquarters and foreign offices.
[3] Included in Internal Revenue excise tax collections reported in table 22.

TABLE 25.—*Summary of customs collections and expenditures, fiscal years 1964 and 1965*

[On basis of Bureau of Customs accounts]

SCHEDULE 1.—COLLECTIONS BY CUSTOMS

Collections	1964	1965	Percentage increase, or decrease (−)
Collections:			
Duties:			
Consumption entries	$1,063,699,694	$1,241,552,607	16.7
Warehouse withdrawals	173,073,954	179,206,399	3.5
Mail entries	13,391,738	16,112,045	20.3
Passenger baggage entries	2,684,406	2,957,438	10.2
Crewmember baggage entries	869,248	962,540	10.7
Informal entries	10,906,258	12,950,353	18.7
Appraisement entries	152,020	154,704	1.8
Supplemental duties	18,651,696	23,204,574	24.4
Withheld duties	190,297	179,412	−5.7
Other duties	557,068	268,748	−51.8
Total duties	1,284,176,379	1,477,548,820	15.1
Miscellaneous:[1]			
Violations of customs laws	2,109,424	2,546,332	20.7
Marine inspection and navigation services	33,634	31,883	−5.2
Testing, inspecting, and grading	547,032	548,555	.3
Miscellaneous taxes	5,401,280	5,540,501	2.6
Fees	269,972	321,263	19.0
Unclaimed funds	60,679	123,665	103.8
Recoveries	14,647	103,602	607.3
All other customs receipts	21,796	33,948	55.8
Total miscellaneous	8,458,464	9,249,749	9.4
Internal revenue taxes	520,558,294	574,744,957	10.4
Total collections	1,813,193,137	2,061,543,526	13.7

[1] Includes miscellaneous customs collections of Puerto Rico and the Virgin Islands and those of other Government agencies.

SCHEDULE 2.—APPROPRIATIONS AND EXPENDITURES

Appropriations and expenditures	1964	1965	Percentage increase
Appropriations:			
For salaries and expenses, Bureau of Customs	$72,485,000	$78,854,000	8.8
Transferred from Department of Commerce for export control	1,450,000	1,708,000	17.8
Transferred from Department of Agriculture for quarantine purposes	1,661,000	1,822,000	9.7
Total	75,596,000	82,384,000	9.0
Expenditures, obligations incurred by:			
Collectors of customs	48,605,996	52,302,163	7.6
Appraisers of merchandise	12,456,970	13,705,278	10.0
Agency Service (investigations)	8,614,622	9,625,655	11.7
Comptrollers of customs	1,102,788	1,195,130	8.4
Chief chemists	1,497,024	1,646,916	10.0
Executive direction	3,305,745	3,814,770	15.4
Total obligations incurred	75,583,145	82,289,912	8.9
Balance of appropriations	12,855	94,088	631.9
Expenditures (refunds):			
Excessive duties and similar refunds	17,036,944	17,619,785	3.4
Drawback payments	15,266,354	17,585,376	15.2
Total	32,303,298	35,205,161	9.0

TABLE 26.—*Postal receipts and expenditures, fiscal years 1926–65*

Year	Postal revolving fund as reported to the Treasury by the Post Office Department				Surplus revenue paid into the Treasury [2]	Advances from the Treasury to cover postal deficiencies [3]
	Postal revenues	Postal expenditures [1]		Surplus, or deficit (−)		
		Extraordinary expenditures as reported under act of June 9, 1930	Other			
1926	$659,819,801		[4] $679,792,180	−$19,972,379		[4] $39,506,490
1927	683,121,989		714,628,189	−31,506,201		27,263,191
1928	693,633,921		725,755,017	−32,121,096		32,080,202
1929	696,947,578		782,408,754	−85,461,176		94,699,744
1930	705,484,098	$39,669,718	764,030,368	−98,215,987		91,714,451
1931	656,463,383	48,047,308	754,482,265	−146,066,190		145,643,613
1932	588,171,923	53,304,423	740,418,111	−205,550,611		202,876,341
1933	587,631,364	61,691,287	638,314,969	−112,374,892		117,380,192
1934	586,733,166	66,623,130	564,143,871	−44,033,835		52,003,296
1935	630,795,302	69,537,252	627,066,001	−65,807,951		63,970,405
1936	665,343,356	68,585,283	685,074,398	−88,316,324		86,038,862
1937	726,201,110	51,587,336	721,228,506	−46,614,732		41,896,945
1938	728,634,051	42,799,687	729,645,920	−43,811,556		44,258,861
1939	745,955,075	48,540,273	736,106,665	−38,691,863		41,237,263
1940	766,948,627	53,331,172	754,401,694	−40,784,239		40,870,336
1941	812,827,736	58,837,470	778,108,078	−24,117,812		30,064,048
1942	859,817,491	73,916,128	800,040,400	−14,139,037		18,308,869
1943	966,227,289	122,343,916	830,191,463	13,691,909		14,620,875
1944	1,112,877,174	126,639,650	942,345,968	43,891,556	$1,000,000	[5] −28,999,995
1945	1,314,240,132	116,198,782	1,028,902,402	169,138,948	188,102,579	649,769
1946	1,224,572,173	100,246,983	1,253,406,696	−129,081,506		160,572,098
1947	1,299,141,041	92,198,225	1,412,600,531	−205,657,715	12,000,000	241,787,174
1948	1,410,971,284	96,222,339	1,591,583,096	−276,834,152		310,213,451
1949	1,571,851,202	120,118,663	2,029,203,465	−577,470,926		524,297,262
1950	1,677,486,967	119,960,324	2,102,988,758	−545,462,114		592,514,046
1951	1,776,816,354	104,895,553	2,236,503,513	−564,582,711		624,169,406
1952	1,947,316,280	107,209,837	2,559,650,534	−719,544,090		740,000,000
1953	2,091,714,112	103,445,741	2,638,680,670	−650,412,299		660,121,483
1954 [6]	2,263,389,229	[7]	2,575,386,760	−311,997,531		521,999,804
1955 [6]	2,336,667,658	[7]	2,692,966,698	−356,299,040		285,261,181
1956 [6]	2,419,211,749	[7]	2,882,291,063	−463,079,314		382,311,040
1957 [6]	2,547,589,618	[7]	3,065,126,065	−517,536,447		516,502,460
1958 [6]	2,583,459,773	[8]	3,257,452,203	−673,992,431		921,750,883
1959 [6]	3,061,110,753	[8]	3,834,997,671	−773,886,918		605,184,335
1960 [6]	3,334,343,038	[8]	3,821,959,408	−487,616,370		569,229,167
1961 [6]	3,482,961,182	[8]	4,347,945,979	−864,984,797		824,989,797
1962 [6]	3,609,260,097	[8]	4,343,436,402	−734,176,305		773,739,374
1963 [6]	3,869,713,783	[8]	4,640,048,550	−770,334,767		817,693,516
1964 [6]	4,393,516,717	[8]	4,971,215,682	−577,698,965		698,626,276
1965 [6]	4,662,663,155	[8]	5,467,205,453	−804,542,298		764,090,520

[1] From 1927 to date includes salary deductions paid to and deposited for credit to the retirement fund.
[2] On basis of warrants-issued adjusted to basis of daily Treasury statements through 1947.
[3] Advances to the Postmaster General to meet estimated deficiencies in postal revenues, reduced by repayments from prior year advances. Excludes allowances for offsets of extraordinary expenditures or the cost of free mailings. Figures are on basis of warrants-issued adjusted to basis of daily Treasury statements through 1953, and thereafter on basis of the central accounts of the U.S. Government maintained by the Treasury Department.
[4] Excludes $10,472,289 transferred to the civil service retirement and disability fund on account of salary deductions.
[5] Repayment of unexpended portion of prior years' advances.
[6] Transactions for 1954–65 are on the basis of cash receipts and expenditures as reported by the Post Office Department. Reports of the Postmaster General are on a modified accrual basis.
[7] See letter of the Postmaster General in exhibits in annual reports prior to 1958.
[8] Under the act of May 27, 1958 (72 Stat. 143), the Postmaster General is no longer required to certify the estimated amounts of postage that would have been collected on certain free or reduced-rate mailings.

NOTE.—For figures from 1789–1925 see annual report for 1946, p. 419.

TABLE 27.—*Increment resulting from reduction in weight of the gold dollar, as of June 30, 1965*

	Allocation of increment [1]	Charges against increment	Unexpended balance of increment
Exchange Stabilization Fund	$2, 000, 000, 000. 00	$2, 000, 000, 000. 00	
Payments to Federal Reserve banks for industrial loans [2]	139, 299, 557. 00	139, 299, 557. 00	
Philippine currency reserve	23, 862, 751. 00	23, 862, 751. 00	
Melting losses on gold	2, 175, 121. 93	1, 857, 771. 96	$317, 349. 97
Retirement of national bank notes	645, 387, 965. 45	645, 387, 965. 45	
Unassigned	8, 789, 561. 79		8, 789, 561. 79
Total	2, 819, 514, 957. 17	2, 810, 408, 045. 41	9, 106, 911. 76

[1] The authority, purpose, and amount of these allocations through 1940 are summarized in the 1940 annual report, pp. 128–30.
[2] Pursuant to the act of Aug. 21, 1958 (12 U.S.C. 352a notes), the $111,753,246.03 unexpended balance of this allocation was covered into the Treasury as miscellaneous receipts; and the $27,546,310.97 which had been advanced to the Federal Reserve banks under this allocation was repaid to a special fund from which it was appropriated to the Small Business Administration. The unused portion of the appropriation was subsequently rescinded (73 Stat. 209) and the balance, $23,653,582.01, covered into the Treasury. Cumulative subsequent rescissions through June 30, 1965, totaled $141,104.72.

TABLE 28.—*Seigniorage on coin and silver bullion, January 1, 1935–June 30, 1965*

Fiscal year	Total seigniorage on coin (silver and minor) and on silver bullion revalued	Potential seigniorage on silver bullion at cost in Treasurer's account, end of fiscal year [1]
Jan. 1, 1935–June 30, 1960, cumulative	$2, 182, 367, 242. 94	[2] $87, 536, 030. 23
1961	55, 378, 802. 51	45, 937, 577. 49
1962	57, 543, 750. 09	16, 693, 959. 11
1963	44, 896, 025. 48	17, 290, 212. 19
1964	68, 745, 284. 41	7, 520, 617. 15
1965	116, 996, 658. 41	6, 560, 393. 72
Jan. 1, 1935–June 30, 1965, cumulative	2, 525, 927, 763. 84	

[1] Not cumulative, as the bullion held by the Treasurer of the United States changes, the potential seigniorage changes accordingly.
[2] Represents potential seigniorage as of June 30, 1960.

NOTE.—For calendar year figures 1935–63, see the *Treasury Bulletin* for July 1964, p. 79.

Public Debt, Guaranteed Debt, Etc.
I.—Outstanding
TABLE 29.—*Principal of the public debt, fiscal years 1790–1965*

[On basis of Public Debt accounts from 1790 through 1915, and on basis of daily Treasury statements from 1916 to date, see "Bases of Tables" and Note]

Date	Total gross debt	Date	Total gross debt	Date	Total gross debt
December 31—		December 31—		December 31—	
1790	$75,463,477	1812	$55,962,828	1833	$4,760,082
1791	77,227,925	1813	81,487,846	1834	37,733
1792	80,358,634	1814	99,833,660	1835	37,513
1793	78,427,405	1815	127,334,934	1836	336,958
1794	80,747,587	1816	123,491,965	1837	3,308,124
1795	83,762,172	1817	103,466,634	1838	10,434,221
1796	82,064,479	1818	95,529,648	1839	3,573,344
1797	79,228,529	1819	91,015,566	1840	5,250,876
1798	78,408,670	1820	89,987,428	1841	13,594,481
1799	82,976,294	1821	93,546,677	1842	20,201,226
1800	83,038,051	1822	90,875,877	June 30—	
1801	80,712,632	1823	90,269,778	1843	32,742,922
1802	77,054,686	1824	83,788,433	1844	23,461,653
1803	86,427,121	1825	81,054,060	1845	15,925,303
1804	82,312,151	1826	73,987,357	1846	15,550,203
1805	75,723,271	1827	67,475,044	1847	38,826,535
1806	69,218,399	1828	58,421,414	1848	47,044,862
1807	65,196,318	1829	48,565,407	1849	63,061,859
1808	57,023,192	1830	39,123,192	1850	63,452,774
1809	53,173,218	1831	24,322,235	1851	68,304,796
1810	48,005,588	1832	7,011,699	1852	66,199,342
1811	45,209,738				

June 30	Interest-bearing [1]	Matured debt on which interest has ceased	Debt bearing no interest	Total gross debt	Gross debt per capita [2]
1853	$59,642,412	$162,249		$59,804,661	$2.32
1854	42,044,517	199,248		42,243,765	1.59
1855	35,418,001	170,498		35,588,499	1.30
1856	31,805,180	168,901		31,974,081	1.10
1857	28,503,377	197,998		28,701,375	.93
1858	44,743,256	170,168		44,913,424	1.59
1859	58,333,156	165,225		58,498,381	1.91
1860	64,683,256	160,575		64,843,831	2.06
1861	90,423,292	159,125		90,582,417	2.80
1862	365,356,045	230,520	$158,591,390	524,177,955	15.79
1863	707,834,255	171,970	411,767,456	1,119,773,681	32.91
1864	1,360,026,914	366,629	455,437,271	1,815,830,814	52.08
1865	2,217,709,407	2,129,425	458,090,180	2,677,929,012	75.01
1866	2,322,116,330	4,435,865	429,211,734	2,755,763,929	75.42
1867	2,238,954,794	1,739,108	409,474,321	2,650,168,223	70.91
1868	2,191,326,130	1,246,334	390,873,992	2,583,446,456	67.61
1869	2,151,495,065	5,112,034	388,503,491	2,545,110,590	65.17
1870	2,035,881,095	3,569,664	397,002,510	2,436,453,269	61.06
1871	1,920,696,750	1,948,902	399,406,489	2,322,052,141	56.72
1872	1,800,794,100	7,926,547	401,270,191	2,209,990,838	52.65
1873	1,696,483,950	51,929,460	402,796,935	2,151,210,345	50.02
1874	1,724,930,750	3,216,340	431,785,640	2,159,932,730	49.05
1875	1,708,676,300	11,425,570	436,174,779	2,156,276,649	47.84
1876	1,696,685,450	3,902,170	430,258,158	2,130,845,778	46.22
1877	1,697,888,500	16,648,610	393,222,793	2,107,759,903	44.71
1878	1,780,735,650	5,594,070	373,088,595	2,159,418,315	44.82
1879	1,887,716,110	37,015,380	374,181,153	2,298,912,643	46.72
1880	1,709,993,100	7,621,205	373,294,567	2,090,908,872	41.60
1881	1,625,567,750	6,723,615	386,994,363	2,019,285,728	39.18
1882	1,449,810,400	16,260,555	390,844,689	1,856,915,644	35.16
1883	1,324,229,150	7,831,165	389,898,603	1,721,958,918	31.83
1884	1,212,563,850	19,655,955	393,087,639	1,625,307,444	29.35
1885	1,182,150,950	4,100,745	392,299,474	1,578,551,169	27.86
1886	1,132,014,100	9,704,195	413,941,255	1,555,659,550	26.85
1887	1,007,692,350	6,114,915	451,678,029	1,465,485,294	24.75
1888	936,522,500	2,495,845	445,613,311	1,384,631,656	22.89
1889	815,853,990	1,911,235	431,705,286	1,249,470,511	20.23
1890	711,313,110	1,815,555	400,267,919	1,122,396,584	17.80
1891	610,529,120	1,614,705	393,662,736	1,005,806,561	15.63
1892	585,029,330	2,785,875	380,403,636	968,218,841	14.74
1893	585,037,100	2,094,060	374,300,606	961,431,766	14.36
1894	635,041,890	1,851,240	380,004,687	1,016,897,817	14.89
1895	716,202,060	1,721,590	378,989,470	1,096,913,120	15.76
1896	847,363,890	1,636,840	373,728,570	1,222,729,350	17.25
1897	847,365,130	1,346,880	378,081,703	1,226,793,713	16.99
1898	847,367,470	1,262,680	384,112,913	1,232,743,063	16.77
1899	1,046,048,750	1,218,300	389,433,654	1,436,700,704	19.21
1900	1,023,478,860	1,176,320	238,761,733	1,263,416,913	16.60

Footnotes at end of table.

TABLE 29.—*Principal of the public debt, fiscal years 1790-1965*—Continued

June 30	Interest-bearing [1]	Matured debt on which interest has ceased	Debt bearing no interest	Total gross debt [3]	Gross debt per capita [2]
1901	$987,141,040	$1,415,620	$233,015,585	$1,221,572,245	$15.74
1902	931,070,340	1,280,860	245,680,157	1,178,031,357	14.88
1903	914,541,410	1,205,090	243,659,413	1,159,405,913	14.38
1904	895,157,440	1,970,920	239,130,656	1,136,259,016	13.83
1905	895,158,340	1,370,245	235,828,510	1,132,357,095	13.51
1906	895,159,140	1,128,135	246,235,695	1,142,522,970	13.37
1907	894,834,280	1,086,815	251,257,098	1,147,178,193	13.19
1908	897,503,990	4,130,015	276,056,398	1,177,690,403	13.28
1909	913,317,490	2,883,855	232,114,027	1,148,315,372	12.69
1910	913,317,490	2,124,895	231,497,584	1,146,939,969	12.41
1911	915,353,190	1,879,830	236,751,917	1,153,984,937	12.29
1912	963,776,770	1,760,450	228,301,285	1,193,838,505	12.52
1913	965,706,610	1,659,550	225,681,585	1,193,047,745	12.27
1914	967,953,310	1,552,560	218,729,530	1,188,235,400	11.99
1915	969,759,090	1,507,260	219,997,718	1,191,264,068	11.85
1916	971,562,590	1,473,100	252,109,877	1,225,145,568	12.02
1917	2,712,549,477	14,232,230	248,836,878	2,975,618,585	28.77
1918	12,197,507,642	20,242,550	237,475,173	12,455,225,365	119.13
1919	25,236,947,172	11,176,250	236,382,738	25,484,506,160	242.56
1920	24,062,500,285	6,745,237	230,075,945	24,299,321,467	228.23
1921	23,738,900,085	10,688,160	227,862,308	23,977,450,553	220.91
1922	22,710,338,105	25,250,880	227,792,723	22,963,381,708	208.65
1923	22,007,043,612	98,738,910	243,924,844	22,349,707,365	199.64
1924	20,981,242,042	30,278,200	239,292,747	21,250,812,989	186.23
1925	20,210,906,915	30,258,980	275,027,993	20,516,193,888	177.12
1926	19,383,770,860	13,359,900	246,085,555	19,643,216,315	167.32
1927	18,252,664,666	14,718,585	244,523,681	18,511,906,932	155.51
1928	17,317,694,182	45,335,060	241,263,959	17,604,293,201	146.09
1929	16,638,941,379	50,749,199	241,397,905	16,931,088,484	139.04
1930	15,921,892,350	31,716,870	231,700,611	16,185,309,831	131.51
1931	16,519,588,640	.51,819,095	229,873,756	16,801,281,492	135.45
1932	19,161,273,540	60,079,385	265,649,519	19,487,002,444	156.10
1933	22,157,643,120	65,911,170	315,118,270	22,538,672,560	179.48
1934	26,480,487,870	54,266,830	518,386,714	27,053,141,414	214.07
1935	27,645,241,089	230,662,155	824,989,381	28,700,892,625	225.55
1936	32,988,790,135	169,363,395	620,389,964	33,778,543,494	263.79
1937	35,800,109,418	118,529,815	505,974,499	36,424,613,732	282.75
1938	36,575,925,880	141,362,460	447,451,975	37,164,740,315	286.27
1939	39,885,969,732	142,283,140	411,279,539	40,439,532,411	308.98
1940	42,376,495,928	204,591,190	386,443,919	42,967,531,038	325.23
1941	48,387,399,539	204,999,860	369,044,137	48,961,443,536	367.09
1942	71,968,418,098	98,299,730	355,727,288	72,422,445,116	537.13
1943	135,380,305,795	140,500,090	1,175,284,445	136,696,090,330	999.83
1944	199,543,355,301	200,851,160	1,259,180,760	201,003,387,221	1,452.44
1945	256,356,615,818	268,667,135	2,056,904,457	258,682,187,410	1,848.60
1946	268,110,872,218	376,406,860	934,820,095	269,422,099,173	1,905.42
1947	255,113,412,039	230,913,536	2,942,057,534	258,286,383,109	1,792.05
1948	250,063,348,379	279,751,730	1,949,146,403	252,292,246,513	1,720.71
1949	250,761,636,723	244,757,458	1,763,965,680	252,770,359,860	1,694.17
1950	255,209,353,372	264,770,705	1,883,228,274	257,357,352,351	ʳ 1,696.67
1951	252,851,765,497	512,046,600	1,858,164,718	255,221,976,815	ʳ 1,654.20
1952	256,862,861,128	418,692,165	1,823,625,492	259,105,178,785	ʳ 1,650.84
1953	263,946,017,740	298,420,570	1,826,623,328	266,071,061,639	ʳ 1,667.48
1954	268,909,766,654	437,184,655	1,912,647,799	271,259,599,108	ʳ 1,670.41
1955	271,741,267,507	588,601,480	2,044,353,816	274,374,222,803	ʳ 1,660.11
1956	269,883,068,041	666,051,697	2,201,693,911	272,750,813,649	ʳ 1,621.38
1957	268,485,562,677	529,241,585	1,512,367,635	270,527,171,896	ʳ 1,579.50
1958	274,697,560,009	597,324,889	1,048,332,847	276,343,217,746	ʳ 1,586.89
1959	281,833,362,429	476,455,003	2,396,089,647	284,705,907,078	ʳ 1,606.11
1960	283,241,182,755	444,608,630	2,644,969,463	286,330,760,848	1,584.70
1961	285,671,608,619	349,355,209	2,949,974,782	288,970,938,610	1,572.58
1962	294,442,000,790	437,627,514	3,321,194,417	298,200,822,721	1,597.60
1963	301,953,730,701	310,415,540	3,595,486,755	305,859,632,996	1,615.10
1964	307,356,561,535	295,293,165	4,061,044,557	311,712,899,257	ʳ 1,622.50
1965	313,112,816,994	292,259,861	3,868,822,129	317,273,898,984	ᵖ 1,630.53

ʳ Revised.
ᵖ Preliminary.

[1] Exclusive of bonds issued to the Pacific railroads (acts of 1862, 1864, and 1878), since statutory provision was made to secure the Treasury against both principal and interest, and the Navy pension fund, which was not a debt as principal and interest were the property of the United States. The Statement of the Public Debt included the railroad bonds from issuance and the Navy fund from September 1, 1866, through June 30, 1890.

[2] See table 30, footnote 3.

[3] Includes certain securities not subject to statutory limitation; see table 1, notes 6 and 7. Public debt includes debt incurred to finance expenditures of wholly owned Government corporations and other business-type activities in exchange for which securities of the corporations and activities were issued to the Treasury (see table 110).

NOTE.—From 1790-1842, the fiscal year ended December 31. Detailed figures for 1790-1852 are not available on a basis comparable with those of later years. For bases prior to 1916, see the 1963 annual report p. 497, Note.

TABLE 30.—*Public debt and guaranteed debt outstanding June 30, 1934–65*

[Gross public debt on basis of daily Treasury statements. Guaranteed debt from 1934 through 1939 on basis of Public Debt accounts, and for 1940 and subsequent years on basis of daily Treasury statements]

June 30	Gross public debt [1]	Guaranteed debt of U.S. Government agencies held outside the Treasury			Gross public debt and guaranteed debt [1]	
		Interest-bearing	Matured [2]	Total	Total	Per capita [3]
1934	$27,053,141,414	$680,767,817		$680,767,817	$27,733,909,231	$219.46
1935	28,700,892,625	4,122,684,692		4,122,684,692	32,823,577,316	257.95
1936	33,778,543,494	4,718,033,242		4,718,033,242	38,496,576,735	300.63
1937	36,424,613,732	4,664,594,533		4,664,604,533	41,089,218,265	318.95
1938	37,164,740,315	4,852,559,151	$10,000	4,852,791,651	42,017,531,967	323.65
1939	40,439,532,411	5,450,012,899	232,500	5,450,834,099	45,890,366,510	350.63
1940	42,967,531,038	5,497,556,555	821,200	5,529,070,655	48,496,601,693	367.08
1941	48,961,443,536	6,359,619,105	31,514,100	6,370,252,580	55,331,696,116	414.85
1942	72,422,445,116	4,548,529,255	10,633,475	4,568,259,630	76,990,704,746	571.02
1943	136,696,090,330	4,091,686,621	19,730,375	4,099,943,046	140,796,033,376	1,029.82
1944	201,003,387,221	1,515,638,626	8,256,425	1,623,069,301	202,626,456,522	1,464.17
1945	258,682,187,410	409,091,867	107,430,675	433,158,392	259,115,345,802	1,851.70
1946	269,422,099,173	466,671,984	24,066,525	476,384,859	269,898,484,033	1,908.79
1947	258,286,383,109	83,212,285	9,712,875	89,520,185	258,375,903,294	1,792.67
1948	252,292,246,513	68,768,043	6,307,900	73,460,818	252,365,707,331	1,721.21
1949	252,770,359,860	23,862,383	4,692,775	27,275,408	252,797,635,268	1,694.93
1950	257,357,352,351	17,077,809	3,413,025	19,503,034	257,376,855,385	r 1,696.80
1951	255,221,976,815	27,364,069	2,425,225	29,227,169	255,251,203,984	r 1,654.39
1952	259,105,178,785	44,092,646	1,863,100	45,565,346	259,150,744,131	r 1,651.13
1953	266,071,061,639	50,881,686	1,472,700	52,072,761	266,123,134,400	r 1,667.80
1954	271,259,599,108	80,415,386	1,191,075	81,441,386	271,341,040,495	r 1,670.91
1955	274,374,222,803	43,257,786	1,026,000	44,142,961	274,418,365,764	r 1,660.37
1956	272,750,813,649	73,100,900	885,175	73,888,475	272,824,702,124	r 1,621.82
1957	270,527,171,896	106,434,150	787,575	107,137,950	270,634,309,846	r 1,580.12
1958	276,343,217,746	100,565,250	703,800	101,220,600	276,444,438,346	r 1,587.47
1959	284,705,907,078	110,429,100	655,350	111,019,150	284,816,926,228	r 1,606.74
1960	286,330,760,848	139,305,000	590,050	139,841,775	286,470,602,623	1,585.48
1961	288,970,938,610	239,694,000	536,775	240,215,450	289,211,154,060	1,573.89
1962	298,200,822,721	443,688,500	521,450	444,218,925	298,645,041,646	1,599.98
1963	305,859,632,996	605,489,600	530,425	606,610,375	306,466,243,371	1,618.30
1964	311,712,899,257	812,272,200	1,120,775	812,991,925	312,525,891,182	r 1,626.73
1965	317,273,898,984	588,900,500	719,725	590,326,050	317,864,225,034	p 1,633.57
			1,425,550			

r Revised.

p Preliminary.

[1] Includes certain securities not subject to statutory limitation. For amounts subject to limitation, see table 1. Public debt includes debt incurred to finance expenditures of wholly owned Government corporations and other business-type activities in exchange for which securities of the corporations and activities were issued to the Treasury (see table 110).

[2] Amounts shown represent outstanding principal on which interest has ceased. The amount of accrued interest as of June 30, 1965, was $125,146, funds for which are on deposit with the Treasurer of the United States.

[3] Based on the Bureau of the Census estimated population. Through 1958 the estimated population is for the conterminous United States (that is, exclusive of Alaska, Hawaii, and the outlying areas, such as Puerto Rico, Guam, and the Virgin Islands). Beginning with 1959 the estimates include Alaska, and with 1960, Hawaii.

TABLE 31.—*Public debt outstanding by classification, June 30, 1955–65*

[In millions of dollars. On basis of daily Treasury statements, see "Bases of Tables"]

Class	1955	1956	1957	1958	1959	1960	1961	1962	1963	1964	1965
Interest-bearing:											
Public:											
Marketable:											
Treasury bills:											
Regular weekly	19,514	20,808	21,919	22,406	25,006	25,903	26,914	32,225	37,729	39,730	43,659
Tax anticipation			1,501		3,002		1,503	1,802	9,501	11,010	10,005
Other					4,009	7,512	8,307	8,009			
Certificates of indebtedness (regular)	13,836	16,303	20,473	32,920	33,843	17,660	13,338	13,547	22,109	22,169	
Treasury notes	40,729	35,952	30,973	20,416	27,314	51,483	56,257	65,464	52,145	67,284	52,549
Bonds:											
Bank eligible	81,057	81,840	80,789	90,883	84,803	81,247	80,830	75,025	81,964	88,464	102,481
Bank restricted											
Panama Canal bonds	50	50	50	50	50	50					
Postal savings bonds	21										
Total marketable issues	155,206	154,963	155,705	166,675	178,027	183,845	187,148	196,072	203,508	206,489	208,695
Certificates of indebtedness:											
Foreign currency series								[2]75	[3]25	[4]30	778
Foreign series								860	465	240	95
Treasury certificates									2	18	59
Depositary bonds	417	310	196	171	183	170	117	138	103	103	
Treasury bonds:											
Foreign currency series									[5]604	[6]802	[7]1,137
Foreign series											204
Investment series	12,589	12,009	11,135	9,621	8,365	6,783	5,830	4,727	3,921	3,546	3,256
R.E.A. series							19	25	27	25	26
Treasury notes, foreign series										20	9
Treasury notes, tax and savings	1,913								183	152	150
U.S. retirement plan bonds									(*)	5	11
U.S. savings bonds	58,365	57,497	54,622	51,984	50,503	47,544	47,514	47,607	48,314	49,299	50,043
Total nonmarketable issues	73,285	69,817	65,953	61,777	59,050	54,497	53,481	53,431	53,645	54,240	55,768
Total public issues	228,491	224,769	221,658	228,452	237,078	238,342	240,629	249,503	257,153	260,729	264,463
Special issues:											
Adjusted service certificate fund certificates	5	5									
Canal Zone Postal Savings System notes	1	1	(*)		(*)						
Civil service retirement fund:											
Notes	4,055	6,051	5,707	4,249	298	186	170	210	80	73	70
Bonds	2,097	596	740	1,540	2,072	1,892	1,608	1,236	1,056	986	1,002
Exchange Stabilization Fund			925	1,925	6,212	7,289	8,604	9,899	11,263	12,432	13,465
Farm mortgage insurance fund notes											
Federal Deposit Insurance Corporation notes	835	673	718	673	629	694	556	500	260	270	312
Federal insurance trust fund:											
Certificates	256		258	638	89	56	34	1	6	1	1
Notes	30		30	150	394	457	464	336	84		
Bonds	38		38	188	1,050	1,474	1,801	1,967	2,076	1,901	1,563

Class	1955	1956	1957	1958	1959	1960	1961	1962	1963	1964	1965
Interest-bearing—Continued											
Special issues—Continued											
Federal home loan banks:											
Certificates	200	2	10	165	165	59	50	74	372	82	100
Notes		50	40								
Federal Housing Administration notes:											
Apartment unit insurance fund		2	3	1	(*)	(*)	26	10	1	14	3
Armed services housing mortgage insurance fund									1	1	1
Experimental housing insurance fund		1	2	1	4	4	4	4	1	2	4
Housing insurance fund				(*)	(*)	(*)		(*)	(*)	(*)	(*)
Housing investment insurance fund											
Military housing insurance fund	2	26	26	18	15	15	15	15	10	10	96
Mutual mortgage insurance fund	16	2	2	2	1	1					
National defense housing insurance fund	2										
Section 203 home improvement account	1	1	1	1	1	1		1	1	1	1
Section 220 home improvement	1	1	1	3	1	1	2	1	1	1	1
Section 220 housing insurance fund	1	1	1	1	2	1	1	1	2	2	1
Section 221 housing insurance fund	1	1	1	1	1	1		1			
Servicemen's mortgage insurance fund	38	43	43	34	29	23	2	2	2	2	10
Title I housing insurance fund	3	8	7	7	6	6	23	23	14	9	1
Title I insurance fund							15	10	8	8	11
War housing insurance fund							1				6
Federal old-age and survivors insurance trust fund:											
Certificates	18,239	19,467	14,963	9,925	400	270	441	1,090	14,221	598	141
Notes			2,000	3,560	4,032	2,428	1,387	257	98	14,201	1,032
Bonds			2,500	4,825	12,795	13,715	14,372	13,737		332	14,088
			103	112	116	104	138	182			287
Federal Savings and Loan Insurance Corporation notes	94	103	22	24	26	29	32	37	38	39	40
Foreign service retirement fund:											
Bills	10	16									
Notes	6	4									
Government life insurance fund:											
Certificates	1,233	1,217	1,200	1,144	1,127	1	222	7	74	1	933
Notes						295	849	142	929	955	265
Bonds						811	234	879	678	609	
Highway trust fund certificates			404	822	429			436			
National service life insurance fund:											
Certificates	5,346	5,481	5,570	5,665	5,742	8	1,168	1	395	8	8
Notes						1,547	4,591	782	5,319	5,775	28
Bonds						4,248		5,021			5,873
								26			
Postal Savings System notes	90	5	5								
Railroad retirement account:											
Certificates	3,486	3,600	3,475	3,531	3,417	3,586	3,504	3,316	2,786	119	208
Notes										686	450
Bonds											
Unemployment trust fund certificates	7,479	7,737	7,996	6,671	5,636	5,580	4,625	4,657	4,803	2,164	2,465
Veterans' special term insurance fund certificates	10	20	34	48	66	85	106	88	101	4,931	5,799
Veterans' reopened insurance fund										123	149
											3
Total special issues	43,250	45,114	46,827	46,246	44,756	44,899	46,043	44,939	44,801	46,627	48,650
Total interest-bearing debt	271,741	269,883	268,486	274,698	281,833	283,241	285,672	294,442	301,954	307,357	313,113
Matured debt on which interest has ceased	589	666	529	597	476	445	349	438	310	295	292

Debt bearing no interest:											
Special notes of the United States:											
International Monetary Fund series	1,567	1,742	1,068	618	1,979	2,238	2,496	2,667	2,922	3,289	3,167
International Development Association							63	115	129	142	138
Inter-American Development Bank series								55	125	150	150
Special notes of the United States:											
U.N. Children's Fund Series										8	8
U.N. Special Series										56	75
U.N./FAO World Food Program Series										2	2
U.S. savings stamps	48	49	51	51	50	53	52	53	54	54	55
Excess profits tax refund series	1	1	1	1	1	1	1	1	1	1	1
U.S. notes (less gold reserve)	191	191	191	191	191	191	191	191	191	191	167
Deposits for retirement of national bank and Federal Reserve bank notes	232	213	196	182	169	157	147	139	116	110	91
Other debt bearing no interest	6	6	6	6	6	6	6	101	59	58	23
Total debt bearing no interest	2,044	2,292	1,512	1,048	2,396	2,645	2,950	3,321	3,595	4,061	3,869
Total gross debt [10]	274,374	272,751	270,527	276,343	284,706	286,331	288,971	298,201	305,860	311,713	317,274

Less than $500,000.

[1] See 1946 annual report, pp. 42, 43, and 654, and 1955 annual report, p. 515, table 5.

[2] Dollar equivalent of securities used and payable in the amount of 46,500,000,000 Italian lire.

[3] Dollar equivalent of securities used and payable in the amount of 110,000,000 Swiss francs.

[4] Dollar equivalent of certificates issued and payable in the amount of 130,000,000 Swiss francs.

[5] Dollar equivalent of securities his issued and payable in the amount of 124,050,000,000 Italian lire, 647,000,000 Swiss francs, 800,000,000 Belgian francs, 660,000,000 Swiss schillings, and 1,500,000,000 Belgian francs.

[6] Dollar equivalent of securities issued and payable in the amount of 1,057,000,000 Swiss francs, 1,900,000,000 Italian schillings, and 1,500,000,000 Belgian francs.

[7] Dollar equivalent of Treasury securities issued and payable in the amount of 1,412,000,000 Swiss francs, 2,700,000,000 Italian Marks, 2,600,000,000 Italian schillings, and 1,500,000,000 Belgian francs.

[8] On October 1, 1942, they had been Postal savings stamps and postal savings stamps and the issuing authority of the Old Series currency with by the Secretary's obligations.

[9] Includes $95,635,198 of old series currency which by the act of June 30, 1961 (31 U.S.C. 912-916), was transferred to public debt Current Act, and See the 60, footnote 7.

[10] Includes securities not subject to statutory limitation; for units subject to limitation, see table 1. Includes public debt incurred to finance activities of certain wholly owned Government and other business-type activities in exchange for which notes of the corporations and notes were issued to the public; see table 110.

NOTE.—For comparable data 1931–43, see 1943 annual report, p. 564, and for 1944–54, see 1954 annual report, p. 472. Composition of the public debt 1916–45, is shown in the 1947 annual report, p. 361. For reconciliation with Public Debt accounts for 1965, see table 35.

TABLE 32.—*Guaranteed securities issued by Government corporations and other business-type activities and held outside the Treasury, June 30, 1955-65*

[Face amount, in thousands of dollars. On basis of daily Treasury statements, see "Bases of Tables"]

Issuing agency	1955	1956	1957	1958	1959	1960	1961	1962	1963	1964	1965
UNMATURED DEBT											
Dist of Col ... ry Board ... tis:					(1)	476	19,800	19,800	19,800	19,800	19,800
Federal Housing ... ion ... t ois:											
Mal ... insurance fnd	9,021	8,471	10,638	9,987	8,699	1,411	25,389	194,716	328,062	499,018	333,523
Armed ser ... the mortgage ... fnd	725	9,695	10,209	8,324	10,466	9,368	62,420	47,277	16,001	5,691	2,576
Housing ... fnd	2,317	5,838	10,135	8,987	9,970	9,232	23,406	35,299	63,445	89,942	76,723
Mal ... thg insurance unfd	1,462	16,103	40,738	47,734	²59,446	7,737	75,393	92,551	98,124	79,354	71,965
Section 203 ... get ... nt						10		66	2		6
Section 220 ... ing insurance fnd				8	9	217	4,780	23,353	9,360	27,547	23,514
Sn 221 ... ing insurance fnd				78	38	680	1,673	12,609	36,558	55,836	31,566
Sals mortgage ... ine unfd			12	377	213	411	186	633	22,746	31,111	22,886
fle I ... ihg ... ine unfd	35	224	482						523	254	373
War housing insurance fund	29,697	32,765	34,220	25,070	21,591	25,762	26,647	17,385	10,869	3,720	5,970
Total unmatured debt	43,258	73,101	106,434	100,565	²110,429	139,305	239,694	443,688	605,490	812,272	588,900
MATURED DEBT ³											
Federal Farm Mortgage Corporation	333	295	265	240	214	193	174	170	161	144	133
Federal Housing Administration						12	25	57	669	299	1,025
Home Owners' Loan Corporation	552	493	438	415	376	331	323	303	291	276	268
Total matured debt ⁴	885	788	704	655	590	537	521	530	1,121	720	1,426
Total ⁴	44,143	73,883	107,138	101,221	²111,019	139,842	240,215	444,219	606,610	812,992	590,326

¹ Excludes guaranteed securities of the District of Columbia Armory Board in the amount of $96 thousand not reported in the daily Treasury statement of June 30, 1959.

² Includes $179 thousand face amount redeemed as of June 30, 1959, but omitted from transactions cleared on that date.

³ Funds are on deposit with the Treasurer of the United States for payment of these securities.

⁴ Consists of principal only.

NOTE.—For figures for 1946-54, see 1958 annual report, p. 474. For securities held by the Treasury, see table 110.

TABLE 33.—*Interest-bearing securities outstanding issued by Federal agencies but not guaranteed by the U.S. Government, fiscal years 1955-65*

[In millions of dollars]

Fiscal year or month	Banks for coopera- tives	Federal home loan banks [1]	Federal inter- mediate credit banks	Federal land banks [2]	Federal National Mortgage Association		Tennes- see Valley Authority	Total
					Manage- ment and liquida- tion program	Second- ary market program		
1955	110	341	793	1,061	570			2,876
1956	133	929	834	1,322	570	100		3,889
1957	179	738	924	1,552	570	1,050		5,013
1958	199	456	1,159	1,646	797	1,165		5,423
1959	284	992	1,456	1,888	797	1,290		6,708
1960	330	1,259	1,600	2,137	797	2,284		8,407
1961	382	1,055	1,723	2,357		2,198	50	7,765
1962	430	1,797	1,855	2,550		2,556	145	9,332
1963	459	2,770	2,133	2,725		1,960	145	10,192
1964	498	4,201	2,315	2,973		1,698	180	11,865
1965	686	4,757	2,462	3,532		1,797	225	13,460
1964—July	498	4,048	2,396	2,973		1,698	180	11,792
August	538	4,194	2,433	3,102		1,696	180	12,142
September	538	4,182	2,424	3,102		1,571	180	11,996
October	576	4,144	2,352	3,169		1,707	180	12,128
November	638	4,369	2,174	3,169		1,701	190	12,241
December	686	4,369	2,112	3,169		1,601	190	12,127
1965—January	686	4,120	2,102	3,169		1,723	190	11,990
February	670	3,905	2,143	3,298		1,739	190	11,945
March	723	4,090	2,206	3,298		1,739	190	12,246
April	696	4,184	2,278	3,415		1,795	190	12,557
May	678	4,484	2,367	3,415		1,898	225	13,067
June	686	4,757	2,462	3,532		1,797	225	13,460

[1] The proprietary interest of the United States in these banks ended in July 1951.
[2] The proprietary interest of the United States in these banks ended in June 1947. Excludes securities which are issued for use as collateral for commercial bank borrowing and not as a part of public offerings. Includes small amounts owned by Federal land banks.

NOTE.—The securities shown in the table are public offerings.

TABLE 34.—*Maturity distribution and average length of marketable interest-bearing public debt,* [1] *June 30, 1946–65*

[Dollar amounts in millions. On basis of daily Treasury statements]

Fiscal year	Within 1 year	1 to 5 years	5 to 10 years	10 to 15 years	15 to 20 years	20 years and over	Total	Average length	
	By call classes (due or first becoming callable)							Years	Months
1946	$62,091	$35,057	$32,847	$16,012	$21,227	$22,372	$189,606	7	4
1947	52,442	42,522	18,932	13,326	27,076	14,405	168,702	7	5
1948	49,870	46,124	10,464	12,407	41,481		160,346	7	1
1949	52,302	39,175	15,067	13,715	34,888		155,147	6	7
1950	42,448	51,802	15,926	19,281	25,853		155,310	6	2
1951	60,860	31,022	16,012	21,226	8,797		137,917	4	10
1952	70,944	29,434	13,321	20,114	6,594		140,407	4	1
1953	76,017	30,162	13,018	26,546		1,592	147,335	3	11
1954	63,291	38,407	27,113	19,937		1,606	150,354	4	3
1955	51,152	46,399	42,755	11,371		3,530	155,206	4	7
1956	64,910	36,942	40,363	8,387		4,351	154,953	4	2
1957	76,697	41,497	26,673	6,488		4,349	155,705	3	7
1958	73,050	39,401	45,705	657	2,258	5,604	166,675	4	2
1959	81,678	58,256	28,075	1,276	2,256	6,485	178,027	3	8
1960	79,182	81,295	14,173	1,123	2,484	5,588	183,845	3	5
1961	84,855	70,760	18,391	1,123	3,125	8,893	187,148	3	9
1962	89,905	67,759	18,655	1,641	4,956	13,157	196,072	4	4
1963	91,202	68,980	20,522	4,304	4,525	13,975	203,508	4	7
1964	92,272	66,954	22,580	5,048	4,524	15,111	206,489	4	6
1965	99,792	51,377	33,053	4,192	3,040	17,241	208,695	4	9
	By maturity classes [2]								
1946	$61,974	$24,763	$41,807	$8,707	$8,754	$43,599	$189,606	9	1
1947	51,211	21,851	35,562	13,009	5,588	41,481	168,702	9	5
1948	48,742	21,630	32,264	14,111	2,118	41,481	160,346	9	2
1949	48,130	32,562	16,746	14,111	8,710	34,888	155,147	8	9
1950	42,338	51,292	7,792	10,289	17,746	25,853	155,310	8	2
1951	43,908	46,526	8,707	8,754	21,226	8,797	137,917	6	7
1952	46,367	47,814	13,933	5,586	20,114	6,594	140,407	5	8
1953	65,270	36,161	15,651	2,117	26,546	1,592	147,335	5	4
1954	62,734	29,866	27,515	8,696	19,937	1,606	150,354	5	6
1955	49,703	39,107	34,253	17,242	11,371	3,530	155,206	5	10
1956	58,714	34,401	28,908	20,192	8,387	4,351	154,953	5	4
1957	71,952	40,669	12,328	19,919	6,488	4,349	155,705	4	9
1958	67,782	42,557	21,476	26,999	654	7,208	166,675	5	3
1959	72,958	58,304	17,052	20,971	654	8,088	178,027	3	7
1960	70,467	72,844	20,246	11,746	884	7,658	183,845	4	4
1961	81,120	58,400	26,435	8,706	1,527	10,960	187,148	4	6
1962	88,442	57,041	26,049	5,957	3,362	15,221	196,072	4	11
1963	85,294	58,026	37,385	2,244	6,115	14,444	203,508	5	1
1964	81,424	65,453	34,929	2,244	6,110	16,328	206,489	5	
1965	87,637	56,198	39,169	2,609	5,841	17,241	208,695	5	4

[1] Includes public debt incurred to finance expenditures of wholly owned Government corporations and other business-type activities in exchange for which securities of the corporations and activities were issued to the Treasury.

[2] All issues are classified to final maturity except partially tax-exempt bonds which have been classified to earliest call date. The last of these bonds were called on Aug. 14, 1962, for redemption on Dec. 15, 1962.

TABLE 35.—*Summary of public debt and guaranteed debt by classification, June 30, 1965*

Classification	Computed rate of interest [1]	Amount outstanding on basis of Public Debt Accounts	Net adjustment to basis of daily Treasury statement [2]	Amount outstanding on basis of daily Treasury statement
PUBLIC DEBT				
INTEREST-BEARING DEBT				
Public issues:				
Marketable:				
·Treasury bills:	*Percent*			
Regular weekly	[3] 4.053	$41,655,928,000		$41,655,928,000
Other	[3] 4.106	12,008,939,000		12,008,939,000
Treasury notes	3.842	52,548,595,000	−$94,000	52,548,501,000
Treasury bonds	3.642	102,477,519,450	3,954,500	102,481,473,950
Subtotal	3.800	208,690,981,450	3,860,500	208,694,841,950

Footnotes at end of table.

TABLE 35.—*Summary of public debt and guaranteed debt by classification, June 30, 1965*—Continued

Classification	Computed rate of interest [1]	Amount outstanding on basis of Public Debt Accounts	Net adjustment to basis of daily Treasury statement [2]	Amount outstanding on basis of daily Treasury statement
Public issues—Continued				
Nonmarketable:				
Certificates of indebtedness, foreign series	*Percent* 3.201	$778,000,000	------------	$778,000,000
Treasury notes, foreign series	3.963	150,000,000	------------	150,000,000
Treasury bonds:				
Foreign series	4.195	203,929,534	------------	203,929,534
Foreign currency series	3.874	1,136,728,521	------------	1,136,728,521
Treasury certificates	3.445	95,286,087	------------	95,286,087
Treasury bonds	4.000	9,094,068	------------	9,094,068
U.S. savings bonds	3.537	50,019,043,262	$23,586,398	50,042,629,660
U.S. retirement plan bonds	3.750	10,851,529	−9,870	10,841,659
Depositary bonds	2.000	58,738,000	750,000	59,488,000
Treasury bonds, REA series	2.000	25,975,000	------------	25,975,000
Treasury bonds, investment series	2.721	3,255,958,000	94,000	3,256,052,000
Subtotal	3.493	55,743,604,001	24,420,528	55,768,024,528
Total public issues	3.735	264,434,585,451	28,281,028	264,462,866,478
Special issues:				
Civil service retirement fund	3.408	14,536,763,000	------------	14,536,763,000
Exchange Stabilization Fund	3.668	231,805,515	------------	231,805,515
Federal Deposit Insurance Corp	2.000	312,398,000	------------	312,398,000
Federal disability insurance trust fund	3.327	1,562,764,000	------------	1,562,764,000
Federal home loan banks	2.251	100,500,000	------------	100,500,000
Federal Housing Administration funds	2.000	135,203,000	------------	135,203,000
Federal old-age and survivors insurance trust fund	3.224	15,261,174,000	------------	15,261,174,000
Federal Savings and Loan Insurance Corp	2.000	287,422,000	------------	287,422,000
Foreign service retirement fund	3.972	40,444,000	------------	40,444,000
Government life insurance fund	3.532	933,454,000	------------	933,454,000
Highway trust fund	3.750	265,394,000	------------	265,394,000
National service life insurance fund	3.205	5,908,757,000	------------	5,908,757,000
Railroad retirement account	4.036	3,123,019,000	------------	3,123,019,000
Unemployment trust fund	3.625	5,799,114,000	------------	5,799,114,000
Veterans' special term insurance fund	3.625	149,134,000	------------	149,134,000
Veterans' reopened insurance fund	4.125	2,605,000	------------	2,605,000
Subtotal	3.372	48,649,950,515	------------	48,649,950,515
Total interest-bearing debt	3.678	313,084,535,966	28,281,028	313,112,816,994
Matured debt on which interest has ceased	----------	262,480,615	29,779,246	292,259,861
DEBT BEARING NO INTEREST				
International Monetary Fund	----------	3,167,000,000	------------	3,167,000,000
International Development Association	----------	138,000,000	------------	138,000,000
Inter-American Development Bank	----------	150,000,000	------------	150,000,000
U.N. Special Fund	----------	74,613,886	------------	74,613,886
U.N./FAO World Food Program	----------	2,361,904	------------	2,361,904
Other	----------	336,478,885	367,454	336,846,339
Total gross public debt	----------	317,215,471,256	58,427,727	317,273,898,984
GUARANTEED DEBT OF U.S. GOVERNMENT AGENCIES				
Interest-bearing debt:				
Federal Housing Administration	3.642	569,100,500	------------	[4] 569,100,500
D.C. Armory Board bonds	4.200	19,800,000	------------	19,800,000
Matured debt on which interest has ceased	----------	1,425,550	------------	1,425,550
Total guaranteed debt	----------	590,326,050	------------	590,326,050
SUMMARY				
Total gross public debt and guaranteed debt	----------	317,805,797,306	58,427,727	317,864,225,034
Deduct debt not subject to statutory limitation	----------	283,364,986	------------	283,364,986
Total debt subject to limitation	----------	317,522,432,320	58,427,727	317,580,860,048

[1] On daily Treasury statement basis.
[2] Items in transit on June 30, 1965.
[3] Included in debt outstanding at face amount, but the annual interest rate is computed on the discount value.
[4] Components shown in table 37.

TABLE 36.—*Description of public debt issues outstanding June 30, 1965*

[On basis of Public Debt accounts, see "Bases of Tables"]

Description	Date	When redeemable or payable[1]	Interest payment date	Average price received (per $100)	Amount issued	Amount retired	Amount outstanding[2]
INTEREST-BEARING DEBT[a]							
Public Issues							
Marketable:							
Treasury bills: Series maturing and approximate yield to maturity (%):[3][a]							
Regular weekly:							
July 1, 1965	Dec. 31, 1964 — 3.957	July 1, 1965		$97.998 {Sh. / Exchange}	$878,464,000.00 / 123,513,000.00		$2,202,143,000.00
	Apr. 1, 1965 — 3.921			99.009 {Cash / Exchange}	1,001,390,000.00 / 198,776,000.00		
	Jan. 7, 1965 — 3.927			98.015 {Sh. / Exchange}	917,910,000.00 / 85,452,000.00		
July 8, 1965	Apr. 8, 1965 — 3.942	July 8, 1965		99.004 {Cash / Exchange}	1,010,487,000.00 / 191,332,000.00		2,205,181,000.00
	Jan. 14, 1965 — 3.942			98.007 {Cash / Exchange}	905,987,000.00 / 95,080,000.00		
July 15, 1965	Apr. 15, 1965 — 3.937	July 15, 1965		99.005 {Cash / Exchange}	1,029,246,000.00 / 11,422,000.00		2,201,735,000.00
	Jan. 21, 1965 — 3.960			97.998 {Cash / Exchange}	877,931,000.00 / 123,120,000.00		
July 22, 1965	Apr. 22, 1965 — 3.946	July 22, 1965		99.003 {Sh. / Exchange}	982,331,000.00 / 219,233,000.00		2,202,615,000.00
	Jan. 28, 1965 — 3.946			98.005 {Cash / Exchange}	871,198,000.00 / 132,035,000.00		
July 29, 1965	Apr. 29, 1965 — 3.916	July 29, 1965		99.010 {Cash / Exchange}	995,602,000.00 / 205,496,000.00		2,204,331,000.00
Other:							
July 31, 1965	Aug. 4, 1964 — 3.644	July 31, 1965		96.346 Cash	1,000,462,000.00		1,000,462,000.00
Regular weekly:							
Aug. 5, 1965	Feb. 4, 1965 — 3.968	Aug. 5, 1965		97.994 {Cash / Exchange}	869,929,000.00 / 133,651,000.00		2,204,116,000.00
	May 6, 1965 — 3.901			99.014 {Cash / Exchange}	971,271,000.00 / 229,265,000.00		
Aug. 12, 1965	Feb. 11, 1965 — 3.987	Aug. 12, 1965		97.984 {Cash / Exchange}	868,314,000.00 / 132,922,000.00		2,202,205,000.00
	May 13, 1965 — 3.893			99.016 {Cash / Exchange}	977,871,000.00 / 223,098,000.00		
Aug. 19, 1965	Feb. 18, 1965 — 4.16	Aug. 19, 1965		97.970 {Cash / Exchange}	998,511,000.00 / 847,000.00		2,201,249,000.00
	May 20, 1965 — 3.897			99.015 {Cash / Exchange}	1,013,276,000.00 / 187,615,000.00		
Aug. 26, 1965	Feb. 25, 1965 — 4.043	Aug. 26, 1965		97.956 {Cash / Exchange}	860,395,000.00 / 142,991,000.00		2,263,046,000.00

Date of maturity group	Rate (pct)	Date of issue	Date payable	Price	Type	Amount	Total amount
Other:							
Aug. 31, 1965	3.688	Aug. 31, 1964	Aug. 31, 1965	96.260	Cash	973,989,000.00	
					Exchange	26,450,000.00	1,000,439,000.00
Regular weekly:							
Sept. 2, 1965	4.037	Mar. 4, 1965	Sept. 2, 1965	97.959	Cash	864,834,000.00	
					Exchange	135,465,000.00	
	3.870	June 3, 1965		99.022	Cash	975,008,000.00	
					Exchange	227,344,000.00	2,202,651,000.00
Sept. 9, 1965	4.001	Mar. 11, 1965	Sept. 9, 1965	97.977	Cash	924,479,000.00	
					Exchange	75,876,000.00	
	3.781	June 10, 1965		99.044	Cash	1,024,630,000.00	
					Exchange	175,624,000.00	2,200,609,000.00
Sept. 16, 1965	3.990	Mar. 18, 1965	Sept. 16, 1965	97.983	Cash	948,352,000.00	
					Exchange	54,174,000.00	
	3.799	June 17, 1965		99.040	Cash	1,015,367,000.00	
					Exchange	185,303,000.00	2,203,196,000.00
Sept. 23, 1965	3.984	Mar. 25, 1965	Sept. 23, 1965	97.986	Cash	859,616,000.00	
					Exchange	140,841,000.00	
	3.789	June 24, 1965		99.042	Cash	1,001,183,000.00	
					Exchange	204,098,000.00	2,205,738,000.00
Other:							
Sept. 30, 1965	3.773	Sept. 30, 1964	Sept. 30, 1965	96.174	Cash	982,146,000.00	
					Exchange	18,393,000.00	1,000,539,000.00
Regular weekly:							
Sept. 30, 1965	3.993	Apr. 1, 1965	Sept. 30, 1965	97.981	Cash	857,619,000.00	
					Exchange	144,444,000.00	1,002,063,000.00
Oct. 7, 1965	3.993	Apr. 8, 1965	Oct. 7, 1965	97.981	Cash	908,731,000.00	
					Exchange	92,530,000.00	1,001,261,000.00
Oct. 14, 1965	3.991	Apr. 15, 1965	Oct. 14, 1965	97.983	Cash	914,277,000.00	
					Exchange	86,422,000.00	1,000,699,000.00
Oct. 21, 1965	4.008	Apr. 22, 1965	Oct. 21, 1965	97.974	Cash	846,264,000.00	
					Exchange	155,258,000.00	1,001,522,000.00
Oct. 28, 1965	3.978	Apr. 29, 1965	Oct. 28, 1965	97.989	Cash	850,075,000.00	
					Exchange	153,200,000.00	1,003,275,000.00
Other:							
Oct. 31, 1965	3.790	Oct. 31, 1964	Oct. 31, 1965	96.158	Cash	896,159,000.00	
					Exchange	103,791,000.00	999,950,000.00
Regular weekly:							
Nov. 4, 1965	3.950	May 6, 1965	Nov. 4, 1965	98.003	Cash	838,522,000.00	
					Exchange	161,892,000.00	1,000,414,000.00
Nov. 12, 1965	3.950	May 13, 1965	Nov. 12, 1965	97.992	Cash	866,647,000.00	
					Exchange	134,210,000.00	1,000,857,000.00
Nov. 18, 1965	3.955	May 20, 1965	Nov. 18, 1965	98.000	Cash	896,771,000.00	
					Exchange	105,007,000.00	1,001,778,000.00
Nov. 26, 1965	3.944	May 27, 1965	Nov. 26, 1965	97.995	Cash	857,411,000.00	
					Exchange	143,374,000.00	1,000,785,000.00
Other:							
Nov. 30, 1965	4.068	Nov. 30, 1964	Nov. 30, 1965	95.876	Cash	937,414,000.00	
					Exchange	63,128,000.00	1,000,542,000.00
Regular weekly:							
Dec. 2, 1965	3.924	June 3, 1965	Dec. 2, 1965	98.016	Cash	884,850,000.00	
					Exchange	116,327,000.00	1,001,177,000.00

Sold at a discount; payable at par on maturity.

Footnotes at end of table.

Table 36.—Description of public debt issues outstanding June 30, 1965—Continued

Description	Date	When redeemable or payable[1]	Interest payment date	Average price received (per $100)	Amount issued	Amount retired	Amount outstanding[2]
INTEREST-BEARING DEBT— Continued							
Public Issues—Continued							
Marketable—Continued							
Treasury bills: Series maturing and approximate yield to maturity (%)[3]—Continued							
Regular weekly—Continued							
Dec. 9, 1965..........3.863	June 10, 1965	Dec. 9, 1965	Sold at a discount; payable at par on maturity.	$98.047 Cash / Exchange	$896,155,000.00 / 104,139,000.00		$1,000,294,000.00
Dec. 16, 1965.........3.873	June 17, 1965	Dec. 16, 1965		98.042 Cash / Exchange	886,590,000.00 / 114,879,000.00		1,001,469,000.00
Dec. 23, 1965.........3.831	June 24, 1965	Dec. 23, 1965		98.063 Cash / Exchange	914,899,000.00 / 86,620,000.00		1,001,519,000.00
Other:							
Dec. 31, 1965.........3.972	Dec. 31, 1964	Dec. 31, 1965		95.972 Cash / Exchange	976,694,000.00 / 26,257,000.00		1,002,951,000.00
Jan. 31, 1966.........3.945	Jan. 31, 1965	Jan. 31, 1966		96.000 Cash / Exchange	897,633,000.00 / 102,754,000.00		1,000,387,000.00
Feb. 28, 1966.........4.062	Feb. 28, 1965	Feb. 28, 1966		95.882 Cash / Exchange	964,106,000.00 / 36,599,000.00		1,000,705,000.00
Mar. 31, 1966.........3.987	Mar. 31, 1965	Mar. 31, 1966		95.957 Cash / Exchange	950,986,000.00 / 49,318,000.00		1,000,304,000.00
Apr. 30, 1966.........3.996	Apr. 30, 1965	Apr. 30, 1966		95.949 Cash / Exchange	880,278,000.00 / 120,884,000.00		1,001,162,000.00
May 31, 1966.........3.954	May 1965	May 31, 1966		95.991 Cash / Exchange	900,604,000.00 / 100,282,000.00		1,000,886,000.00
June 30, 1966........3.807	June 30, 1965	June 30, 1966		96.140 Cash / Exchange	938,511,000.00 / 62,101,000.00		1,000,612,000.00
Total Treasury bills					53,664,867,000.00		53,664,867,000.00
Treasury notes:[4]							
3½% Series B-1965	Nov. 15, 1962	Nov. 15, 1965	May 15-Nov. 15	Exchange at par	3,285,508,000.00	$1,668,904,000.00	1,616,604,000.00
3⅝% Series D-1965 (effective rate 3.9620%)	Feb. 15, 1964	Aug. 13, 1965	Feb. 15-Aug. 15	Exchange at 99.875	6,202,029,000.00		6,202,029,000.00
3⅝% Series D-1965 (effective rate 4.0995%)	Apr. 8, 1964	...do	...do	99.70	1,066,270,000.00		1,066,270,000.00
4% Series E-1965 (effective rate 4.0668%)	May 15, 1964	Nov. 15, 1965	May 15-Nov. 15	Exchange at 99.875	8,559,999,000.00	460,713,000.00	8,099,286,000.00
4% Series A-1966 (effective rate 4.0616%)	Feb. 15, 1962	Aug. 15, 1966	Feb. 15-Aug. 15	Exchange at par / Exchange at 99.85	6,264,789,000.00 / 5,904,242,000.00		
Subtotal					12,169,031,000.00	1,108,561,000.00	11,060,470,000.00

3⅝% Series B-1966 (effective rate 3.6530%).	May 15, 1962	Feb. 15, 1966	Feb. 15-Aug 15	Exchange at par Exchange at 99.80	3, 272, 638, 000. 00 3, 113, 899, 000. 00		
Subtotal					6, 386, 537, 000. 00	4, 191, 470, 000. 00	2, 195, 067, 000. 00
3⅞% Series C-1966	Aug. 15, 1964	Feb. 15, 1966	Feb. 15-Aug. 15	Exchange at par	4, 039, 918, 000 00	1, 443, 323, 000. 00	2, 596, 595, 000. 00
4% Series D-1966	Nov. 15, 1964	May 15, 1966	May 15-Nov. 15	do	9, 518, 942, 000 00		9, 518, 942, 000. 00
4% Series E-1966 (effective rate 4.0898%).	Feb. 15, 1965	Nov. 15, 1966	do	99.85 Exchange at 99.85	1, 735, 350, 000 00 518, 471, 000. 00		
Subtotal					2, 253, 821, 000 00		2, 253, 821, 000. 00
3¾% Series A-1967 [s] (effective rate 3.8353%).	Sept. 15, 1964	Aug. 15, 1967	Feb. 15-Aug. 15	Exchange at 99.00 Exchange at 99.50 Exchange at 99.60 Exchange at 99.90	180, 885, 000. 00 772, 384, 000. 00 3, 234, 798, 000 00 1, 093, 461, 000. 00		
Subtotal					5, 281, 528, 000. 00	2, 352, 168, 000. 00	2, 929, 360, 000. 00
3⅝% Series B-1967 [s] (effective rate 3.6800%).	Mar. 15, 1963	Feb. 15, 1967	Feb. 15-Aug. 15	Exchange at 99.50 Exchange at 99.70 Exchange at 99.90	959, 980, 000. 00 205, 885, 000. 00 3, 120, 670, 000. 00		
Subtotal					4, 286, 535, 000. 00	1, 928, 887, 000. 00	2, 357, 648, 000. 00
1½% Series EO-1965	Oct. 1, 1960	Oct. 1, 1965	Apr. 1-Oct. 1	Exchange at par	315, 094, 000. 00		315, 094, 000. 00
1½% Series EA-1966	Apr. 1, 1961	Apr. 1, 1966	do	do	674, 981, 000. 00		674, 981, 000. 00
1½% Series EO-1966	Oct. 1, 1961	Oct. 1, 1966	do	do	356, 530, 000. 00		356, 530, 000. 00
1½% Series EA-1967	Apr. 1, 1962	Apr. 1, 1967	do	do	270, 496, 000. 00		270, 496, 000. 00
1½% Series EO-1967	Oct. 1, 1962	Oct. 1, 1967	do	do	457, 177, 000. 00		457, 177, 000. 00
1½% Series EA-1968	Apr. 1, 1963	Apr. 1, 68	do	do	212, 127, 000. 00		212, 127, 000 00
1½% Series EO-1968	Oct. 1, 1963	Oct. 1, 1968	do	do	115, 331, 000. 00		115, 331, 000 00
1½% Series EA-1969	Apr. 1, 1964	Apr. 1, 69	do	do	60, 545, 000. 00		60, 545, 000. 00
1½% Series EO-1969	Oct. 1, 1964	Oct. 1, 1969	do	do	158, 926, 000. 00		158, 926, 000. 00
1½% Series EA-1970	Apr. 1, 1965	Apr. 1, 1970	do	do	31, 296, 000. 00		31, 296, 000 00
Total Treasury notes					65, 702, 621, 000. 00	13, 154, 026, 000. 00	52, 548, 595, 000. 00
Treasury bonds: [f]							
2½% of 1962-67	May 5, 1942	On and after Dec. 15, 68; on June 15, 69. [4 5]	June and Dec. 15	Par	2, 118, 164, 500. 00	687, 363, 800. 00	1, 430, 800, 700. 00
2½% of 1963-68	Dec. 1, 1942	On and after Dec. 965; on Dec. 15, 1968 [4 5]	June and Dec. 15	Par	2, 830, 914, 000. 00	1, 038, 678, 000. 00	1, 792, 236, 000. 00
2½% of 1964-69	Apr. 15, 1943	On and after Dec. 15, 68; on June 15, 1969. [4 5]	do	do	3, 761, 904, 000. 00	1, 175, 666, 500. 00	2, 586, 237, 500. 00

Footnotes at end of table.

TABLE 36.—Description of public debt issues outstanding June 30, 1965—Continued

Description	Date	When redeemable or payable [1]	Interest payment date	Average price received (per $100)	Amount issued	Amount retired	Amount outstanding [2]
INTEREST-BEARING DEBT—Continued							
Public Issues—Continued							
Marketable—Continued							
Treasury bonds[1]—Continued							
2½% of 1964-69	Sept. 15, 1943	On and after Dec. 15, 1965; on Dec. 15, 1969.[4][5]	June and Dec. 15	Par Exchange at par	$3,778,754,000.00 59,444,000.00		
Subtotal					3,838,198,000.00	$1,303,286,000.00	$2,534,912,000.00
2½% of 1965-70	Feb. 1, 1944	On and after Mar. 15, 1966; on Mar. 15, 1970.[4][5]	Mar. and Sept. 15	Par Exchange at par	5,120,861,500.00 76,533,000.00		
Subtotal					5,197,394,500.00	2,786,330,500.00	2,411,064,000.00
2½% of 1966-71	Dec. 1, 1944	On and after Mar. 15, 1966; on Mar. 15, 1971.[4][5]	Mar. and Sept. 15	Par Exchange at par	3,447,511,500.00 33,353,500.00		
Subtotal					3,480,865,000.00	2,081,278,500.00	1,399,586,500.00
3¾% of 1966 (effective rate 3.8153%).	Nov. 15, 1960	On May 15, 1966.	May and Nov. 15	Exchange at par Exchange at 99.75.	1,213,109,500.00 2,384,364,000.00		
Subtotal					3,597,473,500.00	1,909,925,500.00	1,687,548,000.00
3% of 1966.[4]	Feb. 28, 1958	On Aug. 15, 1966.[4]	Feb and Aug. 15	Par	1,484,298,000.00	459,895,500.00	1,024,402,500.00
3⅜% of 1966.[4]	Mar. 15, 1961	On Nov. 15, 1966.[4]	May and Nov. 15	Exchange at par	2,437,629,500.00	586,221,500.00	1,851,408,000.00
2½% of 1967-72	June 1, 1945	On and after June 15, 1972.[4]	June and Dec. 15	Par	7,967,261,000.00	6,684,779,500.00	1,282,481,500.00
Subtotal							
2½% of 1967-72	Oct. 20, 1941	On and after Sept. 15, 1967; on Sept. 15, 1972.	Mar. and Sept. 15	do. Exchange at par	2,527,073,950.00 188,971,200.00		
Subtotal					2,716,045,150.00	764,244,400.00	1,951,800,750.00

Description	Date of issue	Redeemable	Interest payable	Exchange terms	Amount issued	Retired	Outstanding
3⅝% of 1967 (effective rate 3.6083%).[8]	Mar. 15, 1961	On Nov. 15, 1967	May and Nov. 15	Exchange at par / Exchange at 100.30	2,426,887,500.00 / 1,176,657,000.00		
Subtotal					3,603,544,500.00	1,585,003,500.00	2,018,541,000.00
2½% of 1967-72	Nov. 15, 1945	On and after Dec. 15, 1967; on Dec. 15, 1972.[4]	June and Dec. 15	Par	11,688,868,500.00	8,989,433,500.00	2,699,435,000.00
3⅞% of 1968 (effective rate 3.9187%).[8]	June 23, 1960	On May 15, 1968.[8]	May and Nov. 15	Par / Exchange at 99.50 / Exchange at 99.375	1,041,697,000.00 / 348,710,500.00 / [e] 320,407,000.00 / 749,121,000.00		
Subtotal					2,459,935,500.00		2,459,935,500.00
3¾% of 1968	Apr. 18, 1962	On Aug. 15, 1968	Feb. and Aug. 15	Par / Exchange at par	1,257,539,500.00 / 2,489,819,000.00		
Subtotal					3,747,358,500.00		3,747,358,500.00
3⅞% of 1968 (effective rate 4.0704%).[8]	Sept. 15, 1963	On Nov. 15, 1968	May and Nov. 15	Exchange at 99.35 / Exchange at 98.40 / Exchange at 99.05	619,595,000.00 / 194,370,000.00 / 777,469,000.00		
Subtotal					1,591,434,000.00		1,591,434,000.00
4% of 1969	Aug. 15, 1962	On Feb. 15, 1969	Feb. and Aug. 15	Par	1,843,615,500.00		
4% of 1969 (effective rate 4.0407%).[8]	Oct. 1, 1957	On Oct. 1, 1969	Apr. and Oct. 1	...do... / Exchange at par / Exchange at 100.50 / Exchange at 99.75 / Exchange at 99.70 / ...at 99.55 / ...at 99.50 / Exchange at 99.35 / Exchange at 99.20 / ...at 99.90 / Exchange at 100.30	656,933,000.00 / 619,461,000.00 / 147,697,000.00 / 1,408,618,500.00 / 634,731,000.00 / 417,882,000.00 / 399,388,000.00 / 178,729,000.00 / 249,658,000.00 / 941,992,000.00 / 578,928,000.00		
Subtotal					6,264,017,500.00	3,103,000.00	6,260,914,500.00
4% of 1970 (effective rate 4.0740%).[8]	Jan. 15, 1965	On Feb. 15, 1970	Feb. and Aug. 15	Exchange at 99.10 / Exchange at 99.30 / Exchange at 99.40 / Exchange at 99.60 / Exchange at 99.55 / Exchange at 99.60 / Exchange at 99.95 / Exchange at 100.30	175,672,000.00 / 378,810,000.00 / 673,631,000.00 / 299,549,000.00 / 639,501,000.00 / 587,544,000.00 / 902,827,000.00 / 723,886,000.00		
Subtotal					4,381,420,000.00		4,381,420,000.00

Footnotes at end of table.

TABLE 36.—Description of public debt issues outstanding June 30, 1965—Continued

Description	Date	When redeemable or payable [1]	Interest payment date	Average price received (per $100)	Amount issued	Amount retired	Amount outstanding [2]
INTEREST-BEARING DEBT—Continued							
Public Issues—Continued							
Marketable—Continued							
Treasury bonds [1]—Continued							
4% of 1970 (effective rate 4.0773%),[5]	June 20, 1963	On Aug. 15, 1970	Feb. and Aug. 15	Par.	$1,905,811,000.00		$4,129,240,000.00
				Exchange at 99.05	972,382,000.00		
				Exchange at 98.35	164,679,000.00		
				Exchange at 98.15	211,391,000 0		
				Exchange at 98.20	221,389,000.00		
				Exchange at 100.25.	653,588,000.00		
Subtotal					4,129,240,000. 0		4,129,240,000.00
4% of 1971 (effective rate 3.8499%),[5]	Mar. 1, 1962	On Aug. 15, 1971	Feb. and Aug. 15	Exchange at par	1,154,257,500. 0		2,805,626,500.00
				Exchange at 102.00.	1,651,369,000. 0		
Subtotal					2,805,626,500.00		2,805,626,500.00
3⅜% of 1971 (effective rate 3.9713%),[5]	May 15, 1962	On Nov. 15, 1971	May and Nov 15	Exchange at 99.50	[8] 1,245,537,000.00		2,760,420,000.00
				Exchange at 98.90	693,473,000.00		
				Exchange at 99.10	93,607,000.00		
				Exchange at 99.30.	727,803,000.00		
Subtotal					2,760,420,000.00		2,760,420,000.00
4% of 1972 (effective rate 4.0840%),[5]	Nov. 15, 1962	On Feb. 15, 1972	Feb. and Aug. 15	Exchange at par.	2,343,511,000.00		2,343,511,000.00
	Sept. 15, 1962	On Aug. 15, 1972	do	Exchange at 98.80	378,792,000.00		
				Exchange at 99.30	370,327,000.00		
				Exchange at 99.40	1,570,407,000.00		
				Exchange at 99.70.	259,021,000.00		
Subtotal					2,578,547,000.00		2,578,547,000.00
4% of 1973 (effective rate 4.1491%),[5]	Sept. 15, 1963	On Aug. 15, 1973	Feb. and Aug. 15	Exchange at 98.85	1,120,883,000.00		3,893,834,000.00
				Exchange at 97.90	213,528,000.00		
				Exchange at 98.55	782,366,000.00		
				Exchange at 98.20	340,079,000.00		
				Exchange at 99.60	720,541,000 0		
				Exchange at 99.30.	716,437,000.00		
Subtotal					3,893,834,000.00		3,893,834,000.00

Description	Date issued	Date redeemable/payable	Interest payable	Issue/exchange terms	Amount		Total
4⅛% of 1973 (effective rate 4.2241%).ᵍ	July 22, 1964	On Nov. 15, 1973	May and Nov. 15	Exchange at 98.75	232,162,000.00		
				Exchange at 98.90	334,055,000.00		
				Exchange at 99.05	769,304,000.00		
				Exchange at 99.10	574,915,000.00		
				Exchange at 99.25	343,825,000.00		
				Exchange at 99.30	296,850,500.00		
				Exchange at 99.45	1,302,758,000.00		
				Exchange at 99.85	503,341,000.00		
Subtotal					4,357,210,500.00	$1,000.00	4,357,209,500.00
4⅝% of 1974 (effective rate 4.1721%).ᵍ	Jan. 15, 1965	On Feb. 15, 1974	Feb. and Aug. 15	Exchange at 99.05	140,326,000.00		
				Exchange at 99.25	399,959,000.00		
				Exchange at 99.35	493,462,000.00		
				Exchange at 99.45	146,917,000.00		
				Exchange at 99.50	415,742,000.00		
				Exchange at 99.55	333,760,000.00		
				Exchange at 99.90	461,289,000.00		
				Exchange at 100.25	738,918,500.00		
Subtotal					3,130,373,500.00		3,130,373,500.00
4¼% of 1974 (effective rate 4.2306%).	May 15, 1964	On May 15, 1974	May and Nov. 15	Exchange at par	1,531,898,500.00		
				Exchange at 100.25	2,061,558,000.00		
Subtotal					3,593,456,500.00		3,593,456,500.00
3⅞% of 1974 (effective rate 3.9516%).ᵍ	Dec. 2, 1957	On Nov. 15, 1974	May and Nov. 15	Par	653,811,500.00		
				Exchange at 98.50	136,239,000.00		
				Exchange at 99.00	517,421,500.00		
				Exchange at 98.30	313,758,000.00		
				Exchange at 99.10	373,227,000.00		
				Exchange at par	250,315,000.00		
Subtotal					2,244,772,000.00	1,244,500.00	2,243,527,500.00
4¾% of 1975-85 (effective rate 4.2631%).ᵍ	Apr. 5, 1960	On and after May 15, 1975; on May 15, 1985.⁴	May and Nov. 15	Par	469,533,000.00		
				Exchange at 101.15	52,853,500.00		
				Exchange at 99.95	397,057,000.00		
				Exchange at 99.25	105,792,000.00		
				Exchange at 99.10	75,642,000.00		
				Exchange at 99.05	116,733,000.00		
Subtotal					1,217,610,500.00	21,000.00	1,217,589,500.00
3¾% of 1978-83.	May 1, 1953	On and after June 15, 1978; on June 15, 1983.⁴	June and Dec. 15	Par	1,188,769,175.00		
				Exchange at par	417,314,825.00		
Subtotal					1,606,084,000.00	22,673,000.00	1,583,411,000.00

Footnotes at end of table.

TABLE 36.—*Description of public debt issues outstanding June 30, 1965*—Continued

Description	Date	When redeemable or payable[1]	Interest payment date	Average price received (per $100)	Amount issued	Amount retired	Amount outstanding[2]
INTEREST-BEARING DEBT—Continued							
Public Issues—Continued							
Marketable—Continued							
Treasury bonds[1]—Continued							
4% of 1980 (effective rate 4.045%).[5]	Jan. 23, 1959	On Feb. 15, 1980[4]	Feb. and Aug. 15	$99.00	$884,115,500.00		
				99.50	[9] 102,000.00		
				Exchange at 99.00	195,465,000.00		
				Exchange at 99.10	17,346,000.00		
				Exchange at 99.30	2,113,000.00		
				Exchange at 99.50	[9] 107,341,500.00		
				Exchange at 99.60	212,994,500.00		
				Exchange at 98.80	420,040,000.00		
				Exchange at 100.25	562,595,500.00		
				Exchange at 100.50	209,580,500.00		
Subtotal					2,611,693,500.00	$3,389,500.00	$2,608,304,000.00
3½% of 1980 (effective rate 3.3817%).[5]	Oct. 3, 1960	On Nov. 15, 1980[4]	May and Nov. 15	Exchange at par	643,406,000.00		
				Exchange at 102.25	1,034,722,000.00		
				Exchange at 103.50	237,815,000.00		
Subtotal					1,915,943,000.00	3,356,000.00	1,912,587,000.00
3¼% of 1985 (effective rate 3.2222%).[5]	June 3, 1958	On May 15, 1985[4]	May and Nov. 15	100.50	1,134,867,500.00	7,709,500.00	1,127,158,000.00
4¼% of 1987-92 (effective rate 4.2340%).[5]	Aug. 15, 1962	On and after Aug. 15, 1987; on Aug. 15, 1992.[4]	Feb. and Aug. 15	101.00	359,711,500.00		
				Exchange at 99.60	118,050,000.00		
				Exchange at 99.75	150,959,000.00		
				Exchange at 99.90	188,007,000.00		
				Exchange at 99.95	486,642,000.00		
				Exchange at 100.10	195,976,000.00		
				Exchange at 100.15	685,356,500.00		
				Exchange at 100.25	641,227,500.00		
				Exchange at 100.30	147,686,000.00		
				Exchange at 100.35	116,072,500.00		
				Exchange at 100.40	281,957,000.00		
				Exchange at 100.45	143,932,000.00		
				Exchange at 100.80	139,738,000.00		
				Exchange at 101.00	5,410,000.00		
				Exchange at 101.15	122,199,500.00		
				Exchange at 100.70	34,928,000.00		
Subtotal					3,817,852,500.00	11,000.00	3,817,841,500.00

Title	Date of issue	Redeemable	Interest payable	Issue price	Amount	Amount	Amount
4% of 1988–93 (effective rate 4.0082%).	Jan. 17, 1963	On and after Feb. 15, 1988; on Feb. 15, 1993.[4]	Feb. and Aug. 15	99.85	250,000,000.00	99,000.00	249,901,000.00
4¼% of 1989–94 (effective rate 4.1905%).[5]	Apr. 18, 1963	On and after May 15, 1989; on May 15, 1994.[4]	May and Nov. 15	100.55; Exchange at 97.70; Exchange at 98.00; Exchange at 98.35; Exchange at 98.65; Exchange at 99.10; Exchange at 99.40	300,000,500.00; 125,623,000.00; 104,739,000.00; 317,182,000.00; 489,896,000.00; 131,877,000.00; 91,149,000.00	------	1,560,394,000.00
Subtotal					1,560,466,500.00	72,000.00	------
3½% of 1990 (effective rate 3.4907%).[5]	Feb. 14, 1958	On Feb. 15, 1990.[4]	Feb. and Aug. 15	Exchange at par; Exchange at 99.00; Exchange at 100.25; Exchange at 101.25; Exchange at 101.50; Exchange at 101.75	2,719,730,000.00; 721,728,000.00; 575,798,500.00; 233,236,000.00; 344,644,000.00; 322,275,000.00	------	4,901,645,000.00
Subtotal					4,917,411,500.00	15,766,500.00	------
3% of 1995	Feb. 15, 1955	On Feb. 15, 1995.[4]	Feb. and Aug. 15	Par; Exchange at par	821,474,500.00; 1,923,642,500.00	------	2,286,890,500.00
Subtotal					2,745,117,000.00	458,226,500.00	------
3½% of 1998 (effective rate 3.5164%).[5]	Oct. 3, 1960	On Nov. 15, 1998.[4]	May and Nov. 15	Exchange at par; Exchange at 98.00; Exchange at 99.00; Exchange at 100.25; Exchange at 100.50	2,523,039,000.00; 494,804,500.00; 692,076,500.00; 419,613,000.00; 333,306,000.00	------	4,420,921,000.00
Subtotal					4,462,839,000.00	41,918,000.00	------
Total Treasury bonds					133,087,216,650.00	30,609,697,200.00	102,477,519,450.00
Total marketable issues					252,454,704,650.00	43,763,723,200.00	208,690,981,450.00
Nonmarketable:[f] Certificates of Indebtedness: 3.95% foreign series.	Apr. 1, 1965	On 2 days' notice; on July 1, 1965.	July 1, 1965	Par	100,000,000.00	------	100,000,000.00
3.75% foreign series.	Apr. 12, 1965	On 2 days' notice; on July 12, 1965.	July 12, 1965	do.	5,000,000.00	------	5,000,000.00
3.90% foreign series.	May 18, 1965	On 2 days' notice; on Aug. 18, 1965.	Aug. 18, 1965	do.	50,000,000.00	------	50,000,000.00
3.90% foreign series.	May 25, 1965	On 2 days' notice; on Aug. 25, 1965.	Aug. 25, 1965	do.	100,000,000.00	------	100,000,000.00
3.80% foreign series.	June 8, 1965	On 2 days' notice; on Sept. 8, 1965.	Sept. 8, 1965	do.	18,000,000.00	------	18,000,000.00

Footnotes at end of table.

Table 36.—Description of public debt issues outstanding June 30, 1965—Continued

Description	Date	When redeemable or payable[1]	Interest payment date	Average price received (per $100)	Amount issued	Amount retired	Amount outstanding[2]
INTEREST-BEARING DEBT— Continued							
Public Issues—Continued							
Nonmarketable[1]—Continued							
Certificates of indebtedness—Con.							
3.75% foreign series	June 22, 1965	On 2 days' notice; on Sept. 22, 1965.	Sept. 22, 1965	Par	$25,000,000.00		$,000,000.00
3.75% foreign series	June 30, 1965	On 2 days' notice; on Sept. 30, 1965.	Sept. 30, 1965	do	20,000,000.00		0,000,000.00
2.00% foreign series	do	do	do	do	275,000,000.00		25,000,000.00
3.784% foreign series	do	On 1 days' notice; on Sept. 30, 1965.	do	do	135,000,000.00		135,000,000.00
3.875% foreign series	June 22, 1965	On 2 days' notice; on Dec. 22, 1965.	Dec. 22, 1965	do	50,000,000.00		6,000,000.00
Total certificates, foreign series.					778,000,000.00		778,000,000.00
Treasury notes:							
4.03% foreign series	Apr. 6, 1964	On July 6, 1965[10]	Jan. and July 6	Par	125,000,000.00		125,000,000.00
3.63% foreign series	July 12, 1963	On 2 days' notice; on Oct. 12, 1965.	Apr. and Oct. 12	do	25,000,000.00		25,000,000.00
Total notes, foreign series.					150,000,000.00		150,000,000.00
Treasury bonds:							
4.00% foreign series	Sept. 16, 1964	On Nov. 1, 1965[11]	May and Nov. 1	Par	30,000,000.00		30,00,000.00
4.125% foreign series	do	On Nov. 1, 1966[11]	do	do	30,000,000.00		30,000,000.00
4.25% foreign series	do	On Nov. 1, 1967[11]	do	do	30,000,000.00		30,000,000.00
4.25% foreign series	do	On Nov. 1, 1968[11]	do	do	30,000,000.00		30,000,000.00
4.25% foreign series	do	On Nov. 1, 1969[11]	do	do	30,000,000.00		30,000,000.00
4.25% foreign series	do	On Nov. 1, 1970[11]	do	do	30,000,000.00		30,000,000.00
4.25% foreign series	do	On Nov. 1, 1971[11]	do	do	23,929,534.25		23,929,534.25
Total bonds, foreign series.					203,929,534.25		203,929,534.25
Treasury bonds:							
3.71% foreign currency series	Mar. 9, 1964	On July, 9, 1965.	Jan. and July 9	432.9000 Swiss francs.	27,720,0.72		27,720,027.72
3.55% foreign currency series	July 11, 1963	On July 11, 1965[12]	Jan. and July 11	398.2100 Deutsche marks.	25,112,2.89		25,112,377.89
3.93% foreign currency series	Apr. 24, 1964	On July 26, 1965[12]	Jan. and July 26	397.3400 Deutsche marks.	50,334,3.93		50,334,725.93
3.37% foreign currency series	May 25, 1964	On Aug. 25, 1965[12]	Feb. and Aug. 25	431.5200 Swiss francs.	69,521,0.77		69,521,690.77
3.56% foreign currency series	Aug. 28, 1963	On Aug. 28, 1965[12]	Feb. and Aug. 28	398.1900 Deutsche marks.	50,227,2.43		50,227,278.43

							₿, 414. 21
3.67% foreign currency series	Aug. 4, 1964	On ep. 7, 1965 [11]	432.2400 Swiss francs.	Mar. and Sept. 7	---	52,054,414.21	30,126,066.00
3.84% foreign currency series	May 25, 1964	On ep. 27, 1965.	431.5200 Swiss francs.	Mar. and Sept. 27	---	30,126,066.00	22,461,502.84
3.81% foreign currency series	July 1, 1964	On Q. 1, 1965 [12].	431.8500 wiss mks.	Apr. and Q. 1	---	22,461,502.84	50,319,529.01
4.04% foreign currency series	Apr. 1, 1964	do	397.4600 Deutsche mks.	do	---	50,319,529.01	50,319,529.01
4.05% foreign currency series	do	On Nov. 1, 195 [12]	397.4600 Deutsche mks.	May and Nov. 1	---	50,319,529.01	50,319,529.01
4.06% foreign currency series	do	On Dec. 1, 1965 [12]	397.4600 marks.	June and Dec. 1	---	50,319,529.01	30,126,066.00
3.87% foreign currency series	Oct. 30, 1964	On Dec. 31, 1965	431.5200 Swiss ds.	June 30 and Dec. 31	---	30,126,066.00	50,319,529.01
4.07% foreign currency series	Apr. 1, 1964	On Jan. 1, 1966 [12]	397.4600 Deutsche ds.	Jan. and July 1	---	50,319,529.01	50,314,465.41
3.83% foreign currency series	July 1, 1964	On e6 [12]	397.5000 Deutsche ms.	Feb. and Aug. 1	---	50,314,465.41	23,141,719.89
3.87% foreign currency series	Sept. 4, 1964	On Feb. 4, 1966.	397.5000 Deutsche ms.	Feb. and Aug. 4	---	23,141,719.89	50,314,465.41
3.84% foreign currency series	July 1, 1964	On Mf. 1, 1966 [12]	397.1200 Swiss francs.	Mf. and Sept. 1	---	50,314,465.41	50,314,465.41
3.85% foreign currency series	do	On Apr. 1, 1966 [12]	397.5000	Apr. and Ot. 1	---	50,314,465.41	25,154,798.76
3.90% foreign currency series	64	On Apr. 26, 1966 [12]	397.5000 Deutsche mks.	Apr. and Oct. 26	---	25,154,798.76	50,322,061.19
3.77% foreign currency series	July 24, 1964	On May 2, 1966 [12]	2,584.0000 Austrian schillings.	May and Nov. 2	---	50,322,061.19	23,174,433.96
3.92% foreign currency series	Nov. 16, 1964	On May 16, 1966.	397.4400 Deutsche mks.	My and Nv. 16	---	23,174,433.96	50,289,162.69
3.90% foreign currency series	Oct. 0, 1 64	On June 1, 1966 [12]	431.5100 Swiss mks.	June and Dec. 1	---	50,289,162.69	50,263,885.38
3.93% foreign currency series	Nov. 16, 1964	On July 1, 1966 [12]	397.7000	Jan. and July 1	---	50,263,885.38	25,491,877.36
3.99% foreign currency series	1, 1965	do	397.9000 Deutsche marks.	do	---	25,491,877.36	23,025,558.37
4.02% foreign currency series	Apr. 20, 1965	On July 20, 1966.	397.9000 Deutsche marks.	Jan. and July 20	---	23,025,558.37	50,238,633.51
4.04% foreign currency series	Feb. 15, 1965	On Ag. 1, 1966 [12]	434.3000 Swiss francs.	Feb. and Aug. 1	---	50,238,633.51	25,154,798.76
4.09% foreign currency series	Feb. 23, 1965	On Aug. 23, 1966 [12]	398.1000 Deutsche mks.	Feb. and Aug. 23	---	25,154,798.76	25,164,537.36
4.11% foreign currency series	Mar. 3, 1965	On e6, 1966 [12]	2,584.0000 Austrian schillings.	Mar. and Sept. 6	---	25,164,537.36	2,176,721.22
4.04% foreign currency series	June 11, 1965	On Dec. 12, 1966 [12]	2,583.0000 Austrian schillings.	June and Dec. 12	---	2,176,721.22	0,150,118.38
4.08% foreign currency series	May 16, 1965	On 7 [12]	2,581.7500 Austrian schillings. 4, 3.7500 Belgian fs.	May and Nov. 16	---	0,150,118.38	

Footnotes at end of table.

TABLE 36.—Description of public debt issues outstanding June 30, 1965—Continued

Description	Date	When redeemable or payable [1]	Interest payment date	Average price received (per $100)	Amount issued	Amount retired	Amount outstanding [3]
INTEREST-BEARING DEBT— Continued **Public Issues—Continued** Nonmarketable [1]—Continued Treasury bonds—Continued 4.09% foreign currency series	May 20, 1965	On May 22, 1967 [12]	May and Nov. 22	4,963.0000 Belgian francs	$10,074,551.68		$10,074,551.68
Total bonds, foreign currency series					1,136,728,520.57		1,136,728,520.57
U.S. retirement plan bonds: (investment yield 3.75% compounded semiannually) [14]	1st day of each month beginning Jan. 1, 1963.	Not ... until ... tains age 59½, except in case of death or disability.	Indeterminate	Par	11,044,775.09	$193,245.84	10,851,529.25
Depositary bonds: 2% First Series	Various dates from July 1953.	At option of U.S. or owner upon 30 to 60 days' notice; 12 ... form issue date.	June and Dec. 1	do	490,024,500.00	431,286,500.00	58,738,000.00
Treasury bonds: 2% REA series	Various dates from July 1, 1960.	do	Jan. and July 1	do	43,578,000.00	17,603,000.00	25,975,000.00
Treasury bonds, investment series: 2½% Series A-1965	Oct. 1, 1947	On and after Apr. 1, 1948, on demand at option of owner on 1 ... ; payable on Oct. 1, 1965.	Apr. and Oct. 1	do	969,960,000.00	589,295,000.00	380,665,000.00
2¾% Series B-1975-80	Apr. 1, 1951	Apr. 1, 1975, except ... at any ... at option of owner for a ... on ... Apr. 1, 1980 [15]	do	do / Exchange at par	451,397,500.00 / 14,879,956,500.00		
Subtotal					15,331,354,000.00	[16]12,456,061,000.00	2,875,293,000.00

	Issue date	Redeemable	Payable	Price			
					16,301,314,000.00	13,045,356,000.00	3,255,958,000.00
Total Treasury bonds, investment series.							
Treasury certificates:							
3.54% certificates	June 30, 1965	On demand; on July 31, 1965.	July 31, 1965	Par	61,606,974.14	....	61,606,974.14
3.784% certificates	do	On demand; on Sept. 30, 1965.	Sept. 30, 1965.	do	27,487,858.09	....	27,487,858.09
1% certificates	Various dates from June 14, 1965.	On demand; on Dec. 15, 1965.	Dec. 15, 1965.	do	6,191,254.40	....	6,191,254.40
Total Treasury certificates.					95,286,086.63	....	95,286,086.63
4% Treasury bonds	Various dates from Dec. 31, 1963.	On ... June 30, 1967.	June 30 and Dec. 31.	do	20,986,315.06	11,892,247.04	9,094,068.02
U.S. savings bonds: Series and approximate yield (%):[17]	First day of each month.	After 2 mos. from issue date on demand at option of owner; 10 yrs. from issue date but may be held for additional period.[18]	Sold at a discount; payable at par on maturity.				
E-1941, 3.29%[19]	May to Dec. 1941	...period.[18]	do	$75.00	1,846,098,932.11	1,586,084,482.73	260,014,449.38
E-1942, 3.59%[19]	Jan. to Dec. 1942	do	do	$75.00	8,149,422,199.86	7,030,466,075.44	1,118,956,124.42
E-1943, 3.277%[19]	Jan. to Dec. 1943	do	do	$75.00	13,118,262,111.86	11,346,308,853.69	1,771,953,258.17
E-1944, 3.298%[19]	Jan. to Dec. 1944	do	do	$75.00	15,289,586,635.06	13,100,931,042.36	2,188,655,592.70
E-1945, 3.316%[19]	Jan. to Dec. 1945	do	do	$75.00	11,988,396,202.73	10,035,664,485.47	1,952,731,717.26
E-1946, 3.22%[19]	Jan. to Dec. 1946	do	do	$75.00	5,396,277,387.87	4,305,335,040.20	1,090,942,347.67
E-1947, 3.346%[19]	Jan. to Dec. 1947	do	do	$75.00	5,691,714,980.57	3,894,450,207.49	1,197,264,773.08
E-1948, 3.366%[19]	Jan. to Dec. 1948	do	do	$75.00	5,252,559,937.92	3,918,631,275.93	1,333,928,661.99
E-1949, 3.344%[19]	Jan. to Dec. 1949	do	do	$75.00	5,173,914,421.65	3,777,944,667.70	1,395,969,753.95
E-1950, 3.347%[19]	Jan. to Dec. 1950	do	do	$75.00	4,516,375,809.06	3,229,486,139.92	1,286,889,669.14
E-1951, 3.3%[19]	Jan. to Dec. 1951	do	do	$75.00	3,911,190,199.39	2,792,547,156.68	1,118,643,042.71
E-1952, 3.400%[19] (Jan. to Apr.)	Jan. to Apr. 1952	do	do	$75.00	1,342,860,028.41	954,620,189.55	388,239,838.86
E-1952, 3.451%[19] (May to Dec.)	May to Dec. 1952	After 2 mos. from issue date at option of 9 mos., 8 mos. from issue date but may be held for additional period.[18]	do	$75.00	2,750,364,279.33	1,928,183,124.95	822,181,154.38
E-1953, 3.468%[19]	Jan. to Dec. 1953	do	do	$75.00	4,666,218,167.67	3,162,838,567.60	1,503,379,600.07
E-1954, 3.497%[19]	Jan. to Dec. 1954	do	do	$75.00	4,745,714,177.46	3,096,267,987.60	1,649,446,189.86
E-1955, 3.522%[19]	Jan. to Dec. 1955	do	do	$75.00	4,934,675,967.59	3,062,129,557.81	1,872,546,409.78
E-1956, 3.546%[19]	Jan. to Dec. 1956	do	do	$75.00	4,712,593,342.95	2,889,734,061.19	1,822,859,281.76
E-1957, 3.560%[19] (Jan.)	Jan. 1957	do	do	$75.00	388,859,690.78	231,890,881.09	156,968,809.66

Footnotes at end of table.

TABLE 36.—*Description of public debt issues outstanding June 30, 1965*—Continued

Description	Date	When redeemable or payable[1]	Interest payment date	Average price received (per $100)	Amount issued	Amount retired	Amount outstanding[2]
INTEREST-BEARING DEBT— Continued							
Public Issues—Continued							
Nonmarketable:—Continued U.S. savings bonds: Series and approximate yield to maturity (%):[1]—Continued	First day of each month.	After 2 mos. from issue date, on redemption at par; 8 yrs., 11 mos. from issue date but may be held for period.[18]	Sold at a discount; payable at par on maturity.				
E-1957, 3.653% (Feb. to Dec.)[19]	Feb. to Dec. 1957.	do	do	$75.00	$4,041,458,611.59	$2,423,828,411.29	$1,617,630,200.30
E-1958, 3.690%[19]	Jan. to Dec. 1958.	do	do	$75.00	4,290,032,537.12	2,437,128,703.24	1,852,903,833.88
E-1959, 3.730% (Jan. to May)[19]	Jan. to May 1959.	do	do	$75.00	1,717,915,022.39	966,429,668.47	751,485,353.92
E-1959, 3.750% (June to Dec.)[19]	June to Dec. 1959.	A after 2 mos. from issue date at option of par; 7 yrs., 9 m. from issue date but may be held for period.[18]	do	$75.00	2,297,224,599.36	1,283,166,973.66	1,014,067,625.70
E-1960, 3.750%	Jan. to Dec. 1960.	do	do	$75.00	4,003,350,316.60	2,114,077,232.45	1,889,273,084.15
E-1961, 3.750%	Jan. to Dec. 1961.	do	do	$75.00	4,019,952,019.04	1,964,308,516.49	2,055,643,502.55
E-1962, 3.750%	Jan. to Dec. 1962.	do	do	$75.00	3,869,262,288.57	1,788,958,741.73	2,080,303,546.84
E-1963, 3.750%	Jan. to Dec. 1963.	do	do	$75.00	4,287,984,157.90	1,718,684,446.20	2,569,299,711.70
E-1964, 3.750%	Jan. to Dec. 1964.	do	do	$75.00	4,190,467,289.55	1,423,785,415.72	2,766,681,873.83
E-1965, 3.750%	Jan. to June 1965.	do	do	$75.00	1,765,465,275.00	270,516,712.50	1,494,948,562.50
Unclassified sales and redemptions.					24,78,804.47	830,465.71	23,842,338.76
Total Series E.					137,782,869,393.86	96,735,229,084.86	41,047,640,309.00
H-1952, 3.392%[19]	June to Dec. 1952.	After 6 mos. from issue date, on demand at option of owner on 1 month's notice; 9 yrs., 8 mos. from issue date.[20]	Semiannually	Par	191,480,500.00	114,726,500.00	76,754,000.00
H-1953, 3.409%[19]	Jan. to Dec. 1953.	do	do	do	470,500,500.00	256,922,500.00	213,578,000.00

	Date issued	Redemption terms	Sale terms	Price	Amount issued	Amount redeemed	Amount outstanding
H-1955, 3.467% [19]	Jan. to Dec. 1955	do.	do.	do.	1,173,084,000.00	561,161,500.00	611,922,500.00
H-1956, 3.496% [19]	Jan. to Dec. 1956	do.	do.	do.	893,176,000.00	334,351,500.00	558,824,500.00
H-1957, 3.520% (Jan.)	Jan. 1957	do.	do.	do.	64,506,000.00	21,506,000.00	43,000,000.00
H-1957, 3.626% (Feb. to Dec.)[19]	Feb. to Dec. 1957	After 6 mos. from issue date at option of owner on 1 mth's toe; 10 yrs. from issue date.	do.	do.	567,682,000.00	173,850,500.00	393,831,500.00
H-1958, 3.679% [19]	Jan. to Dec. 1958	do.	do.	do.	890,252,500.00	261,791,000.00	628,461,500.00
H-1959, 3.720% (Jan. to May)	Jan. to May 1959	do.	do.	do.	356,318,500.00	85,161,000.00	271,157,500.00
H-1959, 3.70% (June to Dec.)	June to Dec. 1959	do.	do.	do.	362,413,000.00	77,064,000.00	285,349,000.00
H-1960, 3.750%	Jan. to Dec. 1960	do.	do.	do.	1,006,767,500.00	159,443,000.00	847,324,500.00
H-1961, 3.750%	Jan. to Dec. 1961	do.	do.	do.	1,041,579,000.00	130,899,000.00	910,680,000.00
H-1962, 3.750%	Jan. to Dec. 1962	do.	do.	do.	856,759,000.00	75,961,000.00	780,798,000.00
943, 3.750%	Jan. to Dec. 1963	do.	do.	do.	772,897,500.00	46,840,000.00	726,057,500.00
H-1964, 3.750%	Jan. to Dec. 1964	do.	do.	do.	671,440,000.00	16,266,000.00	655,174,000.00
H-1965, 3.750%	Jan. to June 1965	do.	do.	do.	296,186,000.00	265,500.00	295,920,500.00
Unclassified sales and redemptions.					8,741,000.00	12,000.00	8,729,000.00
Total Series H					10,501,462,500.00	2,778,183,500.00	7,723,279,000.00
J-1953, 2.76%	Jan. to Dec. 1953	After 6 mos. from issue date on dmd at option of owner on 1 mth's toe; 12 yrs. from issue date.	Sold at a discount; payable at par on maturity.	$72.00	160,728,479.39	113,954,978.39	46,773,501.00
J-1954, 2.76%	Jan. to Dec. 1954	do.	do.	$72.00	384,787,986.40	255,299,942.20	129,488,044.20
J-1955, 2.76%	Jan. to Dec. 1955	do.	do.	$72.00	278,015,567.62	163,478,793.28	114,536,774.34
J-1956, 2.76%	Jan. to Dec. 1956	do.	do.	$72.00	176,645,076.18	84,374,187.13	92,270,889.05
J-1957, 2.76%	Jan. to Apr. 1957	do.	do.	$72.00	37,269,112.94	16,426,161.19	20,842,951.75
Unclassified redemptions.						4,207.40	−4,207.40
Total Series J					1,037,446,222.53	633,538,269.59	403,907,952.94
K-1953, 2.76%	Jan. to Dec. 1953	A fr 6 mos. form issue date on dmd at pwn of owner on 1 mths toe; 12 yrs. form issue da.	Semiannually	Par	302,931,500.00	237,648,000.00	65,283,500.00
K-1954, 2.76%	Jan. to Dec. 1954	do.	do.	do.	981,680,000.00	665,602,000.00	316,078,000.00
K-1955, 2.76%	Jan. to Dec. 1955	do.	do.	do.	633,925,500.00	370,764,500.00	263,171,000.00
K-1956, 2.76%	Jan. to Dec. 1956	do.	do.	do.	318,825,500.00	162,288,500.00	166,537,000.00
K-1957, 2.76%	Jan. to Apr. 1957	do.	do.	do.	53,978,500.00	20,813,000.00	33,165,500.00

Footnotes at end of table.

TABLE 36.—*Description of public debt issues outstanding June 30, 1965*—Continued

Description	Date	When redeemable or payable [1]	Interest payment date	Average price received (per $100)	Amount issued	Amount retired	Amount outstanding [2]
INTEREST-BEARING DEBT [a]—Continued							
Public Issues—Continued							
Nonmarketable [f]—Continued							
U.S. savings bonds [17]—Continued							
Unclassified redemptions						$19,000.00	−$19,000.00
Total Series K					$2,291,341,000.00	1,447,125,000.00	844,216,000.00
Total U.S. savings bonds					151,613,119,116.39	101,594,075,854.45	50,019,043,261.94
Total nonmarketable issues					170,844,010,847.99	115,100,406,847.33	55,743,604,000.66
Total public issues					423,298,715,497.99	158,864,130,047.33	264,434,585,450.66
Special Issues [b]							
Civil service retirement fund:							
Certificates:							
4⅛% Series 1966	June 30, 1965	On demand; on June 30, 1966.	June 30	Par	69,707,000.00		69,707,000.00
Notes:	Various dates from:	Redeemable after 1 yr. from issue date and payable on June 30:					
4⅛% Series 1966	June 30, 1964	1966	do	do	72,775,000.00		72,775,000.00
4⅛% Series 1967	do	1967	do	do	142,474,000.00		142,474,000.00
4⅛% Series 1968	do	1968	do	do	142,474,000.00		142,474,000.00
4⅛% Series 1969	do	1969	do	do	142,474,000.00		142,474,000.00
4⅛% Series 1970	do	1970	do	do	69,699,000.00		69,699,000.00
3⅞% Series 1966	June 30, 1963	1966	do	do	80,227,000.00		80,227,000.00
3⅞% Series 1967	do	1967	do	do	80,227,000.00		80,227,000.00
3⅞% Series 1968	do	1968	do	do	80,227,000.00		80,227,000.00
3¾% Series 1966	June 30, 1962	1966	do	do	60,976,000.00		60,976,000.00
3¾% Series 1967	do	1967	do	do	60,976,000.00		60,976,000.00
2⅞% Series 1966	June 30, 1961	1966	do	do	69,913,000.00		69,913,000.00
Bonds:	Various dates from:	On demand; on June 30:					
4⅛% Series 1970	June 30, 1964	1970	do	do	72,775,000.00		72,775,000.00
4⅛% Series 1971	do	1971	do	do	142,474,000.00		142,474,000.00
4⅛% Series 1972	do	1972	do	do	375,160,000.00		375,160,000.00
4⅛% Series 1973	do	1973	do	do	552,988,000.00		552,988,000.00
4⅛% Series 1974	do	1974	do	do	212,387,000.00		212,387,000.00
4⅛% Series 1975	do	1975	do	do	167,167,000.00		167,167,000.00

%, Series 1976	1a		1976	do	1a	42, 44, 00.00		42, 474, 000.00
%, Series 19	1a		1977	do	do	42, 44, 00.00		42, 44, 00.00
4½%, ds 1978	do		1978	do	do	42, 44, 00.00		42, 44, 00.00
4½%, Series 99	d		1979	do	do	69, 17, 00.00		69, 17, 00.00
½%, Series 80	June 30, 1963		1980	do	1a	80, 227, 00.00		80, 227, 00.00
3%, Series 89	1a		1969	do	do	80, 27, 00.00		80, 27, 00.00
8%, Series 90	d1		1970	do	do	80, 27, 00.00		80, 27, 00.00
%, Series 1971	do		19	do	1a	32, 81, 00.00		32, 81, 00.00
%, Series 1972	do		1972	do	1a	63, 48, 00.00		63, 48, 00.00
3⅞%, Series 91	do		1973	do	do	80, 27, 00.00		80, 27, 00.00
%, Series 1975	do	d	1974	do	d	80, 27, 00.00		80, 27, 00.00
3⅞%, Series 1976	do		1975	do	do	80, 27, 00.00		80, 27, 00.00
3⅞%, Series 79	do		1976	do	do	80, 27, 00.00		80, 27, 00.00
%, Series 1975	1a		1977	1a	1a	85, 63, 00.00		85, 63, 00.00
%, Series 18	June 30, 1962		1968	do	do	60, 96, 000.00		60, 96, 00.00
%, Series 0	1a		(39	do	d	60, 96, 000.00		60, 96, 00.00
%, Series 1970	1a		90	do	do	60, 96, 000.00		60, 96, 00.00
3¾%, Series 91	d		2	do	do	60, 976, 00.00		60, 96, 00.00
3%, Series 93	do		1972	do	d	60, 96, 000.00		60, 96, 00.00
%, Series 1974	do		1973	do	1a	60, 976, 00.00		60, 96, 00.00
%, Series 759	1a		1974	do	do	60, 976, 000.00		60, 976, 00.00
%, Series 1976	do		1975	do	do	60, 976, 000.00		60, 96, 00.00
3⅜%, Series 71	d, 61		1976	do		746, 416, 000.00		746, 416, 000.00
%, Series 18	Jne 8, 61		1977	do	do	69, 913, 000.00		69, 93, 00.00
%, Series 0	do		1968	do	do	69, 913, 000.00		69, 93, 00.00
%, Series 18	do		1969	o d	o d	69, 913, 000.00		69, 93, 00.00
2⅞%, Series 971	1a		1971	do	do	69, 913, 000.00		69, 93, 00.00
2⅞%, Series 759	1a		1975	do	do	65, 40, 00.00	24, 693, 000.00	45, 20, 00.00
%, Series 1	as ds from June 30, 1959.		18	do	do	230, 527, 00.00		30, 37, 00.00
2⅝%, Series 1967	do		1967	1a	1a	230, 527, 00.00		230, 527, 000.00
2⅝%, Series 1968	do		1968	do	do	45, 87, 00.00		415, 527, 000.00
2⅝%, Series 1969	do		1969	do	do	65, 87, 00.00		615, 527, 000.00
2⅝%, Series 1970	do		1970	do	do	65, 87, 00.00		615, 527, 000.00
2⅝%, Series 1971	do		1971	do	do	65, 87, 00.00		615, 527, 000.00
2⅝%, Series 1973	d		1973	do	do	65, 87, 00.00	363, 822, 000.00	251, 705, 000.00
2⅝%, Series 1974	do		1974	do	do	65, 87, 00.00		615, 527, 000.00
2½%, Series 1965	as d, 8, ds from 1	a	1975	do	a	65, 87, 00.00		615, 527, 000.00
2¾%, Series 1967	n8e 8,		1966	42	do	385, 000, 000.00		385, 000, 000.00
2½%, Series 1968	do		68		do	00, 000, 00.00		200, 000, 000.00

Footnotes at end of table.

TABLE 36.—*Description of public debt issues outstanding June 30, 1965*—Continued

Description	Date	When redeemable or payable [1]	Interest payment date	Average price received (per $100)	Amount issued	Amount retired	Amount outstanding [2]
INTEREST-BEARING DEBT— Continued							
Special Issues l—Continued							
Exchange Stabilization Fund:							
Certificates:							
3.65% Series 1965	Various dates from: June 1, 1965	On July 1, ... on	July 1, 1965	Par	$816,789,843.96	$600,484,328.63	$216,305,515.33
3.921% Series 1965	Apr. 1, 1965	On 1 day's ... on	do	do	293,500,000.00	278,000,000.00	15,500,000.00
Federal Deposit Insurance Corporation:							
Notes:							
2% Series 1968	from Dec. 1,	Dec. 1	June 1-Dec. 1	do	463,709,000.00	318,082,000.00	145,627,000.00
2% Series 1969	do		do	do	166,771,000.00		166,771,000.00
Federal disability insurance trust fund:							
Bonds:							
4 1/8% Series 1979	from: June 30,	On ... June 30:	June 30-Dec. 31	do	153,632,000.00		153,632,000.00
4 1/8% Series 1980	do...June 30,		do	do	125,606,000.00		125,606,000.00
3 7/8% Series 1978			do	do	153,632,000.00		153,632,000.00
3 3/4% Series 1970	from: ...	1970	do	do	20,738,000.00		20,738,000.00
3 3/4% Series 1971	do	1971	do	do	20,738,000.00		20,738,000.00
3 3/4% Series 1972	do	1972	do	do	20,738,000.00		20,738,000.00
3 3/4% Series 1973	do	1973	do	do	20,738,000.00		20,738,000.00
3 3/4% Series 1974	do	1974	do	do	20,738,000.00		20,738,000.00
3 3/4% Series 1975	do	1975	do	do	20,738,000.00		20,738,000.00
3 3/4% Series 1976	do	1976	do	do	33,632,000.00		153,632,000.00
3 3/4% Series 1977	do	1977	do	do	33,632,000.00		153,632,000.00
2 5/8% Series 1970	Various from: June 30,	1970	do	do	132,894,000.00	99,162,000.00	33,732,000.00
2 5/8% Series 1971	do	1971	do	do	132,894,000.00		32,894,000.00
2 5/8% Series 1972	do	1972	do	do	132,894,000.00		132,894,000.00
2 5/8% Series 1973	do	1973	do	do	132,894,000.00		132,894,000.00
2 5/8% Series 1974	do	1974	do	do	132,894,000.00		132,894,000.00
2 5/8% Series 1975	do	1975	do	do	132,894,000.00		132,894,000.00
Federal home loan banks:							
Certificates:							
2 3/8% Series 1966	June 30, 1965	1966	do	do	50,500,000.00		50,500,000.00
2 3/8% Series 1966	do	1966	do	do	50,000,000.00		50,000,000.00

Federal Housing Administration: Apartment unit insurance fund (notes):	Date issued	Redeemable after 1 yr. from issue date; payable on June 30:				
2% ... Series	Aug. 21, 1961	1966	do	850,000.00	525,000.00	325,000.00
% Series	June 24, 1965	1969	do	3,300,000.00	3,300,000.00	3,300,000.00
% Series	Various dates from: Aug. 21, 1961	1966	do	850,000.00	125,000.00	725,000.00
% Series	July 23, 1964	1969	do	5,780,000.00	2,242,000.00	3,538,000.00
2% Series ... insurance fund	June 30, 1962	1967	do	90,000.00		90,000.00
... insurance fi % Series 97	do	1967	do	24,209,000.00	18,990,000.00	5,219,000.00
2% Series 99	do	1969	do	90,932,000.00		90,932,000.00
M... housing	Various dates from Aug. 21, 1961	1966	do	860,000.00	770,000.00	90,000.00
% ... f1 ... 2% Series 1967	do	1967	do	340,000.00		340,000.00
Section 203 home improvement account (notes): 2% Series 1966	do	1966	do	850,000.00	325,000.00	525,000.00
Section 220 home improvement account (notes): 2% Series 1966	do	1966	do	850,000.00	325,000.00	525,000.00
Section 220 housing insurance fund (notes): 2% Series 1967	Various dates from June 30, 1969.	1967	do	1,300,000.00		1,08 0.00
2% Series 1968	do	1968	do	140,000.00		140,000.00
Servicemen's mortgage insurance fund (notes): 2% Series 1967	Various dates from June 30, 1962.	1967	do	3,175, 00.00	1,550,000.00	1,625,000.00
2% Series 1969	do	1969	do	8,606,000.00		8,606,000.00
Title I housing insurance fund (notes): 2% Series 1969	June 24, 1965	1969	do	1,150,000.00		1,150,000.00

Footnotes at end of table.

TABLE 36.—*Description of public debt issues outstanding June 30, 1965*—Continued

Description	Date	When redeemable or payable [1]	Interest payment date	Average price received (per $100)	Amount issued	Amount retired	Amount outstanding [2]
INTEREST-BEARING DEBT— Continued							
Special Issues ᵇ—Continued							
Federal Housing Administration—Con.							
Title I insurance fund (notes):							
2% Series 1967	Various dates from June 30, 1962.	Redeemable after 1 yr. from issue date; payable on June 30: 1967	June 30–Dec. 31	Par	$26,549,000.00	$17,926,000.00	$8,623,000.00
2% Series 1969	do	1969	do	do	2,650,000.00		2,650,000.00
War housing insurance fund (notes):							
2% Series 1969	June 24, 1965	1969	do	do	5,500,000.00		5,500,000.00
Federal old-age and survivors insurance trust fund:							
Certificates:							
4⅛% Series 1966	June 30, 1965	On Je 30, 1966.	do	do	141,020,000.00		141,020,000.00
Notes:							
4⅛% Series 1967	do	1 yr. from Jne on Je 8, 61. On ni, on Je 30: 61	do	do	1,032,019,000.00		1,032,019,000.00
Bonds:							
4⅜% Series 1978	Je 8, tis from June 8, 8.		do	do	421, 8, 00.00		421,567,000.00
4⅛% Series 1979	do	1979	do	ai	1,080,011,000.00		1,080,011, 0.00
4⅛% Series 1980	do	1980	do	do	1,080,011,000.00		1,080,011,000.00
3⅞% Series 1977	Je 30, 83	1977	d	a	1, 60, 01, 000.00		1,080,011,000.00
3⅞% Series 1978	do	1978	do	a	658,444,000.00		658,444,000.00
3¾% Series 1976	Je 30, 68.	1975	do	do	97,000.00		160,077,000.00
3¾% Series 1976	do	gd	d	do	1,080,011,000.00		1,080,011,000.00
2⅜% Series 1967	Vas dates from June 8, 8.	1967	do	do	168,000,000.00	120,008,000.00	47,992,000.00
2⅝% Series 1968	do	968	do	a	6000, 00.00	52,989,000.00	688,000, 0.00
2⅝% Series 1969	do	89	do	do	1,33,000.00	52,989,000.00	1,080,011,000.00
2⅝% Series 1970	do	1970	do	ia	1,133,000.00	52,989,000.00	1,080,01,000.00
2⅝% Series 1971	do	9	do	d	1,133,000.00	52,989,000.00	1,080,011,000.00
2⅝% Series 1972	do	1972	ia	do	1,133,000.00	52,989,000.00	1,080,011,000.00
2⅝% Series 1973	do	7	do	ai	1,33,000.00	52,989,000.00	1,080, 0,000.00
2⅝% Series 1974	A	7.	do	do	1,133,000.00	52,989,000.00	1,080, 0,000.00
2⅝% Series 1975	d	1975	do	do	919,934,000.00		919, 4000.00

2½% Series 1968	Various dates from June 30, 1958.	1968	do	do	465,000,000.00	52,989,000.00	412,011,000.00
Federal Savings and Loan Insurance Corporation:							
Notes:	Various dates from:	Redeemable after 1 yr. from issue date; payable on June 30:					
2% Series 1968	Nov. 13, 1963	1968	do	do	300,000,000.00	292,578,000.00	7,422,000.00
2% Series 1969	do	1969	do	do	280,000,000.00		280,000,000.00
Foreign service retirement fund:							
Certificates:							
4% Series 1966	June 30, 1965	On [illegible]; on [illegible]	June 30	do	39,318,000.00		39,318,000.00
3% Series [illegible]	do	do	do	do	1,126,000.00		1,126,000.00
Go[illegible] life [illegible] fund:		On [illegible]; on [illegible]					
[illegible]:							
3¾% Series [illegible]	[illegible]	[illegible]	do	do	670,000.00		[illegible]
[illegible] Series [illegible]	do	[illegible]	do	do	[illegible]		670,000.00
3¾% Series [illegible]	do	[illegible]	do	do	670,000.00		[illegible]
3¾% Series [illegible]	do	[illegible]	do	do	670,000.00		670,000.00
3¾% [illegible]	[illegible]	[illegible]	do	do	670,000.00		670,000.00
3¾% Series [illegible]	[illegible]	[illegible]	do	do	670,000.00		670,000.00
3¾% Series [illegible]	do	[illegible]	do	do	670,000.00		670,000.00
[illegible] [illegible]	[illegible]	[illegible]	do	do	[illegible]		[illegible]
3¾% [illegible]	do	[illegible]	do	do	670,000.00		670,000.00
[illegible] [illegible]	do	[illegible]	do	do	73,770,000.00		73,770,000.00
	[illegible] from:						
3⅝% Series 1976	[illegible]	1976	do	do	5,971,000.00		5,971,000.00
3⅝% Series 1977	do	1977	do	do	23,807,000.00		23,807,000.00
3⅝% Series 1978	do	1978	do	do	48,214,000.00		48,214,000.00
	[illegible] from:						
[illegible] Series [illegible]	Feb. 1, 1960	[illegible]	do	[illegible]	[illegible]		73,100,000.00
[illegible] Series [illegible]	[illegible]	[illegible]	do	[illegible]	73,100,000.00		73,100,000.00
[illegible] Series [illegible]	do	[illegible]	[illegible]	[illegible]	73,100,000.00		73,100,000.00
3½% [illegible]	do	[illegible]	do	do	73,100,000.00		[illegible]
[illegible] Series [illegible]	do	[illegible]	do	[illegible]	73,100,000.00		73,100,000.00
[illegible] Series [illegible]	do	[illegible]	do	[illegible]	73,100,000.00		73,100,000.00
[illegible] Series [illegible]	do	[illegible]	do	do	[illegible]		73,100,000.00
[illegible] Series [illegible]	do	[illegible]	[illegible]	[illegible]	73,100,000.00		73,100,000.00
[illegible]	do	[illegible]	do	[illegible]	73,100,000.00		73,100,000.00
[illegible]	[illegible]	[illegible]	[illegible]	do	67,799,000.00		67,799,000.00
[illegible]	[illegible]	[illegible]	do	[illegible]	49,963,000.00		49,963,000.00
Highway trust fund:							
[illegible]:							
[illegible]	June 30, 1965	1966	June 30–Dec. 31	do	265,394,000.00		265,394,000.00

Footnotes at end of table.

TABLE 36.—*Description of public debt issues outstanding June 30, 1965*—Continued

Description	Date	When redeemable or payable [1]	Interest payment date	Average price received (per $100)	Amount issued	Amount retired	Amount outstanding [2]
INTEREST-BEARING DEBT—Continued							
Special Issues [b]—**Continued**							
National service life insurance fund:							
Certificates:							
3⅝% Series 1966	June 30 1965	On ne 30: 66; on	June 30	Par	$8,418,000.00		$8,418,000.00
3⅝% Series 1967	do	ne after	do	do	6,946,000.00		6,946,000.00
3⅝% Series 1968	do	1 yr. n so	do	do	6,946,000.00		6,946,000.00
3⅝% Series 1969	do	de; payable	do	do	6,946,000.00		6,946,000.00
3⅝% Series 1970	do	1970. on ne 0:	do	do	6,946,000.00		6,946,000.00
Notes:		On ne on					
3¾% Series 1966	ne 30, 6	ne 30:	do	do	7,873,000.00		7,873, 0.00
3¾% Series 1967	do	66.	do	do	7,873,000.00		7,873,000.00
3¾% Series 1968	do	67.	do	do	7,83,00.00		7,873,000.00
3¾% Series 1969	do	68.	do	do	7,873,000.00		7,873,000.00
3¾% Series 1970	do	1969.	do	do	7,873,000.00		7,873, 00
3¾% Series 1971	do	0	do	do	7,873,000.00		7,873,000.00
3¾% Series 1972	do	1971.	do	do	7,873,000.00		7,873,000.00
3¾% Series 1973	do	1972.	do	do	7,873,000.00		7,873,000.00
3¾% Series 1974	do	3	do	do	7,873,000.00		7,873,000.00
3¾% Series 1975	do	94.	do	do	7,873,000.00		7,873,000.00
Bonds:	ne ties	1975.	do	do	386,873,000.00		386,873,000.00
? Series 91	ne 8, 6	1971.	do	do	6,946,000.00		6,946, 00.00
' ? ?	do	1972.	do	do	6,946,000.00		6,946,000.00
? ? 93	do	1973.	do	do	6,946,000.00		6,946,000.00
? ? 94	do	1974.	do	do	6,946,000.00		6,946,000.00
? ? 95	d	1975.	d	do	6,946,000.00		6,946,000.00
? ? 96	do	96.	d	do	6,946,000.00		6, 0.00
3⅝% Series 1977	io	1977.	do	od	7,512,000.00		7, 2,000.00
? ? 99	do	1978.	do	do	95,560,000.00		95,560,000.00
3⅝% ?	do	1979.	do	do	393,819,000.00		393,819,000.00
3⅝% ?	do		do	do	83,819,000.00		393,819,000.00
3¾% ?	ne 30, 61	1978.	do	ol	298,259,000.00		298,259,000.00
3¼% ?	ne 30, 1962.	1976.	od	od	43,724,000.00		43, 24, 00.00
? Series	d	1977.	do	do	386,307,000.00		386,307,000.00
? ?	June 30, 6	1976.	d	d	343,149,000.00		343,149,000.00

3%,	as	0	Feb. 1, 1960	1966	do	do	do	39,000,000.00		39,000,000.00
3%,	as	67	do	1967	do	do	do	39,000,000.00		39,000,000.00
3% Series 1968	as	0	do	1968	do	do	do	39,000,000.00		39,000,000.00
3%, Series	0	do	1969	do	do	do	39,000,000.00		39,000,000.00
3%, Series	92	do	1970	do	do	do	39,000,000.00		39,000,000.00
3% Series	1	do	1971	do	do	do	39,000,000.00		39,000,000.00
3% Series	0	do	1972	do	do	do	39,000,000.00		39,000,000.00
3% Series	94	do	1973	do	do	do	39,000,000.00		39,000,000.00
			1974	do	do	do	39,000,000.00		9,000,000.00
Railroad et account:									
½ % Series 06	Je 8, 1965	06	do	do	do	208,205,000.00		208,205,000.00
Notes:			1 yr. from de						
4¼% Series 1967	as	0	rem:	97	do	do	do	30, 66,000.00		30, 66, 00.00
4¼% Series 1968	as	0	de 8, 0	98	do	do	do	23, 10, 000.00		23, 10, 00.00
4¼% Series 1969	as	92	d	99	do	do	do	23, 10, 000.00		23, 10, 00.00
4¼% Series 1970	as	1	d	20	do	do	do	10, 98, 000.00		10, 98, 00.00
4% Series 1967	as	0	Oct. 5, 63	97	do	do	do	177, 91, 000.00		85, 91, 00.00
4% Series 1968	as	0	as	Je 30: on				85, 0, 000.00		
			from:						
½%:	as	0	Je 8, 1964	9	do	do	do	12, 812, 000.00		12, 8 00.00
½% Series	as	0	do	9	do	do	do	23, 110, 000.00		23, 0 00.00
½% Series	as	92	do	9	do	do	do	23, 10, 000.00		23, 0 00.00
½% Series	as	1	d	9	do	do	do	23, 110, 000.00		23, 10 00.00
½% Series	as	0	d	96	do	do	do	23, 110, 000.00		23, 10 00.00
½% Series	as	0	d	9	do	do	do	23, 10, 000.00		23, 10 00.00
½% Series	as	0	d	99	do	d	do	23, 10, 000.00		23, 0 00.00
½% Series	90	d	9	do	do	do	208, 201, 000.00		208,201, 00.00
			69	do	do	do	208, 201, 000.00		208,201, 00.00
4%	as	0	Oct. 5, 63	1970	do	do	do	185, 091, 00.00		185,091, 00.00
4%	as	91	d	9	do	do	do	185, 091, 000.00		185,091, 00.00
4% Series	93	d	9	do	do	do	185, 091, 000.00		185,091, 00.00
4% Series	94	d	4	do	do	do	185, 091, 000.00		185,091, 00.00
4% Series	as	0	d	9	do	d	do	85, 0, 000.00		85, 0 00.00
4% Series	96	d	9	do	do	do	185, 091, 000.00		185,091, 00.00
4% Series	97	d	9	do	do	do	185, 091, 000.00		185,091, 00.00
				do	do	do	185, 091, 000.00		185,091, 00.00
U ½% Series 0	it fnd:	June 30, 1965	1966	June 30–Dec. 31	do	do	5,799,114,000.00		5,799,114,000. 00

Footnotes at end of table.

TABLE 36.—*Description of public debt issues outstanding June 30, 1965*—Continued

Description	Date	When redeemable or payable [1]	Interest payment date	Average price received (per $100)	Amount issued	Amount retired	Amount outstanding [2]
INTEREST-BEARING DEBT—Continued							
Special Issues [h]—Continued							
Veterans' special term insurance fund:							
Certificates:							
3⅜% Series 1966	June 30, 1965	On demand; on June 30; 1966	June 30	Par	$149,134,000.00		$149,134,000.00
Veterans' reopened insurance fund:							
Certificates:							
4⅛% Series 1966	do	1966	do	do	2,605,000.00		2,605,000.00
Total special issues					51,168,136,843.96	$2,518,186,328.63	48,649,950,515.33
Total interest-bearing debt outstanding					474,466,852,341.95	161,382,316,375.96	313,084,535,965.99

MATURED DEBT ON WHICH INTEREST HAS CEASED

Title	Amount outstanding
Old debt matured (issued prior to Apr. 1, 1917) [21] [b]	[22] $1,503,710.26
2½% postal savings bonds [c]	[22] 272,480.00
First Liberty bonds, at various interest rates [d]	[22] 561,600.00
Other Liberty bonds, and Victory notes, at various interest rates [a]	4,481,950.00
Treasury bonds, at various interest rates [a]	31,264,300.00
Adjusted service bonds of 1945 [a]	1,343,700.00
Treasury notes, at various interest rates [a]	40,531,700.00
Treasury savings notes [a]	511,600.00

MATURED DEBT ON WHICH INTEREST HAS CEASED

Title	Amount outstanding
Treasury notes, tax series [a]	$101,525.00
Certificates of indebtedness, at various interest rates [a]	527,200.00
Treasury bills [a]	66,[22] [a] 00
Treasury savings certificates [a]	8.00
U.S. savings bonds [a]	108,196,550.00
Armed Forces leave bonds [a]	6,626,650.00
Total matured debt on which interest has ceased	262,480,615.26

DEBT BEARING NO INTEREST

Title	Amount outstanding
Obligations of the United States:	
[illegible] United States notes (old issue) (act of July 3, [illegible] 22 U.S.C. 8c), [illegible] (act of [illegible] on demand)	$3,167,000,000.00
[illegible] 22 U.S.C. 8c) [illegible]	138,000,000.00
U.S.C. [illegible]	150,000,000.00
Special [illegible]	74,613,886.00
U.N. [illegible]	2,361,904.00
U.N./FAO [illegible]	54,846,511.56
[illegible]	
[illegible] Series [illegible]	380,216.47
[illegible]	295,611.40
Total excess profits tax refund bonds	675,827.87
Old demand notes (acts of July 17, 1861 (12 Stat. 259); Aug. 5, 1861 (12 Stat. 313); Feb. 12, 1862 (12 Stat. 338)). (The $60,030,000 issued includes $60,000,000 authorized to be outstanding and amounts issued on deposits including reissues.)	[illegible] 3, [illegible] .50
Fractional currency (acts of July 17, 1862 (12 Stat. 592); Mar. 3, 1863 (12 Stat. 711); June 30, 1864 (13 Stat. 220)). (The $368,724,080 issued includes $50,000,000 authorized to be outstanding and amounts issued on deposits including reissues.)	[illegible] 1, 0, .68
Legal tender notes (acts of Feb. 25, 1862 (12 Stat. 345); July 11, 1862 (12 Stat. 532); Mar. 3, 1863 (12 Stat. 719); May 31, 1878 (31 U.S.C. 404); Mar. 14, 1900 (31 U.S.C. 408); Mar. 4, 1907 (31 U.S.C. 403)). (Greatest amount ever authorized to be outstanding $450,000,000.)	322,681,016.00
Less gold reserve	−156,039,430.93
Total legal tender notes less gold reserve	22 166,641,585.07
Old series currency (31 U.S.C. 912–916)	22 23 17,520,573.50
National bank notes, redemption account (act of July 14, 1890 (31 U.S.C. 408))	22 23 22,282,677.00
Federal Reserve bank notes, redemption account (act of Dec. 23, 1913 (12 U.S.C. 467))	22 23 68,793,208.00
Thrift and Treasury savings stamps	22 3,700,395.00
Total debt bearing no interest	3,888,454,675.18

Footnotes at end of table.

TABLE 36.—*Description of public debt issues outstanding June 30, 1965*—Continued

Title	Amount outstanding

SUMMARY

Gross debt (including $28,354,419,064.62 to finance expenditures of Government corporations for which securities of such corporations are held by the Treasury) $317,215,471,256.43

Guaranteed debt of U.S. Government agencies 590,326,050.00

Total gross public debt and guaranteed debt 317,805,797,306.43

Deduct debt not subject to statutory limitation [24] 283,364,986.01

Total debt subject to limitation [24] 317,522,432,320.42

AUTHORIZING ACTS:

(a) Sept. 24, 1917, as amended
(b) Various.
(c) June 25, 1910.
(d) Apr. 24, 1917.

TAX STATUS:

(e) [illegible] bills are not [illegible] capital [illegible] the Internal [illegible] of [illegible]. The [illegible] the price [illegible] the bills and [illegible] at maturity for [illegible] is to be [illegible] as an ordinary [illegible] or [illegible] for [illegible] in [illegible].

(f) [illegible] derived from [illegible] is subject to [illegible] now or [illegible] the [illegible] of [illegible].

(g) [illegible] gain or [illegible] from [illegible] of [illegible] will be [illegible] into [illegible] of the new securities:

New security	Effective date of exchange	Security exchanged
[illegible]	[illegible] 23, [illegible]	[illegible]
[illegible]	Oct. 3, [illegible]	[illegible]-67
[illegible]	Oct. 3, [illegible]	2½% [illegible]
3½% [illegible]	[illegible] 3, [illegible]	[illegible], 1964–69; [illegible], 1964–69
[illegible]	Mar. 15, [illegible]	[illegible]
[illegible] Bonds [illegible]	Mar. 15, 1961	[illegible], 1959–62; [illegible], 1959–62; [illegible]
[illegible]	Sept. 15, 1961	[illegible]; 2½% [illegible] 1966–71
[illegible]	Mar. 1, 1962	[illegible]
[illegible] Bonds [illegible]	Mar. 1, 1962	[illegible]
3½% Bonds [illegible]; [illegible]	Mar. 1, 1962	[illegible]-72; [illegible]; [illegible]-72
3¾% Notes A–1967; 4% Bonds 1972 (9–15–62)	Sept. 15, 1962	[illegible] A– [illegible]; [illegible]–1963; 3¼% [illegible]
3⅝% Notes B–1967; 3⅞% Bonds 1971	Mar. 15, [illegible]	[illegible] C– [illegible]
3⅞% Bonds 1974	Mar. 15, 1963	[illegible]; 3% Bonds 1966; [illegible]

New security	Effective date of exchange	Security exchanged
4% Bonds 1980	Mar. 15, 1963	[illegible] B–1965; [illegible] C– [illegible]; 3⅛% [illegible]; [illegible] Bonds [illegible]
3⅞% Bonds 1968 (9–15–63)	Sept. 18, 1963	[illegible]–1964; [illegible] A–1964; [illegible]
4% Bonds 1973; 4⅛% Bonds 1989–94	Sept. 18, 1963	[illegible] B– [illegible]64; [illegible]; 3¾% [illegible] D–1964; [illegible] B–1967; 3¾% [illegible] A–[illegible]67
4% Bonds 1970; 4¼% Bonds 1975–85	Jan. 29, 1964	[illegible]; 4⅞% [illegible]; 3¾% [illegible]; [illegible] A– [illegible]
4% Bonds 1969 (10–1–57); 4⅛% Bonds 1973; 4⅛% Bonds 1987–92	July 24, 1964	3⅞% [illegible] C– [illegible]; [illegible] A–1966; [illegible] B–1967; [illegible]
4% Bonds 1970 (1–15–65); 4⅛% Bonds 1974; 4¼% Bonds 1987–92	Jan. 19, 1965	[illegible] B– [illegible]; [illegible] A– [illegible]; [illegible] Bonds [illegible]; [illegible] 1967

(h) These issues, being investments of various Government funds and payable only for the account of such funds, have no present tax liability.

MEMORANDUM RELATING TO OTHER SECURITIES:

Securities of the United States payable on presentation:	
U.S. registered interest checks payable	$946, 494, 559. 58
U.S. interest coupons due and outstanding	119, 919, 518. 90
Interest payable with and accrued discount added to principal of U.S. securities	5, 246, 922. 27
Total	1, 071, 661, 000. 75

TABLE 37.—*Description of guaranteed debt held outside the Treasury, June 30, 1965*

[On basis of daily Treasury statements, see "Bases of Tables"]

Securities	Rate of interest	Amount
UNMATURED DEBT		
District of Columbia Armory Board Stadium bonds of 1970–79 issued under the act of September 7, 1957, as amended (2 D.C. Code 1722–1727) [1] [2]	*Percent* 4.20	$19,800,000.00
Federal Housing Administration debentures issued under the act of June 27, 1934, as amended (12 U.S.C. 1701–1750g): [3] [4]		
Mutual mortgage insurance fund:		
Series AA	2½	638,600.00
Series AA	2⅝	919,800.00
Series AA	2¾	647,900.00
Series AA	2⅞	2,118,250.00
Series AA	3	1,835,450.00
Series AA	3⅛	6,455,300.00
Series AA	3¼	1,708,150.00
Series AA	3⅜	6,511,300.00
Series AA	3½	28,067,500.00
Series AA	3¾	58,924,550.00
Series AA	3⅞	49,692,400.00
Series AA	4	61,242,650.00
Series AA	4⅛	114,761,150.00
Armed services housing mortgage insurance fund:		
Series FF	2½	269,650.00
Series FF	2¾	1,459,700.00
Series FF	3⅛	33,050.00
Series FF	3⅜	33,700.00
Series FF	3½	121,550.00
Series FF	3¾	1,350.00
Series FF	3⅞	16,100.00
Series FF	4	557,600.00
Series FF	4⅛	83,050.00
Housing insurance fund:		
Series BB	2½	7,573,050.00
Series BB	2¾	3,027,700.00
Series BB	2⅞	294,050.00
Series BB	3	55,150.00
Series BB	3⅛	2,332,750.00
Series BB	3¼	221,700.00
Series BB	3⅜	1,148,250.00
Series BB	3½	11,486,950.00
Series BB	3¾	13,999,050.00
Series BB	3⅞	8,830,600.00
Series BB	4	7,220,600.00
Series BB	4⅛	20,533,050.00
National defense housing insurance fund:		
Series GG	2½	29,779,150.00
Series GG	2⅝	2,003,900.00
Series GG	2¾	34,431,350.00
Series GG	2⅞	5,240,750.00
Series GG	3	196,650.00
Series GG	3¼	303,750.00
Series GG	3⅜	9,050.00
Section 203 home improvement account:		
Series HH	3⅞	5,800.00
Section 220 housing insurance fund:		
Series CC	3⅛	4,740,000.00
Series CC	3⅜	9,251,200.00
Series CC	3½	2,345,450.00
Series CC	3¾	7,177,200.00
Section 221 housing insurance fund:		
Series DD	3⅛	34,050.00
Series DD	3¼	1,650.00
Series DD	3⅜	1,139,600.00
Series DD	3½	9,315,900.00
Series DD	3¾	13,131,800.00
Series DD	3⅞	5,898,900.00
Series DD	4	391,050.00
Series DD	4⅛	1,652,800.00
Servicemen's mortgage insurance fund:		
Series EE	2⅝	126,700.00
Series EE	2⅞	641,050.00
Series EE	3	653,900.00
Series EE	3⅛	2,794,700.00
Series EE	3¼	669,350.00

Footnotes at end of table.

TABLE 37.—*Description of guaranteed debt held outside the Treasury, June 30, 1965*—
Continued

Securities	Rate of interest	Amount
UNMATURED DEBT—Continued		
Federal Housing Administration debentures issued under the act of June 27, 1934, as amended (12 U.S.C. 1701–1750g): [3] [4]—Continued	*Percent*	
Servicemen's mortgage insurance fund—Continued		
Series EE	3⅜	$2,154,500.00
Series EE	3½	4,818,100.00
Series EE	3¾	1,583,250.00
Series EE	3⅞	2,042,850.00
Series EE	4	2,001,500.00
Series EE	4⅛	5,400,400.00
Title I housing insurance fund:		
Series L	2½	14,350.00
Series R	2¾	129,100.00
Series T	3	229,200.00
War housing insurance fund:		
Series H	2½	5,969,900.00
Subtotal		[5] 569,100,500.00
Total unmatured debt		588,900,500.00
MATURED DEBT [6]		
Commodity Credit Corporation, interest		11.25
District of Columbia Armory Board, interest		3,570.00
Federal Farm Mortgage Corporation:		
Principal		132,900.00
Interest		34,506.89
Federal Housing Administration:		
Principal		1,024,650.00
Interest		23,008.27
Home Owners' Loan Corporation:		
Principal		268,000.00
Interest		64,030.49
Reconstruction Finance Corporation, interest		19.25
Total matured debt (principal and interest)		1,550,696.15
Total		590,451,196.15

[1] Issued on June 1, 1960, at a price to yield 4.1879 percent, but sale was not consummated until Aug. 2, 1960. Interest is payable semiannually on June 1 and December 1. These bonds are redeemable on and after June 1, 1970, and mature on Dec. 1, 1979.

[2] The securities and the income derived therefrom, and gain from the sale or other disposition thereof or transfer as by inheritance or gift, are subject to taxation by the United States, but are exempt both as to principal and interest from all taxation, except estate and inheritance taxes, imposed by the District of Columbia.

[3] Issued and payable on various dates. Interest is payable semiannually on January 1 and July 1. All unmatured debentures are redeemable on any interest day or days, on 3 months' notice.

[4] Under the Public Debt Act of 1941 (31 U.S.C. 742a), income or gain derived from these securities is subject to all Federal taxes now or hereafter imposed. The securities are subject to surtaxes, estate, inheritance, gift, or other excise taxes, whether Federal or State, but are exempt from all taxation now or hereafter imposed on the principal or interest thereof by any State, municipality, or local taxing authority. Debentures issued on contracts entered into before Mar. 1, 1941, are exempt from all taxation except surtaxes, estate, inheritance, and gift taxes.

[5] Includes debentures called for redemption on July 1, 1965, at par plus accrued interest, as follows: Series AA, $138,209,550; Series BB, $12,248,250; Series CC, $3,833,200; Series DD, $17,894,600; Series EE, $2,956,050; and Series FF, $534,400.

[6] Funds are on deposit with the Treasurer of the United States for payment of principal of $1,425,550 and interest of $125,146.15.

NOTE.—For securities held by the Treasury, see table 110.

TABLE 38.—*Postal savings systems' deposits and Federal Reserve notes outstanding, June 30, 1946–65*

[Face amount in thousands of dollars. On basis of reports received by the Treasury]

| June 30 | Deposits in postal savings systems [1] | | | Federal Reserve notes [4] |
	U.S. Postal Savings System [2]	Canal Zone Postal Savings System [3]	Total	
1946	3,119,656	9,612	3,129,268	23,434,613
1947	3,392,773	9,602	3,402,375	23,444,193
1948	3,379,130	9,129	3,388,259	23,136,167
1949	3,277,402	8,943	3,286,346	22,783,823
1950	3,097,316	8,643	3,105,959	22,398,284
1951	2,788,199	7,044	2,795,244	22,975,292
1952	2,617,564	7,005	2,624,569	24,135,367
1953	2,457,548	6,848	2,464,396	25,040,465
1954	2,251,419	6,506	2,257,926	24,726,731
1955	2,007,996	6,290	2,014,286	25,030,031
1956	1,765,470	6,313	1,771,783	25,523,779
1957	1,462,268	6,139	1,468,408	25,836,574
1958	1,212,672	5,713	1,218,385	25,862,932
1959	1,041,792	5,492	1,047,284	26,479,923
1960	835,800	5,067	840,867	26,569,479
1961	699,528	4,695	704,223	26,735,869
1962	581,177	4,275	585,452	27,852,820
1963	483,504	4,023	487,527	29,379,114
1964	414,533	3,781	418,314	31,400,405
1965	[5] 342,274	[6] 3,145	345,419	[7] 33,828,265

[1] The faith of the United States is solemnly pledged to the payment of deposits (plus accrued interest at the rate of 2 percent) made in postal savings depository offices. Interest is payable quarterly from the first day of the month next following date of deposit, and on deposits made after Mar. 1, 1941, under the Public Debt Act of 1941 (31 U.S.C. 742(a)), is subject to all Federal taxes.

[2] Established by the act of June 25, 1910, as amended (39 U.S.C. 5201–5224).

[3] Established by the act of June 13, 1940, as amended (2 Canal Zone Code 1131–1143).

[4] Authority for the issuance of Federal Reserve notes was given under the act of Dec. 23, 1913, as amended (12 U.S.C. 411–416). The notes are obligations of the United States and are receivable by all national and member banks and Federal Reserve banks and for all taxes, customs, and other public dues. They are redeemable in lawful money on demand at the Treasury Department, Washington, D.C., or at any Federal Reserve bank.

[5] Funds due depositors on June 30, 1965, including interest of $46,236,547 totaling $388,510,983, are offset by cash in designated depositary banks amounting to $17,643,624, which is secured by the pledge of collateral as provided in the regulations of the Postal Savings System, having a face value of $18,917,000; Government securities with a face value of $355,579,000; and cash in possession of the System and other net assets of $15,288,359.

[6] Funds due depositors on June 30, 1965, including interest of $210,727 totaling $3,355,772, are offset by Government securities having a face value of $3,600,000 and other assets.

[7] In actual circulation, exclusive of $1,616,842,174 redemption fund deposited in the Treasury and $1,898,364,625 of their own Federal Reserve notes held by the issuing banks. Also excludes $17,995,238 held by the Treasurer of the United States for the redemption of all series of Federal Reserve notes before Series of 1928. See table 62, footnote 9. The collateral security for Federal Reserve notes issued consists of $6,295,000,000 in gold certificates and in credits with the Treasurer of the United States payable in gold certificates, $32,095,000,000 face amount of U.S. Government securities, and $28,373,994 face amount of commercial paper. Notes issued by a Federal Reserve bank are a first lien against the assets of such bank.

TABLE 39.—*Statutory limitation on the public debt and guaranteed debt, June 30, 1965*

[In millions of dollars]

PART I.—STATUS UNDER LIMITATION, JUNE 30, 1965

Maximum amount of securities which may be outstanding at any one time under limitations imposed by section 21 of Second Liberty Bond Act, as amended [1]	324,000
Amount of securities outstanding subject to such statutory debt limitation:	
U.S. Government securities issued under the Second Liberty Bond Act, as amended	316,991
Guaranteed debt held outside the Treasury	590
Total	317,581
Balance issuable under limitation	6,419

PART II.—APPLICATION OF LIMITATION TO PUBLIC DEBT AND GUARANTEED DEBT OUTSTANDING JUNE 30, 1965

Class of securities	Subject to statutory debt limitation	Not subject to statutory debt limitation	Total outstanding
Public debt:			
Interest-bearing securities:			
Marketable:			
Treasury bills	53,665		53,665
Treasury notes	52,549		52,549
Treasury bonds	102,481		102,481
Total marketable	208,695		208,695
Nonmarketable:			
Certificates of indebtedness, foreign series	778		778
Treasury notes, foreign series	150		150
Treasury bonds, foreign series	204		204
Treasury bonds, foreign currency series	1,137		1,137
Treasury certificates	95		95
Treasury bonds	9		9
U.S. savings bonds (current redemption value)	50,043		50,043
U.S. retirement plan bonds	11		11
Depositary bonds	59		59
Treasury bonds, REA series	26		26
Treasury bonds, investment series	3,256		3,256
Total nonmarketable	55,768		55,768
Special issues to Government agencies and trust funds	48,650		48,650
Total interest-bearing securities	313,113		313,113
Matured debt on which interest has ceased	290	2	292
Debt bearing no interest:			
U.S. savings stamps	55		55
Excess profits tax refund bonds	1		1
Special notes of the United States:			
International Monetary Fund Series	3,167		3,167
International Development Association Series	138		138
Inter-American Development Bank Series	150		150
Special bonds of the United States:			
U.N. Special Fund Series	75		75
U.N./FAO World Food Program Series	2		2
U.S. notes (less gold reserve)		167	167
Deposits for retirement of national bank and Federal Reserve bank notes		91	91
Other debt bearing no interest		23	23
Total debt bearing no interest	3,588	281	3,869
Total public debt [2]	316,991	283	317,274
Guaranteed debt held outside the Treasury:			
Interest-bearing	589		589
Matured	1		1
Total guaranteed debt	590		590
Total public debt and guaranteed debt	317,581	283	317,864

[1] The following table details amendments to the act.
[2] Includes public debt incurred to finance expenditures of wholly owned Government corporations and other business-type activities in exchange for which securities of the corporations and activities were issued to the Treasury. See table 110.

TABLE 40.—*Debt limitation under the Second Liberty Bond Act, as amended, 1917–65*

Date and act	History of legislation	Amount of limitation
Sept. 24, 1917 40 Stat. 288_____ 40 Stat. 290_____	Sec. 1 authorized issuance of *bonds* in the amount of_____ Sec. 5 authorized *certificates* of indebtedness outstanding_____	$7, 538, 945, 460 4, 000, 000, 000
Apr. 4, 1918 40 Stat. 502_____ 40 Stat. 504_____	Amended sec. 1, increasing *bond* issuance authority to_____ Amended sec. 5, increasing authority for *certificates* outstanding to____	12, 000, 000, 000 8, 000, 000, 000
July 9, 1918 40 Stat. 844_____	Amended sec. 1, increasing *bond* issuance authority to_____	20, 000, 000, 000
Mar. 3, 1919 40 Stat. 1311_____ 40 Stat. 1309_____	Amended sec. 5, increasing authority for *certificates* outstanding to_____ Added sec. 18, authorizing issuance of *notes* in the amount of_____	10, 000, 000, 000 7, 000, 000, 000
Nov. 23, 1921 42 Stat. 321_____	Amended sec. 18, providing limit on *notes* outstanding_____	7, 500, 000, 000
June 17, 1929 46 Stat. 19_____	Amended sec. 5, authorizing *bills* in addition to certificates of indebtedness outstanding_____	10, 000, 000, 000
Mar. 3, 1931 46 Stat. 1506_____	Amended sec. 1, increasing *bond* issuance authority to_____	28, 000, 000, 000
Jan. 30, 1934 48 Stat. 343_____	Amended sec. 18, increasing authority for *notes* outstanding to_____	10, 000, 000, 000
Feb. 4, 1935 49 Stat. 20_____ 49 Stat. 21_____	Amended sec. 1, providing limit on *bonds* outstanding_____ Added sec. 21, consolidating authority for *certificates* and *bills* (sec. 5) and authority for *notes* (sec. 18) outstanding_____	25, 000, 000. 00 20, 000, 000, 000
May 26, 1938 52 Stat. 447_____	Amended sec. 21, consolidating authority for bonds, notes, certificates of indebtedness, and bills outstanding (*bonds* limited to $30 billion)__	45, 000, 000, 000
July 20, 1939 53 Stat. 1071_____	Amended sec. 21, removing limitation on *bonds* without changing authorized total of bonds, notes, certificates of indebtedness, and bills outstanding_____	45, 000, 000, 000
June 25, 1940 54 Stat. 526_____	Amended sec. 21, adding new authority for issuance of $4 billion National Defense Series obligations outstanding_____	49, 000, 000, 000
Feb. 19, 1941 55 Stat. 7_____	Amended sec. 21, eliminating authority for $4 billion of National Defense Series obligations and increasing limitation to_____	65, 000, 000, 000
Mar. 28, 1942 56 Stat. 189_____	Amended sec. 21, increasing limitation to _____	125, 000, 000, 000
Apr. 11, 1943 57 Stat. 63_____	Amended sec. 21, increasing limitation to _____	210, 000, 000, 000
June 9, 1944 58 Stat. 272_____	Amended sec. 21, increasing limitation to _____	260, 000, 000, 000
Apr. 3, 1945 59 Stat. 47_____	Amended sec. 21, including obligations guaranteed as to principal and interest by the United States and increasing limitation to_____	300, 000, 000, 000
June 26, 1946 60 Stat. 316_____	Amended sec. 21, defining face amount of savings bonds to be current redemption value and decreasing limitation to_____	275, 000, 000, 000

TABLE 40.—*Debt limitation under the Second Liberty Bond Act, as amended, 1917–65*—Continued

Date and act	History of legislation	Amount of limitation
Aug. 28, 1954 68 Stat. 895_____	Increased sec. 21 limitation by $6 billion during period beginning Aug. 28, 1954, and ending June 30, 1955_____	$281, 000, 000. 000
June 30, 1955 69 Stat. 241_____	Amended act of Aug. 28, 1954, extending increase in limitation until June 30, 1956_____	281, 000, 000, 000
July 9, 1956 70 Stat. 519_____	Increased sec. 21 limitation by $3 billion during period beginning July 1, 1956, and ending June 30, 1957_____ Temporary increase terminated July 1, 1957, and limitation reverted to_	278, 000, 000, 000 275, 000, 000, 000
Feb. 26, 1958 72 Stat. 27_____	Increased sec. 21 limitation by $5 billion during period beginning Feb. 26, 1958, and ending June 30, 1959_____	280, 000, 000, 000
Sept. 2, 1958 72 Stat. 1758_____	Amended sec. 21, increasing limitation to $283 billion, which, with temporary increase of Feb. 26, 1958, made limitation_____	288, 000, 000, 000
June 30, 1959 73 Stat. 156_____	Amended sec. 21, increasing limitation to $285 billion, and increased sec. 21 limitation by $10 billion during period beginning July 1, 1959, and ending June 30, 1960_____	295, 000, 000, 000
June 30, 1960 74 Stat. 290_____	Increased sec. 21 limitation by $8 billion during period beginning July 1, 1960, and ending June 30, 1961_____	293, 000, 000, 000
June 30, 1961 75 Stat. 148_____	Increased sec. 21 limitation by $13 billion during period beginning July 1, 1961, and ending June 30, 1962_____	298, 000, 000, 000
Mar. 13, 1962 76 Stat. 23_____	Increased sec. 21 limitation by $2 billion (in addition to temporary increase of $13 billion in act of June 30, 1961) during period beginning Mar. 13, 1962, and ending June 30, 1962_____	300, 000, 000, 000
July 1, 1962 76 Stat. 124_____	Increased sec. 21 limitation during the periods: (1) beginning July 1, 1962 ,and ending Mar. 31, 1963, to_____ (2) beginning Apr. 1, 1963, and ending June 24, 1963, to_____ (3) beginning June 25, 1963, and ending June 30, 1963, to_____	308, 000, 000, 000 305, 000, 000, 000 300, 000, 000, 000
May 29, 1963 77 Stat. 50_____	Increased sec. 21 limitation during the periods: (1) beginning May 29, 1963, and ending June 30, 1963, to_____ (2) beginning July 1, 1963, and ending Aug. 31, 1963, to_____	307, 000, 000, 000 309, 000, 000, 000
Aug. 27, 1963 77 Stat. 131_____	Increased sec. 21 limitation during the period beginning Sept. 1, 1963, and ending Nov. 30, 1963, to_____	309, 000, 000, 000
Nov. 26, 1963 77 Stat. 342_____	Increased sec. 21 limitation during the periods: (1) beginning Dec. 1, 1963, and ending June 29, 1964, to_____ (2) ending June 30, 1964, to_____	315, 000, 000, 000 309, 000, 000, 000
June 29, 1964 78 Stat. 225_____	Increased sec. 21 limitation during the period beginning June 29, 1964, and ending June 30, 1965, to_____	324, 000, 000, 000
June 24, 1965 79 Stat. 172_____	Increased sec. 21 limitation during the period beginning July 1, 1965, and ending June 30, 1966, to_____	328, 000, 000, 000

II. Operations

TABLE 41.—*Public debt receipts and expenditures by classes, monthly for fiscal year 1965 and totals for 1964 and 1965*

[On basis of daily treasury statements, see "Bases of Tables"]

Receipts (issues)	July 1964	August 1964	September 1964	October 1964	November 1964	December 1964	January 1965
Public issues.							
Marketable:							
Treasury bills:							
Regular weekly	$10,306,451,000.00	$7,244,622,000.00	$7,807,397,000.00	$9,814,600,000.00	$7,556,277,000.00	$10,195,529,000.00	$7,369,611,000.00
Tax anticipation			1,000,965,000.00	1,503,195,000.00	1,504,489,000.00		1,758,347,000.00
Other			982,146,000.00		1,833,573,000.00	976,694,000.00	
Treasury notes	1,001,222,000.00	1,974,451,000.00				−172,000.00	
Treasury bonds		2,085,948,000.00			2,893,397,000.00		
Subtotal	11,307,673,000.00	11,305,021,000.00	9,790,508,000.00	11,317,795,000.00	13,787,736,000.00	11,172,051,000.00	9,127,958,000.00
Exchanges:							
Treasury bills:							
Regular weekly	1,203,573,000.00	1,159,141,000.00	900,438,000.00	1,110,744,000.00	1,246,680,000.00	1,022,619,000.00	1,243,723,000.00
Tax anticipation							
Other		26,450,000.00	18,393,000.00		166,919,000.00	26,257,000.00	
Treasury notes	8,352,000.00	1,959,919,000.00	12,827,000.00	23,955,000.00	6,633,509,000.00	53,032,000.00	33,500,000.00
Treasury bonds	9,284,684,500.00	629,500.00	−1,599,000.00	−3,000.00	−103,000.00	−2,564,000.00	9,751,464,000.00
Subtotal	10,496,609,500.00	3,146,139,500.00	930,059,000.00	1,134,696,000.00	8,047,005,000.00	1,099,344,000.00	11,028,687,000.00
Total marketable issues	21,804,282,500.00	14,451,160,500.00	10,720,567,000.00	12,452,491,000.00	21,834,741,000.00	12,271,395,000.00	20,156,645,000.00
Nonmarketable:							
Certificates of indebtedness:	80,000,000.00	30,000,000.00	6, 0, 0. 00	25,000,000.00	60,000,000.00	245,000,000.00	60,000,000.00
Foreign ... series	129,000,000.00		916,000.00				
Depositary ...:		987,000.00		477,000.00	638,000.00	5,545,000.00	85,000.00
Treasury ...:							
Foreign series	223,726,960.26	52,054,414.21	203,929,534.25	105,570,027.45	73,438,319.34	1,824,000.00	25,491,877.36
Foreign currency series	215,000.00	6,000.00	3,141,719.89	80,000.00	845,000.00	1,608,211.27	9,000.00
R.E.A. series	65,837.49	68,406.50	363,000.00	223,122.32	281,800.04	6,075,456.97	2,298,491.17
U.S. retirement plan bonds		50,990.98	134,572.52				
1% ...						408,000.00	
4⅞% Treasury certificates							
3.525% ...							
⅞% Treasury bonds							
3.45% Treasury certificates							
3.555% Treasury certificates			10,364,308.44			10,355,688.18	
3.867% Treasury certificates							
3⅞% Treasury certificates							
3⅞% ...							
3.54% Treasury certificates							
⅞%							

Receipts (issues)	February 1965	March 1965	April 1965	May 1965	June 1965	Total fiscal year 1965	Total fiscal year 1964
Public issues:							
Marketable:							
Treasury bills:							
Regular weekly	$7,732,626,000.00	$7,634,520,000.00	$9,396,022,000.00	$7,404,890,000.00	$7,598,682,000.00	$100,061,227,000.00	[2] $101,128,431,000.00
Tax anticipation						5,766,996,000.00	4,495, ■,000.00
Other	897,633,000.00	1,915,092,000.00	880,278,000.00	3,063,000.00	1,836,052,000.00	12,300,204,000.00	2,001, 88,000.00
Treasury notes	1,735,350,000.00					6,714,523,000.00	4,678, 9,000.00
Treasury bonds							9,000.00
Subtotal	10,365,609,000.00	9,549,612,000.00	10,276,300,000.00	7,407,953,000.00	9,434,734,000.00	124,842,950,000.00	122,303, ■,000.00
Exchanges:							
Treasury bills:							
Regular weekly	1,079,796,000.00	1,173,815,000.00	1,618,113,000.00	1,401,000,000.00	1,214,334,000.00	14,373,976,000.00	9,768, 35,000.00
Tax anticipation							6,635,000.00
Other	102,754,000.00	85,917,000.00	120,884,000.00	5,907,092,000.00	162,383,000.00	709,957,000.00	8,997,000.00
Treasury notes	524,660,000.00	21,820,000.00	36,500,000.00	2,061,342,000.00	25,885,000.00	15,241,051,000.00	2,631,045,000.00
Treasury bonds	21,178,500.00	−7,132,500.00			895,000.00	21,108,792,000.00	1,249,222,500.00
Subtotal	1,728,388,500.00	1,274,419,500.00	1,775,497,000.00	9,369,434,000.00	1,403,497,000.00	51,433,776,000.00	8,664,054,500.00
Total marketable issues	12,093,997,500.00	10,824,031,500.00	12,051,797,000.00	16,777,387,000.00	10,838,231,000.00	176,276,726,000.00	170,967,497,500.00
N ... tle:							
... ks of i ... bs:							
Foreign series	15,000,000.00	140,000,000.00	155,000,000.00	150,000,000.00	523,000,000.00	1,548,000,000.00	1,325,000,000.00
Foreign ... series							30,120,481.92
... ls ... fn ... s							14,745,000.00
... bonds							150,000,000.00
Foreign series	162,000.00	396,000.00	915,000.00	666,000.00	45,500.00	11,011,500.00	
Foreign currency series	5,393,432.27	25,164,537.36	3,025,558.37	30,224,670.06	25,176,721.22	203,929,534.25	5,951,058.84
R.E.A. ... s	250,000.00	269,000.00	225,000.00	275,000.00	245,000.00	682,408,237.79	3,739,000.00
U.S. ... ett ... h bds	9,944.73	108,851.69	129,254.98	108,829.21	270,848.24	4,732,000.00	5,371,165.18
1% Treasury certificates					6,191,254.40	5,473,170.16	12,499,345.83
...% Treasury certificates						16,317,702.35	10,274,942.13
... bonds							10,185,185.19
... bonds					18, 15.06	86, 15.06	20,400,000.00
3.45% Treasury certificates			121,031,737.44	9,915.48		121,041,652.92	
3.5% ... cts						10,364,308.44	
3.867% ... cts						10,365,688.18	
3.9% ... certificates		10,455,801.80				27,435,801.80	
3.41% ... ts			16,980,000.00	45,182.12		120,950,409.63	
3.9% ... cts			120,905,227.51	91,368, 2.18	61,606,974.14	152,975,185.32	
3.784% ... cts					27,487,858.09	27,487,858.09	

Footnotes at end of table.

TABLE 41.—Public debt receipts and expenditures by classes, monthly for fiscal year 1965 and totals for 1964 and 1965—Continued

Receipts (Issues)	July 1964	August 1964	September 1964	October 1964	November 1964	December 1964	January 1965
Public Issues—Continued							
Nonmarketable—Continued							
U.S. savings bonds:							
Issue price	$386,536,307.15	$363,151,479.00	$357,456,468.56	$366,733,339.59	$347,964,725.62	$371,557,169.65	$430,397,982.13
Accrued discount	145,258,398.12	114,436,350.76	126,594,623.00	115,396,218.57	115,258,190.56	137,750,602.31	145,941,986.24
Exchanges, Series H	19,693,000.00	16,557,000.00	14,498,500.00	14,979,000.00	12,64,000.00	13,438,500.00	20,947,500.00
U.S. savings stamps	944,755.65		1,120,936.00	1,497,422.55	1,814,086.95	3,288,463.15	2,014,664.80
Total nonmarketable issues	856,612,258.67	577,391,641.45	803,519,662.66	629,966,130.48	612,944,122.51	800,871,091.53	687,272,501.70
Total public issues	22,660,894,758.67	15,028,552,141.45	11,524,086,662.66	13,082,447,130.48	22,447,685,122.51	13,072,266,091.53	20,843,917,501.70
Special issues:							
Exchange … trust fund	189,692,000.00	170,371,000.00	6,364,000.00	174,342,000.00	13,897,000.00	89,82,000.00	181,956,000.00
…	392,698,596.52	335,066,702.06	460,329,288.80	532,355,043.59	572,963,332.34	612,711,123.87	814,089,069.37
Federal … Insurance …	72,000,000.00	22,000,000.00		5,000,000.00	14,500,00.00	3,00,0.00	44,271,000.00
… surance trust fund	39,179,000.00	151,163,000.00	14, 19,000.00	33,630,000.00	99,076,000.00	3,0,0.00	31,646,000.00
Federal Housing …	101,500,000.00	266,700,000.00	0, 0.00	150,500,000.00	357,600,00.00	8,0,0.00	264,800,000.00
… old-age … reserve …	4,680,000.00						
Federal … insurance fund	500,280,000.00	2,383,877,000.00	1,281,744,000.00	0, 3, 0.00	1,546,883,000.00	1,079,276,000.00	242,163,000.00
… trust fund	12,000,000.00		8,000,000.00	4,00,000.00	16,000,000.00	4,00,000.00	
… life insurance trust fund	683,000.00	700,000.00	832,000.00	639,000.00	839,000.00	690,000.00	753,000.00
						60,000.00	
Highway trust fund	328,202,000.00	380,411,000.00	324,304,000.00	297,602,000.00	8,118,00. 0	8,302,000.00	261,041,000.00
… life insurance fund	15,480,000.00	9,800,000.00	6,830,000.00	9,908,000.00	6,791,000.00	7,350,000.00	13,900,000.00
Railroad …	9,633,000.00	95,621,000.00	93,309,000.00	14,760,000.00	82,389,000.00	81,921,000.00	12,002,000.00
Unemployment trust fund	91,098,000.00	833,820,000.00	80,818,000.00	85,607,000.00	482,952,000.00	158,774,000.00	147,139,000.00
… insurance fund	2,400,000.00	1,750,000.00	1, 0.00	1,900,000.00	853,000.00	2, 0.00	2,850,000.00
Total special issues	1,759,525,596.52	4,651,279,702.06	2,822,099,288.80	1,704,775,043.59	3,690,861,332.34	2, 0, 1.87	2,016,610,069.37
Other issues:							
International Monetary Fund notes	10,000,000.00	9,000,000.00	150,000,000.00	9,000,000.00	40,000,000.00	135,000,000.00	
International Development Association notes					57,652,200.00		

Receipts (issues)	February 1965	March 1965	April 1965	May 1965	June 1965	Total fiscal year 1965	Total fiscal year 1964
Public issues—Continued							
Nonmarketable—Continued							
U.S. savings bonds:							
Issue price	$393,620,154.87	$413,362,871.38	$390,323,666.93	$355,698,902.48	$362,106,779.99	$4,538,909,847.35	$4, 60, 22,307.85
Accrued discount	119,926,880.15	122,106,001.72	117,619,593.18	116,910,436.81	139,716,540.97	1,616,915,822.39	1, 4, 2,499.57
Exchanges, Series H	16,723,500.00	15,988,500.00	15,987,500.00	15,119,500.00	14,561,000.00	192,167,500.00	212,548,000.00
U.S. savings stamps	1,694,572.60	1,663,875.40	2,503,284.60	1,376,828.10	997,249.60	18,916,139.40	18,338,450.00
Total nonmarketable issues	622,862,484.62	730,515,439.35	964,645,823.01	761,803,475.44	1,161,584,041.71	9,209,978,673.13	8, 3, 8,436.51
Total public issues	12,716,859,984.62	11,554,546,939.35	13,016,442,823.01	17,539,190,475.44	11,999,815,041.71	185,486,704,673.13	179,484,633,936.51
Special al service nt f d	164,049,000.00	194,326,000.00	192,914,000.00	170,753,000.00	2,495,244,000.00	4,543,890,000.00	4,389, 82,000.00
Exchange al R	853,680,695.45	1,030,434,076.01	928,858,380.31	1,026,885,334.07	1,088,789,843.96	8,618, 81,486.35	3,003,524,784.48
Federal ght Insurance Corp	94,500,000.00	4,000,000.00	5,000,000.00	14,500,000.00	299,555,000.00	280,271,000.00	393, 89,000.00
Federal ance trust fund	137,654,000.00	125,538,000.00	50,458,000.00	244,516,000.00	412,500,000.00	1,450,588,000.00	1,359,783,000.00
al m g	116,000,000.00	336,500,000.00	109,000,000.00	295,000,000.00	412,600,000.00	2,697,400,000.00	2,915,400,000.00
funds							
Federal old age and res r-					113,238,000.00	117,918,000.00	540,000,000.00
ace al res	2,103,476,000.00	1,420,982,000.00	506,040,000.00	3,559,788,000.00	3,814,574,000.00	18,833,615,000.00	18,032,287,000.00
Federal Savings and Loan Insurance Corp		30,000,000.00	8,000,000.00	5,000,00.00	198,00,000.00	85,00, 0.00	95, 00, 00.00
Foreign nt d	753,000.00	665,000.00	626,000.00	684,000.00	41,012,000.00	48,876,000.00	46,062,00.00
ght life d					45,975,000.00	46,475,000.00	33,017,
N y trust d	175,536,000.00	286,002,000.00	270,602,000.00	33, 0, 0.00	611,985,000.00	3,885,195,000.00	4,187,293,
ce le ace fund	4,997,000.00	6,196,000.00	4,000,000.00	7, 0, 0.00	521,452,000.00	44,471,000.00	524,666,00.00
Railroad cat.	84,768,000.00	107,910,000.00	12,822,000.00	8,450,000.00	1,097,217,000.00	1,785,802,000.00	4,498,001,00.00
nt fund ace fund	861,031,000.00	144,679,000.00	64,297,000.00	1,060,088,000.00	5,892,038,000.00	9,902,341,000.00	9,023,577,00.00
al term ace fund	1,751,000.00	2,285,000.00	2,410,000.00	1,863,000.00	149,804,000.00	171,336,000.00	145,683,00.00
s' gt ce fl				750,000.00	3,755,000.00	4,505,000.00	
Total special issues	4,598,185,695.45	3,690,517,076.01	2,155,027,380.31	6,814,144,334.07	16,756,738,843.96	53,286,544,486.35	48,847,074,784.48
Other issues:							
International Monetary Fund notes		75,000,000.00				428,000,000.00	1,520,000,000.00
International Development Association notes						57,652,200.00	57,652,200.00

Footnotes at end of table.

TABLE 41.—Public debt receipts and expenditures by classes, monthly for fiscal year 1965 and totals for 1964 and 1965—Continued

Receipts (issues) and Expenditures (retirements)	July 1964	August 1964	September 1964	October 1964	November 1964	December 1964	January 1965
RECEIPTS (ISSUES)							
Other issues—Continued							
Inter-American Development Bank notes					$1,649,911.00		
U.N. Children's Fund bonds					14,686,900.00		
U.N. Special Fund bonds							
U.N./FAO World Food Program bonds							
Total other issues	$10,000,000.00	$9,000,000.00	$150,000,000.00	$9,000,000.00	113,989,011.00	$135,000,000.00	$22,860,527,571.07
Total public debt receipts	24,430,420,355.19	19,688,831,843.51	14,496,185,951.46	14,796,222,174.07	26,252,535,465.85	15,834,046,215.40	$22,860,527,571.07
EXPENDITURES (RETIREMENTS)							
Public debt:							
bills:							
Regular weekly	8,981,369,000.00	7,254,004,000.00	7,487,2,000.00	9,64,324,000.00	7,400,82,0.00	9,235,744,000.00	7,187,553,000.00
Other	20,059,000.00	9,000.00	3,000.00		9,0.00	9,000.00	
Certificates of indebtedness	1,996,871,000.00	984,89,000.00	1,004,044,000.00	15,738,000.00	1,978,727,000.00	1,902,9,000.00	23,243,000.00
of	267,000.00	69,00.00	9,000.00	154,000.00	2,000.00	9,000.00	17,000.00
notes	9,0	1,979,409,000.0	9347,500.00	515,417,500.00	2,038,712,000.00	9,851,000.00	16,624,000.00
bonds	31,889,550.00	20,613,90.00	90.00	18,883,050.00	9,8,00	17,373,300.00	29,438,000.00
Other	22,273.75	50,97.00	15,896.25	4,839.75	3,172.25	3,554.75	9,420.75
Subtotal	11,045,9,83.75	10,238,9,9.00	8,636,9,9.25	10,234,9,98.75	11,444,9,9.25	11,205,9,9.75	7,256,9,9.75
Exchanges:							
Treasury bills:							
Regular weekly	1,203,573,000.00	1,159,141,000.00	900,438,000.00	1,110,744,000.00	1,9,60,000.00	1,92,69,0.00	1,243,723,000.00
Other		26,450,000.00	18,393,000.00		9,9,0.00	9,9,0.00	
Treasury certificates, regular					9,3,000.00		
Treasury notes	8,671,293,000.00	1,954,681,000.00	−1,696,000.00	−3,000.00	6,9,68,000.00	−2,026,000.00	5,805,578,000.00
Treasury bonds	613,388,500.00	−81,500.00	−265,000.00		−1,200,000.00	94,000.00	3,945,886,000.00
Subtotal	10,488,254,500.00	3,140,190,500.00	916,870,000.00	1,110,741,000.00	8,039,044,000.00	1,046,944,000.00	10,995,187,000.00
Total marketable issues	21,533,474,323.75	13,379,054,957.00	9,553,736,546.25	11,345,262,389.75	19,483,170,472.25	12,252,190,854.75	18,252,072,320.75

Receipts (issues) and Expenditures (retirements)	February 1965	March 1965	April 1965	May 1965	June 1965	Total fiscal year 1965	Total fiscal year 1964
RECEIPTS (ISSUES)							
Other issues—Continued							
Inter-American Development Bank notes			$5,184,219.00			$6,834,130.00	$5, 00,000.00
U.N. Children's Fund bonds			4,385,685.00			19,072,585.00	19,835,779.00
U.N. Special Fund bonds							55,541,301.00
U.N./FAO World Food Program bonds			1,361,904.00			1,361,904.00	2,400,000.00
Total other issues		$75,000,000.00	10,931,808.00			512,920,819.00	1,680,429,280.00
Total public debt receipts	$17,315,046,680.07	15,320,064,015.36	15,182,402,011.32	$24,353,334,809.51	$28,756,553,885.67	239,286,169,978.48	230,012,138,000.99
EXPENDITURES (RETIREMENTS)							
Public							
M[...]							
[...] ills:							
Regular weekly	7,230,364,000.00	7,351,393,000.00	8,865,609,000.00	7,414,928, 0.00	8,408,310, 0.00	96,501, 2,000.00	100,133, 4,000.00
Tax [...]		2,495,046,000.00	6,347,000.00	2,585,000.00	3,217,890,000.00	5,742,321,000.00	4,487,968,000.00
Other	1,000,694,000.00	1,982,912,000.00	1,011,025,000.00	99,395,000.00	910,421,000.00	12,909,896,000.00	9,492,102,000.00
[...] bds:							
Regular	94,000.00	18,500.00	41,000.00	17,000.00	17,000.00	732,500.00	965, 36, 80.00
[...]	8,050.00						2,000.00
[...] tes.	1,639,116,150.00	6,024,000.00	469,177,000.00	43, 24, 00.00	20, 06,000.00	5, 62, 82,050.00	3,872,413,400.00
Treasury bonds		107,852,900.00	33,298,900.00	36,407,950.00	25,065,450.00	2,011,342,350.00	662,984,400.00
[...]	18,337.25	20,941.00	18,604.50	8, 968.75	39,253.50	215,969.50	203,062.00
Subtotal	9,878,624,537.25	11,943,267,341.00	10,385,516,504.50	7,996,575,918.75	12,582,348,703.50	122,848,283,869.50	119,614,103,162.00
Exchanges:							
Treasury bills:							
Regular weekly	1,079,796,000.00	1,173,815,000.00	1,618,113,000.00	1,401,000,000.00	1,214,334,000.00	14, 33, 96, 00.00	9,768,155,000.00
Other	102,754,000.00	85,917,000.00	120,884,000.00		162,383,000.00	709,957,000.00	15,632,000.00
Treasury certificates, regular						-3,000.00	21,204,457,00.00
Treasury notes, regular	791,000.00	3,957,000.00		7,964,666,000.00	1,134,000.00	31, 05,023,000.00	13,276,328,500.00
Treasury bonds	538,858,500.00	-11,089,500.00		679,000.00		5,086,270,000.00	4,103,875,500.00
Subtotal	1,722,199,500.00	1,252,599,500.00	1,738,997,000.00	9,366,345,000.00	1,377,851,000.00	51,195,223,000.00	48,368,448,000.00
Total marketable issues	11,600,824,037.25	13,195,866,841.00	12,124,513,504.50	17,362,920,918.75	13,960,199,703.50	174,043,506,869.50	167,982,551,162.00

Footnotes at end of table.

TABLE 41.—*Public debt receipts and expenditures by classes, monthly for fiscal year 1965 and totals for 1964 and 1965*—Continued

Expenditures (retirements)	July 1964	August 1964	September 1964	October 1964	November 1964	December 1964	January 1965
Public Issues—Continued							
Civil service bonds	$16,400.00	$13,300.00	$11,250.00	$12,400.00	$5,150.00	$7,000.00	$11,150.00
Armed Forces leave bonds	96,525.00		52,625.00	100,875.00		74,000.00	−75.00
1% notes			1,820,296.06				
3.525% Treasury notes						7,37,768.13	
3.9% notes							
3.47% certificates							
3.479% certificates			10,274,942.13				
3.55% notes				99,845.67			
3.55% notes						10,264,462.77	
3.867% notes							
3.921% Treasury certificates							
4% bonds							
Foreign series notes of	0,000,000.00		30,000,000.00	20,00,000.00	60,000,000.00	165,000,000.00	90,0,000.00
Foreign currency series				30,120,481.92			1, 96,000.00
Depositary bonds	556,000.00	313,000.00	1,121,000.00	1,744,000.00	832,000.00	2,300,000.00	3,84.73
Es profits tax bonds	914.10	673.37	362.82	48.64	280.11	306.05	
bonds							
Int ry notes	72,339,800.00	316,000.00	23,07,500.00	25,154,93.76	73,103,689.59	700,000.00	25,4,722.05
Int series	2,244,000.00	136,000.00	55,000.00	41,765,000.00	100,000.00	459,000.00	81,000.00
R.E.A. notes	175,000.00		63,000.00	186,000.00	140,000.00	925.00	0,000.00
U.S. ax and tax notes	2,550.00	225.00	8,650.00	17,000.00	2,150.00		375.00
U.S. as (int ph bonds	10,087.06	5,673.42	7,068.54	2,699.74	9,936.97	10,645.96	0,155.57
Issue price bonds	111,077,867.00	115,923,423.75	97,285,646.50	125,382,07.75	100,875,386.00	80,824,080.75	103,97,138.25
Series H bonds	59,662,124.91	51,681,772.50	48,466,165.10	68,254,003.92	53,505,1005	42,076,788.20	54,567,528.43
Issue fee notes	3,829,500.00	13,447,500.00	22,573,500.00	5,319,500.00	10,758,000.00	14,250,500.00	13,808,000.00
Int bonds	243,903,421.93	228,695,103.67	35,289,438.36	301,387,408.98	261,417,408.98	211,229,795.42	83,290,432.91
Issue bonds	15,782,033.06	13,705,983.71	13,867,634.44	18,663,247.25	14,856,029.93	11,496,316.31	13,372,552.95
Exchanges:							
Series E, F, ad J, for Series H:							
Issue price	12,371,159.32	10,992,191.08	10,993,440.14	13,558,441.77	10,654,401.77	8,625,231.58	9,231,652.84
Int price	6,546,253.03	5,778,255.99	5,648,649.34	7,197,444.89	5,711,694.50	4,605,937.88	4,914,899.84
Series F and G for bonds							
Exchanges:							
Series E, F, and J, for Series H	31,609,622.23	−14,255,628.20	−6,786,449.72	−111,445,785.69	−86,326,806.30	65,904,234.40	80,705,168.68
	775,244.35	−213,447.07	−2,143,589.48	−5,776,910.73	−3,711,728.90	227,330.54	6,800,947.32

Expenditures (retirements)	February 1965	March 1965	April 1965	May 1965	June 1965	Total fiscal year 1965	Total fiscal year 1964
Public issues—Continued							
Nonmarketable—Continued							
Armed Forces leave bonds	$10,950.00	$17,950.00	$9,000.00	$13,950.00	$13,300.00	$142,200.00	$129,550.00
Armed Forces leave ⋯ series	39,525.00	53,375.00	46,025.00	65,575.00	53,850.00	582,700.00	607,450.00
1% Treasury certificates						1,820,296.06	181,179,703.94
3.% ⋯ certificates						17,613,225.10	2,500,000.00
3.41% ⋯			120,905,227.51		10,075,456.97	120,905,227.51	15,197,753.87
3.45% Treasury certificates				121,086,835.04		121,086,835.04	
3.47% ⋯						10,274,942.13	
3.% ⋯ Treasury certificates					91,368,211.18	91,363,211.18	
3.% ⋯						10,364,308.44	
3.% ⋯		10,355,688.18				10,355,688.18	
3.% ⋯			212,966.47		27,222,835.33	27,435,801.80	
4% ⋯		11,892,247.04				11,892,247.04	
⋯ series	30,000,000.00	120,000,000.00	65,000,000.00	127,000,000.00	113,000,000.00	1,00,000,000.00	1, 50, 00, 00.00
Foreign currency ⋯ series	150,000.00	11,673,000.00	21,899,000.00	11,233,500.00	1,540,000.00	30,120,481.92	25,456,750.00
Depositary ⋯						54,647,500.00	14,735,500.00
Excess profits ⋯	332.40	3,229.55	1,182.73	15.49	1,095.45	11,745.44	8,396.18
Foreign ⋯ series	49, 90, 00.00		23,174,433.96	30,084,487.48	25,162,102.00	347,511,533.84	380, 30,323.70
⋯	40,000.00	44,000.00	4,941,000.00	102,000.00	28,000.00	50,916,000.00	79,884,000.00
REA series ⋯	85,000.00	390,000.00	323,000.00	100,000.00	1,316,000.00	3, 58,200.00	5, 65,000.00
⋯	400.00	4,150.00	1,150.00	11,600.00	9,025.00	58,200.00	297,175.00
U.S. ⋯ tax and savings ⋯	13,885.68	10,655.67	14,633.97	6,806.12	22,481.23	124,729.93	63,296.03
U.S. ⋯							
Issue price ⋯	128,942,877.50	152,380,002.75	112,373,978.00	89,849,642.75	100,913,076.25	1,318,925,821.25	1,329,585,950.00
Series H ⋯	64,593,356.54	85,342,513.17	60,160,556.98	50,083,035.02	53,996,642.35	692,389,600.17	628,139,348.57
Issue price ⋯	12,844,000.00	26,831,000.00	16,253,500.00	5,191,000.00	2, 8, 6.00	172,794,500.00	99,749,500.00
Exchanges:							
Series E, F, and J, for Series H:							
Issue ⋯	197,453,939.03	366,902,583.71	272,226,979.04	213,425,298.92	281,082,813.33	3,096,304,624.28	2,915,559,217.29
Se⋯ and discount ⋯	12,487,686.37	23,571,374.19	16,611,173.52	13,629,001.48	15,233,598.35	183,176,631.56	166,287,371.19
⋯ as F and G for Treasury ⋯	9,779,302.72	16,571,340.04	10,753,862.21	7,965,731.58	9,779,206.17	131,275,961.22	141,074,762.21
⋯	5,347,842.25	9,080,879.77	5,674,270.96	4,312,375.80	5,375,622.23	70,194,126.48	70,826,535.30
							−8,500.00
Exchanges:							
Series E, F, and J, for Series H	29,132,351.45	−167,568,972.00	11,349,207.71	61,040,788.93	−14,803,207.97	−121,445,476.48	18,885,028.58
	1,596,355.03	−8,663,719.81	−440,633.17	2,841,392.62	−593,828.40	−9,302,587.70	646,702.49

Footnotes at end of table.

TABLE 41.—*Public debt receipts and expenditures by classes, monthly for fiscal year 1965 and totals for 1964 and 1965*—Continued

Expenditures (retirements)	July 1964	August 1964	September 1964	October 1964	November 1964	December 1964	January 1965
Public issues—Continued							
Nonmarketable—Continued							
U.S. savings stamps	$1,588,666.30	$1,090,517.45	$931,171.95	$1,070,074.60	$1,047,033.65	$1,546,825.05	$1,522,686.45
Subtotal	752,587,168.29	427,630,544.67	512,647,301.18	542,713,276.47	503,279,739.35	627,141,948.04	668,347,640.02
Exchanges:							
Treasury bonds, investment series	8,355,000.00	5,949,000.00	13,189,000.00	23,965,000.00	7,961,000.00	52,400,000.00	33,500,000.00
Total nonmarketable issues	760,942,168.29	433,579,544.67	525,836,301.18	566,668,276.47	511,240,739.35	679,541,948.04	701,847,640.02
Total public issues	22,294,416,492.04	13,813,634,501.67	10,079,572,847.43	11,911,930,666.22	19,994,411,211.60	12,931,952,802.79	18,953,919,960.77
Special issues:							
	115,000,000.00	17,000,000.00	18,500,000.00	119,60,000.00	17,00,00.00	122,500,000.00	216,96,00.00
Exchange	367,960,180.77	1,088,938.78	9,175,766.99	434,811,684.51	632,120,67.19	600,608,156.41	678,729,880.77
	111,300,000.00	8,000,000.00	4,953,000.00	127,000,000.00	4,000,00.00		131,144,000.00
Federal	123,500,000.00	1,000,00.00	25,910,000.00	148,000,000.00	128,100,00.00	201,223,000.00	202,90,00.00
Housing insurance	100,000.00	1,700,000.00	9,500,00.00	3,900,000.00	31,00,00.00	304,600,000.00	223,900,000.00
trust fund insurance					22,310.00		75,000.00
Corp. Sgs. in insurance	1,275,000,000.00	1,280,000,000.00	1,287,000,000.00	1,275,000,000.00	1,281,000,000.00	1,332,000,000.00	1,489,871,000.00
Foreign		30,00,00.00	57,96,00.00				47,89,00.00
	621,000.00	652,000.00	60,00.00	683,000.00	99,000.00	702,000.00	810,000.00
Highway trust fd	2,965,000.00	4,975,000.00	2,97,00.00	2,965,000.00	3,934,000.00	2,970,000.00	14,90,00.00
N ce fund	378,890,000.00	512,923,000.00	414,058,…	457,647,000.00	476,668,000.00	35,51,00.00	225,304,000.00
				97,000.00			45,000,000.00
Unemployment fud ce fund	96,645,000.00	100,260,00.00	93,90,00.00	100,495,000.00	01,90,000.00	93,96,00.00	103,680,000.00
Veterans ce fund	178,152,000.00	173,293,000.00	186,348,00.00	144,661,000.00	336,069,000.00	239,929,00.00	368,211,000.00
Total special issues	2,650,274,180.77	2,946,471,938.78	2,896,184,766.99	2,814,759,684.51	3,284,642,687.19	3,214,299,156.41	3,857,409,880.77

Expenditures (retirements)	February 1965	March 1965	April 1965	May 1965	June 1965	Total fiscal year 1965	Total fiscal year 1964
Public issues—Continued							
Nonmarketable—Continued							
U.S. savings stamps	$1,867,410.84	$1,430,693.31	$1,820,002.55	$1,686,428.95	$2,200,490.05	$17,802,001.15	$17,938,421.45
Subtotal	544,355,214.81	660,321,990.57	743,310,517.44	739,729,465.18	750,785,269.52	7,472,850,075.54	7,644,869,235.80
Exchanges:							
Treasury bonds, investment series	6,189,000.00	21,820,000.00	36,500,000.00	3,089,000.00	25,646,000.00	238,553,000.00	295,615,000.00
Total nonmarketable issues	550,544,214.81	682,141,990.57	779,810,517.44	742,818,465.18	776,431,269.52	7,711,403,075.54	7,940,484,235.80
Total public issues	12,151,368,252.06	13,878,008,831.57	12,904,324,021.94	18,105,739,383.93	14,736,630,973.02	181,764,909,945.04	175,923,035,397.80
Special issues:							
... tt trl	118,000,000.00	127,000,000.00	22,000,000.00	93, 45,000.00	2,011,881,000.00	3, 96,422,000.00	3, 97,403,000.00
Exchange Stabilization Fund	872,259,934.79	968,291,016.36	951,141,380.71	901,919,734.03	1,597,013,100.25	8,679,120,461.56	2,819,607,268.70
Federal Deposit Insurance	28,085,000.00	653,000.00	700,000.00		39,744,000.00	38,182,000.00	383,343,000.00
Federal ... insurance trust fd	129,900,000.00	130,000,000.00	124,000,000.00	125,000, 00.00	273,006,000.00	1,790,479,000.00	1,622,595,000.00
Federal ...	118,000,000.00	225,500,000.00	233,500,000.00	161,500,000.00	495,600,000.00	2,678,400,000.00	3,205,900,000.00
Federal Housing ...	50,000.00			100,000.00	5,268,000.00	31,803,000.00	5,540,000.00
Federal old-age ... trust fund	1,326,974,000.00	1,333,000,000.00	1,324,000,000.00	1,333,000,000.00	3,834,910,000.00	18,371,755,000.00	17,454,124,000.00
Federal Savings and Loan Insurance	718,000.00	29,808,000.00	87, $5, 00.00	77, 054,000.00		329,672,000.00	61,000,000.00
...		653,000.00	700,000.00	$4,000.00	17,632,000.00	$6, 0.00	45,039,000.00
...	3,995,000.00	4,937,000.00	2,933,000.00	3,878,000.00	639,193,000.00	66, $1, 00.00	80, T9,000.00
Highway ... trust fund	82,143,000.00	266,916,000.00	189,326,000.00	269,980,000.00	331,638,000.00	4,228,829,000.00	4,256,008,000.00
National ... life ... fund		165,000.00			539,502,000.00	488,706,000.00	45, 89, 00.00
Railroad retirement ...	102,950,000.00	94,000,000.00	$4,850,000.00	$0,250,000.00	6,007,248,000.00	1,631,332,000.00	4,315,538,000.00
... trust fund	480,579,000.00	431,611,000.00	271,256,000.00	216,456,000.00	145,375,000.00	9,033,833,000.00	8,895,591,000.00
... employees ... trust fund					1,900,000.00	1, 0.00	123,096,000.00
Total special issues	3,263,613,934.79	3,601,881,016.36	3,411,281,380.71	3,383,286,734.03	15,939,910,100.25	51,264,015,461.56	47,020,554,268.70

Footnotes at end of table.

TABLE 41.—*Public debt receipts and expenditures by classes, monthly for fiscal year 1965 and totals for 1964 and 1965*—Continued

Expenditures (retirements)	July 1964	August 1964	September 1964	October 1964	November 1964	December 1964	January 1965	Total fiscal year 1964
Other issues:								
International Monetary Fund notes.	$10,000,000.00	$23,000,000.00		$40,000,000.00	$49,000,000.00	$212,000,000.00	$5,000,000.00	$1,153,000,000.00
International Development Association notes.	5,000,000.00			3,245,273.00		20,608,800.00	1,649,911.00	44, 87, 90.00
U.N. Children's Fund bonds.								11, 6, 6.00
U.N./FAO World Food Program bonds.	582,730.00	$572,717.00	$112,977.00	606,775.00	73, 85, 96.00	500,000.00	$2,689.00	
Other.						503,050.00		90,000,000.00
Total other issues.	15,582,730.00	23,572,717.00	112,977.00	43,852,048.00	122,385,286.00	233,611,850.00	6,932,600.00	5,943,767.60
Total public debt expenditures.	24,960,273,402.81	16,782,679,157.45	12,975,870,591.42	14,770,542,398.73	23,401,439,184.79	16,379,863,809.20	22,818,262,441.54	1,215,282,073.60
Excess of receipts, or expenditures (−).	−529,853,047.62	2,906,152,686.06	1,520,315,360.04	25,679,775.34	2,851,096,281.06	−545,817,593.80	42,265,129.53	5,853,266,260.89

Expenditures (retirements)	February 1965	March 1965	April 1965	May 1965	June 1965	Total fiscal year 1965
Other issues:						
International Monetary Fund notes.		$5,000,000.00	$6,000,000.00	$200,000,000.00		$550,000,000.00
International Development Association notes.		20,652,200.00		2,500,000.00	$20,652,200.00	61, 93, 200.00
U.N. Children's Fund bonds.					2,684,219.00	15,079,403.00
U.N./FAO World Food Program bonds.				500,000.00		1, 00,000.00
Other.	$270,708.54	534,111.00	670,740.00	373,804.00	356,655.00	478,252,242.54
Total other issues.	270,708.54	26,186,311.00	6,670,740.00	203,373,804.00	23,693,074.00	706,244,845.54
Total public debt expenditures.	15,415,252,895.39	17,506,076,158.93	16,322,276,142.65	21,692,399,921.96	30,700,234,147.27	233,725,170,252.14
Excess of receipts, or expenditures (−).	1,899,792,784.68	−2,186,012,143.57	−1,139,874,131.33	2,660,934,887.55	−1,943,680,261.60	5,560,999,726.34

[1] Includes $1,000,860,000 of 10 series of weekly bills issued in a strip on July 29, 1964.
[2] Includes $1,000,920,000 of 10 series of weekly bills issued in a strip on Oct. 28, 1963.
[3] Redemptions (all series) not yet classified as between matured and unmatured or as between issue price and accrued discount.
[4] Includes the following amounts determined by the Secretary of the Treasury, pursuant to legislation (31 U.S.C. 915(c)), to have been destroyed or irretrievably lost and so will never be presented for redemption: Federal Reserve bank notes, $1,000,000; national bank notes, $13,500,000; United States notes, $24,000,000; Treasury notes, $100,000; gold certificates prior to Series of 1934, $6,000,000; Federal Reserve notes prior to Series of 1928, $14,000,000; and silver certificates issued before Jan. 30, 1934, $14,500,000.

TABLE 42.—*Public debt increases and decreases, and balances in the account of the Treasurer of the United States, fiscal years 1916-65*

[In millions of dollars. On basis of daily Treasury statements, see "Bases of Tables"]

Fiscal year	Public debt outstanding at end of year	Increase, or decrease (−), during year	Analysis of increase or decrease			Balance in Treasurer's account at end of year
			Excess of expenditures (+), or receipts (−)	Increase (+), or decrease (−), in the balance in Treasurer's account	Decreases due to statutory debt retirements [1]	
1916	1,225.1	33.8	−48.5	+82.3		240.4
1917	2,975.6	1,750.5	+853.4	+897.1		1,137.5
1918	12,455.2	9,479.6	+9,033.3	+447.5	1.1	1,585.0
1919	25,484.5	13,029.3	+13,370.6	−333.3	8.0	1,251.7
1920	24,299.3	−1,185.2	−212.5	−894.0	78.7	357.7
1921	23,977.5	−321.9	−86.7	+192.0	427.1	549.7
1922	22,963.4	−1,014.1	−313.8	−277.6	422.7	272.1
1923	22,349.7	−613.7	−309.7	+98.8	402.9	370.9
1924	21,250.8	−1,098.9	−505.4	−135.5	458.0	235.4
1925	20,516.2	−734.6	−250.5	−17.6	466.5	217.8
1926	19,643.2	−873.0	−377.8	−7.8	487.4	210.0
1927	18,511.9	−1,131.3	−635.8	+24.1	519.6	234.1
1928	17,604.3	−907.6	−398.8	+31.5	540.3	265.5
1929	16,931.1	−673.2	−184.8	+61.2	549.6	326.7
1930	16,185.3	−745.8	−183.8	−8.1	553.9	318.6
1931	16,801.3	616.0	+902.7	+153.3	440.1	471.9
1932	19,487.0	2,685.7	+3,153.1	−54.7	412.6	417.2
1933	22,538.7	3,051.7	+3,068.3	+445.0	461.6	862.2
1934	27,053.1	4,514.5	+3,154.6	+1,719.7	359.9	2,581.9
1935	28,700.9	1,647.8	+2,961.9	−740.6	573.6	1,841.3
1936	33,778.5	5,077.7	+4,640.7	+840.2	403.2	2,681.5
1937	36,424.6	2,646.1	+2,878.1	−128.0	104.0	2,553.5
1938	37,164.7	740.1	+1,143.1	−337.6	65.5	2,215.9
1939	40,439.5	3,274.8	+2,710.7	+622.3	58.2	2,838.2
1940	42,967.5	2,528.0	+3,604.7	−947.5	129.2	1,890.7
1941	48,961.4	5,993.9	+5,315.7	+742.4	64.3	2,633.2
1942	72,422.4	23,461.0	+23,197.8	+358.0	94.7	2,991.1
1943	136,696.1	64,273.6	+57,761.7	+6,515.4	3.5	9,506.6
1944	201,003.4	64,307.3	+53,645.3	+10,662.0	(*)	20,168.6
1945	258,682.2	57,678.8	+53,149.6	+4,529.2	(*)	24,697.7
1946	269,422.1	10,739.9	+21,199.8	−10,459.8	(*)	14,237.9
1947	258,286.4	−11,135.7	−206.0	−10,929.7		3,308.1
1948	252,292.2	−5,994.1	−6,606.4	+1,623.9	1,011.6	4,932.0
1949	252,770.4	478.1	+1,947.5	−1,461.6	7.8	3,470.4
1950	257,357.4	4,587.0	+2,592.0	+2,046.7	51.7	5,517.1
1951	255,222.0	−2,135.4	−3,973.6	+1,839.5	1.2	7,356.6
1952	259,105.2	3,883.2	+4,271.8	−387.8	.9	6,968.8
1953	266,071.1	6,965.9	+9,265.0	−2,298.6	.5	4,670.2
1954	271,259.6	5,188.5	+3,092.7	+2,096.2	.4	6,766.5
1955	274,374.2	3,114.6	+3,665.6	−550.8	.2	6,215.7
1956	272,750.8	−1,623.4	−1,190.8	+330.5	763.1	6,546.2
1957	270,527.2	−2,223.6	−1,267.3	−956.2	.1	5,590.0
1958	276,343.2	5,816.0	+1,656.9	+4,159.2		9,749.1
1959	284,705.9	8,362.7	+12,761.4	−4,398.7	2 .1	5,350.4
1960	286,330.8	1,624.9	−1,029.5	+2,654.3		8,004.7
1961	288,970.9	2,640.2	+4,950.8	−1,310.6	1,000.0	6,694.1
1962	298,200.8	9,229.9	+5,494.6	+3,736.3	1.0	10,430.4
1963	305,859.6	7,658.8	+6,031.0	+1,685.8	58.0	12,116.2
1964	311,712.9	5,853.3	+6,933.7	−1,080.4		11,035.7
1965	317,273.9	5,561.0	+4,059.6	+1,574.5	73.1	12,610.3
Total		316,082.5	+314,686.1	+12,452.1	11,055.7	

*Less than $50,000.
[1] Effective with the fiscal year 1948, statutory debt retirements have been excluded from administrative budget expenditures; they are shown here for purposes of comparison.
[2] Adjustment for overstatement of price paid for securities purchased in fiscal 1956 at a discount but previously stated at par value.

TABLE 43.—*Changes in public debt issues, fiscal year 1965*

[On basis of Public Debt accounts, see "Bases of Tables"]

Issues	Outstanding June 30, 1964	Issues during year	Redemptions during year	Transferred to matured debt	Outstanding June 30, 1965 [1]
INTEREST-BEARING DEBT					
Public Issues					
bills, 4s maturing: [2]					
Jly 2, 64	$2, 0, 8, 000. 00		$2, 0, 8, 000. 00		
July 9, 64	2, 0, 95, 000. 00		2, 0, 95, 000. 00	$65, 000. 00	
Other:					
Jly 15, 64	1, 997, 942, 0 0. 00		1, 9, 877, 000. 00		
Regular 6, 64	2, 000, 950, 000. 00		2, 000, 950, 000. 00		
Jly 23, 1964	2, 000, 8, 00. 00		2, 000, 8, 00. 00	8, 0.00	
Jly 30, 64	2, 001, 550, 000. 00		2, 001, 50, 000. 00	8, 0.00	
Ag. 6, 1 64	2, 100, 0. 00		2, 2, 0. 00	5, 0. 00	
Aug. 3, 64	0, 0. 00		2, 2, 0. 00		
Aug. 2, 64	2, 101, 786,		2, 101, 781, 000. 00	5, 0. 00	
Other:					
Aug. 31, 1964	1, 001, 143, 000. 00		1, 0, 111, 0. 00	32, 000. 00	
Regular Sept. 3, 1 64	2, 104, 412, 000. 00		2, 101, 395, 000	2, 000. 00	
Sept. 10, 1964	2, 101, 395, 0. 00		2, 0, 0. 00	8, 0. 00	
Sept. 7, 64	2, 0, 0. 00		2, 101, 505, 000. 00	6, 000. 00	
Other:					
Sept. 6, 64	1, 001, 960, 0. 00		1, 001, 935, 000. 00	25, 0. 00	
Regular Oct. 1, 64	901, 457, 000. 00	$1, 200, 167, 000. 00	2, 101, 624, 000. 00		
Oct. 8, 64	900, 029, 000. 00	201, 238, 0. 00	2, 0, 8, 0. 00	1, 0. 00	
Oct. 15 Dec. 17, 1964		1, 000, 860, 000. 00	1, 000, 860, 000. 00		
Oct. 15, 1964	900, 050, 000. 00	1, 201, 549, 000. 00	2, 101, 585, 000. 00	14, 000. 00	
Oct. 2, 64	0, 0. 00	1, 200, 735, 000. 00	2, 0, 8, 0. 00	129, 000. 00	
Oct. 29, 1964	900, 482, 000. 00	1, 200, 736, 000. 00	2, 101, 207, 000. 00	11, 000. 00	
Regular Oct. 3, 64	1, 000, 23, 000. 00	1, 200, 441, 0. 00	1, 00, 68, 0. 00	5, 0. 00	
Nov. 5, 64	900, 8, 000. 00	1, 793, 000. 00	2, 096, 245, 000. 00	1, 0. 00	
Nov. 12, 18	900, 8, 000. 00	1, 000. 00	2, 100, 666, 000. 00	1, 000. 00	
Nov. 19, 1964	900, 0, 000. 00	1, 0, 177, 000. 00	2, 100, 603, 000. 00	8, 000. 00	
Nov. 27, 1964	900, 091, 000. 00	1, 0, 538, 000. 00			
Other: Nov. 30, 1964	1, 004, 801, 000. 00		1, 004, 796, 000. 00	5, 000. 00	

Mar. 3, 64	----	2,105,407,000.00	1,200, 6 ,00.00	904,729,000.00
Dec. 3, 64	29,000.00	2,202,281,000.00	1,301,793,000.00	900,518,000.00
Dec. 1, 64	6, 00.00	2,202,670,000.00	1,301,621,000.00	901,049,000.00
Dec. 24, 1964		2,201,995,000.00	1,301,980,000.00	900,065,000.00
Other:				
Dec. 31, 1964	34, 00.00	3,201,276,000.00	2,201,282,000.00	1,000,309,000.00
Mar. 7,	30, 00.00	2,100,308,000.00	2,100,338,000.00	
Jan. 7,	3, 00.00	2,114,017,000.00	2,114,060,000.00	
Jan. 14, 1965		2,102,744,000.00	2,102,744,000.00	
Jan. 21,		2,102,144,000.00	2,102,144,000.00	
Jan. 28, 1965				
Other:	17,000.00	1,000,376,000.00		1,000,393,000.00
Feb. 4,	36,000.00	2,101,157,000.00	2,101,193,000.00	
Feb. 11,		2,101,787,000.00	2,101,787,000.00	
Feb. 8,		2,102,387,000.00	2,102,387,000.00	
Feb. 25,	50,000.00	2,102,152,000.00	2,102,202,000.00	
weekly:	90,000.00	1,000,430,000.00		1,000,520,000.00
Mar. 4, 65	43,000.00	2,100,468,000.00	2,100,511,000.00	
Mar. 11, 1965	173,000.00	2,201,666,000.00	2,201,839,000.00	
Mar. 1, 65	46,000.00	2,200,814,000.00	2,200,860,000.00	
Tk Mar. 2, 65	1,000.00	2,504,159,000.00	2,504,160,000.00	
Mar.	21,000.00	2,108,719,000.00	2,108,740,000.00	
Mar. 3, 65				
Other:	95,000.00	1,001,369,000.00		1,001,464,000.00
Apr. 1, 1965	76,000.00	2,100,111,000.00	2,100,187,000.00	
Apr. 8,	63,000.00	2,002,953,000.00	2,003,016,000.00	
Apr. 4,	194,000.00	2,103,923,000.00	2,104,117,000.00	
Apr. 2,	140,000.00	2,200,911,000.00	2,201,051,000.00	
Apr. 29,	25,000.00	2,205,594,000.00	2,205,619,000.00	
Apr. 8 1 65	4, 00.00	1, 00,295, 00.00		1,001,439,000.00
Regular 65:				
May 6,	224, 00.00	2, 02, 33,000.00	2,202,477,000.00	
May 13,	106,000.00	2, 6, 000.00	2,200,674,000.00	
May 20,	209,000.00	2, 00, 65,000.00	2,200,894,000.00	
May 2,	239,000.00	2,200,780,000.00	2,201,019,000.00	
Other:				
May 3,	6, 00.00	999,522,000.00		1,000,141,000.00
Regular 65:				
June 3	622,000.00	2, 99,636,000.00	2,200,248,000.00	
June 10,	904,000.00	2,200,428,000.00	2,201,332,000.00	
June 17,	1,586,000.00	2, 0,011, 0.00	2,201,597,000.00	

Footnotes at end of table.

TABLE 43.—*Changes in public debt issues, fiscal year 1965*—Continued

Issues	Outstanding June 30, 1964	Issues during year	Redemptions during year	Transferred to matured debt	Outstanding June 30, 1965 [1]
INTEREST-BEARING DEBT—Continued					
Public Issues—Continued					
Marketable—Continued					
Tax bills, as maturing [2]—Continued					
		$3, 217, 704, 000. 00		$45, 132, 000. 00	
		2, 205, 814, 000. 00		1, 847, 000. 00	
		989, 551, 000. 00		11, 671, 000. 00	

Qr:					
Nv. 30, 65.	1,000,542,000.00				1,000,542,000.00
3r	1,001,177,000.00				1,001,177,000.00
Dec. 2, 1965	1,000,294,000.00				1,000,294,000.00
Dec. 9, 1965	1,001,469,000.00				1,001,463,000.00
Dec. 16, 1965	1,001,519,000.00				1,001,519,000.00
Dec. 23, 1965					
Other:					
Dec. 31, 1965	1,002,951,00.00				1,002,951,000.00
1966	1,000,387,000.00				1,000,387,000.00
28, 1966	1,000,705,000.00				1,000,705,000.00
Mar. 31, 1966	1,000,304,000.00				1,000,304,000.00
Apr. 30, 1966	1,001,162,000.00				1,001,162,000.00
1966	1,000,886,000.00				1,000,886,000.00
June 30,	1,000,612,000.00				1,000,612,000.00
Total Treasury bills	3, 6,867, 00.00	65,534,000.00	130,221,897,000.00	133,212,360, 00.00	$50,739,938,000.00
Treasury notes:					
% Series B-1 64		11, 6,000.00	2,034,108,000.00		2,045,253,000.00
% Series C- 64		2, 6,000.00	3,864,533,000.00		3,867,196,000.00
% Series E-1964		6,000.00	4,085,335,000.00		4,086,154,000.00
% Series F-1964		9,295,000.00	5,960,370,000.00		5,961,223,000.00
% Series A-	1, 6, 000.00		1,806,415,000.00		2,953,804,000.00
% Series B-1965		2,654,000.00	1,337,200,000.00		7,976,816,000.00
% Series C- 65	6,202,029,000.00		6,162,000.00		6,202,029,000.00
% Series D-1965	1,066,270,000.00		60, 73, 00.00		1,066,270,000.00
% Series D-1965	8,099,286,000.00		663,743,000.00	98,000.00	5,819,971,000.00
% Series E-1965	2,195,067,000.00		3,457,672,000.00	5,904,242,000.00	5,652,739,000.00
% Series A-1966	2,596,595,000.00		1,443,323,000.00	4,039,918,000.00	4,433,214,000.00
% Series B-1966	9,518,942,000.00		1,503,854,000.00	9,518,942,000.00	3,474,845,000.00
% Series C-1966	2,253,821,000.00	279,000.00	1,117,197,000.00	2,253,821,000.00	489,777,000.00
% Series I- 66	2,929,300,000.00	504,000.00	69, 68,000.00		465,673,000.00
% Series V-	2,357,648,000.00		465,169,000.00		315,094,000.00
% Series F-	315,094,000.00				674,981,000.00
% Series EO-	674,981,000.00				356,530,000.00
% Series EA-	356,530,000.00				270,496,00.00
% Series EO-	96,000.00				457,177,000.00
% Series EA-	457,177,000.00				212,127,000.00
% Series EA-	212,127,000.00				115,331,000.00
% Series EA-	115,331,000.00			48,424,000.00	12,121,000.00
% Series EA-1967	60,545,000.00			158,926,000.00	
% Series O	96,926,000.00			31,296,000.00	
% Series	31,296,000.00				
Total Treasury notes	52,548,595,000.00	28,212,000.00	36,663,292,000.00	21,955,667,000.00	67,284,432, 00.00

Footnotes at end of table.

TABLE 43.—*Changes in public debt issues, fiscal year 1965*—Continued

Issues	Outstanding June 30, 1964	Issues during year	Redemptions during year	Transferred to matured debt	Outstanding June 30, 1965 [1]
INTEREST-BEARING DEBT—Continued					
Public Issues—Continued					
Marketable—Continued					
	$1,452,227,100.00				3,430,800,00.00
	1, 8,		2,044,500.00		1,792,236,000.00
of 1963–68	2,627,692,		41 35,000.00		2,586,237,500.00
(di Apr. 15, 1943)	2,539, 01,		500.00	$7,558,500.00	2,534,912,000.00
(di Bt. 15, 1943)	3, 6,				
of 1965–70	1, 6,		3, 8, 0, 0.00		2,411,064,000.00
	1,851,408,000.00				1, 02, 0.00
of 7	3, 8,		1,174,474,500.00		1,687,548,000.00
	1,403,545,		1,585,003, 0.00		89,586,500.00
(di Je 1, 1945)	3, 1, 8,		16,056,000.00		2,018,541,000.00
(di Q. 20,)	2, 1,		8, 5, 0.00		1,282,481,500.00
(dated Nv. 15, 1945)	2, 1,				1,951,800,750.00
(di De 2, 1960)	2, 1,				2,699,435,000.00
(di eß. 5,)	3, eß,				2,459,935,500.00
of 1968	3, 7,				1,591,434, 0.00
of 1957	3, 0,	$3,725,591,000.00	1,747,000.00		3,747,358,500.00
(di Ot. 1, 1957)	4, 9,				6,260,914,500.00
(di Aug. 15,)	2, 9,				1,843,615,500.00
(di Je 0)	4, 9,	4,381,420,000.00			4,381,420,000.00
(di Jan. 15,)	2, 85, 86, 60.00		2,805,626,500.00		2,805,626,500.00
of 1971	2, 8,				2,760,420,000.00
(di Bt. 15)	2, 8,		2,578,547,000.00		2,578,547,000.00
of 1972 (dated Nv. 1,)	3, 8,				2,343,611,000.00
of 1973		4, 3, 8, 0.00			2,893,834, 00
of	1, 31, 0, 60.00	3, 0,			3,357,209,500.00
of	2, 03, 0.00	2, 0.	1,000.00		3,130,373,500.00
1974	1,217,601,500.00				3,593,456,500.00
of 1975–85	1,586,860,000.00		486,000.00		2,243,527,500.00
of 978–83	2,609,982,500.00		12, 00.00		1,217,589,500.00
of	1,913,650,500.00		3,449,000.00		65, 4, 0
of	1, 88,000.00		1,678, 00.00		1,912,587,000.00
of 1987–92	365,121,500.00	3,452,731,000.00	1,063,500.00		1,127,158,500.00
of 1988–93	249,990, 00.00		1,810,000.00		817,841,500.00
of 1989–94	1,560,466,000.00		89,000.00		249,901,000.00
of	4,907,772, 0.00		72,000.00		1,560,394,000.00
of	2, 89, 8, 0.00		6,127,600.00		6, 6, 0.00
			172,500,000.00		2,286,890,500.00

Security					
3½% of 1998	4,420,921,000.00		17,576,500.00		4,438,497,500.00
Total Treasury bonds	102,477,519,450.00	7,658,500.00	7,087,261,400.00	21,108,792,000.00	88,463,547,350.00
Total marketable issues	208,690,981,450.00	101,394,500.00	173,972,450,400.00	176,276,819,000.00	206,487,917,350.00
...tedness:					
2.00% ... series	2 ,000, 00.00			275,000,000.00	50,000,000.00
2.00% ... series			130,000,000.00	000,000.00	
3.25% ... series			60, 00, 00.00	000,000.00	
3.43% ... series			35 000,000.00	35 000,000.00	90,000,000.00
3.50% ... series			120,000,000.00	000,000.00	
3.55% ... series			65,000,000.00	6, 0,	00,000,000.00
3.60% ... series			135,000,000.00	35,000,000.00	
3.75% foreign	50,000,000.00		95,000,000.00	145,000,000.00	
3.78% foreign series	135,000,000.00			135,000,000.00	
3.80% foreign series	18,000,000.00			18,000,000.00	
3.85% ... series			85,000,000.00	85,000,000.00	
3.875% ... series	50,000,000.00		50,000,000.00	100,000,000.00	
3.90% fo ... series	150,000,000.00		100,000,000.00	250,000,000.00	
3.95% fo series	100,000,000.00		95,000,000.00	195,000,000.00	
4 % fo series			50,000,000.00	60,000,000.00	
Total foreign series	778,000,000.00		1,010,000,000.00	1, 8,000,000.00	240,000,000.00
Treasury notes:					
2.125% foreign series	25,000,000.00		1,820,296.06		1,820,296.06
3.63% foreign series					25,000,000.00
4.03% foreign series	125,000,000.00				125,000,000.00
Total foreign series	150,000,000.00		1,820,296.06		151,820,296.06
Treasury bonds:					
4.00% foreign series	30,000,000.00			30,000,000.00	
4.125% foreign series	30,000,000.00			30,000,000.00	
4.25% foreign series	143,929,534.25			143,929,534.25	
Total foreign series	203,929,534.25			203,929,534.25	
Certificates of indebtedness:					
3.54% foreign currency series	30,120,481.92		30,120,481.92		30,120,481.92
Treasury bonds:					
2.82% foreign currency series			45,530,989.59		45,530,989.59
2.83% foreign currency series			23,107,500.00		23,107,500.00
2.89% foreign currency series			25,414,722.05		25,414,722.05
3.09% foreign currency series			49,970,000.00		49,970,000.00
3.14% foreign currency series			49,970,000.00		49,970,000.00
3.18% foreign currency series			49,942,500.00		49,942,500.00
3.22% foreign currency series			10,029,335.81		10,029,335.81

Footnotes at end of table.

TABLE 43.—*Changes in public debt issues, fiscal year 1965*—Continued

Issues	Outstanding June 30, 1964	Issues during year	Redemptions during year	Transferred to matured debt	Outstanding June 30, 1965 [1]

INTEREST-BEARING DEBT—Continued

Public Issues—Continued

Nonmarketable—Continued

Treasury bonds—Continued

3.47% Treasury	10, 274, 942. 13		10, 274, 942. 13		
	7, 486, 777. 15		7, 537, 768. 13		
3.86%		50, 990. 98	10, 364, 308. 44		
3.41%		10, 364, 308. 44	10, 355, 688. 18		
3.45%		10, 355, 688. 18	120, 905, 227. 51		
		120, 905, 227. 51	121, 031, 737. 44		
		121, 031, 737. 44	10, 075, 456. 97		
		10, 075, 456. 97	27, 435, 801. 80		
		27, 435, 801. 80	91, 368, 211. 18		
3.54%		91, 368, 211. 18			61, 606, 974. 14
3.54%		61, 606, 974. 14			27, 487, 858. 09
		27, 487, 858. 09			

| Total foreign currency series | 801, 531, 816. 62 | 2. 79 | 347, 511, 533. 84 | | 1, 136, 728, 520. 57 |

1% Treasury certificates, maturing Dec. 15, 1965	17,761,719.28	6,191,254.40	6,191,254.40
Total Treasury certificates	20,400,000.00	486,873,509.13	409,349,141.78	95,286,086.63
4% Treasury bonds, maturing June 30, 1967		586,315.06	11,892,247.04	9,094,008.02

U.S. savings bonds:

Series				
Series E-1951				
Series E-1952				
Series E-1953				
Series E-1954				
Series E-1955				
Series E-1956				
Series E-1957				
Series E-1957 (February to December)				
Series E-1958				
Series E-1959				
Series E-1960				
Series E-1961				
Series E-1962				
Series E-1963				
Series E-1964				
Series E-1965				
Unclassified				
Total Series E	40,167,872,696.83	5,627,107,269.03	4,747,339,566.86	41,047,640,309.00
Series H-1952				
Series H-1954				
Series H-1955				
Series H-1956				
Series H-1958				
Series I-				
Series I-				
Series				

Footnotes at end of table.

TABLE 43.—Changes in public debt issues, fiscal year 1965—Continued

Issues	Outstanding June 30, 1964	Issues during year	Redemptions during year	Transferred to matured debt	Outstanding June 30, 1965 [1]
INTEREST-BEARING DEBT—Continued					
Public Issues—Continued					
Nonmarketable—Continued					
U.S. savings bonds [1]—Continued					
Series H-1962	68,781. 6.00	$5,000.00	$27,988,500.00		$780,798,000.00
Series H-1963	754,229. 6.00	4,000.00	28,646,000.00		726,057,500.00
Series H-1964	344,178,000.00	326,976,500.00	15,980,500.00		655,174,000.00
Series H-1965		296,186,000.00	265,000.00		295,920,500.00
Unclassified sales and redemptions	12,729,500.00	-3,998,500.00	2,000.00		8,729,000.00
Total Series H	7,552,877,000.00	619,643,000.00	449,241,000.00	13,792,100.00	7,723,279,000.00
Series J-1952	31,086,060.60	64,051.20	28,072,861.80	$3, 57. 30.00	36,498,651.00
Series J-1953	73,234,423.20	2,380,564.80	28,841,487.00	10,274,850.00	129,488,044.20
Series J-1954	135,279,665.12	4,441,223.98	10,232,844.90		114,536,774.34
Series J-1955	119,899,028.80	83,073.71	9,190,328.17		92,270,889.05
Series J-1956	96,104,435.90	2,994,950.00	6,828,496.85		20,842,951.75
Series J-1957	21,819,585.00	699,832.00	1,676,465.25		• -4,207.40
Unclassified redemptions	• -5,000.00		-792.60		
Total Series J	477,418,198.62	14,848,695.69	84,841,691.37	13,792,100.00	393,633,102.94
Series K-1952	81,060,000.00		73,500.00	5, 38. 500.00	55,511,000.00
Series K-1953	139,234,500.00		1,000.00	9,772,500.00	316,078,000.00
Series K-1954	347,300,000.00		27,253,500.00		263,171,000.00
Series K-1955	290,424,500.00		13,000.00		166,537,000.00
Series K-1956	180,005,000.00		2,361,500.00		33,165,500.00
Series K-1957	85,527,000.00		6,500.00		• -19,000.00
Unclassified redemptions	• -12,500.00				
Total Series K	1,073,538,500.00		223,944,000.00	15,151,000.00	834,443,500.00
Total U.S. savings bonds	49,271,706,305.45	6,261,598,964.72	5,505,366,258.23	28,943,100.00	49,998,995,911.94
U.S. retirement plan bonds	5,512,481.81	5,473,745.02	134,697.58		10,851,529.25
Depository bonds:					
First Series	103,299,000.00	11,005,500.00	55,566,500.00		58,738,000.00
Treasury bonds, REA series	24,571,000.00	4,702,000.00	3,298,000.00		25,975,000.00
Treasury bonds, investment series:					
2½% Series A-1965	430,940,000.00		50,275,000.00		380,665,000.00
2¾% Series B-1975-80	3,114,580,000.00		239,287,000.00		2,875,293,000.00

	3,545,520,000.00	9,204,577,805.97	289,562,000.00	28,943,100.00	3,255,958,000.00
Total Treasury bonds investment series	54,212,543,101.14		7,664,621,156.45		55,723,556,650.66
Total nonmarketable	260,700,460,451.14	185,481,396,805.97	181,637,071,556.45	130,247,600.00	264,414,538,100.66
Total public issues					
Special Issues					
Civil ... fund:	72,800,000.00	2,299,783,000.00	2,302,876,000.00		69,707,000.00
...	91,101,000.00	278,96,000.00			569,896,000.00
37⅝% notes	30,908,000.00		80,227,000.00		240,681,000.00
3⅞% notes	82,928,000.00		69,976,000.00		121,952,000.00
...% notes	39,...00		69,913,000.00		69,913,000.00
...	51,3..00	1,965,311,000.00	51,316,000.00		
	93,96,00.00				3,888,607,000.00
	2,024,61,00.00		70,649,000.00		2,024,661,000.00
	1,295,20,00.00		4,165,000.00		1,295,200,000.00
	1,150,94,00.00		385,000,000.00		1,080,225,000.00
	4,683,86,00.00				4,205,921,000.00
	1,355,00,00.00				0, 0, 0.00
Exchange Stabilization fi:		12,000,000.00	12,000,000.00		15,500,000.00
		93,500,000.00	278,000,000.00		
3.75% certificates		1,018,434,076.01	1,904,243,714.38		
3.70% certificates		1,904,243,714.38	2,020,284,521.87		216,305,515.33
3.65% certificates		2,236,590,037.20	853,680,695.45		
3.60% certificates		83,680,695.45	39,500,000.00		
		39,500,000.00	60,000,000.00		
	500,000.00		9,000,000.00		
3.35%		42,500,000.00	567,963,332.34		
		567,963,332.34	959,684,332.39		
		959,684,332.39	982,329,789.12		
3.25% certificates	291,564,490.54	690,765,298.58			
... trust	270,309,000.00	280,271,000.00	238,182,000.00	312,398,000.00	312,398,000.00
3¾% notes	1,349,000.00	1,304,523,00.00	1,304,523,000.00		279,238,000.00
4⅛% bonds	133,173,000.00	146,065,000.00	1,349,000.00		153,632,000.00
3⅞% bonds	153,632,000.00		60,865,000.00		431,692,000.00
3¼% bonds	492,557,000.00		393,742,000.00		698,202,000.00
2⅝%	1,091,944,000.00		30,000,000.00		
2½% notes	30,000,000.00				
Federal ...	31,500,000.00	2,647,400,000.00	2,628,400,000.00		50,500,000.00
	50,000,000.00	50,000,000.00	50,000,000.00		50,000,000.00
...% notes	475,000.00		150,000.00		325,000.00

Footnotes at end of table.

TABLE 43.—*Changes in public debt issues, fiscal year 1965*—Continued

Issues	Outstanding June 30, 1964	Issues during year	Redemptions during year	Transferred to matured debt	Outstanding June 30, 1965 [1]
INTEREST-BEARING DEBT—Continued					
Special Issues—Continued					
Federal Housing					
Armed services ... fund:					
2% ...	$13,675,000.00	$3,300,000.00	$13,675,000.00		$3,300,000.00
Experimental ... fund:					
2% ...	825,000.00		100,000.00		725,000.00
... fund:					
2% ... fund:	1,558,0.00	5,780,000.00	3,800,000.00		3,538,000.00
Housing ... fund:	90,000.00				90,000.00
2% ... fund:	10, 2, 0.00	90,932,000.00	5,018,000.00		96,151,000.00
2% ... fund:	0, 00.00				430,000.00
Section 03 ... cent:	575,000.00		60,000.00		525,000.00
Section 20 ...	0, 0.00		125,000.00		525,000.00
Section 20 ... fund:	1, 0 00.00		250,000.00		1,440,000.00
% notes					
Servicemen's ... fund:	1,625,000.00	8,606,000.00			10,231,000.00
2% notes ...	0, 0.00	1,150,000.00	690,000.00		1,150,000.00
... fund:	8, 0.00	2,650,000.00			11,273,000.00
... fund:	7,945,000.00	0.00	7,945,000.00		5,500,000.00
Federal old-age ... trust fund:					
4% ...	00	16,721,585,000.00	16,580,565,000.00		141,020,000.00
4⅛% notes	0.00	1,032,019,000.00	597,887,000.00		1,032,019,000.00
...	1,738,455,000.00	1,080,011,000.00			2,581,889,000.00
... bonds	1,738,455,000.00				1,738,455,000.00
... bonds	1,240,088,000.00		281,292,000.00		1,240,088,000.00
2⅛% bonds	1,324,022,000.00		912,011,000.00		412,011,000.00
...	3, 0.00	285,000,000.00	0.00		287,422,000.00
... service ... fund:					
4%	37, 0.00	4,692,000.00	46,148,000.00		39,318,000.00
3%	1,140,000.00	1,184,000.00	1,198,000.00		1,126,000.00

...t life ...nce fund:					
3⅜% ...s	670,000.00			1,000,000.00	79,800,000.00
3¾% notes	79,800,000.00	1,000,000.00		670,000.00	77,992,000.00
3¾% bonds	32,517,000.00	45,475,000.00			775,662,000.00
...% ...	842,853,000.00				
3⅜% ...ds					265,394,000.00
Highway trust fund:					
3⅞% ...	609,028,000.00	1,501,689,000.00		67,191,000.00	
3⅞% ...		2,383,506,000.00		1,236,295,000.00	8,418,000.00
N...al service life insurance fund:				2,992,534,000.00	
...% certificates	7,873,000.00	94,771,000.00		86,353,000.00	.00
3½% notes		15,480,000.00		15,480,000.00	27,...
3¾% notes	457,730,000.00	27,784,000.00		7,873,000.00	57,730,000.00
3⅞% notes	455,950,000.00	476,436,000.00			82,386,000.00
3¾% bonds	298,259,000.00				98,259,000.00
3⅞% bonds	430,031,000.00				...031,000.00
3⅞% bonds	343,149,000.00				33,149,000.00
3¾% bonds	3,790,006,000.00			379,000,000.00	3,411,000,000.00
3⅞% bonds					
3% bonds					
Railroad retirement account:					
4⅜% certificates	118,693,000.00	1,426,438,000.00		1,336,926,000.00	208,205,000.00
4% certificates		9,633,000.00		9,633,000.00	
4⅜% notes	51,248,000.00	48,848,000.00		12,812,000.00	87,284,000.00
4% notes	634,487,000.00	300,883,000.00		271,961,000.00	362,526,000.00
4⅛% bonds	313,211,000.00				614,094,000.00
4% bonds	1,850,910,000.00				1,850,910,000.00
3⅞% ... trust fund:					
3⅞% certificates	4,930,606,000.00	8,022,133,000.00		2,223,019,000.00	5,799,114,000.00
3½% certificates		1,880,208,000.00		6,810,814,000.00	
Veterans' special term insurance fund:					
3⅝% ...		138,113,000.00		8,979,000.00	149,134,000.00
3½% certificates	123,173,000.00	13,223,000.00		136,396,000.00	
Veterans' ...ped insurance fund:					
4⅛% certificates		4,505,000.00		1,900,000.00	2,605,000.00
Total special issues	46,627,421,490.54	53,286,544,486.35		51,264,015,461.56	48,649,950,515.33
Total interest-bearing debt	307,327,881,941.68	238,767,941,292.32	$130,247,600.00	232,901,087,018.01	313,064,488,615.99

Footnotes at end of table.

TABLE 43.—*Changes in public debt issues, fiscal year 1965*—Continued

Issues	Outstanding June 30, 1964	Issues during year	Transferred from interest-bearing debt	Redemptions during year	Outstanding June 30, 1965 [1]
MATURED DEBT ON WHICH INTEREST HAS CEASED					
Old debt—Issued prior to Apr. 1, 1917:					
6% compound interest notes 1864–66	$5, 960. 00				$155, 960. 00
3% loan of 1908–18	8, 060. 00			$40. 00	98, 0. 00
2½% postal savings bonds	3, 240. 00			61, 760. 00	272, 480. 00
2% consols of 1930	9, 800. 00				9, 8. 00
4% funded loan of 1907	3, 850. 00				342, 850. 00
3% Panama Canal loan of 1961	3, 900. 00			500. 00	33, 0. 00
All others [7]	8, 680. 26				763, 0. 26
Total old debt—issued prior to Apr. 1, 1917	1, 838, 490. 26			62, 300. 00	1, 776, 190. 26
Liberty loan bonds:					
First Liberty loan:					
First 3½'s	279, 600. 00			3 6. 00	276, 050. 00
First 4's	88, 300. 00			6. 00	87, 750. 00
First 4¼'s	227, 500. 00			31, 750. 00	195, 750. 00
First-Second 4¼'s	3, 050. 00			1, 000. 00	2, 050. 00
Total	598, 450. 00			36, 850. 00	561, 600. 00
Second Liberty loan:					
Second 4's	341, 900. 00			7, 200. 00	334, 700. 00
Second 4¼'s	357, 000. 00			2, 750. 00	354, 250. 00
Total	698, 900. 00			9, 950. 00	688, 950. 00
Third Liberty loan 4¼'s	1, 207, 500. 00			5, 800. 00	1, 201, 700. 00
Fourth Liberty loan 4¼'s	2, 295, 950. 00			98, 550. 00	2, 197, 400. 00
Total Liberty loan bonds	4, 800, 800. 00			151, 150. 00	4, 649, 650. 00
Victory notes:					
Victory 3¾'s	700. 00				700. 00
Victory 4¾'s	394, 500. 00			1, 300. 00	393, 200. 00
Total Victory notes	395, 200. 00			1, 300. 00	393, 900. 00
Treasury bonds:					
3⅜% of 1940–43	11, 450. 00			100. 00	11, 350. 00
3⅜% of 1941–43	29, 350. 00			500. 00	28, 850. 00
3¼% of 1941	15, 200. 00			6, 050. 00	9, 150. 00
3⅜% of 1943–47	51, 450. 00			1, 550. 00	49, 900. 00
3¼% of 1943–45	149, 050. 00			24, 700. 00	124, 350. 00

[illegible]of 1944–46	20, [illegible].00			36 050.00	234, 650.00
4% of 1944–54	[illegible], [illegible].00			( )[illegible]0	183, 300.00
2¾% of 1945–47	129, 950.00			10, 950.00	119, 000.00
2½% of 1945	2, 500.00				2, 500.00
3¾% of 1946–56	[illegible], [illegible].00			3, 000.00	61, 600.00
[illegible]% of 1946–48	52, 00.00			3, 000.00	49, 000.00
[illegible]% of 1946–49	279, 250.00			19, 100.00	260, 150.00
4¼% of 1947–52	358, 500.00			133, 400.00	225, 100.00
2% of 1947	350.00				350.00
2% of 1948–50 (dated Mar. 15, 1941)	2, [illegible].00				2, 300.00
[illegible]% of 1948–51	7, 300.00			1, 000.00	6, 300.00
1¾% of 1948	63, 500.00			9, 0.00	54, 500.00
[illegible]8	4, 050.00				4, 050.00
[illegible]% of [illegible]–50 ([illegible]d [illegible]. 8, [illegible])	2, 750.00			150.00	2, 600.00
[illegible]% of [illegible]1 ([illegible]d [illegible]. [illegible], [illegible])	1, 150.00				1, 150.00
[illegible]% of [illegible]–51 ([illegible]d M[illegible]y [illegible], [illegible])	14, 000.00				14, 000.00
[illegible]% of 9[illegible]1 ([illegible]d [illegible]ly [illegible], [illegible])	9, [illegible].00			5, 300.00	4, 000.00
3⅛% of 1949–52	19, 500.00				19, 500.00
[illegible]3	157, 200.00			25, 650.00	131, 550.00
1½% of 1950	[illegible] 500.00			38, 500.00	462, 000.00
[illegible]% of 1950–52 ([illegible]d [illegible]. [illegible], [illegible])	( )[illegible]0			700.00	19, 300.00
2½% of 1950–52	101, 900.00			5 [illegible]0.00	96, 000.00
[illegible]% of 0[illegible]2 ([illegible]d [illegible]pr. [illegible], 1943)	[illegible]6, 00.00			( )[illegible]0	265, 500.00
[illegible]–53	[illegible], [illegible]0.00				51, 400.00
2% of 1951–[illegible]	719, 000.00			91, 500.00	627, 500.00
2¾% of 1951–[illegible]	124, 000.00			([illegible])00	101, 300.00
2% of 1951–55	28, 450.00			850.00	27, 600.00
3% of 1951–[illegible]5	737, 050.00			[illegible]00.00	685, 150.00
[illegible]% of [illegible]–54	20, [illegible]0.00			2, [illegible]0.00	18, 750.00
[illegible]% of 2[illegible]4 ([illegible]d [illegible]e 26, 1944)	789, 000.00			55, 500.00	[illegible], [illegible].00
[illegible]% of [illegible]4 ([illegible]d [illegible]. 1, [illegible])	1, 565, 000.00			[illegible]3 [illegible]0.00	1, 361, 500.00
2¼% of 1952–55	31, 950.00			, [illegible]0.00	21, 800.00
[illegible]–5	71, 600.00			10, 250.00	61, 350.00
[illegible]of 1954–56	84, 650.00			2, 500.00	82, 150.00
[illegible]of [illegible]–[illegible]	1, 887, 350.00			273, 850.00	1, 613, 500.00
[illegible]of 1956–58	113, 850.00			2, 900.00	110, 950.00
[illegible]of 1956–59	213, 150.00			43, [illegible]0.00	[illegible]0.00
[illegible]of 1956–59	1, 407, 000.00			266, 500.00	1, 140, 500.00
[illegible]of [illegible]–[illegible]	44, 00.00			2, 500.00	41, 500.00
[illegible]of [illegible]	156, 000.00			36, 000.00	[illegible]0, 00.00
[illegible]of [illegible]8	159, 000.00			84, 000.00	75, 000.00
[illegible]of 1958–63	[illegible]4, 750.00			15, 000.00	199, 750.00
[illegible]of [illegible]	138, 000.00			27, 000.00	111, 000.00
[illegible]of [illegible]1	[illegible], [illegible].00			247, 500.00	63, 00.00
[illegible]of [illegible]	1, 751, 000.00			532, 000.00	1, 219, 000.00
[illegible]% of 1959–62 ([illegible] [illegible]e 1, [illegible])	5, 028, 000.00			1, 340, 500.00	3, 687, 500.00
[illegible]of [illegible]–[illegible]2 ([illegible]d N[illegible]v. 15, [illegible])	5, 864, 500.00			1, 854, 000.00	4, 010, 500.00
[illegible]of 1960–65	2, 008, 950.00			881, 800.00	1 [illegible]0.00
[illegible]of [illegible]3	3, 677, 500.00			1, 911, 000.00	[illegible]6, [illegible]0.00

Foo[illegible]notes at end of table.

TABLE 43.—*Changes in public debt issues, fiscal year 1965*—Continued

Issues	Outstanding June 30, 1964	Issues during year	Transferred from interest-bearing debt	Redemptions during year	Outstanding June 30, 1965 [1]
MATURED DEBT ON WHICH INTEREST HAS CEASED—Con.					
Treasury bonds—Continued					
2% of 1964	$6,448,500.00		$7,558,500.00	$4,912,500.00	$1,536,000.00
2⅜% of 1965					7,558,500.00
Total Treasury bonds	36,962,500.00		7,558,500.00	13,256,700.00	31,264,300.00
3% Adjusted service bonds of 1945	1,485,900.00			142,200.00	1,343,700.00
U.S. savings bonds:					
Series A-1935	319,200.00			28,250.00	290,950.00
Series B-1936	614,650.00			53,825.00	60,825.00
Series C-1937	651,775.00			54,750.00	597,025.00
Series C-1938	1,091,425.00			133,850.00	97,575.00
Series D-1939	1,623,550.00			147,250.00	1,476,300.00
Series D-1940	3,470,450.00			398,600.00	3,071,850.00
Series D-1941	3,765,500.00			417,875.00	3,347,625.00
Series E-1941	644,850.00			90,100.00	554,750.00
Series F-1942	2,768,275.00			524,775.00	2,243,500.00
Series F-1943	3,714,600.00			66,000.00	3,048,600.00
Series F-1944	3,413,575.00			537,125.00	2,876,450.00
Series F-1945	2,483,000.00			396,375.00	2, 8.00
Series F-1946	1,516,150.00			31,525.00	1,204,625.00
Series F-1947	1,354,500.00			279,075.00	1,075,425.00
Series F-1948	1,049,450.00			325,300.00	724,150.00
Series F-1950	1,591,425.00			428,250.00	1,163,175.00
Series F-1951	2,262,675.00			1,082,925.00	1,179,750.00
Series F-1952	2,916,025.00			1,664,225.00	1,251,800.00
Series F-1953	2,558,800.00			1,893,961.00	664,775.00
Series F Unclassified	891,566.60	−$64.00		−890,966.60	−600.00
Series G-1941	512,000.00			64,500.00	447,500.00
Series G-1942	2,854,500.00			497,100.00	2,357,400.00
Series G-1943	5,353,900.00			788,700.00	4,595,200.00
Series G-1944	7,248,200.00			1,308,100.00	5,940,100.00
Series G-1945	6,938,200.00			1,369,400.00	5,568,800.00
Series G-1946	6,666,600.00			1,317,300.00	5,349,300.00
Series G-1947	8,559,800.00			1,709,800.00	6,850,000.00
Series G-1948	8,733,400.00			2,117,300.00	6,616,100.00
Series G-1949	11,832,800.00			3,459,800.00	8,373,000.00
Series G-1950	13,827,900.00			4,488,300.00	9,339,600.00
Series G-1951	17,275,200.00			7,903,900.00	9,371,300.00
Series G-1952	10,414,700.00			6,314,300.00	4,100,400.00
Series G	−29,200.00			−18,000.00	−11,200.00
Series J-1952	3,687,025.00		3,517,250.00	3,068,900.00	4,135,375.00

Series J-1953				10,274,850.00
Series K-1952				6,788,500.00
Series K-1953				9,772,500.00
Total U.S. savings bonds	148,405,833.40	−64.00	8,943,100.00	49,104,969.40	128,243,900.00

Armed Forces leave bonds:

Apr. 1, 1943	0.00			0.00	0.00
July 1, 1943	0.00			0.00	0.00
Oct. 1, 1943	0.00			3,200.00	0.00
1944:					
Jan. 1, 1944	0.00			0.00	0.00
Apr. 1, 1944	0.00			0.00	0.00
July 1, 1944	0.00			0.00	39,925.00
Oct. 1, 1944	0.00			0.00	0.00

Series 1945:

Jan. 1, 1945	0.00			0.00	0.00
Apr. 1, 1945	0.00			0.00	0.00
July 1, 1945	0.00			0.00	0.00
Oct. 1, 1945	3,003,125.00			236,275.00	2,766,850.00
1946	0.00			0.00	0.00
July 1, 1946	0.00			0.00	0.00
Oct. 1, 1946	657,075.00			0.00	600,900.00

Total Armed Forces leave bonds | 7, 0.00 | | | 0.00 | 6, 0.00

Treasury

6, 00.00			6, 00.00
1, 0.00			1, 00.00
6, 5,700.00			6, 00.00
2, 0.00			5, 00.00
2, 00.00			2, 00.00
9, 00.00			9, 00.00
80, 00.00			80, 00.00
6, 00.00			9, 50.00
6, 00.00			6, 00.00
3, 00.00			3, 00.00
5, 00.00	50.00		5, 00.00
11, 00.00			11, 00.00
2, 00.00			25, 00.00
5, 00.00			5, 00.00
1, 400.00			1, 00.00
30, 200.00	20, 00.00		10, 00.00
1, 00.00			1, 00.00

Footnotes at end of table.

TABLE 43.—Changes in public debt issues, fiscal year 1965—Continued

Issues	Outstanding June 30, 1964	Issues during year	Transferred from interest-bearing debt	Redemptions during year	Outstanding June 30, 1965 [1]
MATURED DEBT ON WHICH INTEREST HAS CEASED—Con.					
Treasury notes—Continued					
A series—Continued					
1⅝% A-1940	$150.00				$150.00
2% J- 42	2,000.00				2,000.00
1% C-1 43	3,6.00				3,6.00
1% A-1945	300.00				80.00
⅞% J- 94	300.00				300.00
⅝% B-1947	1,500.00			$1,000.00	500.00
⅝% C-	500.00				500.00
1¼% A-	26,000.00				26,000.00
1⅜% A-	59,000.00			6,000.00	39,000.00
⅝% E-	8,000.00				8,000.00
⅝% A-	37,000.00			27,000.00	10,000.00
⅝% 34	4,000.00				4,00.00
⅝% 59	36,000.00				36,000.00
3⅝% J-1955	1,000.00				1,000.00
⅝% A- 0	15,000.00			5,000.00	15,000.00
⅝% A- 1	11,000.00				6,000.00
⅝% C-	1,000.00				1,000.00
⅞% J- 4	5,000.00			2,000.00	5,000.00
⅞% J- 1	34,000.00			5,000.00	32,000.00
⅝% B-1960	5,000.00				75,000.00
⅝% C- 0	75,000.00			1,000.00	30,000.00
4% J- 94	30,000.00			39,000.00	16,000.00
5% J- 11	17,000.00			10,000.00	91,00.00
4% J- 02	230,000.00			12,000.00	6? 000.00
4% E- 02	72,000.00			129,000.00	8,0.00
⅝% 58	108,000.00			69,000.00	60,0.00
⅝% A-	4,000.00			130,000.00	62,000.00
4% B-1963	129,000.00			252,000.00	8,000.00
1⅞% J- 18	192,000.00			76,000.00	197,000.00
⅝% J- 58	562,000.00			72,000.00	122,000.00
4¾% A-	273,000.00			8,0.00	130,000.00
⅝% J-1 0	194,000.00			12,0.00	128,000.00
	228,000.00			24,0.00	21,000.00
	140,000.00				23,000.00
	45,000.00				176,000.00
	23,000.00			201,000.00	845,000.00
	377,000.00			1,056,000.00	1,729,000.00
	1,901,000.00			3,044,000.00	89,000.00
	4,773,000.00			79,000.00	27,000.00
	168,000.00			18,000.00	6,439,000.00
	45,000.00			9,9,0.00	11,145,000.00
	38,346,000.00		$11,145,000.00		

				2, 663, 000. 00
				470, 000. 00
½% E—			2, 63, 000. 00	7, 06, 0. 00	6, 936, 000. 00
½% J—			819, 000. 00	00. 00	819, 000. 00
½% F—			853, 000. 00	1, 000. 00	853, 000. 00
½% A—			9, 295, 000. 00	10, 000. 00	9, 295, 000. 00
½% C–1965			2, 64, 000. 00	12, 000. 00	2, 654, 000. 00
1½% EA–1956				1, 000. 00	1, 000. 00
½% G—				10, 000. 00	10, 000. 00
½% I—				8, 000. 00	12, 000. 00
½% J—				35, 000. 00	1, 000. 00
½% EA–1962					10, 000. 00
1½% EO–1962				53, 000. 00	8, 000. 00
½% EA–1963			279, 000. 00	0. 00	29, 000. 00
1½% EO—			0, 0. 00	500, 000. 00	5, 000. 00
					17, 000. 00
					238, 000. 00
					279, 000. 00
					504, 000. 00
Tax series:					
J—			1, 525. 00	8, 725. 00	7, 200. 00
B—			4, 000. 00	5, 600. 00	1, 600. 00
J–04			50. 00	7, 875. 00	7, 825. 00
J–1944				2, 000. 00	2, 000. 00
V–05			2, 675. 00	85, 575. 00	82, 900. 00
Savings					
J—			6, 000. 00	61, 300. 00	55, 300. 00
J–07			29, 400. 00	159, 300. 00	129, 900. 00
J–98			3, 300. 00	92, 300. 00	88, 700. 00
J–99			15, 000. 00	26, 500. 00	11, 000. 00
J–01				7, 100. 00	7, 100. 00
J—			900. 00	5, 200. 00	900. 00
J–2			00. 00	15, 00. 00	0. 00
J–93			500. 00	80, 400. 00	15, 800. 00
V–1954				2, 000. 00	9, 900. 00
V–1954				26, 500. 00	2, 000. 00
V–05			500. 00	57, 100. 00	67, 000. 00
J—				10, 000. 00	9, 500. 00
J–¥				1, 800. 00	1, 800. 00
V–96			−4, 100. 00	16, 300. 00	1, 000. 00
Total Treasury notes		28, 212, 000. 00	42, 992, 100. 00	55, 924, 925. 00	41, 14, 825. 00
Certificates of indebtedness:					
Tax series:					
4½% T–10				1, 000. 00	1, 000. 00
4¾% TM–1921				500. 00	500. 00
6% TI–1921				1, 500. 00	1, 500. 00
6% TS–1921				1, 500. 00	1, 500. 00
6% TD–1921				2, 000. 00	2, 000. 00
5½% TS2–1921				1, 000. 00	1, 000. 00
5¾% TM–922				1, 000	1, 000. 00

Footnotes at end of table.

TABLE 43.—Changes in public debt issues, fiscal year 1965—Continued

Issues	Outstanding June 30, 1964	Issues during year	Transferred from interest-bearing debt	Redemptions during year	Outstanding June 30, 1965[1]
MATURED DEBT ON WHICH INTEREST HAS CEASED—Con.					
Certificates of indebtedness—Continued					
Tax series—Continued					
% TM–	$500.00				$500.00
% TM–1923	1,000.00				1,000.00
3¾% TS–1923	500.00				500.00
% TM–1924	1,000.00				1,000.00
4% TM–1925	1,000.00				1,000.00
	1,100.00				1,100.00
% TM–1930	2,00.00				2,000.00
%	3,500.00				3,500.00
3¾%	12,500.00				12,500.00
% Mar. 15,	4,600.00			$500.00	4,100.00
	1,000.00				1,000.00
Regular:					
% IVA–1918	500.00				500.00
5¼% H–	1,000.00				1,000.00
%	1,00.00				1,000.00
3	500.00				500.00
% B–	22,000.00				22,000.00
% E–1944	23,000.00			7,000.00	16,000.00
% A–	70,000.00			7,000.00	63,000.00
% C–	20,000.00			9,000.00	11,000.00
% I–	8,000.00				
% B–1946	0.00				
% E–	16,000.00			1,000.00	16,000.00
% K–1946	9,000.00			11,000.00	9,000.00
% E–	51,000.00			7,000.00	51,000.00
% F–1947	1,000.00				2,000.00
% C–1948					4,000.00
1¼% A–1950	4,000.00			1, 0. 0	1, 0.00
% B–1954	2,000.00				18,000.00
% I–	18,000.00			1,000.00	
% E–1954	6,000.00				6,000.00
% C–1958	15,000.00			2,000.00	15,000.00
% B–1959	8,000.00				6,000.00
% E–1959	10,000.00				10,000.00
3¾% A–	9,000.00				4,000.00
% B–1960	1,000.00			7,000.00	2,000.00
% C–1960	97,000.00			11,000.00	86,000.00
% B–1961	40,000.00			1,000.00	39,000.00
% C–1961	13,000.00			3,000.00	10,000.00
	16,000.00			13,000.00	3,000.00

3% A-1962	15,000.00	14,000.00		0.00
3¼% B-1963	45,000.00	36,000.00		9,000.00
3½% C-1963	70,000.00	21,000.00		49,000.00
3⅛% D-1963	67,000.00	47,000.00		20,000.00
3¼% A-1964	0.00	89,000.00		7,000.00
3¼% B-1964	427,000.00	421,000.00		6,000.00
Total certificates of indebtedness	1,245,700.00	718,500.00		527,200.00
Tre by de:				
Regular:				
June 5, 1942	30,000.00			30,000.00
Jan. 14, 1942	4,000.00			4,000.00
3,	1,000.00			1,000.00
July 29, 1954	5,000.00			5,000.00
May 19, 5	1,000.00			1,000.00
Aug. 7	5,000.00			
Oct. 24, 1957	8,000.00	5,000.00		8,000.00
,	15,000.00			15,000.00
May 15, 1959	0.00			11,000.00
Regular:				
Sept. 3, 1959	20,000.00			20,000.00
Dec. 10, 1959	3,000.00	1,000.00		2,000.00
Jan. 4,	1,000.00			1,000.00
Mr. 2, 0	30,000.00			30,000.00
, 5,	4,000.00			44,000.00
e 22, 6	7,000.00			7,000.00
Other:				
July 15, 1960	42,000.00	6,000.00		36,000.00
Regular:				
21, 0	5,000.00			5,000.00
8, 0	6,000.00			6,000.00
Aug. 4, 1960	12,000.00			12,000.00
Aug. 11, 1960	0			3, 0.00
Sept. 29, 1960	20,000.00			0.00
Oct. 17, 1960	13,000.00			13,000.00
Jan. ,	81,000.00	61,000.00		120,000.00
Regular:				
Jan. 26, 1961	1,000.00			1,000.00
Feb. 16, 9	18,000.00	18,000.00		
Mar. 23, 1961	37,000.00	37,000.00		
July 27, 1961	1,000.00			1,000.00
Oct. 5, 1961	10,000.00			10,000.00
Dec. 28, 1961	100,000.00			100,000.00
,	15,000.00	15,000.00		
n. 15, 1962	9,000.00	2,000.00		7,000.00

Footnotes at end of table.

Table 43.—Changes in public debt issues, fiscal year 1965—Continued

Issues	Outstanding June 30, 1964	Issues during year	Transferred from interest-bearing debt	Redemptions during year	Outstanding June 30, 1965 [1]
MATURED DEBT ON WHICH INTEREST HAS CEASED—Con.					
Treasury bills, maturity date—Continued					
Apr. 1, 1962	$6,000.00				$6,000.00
Mar. 1, 1962	7,0.00				7,000.00
Tax:					
Mar. 23, 1962	25,000.00				25,000.00
July 5, 1962	50,000.00			$50,000.00	
Tax:					
July 15, 1962	12,000.00				12,000.00
Oct. 1, 1962	8,000.00			18,000.00	
Tax:					
Nov. 1, 1962	11,00.00			1,000.00	
Jan. 31, 1963	5,000.00			5,000.00	
Feb. 7, 1963	1,000.00				1,000.00
Mar. 7, 1963	27,000.00			27,000.00	
Regular:					
Apr. 15, 1963	2,000.00			2,000.00	
Apr. 18, 1963	21,00.00			1,000.00	20,000.00
May 9, 1963	20,000.00				20,000.00
May 6, 1963	5,000.00			5,000.00	
May 23, 1963	5,000.00			5,000.00	
June 1, 1963	20,000.00			20,000.00	
June 9, 1963	31,000.00			31,000.00	
July 5, 1963	13,000.00			13,000.00	
Other:					
July 15, 1963	50,000.00			50,000.00	
Aug. 8, 1963	2,000.00			2,000.00	
Aug. 15, 1963	10,000.00			10,000.00	
Sept. 5, 1963	20,000.00			20,000.00	
Sept. 12, 1963	1,000.00			1,000.00	
Sept. 26, 1963	1,000.00			3,000.00	
Oct. 10, 1963	7,000.00			7,000.00	
Other:					
Oct. 15, 1963	18,000.00			13,000.00	5,000.00
Regular:					
Oct. 31, 1963	10,000.00			10,000.00	
Nov. 7, 1963	49,000.00			10,000.00	39,000.00
Nov. 21, 1963	32,000.00			10,000.00	22,000.00
Nov. 29, 1963	10,000.00			10,000.00	
Dec. 5, 1963	85,000.00			85,000.00	
Dec. 12, 1963	6,000.00			6,000.00	3,000.00
Jan. 2, 1964	63,000.00			60,000.00	

ter:				
th. 15, 1964	238,000.00		80,000.00	58,000.00
Regular:				
J a. 6, 64	26,000.00		26,000.00	
Jn. 2, 1964	0, 0.00		10,000.00	
Jn. 6,	70,000.00		70,000.00	
Feb. 6,	75,000.00		66,000.00	
Feb. 3, or 4	80,000.00		80,000.00	9,000.00
Feb. 2, 0,	39,000.00		39,000.00	
Feb. 2,	8, 0.00		39, 00.00	
Mar. 5, 1964	56,000.00		66,000.00	
Mar. 2, 1964	3,000.00		3,000.00	
Mar. 8, 68	33,000.00		133,000.00	
Mar. 8,	102,000.00		102,000.00	
A a. 2, 64	44,000.00		44,000.00	
Apr. 0, 1964	34,000.00		34,000.00	
Apr. 15, 1964	291,000.00		203,000.00	88,000.00
Regular:				
Apr. 16, 1964	7, 00.00		7,000.00	
Apr. 23, 1964	83,000.00		83,000.00	
Apr. 30, 1964	33,000.00		33,000.00	
May 7,	16,000.00		145,000.00	
May 14, 1964	549,000.00		549,000.00	
May 21, 1964	357,000.00		357,000.00	
May 8, 1964	192, 00.00		492,000.00	
he 1,	538,000.00		538,000.00	
ube 8,	904,000.00		899,000.00	5,000.00
Th ube 2, 64	1,407,000.00		1,287,000.00	120,000.00
3, 64	20,458,000.00		20,458,000.00	
ube 9, 64	2,963,000.00		2,963,000.00	
Qtr:				
July 4, 64		$65,000.00		65,000.00
Regular:				
A 6, 1964		25,000.00		25,000.00
Aug. 13, 1964		40,000.00		40,000.00
Aug. 27, 94		5,000.00		5,000.00
Ag. 3, 1964		32,000.00		32,000.00
Regular:				
Sept. 3, 1964		300,000.00		2, 0.00
Sept. 17, 1964		6,000.00		300,000.00
Sept. 24				6,000.00
Other:				
Sept. 30, 1964		25, 00.00		25,000.00
Regular:				
Oct. 8,		1,000.00		1,000.00
Oct. 15, 1964		14,000.00		4,000.00
Oct. 22, 1964		11,000.00		9,000.00
Oct. 29, 1964				1,000.00
Other:				
Oct. 31, 1964		5,000.00		5,000.00

Footnotes at end of table.

TABLE 43.—*Changes in public debt issues, fiscal year 1965*—Continued

Issues	Outstanding June 30, 1964	Issues during year	Transferred from interest-bearing debt	Redemptions during year	Outstanding June 30, 1965 [1]
MATURED DEBT ON WHICH INTEREST HAS CEASED—Con.					
By tax, maturity date—Continued					
Regular:					
Nov. 5, 1964			$1,000.00		$11,000.00
Nov. 19, 1964			1,000.00		1,000.00
Nov. 2, 1964			26,000.00		26,000.00
Other:					
Nov. 8, 1964			5,000.00		5,000.00
Regular:					
Dec. 10, 1964			20,000.00		20,000.00
Dec. 24, 1964			50,000.00		50,000.00
Other:					
Dec. 31, 1964			315,000.00		315,000.00
Regular:					
Jan. 7, 1965			30,000.00		30,000.00
Jan. 14, 1965			43,000.00		43,000.00
Other:					
Jan. 31, 1965			7,000.00		17,000.00
Regular:					
Feb. 4, 1965			36,000.00		36,000.00
Feb. 25, 1965			50,000.00		50,000.00
Other:					
Feb. 8, 1965			90,000.00		0, 0.00
Regular:					
Mar. 4, 1965			43,000.00		43,000.00
Mar. 11, 1965			173,000.00		173,000.00
Mar. 18, 1965			46,000.00		46,000.00
Tax:					
Mar. 22, 1965			1,000.00		1,000.00
Regular:					
Mar. 25, 1965			21,000.00		21,000.00
Other:					
Mar. 31, 1965			95,000.00		95,000.00
Regular:					
Mar. 1, 1965			76,000.00		76,000.00
Mar. 8, 1965			63,000.00		63,000.00
Mar. 15, 1965			194,000.00		194,000.00
Mar. 22, 1965			140,000.00		140,000.00
Mar. 29, 1965			25,000.00		25,000.00
Other:					
Apr. 6, 1965			144,000.00		144,000.00
Regular:					
May 6, 1965			224,000.00		224,000.00
May 3, 1965			106,000.00		106,000.00
May 6, 1965			209,000.00		99,000.00
May 27, 1965			239,000.00		239,000.00
Other:					
May 3, 1965			0, 000.00		0, 000.00

Regular:					
June 3, 1965					622,000.00
June 10, 1965		904,000.00		904,000.00	904,000.00
June 17, 1965		1,586,000.00		1,586,000.00	1,586,000.00
Tax anticipation:					
June 22, 1965		45,132,000.00		45,132,000.00	45,132,000.00
Regular:					
June 24, 1965		1,847,000.00		1,847,000.00	1,847,000.00
Other:					
June 30, 1965		11,671,000.00		11,671,000.00	11,671,000.00
Total Treasury bills	$30,549,000.00			$29,596,000.00 65,534,000.00	66,487,000.00
Treasury savings certificates:					
Issued Dec. 15, 1921	7,925.00			25.00	7,900.00
Issued Sept. 30, 1922	47,650.00			175.00	47,475.00
Issued Dec. 1, 1923	15,450.00			175.00	15,275.00
Total Treasury savings certificates	71,025.00			375.00	70,650.00
Total matured debt on which interest has ceased	288,866,773.66	−$64.00		136,588,344.40 130,247,600.00	282,527,965.26

DEBT BEARING NO INTEREST

U.S.	53, 0.86	18,916,139.40		17, 31.70	54,846,511.56
					8,216.47
Second Series	387,586.51			7,370.04	295,611.40
	299,986.80			4,375.40	
Special					
U.S.	3,289,000,000.00	428,000,000.00		550,000,000.00	3,167,000,000.00
	142,261,000.00	57,652,200.00		61,913,200.00	138,000,000.00
	150,000,000.00				150,000,000.00
U.N. Children's Series	45,273.00	6,834,130.00		15,079,403.00	74,613,886.00
U.N. Series	55,541,301.00	19,02,585.00		1,000,000.00	2,361,904.00
U.N./FAO Series	2,000,000.00	1,361,904.00		4,000.00	166,641,585.07
U.S.	90,641,585.07				52,917.50
N Reserve bk notes	110,322,462.00			9,577.00	91,075,885.00
Fractional	1,965,245.22			55.54	1,965,189.68
Old	52,526,183.50			36,005,610.00	17,520,573.50
	3,701,187.60			792.50	3,700,395.00
Total debt bearing no interest	4,060,787,231.96	531,836,958.40		724,169,515.18	3,868,454,675.18
Total gross public debt	311,677,537,947.30	239,299,778,186.72		233,761,844,877.59	317,215,471,256.43

1 Reconciliation by classes to the basis of the daily Treasury statement is shown in summary table 35.
2 Treasury bills are shown at maturity value.
3 Consists of a strip issued on July 29, 1964, of additional amounts of 10 series of outstanding Treasury bills dated from Apr. 16, through June 18, 1964, and maturing each week Oct. 15 through Dec. 17, 1964.
4 Excludes $100,086,000 issued July 29, 1964 (see footnote 3).
5 Amounts issued and retired for Series E and J include accrued discount; amounts outstanding are stated at current redemption values. Amounts issued, retired, and outstanding for Series H and K are stated at par value.
6 Excess of unclassified redemptions over unclassified sales.
7 Consists of issues in which there have been no transactions since the fiscal year 1956; for amount of each issue outstanding (unchanged since June 30, 1956) see 1956 annual report, page 435.
8 Includes public debt incurred to finance expenditures of wholly owned Government corporations and other business-type activities in exchange for which their securities were issued to the Treasury (see table 110).

TABLE 44.—*Issues, maturities, and redemptions of interest-bearing public debt securities, excluding special issues, July 1964–June 1965*

[On basis of daily Treasury statements, supplemented by special statements by the Bureau of the Public Debt on public debt transactions]

Date	Securities	Rate of interest [1]	Amount issued [2]	Amount matured or called or redeemed prior to maturity [3]
1964		*Percent*		
July 1	Treasury bonds, foreign currency series, maturing:			
	July 1, 1964	2.82		$22,397,300.00
	Oct. 1, 1965	3.81	$22,461,502.84	
	Feb. 1, 1966	3.83	50,314,465.41	
	Mar. 1, 1966	3.84	50,314,465.41	
	Apr. 1, 1966	3.85	50,314,465.41	
	Treasury bills:			
	Regular weekly:			
2	Dated Jan. 2, 1964	[4] 3.573		
	Redeemed in exchange for series issued July 2, 1964, due Oct. 1, 1964			163,969,000.00
	Redeemed in exchange for series dated July 2, 1964, due Dec. 31, 1964			92,408,000.00
	Redeemable for cash			1,844,649,000.00
2	Maturing Oct. 1, 1964	3.479		
	Issued in exchange for series dated Jan. 2, 1964		163,969,000.00	
	Issued for cash		1,036,198,000.00	
2	Maturing Dec. 31, 1964	3.528		
	Issued in exchange for series dated Jan. 2, 1964		92,408,000.00	
	Issued for cash		807,994,000.00	
	Other:			
7	Maturing June 30, 1965	3.691		
	Issued for cash		1,001,222,000.00	
	Regular weekly:			
9	Dated Jan. 9, 1964	[4] 3.614		
	Redeemed in exchange for series issued July 9, 1964, due Oct. 8, 1964			172,146,000.00
	Redeemed in exchange for series dated July 9, 1964, due Jan. 7, 1965			51,455,000.00
	Redeemable for cash			1,877,394,000.00
9	Maturing Oct. 8, 1964	3.492		
	Issued in exchange for series dated Jan. 9, 1964		172,146,000.00	
	Issued for cash		1,029,092,000.00	
9	Maturing Jan. 7, 1965	3.544		
	Issued in exchange for series dated Jan. 9, 1964		51,455,000.00	
	Issued for cash		848,591,000.00	
	Other:			
15	Issued July 15, 1963	3.582		
	Redeemable for cash			1,997,942,000.00
	Regular weekly:			
16	Dated Jan. 16, 1964	[4] 3.562		
	Redeemed in exchange for series issued July 16, 1964, due Oct. 15, 1964			16,450,000.00
	Redeemed in exchange for series dated July 16, 1964, due Jan. 14, 1965			4,398,000.00
	Redeemable for cash			1,980,102,000.00
16	Maturing Oct. 15, 1964	3.448		
	Issued in exchange for series dated Jan. 16, 1964		16,450,000.00	
	Issued for cash		1,185,099,000.00	
16	Maturing Jan. 14, 1965	3.549		
	Issued in exchange for series dated Jan. 16, 1964		4,398,000.00	
	Issued for cash		898,097,000.00	
16	Certificates of indebtedness, foreign series, maturing:			
	Sept. 29, 1964	3.50		40,000,000.00
	Dec. 29, 1964	3.60		100,000,000.00
22	Treasury notes, Series B–1964	5.00		
	Redeemed in exchange for:			
	4¼% Treasury bonds of 1987–92			196,916,000.00
	4½% Treasury bonds of 1973			362,299,000.00
	4% Treasury bonds of 1969			287,581,000.00
22	Treasury notes, Series C–1964	4⅞		
	Redeemed in exchange for:			
	4¼% Treasury bonds of 1987–92			118,176,000.00
	4½% Treasury bonds of 1973			232,444,000.00
	4% Treasury bonds of 1969			249,728,000.00

Footnotes at end of table.

TABLE 44.—*Issues, maturities, and redemptions of interest-bearing public debt securities, excluding special issues, July 1964–June 1965*—Continued

Date	Securities	Rate of interest [1]	Amount issued [2]	Amount matured or called or redeemed prior to maturity [3]
1964		*Percent*		
July 22	Treasury notes, Series E–1964	3¾		
	Redeemed in exchange for:			
	4¼% Treasury bonds of 1987–92			$195,991,000.00
	4⅛% Treasury bonds of 1973			342,699,000.00
	4% Treasury bonds of 1969			637,270,000.00
22	Treasury notes, Series F–1964	3¾		
	Redeemed in exchange for:			
	4¼% Treasury bonds of 1987–92			145,016,000.00
	4⅛% Treasury bonds of 1973			212,929,000.00
	4% Treasury bonds of 1969			161,955,000.00
22	Treasury notes, Series C–1965	3⅞		
	Redeemed in exchange for:			
	4¼% Treasury bonds of 1987–92			188,007,000.00
	4⅛% Treasury bonds of 1973			769,509,000.00
	4% Treasury bonds of 1969			400,013,000.00
22	Treasury notes, Series A–1966	4.00		
	Redeemed in exchange for:			
	4¼% Treasury bonds of 1987–92			150,984,000.00
	4⅛% Treasury bonds of 1973			334,464,000.00
	4% Treasury bonds of 1969			178,933,000.00
22	Treasury notes, Series B–1966	3⅝		
	Redeemed in exchange for:			
	4¼% Treasury bonds of 1987–92			146,678,000.00
	4⅛% Treasury bonds of 1973			1,302,727,000.00
	4% Treasury bonds of 1969			942,287,000.00
22	Treasury bonds of 1966	3¾		
	Redeemed in exchange for:			
	4¼% Treasury bonds of 1987–92			17,656,500.00
	4⅛% Treasury bonds of 1973			300,765,000.00
	4% Treasury bonds of 1969			294,967,000.00
22	Treasury notes, Series B–1967	3⅝		
	Redeemed in exchange for:			
	4¼% Treasury bonds of 1987–92			34,914,000.00
	4⅛% Treasury bonds of 1973			501,559,000.00
	4% Treasury bonds of 1969			578,205,000.00
22	Treasury bonds of 1987–92	4¼		
	Issued in exchange for:			
	5% Treasury notes, Series B–1964		$196,916,000.00	
	4⅞% Treasury notes, Series C–1964		118,176,000.00	
	3¾% Treasury notes, Series E–1964		195,991,000.00	
	3¾% Treasury, notes, Series F–1964		145,016,000.00	
	3⅞% Treasury notes, Series C–1965		188,007,000.00	
	4% Treasury notes, Series A–1966		150,984,000.00	
	3⅝% Treasury notes, Series B–1966		146,678,000.00	
	3¾% Treasury bonds of 1966		17,656,500.00	
	3⅝% Treasury notes, Series B–1967		34,914,000.00	
22	Treasury bonds of 1973	4⅛		
	Issued in exchange for:			
	5% Treasury notes, Series B–1964		362,299,000.00	
	4⅞% Treasury notes, Series C–1964		232,444,000.00	
	3¾% Treasury notes, Series E–1964		342,699,000.00	
	3¾% Treasury notes, Series F–1964		212,929,000.00	
	3⅞% Treasury notes, Series C–1965		769,509,000.00	
	4% Treasury notes, Series A–1966		334,464,000.00	
	3⅝% Treasury notes, Series B–1966		1,302,727,000.00	
	3¾% Treasury bonds of 1966		300,765,000.00	
	3⅝% Treasury notes, Series B–1967		501,559,000.00	
22	Treasury bonds of 1969	4.00		
	Issued in exchange for:			
	5% Treasury notes, Series B–1964		287,581,000.00	
	4⅞% Treasury notes, Series C–1964		249,728,000.00	
	3¾% Treasury notes, Series E–1964		637,270,000.00	
	3¾% Treasury notes, Series F–1964		161,955,000.00	
	3⅞% Treasury notes, Series C–1965		400,013,000.00	
	4% Treasury notes, Series A–1966		178,933,000.00	
	3⅝% Treasury notes, Series B–1966		942,287,000.00	
	3¾% Treasury bonds of 1966		294,967,000.00	
	3⅝% Treasury notes, Series B–1967		578,205,000.00	
	Treasury bills:			
	Regular weekly:			
23	Dated Jan. 23, 1964	[4]3.537		
	Redeemed in exchange for series issued July 23, 1964, due Oct. 22, 1964			271,990,000.00
	Redeemed in exchange for series dated July 23, 1964, due Jan. 21, 1965			111,904,000.00
	Redeemable for cash			1,616,799,000.00

Footnotes at end of table.

TABLE 44.—*Issues, maturities, and redemptions of interest-bearing public debt securities, excluding special issues, July 1964–June 1965*—Continued

Date	Securities	Rate of interest [1]	Amount issued [2]	Amount matured or called or redeemed prior to maturity [3]
	Treasury bills—Continued	*Percent*		
1964	Regular weekly—Continued			
July 23	Maturing Oct. 22, 1964	3.502		
	Issued in exchange for series dated Jan. 23, 1964		$271,990,000.00	
	Issued for cash		928,745,000.00	
23	Maturing Jan. 21, 1965	3.619		
	Issued in exchange for series dated Jan. 23, 1964		111,904,000.00	
	Issued for cash		787,923,000.00	
24	Treasury bonds, foreign currency series, maturing:			
	July 24, 1964	3.18		$49,942,500.00
	May 2, 1966	3.77	50,322,061.19	
	Treasury bills:			
	Regular weekly:			
29	Maturing Oct. 15, 1964–Dec. 17, 1964 [5]	3.505		
	Issued for cash		1,000,860,000.00	
30	Dated Jan. 30, 1964	[4] 3.512		
	Redeemed in exchange for series issued July 30, 1964, due Oct. 29, 1964			207,249,000.00
	Redeemed in exchange for series dated July 30, 1964, due Jan. 28, 1965			111,559,000.00
	Redeemable for cash			1,682,742,000.00
30	Maturing, Oct. 29, 1964	3.475		
	Issued in exchange for series dated Jan. 30, 1964		207,249,000.00	
	Issued for cash		993,487,000.00	
30	Maturing Jan. 28, 1965	3.591		
	Issued in exchange for series dated Jan. 30, 1964		111,559,000.00	
	Issued for cash		790,410,000.00	
30	Certificates of indebtedness, foreign series, maturing:			
	July 30, 1964	3.00		50,000,000.00
	Oct. 30, 1964	3.00	50,000,000.00	
31	Nov. 2, 1964	3.00	30,000,000.00	
31	U.S. savings bonds: [6]			
	Series E-1941	[7] 3.223	611,033.48	2,334,933.05
	Series E-1942	[7] 3.252	4,729,189.89	9,935,843.42
	Series E-1943	[7] 3.277	5,069,013.83	16,891,763.98
	Series E-1944	[7] 3.298	10,732,215.36	23,268,499.85
	Series E-1945	[7] 3.316	5,658,362.39	16,089,180.83
	Series E-1946	[7] 3.327	4,286,895.70	8,140,029.47
	Series E-1947	[7] 3.346	4,922,889.49	8,629,592.82
	Series E-1948	[7] 3.366	5,326,715.97	9,743,920.41
	Series E-1949	[7] 3.344	5,637,895.59	9,902,599.53
	Series E-1950	[7] 3.347	5,470,952.47	10,080,083.15
	Series E-1951	[7] 3.378	4,274,593.72	9,161,678.21
	Series E-1952 (January to April)	3.400	2,418,542.08	3,234,417.86
	Series E-1952 (May to December)	[7] 3.451	3,519,206.71	7,489,537.52
	Series E-1953	[7] 3.468	4,180,194.24	15,526,420.67
	Series E-1954	[7] 3.497	4,922,846.19	20,913,102.16
	Series E-1955	[7] 3.522	8,043,802.67	10,973,250.11
	Series E-1956	[7] 3.546	7,921,883.94	10,097,801.78
	Series E-1957 (January)	3.560	2,950,967.43	801,253.87
	Series E-1957 (February to December)	[7] 3.653	3,333,794.89	9,875,462.49
	Series E-1958	[7] 3.690	7,358,994.61	12,933,398.34
	Series E-1959 (January to May)	3.730	3,940,272.25	4,878,669.69
	Series E-1959 (June to December)	3.750	3,084,378.38	6,805,452.78
	Series E-1960	3.750	7,737,270.58	14,911,572.88
	Series E-1961	3.750	8,013,626.76	16,913,811.66
	Series E-1962	3.750	8,059,810.15	22,729,831.99
	Series E-1963	3.750	9,131,578.82	59,670,130.02
	Series E-1964	3.750	406,501,186.27	86,806,500.00
	Unclassified sales and redemptions		[8] −59,338,367.85	[8] −22,221,453.64
	Series H-1952	[7] 3.392		38,000.00
	Series H-1953	[7] 3.409		135,500.00
	Series H-1954	[7] 3.438		3,697,000.00
	Series H-1955	[7] 3.467		198,000.00
	Series H-1956	[7] 3.496		240,500.00
	Series H-1957 (January)	3.520		3,000.00
	Series H-1957 (February to December)	[7] 3.626		96,500.00
	Series H-1958	[7] 3.679		364,500.00
	Series H-1959 (January to May)	3.720		42,500.00
	Series H-1959 (June to December)	3.750		103,500.00
	Series H-1960	3.750		242,000.00
	Series H-1961	3.750		249,500.00
	Series H-1962	3.750		207,000.00

Footnotes at end of table.

TABLE 44.—*Issues, maturities, and redemptions of interest-bearing public debt securities, excluding special issues, July 1964–June 1965*—Continued

Date	Securities	Rate of interest [1]	Amount issued [2]	Amount matured or called or redeemed prior to maturity [3]
1964		*Percent*		
July 31	U.S. savings bonds [4]—Continued			
	Series H-1963	3.750	$191,500.00	$210,500.00
	Series H-1964	3.750	52,964,000.00	72,500.00
	Unclassified sales and redemptions		8,271,000.00	30,817,500.00
	Series J-1952	2.76	78,652.80	2,485,471.20
	Series J-1953	2.76	219,974.40	20,148.00
	Series J-1954	2.76	397,237.89	56,536.26
	Series J-1955	2.76	401,720.80	59,465.35
	Series J-1956	2.76	355,682.60	47,939.90
	Series J-1957	2.76	108,254.77	5,185.00
	Unclassified redemptions			4,027,584.22
	Series K-1952	2.76		8,425,000.00
	Series K-1953	2.76		41,000.00
	Series K-1954	2.76		150,000.00
	Series K-1955	2.76		146,000.00
	Series K-1956	2.76		111,500.00
	Series K-1957	2.76		12,500.00
	Unclassified redemptions			20,842,500.00
31	Treasury notes, Series E-1965	4.00		
	Adjustments of issues [9]		−3,000.00	
31	Treasury bonds of 1974	4¼		
	Adjustments of issues [9]		12,000.00	
31	U.S. retirement plan bonds	3.75	108,837.49	10,087.06
31	Depositary bonds, First Series	2.00	129,000.00	556,000.00
31	Treasury bonds, REA Series	2.00	215,000.00	175,000.00
31	Treasury bonds, Investment Series B-1975-80	2¾		
	Redeemed in exchange for Treasury notes, Series EA-1969			8,355,000.00
31	Treasury notes, Series EA-1969	1½	8,355,000.00	
31	Miscellaneous			31,673,100.00
	Total July		22,659,950,067.02	22,270,603,601.89
Aug. 3	Certificates of indebtedness, foreign series, maturing Nov. 4, 1964	3.50	20,000,000.00	
4	Treasury bonds, foreign currency series, maturing Sept. 7, 1965	3.67	52,054,414.21	
	Treasury bills:			
	Other:			
4	Maturing July 31, 1965	3.644		
	Issued for cash		1,000,462,000.00	
	Regular weekly:			
6	Dated Feb. 6, 1964	[4] 3.539		
	Redeemed in exchange for series issued Aug. 6, 1964, due Nov. 5, 1964			189,878,000.00
	Redeemed in exchange for series dated Aug. 6, 1964, due Feb. 4, 1965			111,941,000.00
	Redeemable for cash			1,798,883,000.00
6	Maturing Nov. 5, 1964	3.489		
	Issued in exchange for series dated Feb. 6, 1964		189,878,000.00	
	Issued for cash		1,010,563,000.00	
6	Maturing Feb. 4, 1965	3.588		
	Issued in exchange for series dated Feb. 6, 1964		111,941,000.00	
	Issued for cash		788,675,000.00	
10	Certificates of indebtedness, foreign series, maturing Nov. 10, 1964	3.50	10,000,000.00	
12	Treasury certificates, maturing Dec. 15, 1964	1.00	50,990.98	
	Treasury bills:			
	Regular weekly:			
13	Dated Feb. 13, 1964	[4] 3.563		
	Redeemed in exchange for series issued Aug. 13, 1964, due Nov. 12, 1964			66,863,000.00
	Redeemed in exchange for series dated Aug. 13, 1964, due Feb. 11, 1965			53,182,000.00
	Redeemable for cash			1,981,389,000.00
13	Maturing Nov. 12, 1964	3.510		
	Issued in exchange for series dated Feb. 13, 1964		66,863,000.00	
	Issued for cash		1,128,930,000.00	
13	Maturing Feb. 11, 1965	3.611		
	Issued in exchange for series dated Feb. 13, 1964		53,182,000.00	
	Issued for cash		848,664,000.00	

Footnotes at end of table.

TABLE 44.—*Issues, maturities, and redemptions of interest-bearing public debt securities, excluding special issues, July 1964–June 1965*—Continued

Date	Securities	Rate of interest [1]	Amount issued [2]	Amount matured or called or redeemed prior to maturity [3]
1964		*Percent*		
Aug. 15	Treasury notes, Series B-1964	5.00		
	Redeemed in exchange for 3⅛% Treasury notes, Series C-1966			$137,430,000.00
	Redeemable for cash			1,061,119,000.00
15	Treasury notes, Series E-1964	3¾		
	Redeemed in exchange for 3⅛% Treasury notes, Series C-1966			1,816,540,000.00
	Redeemable for cash			1,092,307,000.00
15	Treasury notes, Series C-1966	3⅛		
	Issued in exchange for:			
	5% Treasury notes, Series B-1964		$137,430,000.00	
	3¾% Treasury notes, Series E-1964		1,816,540,000.00	
	Issued for cash		2,085,948,000.00	
	Treasury bills:			
	Regular weekly:			
20	Dated Feb. 20, 1964	[4] 3.566		
	Redeemed in exchange for series issued Aug. 20, 1964, due Nov. 19, 1964			268,685,000.00
	Redeemed in exchange for series dated Aug. 20, 1964, due Feb. 18, 1965			122,293,000.00
	Redeemable for cash			1,712,058,000.00
20	Maturing Nov. 19, 1964	3.512		
	Issued in exchange for series dated Feb. 20, 1964		268,685,000.00	
	Issued for cash		931,492,000.00	
20	Maturing Feb. 18, 1965	3.634		
	Issued in exchange for series dated Feb. 20, 1964		122,293,000.00	
	Issued for cash		779,053,000.00	
27	Dated Feb. 27, 1964	[4] 3.573		
	Redeemed in exchange for series issued Aug. 27, 1964, due Nov. 27, 1964			234,238,000.00
	Redeemed in exchange for series dated Aug. 27, 1964, due Feb. 25, 1965			112,106,000.00
	Redeemable for cash			1,755,442,000.00
27	Maturing Nov. 27, 1964	3.513		
	Issued in exchange for series dated Feb. 27, 1964		234,238,000.00	
	Issued for cash		967,300,000.00	
27	Maturing Feb. 25, 1965	3.639		
	Issued in exchange for series dated Feb. 27, 1964		112,106,000.00	
	Issued for cash		789,900,000.00	
	Other:			
31	Issued Sept. 3, 1963	3.575		
	Redeemed in exchange for series dated Aug. 31, 1964, due Aug. 31, 1965			26,450,000.00
	Redeemable for cash			974,693,000.00
31	Maturing Aug. 31, 1965	3.688		
	Issued in exchange for series dated Sept. 3, 1963		26,450,000.00	
	Issued for cash		973,989,000.00	
31	U.S. savings bonds: [5]			
	Series E-1941	[7] 3.223	387,312.70	1,892,964.61
	Series E-1942	[7] 3.252	2,822,469.75	8,127,710.24
	Series E-1943	[7] 3.277	3,899,080.03	13,386,180.23
	Series E-1944	[7] 3.298	7,607,887.02	21,895,760.32
	Series E-1945	[7] 3.316	3,804,069.35	13,028,403.47
	Series E-1946	[7] 3.327	3,227,123.78	6,910,763.40
	Series E-1947	[7] 3.346	3,409,191.60	7,267,664.43
	Series E-1948	[7] 3.366	3,863,860.75	8,588,781.63
	Series E-1949	[7] 3.344	4,213,331.75	8,818,320.87
	Series E-1950	[7] 3.347	3,955,552.24	8,405,521.74
	Series E-1951	[7] 3.378	3,322,113.08	7,814,615.62
	Series E-1952 (January to April)	3.400	1,803,695.39	2,780,226.06
	Series E-1952 (May to December)	[7] 3.451	4,406,105.05	6,198,267.76
	Series E-1953	[7] 3.468	4,969,401.45	12,703,498.38
	Series E-1954	[7] 3.497	4,451,016.44	18,562,757.09
	Series E-1955	[7] 3.522	6,250,949.69	9,075,627.04
	Series E-1956	[7] 3.546	6,322,459.03	8,611,846.62
	Series E-1957 (January)	3.560	-172.61	746,919.84
	Series E-1957 (February to December)	3.653	5,613,479.34	8,048,966.80
	Series E-1958	[7] 3.690	5,757,201.98	10,305,836.89
	Series E-1959 (January to May)	3.730	3,031,925.69	4,067,061.94
	Series E-1959 (June to December)	3.750	2,505,365.61	5,816,704.31
	Series E-1960	3.750	6,315,460.97	12,073,077.50
	Series E-1961	3.750	6,370,205.59	14,180,377.96
	Series E-1962	3.750	6,216,285.92	18,408,389.71

Footnotes at end of table.

TABLE 44.—*Issues, maturities, and redemptions of interest-bearing public debt securities, excluding special issues, July 1964–June 1965*—Continued

Date	Securities	Rate of interest [1]	Amount issued [2]	Amount matured or called or redeemed prior to maturity [3]
1964		*Percent*		
Aug. 31	U.S. savings bonds [4]—Continued			
	Series E–1963	3.750	$6,454,755.71	$44,590,002.75
	Series E–1964	3.750	297,823,588.16	78,693,323.71
	Unclassified sales and redemptions		33,163,771.50	1,582,354.93
	Series H–1952	[7] 3.392		526,500.00
	Series H–1953	[7] 3.409		1,629,000.00
	Series H–1954	[7] 3.438		8,446,500.00
	Series H–1955	[7] 3.467		3,267,000.00
	Series H–1956	[7] 3.496		2,671,500.00
	Series H–1957 (January)	3.520		174,500.00
	Series H–1957 (February to December)	[7] 3.626		1,893,500.00
	Series H–1958	[7] 3.679		3,171,500.00
	Series H–1959 (January to May)	3.720		1,300,000.00
	Series H–1959 (June to December)	3.750		1,282,000.00
	Series H–1960	3.750		2,981,500.00
	Series H–1961	3.750		3,193,000.00
	Series H–1962	3.750	5,000.00	2,697,500.00
	Series H–1963	3.750	51,000.00	3,142,500.00
	Series H–1964	3.750	60,800,000.00	312,500.00
	Unclassified sales and redemptions		[8] −9,910,000.00	[8] −734,000.00
	Series J–1952	2.76	60,826.80	3,737,633.00
	Series J–1953	2.76	168,469.20	306,893.00
	Series J–1954	2.76	350,150.30	1,173,854.06
	Series J–1955	2.76	260,198.55	927,816.27
	Series J–1956	2.76	310,557.45	408,520.50
	Series J–1957	2.76	81,140.50	54,467.95
	Unclassified redemptions			[8] −1,435,605.20
	Series K–1952	2.76		17,037,000.00
	Series K–1953	2.76		1,606,500.00
	Series K–1954	2.76		4,696,000.00
	Series K–1955	2.76		5,099,000.00
	Series K–1956	2.76		1,589,500.00
	Series K–1957	2.76		230,000.00
	Unclassified redemptions			[8] −12,641,000.00
31	Treasury notes, Series B–1964	5.00		
	Adjustments of redemptions [9]			−92,000.00
31	Treasury notes, Series C–1964	4⅞		
	Adjustments of redemptions [9]			−280,000.00
31	Treasury notes, Series E–1964	3¾		
	Adjustments of redemptions [9]			1,347,000.00
31	Treasury notes, Series F–1964	3¾		
	Adjustments of redemptions [9]			−477,000.00
31	Treasury notes, Series C–1965	3⅞		
	Adjustments of redemptions [9]			−630,000.00
31	Treasury notes, Series A–1966	4.00		
	Adjustments of redemptions [9]			−655,000.00
31	Treasury notes, Series B–1966	3⅝		
	Adjustments of redemptions [9]			138,000.00
31	Treasury bonds of 1966	3¾		
	Adjustments of redemptions [9]			−81,500.00
31	Treasury notes, Series B–1967	3⅝		
	Adjustments of redemptions [9]			1,360,000.00
31	Treasury bonds of 1969 (Oct. 1, 1957)	4.00		
	Adjustments of issues [9]		−1,934,000.00	
31	Treasury bonds of 1973	4⅛		
	Adjustments of issues [9]		−1,610,500.00	
31	Treasury bonds of 1987–92	4¼		
	Adjustments of issues [9]		4,174,000.00	
31	U.S. retirement plan bonds	3.75	108,406.50	5,673.42
31	Depositary bonds, First Series	2.00	987,000.00	313,000.00
31	Treasury bonds, REA Series	2.00	46,000.00	136,000.00
31	Treasury bonds, Investment Series B–1975–80	2¾		
	Redeemed in exchange for Treasury notes, Series EA–1969			5,949,000.00
31	Treasury notes, Series EA–1969	1½	5,949,000.00	
31	Miscellaneous			19,375,200.00
	Total August		15,028,552,141.45	13,963,232,878.85
	Treasury bills:			
	Tax anticipation:			
Sept. 2	Maturing Mar. 22, 1965	3.580		
	Issued for cash		1,000,965,000.00	

Footnotes at end of table.

TABLE 44.—*Issues, maturities, and redemptions of interest-bearing public debt securities, excluding special issues, July 1964–June 1965*—Continued

Date	Securities	Rate of interest [1]	Amount issued [2]	Amount matured or called or redeemed prior to maturity [3]
1964 Sept. 3	Treasury bills—Continued Regular weekly: Dated Mar. 5, 1964	*Percent* [4] 3.606		
	Redeemed in exchange for series issued Sept. 3, 1964, due Dec. 3, 1964			$222,308,000.00
	Redeemed in exchange for series dated Sept. 3, 1964, due Mar. 4, 1965			115,425,000.00
	Redeemable for cash			1,766,679,000.00
3	Maturing Dec. 3, 1964	3.512		
	Issued in exchange for series dated Mar. 5, 1964		$222,308,000.00	
	Issued for cash		978,370,000.00	
3	Maturing Mar. 4, 1965	3.629		
	Issued in exchange for series dated Mar. 5, 1964		115,425,000.00	
	Issued for cash		784,862,000.00	
4	Treasury bonds, foreign currency series, maturing: Sept. 4, 1964	2.83		23,107,500.00
	Feb. 4, 1966	3.87	23,141,719.89	
9	Certificates of indebtedness, foreign series, maturing Dec. 9, 1964	3.55	30,000,000.00	
10	Treasury bills: Regular weekly: Dated Mar. 12, 1964	[4] 3.570		
	Redeemed in exchange for series issued Sept. 10, 1964, due Dec. 10, 1964			80,969,000.00
	Redeemed in exchange for series dated Sept. 10, 1964, due Mar. 11, 1965			32,178,000.00
	Redeemable for cash			1,988,248,000.00
10	Maturing Dec. 10, 1964	3.514		
	Issued in exchange for series dated Mar. 12, 1964		80,969,000.00	
	Issued for cash		1,220,814,000.00	
10	Maturing Mar. 11, 1965	3.649		
	Issued in exchange for series dated Mar. 12, 1964		32,178,000.00	
	Issued for cash		868,644,000.00	
16	Certificates of indebtedness, foreign series, maturing Dec. 16, 1964	3.55	30,000,000.00	
16	Treasury bonds, foreign series, maturing: Nov. 1, 1965	4.00	30,000,000.00	
	Nov. 1, 1966	4.125	30,000,000.00	
	Nov. 1, 1967	4.25	30,000,000.00	
	Nov. 1, 1968	4.25	30,000,000.00	
	Nov. 1, 1969	4.25	30,000,000.00	
	Nov. 1, 1970	4.25	30,000,000.00	
	Nov. 1, 1971	4.25	23,929,534.25	
17	Treasury bills: Regular weekly: Dated Mar. 19, 1964	[4] 3.595		
	Redeemed in exchange for series issued Sept. 17, 1964, due Dec. 17, 1964			138,652,000.00
	Redeemed in exchange for series dated Sept. 17, 1964, due Mar. 18, 1965			63,828,000.00
	Redeemable for cash			1,896,985,000.00
17	Maturing Dec. 17, 1964	3.541		
	Issued in exchange for series dated Mar. 19, 1964		138,652,000.00	
	Issued for cash		1,162,969,000.00	
17	Maturing Mar. 18, 1965	3.693		
	Issued in exchange for series dated Mar. 19, 1964		63,828,000.00	
	Issued for cash		836,192,000.00	
21	Certificates of indebtedness, foreign series, maturing Dec. 21, 1964	3.55	5,000,000.00	
23	Treasury notes, foreign series, maturing Jan. 21, 1968	3.125		1,820,296.06
24	Treasury bills: Regular weekly: Dated Mar. 26, 1964	[4] 3.590		
	Redeemed in exchange for series issued Sept. 24, 1964, due Dec. 24, 1964			162,444,000.00
	Redeemed in exchange for series dated Sept. 24, 1964, due Mar. 25, 1965			84,634,000.00
	Redeemable for cash			1,854,433,000.00
24	Maturing Dec. 24, 1964	3.542		
	Issued in exchange for series dated Mar. 26, 1964		162,444,000.00	
	Issued for cash		1,139,536,000.00	

Footnotes at end of table.

TABLE 44.—*Issues, maturities, and redemptions of interest-bearing public debt securities, excluding special issues, July 1964–June 1965*—Continued

Date	Securities	Rate of interest [1]	Amount issued [2]	Amount matured or called or redeemed prior to maturity [3]
1964	Treasury bills—Continued	*Percent*		
Sept. 24	Regular weekly—Continued			
	Maturing Mar. 25, 1965	3.692		
	Issued in exchange for series dated Mar. 26, 1964		$84,634,000.00	
	Issued for cash		816,010,000.00	
30	Other:			
	Issued Oct. 1, 1963	3.586		
	Redeemed in exchange for series dated Sept. 30, 1964, due Sept. 30, 1965			$18,393,000.00
	Redeemable for cash			983,567,000.00
30	Maturing Sept. 30, 1965	3.773		
	Issued in exchange for series dated Oct. 1, 1963		18,393,000.00	
	Issued for cash		982,146,000.00	
30	Treasury certificates, maturing Sept. 30, 1964	3.479		10,274,942.13
30	Treasury certificates, maturing Dec. 31, 1964	3.555	10,364,308.44	
30	Certificates of indebtedness, foreign series, maturing Oct. 30, 1964	3.00		30,000,000.00
30	U.S. savings bonds: [6]			
	Series E–1941	[7] 3.223	419,461.70	1,752,300.45
	Series E–1942	[7] 3.252	3,155,751.87	7,811,168.13
	Series E–1943	[7] 3.277	9,715,846.47	12,611,303.35
	Series E–1944	[7] 3.298	3,865,378.99	19,613,649.00
	Series E–1945	[7] 3.316	3,732,623.78	12,360,399.05
	Series E–1946	[7] 3.327	3,121,757.70	6,607,205.80
	Series E–1947	[7] 3.346	3,458,319.45	7,198,960.27
	Series E–1948	[7] 3.366	3,655,024.15	7,750,892.34
	Series E–1949	[7] 3.344	4,092,078.87	8,221,450.32
	Series E–1950	[7] 3.347	3,910,618.80	7,921,708.27
	Series E–1951	[7] 3.378	3,323,908.14	7,300,466.04
	Series E–1952 (January to April)	3.400	1,719,757.50	2,720,651.59
	Series E–1952 (May to December)	[7] 3.451	2,013,183.44	5,909,435.33
	Series E–1953	[7] 3.468	5,651,327.76	11,900,820.03
	Series E–1954	[7] 3.497	6,264,003.57	17,454,190.50
	Series E–1955	[7] 3.522	15,255,922.54	8,954,529.17
	Series E–1956	[7] 3.546	6,064,378.31	8,379,369.77
	Series E–1957 (January)	3.560		781,190.34
	Series E–1957 (February to December)	[7] 3.653	5,521,075.38	7,976,483.20
	Series E–1958	[7] 3.690	5,834,598.70	9,717,317.46
	Series E–1959 (January to May)	3.730	2,899,379.96	4,199,716.12
	Series E–1959 (June to December)	3.750	2,753,008.50	5,591,596.83
	Series E–1960	3.750	6,380,522.43	11,629,457.26
	Series E–1961	3.750	6,572,063.37	13,209,780.97
	Series E–1962	3.750	6,649,097.53	17,439,739.67
	Series E–1963	3.750	6,994,211.81	39,955,686.55
	Series E–1964	3.750	322,312,999.31	81,872,607.65
	Unclassified sales and redemptions		1,382,156.06	26,209,407.46
	Series H–1952	[7] 3.392		1,077,500.00
	Series H–1953	[7] 3.409		3,231,000.00
	Series H–1954	[7] 3.439		14,590,000.00
	Series H–1955	[7] 3.467		8,477,500.00
	Series H–1956	[7] 4.496		4,539,500.00
	Series H–1957 (January)	3.520		431,500.00
	Series H–1957 (February to December)	[7] 3.626		3,473,500.00
	Series H–1958	[7] 3.679		5,588,000.00
	Series H–1959 (January to May)	3.720		2,247,500.00
	Series H–1959 (June to December)	3.750		2,180,500.00
	Series H–1960	3.750		6,356,500.00
	Series H–1961	3.750		5,908,500.00
	Series H–1962	3.750		4,630,500.00
	Series H–1963	3.750	134,000.00	4,813,000.00
	Series H–1964	3.750	51,900,500.00	1,277,500.00
	Unclassified sales and redemptions		[8] −1,465,500.00	[8] −25,902,000.00
	Series J–1952	2.76	78,207.20	2,920,837.00
	Series J–1953	2.76	189,928.40	664,041.60
	Series J–1954	2.76	326,925.17	1,678,144.36
	Series J–1955	2.76	330,609.20	1,493,576.21
	Series J–1956	2.76	253,717.10	1,385,221.20
	Series J–1957	2.76	82,748.40	255,278.05
	Unclassified redemptions			[8] −1,479,446.66
	Series K–1952	2.76		13,127,500.00
	Series K–1953	2.76		1,840,000.00
	Series K–1954	2.76		4,521,500.00
	Series K–1955	2.76		3,403,500.00
	Series K–1956	2.76		2,384,000.00
	Series K–1957	2.76		257,000.00
	Unclassified redemptions			[8] −7,860,000.00
30	Treasury notes, Series C–1964	4⅞		
	Adjustments of redemptions [9]			−86,000.00

Footnotes at end of table.

TABLE 44.—*Issues, maturities, and redemptions of interest-bearing public debt securities, excluding special issues, July 1964–June 1965*—Continued

Date	Securities	Rate of interest [1]	Amount issued [2]	Amount matured or called or redeemed prior to maturity [3]
1964		*Percent*		
Sept. 30	Treasury notes, Series B-1966	3⅝		
	Adjustments of redemptions [9]			—$517,000.00
30	Treasury notes, Series A-1966	4.00		
	Adjustments of redemptions [9]			—169,000.00
30	Treasury notes, Series B-1967	3⅝		
	Adjustments of redemptions [9]			158,000.00
30	Treasury notes, Series F-1964	3¾		
	Adjustments of redemptions [9]			555,000.00
30	Treasury notes, Series C-1965	3⅞		
	Adjustments of redemptions [9]			—200,000.00
30	Treasury bonds of 1966	3¾		
	Adjustments of redemptions [9]			—265,000.00
30	Treasury notes, Series E-1965	4.00		
	Adjustments of issues [9]		—$362,000.00	
30	Treasury bonds of 1974	4¼		
	Adjustments of issues [9]		—101,000.00	
30	Treasury bonds of 1969 (Oct. 1, 1957)	4.00		
	Adjustments of issues [9]		—689,000.00	
30	Treasury bonds of 1987-92	4¼		
	Adjustments of issues [9]		—145,000.00	
30	Treasury bonds of 1973	4⅛		
	Adjustments of issues [9]		—664,000.00	
30	U.S. retirement plan bonds	3.75	134,572.52	7,068.54
30	Depositary bonds, First Series	2.00	916,000.00	1,121,000.00
30	Treasury bonds, REA Series	2.00	363,000.00	63,000.00
30	Treasury bonds, Investment Series B-1975-80	2¾		
	Redeemed in exchange for Treasury notes Series EA-1969			13,189,000.00
30	Treasury notes, Series EA-1969	1½	13,189,000.00	
30	Miscellaneous			23,593,600.00
	Total September		11,522,965,726.66	9,951,958,541.41
Oct. 1	Treasury notes, Series EO-1964	1½		
	Redeemable for cash			489,777,000.00
	Treasury bills:			
	Regular weekly:			
1	Dated Apr. 2, 1964	[4] 3.578		
	Redeemed in exchange for series issued Oct. 1, 1964, due Dec. 31, 1964			160,403,000.00
	Redeemed in exchange for series dated Oct. 1, 1964, due Apr. 1, 1965			73,165,000.00
	Redeemable for cash			1,868,056,000.00
1	Maturing Dec. 31, 1964	3.555		
	Issued in exchange for series dated Apr. 2, 1964		160,403,000.00	
	Issued for cash		1,140,477,000.00	
1	Maturing Apr. 1, 1965	3.711		
	Issued in exchange for series dated Apr. 2, 1946		73,165,000.00	
	Issued for cash		827,168,000.00	
8	Dated Apr. 9, 1964	[4] 3.583		
	Redeemed in exchange for series issued Oct. 8, 1964, due Jan. 7, 1965			159,243,000.00
	Redeemed in exchange for series dated Oct. 8, 1964, due Apr. 8, 1965			73,130,000.00
	Redeemable for cash			1,868,894,000.00
8	Maturing Jan. 7, 1965	3.583		
	Issued in exchange for series dated Apr. 9, 1964		159,243,000.00	
	Issued for cash		1,041,049,000.00	
8	Maturing Apr. 8, 1965	3.744		
	Issued in exchange for series dated Apr. 9, 1964		73,130,000.00	
	Issued for cash		828,046,000.00	
15	Dated Apr. 16, 1964	[4] 3.548		
	Redeemed in exchange for series issued Oct. 15, 1964, due Jan. 14, 1965			13,805,000.00
	Redeemed in exchange for series dated Oct. 15, 1964, due Apr. 15, 1965			5,619,000.00
	Redeemable for cash			2,182,261,000.00
15	Maturing Jan. 14, 1965	3.580		
	Issued in exchange for series dated Apr. 16, 1964		13,805,000.00	
	Issued for cash		1,197,760,000.00	

Footnotes at end of table.

TABLE 44.—*Issues, maturities, and redemptions of interest-bearing public debt securities, excluding special issues, July 1964–June 1965*—Continued

Date	Securities	Rate of interest [1]	Amount issued [2]	Amount matured or called or redeemed prior to maturity [3]
	Treasury bills—Continued			
1964	Regular weekly—Continued	*Percent*		
Oct. 15	Maturing Apr. 15, 1965_____	3.726		
	Issued in exchange for series dated Apr. 16, 1964_____		$5,619,000.00	
	Issued for cash_____		998,864,000.00	
16	Certificates of indebtedness, foreign series, maturing Jan. 18, 1965_____	3.60	5,000,000.00	
16	Treasury certificates, maturing Dec. 31, 1964	3.555		$99,845.67
	Treasury bills:			
	Regular weekly:			
22	Dated Apr. 23, 1964_____	[4] 3.568		
	Redeemed in exchange for series issued Oct. 22, 1964, due Jan. 21, 1965_____			193,385,000.00
	Redeemed in exchange for series dated Oct. 22, 1964, due Apr. 22, 1965_____			114,172,000.00
	Redeemable for cash_____			1,894,057,000.00
22	Maturing Jan. 21, 1965_____	3.592		
	Issued in exchange for series dated Apr. 23, 1964_____		193,385,000.00	
	Issued for cash_____		1,009,532,000.00	
22	Maturing Apr. 22, 1965_____	3.738		
	Issued in exchange for series dated Apr. 23, 1964_____		114,172,000.00	
	Issued for cash_____		886,597,000.00	
	Tax anticipation:			
26	Maturing Mar. 22, 1965_____	3.518		
	Issued for cash_____		1,503,195,000.00	
26	Certificates of indebtedness, foreign series, maturing Jan. 26, 1965_____	3.25	20,000,000.00	
26	Treasury bonds, foreign currency series, maturing:			
	Oct. 26, 1964_____	3.23		25,154,798.76
	Apr. 26, 1966_____	3.90	25,154,798.76	
	Treasury bills:			
	Regular weekly:			
29	Dated Apr. 30, 1964_____	[4] 3.534		
	Redeemed in exchange for series issued Oct. 29, 1964, due Jan. 28, 1965_____			215,120,000.00
	Redeemed in exchange for series dated Oct. 29, 1964, due Apr. 29, 1965_____			102,702,000.00
	Redeemable for cash_____			1,883,482,000.00
29	Maturing Jan. 28, 1965_____	3.568		
	Issued in exchange for series dated Apr. 30, 1964_____		215,120,000.00	
	Issued for cash_____		985,055,000.00	
29	Maturing Apr. 29, 1965_____	3.724		
	Issued in exchange for series dated Apr. 30, 1964_____		102,702,000.00	
	Issued for cash_____		900,052,000.00	
30	Certificates of indebtedness, foreign series, maturing Oct. 30, 1964_____	3.00		20,000,000.00
30	Certificates of indebtedness, foreign currency series, maturing Oct. 30, 1964_____	3.54		30,120,481.92
30	Treasury bonds, foreign currency series, maturing:			
	Dec. 31, 1965_____	3.87	30,126,066.00	
	June 1, 1966_____	3.90	50,289,162.69	
31	U.S. savings bonds: [6]			
	Series E–1941_____	[7] 3.223	471,588.34	2,290,584.94
	Series E–1942_____	[7] 3.252	3,201,463.57	10,506,259.55
	Series E–1943_____	[7] 3.277	7,398,399.87	17,621,596.28
	Series E–1944_____	[7] 3.298	3,358,959.40	25,066,845.28
	Series E–1945_____	[7] 3.316	4,459,163.14	16,419,559.61
	Series E–1946_____	[7] 3.327	3,158,388.98	9,316,870.79
	Series E–1947_____	[7] 3.346	3,231,615.43	9,987,124.66
	Series E–1948_____	[7] 3.366	3,448,827.63	11,064,378.71
	Series E–1949_____	[7] 3.344	3,749,258.35	11,929,036.36
	Series E–1950_____	[7] 3.347	3,534,994.81	11,279,529.80
	Series E–1951_____	[7] 3.378	3,313,962.48	10,348,551.08
	Series E–1952 (January to April)_____	3.400	1,515,184.41	3,657,111.92
	Series E–1952 (May to December)_____	[7] 3.451	1,772,501.98	8,569,196.72
	Series E–1953_____	[7] 3.468	4,339,578.88	16,955,353.74
	Series E–1954_____	[7] 3.497	2,074,160.76	25,722,728.47
	Series E–1955_____	[7] 3.522	12,364,349.09	14,711,124.29
	Series E–1956_____	[7] 3.546	5,932,737.49	11,961,888.13
	Series E–1957 (January)_____	3.560	−28,791.33	952,220.64
	Series E–1957 (February to December)___	[7] 3.653	5,663,106.12	11,175,037.10
	Series E–1958_____	[7] 3.690	5,799,021.98	14,167,374.13
	Series E–1959 (January to May)_____	3.730	2,771,910.71	5,424,268.84

Footnotes at end of table.

TABLE 44.—*Issues, maturities, and redemptions of interest-bearing public debt securities, excluding special issues, July 1964–June 1965*—Continued

Date	Securities	Rate of interest [1]	Amount issued [2]	Amount matured or called or redeemed prior to maturity [3]
1964 Oct. 31	U.S. savings bonds [6]—Continued	*Percent*		
	Series E-1959 (June to December)_____	3.750	$3,243,521.19	$7,947,216.26
	Series E-1960_____	3.750	6,400,768.39	16,626,461.11
	Series E-1961_____	3.750	6,589,152.60	19,321,892.81
	Series E-1962_____	3.750	6,800,467.09	24,364,856.26
	Series E-1963_____	3.750	7,445,277.07	52,059,623.51
	Series E-1964_____	3.750	457,179,266.47	140,923,031.42
	Unclassified sales and redemptions_____		[5] −121,885,929.16	[5] −154,445,242.11
	Series H-1952_____	[7] 3.392		34,000.00
	Series H-1953_____	[7] 3.409		88,000.00
	Series H-1954_____	[7] 3.439		1,620,500.00
	Series H-1955_____	[7] 3.467		6,918,500.00
	Series H-1956_____	[7] 3.496		247,000.00
	Series H-1957 (January)_____	3.520		10,500.00
	Series H-1957 (February to December)___	[7] 3.626		125,500.00
	Series H-1958_____	[7] 3.679		189,000.00
	Series H-1959 (January to May)_____	3.720		75,000.00
	Series H-1959 (June to December)_____	3.750		90,500.00
	Series H-1960_____	3.750		332,500.00
	Series H-1961_____	3.750		224,500.00
	Series H-1962_____	3.750		150,500.00
	Series H-1963_____	3.750	150,500.00	170,500.00
	Series H-1964_____	3.750	51,316,500.00	103,500.00
	Unclassified sales and redemptions_____		[5] −2,860,000.00	26,280,000.00
	Series J-1952_____	2.76	88,105.60	3,767,951.00
	Series J-1953_____	2.76	175,070.80	53,945.40
	Series J-1954_____	2.76	328,891.47	33,436.20
	Series J-1955_____	2.76	332,616.80	41,741.75
	Series J-1956_____	2.76	186,784.15	156,100.20
	Series J-1957_____	2.76	87,183.60	2,351.60
	Unclassified redemptions_____			3,629,895.69
	Series K-1952_____	2.76		9,283,000.00
	Series K-1953_____	2.76		23,500.00
	Series K-1954_____	2.76		622,000.00
	Series K-1955_____	2.76		166,500.00
	Series K-1956_____	2.76		118,000.00
	Series K-1957_____	2.76		3,500.00
	Unclassified redemptions_____			7,509,000.00
31	Treasury bonds of 1969_____	4.00		
	Adjustments of issues [5]_____		−3,000.00	
31	U.S. retirement plan bonds_____	3.75	223,122.32	2,699.74
31	Depositary bonds, First Series_____	2.00	477,000.00	1,744,000.00
31	Treasury bonds, REA Series_____	2.00	80,000.00	186,000.00
31	Treasury bonds, Investment Series B-1975-80	2¾		
	Redeemed in exchange for Treasury notes:			
	Series EA-1969_____			20,932,000.00
	Series EO-1969_____			3,023,000.00
31	Treasury notes, Series EA-1969_____	1½	20,932,000.00	
31	Treasury notes, Series EO-1969_____	1½	3,023,000.00	
31	Miscellaneous_____			59,463,400.00
	Total October_____		13,080,949,707.93	11,875,992,628.23
	Treasury bills:			
	Other:			
Nov. 2 [10]	Issued Nov. 4, 1963_____	3.633		
	Redeemed in exchange for series dated Oct. 31, 1964, due Oct. 31, 1965_____			103,791,000.00
	Redeemable for cash_____			896,482,000.00
2	Maturing Oct. 31, 1965_____	3.790		
	Issued in exchange for series dated Nov. 4, 1963_____		103,791,000.00	
	Issued for cash_____		896,159,000.00	
2	Certificates of indebtedness, foreign series, maturing:			
	Nov. 2, 1964_____	3.00		30,000,000.00
	Feb. 2, 1965_____	3.25	15,000,000.00	
4	Nov. 4, 1964_____	3.50		20,000,000.00
	Feb. 4, 1965_____	3.60	20,000,000.00	
	Treasury bills:			
	Regular weekly:			
5	Dated May 7, 1964_____	[4] 3.547		
	Redeemed in exchange for series issued Nov. 5, 1964, due Feb. 4, 1965_____			205,253,000.00
	Redeemed in exchange for series dated Nov. 5, 1964, due May 6, 1965_____			113,347,000.00
	Redeemable for cash_____			1,882,320,000.00

Footnotes at end of table.

Tᴀʙʟᴇ 44.—*Issues, maturities, and redemptions of interest-bearing public debt securities, excluding special issues, July 1964–June 1965*—Continued

Date	Securities	Rate of interest [1]	Amount issued [2]	Amount matured or called or redeemed prior to maturity [3]
1964	Treasury bills—Continued Regular weekly—Continued	*Percent*		
Nov. 5	Maturing Feb. 4, 1965	3. 561		
	Issued in exchange for series dated May 7, 1964		$205, 253, 000. 00	
	Issued for cash		995, 324, 000. 00	
5	Maturing May 6, 1965	3. 718		
	Issued in exchange for series dated May 7, 1964		113, 347, 000. 00	
	Issued for cash		886, 613, 000. 00	
10	Certificates of indebtedness, foreign series, maturing:			
	Nov. 10, 1964	3. 50		$10, 000, 000. 00
	Feb. 10, 1965	3. 60	10, 000, 000. 00	
	Treasury bills: Regular weekly:			
12	Dated May 14, 1964	[4] 3. 557		
	Redeemed in exchange for series issued Nov. 12, 1964, due Feb. 11, 1965			149, 663, 000. 00
	Redeemed in exchange for series dated Nov. 12, 1964, due May 13, 1965			74, 301, 000. 00
	Redeemable for cash			1, 972, 367, 000. 00
12	Maturing Feb. 11, 1965	3. 574		
	Issued in exchange for series dated May 14, 1964		149, 663, 000. 00	
	Issued for cash		1, 050, 278, 000. 00	
12	Maturing May 13, 1965	3. 742		
	Issued in exchange for series dated May 14, 1964		74, 301, 000. 00	
	Issued for cash		926, 016, 000. 00	
15	Treasury notes, Series C-1964	4⅞		
	Redeemed in exchange for 4% Treasury notes, Series D-1966			2, 365, 995, 000. 00
	Redeemable for cash			901, 314, 000. 00
15	Treasury notes, Series F-1964	3¾		
	Redeemed in exchange for 4% Treasury notes, Series D-1966			4, 259, 550, 000. 00
	Redeemable for cash			1, 181, 700, 000. 00
15	Treasury notes, Series D-1966	4. 00		
	Issued in exchange for:			
	4⅞% Treasury notes, Series C-1964		2, 365, 995, 000. 00	
	3¾% Treasury notes, Series F-1964		4, 259, 550, 000. 00	
	Issued for cash		2, 893, 397, 000. 00	
16	Treasury bonds, foreign currency series, maturing:			
	Nov. 16, 1964	3. 09		49, 970, 000. 00
	Nov. 16, 1964	2. 82		23, 133, 689. 59
	May 16, 1966	3. 92	23, 174, 433. 96	
	July 1, 1966	3. 93	50, 263, 885. 38	
	Treasury bills: Regular weekly:			
19	Dated May 21, 1964	[4] 3. 547		
	Redeemed in exchange for series issued Nov. 19, 1964, due Feb. 18, 1965			230, 220, 000. 00
	Redeemed in exchange for series dated Nov. 19, 1964, due May 20, 1965			133, 325, 000. 00
	Redeemable for cash			1, 837, 208, 000. 00
19	Maturing Feb. 18, 1965	3. 600		
	Issued in exchange for series dated May 21, 1964		230, 220, 000. 00	
	Issued for cash		970, 821, 000. 00	
19	Maturing May 20, 1965	3. 772		
	Issued in exchange for series dated May 21, 1964		133, 325, 000. 00	
	Issued for cash		867, 498, 000. 00	
20	Certificates of indebtedness, foreign series, maturing Feb. 19, 1965	3. 25	15, 000, 000. 00	
	Treasury bills: Tax anticipation:			
24	Maturing June 22, 1965	3. 639		
	Issued for cash		1, 504, 489, 000. 00	
	Regular weekly:			
27	Dated May 28, 1964	[4] 3. 547		
	Redeemed in exchange for series issued Nov. 27, 1964, due Feb. 25, 1965			217, 832, 000. 00
	Redeemed in exchange for series dated Nov. 27, 1964, due May 27, 1965			122, 739, 000. 00
	Redeemable for cash			1, 861, 144, 000. 00

Footnotes at end of table.

TABLE 44.—*Issues, maturities, and redemptions of interest-bearing public debt securities, excluding special issues, July 1964–June 1965*—Continued

Date	Securities	Rate of interest [1]	Amount issued [2]	Amount matured or called or redeemed prior to maturity [3]
1964	Treasury bills—Continued Regular weekly—Continued	*Percent*		
Nov. 27	Maturing Feb. 25, 1965	3.757		
	Issued in exchange for series dated May 28, 1964		$217,832,000.00	
	Issued for cash		982,364,000.00	
27	Maturing May 27, 1965	3.942		
	Issued in exchange for series dated May 28, 1964		122,739,000.00	
	Issued for cash		877,363,000.00	
	Other:			
30	Issued Dec. 3, 1963	3.590		
	Redeemed in exchange for series dated Nov. 30, 1964, due Nov. 30, 1965			$63,128,000.00
	Redeemable for cash			941,673,000.00
30	Maturing Nov. 30, 1965	4.068		
	Issued in exchange for series dated Dec. 3, 1963		63,128,000.00	
30	Issued for cash		937,414,000.00	
	U.S. savings bonds: [5]			
	Series E–1941	[7] 3.223	860,058.08	1,806,632.10
	Series E–1942	[7] 3.252	3,413,812.31	8,271,509.34
	Series E–1943	[7] 3.277	3,966,487.78	14,445,155.70
	Series E–1944	[7] 3.298	5,892,724.52	19,083,111.14
	Series E–1945	[7] 3.316	10,857,344.76	12,990,122.67
	Series E–1946	[7] 3.327	3,149,610.11	7,252,826.55
	Series E–1947	[7] 3.346	2,967,583.28	7,792,564.70
	Series E–1948	[7] 3.366	3,467,622.08	8,222,005.84
	Series E–1949	[7] 3.344	3,689,045.47	8,689,057.87
	Series E–1950	[7] 3.347	3,440,662.55	8,713,315.51
	Series E–1951	[7] 3.378	3,110,728.88	7,855,620.82
	Series E–1952 (January to April)	3.400	−27,232.25	2,749,756.64
	Series E–1952 (May to December)	[7] 3.451	1,742,483.00	6,370,289.02
	Series E–1953	[7] 3.468	4,321,653.37	12,647,627.39
	Series E–1954	[7] 3.497	720,820.00	19,668,712.29
	Series E–1955	[7] 3.522	12,493,691.18	11,635,600.01
	Series E–1956	[7] 3.546	5,753,720.23	9,182,193.35
	Series E–1957 (January)	3.560	488.89	725,703.38
	Series E–1957 (February to December)	[7] 3.653	5,889,838.42	8,866,054.91
	Series E–1958	[7] 3.690	5,440,597.28	10,590,718.35
	Series E–1959 (January to May)	3.730	2,608,404.58	4,070,771.93
	Series E–1959 (June to December)	3.750	2,991,238.11	6,025,463.03
	Series E–1960	3.750	5,903,066.80	12,490,759.32
	Series E–1961	3.750	6,282,768.41	15,128,596.85
	Series E–1962	3.750	6,578,260.70	18,253,754.22
	Series E–1963	3.750	6,504,663.12	36,625,219.16
	Series E–1964	3.750	371,906,702.33	115,991,561.78
	Unclassified sales and redemptions		[8] −51,347,730.63	[8] −87,015,375.58
	Series H–1952	[7] 3.392		501,000.00
	Series H–1953	[7] 3.409		1,343,000.00
	Series H–1954	[7] 3.439		4,583,500.00
	Series H–1955	[7] 3.467		8,584,500.00
	Series H–1956	[7] 3.496		2,248,500.00
	Series H–1957 (January)	3.520		140,500.00
	Series H–1957 (February to December)	[7] 3.626		1,556,000.00
	Series H–1958	[7] 3.679		2,818,000.00
	Series H–1959 (January to May)	3.720		1,215,500.00
	Series H–1959 (June to December)	3.750		1,152,000.00
	Series H–1960	3.750		2,880,000.00
	Series H–1961	3.750		2,841,500.00
	Series H–1962	3.750		2,310,500.00
	Series H–1963	3.750	32,000.00	2,463,000.00
	Series H–1964	3.750	39,618,000.00	878,500.00
	Unclassified sales and redemptions		2,526,500.00	[8] −1,384,000.00
	Series J–1952	2.76	87,479.20	4,242,189.00
	Series J–1953	2.76	190,161.60	366,410.20
	Series J–1954	2.76	366,523.54	756,249.98
	Series J–1955	2.76	289,246.53	773,360.38
	Series J–1956	2.76	188,549.20	468,233.25
	Series J–1957	2.76	−656.95	255,268.80
	Unclassified redemptions			446,259.13
	Series K–1952	2.76		10,662,500.00
	Series K–1953	2.76		599,000.00
	Series K–1954	2.76		2,254,000.00
	Series K–1955	2.76		1,807,000.00
	Series K–1956	2.76		649,500.00
	Series K–1957	2.76		66,000.00
	Unclassified redemptions			[8] −1,830,500.00
30	Treasury notes, Series A–1966	4.00		
	Adjustments of redemptions [9]			176,000.00

Footnotes at end of table.

TABLE 44.—*Issues, maturities, and redemptions of interest-bearing public debt securities, excluding special issues, July 1964–June 1965*—Continued

Date	Securities	Rate of interest [1]	Amount issued [2]	Amount matured or called or redeemed prior to maturity [3]
1964		*Percent*		
Nov. 30	Treasury notes, Series B–1966	3⅝		
	Adjustments of redemptions [9]			$1,002,000.00
30	Treasury notes, Series B–1967	3⅝		
	Adjustments of redemptions [9]			11,000.00
30	Treasury notes, Series C–1964	4⅞		
	Adjustments of redemptions [9]			−95,000.00
30	Treasury notes, Series F–1964	3¾		
	Adjustments of redemptions [9]			−5,000.00
30	Treasury bonds of 1966	3¾		
	Adjustments of redemptions [9]			−1,200,000.00
30	Treasury notes, Series E–1965	4.00		
	Adjustments of issues [9]		$3,000.00	
30	Treasury bonds of 1974	4¼		
	Adjustments of issues [9]		−3,000.00	
30	Treasury bonds of 1969 (Oct. 1, 1957)	4.00		
	Adjustments of issues [9]		−36,000.00	
30	Tresury bonds of 1973	4⅛		
	Adjustments of issues [9]		−64,000.00	
30	U.S. retirement plan bonds	3.75	281,800.04	9,936.97
30	Depositary bonds, First Series	2.00	688,000.00	832,000.00
30	Treasury bonds, REA Series	2.00	845,000.00	140,000.00
30	Treasury bonds, Investment Series B–1975–80	2¾		
	Redeemed in exchange for Treasury notes, Series EO–1969			7,961,000.00
30	Treasury notes, Series EO–1969	1½	7,961,000.00	
30	Miscellaneous			25,855,200.00
	Total November		22,445,871,035.56	20,045,919,625.59
Dec. 1	Certificates of indebtedness, foreign series, maturing:			
	Feb. 2, 1965	3.25		15,000,000.00
	Feb. 19, 1965	3.25		15,000,000.00
2	Jan. 26, 1965	3.25		20,000,000.00
	Treasury bills:			
	Regular weekly:			
3	Dated June 4, 1964	[4] 3.543		
	Redeemed in exchange for series issued Dec. 3, 1964, due Mar. 4, 1965			192,655,000.00
	Redeemed in exchange for series dated Dec. 3, 1964, due June 3, 1965			132,225,000.00
	Redeemable for cash			1,880,613,000.00
3	Maturing Mar. 4, 1965	3.868		
	Issued in exchange for series dated June 4, 1964		192,655,000.00	
	Issued for cash		1,007,569,000.00	
3	Maturing June 3, 1965	4.030		
	Issued in exchange for series dated June 4, 1964		132,225,000.00	
	Issued for cash		867,826,000.00	
9	Certificates of indebtedness, foreign series, maturing:			
	Dec. 9, 1964	3.55		30,000,000.00
	Mar. 9, 1965	3.85	30,000,000.00	
	Treasury bills:			
	Regular weekly:			
10	Dated June 11, 1964	[4] 3.529		
	Redeemed in exchange for series issued Dec. 10, 1964, due Mar. 11, 1965			15,120,000.00
	Redeemed in exchange for series dated Dec. 10, 1964, due June 10, 1965			4,997,000.00
	Redeemable for cash			2,282,270,000.00
10	Maturing Mar. 11, 1965	3.815		
	Issued in exchange for series dated June 11, 1964		15,120,000.00	
	Issued for cash		1,285,897,000.00	
10	Maturing June 10, 1965	3.944		
	Issued in exchange for series dated June 11, 1964		4,997,000.00	
	Issued for cash		995,581,000.00	
15	Treasury certificates, maturing Dec. 15, 1964	1.00		7,537,768.13
15	Treasury certificates, maturing June 15, 1965	1.00	10,075,456.97	

Footnotes at end of table.

TABLE 44.—*Issues, maturities, and redemptions of interest-bearing public debt securities, excluding special issues, July 1964-June 1965*—Continued

Date	Securities	Rate of interest [1]	Amount issued [2]	Amount matured or called or redeemed prior to maturity [3]
1964 Dec. 16	Certificates of indebtedness, foreign series, maturing:	*Percent*		
	Dec. 16, 1964	3.55		$30,000,000.00
	Mar. 16, 1965	3.90	$30,000,000.00	
17	Treasury bills: Regular weekly: Dated June 18, 1964	[4] 3.559		
	Redeemed in exchange for series issued Dec. 17, 1964, due Mar. 18, 1965			17,974,000.00
	Redeemed in exchange for series dated Dec. 17, 1964, due June 17, 1965			7,453,000.00
	Redeemable for cash			2,277,329,000.00
17	Maturing Mar. 18, 1965	3.864		
	Issued in exchange for series dated June 18, 1964		17,974,000.00	
	Issued for cash		1,282,866,000.00	
17	Maturing June 17, 1965	3.965		
	Issued in exchange for series dated June 18, 1964		7,453,000.00	
	Issued for cash		993,151,000.00	
21	Certificates of indebtedness, foreign series, maturing:			
	Dec. 21, 1964	3.55		5,000,000.00
	Mar. 22, 1965	3.90	5,000,000.00	
22	Dec. 22, 1964	3.50		50,000,000.00
	Mar. 22, 1965	3.75	25,000,000.00	
	June 22, 1965	3.875	50,000,000.00	
23	Mar. 23, 1965	3.90	30,000,000.00	
24	Mar. 24, 1965	3.90	20,000,000.00	
24	Treasury bills: Regular weekly: Dated June 25, 1964	[4] 3.547		
	Redeemed in exchange for series issued Dec. 24, 1964, due Mar. 25, 1965			192,212,000.00
	Redeemed in exchange for series dated Dec. 24, 1964, due June 24, 1965			134,800,000.00
	Redeemable for cash			1,875,033,000.00
24	Maturing Mar. 25, 1965	3.868		
	Issued in exchange for series dated June 25, 1964		192,212,000.00	
	Issued for cash		1,015,884,000.00	
24	Maturing June 24, 1965	3.960		
	Issued in exchange for series dated June 25, 1964		134,800,000.00	
	Issued for cash		870,107,000.00	
28	Certificates of indebtedness, foreign series, maturing:			
	Jan. 28, 1965	3.43	35,000,000.00	
30	Mar. 30, 1965	3.75	20,000,000.00	
31	Treasury bills: Regular weekly: Dated Jan. 3, 1964	[4] 3.544		
	Redeemed in exchange for series issued Dec. 31, 1964, due Apr. 1, 1965			201,670,000.00
	Redeemed in exchange for series dated Dec. 31, 1964, due July 1, 1965			123,513,000.00
	Redeemable for cash			1,876,099,000.00
31	Maturing Apr. 1, 1965	3.866		
	Issued in exchange for series dated Jan. 3, 1964		201,670,000.00	
	Issued for cash		998,184,000.00	
31	Maturing July 1, 1965	3.957		
	Issued in exchange for series dated Jan. 3, 1964		123,513,000.00	
	Issued for cash		878,464,000.00	
31	Other: Issued Jan. 3, 1964	3.707		
	Redeemed in exchange for series dated Dec. 31, 1964, due Dec. 31, 1965			26,257,000.00
	Redeemable for cash			974,052,000.00
31	Maturing Dec. 31, 1965	3.972		
	Issued in exchange for series dated Jan. 3, 1964		26,257,000.00	
	Issued for cash		976,694,000.00	
31	Treasury certificates, maturing Dec. 31, 1964	3.555		10,264,462.77
31	Treasury certificates, maturing Mar. 31, 1965	3.867	10,355,688.18	
31	Treasury bonds, maturing June 30, 1967	4.00	408,000.00	

Footnotes at end of table.

TABLE 44.—*Issues, maturities, and redemptions of interest-bearing public debt securities, excluding special issues, July 1964–June 1965*—Continued

Date	Securities	Rate of interest [1]	Amount issued [2]	Amount matured or called or redeemed prior to maturity [3]
1964		*Percent*		
Dec. 31	U.S. savings bonds: [5]			
	Series E-1941	[7] 3.223	$2,270,841.44	$1,520,427.95
	Series E-1942	[7] 3.252	4,322,549.34	6,538,176.31
	Series E-1943	[7] 3.277	4,254,093.86	10,781,735.54
	Series E-1944	[7] 3.298	13,364,527.56	15,649,523.26
	Series E-1945	[7] 3.316	10,957,205.62	10,564,027.23
	Series E-1946	[7] 3.327	4,041,283.08	5,564,465.02
	Series E-1947	[7] 3.346	3,871,313.70	5,549,893.35
	Series E-1948	[7] 3.366	4,734,797.29	6,325,421.11
	Series E-1949	[7] 3.344	4,970,341.58	6,409,083.77
	Series E-1950	[7] 3.347	4,096,442.06	6,499,359.66
	Series E-1951	[7] 3.378	3,713,929.73	5,927,316.20
	Series E-1952 (January to April)	3.400	−25,307.53	2,106,359.58
	Series E-1952 (May to December)	[7] 3.451	1,878,501.06	4,971,114.51
	Series E-1953	[7] 3.468	4,342,871.37	9,576,402.66
	Series E-1954	[7] 3.497	4,513,281.32	14,901,554.92
	Series E-1955	[7] 3.522	8,595,927.38	9,567,809.41
	Series E-1956	[7] 3.546	6,496,920.47	7,042,831.20
	Series E-1957 (January)	3.560	90.95	564,158.98
	Series E-1957 (February to December)	[7] 3.653	6,787,243.31	6,856,130.49
	Series E-1958	[7] 3.690	6,434,086.02	8,011,549.17
	Series E-1959 (January to May)	3.730	−33,477.06	3,203,947.61
	Series E-1959 (June to December)	3.750	6,561,406.31	4,421,076.53
	Series E-1960	3.750	6,831,004.41	9,210,102.31
	Series E-1961	3.750	6,852,572.99	10,803,919.00
	Series E-1962	3.750	7,564,328.17	13,406,893.49
	Series E-1963	3.750	6,882,828.42	26,569,856.91
	Series E-1964	3.750	318,988,799.35	101,069,049.59
	Unclassified sales and redemptions		21,019,666.04	61,562,650.13
	Series H-1952	[7] 3.392		560,000.00
	Series H-1953	[7] 3.409		1,326,500.00
	Series H-1954	[7] 3.439		4,831,500.00
	Series H-1955	[7] 3.467		9,299,500.00
	Series H-1956	[7] 3.496		2,073,500.00
	Series H-1957 (January)	3.520		76,500.00
	Series H-1957 (February to December)	[7] 3.626		1,629,500.00
	Series H-1958	[7] 3.679		2,230,000.00
	Series H-1959 (January to May)	3.720		1,043,000.00
	Series H-1959 (June to December)	3.750		950,000.00
	Series H-1960	3.750		2,542,500.00
	Series H-1961	3.750		2,656,500.00
	Series H-1962	3.750		2,215,500.00
	Series H-1963	3.750	42,000.00	1,952,000.00
	Series H-1964	3.750	44,020,000.00	1,047,000.00
	Unclassified sales and redemptions		3,034,000.00	[8] −93,500.00
	Series J-1953	2.76	260,489.60	477,262.20
	Series J-1954	2.76	468,750.14	908,593.70
	Series J-1955	2.76	310,589.97	646,662.58
	Series J-1956	2.76	233,022.65	683,133.05
	Series J-1957	2.76	−280.70	174,355.20
	Unclassified redemptions			244,740.80
	Series K-1953	2.76		739,000.00
	Series K-1954	2.76		1,786,000.00
	Series K-1955	2.76		1,491,000.00
	Series K-1956	2.76		785,000.00
	Series K-1957	2.76		124,500.00
	Unclassified redemptions			4,080,000.00
31	Treasury notes, Series B-1966	3⅝		
	Adjustments of redemptions [9]			121,000.00
31	Treasury notes, Series A-1966	4.00		
	Adjustments of redemptions [9]			10,000.00
31	Treasury notes, Series B-1967	3⅝		
	Adjustments of redemptions [9]			990,000.00
31	Treasury bonds of 1966	3¾		
	Adjustments of redemptions [9]			94,000.00
31	Treasury notes, Series E-1965	4.00		
	Adjustments of issues [9]		460,000.00	
31	Treasury bonds of 1969 (Oct. 1, 1957)	4.00		
	Adjustments of issues [9]		−2,686,000.00	
31	Treasury bonds of 1973	4⅛		
	Adjustments of issues [9]		154,000.00	
31	Treasury bonds of 1987–92	4¼		
	Adjustments of issues [9]		−32,000.00	
31	U.S. retirement plan bonds	3.75	1,608,211.27	10,645.96
31	Depositary bonds, First Series	2.00	5,545,000.00	2,300,000.00
31	Treasury bonds, REA Series	2.00	1,824,000.00	459,000.00

Footnotes at end of table.

TABLE 44.—*Issues, maturities, and redemptions of interest-bearing public debt securities, excluding special issues, July 1964–June 1965*—Continued

Date	Securities	Rate of interest [1]	Amount issued [2]	Amount matured or called or redeemed prior to maturity [3]
		Percent		
1964 Dec. 31	Treasury bonds, Investment Series B–1975–80.	2¾		
	Redeemed in exchange for Treasury notes, Series EO–1969			$52,400,000.00
31	Treasury notes, Series EO–1969	1½	$52,400,000.00	
31	Miscellaneous			17,052,100.00
	Total December		13,068,867,996.32	12,892,166,060.28
1965 Jan. 1	Treasury bonds, foreign currency series, maturing:			
	Jan. 1, 1965	2.89		25,414,722.05
	July 1, 1966	3.99	25,491,877.36	
	Treasury bills:			
	Regular weekly:			
7	Dated July 9, 1964	[4] 3.566		
	Redeemed in exchange for series issued Jan. 7, 1965, due Apr. 8, 1965			213,375,000.00
	Redeemed in exchange for series dated Jan. 7, 1965, due July 8, 1965			85,452,000.00
	Redeemable for cash			1,801,511,000.00
7	Maturing Apr. 8, 1965	3.829		
	Issued in exchange for series dated July 9, 1964		213,375,000.00	
	Issued for cash		888,465,000.00	
7	Maturing July 8, 1965	3.927		
	Issued in exchange for series dated July 9, 1964		85,452,000.00	
	Issued for cash		917,910,000.00	
11	Certificates of indebtedness, foreign series, maturing:			
	Jan. 28, 1965	3.43		35,000,000.00
12	Apr. 12, 1965	3.75	5,000,000.00	
	Treasury bills:			
	Regular weekly:			
14	Dated July 16, 1964	[4] 3.567		
	Redeemed in exchange for series issued Jan. 14, 1965, due Apr. 15, 1965			181,686,000.00
	Redeemed in exchange for series dated Jan. 14, 1965, due July 15, 1965			95,380,000.00
	Redeemable for cash			1,836,994,000.00
14	Maturing Apr. 15, 1965	3.814		
	Issued in exchange for series dated July 16, 1964		181,686,000.00	
	Issued for cash		917,948,000.00	
14	Maturing July 15, 1965	3.942		
	Issued in exchange for series dated July 16, 1964		95,380,000.00	
	Issued for cash		905,687,000.00	
15	Treasury bonds of 1965	2⅝		
	Redeemed in exchange for:			
	4% Treasury bonds of 1970 (Jan. 15, 1965)			674,117,500.00
	4⅛% Treasury bonds of 1974			489,281,000.00
	4¼% Treasury bonds of 1987–92			641,970,000.00
15	Treasury notes, Series B–1965	3½		
	Redeemed in exchange for:			
	4% Treasury bonds of 1970 (Jan. 15, 1965)			639,939,000.00
	4⅛% Treasury bonds of 1974			415,654,000.00
	4¼% Treasury bonds of 1987–92			283,029,000.00
15	Treasury notes, Series E–1965	4.00		
	Redeemed in exchange for:			
	4% Treasury bonds of 1970 (Jan. 15, 1965)			175,641,000.00
	4⅛% Treasury bonds of 1974			140,413,000.00
	4¼% Treasury bonds of 1987–92			144,906,000.00
15	Treasury notes, Series B–1966	3⅝		
	Redeemed in exchange for:			
	4% Treasury bonds of 1970 (Jan. 15, 1965)			587,445,000.00
	4⅛% Treasury bonds of 1974			332,810,000.00
	4¼% Treasury bonds of 1987–92			144,282,000.00
15	Treasury notes, Series C–1966	3⅞		
	Redeemed in exchange for:			
	4% Treasury bonds of 1970 (Jan. 15, 1965)			379,285,000.00
	4⅛% Treasury bonds of 1974			400,674,000.00
	4¼% Treasury bonds of 1987–92			660,315,000.00

Footnotes at end of table.

TABLE 44.—*Issues, maturities, and redemptions of interest-bearing public debt securities, excluding special issues, July 1964–June 1965*—Continued

Date	Securities	Rate of interest [1]	Amount issued [2]	Amount matured or called or redeemed prior to maturity [3]
1965		*Percent*		
Jan. 15	Treasury bonds of 1966	3¾		
	Redeemed in exchange for:			
	4% Treasury bonds of 1970 (Jan. 15, 1965)			$302,253,500.00
	4⅛% Treasury bonds of 1974			136,905,000.00
	4¼% Treasury bonds of 1987–92			126,079,500.00
15	Treasury notes, Series A-1967	3¾		
	Redeemed in exchange for:			
	4% Treasury bonds of 1970 (Jan. 15, 1965)			902,190,000.00
	4⅛% Treasury bonds of 1974			459,060,000.00
	4¼% Treasury bonds of 1987–92			139,985,000.00
15	Treasury bonds of 1967	3⅝		
	Redeemed in exchange for:			
	4% Treasury bonds of 1970 (Jan. 15, 1965)			723,429,000.00
	4⅛% Treasury bonds of 1974			727,841,000.00
	4¼% Treasury bonds of 1987–92			124,009,500.00
15	Treasury bonds of 1970 (Jan. 15, 1965)	4.00		
	Issued in exchange for:			
	2⅝% Treasury bonds of 1965		$674,117,500.00	
	3½% Treasury notes, Series B-1965		639,939,000.00	
	4% Treasury notes, Series E-1965		175,641,000.00	
	3⅝% Treasury notes, Series B-1966		587,445,000.00	
	3⅞% Treasury notes, Series C-1966		379,285,000.00	
	3¾% Treasury bonds of 1966		302,253,500.00	
	3¾% Treasury notes, Series A-1967		902,190,000.00	
	3⅝% Treasury bonds of 1967		723,429,000.00	
15	Treasury bonds of 1974	4⅛		
	Issued in exchange for:			
	2⅝% Treasury bonds of 1965		489,281,000.00	
	3½% Treasury notes, Series B-1965		415,654,000.00	
	4% Treasury notes, Series E-1965		140,413,000.00	
	3⅝% Treasury notes, Series B-1966		332,810,000.00	
	3⅞% Treasury notes, Series C-1966		400,674,000.00	
	3¾% Treasury bonds of 1966		136,905,000.00	
	3¾% Treasury notes, Series A-1967		459,060,000.00	
	3⅝% Treasury bonds of 1967		727,841,000.00	
15	Treasury bonds of 1987–92	4¼		
	Issued in exchange for:			
	2⅝% Treasury bonds of 1965		641,970,000.00	
	3½% Treasury notes, Series B-1965		283,029,000.00	
	4% Treasury notes, Series E-1965		144,906,000.00	
	3⅝% Treasury notes, Series B-1966		144,232,000.00	
	3⅞% Treasury notes, Series C-1966		660,315,000.00	
	3¾% Treasury bonds of 1966		126,079,500.00	
	3¾% Treasury notes, Series A-1967		139,985,000.00	
	3⅝% Treasury bonds of 1967		124,009,500.00	
18	Certificates of indebtedness, foreign series, maturing:			
	Jan. 18, 1965	3.60		5,000,000.00
	Apr. 20, 1965	3.85	5,000,000.00	
	Treasury bills:			
	Tax anticipation:			
18	Maturing June 22, 1965	3.711		
	Issued for cash		1,758,347,000.00	
	Regular weekly:			
21	Dated July 23, 1964	[4] 3.604		
	Redeemed in exchange for series issued Jan. 21, 1965, due Apr. 22, 1965			199,823,000.00
	Redeemed in exchange for series dated Jan. 21, 1965, due July 22, 1965			123,120,000.00
	Redeemable for cash			1,779,801,000.00
21	Maturing Apr. 22, 1965	3.821		
	Issued in exchange for series dated July 23, 1964		199,823,000.00	
	Issued for cash		1,000,459,000.00	
21	Maturing July 22, 1965	3.960		
	Issued in exchange for series dated July 23, 1964		123,120,000.00	
	Issued for cash		877,931,000.00	
22	Certificates of indebtedness, foreign series, maturing:			
	Apr. 22, 1965	3.85	50,000,000.00	
28	Mar. 24, 1965	3.90		20,000,000.00

Footnotes at end of table.

TABLE 44.—*Issues, maturities, and redemptions of interest-bearing public debt securities, excluding special issues, July 1964–June 1965*—Continued

Date	Securities	Rate of interest [1]	Amount issued [2]	Amount matured or called or redeemed prior to maturity [3]
	Treasury bills:	*Percent*		
1965 Jan. 28	Regular weekly: Dated July 30, 1964	[4] 3. 578		
	Redeemed in exchange for series issued Jan. 28, 1965, due Apr. 29, 1965			$213, 152, 000. 00
	Redeemed in exchange for series dated Jan. 28, 1965, due July 29, 1965			132, 035, 000. 00
	Redeemable for cash			1, 756, 957, 000. 00
28	Maturing Apr. 29, 1965	3. 848		
	Issued in exchange for series dated July 30, 1964		$213, 152, 000. 00	
	Issued for cash		989, 713, 000. 00	
28	Maturing July 29, 1965	3. 946		
	Issued in exchange for series dated July 30, 1964		132, 035, 000. 00	
	Issued for cash		871, 198, 000. 00	
29	Certificates of indebtedness, foreign series, maturing Mar. 23, 1965	3. 90		30, 000, 000. 00
31	U.S. savings bonds: [5]			
	Series E-1941	[7] 3. 223	587, 151, 24	2, 070, 878. 91
	Series E-1942	[7] 3. 252	4, 651, 589. 52	8, 080, 339. 74
	Series E-1943	[7] 3. 277	4, 996, 604. 64	13, 387, 937. 95
	Series E-1944	[7] 3. 298	9, 911, 885. 30	21, 808, 256, 44
	Series E-1945	[7] 3. 316	5, 711, 145. 70	13, 637, 651. 10
	Series E-1946	[7] 3. 327	4, 324, 063. 17	6, 831, 607. 65
	Series E-1947	[7] 3. 346	4, 896, 043. 98	7, 207, 037. 84
	Series E-1948	[7] 3. 366	5, 283, 753. 89	7, 899, 227. 27
	Series E-1949	[7] 3. 344	5, 548, 759. 53	8, 410, 289. 85
	Series E-1950	[7] 3. 347	5, 422, 886. 13	7, 982, 081. 94
	Series E-1951	[7] 3. 378	4, 184, 833. 66	7, 165, 892. 51
	Series E-1952 (January to April)	3. 400	2, 327, 290. 36	2, 348, 799. 76
	Series E-1952 (May to December)	[7] 3. 451	3, 438, 896. 20	5, 751, 283. 81
	Series E-1953	[7] 3. 468	4, 078, 020. 77	11, 139, 213. 98
	Series E-1954	[7] 3. 497	4, 453, 308. 30	18, 925, 206. 87
	Series E-1955	[7] 3. 522	5, 891, 230. 05	11, 244, 205. 40
	Series E-1956	[7] 3. 546	7, 710, 443. 90	8, 127, 942. 68
	Series E-1957 (January)	3. 560	3, 349, 367. 34	656, 963. 28
	Series E-1957 (February to December)	[7] 3. 653	3, 301, 977. 82	8, 010, 846. 30
	Series E-1958	[7] 3. 690	7, 568, 779. 95	9, 537, 183. 21
	Series E-1959 (January to May)	3. 730	3, 828, 253. 79	3, 659, 627. 15
	Series E-1959 (June to December)	3. 750	3, 051, 959. 42	5, 368, 122. 85
	Series E-1960	3. 750	7, 659, 757. 63	10, 415, 090. 18
	Series E-1961	3. 750	8, 228, 598. 38	12, 288, 143. 40
	Series E-1962	3. 750	7, 638, 837. 04	15, 308, 670. 45
	Series E-1963	3. 750	9, 723, 911. 25	30, 358, 672. 33
	Series E-1964	3. 750	362, 925, 209. 12	140, 556, 199. 30
	Unclassified sales and redemptions		26, 441, 114. 49	79, 040, 575. 97
	Series H-1952	[7] 3. 392		420, 000. 00
	Series H-1953	[7] 3. 409		1, 487, 500. 00
	Series H-1954	[7] 3. 439		4, 174, 000. 00
	Series H-1955	[7] 3. 467		9, 317, 500. 00
	Series H-1956	[7] 3. 496		2, 236, 500. 00
	Series H-1957 (January)	3. 520		66, 000. 00
	Series H-1957 (February to December)	[7] 3. 626		1, 648, 000. 00
	Series H-1958	[7] 3. 679		2, 261, 500. 00
	Series H-1959 (January to May)	3. 720		913, 000. 00
	Series H-1959 (June to December)	3. 750		1, 250, 500. 00
	Series H-1960	3. 750		2, 606, 500. 00
	Series H-1961	3. 750		2, 875, 500. 00
	Series H-1962	3. 750		1, 860, 500. 00
	Series H-1963	3. 750	20, 000. 00	2, 216, 000. 00
	Series H-1964	3. 750	48, 010, 000. 00	1, 035, 000. 00
	Unclassified sales and redemptions		20, 671, 500. 00	[8] −1, 327, 000. 00
	Series J-1953	2. 76	217, 447. 60	143, 992. 40
	Series J-1954	2. 76	388, 111. 81	971, 698. 80
	Series J-1955	2. 76	391, 833. 40	624, 610. 77
	Series J-1956	2. 76	347, 645. 20	414, 492. 30
	Series J-1957	2. 76	105, 376. 25	48, 988. 80
	Unclassified redemptions			1, 495, 750. 24
	Series K-1953	2. 76		730, 500. 00
	Series K-1954	2. 76		2, 607, 000. 00
	Series K-1955	2. 76		1, 605, 000. 00
	Series K-1956	2. 76		892, 000. 00
	Series K-1957	2. 76		98, 500. 00
	Unclassified redemptions			8, 547, 500. 00
31	U.S. retirement plan bonds	3. 75	2, 298, 491. 17	10, 155. 57
31	Depositary bonds, First Series	2. 00	85, 000. 00	1, 286, 000. 00
31	Treasury bonds, REA Series	2. 00	95, 000. 00	130, 000. 00

Footnotes at end of table.

TABLE 44.—*Issues, maturities, and redemptions of interest-bearing public debt securities, excluding special issues, July 1964–June 1965*—Continued

Date	Securities	Rate of interest [1]	Amount issued [2]	Amount matured or called or redeemed prior to maturity [3]
1965		*Percent*		
Jan. 31	Treasury bonds, Investment Series B-1975-80.	2¾		
	Redeemed in exchange for Treasury notes, Series EO-1969.			$33, 500, 000. 00
31	Treasury, notes, Series EO-1969	1½	$33, 500, 000. 00	
31	Miscellaneous			28, 566, 200. 00
	Total January		20, 841, 902, 955. 36	18, 878, 096, 059. 05
	Treasury bills:			
	Other:			
Feb. 1 [10]	Issued Feb. 6, 1964	3. 680		
	Redeemed in exchange for series dated Jan. 31, 1965 due Jan. 31, 1966			102, 754, 000. 00
	Redeemable for cash			897, 639, 000. 00
1	Maturing Jan. 31, 1966	3. 945		
	Issued in exchange for series dated Feb. 6, 1964		102, 754, 000. 00	
	Issued for cash		897, 633, 000. 00	
	Regular weekly:			
4	Dated Aug. 6, 1964	[4] 3. 573		
	Redeemed in exchange for series issued Feb. 4, 1965 due May 6, 1965			242, 072, 000. 00
	Redeemed in exchange for series dated Feb. 4, 1965 due Aug. 5, 1965			133, 651, 000. 00
	Redeemable for cash			1, 725, 470, 000. 00
4	Maturing May 6, 1965	3. 888		
	Issued in exchange for series dated Aug. 6, 1964		242, 072, 000. 00	
	Issued for cash		960, 445, 000. 00	
4	Maturing Aug. 5, 1965	3. 968		
	Issued in exchange for series dated Aug. 6, 1964		133, 651, 000. 00	
	Issued for cash		869, 929, 000. 00	
4	Certificates of indebtedness, foreign series, maturing:			
	Feb. 4, 1965	3. 60		20, 000, 000. 00
8	May 10, 1965	3. 90	15, 000, 000. 00	
10	Feb. 10, 1965	3. 60		10, 000, 000. 00
	Treasury bills:			
	Regular weekly:			
11	Dated Aug. 13, 1964	[4] 3. 590		
	Redeemed in exchange for series issued Feb. 11, 1965, due May 13, 1965			179, 629, 000. 00
	Redeemed in exchange for series dated Feb. 11, 1965, due Aug. 12, 1965			132, 922, 000. 00
	Redeemable for cash			1, 789, 236, 000. 00
11	Maturing May 13, 1965	3. 903		
	Issued in exchange for series dated Aug. 13, 1964		179, 629, 000. 00	
	Issued for cash		1, 020, 728, 000. 00	
11	Maturing Aug. 12, 1965	3. 987		
	Issued in exchange for series dated Aug. 13, 1964		132, 922, 000. 00	
	Issued for cash		868, 314, 000. 00	
15	Treasury bonds, foreign currency series, maturing:			
	Feb. 15, 1965	3. 14		49, 970, 000. 00
	Aug. 1, 1966	4. 04	50, 238, 633. 51	
15	Treasury bonds of 1965	2⅝		
	Redeemed in exchange for 4% Treasury notes, Series E-1966			518, 471, 000. 00
	Redeemable for cash			1, 649, 096, 500. 00
15	Treasury notes, Series E-1966	4. 00		
	Issued in exchange for 2⅝% Treasury bonds of 1965		518, 471, 000. 00	
	Issued for cash		1, 735, 350, 000. 00	
	Treasury bills:			
	Regular weekly:			
18	Dated Aug. 20, 1964	[4] 3. 615		
	Redeemed in exchange for series issued Feb. 18, 1965, due May 20, 1965			12, 338, 000. 00
	Redeemed in exchange for series dated Feb. 18, 1965, due Aug. 19, 1965			1, 847, 000. 00
	Redeemable for cash			2, 088, 202, 000. 00
18	Maturing May 20, 1965	3. 936		
	Issued in exchange for series dated Aug. 20, 1964		12, 338, 000. 00	
	Issued for cash		1, 187, 733, 000. 00	

Footnotes at end of table.

TABLE 44.—*Issues, maturities, and redemptions of interest-bearing public debt securities, excluding special issues, July 1964–June 1965*—Continued

Date	Securities	Rate of interest [1]	Amount issued [2]	Amount matured or called or redeemed prior to maturity [3]
	Treasury bills—Continued			
1965	Regular weekly—Continued	*Percent*		
Feb. 18	Maturing Aug. 19, 1965	4. 015		
	Issued in exchange for series dated Aug. 20, 1964		$1, 847, 000. 00	
	Issued for cash		998, 511, 000. 00	
23	Treasury bonds, foreign currency series, maturing Aug. 23, 1966	4. 09	25, 154, 798. 76	
	Treasury bills:			
	Regular weekly:			
25	Dated Aug. 27, 1964	[4] 3. 706		
	Redeemed in exchange for series issued Feb. 25, 1965, due May 27, 1965			$234, 346, 000. 00
	Redeemed in exchange for series dated Feb. 25, 1965, due Aug. 26, 1965			142, 991, 000. 00
	Redeemable for cash			1, 724, 865, 000. 00
25	Maturing May 27, 1965	3. 989		
	Issued in exchange for series dated Aug. 27, 1964		234, 346, 000. 00	
	Issued for cash		966, 571, 000. 00	
25	Maturing Aug. 26, 1965	4. 043		
	Issued in exchange for series dated Aug. 27, 1964		142, 991, 000. 00	
	Issued for cash		860, 395, 000. 00	
28	U.S. savings bonds: [6]			
	Series E-1941	[7] 3. 223	405, 379. 80	2, 194, 589. 80
	Series E-1942	[7] 3. 252	2, 846, 060. 21	9, 182, 200. 08
	Series E-1943	[7] 3. 277	3, 922, 561. 89	14, 668, 054. 15
	Series E-1944	[7] 3. 298	7, 342, 641. 77	23, 688, 293. 97
	Series E-1945	[7] 3. 316	4, 016, 460. 42	16, 770, 420. 48
	Series E-1946	[7] 3. 327	3, 325, 833. 85	8, 015, 183. 84
	Series E-1947	[7] 3. 346	3, 440, 408. 50	9, 189, 637. 25
	Series E-1948	[7] 3. 366	3, 898, 854. 19	9, 920, 996. 31
	Series E-1949	[7] 3. 344	4, 211, 253. 13	10, 122, 010. 21
	Series E-1950	[7] 3. 347	3, 978, 376. 59	9, 461, 947. 90
	Series E-1951	[7] 3. 378	3, 316, 028. 85	8, 480, 788. 94
	Series E-1952 (January to April)	3. 400	1, 734, 945. 44	2, 853, 584. 68
	Series E-1952 (May to December)	[7] 3. 451	4, 441, 099. 34	6, 602, 468. 88
	Series E-1953	[7] 3. 468	4, 963, 532. 58	12, 860, 988. 62
	Series E-1954	[7] 3. 497	5, 565, 098. 03	20, 590, 017. 18
	Series E-1955	[7] 3. 522	5, 938, 402. 16	14, 650, 124. 04
	Series E-1956	[7] 3. 546	6, 212, 084. 50	8, 493, 429. 52
	Series E-1957 (January)	3. 560	−17. 52	720, 783. 28
	Series E-1957 (February to December)	[7] 3. 653	5, 657, 865. 87	7, 415, 411. 00
	Series E-1958	[7] 3. 690	5, 998, 647. 88	8, 573, 628. 79
	Series E-1959 (January to May)	3. 730	2, 936, 286. 81	3, 353, 048. 14
	Series E-1959 (June to December)	3. 750	2, 564, 401. 48	4, 737, 929. 22
	Series E-1960	3. 750	6, 352, 110. 56	9, 176, 617. 28
	Series E-1961	3. 750	6, 647, 709. 13	10, 876, 155. 98
	Series E-1962	3. 750	6, 026, 763. 06	12, 069, 484. 84
	Series E-1963	3. 750	7, 496, 894. 73	20, 669, 299. 41
	Series E-1964	3. 750	240, 268, 771. 54	89, 871. 598. 29
	Series E-1965	3. 750	19, 570, 593. 75	750. 00
	Unclassified sales and redemptions		103, 518, 423. 62	44, 410, 127. 05
	Series H-1952	[7] 3. 392		425, 000. 00
	Series H-1953	[7] 3. 409		1, 327, 500. 00
	Series H-1954	[7] 3. 439		4, 497, 000. 00
	Series H-1955	[7] 3. 467		7, 956, 500. 00
	Series H-1956	[7] 3. 496		2, 142, 500. 00
	Series H-1957 (January)	3. 520		248, 500. 00
	Series H-1957 (February to December)	[7] 3. 626		1, 583, 500. 00
	Series H-1958	[7] 3. 679		2, 311, 500. 00
	Series H-1959 (January to May)	3. 720		1, 037, 000. 00
	Series H-1959 (June to December)	3. 750		964, 500. 00
	Series H-1960	3. 750	2, 000. 00	2, 748, 500. 00
	Series H-1961	3. 750		2, 872, 000. 00
	Series H-1962	3. 750		2, 275, 000. 00
	Series H-1963	3. 750		2, 069, 000. 00
	Series H-1964	3. 750	28, 825, 500. 00	1, 422, 000. 00
	Series H-1965	3. 750	42, 529, 500. 00	
	Unclassified sales and redemptions		[8] −18, 844, 000. 00	151, 000. 00
	Series J-1953	2. 76	169, 685. 20	4, 292, 740. 20
	Series J-1954	2. 76	351, 806. 23	987, 451. 80
	Series J-1955	2. 76	265, 193. 63	819, 023. 43
	Series J-1956	2. 76	297, 159. 80	591, 180. 75
	Series J-1957	2. 76	76, 344. 80	57, 590. 75
	Unclassified redemptions			[8] −3, 070, 140. 77
	Series K-1953	2. 76		18, 505, 000. 00
	Series K-1954	2. 76		2, 189, 500. 00

Footnotes at end of table.

TABLE 44.—*Issues, maturities, and redemptions of interest-bearing public debt securities, excluding special issues, July 1964–June 1965*—Continued

Date	Securities	Rate of interest [1]	Amount issued [2]	Amount matured or called or redeemed prior to maturity [3]
1965		*Percent*		
Feb. 28	U.S. savings bonds [4]—Continued			
	Series K-1955	2.76		$2,233,000.00
	Series K-1956	2.76		1,463,000.00
	Series K-1957	2.76		192,500.00
	Unclassified redemptions			[5] —9,576,000.00
28	Treasury notes, Series B-1966	3⅝		
	Adjustments of redemptions [6]			125,000.00
28	Treasury bonds of 1966	3¾		
	Adjustments of redemptions [6]			8,305,000.00
28	Treasury notes, Series C-1966	3⅞		
	Adjustments of redemptions [6]			—340,000.00
28	Treasury bonds of 1965	2⅝		
	Adjustments of redemptions [6]			2,832,000.00
28	Treasury notes, Series A-1967	3¾		
	Adjustments of redemptions [6]			1,449,000.00
28	Treasury notes, Series B-1965	3½		
	Adjustments of redemptions [6]			—443,000.00
28	Treasury bonds of 1967	3⅝		
	Adjustments of redemptions [6]			9,250,500.00
28	Treasury bonds of 1970	4.00		
	Adjustments of issues [6]		—$2,398,000.00	
28	Treasury bonds of 1974	4⅛		
	Adjustments of issues [6]		23,579,500.00	
28	Treasury bonds of 1987-92	4¼		
	Adjustments of issues [6]		—3,000.00	
28	U.S. retirement plan bonds	3.75	91,944.73	13,885.68
28	Depositary bonds, First Series	2.00	162,000.00	150,000.00
28	Treasury bonds, REA Series	2.00	250,000.00	85,000.00
28	Treasury bonds, Investment Series B-1975-80	2¾		
	Redeemed in exchange for Treasury notes, Series EO-1969			6,189,000.00
28	Treasury notes, Series EO-1969	1½	6,189,000.00	
28	Miscellaneous			45,299,100.00
	Total February		12,715,165,538.82	12,180,750,900.97
	Treasury bills:			
	Other:			
Mar. 1 [10]	Issued, Mar. 3, 1964	3.765		
	Redeemed in exchange for series dated Feb. 28, 1965, due Feb. 28, 1966			36,599,000.00
	Redeemable for cash			963,921,000.00
1	Maturing Feb. 28, 1966	4.062		
	Issued in exchange for series dated Mar. 3, 1964		36,599,000.00	
	Issued for cash		964,106,000.00	
3	Treasury bonds, foreign currency series, maturing Sept. 6, 1966	4.11	25,164,537.36	
	Treasury bills:			
	Regular weekly:			
4	Dated Sept. 3, 1964	[4] 3.765		
	Redeemed in exchange for series issued Mar. 4, 1965, due June 3, 1965			228,534,000.00
	Redeemed in exchange for series dated Mar. 4, 1965, due Sept. 2, 1965			135,465,000.00
	Redeemable for cash			1,736,512,000.00
4	Maturing June 3, 1965	3.982		
	Issued in exchange for series dated Sept. 3, 1964		228,534,000.00	
	Issued for cash		971,663,000.00	
4	Maturing Sept. 2, 1965	4.037		
	Issued in exchange for series dated Sept. 3, 1964		135,465,000.00	
	Issued for cash		864,834,000.00	
8	Certificates of indebtedness, foreign series maturing:			
	June 8, 1965	4.00	50,000,000.00	
9	Mar. 9, 1965	3.85		30,000,000.00
	June 9, 1965	3.95	15,000,000.00	
	Treasury bills:			
	Regular weekly:			
11	Dated Sept. 10, 1964	[4] 3.747		
	Redeemed in exchange for series issued Mar. 11, 1965, due June 10, 1965			184,384,000.00
	Redeemed in exchange for series dated Mar. 11, 1965, due Sept. 9, 1965			75,876,000.00
	Redeemable for cash			1,941,579,000.00

Footnotes at end of table.

TABLE 44.—*Issues, maturities, and redemptions of interest-bearing public debt securities, excluding special issues, July 1964-June 1965*—Continued

Date	Securities	Rate of interest [1]	Amount issued [2]	Amount matured or called or redeemed prior to maturity [3]
	Treasury bills—Continued			
1965	Regular weekly—Continued	*Percent*		
Mar. 11	Maturing June 10, 1965	3. 948		
	Issued in exchange for series dated Sept. 10, 1964		$184,384,000.00	
	Issued for cash		1,016,370,000.00	
11	Maturing Sept. 9, 1965	4. 001		
	Issued in exchange for series dated Sept. 10, 1964		75,876,000.00	
	Issued for cash		924,479,000.00	
16	Certificates of indebtedness, foreign series, maturing:			
	Mar. 16, 1965	3. 90		$30,000,000.00
	June 16, 1965	3. 95	30,000,000.00	
	Mar. 22, 1965	3. 90		5,000,000.00
	Treasury bills:			
	Regular weekly:			
18	Dated Sept. 17, 1964	[4] 3. 794		
	Redeemed in exchange for series issued Mar. 18, 1965, due June 17, 1965			188,121,000.00
	Redeemed in exchange for series dated Mar. 18, 1965, due Sept. 16, 1965			54,174,000.00
	Redeemable for cash			1,958,565,000.00
18	Maturing June 17, 1965	3. 917		
	Issued in exchange for series dated Sept. 17, 1964		188,121,000.00	
	Issued for cash		1,012,872,000.00	
18	Maturing Sept. 16, 1965	3. 990		
	Issued in exchange for series dated Sept. 17, 1964		54,174,000.00	
	Issued for cash		948,352,000.00	
	Tax anticipation:			
22	Dated Sept. 2, 1964	[4] 3. 542		
	Redeemable for cash			2,504,160,000.00
22	Certificates of indebtedness, foreign series, maturing:			
	Mar. 22, 1965	3. 75		25,000,000.00
	June 22, 1965	3. 75	25,000,000.00	
23	Treasury bonds, maturing June 30, 1967	4. 00		11,892,247.04
25	Certificates of indebtedness, foreign series, maturing May 10, 1965	3. 90		10,000,000.00
	Regular weekly:			
25	Dated Sept. 24, 1964	[4] 3. 793		
	Redeemed in exchange for series dated Mar. 25, 1965, due June 24, 1965			166,420,000.00
	Redeemed in exchange for series issued Mar. 25, 1965, due Sept. 23, 1965			140,841,000.00
	Redeemable for cash			1,801,479,000.00
25	Maturing June 24, 1965	3. 922		
	Issued in exchange for series dated Sept. 24, 1964		166,420,000.00	
	Issued for cash		1,036,334,000.00	
25	Maturing Sept. 23, 1965	3. 984		
	Issued in exchange for series dated Sept. 24, 1964		140,841,000.00	
	Issued for cash		859,616,000.00	
30	Certificates of indebtedness, foreign series, maturing:			
	Mar. 30, 1965	3. 75		20,000,000.00
	June 30, 1965	3. 75	20,000,000.00	
31	Treasury certificates, maturing:			
	Mar. 31, 1965	3. 867		10,355,688.18
	June 30, 1965	3. 921	10,455,801.80	
	Treasury bills:			
	Other:			
31	Dated Apr. 8, 1964	3. 719		
	Redeemed in exchange for series issued Mar. 31, 1965, due Mar. 31, 1966			49,318,000.00
	Redeemable for cash			952,146,000.00
31	Maturing Mar. 31, 1966	3. 987		
	Issued in exchange for series dated Apr. 8, 1964		49,318,000.00	
	Issued for cash		950,986,000.00	
31	U.S. savings bonds: [6]			
	Series E-1941	[7] 3. 223	378,183.10	2,772,557.90
	Series E-1942	[7] 3. 252	3,041,660.74	12,490,479.05
	Series E-1943	[7] 3. 277	9,417,308.65	20,380,766.00

Footnotes at end of table.

TABLE 44.—*Issues, maturities, and redemptions of interest-bearing public debt securities, excluding special issues, July 1964–June 1965*—Continued

Date	Securities	Rate of interest [1]	Amount issued [2]	Amount matured or called or redeemed prior to maturity [3]
1965		*Percent*		
Mar. 31	U.S. savings bonds [4]—Continued			
	Series E-1944	[7] 3.298	$3,397,039.46	$30,029,914.53
	Series E-1945	[7] 3.316	3,662,355.75	23,279,228.43
	Series E-1946	[7] 3.327	3,114,980.37	10,986,553.51
	Series E-1947	[7] 3.346	3,399,194.79	11,989,228.44
	Series E-1948	[7] 3.366	3,584,796.19	13,122,967.04
	Series E-1949	[7] 3.344	3,979,295.65	13,570,756.67
	Series E-1950	[7] 3.347	3,827,289.04	13,345,111.79
	Series E-1951	[7] 3.378	3,220,759.11	11,884,380.62
	Series E-1952 (January to April)	3.400	1,654,069.88	4,332,511.33
	Series E-1952 (May to December)	[7] 3.451	1,979,948.37	9,219,769.00
	Series E-1953	[7] 3.468	5,520,094.93	18,270,581.35
	Series E-1954	[7] 3.497	5,889,079.57	26,105,843.46
	Series E-1955	[7] 3.522	10,447,841.88	23,342,598.67
	Series E-1956	[7] 3.546	5,845,232.12	13,659,081.43
	Series E-1957 (January)	3.560	8.66	1,261,116.97
	Series E-1957 (February to December)	[7] 3.653	5,413,032.06	12,790,418.05
	Series E-1958	[7] 3.690	5,909,376.52	15,172,804.51
	Series E-1959 (January to May)	3.730	2,812,738.62	9,167,044.83
	Series E-1959 (June to December)	3.750	2,660,653.02	13,201,585.08
	Series E-1960	3.750	6,214,350.61	16,574,433.77
	Series E-1961	3.750	6,639,748.56	24,354,684.95
	Series E-1962	3.750	6,138,752.09	23,209,414.78
	Series E-1963	3.750	7,443,223.48	35,075,607.08
	Series E-1964	3.750	169,516,912.59	162,540,566.30
	Series E-1965	3.750	370,402,293.69	113,756.25
	Unclassified sales and redemptions		[8] −159,923,434.87	[8] −142,398,106.00
	Series H-1952	[7] 3.392		1,102,500.00
	Series H-1953	[7] 3.409		3,021,000.00
	Series H-1954	[7] 3.439		9,024,000.00
	Series H-1955	[7] 3.467		14,732,500.00
	Series H-1956	[7] 3.496		4,697,000.00
	Series H-1957 (January)	3.526		350,000.00
	Series H-1957 (February to December)	[7] 3.626		3,292,000.00
	Series H-1958	[7] 3.679		5,048,500.00
	Series H-1959 (January to May)	3.720		2,058,500.00
	Series H-1959 (June to December)	3.750		2,134,500.00
	Series H-1960	3.750		5,538,000.00
	Series H-1961	3.750		5,801,500.00
	Series H-1962	3.750		4,549,500.00
	Series H-1963	3.750	22,000.00	4,543,500.00
	Series H-1964	3.750	1,821,000.00	3,317,000.00
	Series H-1965	3.750	54,592,000.00	64,000.00
	Unclassified sales and redemptions		[8] −704,000.00	[8] −24,984,500.00
	Series J-1953	2.76	181,964.40	4,700,823.00
	Series J-1954	2.76	315,991.52	1,281,355.40
	Series J-1955	2.76	319,405.80	1,268,314.44
	Series J-1956	2.76	240,820.30	1,135,641.15
	Series J-1957	2.76	81,566.45	449,053.85
	Unclassified redemptions			[8] −1,588,053.06
	Series K-1953	2.76		13,102,000.00
	Series K-1954	2.76		5,055,000.00
	Series K-1955	2.76		3,973,500.00
	Series K-1956	2.76		2,114,500.00
	Series K-1957	2.76		615,500.00
	Unclassified redemptions			[8] −7,629,500.00
31	Treasury bonds of 1966	3¾		−11,004,500.00
	Adjustments of redemptions [9]			
31	Treasury bonds of 1967	3⅝		−91,500.00
	Adjustments of redemptions [9]			
31	Treasury notes, Series B-1965	3½		−979,000.00
	Adjustments of redemptions [9]			
31	Treasury notes, Series E-1965	4.00		−247,000.00
	Adjustments of redemptions [9]			
31	Treasury notes, Series B-1966	3⅝		624,000.00
	Adjustments of redemptions [9]			
31	Treasury notes, Series C-1966	3⅞		3,389,000.00
	Adjustments of redemptions [9]			
31	Treasury notes, Series A-1967	3¾		1,170,000.00
	Adjustments of redemptions [9]			
31	Treasury bonds of 1970	4.00		
	Adjustments of issues [9]		−482,000.00	
31	Treasury bonds of 1974	4⅛		
	Adjustments of issues [9]		3,477,000.00	
31	Treasury bonds of 1987–92	4¼		
	Adjustments of issues [9]		−10,127,500.00	
31	U.S. retirement plan bonds	3.75	108,851.69	10,655.67
31	Depositary bonds, First Series	2.00	396,000.00	11,673,000.00

Footnotes at end of table

TABLE 44.—*Issues, maturities, and redemptions of interest-bearing public debt securities, excluding special issues, July 1964–June 1965*—Continued

Date	Securities	Rate of interest [1]	Amount issued [2]	Amount matured or called or redeemed prior to maturity [3]
1965		*Percent*		
Mar. 31	Treasury bonds, REA Series_____	2.00	$269,000.00	$390,000.00
31	Treasury bonds, Investment Series B–1975–80_	2¾	_____	_____
	Redeemed in exchange for 1½% Treasury notes, Series EO–1969_____		_____	21,820,000.00
31	Treasury notes, Series EO–1969_____	1½	21,820,000.00	_____
31	Miscellaneous_____		_____	69,212,800.00
	Total March_____		11,552,883,223.95	13,854,922,681.46
Apr. 1	Treasury notes, Series EA–1965_____	1½	_____	_____
	Redeemable for cash_____		_____	465,673,000.00
1	Treasury certificates, maturing June 30, 1965__	3.921	16,980,000.00	_____
1	Certificates of indebtedness, foreign series, maturing July 1, 1965_____	3.95	100,000,000.00	_____
	Treasury bills:			
	Regular weekly:			
1	Dated Oct. 1, 1964_____	[4] 3.800	_____	_____
	Redeemed in exchange for series issued Apr. 1, 1965, due July 1, 1965_____		_____	198,776,000.00
	Redeemed in exchange for series dated Apr. 1, 1965, due Sept. 30, 1965_____		_____	144,444,000.00
	Redeemable for cash_____		_____	1,756,967,000.00
1	Maturing July 1, 1965_____	3.921	_____	_____
	Issued in exchange for series dated Oct. 1, 1964_____		198,776,000.00	_____
	Issued for cash_____		1,001,390,000.00	_____
1	Maturing Sept. 30, 1965_____	3.993	_____	_____
	Issued in exchange for series dated Oct. 1, 1964_____		144,444,000.00	_____
	Issued for cash_____		857,619,000.00	_____
8	Dated Oct. 8, 1964_____	[4] 3.791	_____	_____
	Redeemed in exchange for series issued Apr. 8, 1965, due July 8, 1965_____		_____	191,332,000.00
	Redeemed in exchange for series dated Apr. 8, 1965, due Oct. 7, 1965_____		_____	92,530,000.00
	Redeemable for cash_____		_____	1,719,154,000.00
8	Maturing July 8, 1965_____	3.942	_____	_____
	Issued in exchange for series dated Oct. 8, 1964_____		191,332,000.00	_____
	Issued for cash_____		1,010,487,000.00	_____
8	Maturing Oct. 7, 1965_____	3.993	_____	_____
	Issued in exchange for series dated Oct. 8, 1964_____		92,530,000.00	_____
	Issued for cash_____		908,731,000.00	_____
12	Treasury certificates, maturing June 30, 1965_	3.921	_____	212,966.47
12	Certificates of indebtedness, foreign series, maturing:			
	Apr. 12, 1965_____	3.75	_____	5,000,000.00
	July 12, 1965_____	3.75	5,000,000.00	_____
14	May 10, 1965_____	3.90	_____	5,000,000.00
14	Treasury certificates, maturing Apr. 30, 1965_	3.41	120,905,227.51	_____
	Treasury bills:			
	Regular weekly:			
15	Dated Oct. 15, 1964_____	[4] 3.772	_____	_____
	Redeemed in exchange for series issued Apr. 15, 1965, due July 15, 1965_____		_____	171,422,000.00
	Redeemed in exchange for series dated Apr. 15, 1965, due Oct. 14, 1965_____		_____	86,422,000.00
	Redeemable for cash_____		_____	1,846,273,000.00
15	Maturing July 15, 1965_____	3.937	_____	_____
	Issued in exchange for series dated Oct. 15, 1964_____		171,422,000.00	_____
	Issued for cash_____		1,029,246,000.00	_____
15	Maturing Oct. 14, 1965_____	3.991	_____	_____
	Issued in exchange for series dated Oct. 15, 1964_____		86,422,000.00	_____
	Issued for cash_____		914,277,000.00	_____
20	Treasury bonds, foreign currency series, maturing:			
	Apr. 20, 1965_____	3.61	_____	23,174,433.96
	July 20, 1966_____	4.02	23,025,558.37	_____
20	Certificates of indebtedness, foreign series, maturing:			
	Apr. 20, 1965_____	3.85	_____	5,000,000.00
22	Apr. 22, 1965_____	3.85	_____	50,000,000.00
	July 22, 1965_____	3.95	50,000,000.00	_____

Footnotes at end of table.

TABLE 44.—*Issues, maturities, and redemptions of interest-bearing public debt securities, excluding special issues, July 1964–June 1965*—Continued

Date	Securities	Rate of interest [1]	Amount issued [2]	Amount matured or called or redeemed prior to maturity [3]
	Treasury bills:			
1965	Regular weekly:	*Percent*		
Apr. 22	Dated Oct. 22, 1964_____	[4] 3.784	_____	_____
	Redeemed in exchange for series issued Apr. 22, 1965, due July 22, 1965__	_____	_____	$219,233,000.00
	Redeemed in exchange for series dated Apr. 22, 1965 due Oct. 21, 1965_____	_____	_____	155,258,000.00
	Redeemable for cash_____	_____	_____	1,826,560,000.00
22	Maturing July 22, 1965_____	3.946	_____	_____
	Issued in exchange for series dated Oct. 22, 1964_____	_____	$219,233,000.00	_____
	Issued for cash_____	_____	982,331,000.00	_____
22	Maturing Oct. 21, 1965_____	4.008		_____
	Issued in exchange for series dated Oct. 22, 1964_____	_____	155,258,000.00	_____
	Issued for cash_____	_____	846,264,000.00	_____
29	Dated Oct. 29, 1964_____	[4] 3.792		205,496,000.00
	Redeemed in exchange for series issued Apr. 29, 1965, due July 29, 1965_____	_____	_____	205,496,000.00
	Redeemed in exchange for series dated Apr. 29, 1965, due Oct. 28, 1965_____	_____	_____	153,200,000.00
	Redeemable for cash_____	_____	_____	1,846,923,000.00
29	Maturing July 29, 1965_____	3.916		_____
	Issued in exchange for series dated Oct. 29, 1964_____	_____	205,496,000.00	_____
	Issued for cash_____	_____	995,602,000.00	_____
29	Maturing Oct. 28, 1965_____	3.978		_____
	Issued in exchange for series dated Oct. 29, 1964_____	_____	153,200,000.00	_____
	Issued for cash_____	_____	850,075,000.00	_____
	Other:			
30	Dated May 6, 1964_____	3.705		_____
	Redeemed in exchange for series dated Apr. 30, 1965, due Apr. 30, 1966_____	_____	_____	120,884,000.00
	Redeemable for cash_____	_____	_____	880,555,000.00
30	Maturing Apr. 30, 1966_____	3.996		_____
	Issued in exchange for series dated May 6, 1964_____	_____	120,884,000.00	_____
	Issued for cash_____	_____	880,278,000.00	_____
30	Treasury certificates, maturing Apr. 30, 1965__	3.41		120,905,227.51
30	Treasury certificates, maturing May 31, 1965__	3.45	121,031,737.44	
30	U.S. savings bonds: [5]			
	Series E-1941_____	[7] 3.223	453,053.85	1,956,179.21
	Series E-1942_____	[7] 3.252	3,139,030.49	8,618,291.68
	Series E-1943_____	[7] 3.277	7,260,708.20	14,579,179.92
	Series E-1944_____	[7] 3.298	3,098,967.94	18,435,988.17
	Series E-1945_____	[7] 3.316	4,502,051.95	16,074,877.14
	Series E-1946_____	[7] 3.327	3,199,852.23	7,380,150.72
	Series E-1947_____	[7] 3.346	3,203,827.06	7,979,348.50
	Series E-1948_____	[7] 3.366	3,426,583.64	8,686,884.11
	Series E-1949_____	[7] 3.344	3,685,727.17	9,414,588.49
	Series E-1950_____	[7] 3.347	3,503,100.07	8,988,513.47
	Series E-1951_____	[7] 3.378	3,258,346.88	8,266,528.63
	Series E-1952 (January to April)_____	3.400	1,460,897.58	3,070,425.06
	Series E-1952 (May to December)_____	[7] 3.451	1,773,410.75	6,087,357.08
	Series E-1953_____	[7] 3.468	4,297,371.72	12,540,252.50
	Series E-1954_____	[7] 3.497	4,742,899.50	16,755,241.80
	Series E-1955_____	[7] 3.522	8,874,748.37	19,684,040.47
	Series E-1956_____	[7] 3.546	5,772,160.87	10,157,149.92
	Series E-1957 (January)_____	3.560	−27,844.74	858,835.53
	Series E-1957 (February to December)____	[7] 3.653	5,617,058.08	9,328,247.61
	Series E-1958_____	[7] 3.690	5,951,692.39	10,546,509.85
	Series E-1959 (January to May)_____	3.730	2,685,332.68	5,374,350.97
	Series E-1959 (June to December)_____	3.750	3,213,345.14	7,407,343.27
	Series E-1960_____	3.750	6,341,837.31	12,032,464.77
	Series E-1961_____	3.750	6,766,185.18	17,539,392.63
	Series E-1962_____	3.750	6,451,891.21	16,780,321.91
	Series E-1963_____	3.750	8,271,276.30	26,891,570.33
	Series E-1964_____	3.750	11,614,430.90	100,734,990.88
	Series E-1965_____	3.750	357,273,562.50	38,371,462.50
	Unclassified sales and redemptions_____	_____	[8] −8,535,058.07	16,560,693.64
	Series H-1952_____	[7] 3.392	_____	552,000.00
	Series H-1953_____	[7] 3.409	_____	1,433,500.00
	Series H-1954_____	[7] 3.439	_____	4,025,500.00
	Series H-1955_____	[7] 3.467	_____	10,963,500.00
	Series H-1956_____	[7] 3.496	_____	2,239,000.00
	Series H-1957 (January)_____	3.520	_____	175,500.00

Footnotes at end of table.

TABLE 44.—*Issues, maturities, and redemptions of interest-bearing public debt securities, excluding special issues, July 1964–June 1965*—Continued

Date	Securities	Rate of interest [1]	Amount issued [2]	Amount matured or called or redeemed prior to maturity [3]
1965		*Percent*		
Apr. 30	U.S. savings bonds [6]—Continued			
	Series H-1957 (February to December)___	[7] 3.626	------------------	$1,796,000.00
	Series H-1958_____	[7] 3.679	------------------	2,465,500.00
	Series H-1959 (January to May)_____	3.720	------------------	1,067,500.00
	Series H-1959 (June to December)_____	3.750	------------------	1,065,500.00
	Series H-1960_____	3.750	------------------	3,343,000.00
	Series H-1961_____	3.750	------------------	2,839,500.00
	Series H-1962_____	3.750	------------------	2,296,000.00
	Series H-1963_____	3.750	$10,500.00	2,117,000.00
	Series H-1964_____	3.750	436,000.00	1,860,500.00
	Series H-1965_____	3.750	54,429,500.00	92,500.00
	Unclassified sales and redemptions_____	---------	[8] —3,313,500.00	[8] —1,951,000.00
	Series J-1953_____	2.76	168,103.60	5,375,290.00
	Series J-1954_____	2.76	326,241.60	853,244.00
	Series J-1955_____	2.76	333,495.96	686,979.14
	Series J-1956_____	2.76	181,256.95	593,479.10
	Series J-1957_____	2.76	82,714.45	217,185.10
	Unclassified redemptions_____	----------	------------------	[8] —807,657.30
	Series K-1953_____	2.76	------------------	11,564,000.00
	Series K-1954_____	2.76	------------------	2,586,500.00
	Series K-1955_____	2.76	------------------	2,692,000.00
	Series K-1956_____	2.76	------------------	1,040,000.00
	Series K-1957_____	2.76	------------------	218,500.00
	Unclassified redemptions_____	----------	------------------	[8] —2,646,000.00
30	U.S. retirement plan bonds_____	3.75	129,254.98	14,633.97
30	Depositary bonds, First Series_____	2.00	915,000.00	21,899,000.00
30	Treasury bonds, REA Series_____	2.00	225,000.00	323,000.00
30	Treasury bonds, Investment Series B-1975-80_____	2¾	------------------	------------------
	Redeemed in exchange for Treasury notes:			
	Series EO-1969_____	----------	------------------	34,033,000.00
	Series EA-1970_____	----------	------------------	2,467,000.00
30	Treasury notes, Series EO-1969_____	1½	34,033,000.00	------------------
30	Treasury notes, Series EA-1970_____	1½	2,467,000.00	------------------
30	Miscellaneous_____	----------	------------------	31,574,500.00
	Total April_____	----------	13,013,939,538.01	12,880,561,462.71
	Treasury bills:			
	Regular weekly:			
May 6	Dated Nov. 5, 1964_____	[4] 3.811	------------------	------------------
	Redeemed in exchange for series issued May 6, 1965, due Aug. 5, 1965_____	----------	------------------	229,265,000.00
	Redeemed in exchange for series dated May 6, 1965, due Nov. 4, 1965_____	----------	------------------	161,892,000.00
	Redeemable for cash_____	----------	------------------	1,811,320,000.00
6	Maturing Aug. 5, 1965_____	3.901	------------------	------------------
	Issued in exchange for series dated Nov. 5, 1964_____	----------	229,265,000.00	------------------
	Issued for cash_____	----------	971,271,000.00	------------------
6	Maturing Nov. 4, 1965_____	3.950	------------------	------------------
	Issued in exchange for series dated Nov. 5, 1964_____	----------	161,892,000.00	------------------
	Issued for cash_____	----------	838,522,000.00	------------------
13	Dated Nov. 12, 1964_____	[4] 3.830	------------------	------------------
	Redeemed in exchange for series issued May 13, 1965, due Aug. 12, 1965_____	----------	------------------	223,098,000.00
	Redeemed in exchange for series dated May 13, 1965, due Nov. 12, 1965____	----------	------------------	134,210,000.00
	Redeemable for cash_____	----------	------------------	1,843,366,000.00
13	Maturing Aug. 12, 1965_____	3.893	------------------	------------------
	Issued in exchange for series dated Nov. 12, 1964_____	----------	223,098,000.00	------------------
	Issued for cash_____	----------	977,871,000.00	------------------
13	Maturing Nov. 12, 1965_____	3.950	------------------	------------------
	Issued in exchange for series dated Nov. 12, 1964_____	----------	134,210,000.00	------------------
	Issued for cash_____	----------	866,647,000.00	------------------
17	Treasury notes, Series A-1965_____	4⅝	------------------	------------------
	Redeemed in exchange for:			
	4% Treasury notes, Series A-1966_____	----------	------------------	796,594,000.00
	4¼% Treasury bonds of 1974 (additional issue)_____	----------	------------------	733,811,000.00
	Redeemable for cash_____	----------	------------------	285,305,000.00

Footnotes at end of table.

TABLE 44.—*Issues, maturities, and redemptions of interest-bearing public debt securities, excluding special issues, July 1964–June 1965*—Continued

Date	Securities	Rate of interest [1]	Amount issued [2]	Amount matured or called or redeemed prior to maturity [3]
1965		*Percent*		
May 17	Treasury notes, Series C-1965	3⅞		
	Redeemed in exchange for:			
	4% Treasury notes, Series A-1965			$5,107,409,000.00
	4¼% Treasury bonds of 1974 (additional issue)			1,326,852,000.00
	Redeemable for cash			185,856,000.00
17	Treasury notes, Series A-1966	4.00		
	Issued in exchange for:			
	4⅝% Treasury notes, Series A-1965		$796,594,000.00	
	3⅞% Treasury notes, Series C-1965		5,107,409,000.00	
17	Treasury bonds of 1974 (additional issue)	4¼		
	Issued in exchange for:			
	4⅝% Treasury notes, Series A-1965		733,811,000.00	
	3⅞% Treasury notes, Series C-1965		1,326,852,000.00	
17	Treasury bonds, foreign currency series, maturing:			
	May 16, 1965	3.26		20,055,151.67
	May 16, 1967	4.08	20,150,118.38	
18	Certificates of indebtedness, foreign series, maturing Aug. 18, 1965	3.90	50,000,000.00	
	Treasury bills:			
	Regular weekly:			
20	Dated Nov. 19, 1964	[4] 3.861		
	Redeemed in exchange for series issued May 20, 1965, due Aug. 19, 1965			187,615,000.00
	Redeemed in exchange for series dated May 20, 1965 due Nov. 18, 1965			105,007,000.00
	Redeemable for cash			1,908,272,000.00
20	Maturing Aug. 19, 1965	3.897		
	Issued in exchange for series dated Nov. 19, 1964		187,615,000.00	
	Issued for cash		1,013,276,000.00	
20	Maturing Nov. 18, 1965	3.955		
	Issued in exchange for series dated Nov. 19, 1964		105,007,000.00	
	Issued for cash		896,771,000.00	
20	Treasury bonds, foreign currency series, maturing:			
	May 20, 1965	3.22		10,029,335.81
	May 22, 1967	4.09	10,074,551.68	
25	Certificates of indebtedness, foreign series, maturing:			
	June 8, 1965	4.00		32,000,000.00
	June 9, 1965	3.95		15,000,000.00
	June 16, 1965	3.95		30,000,000.00
	July 22, 1965	3.95		50,000,000.00
	Aug. 25, 1965	3.90	100,000,000.00	
	Treasury bills:			
	Regular weekly:			
27	Dated Nov. 27, 1964	[4] 3.968		
	Redeemed in exchange for series issued May 27, 1965, due Aug. 26, 1965			216,539,000.00
	Redeemed in exchange for series dated May 27, 1965, due Nov. 26, 1965			143,374,000.00
	Redeemable for cash			1,841,106,000.00
27	Maturing Aug. 26, 1965	3.889		
	Issued in exchange for series dated Nov. 27, 1964		216,539,000.00	
	Issued for cash		983,121,000.00	
27	Maturing Nov. 26, 1965	3.944		
	Issued in exchange for series dated Nov. 27, 1965		143,374,000.00	
	Issued for cash		857,411,000.00	
	Other:			
31	Dated June 2, 1964	3.719		
	Redeemed for cash			[11] 90,993,000.00
31	Maturing May 31, 1966	3.954		
	Issued for cash		[12] 3,063,000.00	
31	Treasur certificates maturing:			
	May 31, 1965	3.45		121,031,737.44
	June 30, 1965	3.54	91,368,211.16	
31	U.S. savings bonds: [6]			
	Series E-1941	[7] 3.223	834,272.88	1,449,958.46
	Series E-1942	[7] 3.252	3,311,082.02	7,219,804.90
	Series E-1943	[7] 3.277	3,877,470.76	12,352,793.20
	Series E-1944	[7] 3.298	5,285,236.70	14,631,132.01
	Series E-1945	[7] 3.316	10,896,437.48	13,563,800.01
	Series E-1946	[7] 3.327	3,179,097.42	6,276,058.26

Footnotes at end of table.

TABLE 44.—*Issues, maturities, and redemptions of interest-bearing public debt securities, excluding special issues, July 1964–June 1965*—Continued

Date	Securities	Rate of interest [1]	Amount issued [2]	Amount matured or called or redeemed prior to maturity [3]
1965		*Percent*		
May 31	U.S. savings bonds [6]—Continued			
	Series E-1947	[7] 3.346	$2, 925, 729. 00	$6, 458, 987. 03
	Series E-1948	[7] 3.366	3, 427, 495. 18	7, 309, 083. 02
	Series E-1949	[7] 3.344	3, 607, 592. 41	7, 523, 328. 16
	Series E-1950	[7] 3.347	3, 392, 129. 13	7, 270, 475. 42
	Series E-1951	[7] 3.378	3, 041, 060. 76	6, 508, 539. 63
	Series E-1952 (January to April)	3. 400	−27, 200. 52	2, 867, 217. 22
	Series E-1952 (May to December)	[7] 3.451	1, 724, 240. 70	4, 974, 499. 85
	Series E-1953	[7] 3.468	4, 249, 388. 50	10, 294, 186. 43
	Series E-1954	[7] 3.497	4, 492, 075. 05	13, 195, 918. 08
	Series E-1955	[7] 3.522	8, 298, 758. 54	16, 979, 413. 84
	Series E-1956	[7] 3.546	5, 588, 925. 97	8, 449, 475. 13
	Series E-1957 (January)	3. 560	−24. 38	633, 653. 02
	Series E-1957 (February to December)	[7] 3.653	5, 830, 562. 42	7, 963, 154. 03
	Series E-1958	[7] 3.690	5, 565, 617. 59	8, 885, 405. 12
	Series E-1959 (January to May)	3. 730	2, 508, 827, 84	4, 464, 639. 74
	Series E-1959 (June to December)	3. 750	2, 940, 197. 60	6, 335, 545. 01
	Series E-1960	3. 750	5, 834, 850. 19	10, 090, 389, 99
	Series E-1961	3. 750	6, 420. 067. 62	13, 416, 193. 58
	Series E-1962	3. 750	6, 219, 199. 41	14, 081, 614. 58
	Series E-1963	3. 750	7, 241, 334. 27	22, 464, 326. 98
	Series E-1964	3. 750	5, 851, 582. 94	71, 740, 103. 65
	Series E-1965	3. 750	298, 182, 756. 75	55, 307, 512. 50
	Unclassified sales and redemptions		27, 817, 558. 73	19, 436, 542. 14
	Series H-1952	[7] 3.392		45, 500. 00
	Series H-1953	[7] 3.409		141, 000. 00
	Series H-1954	[7] 3.439		387, 000. 00
	Series H-1955	[7] 3.467		4, 671, 000. 00
	Series H-1956	[7] 3.496		207, 500. 00
	Series H-1957 (January)	3. 520		5, 500. 00
	Series H-1957 (February to December)	[7] 3.626		129, 500. 00
	Series H-1958	[7] 3.679		187, 500. 00
	Series H-1959 (January to May)	3. 720		86, 500. 00
	Series H-1959 (June to December)	3. 750		89, 000. 00
	Series H-1960	3. 750		220, 500. 00
	Series H-1961	3. 750		118, 000. 00
	Series H-1962	3. 750		160, 500. 00
	Series H-1963	3. 750		190, 000. 00
	Series H-1964	3. 750	112, 500. 00	172, 500. 00
	Series H-1965	3. 750	51, 585, 500. 00	53, 000. 00
	Unclassified sales and redemptions		[8] −7, 495, 000. 00	33, 763, 000. 00
	Series J-1953	2. 76	183, 772. 00	3, 663, 263. 60
	Series J-1954	2. 76	362, 238. 80	15, 730. 80
	Series J-1955	2. 76	285, 102. 15	95, 334. 15
	Series J-1956	2. 76	178, 713. 15	101, 389. 80
	Series J-1957	2. 76	−309. 75	9, 833. 60
	Unclassified redemptions			2, 088, 414. 66
	Series K-1953	2. 76		6, 511, 000. 00
	Series K-1954	2. 76		113, 500. 00
	Series K-1955	2. 76		235, 000. 00
	Series K-1956	2. 76		112, 500. 00
	Series K-1957	2. 76		7, 000. 00
	Unclassified redemptions			9, 119, 000. 00
31	Treasury bonds of 1967	3⅝		
	Adjustments of redemptions [9]			565, 000. 00
31	Treasury bonds of 1974	4⅛		
	Adjustments of issues [9]		679, 000. 00	
31	U.S. retirement plan bonds	3. 75	108, 829. 21	6, 806. 12
31	Depositary bonds, First Series	2. 00	666, 000. 00	11, 233, 500. 00
31	Treasury bonds, REA Series	2. 00	275, 000. 00	100, 000. 00
31	Treasury bonds, Investment Series, B-1975–80	2¾		
	Redeemed in exchange for 1½% Treasury notes, Series EA-1970			3, 089, 000. 00
31	Treasury notes, Series EA-1970	1½	3, 089, 000. 00	
31	Miscellaneous			33, 016, 600. 00
	Total May			17, 537, 758, 549. 74	18, 102, 854, 348. 64

Footnotes at end of table.

TABLE 44.—*Issues, maturities, and redemptions of interest-bearing public debt securities, excluding special issues, July 1964–June 1965*—Continued

Date	Securities	Rate of interest [1]	Amount issued [2]	Amount matured or called or redeemed prior to maturity [3]
	Treasury bills:			
1965	Other:	*Percent*		
June 1	Dated June 2, 1964	3. 719		
	Redeemed in exchange for series dated May 31, 1965, due May 31, 1966			[11] $100, 282, 000. 00
	Redeemable for cash			[11] 808, 866, 000. 00
1	Maturing May 31, 1966	3. 954		
	Issued in exchange for series dated June 2, 1964		[12] $100, 282, 000. 00	
	Issued for cash		[12] 897, 541, 000. 00	
	Regular weekly:			
3	Dated Dec. 3, 1964	[4] 4. 004		
	Redeemed in exchange for series issued June 3, 1965, due Sept. 2, 1965			227, 344, 000. 00
	Redeemed in exchange for series dated June 3, 1965, due Dec. 2, 1965			116, 327, 000. 00
	Redeemable for cash			1, 856, 577, 000. 00
3	Maturing Sept. 2, 1965	3. 870		
	Issued in exchange for series dated Dec. 3, 1964		227, 344, 000. 00	
	Issued for cash		975, 008, 000. 00	
3	Maturing Dec. 2, 1965	3. 924		
	Issued in exchange for series dated Dec. 3, 1964		116, 327, 000. 00	
	Issued for cash		884, 850, 000. 00	
8	Certificates of indebtedness, foreign series, maturing:			
	June 8, 1965	4. 00		18, 000, 000. 00
	Sept. 8, 1965	3. 80	18, 000, 000. 00	
	Treasury bills:			
	Regular weekly:			
10	Dated Dec. 10, 1964	[4] 3. 946		
	Redeemed in exchange for series issued June 10, 1965, due Sept. 9, 1965			175, 624, 000. 00
	Redeemed in exchange for series dated June 10, 1965, due Dec. 9, 1965			104, 139, 000. 00
	Redeemable for cash			1, 921, 569, 000. 00
10	Maturing Sept. 9, 1965	3. 781		
	Issued in exchange for series dated Dec. 10, 1964		175, 624, 000. 00	
	Issued for cash		1, 024, 630, 000. 00	
10	Maturing Dec. 9, 1965	3. 863		
	Issued in exchange for series dated Dec. 10, 1964		104, 139, 000. 00	
	Issued for cash		896, 155, 000. 00	
11	Treasury bonds, foreign currency series, maturing:			
	June 11, 1965	3. 83		25, 162, 102. 00
	Dec. 12, 1966	4. 04	25, 176, 721. 22	
	Treasury certificates, maturing:			
14	Dec. 15, 1965	1. 00	2, 500, 000. 00	
15	June 15, 1965	1. 00		10, 075, 456. 97
15	Dec. 15, 1965	1. 00	3, 691, 254. 40	
	Treasury bills:			
	Regular weekly:			
17	Dated Dec. 17, 1964	[4] 3. 939		
	Redeemed in exchange for series issued June 17, 1965, due Sept. 16, 1965			185, 303, 000. 00
	Redeemed in exchange for series dated June 17, 1965, due Dec. 16, 1965			114, 879, 000. 00
	Redeemable for cash			1, 901, 415, 000. 00
17	Maturing Sept. 16, 1965	3. 799		
	Issued in exchange for series dated Dec. 17, 1964		185, 303, 000. 00	
	Issued for cash		1, 015, 367, 000. 00	
17	Maturing Dec. 16, 1965	3. 873		
	Issued in exchange for series dated Dec. 17, 1964		114, 879, 000. 00	
	Issued for cash		886, 500, 000. 00	

Footnotes at end of table.

TABLE 44.—*Issues, maturities, and redemptions of interest-bearing public debt securities, excluding special issues, July 1964–June 1965*—Continued

Date	Securities	Rate of interest [1]	Amount issued [2]	Amount matured or called or redeemed prior to maturity [3]
1965		*Percent*		
June 22	Certificates of indebtedness, foreign series, maturing:			
	June 22, 1965	3.75		$25,000,000.00
	June 22, 1965	3.875		50,000,000.00
	Sept. 22, 1965	3.75	$25,000,000.00	
	Dec. 22, 1965	3.875	50,000,000.00	
	Treasury bills:			
	Tax anticipation:			
22	Dated Nov. 24, 1964	[4] 3.671		
	Redeemable for cash			3,262,836,000.00
	Regular weekly:			
24	Dated Dec. 24, 1964	[4] 3.939		
	Redeemed in exchange for series issued June 24, 1965, due Sept. 23, 1965			204,098,000.00
	Redeemed in exchange for series dated June 24, 1965, due Dec. 23, 1965			86,620,000.00
	Redeemable for cash			1,916,943,000.00
24	Maturing Sept. 23, 1965	3.789		
	Issued in exchange for series dated Dec. 24, 1964		204,098,000.00	
	Issued for cash		1,001,183,000.00	
24	Maturing Dec. 23, 1965	3.831		
	Issued in exchange for series dated Dec. 24, 1964		86,620,000.00	
	Issued for cash		914,899,000.00	
	Other:			
30	Dated July 7, 1964	3.691		
	Redeemed in exchange for series dated June 30, 1965, due June 30, 1966			62,101,000.00
	Redeemable for cash			939,121,000.00
30	Maturing June 30, 1966	3.807		
	Issued in exchange for series dated July 7, 1964		62,101,000.00	
	Issued for cash		938,511,000.00	
	Certificates of indebtedness, foreign series, maturing:			
30	June 30, 1965	3.75		20,000,000.00
	Sept. 30, 1965	3.75	20,000,000.00	
	Sept. 30, 1965	2.00	275,000,000.00	
	Sept. 30, 1965	3.784	135,000,000.00	
30	Treasury bonds, maturing June 30, 1967	4.00	178,315.06	
	Treasury certificates, maturing:			
30	June 30, 1965	3.921		27,222,835.33
	June 30, 1965	3.54		91,368,211.18
	July 31, 1965	3.54	61,606,974.14	
	Sept. 30, 1965	3.784	27,487,858.09	
30	U.S. savings bonds: [6]			
	Series E–1941	[7] 3.223	2,207,809.89	1,709,012.42
	Series E–1942	[7] 3.252	4,186,990.98	7,544,967.61
	Series E–1943	[7] 3.277	4,126,464.79	12,634,188.34
	Series E–1944	[7] 3.298	12,299,456.29	15,624,410.65
	Series E–1945	[7] 3.316	10,913,204.80	16,911,196.46
	Series E–1946	[7] 3.327	4,191,760.92	6,609,820.05
	Series E–1947	[7] 3.346	3,778,257.54	7,023,137.84
	Series E–1948	[7] 3.366	4,578,450.91	8,051,015.06
	Series E–1949	[7] 3.344	4,947,746.62	7,894,359.86
	Series E–1950	[7] 3.347	4,036,335.15	7,763,660.92
	Series E–1951	[7] 3.378	3,665,933.81	7,071,328.16
	Series E–1952 (January to April)	3.400	−26,459.59	2,632,569.92
	Series E–1952 (May to December)	[7] 3.451	1,867,117.25	5,573,884.46
	Series E–1953	[7] 3.468	4,261,925.68	10,831,897.29
	Series E–1954	[7] 3.497	4,333,285.50	14,047,509.51
	Series E–1955	[7] 3.522	8,748,539.52	17,843,134.30
	Series E–1956	[7] 3.546	6,495,351.75	8,827,921.68
	Series E–1957 (January)	3.560	−2.24	705,153.91
	Series E–1957 (February to December)	[7] 3.653	6,846,994.13	8,671,740.85
	Series E–1958	[7] 3.690	6,644,103.93	9,591,912.12
	Series E–1959 (January to May)	3.730	−39,032.64	4,374,236.24
	Series E–1959 (June to December)	3.750	6,385,998.86	5,874,610.51
	Series E–1960	3.750	6,759,168.10	10,672,013.25
	Series E–1961	3.750	6,973,568.60	13,674,688.12
	Series E–1962	3.750	7,136,799.80	14,719,865.12
	Series E–1963	3.750	7,616,732.70	23,409,824.25
	Series E–1964	3.750	6,055,499.83	61,717,773.36
	Series E–1965	3.750	332,620,737.06	71,373,937.50
	Unclassified sales and redemptions		[5] −1,501,807.51	30,739,357.15

Footnotes at end of table.

TABLE 44.—*Issues, maturities, and redemptions of interest-bearing public debt securities, excluding special issues, July 1964–June 1965*—Continued

Date	Securities	Rate of interest [1]	Amount issued [2]	Amount matured or called or redeemed prior to maturity [3]
1965		*Percent*		
June 30	U.S. savings bonds [6]—Continued			
	Series H-1952	[7] 3.392		$960,500.00
	Series H-1953	[7] 3.409		2,875,500.00
	Series H-1954	[7] 3.439		6,721,500.00
	Series H-1955	[7] 3.467		17,926,500.00
	Series H-1956	[7] 3.496		5,051,000.00
	Series H-1957 (January)	3.520		208,000.00
	Series H-1957 (February to December)	[7] 3.626		3,355,500.00
	Series H-1958	[7] 3.679		5,217,000.00
	Series H-1959 (January to May)	3.720		2,360,000.00
	Series H-1959 (June to December)	3.750		2,591,500.00
	Series H-1960	3.750		5,889,000.00
	Series H-1961	3.750		6,534,000.00
	Series H-1962	3.750		4,626,000.00
	Series H-1963	3.750	$4,500.00	4,781,500.00
	Series H-1964	3.750	98,500.00	4,368,500.00
	Series H-1965	3.750	46,156,500.00	29,000.00
	Unclassified sales and redemptions		[8] −1,055,000.00	[8] −33,561,000.00
	Series J-1953	2.76	248,160.40	4,970,573.60
	Series J-1954	2.76	466,722.00	1,536,016.60
	Series J-1955	2.76	308,523.23	1,612,995.67
	Series J-1956	2.76	225,256.15	882,031.40
	Series J-1957	2.76	−173.25	148,096.65
	Unclassified redemptions			[8] −1,795,177.25
	Series K-1953	2.76		12,841,500.00
	Series K-1954	2.76		4,643,500.00
	Series K-1955	2.76		4,437,500.00
	Series K-1956	2.76		2,165,500.00
	Series K-1957	2.76		542,000.00
	Unclassified redemptions			[8] −10,394,500.00
30	Treasury notes, Series A-1966	4.00		
30	Adjustments of issues [9]		239,000.00	
30	Treasury bonds of 1974	4¼		
	Adjustments of issues [9]		895,000.00	
30	U.S. retirement plan bonds	3.75	270,848.24	22,481.23
30	Depositary bonds, First Series	2.00	45,500.00	1,540,000.00
30	Treasury bonds, REA Series	2.00	245,000.00	1,316,000.00
30	Treasury bonds, Investment Series B-1975-80	2¾		
	Redeemed in exchange for 1½% Treasury notes, Series EA-1970			25,646,000.00
30	Treasury notes, Series EA-1970	1½	25,646,000.00	
30	Miscellaneous			22,762,000.00
	Total June		11,998,817,792.11	14,777,802,250.29
	Total fiscal year 1965		185,467,624,272.93	181,674,861,039.37

[1] For Treasury bills, average rate on bank discount basis is shown; for savings bonds, approximate yield to maturity is shown.

[2] Since May 1, 1957, Series E and H bonds have been the only savings bonds on sale. Amounts shown for Series E and J represent issue price plus accrued discount, and amounts shown for Series H represent issue price at par.

[3] For savings bonds of Series E and J, amounts represent current redemption value (issue price plus accrued discount); and for Series H and K, amounts represent redemption value at par.

[4] Average interest rate for combined original and additional issues.

[5] Represents an additional $100,086,000 of each of 10 series of outstanding Treasury bills issued in a strip to mature each week from Oct. 15, to Dec. 17, 1964.

[6] At option of owner, Series E bonds dated May 1, 1941, through May 1, 1949, may be held and will accrue interest for additional 20 years; bonds dated on and after June 1, 1949, may be held and will accrue interest for additional 10 years. At option of owner, Series H bonds dated June 1, 1952, through Jan. 1, 1957, may be held and will accrue interest for additional 10 years.

[7] Represents a weighted average of the approximate yields of bonds of various issue dates within the yearly series if held to maturity or if held from issue date to end of applicable extension period, computed on the basis of bonds outstanding June 30, 1964. (See Treasury Circulars Nos. 653 (Sixth Revision) and 905 (Third Revision) for details of yields by issue dates, for Series E and Series H savings bonds, respectively.) (Circulars dated Dec. 23, 1964, and printed as exhibits 8 and 10 of this report.)

[8] Amounts transferred from unclassified sales or redemptions to sales or redemptions of designated series.

[9] Adjustments of amounts originally reported on date of issue or exchange.

[10] Settlement made subsequent to last day of month in which bills matured.

[11] Partial settlement of $90,993,000 made May 31, 1965; final settlement of $909,148,000 made June 1, 1965.

[12] Partial settlement of accepted tenders for $3,063,000 made May 31, 1965; final settlement of accepted tenders for $997,823,000 made June 1, 1965.

TABLE 45.—*Allotments by investor classes on subscriptions for public marketable securities other than regular weekly Treasury bills, fiscal year 1965*

[In millions of dollars. On basis of subscription and allotment reports]

Date of financing	Description [1]	Amount issued		U.S. Government investment accounts and Federal Reserve banks	Allotments by investor classes											
		For cash	In exchange for other securities		Commercial banks [2]	Individuals [3]	Insurance companies	Mutual savings banks	Corporations [4]	Private pension and retirement funds	State and local governments [4]		Dealers and brokers	All other [5]
											Pension and retirement funds	Other funds		
1964															
July 7	3% bill, June 8, 66 [8]	[7] 1,001		20	287	2	1	(*)	86		(*)	2	540	63
July 22	¾% ctf, Oct. 1, 66 [8]		3,726		2,392	132	60	67	150	14	3	114	221	573
	¾% ctf, Nov. 1, 66 [8]		4,357	4	2,582	161	225	136	134	39	8	227	534	307
	4¼% ctf, Aug. 8		1,198	22	527	20	41	37	5	72	7	81	331	55
Aug. 29	3.6% bill {Oct. 5, 1964} {Oct. 7, 1964}	1,001			308	(*)			30			11	650	2
Aug. 4	3.644% bill, July 1965	[7] 1,000		(*)	621	1	(*)	(*)	102	(*)		(*)	232	44
Aug. 15	4% note, Feb. 4, 1966-C [10]	2,086	1,954	1,867	1,218	65	26	37	249	10	11	96	341	120
Aug. 31	3% bill, Aug. 1965	1,001		49	400	4		(*)	66			7	425	49
Sept. 2	3% bill, Mar. 2, 66 [12]	1,001			232	1	1		371	(*)		4	389	4
Sept. 30	3% bill, Mar. 2, 66 [8]	1,503			514	6	1		48			10	323	67
Oct. 26	3% bill, Oct. 66 [12] [8]	1,000		32	367	1			3	(*)	(*)		(*)	13
Oct. 31	4% note, May 8, 1966-D [10]	2,893	6,626	112	1,670	9	120	87	303	31	1	11	408	72
Nov. 15	3.639% bill, 66 [12]	2,504		6,442	1,487	129			20			212	264	260
Nov. 8	4.068% bill, Nov. 8, 66 [8]	1,001			354	5	1	1	35	3		(*)	418	83
Nov. 30	3.972% bill, ctf 31, 66	1,003		92	458	5	(*)	2	69	1		9	282	147
1965				30										
Jan. 15	{4% bond, Feb 8, 1970.} {4¾% bond, ctf 8, 1974.}		4,381	322	2,883	111	137	63	137	19	3	172	186	348
	4¾% b ord, Aug. 82 [8]		3,130	325	1,792	54	171	54	67	28	6	69	266	298
			2,254	55	975	10	68	31	10	7	65	21	974	38
Jan. 18	3% bill, Jan. 4, 66 [12] [8]	[11] 1,758			1,742	(*)	1		2		1		342	13
Jan. 31	3.945% bill, Jan. [8]	[11] 1,000		102	374	12	3	(*)	87			5	196	74
Feb. 15	4% ctfs, Nov. 15, 1966-E [10]	[11] 1,735	518	487	1,018	51	43	33	165	11		57	355	192
Feb. 28	4.062% bill, ctf 8, 66	[11] 1,001		42	473	6	2	(*)	40			6	420	77
Mar. 31	3.987% bill, Mar. 66	[11] 1,000		73	385	12	1	(*)	15	23		14	650	76
Apr. 30	3% bill, Apr. 66	[11] 1,001		154	98	3	2	1	8	6		4	47	76
May 15	{4% nd, Aug. 8, 1966-A [8]} {4¾% ctf, May 8, 1974 [8]}		5,904	4,253	944	116	27	18	149	19	1	127	555	203
May 31	3.954% ctf, May 66	[11] 1,001	2,062	65	1,078	43	41	45	22	12	11	99	724	47
June 30	3% bil, June 6, 66	[11] 1,001		136	55	5	(*)	1	55	(*)		15	61	91
				111	378	8			47	16		26	349	65

* Less th... 00, 00.

1 ... 1½ ... Treasury ... issued in exchange for nonmarket-... Series B-1975-80.

2 ... Treasury ... savings banks ... trust accounts.

3 ...

4 ... of trust ... of State and local governments and ...

5 ...

6 ... institutions, and investments of foreign ... country.

7 ... -year bills ... Sept. 3, 1963, to replace the existing ... cycle.

8 ... of earlier issue.

9 Offering consisted of an additional $100 million each of ten series of outstanding weekly bills issued in a strip on July 29, 1964.

10 Offerings of these securities, subject to allotments, were made for the purpose of paying off maturing securities in cash. Holders of the maturing securities were not offered preemptive rights to exchange their holdings but were permitted to present them in payment or exchange, in whole or in part, for the new issues.

11 Issued as a rollover of monthly one-year bills.

12 Tax anticipation security.

NOTE.—Allotments from July 15, 1953, through May 15, 1959, will be found in the 1959 annual report, pp. 528–530. For the fiscal year 1960 see 1960 annual report, p. 573, for fiscal 1961, see 1961 annual report, p. 604, for fiscal 1962, see 1962 annual report, p. 722, for fiscal 1963, see 1963 annual report, p. 606, for fiscal 1964, see 1964 annual report, p. 570, and for current figures see monthly *Treasury Bulletin*.

TABLE 46.—*Statutory debt retirements, fiscal years 1918–65*

[In thousands of dollars. On basis of par amounts and of daily Treasury statements through 1947, and on basis of Public Debt accounts thereafter, see "Bases of Tables"]

Fiscal year	Cumulative sinking fund	Repayments of foreign debt	Bonds and notes received for estate taxes	Bonds received for loans from Public Works Administration	Franchise tax receipts, Federal Reserve banks	Payments from net earnings, Federal intermediate credit banks	Commodity Credit Corporation capital repayments	Miscellaneous gifts, forfeitures, etc.	Total
1918					1,134				1,134
1919		7,922	93						8,015
1920		72,670	3,141		2,922			13	78,746
1921	261,100	73,939	26,349		60,724			[1] 5,010	427,123
1922	276,046	64,838	21,085		60,333			393	422,695
1923	284,019	100,893	6,569		10,815			555	402,850
1924	295,987	149,388	8,897		3,635			93	458,000
1925	306,309	159,179	47		114	680		208	466,538
1926	317,092	169,654			59	509		63	487,376
1927	333,528	179,216			818	414		5,578	519,555
1928	354,741	181,804		2	250	369		3,090	540,255
1929	370,277	176,213		20	2,667	266		160	549,604
1930	388,369	160,926		73	4,283	172		61	553,884
1931	391,660	48,246			18	74		85	440,082
1932	412,555		1			21		53	412,630
1933	425,660	33,887			2,037	21		21	461,605
1934	359,492	357						15	359,864
1935	573,001			1				556	573,558
1936	403,238							1	403,240
1937	103,815	142						14	103,971
1938	65,116	210						139	65,465
1939	48,518	120			8,095	1,501		12	58,246
1940	128,349				134	685		16	129,184
1941	37,011				1,321	548	25,364	16	64,260
1942	75,342				668	315	18,393	5	94,722
1943	3,460							4	3,463
1944	−1							3	2
1945								2	2
1946								4	4
1947								(²)	
1948	746,636				8,028	1,634	45,509	[3] 209,828	1,011,636
1949	7,498					178		[3] 81	7,758
1950	1,815					261	48,943	[3] 690	51,709
1951	839					394			1,232
1952	551					300			851
1953	241					285			526
1954						387			387
1955						231			231
1956	762,627					462			763,089
1957						139			139
1958									
1959	−57								−57
1960									
1961	1,000,000								1,000,000
1962								[4] 1,000	1,000
1963								[5] 58,000	58,000
1964									
1965								[6] 73,100	[6] 73,100
Total	8,734,833	1,579,605	66,278	18,246	149,809	9,825	138,209	358,869	11,055,675

[1] Includes $4,842,066.45 written off the debt Dec. 31, 1920, for fractional currency estimated to have been lost or destroyed in circulation.

[2] Beginning with 1947, bonds acquired through gifts, forfeitures, and estate taxes are redeemed prior to maturity from regular public debt receipts.

[3] Represents payments from net earnings, War Damage Corporation.

[4] Represents Treasury notes of 1890 determined by the Secretary of the Treasury on Oct. 20, 1961, pursuant to the Old Series Currency Adjustment Act approved June 30, 1961 (31 U.S.C. 912-916) to have been destroyed or irretrievably lost and so will never be presented for redemption.

[5] Represents $15,000,000 national bank notes, $1,000,000 Federal Reserve bank notes, and $15,000,000 silver certificates, all issued prior to July 1, 1929; $18,000,000 Federal Reserve notes issued prior to the series of 1928; $9,000,000 gold certificates issued prior to Jan. 30, 1934; all of which have been determined by the Secretary of the Treasury pursuant to the Old Series Currency Adjustment Act approved June 30, 1961 (31 U.S.C. 912-916) to have been destroyed or irretrievably lost and so will never be presented for redemption.

[6] Represents $24,000,000 U.S. notes, $1,000,000 Federal Reserve bank notes, $13,500,000 national bank notes, and $14,500,000 silver certificates, all issued before July 1, 1929; $6,000,000 gold certificates prior to 1934 series; $100,000 Treasury notes of 1890; and $14,000,000 Federal Reserve notes (prior to series of 1928); all of which were e e m ne on Nov. 16, 1964, pursuant to 31 U.S.C. 912-916, to have been destroyed or irretrievably lostd t r i d

TABLE 47.—*Cumulative sinking fund, fiscal years 1921-65*

PART I—APPROPRIATIONS AND EXPENDITURES

[In millions of dollars. On basis of Public Debt accounts. see "Bases of Tables"]

Fiscal year	Appropriations	Available for expenditure during year [1]	Debt retired [2]	
			Par amount	Cost (principal)
1921–1940	8, 208. 6	2, 117. 3	6, 099. 0	6, 091. 3
1941	585. 8	2, 703. 2	37. 0	37. 0
1942	586. 9	3, 253. 1	75. 3	75. 3
1943	587. 8	3, 765. 6	3. 4	3. 4
1944	587. 6	4, 349. 7		
1945	587. 6	4, 937. 4		
1946	587. 6	5, 525. 0		
1947	587. 6	6, 112. 6		
1948	603. 5	6, 716. 0	746. 6	746. 6
1949	619. 6	6, 589. 0	7. 5	7. 5
1950	619. 7	7, 201. 2	1. 8	1. 8
1951	619. 8	7, 819. 2	. 8	. 8
1952	619. 8	8, 438. 1	. 6	. 6
1953	619. 8	9, 057. 4	. 2	. 2
1954	619. 8	9, 676. 9		
1955	619. 8	10, 296. 7		
1956	623. 8	10, 920. 5	762. 6	762. 6
1957	633. 3	10, 791. 2		
1958	633. 3	11, 424. 5		
1959	633. 3	12, 057. 9		
1960	633. 3	12, 691. 3		
1961	657. 1	13, 348. 4	1, 000. 0	1, 000. 0
1962	680. 8	13, 029. 3		
1963	680. 8	13, 710. 1		
1964	680. 8	14, 391. 0		
1965	680. 8	15, 071. 8		
Total	23, 798. 9		8, 734. 8	8, 727. 1
Deduct cumulative expenditures	8, 727. 1			
Unexpended balance	15, 071. 8			

PART II.—TRANSACTIONS ON ACCOUNT OF THE CUMULATIVE SINKING FUND
FISCAL YEAR 1965

[On basis of Public Debt accounts, see "Bases of Tables"]

Unexpended balance July 1, 1964		$14, 390, 961, 975. 31
Appropriation for 1965:		
Initial credit:		
(a) Under the Victory Loan Act (2½ percent of the aggregate amount of Liberty bonds and Victory notes outstanding on July 1, 1920, less an amount equal to the par amount of any obligation of foreign governments held by the United States on July 1, 1920)	$253, 404, 864. 87	
(b) Under the Emergency Relief and Construction Act of 1932 (2½ percent of the aggregate amount of expenditures from appropriations made or authorized under this act)	7, 860, 606. 83	
(c) Under the National Industrial Recovery Act (2½ percent of the aggregate amount of expenditures from appropriations made or authorized under this act)	80, 164, 079. 53	
Total initial credit	341, 429, 551. 23	
Secondary credit (the interest which would have been payable during the fiscal year for which the appropriation is made on the bonds and notes purchased, redeemed, or paid out of the sinking fund during such year or in previous years)	339, 419, 534. 24	680, 849, 085. 47
Total available 1965		15, 071, 811, 060. 78
Unexpended balance June 30, 1965 [2]		15, 071, 811, 060. 78

[1] Represents appropriations authorized by Congress. There are no specific funds set aside for this account since any retirements of public debt charged to this account are made from cash balances to the credit of the Treasurer of the United States.

[2] Net discount on debt retired through June 30, 1965, is $7.7 million.

NOTE.—Comparable annual data for 1921 through 1940 are shown in the 1962 annual report. p. 726.

III.—United States savings bonds

TABLE 48.—*Sales and redemptions of Series E through K savings bonds by series, fiscal years 1941-65 and monthly 1965* [1][2]

[In millions of dollars]

Fiscal year or month	Sales	Accrued discount	Sales plus accrued discount	Redemptions			Amount outstanding [3]	
				Total	Original purchase price	Accrued discount	Interest-bearing	Matured non-interest-bearing
			Series E and H					
1941-55	79,203.6	9,183 8	88,387.4	49,102.2	45,969.3	3,132.9	39,285.1	....
1956	5,259.9	1,114.1	6,374.0	4,730.1	4,069.1	660.9	40,929.1	....
1957	4,613.0	1.132.6	5,745.5	5,176.2	4,444.0	732.2	41,498.5	....
1958	4,670.1	1,160.7	5,830.8	5.187.1	4,431.9	755.3	42,142.2	....
1959	4,506.0	1,174 5	5,680.4	5,106.8	4,309.8	797.0	42,715.8	....
1960	4,307.0	1,194.2	5,501.2	5.502 2	4,616.3	885.9	42,714.8	....
1961	4,463.7	1,253.7	5,717.4	4.626.7	3,905.8	720.8	43,805.6	....
1962	4,421.5	1,331.0	5,752.5	4.603.3	3,872.7	730.6	44,954.8	....
1963	4,518.0	1,386.5	5,904.5	4,500 5	3,758.5	742.0	46,358.8	....
1964	4,656.4	1,458.0	6,114.4	4.736 3	3,981.8	754.5	47,736.9	....
1965	4,543.0	1,502.1	6,045.1	4,987.4	4,154.1	833.3	48,794.5	....
Total through June 30, 1965	125,162.3	21,891.0	147,053.3	98,258.8	87,513.4	10,745.4	48,794.5	....
1964—July	387.1	143.7	530.8	424.1	356.7	67.4	47,843.6	....
August	363.6	113.2	476.8	382.4	324.9	57.5	47,937.9	....
September	357.8	125.3	483.2	401.8	338.3	63.5	48,019.2	....
October	366.8	114.2	481.0	377.7	316.3	61.4	48,122.6	....
November	348.4	114.1	462.5	331.0	278.5	52.6	48,254.1	....
December	372.0	136.4	508.4	396.5	330.9	65.5	48,365.9	....
1965—January	430.8	144.5	575.3	489.7	393.8	95.9	48,451.5	....
February	393.9	118.8	512.7	417.2	344.8	72.4	48,547.0	....
March	413.8	121.0	534.7	457.5	380.7	76.9	48,624.2	....
April	390.6	116.5	507.1	461.8	383.5	78.3	48,669.5	....
May	356.0	115.9	471.9	407.9	340.3	67.6	48,733.5	....
June	362.3	138.5	500.8	439.7	365.3	74.4	48,794.5	....
			Series F, G, J, and K					
1941-55	31,096.5	836.9	31,933.3	12,634.4	12,298.8	335.6	19,080.3	218.7
1956	586.3	99.6	686.0	3,104.8	2,940.6	164.2	16,567.6	312.4
1957	268.4	83.4	351.8	3,773.5	3,605.0	168.5	13,123.5	334.8
1958	(*)	65.2	65.2	3,350.5	3,234.6	115.9	9,842.2	331.0
1959	(*)	53.6	53.6	2,137.2	2,063.4	73.8	7,786.7	302.8
1960	(*)	46.0	46.0	3,049.3	2 921.2	128.1	4,829.0	257.3
1961	(*)	32.1	32.1	1,188.0	1,128.8	59.1	3,708.7	221.6
1962	....	27.4	27.4	1,109.9	1,059.0	50.9	2,651.9	195.8
1963	....	21.6	21.6	770.7	721.7	49.0	1,954.9	143.7
1964	....	17.7	17.7	426.3	399.8	26.6	1,562.6	127.4
1965	....	14.9	14.9	357.5	333.1	24.4	1,248.1	99.3
Total through June 30, 1965	31,951.2	1,298.3	33,249.6	31,902.2	30,706.1	1,196.1	1,248.1	99.3
1964—July	....	1.6	1.6	42.2	40.3	1.8	1,527.8	121.7
August	....	1.2	1.2	27.1	25.6	1.5	1,506.2	117.4
September	....	1.3	1.3	29.1	27.1	2.0	1,482.9	112.9
October	....	1.2	1.2	29.7	27.6	2.2	1,458.7	108.6
November	....	1.1	1.1	24.4	22.3	2.0	1,438.3	105.7
December	....	1.4	1.4	29.7	27.4	2.2	1,368.4	147.3
965—January	....	1.5	1.5	39.4	36.9	2.5	1,351.6	126.1
February	....	1.2	1.2	28.4	26.6	1.9	1,334.1	116.3
March	....	1.1	1.1	30.1	27.9	2.3	1,310.8	110.7
April	....	1.1	1.1	27.4	25.3	2.1	1,289.5	105.6
May	....	1.0	1.0	25.5	23.7	1.8	1,268.4	102.3
June	....	1.2	1.2	24.5	22.4	2.1	1,248.1	99.3

Footnotes at end of table.

TABLE 48.—*Sales and redemptions of Series E through K savings bonds by series, fiscal years 1941–65 and monthly 1965* [1][2]—Continued

[In millions of dollars]

Fiscal year or month	Sales	Accrued discount	Sales plus accrued discount	Redemptions			Exchanges of E bonds for H bonds	Amount outstanding (interest-bearing)
				Total	Original purchase price	Accrued discount		
Series E								
1941–55	77,018.7	9,183.8	86,202.5	49,016.1	45,883.2	3,132.9		37,186.4
1956	4,2██.█	1,114.1	5,██3.█	4,622.0	3,961.█	660.9		37,897.8
1957	█,9	1,13█.6	5,1.	4,980.6	4,248.	732.2		37,969.0
1958	.88	1,160.7	5,9.	4,951.0	4,195.	755.3		38,067.2
1959	.68	1,174.5	4,2.	4,██8.4	4,092.	797.0		38,040.3
1960	.60	1,19█.2	4,7.	5,.6	4,294.	885.9	201.3	37,455.7
1961	.68	1,25.7	4,2.	4,.8	3,672.	720.8	188.3	37,816.6
1962	.6	1,33.0	5,005.	4,.3	3,612.	730.6	218.6	38,260.1
1963	.9	1,38.5	5,300.	4,.9	3,461.	742.0	191.3	39,166.2
1964	.1	1,458.0	5,6█3.	4,.1	3,608.	754.5	206.3	40,190.4
1965	1	1,502.1	5,4.	4,.4	3,705.	833.3	188.1	41,078.4
Total through June 30, 1965	115,862.4	21,891.0	137,753.5	95,481.1	84,735.7	10,745.4	1,193.9	41,078.4
1964—July	344.8	143.7	488.5	387.4	320.0	67.4	19.1	40,272.4
August	328.8	113.2	442.0	346.5	288.9	57.5	16.1	40,351.8
September	321.4	125.3	446.7	358.9	295.4	63.5	14.1	40,425.5
October	333.1	114.2	447.3	341.0	279.7	61.4	14.9	40,516.9
November	318.4	114.1	432.6	296.9	244.3	52.6	12.2	40,640.3
December	337.9	136.4	474.3	362.1	296.6	65.5	13.0	40,739.4
1965—January	382.6	144.5	527.1	456.6	360.7	95.9	20.6	40,816.6
February	357.8	118.8	476.6	383.2	310.7	72.4	16.5	40,866.3
March	374.6	121.0	495.6	413.3	336.4	76.9	16.6	40,932.1
April	354.7	116.5	471.3	425.4	347.1	78.3	15.7	40,962.2
May	326.6	115.9	442.5	367.3	299.7	67.6	14.9	41,022.6
June	331.5	138.5	469.9	399.7	325.4	74.4	14.4	41,078.4
Series H								
1952–55	2,184.9		2,184.9	86.1	86.1			2,098.7
1956	1,040.6		1,040.6	108.1	108.1			3,031.2
1957	693.8		693.8	195.5	195.5			3,529.5
1958	781.6		781.6	236.1	236.1			4,075.0
1959	818.0		818.0	217.4	217.4			4,675.5
1960	703.9		703.9	321.6	321.6		201.3	5,259.1
1961	774.5		774.5	232.9	232.9		188.3	5,989.0
1962	747.2		747.2	260.1	260.1		218.6	6,694.7
1963	604.1		604.1	297.5	297.5		191.3	7,192.5
1964	520.8		520.8	373.3	373.3		206.3	7,546.4
1965	430.7		430.7	449.0	449.0		188.1	7,716.1
Total through June 30, 1965	9,299.9		9,299.9	2,777.7	2,777.7		1,193.9	7,716.1
1964—July	42.3		42.3	36.7	36.7		19.1	7,571.1
August	34.8		34.8	36.0	36.0		16.1	7,586.1
September	36.4		36.4	42.9	42.9		14.1	7,593.8
October	33.7		33.7	36.7	36.7		14.9	7,605.7
November	29.9		29.9	34.1	34.1		12.2	7,613.8
December	34.1		34.1	34.3	34.3		13.0	7,626.5
1965—January	48.1		48.1	33.0	33.0		20.6	7,662.2
February	36.1		36.1	34.0	34.0		16.5	7,680.7
March	39.1		39.1	44.3	44.3		16.6	7,692.1
April	35.9		35.9	36.4	36.4		15.7	7,707.3
May	29.3		29.3	40.6	40.6		14.9	7,710.9
June	30.8		30.8	39.9	39.9		14.4	7,716.1

Footnotes at end of table.

TABLE 48.—*Sales and redemptions of Series E through K savings bonds by series, fiscal years 1941–65 and monthly 1965* [1] [2]—Continued

[In millions of dollars]

Fiscal year or month	Sales	Accrued discount	Sales plus accrued discount	Redemptions			Amount outstanding [3]	
				Total	Original purchase price	Accrued discount	Interest-bearing	Matured non-interest-bearing
				Series F				
1941–55	4,957.6	826.9	5,784.5	2,800.0	2,464.8	335.1	2,876.9	107.6
1956	(*)	87.7	87.7	665.3	502.3	163.0	2,249.9	157.1
1957	(*)	67.5	67.5	709.3	544.8	164.6	1,598.3	166.8
1958	(*)	47.1	47.1	487.9	377.6	110.3	1,169.1	155.3
1959	(*)	35.7	35.7	285.2	215.3	69.9	943.9	131.0
1960	(*)	27.8	27.8	483.5	370.3	113.1	508.2	111.1
1961		15.4	15.4	212.3	157.9	54.4	331.2	91.2
1962		10.6	10.6	177.9	132.5	45.4	182.9	72.1
1963		5.0	5.0	167.4	124.3	43.1	57.8	34.9
1964		1.4	1.4	67.3	49.9	17.5		26.8
1965		(*)	(*)	8.6	6.4	2.2		18.1
Total through June 30, 1965	4,957.7	1,125.1	6,082.8	6,064.6	4,946.1	1,118.5		18.1
1964—July		(*)	(*)	1.7	1.3	.4		25.0
August				1.2	.9	.3		23.9
September				.8	.6	.2		23.0
October				.8	.6	.2		22.2
November				.6	.5	.2		21.6
December				1.0	.7	.3		20.6
1965—January				.3	.3	.1		20.3
February				.5	.4	.1		19.8
March				.6	.4	.1		19.2
April				.5	.3	.1		18.7
May				.4	.3	.1		18.4
June				.3	.2	.1		18.1
				Series G				
1941–55	23,437.9		23,437.9	9,743.5	9,743.5		13,583.3	111.1
1956				2,300.5	2,300		11,238.5	155.4
1957				2,719.5	2,719		8,506.3	168.0
1958				2,506.5	2,506		5,992.1	175.7
1959				1,668.6	1,668		4,327.4	171.8
1960				2,055.9	2,055		2,297.2	146.2
1961				843.9	843		1,469.0	130.5
1962				805.4	805		670.4	123.7
1963				496.6	496		188.7	108.8
1964				196.8	196			100.7
1965				31.5	31			69.2
Total through June 30, 1965	23,437.9		23,437.9	23,368.7	23,368.7			69.2
1964—July				4.0	4.0			96.6
August				3.1	3.1			93.5
September				3.7	3.7			89.8
October				3.5	3.5			86.4
November				2.2	2.2			84.1
December				2.3	2.3			81.8
1965—January				2.5	2.5			79.3
February				2.2	2.2			77.1
March				2.5	2.5			74.6
April				2.3	2.3			72.3
May				1.7	1.7			70.6
June				1.4	1.4			69.2

Footnotes at end of table.

TABLE 48.—*Sales and redemptions of Series E through K savings bonds by series, fiscal years 1941–65 and monthly 1965* [1] [2]—Continued

[In millions of dollars]

| Fiscal year or month | Sales | Accrued discount | Sales plus accrued discount | Redemptions | | | Amount outstanding [3] | |
				Total	Original purchase price	Accrued discount	Interest-bearing	Matured non-interest-bearing
				Series J				
1952–55	696.8	10.0	706.8	33.7	33.2	.5	673.1	
1956	183.2	11.9	195.2	59.6	58.4	1.3	808.6	
1957	92.4	15.9	108.3	106.5	102.5	3.9	810.4	
1958	(*)	18.1	18.1	98.4	92.8	5.6	730.2	
1959	(*)	17.8	17.8	51.2	47.3	3.9	696.9	
1960		18.2	18.2	144.2	129.2	15.0	570.8	
1961	(*)	16.7	16.7	39.1	34.4	4.8	548.4	
1962		16.8	16.8	37.2	31.7	5.5	527.9	
1963		16.6	16.6	33.2	27.4	5.9	511.3	
1964		16.3	16.3	46.2	37.1	9.1	481.4	
1965		14.9	14.9	87.6	65.4	22.2	403.8	4.8
Total through June 30, 1965	972.4	173.2	1,145.7	737.1	659.5	77.6	403.8	4.8
1964—July		1.6	1.6	6.7	5.3	1.4	476.2	
August		1.2	1.2	5.2	4.0	1.2	472.3	
September		1.3	1.3	6.9	5.2	1.8	466.6	
October		1.2	1.2	7.7	5.7	1.9	460.1	
November		1.1	1.1	7.3	5.4	1.9	453.9	
December		1.4	1.4	7.8	5.8	2.0	431.6	16.0
1965—January		1.5	1.5	9.4	7.0	2.4	429.3	10.3
February		1.2	1.2	6.7	5.0	1.8	426.8	7.3
March		1.1	1.1	8.1	6.0	2.1	420.7	6.4
April		1.1	1.1	7.5	5.5	2.0	414.9	5.8
May		1.0	1.0	6.5	4.8	1.7	409.9	5.3
June		1.2	1.2	7.8	5.8	2.1	403.8	4.8
				Series K				
1952–55	2,004.2		2,004.2	57.2	57.2		1,947.0	
1956	403.1		403.1	79.5	79.5		2,270.6	
1957	176.0		176.0	238.2	238.2		2,208.5	
1958	(*)		(*)	257.7	257.7		1,950.7	
1959	(*)		(*)	132.2	132.2		1,818.6	
1960				365.8	365.8		1,452.8	
1961				92.7	92.7		1,360.1	
1962				89.4	89.4		1,270.7	
1963				73.5	73.5		1,197.2	
1964				116.0	116.0		1,081.3	
1965				229.8	229.8		844.3	7.2
Total through June 30, 1965	2,583.3		2,583.3	1,731.8	1,731.8		844.3	7.2
1964—July				29.7	29.7		1,051.5	
August				17.6	17.6		1,033.9	
September				17.7	17.7		1,016.3	
October				17.7	17.7		998.5	
November				14.2	14.2		984.3	
December				18.6	18.6		936.8	28.9
1965—January				27.2	27.2		922.3	16.2
February				19.0	19.0		907.3	12.2
March				18.9	18.9		890.1	10.5
April				17.1	17.1		874.6	8.8
May				16.9	16.9		858.5	8.0
June				15.1	15.1		844.3	7.2

*Less than $50,000.

[1] Sales and redemption figures include exchanges of minor amounts of matured Series E for Series G and K bonds from May 1951 through April 1957, and Series F and J for Series H bonds beginning January 1960; they exclude exchanges of Series E for Series H bonds. Redemption figures for fiscal 1953–54 and fiscal years 1960–63 also include the maturing Series F and G savings bonds exchanged for marketable Treasury securities during special exchange offerings. The amounts involved were $416.6 million in 1953, $.7 million in 1954, $745.4 million in 1960, $147.3 million in 1961, $320.1 million in 1962, and $75.1 million in 1963.

[2] Sales of Series E, F, and J bonds are included at issue price, and their redemptions and amounts outstanding at current redemption value. Series G, H, and K bonds are included at face value throughout.

[3] Matured F, G, J, and K bonds outstanding are included in the interest-bearing debt until all bonds of the annual series have matured, and are then transferred to matured debt on which interest has ceased.

NOTE.—Series E and H are the only savings bonds now being sold. Series A–D, sold from Mar. 1, 1935 through Apr. 30, 1941, have all matured and are no longer reflected in these tables. Series F and G were sold from May 1, 1941, through Apr. 30, 1952. Series J and K were sold from May 1, 1952, through Apr. 30, 1957. Sales figures for Series F, G, J, and K after fiscal 1957, represent adjustments. Details by months for Series E, F, and G from May 1941 will be found on p. 608 of the 1943 annual report, and in corresponding tables in subsequent reports. Monthly detail for Series H, J, and K bonds will be found in the 1952 annual report, pp. 629 and 630, and in corresponding tables in subsequent reports.

TABLE 49.—Sales and redemptions of Series E and H savings bonds by denominations, fiscal years 1941–65 and monthly 1965 [1]

[In thousands of pieces. Estimated on basis of daily Treasury statements and reports from Bureau of the Public Debt]

Fiscal year or month	Total, all denominations [2]	$25	$50	$75	$100	$200 [4]	$500	$1,000	$5,000	$10,000 [6]
Sales [7]										
	1,696,608	1,155,275	267,768		189,89	8	26,20	27,519	106	48
	90,63	56,79	18,784		10,000	98	1,608	1,854	48	21
	90,160	56,327	20,043		10,969	99	1,320	96	29	12
	89,81	54,908	20,108		9,824	81	1,304	413	33	14
	85,882	52,805	20,20		9,477	83	1,212	30	35	16
	85,07	52,92	20,434		9,208	98	1,165	1,230	27	11
	86,495	53,453	20,901		23	74	01	1,299	31	15
	86,39	53,00	21,903		9,286	89	1,186	37	30	16
	89,627	54,629	23,42		9,623	83	33	1,270	25	16
July	96,609	59,230	23,947	135	10,34	98	1,220	1,214	22	16
	99,560	60,928	1,915	1,141	10,409	1,06	1,067	63	18	14
	8,30	5,116	1,845	77	85	92	97	96	2	1
	7,505	4,483	1,924	77	89	82	96	92	2	1
	7,853	4,76	1,99	79	86	78	83	78	2	1
	8,415	5,249	1,967	80	86	74	85	70	1	1
December	8,003	4,881	2,66	90	88	77	80	75	1	1
1965—January	8,422	5,151	2,062	93	80	79	85	13	1	1
	8,936	5,545	1,956	101	96	88	109	65	2	2
	8,18	4,902	2,90	97	83	81	101	88	2	1
	9,215	5,601	2,013	113	94	92	94	91	2	1
	8,65	5,313	1,922	111	84	88	93	76	2	1
June	7,922	4,811	2,030	109	84	83	84	70	1	1
	8,346	5,100		114	84	85	80			
Redemptions [7]										
1941–55	1,29,60	82,30	182,05		89,62	3,61	12,65	11,89		
1956	89,953	60,014	16,503		9,925	87	1,255	1,281	4	2
1957	93,175	60,612	18,165		10,590	63	1,354	1,485	5	3
1958	93,452	59,80	19,467		10,433	89	1,320	64	9	6
1959	88,647	56,036	19,507		10,394	675	81	1,451	11	5
1960	90,748	56,796	18,654	(*)	84	725	1,351	67	15	8
1961	85,07	54,280	18,746		9,197	616	1,076	1,139	10	4
1962	83,804	52,98	19,02		9,150	653	07	1,126	10	5
1963	83,69	53,018	20,034		8,75	601	1,005	08	12	5
1964	87,242	55,264			9,080	648	1,051	1,088	15	7

Period										
1965	90,012	56,736	20,74	245	9,322	694	1,80	1,122	19	9
1964—July	7,600	4,784	1,737	2	83	62	95	100	2	1
Aug.	7,100	4,534	1,607	5	23	54	84	87	1	1
Sept.	7,264	4,567	1,696	9	34	56	88	90	2	1
October	6,906	4,384	1,61	12	66	52	82	83	2	1
Nov.	6,151	3,946	1,385	15	63	45	71	72	1	1
Dec.	7,555	4,885	1,701	21	27	51	80	83	1	1
196_—Jan.	7,772	4,733	1,80	21	91	70	88	127	1	1
Feb.	7,538	4,718	1,783	24	88	56	86	94	2	1
March	8,246	5,182	1,96	30	80	63	96	102	2	1
April	8,494	5,286	2,015	36	80	67	94	99	2	1
May	7,390	4,688	1,68	32	90	56	88	91	2	1
June	7,997	5,030	1,837	37	87	62	92	95	2	1

* Less than 500 pieces.

1 Sales of Series H began on June 1, 1952, the denominations authorized were: $500, $1,000, $5,000, and $10,000.

2 Totals include $10 denomination Series E bonds sold to Armed Forces only from June 1944–March 1950. Details by years will be found in the 1952 annual report, pp. 631, 633; thereafter, monthly detail for each fiscal year appears in a footnote to the redemptions by denominations table of successive annual reports. Details in thousands of pieces by months in fiscal year 1965 follow:

3 Sales of $75 denomination Series E bonds began in May 1964.

4 Sales of $200 denomination Series E bonds began in October 1945.

5 Sales of $10,000 denomination Series E bonds were authorized on May 1, 1952.

6 Includes sales of $100,000 denomination Series E bonds which are purchasable only by trustees of employees' savings plans beginning April 1954, and personal trust accounts beginning January 1955.

7 See table 48, footnote 1.

Fiscal year	July	Aug.	Sept.	Oct.	Nov.	Dec.	Jan.	Feb.	Mar.	Apr.	May	June	Total
1965	4	4	4	4	3	3	5	5	5	5	4	4	51

TABLE 50.—*Sales of Series E and H savings bonds by States, fiscal years 1964, 1965, and cumulative* [1]

[In thousands of dollars, at issue price. On basis of reports received by the Treasury Department, with totals adjusted to basis of daily Treasury statements]

State	Fiscal year 1964	Fiscal year 1965	May 1941–June 1965
Alabama	36, 489	37, 793	1, 196, 074
Alaska	3, 291	3, 764	[2] 58, 356
Arizona	19, 609	18, 559	460, 236
Arkansas	18, 028	17, 437	702, 972
California	287, 769	278, 144	8, 482, 060
Colorado	32, 361	28, 250	936, 237
Connecticut	70, 682	68, 101	1, 935, 866
Delaware	19, 225	19, 505	344, 707
District of Columbia	41, 154	40, 675	1, 294, 602
Florida	76, 231	75, 399	1, 646, 682
Georgia	42, 227	43, 048	1, 334, 785
Hawaii	11, 653	11, 811	458, 841
Idaho	6, 081	5, 880	294, 885
Illinois	339, 931	322, 746	10, 009, 534
Indiana	127, 905	117, 200	3, 497, 095
Iowa	108, 511	104, 367	3, 408, 483
Kansas	62, 559	54, 547	2, 002, 908
Kentucky	46, 956	45, 847	1, 370, 648
Louisiana	35, 723	37, 037	1, 174, 995
Maine	13, 811	12, 978	463, 312
Maryland	68, 551	70, 542	1, 580, 778
Massachusetts	115, 873	112, 166	3, 462, 500
Michigan	259, 724	276, 808	6, 889, 706
Minnesota	62, 420	62, 553	2, 302, 663
Mississippi	13, 204	12, 369	673, 421
Missouri	133, 168	129, 997	3, 502, 434
Montana	16, 297	14, 554	600, 504
Nebraska	76, 366	69, 668	1, 990, 795
Nevada	6, 279	6, 376	150, 859
New Hampshire	9, 502	8, 753	286, 791
New Jersey	183, 261	174, 339	4, 672, 063
New Mexico	10, 988	10, 334	302, 157
New York	546, 128	494, 504	13, 919, 101
North Carolina	43, 380	42, 739	1, 371, 703
North Dakota	16, 053	14, 904	603, 818
Ohio	288, 298	279, 608	7, 767, 005
Oklahoma	49, 450	48, 118	1, 517, 838
Oregon	29, 508	27, 342	1, 156, 690
Pennsylvania	431, 161	404, 809	10, 378, 485
Rhode Island	14, 911	14, 701	536, 030
South Carolina	21, 669	21, 604	698, 779
South Dakota	21, 422	18, 686	735, 125
Tennessee	r 36, 760	37, 058	1, 258, 876
Texas	121, 559	123, 619	4, 311, 292
Utah	17, 898	18, 209	483, 884
Vermont	4, 462	4, 270	155, 150
Virginia	72, 152	73, 207	2, 039, 252
Washington	53, 468	50, 890	1, 983, 452
West Virginia	46, 578	41, 259	1, 257, 907
Wisconsin	84, 530	83, 916	2, 761, 768
Wyoming	5, 824	5, 695	234, 074
Canal Zone	3, 467	3, 605	76, 024
Puerto Rico	3, 130	3, 417	69, 570
Virgin Islands	269	250	3, 774
Undistributed and adjustment to daily Treasury statement	r +388, 516	+439, 061	3 +4, 354, 734
Total	4, 656, 422	4, 543, 018	125, 162, 280

r Revised.

[1] Figures include exchanges of minor amounts of Series F and J bonds for Series H bonds beginning January 1960; however, they exclude exchanges of Series E bonds for Series H bonds, which are reported in table 48.

[2] Excludes data for period April 1947 through December 1956, when reports were not available. In the annual reports for 1952-58 data for period May 1941 through March 1947 were included with "Other possessions."

[3] Includes a small amount for other possessions.

NOTE.—Sales by States of the various series of savings bonds were published in the annual report for 1943, pp. 614-621, and in subsequent reports; and by months at intervals in the *Treasury Bulletin*, beginning with the issue of July 1946. Since Apr. 30, 1953, figures for sales of Series E and H bonds only have been available by States.

IV.—Interest

TABLE 51.—*Amount of interest-bearing public debt outstanding, the computed annual interest charge, and the computed rate of interest, June 30, 1939–65, and at the end of each month during 1965*

[On basis of daily Treasury statements, see "Bases of Tables"]

End of fiscal year or month	Interest-bearing debt [1]	Computed annual interest charge [2]	Computed rate of interest [2]
			Percent
1939	$39, 885, 969, 732	$1, 036, 937, 397	2. 600
1940	42, 376, 495, 928	1, 094, 619, 914	2. 583
1941	48, 387, 399, 539	1, 218, 238, 845	2. 518
1942	71, 968, 418, 098	1, 644, 476, 360	2. 285
1943	135, 380, 305, 795	2, 678, 779, 036	1. 979
1944	199, 543, 355, 301	3, 849, 254, 656	1. 929
1945	256, 356, 615, 818	4, 963, 730, 414	1. 936
1946	268, 110, 872, 218	5, 350, 772, 231	1. 996
1947	255, 113, 412, 039	5, 374, 409, 074	2. 107
1948	250, 063, 348, 379	5, 455, 475, 791	2. 182
1949	250, 761, 636, 723	5, 605, 929, 714	2. 236
1950	255, 209, 353, 372	5, 612, 676, 516	2. 200
1951	252, 851, 765, 497	5, 739, 615, 990	2. 270
1952	256, 862, 861, 128	5, 981, 357, 116	2. 329
1953	263, 946, 017, 740	6, 430, 991, 316	2. 438
1954	268, 909, 766, 654	6, 298, 069, 299	2. 342
1955	271, 741, 267, 507	6, 387, 225, 600	2. 351
1956	269, 883, 068, 041	6, 949, 699, 625	2. 576
1957	268, 485, 562, 677	7, 325, 146, 596	2. 730
1958	274, 697, 560, 009	7, 245, 154, 946	2. 638
1959	281, 833, 362, 429	8, 065, 917, 424	2. 867
1960	283, 241, 182, 755	9, 316, 066, 872	3. 297
1961	285, 671, 608, 619	8, 761, 495, 974	3. 072
1962	294, 442, 000, 790	9, 518, 857, 333	3. 239
1963	301, 953, 730, 701	10, 119, 294, 547	3. 360
1964	307, 356, 561, 535	10, 900, 360, 741	3. 560
1965	313, 112, 816, 994	11, 466, 618, 472	3. 678
1964—July	306, 855, 159, 416	10, 897, 100, 894	3. 565
August	309, 625, 286, 442	10, 993, 886, 433	3. 565
September	311, 122, 208, 149	11, 054, 541, 853	3. 567
October	311, 217, 180, 588	11, 073, 637, 107	3. 573
November	314, 023, 350, 643	11, 183, 983, 274	3. 576
December	313, 553, 496, 747	11, 216, 650, 276	3. 593
1965—January	313, 676, 503, 832	11, 324, 398, 508	3. 626
February	315, 545, 490, 230	11, 461, 514, 657	3. 649
March	313, 332, 086, 832	11, 408, 476, 673	3. 657
April	312, 209, 210, 907	11, 401, 275, 983	3. 668
May	314, 165, 824, 708	11, 494, 398, 991	3. 672
June	313, 112, 816, 994	11, 466, 618, 472	3. 678

[1] Includes discount on Treasury bills; the current redemption value of savings bonds of Series C–F and J; and beginning August 1941, the face amount of Treasury tax and savings notes. The face value of matured savings bonds and notes outstanding is included until all of the annual series have matured, when they are transferred to matured debt on which interest has ceased.

[2] Comparable annual data 1916–38 are contained in 1962 annual report, p. 735. Current monthly figures are published in the *Treasury Bulletin.* Comparable monthly data 1929–36 appear in 1936 annual report, p. 442, and from 1937 in later reports. Annual interest charge monthly 1916–29 appears in 1929 annual report, p. 509.

NOTE.—The computed annual interest charge represents the amount of interest that would be paid if each interest-bearing issue outstanding at the end of the month or year should remain outstanding for a year at the applicable annual rate of interest. The charge is computed for each issue by applying the appropriate annual interest rate to the amount outstanding on that date.

Beginning Dec. 31, 1958, the computed average rate is based upon the rate of effective yield for issues sold at premiums or discounts. Before that date the computed average rate was based upon the coupon rates of the securities. That rate did not materially differ from the rate on the basis of effective yield. The "effective yield" method of computing the average interest rate on the public debt more accurately reflects the interest cost to the Treasury, and is believed to be in accord with the intent of Congress where legislation has required the use of the rate of effective yield for various purposes.

Table 52.—*Computed annual interest rate and computed annual interest charge on the public debt by classes, June 30, 1939–65*

[Dollar amounts in millions. On basis of daily Treasury statements, see "Bases of Tables"]

Computed annual interest rate

End of fiscal year or month	Total public debt	Marketable issues					Nonmarketable issues				
		Total [1]	Bills [2]	Certificates	Notes	Treasury bonds	Total	Savings bonds [3]	Tax and savings notes	Other	Special issues
1939	2.600	2.525	0.010	------	1.448	2.964	2.913	2.900	------	3.000	3.091
1940	2.583	2.492	.038	------	1.256	2.908	2.908	2.900	------	3.000	3.026
1941	2.518	2.413	.089	------	1.075	2.78	2.865	2.858	------	3.000	2.904
1942	2.285	2.225	.360	.564	1.092	2.680	2.277	2.787	.506	2.743	2.681
1943	1.979	1.822	.380	.875	1.165	2.494	2.330	2.782	1.040	2.495	2.408
1944	1.929	1.725	.381	.875	1.281	2.379	2.417	2.738	1.080	2.314	2.405
1945	1.936	1.718	.381	.875	1.204	2.314	2.473	2.789	1.076	2.000	2.436
1946	1.996	1.773	.381	.875	1.289	2.307	2.567	2.777	1.070	2.000	2.448
1947	2.107	1.871	.382	.875	1.448	2.30	2.593	2.765	1.070	2.423	2.510
1948	2.182	1.942	1.014	1.042	1.204	2.309	2.623	2.759	1.070	2.414	2.588
1949	2.236	2.001	1.176	1.225	1.375	2.313	2.623	2.751	1.070	2.393	2.596
1950	2.200	1.958	1.187	1.163	1.344	2.322	2.629	2.748	1.290	2.407	2.589
1951	2.270	1.981	1.569	1.875	1.399	2.327	2.623	2.742	1.383	2.717	2.606
1952	2.329	2.051	1.711	1.875	1.560	2.317	2.623	2.745	1.567	2.714	2.675
1953	2.438	2.207	2.254	2.319	1.754	2.342	2.659	2.760	1.785	2.708	2.746
1954	2.342	2.043	.843	1.928	1.838	2.440	2.720	2.793	2.231	2.709	2.671
1955	2.351	2.079	1.539	1.173	1.846	2.480	2.751	2.821	2.377	2.708	2.585
1956	2.576	2.427	2.654	2.625	2.075	2.485	2.789	2.848	2.359	2.713	2.705
1957	2.730	2.707	3.197	3.345	2.504	2.482	2.824	2.880	------	2.718	2.635
1958	2.638	2.546	1.033	3.330	2.806	2.576	2.853	2.925	------	2.718	2.630
1959	2.867	2.891	3.316	2.842	2.304	2.619	2.892	2.961	------	2.714	2.694
1960	3.072	3.449	3.815	4.721	4.058	2.829	2.925	3.293	------	2.715	2.772
1961	3.239	3.043	2.584	3.073	3.704	3.122	3.219	3.408	------	2.713	2.803
1962	3.360	3.285	2.926	3.377	3.680	3.344	3.330	3.449	------	2.670	2.891
1963	3.560	3.425	3.081	3.283	3.921	3.471	3.364	3.482	------	2.770	3.003
July	3.565	3.659	3.729	------	3.854	3.642	3.412	3.517	------	2.917	3.238
August	3.565	3.666	3.718	------	3.842	3.535	3.462	3.519	------	2.938	3.228
September	3.567	3.662	3.720	------	3.838	3.535	3.493	3.521	------	2.949	3.253
October	3.573	3.663	3.722	------	3.821	3.536	3.466	3.522	------	3.009	3.258
November	3.576	3.672	3.736	------	3.821	3.535	3.468	3.524	------	3.030	3.240
December	3.593	3.675	3.773	------	3.839	3.536	3.472	3.526	------	3.045	3.243
January	3.626	3.593	3.854	------	3.813	3.536	3.477	3.528	------	3.070	3.248
February	3.649	3.738	3.900	------	3.811	3.607	3.480	3.529	------	3.095	3.261
March	3.65	3.769	3.957	------	3.815	3.629	3.484	3.531	------	3.089	3.279
April	3.668	3.782	4.013	------	3.826	3.630	3.488	3.533	------	3.100	3.282
May	3.675	3.797	4.053	------	3.825	3.642	3.489	3.535	------	3.144	3.320
June	3.678	3.803	4.064	------	3.844	3.642	3.492	3.537	------	3.105	3.372

Computed annual interest charge

1939	$1,037	$8			$05	$7	63	$54		$8	$7
1940	1,095	88			80	772	92	84		8	15
1941	1,218	90			61	82	30	123		7	78
1942	1,644	1,125	$1	$17	73	1,021	60	284	$15	8	71
1943	2,679	1,737	9	145	07	1,435	87	591	78	11	62
1944	3,849	2,422	45	252	23	1,885	1,084	965	63	16	84
1945	4,964	3,115	56	299	83	2,463	1,390	1,271	109	10	48
1946	5,351	3,362	65	305	35	2,753	1,442	1,362	72	9	57
1947	5,374	3,156	65	221	18	2,753	1,530	1,420	59	51	67
1948	5,455	3,113	60	235	57	2,597	1,561	1,470	47	44	32
1949	5,606	3,103	39	361	49	2,554	1,652	1,548	63	41	81
1950	5,613	3,040	35	214	24	2,387	1,735	1,581	117	37	88
1951	5,740	2,731	60	178	61	1,835	2,106	1,579	123	405	83
1952	5,981	2,879	23	533	96	1,753	2,093	1,583	118	391	00
1953	6,431	3,249	93	368	34	1,903	2,069	1,598	99	372	15
1954	6,298	3,071	42	355	88	1,962	2,099	1,622	121	357	28
1955	6,387	3,225	64	162	82	2,010	2,044	1,647	45	352	18
1956	6,950	3,758	99	428	36	2,034	1,972	1,637		334	20
1957	7,325	4,210	49	685	76	2,005	1,881	1,573		308	34
1958	7,245	4,242	31	1,096	53	2,341	1,787	1,520		266	26
1959	8,066	5,133	06	962	02	2,221	1,728	1,496		232	06
1960	9,316	6,317	89	833	2,088	2,145	1,754	1,566		189	1,245
1961	8,761	5,718	97	410	2,084	2,288	1,781	1,619		162	1,263
1962	9,619	6,422	1,212	457	2,408	2,344	1,798	1,642		156	1,299
1963	10,119	6,944	1,433	728	2,043	2,740	1,830	1,682		148	1,345
1964	10,00	7,513	85		81	07	878	1,734		144	1,509
	10,467	7,878	2,135		2,017	3,727	948	1,770		178	641
1964—July	10,897	7,537	1,861		248	3,428	883	1,737		146	476
August	10,994	7,561	1,898		236	3,427	890	1,741		149	543
September	11,055	7,609	1,946		229	3,426	902	1,744		158	43
October	11,074	7,668	2,013		245	3,425	907	1,747		160	89
November	11,184	7,759	2,088		98	3,425	912	1,752		160	53
December	11,217	7,803	2,133		028	3,701	917	1,755		162	47
1965—January	11,324	62	2,232		121	3,644	919	1,758		161	42
February	11,462	8,044	2,290		121	3,642	923	1,761		162	84
March	11,408	7,983	2,221		114	3,641	927	1,764		163	98
April	11,401	8,014	2,258		016	3,727	935	1,766		169	62
May	11,494	7,969	2,226		017	3,727	1,948	1,768		169	88
June	1,67	7,878	2,135					1,770		178	61

*Less than $500,000.

1 Total includes Panama Canal bonds prior to 1961, postal savings bonds prior to 1956, and conversion bonds prior to 1947.

2 Included in debt outstanding at face amount, but the annual interest charge and the annual interest rate are computed on the discount value.

3 The annual interest charge and annual interest rate on United States savings bonds are computed on the basis of the rate to maturity applied against the amount outstanding.

NOTE.—For methods of computing annual interest rate and charge see note to table 51. See table 35 for amounts of public debt outstanding by classification.

TABLE 53.—*Interest on the public debt by classes, fiscal years 1961–65*

[In millions of dollars, on an accrual basis. On basis of Public Debt accounts, see "Bases of Tables"]

Class of securities	1961	1962	1963	1964	1965
Public issues:					
Marketable:					
Treasury bills [1]	1,108.7	1,149.3	1,392.4	1,763.9	2,099.0
Certificates of indebtedness	712.3	282.5	682.4	343.3	
Treasury notes	1,951.8	2,417.9	2,127.4	2,302.9	2,194.4
Treasury bonds	2,214.1	2,216.8	2,554.1	2,944.3	3,508.7
Panama Canal bonds	1.4				
Total marketable issues	5,988.3	6,066.5	6,756.3	7,354.4	7,802.2
Nonmarketable:					
Depositary bonds	2.6	2.9	2.1	2.0	1.9
Foreign currency series:					
Certificates of indebtedness		.9	1.9	.7	.4
Treasury bonds			8.2	23.3	40.3
Foreign series:					
Certificates of indebtedness		10.7	11.3	11.1	9.0
Treasury notes			2.7	5.6	6.0
Treasury bonds					6.7
Treasury bonds, investment series	169.1	140.2	118.7	100.4	92.2
Treasury bonds, REA series	.2	.5	.5	.5	.5
U.S. savings bonds:					
Series E, F, and J [1]	1,285.8	1,358.3	1,404.5	1,466.7	1,515.8
Series G, H, and K	261.1	277.7	298.1	313.6	324.9
U.S. retirement plan bonds				.1	.3
Treasury certificates				.1	1.5
Treasury bonds				.4	.6
Other [2]	(*)	(*)	(*)	(*)	
Total nonmarketable issues	1,718.8	1,791.2	1,848.0	1,924.5	2,000.0
Total public issues	7,707.1	7,857.7	8,604.3	9,278.9	9,802.1
Special issues:					
Certificates of indebtedness	243.6	228.6	248.9	264.5	312.3
Treasury notes	265.7	204.6	167.6	95.6	68.1
Treasury bonds	740.8	828.9	874.5	1,025.6	1,162.2
Total special issues	1,250.1	1,262.1	1,291.0	1,385.7	1,542.6
Total interest on public debt	8,957.2	9,119.8	9,895.3	10,664.6	11,344.7
Other [3]				1.3	1.8
Total interest and charges	8,957.2	9,119.8	9,895.3	10,665.9	11,346.5

*Less than $50,000.
[1] Amounts represent discount treated as interest.
[2] Includes Armed Forces leave bonds and adjusted service bonds.
[3] Charges for gold and foreign currency purchases authorized by act of June 19, 1962 (22 U.S.C. 286e-2(c)) and act of Oct. 23, 1962 (76 Stat. 1168).

V.—Prices and yields of securities

TABLE 54.—*Average yields of taxable* [1] *long-term Treasury bonds by months, October 1941–June 1965* [2]

[Averages of daily figures. Percent per annum compounded semiannually]

Year	Jan.	Feb.	Mar.	Apr.	May	June	July	Aug.	Sept.	Oct.	Nov.	Dec.	Average
1941										*2.34	2.34	2.47	2.46
1942	2.48	2.48	2.46	2.44	2.45	2.43	2.46	2.47	2.46	2.48	2.47	2.49	2.47
1943	2.46	2.46	2.48	2.48	2.46	2.45	2.45	2.46	2.48	2.48	2.48	2.49	2.47
1944	2.49	2.49	2.48	2.48	2.49	2.49	2.49	2.48	2.47	2.48	2.48	2.48	2.48
1945	2.44	2.38	2.40	2.39	2.39	2.35	2.34	2.36	2.37	2.35	2.33	2.33	2.37
1946	2.21	2.12	2.09	2.08	2.19	2.16	2.18	2.23	2.28	2.26	2.25	2.24	2.19
1947	2.21	2.21	2.19	2.19	2.19	2.22	2.25	2.24	2.24	2.27	2.36	2.39	2.25
1948	2.45	2.45	2.44	2.44	2.42	2.41	2.44	2.45	2.45	2.45	2.44	2.44	2.44
1949	2.42	2.39	2.38	2.38	2.38	2.38	2.27	2.24	2.22	2.22	2.20	2.19	2.31
1950	2.20	2.24	2.27	2.30	2.31	2.33	2.34	2.33	2.36	2.38	2.38	2.39	2.32
1951	2.39	2.40	2.47	2.56	2.63	2.65	2.63	2.57	2.56	2.61	2.66	2.70	2.57
1952	2.74	2.71	2.70	*2.64	2.57	2.61	2.61	2.70	2.71	2.74	2.71	2.75	2.68
1953	2.80	2.83	2.89	*2.97	3.11	3.13	3.02	3.02	2.98	2.83	2.86	2.79	2.94
1954	2.69	2.62	2.53	2.48	2.54	2.55	2.47	2.48	2.52	2.54	2.57	2.69	2.55
1955	2.68	2.78	2.78	2.82	2.81	2.82	2.91	2.95	2.92	2.87	2.89	2.91	2.84
1956	2.88	2.85	2.93	3.07	2.97	2.93	3.00	3.17	3.21	3.20	3.30	3.40	3.08
1957	3.34	3.22	3.26	3.32	3.40	3.58	3.60	3.66	3.66	3.73	3.57	3.30	3.47
1958	3.24	3.25	3.25	3.12	3.14	3.20	3.36	3.60	3.75	3.76	3.70	3.80	3.43
1959	3.91	3.92	3.92	4.01	4.08	4.09	4.11	4.10	4.26	4.11	4.12	4.27	4.08
1960	4.37	4.22	4.08	4.18	4.16	3.98	3.86	3.79	3.84	3.91	3.93	3.88	4.02
1961	3.89	3.81	3.78	3.80	3.73	3.88	3.90	4.00	4.02	3.98	3.98	4.06	3.90
1962	4.08	4.09	4.01	3.89	3.88	3.90	4.02	3.98	3.94	3.89	3.87	3.87	3.95
1963	3.89	3.92	3.93	3.97	3.97	4.00	4.01	3.99	4.04	4.07	4.11	4.14	4.00
1964	4.15	4.14	4.18	4.20	4.16	4.13	4.13	4.14	4.16	4.16	4.12	4.14	4.15
1965	4.14	4.16	4.15	4.15	4.14	4.14							

[1] Taxable bonds are those on which the interest is subject to both the normal and surtax rates of the Federal income tax. This average commenced Oct. 20, 1941.

[2] Prior to October 1941 yields were on partially tax-exempt long-term bonds. For January 1920 through December 1945, see the 1956 annual report, page 492, and for January 1919 through December 1929, see the 1943 annual report, p. 662.

[3] Beginning Oct. 20, 1941, through Mar. 31, 1962, yields are based on bonds neither due nor callable for 15 years; beginning Apr. 1, 1962, through Mar. 31, 1963, on bonds neither due nor callable for 12 years; beginning Apr. 1, 1963, on bonds neither due nor callable for 10 years.

NOTE.—For bonds selling above par and callable at par before maturity, the yields are computed on the basis of redemption at first call date; while for bonds selling below par, yields are computed to maturity. Monthly averages are averages of daily figures. Each daily figure is an unweighted average of the yields of the individual issues. Yields before 1953 are computed on the basis of the mean of closing bid and ask quotations in the over-the-counter market. Commencing April 1953, yields, as reported by the Federal Reserve Bank of New York, are based on over-the-counter closing bid quotations. See *Treasury Bulletin* for current monthly yields.

TABLE 55.—*Prices and yields of taxable public debt marketable issues June 30, 1964, and June 30, 1965, and price range since first traded*

[Price decimals are thirty-seconds and + indicates additional sixty-fourth]

Issue [1]	June 30, 1964			June 30, 1965			Price range since first traded [2]			
	Price		Yield to call or to maturity [3]	Price		Yield to call or to maturity [3]	High		Low	
	Bid	Ask		Bid	Ask		Price	Date	Price	Date
Treasury bonds:			*Percent*			*Percent*				
3% May 15, 1965	99.15+	99.17+	3.47	99.26+	99.28+	3.95	100.13	June 5, 1958	89.00	Apr. 6, 1960
3% May 15, 1966	99.26	99.28	3.85	99.04	99.06	3.80	102.11	May 15, 1961	99.07	Apr. 7, 1960
3% Aug. 15, 1962-67	98.15	98.19	3.76	99.09	99.11	3.92	103.20	Apr. 21, 1958	89.24	Apr. 6, 1960
3% Nov. 15, 1967	99.00	99.02	3.82	97.22	97.26	3.92	100.06	May 15, 1961	97.10	Dec. 12, 1961
3% Nov. 15, 1962-67	96.18	96.22	3.74	99.06	99.08	3.74	108.12	Apr. 6, 1946	84.22	Nov. 15, 1959
3% Nov. 15, 1967	98.29	98.31	3.97	99.06	99.08	3.99	108.26	Dec. 24, 1962	97.18	Aug. 8, 1961
3% May 15	99.17	99.21	4.01	99.16	99.20	4.06	102.04	May 12, 1961	98.11	Aug. 9, 1960
3% Aug. 15	98.29	99.01	4.04	99.02	99.06	4.07	101.06	Dec. 26, 1962	97.29	Dec. 24, 1964
3% May 15, 1968	99.12	99.14	4.03	99.12	99.16	4.08	99.19	Nov. 26, 1964	98.13	Dec. 24, 1964
3% Feb. 15, 1964-69	94.14	94.20	3.87	95.21	95.25	3.86	108.03	Apr. 6, 1946	82.08	Apr. 24, 1960
2½% Oct. 1, 1969	99.31	100.03	4.01	99.29	100.01	4.03	102.08	Dec. 24, 1962	99.07	Apr. 24, 1964
2½% Oct. 1, 1969	93.15	93.21	3.97	94.31	94.31	4.01	107.25	Apr. 21, 1958	81.10	Apr. 6, 1960
4% Mar. 15, 1965-70	99.31	100.03	4.01	99.26	99.26	4.08	110.14	Apr. 6, 1946	94.04	Oct. 30, 1959
4% Aug. 15	92.28	93.02	3.97	94.08	94.08	3.92	107.24	Apr. 6, 1946	81.04	Apr. 6, 1960
4% Mar. 15, 1971	92.17	92.21	3.98	93.29	94.16	4.13	99.19	Jan. 22, 1965	99.05	Mar. 2, 1965
4% Aug. 15	99.19	99.23	4.08	93.11	94.15	3.93	107.23	Aug. 2, 1963	80.10	Jan. 24, 1964
4% Nov. 15, 1971	91.19	91.23	3.94	92.23	92.27	3.94	100.14	Apr. 6, 1946	79.28	Mar. 3, 1964
4% Feb. 15, 1972	99.13	99.17	4.10	98.09	99.13	4.13	107.27	Dec. 26, 1962	98.14	Apr. 3, 1964
4% June 15, 1972	98.15	98.19	4.13	98.11	98.15	4.17	101.27	Dec. 26, 1962	97.16	Mar. 3, 1964
4% Aug. 15, 1972	99.06	99.10	3.98	91.07	91.11	4.16	101.20	Dec. 26, 1962	98.06	Mar. 4
4% June 15	99.06	99.10	3.12	91.02	99.06	3.96	106.16	Apr. 6, 1946	79.12	Dec. 26, 1962
2½% Feb. 15, 1967-72	89.14	89.27	3.99	90.30	100.02	3.96	101.20	Dec. 26, 1962	98.06	Apr. 24, 1964
2½% Nov. 15	89.14	89.27	3.98	90.20	90.26	3.95	109.18	Apr. 6, 1946	78.24	Apr. 6, 1960
4% Nov. 15, 1973	98.29	99.01	4.15	98.20	98.24	4.20	106.16	Apr. 6, 1946	79.06	Apr. 6, 1960
4% Nov. 15				99.14	99.16	4.21	99.06	Nov. 12, 1964	98.01	Apr. 25
4% Feb. 15	0.21	100.23	4.17	99.13	99.17	4.20	100.01	Jan. 22, 1965	99.04	Mar. 2, 1965
4¼% Feb. 15, 1975-85	97.22	97.28	4.15	100.11	100.13	4.18	101.07	Nov. 12, 1964	100.04	June 2, 1965
4% Nov. 15	0.20	100.28	4.15	97.22	97.26	4.22	110.24	Apr. 22, 1958	92.08	Dec. 6, 1960
4% Feb. 15, 1978-83	98.10	98.18	4.15	100.15	100.15	4.17	105.28	May 5, 1961	98.10	July 19, 1960
3% Nov. 15	98.16	98.24	4.14	98.04	98.12	4.18	103.18	May 12, 1961	93.08	Dec. 6, 1960
3% June 15, 1978-83	8.22	88.30	4.12	92.10	92.18	4.16	97.17	Aug. 4, 1954	91.02	Jan. 14, 1964
3% May 15	87.28	88.02	4.11	88.18	88.26	4.12	111.28	May 12, 1961	82.06	Dec. 6, 1960
3% Feb. 15	0.02	90.10	4.13	88.08	88.16	4.12	101.04	June 4, 1954	82.04	June 6, 1960
3% Feb. 15, 1987-92	101.04	101.12	4.17	89.23	89.31	4.17	106.26	Apr. 21, 1958	84.08	Dec. 6, 1960
3% Feb. 15, 1988-93	97.10	97.18	4.16	100.00	100.13	4.23	104.10	Dec. 26, 1962	99.30	May 2, 1965
				96.22	96.30	4.20	100.11	Jan. 16, 1963	96.17	June 1, 1965

	Price[2]		Yield[3]	Price[2]		Yield[3]	Price[2]	Date	Price[2]	Date
2% May 5, 90	9.02	9.10	4.18	98.18	98.26	4.21	100.26	Aug. 28, 1963	98.00	Mar. 30, 1964
2% Feb. 15, 95	8.12	8.20	3.75	86.10	86.18	3.77	101.12	June 8, 1955	79.08	Jan. 6, 1960
3½% Nov. 15, 2	8.02	8.10	4.10	88.14	88.22	4.14	95.14	May 12, 1961	87.06	Mar. 30, 1964
Treasury notes.										
2⅝B, Aug. 15, 1964	0+	0. 0+	3.51				105.28	May 12, 1961	99.31	Aug. 12, 1964
3¾% E, Aug. 15, 2	100.00+	00+	3.57				101.08	Oct. 4, 1962	99.23	Aug. 14, 1961
2% C, Nov. 15, 1964	0.17	0.19	3.40				105.22	May 15, 1961	99.25	Feb. 2, 1960
2% F, Nov. 15, 1964	100.04+	100.06+	3.35							
2% A, May 5, 2	0.22	0.24	3.81				105.07	May 12, 1961	99.25	May 18, 1960
3% C, May 15, 65	0.03	0.05	3.76							
2% D, Aug. 15, 2	0.02	0.04	3.82	0+	0.00+	3.95				
3½% B, Nov. 15, 1965	9.20	9.22	3.78	99.28	9.30	3.83	100.17	eB. 21, 1963	9.01	Mar. 30, 94
2% E, Nov. 15, 1965	100.08	100.09	3.81	.00+	100.03+	3.85				
3⅝% B, Feb. 15, 66	9.21	9.23	3.85	9.26	99.28	3.93	0.25	ed. 24, 1962	9.00	Mar. 24, 94
2% C, Feb. 15, 66				9.31	0.01	3.93				
2% D, May 15, 66				0.01	0.03	3.96				
2% A, Aug. 15, 66	0.08	0.10	3.88	0.01	0.03	3.97	0.04	ed. 26, 62	9.22	Mar. 24, 94
4% E, Nov. 15, 66				0.01	0.03	3.98				
4% B, Feb. 15, 67	9.08	9.10	3.93	99 16	9.18	3.95	0.02+	aB. 20, 1963	8.11	Mar. 24, 94
3¾% A, Apr. 15, 67	9.13	9.17	3.95	9.16	9.18	4.00	0.06	ed. 24, 1962	8.13	Mar. 24, 94
2% EO, Oct. 1, 67	9.19	9.21	3.13				9.31	eB. 29, 1964	8.00	eB. 30, 99
2% EA, Apr. 1, 65	8.25	8.29	3.16				9.30	aB. 29, 1965	8.12	My 24, 1960
2% EO, O. 1, 65	9.29	8.05	3.22	9.12	99.16	4.02	99 12	Je 6, 65	0.06	Nov. 29, 1960
1½% EA, Apr. 1, 66	9.26	9.00	3.39	8.19	8.23	3.42	8.19	ule 30, 1965	8.06	Bt. 8, 1961
2% EO, O. 1, 66	9.26	9.00	2.45	9.23	9.29	3.38	97.24	nle 24, 1965	89 12	Oct. 11, 1961
2% EA, Apr. 1, 6	94.24	9.00	3.52	9.24	9.30	3.43	9.26	nle 24, 1965	9.09	Jy 9, 1962
1½% EO, O. 1, 6	9.24	9.00	3.55	9.24	9.30	3.48	9.24	ule 30, 1965	9.00	Oct. 1, 1962
1½% EA, Apr. 1, 68	9.28	9.04	3.55	9.25	94 31	3.51	9.26	ule 24, 1965	9.02	Jy 17, 1963
1% EO, O. 1, 68	9.28	9.04	3.58	9.27	9.01	3.52	8.28	nle 24, 1965	9.08	aB. 25, 1964
1½% EA, Apr. 1, 9	9.02	9.10	3.56	9.21	92.27	3.61	9.22	ule 24, 1965	8.25	Jo. 6, 1964
1% EO, Oct. 1, 9				9.20	9.26	3.65	9.22	Jne 24, 1965	9.00	Nov. 30, 1964
1½% EA, Apr. 1, 9				9.20	9.28	3.67	9.22	Jne 24, 1965	90.12	My 24, 1965

[1] Excludes Treasury bills, which are fully taxable. For description and amount of each issue outstanding on June 30, 1965, see table 36; for information as of June 30, 1964, see 1964 annual report, p. 470.

[2] Beginning April 1953, prices are closing bid quotations. Prices for prior dates are the means of closing bid and ask quotations; "when issued" prices are included in price range. Dates of highs and lows in case of recurrence are the latest dates. Issues with original maturity of less than two years are excluded.

[3] Yields are computed to earliest call date when prices are above par and to maturity date when prices are at par or below.

NOTE.—Prices and yields (based on closing bid prices) on June 30, 1964 and 1965, are over-the-counter quotations, as reported to the Treasury Department by the Federal Reserve Bank of New York. Yields are percent per annum compounded semiannually except that those for securities having only one interest payment are computed on a simple interest basis.

TREASURY DEP

VI.—Ownership of governmental securities

TABLE 56.—*Estimated ownership of interest-bearing governmental securities outstanding June 30, 1954–65, by type of issuer*

[Par value.[1] In billions of dollars]

June 30	Total amount outstanding	Held by banks			Held by U.S. Government investment accounts	Held by private nonbank investors						
		Total	Commercial banks	Federal Reserve banks		Total	Individuals[2]	Insurance companies	Mutual savings banks	Corporations[3]	State, local, and Territorial governments[4]	Miscellaneous investors[5]
I. Securities of U.S. Government and Federal instrumentalities guaranteed by United States[6]												
1954	269.0	88.7	63.6	25.0	49.3	131.0	r 63.8	15.4	9.1	r 16.5	13.9	12.2
1955	271.8	87.1	63.5	23.6	50.5	134.1	r 64.2	15.0	8.7	r 18.6	14.7	12.8
1956	270.0	81.0	57.3	23.8	53.5	135.4	r 65.5	13.6	8.4	r 17.3	16.1	14.6
1957	268.6	79.2	56.2	23.0	55.6	133.8	r 65.3	12.7	7.9	r 16.1	16.8	14.9
1958	274.8	90.7	65.3	25.4	55.9	128.2	r 63.4	12.2	7.4	r 14.1	16.3	14.7
1959	281.9	87.6	61.5	26.0	54.6	139.7	r 65.4	12.6	7.3	r 19.8	16.9	17.7
1960	283.4	81.8	55.3	26.5	55.3	146.2	r 68.8	12.0	6.6	r 19.5	18.8	20.4
1961	285.9	89.8	62.5	27.3	56.1	140.0	r 63.9	11.4	6.3	r 18.5	19.3	20.6
1962	294.9	94.8	65.2	29.7	56.5	143.6	r 64.8	11.4	6.3	r 18.2	20.1	22.9
1963	302.6	96.4	64.4	32.0	58.4	147.8	r 65.3	11.0	6.1	r 18.7	21.5	25.2
1964	308.2	95.0	60.2	34.8	61.1	152.0	r 68.5	10.9	6.0	r 18.5	22.5	25.7
1965	313.7	97.4	58.3	39.1	63.4	153.0	70.5	10.6	5.8	15.1	24.1	27.0
II. Securities of Federal instrumentalities not guaranteed by United States[7]												
1954	2.0	1.3	1.3	--------	(*)	.7	.2	.1	.1	.1	.1	.1
1955	2.9	1.8	1.8	--------	(*)	1.1	.4	.1	.1	.2	.1	.2
1956	3.9	1.6	1.6	--------	(*)	2.3	1.0	.1	.2	.4	.2	.4
1957	5.0	1.7	1.7	--------	(*)	3.3	1.3	.1	.3	.7	.3	.6
1958	5.4	2.2	2.2	--------	(*)	3.2	.9	.2	.3	.7	.3	.8
1959	6.7	1.9	1.9	--------	(*)	4.8	1.9	.2	.4	1.0	.4	.9
1960	8.4	1.6	1.6	--------	(*)	6.8	2.7	.3	.5	1.7	.6	1.0
1961	7.8	1.8	1.8	--------	(*)	6.0	1.9	.3	.5	1.5	.7	1.1
1962	9.3	2.3	2.3	--------	(*)	7.0	2.5	.4	.6	1.5	.8	1.2
1963	10.2	2.9	2.9	--------	.1	7.3	2.6	.4	.6	1.6	.9	1.1
1964	11.9	3.1	3.1	--------	(*)	8.8	3.6	.5	.7	1.7	1.0	1.3
1965	13.5	3.5	3.5	--------	(*)	10.0	4.0	.6	.8	1.3	1.7	1.6
III. Securities of State and local governments, Territories, and possessions[8]												
1954	37.4	12.0	12.0	--------	.3	25.1	13.8	4.6	.5	.9	4.5	.7
1955	42.8	12.8	12.8	--------	.3	29.7	16.4	5.8	.7	1.1	4.9	.8
1956	47.6	13.0	13.0	--------	.2	34.5	19.5	6.6	.7	1.4	5.3	.9
1957	52.1	13.4	13.4	--------	.2	38.4	22.0	7.4	.7	1.5	5.8	1.0
1958	56.8	15.8	15.8	--------	.3	40.7	22.8	8.2	.7	1.5	6.4	1.1
1959	62.0	17.0	17.0	--------	.3	44.6	24.6	9.5	.7	1.7	6.8	1.3
1960	66.4	16.8	16.8	--------	.3	49.2	27.2	11.1	.7	1.7	7.1	1.5
1961	71.7	18.8	18.8	--------	.4	52.5	28.3	12.6	.7	1.9	7.4	1.6
1962	80.1	23.2	23.2	--------	.5	56.4	30.7	13.7	.6	2.4	7.2	1.8
1963	85.9	27.9	27.9	--------	.6	57.5	31.7	14.5	.5	2.6	6.4	1.8
1964	91.3	31.5	31.5	--------	.6	59.2	r 33.7	r 15.0	.4	2.7	5.6	1.8
1965	97.8	36.6	36.6	--------	.8	60.4	35.0	15.2	.4	3.0	5.0	1.8

*Less than $50 million.
r Revised.
[1] Except data including U.S. savings bonds of Series A–F and J, which are on the basis of current redemption value.
[2] Includes partnerships and personal trust accounts.
[3] Exclusive of banks and insurance companies.
[4] Comprises trust, sinking, and investment funds of State and local governments, Territories, and possessions.
[5] Includes savings and loan associations, nonprofit associations, corporate pension trust funds, dealers and brokers, and investments of foreign balances and international accounts in this country.
[6] On daily Treasury statement basis. Since noninterest-bearing debt is excluded the figures differ slightly from those in discussion of debt ownership. Special issues to Federal agencies and trust funds are included and guaranteed securities held by the Treasury are excluded.
[7] Excludes stocks and interagency loans. Series revised to include Federal land bank securities.
[8] Excludes obligations of Puerto Rico.

NOTE.—For data from 1937–51, see the 1952 annual report, pp. 764 and 765; and for 1952 and 1953, the 1962 annual report, page 745. The 1963 and earlier reports exclude Federal land banks for the years 1947–63 in the series for Federal instrumentalities not guaranteed by the United States.

TABLE 57.—*Summary of Treasury survey of ownership of interest-*

[Par value. In

Classification	Total amount outstanding		Held by investors							
			Commercial banks [2][3]		Mutual savings banks [2]		Insurance companies			
							Life		Fire, casualty, and marine	
	June 30		June 30		June 30		June 30		June 30	
	1964	1965	1964	1965	1964	1965	1964	1965	1964	1965
Number of institutions or funds_			6,039	5,978	502	501	297	296	488	482
TYPE OF SECURITY										
Public marketable:										
Treasury bills_____	50,740	53,665	7,505	7,058	374	568	106	92	240	255
Treasury notes_____	67,284	52,549	20,545	12,850	921	450	147	67	1,093	572
Treasury bonds_____	88,464	102,481	23,058	28,574	4,363	4,508	4,402	4,358	2,946	3,508
Guaranteed securities held outside the Treasury____	812	589	72	48	176	114	104	93	12	6
Total public marketable___	207,301	209,284	51,180	48,530	5,834	5,641	4,758	4,610	4,291	4,342
Public nonmarketable: [5]										
U.S. savings bonds [5]_____	49,299	50,043	1	1	6	5	5	4	18	13
Investment series bonds_____	3,546	3,256	157	134	113	100	369	190	57	54
Depositary bonds_____	103	59	[7] 103	[7] 59	(*)	(*)				
All other [4]_____	1,292	2,410								
Total public nonmarketable_____	54,240	55,768	261	194	119	105	374	194	74	67
Special issues_____	46,627	48,650								
Grand total_____	308,169	313,702	51,441	48,724	5,953	5,746	5,133	4,804	4,365	4,409
MATURITY CLASSES [9]										
Public marketable:										
Within 1 year_____	81,424	87,637	14,549	13,945	829	766	130	136	770	526
1 to 5 years_____	65,453	56,198	25,392	20,672	1,401	1,384	352	344	1,684	1,646
5 to 10 years_____	34,929	39,169	10,208	12,827	1,857	1,814	841	740	1,407	1,644
10 to 15 years_____	2,244	2,609	311	79	88	84	44	178	66	57
15 to 20 years_____	6,110	5,841	183	255	272	248	674	759	134	125
20 years and over_____	16,328	17,241	466	705	1,211	1,231	2,614	2,362	218	338
Guaranteed securities_____	812	589	72	48	176	114	104	93	12	6
Total public marketable___	207,301	209,284	51,180	48,530	5,834	5,641	4,758	4,610	4,291	4,342

*Less than $500,000.
[1] Banks and insurance companies covered in the Treasury survey of ownership of securities issued or guaranteed by the U.S. Government, account for approximately 90 percent of the amount of such securities owned by all banks and insurance companies in the United States. The savings and loan associations and corporations account for about half of the Federal securities held by these investor classes. State and local government funds account for about 70 percent. Details as to the ownership of each security are available in the *Treasury Bulletin* monthly for the above investors and semiannually for commercial banks classified by membership in the Federal Reserve System.
[2] Securities held in trust departments are excluded.
[3] Includes trust companies and stock savings banks.
[4] Included with all other investors are those banks, insurance companies, savings and loan associations, corporations, and State and local government funds not reporting in the Treasury survey.
[5] Consists of corporate pension trust funds and profit-sharing plans which involve retirement benefits.

bearing public debt and guaranteed securities, June 30, 1964 and 1965

millions of dollars]

covered in Treasury survey [1]													
Savings and loan associations		Corporations		State and local governments				U.S. Government investment accounts and Federal Reserve banks		Held by all other investors [4]		Memorandum: Held by corporate pension trust funds [5]	
				General funds		Pension and retirement funds							
June 30		June 30		June 30		June 30		June 30		June 30		June 30	
1964	1965	1964	1965	1964	1965	1964	1965	1964	1965	1964	1965	1964	1965
488	488	469	469	315	316	191	191	-------	-------	-------	-------	16,904	18,387
252	314	5,845	4,270	4,729	5,261	407	430	6,631	8,993	24,651	26,422	653	565
502	234	2,675	2,128	1,987	1,560	101	11	25,818	26,266	13,496	8,410	444	218
2,534	3,033	1,685	1,304	3,517	3,852	5,325	5,840	14,465	16,216	26,169	31,290	1,128	1,390
106	73	-------	-------	(*)	1	22	26	159	139	162	88	8	8
3,394	3,655	10,205	7,701	10,234	10,673	5,855	6,307	47,073	51,614	64,477	66,210	2,233	2,180
28	21	2	1	33	25	26	19	7	7	49,175	49,948	130	138
49	40	5	1	124	89	186	169	2,210	2,204	275	274	17	17
-------	-------	-------	-------	-------	-------	-------	-------	-------	-------	1,292	2,410	-------	-------
77	61	7	2	157	114	212	188	2,217	2,211	50,742	52,632	146	155
-------	-------	-------	-------	-------	-------	-------	-------	46,627	48,650	-------	-------	-------	-------
3,471	3,715	10,212	7,703	10,391	10,787	6,066	6,495	95,918	102,475	115,220	118,842	2,379	2,336
447	432	7,688	5,482	5,602	6,218	507	439	19,851	28,415	31,052	31,279	880	684
962	950	2,078	1,845	1,846	1,609	175	281	16,639	12,416	14,924	15,052	480	453
1,191	1,492	319	249	1,087	1,210	803	752	4,839	4,996	12,377	13,446	530	572
106	66	8	1	111	207	127	354	671	726	713	858	32	59
135	181	2	52	541	576	933	882	1,618	1,473	1,619	1,290	111	88
448	461	110	73	1,047	852	3,289	3,573	3,297	3,449	3,630	4,198	191	316
106	73	-------	-------	(*)	1	22	26	159	139	162	88	8	8
3,394	3,655	10,205	7,701	10,234	10,673	5,855	6,307	47,073	51,614	64,477	66,210	2,233	2,180

Quarterly data are presented in the *Treasury Bulletin* as supplemental information in a memorandum column accompanying the Survey of Ownership for each reporting date, beginning with Dec. 31, 1953. The corresponding information from earlier reports, beginning with Dec. 31, 1949, is summarized in the March 1954 *Treasury Bulletin*, p. 30.

[6] U.S. savings bonds Series E, F, and J are reported at maturity value by the investors covered in the Treasury survey and have been adjusted to current redemption value for this table.

[7] Includes depositary bonds held by commercial banks not included in the survey: $52 million in 1964 and $19 million in 1965.

[8] For details see table 35.

[9] All issues classified to final maturity. Table 34 shows from 1946–65 the maturity distribution of marketable, interest-bearing public debt by call classes and by maturity classes.

Account of the Treasurer of the United States

TABLE 58.—*Assets and liabilities in the account of the Treasurer of the United States, June 30, 1964 and 1965*

[On basis of daily Treasury statements, see "Bases of Tables"]

	June 30, 1964	June 30, 1965	Increase, or decrease (−)
GOLD			
Assets: Gold	$15,461,239,587.26	$13,934,074,997.61	−$1,527,164,589.65
Liabilities:			
Gold certificates, Series of 1934, outstanding	2,816,055,600.00	1,277,800.00	[1]−2,814,777,800.00
Gold certificates fund-Board of Governors, Federal Reserve System	10,936,087,296.12	12,052,115,092.09	1,116,027,795.97
Redemption fund-Federal Reserve notes	1,433,306,749.26	1,616,842,174.26	183,535,425.00
Reserve against U.S. notes outstanding	156,039,430.93	156,039,430.93	
Gold balance	119,750,510.95	107,800,500.33	−11,950,010.62
Total	15,461,239,587.26	13,934,074,997.61	−1,527,164,589.65
SILVER			
Assets:			
Silver bullion (monetary value) [2]	1,846,779,522.69	1,267,428,614.02	−579,350,908.67
Silver dollars	2,943,295.00	2,971,079.00	27,784.00
Total	1,849,722,817.69	1,270,399,693.02	−579,323,124.67
Liabilities:			
Silver certificates (issued after June 30, 1929) outstanding	ʳ 1,822,516,364.00	888,750,703.00	−933,765,661.00
Silver balance	ʳ 27,206,453.69	381,648,990.02	354,442,536.33
Total	1,849,722,817.69	1,270,399,693.02	−579,323,124.67
GENERAL ACCOUNT			
Assets:			
In Treasury offices:			
Gold balance (as above)	119,750,510.95	107,800,500.33	−11,950,010.62
Silver:			
At monetary value, balance (as above)	ʳ 27,206,453.69	381,648,990.02	354,442,536.33
Subsidiary coin	5,840,527.84	9,455,423.56	3,614,895.72
Bullion:			
At recoinage value	144,358.53		−144,358.53
At cost value	10,223,898.49	8,848,785.75	−1,375,112.74
At monetary value [3]	1,410,130.90	9,921,208.46	8,511,077.56
Minor coin	801,606.39	6,342,987.34	5,541,380.95
U.S. notes	1,716,119.00	1,551,521.00	−164,598.00
Silver certificates	ʳ 12,062,693.00	5,841,222.00	−6,221,471.00
Federal Reserve notes	85,295,818.00	109,559,653.00	24,263,835.00
Other currencies, unassorted money, etc.	642,735.00	530,378.00	−112,357.00
Unclassified collections, uncollected items, exchanges, etc. (net)	58,288,291.80	54,584,370.28	−3,703,921.52
Subtotal	323,383,143.59	696,085,039.74	372,701,896.15
Deposits in:			
Federal Reserve banks:			
Available funds	939,014,001.67	672,043,715.74	−266,970,285.93
In process of collection	233,819,839.40	233,455,908.51	−363,930.89
Special depositaries, Treasury tax and loan accounts	9,179,608,424.92	10,688,996,286.68	1,509,387,861.76
National and other bank depositaries	305,946,040.26	263,564,759.56	−42,381,280.70
Foreign depositaries	53,959,759.23	56,118,925.14	2,159,165.91
Subtotal	10,712,348,065.48	11,914,179,595.63	1,201,831,530.15
Total assets, Treasurer's account	11,035,731,209.07	12,610,264,635.37	1,574,533,426.30
General account balance	11,035,731,209.07	12,610,264,635.37	1,574,533,426.30

ʳ Revised.

[1] Decrease represents retirement of certificates held by Federal Reserve banks with corresponding credit in gold certificate fund—Board of Governors, Federal Reserve System.

[2] The Atomic Energy Commission held 64,751,316.1 ounces on June 30, 1964 and 1965.

[3] Consists of silver bullion previously revalued and held to secure outstanding silver certificates, which has been released for use in coinage, pursuant to the President's directive to the Secretary of the Treasury, dated Nov. 28, 1961.

TABLE 59.—*Analysis of changes in tax and loan account balances, fiscal years 1955–65*

[In millions of dollars. On basis of telegraphic reports]

Fiscal year or month	Credits							Withdrawals	Balance			
	Proceeds from sales of securities[1]				Taxes		Total credits		End of period	During period		
	Savings bonds	Retirement plan bonds[2]	Tax anticipation securities	Other	Withheld and excise[3]	Income (by special arrangement)[4]				High	Low	Average
1955	4,424		5,977	8,167	20,538	2,967	42,074	42,545	4,365	7,299	1,910	3,991
1956	3,810		6,035	786	23,897	4,611	39,140	38,871	4,633	5,486	1,103	3,373
1957	2,976		5,043	6,568	26,709	4,152	45,448	46,000	4,082	6,078	813	2,987
1958	2,824		2,922	13,513	27,881	7,903	55,044	50,908	3,744	8,869	1,078	3,246
1959	2,668		7,581	13,164	29,190	5,919	58,520	62,994	6,458	8,055	912	3,638
1960	2,679		7,784	7,920	33,059	6,053	57,496	54,782	6,458	6,458	1,390	4,103
1961	2,787		7,613	1,788	34,511	9,142	55,842	56,847	5,453	7,653	1,161	4,151
1962	2,725	(*)	5,898	3,774	37,519	6,521	56,438	53,076	8,815	8,889	1,531	4,457
1963	2,699	(*)	2,963	3,830	41,267	6,835	57,595	56,085	10,324	10,324	2,635	5,325
1964	2,760	(*)		2,014	43,580	9,921	58,277	59,421	9,180	10,257	1,577	4,747
1965	2,635	(*)	2,340		42,475	12,598	60,050	58,540	10,689	10,872	1,844	6,165
65—												
July	235	(*)			1,546	63	1,844	6,519	4,505	9,155	3,732	5,109
August	219	(*)			4,875		5,094	4,514	5,085	5,899	4,411	5,529
September	204	(*)			3,911	4,019	8,134	4,880	8,339	8,519	2,742	4,789
October	210	(*)	740		1,196	105	2,250	6,434	4,155	7,707	3,320	4,639
November	198		735		4,488		5,421	3,394	6,182	6,329	3,339	4,438
December	217	(*)			3,816	1,860	5,894	6,699	5,377	6,076	2,221	3,450
1965—January	274		865		1,259	35	2,433	4,198	3,612	5,514	1,844	4,478
February	219	(*)			5,088		5,307	3,119	5,800	5,822	3,447	5,599
March	238	(*)			4,640	2,038	6,915	5,444	7,271	7,960	3,111	4,826
April	220	(*)			1,503	2,022	3,745	4,082	6,934	6,934	3,368	8,183
May	196	(*)			5,498	412	6,106	4,218	8,822	9,272	6,901	7,968
June	207				4,655	2,044	6,906	5,040	10,689	10,872	5,766	

*Less than $500,000.

[1] Special depositaries are permitted to make payment in the form of a deposit credit for the purchase price of U.S. Government securities purchased by them for their own account, or for the account of their customers who enter subscriptions through them, when this method of payment is permitted under the terms of the circulars inviting subscriptions to the issues.

[2] Retirement plan bonds were first offered for sale as of Jan. 1, 1963.

[3] Taxes eligible for credit consist of those deposited by taxpayers in the depositary banks, as follows: Withheld income tax beginning March 1948; taxes on employers and employees under the Federal Insurance Contributions Act beginning January 1950, and under the Railroad Retirement Tax Act beginning July 1951; and a number of excise taxes beginning July 1953.

[4] Under a special procedure begun in Mar. 1951, authorization may be given for income tax payments, or a portion of them, made by checks of $10,000 or more drawn on a special depositary bank to be credited to the tax and loan account in that bank. This procedure is followed during some of the periods of heavy tax payments.

Stock and Circulation of Money in the United States

TABLE 60.—*Stock of money, money in the Treasury, in the Federal Reserve banks, and in circulation, by kinds, June 30, 1965*

[In thousands of dollars, except per capita figures. On basis of reports received from various Treasury offices and Federal Reserve banks which take into account those transactions in transit to the Treasurer's Office as of June 30, supplemented by information taken from the Treasurer's accounts. Therefore, the figures shown in this table may differ from similar figures in other tables prepared on basis of daily Treasury statements. See *Circulation Statement of United States Money* published monthly]

Kind of money	Stock of money [1]	Money held in the Treasury					Money outside of the Treasury			
		Total	Amount held as security against gold and silver certificates	Reserve against U.S. notes	Held for Federal Reserve banks and agents	All other money	Total	Held by Federal Reserve banks and agents	In circulation Amount	Per capita [2]
Gold	[3]13,934,083	13,934,063	13,670,235	156,039		107,808	1,278	1,278		
Gold certificates—Series of 1934	[4](13,670,235)	[4](13,668,957)			[4][5](13,668,957)		481,749	51	481,698	2.48
Standard silver dollars	484,720	2,971				2,971				
Silver bullion	1,267,417	1,267,417	888,751			378,666				
Silver certificates—issued after June 30, 1929	[4](888,751)	[4](4,385)				[4](4,385)	884,365	55,611	828,755	4.26
Subsidiary silver	2,375,327	2,056				2,056	2,373,271	17,891	2,355,380	12.11
Minor coin	853,388	4,753				4,753	848,635	24,050	824,585	4.24
U.S. notes	322,681	1,530				1,530	321,151	19,173	301,973	1.55
Federal Reserve notes—1928 and subsequent series	37,343,472	88,267				88,267	37,255,205	2,435,669	34,819,536	178.94
Subtotal	56,581,087	15,301,077	14,558,986	156,039	[4][5](13,668,957)	[6]586,051	[7]42,165,653	2,553,723	39,611,930	203.58
In process of mint (recoinage) from general fund of the Treasury):										
Federal Reserve bank notes	68,793	196				196	68,597	265	68,333	.35
National bank notes	22,283	84				84	22,199	32	22,167	.11
Gold certificates—prior to Series of 1934	13,340	131				131	13,209		13,209	.07
Federal Reserve notes—prior to Series of 1928	3,714	16				16	3,697		3,697	.02
Silver certificates—issued before July 1, 1929	425	3				3	422		422	(*)
Treasury notes of 1890	42						42		42	(*)
Total	56,689,683	15,301,506	14,558,986	156,039	[4](13,668,957)	[6]586,481	[7]42,273,821	2,554,020	39,719,801	204.13

Denomination	Gold certificates	Silver certificates	U.S. notes	Federal Reserve notes	Federal Reserve bank notes	National bank notes	Treasury notes of 1890	Total
$1	---	617,416	188	1,134,418	68	12	7	1,752,108
$2	---	39	115,474	---	15	5	6	115,541
$5	---	175,509	186,226	2,081,023	1,264	2,618	7	2,446,647
$10	3,347	36,137	58	7,437,005	5,359	6,716	6	7,488,629
$20	5,062	9	21	12,695,819	13,552	8,628	6	12,723,097
$50	1,327	2	1	3,341,730	15,771	1,807	(**)	3,360,639
$100	2,183	50	3	7,598,289	32,304	2,368	4	7,635,200
$500	594	7	3	242,868		3		243,475
$1,000	565	8	3	286,136		10	5	286,727
$5,000	50			2,455				2,505
$10,000	80			3,490				3,570
Fractional parts	---	---	---		(**)	(**)		(**)
Total	13,209	829,177	301,978	34,823,233	68,333	22,167	42	36,058,139

Comparative totals of money in circulation

Date	Amount	Per capita [2]
June 30, 1965	$39,719,801	204.13
May 31, 1965	39,206,755	201.69
June 30, 1964	37,733,694	r 196.41
June 30, 1960	32,064,619	177.47
June 30, 1955	30,229,323	182.90
June 30, 1950	27,156,290	179.03
June 30, 1945	26,746,438	191.14
June 30, 1940	7,847,501	59.40
June 30, 1935	5,567,093	43.75
June 30, 1930	4,521,988	36.74
June 30, 1925	4,815,208	41.56
Oct. 31, 1920	5,698,215	53.18
Mar. 31, 1917	4,172,946	40.49
June 30, 1914	3,459,434	34.90
Jan. 1, 1879	816,267	16.76

r Revised.
**Less than $500.
1 For a ...
2 ...

TABLE 61.—*Stock of money, money in the Treasury, in the Federal Reserve banks, and in circulation, selected years, June 30, 1930–65*

[In thousands of dollars, except per capita figures. For basis of data see headnote to table 60]

June 30	Stock of money [1]	Money held in the Treasury					Money outside of the Treasury			
		Total	As security against gold and silver certificates, etc.[2]	As reserve against United States notes [3]	For Federal Reserve banks and agents [4]	All other money	Total	Held by Federal Reserve banks and agents	In circulation Amount [5]	Per capita [6]
1930	8,306,564	4,021,937	1,978,448	156,039	1,796,239	91,211	6,263,076	1,741,087	4,521,988	36.74
1935	15,113,035	9,997,362	7,131,431	156,039	5,832,580	2,709,891	6,714,514	1,147,422	5,567,093	43.75
1940	28,457,960	21,836,936	19,651,667	156,039	14,938,895	2,029,829	11,333,196	3,485,695	7,847,501	59.40
1945	48,009,400	22,202,115	19,923,738	156,039	15,239,072	2,152,338	30,491,980	3,745,512	26,746,438	191.14
1950	52,440,353	26,646,409	23,448,025	156,039	20,166,524	1,141,744	30,976,045	3,819,755	27,156,290	179.03
1955	53,306,618	24,250,685	23,438,908	156,039	18,178,115	635,737	34,318,726	4,089,403	30,229,323	182.90
1960	53,070,922	21,850,109	21,455,014	156,039	16,213,467	239,056	36,462,360	4,397,741	32,064,619	177.47
1963	53,334,680	17,953,822	17,584,879	156,039	12,641,164	212,903	40,324,573	4,854,775	35,469,798	187.30
1964	55,450,634	17,388,137	16,997,358	156,039	12,369,394	234,740	42,690,461	4,956,767	37,733,694	196.41
1965	56,689,683	15,301,506	14,558,086	156,039	13,668,957	586,481	42,273,821	2,554,020	39,719,801	204.11

r Revised.

[3] Until the Old Series Currency Adjustment Act (31 U.S.C. 911–916) was approved June 30, 1961, this gold reserve was also security for the Treasury notes of 1890.

[4] Represents gold earmarked for account of Federal Reserve System. Beginning with 1934 these amounts have been construed as gold certificates issued to the System but held in the Treasury and excluded from total stock of money.

[5] Composition of money in circulation is shown in table 63.

[6] Based on Bureau of Census estimated population, see table 60, footnote 2.

NOTE.—Figures for years not shown appeared in the following annual reports: 1860–1947 in the 1947 report, page 478; 1948 and 1949 in the 1956 report, page 540; 1951–61 in the 1961 report, page 634; and 1962 in the 1964 report, page 595.

TABLE 62.—Stock of money by kinds, selected years, June 30, 1930–65

[In thousands of dollars, except percentage of gold to total stock of money. For basis of data see headnote to table 60]

Kind of money	1930	1935	1940	1945	1950	1955	1960	1963	1964	1965
Bullion and coin:										
Gold	4,534,866	9,115,643	19,963,091	20,212,973	24,230,720	21,677,575	19,322,238	15,733,309	15,461,436	13,934,063
Silver bullion (at monetary value)		313,309	1,353,162	1,520,295	2,022,835	2,187,429	2,252,075	[1] 2,078,399	[1] 1,846,780	[1] 1,267,417
Standard silver dollars	539,960	545,642	547,078	493,943	492,583	490,347	487,773	486,017	484,722	484,720
Subsidiary silver coin	310,978	312,416	402,261	825,798	1,001,574	1,296,140	1,552,106	1,824,878	1,999,475	2,376,327
Minor coin	126,001	133,040	173,909	303,539	378,463	449,625	559,148	681,787	737,665	853,388
Subtotal	5,511,805	10,420,050	22,439,501	23,356,548	28,126,175	26,101,115	24,173,340	20,804,391	20,530,078	18,914,934
Less: Gold, silver bullion, and standard silver dollars held as security for, or redemption of outstanding paper currencies [3]	3,967,402	7,287,471	19,807,106	20,079,777	25,504,665	23,594,948	21,611,053	17,740,919	17,153,397	14,715,025
Total bullion and coin (net)	1,544,403	3,132,579	2,632,395	3,276,771	2,621,510	2,506,168	2,562,287	3,063,472	3,376,681	4,199,909
Paper currency:										
Gold certificates, and credits payable therein [3]	3,322,904	6,320,236	17,821,133	18,106,600	23,022,852	21,028,137	19,059,416	15,457,220	15,185,450	13,670,235
Less: Amount included in collateral held by Federal Reserve agents for Federal Reserve notes	1,596,214	3,294,639	5,557,500	10,968,000	14,349,000	11,108,000	10,565,000	7,243,000	6,542,000	6,295,000
Subtotal	1,726,690	3,025,597	12,263,633	7,138,600	8,673,851	9,920,137	8,494,416	8,214,220	8,643,450	7,375,235
Gold certificates—prior to Series of 1934 [4]								19,982	19,624	13,340
Silver certificates [5]	487,198	810,014	1,828,771	1,815,988	2,324,628	2,409,630	2,394,456	2,142,599	1,826,840	889,176
Treasury notes of 1890 [6]	1,260	1,182	1,163	1,150	1,150	1,142	1,142	142	142	42
United States notes [7]	346,681	346,681	346,681	346,681	346,681	346,681	346,681	346,681	346,681	346,681
Federal Reserve notes [8]	1,746,501	3,492,854	5,481,778	23,650,975	23,602,680	26,629,030	28,394,186	32,032,811	34,428,856	37,347,185
Federal Reserve bank notes [9]	3,260	84,354	22,809	533,979	277,202	164,412	100,736	78,501	73,929	68,093
National bank notes [10]	698,317	769,096	167,190	121,215	87,615	67,379	55,979	37,233	36,393	22,283
Total paper currency (net)	5,009,907	8,529,778	20,112,025	33,608,588	35,313,803	39,538,411	39,787,595	42,872,169	45,375,915	46,038,735
Total stock of money	6,554,310	11,662,357	22,744,420	36,885,360	37,935,313	42,044,579	42,349,882	45,935,641	48,752,595	50,238,644
Percentage of gold to total stock of money	69.19	78.16	87.77	54.80	63.87	51.56	45.63	34.25	31.71	27.74

Footnotes on page 694.

Footnotes to table 62

[1] Excludes bullion carried at monetary value but released for coinage use (see table 58, footnote 3).

[2] Comprises the security for: Gold certificates and credits payable therein (100% in gold); U.S. notes (gold to the extent of the reserve required by law (31 U.S.C. 408)); and silver certificates and Treasury notes of 1890 (100% in silver bullion or standard silver dollars). Since enactment of the Old Series Currency Adjustment Act (31 U.S.C. 912–916) on June 30, 1961, gold certificates prior to the Series of 1934, silver certificates issued before July 1, 1929, and Treasury notes of 1890 have been payable from the general fund. The amount of security shown on this line for years after 1961 has been reduced accordingly.

[3] Consists of: Gold certificates outside of the Treasury (issues prior to Series of 1934 are included through 1961); credits with Treasurer of the United States payable to Board of Governors, Federal Reserve System, in gold certificates (gold or gold certificates prior to Gold Reserve Act of 1934) and 5 percent redemption fund with the Treasurer of the United States for Federal Reserve notes. These obligations are fully secured by gold in the Treasury.

[4] Pursuant to the Old Series Currency Adjustment Act are redeemable from the general fund of the Treasury and upon redemption will be retired.

[5] Silver certificates are secured by silver bullion at monetary value ($1.29+ per fine ounce) and standard silver dollars held in the Treasury. Those certificates issued before July 1, 1929 (of which $425,003 remained outstanding on June 30, 1965) are redeemable from the general fund and upon redemption will be retired (31 U.S.C. 912–916).

[6] Treasury notes of 1890 have been in process of retirement since March 1900 (31 U.S.C. 411) upon receipt by the Treasury. Until June 30, 1961, secured by silver and by gold reserve; thereafter redeemable from general fund.

[7] U.S. notes are secured by the gold reserve (31 U.S.C. 408). This reserve, which was also a reserve for Treasury notes of 1890 until June 30, 1961, amounted to $156,039,088 in 1930, and $156,039,431 for subsequent dates in this table. The act of May 31, 1878 (31 U.S.C. 404) required that the amount of U.S. notes then outstanding, $346,681,016, be kept in circulation. The Old Series Currency Adjustment Act provided that this amount should be reduced by such amounts of notes as the Secretary of the Treasury might determine to have been destroyed or irretrievably lost. On Nov. 16, 1964, the Secretary made such a determination with respect to $24,000,000 of the U.S. notes issued prior to July 1, 1929.

[8] Federal Reserve banks secure Federal Reserve notes by depositing like amounts of collateral with Federal Reserve agents. Such collateral may consist of (a) gold certificates or gold certificate credits (also gold prior to conservation actions of 1933 and 1934), (b) such discounted or purchased paper as is eligible under terms of the Federal Reserve Act, as amended, or (c) since Feb. 27, 1932, securities issued by the United States. Federal Reserve banks must maintain reserves in gold certificates or gold certificate credits (gold for 1933 and preceding years), which may include the 5 percent redemption fund deposited with the Treasurer of the United States, equal to a specified percentage of their notes in actual circulation (40 percent before act of June 12, 1945 (12 U.S.C. 413) and 25 percent thereafter). Federal Reserve notes are obligations of the United States and are a first lien on all assets of the issuing Federal Reserve bank.

Pursuant to the Old Series Currency Adjustment Act of 1961, funds were deposited by the Federal Reserve banks on July 28, 1961, with the Treasurer of the United States for the redemption of all series of Federal Reserve notes issued before the Series of 1928. The amount shown for 1965 includes $3,713,658 for such series.

[9] Federal Reserve bank notes at issuance were secured by direct obligations of the United States or commercial paper. Since termination of their issuance on June 12, 1945 (12 U.S.C. 445 note), the notes have been in process of retirement, and lawful money has been deposited with the Treasurer of the United States for their redemption.

[10] National bank notes at issuance were secured by direct obligations of the United States. From Dec. 23, 1915 (12 U.S.C. 441) these notes have been in process of retirement, and lawful money has been deposited with the Treasurer of the United States for their redemption.

NOTE.—Figures for years not shown appeared in the following annual reports: 1860–1947 in the 1947 report, page 482; 1948 and 1949 in the 1956 report, page 542; 1951–61 in the 1961 report, page 634; and 1962 in the 1964 report, page 596.

TABLE 63.—*Money in circulation by kinds, selected years, June 30, 1930–65*

[In thousands of dollars. On basis of reports received from various Treasury offices, from the Federal Reserve banks, and from the accounts of the Treasurer of the United States]

June 30	Gold coin	Gold certificates[1]	Standard silver dollars	Silver certificates[1]	Treasury notes of 1890[1]	Subsidiary silver	Minor coin	United States notes[1]	Federal Reserve notes[1]	Federal Reserve bank notes[1]	National bank notes[1]	Total
1930	357,236	994,841	38,629	386,915	1,260	281,231	117,436	288,389	1,402,066	3,206	650,779	4,621,988
1935	(²)	117,167	32,308	701,474	1,182	295,773	125,125	285,417	3,222,913	81,470	704,263	5,567,063
1940	(²)	66,793	46,020	1,581,662	1,163	384,187	168,977	247,887	5,163,284	22,373	165,155	7,847,501
1945	(²)	52,084	125,178	1,650,689	1,150	788,283	291,996	322,587	22,867,459	527,001	120,012	26,746,438
1950	(²)	40,772	170,185	2,177,251	1,145	964,709	360,886	320,781	22,760,285	273,788	86,488	27,156,290
●	(²)	34,466	223,047	2,169,726	1,142	1,202,209	432,512	319,064	25,617,775	162,573	66,810	30,229,323
●	(²)	30,394	305,083	2,126,833	1,142	1,484,033	549,367	318,436	27,093,693	99,987	55,652	32,064,619
●	(²)	19,858	411,489	1,846,537	142	1,789,924	676,291	318,537	30,291,625	78,247	37,148	35,469,798
●	(²)	19,379	481,721	1,722,995	142	1,987,138	736,049	320,721	32,355,954	73,276	36,320	37,733,694
●	(²)	13,209	481,698	829,177	42	2,355,380	824,585	301,978	34,823,233	68,333	22,167	39,719,801

[1] For description of security required to be held against the various kinds of paper currency, and for retirement provisions, see footnotes to table 62.

[2] Gold Reserve Act of 1934, which was the culmination of gold actions of 1933, vested in the United States title to all gold coin and gold bullion. Gold coin was withdrawn from circulation and formed into bars. Gold coin ($287,000,000) shown on Treasury records as being then outstanding was dropped from monthly circulation statement as of Jan. 31, 1934.

NOTE.—Figures for years not shown appeared in the following annual reports: 1860–1947 in the 1947 report, page 485; 1948–49 in the 1956 report, page 543; and 1951–61 in the 1961 report, page 636; and 1962 in the 1964 report, page 598.

TABLE 64.—*Location of gold, silver bullion at monetary value, and coin held by the Treasury on June 30, 1965*

[In thousands of dollars. On basis of reports received from various Treasury offices and Federal Reserve banks which take into account those transactions in transit to the Treasurer's Office as of June 30, supplemented by information taken from the Treasurer's accounts. Therefore, the figures shown in this table may differ from figures in other tables prepared on basis of daily Treasury statements]

Location	Gold	Silver bullion at monetary value [1]	Standard silver dollars	Subsidiary silver coin	Minor coin
U.S. mints:					
Denver	2,412,362	20,359	23	12	[2] 6,305
Philadelphia	1,288	35,026	27	12	[2] 6,089
U.S. assay offices:					
New York [3]	805,222	743,677			
San Francisco	332,238	384,636		16	
Bullion depository, Fort Knox	10,101,840				
Treasurer of United States, Washington	11		2,921	1,719	551
Custody accounts:					
Federal Reserve Bank of New York	[4] 281,109				
Other banks, etc., various locations	13	83,719		297	205
Total	13,934,083	1,267,417	2,971	2,056	[5] 13,150

[1] Held to secure silver certificates. Excludes certain silver at monetary value held for coinage.
[2] Includes metals and alloys in process of manufacture into minor coins and finished coins in transit to Federal Reserve banks.
[3] Includes bullion depository at West Point, N.Y.
[4] Physically located as follows: At Bank of Canada, Ottawa, $135,032,675; at Bank of England, London, $50,546,602; at New York Assay Office, $34,714,178; and in Federal Reserve Bank's own vaults, $60,815,049.
[5] Minor coin held in the Treasury, $4,753,364, as shown rounded in table 60, consists of this amount, $13,149,587, less $8,396,223 payable to vendors of coinage metal.

TABLE 65.—*Paper currency issued and redeemed during the fiscal year 1965 and outstanding June 30, 1965, by classes and denominations*

[For basis of data, see headnote to table 64]

	Issued during 1965	Redeemed during 1965 [1]	Outstanding June 30, 1965		
			In Treasury	In Federal Reserve banks	In circulation
CLASS					
Gold certificates—Series of 1934	------------	$2, 814, 777, 800	------------	$1, 277, 800	------------
Silver certificates—issued after June 30, 1929	$85, 468, 000	1, 019, 233, 661	$4, 385, 391	55, 610, 798	$828, 754, 514
U. S. notes	100, 961, 873	124, 961, 873	1, 530, 028	19, 173, 464	301, 977, 524
Federal Reserve notes—1928 and subsequent series	9, 640, 532, 920	6, 708, 088, 275	88, 267, 072	2, 435, 668, 917	34, 819, 535, 701
In process of retirement:					
Federal Reserve bank notes	------------	5, 136, 256	195, 725	264, 505	68, 332, 978
National bank notes	------------	14, 110, 321	83, 646	31, 750	22, 167, 281
Gold certificates—prior to 1934 Series		6, 283, 850	131, 010	------------	13, 209, 369
Federal Reserve notes— prior to 1928 Series	------------	14, 115, 070	16, 280	------------	3, 697, 378
Silver certificates—issued before July 1, 1929	------------	14, 506, 690	2, 716	------------	422, 287
Treasury notes of 1890	------------	100, 000	------------	------------	41, 534
Total	9, 826, 962, 793	10, 721, 313, 796	94, 611, 868	2, 512, 027, 234	36, 058, 138, 566
DENOMINATION					
$1	1, 246, 284, 000	902, 167, 420	17, 442, 283	521, 675, 460	1, 752, 107, 881
$2	18, 031, 828	12, 062, 698	1, 285, 830	9, 558, 064	115, 540, 706
$5	1, 448, 610, 045	1, 382, 613, 305	9, 987, 480	289, 712, 540	2, 446, 647, 008
$10	2, 698, 561, 920	2, 436, 213, 316	17, 833, 355	660, 076, 620	7, 488, 629, 370
$20	3, 053, 120, 000	2, 439, 233, 882	32, 981, 120	705, 247, 600	12, 723, 097, 364
$50	453, 400, 000	296, 896, 075	5, 250, 550	120, 627, 150	3, 360, 638, 950
$100	883, 200, 000	406, 815, 600	6, 762, 750	161, 755, 300	7, 635, 200, 300
$500	9, 950, 000	13, 210, 500	1, 015, 000	9, 097, 500	243, 475, 000
$1,000	14, 940, 000	16, 516, 000	1, 963, 500	22, 157, 000	286, 726, 500
$5,000	415, 000	265, 000	20, 000	2, 790, 000	2, 505, 000
$10,000	450, 000	5, 920, 000	70, 000	8, 130, 000	3, 570, 000
$100,000	------------	2, 809, 400, 000	------------	1, 200, 000	------------
Fractional parts	------------	------------	------------	------------	487
Total	9, 826, 962, 793	10, 721, 313, 796	94, 611, 868	2, 512, 027, 234	36, 058, 138, 566

[1] Includes old series currencies totaling $73,100,000 written off on Nov. 16, 1964, pursuant to the Old Series Currency Adjustment Act (31 U.S.C. 915c). The act permits this action when the Secretary of the Treasury determines that such currencies have been destroyed or irretrievably lost and so will never be presented for redemption. The distribution by classes is: U.S. notes $24,000,000, Federal Reserve bank notes $1,000,000, national bank notes $13,500,000, gold certificates prior to 1934 series $6,000,000, Federal Reserve notes prior to 1928 series $14,000,000, silver certificates issued before July 1, 1929 $14,500,000, and Treasury notes of 1890 $100,000.

Trust and Other Funds

TABLE 66.—*Holdings of public debt and agency securities by Government agencies and accounts, June 30, 1961–65*

[Par value. In thousands of dollars]

Investments of agencies	1961	1962	1963	1964	1965
GOVERNMENT INVESTMENT ACCOUNTS					
HANDLED BY THE TREASURY [1]					
Major trust funds and accounts:					
Civil Service Commission:					
Employees health benefits fund	12,324	23,499	37,924	53,028	61,948
Employees' life insurance fund	[2] 196,625	[2] 247,570	[3] 303,406	352,910	379,524
Retired employees health benefits fund		1,631	100	100	1,325
Federal Deposit Insurance Corporation	2,439,517	2,593,817	2,754,363	2,937,229	3,117,186
Federal disability insurance trust fund	2,386,452	2,406,992	2,277,967	2,140,925	1,877,759
Unamortized premium or discount [4]	−877	−855	−723	−2,416	−2,193
Federal employees' retirement funds:					
Civil service retirement and disability	11,051,014	12,080,760	13,154,721	14,279,250	15,491,646
Foreign service retirement and disability	32,180	36,710	37,891	38,914	40,444
Judicial survivors annuity	1,556	1,772	2,012	2,238	2,668
Federal Housing Administration funds:					
Apartment unit		850	625	475	325
Armed services housing mortgage insurance	36,285	20,285	27,255	26,105	13,850
Experimental housing		850	900	825	725
Housing insurance	7,318	8,068	5,758	6,858	6,838
Housing investment insurance	910	915	935	971	907
Mutual mortgage insurance	556,223	532,766	520,549	558,194	488,618
National defense housing insurance	530	490	830	4,440	830
Section 203 home improvement		850	625	575	525
Section 220 home improvement		850	700	650	525
Section 220 housing insurance	4,300	2,940	3,660	3,375	1,440
Section 221 housing insurance	100				
Servicemen's mortgage insurance	10,413	8,132	8,902	16,887	10,331
Title I housing insurance	2,200	2,045	2,060	5,140	2,100
Title I insurance	103,523	103,678	107,442	80,810	33,995
War housing insurance	35,232	42,118	39,630	76,876	26,112
Federal old-age and survivors insurance trust fund	19,552,914	18,455,510	17,633,024	18,325,487	18,783,222
Unamortized premium or discount [4]	−29,398	−20,845	−19,835	−20,618	−17,498
Federal Savings and Loan Insurance Corporation	363,500	592,500	861,094	1,105,094	1,312,622
Highway trust fund	234,034	435,935	677,743	609,028	265,394
Railroad retirement account	3,759,509	3,696,960	3,697,461	3,766,424	3,915,705
Unemployment trust fund	5,719,956	5,791,982	6,245,191	6,827,077	7,793,935
Unamortized premium or discount [4]	−3,433	−3,327	−58	−8,722	−8,816
Veterans' life insurance funds:					
Government life insurance:					
Public debt securities	1,071,433	1,027,809	1,003,002	955,840	933,454
Nonguaranteed securities				25,000	25,000
National service life insurance	5,759,371	5,803,529	5,713,915	5,782,992	5,908,757
Special term insurance	106,280	87,956	100,588	123,173	149,134
Veterans' reopened insurance					2,605
Other trust funds and accounts:					
Ainsworth Library fund, Walter Reed General Hospital	10	11	11	11	11
Bequest of George C. Edgeter, relief of indigent American Indians, Bureau of Indian Affairs	31	31	31	31	31
District of Columbia:					
Fees and other collections, Recreation Board	10	20	20	20	21
General funds	9,213	9,213	9,213	9,213	
Highway fund			3,700	6,000	
Judicial retirement and survivors annuity fund					100
Miscellaneous trust funds	34	96	115	87	2,335
Motor vehicle parking, highway fund	3,378	4,122	2,954	743	743
Redevelopment program, Redevelopment Land Agency:					
Public debt securities	409	725			
Nonguaranteed securities	5,750	4,365	7,640	5,325	12,360

Footnotes at end of table.

TABLE 66.—*Holdings of public debt and agency securities by Government agencies and accounts, June 30, 1961–65*—Continued

[Par value. In thousands of dollars]

Investments of agencies	1961	1962	1963	1964	1965
GOVERNMENT INVESTMENT ACCOUNTS—Continued					
HANDLED BY THE TREASURY [1]—Con.					
Other trust funds and accounts:—Con.					
District of Columbia—Continued					
Sanitary sewage works fund	2,429		150		235
Stadium fund, Armory Board	10,140	590			
Teachers' retirement and annuity fund	37,088	39,970	43,326	47,108	50,986
Welfare funds	10	10		10	
Working capital fund, Armory Board				50	125
Esther Cattell Schmitt gift fund				417	414
Exchange Stabilization Fund	46,000	72,250	153,147	317,064	256,806
Federal ship mortgage insurance escrow fund, maritime activities	35,232	8,822	13,618	22,398	10,988
Federal ship mortgage insurance fund, revolving fund			3,543	758	758
General post fund, Veterans' Administration	1,288	1,597	1,835	2,135	2,185
Gifts and bequests, Commerce [6]				5	6
Longshoremen's and Harbor Workers' Compensation Act, relief and rehabilitation	588	588	466	408	312
National Archives gift fund					1,824
National Archives trust fund	102	102	102	102	102
National Capital Housing Authority	1,031	1,761	3,861	3,311	4,011
National park trust fund	21	69	73	578	592
Navajo and Ute Mountain Ute Indians, New Mexico	200	356	436	729	830
Office of Naval Records and History fund	153	153	153	212	212
Pershing Hall Memorial fund	211	211	211	211	211
Philippine Government pre-1934 bond account	1,571	916	919	292	295
Preservation of Birthplace of Abraham Lincoln, National Park Service	64	64	64	64	64
Public Health Service:					
Gift funds	166	176	166	156	156
Patients' benefit fund, Public Health Service hospitals	7	6	5	2	2
Public Housing Administration				24,500	7,500
Saint Elizabeths Hospital unconditional gift fund	1	1	1	1	1
Tennessee Valley Authority	28,500	10,000			
U.S. Department of the Air Force—general gift fund	5	6	6	6	6
U.S. Department of the Army—general gift fund	31	31	205	189	192
U.S. Naval Academy—general gift fund	109	109	109	109	109
U.S. Naval Academy—museum fund	1	1	1	1	1
War risk insurance revolving fund			3,153	3,365	3,461
Workmen's Compensation Act within the District of Columbia, relief and rehabilitation	126	126	126	126	126
HANDLED BY THE AGENCIES					
Banks for cooperatives	45,990	43,000	43,051	44,459	44,368
District of Columbia: Miscellaneous trust funds	116	117	102	108	116
Farmers Home Administration, State rural rehabilitation funds	856	1,083	1,634	1,477	1,646
Federal home loan banks	1,454,060	1,332,065	1,944,000	1,803,256	1,699,410
Federal Housing Administration, mutual mortgage insurance fund:					
Guaranteed securities	6,493	6,493	47,815	123,868	125,561
Federal intermediate credit banks	107,800	110,603	111,384	111,331	109,604
Federal land banks	105,800	103,600	101,667	101,588	99,482

Footnotes at end of table.

TABLE 66.—*Holdings of public debt and agency securities by Government agencies and accounts, June 30, 1961-65*—Continued

[Par value. In thousands of dollars]

Investments of agencies	1961	1962	1963	1964	1965
GOVERNMENT INVESTMENT ACCOUNTS—Continued					
HANDLED BY THE AGENCIES—Con.					
Federal National Mortgage Association:					
Public debt securities:					
Government mortgage liquidation fund					5, 794
Secondary market operations			91, 500		
Guaranteed securities:					
Management and liquidating functions	69, 008	84, 124	79, 233	23, 558	1, 852
Secondary market operations	746	38, 673	23, 250	4, 986	5, 993
Special assistance functions	10, 448	37, 424	14, 980	6, 928	5, 967
Nonguaranteed securities:					
Government mortgage liquidation fund					19, 115
Secondary market operations			59, 570		
Housing and Home Finance Administrator liquidating programs:					
Guaranteed securities		4			
Tennessee Valley Authority:					
Nonguaranteed securities	10, 700				
Total	55, 405, 917	55, 898, 425	57, 967, 204	60, 742, 428	63, 097, 958
OTHER ACCOUNTS					
HANDLED BY THE TREASURY					
Alien property trust fund	570	569	544	614	608
Canal Zone Postal Savings System [6]	5, 050	4, 750	4, 400	4, 100	3, 600
Central hospital fund, U.S. Army, Office of The Surgeon General	1, 945	1, 945	1, 945	1, 945	1, 945
Comptroller of the Currency	4, 749	4, 548	6, 742	8, 357	10, 054
Individual Indian money deposit fund [5]	38, 128	36, 162	35, 971	35, 046	34, 160
U.S. Department of the Air Force—cadet fund [6]	1				
U.S. Postal Savings System	720, 703	599, 017	502, 866	432, 079	355, 579
HANDLED BY THE AGENCIES					
General Services Administration, Public Works Administration (in liquidation)		497	887	440	
Panama Canal Company	25				
Total	771, 170	647, 488	553, 355	482, 581	405, 946
Grand total	56, 177, 087	56, 545, 913	[7] 58, 520, 558	[7] 61, 225, 009	[7] 63, 503, 904

[1] For further details of these accounts, see tables 67 through 83.
[2] Includes Series F and J savings bonds at current redemption value.
[3] Includes Series J savings bonds at current redemption value.
[4] Includes accrued interest purchased.
[5] Securities reported under the Merchant Marine Academy general gift fund, on page 601, 1964 annual report, were transferred to this fund by authorization of an act approved October 2, 1964 (5 U.S.C. 608a-c).
[6] Handled as Government investment accounts for the fiscal year 1961.
[7] Excludes securities in the amounts of $17,757,000, $17,671,000, and $12,459,000 held by the Atomic Energy Commission as of June 30, 1963, 1964, and 1965, respectively, which in turn are held by trustees for the protection of certain contractors against financial loss in event of a catastrophe.

NOTE.—For comparable data 1939-49, see 1949 annual report, p. 492-493, and for 1950-58, see 1958 annual report, p. 586-589, and for 1959-60, see 1963 annual report, p. 637-639.

TABLE 67.—*Civil service retirement and disability fund, June 30, 1965*

[This trust fund was established in accordance with the provisions of the act of May 22, 1920, as amended (5 U.S.C. 2267). For further details see annual report of the Secretary for 1941, p. 136]

I. RECEIPTS AND EXPENDITURES (EXCLUDING INVESTMENT TRANSACTIONS)

	Cumulative through June 30, 1964	Fiscal year 1965	Cumulative through June 30, 1965
Receipts:			
Deductions from salaries, service credit payments, and voluntary contributions of employees subject to retirement act [1]	$12,107,633,904.45	$1,066,846,060.20	$13,174,479,964.65
Federal contributions [2]	4,324,352,923.21	65,000,000.00	4,389,352,923.21
Payments by employing agencies [2]	5,678,211,506.14	1,050,356,476.70	6,728,567,982.84
Interest and profits on investments	4,426,593,521.57	482,170,944.47	4,908,764,466.04
Transfer from the Comptroller of the Currency retirement fund [3]	5,050,000.00		5,050,000.00
Total receipts	26,541,841,855.37	2,664,373,481.37	29,206,215,336.74
Expenditures:			
Annuity payments, refunds, etc	12,155,870,734.05	1,438,114,294.78	13,593,985,028.83
Transfers to policemen's and firemen's relief fund, D.C., deductions and accrued interest thereon	250,747.42	32,544.49	283,291.91
Total expenditures	12,156,121,481.47	1,438,146,839.27	13,594,268,320.74
Balance	14,385,720,373.90	1,226,226,642.10	15,611,947,016.00

II. ASSETS HELD BY THE TREASURY DEPARTMENT

Assets	June 30, 1964	Fiscal year 1965, increase, or decrease (−)	June 30, 1965
Investments in public debt securities:			
Special issues, civil service retirement fund series maturing June 30:			
Treasury certificates of indebtedness:			
4⅛% of 1965	$72,800,000.00	−$72,800,000.00	
4⅛% of 1966		69,707,000.00	$69,707,000.00
Treasury notes:			
2⅝% of 1965	51,316,000.00	−51,316,000.00	
2⅞% of 1965	69,913,000.00	−69,913,000.00	
3¾% of 1965	60,976,000.00	−60,976,000.00	
3⅞% of 1965	80,227,000.00	−80,227,000.00	
2⅞% of 1966	69,913,000.00		69,913,000.00
3¾% of 1966	60,976,000.00		60,976,000.00
3⅞% of 1966	80,227,000.00		80,227,000.00
4⅛% of 1966	72,775,000.00		72,775,000.00
3¾% of 1967	60,976,000.00		60,976,000.00
3⅞% of 1967	80,227,000.00		80,227,000.00
4⅛% of 1967	72,775,000.00	69,699,000.00	142,474,000.00
3⅞% of 1968	80,227,000.00		80,227,000.00
4⅛% of 1968	72,775,000.00	69,699,000.00	142,474,000.00
4⅛% of 1969	72,775,000.00	69,699,000.00	142,474,000.00
4⅛% of 1970		69,699,000.00	69,699,000.00
Treasury bonds:			
2½% of 1965	385,000,000.00	−385,000,000.00	
2⅝% of 1965	179,211,000.00	−179,211,000.00	
2½% of 1966	385,000,000.00		385,000,000.00
2⅝% of 1966	230,527,000.00		230,527,000.00
2½% of 1967	385,000,000.00		385,000,000.00
2⅝% of 1967	230,527,000.00		230,527,000.00
2⅞% of 1967	69,913,000.00		69,913,000.00
2½% of 1968	200,000,000.00		200,000,000.00
2⅝% of 1968	415,527,000.00		415,527,000.00
2⅞% of 1968	69,913,000.00		69,913,000.00
3¾% of 1968	60,976,000.00		60,976,000.00
2⅝% of 1969	615,527,000.00		615,527,000.00
2⅞% of 1969	69,913,000.00		69,913,000.00
3¾% of 1969	60,976,000.00		60,976,000.00
3⅞% of 1969	80,227,000.00		80,227,000.00
2⅝% of 1970	615,527,000.00		615,527,000.00
2⅞% of 1970	69,913,000.00		69,913,000.00
3¾% of 1970	60,976,000.00		60,976,000.00

Footnotes at end of table.

TABLE 67.—*Civil service retirement and disability fund, June 30, 1965*—Continued

II. ASSETS HELD BY THE TREASURY DEPARTMENT—Continued

Assets	June 30, 1964	Fiscal year 1965, increase, or decrease (−)	June 30, 1965
Investments in public debt securities—Con.			
Special issues, civil service retirement fund series maturing June 30—Con.			
Treasury bonds—Continued			
3⅞% of 1970	$80,227,000.00		$80,227,000.00
4⅛% of 1970	72,775,000.00		72,775,000.00
2⅝% of 1971	615,527,000.00		615,527,000.00
2⅞% of 1971	69,913,000.00		69,913,000.00
3¾% of 1971	60,976,000.00		60,976,000.00
3⅞% of 1971	80,227,000.00		80,227,000.00
4⅛% of 1971	72,775,000.00	$69,699,000.00	142,474,000.00
3¾% of 1972	60,976,000.00		60,976,000.00
3⅞% of 1972	532,981,000.00		532,981,000.00
4⅛% of 1972	305,461,000.00	69,699,000.00	375,160,000.00
2⅝% of 1973	549,959,000.00	−298,254,000.00	251,705,000.00
3¾% of 1973	60,976,000.00		60,976,000.00
3⅞% of 1973	103,448,000.00		103,448,000.00
4⅛% of 1973	185,035,000.00	367,953,000.00	552,988,000.00
2⅝% of 1974	615,527,000.00		615,527,000.00
2⅞% of 1974	45,956,000.00	−45,956,000.00	
3¾% of 1974	60,976,000.00		60,976,000.00
3⅞% of 1974	80,227,000.00		80,227,000.00
4⅛% of 1974	96,732,000.00	115,655,000.00	212,387,000.00
2⅝% of 1975	615,527,000.00		615,527,000.00
2⅞% of 1975	69,913,000.00	−24,693,000.00	45,220,000.00
3¾% of 1975	60,976,000.00		60,976,000.00
3⅞% of 1975	80,227,000.00		80,227,000.00
4⅛% of 1975	72,775,000.00	94,392,000.00	167,167,000.00
2⅞% of 1976	685,440,000.00		685,440,000.00
3¾% of 1976	60,976,000.00		60,976,000.00
3⅞% of 1976	80,227,000.00		80,227,000.00
4⅛% of 1976	72,775,000.00	69,699,000.00	142,474,000.00
3¾% of 1977	746,416,000.00		746,416,000.00
3⅞% of 1977	80,227,000.00		80,227,000.00
4⅛% of 1977	72,775,000.00	69,699,000.00	142,474,000.00
3⅞% of 1978	826,643,000.00		826,643,000.00
4⅛% of 1978	72,775,000.00	69,699,000.00	142,474,000.00
4⅛% of 1979	899,418,000.00	69,699,000.00	969,117,000.00
4⅛% of 1980		969,117,000.00	969,117,000.00
Total special issues	13,491,295,000.00	1,045,468,000.00	14,536,763,000.00
Public issues:			
Treasury notes:			
4⅞%, Series C-1964	2,472,000.00	−2,472,000.00	
4⅝%, Series A-1965	610,000.00	−610,000.00	
Treasury bonds:			
2½% of 1964-69 (Apr. 15, 1943)	10,000,000.00		10,000,000.00
2½% of 1964-69 (Sept. 15, 1943)	16,400,000.00		16,400,000.00
3⅝% of 1967	48,400,000.00	−48,400,000.00	
3¾% of 1968	2,800,000.00		2,800,000.00
3⅞% of 1968	11,400,000.00		11,400,000.00
4% of 1969 (Aug. 15, 1962)	10,000,000.00		10,000,000.00
4% of 1969 (Oct. 1, 1957)	59,400,000.00		59,400,000.00
4% of 1970	46,000,000.00		46,000,000.00
4% of 1972	25,000,000.00		25,000,000.00
4% of 1973	12,000,000.00		12,000,000.00
4⅛% of 1973		5,400,000.00	5,400,000.00
3⅞% of 1974	47,650,000.00		47,650,000.00
4⅛% of 1974		51,400,000.00	51,400,000.00
4¼% of 1974	10,550,000.00	61,610,000.00	72,160,000.00
4¼% of 1975-85	49,605,000.00		49,605,000.00
3¼% of 1978-83	5,600,000.00		5,600,000.00
3½% of 1980	15,700,000.00		15,700,000.00
4% of 1980	102,394,000.00		102,394,000.00
3¼% of 1985	77,900,000.00		77,900,000.00
4¼% of 1987-92	10,000,000.00	100,000,000.00	110,000,000.00
3½% of 1990	85,600,000.00		85,600,000.00
3% of 1995	55,205,000.00		55,205,000.00
3½% of 1998	83,269,000.00		83,269,000.00
Total public issues	787,955,000.00	166,928,000.00	954,883,000.00
Total investments	14,279,250,000.00	1,212,396,000.00	15,491,646,000.00
Undisbursed balance	106,470,373.90	13,830,642.10	120,301,016.00
Total assets	14,385,720,373.90	1,226,226,642.10	15,611,947,016.00

Footnotes on page 703.

Footnotes to table 67.

[1] Basic compensation deductions have been at the rate of 6½ percent since the day before the first pay period which began after Sept. 30, 1956. Since 1958 District of Columbia and Government corporations' contributions have been included with contributions from agency salary funds.

[2] Beginning July 1, 1957, appropriations are not made directly to the fund. Instead, in accordance with the act approved July 31, 1956 (5 U.S.C. 2254(a)), the employing agency contributes (from appropriations or funds from which the salaries are paid) amounts equal to the deductions from employees' salaries.

[3] The act of June 30, 1948, as amended (5 U.S.C. 2259 note), abolished the separate retirement fund for employees of the Office of the Comptroller of the Currency and directed transfer of its assets to the civil service retirement and disability fund. Amount comprises cash derived from sale of securities.

TABLE 68.—*District of Columbia teachers' retirement and annuity fund, June 30, 1965*

[This fund was established in accordance with the provisions of the act of Aug. 7, 1946 (31 D.C.C. 702, 707 772), as successor to the District of Columbia teachers' retirement fund established under the act of Jan. 15 1920, as amended, effecting the consolidation of the deductions fund and the Government reserve fund as of July 1, 1945]

I. RECEIPTS AND EXPENDITURES (EXCLUDING INVESTMENT TRANSACTIONS)

	Cumulative through June 30, 1964	Fiscal year 1965	Cumulative through June 30, 1965
Receipts:			
Deductions from salaries	$29,179,252.94	$2,235,993.38	$31,415,246.32
Voluntary contributions	196,465.55	975.00	197,440.55
Interest and profits on investments	18,903,369.69	1,647,891.22	20,551,260.91
Appropriations from District of Columbia revenues	61,699,942.84	6,544,700.00	68,244,642.84
Total receipts	109,979,031.02	10,429,559.60	120,408,590.62
Expenditures:			
Annuities, refunds, etc	62,765,239.39	6,531,957.41	69,297,196.80
Balance	47,213,791.63	3,897,602.19	51,111,393.82

II. ASSETS HELD BY THE TREASURY DEPARTMENT

Assets	June 30, 1964	Fiscal year 1965, increase, or decrease (−)	June 30, 1965
Investments in public debt securities:			
Public issues:			
Treasury bills	$250,000.00	−$250,000.00	
Treasury notes:			
4⅝%, Series A-1965	33,000.00	−33,000.00	
4%, Series A-1966	475,000.00	−475,000.00	
Treasury bonds:			
2½% of 1965-70	1,000,000.00		$1,000,000.00
2½% of 1966-71	1,000,000.00		1,000,000.00
2½% of 1967-72 (dated June 1, 1945)	1,247,500.00		1,247,500.00
3⅞% of 1968	1,056,500.00		1,056,500.00
3⅞% of 1971	3,256,000.00		3,256,000.00
4⅛% of 1973		475,000.00	475,000.00
3⅞% of 1974	2,388,500.00		2,388,500.00
4¼% of 1974	2,617,000.00	33,000.00	2,650,000.00
4¼% of 1975-85	1,167,000.00	196,000.00	1,363,000.00
3¼% of 1978-83	1,777,500.00		1,777,500.00
4% of 1980	956,500.00		956,500.00
3¼% of 1985	1,077,500.00		1,077,500.00
4¼% of 1987-92		3,932,500.00	3,932,500.00
4% of 1988-93	1,000,000.00		1,000,000.00
4⅛% of 1989-94	2,531,500.00		2,531,500.00
3½% of 1990	3,000,000.00		3,000,000.00
3% of 1995	3,599,500.00		3,599,500.00
3½% of 1998	4,100,000.00		4,100,000.00
2½% Investment Series A-1965	250,000.00		250,000.00
2¾% Investment Series B-1975-80	14,325,000.00		14,325,000.00
Total investments	47,108,000.00	3,878,500.00	50,986,500.00
Undisbursed balance	105,791.63	19,102.19	124,893.82
Total assets	47,213,791.63	3,897,602.19	51,111,393.82

TABLE 69.—*Employees health benefits fund, Civil Service Commission, June 30, 1965*

[On basis of reports from the Civil Service Commission. This trust revolving fund was established in accordance with the provisions of the act of Sept. 28, 1959, as amended (5 U.S.C. 3007)]

I. RECEIPTS AND EXPENDITURES (EXCLUDING INVESTMENT TRANSACTIONS)

	Cumulative through June 30, 1964	Fiscal year 1965	Cumulative through June 30, 1965
Receipts:			
Direct appropriations	$21, 666, 000. 00	$12, 210, 000. 00	$33, 876, 000. 00
Employees' and annuitants' withholdings	888, 317, 682. 18	311, 178, 467. 19	1, 199, 496, 149. 37
Agency contributions	495, 799, 894. 56	139, 003, 863. 32	634, 803, 757. 88
Interest and profits on investments	3, 020, 165. 43	1, 829, 255. 15	4, 849, 420. 58
Total receipts	1, 408, 803, 742 17	464, 221, 585. 66	1, 873, 025, 327. 83
Expenditures:			
Subscription charges paid to carriers	1, 343, 903, 579. 29	444, 250, 815. 31	1, 788, 154, 394. 60
Contingency reserve paid to carriers	861, 483. 24	9, 719, 023. 15	10, 580, 506. 39
Carrier refunds	—253, 285. 51	—3. 89	—253, 289. 40
Administrative expenses	4, 614, 758. 92	1, 170, 787. 40	5, 785, 546. 32
Interest on administrative expenses paid by employees' life insurance fund [1]	43, 625. 79		43, 625. 79
Other [2]	—1, 332, 762. 45	—196, 551. 73	—1, 529, 314. 18
Total expenditures	1, 347, 837, 399. 28	454, 944, 070. 24	1, 802, 781, 469. 52
Balance	60, 966, 342. 89	9, 277, 515. 42	70, 243, 858. 31

II. ASSETS HELD BY THE TREASURY DEPARTMENT

Assets	June 30, 1964	Fiscal year 1965, increase, or decrease (—)	June 30, 1965
Investments in public debt securities:			
Public issues:			
Treasury bills	$8, 374, 000. 00	—$6, 959, 000. 00	$1, 415, 000. 00
Treasury notes:			
4⅞%, Series C-1964	591, 000. 00	—591, 000. 00	
3¾%, Series F-1964	3, 172, 000. 00	—3, 172, 000. 00	
4%, Series E-1965	1, 000, 000. 00	—1, 000, 000. 00	
4%, Series D-1966		763, 000. 00	763, 000. 00
4%, Series A-1966	599, 000. 00		599, 000. 00
3⅝%, Series B-1966	1, 120, 000. 00	—1, 120, 000. 00	
3⅝%, Series B-1967		9, 729, 000. 00	9, 729, 000. 00
Treasury bonds:			
2½% of 1964–69 (dated Apr. 15, 1943)	875, 000. 00		875, 000. 00
3¾% of 1966	1, 751, 000. 00	—1, 751, 000. 00	
3⅝% of 1967	1, 698, 000. 00	—1, 698, 000. 00	
3⅞% of 1968	1, 000, 000. 00		1, 000, 000. 00
3¾% of 1968	1, 298, 000. 00		1, 298, 000. 00
4% of 1969 (dated Oct. 1, 1957)	1, 000, 000. 00		1, 000, 000. 00
3⅞% of 1971	5, 804, 000. 00		5, 804, 000. 00
4% of 1971	3, 732, 000. 00		3, 732, 000. 00
4% of 1972 (dated Sept. 15, 1962)	4, 410, 500. 00		4, 410, 500. 00
4% of 1972 (dated Nov. 15, 1962)	3, 792, 500. 00		3, 792, 500. 00
4% of 1973	2, 016, 500. 00		2, 016, 500. 00
4⅛% of 1973		1, 796, 000. 00	1, 796, 000. 00
3⅞% of 1974	3, 785, 500. 00		3, 785, 500. 00
4⅛% of 1974		9, 923, 500. 00	9, 923, 500. 00
3¼% of 1978–83	190, 000. 00		190, 000. 00
3½% of 1980	738, 000. 00		738, 000. 00
4¼% of 1987–92		3, 000, 000. 00	3, 000, 000. 00
3½% of 1990	2, 130, 500. 00		2, 130, 500. 00
3½% of 1998	3, 950, 000. 00		3, 950, 000. 00
Total investments	53, 027, 500. 00	8, 920, 500. 00	61, 948, 000. 00
Undisbursed balance	7, 938, 842. 89	357, 015. 42	8, 295, 858. 31
Total assets	60, 966, 342. 89	9, 277, 515. 42	70, 243, 858. 31

[1] As provided in the act (5 U.S.C. 3008(a)).
[2] Difference between cost and face value of investments.

Table 70.—*Retired employees health benefits fund, Civil Service Commission, June 30, 1965*

[On basis of reports from the Civil Service Commission. This trust revolving fund was established in accordance with the provisions of the act of September 8, 1960 (5 U.S.C. 3057)]

I. RECEIPTS AND EXPENDITURES (EXCLUDING INVESTMENT TRANSACTIONS)

	Cumulative through June 30, 1964	Fiscal year 1965	Cumulative through June 30, 1965
Receipts:			
Direct appropriations (Government contribution)	$43,425,000.00	$14,800,000.00	$58,225,000.00
Annuitants withholdings	38,628,208.53	13,068,118.62	51,696,327.15
Interest and profits on investments	8,736.26	4,000.00	12,736.26
Total receipts	82,061,944.79	27,872,118.62	109,934,063.41
Expenditures:			
Subscription charges paid to carrier	60,100,052.70	20,451,958.63	80,552,011.33
Government contributions paid to annuitants [1]	18,971,645.44	6,608,549.49	25,580,194.93
Administrative expenses	1,306,286.87	230,377.42	1,536,664.29
Interest on loans	6,409.00		6,409.00
Other [2]	−294,092.95	−201,268.48	−495,361.43
Total expenditures	80,090,301.06	27,089,617.06	107,179,918.12
Balance	1,971,643.73	782,501.56	2,754,145.29

II. ASSETS HELD BY THE TREASURY DEPARTMENT

Assets	June 30, 1964	Fiscal year 1965, increase, or decrease (−)	June 30, 1965
Investments in public debt securities:			
Public issues:			
Treasury bills		$1,225,000.00	$1,225,000.00
Treasury bonds, 4% of 1969	$100,000.00		100,000.00
Total investments	100,000.00	1,225,000.00	1,325,000.00
Undisbursed balance	1,871,643.73	−442,498.44	1,429,145.29
Total assets	1,971,643.73	782,501.56	2,754,145.29

[1] In accordance with 5 U.S.C. 3055(a), subject to specified restrictions, a retired employee who elects to obtain or retain a health benefits plan other than the uniform Government-wide health benefits plan directly with a carrier, shall be paid a Government contribution toward the cost of his plan which shall be equal in amount to the appropriate Government contribution.
[2] Difference between cost and face value of investments.

TABLE 71.—*Employees' life insurance fund, Civil Service Commission, June 30, 1965*

[On basis of reports from the Civil Service Commission. This trust revolving fund was established in accordance with the provisions of the act of August 17, 1954, as amended (5 U.S.C. 2091(c))]

I. RECEIPTS AND EXPENDITURES (EXCLUDING INVESTMENT TRANSACTIONS)

	Cumulative through June 30, 1964	Fiscal year 1965	Cumulative through June 30, 1965
Receipts:			
Employees' withholdings	$796, 979, 415. 36	$110, 165, 786. 01	$907, 145, 201. 37
Government contributions	398, 494, 235. 54	55, 080, 341. 44	453, 574, 576. 98
Premiums collected from beneficial association members	23, 295, 055. 96	3, 141, 271. 75	26, 436, 327. 71
Interest and profits on investments	39, 643, 081. 95	13, 414, 253. 71	53, 057, 335. 66
Other	3, 666. 09		3, 666. 09
Assets acquired from beneficial associations:			
U.S. securities	13, 958, 336. 40		13, 958, 336. 40
Other	7, 922, 934. 40	87, 067. 95	8, 010, 002. 35
Total receipts	1, 280, 296, 725. 70	181, 888, 720. 86	1, 462, 185, 446. 56
Expenditures:			
Premiums paid to insurance companies:			
For Federal employees generally	1, 172, 922, 178. 10	163, 216, 031. 38	1, 336, 138, 209. 48
Less return of premiums paid	266, 096, 878. 69	[1] 14, 015, 690. 64	280, 112, 569. 33
For beneficial association members	37, 172, 754. 95	5, 800, 926. 13	42, 973, 681. 08
Less return of premiums paid	5, 626, 936. 10	[2] 15, 339. 74	5, 642, 275. 84
Administrative expenses	1, 917, 297. 51	286, 269. 08	2, 203, 566. 59
Other	−16, 046, 135. 31	[3] 255, 490. 24	−15, 790, 645. 07
Total expenditures	924, 242, 280. 46	155, 527, 686. 45	1, 079, 769, 966. 91
Balance	356, 054, 445. 24	26, 361, 034. 41	382, 415, 479. 65

Footnotes at end of table.

TABLE 71.—*Employees' life insurance fund, Civil Service Commission, June 30, 1965*—Continued

II. ASSETS HELD BY THE TREASURY DEPARTMENT

Assets	June 30, 1964	Fiscal year 1965, increase, or decrease (−)	June 30, 1965
Investments in public debt securities:			
Public issues:			
Treasury bills	$3,000,000.00		$3,000,000.00
Treasury notes:			
4⅝%, Series A-1965	838,000.00	−$838,000.00	
4%, Series A-1966	17,165,000.00	−17,165,000.00	
Treasury bonds:			
2½% of 1962-67	15,015,000.00	−14,000,000.00	1,015,000.00
2½% of 1963-68	3,000,000.00		3,000,000.00
2½% of 1964-69 (dated April 15, 1943)	5,500,000.00		5,500,000.00
2½% of 1964-69 (dated Sept. 15, 1943)	5,000,000.00		5,000,000.00
3¾% of 1966	5,000,000.00	−5,000,000.00	
2½% of 1966-71	3,864,500.00		3,864,500.00
3⅝% of 1967	5,000,000.00	−5,000,000.00	
3⅞% of 1968	22,105,000.00		22,105,000.00
3¾% of 1968	1,500,000.00		1,500,000.00
4% of 1969	15,330,000.00		15,330,000.00
3⅞% of 1971	2,806,500.00		2,806,500.00
4% of 1971	15,000,000.00		15,000,000.00
4% of 1972 (dated Sept. 15, 1962)	10,000,000.00		10,000,000.00
4% of 1972 (dated Nov. 15, 1962)	5,783,000.00		5,783,000.00
4⅛% of 1973		4,000,000.00	4,000,000.00
4⅛% of 1974		15,000,000.00	15,000,000.00
4¼% of 1974	15,000,000.00	838,000.00	15,838,000.00
3⅞% of 1974	20,220,000.00		20,220,000.00
4¼% of 1975-85	16,012,500.00	11,096,500.00	27,109,000.00
3¼% of 1978-83	9,330,500.00	222,000.00	9,552,500.00
3½% of 1980	11,272,500.00		11,272,500.00
4% of 1980	39,942,500.00		39,942,500.00
3¼% of 1985	8,486,500.00		8,486,500.00
4¼% of 1987-92	3,772,000.00	36,576,500.00	40,348,500.00
4% of 1988-93	15,197,000.00		15,197,000.00
4⅛% of 1989-94	24,198,500.00	904,000.00	25,102,500.00
3½% of 1990	31,276,000.00		31,276,000.00
3% of 1995	135,500.00		135,500.00
3½% of 1998	21,358,500.00		21,358,500.00
2¾% Investment Series B-1975-80	179,000.00		179,000.00
U.S. savings bonds.			
Series J (2.76%)	606,900.00	−20,000.00	586,900.00
Series K (2.76%)	15,000.00		15,000.00
Total investments	352,909,900.00	26,614,000.00	379,523,900.00
Undisbursed balance	3,144,545.24	−252,965.59	2,891,579.65
Total assets	356,054,445.24	26,361,034.41	382,415,479.65

[1] Premium payments in excess of the $100 million contingency reserve set by the Civil Service Commission, which are required to be returned to the fund by the insuring companies (5 U.S.C. 2097(d)).
[2] Return of premium payments in excess of annual claims paid, expenses, and other costs.
[3] Difference between cost and face value of investments.

TABLE 72.—*Federal disability insurance trust fund, June 30, 1965*

[This trust fund was established in accordance with the provisions of the Social Security Act amendments approved Aug. 1, 1956 (42 U.S.C. 401(b))]

I. RECEIPTS AND EXPENDITURES (EXCLUDING INVESTMENT TRANSACTIONS)

	Cumulative through June 30, 1964	Fiscal year 1965	Cumulative through June 30, 1965
Receipts:			
Appropriations [1]	$6,976,286,402.24	$1,095,087,773.24	$8,071,374,175.48
Less refund of internal revenue collections	−65,812,500.00	−13,064,500.00	−78,877,000.00
Deposits by States	497,852,614.58	93,220,620.11	591,073,234.69
Interest and profits on investments	367,601,474.81	65,247,217.77	432,848,692.58
Payments from railroad retirement account	26,831,000.00		26,831,000.00
Other (HEW)		16,970.23	16,970.23
Total receipts	7,802,758,991.63	1,240,508,081.35	9,043,267,072.98
Expenditures:			
Benefit payments	5,173,211,198.07	1,392,190,264.93	6,565,401,463.00
To railroad retirement account	54,926,000.00	23,615,000.00	78,541,000.00
Administrative expenses:			
To general fund	25,487,255.08	3,767,958.52	29,255,213.60
To Federal old-age and survivors insurance trust fund	285,147,054.00	[2] 78,223,221.00	363,370,275.00
Total expenditures	5,538,771,507.15	1,497,796,444.45	7,036,567,951.60
Balance	2,263,987,484.48	−257,288,363.10	2,006,699,121.38

II. ASSETS HELD BY THE TREASURY DEPARTMENT

Assets	June 30, 1964	Fiscal year 1965, increase, or decrease (−)	June 30, 1965
Investments in public debt securities:			
Special issues, Federal disability insurance trust fund series maturing June 30:			
Treasury notes:			
3¾% of 1967	$1,349,000.00	−$1,349,000.00	
Treasury bonds:			
2⅝% of 1967	58,792,000.00	−58,792,000.00	
3¾% of 1967	19,389,000.00	−19,389,000.00	
2½% of 1968	30,000,000.00	−30,000,000.00	
2⅝% of 1968	102,894,000.00	−102,894,000.00	
3¾% of 1968	20,738,000.00	−20,738,000.00	
2⅝% of 1969	132,894,000.00	−132,894,000.00	
3¾% of 1969	20,738,000.00	−20,738,000.00	
2⅝% of 1970	132,894,000.00	−99,162,000.00	$33,732,000.00
3¾% of 1970	20,738,000.00		20,738,000.00
2⅝% of 1971	132,894,000.00		132,894,000.00
3¾% of 1971	20,738,000.00		20,738,000.00
2⅝% of 1972	132,894,000.00		132,894,000.00
3¾% of 1972	20,738,000.00		20,738,000.00
2⅝% of 1973	132,894,000.00		132,894,000.00
3¾% of 1973	20,738,000.00		20,738,000.00
2⅝% of 1974	132,894,000.00		132,894,000.00
3¾% of 1974	20,738,000.00		20,738,000.00
2⅝% of 1975	132,894,000.00		132,894,000.00
3¾% of 1975	20,738,000.00		20,738,000.00
3¾% of 1976	153,632,000.00		153,632,000.00
3¾% of 1977	153,632,000.00		153,632,000.00
3⅞% of 1978	153,632,000.00		153,632,000.00
4⅛% of 1979	133,173,000.00	20,459,000.00	153,632,000.00
4⅛% of 1980		125,606,000.00	125,606,000.00
Total special issues	1,902,655,000.00	−339,891,000.00	1,562,764,000.00

Footnotes at end of table.

TABLE 72.—*Federal disability insurance trust fund, June 30, 1965*—Continued

II. ASSETS HELD BY THE TREASURY DEPARTMENT—Continued

Assets	June 30, 1964	Fiscal year 1965, increase, or decrease (−)	June 30, 1965
Investments in public debt securities—Con.			
Public issues:			
Treasury notes:			
5%, Series B-1964	$825,000.00	−$825,000.00	
Treasury bonds:			
3⅝% of 1967	10,000,000.00	−$10,000,000.00	
3⅞% of 1968 (dated June 23, 1960)	3,750,000.00		$3,750,000.00
3⅞% of 1968 (dated Sept. 15, 1963)	5,000,000.00		5,000,000.00
3¾% of 1968	5,000,000.00		5,000,000.00
4% of 1969 (dated Aug. 15, 1962)	10,000,000.00		10,000,000.00
4% of 1969 (dated Oct. 1, 1957)	26,000,000.00		26,000,000.00
4% of 1970	14,000,000.00		14,000,000.00
4% of 1972 (dated Nov. 15, 1962)	2,000,000.00		2,000,000.00
4% of 1972 (dated Sept. 15, 1962)	2,000,000.00		2,000,000.00
4% of 1973	16,500,000.00		16,500,000.00
3⅞% of 1974	5,000,000.00		5,000,000.00
4⅛% of 1974		10,000,000.00	10,000,000.00
4¼% of 1975-85	19,045,000.00	1,750,000.00	20,795,000.00
4% of 1980	30,250,000.00		30,250,000.00
4¼% of 1987-92	5,000,000.00	75,800,000.00	80,800,000.00
4⅛% of 1989-94	68,400,000.00		68,400,000.00
3½% of 1990	10,500,000.00		10,500,000.00
3½% of 1998	5,000,000.00		5,000,000.00
Total public issues	238,270,000.00	76,725,000.00	314,995,000.00
Total investments—par value	2,140,925,000.00	−263,116,000.00	1,877,759,000.00
Unamortized discount and premium on investments (net)	−2,470,562.05	270,150.60	−2,200,411.45
Accrued interest purchased	54,615.38	−47,006.68	7,608.70
Total investments	2,138,509,053.33	−262,942,856.08	1,875,566,197.25
Undisbursed balance	125,478,431.15	5,654,492.98	131,132,924.13
Total assets	2,263,987,484.48	−257,288,363.10	2,006,699,121.38

[1] Appropriations are equal to the amount of employment taxes collected as estimated by the Secretary of the Treasury and adjusted in accordance with wage reports certified by the Secretary of Health, Education, and Welfare for distribution to this fund and the Federal old-age and survivors insurance trust fund.

[2] Reimbursement covering the fiscal year 1964 including $3,112,262.00 interest.

TABLE 73.—*Federal old-age and survivors insurance trust fund, June 30, 1965*

[This trust fund, the successor of the old-age reserve account, was established in accordance with the provisions of the Social Security Act Amendments (42 U.S.C. 401). For further details see annual reports of the Secretary for 1940, p. 212, and 1950, p. 42]

I. RECEIPTS AND EXPENDITURES (EXCLUDING INVESTMENT TRANSACTIONS)

	Cumulative through June 30, 1964	Fiscal year 1965	Cumulative through June 30, 1965
Receipts:			
Appropriations [1]	$119, 713, 870, 201. 85	$14, 777, 984, 820. 93	$134, 491, 855, 022. 78
Less refund of internal revenue collections	−973, 595, 000. 00	−178, 625, 500. 00	−1, 152, 220, 500. 00
Deposits by States	6, 114, 715, 147. 43	1, 257, 853, 080. 87	7, 372, 568, 228. 30
Interest and profits on investments	8, 180, 061, 742. 01	583, 124, 534. 10	8, 763, 186, 276. 11
Transfers from general fund [2]	15, 386, 400. 00		15, 386, 400. 00
Payments from railroad retirement account	35, 393, 000. 00		35, 393, 000. 00
Other [3]	10, 827, 061. 30	3, 189, 891. 22	14, 016, 952. 52
Total receipts	[4] 133, 096, 658, 552. 59	16, 443, 526, 827. 12	149, 540, 185, 379. 71
Expenditures:			
Benefit payments	108, 427, 294, 887. 26	15, 225, 894, 365. 63	123, 653, 189, 252. 89
Construction of buildings	35, 349, 961. 30	305, 245. 52	35, 655, 206. 82
To railroad retirement account	2, 242, 559, 000. 00	435, 638, 000. 00	2, 678, 197, 000. 00
Administrative expenses:			
Salaries and expenses [5]	2, 236, 144, 888. 31	322, 787, 831. 11	2, 558, 932, 719. 42
To general fund	706, 749, 221. 22	49, 712, 198. 83	756, 461, 420. 05
To Department of Health, Education, and Welfare	25, 400, 625. 00	2, 666, 000. 00	28, 066, 625. 00
From Federal disability insurance trust fund	−275, 690, 818. 00	−75, 110, 959. 00	−350, 801, 777. 00
Total expenditures	113, 397, 807, 765. 09	15, 961, 892, 682. 09	129, 359, 700, 447. 18
Balance	19, 698, 850, 787. 50	481, 634, 145. 03	20, 180, 484, 932. 53

II. ASSETS HELD BY THE TREASURY DEPARTMENT

Assets	June 30, 1964	Fiscal year 1965, increase, or decrease (−)	June 30, 1965
Investments in public debt securities:			
Special issues, Federal old-age and survivors insurance trust fund series maturing June 30:			
Certificates of indebtedness:			
4⅛% of 1966		$141, 020, 000. 00	$141, 020, 000. 00
Treasury notes:			
4⅛% of 1966	$597, 887, 000. 00	−597, 887, 000. 00	
4⅛% of 1967		1, 032, 019, 000. 00	1, 032, 019, 000. 00
Treasury bonds:			
2⅝% of 1966	161, 284, 000. 00	−161, 284, 000. 00	
2½% of 1967	912, 011, 000. 00	−912, 011, 000. 00	
2⅝% of 1967	168, 000, 000. 00	−120, 008, 000. 00	47, 992, 000. 00
2½% of 1968	412, 011, 000. 00		412, 011, 000. 00
2⅝% of 1968	668, 000, 000. 00		668, 000, 000. 00
2⅝% of 1969	1, 080, 011, 000. 00		1, 080, 011, 000. 00
2⅝% of 1970	1, 080, 011, 000. 00		1, 080, 011, 000. 00
2⅝% of 1971	1, 080, 011, 000. 00		1, 080, 011, 000. 00
2⅝% of 1972	1, 080, 011, 000. 00		1, 080, 011, 000. 00
2⅝% of 1973	1, 080, 011, 000. 00		1, 080, 011, 000. 00
2⅝% of 1974	1, 080, 011, 000. 00		1, 080, 011, 000. 00
2⅝% of 1975	919, 934, 000. 00		919, 934, 000. 00
3¾% of 1975	160, 077, 000. 00		160, 077, 000. 00
3¾% of 1976	1, 080, 011, 000. 00		1, 080, 011, 000. 80
3⅞% of 1977	1, 080, 011, 000. 00		1, 080, 011, 000. 00
3⅞% of 1978	658, 444, 000. 00		658, 444, 000. 00
4⅛% of 1978	421, 567, 000. 00		421, 567, 000. 00
4⅛% of 1979	1, 080, 011, 000. 00		1, 080, 011, 000. 00
4⅛% of 1980		1, 080, 011, 000. 00	1, 080, 011, 000. 00
Total special issues	14, 799, 314, 000. 00	461, 860, 000. 00	15, 261, 174, 000. 00

Footnotes at end of table.

TABLE 73.—*Federal old-age and survivors insurance trust fund, June 30, 1965*—Con.

II. ASSETS HELD BY THE TREASURY DEPARTMENT—Continued

Assets	June 30, 1964	Fiscal year 1965, increase, or decrease (−)	June 30, 1965
Investments in public debt securities—Con.			
Public issues:			
Treasury notes:			
5%, Series B–1964_____	$4,125,000.00	−$4,125,000.00	_____
4⅝%, Series A–1965_____	6,352,000.00	−6,352,000.00	_____
Treasury bonds:			
2½% of 1964–69 (dated Apr. 15, 1943)_____	22,180,000.00	_____	$22,180,000.00
2½% of 1964–69 (dated Sept. 15, 1943)_____	33,000,000.00	_____	33,000,000.00
3¾% of 1966_____	27,729,000.00	−27,729,000.00	_____
2½% of 1967–72 (dated Oct. 20, 1941)_____	250.00	_____	250.00
3⅝% of 1967_____	34,205,000.00	−34,205,000.00	_____
3¾% of 1968_____	7,000,000.00	_____	7,000,000.00
3⅞% of 1968_____	17,450,000.00	_____	17,450,000.00
4% of 1969 (dated Aug. 15, 1962)_____	20,000,000.00	−15,000,000.00	5,000,000.00
4% of 1969 (dated Oct. 1, 1957)_____	57,500,000.00	_____	57,500,000.00
4% of 1970_____	_____	15,000,000.00	15,000,000.00
4% of 1971_____	100,000,000.00	_____	100,000,000.00
4% of 1973_____	38,000,000.00	_____	38,000,000.00
3⅞% of 1974_____	32,500,000.00	−8,000,000.00	24,500,000.00
4⅛% of 1974_____	_____	61,934,000.00	61,934,000.00
4¼% of 1974_____	_____	6,352,000.00	6,352,000.00
4¼% of 1975–85_____	78,023,000.00	_____	78,023,000.00
3¼% of 1978–83_____	60,200,000.00	_____	60,200,000.00
4% of 1980_____	153,100,000.00	_____	153,100,000.00
3½% of 1980_____	449,450,000.00	_____	449,450,000.00
3¼% of 1985_____	25,700,000.00	_____	25,700,000.00
4¼% of 1987–92_____	10,000,000.00	23,000,000.00	33,000,000.00
4⅛% of 1989–94_____	91,300,000.00	_____	91,300,000.00
3½% of 1990_____	556,250,000.00	_____	556,250,000.00
3% of 1995_____	85,170,000.00	−15,000,000.00	70,170,000.00
3½% of 1998_____	552,037,000.00	_____	552,037,000.00
2¾% Investment Series B–1975–80__	1,064,902,000.00	_____	1,064,902,000.00
Total public issues_____	3,526,173,250.00	−4,125,000.00	3,522,048,250.00
Total investments, par value_____	18,325,487,250.00	457,735,000.00	18,783,222,250.00
Unamortized premium and discount (net)_____	−20,618,109.13	3,104,387.93	−17,513,721.20
Accrued interest purchased_____	_____	15,756.96	15,756.96
Total investments_____	18,304,869,140.87	460,855,144.89	18,765,724,285.76
Undisbursed balance⁶_____	1,393,981,646.63	20,779,000.14	1,414,760,646.77
Total assets_____	19,698,850,787.50	481,634,145.03	20,180,484,932.53

¹ Appropriations are equal to the amount of employment taxes collected as estimated by the Secretary of the Treasury and adjusted in accordance with wage reports certified by the Secretary of Health, Education, and Welfare for distribution to this fund and the Federal disability insurance trust fund.

² In connection with payments of benefits to survivors of certain World War II veterans who died within three years after separation from active service.

³ Incidental recoveries, and, beginning with the fiscal year 1958, includes reimbursement of interest in the amount of $12,568,498 transferred from the Federal disability insurance trust fund pursuant to 42 U.S.C. 201(g)(1).

⁴ Excludes unappropriated receipts of $27,000,000.

⁵ Paid directly from the trust fund beginning with the fiscal year 1947 under annual appropriation acts.

⁶ Includes the following balances in accounts as of June 30:

	1964	1965
Benefit payments_____	$1,380,603,694.51	$1,413,151,272.04
Salaries and expenses_____	13,347,072.24	1,178,240.37
Construction of buildings_____	30,879.88	431,134.36

TABLE 74.—*Foreign service retirement and disability fund, June 30, 1965*

[This trust fund was established in accordance with the provisions of the act of May 24, 1924, and the act of Aug. 13, 1946 (22 U.S.C. 1062). For further details, see annual report of the Secretary for 1941, p. 138]

I. RECEIPTS AND EXPENDITURES (EXCLUDING INVESTMENT TRANSACTIONS)

	Cumulative through June 30, 1964	Fiscal year 1965	Cumulative through June 30, 1965
Receipts:			
Deductions from salaries, service credit payments, and voluntary contributions of employees subject to retirement act	$39,760,403.52	$3,877,557.80	$43,637,961.32
Appropriations [1]	25,815,900.00		25,815,900.00
Payments by employing agency [1]	9,296,936.33	3,686,757.02	12,983,693.35
Receipts from civil service retirement and disability fund	3,557,225.55	795,896.16	4,353,121.71
Interest and profits on investments	18,195,843.95	1,577,255.77	19,773,099.72
Total receipts	96,626,309.35	9,937,466.75	106,563,776.10
Expenditures:			
Annuity payments and refunds	57,123,588.70	8,306,582.54	65,430,171.24
Balance	39,502,720.65	1,630,884.21	41,133,604.86

II. ASSETS HELD BY THE TREASURY DEPARTMENT

Assets	June 30, 1964	Fiscal year 1965, increase, or decrease (−)	June 30, 1965
Investments in public debt securities:			
Special issues, Treasury certificates of indebtedness, foreign service retirement fund series maturing June 30:			
4% of 1965	$37,774,000.00	−$37,774,000.00	
3% of 1965	1,140,000.00	−1,140,000.00	
3% of 1966		1,126,000.00	$1,126,000.00
4% of 1966		39,318,000.00	39,318,000.00
Total	38,914,000.00	1,530,000.00	40,444,000.00
Undisbursed balance	588,720.65	100,884.21	689,604.86
Total assets	39,502,720.65	1,630,884.21	41,133,604.86

[1] Beginning July 1, 1961, appropriations are not made directly to the fund. Instead, in accordance with the act approved Sept. 8, 1960 (22 U.S.C. 1071(a)), the employing agency contributes (from appropriations or funds from which the salaries are paid) amounts equal to the deductions from employee's salaries.

TABLE 75.—*Highway trust fund, June 30, 1965*

[This trust fund was established in accordance with the provisions of section 209(a) of the Highway Revenue Act of 1956 (23 U.SC. 120 note)]

I. RECEIPTS AND EXPENDITURES (EXCLUDING INVESTMENT TRANSACTIONS)

	Cumulative through June 30, 1964	Fiscal year 1965	Cumulative through June 30, 1965
Receipts:			
Excise taxes: [1]			
Gasoline [2]	$16, 626, 725, 484. 41	$2, 720, 696, 170. 12	$19, 347, 421, 654. 53
Diesel and special motor fuels	646, 068, 900. 31	143, 675, 108. 28	789, 744, 008. 59
Tires [2]	1, 890, 077, 996. 80	381, 539, 560. 92	2, 271, 617, 557. 72
Tread rubber [2]	136, 565, 691. 28	24, 160, 662. 81	160, 726, 354. 09
Trucks, buses, and trailers [2]	1, 306, 348, 438. 06	393, 304, 162. 28	1, 699, 652, 600. 34
Truck use	459, 980, 677. 29	99, 278, 933. 75	559, 259, 611. 04
Inner tubes [2]	124, 027, 090. 77	23, 752, 914. 01	147, 780, 004. 78
Other tires	272, 718, 179. 33		272, 718, 179. 33
Total taxes	21, 462, 512, 458. 25	3, 786, 407, 512. 17	25, 248, 919, 970. 42
Deduct—Reimbursement to general fund—refund of tax receipts:			
Gasoline used on farms	647, 037, 663. 91	101, 023, 407. 29	748, 061, 071. 20
Gasoline for nonhighway purposes or local transit systems	152, 959, 562. 59	22, 474, 686. 13	175, 434, 248. 72
Gasoline, other	102, 736. 97	247. 99	102, 984. 96
Tires and tread rubber	97, 416. 90		97, 416. 90
Trucks, buses, and trailers	66, 650. 55		66, 650. 55
Total refunds of taxes	800, 264, 030. 92	123, 498, 341. 41	923, 762, 372. 33
Transfers to land and water conservation fund		4, 400, 000. 00	4, 400, 000. 00
Net taxes	20, 662, 248, 427. 33	3, 658, 509, 170. 76	24, 320, 757, 598. 09
Interest on investment	79, 637, 907. 39	11, 034, 928. 41	90, 672, 835. 80
Advances from general fund	419, 000, 000. 00		419, 000, 000. 00
Less return of advances to general fund	−419, 000, 000. 00		−419, 000, 000. 00
Net receipts	20, 741, 886, 334. 72	3, 669, 544, 099. 17	24, 411, 430, 433. 89
Expenditures:			
Highway program:			
Reimbursement to general fund	501, 018, 553. 13		501, 018, 553. 13
Federal Aid Highway Act of 1956	19, 591, 971, 613. 73	4, 025, 483, 540. 38	23, 617, 455, 154. 11
Pentagon road network	1, 486, 895. 98	633, 931. 53	2, 120, 827. 51
Total highway program	20, 094, 477, 062. 84	4, 026, 117, 471. 91	24, 120, 594, 534. 75
Services of Department of Labor (administration and enforcement of labor standards)	368, 225. 00		368, 225. 00
Interest on advances from general fund	5, 610, 162. 02		5, 610, 162. 02
Total expenditures	20, 100, 455, 449. 86	4, 026, 117, 471. 91	24, 126, 572, 921. 77
Balance	641, 430, 884. 86	−356, 573, 372. 74	284, 857, 512. 12

II. ASSETS HELD BY THE TREASURY DEPARTMENT

Assets	June 30, 1964	Fiscal year 1965, increase, or decrease (−)	June 30, 1965
Investments in public debt securities:			
Special issues, Treasury certificates of indebtedness, highway trust fund series, maturing June 30:			
3⅜% of 1965	$609, 028, 000. 00	−$609, 028, 000. 00	
3¾% of 1966		265, 394, 000. 00	$265, 394, 000. 00
Total investments	609, 028, 000. 00	−343, 634, 000. 00	265, 394, 000. 00
Undisbursed balances	32, 402, 884. 86	−12, 939, 372. 74	19, 463, 512. 12
Total assets	641, 430, 884. 86	−356, 573, 372. 74	284, 857, 512. 12

[1] Amounts equivalent to specified percentages of receipts from certain taxes on motor fuels, vehicles, tires and tubes, and use of certain vehicles are appropriated and transferred monthly from general fund receipts to the trust fund on the basis of estimates by the Secretary of the Treasury, with proper adjustments to be made in subsequent transfers as required by section 209(c) of the Highway Revenue Act of 1956, as amended (23 U.S.C. 120 note). See also the annual report to Congress on the financial condition and fiscal operations of the highway trust fund.
[2] Includes floor stocks taxes.

TABLE 76.—*Judicial survivors annuity fund, June 30, 1965*

[This fund was established in accordance with the provisions of the act of Aug. 3, 1956 (28 U.S.C. 376(b))]

I. RECEIPTS AND EXPENDITURES (EXCLUDING INVESTMENT TRANSACTIONS)

	Cumulative through June 30, 1964	Fiscal year 1965	Cumulative through June 30, 1965
Receipts:			
Deductions from salaries and contributions	$4,748,220.20	$790,371.42	$5,538,591.62
Interest and profits on investments	343,982.89	89,797.17	433,780.06
Total receipts	5,092,203.09	880,168.59	5,972,371.68
Expenditures:			
Annuity payments, refunds, etc	2,813,216.14	487,789.49	3,301,005.63
Balance	2,278,986.95	392,379.10	2,671,366.05

II. ASSETS HELD BY THE TREASURY DEPARTMENT

Assets	June 30, 1964	Fiscal year 1965, increase, or decrease (−)	June 30, 1965
Investments in public debt securities:			
Public issues:			
Treasury notes:			
5%, Series B-1964	$10,000.00	−$10,000.00	
4⅝%, Series A-1965	16,000.00	−16,000.00	
4%, Series A-1966	60,000.00	−60,000.00	
Treasury bonds:			
3⅞% of 1968	195,000.00		$195,000.00
4% of 1969	40,500.00		40,500.00
4% of 1971	240,000.00		240,000.00
4% of 1972 (dated Sept. 15, 1962)	150,000.00		150,000.00
4⅛% of 1973		70,000.00	70,000.00
3⅞% of 1974	169,000.00		169,000.00
4¼% of 1974	106,000.00	16,000.00	122,000.00
4¼% of 1975-85	137,000.00	156,000.00	293,000.00
3¼% of 1978-83	93,500.00		93,500.00
4% of 1980	500,500.00		500,500.00
4¼% of 1987-92		274,000.00	274,000.00
4⅛% of 1989-94	167,000.00		167,000.00
3½% of 1990	188,500.00		188,500.00
3% of 1995	51,000.00		51,000.00
3½% of 1998	113,500.00		113,500.00
Total investments	2,237,500.00	430,000.00	2,667,500.00
Undisbursed balance	41,486.95	−37,620.90	3,866.05
Total assets	2,278,986.95	392,379.10	2,671,366.05

TABLE 77.—*Library of Congress trust funds, June 30, 1965*

[Established in accordance with provisions of the act of Mar. 3, 1925, as amended (2 U.S.C. 154–161). For further details see 1941 annual report, p. 149]

Name of donor	Permanent loan account						Income from donated securities, etc.		
	Funds on deposit with Treasurer of the United States			Interest at 4 percent paid by U.S. Treasury					
	June 30, 1964	Fiscal year 1965	June 30, 1965	Cumulative through June 30, 1964	Fiscal year 1965	Cumulative through June 30, 1965	Cumulative through June 30, 1964	Fiscal year 1965	Cumulative through June 30, 1965
Ba..be, Axis V.	$6,684.74		$6,684.74	$7,214.16	$267.40	$7,481.56	$1,785.58		$1,785.58
Benjamin, William R.	83,083.31		83,083.31	56,281.91	3,323.34	59,605.25	49,744.50		49,744.50
Bowker, Richard R.	14,843.15		14,843.15	6,451.46	593.72	7,045.18	8,024.80		8,024.80
Carnegie ...tion of New York	93,307.98		93,307.98	98,168.82	3,732.32	101,901.14	37,838.36		37,838.36
Coolidge, Elizabeth S.	804,444.26		804,444.26	365,329.13	32,177.78	397,506.91	131,904.76		131,904.76
...un, Louis C., ...al fund	12,585.03		12,585.03	9,636.91	503.40	10,140.31			
Friends of ...sic in the Library of Congress				4,614.66	290.25	4,904.91	318.22		318.22
Guggenheim, Daniel	6,609.09	$1,400.00	8,009.09	93,922.10	3,636.16	97,548.26	32,759.36		32,759.36
Hanks, Nymphus Corridon	90,654.22		90,654.22	1,765.86	209.10	1,974.96			
Huntington, Archer M.	5,227.31		5,227.31	183,662.69	10,423.10	194,085.79			
Koussevitzky ...sic Foundation, Inc	260,577.66		260,577.66	88,550.68	7,390.61	95,941.29	[1] 396,497.26	[1] $19,798.45	416,295.71
Longw...th, ...his Foundation	176,103.58	31,995.83	208,099.41	9,439.30	387.66	9,826.96			
...ur, Dayton C.	9,691.59		9,691.59	16,009.21	821.92	16,831.13	757.02		757.02
...dial ...ty for the ...Bld, Inc	20,548.18		20,548.18	16,821.27	1,440.60	18,261.87	412.50		412.50
Pennell, Joseph	36,015.00		36,015.00	280,139.42	12,130.02	292,269.44	85,487.80		85,487.80
Porter, Henry K., memorial fund	303,250.46		303,250.46	208,048.04	11,620.00	219,668.04	25,369.03		25,369.03
Roberts fund	290,600.00		290,600.00	33,048.45	2,508.16	35,556.61			
Sonneck memorial fund	62,703.75		62,703.75	12,521.18	483.52	13,004.70	4,429.73		4,429.73
Stern memorial fund	12,088.13		12,088.13						
...l, Gertrude C.; ...ion of Stradivari instr...ents and Tourte bows	14,452.64	2,000.00	16,452.64	534.75	614.12	1,148.87	75.00		75.00
Poetry fund	1,225,060.97		1,225,060.97	701,985.01	49,002.44	750,987.45			
General ...ure	101,149.73		101,149.73	54,653.71	4,045.98	58,699.69	3,382.00		3,382.00
Appreciation and understanding of good ...ure	393,279.59		393,279.59	95,894.14	15,731.18	111,625.32	2,168.26		2,168.26
Wilbur, Ja...es B.	150,000.00		150,000.00	61,898.31	6,000.00	67,898.31			
	305,813.57		305,813.57	325,527.76	12,232.56	337,760.32	107,345.09		107,345.09
Donations and investment income	4,478,673.94	35,395.83	4,614,069.77	2,732,118.93	179,555.34	2,911,674.27	888,299.27	19,798.45	908,097.72
Expenditures from investment income				2,459,649.86	212,419.25	2,672,069.11	884,422.66	7,103.81	891,526.47
Balances in the accounts	4,478,673.94	35,395.83	4,614,069.77	272,469.07	−32,863.91	239,605.16	3,876.61	12,694.64	16,571.25

[1] Includes income from securities held as investment under deed of trust dated Nov. 17, 1936, administered by designated trustees including the Bank of New York.

TABLE 78.—*National service life insurance fund, June 30, 1965*

[This trust fund was established in accordance with the provisions of the act of Oct. 8, 1940 (38 U.S.C. 720).
For further details, see annual report of the Secretary for 1941, p. 143]

I. RECEIPTS AND EXPENDITURES (EXCLUDING INVESTMENT TRANSACTIONS)

	Cumulative through June 30, 1964	Fiscal year 1965	Cumulative through June 30, 1965
Receipts:			
Premiums and other receipts	$10,833,976,352.81	$472,983,649.66	$11,306,960,002.47
Interest on investments	3,312,058,799.15	182,144,899.82	3,494,203,698.97
Payments from general fund	4,752,819,262.82	7,028,552.70	4,759,847,815.52
Total receipts	18,898,854,414.78	662,157,102.18	19,561,011,516.96
Expenditures:			
Benefit payments, dividends, and refunds	13,102,075,624.12	544,995,877.93	13,647,071,502.05
Balance	5,796,778,790.66	117,161,224.25	5,913,940,014.91

II. ASSETS HELD BY THE TREASURY DEPARTMENT

Assets	June 30, 1964	Fiscal year 1965, increase, or decrease (−)	June 30, 1965
Investments in public debt securities: Special issues, national service life insurance fund series maturing June 30:			
Certificates of indebtedness:			
3⅝% of 1966		$8,418,000.00	$8,418,000.00
Treasury notes:			
3¾% of 1965	$7,873,000.00	−7,873,000.00	
3⅝% of 1967		6,946,000.00	6,946,000.00
3⅝% of 1968		6,946,000.00	6,946,000.00
3⅝% of 1969		6,946,000.00	6,946,000.00
3⅝% of 1970		6,946,000.00	6,946,000.00
Treasury bonds:			
3% of 1965	379,000,000.00	−379,000,000.00	
3% of 1966	379,000,000.00		379,000,000.00
3¾% of 1966	7,873,000.00		7,873,000.00
3% of 1967	379,000,000.00		379,000,000.00
3¾% of 1967	7,873,000.00		7,873,000.00
3% of 1968	379,000,000.00		379,000,000.00
3¾% of 1968	7,873,000.00		7,873,000.00
3% of 1969	379,000,000.00		379,000,000.00
3¾% of 1969	7,873,000.00		7,873,000.00
3% of 1970	379,000,000.00		379,000,000.00
3¾% of 1970	7,873,000.00		7,873,000.00
3% of 1971	379,000,000.00		379,000,000.00
3⅝% of 1971		6,946,000.00	6,946,000.00
3¾% of 1971	7,873,000.00		7,873,000.00
3% of 1972	379,000,000.00		379,000,000.00
3⅝% of 1972		6,946,000.00	6,946,000.00
3¾% of 1972	7,873,000.00		7,873,000.00
3% of 1973	379,000,000.00		379,000,000.00
3⅝% of 1973		6,946,000.00	6,946,000.00
3¾% of 1973	7,873,000.00		7,873,000.00
3% of 1974	379,000,000.00		379,000,000.00
3⅝% of 1974		6,946,000.00	6,946,000.00
3¾% of 1974	7,873,000.00		7,873,000.00
3⅝% of 1975		6,946,000.00	6,946,000.00
3¾% of 1975	386,873,000.00		386,873,000.00
3⅛% of 1976	343,149,000.00		343,149,000.00
3¼% of 1976	43,724,000.00		43,724,000.00
3⅝% of 1976		6,946,000.00	6,946,000.00
3¼% of 1977	386,307,000.00		386,307,000.00
3⅝% of 1977	566,000.00	6,946,000.00	7,512,000.00
3⅜% of 1978	298,259,000.00		298,259,000.00
3⅝% of 1978	88,614,000.00	6,946,000.00	95,560,000.00
3⅝% of 1979	366,770,000.00	27,049,000.00	393,819,000.00
3⅝% of 1980		393,819,000.00	393,819,000.00
Total investments	5,782,992,000.00	125,765,000.00	5,908,757,000.00
Undisbursed balance	13,786,790.66	−8,603,775.75	5,183,014.91
Total assets	5,796,778,790.66	117,161,224.25	5,913,940,014.91

NOTE.—Policy loans outstanding, on basis of information furnished by the Veterans' Administration,
amounted to $550,141,862.14 as of June 30, 1965.

TABLE 79.—*Pershing Hall Memorial fund, June 30, 1965*

[This special fund was established in accordance with the provisions of the act of June 28, 1935, as amended (36 U.S.C. 491). For further details, see annual report of the Secretary for 1941, p. 155]

I. RECEIPTS AND EXPENDITURES (EXCLUDING INVESTMENT TRANSACTIONS)

	Cumulative through June 30, 1964	Fiscal year 1965	Cumulative through June 30, 1965
Receipts:			
Appropriations	$482,032.92		$482,032.92
Profits on investments	5,783.21		5,783.21
Net increase in book value of bonds	12,000.35		12,000.35
Interest earned	152,228.88	$7,385.00	159,613.88
Total receipts	652,045.36	7,385.00	659,430.36
Expenditures:			
Claims and expenses	288,629.70		288,629.70
National Treasurer, American Legion	144,843.88	11,077.50	155,921.38
Total expenditures	433,473.58	11,077.50	444,551.08
Balance	218,571.78	−3,692.50	214,879.28

II. ASSETS HELD BY THE TREASURY DEPARTMENT

Assets	June 30, 1964	Fiscal year 1965 increase, or decrease (−)	June 30, 1965
Investments in public debt securities:			
Public issues:			
Treasury bonds, 3½% of 1990	$211,000.00		$211,000.00
Undisbursed balance	7,571.78	−$3,692.50	3,879.28
Total assets	218,571.78	−3,692.50	214,879.28

TABLE 80.—*Philippine Government pre-1934 bond account, June 30, 1965*

[This special trust account was established in accordance with the provisions of the act of Aug. 7, 1939 (22 U.S.C. 1393), for the payment of bonds issued prior to May 1, 1934, by provinces, cities, and municipalities of the Philippines].

I. RECEIPTS AND EXPENDITURES (EXCLUDING INVESTMENT TRANSACTIONS)

	Cumulative through June 30, 1964	Fiscal year 1965	Cumulative through June 30, 1965
Receipts:			
Taxes on exports	$1,586,135.92		$1,586,135.92
Interest and profits on investments [1]	3,722,549.74	$11,306.40	3,733,856.14
Sale of stock of Bank of Philippine Islands	43,100.00		43,100.00
Deposit of the Philippine Government	13,141.85		13,141.85
U.S. Treasury bonds from the Philippine Government	6,269,750.00		6,269,750.00
Annual payments by the Philippine Government	15,646,589.37		15,646,589.37
Total receipts	27,281,266.88	11,306.40	27,292,573.28
Expenditures:			
Interest on outstanding Philippine bonds	2,441,371.31	1,747.50	2,443,118.81
Return of excess cash to the Philippine Government	1,600,000.00		1,600,000.00
Payment of matured bonds of the Philippine Government	19,173,425.00	8,050.00	19,181,475.00
Cancellation of Philippine bonds at cost [2]	3,533,585.13		3,533,585.13
Losses on securities sold	153,752.03		153,752.03
Unamortized discount on investments	−1,687.68	−2,181.12	−3,868.80
Total expenditures	26,900,445.79	7,616.38	26,908,062.17
Balance	380,821.09	3,690.02	384,511.11

II. ASSETS HELD BY THE TREASURY DEPARTMENT

Assets	June 30, 1964	Fiscal year 1965, increase, or decrease (−)	June 30, 1965
Investments in public debt securities:			
Public issues:			
Treasury bills	$192,000.00	$3,000.00	$195,000.00
Treasury notes, 4%, Series E-1965	100,000.00		100,000.00
Total investments	292,000.00	3,000.00	295,000.00
Undisbursed balance	88,821.09	690.02	89,511.11
Total assets	380,821.09	3,690.02	384,511.11

[1] Losses were netted against profits through fiscal 1957.
[2] The face value of the bonds canceled was $3,436,000.

NOTE.—As of June 30, 1964, the total principal and interest of pre-1934 bonds had matured.

TABLE 81.—*Railroad retirement account, June 30, 1965*

[This trust account was established in accordance with the provisions of the act of June 24, 1937 (45 U.S.C. 228o). For further details, see annual report of the Secretary for 1941, p. 148]

I. RECEIPTS AND EXPENDITURES (EXCLUDING INVESTMENT TRANSACTIONS)

	Cumulative through June 30, 1964	Fiscal year 1965	Cumulative through June 30, 1965
Receipts:			
Tax collections:			
Appropriated [1]	$12,459,504,789.55	$644,263,539.27	$13,103,768,328.82
Unappropriated	1,236,977.71	5,115,907.81	6,352,885.52
Fines and penalties	450.00		450.00
Interest and profits on investments	1,680,738,783.06	143,133,662.01	1,823,872,445.07
Payments from Federal old-age and survivors and Federal disability insurance trust funds [2]	2,297,485,000.00	459,253,000.00	2,756,738,000.00
Railroad unemployment insurance account:			
Interest on advances	32,763,471.93	12,167,342.48	44,930,814.41
Repayment of advances	178,715,000.00	77,935,000.00	256,650,000.00
Total receipts	16,650,444,472.25	1,341,868,451.57	17,992,312,923.82
Expenditures:			
Benefit payments, etc	12,124,159,589.42	1,116,369,550.16	13,240,529,139.58
Administrative expenses [3]	114,628,094.75	10,342,427.72	124,970,522.47
Federal old-age and survivors and Federal disability insurance trust funds:			
Payments	26,831,000.00		26,831,000.00
Interest payments	35,393,000.00		35,393,000.00
Advances to railroad unemployment insurance account	490,431,000.00	58,230,000.00	548,661,000.00
Interest on refunds of taxes	5,576.97	9,281.53	14,858.50
Total expenditures	12,791,448,261.14	1,184,951,259.41	13,976,399,520.55
Balance	3,858,996,211.11	156,917,192.16	4,015,913,403.27

II. ASSETS HELD BY THE TREASURY DEPARTMENT

Assets	June 30, 1964	Fiscal year 1965, increase, or decrease (−)	June 30, 1965
Investments in public debt securities:			
Special issues, railroad retirement series, maturing June 30			
Treasury certificates of indebtedness:			
4¼% of 1965	$118,693,000.00	−$118,693,000.00	
4⅛% of 1966		208,205,000.00	$208,205,000.00
Treasury notes:			
4% of 1965	79,214,000.00	−79,214,000.00	
4% of 1966	185,091,000.00	−185,091,000.00	
4⅛% of 1966	12,812,000.00	−12,812,000.00	
4% of 1967	185,091,000.00	−7,656,000.00	177,435,000.00
4⅛% of 1967	12,812,000.00	17,954,000.00	30,766,000.00
4% of 1968	185,091,000.00		185,091,000.00
4⅛% of 1968	12,812,000.00	10,298,000.00	23,110,000.00
4⅛% of 1969	12,812,000.00	10,298,000.00	23,110,000.00
4⅛% of 1970		10,298,000.00	10,298,000.00

Footnotes at end of table.

TABLE 81.—*Railroad retirement account, June 30, 1965*—Continued

II. ASSETS HELD BY THE TREASURY DEPARTMENT—Continued

Assets	June 30, 1964	Fiscal year 1965, increase, or decrease (—)	June 30, 1965
Investments in public debt securities—Con.			
Special issues, railroad retirement series, maturing June 30—Continued			
Treasury bonds:			
4% of 1969	$185, 091, 000. 00		$185, 091, 000. 00
4% of 1970	185, 091, 000. 00		185, 091, 000. 00
4⅛% of 1970	12, 812, 000. 00		12, 812, 000. 00
4% of 1971	185, 091, 000. 00		185, 091, 000. 00
4⅛% of 1971	12, 812, 000. 00	$10, 298, 000. 00	23, 110, 000. 00
4% of 1972	185, 091, 000. 00		185, 091, 000. 00
4⅛% of 1972	12, 812, 000. 00	10, 298, 000. 00	23, 110, 000. 00
4% of 1973	185, 091, 000. 00		185, 091, 000. 00
4⅛% of 1973	12, 812, 000. 00	10, 298, 000. 00	23, 110, 000. 00
4% of 1974	185, 091, 000. 00		185, 091, 000. 00
4⅛% of 1974	12, 812, 000. 00	10, 298, 000. 00	23, 110, 000. 00
4% of 1975	185, 091, 000. 00		185, 091, 000. 00
4⅛% of 1975	12, 812, 000. 00	10, 298, 000. 00	23, 110, 000. 00
4% of 1976	185, 091, 000. 00		185, 091, 000. 00
4⅛% of 1976	12, 812, 000. 00	10, 298, 000. 00	23, 110, 000. 00
4% of 1977	185, 091, 000. 00		185, 091, 000. 00
4⅛% of 1977	12, 812, 000. 00	10, 298, 000. 00	23, 110, 000. 00
4% of 1978	185, 091, 000. 00		185, 091, 000. 00
4⅛% of 1978	12, 812, 000. 00	10, 298, 000. 00	23, 110, 000. 00
4⅛% of 1979	197, 903, 000. 00	10, 298, 000. 00	208, 201, 000. 00
4⅛% of 1980		208, 201, 000. 00	208, 201, 000. 00
Total special issues	2, 968, 549, 000. 00	154, 470, 000. 00	3, 123, 019, 000. 00
Public issues:			
Treasury notes:			
4%, Series A-1966	6, 000, 000. 00		6, 000, 000. 00
3⅝%, Series B-1966	30, 500, 000. 00		30, 500, 000. 00
3¾%, Series A-1967	10, 000, 000. 00		10, 000, 000. 00
3⅝%, Series B-1967	18, 000, 000. 00		18, 000, 000. 00
Treasury bonds:			
2⅝% of 1965	5, 189, 000. 00	—5, 189, 000. 00	
3¾% of 1966	5, 500, 000. 00		5, 500, 000. 00
3¾% of 1968	14, 000, 000. 00		14, 000, 000. 00
3⅞% of 1968	7, 000, 000. 00		7, 000, 000. 00
4% of 1969 (dated Oct. 1, 1957)	57, 000, 000. 00		57, 000, 000. 00
4% of 1969 (dated Aug. 15, 1962)	51, 000, 000. 00		51, 000, 000. 00
4% of 1970	35, 000, 000. 00		35, 000, 000. 00
3⅞% of 1971	46, 500, 000. 00		46, 500, 000. 00
4% of 1971	8, 500, 000. 00		8, 500, 000. 00
4% of 1972 (dated Sept. 15, 1962)	33, 500, 000. 00		33, 500, 000. 00
4% of 1972 (dated Nov. 15, 1962)	21, 000, 000. 00		21, 000, 000. 00
3⅞% of 1974	156, 700, 000. 00		156, 700, 000. 00
4¼% of 1975-85	47, 261, 000. 00		47, 261, 000. 00
3½% of 1980	6, 000, 000. 00		6, 000, 000. 00
4% of 1980	125, 550, 000. 00		125, 550, 000. 00
3¼% of 1985	6, 900, 000. 00		6, 900, 000. 00
4¼% of 1987-92	14, 000, 000. 00		14, 000, 000. 00
4% of 1988-93	6, 000, 000. 00		6, 000, 000. 00
4⅛% of 1989-94	13, 100, 000. 00		13, 100, 000. 00
3½% of 1990	38, 925, 000. 00		38, 925, 000. 00
3% of 1995	3, 200, 000. 00		3, 200, 000. 00
3½% of 1998	31, 550, 000. 00		31, 550, 000. 00
Total public issues	797, 875, 000. 00	—5, 189, 000. 00	792, 686, 000. 00
Total investments	3, 766, 424, 000. 00	149, 281, 000. 00	3, 915, 705, 000. 00
Undisbursed balance	92, 572, 211. 11	7, 636, 192. 16	100, 208, 403. 27
Total assets	3, 858, 996, 211. 11	156, 917, 192. 16	4, 015, 913, 403. 27

[1] Includes the Government's contribution for creditable military service under the act of Apr. 8, 1942, as amended by the act of Aug. 1, 1956 (45 U.S.C. 228c-1(n)(p)). Effective July 1, 1951, appropriations of receipts are equal to the amount of taxes deposited in the Treasury (less refunds) under the Railroad Retirement Tax Act (26 U.S.C. 3201-3233).

[2] Pursuant to act of June 24, 1937 (45 U.S.C. 228c(k)).

[3] Beginning Aug. 1, 1949, paid from the trust fund under Title IV, act of June 29, 1949 (45 U.S.C. 228 p), and subsequent annual appropriations acts.

TABLE 82.—*Unemployment trust fund, June 30, 1965*

[This trust fund was established in accordance with the provisions of Sec. 904(a) of the Social Security Act of August 14, 1935 (42 U.S.C. 1104). For further details see annual report of the Secretary for 1941, p. 145]

I. RECEIPTS AND EXPENDITURES (EXCLUDING INVESTMENT TRANSACTIONS)

	Cumulative through June 30, 1964	Fiscal year 1965	Cumulative through June 30, 1965
STATE UNEMPLOYMENT ACCOUNTS			
Receipts:			
Appropriations from general fund [1]	$138,024,733.38		$138,024,733.38
Deposits by States	39,629,818,338.20	$3,051,539,275.85	42,681,357,614.05
Interest earned:			
Collected	3,805,574,526.04	240,795,448.29	4,046,369,974.33
Accrued	15,742,137.77	2,954,567.06	18,696,704.83
Total receipts	43,589,159,735.39	3,295,289,291.20	46,884,449,026.59
Expenditures:			
Withdrawals by States	37,026,622,248.27	2,386,478,698.62	39,413,100,946.89
Advances to States	1,167,074.12	−1,167,074.12	
Total expenditures	37,027,789,322.39	2,385,311,624.50	39,413,100,946.89
Transfers:			
From Employment Security Administration Account (1958 Act)		[2] 6,165,915.22	6,165,915.22
To the railroad unemployment insurance account	−107,226,931.89		−107,226,931.89
From Federal unemployment account	236,765,000.00		236,765,000.00
From Federal extended compensation account (reimbursement)	46,282,805.47		46,282,805.47
To Federal unemployment account	−15,551,000.00	[3] −20,749,500.00	−36,300,500.00
Net transfers	160,269,873.58	−14,583,584.78	145,686,288.80
Balance	6,721,640,286.58	895,394,081.92	7,617,034,368.50
RAILROAD UNEMPLOYMENT INSURANCE ACCOUNT			
BENEFIT PAYMENTS ACCOUNT			
Receipts:			
Deposits by Railroad Retirement Board	2,001,378,948.02	142,780,563.16	2,144,159,511.18
Advances from the railroad retirement account	490,431,000.00	58,230,000.00	548,661,000.00
From the railroad unemployment insurance administration fund	106,187,199.00		106,187,199.00
Advance by Secretary of Treasury	15,000,000.00		15,000,000.00
Interest earned:			
Collected	221,726,504.58	125,880.29	221,852,384.87
Accrued	24,393.14	1,544.55	25,937.69
Total receipts	2,834,748,044.74	201,137,988.00	3,035,886,032.74
Expenditures:			
Benefit payments	2,675,713,532.08	115,243,038.35	2,790,956,570.43
To the railroad unemployment insurance administration fund	12,338,198.54		12,338,198.54
Repayment of advances to railroad retirement account	178,715,000.00	77,935,000.00	256,650,000.00
Repayment of advance to the Secretary of the Treasury	15,000,000.00		15,000,000.00
Repayment of advances from general fund for temporary unemployment compensation benefits	19,398,592.24		19,398,592.24
Payment of interest on advances from railroad retirement account	32,763,471.93	12,167,342.48	44,930,814.41
Total expenditures	2,933,928,794.70	205,345,380.83	3,139,274,175.62
Transfers:			
To the railroad unemployment insurance administration fund [4]	−3,464,997.48		−3,464,997.48
From State unemployment funds	107,226,931.89		107,226,931.89
From the railroad unemployment insurance administration fund [5]	755,906.78	1,906,698.62	2,662,605.40
Net transfers	104,517,841.19	1,906,698.62	106,424,539.81
Balance	5,337,091.14	−2,300,694.21	3,036,396.93

Footnotes at end of part I.

782–556—66——46

TABLE 82.—*Unemployment trust fund, June 30, 1965*—Continued

I. RECEIPTS AND EXPENDITURES (EXCLUDING INVESTMENT TRANSACTIONS)—Con.

	Cumulative through June 30, 1964	Fiscal year 1965	Cumulative through June 30, 1965
RAILROAD UNEMPLOYMENT INSURANCE ACCOUNT—Continued			
ADMINISTRATIVE EXPENSE FUND			
Receipts:			
Deposits by Railroad Retirement Board	$50,680,173.70	$9,519,774.84	$60,199,948.54
Adjusted for prior year (unexpended balance)	7,237,031.36		7,237,031.36
Interest earned:			
Collected	771,430.55	231,626.75	1,003,057.30
Accrued	11,589.23	2,842.07	14,431.30
Total receipts	58,700,224.84	9,754,243.66	68,454,468.50
Expenditures:			
Administrative expenses	55,096,890.10	7,860,863.00	62,957,753.10
Transfers:			
From railroad unemployment insurance account [4]	3,464,997.48		3,464,997.48
To railroad unemployment insurance account [5]	−755,906.78	−1,906,698.62	−2,662,605.40
Net transfers	2,709,090.70	−1,906,698.62	802,392.08
Balance	6,312,425.44	−13,317.96	6,299,107.48
FEDERAL EXTENDED COMPENSATION ACCOUNT			
Receipts:			
Advances from general fund	[6] 814,094,450.04		814,094,450.04
Expenditures:			
Temporary extended unemployment compensation payments	767,811,644.57	−467,472.40	767,344,172.17
Repayment of advances from general fund	772,370,555.39	466,302.41	772,836,857.80
Total expenditures	1,540,182,199.96	−1,169.99	1,540,181,029.97
Transfers:			
From employment security administration account	772,370,555.39	−655.59	772,369,899.80
Reimbursement to State accounts	−46,282,805.47		−46,282,805.47
Net transfers	726,087,749.92	−655.59	726,087,094.33
Balance		514.40	514.40
EMPLOYMENT SECURITY ADMINISTRATION ACCOUNT			
Receipts:			
Transfers (Federal unemployment taxes):			
Appropriated [7]	2,605,881,457.46	622,037,760.27	3,227,919,217.73
Less refund of taxes	−14,574,604.91	−7,608,577.12	−22,183,182.03
Advance from general (revolving) fund	1,035,016,596.38	194,968,108.75	1,229,984,705.13
Less return of advances to general fund	−1,035,016,596.38	−194,968,108.75	−1,229,984,705.13
Interest earned:			
Collected	5,775,628.70	2,729,050.95	8,504,679.65
Accrued	140,092.64	34,350.62	174,443.26
Total receipts	2,597,222,573.89	617,192,584.72	3,214,415,158.61

Footnotes at end of part I.

TABLE 82.—*Unemployment trust fund, June 30, 1965*—Continued

I. RECEIPTS AND EXPENDITURES (EXCLUDING INVESTMENT TRANSACTIONS)—Con.

	Cumulative through June 30, 1964	Fiscal year 1965	Cumulative through June 30, 1965
EMPLOYMENT SECURITY ADMINISTRATION ACCOUNT—Continued			
Expenditures:			
Administrative expenses to Department of Labor	$525, 650. 00	$276, 000. 00	$801, 650. 00
Salaries and expenses, Bureau of Employment Security	42, 147, 889. 61	13, 356, 526. 34	55, 504, 415. 95
Grants to States for unemployment compensation and employment service administration	1, 591, 695, 478. 33	399, 396, 202. 56	1, 991, 091, 680. 89
Payments to general fund:			
Temporary unemployment compensation—1958	48, 371, 925. 30	105, 859, 057. 48	154, 230, 982. 78
Reimbursement for administrative expenses	21, 469, 157. 97	5, 882, 590. 71	27, 351, 748. 68
Interest on advances from general (revolving) fund	12, 653, 040. 21	2, 225, 696. 30	14, 878, 736. 51
Interest on refund of taxes	273, 169. 13	172, 046. 51	445, 215. 64
Total expenditures	1, 717, 136, 310. 55	527, 168, 119. 90	2, 244, 304, 430. 45
Transfers:			
To State accounts		[2] −6, 165, 915. 22	−6, 165, 915. 22
To Federal unemployment account:			
Excess [8]	−32, 535, 300. 00	−36, 205, 636. 25	−68, 740, 936. 25
Reduced tax credits:			
Alaska	−675, 706. 98	−128, 769. 14	−804, 476. 12
Michigan	−15, 170, 073. 57	−211, 128. 79	−15, 381, 202. 36
To Federal extended compensation account	−772, 370, 555. 39	655. 59	−772, 369, 899. 80
Net transfers	−820, 751, 635. 94	−42, 710, 793. 81	−863, 462, 429. 75
Balance	59, 334, 627. 40	47, 313, 671. 01	106, 648, 298. 41
FEDERAL UNEMPLOYMENT ACCOUNT			
Receipts:			
Appropriations from general fund [1]	207, 350, 872. 17		207, 350, 872. 17
Interest earned:			
Collected	55, 930, 068. 32	11, 382, 830. 77	67, 312, 899. 09
Accrued	654, 327. 32	139, 667. 66	793, 994. 98
Total receipts	263, 935, 267. 81	11, 522, 498. 43	275, 457, 766. 24
Expenditures:			
To Bureau of Employment Security, Department of Labor	6, 070, 914. 73	−127. 65	6, 070, 787. 08
Transfers:			
To State unemployment accounts	−236, 765, 000. 00		−236, 765, 000. 00
From State unemployment accounts	15, 551, 000. 00	[3] 20, 749, 500. 00	36, 300, 500. 00
From employment security administration account—reduced tax credits	15, 845, 780. 55	339, 897. 93	16, 185, 678. 48
From employment security administration account—excess [8]	32, 535, 300. 00	36, 205, 636. 25	68, 740, 936. 25
Net transfers	−172, 832, 919. 45	57, 295, 034. 18	−115, 537, 885. 27
Balance	85, 031, 433. 63	68, 817, 660. 26	153, 849, 093. 88

Footnotes at end of part I.

TABLE 82.—*Unemployment trust fund, June 30, 1965*—Continued

I. RECEIPTS AND EXPENDITURES (EXCLUDING INVESTMENT TRANSACTIONS)—Con.

	Cumulative through June 30, 1964	Fiscal year 1965	Cumulative through June 30, 1965
SUMMARY OF BALANCES			
State unemployment accounts..............	$6,721,640,286.58	$895,394,081.92	$7,617,034,368.50
Railroad unemployment insurance accounts:			
Benefit payments account..............	5,337,091.14	−2,300,694.21	3,036,396.93
Administrative expense fund.............	6,312,425.44	−13,317.96	6,299,107.48
Federal extended compensation account....	....	514.40	514.40
Employment security administration account..	59,334,627.40	47,313,671.01	106,648,298.41
Federal unemployment account.............	85,031,433.63	68,817,660.26	153,849,093.89
Total balances......................	6,877,655,864 19	1,009,211,915.42	7,886,867,779.61
Cash advance repayable to trust fund.......	1,167,074.12	−1,167,074.12	....
Total assets......................	6,878,822,938.31	1,008,044,841.30	7,886,867,779.61

[1] Amounts appropriated to the unemployment trust fund prior to enactment of the Employment Security Act of 1960 representing the excess of collections from Federal unemployment tax over employment security expenses (42 U.S.C. 1101(b)).

[2] Represents transfer of $5,550,448.12 to California, $153,928.22 to Delaware, and $461,538.88 to Minnesota.

[3] Represents partial repayment by Pennsylvania and Michigan of advances from the Federal unemployment account.

[4] Amount transferred pursuant to Public Law 88–133, approved Oct. 5, 1963 (77 Stat. 219).

[5] Represents the excess in the administrative expense fund transferred pursuant to section 11(d) of the Railroad Unemployment Insurance Act (45 U.S.C. 361(d)).

[6] Includes $36,274,621.83 not repayable to general fund pursuant to section 905(a) of the Social Security Act, as amended.

[7] Excludes unappropriated receipts of −$1,896,326.43.

[8] Represents excess in the employment security administration account transferred pursuant to 42 U.S.C. 1102.

TABLE 82.—*Unemployment trust fund, June 30, 1965*—Continued

II. ASSETS HELD BY THE TREASURY DEPARTMENT (ACCRUAL BASIS)

Assets	June 30, 1964	Fiscal year 1965, increase, or decrease (−)	June 30, 1965
Investments in public debt securities:			
Special issues, Treasury certificates of indebtedness, unemployment trust fund series maturing June 30:			
3½% of 1965	$4,930,606,000.00	−$4,930,606,000.00	
3⅝% of 1966		5,799,114,000.00	$5,799,114,000.00
Total special issues	4,930,606,000.00	868,508,000.00	5,799,114,000.00
Public issues:			
Treasury notes:			
5% Series B-1964	1,650,000.00	−1,650,000.00	
4⅝% Series A-1965	2,640,000.00	−2,640,000.00	
3⅝% Series B-1966	146,000,000.00	−146,000,000.00	
4% Series A-1966	15,750,000.00	−10,000,000.00	5,750,000.00
3¾% Series A-1967	51,500,000.00	−51,500,000.00	
3⅝% Series B-1967	7,000,000.00		7,000,000.00
Treasury bonds:			
2½% of 1964–69 (dated Apr. 15, 1943)	1,000,000.00		1,000,000.00
2½% of 1964–69 (dated Sept. 15, 1943)	5,600,000.00		5,600,000.00
2½% of 1965–70	15,000,000.00		15,000,000.00
3⅜% of 1966	1,000,000.00		1,000,000.00
3¾% of 1966	27,750,000.00	−27,750,000.00	
3⅝% of 1967	14,000,000.00	−14,000,000.00	
3⅞% of 1968	3,000,000.00		3,000,000.00
3¾% of 1968	31,500,000.00		31,500,000.00
4% of 1969 (dated Aug. 15, 1962)	19,000,000.00		19,000,000.00
4% of 1969 (dated Oct. 1, 1957)	26,100,000.00		26,100,000.00
4% of 1970 (dated Jan. 1, 1965)		119,250,000.00	119,250,000.00
4% of 1970 (dated June 20, 1963)	3,000,000.00		3,000,000.00
4% of 1971	10,000,000.00		10,000,000.00
3⅞% of 1971	12,000,000.00		12,000,000.00
4% of 1972 (dated Sept. 15, 1962)	46,500,000.00		46,500,000.00
4% of 1972 (dated Nov. 15, 1962)	31,500,000.00		31,500,000.00
4% of 1973	48,000,000.00		48,000,000.00
4⅛% of 1973		9,000,000.00	9,000,000.00
3⅞% of 1974	16,000,000.00		16,000,000.00
4⅛% of 1974		127,000,000.00	127,000,000.00
4¼% of 1974		2,640,000.00	2,640,000.00
4¼% of 1975–85	32,710,000.00		32,710,000.00
3¼% of 1978–83	53,050,000.00		53,050,000.00
4% of 1980	106,000,000.00		106,000,000.00
3½% of 1980	53,000,000.00		53,000,000.00
3¼% of 1985	14,000,000.00		14,000,000.00
4¼% of 1987–92	10,000,000.00	94,000,000.00	104,000,000.00
4% of 1988–93	17,500,000.00		17,500,000.00
4⅛% of 1989–94	174,300,000.00		174,300,000.00
3½% of 1990	94,221,000.00	18,000,000.00	112,221,000.00
3½% of 1998	61,200,000.00	−18,000,000.00	43,200,000.00
2¾% Investment Series B-1975–80	745,000,000.00		745,000,000.00
Total public issues	1,896,471,000.00	98.350,000.00	1,994,821,000.00
Total investments, par value	6,827,077,000.00	966,858,000.00	7,793,935,000.00
Unamortized discount	−9,792,800.97	69,587.85	−9,723,213.12
Unamortized premium	1,071,166.38	−213,441.75	857,724.63
Accrued interest purchased		49,507.06	49,507.06
Total investments	6,818,355,365.41	966,763,653.16	7,785,119,018.57
Unexpended balances:			
Trust account	19,234,906.45	−9,190,909.95	10,043,996.50
Railroad Unemployment Insurance Accounts:			
Benefits payments account	188,467.92	211,961.65	400,429.57
Administrative expense fund	200,808.08	−40,863.00	159,945.08
Federal extended compensation account		514.40	514.40
Employment security administration account	22,903,776.23	44,034,578.50	66,038,354.82
Subtotal	6,860,883,324.09	1,001,778,934.85	7,862,662,258.94
Accrued interest on investments	16,572,540.10	3,132,980.57	19,705,520.67
Cash advance repayable to trust fund	1,167,074.12	−1,167,074.12	
Accounts receivable	200,000.00	4,300,000.00	4,500,000.00
Total assets	6,878,822,938.31	1,008,044,841.30	7,886,867,779.61

TABLE 82.—*Unemployment trust fund, June 30, 1965*—Continued

III. BALANCE OF UNEMPLOYMENT TRUST FUND BY STATES AND OTHER ACCOUNTS AS OF JUNE 30, 1964, OPERATIONS IN 1965, AND BALANCE JUNE 30, 1965

States and other accounts	Balance June 30, 1964	Operations in fiscal 1965				Balance June 30, 1965
		Deposits	Earnings	Transfers	Withdrawals	
Alabama	$75,708,694.63	$28,168,366.00	$2,96,518.83		$0,612,000.00	$86,061,579.46
Alaska	6,922,218.90	9,473,246.68	81,186.80		4,980,000.00	11,496,652.38
Ai	65,847,911.91	12,4,052.28	2,90,487.21		14,370,000.00	64,3,451.40
4	27,83,745.96	13,830,085.04	989,166.24		14,745,781.00	28,007,216.24
4	626,199,926.66	504,007,208.57	22,234,749.27	1 $5,550,448.12	542,178,964.97	615,813,367.65
4 1	52,026,123.36	17,050,00.00	6 201,568.27		4,090,000.00	56,932,129.12
Delaware	170,448,815.82	52,306,000.00	60,035.20		41,150,000.00	187,866,384.09
District of Columbia	16,459,565.45	9,810,000.00	2,184,875.90	1 153,928.22	5,250,000.00	21,823,528.87
Florida	62,634,676.33	8,598,104.63	6 029,841.40		10,065,000.00	63,352,657.46
63	147,339,455.92	40,811,833.82	6 045.33		21,702,500.00	71,931,898.83
Hawaii	62,952,785.60	32,224,650.88	98,894.58		6,700,000.00	184,201,277.88
I	15,784,558.30	10,599,025.83	16,678,991.77		6,25,000.00	20,333,629.46
India b	89,684,726.73	8,908,400.00	5,68,741.68		96,210,000.00	28,297,832.16
Iowa	150,920,717.74	145,552,520.68	3,836,543.89		2,60,0.00	505,706,239.18
Kansas	107,585,094.24	44,701,232.03	3,121,468.55		8,845,00.00	173,520,691.45
Kentucky	59,37,372.93	10,85,173.81	3,804,137.50		15,960,300.00	112,841,811.94
Louisia a	103,810,499.26	15,475,000.00	3,915,958.92		0,90.0	60,93,541.48
M	105,113,744.92	27,50,00.00	5,030,327.23		24,100,000.00	114,084,636.76
Maryland	26,536,588.30	33,371,135.93	5,152,438.53		36,524,000.00	118,300,839.77
	34,074,602.58	10,97,070.00	6,626,090.93		114,800,000.00	31,88,985.53
M	172,361,289.65	59,519,491.26	11 304,152.10	2 −8,131,500.00	63,925,000.00	162,222,532.37
Msippi	355,158,319.98	134,893,933.04	67,782.21	1 461,538.88	30,975,000.00	199,081,313.62
Montana	19,230,782.04	181,149,029.45	1,700,771.23		8,665,000.00	475,555,001.53
	42,015,933.75	30,040,00.00	7,594,143.73		33,800,00.0	19,455,103.13
N da	208,522,787.30	19,28,000.00	1,418,378.70		0,40.0	54,269,704.98
New	18,642,177.95	43,551,104.08	9,881,625.11		10,60,000.00	225,868,035.11
New	39,128,828.39	5,326,700.00	887,254.80		8,285,000.00	18,178,331.29
New	26,578,514.34	8,362,456.00	9,8,380.82		5,170,000.00	40,624,663.38
North	23,788,559.61	491,485.66	40,865,105.66		133,080,000.00	27,128,814.41
6th Dakota	279,378,846.76	7,61,000.00	7,479,886.21		7,925,000.00	291,624,471.87
	34,426,161.30	135,444,000.00	226,906.09		429,392,401.53	1,24,338,059.35
	1,158,386,976.05	444,626,347.00	7,705,83 14		29,650,000.00	225,393,036.69
Pennsylvania	5,460,210.22	44,565,781.91	6,6,380.82		5,800,000.00	5,467,297.38
Puerto Rico	155,058,777.98	5,580,181.07	2,6,8.16		82,327,00.00	6,217,764.33
e Island	40,942,902.83	20,80,453.27	1,794,189.60	3 −12,618,000.00	14,410,000.00	45,337,609.21
	72,871,949.30	17,287,000.00	1,594,491.66		23,550,000.00	86,727,975.99
	172,076,507.45	34,529,645.87			156,236,000.00	311,801,069.61
	52,182,526.39	303,520,00.00			17,6,0.00	55,266,013.95
	41,943,727.54	8,889,297.96			14,2,0.00	49,687,219.20
		0,876,000.00				

[North] Dakota	81, 40,427.04	19, 65, 0.00	3 02, 2 10	----	12, 90,000.00	90,607,739.14
Tennessee	14,140,498.98	2,251,000.00	65, 032.88	----	2,650,000.00	14,246,531.86
Texas	74,711, 39.72	41,135,000.00	2, 96, 1.79	----	24,809,000.00	94, 03,854.51
Utah	29,306,196.47	56,105,867.96	8,193,759.92	----	51,985,412.71	241,620,411.64
	37,411,461.84	9, 8, 0.00	1 302,288.22	----	12,915,000.00	35, 61,740.06
	5, 61,711.31	6,074,176.13	2, 180.10	----	4,660,000.00	6, 37,067.54
	27,434,456.12	20,638,000.00	69 8.35	----	10,870,000.00	42, 92,098.47
	96,014,576.93	53, 89,580.56	6,947,349.48	----	53,800,000.00	03, 81, 66.97
Vt	56,513,527.16	13,484,000.00	2,030,322.10	----	12,925,000.00	59, 92,849.26
	89,498,704.12	44,119,672.05	6,840,778.02	----	38,450,264.29	02, 08,889.90
Wyoming	5,835,763.86	6,404,966.46	274,944.63	----	2,910,000.00	8, 65,674.85
Subtotal	6, 27,640,286.58	3,051,539,275.85	243, 56,015.35	−14,683,664.78	2,385,311,624.50	7,617,034,368.50
Railroad unemployment insurance accounts:						
Benefits and refunds	5,148,623.22	142,780,563.16	127,424.84	3 60,136,098.62	4 205,557,342.48	2,635,967.36
Administrative expense fund	6,111,617.36	9,510,774.84	234,468.82	5 −1,906,698.62	7,820,000.00	6,139,162.40
Federal unemployment account	85,031,433.63		11,522,498.43	57,295,034. B		153,849,093.89
Employment security administration account	36,430,851.17	621,967,256.51	2,833,905.33	−605,357,158.78	16,164,910.64	39,709,943.59
Federal extended compensation account						
Subtotal	6,854,362,811.96	3,825,806,998.01	258,468,312.77	−504,415,709.38	2,614,853,877.62	7,819,368,535.74
Balances of transfers to other agencies:						
Railroad unemployment insurance accounts:						
Benefits and refunds	188,467.92				−211,961.65	90,429.57
Administrative expense fund	200,808.08				40,863.00	159 945.08
Federal extended compensation account					−514.40	54 40
Employment security administration account	22,903,776.23				−44,034,578.59	66,938,354.82
Total	6,877,655,864.19	3,825,806,998.01	258,468,312.77	−504,415,709.38	2,570,647,685.98	7,886,867,779.61
Cash advance repayable to trust fund	1,167,074.12				1,167,074.12	
Total as shown in parts I and II	6,878,822,938.31	3,825,806,998.01	258,468,312.77	−504,415,709.38	2,571,814,760.10	7,886,867,779.61

1 Transfers to State accounts due to excess receipts in repayment of advances under Temporary Unemployment Compensation Act of 1958.
2 Partial repayment of advances made pursuant to the provisions of title XII of the Social Security Act.
3 Represents advances from the railroad retirement account of $58,230,000.00 and transfers from the railroad unemployment insurance administration fund of $1,906,698.62.
4 Includes repayment of advances to the railroad retirement account: principal $77,935,000.00 and interest $12,167,342.48.
5 Transferred to the railroad unemployment insurance account in accordance with section 11(d) of the Railroad Unemployment Insurance Act.

TABLE 83.—*U.S. Government life insurance fund, June 30, 1965*

[This trust fund operates in accordance with the provisions of the act of June 7, 1924, as amended (38 U.S.C. 755). For further details, see annual report of the Secretary for 1941, p. 142]

I. RECEIPTS AND EXPENDITURES (EXCLUDING INVESTMENT TRANSACTIONS)

	Cumulative through June 30, 1964	Fiscal year 1965	Cumulative through June 30, 1965
Receipts:			
Premiums and other receipts	$2,075,559,932.42	$14,732,515.89	$2,090,292,448.31
Interest and profits on investments	1,198,661,348.10	33,761,925.48	1,232,423,273.58
Payments from general fund [1]	−216,497.03	−119,011.31	−335,508.34
Total receipts	3,274,004,783.49	48,375,430.06	3,322,380,213.55
Expenditures:			
Benefit payments, dividends, and refunds	2,291,292,069.55	70,528,299.41	2,361,820,368.96
Balance	982,712,713.94	−22,152,869.35	960,559,844.59

II. ASSETS HELD BY THE TREASURY DEPARTMENT

Assets	June 30, 1964	Fiscal year 1965, increase, or decrease (−)	June 30, 1965
Investments in public debt securities:			
Special issues, U.S. Government life insurance fund series maturing June 30:			
Treasury notes:			
3¾% of 1965	$670,000.00	−$670,000.00	
Treasury bonds:			
3½% of 1965	67,191,000.00	−67,191,000.00	
3½% of 1966	73,100,000.00		$73,100,000.00
3¾% of 1966	670,000.00		670,000.00
3½% of 1967	73,100,000.00		73,100,000.00
3¾% of 1967	670,000.00		670,000.00
3½% of 1968	73,100,000.00		73,100,000.00
3¾% of 1968	670,000.00		670,000.00
3½% of 1969	73,100,000.00		73,100,000.00
3¾% of 1969	670,000.00		670,000.00
3½% of 1970	73,100,000.00		73,100,000.00
3¾% of 1970	670,000.00		670,000.00
3½% of 1971	73,100,000.00		73,100,000.00
3¾% of 1971	670,000.00		670,000.00
3½% of 1972	73,100,000.00		73,100,000.00
3¾% of 1972	670,000.00		670,000.00
3½% of 1973	73,100,000.00		73,100,000.00
3¾% of 1973	670,000.00		670,000.00
3½% of 1974	73,100,000.00		73,100,000.00
3¾% of 1974	670,000.00		670,000.00
3¾% of 1975	73,770,000.00		73,770,000.00
3½% of 1976	67,799,000.00		67,799,000.00
3⅝% of 1976	5,971,000.00		5,971,000.00
3½% of 1977	49,963,000.00		49,963,000.00
3⅝% of 1977	23,807,000.00		23,807,000.00
3⅝% of 1978	2,739,000.00	45,475,000.00	48,214,000.00
Total special issues	955,840,000.00	−22,386,000.00	933,454,000.00
Investment in nonguaranteed securities:			
Consolidated Federal farm loan bonds:			
4% of 1965	25,000,000.00		25,000,000.00
Total investments	980,840,000.00	−22,386,000.00	958,454,000.00
Undisbursed balance	1,872,713.94	233,130.65	2,105,844.59
Total	982,712,713.94	−22,152,869.35	960,559,844.59

[1] Included under premiums and other receipts prior to fiscal 1962. Negative amounts result from adjustments of prior years' receipts.

NOTE.—Policy loans outstanding on basis of information furnished by the Veterans' Administration amounted to $87,561,974.14 as of June 30, 1965.

Federal Aid To States

TABLE 84.—*Federal grants in aid to State and local governments and to individuals and private institutions within the States, fiscal year 1965*

[On a checks-issued basis except where this detail is not available for all payments. Wherever feasible adjustment to a checks-issued basis has been made, footnoted, and reported under "Adjustments or undistributed to States."]

PART A. FEDERAL AID PAYMENTS TO STATES AND LOCAL UNITS

States, Territories, etc.	Basic scientific research grants[1]	Commodity Credit Corporation Price-support donations[2]	Cooperative agricultural extension work	Cooperative projects in marketing[3]	Cooperative State research service[4]	Food stamp program[5]	Forest protection, utilization, and restoration[6]
	(1)	(2)	(3)	(4)	(5)	(6)	(7)
Alabama		$2,830,541	$2,403,662	$64,229	$1,213,585	$1,576,324	$449,879
Alaska	$30,400	176,672	190,378	11,500	302,187		61,618
Arizona	54,342	1,091,868	489,010	7,000	547,163		
Arkansas	27,000	2,924,967	1,935,127	35,900	986,337	264,575	434,787
California	180,888	5,023,878	1,849,025	144,000	1,425,516	78,877	1,174,644
Colorado	15,000	1,301,161	760,562	56,459	701,574	170,458	86,400
Connecticut	47,300	691,383	421,942	12,901	505,233	9,988	126,043
Delaware		377,922	224,102	24,000	410,198		21,935
District of Columbia		428,819					
Florida	14,443	3,017,535	909,823	95,621	753,874		753,921
Georgia	36,000	2,774,241	2,520,297	74,996	1,291,910	13,012	710,200
Hawaii		333,061	335,669	33,400	417,490		65,635
Idaho		331,424	599,278	7,898	562,761		252,775
Illinois	81,473	3,728,783	2,190,231	53,400	1,279,574	1,326,892	96,237
Indiana	18,000	2,301,298	1,855,601	93,991	1,158,645	384,358	109,789
Iowa	87,500	2,025,673	1,981,065	67,290	1,203,960		101,847
Kansas	20,000	1,169,399	1,366,515	105,873	836,425	31,131	95,824
Kentucky	25,600	3,878,737	2,459,533	88,047	1,241,058	2,260,630	347,812
Louisiana	23,160	3,755,505	1,582,136	105,730	879,493	2,209,657	543,635
Maine		528,986	495,362	66,708	531,930		427,283
Maryland	10,000	1,286,028	728,732	68,924	650,470		210,852
Massachusetts	47,500	1,982,079	570,080	69,653	615,954		165,075
Michigan	8,000	4,443,978	2,029,154	163,819	1,160,875	3,584,165	92,147
Minnesota	25,300	2,241,920	1,907,276	73,321	1,093,467	628,767	438,458
Mississippi	15,000		2,502,516	101,566	1,211,362		545,245
Missouri		2,309,432	2,208,711	116,050	1,141,051	1,108,893	378,697
Montana	20,000	296,428	588,265	22,900	560,083	90,814	201,789
Nebraska	66,260	768,823	1,139,669	15,950	796,429	5,517	40,000
Nevada		101,569	251,705		366,841		94,574
New Hampshire	18,000	317,756	279,163	17,660	421,802		170,285
New Jersey	63,409	1,469,359	562,369	68,890	673,870		175,267
New Mexico		1,190,380	547,288	50,760	477,980	703,100	76,938
New York	45,050	8,889,742	1,941,354	125,129	1,394,620		479,236
North Carolina	80,107	3,781,995	3,397,641	116,478	1,749,560	636,535	591,191
North Dakota		381,478	821,067	58,271	615,301		45,245
Ohio	73,300	5,089,659	2,507,360	42,665	1,358,918	6,539,470	229,896
Oklahoma	14,000	4,306,911	1,624,702	84,858	924,624		187,348
Oregon		1,338,914	799,895	70,132	789,251	623,061	692,913
Pennsylvania	35,000	6,835,492	2,512,607	60,870	1,521,588	5,839,315	440,275
Rhode Island		301,553	196,102	4,060	382,389		70,273
South Carolina	26,000	1,217,413	1,828,852	30,500	988,275	32,948	536,143
South Dakota	50,000	513,502	799,128	17,050	619,869		80,193
Tennessee		3,191,139	2,503,308	50,819	1,263,702	1,507,682	439,824
Texas	34,660	4,815,200	3,894,923	54,069	1,681,137		424,140
Utah	29,500	748,109	455,090	18,998	520,524	11,289	61,104
Vermont	5,000	346,346	348,083	24,288	413,388		136,795
Virginia		1,863,428	2,033,545	92,630	1,116,622	694,272	534,921
Washington	37,027	2,461,945	896,620	52,522	874,257	93,269	804,119
West Virginia		2,826,511	1,296,467	45,506	807,659	2,314,840	291,984
Wisconsin	105,647	2,093,588	1,911,725	61,721	1,102,900	178,473	699,275
Wyoming	21,700	202,299	383,290	5,230	448,622	8,682	67,589
Puerto Rico		5,517,059	1,783,343		1,178,452		21,766
Virgin Islands		63,232					
Other Territories, etc.[7]		124,076					
Adjustments or undistributed to States		[8]4,358,274	[9]10,552,164	109,552	[10]278,365	[8]—1,165,037	
Total	1,491,566	120,122,327	80,371,512	3,043,784	45,449,120	31,761,957	15,283,821

Footnotes at end of table.

TABLE 84.—*Federal grants in aid to State and local governments and to individuals and private institutions within the States, fiscal year 1965*—Continued

PART A. FEDERAL AID PAYMENTS TO STATES AND LOCAL UNITS—Continued

States, Territories, etc.	Department of Agriculture—Continued						Department of Commerce
	National forest and school funds-shared revenues [11]	National grass-lands-shared revenues	Removal of surplus agricultural commodities — Value of commodities distributed	School lunch program [12]	Special milk program [13]	Watershed protection, flood prevention, and resource conservation and development [14]	Bureau of Public Roads — Highway trust fund
	(8)	(9)	(10)	(11)	(12)	(13)	(14)
Alabama	$218,213		$8,652,855	$4,351,035	$1,128,589	$821,994	$90,469,403
Alaska	236,988		540,079	224,949	33,992		50,697,266
Arizona	552,587		3,337,799	1,463,853	467,818	775,509	63,745,701
Arkansas	748,032	$1,757	8,941,513	2,979,418	1,162,302	3,003,589	37,881,444
California	5,190,349	507	15,357,804	8,283,166	7,748,441	4,003,778	318,311,415
Colorado	211,612	31,872	3,977,601	1,930,879	835,222	457,447	58,922,576
Connecticut			2,113,531	1,717,402	1 ʼ316ʼ 790	1,390,270	48,416,556
Delaware			1,155,294	325,886	274,733	243,114	16,677,024
District of Columbia.			1,310,885	257,791	609,404		26,404,142
Florida	272,949	17,454	9,224,488	6,460,491	1,243,663	683,916	87,321,854
Georgia	257,507		8,480,747	6,245,663	1,062,046	3,380,491	80,504,234
Hawaii			1,018,154	1,098,756	146,676	911,639	9,731,419
Idaho	1,134,782	2,234	1,013,151	835,749	202,076	107,473	35,116,139
Illinois	18,537		11,398,748	6,369,980	5,560,782	407,812	208,961,769
Indiana	9,690		7,034,982	4,286,095	2,369,795	867,852	92,877,554
Iowa	65	125	6,192,405	3,475,822	1,722,354	1,870,235	53,436,978
Kansas		17,873	3,574,809	2,235,634	1,056,657	3,838,131	50,841,936
Kentucky	92,349	1,645	11,857,151	4,920,203	1,701,558	1,370,041	59,943,553
Louisiana	246,165		11,480,434	6,201,996	630,055	781,097	102,786,735
Maine	4,831		1,617,090	1,031,201	437,341	289,594	23,793,441
Maryland		13,910	3,931,340	2,439,217	1,983,929	537,133	49,723,232
Massachusetts			6,059,139	4,140,300	2,915,634	307,433	77,600,608
Michigan	222,869	2,425	13,585,073	5,164,706	5,205,853	418,314	132,366,583
Minnesota	235,950		6,853,463	4,155,361	2,411,766	399,192	104,547,350
Mississippi	691,387		13,006,937	4,525,838	1,460,536	5,682,463	57,608,448
Missouri	79,149	743	7,059,845	4,320,113	1,988,296	626,614	113,946,603
Montana	1,010,574		906,169	652,015	200,233	17,005	56,431,894
Nebraska	15,115	5,707	2,350,261	1,388,410	625,117	1,396,916	37,179,616
Nevada	43,094		310,492	166,338	102,418	13,599	40,800,086
New Hampshire	69,071		971,367	467,881	351,158	298,176	16,053,396
New Jersey			4,491,774	2,616,748	3,066,779	340,665	65,103,810
New Mexico	172,166	8,909	3,638,945	1,298,857	729,684	535,493	46,616,494
New York		1,806	25,647,120	12,425,320	7,434,973	407,147	197,519,605
North Carolina	195,436		11,561,415	8,115,738	1,985,884	712,730	50,739,507
North Dakota	79	211,950	1,166,163	950,314	367,842	552,901	31,017,035
Ohio	12,311	1,096	15,558,895	7,473,982	5,669,566	656,923	185,750,829
Oklahoma	101,532	7,773	13,166,062	2,757,648	1,033,814	8,376,960	57,101,018
Oregon	13,654,118	2,437	4,093,008	1,768,501	532,751	361,070	71,991,283
Pennsylvania	216,473	14,084	20,895,837	7,557,184	3,955,901	417,725	141,924,145
Rhode Island			921,835	441,907	387,583		24,812,429
South Carolina	421,393		3,721,586	4,528,917	651,082	754,776	34,688,573
South Dakota	57,126	44,600	1,569,757	728,511	408,879	154,105	45,316,296
Tennessee	89,020		9,755,189	4,937,894	1,807,316	1,384,763	108,187,171
Texas	481,316	15,862	14,719,884	8,738,620	3,269,226	4,682,699	216,233,428
Utah	123,212		2,286,940	1,234,563	373,492	451,570	58,577,879
Vermont	68,479		1,058,765	352,507	190,837		24,274,357
Virginia	101,961	103	5,696,427	5,282,607	1,647,871	911,412	[15] 163,050,684
Washington	5,441,835		7,526,070	2,741,466	1,481,578	488,560	73,295,168
West Virginia	137,060		8,640,537	2,073,191	562,593	1,451,484	55,397,803
Wisconsin	119,324		6,400,020	3,578,071	3,262,983	696,550	53,682,362
Wyoming	126,959	44,038	618,420	3,645,337	128,145	104,754	46,955,210
Puerto Rico	1,719		16,865,439	4,731,800		97,838	6,888,594
Virgin Islands			193,299	127,791			
Other Territories, etc.[7]			379,298	142,829			
Adjustments or undistributed to States			[8] −86,810,214	−119,415	139,317		[16] 17,317,260
Total	33,083,384	448,910	267,076,077	176,930,811	86,043,330	[17] 58,440,952	3,979,539,895

Footnotes at end of table.

TABLE 84.—*Federal grants in aid to State and local governments and to individuals and private institutions within the States, fiscal year 1965*—Continued

PART A. FEDERAL AID PAYMENTS TO STATES AND LOCAL UNITS—Continued

States, Territories, etc.	Department of Commerce—Continued			Department of Defense			Federal Aviation Agency
	Bureau of Public Roads—Continued	Public facilities grants and area redevelopment assistance	State marine schools	Army			Federal airport program [19]
				Civil defense	Flood control lands-shared revenues	National Guard centers, construction	
	Other [18]						
	(15)	(16)	(17)	(18)	(19)	(20)	(21)
Alabama	$60,159	$126,407		$397,649	$2,783	$293,530	$1,410,120
Alaska	2,647,396	2,050		108,225		3,417	2,941,270
Arizona	2,592,637			164,286	19	22,240	1,412,860
Arkansas	885,244	832,054		337,262	94,232	59,138	455,836
California	5,969,466	60,000	$146,402	3,529,456	87,888	1,104,337	5,196,081
Colorado	1,648,009			271,157	10,054	126,703	1,265,541
Connecticut				237,552	1,428	92,156	309,540
Delaware				90,817	3,974		
District of Columbia				111,714			
Florida	256,699			551,501	7,361	5,260	2,197,880
Georgia	677,474	933,278		592,576	49,579	826,352	9,452,846
Hawaii				280,940		295,750	2,097,165
Idaho	4,440,360			82,701	81	8,811	130,878
Illinois	10,530	57,248		627,004	82,774		2,809,416
Indiana	33,300	320,687		111,550	568	346,853	887,927
Iowa	5,991			253,818	115,102	47,202	696,365
Kansas				305,002	194,191	128,297	572,310
Kentucky	108,637	22,533		180,938	36,438	400,358	753,150
Louisiana	131,340			366,455	21,540	126,844	1,630,707
Maine			151,130	249,974		13,824	68,991
Maryland	7	50,000		451,133	791	233,413	864,097
Massachusetts		59,653	140,991	641,332	2,882	51,690	1,401,344
Michigan	411,049	188,000		719,885	722	719,691	1,523,331
Minnesota	499,425	123,660		515,699	2,425	234,531	1,284,162
Mississippi	145,723			152,679	103,836	565,532	1,411,311
Missouri		493,000		396,430	94,402	194,916	917,231
Montana	2,650,396	191,000		74,137	6,108	216,237	615,846
Nebraska	71,348			198,685	45,421	84,807	515,601
Nevada	659,664	5,944		113,143		585	560,504
New Hampshire	88,572			77,222	1,825	162,417	31,208
New Jersey				496,835	1,620	180,442	1,283,956
New Mexico	1,207,437	5,769		76,513	83	441,864	597,592
New York	25,646		147,601	3,465,807	1,317	55,129	5,471,260
North Carolina	362,644	55,164		519,398	1,435	464,863	1,323,758
North Dakota	115,356			160,686	136,704	124,214	274,775
Ohio	31,870	4,600		263,810	11,269	398,290	1,979,423
Oklahoma	360,389	1,084,828		609,390	256,938	26,766	2,101,113
Oregon	4,802,246	345,610		42,657	24,340	5,351	425,103
Pennsylvania		649,037		659,378	7,485	239,680	2,368,337
Rhode Island		23,567		126,334			325,617
South Carolina	38,100	54,029		277,041	1,889	376,221	640,464
South Dakota	67,774			178,864	44,789	149,903	315,010
Tennessee	224,916	545,568		213,186	37,823	28,571	563,404
Texas	62,800	52,980	75,000	573,611	206,074	175,779	4,976,631
Utah	2,347,717			77,559		4,731	796,513
Vermont	390,065			50,179	86	1,020	159,255
Virginia	353,408	827		243,288	6,761	285,202	1,027,282
Washington	1,897,183	120,000		388,777	10,507	134,761	695,382
West Virginia	449,480	1,995,637		71,983	1,524	413,352	723,005
Wisconsin	34,995	4,100		667,352	3,674	397,496	773,667
Wyoming	1,385,608			87,512		222,196	119,003
Puerto Rico	43,868			160,978		569,318	150,083
Virgin Islands				11,645			93,938
Other Territories, etc.[7]				17,534			
Adjustments or undistributed to States	1,018		−50,000				
Total	38,195,946	8,407,230	611,127	21,631,239	1,720,742	11,060,040	70,598,089

Footnotes at end of table.

TABLE 84.—*Federal grants in aid to State and local governments and to individuals and private institutions within the States, fiscal year 1965*—Continued

PART A. FEDERAL AID PAYMENTS TO STATES AND LOCAL UNITS—Continued

States, Territories, etc.	Federal Power Commission	Funds appropriated to the President					
	Payments to States under Federal Power Act-shared revenues	Accelerated public works program [20]	Disaster relief, and State and local preparedness [21][22]	Office of Economic Opportunity			
				Adult basic education [23]	Community action programs	Neighborhood Youth Corps [24]	Work experience and training programs [23]
	(22)	(23)	(24)	(25)	(26)	(27)	(28)
Alabama	$2,084	$10,209,554			$651,508	$97,485	
Alaska	691	1,599,052	$9,704,849		473,592	456,408	$28,247
Arizona	397	157,318	21,919		835,619	2,162,398	6,569
Arkansas	4	6,219,304	151,354		937,629	3,673,417	1,489,717
California	33,000	7,984,690	7,012,227	$225,311	2,803,882	3,482,878	1,200,049
Colorado	439	103,788	15,813		531,310	903,953	382,429
Connecticut		1,405,160	6,000	90,000	957,411	456,408	209,754
Delaware		370,006	16,404		131,955	88,623	4,435
District of Columbia					1,233,562	1,293,894	79,200
Florida	3	3,438,038	3,988,546	515,172	1,510,231	1,169,822	137,589
Georgia	36	5,129,602	1,276,571		1,696,823	1,360,361	285,302
Hawaii		1,767,879	204,021	27,000	227,320	451,976	9,173
Idaho	33,484	493,118	283,400		34,998	22,156	4,415
Illinois		5,481,358	18,767		3,548,335	1,927,547	307,875
Indiana		4,566,119	432,736		396,121	638,085	101,000
Iowa		35,865	24,859	35,316	257,546	270,300	119,301
Kansas		410,935	16,255		196,844	279,162	
Kentucky		18,710,922	629,805	482,945	2,324,336	881,797	5,036,907
Louisiana		14,444,567	1,775,245		365,340	110,779	238,703
Maine		1,557,303	11,245		210,305	137,365	90,188
Maryland		1,519,652	23,058		412,500	70,898	9,210
Massachusetts		9,960,196	23,425		1,157,999	1,298,325	1,021,636
Michigan	105	21,972,295	706,765		1,739,321	717,845	891,460
Minnesota	11	4,204,894	2,135,416		232,594	1,165,391	844,415
Mississippi	24	4,603,984	453		1,693,048	540,599	5,229
Missouri		3,802,937	209,921	42,883	1,698,398	2,991,021	848,039
Montana	11,221	524,210	2,439,737		72,659	44,311	
Nebraska		87,503	289,530		89,208	70,898	
Nevada	904	9,375	−22,103		81,487	88,623	4,908
New Hampshire		625,347			159,067	8,862	5,050
New Jersey		16,202,007	316,700	107,577	1,770,087	1,816,769	668,782
New Mexico	3	1,624,691	16,113		392,410	323,473	93,899
New York		15,206,159	472,415	828,000	1,369,687	3,894,975	593,619
North Carolina	31	8,401,311	235,722	831,799	1,931,371	638,085	70,767
North Dakota		360,889	17,954		104,107	53,174	136,258
Ohio		8,390,529	344,007		2,023,635	1,683,834	1,111,521
Oklahoma		5,255,865	12,634	18,000	749,885	1,019,163	178,939
Oregon	33,448	1,635,672	7,813,072		403,640	314,611	59,491
Pennsylvania	3	36,505,066			1,969,459	1,834,493	258,217
Rhode Island		5,096,743	2,300	28,319	139,719	434,252	309,298
South Carolina	194	3,166,946	18,062		423,898	70,898	
South Dakota		384,139	23,272		84,921	97,485	
Tennessee		6,512,597	12,493		2,310,945	1,329,343	26,823
Texas		10,687,796	22,526		2,280,842	899,522	4,400
Utah	1,370	1,388,017		19,996	45,189	265,869	79,433
Vermont		461,863	7,100		195,702	39,880	3,350
Virginia	16	2,496,653	116,232		825,459	274,731	
Washington	6,454	2,422,285	1,212,060	64,338	396,092	203,833	61,845
West Virginia	3	17,304,743	254,393		1,682,165	509,581	1,481,013
Wisconsin	66	2,399,023	215,238		313,660	1,271,738	116,000
Wyoming	65	213,758	66,710		28,776		136,625
Puerto Rico	13	10,717,062	569,948		946,994	474,132	1,425,977
Virgin Islands		139,404	79,945				7,446
Other Territories, etc.[7]		17,309	225,654		104,489		
Adjustments or undistributed to States							
Total	124,069	288,385,498	43,450,768	3,316,656	47,154,080	44,311,428	20,184,503

Footnotes at end of table.

TABLE 84.—*Federal grants in aid to State and local governments and to individuals and private institutions within the States, fiscal year 1965*—Continued

PART A. FEDERAL AID PAYMENTS TO STATES AND LOCAL UNITS—Continued

States, Territories, etc.	Department of Health, Education, and Welfare						
	American Printing House for the Blind	Office of Education					
		Colleges of agriculture and the mechanical arts	Construction		Cooperative vocational education	Defense educational activities	Educational improvement for the handicapped [26]
			Assistance for public schools	Higher educational facilities			
	(29)	(30)	(31)	(32)	(33)	(34)	(35)
Alabama	$14,547	$277,647	$122,206	$13,600	$963,454	$1,786,159	$68,000
Alaska	88	205,376	329,180	2,832	281,156	210,904	25,100
Arizona	6,898	230,951	2,202,375	701	1,264,524	1,140,807	60,000
Arkansas	8,224	242,458	48,804	28,959	1,715,648	867,144	62,240
California	78,218	573,580	4,487,013	62,610	4,998,683	6,886,829	100,000
Colorado	9,551	241,689	1,772,754	21,359	1,433,997	1,779,376	63,000
Connecticut	17,200	260,260	145,188	16,669	1,683,965	1,171,160	67,200
Delaware	2,388	210,608		28,000	188,988	244,130	32,838
District of Columbia	1,813			28,280	486,835	196,455	
Florida	23,125	317,693	2,542,176	45,447	4,331,715	1,430,705	81,920
Georgia	19,057	293,723	1,907,177	19,835	4,311,053	3,055,827	70,400
Hawaii	3,405	215,040	201,656	2,473	637,249	810,541	43,068
Idaho	1,194	215,858	52,510	19,755	777,473	418,334	45,050
Illinois	34,886	439,618	219,047	25,964	6,380,914	3,351,567	90,600
Indiana	15,741	310,822	250,196	16,828	3,772,448	2,101,360	75,000
Iowa	11,452	265,544	39,901	42,505	2,648,898	1,832,582	66,860
Kansas	15,343	251,783	397,612	32,000	1,926,940	1,558,806	64,400
Kentucky	10,037	272,213		42,414	3,465,197	1,116,816	68,250
Louisiana	14,105	277,416		20,751	3,257,461	980,418	69,400
Maine	3,228	223,038	21,457		923,375	520,126	52,000
Maryland	18,084	273,700	3,565,483	17,162	2,251,179	1,774,223	67,700
Massachusetts	27,679	322,376	105,137	51,652	3,193,536	1,006,295	76,494
Michigan	31,438	385,949	2,009,206	23,474	5,942,366	3,279,478	85,340
Minnesota	13,707	281,144	35,280	9,885	2,180,078	2,342,882	70,880
Mississippi	8,445	251,772	11,515	19,547	2,528,023	643,560	64,500
Missouri	12,027	302,677	63,408	28,400	3,216,676	1,276,728	73,600
Montana	2,565	216,038	143,703	14,638	259,424	329,016	44,800
Nebraska	4,731	233,546	365,918	5,325	1,353,737	802,627	58,170
Nevada	1,857	206,781	357,436		376,999	199,100	25,000
New Hampshire	3,139	214,426		242	584,576	320,106	41,650
New Jersey	33,869	344,201	449,058	25,445	3,906,261	2,414,657	80,700
New Mexico	5,129	222,605	124,607	26,022	963,492	621,761	52,800
New York	78,130	598,897	430,692	89,196	5,870,584	3,828,957	99,900
North Carolina	23,125	308,295	173,997	49,980	5,423,408	3,396,226	75,200
North Dakota	1,769	215,032	1,191,196	11,540	795,270	424,904	41,200
Ohio	36,920	430,710	425,046	59,139	7,346,515	4,560,923	91,300
Oklahoma	6,367	255,341	602,785	45,000	2,419,439	1,611,758	65,400
Oregon	11,762	242,040	62,085	10,107	1,288,153	974,283	63,799
Pennsylvania	58,144	469,049	4,277	45,041	8,445,289	3,261,439	86,656
Rhode Island	4,422	220,429	37,066	8,201	715,444	422,861	49,983
South Carolina	9,683	256,632	36,739	24,942	2,732,597	1,389,947	66,300
South Dakota	2,432	216,175	255,950	8,688	794,562	467,586	45,023
Tennessee	14,370	284,786	66,559	22,094	3,937,415	796,400	71,656
Texas	30,553	427,698	702,474	63,362	4,656,357	2,459,608	91,800
Utah	4,068	221,169	1,054,282	14,252	894,633	707,858	52,100
Vermont	884	209,267		12,500	453,222	260,566	22,000
Virginia	20,030	294,290	1,282,777	23,772	3,699,627	2,145,264	73,945
Washington	13,397	267,818	334,210	30,737	2,294,866	2,571,049	44,000
West Virginia	11,761	244,220	30,000	21,850	1,601,107	1,340,611	61,200
Wisconsin	13,309	293,929	103,440	25,398	2,750,953	2,037,582	72,095
Wyoming	1,592	207,845	257,083	15,033	178,589	231,864	24,300
Puerto Rico	4,068	255,846		2,385	2,893,876	1,226,194	
Virgin Islands			201,140	2,013	46,754	105,613	
Other Territories, etc.[7]	44		7,015		80,000	11,670	
Adjustments or undistributed to States							
Total	800,000	14,500,000	29,228,816	1,278,004	131,524,980	80,703,642	3,144,817

Footnotes at end of table.

TABLE 84.—*Federal grants in aid to State and local governments and to individuals and private institutions within the States, fiscal year 1965*—Continued

PART A.   FEDERAL AID PAYMENTS TO STATES AND LOCAL UNITS—Continued

States, Territories. etc.	Department of Health, Education, and Welfare—Continued						
	Office of Education—Con.		Public Health Service				
	Library services	Maintenance and operation of schools	Air pollution	Chronic diseases and health of the aged [26]	Communicable disease activities [27]	Community health practice and research [28]	Construction: Hospital and health research facilities [29]
	(36)	(37)	(38)	(39)	(40)	(41)	(42)
Alabama	$507,452	$4,221,434	$110,901	$610,816	$178,592	$256,491	$5,784,846
Alaska	92,663	7,949,703		10,300	78,633	28,800	306,647
Arizona	244,026	5,865,597	126,291	215,883		81,830	1,607,812
Arkansas	361,066	1,603,938	9,670	304,105	77,263	159,989	3,273,778
California	2,070,828	52,299,893	184,409	2,146,391	1,589,427	685,672	12,046,879
Colorado	304,092	9,116,929	63,882	631,522	100,644	111,425	1,324,996
Connecticut	471,081	2,601,422	36,903	450,046	108,961	93,278	909,621
Delaware	149,960	1,090,954		165,828		19,119	395,431
District of Columbia	407,660	3,053,790	5,250	531,499	127,026	28,691	2,361,431
Florida	697,490	9,004,685	57,563	873,819	215,432	312,392	7,105,441
Georgia	667,141	7,689,317	40,327	681,028	54,664	282,210	9,713,755
Hawaii	168,658	6,170,356	11,937	260,509	39,976	1,232,373	424,759
Idaho	184,090	2,170,176		186,545	26,617	61,342	1,073,271
Illinois	617,650	5,548,652	400,125	1,292,938	445,961	408,671	4,770,180
Indiana	521,457	1,669,555	89,446	486,603		216,703	4,521,756
Iowa	403,731	1,278,208	6,450	347,622	64,694	152,976	3,964,577
Kansas	413,934	6,979,050	12,186	342,900	129,149	129,740	1,680,002
Kentucky	716,837	1,427,820	47,064	837,541	99,253	216,004	3,005,006
Louisiana	616,429	1,350,764	20,905	294,199	139,185	221,052	5,072,557
Maine	223,590	2,642,115		195,241		72,967	1,146,805
Maryland	603,628	13,308,989		443,109	11,025	145,698	3,595,132
Massachusetts	549,799	8,995,130	126,064	1,164,272	291,978	212,046	4,490,055
Michigan	986,634	2,904,242	103,503	1,207,838	123,697	357,463	7,187,446
Minnesota	560,415	648,165	30,902	806,295	28,411	187,202	4,229,950
Mississippi	484,704	1,587,481		547,082	181,170	211,479	4,052,298
Missouri	352,936	3,817,819	78,842	959,707	233,425	211,979	4,899,079
Montana	242,520	2,604,354	2,514	152,308	92,563	56,179	969,343
Nebraska	267,506	3,538,369	5,308	125,790	47,183	87,980	1,568,672
Nevada	132,440	2,161,540	25,117	125,167	34,366	30,829	357,241
New Hampshire	187,081	1,691,575	3,170	132,893	38,509	34,975	419,075
New Jersey	925,342	7,667,027	194,157	690,059	168,350	251,904	3,331,563
New Mexico	230,494	6,416,076	15,212	173,000	80,862	79,946	1,523,882
New York	1,555,013	7,929,340	218,063	2,698,935	544,047	670,700	10,686,788
North Carolina	657,653	3,794,313	62,267	805,853	104,400	299,245	7,007,326
North Dakota	171,750	1,758,322	5,000	161,340	17,389	56,250	1,468,572
Ohio	1,246,225	7,001,868	103,468	1,405,329		441,907	8,120,851
Oklahoma	132,369	8,808,053	16,828	520,409	164,827	155,729	2,937,958
Oregon	287,096	1,476,707	46,127	302,300	78,742	99,653	2,285,411
Pennsylvania	1,650,524	6,626,442	216,302	2,069,520	374,833	544,547	10,728,729
Rhode Island	293,807	2,485,162	5,214	294,065		43,026	933,176
South Carolina	358,519	4,266,019	5,015	452,807	304,306	197,159	3,571,758
South Dakota	213,310	2,941,219		61,391	51,538	63,475	1,404,282
Tennessee	578,145	2,992,540	26,607	531,106	207,718	245,724	6,841,324
Texas	824,486	17,449,556	13,481	1,403,891	293,495	582,625	10,434,772
Utah	196,636	3,277,092		196,265	91,076	72,500	1,528,202
Vermont	169,164	54,664		151,574	36,458	32,783	1,219,783
Virginia	585,445	19,826,009	26,368	683,343	47,825	253,962	5,327,182
Washington	414,230	11,616,850		736,775	74,862	152,336	3,029,540
West Virginia	305,287	170,274	84,914	468,092	251,020	116,201	618,101
Wisconsin	530,130	864,746		626,854	73,713	208,492	4,326,437
Wyoming	174,852	1,144,560		76,548		32,110	171,682
Puerto Rico	354,933		28,587	843,890	197,550	219,865	5,411,732
Virgin Islands	25,000	58,488		107,777	24,285	7,174	90,833
Other Territories, etc.[7]	22,807	1,129,199		96,177		7,133	3,668
Adjustments or undistributed to States		16,643,301					
Total	26,110,985	311,389,849	2,666,339	32,087,096	7,745,100	11,142,001	195,266,393

Footnotes at end of table.

TABLE 84.—*Federal grants in aid to State and local governments and to individuals and private institutions within the States, fiscal year 1965*—Continued

PART A. FEDERAL AID PAYMENTS TO STATES AND LOCAL UNITS—Continued

States Territories, etc.	Construction—Con. Waste treatment works	Control of tuberculosis [30]	Control of venereal disease [31]	Dental services and resources	National Institute of Mental Health	Radiological health	Water supply and pollution control
	(43)	(44)	(45)	(46)	(47)	(48)	(49)
Alabama	$2,841,118	$212,790	$84,955	$10,000	$203,959	$47,190	$102,105
Alaska	210,600	49,973	7,892		125,816	3,450	12,671
Arizona	682,020	168,753	84,898	10,000	108,055	19,373	41,025
Arkansas	1,545,829	122,893	82,555	10,000	119,685	27,561	62,933
California	3,988,687	516,874	677,700	10,000	973,594	215,061	419,791
Colorado	1,502,140	36,238	68,962	10,000	110,869	38,054	47,215
Connecticut	400,048	27,898	24,130	10,000	111,790	24,349	49,000
Delaware	615,127	34,731	20,207	10,000	112,722	11,366	46,502
District of Columbia	643,800	221,031	78,927	5,000	106,434	16,629	59,921
Florida	1,806,027	253,281	323,238	10,000	280,882	65,507	150,900
Georgia	1,690,320	212,043	329,903	10,000	245,524	59,533	112,534
Hawaii	370,990	44,781	5,457	10,000	114,822	16,599	39,578
Idaho	208,764	13,150	6,463	10,000	116,414	13,624	27,694
Illinois	2,666,129	207,328	414,269	10,000	538,483	106,811	185,534
Indiana	1,552,007	52,259	2,600	10,000	221,605	40,920	115,428
Iowa	1,623,747	26,442	20,436		136,561	39,143	56,520
Kansas	909,862	22,988	26,704	2,220	118,488	27,431	54,200
Kentucky	1,809,323	141,559	98,745	10,000	168,100	45,416	90,007
Louisiana	1,816,333	58,522	139,921		180,899	39,770	104,046
Maine	973,497	17,696	9,096	10,000	108,945	15,732	37,718
Maryland	962,145	140,254	70,800		150,200	40,021	88,974
Massachusetts	1,299,561	174,710	64,198	10,000	235,975	73,366	139,569
Michigan	1,485,495	227,235	187,550	9,965	367,299	101,736	249,390
Minnesota	1,123,127	74,999	36,775	6,600	144,106	37,500	106,207
Mississippi	1,420,106	143,211	56,822	6,000	128,347	30,040	77,018
Missouri	2,072,591	141,615	169,290	10,000	229,325	25,079	98,306
Montana	476,324	23,766	18,872	10,000	110,389	11,000	25,731
Nebraska	794,324	12,553	25,851	2,652	112,425	15,192	19,497
Nevada	10,480	11,254	19,800	7,082	88,755	4,900	16,250
New Hampshire	1,019,334	11,063	2,613	10,000	106,503	5,615	35,445
New Jersey	2,269,513	255,570	317,668	10,000	289,685	69,281	167,601
New Mexico	687,292	41,682	77,746	10,000	116,414	20,074	32,965
New York	3,769,284	781,637	873,482	7,500	773,582	223,500	367,158
North Carolina	1,631,535	149,973	194,966	7,000	279,928	61,804	125,520
North Dakota	151,081	12,946	15,044	10,000	113,689	15,000	29,286
Ohio	3,513,086	209,447	142,703	10,000	470,841	65,182	216,705
Oklahoma	1,506,554	68,928	74,867	10,000	129,589	26,182	74,970
Oregon	1,415,600	47,331	121,553	10,000	110,131	24,300	57,614
Pennsylvania	2,548,656	457,452	353,844	10,000	546,836	161,305	262,101
Rhode Island	1,042,968	90,979	900	10,000	95,237	16,291	58,814
South Carolina	1,426,170	91,259	147,697	10,000	143,747	23,363	84,013
South Dakota	260,410	4,959	15,890		117,516	9,549	27,384
Tennessee	1,279,283	243,683	104,389		195,933	28,494	130,398
Texas	3,111,865	279,138	262,797	10,000	508,786	121,471	211,015
Utah	699,115	47,562	1,671	10,000	101,823	21,272	31,500
Vermont	572,312	12,262	4,521	6,000	107,696	1,643	26,661
Virginia	1,604,568	140,200	105,657	10,000	196,578	13,489	105,541
Washington	1,325,626	57,895	55,000	10,000	143,135	47,338	68,513
West Virginia	1,017,869	124,563	50,094	10,000	111,215	6,159	65,840
Wisconsin	1,179,670	132,487	10,150	6,900	196,669	53,547	104,752
Wyoming	39,582	5,795	5,207		116,990	10,310	18,497
Puerto Rico	183,120	216,546	25,000	5,000	154,261	15,832	64,463
Virgin Islands		3,450	8,898	5,000	113,772		
Other Territories, etc.[7]		11,863		5,000	52,757		
Adjustments or undistributed to States							[12] 260,048
Total	69,755,014	6,889,497	6,129,373	411,919	11,063,781	2,253,354	5,263,968

Footnotes at end of table

TABLE 84.—*Federal grants in aid to State and local governments and to individuals and private institutions within the States, fiscal year 1965*—Continued

PART A. FEDERAL AID PAYMENTS TO STATES AND LOCAL UNITS—Continued

States, Territories, etc.	Office of the Secretary — Educational television	Vocational Rehabilitation Administration	Welfare Administration — Bureau of Family Services				
			Aid to dependent children	Aid to the aged, bhud, and disabled	Aid to the blind	Aid to the permanently and totally disabled	Medical assistance for the aged
	(50)	(51)	(52)	(53)	(54)	(55)	(56)
Alabama	$270,592	$4,195,369	$9,580,100		$1,081,963	$6,342,376	$607,304
Alaska		264,842	1,111,557	$931,719			
Arizona	70,147	1,197,451	9,934,019		567,762	1,956,232	
Arkansas		3,731,330	5,276,603		1,222,829	5,377,277	1,656,690
California	413,725	5,772,849	163,986,790		8,107,266	41,435,862	59,289,464
Colorado	17,809	1,440,246	9,889,490		129,312	3,815,475	4,358,078
Connecticut		626,402	16,351,975		179,140	4,257,786	7,599,157
Delaware		257,850	3,271,601		178,075	262,978	86,507
District of Columbia	170,981	690,171	6,748,324		132,451	2,195,131	1,329,187
Florida	35,803	3,527,815	17,544,581	55,093,578			1,875,697
Georgia		6,406,022	14,629,616		1,649,914	14,108,447	
Hawaii		451,856	3,397,601	1,463,116			928,662
Idaho	48,150	294,655	2,847,426		87,446	1,687,031	2,744,426
Illinois		3,134,269	76,800,168	62,113,433			3,433,742
Indiana		947,843	12,475,248		1,051,823	886,412	163,227
Iowa	35,040	1,276,979	11,043,231		673,379	735,827	4,351,597
Kansas	114,724	624,953	9,521,843	10,543,727	124,812	1,228,206	3,836,406
Kentucky		2,012,663	20,714,937	40,055,508			2,922,384
Louisiana	93,117	2,088,168	26,751,923		1,813,472	11,373,630	1,026,177
Maine		418,234	4,873,862	9,411,415			779,154
Maryland		1,311,152	19,671,562	10,350,948			2,474,959
Massachusetts		1,902,153	26,015,318		1,316,608	7,652,032	27,311,478
Michigan		2,472,043	39,237,819		888,019	5,340,113	10,964,726
Minnesota	77,127	1,829,144	13,879,543		619,483	1,944,468	15,952,462
Mississippi		1,710,548	8,141,863		1,090,351	7,565,171	
Missouri	85,435	1,693,188	25,564,825		2,262,791	9,057,352	
Montana		423,039	2,192,337		168,567	933,695	
Nebraska	90,000	598,714	4,215,246		368,453	1,584,773	608,964
Nevada		261,983	1,480,632		109,495		
New Hampshire		154,046	1,312,266		163,657	379,266	573,766
New Jersey		2,065,136	27,013,945		549,715	5,350,051	7,435,372
New Mexico		412,184	9,546,409	10,961,622			
New York	81,813	7,124,388	166,023,195	46,125,150	1,124,315	11,722,449	73,661,270
North Carolina		4,089,704	27,734,853		2,971,490	14,430,382	1,206,974
North Dakota	65,086	417,905	2,591,160	3,472,543	24,858	469,767	2,510,942
Ohio	199,673	2,715,171	46,123,695		2,247,300	12,263,444	
Oklahoma		2,287,864	20,008,524	68,740,389			1,106,266
Oregon		1,019,933	8,225,443		260,591	4,594,319	3,331,374
Pennsylvania	200,000	7,964,880	81,259,393		2,677,937	11,942,798	14,525,699
Rhode Island		721,674	7,092,689	6,429,894			2,614,521
South Carolina	123,351	2,578,003	5,203,830		1,086,399	4,682,176	2,300,546
South Dakota	5,310	577,586	3,273,149		78,195	737,572	259,513
Tennessee		2,376,275	15,996,699		1,003,715	6,236,028	2,804,367
Texas	147,498	3,637,335	18,696,901		2,934,325	5,351,712	
Utah	142,932	577,434	7,221,560		107,847	3,234,419	1,843,918
Vermont		387,908	1,694,545	5,208,932			285,121
Virginia		2,035,866	10,845,994		706,859	4,282,709	1,470,306
Washington	298,471	1,300,603	21,007,662		401,693	9,612,749	8,811,689
West Virginia		3,060,552	30,078,332		423,044	3,012,260	2,797,504
Wisconsin	83,737	2,132,994	11,376,323		469,513	3,695,308	3,511,501
Wyoming		354,180	950,587		34,000	365,228	72,843
Puerto Rico		1,796,966	4,360,699	2,354,406			422,546
Virgin Islands		55,778	104,503		3,529	16,756	7,697
Other Territories, etc.[1]		59,683	30,597		504	5,254	7,005
Adjustments or undistributed to States			−6,155,000	−1,873,585	−231,000	−1,305,000	−1,607,000
Total	2,870,521	101,465,991	1,088,767,993	331,382,795	40,861,897	230,819,921	284,254,188

Footnotes at end of table.

TABLE 84.—*Federal grants in aid to State and local governments and to individuals and private institutions within the States, fiscal year 1965*—Continued

PART A. FEDERAL AID PAYMENTS TO STATES AND LOCAL UNITS—Continued

States, Territories, etc.	Department of Health, Education, and Welfare—Continued				Housing and Home Finance Agency		
	Welfare Administration—Continued				Office of the Administrator		
	Bureau of Family Services—Continued	Children's Bureau			Low-income housing demonstration programs	Open space land grants	Urban planning grants
	Old-age assistance	Child welfare services	Maternal and child health services	Services for crippled children			
	(57)	(58)	(59)	(60)	(61)	(62)	(63)
Alabama	$65,108,259	$862,062	$890,076	$808,571	--------	--------	$42,914
Alaska	--------	112,319	173,418	133,136	$43,348	--------	108,915
Arizona	7,939,904	355,648	332,339	--------	27,646	--------	33,297
Arkansas	35,777,003	513,766	498,803	476,697	--------	$8,575	219,546
California	184,844,105	2,183,262	1,668,003	1,417,565	154,853	440,027	1,630,224
Colorado	24,529,128	372,467	546,652	352,781	--------	--------	198,394
Connecticut	3,922,312	351,595	492,205	353,990	34,148	222,679	666,966
Delaware	876,512	124,558	153,325	150,654	--------	--------	101,008
District of Columbia	1,886,544	132,869	361,889	291,950	149,401	--------	--------
Florida	--------	972,676	1,205,815	769,349	22,778	--------	432,799
Georgia	46,866,665	984,055	964,315	980,947	--------	48,682	264,216
Hawaii	--------	187,934	260,200	207,287	--------	--------	171,513
Idaho	2,828,698	195,841	239,407	207,034	--------	--------	--------
Illinois	--------	1,309,867	909,453	1,039,210	201,423	1,348,286	784,035
Indiana	14,133,510	828,898	537,776	748,418	39,249	73,259	220,532
Iowa	18,222,725	529,168	406,468	886,678	--------	54,179	235,348
Kansas	6,496,340	439,110	262,425	363,613	--------	--------	160,636
Kentucky	--------	788,039	889,446	1,018,806	--------	--------	297,844
Louisiana	101,442,400	810,933	730,404	731,563	--------	--------	134,074
Maine	--------	235,615	232,977	208,390	--------	--------	143,279
Maryland	--------	547,257	542,129	576,487	--------	589,858	332,471
Massachusetts	33,060,850	790,803	615,538	560,703	156,868	102,000	935,496
Michigan	30,008,329	1,278,432	1,186,566	1,287,553	18,903	34,733	1,109,786
Minnesota	21,329,864	730,728	688,908	835,606	--------	--------	478,426
Mississippi	26,881,945	651,751	721,936	645,462	--------	--------	39,388
Missouri	60,208,261	701,292	666,521	634,551	--------	--------	111,313
Montana	3,294,918	182,189	167,271	200,644	--------	3,210	22,521
Nebraska	7,967,532	307,729	214,970	262,744	--------	28,425	43,646
Nevada	1,820,018	113,768	169,062	192,153	--------	--------	45,101
New Hampshire	3,053,739	157,750	139,507	155,811	--------	--------	192,405
New Jersey	8,295,387	813,671	535,732	498,094	11,250	1,072,570	786,556
New Mexico	--------	284,742	460,108	311,532	--------	--------	101,064
New York	20,444,282	1,893,320	1,604,163	1,361,828	152,868	483,723	612,999
North Carolina	25,100,231	1,145,522	1,264,519	1,220,106	--------	135,180	379,226
North Dakota	1,789,774	208,257	167,586	181,797	--------	--------	40,000
Ohio	48,136,037	1,587,177	1,327,765	1,315,709	86,519	350,225	742,270
Oklahoma	--------	541,217	463,128	426,059	22,449	24,065	267,361
Oregon	5,644,225	308,887	429,022	378,013	--------	38,949	450,496
Pennsylvania	29,252,798	1,630,976	1,322,183	1,750,638	84,514	1,000	1,117,940
Rhode Island	--------	199,184	307,558	186,187	--------	--------	136,584
South Carolina	13,504,185	632,171	654,243	725,013	--------	--------	163,100
South Dakota	5,448,025	212,519	74,358	155,205	--------	--------	81,783
Tennessee	22,953,972	864,767	940,045	888,630	49,010	99,807	158,969
Texas	147,353,762	1,759,432	1,340,301	1,691,611	--------	11,972	256,186
Utah	2,832,003	284,736	200,533	260,788	--------	--------	105,510
Vermont	--------	138,449	137,635	172,121	--------	--------	48,166
Virginia	7,814,513	823,435	1,050,113	903,446	--------	205,375	137,282
Washington	21,305,368	531,954	570,156	478,059	--------	508,040	471,414
West Virginia	7,230,149	385,845	512,962	467,041	--------	--------	101,194
Wisconsin	18,259,357	777,950	580,838	663,439	27,212	53,887	887,932
Wyoming	1,563,433	124,757	126,708	105,929	--------	--------	1,896
Puerto Rico	--------	797,190	864,513	879,221	--------	--------	314,788
Virgin Islands	85,691	88,467	72,789	96,878	--------	--------	43,729
Other Territories, etc.[1]	23,523	70,328	84,207	42,679	--------	--------	--------
Adjustments or undistributed to States	-6,125,000	--------	--------	--------	--------	--------	--------
Total	1,083,411,276	33,857,334	31,948,969	31,658,376	1,282,439	5,938,706	16,562,538

Footnotes at end of table.

TABLE 84.—*Federal grants in aid to State and local governments and to individuals and private institutions within the States, fiscal year 1965*—Continued

PART A.   FEDERAL AID PAYMENTS TO STATES AND LOCAL UNITS—Continued

States, Territories, etc.	Housing and Home Finance Agency—Continued		Department of Interior				
	Office of the Administrator—Con. / Urban renewal and urban mass transportation funds [33]	Public Housing Administration / Low-rent public housing program	Bureau of Indian Affairs [34]	Certain special funds – shared revenues [35]	Fish and wildlife restoration and management [36]	Mineral Leasing Act payments-shared revenues	Migratory Bird Conservation Act and Alaska game law-shared revenues
	(64)	(65)	(66)	(67)	(68)	(69)	(70)
Alabama	$2,281,645	$8,632,318	----------	$138	$458,045	$372	$1,266
Alaska	185,008	182,053	$600,016	974,281	923,068	8,342,615	364
Arizona	----------	621,646	3,293,026	360,460	517,504	135,476	----------
Arkansas	5,854,611	1,654,433	----------	45	211,083	77,771	78,186
California	22,455,085	7,848,105	----------	334,570	959,020	3,094,150	13,094
Colorado	892,033	1,312,407	155,079	34,571	378,002	3,383,740	3,296
Connecticut	21,785,192	3,047,596	----------	----------	168,893	----------	----------
Delaware	613,000	606,210	----------	----------	100,763	----------	502
District of Columbia	1,307,975	3,577,016	----------	----------	----------	----------	----------
Florida	778,271	4,237,496	24,200	53	371,871	123	4,597
Georgia	4,578,480	9,569,336	----------	----------	374,290	----------	38,798
Hawaii	2,799,903	704,977	----------	----------	130,622	----------	----------
Idaho	----------	35,173	153,000	55,806	321,608	421,146	3,137
Illinois	17,402,792	19,476,342	----------	----------	636,003	----------	11,642
Indiana	3,871,842	1,354,095	----------	----------	431,967	----------	----------
Iowa	1,338,566	----------	62,000	----------	328,513	----------	759
Kansas	4,038,905	294,466	11,300	36	256,591	124,248	1,757
Kentucky	3,716,657	3,349,746	----------	----------	309,846	----------	2,768
Louisiana	248,175	5,336,937	----------	759	338,454	66,993	12,779
Maine	935,516	100,957	----------	----------	213,895	----------	1,866
Maryland	6,746,677	4,222,319	----------	----------	149,457	----------	432
Massachusetts	26,779,168	7,068,140	----------	----------	178,185	----------	243
Michigan	12,932,827	3,606,521	----------	56	711,754	3,052	9,871
Minnesota	8,097,256	2,386,881	460,611	137	699,174	----------	2,871
Mississippi	259,166	2,135,276	----------	174	337,043	5,685	12,881
Missouri	5,052,740	5,419,935	----------	14	568,699	----------	4,579
Montana	----------	236,020	163,470	163,846	643,750	2,025,187	11,776
Nebraska	45,170	623,270	170,000	161	529,120	2,847	37,055
Nevada	172,092	362,936	106,885	391,127	312,797	434,117	5,289
New Hampshire	597,920	670,802	----------	----------	106,270	----------	----------
New Jersey	17,512,247	13,946,304	----------	----------	124,903	----------	1,252
New Mexico	----------	259,595	2,043,919	74,665	315,148	10,102,974	698
New York	34,844,687	34,405,102	----------	----------	510,499	----------	815
North Carolina	5,036,184	3,679,221	14,580	----------	381,648	----------	553
North Dakota	99,807	54,313	401,389	2,214	301,540	177,759	15,886
Ohio	14,790,841	5,890,345	----------	----------	415,382	----------	87
Oklahoma	660,817	----------	586,565	5,120	343,614	93,651	12,115
Oregon	629,731	384,521	23,960	21,453,244	596,857	2,213	47,950
Pennsylvania	30,155,306	13,823,698	----------	----------	648,316	----------	530
Rhode Island	1,043,817	1,654,643	----------	----------	170,778	----------	----------
South Carolina	338,300	1,361,847	----------	----------	289,908	----------	2,441
South Dakota	----------	89,939	765,000	13,976	518,403	148,339	5,554
Tennessee	10,891,458	6,842,014	----------	----------	416,290	----------	736
Texas	7,747,507	9,286,785	----------	888	1,067,217	----------	14,497
Utah	----------	----------	110,603	41,547	437,518	3,729,091	408
Vermont	----------	----------	----------	----------	169,669	----------	235
Virginia	5,276,151	4,536,148	----------	----------	261,559	----------	698
Washington	855,338	1,284,982	126,000	17,774	358,842	4,040	6,815
West Virginia	1,351,047	563,104	----------	----------	194,449	----------	----------
Wisconsin	1,494,074	770,398	223,000	49	747,715	----------	6,040
Wyoming	----------	----------	48,530	144,136	244,564	14,976,446	162
Puerto Rico	2,367,822	8,183,186	----------	----------	15,733	----------	----------
Virgin Islands	442,346	573,553	----------	8,313,413	12,489	----------	----------
Other Territories, etc [7]	----------	----------	----------	----------	22,014	----------	----------
Adjustment or undistributed to States	[37] 349,619	----------	----------	----------	----------	----------	----------
Total	291,653,771	206,263,107	9,543,133	32,383,268	20,231,342	47,352,035	377,280

Footnotes at end of table.

TABLE 84.—*Federal grants in aid to State and local governments and to individuals and private institutions within the States, fiscal year 1965*—Continued

PART A. FEDERAL AID PAYMENTS TO STATES AND LOCAL UNITS—Continued

States, Territories, etc.	Department of Labor		Small Business Administration	Tennessee Valley Authority	Veterans' Administration [39]	Miscellaneous grants [22]	Total grant payments, (Part A)
	Manpower development and training activities	Unemployment compensation and employment service administration (trust fund)	Grants for research and management counseling [22]	Shared revenues [38]			
	(71)	(72)	(73)	(74)	(75)	(76)	(77)
Alabama	$284,089	$5,009,115		$1,997,420	$1,948		$254,305,792
Alaska	212,564	3,408,164				[40] $522,118	98,632,515
Arizona	289,833	3,291,133	$5,896		4,153		125,004,303
Arkansas	149,606	3,698,013	4,295		8,868		153,692,711
California	2,504,313	55,013,544	3,851		1,567,397	[41] 11,908,778	1,079,665,996
Colorado	651,175	4,108,015	4,000		74,532		150,153,395
Connecticut	356,966	6,415,130	4,000		637,671		136,688,720
Delaware	64,354	919,973	7,950				31,595,141
District of Columbia	16,990	3,319,868	−952			[42] 39,377,303	101,776,981
Florida	454,516	6,806,159	3,422		16,539		248,655,710
Georgia	335,685	5,160,751	2,930	85,054	283,228		268,428,946
Hawaii	68,945	1,491,471				[43] 4,385,375	46,926,812
Idaho	84,853	2,378,813	4,000		48,731	[44] 6,180	66,021,027
Illinois	1,230,293	17,728,369	7,789		494,760		492,562,275
Indiana	513,850	6,544,226	5,836		198,418		182,271,759
Iowa	148,166	3,616,126	3,998		279,311		131,283,891
Kansas	200,599	3,300,615			58,767		124,393,020
Kentucky	612,919	3,905,646		1,326,034	9,235		215,376,783
Louisiana	212,752	5,491,725	9,072		13,205		323,838,163
Maine	123,150	1,835,326	4,000			[44] 2,500	58,430,854
Maryland	252,692	6,416,401					146,930,833
Massachusetts	652,939	14,196,158			749,413		282,886,913
Michigan	946,956	16,847,023	11,437		637,569		354,829,262
Minnesota	793,699	4,973,144	2,350		279,956	[44] 14,755	225,285,317
Mississippi	157,938	3,624,161		365,553	6,093		167,634,078
Missouri	567,740	6,467,794	2,965		79,251		284,396,130
Montana	155,250	1,967,461	983		46,141		86,662,353
Nebraska	209,722	1,883,231	1,498		193,597		76,681,014
Nevada	135,365	1,756,245	3,475				55,818,684
New Hampshire	77,369	1,577,153			31,112		34,800,114
New Jersey	578,518	13,117,833	5,750		212,314		225,266,226
New Mexico	135,710	2,228,127	4,000		5,267	[44] 4,987	109,601,663
New York	2,205,520	52,416,273	16,923		15,147	[44] 13,903	786,282,737
North Carolina	217,525	6,436,818	6,255	127,582	21,172		218,732,304
North Dakota	126,642	1,465,659	7,587		72,708		59,003,522
Ohio	1,164,989	15,095,207			403,111		437,960,778
Oklahoma	406,677	5,203,663	7,125		485,068		222,686,250
Oregon	324,531	4,909,082			2,811		174,693,521
Pennsylvania	1,053,819	28,703,470			185,195	[45] 441,904	504,381,631
Rhode Island	252,682	3,568,912	10,409		170,995		65,397,852
South Carolina	335,131	3,527,683			5,448		107,606,647
South Dakota	62,774	1,253,273	5,000		133,287	[46] −596	72,564,688
Tennessee	367,499	5,044,653		5,115,930	12,508		248,585,762
Texas	715,591	15,906,156	3,945		7,495		540,933,471
Utah	241,387	3,474,629	6,000				103,994,603
Vermont	84,494	1,201,044			44,885		41,454,509
Virginia	302,376	4,374,350	4,365	30,764	7,365	[44] 13,500	270,205,388
Washington	402,213	7,209,998			345,927		203,005,917
West Virginia	343,232	2,687,371			7,147		160,658,125
Wisconsin	375,807	6,307,384	4,000		245,028		146,394,387
Wyoming	94,445	1,139,685	5,292		13,559		74,783,122
Puerto Rico	245,586	3,155,356	−2			[47] 58,691,220	148,486,761
Virgin Islands	27,421	126,412	2,530			[48] 1,475,000	13,065,878
Other Territories, etc.[7]	19,221	20,157				[49] 13,352,305	16,175,999
Adjustments or undistributed to States		[50] 1,527,176				[50a] 74,000	−53,830,257
Total	22,549,078	393,251,324	181,974	9,048,337	8,116,332	130,283,232	10,903,910,946

Footnotes at end of table.

TABLE 84.—*Federal grants in aid to State and local governments and to individuals and private institutions within the States, fiscal year 1965*—Continued

PART B. FEDERAL AID PAYMENTS TO INDIVIDUALS AND PRIVATE INSTITUTIONS IN THE STATES

States, Territories, etc.	Department of Agriculture						
	Agricultural conservation program	Commodity Credit Corporation				Conservation reserve program	Cropland conversion program [22][55]
		Cotton domestic allotment program [51]	Feed grain program [52]	Wheat program [53]	Wool act program [54]		
	(78)	(79)	(80)	(81)	(82)	(83)	(84)
Alabama	$5,734,294	$5,695,385	$15,099,219	$178,362	$5,621	$3,827,613	$73,849
Alaska	56,723				128		
Arizona	1,534,288	1,065,718	2,998,908	262,288	248,358	24,825	
Arkansas	5,001,791	3,938,662	2,661,992	190,879	7,938	3,767,742	88,299
California	5,640,517	1,076,578	11,467,313	2,467,276	1,294,433	1,066,413	145,619
Colorado	3,418,043		13,063,639	22,368,874	1,096,634	7,455,198	159,364
Connecticut	455,113		172,097	215	2,665	27,454	−45
Delaware	337,555		1,389,032	150,315	1,155	141,955	
District of Columbia							
Florida	3,213,915	192,464	4,828,078	27,292	969	1,905,768	111,544
Georgia	8,040,028	3,874,036	20,741,549	609,864	3,166	10,374,068	130,381
Hawaii	148,253				1,550		
Idaho	1,828,569		2,485,539	13,264,100	884,893	1,975,385	210,612
Illinois	8,356,262	8,392	99,062,105	7,774,510	319,561	2,339,284	94,829
Indiana	6,138,628		68,189,320	5,104,433	229,745	3,390,671	127,726
Iowa	9,258,761		191,285,248	664,408	775,989	3,566,598	363,169
Kansas	6,228,056	31	66,563,627	106,813,209	322,251	10,860,802	723,204
Kentucky	7,594,534	31,878	25,812,707	813,170	139,263	3,137,676	63,786
Louisiana	4,288,769	2,247,625	3,055,805	159,411	13,024	2,035,836	431,413
Maine	1,235,927		42,638	1,247	15,509	966,736	262,769
Maryland	1,325,600		3,452,829	490,378	13,562	440,148	
Massachusetts	571,765		55,458	691	5,547	18,514	2,318
Michigan	4,895,255		27,339,978	5,719,881	223,395	4,553,394	68,297
Minnesota	5,801,132		87,913,693	7,049,000	508,058	10,196,894	326,311
Mississippi	6,851,669	5,017,618	10,505,518	158,790	10,139	1,826,386	57,188
Missouri	8,921,110	1,395,217	77,433,936	8,047,583	310,583	6,218,237	292,792
Montana	3,951,452		5,472,365	28,940,849	1,177,568	3,947,713	174,710
Nebraska	6,904,398		117,937,167	30,323,305	274,858	5,438,220	411,440
Nevada	478,361	48,548	41,649	132,840	175,328	−4,337	
New Hampshire	517,238		4,062		2,985	130,586	−137
New Jersey	707,590		3,268,695	284,359	5,067	302,941	
New Mexico	2,189,404	607,671	7,429,339	2,810,496	661,495	5,705,167	182,564
New York	5,108,731		8,548,717	2,237,373	82,808	3,695,598	124,213
North Carolina	6,985,743	2,731,735	23,792,074	1,238,141	16,316	2,814,518	667,771
North Dakota	3,684,641		25,186,980	57,078,999	426,645	18,423,383	1,434,579
Ohio	5,979,171		42,731,897	6,900,131	631,748	3,815,979	41,607
Oklahoma	6,813,386	2,115,401	11,976,136	41,464,012	73,046	9,324,253	246,173
Oregon	2,425,897		2,590,933	10,550,839	515,870	1,555,195	69,877
Pennsylvania	4,906,668		11,206,461	1,547,975	119,010	2,754,908	31,652
Rhode Island	78,209		4,097		681	663	
South Carolina	3,760,276	3,244,677	8,863,838	604,422	1,536	7,116,249	172,975
South Dakota	4,653,267		30,534,065	18,630,950	1,201,025	11,586,966	881,387
Tennessee	5,705,548	4,421,470	18,518,797	551,044	55,655	4,500,122	253,631
Texas	20,913,827	13,355,162	89,607,274	29,986,123	2,925,527	21,613,739	899,965
Utah	1,434,252		1,417,179	1,681,225	862,441	1,391,792	122,922
Vermont	1,214,376		116,602	69	4,047	363,975	1,510
Virginia	4,705,863	146,482	8,019,675	960,003	164,684	868,354	2,115
Washington	2,594,185		2,633,203	21,910,003	172,507	2,374,534	76,527
West Virginia	1,648,192		1,168,112	66,002	143,828	467,624	
Wisconsin	5,713,010		38,643,931	167,620	130,673	4,774,092	53,139
Wyoming	2,155,579		919,867	1,996,129	1,641,139	633,179	84,654
Puerto Rico	999,506						
Virgin Islands	13,026						
Other Territories, etc.[7]							
Adjustments or undistributed to States, etc.	4,344	158			56	−345	
Total	213,122,697	51,214,908	1,196,253,343	442,379,055	17,900,679	193,712,165	9,666,699

Footnotes at end of table.

TABLE 84.—*Federal grants in aid to State and local governments and to individuals and private institutions within the States, fiscal year 1965*—Continued

PART B. FEDERAL AID PAYMENTS TO INDIVIDUALS AND PRIVATE INSTITUTIONS IN THE STATES—Continued

States, Territories, etc.	Department of Agriculture—Continued					Atomic Energy Commission	Department of Commerce
	Emergency conservation measures [22]	Great Plains Conservation program	Indemnity payments to dairy farmers	Rural housing grants	Sugar Act program	Grants, fellowships, and other aid [86]	State marine schools (subsistence to cadets) [87]
	(85)	(86)	(87)	(88)	(89)	(90)	(91)
Alabama	$376,892			$76,740		$67,530	
Alaska	5,389					7	
Arizona	131,610			1,000		66,125	
Arkansas	445,878			66,460		29,829	
California	320,408			5,190	$14,873,769	694,929	$129,443
Colorado	669,300	$1,087,731		4,990	6,880,518	119,031	
Connecticut						65,389	
Delaware						1,351	
District of Columbia						132,162	
Florida	161,716			57,430	5,653,990	166,952	
Georgia	107,004			163,920		85,074	
Hawaii					10,559,545	5,305	
Idaho	81,697			2,000	7,052,571	52,709	
Illinois			$227	67,550	51,308	1,209,766	
Indiana	644,052			21,840		229,088	
Iowa				20,270	97,761	221,587	
Kansas		902,509		42,670	845,440	141,321	
Kentucky	927,567			547,870		71,369	
Louisiana	19,699		7,469	20,770	8,908,544	86,754	
Maine				54,900	1,048	19,216	244,631
Maryland			121,806	780		88,664	
Massachusetts						437,178	100,880
Michigan	7,094		215	5,810	3,067,406	360,109	
Minnesota			619	12,870	3,069,402	115,363	
Mississippi				257,470		38,945	
Missouri	1,461,542			132,880		138,619	
Montana	297,987	584,542		2,250	2,409,826	8,248	
Nebraska	634	1,266,213		10,520	3,427,543	29,509	
Nevada	58,768			1,000	86,063	27,196	
New Hampshire	3,036			300		11,635	
New Jersey				4,000		271,990	
New Mexico	74,041	773,146		12,950	97,211	32,374	
New York	1,076			29,450	1,671	1,121,796	338,345
North Carolina	586,163		602	130,720		189,081	
North Dakota	-160	550,429		52,750	1,367,578	11,873	
Ohio	415,039			430	994,677	298,331	
Oklahoma	148,597	562,725		46,940		61,921	
Oregon	1,384,832			1,810	1,101,070	43,927	
Pennsylvania	29,499		52,678	14,120		439,180	
Rhode Island						44,872	
South Carolina	7,756			71,680		98,177	
South Dakota		530,146		2,760	295,347	12,706	
Tennessee	557,658		4,565	29,990		693,598	
Texas	100,528	2,797,258		57,320	1,249,310	247,561	29,470
Utah	-596		29,897	9,590	1,123,966	26,766	
Vermont				13,850		5,263	
Virginia	429,187		23,300	14,260		183,479	
Washington	98,490			260	3,131,297	280,587	
West Virginia	415,739		13,740	151,470		32,642	
Wisconsin			5,819	28,520		174,738	
Wyoming	30,861	190,038		4,810	2,122,282	26,854	
Puerto Rico				36,420	13,639,065	1,350,308	
Virgin Islands							
Other Territories, etc.[7]							
Adjustments or undistributed to States	8,553						
Total	10,007,536	9,244,737	260,937	2,291,580	92,108,208	10,368,984	842,769

Footnotes at end of table.

TABLE 84.—*Federal grants in aid to State and local governments and to individuals and private institutions within the States, fiscal year 1965*—Continued

PART B. FEDERAL AID PAYMENTS TO INDIVIDUALS AND PRIVATE INSTITUTIONS IN THE STATES—Continued

States, Territories, etc.	Department of Defense			Funds appropriated to the President	General Services Administration	Department of Health, Education, and Welfare	
	Air Force National Guard	Army National Guard	Civil Defense [22] [58]	Office of Economic Opportunity	National historical grants	Office of Education	
				College work study [23]		Cooperative research	Defense educational activities [59]
	(92)	(93)	(94)	(95)	(96)	(97)	(98)
Alabama	$3,452,518	$7,547,950	$115,927	$980,405		$26,552	$744,515
Alaska	1,345,268	1,778,860	42,236	41,818		13,311	168,283
Arizona	3,664,361	1,397,947	137,439	233,999		42,978	770,759
Arkansas	2,748,597	4,571,504	142,774	562,148			262,797
California	9,270,084	13,946,794	297,262	4,302,698		1,656,060	5,784,618
Colorado	3,605,233	1,573,112	81,735	486,692		153,424	1,248,118
Connecticut	2,228,083	5,031,554	67,948	611,856		83,242	948,466
Delaware	1,690,777	1,946,354	50,195	42,605		38,563	139,390
District of Columbia	2,593,705	1,052,222	73,705	313,867		108,309	1,190,979
Florida	1,983,705	4,376,991	253,183	606,882		256,188	1,234,629
Georgia	4,881,560	4,421,542	101,866	403,473		165,774	1,569,597
Hawaii	4,310,571	5,432,470	54,079	172,826		6,666	334,224
Idaho	2,041,400	2,385,891	75,153	178,698			152,348
Illinois	4,605,809	7,352,720	165,720	847,951	$7,500	1,411,765	2,774,185
Indiana	3,430,697	5,429,967	134,084	287,944	17,630	282,459	2,526,203
Iowa	3,907,873	3,889,935	115,753	153,654		238,631	821,367
Kansas	2,970,829	3,774,406	114,476	484,826	2,721	111,601	1,286,562
Kentucky	1,680,061	3,135,708	126,487	926,336	11,450	79,108	829,128
Louisiana	2,169,459	4,706,375	−4,943	376,345		32,874	760,594
Maine	1,987,022	2,427,663	45,790	199,841		7,989	331,130
Maryland	2,291,432	5,426,554	50,659	351,839		67,821	761,901
Massachusetts	4,153,957	7,917,645	103,806	1,022,606	11,050	840,922	2,505,056
Michigan	4,223,733	7,521,435	1,393	1,017,647	6,700	964,314	2,665,873
Minnesota	3,789,672	5,885,396	176,552	1,410,108	18,300	365,663	1,118,843
Mississippi	3,090,650	5,588,300	1,690	929,272		17,133	245,907
Missouri	4,779,131	5,823,723	111,695	763,213	5,000	294,169	1,234,138
Montana	2,095,262	1,897,017	35,705	397,360			377,353
Nebraska	1,650,974	2,234,362	83,537	536,495		80,337	501,598
Nevada	1,289,413	796,636	20,459	64,230		27,498	183,973
New Hampshire	1,473,604	1,199,174	16,206	70,668	10,789	28,267	472,759
New Jersey	4,940,273	9,642,009	151,048	457,019	15,356	83,238	1,383,399
New Mexico	1,675,622	2,576,491	115,997	238,266		27,640	367,157
New York	8,576,337	15,086,474	4,808	1,961,560	1,690	1,437,208	6,157,855
North Carolina	1,804,920	5,232,169	89,321	959,400	10,500	398,616	1,178,026
North Dakota	2,114,738	1,414,790	64,144	307,747		23,924	626,108
Ohio	7,797,451	8,641,381	151,301	634,796		650,612	2,468,663
Oklahoma	3,795,067	4,276,233	171,351	603,921		41,036	1,112,495
Oregon	2,416,686	2,903,657	106,711	1,185,016		623,222	1,489,813
Pennsylvania	6,748,752	11,772,303	259,882	661,250	4,836	1,420,320	2,612,796
Rhode Island	1,485,503	2,320,281	35,399	63,645		58,846	462,659
South Carolina	2,052,796	4,512,193	78,983	141,971	21,250	965	596,491
South Dakota	2,013,516	2,167,327	60,557	239,274		4,968	284,393
Tennessee	5,686,836	5,675,618	113,481	992,399	23,098	35,984	1,350,309
Texas	6,243,665	10,210,642	232,239	1,384,110	3,000	258,500	2,636,237
Utah	2,238,765	2,530,300	747	421,316		70,290	662,379
Vermont	2,350,224	2,213,334	33,180	76,767		27,520	214,121
Virginia	1,296,927	6,246,583	60,702	402,866	5,044	44,416	1,070,842
Washington	3,473,400	4,403,534	83,132	388,328	8,285	92,940	956,407
West Virginia	2,758,841	1,979,530	18,858	298,157		21,066	364,174
Wisconsin	4,344,565	4,273,054	116,232	1,676,291		491,858	1,286,173
Wyoming	1,350,115	1,208,595	92,861	127,740		6,000	557,947
Puerto Rico	2,264,325	3,485,885	168,951	269,738		79,621	430,554
Virgin Islands				8,482			41,620
Other Territories, etc.[7]				6,237		1,625	56,894
Adjustments or undistributed to States	[60]127,693,346	153,491,145		−9,715,100			
Total	299,527,810	396,733,735	5,002,456	22,569,498	184,199	13,302,033	62,312,805

Footnotes at end of table.

TABLE 84.—*Federal grants in aid to State and local governments and to individuals and private institutions within the States, fiscal year 1965*—Continued

PART B. FEDERAL AID PAYMENTS TO INDIVIDUALS AND PRIVATE INSTITUTIONS IN THE STATES—Continued

States, Territories, etc.	Department of Health, Education, and Welfare—Continued						
	Office of Education—Continued			Public Health Service			
	Educational improvement for the handicapped [25]	Equal education opportunities program	Foreign language and area studies	Accident prevention [22]	Air pollution [22]	Allergy and infectious disease activities	Arthritis and metabolic disease activities
	(99)	(100)	(101)	(102)	(103)	(104)	(105)
Alabama	$200,993	$78,040	$2,435		$6,820	$173,445	$571,549
Alaska							
Arizona	147,882		1,291			99,103	59,323
Arkansas	47,783		7,411			39,110	335,490
California	661,665	42,150	183,488	$389,861	1,216,538	5,935,506	8,085,637
Colorado	217,998		12,475		170,527	1,063,004	683,079
Connecticut	90,000		13,135		4,579	810,397	950,980
Delaware		21,045	535			20,402	
District of Columbia	244,441		4,408	73,087	20,944	382,568	1,130,421
Florida	177,400	232,796	37,589	13,849	41,910	904,064	1,127,168
Georgia	226,211		1,905		28,716	459,957	771,995
Hawaii	20,000		10,390			266,047	52,312
Idaho	37,300					10,284	
Illinois	482,133		79,762		171,287	2,941,797	3,954,446
Indiana	294,598		56,007	89,653	7,539	376,809	812,653
Iowa	242,825		13,567	32,070		341,403	834,368
Kansas	389,946		6,415		13,440	719,525	534,226
Kentucky	43,604	33,000		22,679		164,939	597,686
Louisiana	18,000		892	49,962	26,239	798,293	531,918
Maine			3,086		26,486	6,552	53,202
Maryland	217,025	16,400	13,315		210,473	1,427,036	2,837,995
Massachusetts	324,738		74,245	55,873	149,028	3,153,881	9,313,997
Michigan	992,447		58,790	125,962	259,193	832,924	2,892,411
Minnesota	284,931		4,366	9,625	103,216	1,144,993	2,675,246
Mississippi	108,000	40,000		36,780		195,085	227,613
Missouri	199,998	30,839	13,358	38,367	−660	610,388	1,780,042
Montana	39,000		7,187			220,797	14,347
Nebraska	99,684		535		26,036	92,948	277,251
Nevada					14,956		10,500
New Hampshire	34,096			3,233	12,635	59,037	295,841
New Jersey	211,760		87,231	19,336	108,773	769,927	911,138
New Mexico	51,203				65,359	102,436
New York	1,133,861	81,700	172,081	442,061	698,215	5,819,204	14,056,920
North Carolina	107,030	73,779	24,903		63,663	766,594	1,891,572
North Dakota	93,600					11,812	85,726
Ohio	315,270		23,180	28,728	109,002	921,146	2,329,210
Oklahoma	112,143	42,005	678			334,146	622,671
Oregon	280,741		21,563	13,528	53,127	378,877	1,133,180
Pennsylvania	493,423		69,952	210,610	396,570	2,509,540	4,549,208
Rhode Island	75,400		5,905			53,127	70,833
South Carolina	50,400		1,370		17,241	2,021	79,008
South Dakota	41,600			15,105		48,140	44,075
Tennessee	548,816	199,669	1,370		39,035	705,339	1,523,077
Texas	353,527	27,700	73,817		183,019	1,309,659	2,161,270
Utah	98,000		20,303		92,947	155,042	961,961
Vermont	17,400			3,394		23,359	293,977
Virginia	157,050		13,314		41,028	136,395	434,975
Washington	127,859		29,213	−2,710	201,451	764,517	2,658,756
West Virginia	62,400		1,070		35,536	163,697	422,921
Wisconsin	472,259		46,079	3,696	53,253	1,318,663	1,767,618
Wyoming	14,000		1,913			18,928	
Puerto Rico	20,000		535	78,213		208,097	292,770
Virgin Islands							
Other Territories, etc.[7]					73,841	2,286,883	2,431,435
Adjustments or undistributed to States			154,676	−139,500	−650,000	−4,310,000	−8,764,800
Total	10,680,440	919,123	1,355,740	1,613,462	4,026,603	37,700,766	71,421,632

Footnotes at end of table.

TABLE 84.—*Federal grants in aid to State and local governments and to individuals and private institutions within the States, fiscal year 1965*—Continued

PART B. FEDERAL AID PAYMENTS TO INDIVIDUALS AND PRIVATE INSTITUTIONS IN THE STATES—Continued

States, Territories, etc.	Department of Health, Education, and Welfare—Continued					
	Public Health Service—Continued					
	Child health and human development	Chronic disease and health of the aged	Communicable disease activities [22]	Community health practice and research [22]	Construction of health research facilities	Dental services and resources
	(106)	(107)	(108)	(109)	(110)	(111)
Alabama	$113,988	$383,475		$12,877	$11,061	$107,608
Alaska						
Arizona	4,612		$42,819	215,055	180,000	
Arkansas	100,139			11,500		
California	4,066,409	884,529	168,173	2,660,202	4,708,880	178,472
Colorado	921,255	2,164		102,169	717,088	
Connecticut	426,720	85,240	39,907	403,125	1,841,628	
Delaware	5,760			9,025		10,380
District of Columbia	126,144	348,322	7,764	21,430	115,100	57,462
Florida	939,257	85,754	72,827	272,304	196,926	
Georgia	219,729	223,275	34,387	93,250	1,301,474	29,043
Hawaii	84,615	10,454		2,216	12,500	
Idaho				6,800		
Illinois	1,377,428	283,972	340,258	353,402	2,006,650	161,085
Indiana	239,878	234,340		174,652	27,986	68,966
Iowa	252,424	30,993	55,807	123,334	89,897	26,130
Kansas	468,059	103,903	9,652	75,938	140,873	
Kentucky	205,849	8,587		51,526		27,096
Louisiana	208,807	144,838	93,252	290,803	147,969	17,954
Maine	197,740				22,428	
Maryland	1,071,991	206,742		693,337	277,531	49,650
Massachusetts	2,945,775	537,344	28,206	867,081	4,370,011	139,890
Michigan	656,601	341,377		1,411,340	1,821,129	203,293
Minnesota	512,124	157,751	5,340	552,045	267,135	32,209
Mississippi	29,119			11,188		
Missouri	499,968	154,738	25,802	166,453	1,215,032	130,504
Montana	16,932		−4,700	4,031	82,500	
Nebraska	438,770	27,604		19,300	29,325	62,941
Nevada	55,726			1,233	2,831	
New Hampshire	57,300			13,206		
New Jersey	122,358		54,678	264,090	37,082	29,543
New Mexico	194,308			29,230		
New York	3,709,688	723,214	139,888	856,730	4,334,722	128,664
North Carolina	835,637	181,524	6,050	798,669	150,107	117,243
North Dakota					149,268	4,766
Ohio	1,251,900	197,359	30,953	292,231	415,204	81,519
Oklahoma	241,561	83,340	6,372	115,091	650,170	
Oregon	158,956	74,412		170,730	191,328	40,673
Pennsylvania	2,091,088	301,634	52,006	678,137	2,423,348	142,046
Rhode Island	368,701			158,653	356,129	
South Carolina	13,182			50,514		
South Dakota	6,763			18,687		
Tennessee	722,140	150,125	28,098	30,810	746,888	36,365
Texas	585,915	209,198	91,477	270,259	1,586,001	53,361
Utah	111,950	23,960		70,103	917,443	
Vermont	94,638			−35,045	35,361	
Virginia	94,249		16,530	74,670	125,643	30,078
Washington	654,806	251,595	33,461	261,820	881,698	26,985
West Virginia	48,742	7,252	10,520	15,903		19,674
Wisconsin	444,095	209,254	27,835	44,797	476,587	25,971
Wyoming				5,350		
Puerto Rico		21,181	6,341	344,804		56,263
Virgin Islands						
Other Territories, etc.[7]	710,392	4,449	13,000	61,550		
Adjustments or undistributed to States [81]	−3,097,600	−899,100	−197,200	−1,373,900		−81,100
Total	25,606,568	5,794,799	1,239,503	11,822,705	33,062,933	2,014,734

Footnotes at end of table.

TABLE 84.—*Federal grants in aid to State and local governments and to individuals and private institutions within the States, fiscal year 1965*—Continued

PART B. FEDERAL AID PAYMENTS TO INDIVIDUALS AND PRIVATE INSTITUTIONS IN THE STATES—Continued

States, Territories, etc.	Department of Health, Education, and Welfare—Continued						
	Public Health Service—Continued						
	Environmental engineering and sanitation	Environmental health sciences	General research and services	General research support grants	Hospital and medical facilities research and National Library of Medicine [22]	Hospital construction activities	National Cancer Institute
	(112)	(113)	(114)	(115)	(116)	(117)	(118)
Alabama	$100,367		$1,227,898	$117,424		$50,064	$172,546
Alaska		$44,638	285,773				
Arizona	94,671		309,012				80,774
Arkansas			726,095	68,447		315,316	58,640
California	439,555	436,780	16,612,470	2,103,714	[62] −$9,271	258,361	5,527,240
Colorado	21,725		1,691,389	288,560		8,685	422,461
Connecticut			3,285,007	200,318		46,115	1,365,568
Delaware			36,945				45,406
District of Columbia	152,732	11,004	954,262	499,796		188,292	394,578
Florida	47,979	249,644	1,674,266	257,621	[63] 2,065		852,044
Georgia	90,351		2,243,274	220,566			318,465
Hawaii	154,437		486,810			73,056	
Idaho			22,052				5,563
Illinois	201,492	61,445	7,888,948	1,256,149	[63] 2,118	152,252	2,938,165
Indiana	79,026	25,744	2,274,280	229,493		12,182	510,915
Iowa	141,397		1,733,995	171,952		138,096	139,013
Kansas	38,550	16,120	1,131,296	119,832	18,879		175,058
Kentucky			571,629	197,011			238,478
Louisiana	44,106	37,077	2,840,930	255,059		83,760	923,215
Maine			106,595	68,645		14,259	590,216
Maryland		93,420	5,976,405	333,779		19,655	1,301,042
Massachusetts	332,979	351,961	8,971,985	1,601,087		85,929	5,552,809
Michigan	97,636	124,713	4,126,821	555,576	[62] 4,636	146,853	1,509,125
Minnesota	93,048	23,849	2,093,421	418,580	[62] 13,420	108,941	917,537
Mississippi	9,812	15,750	423,344	72,747			81,343
Missouri	80,487	86,851	2,335,964	381,601	[63] 369	85,349	1,037,526
Montana	15,668		98,414				41,477
Nebraska	11,881		157,821	111,778			148,092
Nevada							
New Hampshire	7,158		895,658	83,117			215,529
New Jersey	22,954	217,533	1,818,317	213,534	[63] 3,164	60,674	653,904
New Mexico	8,599		25,997	37,137			124,739
New York	254,653	532,677	16,757,187	3,049,107	[62] 27,212	192,183	13,118,646
North Carolina	107,323	265,218	3,939,892	327,000	[62] 24,000	24,526	831,309
North Dakota			93,310	29,704			16,576
Ohio	114,973	82,851	4,986,900	576,612	[63] 35,148	161,847	1,100,014
Oklahoma	2,793	67,102	1,154,608	254,133			351,945
Oregon	246,905	238,656	2,861,099	85,817	[62] 11,862	70,680	1,025,985
Pennsylvania	224,620		7,657,356	1,476,154	[64] −20,288	19,014	4,581,339
Rhode Island		9,078	542,738				442,835
South Carolina		2,291	72,584	42,573			48,495
South Dakota	16,860		42,606	27,399			5,000
Tennessee	27,674	6,256	2,330,605	281,563			691,645
Texas	39,762	78,899	4,082,595	693,269		77,764	4,706,128
Utah	78,700		961,910	93,930			385,819
Vermont		5,904	355,006	57,147			125,938
Virginia	5,868	43,876	644,053	161,868		23,500	132,861
Washington	123,735	84,492	4,068,763	187,292		37,950	789,444
West Virginia	23,290		123,440	69,639		54,765	90,378
Wisconsin	195,546	46,900	3,993,559	290,507	[62] 2,301		4,661,894
Wyoming			44,785				
Puerto Rico	16,958		224,684	171,881			124,684
Virgin Islands							
Other Territories, etc.[7]	317,550		2,666,690				1,567,316
Adjustments or undistributed to States [61]	−496,700	−387,100	−12,855,800	−1,636,100	[63] −3,600	−179,000	−7,231,000
Total	3,587,120	2,873,629	117,775,643	16,103,018	112,015	2,331,068	53,908,719

Footnotes at end of table.

TABLE 84.—*Federal grants in aid to State and local governments and to individuals and private institutions within the States, fiscal year 1965*—Continued

PART B. FEDERAL AID PAYMENTS TO INDIVIDUALS AND PRIVATE INSTITUTIONS IN THE STATES—Continued

States, Territories, etc.	Department of Health, Education, and Welfare—Continued						
	Public Health Service—Continued						
	National Heart Institute	National Institute of Dental Research [22]	National Institute of Mental Health	Neurology and blindness activities	Nursing services and resources	Occupational health	Radiological health
	(119)	(120)	(121)	(122)	(123)	(124)	(125)
Alabama	$724,626	$413,218	$474,664	$156,602	$199,677		$37,681
Alaska			25,000				
Arizona	9,000	62,446	258,180	175,242	28,400		
Arkansas	245,982		497,851	182,596	32,398		124,389
California	8,601,311	699,434	15,475,008	6,287,161	897,509	$83,121	154,804
Colorado	821,643	43,320	1,877,713	307,375	507,938	36,072	170,690
Connecticut	884,147	23,077	3,401,547	780,532	270,573	48,241	49,572
Delaware			159,893	6,966			
District of Columbia	1,596,904	99,508	2,632,466	496,091	351,224	5,497	39,326
Florida	1,003,416	156,473	1,370,476	1,420,409	111,102	14,773	324,120
Georgia	2,337,623	158,028	910,736	550,870	216,531	47,230	273,345
Hawaii	102,668		421,751	66,105	5,486		
Idaho			261,998				40,067
Illinois	4,465,744	1,043,490	6,855,684	3,191,297	223,405	33,048	222,330
Indiana	1,633,365	302,211	1,637,793	513,683	281,901	17,238	191,748
Iowa	491,637	134,605	857,581	933,656	77,923		34,517
Kansas	213,269	20,951	1,757,079	380,041	39,444	18,846	23,948
Kentucky	626,897	23,791	1,229,784	282,458	44,308		3,420
Louisiana	1,852,426	23,384	1,158,417	1,430,368	42,721		27,729
Maine	112,878		227,768	364	7,750		21,812
Maryland	2,235,178	298,836	4,177,067	2,899,636	282,075	35,850	216,828
Massachusetts	7,770,862	1,289,183	10,611,316	5,557,388	841,211	147,336	263,944
Michigan	2,053,674	565,820	5,063,232	2,050,563	463,371	71,614	296,940
Minnesota	3,999,949	279,399	2,574,391	2,611,327	285,860	43,631	85,637
Mississippi	613,920		474,916	176,612	29,654		6,460
Missouri	1,472,557	248,027	2,871,912	1,842,673	339,450		64,523
Montana	63,026		280,206	19,159	86,745		
Nebraska	362,141	42,035	908,742	63,324	34,500		
Nevada			113,830		2,286		
New Hampshire	233,283		154,178	197,090	29,720		
New Jersey	747,637	39,452	2,158,066	484,161	37,260		70,223
New Mexico	243,499	14,424	462,316	93,425	3,000		6,515
New York	10,030,832	1,924,162	20,937,205	12,114,439	1,325,185	308,805	624,409
North Carolina	2,575,556	235,509	3,076,071	805,570	286,100	13,800	68,761
North Dakota	60,025	-618	156,414		2,250		20,217
Ohio	3,522,338	228,934	2,957,124	1,579,457	652,538	150,717	137,166
Oklahoma	1,608,244	8,716	994,833	351,027	18,812	28,232	125,883
Oregon	1,275,139	272,045	1,423,876	1,536,759	137,280	33,414	45,037
Pennsylvania	6,934,155	1,419,498	6,390,207	3,516,181	993,927	190,808	371,766
Rhode Island	49,068	27,949	852,770	437,808	7,110		12,313
South Carolina	401,749	8,122	284,278	144,251	85,225		
South Dakota	67,328	12,757	244,216	7,128	21,259		
Tennessee	1,727,891	129,641	1,527,688	775,118	41,668	20,784	81,371
Texas	3,592,477	340,405	2,397,842	791,080	202,355	112,173	116,555
Utah	502,570	33,366	852,581	598,364	58,661		44,333
Vermont	315,467		439,220	163,357	16,532		
Virginia	1,100,706	107,092	630,472	496,107	10,260		6,032
Washington	3,005,620	348,426	1,948,605	1,180,187	330,666	78,678	142,013
West Virginia	246,516	2,842	410,761	177,923	27,770		
Wisconsin	1,916,967	243,039	1,832,165	1,113,725	181,928	108,667	
Wyoming			197,643				
Puerto Rico	156,451	17,040	493,981	231,284	78,130		
Virgin Islands							
Other Territories, etc.[7]	2,180,290	245,645	1,161,742	1,643,898		37,440	124,136
Adjustments or undistributed to States [81]	-9,276,800	-979,500	-5,990,000	-6,720,400	-1,096,300	-244,000	-431,000
Total	77,511,851	10,606,182	114,561,255	54,100,437	9,154,778	1,442,015	4,239,560

Footnotes at end of table.

TABLE 84.—*Federal grants in aid to State and local governments and to individuals and private institutions within the States, fiscal year 1965*—Continued

PART B. FEDERAL AID PAYMENTS TO INDIVIDUALS AND PRIVATE INSTITUTIONS IN THE STATES—Continued

States, Territories, etc.	Public Health Service—Con.	Vocational Rehabilitation Administration		Welfare Administration			
				Bureau of Family Services	Children's Bureau		
	Water supply and pollution control	Grants for special projects [22]	Training and traineeships [22]	Aid for repatriated U.S. nationals	Child welfare research and demonstration grants [22]	Child welfare training grants	Maternal and child health services
	(126)	(127)	(128)	(129)	(130)	(131)	(132)
Alabama	$38,468	$211,654	$119,459		−$3,500		
Alaska	34,331	115,457					
Arizona	34,162	129,188	203,820			$34,105	
Arkansas	35,413	20,288	36,907				
California	746,912	1,768,198	1,926,595	$8,277	328,253	379,563	$316,642
Colorado	149,560	212,608	411,310		72,185	93,631	
Connecticut	15,424	418,105	132,851		72,762	65,565	
Delaware		44,100			38,730		5,614
District of Columbia	109,661	867,788	664,987	233,139	669,660	184,020	19,154
Florida	360,331	229,730	360,573	14,568		58,301	
Georgia	67,586	262,152	242,696	543	24,474	106,118	24,810
Hawaii	38,883		52,846			24,647	
Idaho	5,600	84,562					
Illinois	291,024	904,330	1,253,535	4,077	590,871	232,972	
Indiana	31,292	47,800	249,542			61,176	
Iowa	153,203	49,218	230,575		109,601	58,925	6,425
Kansas	91,097	273,748	234,263			55,285	
Kentucky	75,192	153,067	148,940	157	146,310	84,594	
Louisiana	36,480	119,918	233,663	140		135,465	47,914
Maine	66,515	116,511					
Maryland	81,124	165,469	131,924	913		71,376	218,209
Massachusetts	434,456	638,471	1,240,111		90,289	381,916	397,800
Michigan	657,354	388,771	913,112	502	33,290	192,541	115,120
Minnesota	126,742	1,154,258	518,543			87,144	68,315
Mississippi		−81	5,488	198			
Missouri	169,312	384,252	432,057			202,778	
Montana	81,778	49,258	15,648				
Nebraska	3,633	61,435	140,116			62,157	
Nevada		−1,921					
New Hampshire	15,282	71,700	6,553				
New Jersey	80,130	207,498	190,486	1,942		106,455	
New Mexico	58,148	28,425	24,813				
New York	464,188	4,645,440	4,291,165	44,309	998,596	516,360	388,944
North Carolina	138,877	253,357	374,243	74		53,933	67,626
North Dakota	23,069	43,555	28,234				
Ohio	150,239	1,625,570	611,593		39,046	170,823	29,370
Oklahoma	160,536	27,981	296,362			64,853	
Oregon	380,990	179,683	270,086	1,117	25,655	41,438	
Pennsylvania	148,340	871,946	1,203,023	3,206	79,777	218,659	184,343
Rhode Island	34,243	51,450			46,800		
South Carolina	155,605	41,109	13,761				
South Dakota	19,037	−729	800				
Tennessee	53,115	513,110	309,852		68,466	108,686	55,095
Texas	244,036	811,134	444,196	10,175	−2,856	152,388	105,185
Utah	92,715	91,502	168,689	358		67,605	20,493
Vermont		82,766	−9,494			4,376	
Virginia	59,091	72,538	353,388	535		52,890	
Washington	253,048	532,957	170,483	1,294		40,819	36,979
West Virginia	63,110	4,497	150,373			37,470	
Wisconsin	298,520	604,369	721,973		109,197	97,573	
Wyoming							34,667
Puerto Rico		31,680	246,798	20,000		79,112	
Virgin Islands		14,980					
Other Territories, etc.[7]	68,620						
Adjustments or undistributed to States [61]	−759,600	−5,169,436	−3,168,364		−1,580,000	−2,546,000	−1,054,000
Total	6,136,872	14,505,416	16,598,574	345,524	1,957,606	1,839,719	1,088,705

Footnotes at end of table.

TABLE 84.—*Federal grants in aid to State and local governments and to individuals and private institutions within the States, fiscal year 1965*—Continued

PART B. FEDERAL AID PAYMENTS TO INDIVIDUALS AND PRIVATE INSTITUTIONS IN THE STATES—Continued

States, Territories, etc.	Department of Health, Education, and Welfare—Continued						Department of Labor
	Welfare Administration—Continued						
	Children's Bureau—Continued						Area Redevelopment Act [65]
	Research projects, all Bureau services	Services for crippled children	Special projects, grants for maternity and infant care	Cooperative research	Office of Juvenile Delinquency and Youth Development	Refugees in the United States, aid to	
	(133)	(134)	(135)	(136)	(137)	(138)	(139)
Alabama		$29,438				$1,372	$35,462
Alaska							113,331
Arizona			$32,900		$116,935		−3,899
Arkansas			112,985				142,868
California	$687,284	410,570	12,252	$123,962	743,228	437,377	195,904
Colorado	24,578	39,429			37,568	33,636	5,626
Connecticut	31,834				693,535	69,690	43,412
Delaware				20,733			
District of Columbia	49,275	252,610		189,716	1,089,900	26,818	
Florida	79,182	57,609	110,646	112,528	32,842	23,941,352	1,925
Georgia	96,686		197,727			10,189	24,307
Hawaii					50,216		86,729
Idaho							30,485
Illinois	258,682	149,301	920,670	330,468	249,819	399,710	45,181
Indiana						147,022	−9,205
Iowa				56,125		53,012	45,809
Kansas				60,742	21,743	113,993	1,875
Kentucky			32,779	9,649	99,551	828	178,729
Louisiana	259,105	11,416				96,649	23,330
Maine							213,794
Maryland	592,852	296,989	375,251	37,960	31,656	12,589	54,436
Massachusetts	589,436			16,066	496,342	40,671	307,576
Michigan	372,240	746	252,442	165,156	140,750	86,084	934,647
Minnesota	16,835		48,981		236,043	3,939	45,239
Mississippi		11,633				340	5,025
Missouri		190,803	100,811		361,972	18,502	36,943
Montana						124,432	45,447
Nebraska		122,018				2,500	
Nevada				55,775		12,064	5,217
New Hampshire					41,870	248	
New Jersey			75,398	231,470	214,901	978,728	373,919
New Mexico						2,236	177,103
New York	632,969	281,336	815,839	428,980	2,720,265	920,349	117,423
North Carolina	165,773				51,248	4,237	289,405
North Dakota				21,383		30	52,235
Ohio	28,231	126,937		289,014	1,047,301	6,086	589,890
Oklahoma						12,544	37,532
Oregon	32,453	245,696	50,000		393,587	168,733	32,743
Pennsylvania	222,752		302,609	8,379	51,418	77,821	700,602
Rhode Island	30,331				236,746		271,496
South Carolina							4,400
South Dakota							75,983
Tennessee		114,810				2,227	394,626
Texas		40,610			230,166	30,200	252,180
Utah					61,916	50	12,110
Vermont							53,702
Virginia		6,347				8,956	3,525
Washington	39,446	29,324		41,959	−423		217,751
West Virginia			76,447		275,000		24,192
Wisconsin				66,167	74,032	4,109	329,292
Wyoming							13,538
Puerto Rico	284,690		614,808	59,198			75,891
Virgin Islands							
Other Territories, etc.[7]							
Adjustments or undistributed to States [81]	−2,633,500	−966,000		−1,023,100	−755,400		
Total	1,861,134	1,451,622	4,132,545	1,302,330	9,044,727	27,849,323	6,709,731

Footnotes at end of table.

TABLE 84.—*Federal grants in aid to State and local governments and to individuals and private institutions within the States, fiscal year 1965*—Continued

PART B. FEDERAL AID PAYMENTS TO INDIVIDUALS AND PRIVATE INSTITUTIONS IN THE STATES—Continued

States, Territories, etc.	Department of Labor—continued		National Science Foundation	Veterans' Administration [57]		Total payments within States (Part B)	Grand total (Parts A and B)
	Manpower development and training activities [66]	Unemployment compensation for Federal employees and ex-servicemen	Research grants and fellowship awards	Automobiles, etc., for disabled veterans	Readjustment benefits and vocational rehabilitation		
	(140)	(141)	(142)	(143)	(144)	(145)	(146)
Alabama	$4,660,043	$1,634,100	$975,914	$17,600	$1,048,647	$58,109,087	$312,414,879
Alaska	1,417,444	1,044,393	1,112,234	1,600	17,438	7,663,662	106,296,177
Arizona	2,540,942	1,773,136	3,389,043	11,077	781,339	23,391,161	148,395,464
Arkansas	967,112	865,775	802,962	28,800	684,722	30,978,269	184,670,980
California	13,986,504	28,888,653	35,423,885	67,777	5,589,012	253,228,959	1,332,894,955
Colorado	3,100,731	1,120,224	6,139,177	16,000	893,185	85,908,414	236,061,809
Connecticut	2,135,638	659,314	4,589,669	16,000	447,056	34,105,300	170,794,020
Delaware	701,146	180,843	666,385	3,200	79,770	7,986,125	39,581,266
District of Columbia	925,426	2,611,034	7,587,371	31,735	691,817	31,622,831	133,399,812
Florida	5,034,303	1,623,458	5,789,692	92,783	2,588,794	77,106,545	325,762,255
Georgia	2,707,952	1,516,898	2,364,220	16,000	1,284,969	75,377,190	343,806,136
Hawaii	342,125	1,162,142	1,947,009	----------	108,191	26,597,124	73,523,936
Idaho	533,008	875,959	454,941	----------	162,634	35,202,818	101,223,845
Illinois	11,238,483	3,068,662	16,655,249	70,195	1,469,712	215,270,172	707,832,447
Indiana	4,560,001	1,015,008	7,350,893	15,945	852,976	120,599,597	302,871,356
Iowa	2,100,763	456,251	4,020,417	12,800	601,267	230,232,585	361,516,476
Kansas	2,713,857	992,868	2,633,856	4,800	579,426	216,381,384	340,774,404
Kentucky	8,807,070	2,230,591	1,151,614	17,600	670,048	64,107,559	279,484,322
Louisiana	1,160,720	1,304,012	2,542,460	12,800	841,949	47,189,463	371,027,626
Maine	763,307	409,131	753,845	3,200	196,126	11,826,266	70,257,120
Maryland	1,347,394	1,150,522	4,987,442	11,200	673,905	50,016,150	196,946,983
Massachusetts	6,541,525	5,213,008	26,067,255	52,700	1,367,100	126,960,174	409,847,087
Michigan	10,768,216	2,259,882	9,422,787	54,400	1,352,290	117,478,300	472,307,562
Minnesota	2,274,721	2,390,743	5,581,912	26,933	932,867	160,569,061	385,854,378
Mississippi	1,528,577	616,679	972,065	12,793	706,175	40,933,912	208,567,990
Missouri	4,515,950	1,947,638	4,678,511	30,195	1,159,292	147,254,702	431,650,832
Montana	955,243	823,489	737,731	----------	145,808	55,733,830	142,386,183
Nebraska	2,268,515	465,513	717,598	11,095	447,223	178,327,621	255,008,635
Nevada	1,530,052	373,105	479,778	4,800	47,275	6,135,132	61,953,816
New Hampshire	1,231,104	628,902	1,744,201	12,710	211,097	10,195,920	44,996,034
New Jersey	2,293,601	3,126,068	8,166,201	30,390	893,720	47,630,686	272,896,912
New Mexico	806,553	1,238,796	2,339,546	20,710	377,568	32,113,086	141,714,739
New York	16,606,724	7,741,393	28,507,332	102,400	2,954,902	241,188,224	1,027,470,961
North Carolina	1,968,290	1,575,549	5,997,537	14,400	1,121,763	78,499,534	297,231,838
North Dakota	940,498	590,148	998,001	----------	131,280	116,320,031	175,324,153
Ohio	7,698,163	3,572,057	7,191,969	46,145	1,681,834	129,339,803	567,300,581
Oklahoma	1,699,536	1,466,010	3,970,699	9,595	934,263	98,687,139	321,373,389
Oregon	2,436,092	1,696,143	4,440,381	11,200	501,810	51,654,831	226,348,352
Pennsylvania	8,603,621	7,460,723	13,760,019	63,835	2,593,958	128,809,620	633,191,251
Rhode Island	910,663	498,194	2,840,937	3,200	168,155	13,117,487	78,515,339
South Carolina	3,898,116	851,923	917,148	3,200	635,826	39,170,627	146,777,274
South Dakota	573,539	437,222	929,739	----------	134,333	75,887,501	148,452,189
Tennessee	4,207,688	2,729,000	2,132,986	12,797	992,360	73,238,257	321,824,019
Texas	3,849,931	5,497,815	7,001,961	50,112	3,530,684	251,135,881	792,069,352
Utah	952,381	1,368,920	1,872,572	1,600	457,762	25,253,847	129,248,450
Vermont	872,214	214,987	459,477	1,600	133,219	10,359,340	51,813,849
Virginia	2,844,276	1,314,638	2,697,414	25,585	882,971	37,430,063	307,635,451
Washington	3,625,660	6,258,000	4,818,603	22,400	1,021,197	77,987,988	280,993,905
West Virginia	2,155,634	1,566,718	647,135	23,295	437,511	17,007,581	177,665,706
Wisconsin	3,271,753	1,847,315	5,966,150	33,600	728,054	95,563,889	241,958,276
Wyoming	396,936	307,358	227,069	3,200	90,482	14,504,519	89,287,641
Puerto Rico	3,376,878	1,718,576	666,589	8,000	412,504	32,862,394	181,549,155
Virgin Islands	98,691	18,200	8,000	----------	----------	202,999	13,268,877
Other Territories, etc. [7]	117,154	----------	20,395	----------	807,517	16,604,699	32,780,698
Adjustments or undistributed to States						184,940,933	131,110,676
Total	177,562,464	122,397,686	268,317,976	1,144,004	48,181,783	4,436,000,872	15,339,911,818

Footnotes on pages 750–1.

Footnotes to table 84

[1] Includes: $1,057,474 Commodity Credit Corp.; $295,692, Agriculture Research Service; $13,400, Economic Research Service; and $125,000, Forest Service.

[2] Cost of food commodities acquired through price support operations.

[3] Consists of: $1,543,784 Cooperative extension work, payments and expenses, Extension Service; $1,500,000 payments to States and possessions, Agricultural Consumer and Marketing Service.

[4] Formerly reported as agricultural experiment stations. Includes $102,409 paid to State institutions other than land-grant colleges and universities.

[5] Federal share of the value of food stamps issued ($31,339,792) and Federal payment to State agencies for certification assistance ($422,165).

[6] Consists of: $14,363,592, forest protection and utilization, Forest Service and $920,229, assistance to States for tree planting, Forest Service.

[7] Includes: Guam, American Samoa, Trust Territory of the Pacific, and certain foreign countries.

[8] Represents adjustment to a checks-issued basis.

[9] Consists of: $3,191,500, penalty mail costs for State extension directors and cooperative extension agents; $7,352,606 retirement costs of cooperative extension agents; $21,749 reimbursement for benefits paid from the employees' compensation fund; and −$13,691 undistributed to States.

[10] Consists of: $232,500, penalty mail costs of State experiment station directors and $45,865, undistributed to States.

[11] Consists of: $32,837,416, payments to States, National forests fund; $137,763, payment to Minnesota (Cook, Lake, and St. Louis counties) National forests fund; and $108,205, payments to school funds, Arizona ($107,851) and New Mexico ($354).

[12] Includes $5,309,478 paid directly to participating private schools. In addition the program receives some of the commodities distributed or donated under columns 1 and 10 of this table.

[13] Cash payments to increase consumption of fluid milk by children in nonprofit schools. Net of refunds of $234,987 received from States. Includes $7,680,986 paid directly to private schools and other outlets.

[14] Soil Conservation Service, consists of $44,913,392, watershed protection; $13,363,104, flood prevention; and $164,456 resource conservation and development. (Total represents grants-in-kind of $27,093,242 and contributions of $31,347,710.)

[15] Includes $588,076 for improvement of the Pentagon road network.

[16] $17,273,374 flood relief and $43,886 bridges over Federal dams.

[17] $27,093,242 grants-in-kind and $31,347,710 contributions.

[18] Consists of: $31,726,228 forest highways, $6,339,240 public lands highways, $128,147 highway beautification and control of outdoor advertising, and $2,330 Appalachian development highway system.

[19] Consists of: $61,000,592 grants in aid for airports and $9,597,494 grants in aid for airports, liquidation of contract authority.

[20] Consists of: $188,624,048, disbursed by the Department of Agriculture and the Housing and Home Finance Agency; $3,291,569 by Bureau of Public Roads, Department of Commerce; $92,696,541, by the Department of Health, Education, and Welfare; and $3,773,339 by the Department of Interior.

[21] Consists of: $42,811,858 disaster relief and $638,907 State and local preparedness.

[22] Credit amounts (−) other than "Adjustments or undistributed to States" are refunds of advances from prior years.

[23] Administered by the Department of Health, Education, and Welfare.

[24] Administered by the Department of Labor.

[25] Program beginning fiscal 1965 applies to all categories of children who, by reason of health impairments, require special education including the mentally retarded, deaf, speech impaired, emotionally disturbed, and otherwise health impaired.

[26] Consists of: $3,366,394, cancer; $6,276,529 heart; and $22,444,173 other diseases. $20,254 represents grants-in-kind (supplies and services).

[27] Includes $918,159 grants-in-kind (supplies and services).

[28] Includes $1,194,460 hospital and medical care and $29,289 grants-in-kind (supplies and services).

[29] Includes $32,103, construction of Indian health facilities; $1,249,375 construction of health research facilities, NIH; $192,486,315, hospital construction activities; $50,000 construction mental health activities, Alaska; $767,798 George Washington University Hospital construction in the District of Columbia; and $680,802 cancer research facilities construction, NIH.

[30] Includes $281,543 grants-in-kind (supplies and services).

[31] Includes $3,202,158 grants-in-kind (supplies and services).

[32] Consists of amounts paid to following Interstate agencies: Interstate Sanitation Commission $69,323; Interstate Commission on the Potomac River Basin $24,917; Ohio River Valley Sanitation Commission $100,654; New England Interstate Water Pollution Control Commission $16,613; Delaware River Basin Commission $45,452; and Klamath River Compact $3,989.

[33] Consists of: $280,589,473 urban renewal and $11,064,298 urban mass transportation.

[34] Consists of: $8,685,337 education and welfare services, $769,796 resources management, and $88,000 Menominee educational grants.

Footnotes to table 84—Continued

[35] Consists of: $229,477 payments to States (proceeds of sales receipt limitation); $2,514 payments to Oklahoma (royalties); $265,606 payments to States from grazing receipts, public lands (outside grazing districts); $298,336 payments to States from grazing receipts, etc., public lands (within grazing districts); $1,123 payments to States (grazing fees); $3,443 payments to States from grazing receipts, etc., public lands (within grazing districts miscellaneous); $21,136,029 payments to counties, Oregon and California grant lands; $100,915 payments due counties national grasslands; $223,630 payments to Coos and Douglas counties, Oregon, in lieu of taxes on Coos Bay Wagon Road grant lands; $2,322 payments to counties, national grassland, Bureau of Sport Fisheries and Wildlife; $24,755 payment to Wyoming in lieu of taxes on lands in Grand Teton National Park, National Park Service; $963,635 payment to Alaska from Pribilof Islands fund, Bureau of Commercial Fisheries; $600,000 payments to Arizona and Nevada, Colorado River Dam fund, Boulder Canyon project; $20,754 operation and maintenance, $197,315 payments to local units, Klamath recreation area; and $8,313,413 internal revenue collections for the Virgin Islands.

[36] Consists of: $5,714,764 fish restoration and management, Bureau of Sport Fisheries and Wildlife (receipt limitation) and $14,516,576 wildlife restoration, Bureau of Sport Fisheries and Wildlife.

[37] Illinois-Missouri joint mass transportation projects.

[38] Payments in lieu of taxes.

[39] On an accrual basis; consists of $7,720,214 State homes for disabled soldiers and sailors and $396,118 approval and supervision of training establishments.

[40] Transitional grants to Alaska, Executive Office of the President.

[41] General construction, civil, Corps of Engineers.

[42] Consists of $37,500,000 Federal payment to D.C., Treasury Department and $1,877,303 hospital facilities, General Services Administration.

[43] Center for cultural and technical interchange between East and West, Department of State.

[44] Land and water conservation fund, Bureau of Outdoor Recreation, Department of Interior, totaling $55,825 for the six States represented.

[45] Drainage of anthracite mines, Bureau of Mines, Department of Interior.

[46] White House Conference on Aging.

[47] Consists of $42,941,231 internal revenue collections for Puerto Rico, and $15,750,000 transfers and expenses of operation, Bureau of Customs, and −$11 White House Conference on Aging.

[48] Transfers and expenses of operation, Bureau of Customs, Treasury Department.

[49] Consists of $593,870 administration of Guam, $12,478,435 Trust Territory of the Pacific Islands, Office of the Territories, Department of Interior, and $280,000 grant to Government of the Trust Territory of the Pacific for use as development funds, pursuant to PL 88-487, Aug. 22, 1964.

[50] Net of $3,969,914 penalty mail, $5,920 Veterans' Administration, $286,702 Federal rents, and −$2,735,360 adjustment.

[50a] For Civilian Industrial Technology, National Bureau of Standards, Department of Commerce, for which no State distribution is available.

[51] Price support payments.

[52] Consists of $914,104,854 acreage diversion payments and $282,148,489 price support payments.

[53] Consists of: $32,540,015 acreage diversion payments, −$19,456 price support payments, and $409,858,496 value of wheat marketing certificates issued to producers.

[54] Net of deductions made from producer payments for promotional and advertising programs.

[55] Formerly reported as land-use adjustment program.

[56] On an accrual basis. Consists of: $1,398,696 equipment grants, $2,690,803 student fellowships, $2,588,489 faculty training, and $3,690,996 for materials, services, and other costs.

[57] Figures on an accrual basis.

[58] Includes $4,940,369 transferred from Office of Education, Department of Health, Education, and Welfare, for civil defense adult education.

[59] Includes loans of $4,123,816 made in prior years which due to cancellation of the loans became grants in fiscal 1965.

[60] On an obligations basis.

[61] Negative amounts represent returns to agencies within the Department of Health, Education, and Welfare as of June 30, 1965, from deposits, research and training grantee institutions, NIH, PHS. The amounts returned could not be identified by State of original payment.

[62] Payments for hospital and medical facilities research.

[63] Payments for National Library of Medicine.

[64] Consists of −$21,684 hospital and medical facilities research and $1,396 National Library of Medicine.

[65] Consists of $2,923,657 administered by the Department of Health, Education, and Welfare and $3,786,074 administered by the Department of Labor.

[66] Consists of $89,100,184 administered by the Department of Health, Education, and Welfare and $88,462,280 administered by the Department of Labor.

NOTE.—Compiled from figures furnished by the departments and agencies, pursuant to Treasury Department Circular No. 1014, Aug. 8, 1958 (see 1958 annual report, exhibit 70, page 381).

Customs Operations

TABLE 85.—*Merchandise entries, fiscal years 1964 and 1965*

	1964	1965	Percentage increase, or decrease (−)
Entries:			
Consumption free	345, 830	364, 755	5. 5
Consumption dutiable	1, 276, 022	1, 375, 471	7. 8
Warehouse and rewarehouse	79, 453	80, 972	1. 9
Other formal	12, 864	9, 387	−27. 0
Total formal entries	1, 714, 169	1, 830, 585	6. 8
Warehouse withdrawals	383, 538	396, 829	3. 5
Appraisement	2, 141	1, 762	−17. 7
Drawback	23, 210	24, 464	5. 4
Outbound-immediate transportation; transportation and exportation; etc	576, 200	636, 164	10. 4
Mail	1, 303, 731	1, 365, 125	4. 7
Informal	681, 502	729, 511	7. 0
Passenger declarations—total	2, 908, 357	3, 491, 858	20. 1
Crew declarations—total	894, 826	905, 335	1. 2
Military declarations—total	1, 039, 748	1, 048, 347	. 8
Passenger declarations—dutiable	131, 367	146, 165	11. 3
Crew declarations—dutiable	186, 041	193, 109	3. 8
Military declarations—dutiable	32, 438	38, 617	19. 0
Other informal	1, 341, 443	1, 633, 901	22. 2

TABLE 86.—*Principal commodities on which drawback was paid, fiscal years 1964 and 1965*

Commodity	1964	1965	Percentage increase, or decrease (−)
Aluminum	$706, 585	$1, 417, 708	100. 6
Automobiles, aircraft, and parts	194, 111	175, 580	−9. 6
Barley		50, 903	
Brass and bronze manufactures	16, 599	18, 694	12. 6
Burlap	130, 891	104, 719	−20. 0
Chemicals	1, 528, 964	2, 468, 880	61. 5
Chromium and alloys	187, 539	245, 028	30. 7
Citrus fruit juices	188, 427	1, 598, 661	748. 4
Coal-tar products	565, 339	497, 822	−12. 0
Copper and manufactures	307, 421	379, 042	23. 3
Cork and manufactures	127	2, 647	1, 984. 3
Cotton cloth	208, 734	364, 656	74. 7
Cotton, unmanufactured	49, 808	10, 154	−79. 6
Electrical machinery and apparatus		240, 415	
Ferroalloying ores and metals	66, 283	82, 492	24. 5
Glass and glass products	121, 197	157, 065	29. 6
Iron and steel semimanufactures	452, 900	71, 150	−84. 3
Knit fabrics, cotton	19, 712	12, 762	−35. 3
Lead ore, matte, pigs, and bars	418, 846	729, 464	74. 2
Leather and leather products		5, 165	
Magnesite	24, 490	65, 604	167. 9
Manganese ore	59, 230	83, 368	40. 8
Medicinal preparations	368, 287	111, 748	−69. 7
Nickel	108, 567	173, 975	60. 2
Paper and manufactures	156, 135	36, 846	−76. 4
Petroleum and products	1, 520, 266	823, 363	−45. 9
Quicksilver or mercury	35, 377	26, 006	−26. 5
Rayon and other synthetic textiles	45, 483	29, 123	−36. 0
Steel mill products	1, 298, 123	2, 895, 421	123. 0
Sugar	720, 460	776, 939	7. 8
Tire cord fabric, rayon	2, 317	17, 510	655. 7
Tires and tubes, rubber and synthetic	57, 363	51, 496	−10. 2
Tobacco, unmanufactured	1, 166, 416	841, 526	−27. 9
Tungsten ore	192, 841	191, 312	−. 8
Watch movements	938, 255	610, 707	−34. 9
Whiskey		181, 641	
Wool and semimanufactures	14, 894	17, 940	20. 5
Wool fabrics	40, 807	57, 281	40. 4
Zinc ore and manufactures	368, 622	197, 587	−46. 4
Other	2, 984, 938	1, 762, 976	−40. 9
Total	15, 266, 354	17, 585, 376	15. 2

NOTE.—Includes Puerto Rico.

TABLE 87.—*Carriers and persons arriving in the United States fiscal years 1964 and 1965* [1]

Type of entrant	1964	1965	Percentage increase, or decrease (—)
Carriers arriving:			
Vessels entering direct from foreign ports	48, 651	49, 426	1. 6
Vessels entering via U.S. ports	[2] (40, 172)	[2] (38, 071)	—5. 2
Vessels reporting only from foreign ports:			
Government	1, 661	1, 799	8. 3
Ferries	64, 631	60, 033	—7. 1
Other	r 47, 403	48, 219	1. 7
Commercial planes	97, 755	107, 601	10. 1
Commercial planes entering via U.S. ports	[2] (9, 244)	(9, 920)	7. 3
Military planes	33, 567	36, 971	10. 1
Private planes	60, 738	65, 654	8. 1
Autos, empty trucks	47, 132, 060	49, 909, 968	5. 9
Buses	226, 633	255, 863	12. 9
Trucks	742, 653	777, 019	4. 6
Other vehicles	453, 914	470, 378	3. 6
Passenger trains	14, 585	14, 349	—1. 6
Freight cars	2, 013, 719	2, 039, 181	1. 3
Total carriers	r 50, 937, 970	53, 836, 461	5. 7
Persons arriving:			
Passengers arriving on:			
Vessels entering direct from foreign ports	772, 543	704, 744	—8. 8
Vessels entering via U.S. ports	74, 402	77, 689	4. 4
Vessels reporting only from foreign ports:			
Government	417, 777	398, 606	—4. 6
Ferries	1, 167, 859	1, 116, 634	—4. 4
Other	221, 351	210, 887	—4. 7
Commercial planes	4, 228, 782	4, 940, 805	16. 8
Military planes	803, 058	833, 565	3. 8
Private planes	178, 243	197, 285	10. 7
Autos, empty trucks	126, 624, 321	132, 954, 952	5. 0
Buses	4, 112, 394	5, 020, 158	22. 1
Trucks	208, 981	162, 551	—22. 2
Other vehicles	4, 470, 863	772, 876	—82. 7
Passenger trains	543, 136	501, 581	—7. 7
Pedestrians	30, 442, 707	33, 291, 861	9. 4
Total persons	174, 266, 417	181, 184, 194	4. 0

r Revised.
[1] Excludes Puerto Rico.
[2] Not included in totals, already counted under entering direct from foreign ports.

TABLE 88.—*Aircraft and aircraft passengers entering the United States, fiscal years 1964 and 1965*

District	Aircraft		Aircraft passengers		Percentage increase, or decrease (−)	
	1964	1965	1964	1965	Aircraft	Passengers
Maine and New Hampshire	3,239	3,177	26,059	23,280	−1.9	−10.7
Vermont	1,570	1,803	291,579	334,368	14.8	14.7
Massachusetts	4,795	5,037	110,703	128,066	5.0	15.7
Rhode Island	616	626	13,165	11,984	1.6	−9.0
St. Lawrence	1,799	1,856	8,014	4,863	3.2	−39.3
Rochester	1,181	1,384	14,132	13,542	17.2	−4.2
Buffalo	4,251	4,534	450,484	518,931	6.7	15.2
New York	38,373	42,225	1,703,248	2,033,908	10.0	19.4
Philadelphia	7,514	6,457	302,159	257,269	−14.1	−14.9
Maryland	1,700	2,148	43,652	56,786	26.4	30.1
Virginia	1,405	1,343	29,135	22,823	−4.4	−21.7
North Carolina	708	812	12,666	18,205	14.7	43.7
South Carolina	1,832	2,014	56,446	57,112	9.9	1.2
Georgia	404	886	5,932	2,736	119.3	−53.9
Florida	42,157	45,453	705,771	866,721	7.8	22.8
New Orleans	1,481	1,641	52,120	71,712	10.8	37.6
Galveston	1,447	1,378	46,908	51,323	−4.8	9.4
Laredo	8,210	8,151	96,992	87,988	−.7	−9.3
El Paso	1,685	1,798	4,936	5,334	6.7	8.1
San Diego	6,487	6,505	25,744	27,316	.3	6.1
Arizona	4,613	5,114	18,441	19,856	10.9	7.7
Los Angeles	2,823	3,472	187,458	220,777	23.0	17.8
San Francisco	2,158	6,382	67,770	248,719	195.7	267.0
Washington	8,544	9,639	150,657	174,689	12.8	16.0
Alaska	3,275	4,053	94,183	26,215	23.8	−72.2
Hawaii	8,764	10,252	370,723	335,623	17.0	−9.5
Montana and Idaho	2,635	2,183	25,245	23,995	−17.2	−5.0
Dakota	3,092	3,356	31,923	35,766	8.5	12.0
Minnesota	451	443	3,632	3,716	−1.8	2.3
Duluth and Superior	5,985	6,296	17,276	16,904	5.2	−2.2
Michigan	5,414	5,812	44,555	44,125	7.4	−1.0
Chicago	4,545	5,255	130,647	163,632	15.6	25.2
Ohio	5,898	5,931	36,525	35,899	.6	−1.7
St. Louis	734	428	11,206	6,919	−41.7	−38.3
Other	2,275	2,382	19,997	20,553	4.7	2.8
Total	192,060	210,226	5,210,083	5,971,655	9.5	14.6

TABLE 89.—*Seizures for violations of customs laws, fiscal years 1964 and 1965* [1]

Seizures	Total 1964	1965			
		Seizures by Customs	Seizures by other agencies	Joint seizures by Customs and other agencies	Total
Automobiles:					
Number	785	711	108	25	844
Value	$702, 008	$599, 452	$141, 537	$24, 273	$765, 262
Trucks:					
Number	119	114	9	3	126
Value	$369, 187	$413, 238	$14, 781	$3, 785	$431, 804
Aircraft:					
Number	11	15	1		16
Value	$6, 679, 200	$927, 400	$12, 000		$939, 400
Boats:					
Number	67	51	1		52
Value	$31, 546, 442	$18, 245, 320	$3, 800		$18, 249, 120
Narcotics:					
Number	1, 295	1, 394	7	16	1, 417
Value	$989, 154	$472, 431	$46	$8, 860	$481, 337
Liquors·					
Number	6, 780	7, 044	103	62	7, 209
Gallons	17, 869	19, 530	127	138	19, 795
Value	$247, 814	$327, 724	$2, 015	$2, 567	$332, 306
Prohibited articles (obscene, lottery, etc.):					
Number	4, 646	4, 975	39	24	5, 038
Value	$56, 909	$96, 493	$1, 922	$584	$98, 999
Other seizures:					
Number	9, 191	8, 567	168	90	8, 825
Value:					
Cameras	$31, 301	$41, 716			$41, 716
Edibles and farm products	166, 684	188, 572	$2, 196	$900	191, 668
Furs—skins and manufactures	27, 998	51, 476			51, 476
Guns and ammunition	64, 941	124, 945	69	961	125, 975
Jewelry, including gems	681, 490	664, 179	350	7, 353	671, 882
Livestock	25, 864	6, 411	5, 809	814	13, 034
Tobacco and manufactures	20, 409	40, 607	22	124	40, 753
Watches and parts	219, 045	186, 638		614	187, 252
Wearing apparel	213, 139	260, 103	98	259	260, 460
Miscellaneous	3, 762, 456	2, 623, 489	74, 929	25, 949	2, 724, 367
Total value of other seizures	5, 213, 327	4, 188, 136	83, 473	36, 974	4, 308, 583
Grand total:					
Number [2]	21, 912	21, 980	317	192	22, 489
Value	$45, 804, 041	$25, 270, 194	$259, 574	$77, 043	$25, 606, 811

[1] Includes Puerto Rico and the Virgin Islands.
[2] Excludes number of carriers confiscated in connection with seizures of liquor, narcotics, etc.

TABLE 90.—*Investigative activities, fiscal years 1964 and 1965*

Activity	1964	1965	Percentage increase, or decrease (−)
Drawback	1,179	1,095	−7.1
Classification	312	196	−37.2
Market value	584	725	24.1
Smuggling, narcotics	5,553	4,849	−12.7
Smuggling, all other	2,176	2,064	−5.2
Undervaluation, false invoicing	2,227	2,314	3.9
Prohibited importations	235	337	43.4
Navigation, aircraft, and vehicle violations	1,218	1,093	−10.3
Baggage declarations	1,363	1,877	37.7
Customs brokers, cartmen, and lightermen	611	413	−32.4
Petitions for relief	1,473	1,231	−16.4
Personnel	1,232	1,963	59.3
Customs procedure	320	354	10.6
Collection of duties and penalties	187	220	17.6
Cooperation with other agencies	750	779	3.9
Neutrality	354	337	−4.8
Pilferages and shortages	374	380	1.6
Export control	444	454	2.3
Federal tort claims	161	188	16.8
Miscellaneous	120	100	−16.7
Dumping	59	48	−18.7
Port security	5	2	−60.0
Total	20,937	21,019	.4

Engraving and Printing Production

TABLE 91.—*New postage stamp issues delivered, fiscal year 1965*

Issues	Denominations (cents)	Number of stamps delivered
Commemoratives:		
Nevada Statehood	5	121,825,000
Register and Vote	5	215,000,000
400th Anniversary of the Birth of William Shakespeare	5	121,460,000
Mayo Brothers	5	117,645,000
Robert H. Goddard—air mail	8	62,255,000
American Music	5	126,640,000
Homemakers	5	121,250,000
Verrazano-Narrows Bridge	5	116,655,000
Art, the International Language	5	120,700,000
Amateur Radio	5	115,695,000
Battle of New Orleans	5	115,695,000
Physical Fitness—Sokol	5	115,095,000
Crusade Against Cancer	5	119,560,000
Appomattox, Civil War Centennial	5	112,345,000
Winston Churchill	5	113,200,000
Magna Carta	5	118,925,000
International Cooperation Year—United Nations	5	112,040,000
Special issue:		
Christmas stamp—Series 1964	5	1,407,760,000
Ordinary:		
432 Subject	25	3,584,000
Canal Zone:		
Air mail, Golden Anniversary—Series 1964	6	480,000
	8	5,450,000
	15	500,000
	20	460,000
	30	610,000
	80	440,000
Air mail—Series 1965	6	430,000
	8	6,195,000
	15	550,000
	20	410,000
	30	455,000
	80	465,000

TABLE 92.—*Deliveries of finished work by the Bureau of Engraving and Printing, fiscal years 1964 and 1965*

Class	Number of pieces 1964	Number of pieces 1965	Face value 1965
Currency:			
U.S. notes	86, 360, 000		
Silver certificates	483, 120, 000	11, 880, 000	$59, 400, 000
Federal Reserve notes	1, 153, 168, 000	2, 041, 224, 192	11, 314, 681, 920
Specimens	42	1, 950	
Total	1, 722, 648, 042	2, 053, 106, 142	11, 374, 081, 920
Military payment certificates, Series 641		24, 688, 000	53, 004, 800
Specimens		1, 596	
Total		24, 689, 596	53, 004, 800
Bonds, notes, bills, certificates, and debentures:			
Bonds:			
Treasury	766, 657	871, 421	34, 134, 479, 000
Treasury, special series	603	702	
U.S. savings, registered	408, 201		
Consolidated Federal Farm Loan Bonds	85, 208	166, 533	2, 501, 250, 000
Consolidated bonds of the Federal home loan banks	24, 401	35, 428	1, 127, 350, 000
Notes:			
Treasury	711, 634	384, 422	33, 276, 210, 000
Tennessee Valley Authority	10, 016	6, 004	1, 500, 000, 000
Treasury, special series	425	100	
Consolidated notes of the Federal home loan banks, bearer	105, 120	114, 500	4, 175, 500, 000
Bills:			
Treasury	2, 790, 000	3, 807, 000	185, 328, 000, 000
Certificates:			
Treasury certificate of indebtedness, special series	1, 302	1, 600	
Participation certificates in Government mortgage liquidation trust		53, 119	4, 762, 500, 000
Debentures:			
Consolidated collateral trust for the:			
Twelve Federal intermediate credit banks	119, 000	105, 700	3, 485, 000, 000
Thirteen banks for cooperatives, no coupons	48, 800	54, 000	1, 725, 000, 000
Federal National Mortgage Association secondary market operations	5, 300		
Federal Housing Administration	430, 230	473, 400	755, 900, 000
Total	5, 506, 897	6, 073, 929	272, 771, 189, 000
Stamps:			
Customs	5, 823, 000	570, 000	
U.S. Internal Revenue			
To Office of Issue	1, 976, 795, 415	2, 152, 364, 755	109, 859, 330
To Smithsonian Institution	2, 600	21, 125	431
Puerto Rican Internal Revenue	207, 483, 175	224, 626, 750	
Virgin Islands Internal Revenue	141, 700	154, 100	
U.S. postage:			
Ordinary	18, 762, 407, 264	17, 569, 118, 664	977, 867, 797
Air mail	1, 080, 248, 800	967, 741, 000	88, 158, 130
Commemoratives	4, 662, 672, 600	4, 000, 960, 200	201, 973, 344
Special delivery	34, 055, 000	35, 425, 000	10, 627, 500
Postage due	154, 730, 000	117, 870, 000	14, 739, 600
Canal Zone postage:			
Ordinary	3, 690, 000	1, 433, 840	110, 682
Air mail	3, 080, 000	8, 507, 400	1, 195, 036
Commemoratives	8, 347, 800		
Postal cards		315, 500	12, 620
U.S. savings	117, 973, 500	112, 785, 000	18, 935, 000
Federal migratory bird hunting	3, 426, 240	3, 096, 240	9, 288, 000
Food coupons	49, 098, 500	76, 637, 000	111, 225, 250
Total	27, 069, 975, 594	25, 271, 626, 574	1, 543, 992, 720
Miscellaneous, checks, certificates, etc.:			
To office of issue	4, 551, 540	3, 545, 099	
Grand total	28, 802, 682, 073	27, 359, 041, 340	285, 742, 268, 440

International Claims

TABLE 93.—*Status of Class III awards of the Mixed Claims Commission, United States and Germany, and Private Law 509 as of June 30, 1965*

Description	Class III awards—over $100,000	Private Law 509, approved July 19, 1940
AWARDS [1]		
Principal of awards	$117,387,252.24	$160,000.00
Less amounts paid by Alien Property and others	266,072.77	
Interest to Jan. 1, 1928, as specified in awards	53,245,392.03	64,000.00
Interest thereon to date of payment or, if unpaid, to June 30, 1965, at 5 percent per annum, as specified in the Settlement of War Claims Act of 1928	81,519,235.26	178,192.02
Total due claimants	251,885,806.76	402,192.02
PAYMENTS		
Principal of awards	76,955,283.40	101,053.06
Interest at Jan. 1, 1928	53,245,392.03	64,000.00
Interest at 5 percent from Jan. 1, 1928, to date of payment	55,351,805.93	124,256.61
Total payments [2]	185,552,481.36	289,309.67
BALANCE DUE		
Principal of awards	40,165,896.07	58,946.94
Interest to Jan. 1, 1928		
Accrued interest from Jan. 1, 1928, through June 30, 1965	26,167,429.33	53,935.41
Balance due claimants	66,333,325.40	112,882.35
Total reimbursement for administrative expenses [3]	927,763.13	1,446.53

[1] Excludes Class I awards (on account of death and personal injury) which have been paid in full; and also Class II awards on which there remain balances totaling $42,830.84. For details concerning all classes of awards, including claims of U.S. Government, see 1962 annual report, pp. 138 and 826.

[2] Amounts shown are gross; deductions for administrative expenses are shown below (see footnote 3).

[3] Deductions of ½ of 1 percent are made from each payment to cover administrative expenses. These amounts are covered into the Treasury as miscellaneous receipts.

NOTE.—Ou Feb. 27, 1953, the German Government agreed to pay $97,500,000 (U.S. dollars) over a period of 25 years in full settlement of Germany's obligations on account of Class III awards and the award under Private Law 509. Through June 30, 1965, $45,500,000 had been paid under the agreement.

TABLE 94.—*Status of claims of American nationals against certain foreign governments as of June 30, 1965*

	Bulgaria	Hungary	Rumania	Poland	War Claims Fund
Awards certified to the Treasury: Number of awards	231	1,301	565	3,470	454
Amount of awards:					
Principal	$4,684,186.46	$58,181,408.34	$60,011,347.78	$34,030,549.35	$2,095,016.04
Interest	1,887,637.43	22,114,638.98	24,717,942.92	14,363,203.40	
Total	6,571,823.89	80,296,047.32	84,729,290.70	48,393,752.75	2,095,016.04
Deposits in claims funds	2,816,146.84	1,798,154.90	21,135,056.49	10,000,000.00 [1]	75,000,000.00 [2]
Statutory deduction for administrative expenses	140,807.34	89,907.79	1,056,752.81		
Amounts available for payment on awards	2,675,339.50	1,708,247.11	20,077,303.68	10,000,000.00	75,000,000.00
Payments on awards:					
Principal	2,672,854.30	1,639,097.23	20,048,525.97	2,279,746.72	90,200.00
Interest					
Combined principal and interest					
Balances in claims funds	2,485.20	69,149.88	29,777.71	7,720,253.28	74,909,800.00

[1] Statutory deductions of 5 percent are made from each payment to cover administrative expenses.

[2] Statutory deductions of 5 percent are made by the Foreign Claims Settlement Commission prior to the funds being transferred to the Treasury.

International Financial Transactions

TABLE 95.—*U.S. net monetary gold transactions with foreign countries and international institutions, fiscal years 1945–65*

[In millions of dollars at $35 per ounce. Negative figures represent net sales by the United States; positive figures, net purchases]

Country, etc.	1945-60	1961	1962	1963	1964	1965
Afghanistan	−5.3				(*)	(*)
Algeria					−15.0	
Argentina	914.9	−140.0	85.0		−30.0	
Austria	−174.2		−56.3	−136.3	−87.5	−62.5
Bank for International Settlements	−454.3	−59.0				
Belgium	−277.0	−90.1	−207.4			−101.7
Bolivia	18.8				−.1	−.1
Brazil	−25.4			103.6	54.4	54.3
Burma		−3.8	−5.0	−16.0		
Cambodia		−12.0	−3.1	−4.0	3.2	
Cameroon Republic				−1.9		
Canada	606.3		190.0			
Central African Republic				−.7		
Ceylon	−7.5				(*)	−4.3
Chad				−.7		
Chile	26.7	−8.6				−3.3
Colombia	69.1	−6.3		37.8	(*)	40.0
Congo (Leopoldville)			28.8		−3.1	1.6
Costa Rica			−2.3	−.6	−.6	−1.9
Cyprus			−2.0			
Dahomey				−.8		
Denmark	−63.4	−50.0		15.0		
Dominican Republic	−13.2		−3.1	−.2	−2.5	−.2
Ecuador	2.1			−5.5		
Egypt	−128.3		−8.5	−1.6	−10.4	−3.7
El Salvador	−21.6	6.4	−5.7		−2.2	−1.5
Finland	−13.7	−3.0			−5.0	
France	−63.4	−173.0	−140.6	−517.6	−517.7	−832.5
Gabon				−.7		
Germany, Federal Republic of	−375.6	−56.3			−200.0	−25.0
Ghana		−5.6				
Greece	−60.2	−47.0	−29.2			
Guinea					−2.8	
Iceland	−2.4		−7.1		(*)	
Indonesia	−88.0	−24.9	−.2			−.4
International Bank	18.8					
International Monetary Fund [1]	2 689.4	300.0	150.0			3 −258.8
Iran			−16.2	−5.9		−.1
Iraq		−29.8				−10.0
Ireland				(*)	(*)	−2.3
Israel	−5.5		−10.0		−9.0	
Italy	−463.1	100.0			200.0	−80.0
Ivory Coast				−1.5		
Japan	−187.5	−15.2				
Korea	−3.5					
Kuwait		−9.8		−12.5		

Footnotes at end of table.

TABLE 95.—*U.S. net monetary gold transactions with foreign countries and international institutions, fiscal years 1945-65*—Continued

[In millions of dollars at $35 per ounce]

Country, etc.	1945-60	1961	1962	1963	1964	1965
Laos		-1.9				
Lebanon	-21.8		-32.1	-21.0		-10.5
Madagascar					-2.3	
Mauretania					-.8	
Mexico	34.9	-20.0			-4.0	
Morocco		-21.0			-.1	
Netherlands	-402.0	-214.4	-24.9			-95.0
Nicaragua	19.9					-.1
Niger				-.8		
Nigeria			-20.0			
Norway	11.7					
Panama	-.1					-2.7
Peru	-7.2	-20.0		-.6	-10.6	
Philippines	38.8			24.6	9.6	9.7
Portugal	-41.6			-.7		
Republic of Congo (Brazzaville)						
Saudi Arabia	-4.1	-35.0	-25.1			
Senegal			-.8	-1.7		
Somalia				-1.9	(*)	-.1
South Africa	1,121.3					
Spain	63.2	-171.5	-204.1	-170.0	-2.0	-180.0
Sudan			-.1	(*)		-7.6
Surinam	-2.5	-2.5		2.5	2.5	
Sweden	246.4					
Switzerland	-412.5	-399.1	46.9	5.0	-30.0	-101.0
Syria	-10.4		-1.1	-.3	-3.0	-.7
Togo			-1.1			
Tunisia			-.5	-.5	-.5	-.1
Turkey	57.9	-8.6	-1.1	6.0	9.8	-30.7
United Kingdom	-202.5	-475.4	-711.6	63.8	535.0	241.2
Upper Volta				-.8		
Uruguay	-7.9	-3.8		8.0	-.1	-.2
Vatican City	5.4	-7.0			1.0	
Venezuela	-360.9					
Yugoslavia	-1.5	-15.9	-.7	-1.6	-2.3	-2.3
All other	-143.3	-6.3	r -6.7	-1.4	-1.9	-.6
Total	-105.8	-1,730.4	-1,025.7	-636.2	-128.0	-1,472.8

r Revised.
*Less than $50,000.
1 International Monetary Fund (IMF) figures prior to 1961 include gold purchases by the IMF on behalf of member countries for their payments to the IMF.
2 Includes $343.8 million payment to the International Monetary Fund. Pursuant to an act approved June 17, 1959 (22 U.S.C. 286e-1), the United States made payment of its increase in quota to the IMF, amounting to $1,375,000,000 on June 23, 1959. The payment was made in gold in the amount of $343,750,000.40, and in nonnegotiable, noninterest-bearing notes of the United States amounting to $1,031,249,999.60, in place of a like amount of currency.
3 Public Law 89-31, approved June 2, 1965, authorized an increase of $1,035 million in the quota of the United States in the IMF. On June 30, 1965, the United States made the required payment of 25 percent of its quota increase in gold in the amount of $258,750,004.03.

TABLE 96.—*Estimated gold reserves and dollar holdings of foreign countries and international institutions as of June 30, 1964, December 31, 1964, and June 30, 1965*

[In millions of dollars]

Area and country	June 30, 1964		December 31, 1964		June 30, 1965			
	Total gold and short-term dollars	U.S. Government bonds and notes	Total gold and short-term dollars	U.S. Government bonds and notes	Gold	Short-term dollar holdings	Total gold and short-term dollars	U.S. Government bonds and notes
Western Europe:								
Austria	902	3	923	3	663	222	885	3
Belgium	1,832	(*)	1,887	(*)	1,563	420	1,983	(*)
Denmark	r 289	14	428	14	97	271	368	14
Finland	167	1	212	1	85	104	189	1
France	5,003	7	5,392	7	4,433	1,213	5,646	7
Germany, Federal Republic of	6,616	1	6,258	1	4,378	1,540	5,918	1
Greece	r 227	(*)	252	(*)	84	151	235	(*)
Italy	3,039	1	3,729	1	2,384	1,440	3,824	1
Netherlands	r 1,824	5	2,055	5	1,756	278	2,034	5
Norway	188	131	215	98	31	232	263	68
Portugal	698	(*)	780	(*)	547	248	796	(*)
Spain	839	2	1,010	2	780	231	1,011	2
Sweden	615	130	833	40	202	719	921	24
Switzerland	3,737	77	4,095	79	2,789	1,299	4,088	87
Turkey	129	(*)	140	(*)	126	19	145	(*)
United Kingdom	r 4,153	402	4,020	414	2,226	2,489	4,715	502
Yugoslavia[1]	29		49		18	18	36	
Other[1]	485	48	459	49	−87	392	305	60
Total Western Europe	r 30,772	822	32,737	714	22,075	11,289	33,361	765
Canada	3,674	686	4,010	690	1,089	2,403	3,492	727
Latin American Republics:								
Argentina	424	(*)	362	(*)	68	310	378	(*)
Bolivia[2]	38	(*)	48	(*)	6	53	59	(*)
Brazil	r 294	(*)	350	(*)	62	340	402	(*)
Chile	227		219		42	198	240	
Colombia	r 238		267		31	159	190	
Costa Rica[2]	38	1	33	1	2	29	31	1
Cuba	11	(*)	12	(*)	n.a.		11	(*)
Dominican Republic[3]	44	(*)	59	(*)	3	47	50	(*)
Ecuador[2]	73		78		11	65	76	
El Salvador[2]	76		74		19	72	91	
Guatemala[2]	88		72		23	72	95	
Haiti[1][2]	18	(*)	15	(*)	1	15	16	(*)

Honduras [2]	26	(*)	26	(*)	(*)	33	33	1
Jamaica [2]	5	1	7	1	n.a.	8	8	(*)
Mexico [2]	817	1	904	1	165	687	852	1
Nicaragua [2]	52	(*)	42	(*)	(*)	67	67	(*)
Panama	105	(*)	99	(*)	(*)	124	124	(*)
Paraguay [2]	8	(*)	11	(*)	67	12	12	1
Peru	271	(*)	273	1	n.a.	263	330	(*)
Trinidad and Tobago [2]	5	(*)	7	(*)		9	9	(*)
Uruguay [2]	276	(*)	282	(*)	171	124	295	(*)
Venezuela	1,057	(*)	1,135	(*)	401	696	1,097	1
Unidentified [3]	16	1	6	1		−9	−9	
Total Latin American Republics	4,207	4	4,381	6	1,072	3,385	4,457	5
Asia:								
India	311	(*)	306	(*)	281	72	353	1
Indonesia	r77	1	73	1	35	23	58	(*)
Iran [3]	174	(*)	164	(*)	141	62	203	(*)
Israel [3]	191	2	189	5	56	111	167	(*)
Japan	r2,757	5	3,044	2	327	2,803	3,130	9
Korea	108	(*)	107	(*)	3	88	91	2
Pakistan [2]	69	(*)	76	(*)	53	25	78	
Philippines [2]	r230	2	256	(*)	31	250	281	
Syria [2]	25	(*)	27	(*)	19	3	22	
Thailand	529	(*)	562	(*)	96	496	592	
Other and unidentified [3][4]	r1,376	38	1,496	41	660	1,014	1,674	41
Total Asia [4]	r5,847	48	6,300	49	1,702	4,947	6,649	53
Africa:								
South Africa	645	(*)	621	(*)	375	49	424	(*)
United Arab Republic (Egypt)	196		163		139	22	161	
Other and unidentified [3]	r287	10	283	16	167	206	373	16
Total Africa	r1,128	10	1,067	16	681	277	958	16
Other countries:								
Australia	384	(*)	402	(*)	230	203	433	(*)
New Zealand [2]	20	(*)	13	1	1	20	21	1
Other and unidentified [3][4]	r330	26	361	25	27	366	393	27
Total other countries [4]	r734	26	776	26	258	589	847	28
Total foreign countries [4]	r46,362	1,596	49,271	1,501	26,877	22,887	49,764	1,594
International and regional [5]	7,294	1,068	7,162	904	r1,841	4,848	r6,689	799

Footnotes on next page.

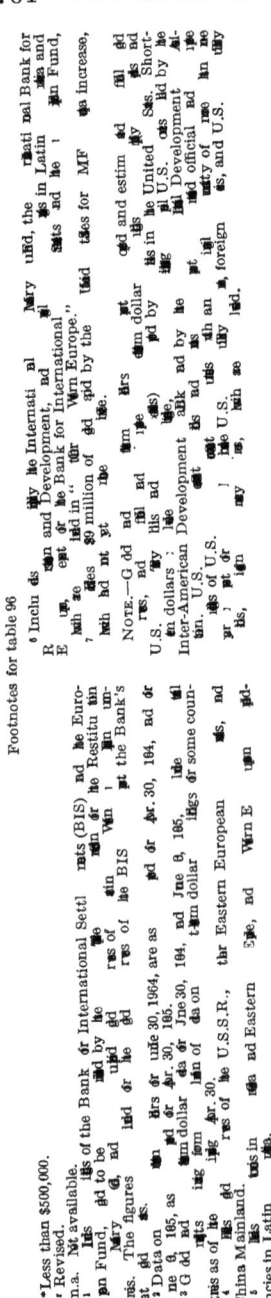

Footnotes for table 96

*Less than $500,000.
ʳ Revised.
n.a. Not available.

TABLE 97.—*U.S. gold stock, and holdings of convertible foreign currencies by U.S. monetary authorities, fiscal years 1952-65*

[In millions of dollars]

End of fiscal year or month	Total gold stock and foreign currency holdings	Gold stock [1]		Foreign currency holdings [3]
		Treasury	Total [2]	
1952	23,533	23,346	23,533	
1953	22,521	22,463	22,521	
1954	22,027	21,927	22,027	
1955	21,730	21,678	21,730	
1956	21,868	21,799	21,868	
1957	22,732	22,623	22,732	
1958	21,412	21,356	21,412	
1959	19,746	19,705	19,746	
1960	19,363	19,322	19,363	
1961	17,789	17,550	17,603	186
1962	17,081	16,435	16,527	554
1963	15,956	15,733	15,830	126
1964	15,805	15,461	15,623	182
1965	14,595	13,934	14,049	546
1964—July	15,840	15,462	15,629	211
August	15,890	15,460	15,657	233
September	15,870	15,463	15,643	227
October	15,702	15,461	15,606	96
November	16,324	15,386	15,566	758
December	15,903	15,388	15,471	432
1965—January	15,572	15,185	15,208	364
February	15,220	14,937	14,993	227
March	15,129	14,563	14,639	490
April	14,884	14,410	14,480	404
May	14,511	14,290	14,362	149
June	14,595	13,934	14,049	546

[1] Includes gold sold to the United States by the International Monetary Fund with the right of repurchase, the proceeds of which are invested by the Fund in U.S. Government securities; as of June 30, 1965, this amounted to $800 million. Of this amount, the United States purchased $200 million in 1956, $300 million in 1959, and $300 million in 1960.

[2] Includes gold in Exchange Stabilization Fund, which is not included in Treasury gold figures shown in the daily Treasury statement or in the *Circulation Statement of United States Money.*

[3] Includes holdings of Treasury and Federal Reserve System.

NOTE.—The United States also had a gold tranche position in the International Monetary Fund, amounting to $907.8 million as of June 30, 1965. In accordance with Fund policies the United States had the right to draw foreign currencies equivalent to this amount from the Fund virtually automatically if needed. Under appropriate circumstances, the United States could draw additional amounts equal to the U.S. quota of $4,125 million. In addition, the United States had a $258.8 million gold claim on the Fund a s n from a gold subscription to the Fund in June 1965, for a U.S. quota increase which had not yet become effective.

TABLE 98.—*International investment position of the United States, total December 31, 1950; by area, December 31, 1963 and 1964*

[In millions of dollars]

Type of investment	Total 1950	Total 1963	Total 1964	Western Europe 1963	Western Europe 1964	Canada 1963	Canada 1964	Latin American Republics 1963	Latin American Republics 1964	Other foreign countries 1963	Other foreign countries 1964	International institutions and unallocated 1963	International institutions and unallocated 1964
U.S. assets and investments abroad, total	31,539	88,301	98,720	24,825	27,801	21,712	24,596	15,727	17,335	21,127	24,211	4,910	4,777
Gold stock (not included in total)	22,820	15,596	15,471										
Private investments	19,004	66,513	75,419	17,000	19,529	21,706	24,591	12,352	13,798	12,647	14,598	2,808	2,903
Long-term	17,488	58,330	64,731	15,343	17,484	20,316	22,597	10,386	11,218	9,478	10,629	2,807	2,903
Direct	11,788	40,686	44,343	10,340	12,067	13,044	13,820	8,662	8,932	6,907	7,661	1,733	1,863
Foreign dollar bonds	1,692	7,335	8,218	60	30	3,835	4,710	24	556	1,286	1,369	1,074	1,040
Other foreign bonds	1,466	819	978	781	779	640	³106	65	167	95	71		
Foreign corporate stocks	1,175	5,145	5,270	2,319	2,065	2,461	2,948	965	67	300	190		
Banking loans	390	³2,830	4,051	1,081	1,699	³190	106	311	1,197	694	1,049		(⁶)
Other	977	1,615	1,871	762	844	246	539	1,966	299	196	189	1	(⁸)
Short-term assets and claims	1,516	8,183	10,688	1,657	2,045	1,390	1,994	1,689	2,380	2,737	4,069		(⁸)
Reported by banks	886	5,887	⁵7,846	923	1,210	638	913	377	2,126		3,597		
Other	630	2,296	2,842	734	835	752	1,081	3,375	454	432	472	1	1,874
U.S. Government credits and claims	12,535	21,788	23,301	7,825	8,272	6	5	3,134	3,537	8,480	9,613	2,102	1,874
Long-term debts	10,768	17,149	18,772	7,029	7,356			2,872	3,298	5,944	7,018	1,042	1,100
Repayable in dollars	n.a.	17,162	13,401	5,992	6,199			262	2,972	3,256	3,700	1,042	1,100
Repayable in foreign monies, etc.	n.a.	3,987	4,801	1,037	1,157			241	326	2,688	3,318		
Foreign currencies and claims	322	3,392	3,328	887	488	3	2		239	2,536	2,594	25	5
IMF gold tranche position and monetary authorities' holdings of dollars	1,445	1,247	1,201	209	428	3	3				1	1,035	769

Foreign assets and liabilities in the United States, total

Foreign assets and liabilities in the United States, total	17,635	51,486	56,842	16,237	33,363	7,772	8,304	4,792	5,461	6,129	6,976	2,937	2,38
Long-term	7,997	22,791	24,979	5,491	17,726	2,183	2,284	112	134	1,095	1,168	184	212
Direct	3,391	7,944	8,363	9,307	5,819	2,183	2,284	935	1,077	158	126	66	80
	2,925	702	13,835	460	10,159	1,490	1,726	77	80	687	793	117	130
	181	1,660	1,922	979	663	(*)	(*)	269	395	48	49	1	2
	1,500		1,859		1,085	209	77			202	200		
	9,638	28,695	31,863	13,619	15,637	3,890	4,117	3,399	3,775	5,034	5,808	2,753	2,526
Reported by banks	6,477	14,82	17,499	5,815	7,089	2,08	2,202	2,900	3,340	3,702	4,442	457	426
	5,751	14,157	16,688	5,415	6,656	1,937	2,117	2,786	3,226	3,562	4,263	457	426
	5,726	735	811	400	433	81	85	114	140	140	179		
	3,161	13,903	14,364	84	8,548	82	1,915	499	435	1,332	1,366	2,296	2,100
	1,508	8,720	8,799	71	5,585	61	867	225	170	1,143	1,157	954	1,020
	1,470	2,742	2,405	68	74	687	690	98	81	81	93	1,135	827
		893	2,440	98	1,111	25	329						
	183	1,448	1,720		1,138	9	29	176	184	108	116	207	253
	n.a.	18,756	20,029	9,600	10,540	1,798	1,841	1,436	1,647	3,169	3,475	2,753	2,526
	n.a.	5,713	7,179	2,360	3,274	1,688	1,836	377	404	1,308	1,665	(*)	(*)
	n.a.	4,226	4,655	1,659	1,823	424	440	1,886	1,724	557	668		

SOURCE.—Department of Commerce, *Survey of Current Business*, September 1965.

TABLE 99.—U.S. balance of payments, calendar year 1964 and January–June 1965

[In millions of dollars]

PART I—SEASONALLY ADJUSTED

	Total	1964				1965	
		Jan.-Mar.	Apr.-June	July-Sept.	Oct.-Dec.	Jan.-Mar.	Apr.-June
Goods and services, net balance	8,560	2,206	1,930	2,199	2,225	1,518	2,006
(Commercial goods and services balance)	(5,170)	(1,394)	(1,085)	(1,325)	(1,366)	(756)	(1,096)
Exports	25,288	6,149	6,067	6,382	6,690	5,586	6,762
(Commercial exports)	(22,476)	(5,478)	(5,384)	(5,640)	(5,974)	(5,012)	(6,071)
Imports	-18,619	-4,410	-4,599	-4,709	-4,901	-4,663	-5,469
(Trade balance)	(6,609)	(1,739)	(1,468)	(1,673)	(1,789)	(923)	(1,293)
(Commercial trade balance)	(3,857)	(1,068)	(785)	(931)	(1,073)	(349)	(578)
Military expenditures (net)	-2,062	-538	-529	-523	-472	488	-462
Investment income (net)	4,053	1,055	1,050	1,045	903	1,177	1,182
Other services	-100	-50	-59	4	5	-94	-87
Transfers and U.S. Government capital, net balance	-4,472	-1,018	-1,092	-1,128	-1,234	-1,028	-936
Remittances and pensions	-839	-209	-203	-207	-220	-224	-288
Government grants and capital, net	-4,208	-970	-1,049	-1,081	-1,108	-968	-1,132
(Dollar outflow)	(-702)	(-185)	(-186)	(-183)	(-198)	(-182)	(-178)
Repayments of Government loans, scheduled	575	161	160	160	94	164	184
U.S. private capital	-6,462	-1,327	-1,344	-1,569	-2,222	-1,533	-264
Direct investment	-2,376	-464	-540	-551	-821	-1,159	-882
New foreign securities	-1,063	-124	-183	-157	-599	-299	-217
Outstanding foreign securities and redemptions	386	148	78	73	87	89	96
Bank claims	-2,465	-655	-616	-426	-768	-435	369
Nonbank long-term	-356	-26	-58	-264	-8	6	60
Nonbank short-term	-588	-206	-25	-244	-113	265	310
Foreign capital	429	10	113	196	110	273	-221
Errors and omissions	-1,161	-288	-152	-291	-430	-10	-166
Balance on regular transactions [1]	-3,106	-417	-545	-593	-1,551	-780	119
Balance on overall transactions [1]	-2,798	-257	-582	-593	-1,366	-701	249
Less: net seasonal adjustments	----	-481	50	428	3	-521	47
Balance on overall transactions, seasonally unadjusted	-2,798	224	-632	-1,021	-1,369	-180	202

PART II—SEASONALLY UNADJUSTED

	1964					1965	
	Total	Jan.-Mar.	Apr.-June	July-Aug.	Sept.-Dec.	Jan.-Mar.	Apr.-June
Financing of overall balance: (seasonally unadjusted)	2,798	−224	632	1,021	1,369	180	−202
Increase in short-term official and banking liabilities and in foreign holdings of marketable U.S. Government bonds and notes	2,252	−173	207	748	1,470	−713	−270
Foreign holders other than official	1,554	227	114	562	651	199	−156
Foreign official holders	698	−400	93	186	819	−912	−114
Net sales of nonmarketable, medium-term, convertible securities	375	----	122	203	50	51	----
Decrease in U.S. monetary reserve assets	171	−51	303	70	−151	842	68
IMF gold tranche position	266	131	118	135	−118	68	−466
Convertible currencies	−220	−228	258	−45	−205	−58	−56
Gold	125	46	−73	−20	172	832	590

Source.—Department of Commerce, *Survey of Current Business*, September 1965.

[1] The overall deficit includes as receipts, in addition to those shown for regular transactions, sales of special nonmarketable, nonconvertible U.S. Treasury bonds to official foreigners, prepayments to the U.S. Government of official foreign debts, and prepayments for U.S. Government military exports.

TABLE 100.—*Assets and liabilities of the Exchange Stabilization Fund as of June 30, 1964 and 1965*

Assets and liabilities	June 30, 1964	June 30, 1965 ᵖ	Fiscal year 1965, increase, or decrease (−)
ASSETS			
Cash:			
Treasurer of the United States, checking account_____	$366, 183. 97	$1, 125, 668. 72	$759, 484. 75
Federal Reserve Bank of New York, special account__			
Imprest fund_____	500. 00	500. 00	
Total cash_____	366, 683. 97	1, 126, 168. 72	759, 484. 75
Special account of the Secretary of the Treasury in the Federal Reserve Bank of New York-gold (schedule 1)_	161, 614, 526. 20	115, 194, 324. 01	−46, 420, 202. 19
Foreign exchange due from foreign banks:			
Banco Central de la Republica Argentina_____	30, 100, 000. 00		−30, 100, 000. 00
Oesterreichische Nationalbank_____		3, 959. 41	3, 959. 41
Banque Nationale de Belgique_____	11, 412. 09	16, 102. 76	4, 690. 67
Banco do Brasil_____	25, 340, 000. 00	22, 340, 000. 00	−3, 000, 000. 00
Bank of Canada_____	568, 653. 64	717, 590. 35	148, 936. 71
Bank of Canada (IMF)_____		6, 000, 000. 00	6, 000, 000. 00
Banco Central de Chile_____	17, 400, 000. 00	23, 565, 000. 00	6, 165, 000. 00
Deutsche Bundesbank_____	1, 654, 587. 89	2, 517, 722. 97	863, 135. 08
Deutsche Bundesbank (IMF)_____	17, 409. 81	14, 787. 04	−2, 622. 77
Banco Central de la Republic Dominicana_____		6, 250, 000. 00	6, 250, 000. 00
Bank of England_____	3, 495, 856. 44	3, 490, 710. 91	−5, 145. 53
Banque de France (IMF)_____	1, 427, 033. 68		−1, 427, 033. 68
Banca d'Italia_____	63, 681. 37	63, 681. 37	
Banca d'Italia (IMF)_____		11, 500, 000. 00	11, 500, 000. 00
De Nederlandsche Bank_____	514, 833. 17	784, 598. 53	269, 765. 36
Sveriges Riksbank_____		4, 952. 77	4, 952. 77
Banque Nationale Suisse_____	153, 730. 43	347, 293. 86	193, 563. 43
Bank for International Settlements_____	21, 175. 47	3, 050, 583. 82	3, 029, 408. 35
Investments in U.S. Government securities (schedule 2)_	317, 064, 490. 54	256, 805, 515. 33	−60, 258, 975. 21
Investments in foreign securities (schedule 2)_____	49, 772, 557. 59	60, 752, 715. 32	10, 980, 157. 73
Accrued interest receivable_____	745, 646. 91	2, 347, 299. 71	1, 601, 652. 80
Accounts receivable_____	ʳ 428, 838. 88	220, 555. 21	−208, 283. 67
Deferred charges_____	191, 261. 90	70, 123. 52	−121, 138. 38
Office equipment and fixtures, less allowance for depreciation_____	55, 909. 20	60, 545. 52	4, 636. 32
Land and structures_____	150, 000. 00	150, 000. 00	
Total assets_____	ʳ611, 158, 289. 18	517, 394, 231. 13	−93, 764, 058. 05
LIABILITIES AND CAPITAL			
Liabilities: ¹			
Vouchers payable_____		30, 890. 04	30, 890. 04
Employees' payroll allotment account, U.S. savings bonds_____	3, 593. 62	3, 495. 01	−98. 61
Accounts payable_____	ʳ 329, 645. 77	324, 960. 64	−4, 685. 13
Special Deposit Accounts_____	ʳ 5, 730, 956. 25	15, 500, 000. 00	9, 769, 043. 75
Advance from U.S. Treasury (U.S. drawing on IMF)_	250, 000, 000. 00	126, 000, 000. 00	−124, 000, 000. 00
Total liabilities_____	ʳ256, 064, 195. 64	141, 859, 345. 69	−114, 204, 849. 95
Capital:			
Capital account_____	200, 000, 000. 00	200, 000, 000. 00	
Cumulative net income (schedule 3)_____	ʳ155, 094, 093. 54	175, 534, 885. 44	20, 440, 791. 90
Total capital_____	ʳ355, 094, 093. 54	375, 534, 885. 44	20, 440, 791. 90
Total liabilities and capital_____	ʳ611, 158, 289. 18	517, 394, 231. 13	−93, 764, 058. 05

¹ For contingent liabilities under outstanding stabilization agreements, see schedule 4.
ᵖ Preliminary.
ʳ Revised.

TABLE 100.—*Assets and liabilities of the Exchange Stabilization Fund as of June 30, 1964 and 1965*—Continued

SCHEDULE 1.—SPECIAL ACCOUNT OF THE SECRETARY OF THE TREASURY IN THE FEDERAL RESERVE BANK OF NEW YORK—GOLD

Gold accounts	June 30, 1964		June 30, 1965 ᵖ	
	Ounces	Dollars	Ounces	Dollars
Federal Reserve Bank of New York___	460, 147. 948	$16, 105, 178. 18	352, 544. 881	$12, 339, 070. 86
U.S. Assay Offioe, New York_____	1, 595. 513	55, 847. 86	2, 904, 463. 905	101, 656, 241. 61
Federal Reserve Bank of New York, Account No. 4_____	4, 147, 511. 943	145, 453, 500. 16	34, 210. 013	1, 199, 011. 54
Total gold_____	4, 609, 255. 404	161, 614, 526. 20	3, 291, 218. 799	115, 194, 324. 01

ᵖ Preliminary.

SCHEDULE 2.—INVESTMENTS HELD BY THE EXCHANGE STABILIZATION FUND, JUNE 30, 1965 ᵖ

Securities	Face value	Cost (in dollars)	Average price	Accrued interest
U.S. Government securities, public issues:				
Treasury bonds:				
2½% of 1964–69 (dated Apr. 15, 1943)___	$2, 200, 000. 00	$2, 199, 625. 00	99. 98295	$2, 254. 10
2½% of 1964–69 (dated Sept. 15, 1943)___	400, 000. 00	399, 875. 00	99. 96875	409. 83
2½% of 1965–70_____	10, 000, 000. 00	10, 000, 000. 00	100. 00000	72, 690. 21
2½% of 1966–71_____	2, 400, 000. 00	2, 398, 843. 75	99. 95182	17, 445. 65
2½% of 1967–72 (dated Nov. 15, 1945)___	10, 000, 000. 00	10, 000, 000. 00	100. 00000	10, 245. 90
Total public issues_____	25, 000, 000. 00	24, 998, 343. 75	_____	103, 045. 69
Special issues, Exchange Stabilization Fund series:				
3.65% maturing July 1, 1965_____	216, 305, 515. 33	216, 305, 515. 33	_____	2, 244, 254. 02
3.921% maturing July 1, 1965_____	15, 500, 000. 00	15, 500, 000. 00	_____	_____
Total special issues_____	231, 805, 515. 33	231, 805, 515. 33	_____	2, 244, 254. 02
Total_____	256, 805, 515. 33	256, 803, 859. 08	_____	2, 347, 299. 71
Foreign securities:				
British Government, Treasury bills_____	£ 8, 915, 000/0/0	24, 500, 454. 22	_____	_____
Republic of Germany, Treasury bills____	DM 128, 400, 000. 00	31, 929, 071. 00	_____	_____
Republic of Germany, Treasury bills (IMF)_____	DM 17, 400, 000. 00	4, 323, 190. 10	_____	_____
Total foreign securities_____	_____	60, 752, 715. 32	_____	_____

ᵖ Preliminary.

TABLE 100.—*Assets and liabilities of the Exchange Stabilization Fund as of June 30, 1964 and 1965*—Continued

SCHEDULE 3.—INCOME AND EXPENSE

Classification	Jan. 31, 1934, through—	
	June 30, 1964	June 30, 1965 ᵖ
Income:		
Profits on transactions in:		
Gold and exchange (including profits from handling charges on gold)..	$138, 507, 284. 87	$138, 704, 308. 37
Sale of silver to U.S. Treasury	3, 473, 362. 29	3, 473, 362. 29
Silver	102, 735. 27	102, 735. 27
Investments	2, 638, 546. 28	2, 638, 546. 28
Miscellaneous	ʳ 117, 155. 70	132, 850. 91
Interest on:		
Investments	ʳ 31, 433, 158. 99	51, 356, 155. 59
Foreign balances	16, 200, 776. 18	20, 572, 512. 96
Total income	ʳ 192, 473, 019. 58	216, 980, 471. 67
Expense:		
Personnel compensation and benefits	ʳ 28, 474, 358. 64	31, 590, 356. 23
Travel	1, 748, 056. 96	1, 973, 064. 47
Transportation of things	2, 169, 165. 65	2, 308, 880. 07
Rent, communications, and utilities	871, 452. 39	942, 213 09
Supplies and materials	235, 071. 78	266, 131. 83
Other	ʳ 3, 880, 820. 62	4, 364, 940. 54
Total expense	ʳ 37, 378, 926. 04	41, 445, 586. 23
Cumulative net income	ʳ 155, 094, 093. 54	175, 534, 885. 44

ᵖ Preliminary.　ʳ Revised.

SCHEDULE 4.—CURRENT U.S. STABILIZATION AGREEMENTS, JUNE 30, 1965

Country	Effective dates			Amounts (in millions)		
	Original	Renewal	Expiration	Original agreement	Advances	Repayments
Argentina	June 7, 1962 ¹	Mar. 27, 1963	Oct. 6, 1963 ²	$50	$50	$50
Brazil	May 16, 1961		May 15, 1963 ³	70	130	107. 7
Brazil	Feb. 23, 1965		Jan. 12, 1966	53. 7		
Chile	Jan. 31, 1963		Jan. 30, 1964 ²	10	10	6. 4
Chile	Mar. 13, 1964		Feb. 4, 1965 ²	15	12	1. 4
Chile	Feb. 4, 1965		Jan. 5, 1966	16. 1	9. 4	
Dominican Republic.	Aug. 10, 1964		Aug. 10, 1965	6. 3	6. 3	
Mexico	Jan. 1, 1964		Dec. 31, 1965	75		

¹ Agreement dated Jan. 1, 1959 terminated.　² No further drawings permitted after expiration.

TABLE 101.—*Summary of receipts, withdrawals, and balances of foreign currencies acquired by the United States without purchase with dollars, fiscal year 1965*

[In U.S. dollar equivalents]

Balance held by Treasury Department, July 1, 1964		$1,627,675,015.55
Receipts:		
Sale of surplus agricultural commodities pursuant to:		
Title I, Public Law 480, Agricultural Trade Development and Assistance Act of 1954, as amended (7 U.S.C. 1704-5)	$1,189,075,572.06	
Commodity Credit Corporation Charter Act (15 U.S.C. 713a)	475,087.89	
Loans and other assistance:		
Title I, Public Law 480, loan repayments, including interest:		
Section 104(e), loans to private enterprises	18,170,354.67	
Section 104(g), loans to foreign governments	75,077,170.99	
Section 612, Foreign Assistance Act of 1961 (22 U.S.C. 2362) loan repayments including interest:		
Development Loan Fund and Mutual Security Program	132,129,334.88	
Informational media guaranties (22 U.S.C. 1442), principal	2,623,549.38	
Lend-lease and surplus property agreements (22 U.S.C. 412b), and (50 App. U.S.C. 1641(b) (1), 1946 ed.) [1]	13,126,071.85	
Bilateral agreements 5% and 10% counterpart funds (22 U.S.C. 1852(b)) [1]	7,788,541.61	
Interest on public deposits	28,418,365.96	
All other sources	45,415,118.22	
Total collections		1,512,299,167.51
Total available		3,139,974,183.06
Withdrawals:		
Sold for dollars, proceeds credited to: [2]		
Miscellaneous receipts of the general fund	129,536,074.11	
Commodity Credit Corporation, Agriculture	193,042,120.09	
Informational media guaranties fund, USIA	2,632,273.89	
Other fund accounts	16,005,651.92	
Total sold for dollars	341,216,120.01	
Requisitioned for use without reimbursement to the Treasury pursuant to:		
Section 104, Public Law 480, as amended (7 U.S.C. 1704)	1,200,084,603.56	
Other authority	90,082.32	
Total requisitioned without reimbursement	1,200,174,685.88	
Total withdrawals		1,541,390,805.89
Adjustment for rate differences		−14,736,978.32
Balances held by Treasury Department, June 30, 1965		1,583,846,398.85
Analysis of balance held by Treasury Department June 30, 1965:		
Proceeds for credit to miscellaneous receipts of the general fund		478,869,257.22
Proceeds for credit to agency accounts.		
Commodity Credit Corporation, Agriculture		423,246,754.87
Informational media guaranties fund, USIA		322,651.22
Other		92,861.29
For program allocations:		
Section 104, Title I, Public Law 480, as amended		679,939,366.80
Section 612, Foreign Assistance Act of 1961 (22 U.S.C. 2362)		1,375,507.45
Total		[3] 1,583,846,398.85

Footnotes at end of table.

TABLE 101.—*Summary of receipts, withdrawals, and balances of foreign currencies acquired by the United States without purchase with dollars, fiscal year 1965*—Con.

[In U.S. dollar equivalents]

Balances held by other executive agencies June 30, 1965, for purpose of:	
Economic and technical assistance under Mutual Security Act_____	$33, 585, 995. 06
Programmed uses under Agricultural Trade Development and Assistance Act____	274, 253, 582. 30
Military family housing in foreign countries_____	5, 031, 631. 71
Trust agreements with foreign countries_____	20, 664, 627. 56
Other_____	914, 913, 089. 78
Total_____	1, 248, 448, 926. 41
Grand total_____	2, 832, 295, 325. 26

¹ Collections under lend-lease and surplus property agreements will continue to be made until such agreements are satisfied, although the act originally authorizing such action has been repealed.
² Dollars acquired from the sale of foreign currencies are derived from charges against the dollar appropriations of the Federal agencies which use the currencies. These dollar proceeds are credited to either miscellaneous receipts or other appropriate accounts on the books of the Treasury.
³ Represents the dollar value of currencies held in the accounts of the Treasury Department only. Currencies transferred to agency accounts pursuant to requisitions submitted to the Treasury Department, or as otherwise authorized, are accounted for by the U.S. Government agencies. Balances held by executive departments and agencies as of June 30, 1965, are stated at end of summary.

NOTE.—For the purpose of providing a common denominator, the currencies of 82 foreign countries are herein stated in U.S. dollar equivalents. It should not be assumed that dollars in amounts equal to the balances shown are actually available. The dollar equivalents are calculated at varying rates of exchange. Foreign currencies deposited under certain provisions of Public Law 480 and the Mutual Security Act were converted at deposit rates provided for in the international agreements with the respective countries. The greater portion of these currencies is available to agencies, without reimbursement pursuant to legislative authority and, when disbursed to the foreign governments, will generally be accepted by them at the deposit or collection rates. Currencies available for sale for dollars and certain other U.S. uses were converted at market rates of exchange in effect on the date of the sale and market rates in effect at the end of the month for transactions during the month, these market rates being those used to pay U.S. obligations. The closing balances were converted at the June 30, 1965, market rates.
For detailed data on collections and withdrawals by country and program, see Part V of the *Combined Statement of Receipts, Expenditures and Balances of the United States Government for the Fiscal Year Ended June 30, 1965.*

TABLE 102.—*Balances of foreign currencies acquired by the United States without purchase with dollars, June 30, 1965*

Country	Currency	In Treasury accounts		In agency accounts	
		Foreign currency	Dollar equivalent	Foreign currency	Dollar equivalent
Afghanistan_____	Afghani_____	189, 000. 08	$2, 625. 00	30, 345, 416. 39	$421, 464. 12
Argentina_____	Peso_____	69, 777, 918. 48	408, 058. 00	102, 804. 64	601. 19
Australia_____	Pound_____	_____	_____	854. 12	1, 913. 36
Austria_____	Schilling_____	−111, 070. 48	−4, 315. 09	169, 292. 82	6, 577. 03
Belgium_____	Franc_____	−671, 111. 00	−13, 516. 84	671, 111. 00	13, 516. 84
Bermuda_____	Pound_____	−294. 21	−821. 81	299. 21	835. 78
Bolivia_____	Peso_____	9, 829, 531. 19	827, 401. 61	134, 681, 623. 80	11, 336, 837. 03
Brazil_____	Cruzeiro_____	22, 165, 105, 726. 10	12, 145, 263. 42	100, 172,646,913.60	54, 889, 121. 60
Burma_____	Kyat_____	120, 312, 692. 79	25, 446, 847. 03	65, 616, 502. 68	13, 878, 278. 91
Cambodia_____	Riel_____	−293, 398. 80	−8, 506. 78	11, 228, 338. 22	325, 553. 44
Ceylon_____	Rupee_____	12, 302, 755. 88	2, 585, 699. 01	58, 462, 136. 41	12, 287, 124. 09
Chile_____	Escudo_____	1, 879. 60	69, 889. 15	1, 140, 185. 77	314, 968. 44
China_____	N.T. Dollar___	624, 319, 132. 18	15, 607, 978. 30	967, 262, 860. 90	24, 181, 571. 53
Colombia_____	Peso_____	8, 571, 803. 19	502, 745. 05	5, 847, 113. 60	342, 939. 50
Congo, Republic of the.	Franc_____	1, 028, 226, 496. 00	6, 854, 843. 30	933, 353, 862. 00	6, 222, 359. 08
Costa Rica_____	Colon_____	_____	_____	161, 870. 61	24, 451. 75
Cyprus_____	Pound_____	−327. 41	−918. 40	552, 920. 15	1, 550, 968. 21
Czechoslovakia___	Koruna_____	7, 161, 557. 00	994, 660. 69	11, 354. 56	791. 26
Denmark_____	Krone_____	_____	_____	28, 608. 63	4, 133. 00
Dominican Republic.	Peso_____	−4, 602. 94	−4, 602. 94	4, 602. 94	4, 602. 94
Ecuador_____	Sucre_____	3, 953, 801. 90	213, 719. 02	1, 227, 312. 84	66, 341. 23
Ethiopia_____	E. Dollar_____	21, 238. 68	8, 560. 53	2, 387, 370. 00	962, 261. 56
Finland_____	New Markka__	5, 103, 052. 36	1, 590, 231. 34	6, 872, 190. 34	2, 141, 536. 41
France_____	Franc_____	1, 772, 095. 12	361, 652. 07	343, 476. 73	70, 097. 29
Germany, Federal Republic of.	W.D. Mark___	−3, 134, 061. 76	−788, 244. 91	16, 729, 956. 48	4, 489, 000. 18

TABLE 102.—*Balances of foreign currencies acquired by the United States without purchase with dollars, June 30, 1965*—Continued

| Country | Currency | In Treasury accounts | | In agency accounts | |
		Foreign currency	Dollar equivalent	Foreign currency	Dollar equivalent
Germany, East...	E.D. Mark...	32,042.69	$2,584.09		
Ghana...........	Pound.........	−528.57	−1,483.90	528.57	$1,483 90
Greece..........	Drachma......	15,384,799.35	512,826.64	527,915,191.80	17,597,173.06
Guatemala......	Quetzal.......			52,627.94	52,627.94
Guinea..........	Franc.........	1,216,464,498.00	4,934,947.26	4,192,397,364.00	17,007,697.20
Hong Kong......	H.K. Dollar...	−77,910.33	−13,568.50	77,910.33	13,568.50
Hungary........	Forint........	670,560.00	13,970.00	52,549.00	1,094.77
Iceland.........	Krona........	56,217,449.00	1,308,904.52	7,935,915.95	184,771.03
India...........	Rupee........	2,770,126,086.62	582,571,206.45	2,416,419,522.65	508,184,967.97
(Nepal, U.S.D.O.).	Indian Rupee_	1,211,022.38	254,683.99	9,835,841.98	2,068,526.18
Indonesia.......	Rupiah.......	2,955,726,510.79	5,718,178.58	14,993,117,704.81	29,005,838.08
Iran............	Rial.........	332,120,705.45	4,428,276.07	850,779,307.75	11,343,724.10
Iraq............	Dinar........	−113.08	−316.22	113.08	316.22
Ireland.........	Pound........			645.48	1,805.02
Israel..........	Pound........	105,688,147.80	35,229,382.58	60,736,091.89	20,245,363.97
Italy...........	Lira.........	−162,932,554.00	−260,692.09	1,644,196,117.00	2,630,713.79
Ivory Coast.....	CFA Franc...	16,147,650.00	65,908.78	463,536,558.00	1,891,985.96
Jamaica.........	Pound........	−302.64	−846.79	450.68	1,260.99
Japan..........	Yen..........	9,355,197,280.33	25,986,659.11	5,193,923.85	14,427.57
Jordan.........	Dinar........	−562.67	−1,578.75	779.88	2,188.21
Kenya..........	E.A. Shilling_	−233,125.60	−32,728.57	233,125.60	32,728.57
Korea..........	Won..........	1,582,385,927.70	5,834,756.36	1,463,334,051.05	5,395,774.52
Laos...........	Kip..........			376,707,365.12	1,569,614.02
Lebanon........	Pound........	557,728.88	181,080.80	12,731.26	4,133.53
Libya..........	Pound........	37,816.67	105,485.83	44,299.99	123,570.40
Malaysia........	Malayan Dollar.	−6,993.36	−2,298.93	6,993.36	2,298.93
Mali...........	Franc........	1,123,077.00	4,612.23	10,690,888.00	43,905.08
Mexico.........	Peso.........	−46,277.67	−3,705.18	46,277.67	3,705.18
Morocco........	Dirham.......	16,603,278.94	3,308,085.06	9,978,828.92	1,988,210.58
Nepal..........	Nepalese Rupee.	348,760.10	46,040.94		
Netherlands.....	Guilder......	6,801,996.31	1,889,443.45	3,282,806.42	911,890.68
New Zealand.....	Pound........	−226.14	−631.85	226.14	631.85
Nigeria.........	Pound........	47,623.42	133,175.11	573.42	1,603.53
Norway.........	Krone........			11,730.79	1,644.12
Pakistan........	Rupee........	763,526,614.18	158,803,372.33	256,311,941.60	53,309,472.04
(Afghanistan, U.S.D.O.).	Pakistan Rupee.			427,465.15	88,907.06
Paraguay........	Guarani......	55,660,525.07	441,750.20	859,559,460.92	6,821,900.49
Peru...........	Sol..........	16,179,286.85	603,704.73	220,400,112.04	8,223,884.78
Philippines.....	Peso.........	−2,120,455.75	−543,706.60	49,231,838.37	12,623,548.31
Poland.........	Zloty........	11,869,025,379.01	494,542,724.13	248,444.96	10,351.87
Portugal........	Escudo.......	1,467,328.26	51,144.24	99,721.74	3,475.84
Senegal........	C.F.A. Franc_	115,086,475.00	469,740.71	359,753,373.00	1,468,381.12
Somali.........	Somalo.......			10,561.65	1,487.56
South Africa....	Rand........	−34.45	−48.32	34.45	48.32
Southern Rhodesia.	Pound........	−539.13	−1,518.26	16,195.56	45,608.45
Spain..........	Peseta.......	−95,210,388.78	−1,589,223.64	346,241,050.68	5,787,926.37
Sudan..........	Pound........	1,447,086.60	4,178,708.05	3,770,328.68	10,887,463.69
Sweden.........	Krona........	−19,887.54	−3,855.67	19,887.54	3,855.67
Switzerland.....	Franc........	1,120.31	258.13	74,622.22	17,194.06
Syrian Arab Republic.	Pound........	5,890,042.94	1,419,287.45	47,748,880.36	11,505,754.30
Thailand........	Baht.........	−230,172.04	−11,146.35	19,646,274.40	951,393.44
Tunisia.........	Dinar........	4,234,762.96	8,128,143.89	4,931,125.58	9,464,732.40
Turkey.........	Lira.........	118,757,450.09	13,195,272.23	209,832,990.29	23,314,776.68
United Arab Republic.	Pound........	45,340,263.38	104,494,730.09	66,712,374.22	153,750,574.37
United Kingdom.	Pound........	−1,450,643.84	−4,052,077.78	2,784,082.49	7,776,766.73
Uruguay........	Peso.........	6,583,641.13	112,540.88	2,071,832.83	35,415.95
Venezuela.......	Bolivar......	1,515,034.80	338,177.41		
Vietnam........	Piastre......	−80,748,196.90	−1,109,635.80	698,688,645.54	9,601,328.09
Yugoslavia......	Dinar........	49,024,839,726.00	65,366,452.97	134,165,690,697.00	178,857,587.60
Total........			[1]1,583,846,398.84		[1]1,248,448,926.41

[1] For the purpose of providing a common denominator, the currencies of 82 foreign countries are herein stated in U.S. dollar equivalents. It should not be assumed that dollars in amounts equal to the balances shown are actually available.

Indebtedness of Foreign Governments

TABLE 103.—*Status of indebtedness of foreign governments to the United States arising from World War I as of June 30, 1965*

	Original Indebtedness	Interest through June 30, 1965	Total	Cumulative payments		Amount due June 30, 1965		
				Principal	Interest	Total	Unmatured principal	Principal and interest due and unpaid
Armenia	$11,959,917.49	$27,391,079.24	$39,350,996.73			$39,350,996.73		$39,350,996.73
Austria [1]	26,843,148.66	44,058.93	26,887,207.59			26,024,539.59	$2,647,878.93	23,376,660.66
Belgium	419,837,630.37	302,252,720.47	722,090,350.84	$862,668.00	$33,033,642.87	669,899,077.60	212,680,000.00	457,219,077.60
Cuba	10,000,000.00	2,286,751.58	12,286,751.58	19,167,630.37	2,286,751.58			
Czechoslovakia	185,071,023.07	101,885,121.53	286,956,144.60	10,000,000.00	304,178.09	266,822,052.34	89,210,000.00	177,612,052.34
Estonia	16,466,012.87	20,724,720.01	37,190,732.88	19,829,914.17	1,248,432.07	35,942,300.81	9,705,000.00	26,237,300.81
Finland	8,999,999.97	11,134,230.96	20,134,230.93	[2]3,928,999.97	[2]11,134,230.96	5,071,000.00	5,071,000.00	
France	4,089,689,588.18	2,977,318,798.39	7,067,008,386.57	226,039,588.18	260,036,302.82	6,580,932,495.57	1,892,453,655.80	4,688,478,839.77
Great Britain	4,802,181,641.56	6,676,331,958.11	11,478,513,599.67	434,181,641.56	1,590,672,656.18	9,453,659,301.93	2,616,000,000.00	6,837,659,301.93
Greece [3]	32,499,922.67	17,217,468.44	49,717,391.11	983,922.67	3,143,133.34	45,590,335.10	8,750,000.00	36,840,335.10
Hungary [4]	1,982,555.50	2,642,705.46	4,625,260.96	73,995.50	482,924.26	4,068,341.20	1,175,270.00	2,893,071.20
Italy	2,042,364,319.28	309,948,970.22	2,352,313,289.50	37,464,319.28	63,365,560.88	2,251,483,409.34	1,246,400,000.00	1,005,083,409.34
Latvia	6,888,664.20	8,772,224.91	15,660,889.11	9,200.00	752,349.07	14,899,340.04	4,091,800.00	10,807,540.04
Liberia	26,000.00	10,471.56	36,471.56	26,000.00	10,471.56			
Lithuania	6,432,465.00	8,180,979.48	14,613,444.48	234,783.00	1,003,173.58	13,375,487.90	3,739,352.00	9,636,135.90
Nicaragua [5]	141,950.36	26,625.48	168,575.84	141,950.36	26,625.48			
Poland	207,344,297.37	265,112,224.38	472,456,521.75	[6]1,287,297.37	21,359,000.18	449,810,224.20	124,269,000.00	325,541,224.20
Rumania	68,359,192.45	47,631,425.46	115,990,617.91	[7]4,498,632.02	[7]292,375.20	111,199,610.69	34,066,000.00	77,133,610.69
Russia	192,601,297.37	456,829,549.79	649,430,847.16		[8]8,750,311.88	640,680,535.28		640,680,535.28
Yugoslavia	63,577,712.55	21,511,527.92	85,089,240.47	1,952,712.55	636,059.14	82,500,468.78	37,766,000.00	44,734,468.78
Total	12,193,267,338.92	11,257,253,612.32	23,450,520,951.24	760,673,255.00	1,998,538,179.14	20,691,309,517.10	6,288,024,956.73	14,403,284,560.37

[1] The Federal Republic of Germany has recognized liability for securities falling due between Mar. 12, 1938, and May 8, 1945.

[2] $6,360,250.26 has been made available for educational exchange programs with Finland pursuant to 20 U.S.C. 222–224.

[3] Includes $11,336,000.00 of this debt which has been refunded by the agreement of May 28, 1964. The agreement has not been ratified by Congress.

[4] Interest payments from Dec. 15, 1932, to June 15, 1937, were paid in pengo equivalent.

[5] The indebtedness of Nicaragua was canceled pursuant to the agreement of Apr. 14, 1938.

[6] Excludes claim allowance of $1,813,428.69 dated Dec. 15, 1929.

[7] Excludes payment of $100,000.00 on June 14, 1940, as a token of good faith.

[8] Principally proceeds from liquidation of Russian assets in the United States.

TABLE 104.—*Status of German World War I indebtedness as of June 30, 1965*

	Funded indebtedness	Interest	Total	Payments	Amount due June 30, 1965		
					Principal	Interest	Total
Agreements of June 23, 1930, and May 26, 1932:							
Mixed claims (reichsmarks)	[1] 1,632,000,000.00	488,070,000.00	2,120,070,000.00	87,210,000.00	1,550,400,000.00	482,460,000.00	[2] 2,032,860,000.00
Army costs (reichsmarks)	1,048,100,000.00	504,031,145.25	1,552,131,145.25	51,456,406.25	997,500,000.00	503,174,739.00	[2] 1,500,674,739.00
Total (reichsmarks)	2,680,100,000.00	962,101,145.25	3,672,201,145.25	138,666,406.25	2,547,900,000.00	985,634,739.00	[3] 3,533,534,739.00
U.S. dollar equivalent	[4] $1,080,884,330.00	$399,554,704.09	$1,480,439,034.09	[5] $333,587,809.69	$1,027,568,070.00	$397,506,490.24	$1,425,074,560.24
Agreement of February 27, 1953—							
Mixed claims (U.S. dollars)	[1] 97,500,000.00	------	97,500,000.00	45,500,000.00	52,000,000.00	------	52,000,000.00

[1] Agreement of Feb. 27, 193, provided for cancellation of 24 bonds totaling 489,600,000 reichs mks and is sue of 26 dollar bns his bmg $97,500,000.00. The dollar bonds mre serially over 25 years beginning Apr. 1, 1953. All unmatured bonds are of $4,000,000.00 denomination.

[2] Includes past due amounts (in reichsmarks) as follows:

	Principal	Interest
Mixed claims	897,600,000.00	482,460,000.00
Army costs	936,900,000.00	497,884,750.00
Moratorium on Army costs	25,300,000.00	5,289,989.00

[3] Includes 4,027,611.95 reichsmarks paid in lieu of dollars.
[4] Converted to U.S. dollars at 40.33 cents to the reichsmark.
[5] Payments converted to U.S. dollars at rate applicable at the time of payment, i.e., 40.33 or 23.82 cents to the reichsmark.

TABLE 105.—*Outstanding indebtedness of foreign countries on U.S. Government credits (exclusive of indebtedness arising from World War I) as of June 30, 1965, by area, country, and major program* [1]

[In millions of dollars]

Area and country	Under Export-Import Bank Act	Under foreign assistance (and related) acts	Under Agricultural Trade Development and Assistance Act			Lend-lease, surplus property, and grant settlements[2]	Other credits	Total
			Loans of foreign currencies		Long-term dollar credits			
			To foreign governments	To private enterprises				
Western Europe:								
Austria	28		25			(*)		53
Belgium and Luxembourg	23	51				6		80
Cyprus								(*)
Denmark	1	31	(*)					33
Finland	47		19	2		7		75
France	186	5		2		414		607
Germany, Federal Republic of		14				211		225
Greece	13	82	49	4	15	10		174
Iceland	(*)	19	10		1	(*)		31
Ireland		113						113
Italy	111	(*)		2		18		130
Liechtenstein	(*)							(*)
Netherlands		66						66
Norway	4	25						29
Portugal	55	27	3		19			105
Spain	146	67	198					411
Turkey	16	424	144	39				623
United Kingdom		344				494	3,149	3,987
Yugoslavia	61	163	264		142	(*)		629
European Atomic Energy Community	19						20	39
European Coal and Steel Community		73						73
North Atlantic Treaty Organization (Maintenance Supply Services Agency)		(*)						(*)
Total Western Europe	710	1,505	713	48	178	1,161	3,169	7,484
Other Europe:								
Czechoslovakia						5		5
Hungary						7		7
Poland	16	56				15		86
Soviet Union						195		195
Total other Europe	16	56				222		293
Asia:								
Afghanistan	32	15						47
Burma		24	8			1		33
Ceylon		5	5					10
China-Taiwan	28	150	19	3	17	116		334
India	266	1,538	999	52		3		2,858
Indonesia	86	43	15			33		177
Iran	25	161	23	2	8	24		243
Iraq	5				11			16
Israel	58	158	163	12				391
Japan	274		103			409		787
Jordan	2	1						2
Korea		37		(*)		21		58
Lebanon	2	4						6
Malaysia	(*)	16						16
Nepal	(*)	(*)	2					2
Pakistan	22	708	216	9				955
Philippines	45	40	7	3		(*)		96
Ryukyu Islands					8		9	17
Saudi Arabia		2						2
Syria		3	7		(*)			10
Thailand	23	51	4					77
Vietnam		79		1				79
Total Asia	868	3,033	1,571	82	45	607	9	6,215
Latin America:								
Argentina	281	64	2					347
Bolivia	34	30	8		4			76
Brazil	723	245	44			1		1,014
Chile	181	273	30	(*)	33			517
Colombia	69	181	11	2	5			269

Footnotes at end of table.

TABLE 105.—*Outstanding indebtedness of foreign countries on U.S. Government credits (exclusive of indebtedness arising from World War I) as of June 30, 1965, by area, country, and major program* [1]—Continued

[In millions of dollars]

Area and country	Under Export-Import Bank Act	Under foreign assistance (and related) acts	Under Agricultural Trade Development and Assistance Act			Lend-lease, surplus property, and grant settlements [2]	Other credits	Total
			Loans of foreign currencies		Long-term dollar credits			
			To foreign governments	To private enterprises				
Latin America—Continued								
Costa Rica	16	19						34
Cuba	36							36
Dominican Republic	5	37			12			55
Ecuador	11	39	6	1	4			61
El Salvador	5	17			(*)			23
Guatemala	5	14						19
Haiti	27	5				(*)		32
Honduras	1	14						15
Jamaica		1						1
Mexico	205	29	11	(*)				245
Nicaragua	6	14						20
Panama	15	26						41
Paraguay	7	15	4	1	(*)			27
Peru	73	42	15	1	2			133
Trinidad and Tobago	11							11
Uruguay	3	15	1	(*)				19
Venezuela	26	80						106
Central American Bank for Economic Integration		4						4
Unspecified Latin America	22						7	29
Total Latin America	1,764	1,163	133	6	60	8		3,135
Africa:								
Cameroon		3						3
Congo (Brazzaville)	(*)							(*)
Ethiopia	4	26			1			32
Ghana	8	9						17
Guinea		2						2
Ivory Coast	2		(*)		1			3
Kenya					2			2
Liberia	70	7			1	19		96
Libya		6						6
Mali		(*)						(*)
Morocco		230	13					243
Nigeria	2	5						7
Senegal	(*)							(*)
Sierra Leone	3				1			4
Somali Republic		1						1
South Africa	19							19
Sudan		10		(*)				10
Tanzania		5						5
Tunisia	2	59	11	(*)				73
Uganda		1						1
United Arab Republic	27	76	418	(*)				521
Unspecified Africa		5						5
Total Africa	137	446	442	1	6	19		1,051
Oceania:								
Australia	1							1
New Zealand	1	1				(*)		2
Total Oceania	2	1				(*)		3
United Nations							107	107
Unspecified		27						27
Total all areas	3,497	6,230	2,859	137	289	2,017	3,285	18,315

[1] Includes estimates for the U.S. dollar equivalent of receivables denominated in other than dollars and/or payable at the option of the debtor in foreign currencies, goods, or services. The total amount of such estimates approximates $5,158,000,000.

[2] Data on lend-lease, surplus property, and settlements for grants include $609,000,000 for settlements for grants and $1,500,000,000 for surplus property credits administered by Federal agencies other than the Treasury Department and not included in the "Status of accounts under lend-lease and surplus property agreements" in table 106. Data exclude about $88,000,000 in defaulted short-term "cash" credits and deferred and otherwise past-due interest.

*Less than $500,000.

SOURCE.—U.S. Department of Commerce, Office of Business Economics, from information made available by operating agencies.

TABLE 106.—Status of accounts under lend-lease and surplus property agreements (World War II) as of June 30, 1965

Country, etc.	Settlement obligation and interest billed (net)[1]	Collections — U.S. dollars	Collections — Foreign currency (in U.S. dollar equivalent)	Other credits	Total outstanding	Amounts past due[3]	Due over a period of years by agreement
Australia	$43,696,716.83	$34,170,930.90	$8,662,268.75	$863,517.18			
Austria	10,579,695.13	3,016,749.25	6,677,500.00	556,807.01	$328,638.87		$328,638.87
Belgium	116,291,702.79	37,622,889.41	11,601,267.53	61,340,822.18	5,726,723.67		5,726,723.67
Burma	6,690,068.40	482,691.58	5,560,577.14	142,077.32	504,722.36		504,722.36
Canada	388,765,007.77	388,765,007.77					
China	178,579,276.84	16,062,109.14	1,591,795.64	8,521,770.94	155,988,036.85; [3] -3,384,435.73	$69,208,818.17	86,779,218.68; [3] -3,384,435.73
Czechoslovakia	10,027,310.98	596,730.50	1,062,961.45	1,990,965.94	6,376,653.09	4,039,116.51	2,337,536.58
Denmark	5,240,272.66	4,266,935.24	931,000.00	42,337.42			
Ethiopia	4,558,988.36	3,899,523.26	23,620.60	635,814.50			
Finland	24,410,478.38	14,029,390.16	2,271,136.46	697,805.34	7,412,146.42		7,412,146.42
France	1,233,362,961.23	716,335,892.66	51,445,798.03	51,402,738.29	414,178,522.25		414,178,522.25
Germany, Federal Republic of	224,295,811.06	3,248,975.25	210,455,344.92		10,591,490.89		10,591,490.89
Greece	71,505,779.41	39,058,846.41	21,229,123.98	1,156,763.08	10,062,812.56; [3] -1,766.62		10,062,812.56; [3] -1,766.62
Greenland	8,351.28	8,351.28					
Hungary	20,974,387.78		12,202,500.10	1,818,002.31	6,953,885.37	3,616,020.46	3,337,864.91
Iceland	4,855,981.42	4,496,553.29	250,198.40	287,954.38	109,229.73		109,229.73
India	[4]199,291,238.43	184,777,327.13	6,943,494.63	904,647.09	[4]7,282,552.29	7,282,552.29	
Indonesia	81,032,580.51	43,024,232.71	3,765,000.00		33,338,700.71		33,338,700.71
Iran	42,904,203.98	3,027,367.45	7,829,287.39		32,047,649.14	32,047,649.14	
Iraq	54.00	54.00					
Italy	266,217,796.67	159,119,022.42	85,669,772.70	3,541,571.44	17,887,430.11		17,887,430.11
Japan	13,728,409.82		2,971,483.00	756,926.82	10,000,000.00		10,000,000.00
Korea	32,925,096.06		2,524,307.70	3,977,576.38	26,423,211.98	5,473,192.56	20,950,019.42
Liberia	19,440,619.66	517,937.27			18,922,682.39	225,000.00	18,697,682.39
Lebanon	1,656,638.01		521,818.51	1,134,819.50			
Luxembourg	120.00	120.00					
Middle East	50,377,089.88	11,142,266.72	39,234,823.16	28,383,412.29			
Netherlands	176,795,845.11	103,219,746.41	45,192,686.41	644,920.86			
New Zealand	4,935,288.23	2,071,022.59	1,813,007.28	1,580,637.90	406,337.50		406,337.50
Norway	21,277,848.08	11,262,135.23	8,435,074.95				
Pakistan	[6]40,308,976.14	40,308,976.14					
Philippines	5,000,000.00		2,005,855.29	2,988,158.91	5,985.80		5,985.80
Poland	49,520,355.99	24,624,287.93	10,385,744.17		14,510,323.89		14,510,323.89
Saudi Arabia	21,427,119.60	21,427,119.60					
Southern Rhodesia	1,415,510.78	1,371,931.69			43,579.09	43,579.09	
Sweden	2,115,455.91	240,659.98	1,824,653.33	50,112.60			

Thailand	7,064,989.28	2,235,736.09	4,178,321.72	650,931.47		
Turkey	14,474,333.51	116,082,482.30	2,110,714.28	1,281,136.93		
Union of South Africa	117,774,297.35	116,608,622.69	242,487.98	923,186.68		
United Kingdom	1,092,797,478.74	374,288,008.23	37,767,414.74	154,635,335.62	526,106,720.15	6 526,106,720.15
U.S.S.R.	326,405,313.28	130,806,352.50		195,598,961.23		139,059,108.76
Yugoslavia	720,117.35	63,376.50	16,300.00	623,065.20	17,375.65	17,375.65
American Republics	136,685,117.19	114,365,404.88	11,921,129.75	3,154,183.21	7,244,399.35	494,399.35
American Red Cross	2,023,386.90	2,023,386.90				7 6,750,000.00
Federal agencies	243,114,726.52	243,092,796.09			21,930.43	21,930.43
Military withdrawals	187,629.76	649.00	186,980.76			
Miscellaneous items	1,472,077.38	1,136,573.15	335,504.23			
United Nations Relief and Rehabilitation Administration	7,226,762.25	7,226,762.25				
Total	5,324,159,226.69	2,875,125,663.50	619,840,864.98	334,687,998.79	1,494,504,499.42	178,992,110.47	1,315,512,388.95

NOTE.—No settlement agreement for lend-lease has been reached with China, Greece, and U.S.S.R. See page 65 for lend-lease silver indebtedness.

1 Excludes accrued interest due July 1, 1965, except for Austria who paid amounts due July 1 in June. Accrued interest due July 1 had previously been included in this report.

2 Principal and interest considered past due as of June 30, 1965, and items subject to negotiation.

3 Credit. Represents amounts collected under advance payment agreements not applied to outstanding indebtedness.

4 ...ent provides for repayment of 37,099,999.99 rupees.

5 Principal obligation ...nd $2,294,542.72 to give effect to U.S. dollar payment in lieu of silver.

6 ...udes $47,437,824.03 ... ...al and ... ...st postponed pursuant to agreement.

7 Represents amount ...ich is postponed by agreement pending settlement of certain claims.

8 Represents $456,479,091.89 due ...uter surplus property agr...ents, $710,525,721.06 due ...uter ...ase settlement agreements, and $311,175,888.82 due ...uter other lend-lease agreements.

Corporations and Other Business-Type Activities of the United States Government

TABLE 107.—*Comparative statement of securities of Government corporations and other business-type activities held by the Treasury, June 30, 1955–65*

[Face amount, in millions of dollars.   On basis of daily Treasury statements, see "Bases of Tables"]

Agency	1955	1956	1957	1958	1959	1960	1961	1962	1963	1964	1965
Agency for International Development	1,209	1,213	1,198	1,188	1,164	1,138	1,107	1,062	807	735	712
Export-Import Bank of Washington	7,608	11,190	13,383	11,523	12,874	12,704	11,534	12,990	13,604	13,990	13,111
	1,310	1,239	1,205	1,528	1,937	1,636	1,698	1,830	1,476	830	513
Commodity Credit Corporation loans	1,966	1,860	1,716	1,348	1,140	719	1,441	1,323	1,172	993	881
Secondary		94	3		42					4	
Special	(*)	(*)	22	154	1,170	1,619	1,762	1,843	1,544	1,395	1,018
Housing and Home Finance Administration:											
loans	82	116	228	389	594	779	988	1,227	1,532	1,746	1,983
			1	14	38	43	60	90	113	161	195
Urban	48	48	53	73	98	150	165	290	360	1410	575
Public	61	38	41	35	27	29	32	32	25		
Rural	2,207	2,343	2,519	2,728	2,923	3,155	3,332	3,484	3,657	3,828	4,075
	3	16	48	97	112	118	121	121	123	123	124
Saint Lawrence Seaway Development											
Secretary of the Treasury, Farmers Home loan program	162	5	41	31	77	104	154	232	391	492	551
loan		146	212	223	216	229	272	698	598	698	598
	(*)	(*)	8	2	29	35	29	23	38	81	86
Secretary of the, Maritime											
Federal ship				1	1	1	1		6	10	5
Secretary of the						1				2	22
Secretary of the Treasury (Federal Civil Defense Act of 1950)			1								
Small Business Administration	2	2	1								
Tennessee Valley Authority	11	9	7				(*)	(*)	(*)	(*)	(*)
U.S. (farmers' direct loan program)	14										
Veterans' Administration	491	584	13	17	20	19	20	20	50	85	95
Virgin Islands			733	780	930	1,180	1,330	1,530	21	21	22
			1			(*)	1	1	1,730	1,730	1,730
Defense Plant, Act of 1940, as amended	22	29	35	30	25	20	10	1,790	1	1	1
	794	869	1,019	1,439	1,684	1,715	1,765	65	1,804	1,921	1,945
	2	47	47	59	69	64	65		66	66	78
Secretary of the Interior, Defense Minerals	18	22	26	30	32	32	32	31	32	32	33
Secretary of the Treasury	166	177	168	167	151	140	93	91	21		
D.C. Stadium Board, D.C.			1					(*)	1	1	1
Total	16,175	20,049	22,727	21,859	25,343	25,636	26,011	28,634	29,172	1 29,256	28,354

*Less than $500,000.

1 Includes $15 million advanced to the urban renewal fund as of June 30, 1964, after publication of the daily Treasury statement.

TABLE 108.—*Capital stock, notes, bonds, and other securities of Government agencies held by the Treasury or other Government agencies, June 30, 1964 and 1965, and changes during 1965*

Class and issuing agent	Date of authorizing act	Amount owned June 30, 1964	Advances [1]	Repayments and other reductions [1]	Amount owned June 30, 1965
Capital stock:					
Held by the Secretary of the Treasury	June 16, 1933, as amended	$1,000,000,000.00			$1,000,000,000.00
	Feb. 16, 1938, as amended	40,000,000.00			40,000,000.00
...by market	Aug. 2, 1954, as amended	88,000,000.00		[1] $38,000,000.00	50,000,000.00
Held by the Secretary of the...	Sept. 1, 1937, as amended	1,000,000.00			1,000,000.00
Held by the Secretary of Farm Credit	June 16, 1933, as amended	100,000,000.00			100,000,000.00
Banks for ...	do	80,911,100.00	$2,900,000.00		60,634,100.00
...the credit banks	July 26, 1956	120,589,120.00		20,287,000.00	123,489,120.00
Total capital stock		1,430,500,220.00	2,900,000.00	58,287,000.00	1,375,113,220.00
Bonds and notes of Government corporations and other agencies held by the Treasury: [3]					
Agency for International Development	Apr. 3, 1948, as amended, and June 15, 1951.	735,329,391.08		23,140,307.52	712,189,083.56
Export-Import Bank of Washington	Mar. 8, 1938, as amended	13,900,000,000.00	4,449,000,000.00	5,328,000,000.00	13,111,000,000.00
Federal National Mortgage Association:	July 31, 1945, as amended	830,000,000.00	697,600,000.00	1,014,500,000.00	513,100,000.00
Management and liquidating functions	Aug. 2, 1954, as amended	993,470,000.00	254,157,913.36	366,467,913.36	881,160,000.00
Secondary market operations	do	4,460,000.00	562,360,000.00	566,820,000.00	
Special assistance functions	do	1,394,740,000.00	138,612,000.00	515,420,000.00	1,017,932,000.00
Housing and Home Finance Administrator:					
College housing loans	Apr. 20, 1950, as amended	1,746,880,000.00	260,780,000.00	24,400,000.00	1,982,768,000.00
Public facility loans	Aug. 11, 1955	160,728,900.00	49,839,500.00	16,000,000.00	94,568,400.00
Urban renewal fund	July 15, 1949, as amended	410,240,000.00	165,000,000.00		575,240,000.00
Rural Electrification Administration	May 20, 1936, as amended	3,388,420,605.36	430,500,000.01	183,919,870.24	4,635,000,735.12
Saint Lawrence Seaway Development Corporation	May 13, 1964, as amended	122,676,050.53	1,000,000.00		123,676,050.53
Secretary of the..., Farmers Home Administration:					
Rural housing loan program	Aug. 7, 1956, as amended; July 8, 1959, June 29, 1960, and June 30, 1961.	491,619,832.76	100,000,000.00	40,901,860.22	50,717,972.54
Direct loan		597,959,607.34			597,959,607.34
Agricultural credit insurance fund	Aug. 14, 1946, as amended	80,645,000.00	141,610,000.00	135,765,000.00	86,190,000.00
Secretary of Commerce, Maritime Administration: Federal ship mortgage insurance fund	July 15, 1958, as amended	9,900,000.00		4,595,000.00	5,305,000.00
Secretary of the Interior, Bureau of Mines: Development and operation of helium properties	Sept. 13, 1960	2,000,000.00	20,000,000.00		22,000,000.00

Footnotes at end of table.

TABLE 108.—Capital stock, notes, bonds, and other securities of Government agencies held by the Treasury or other Government agencies, June 30, 1964 and 1965, and changes during 1965—Continued

Class and issuing agent	Date of authorizing act	Amount owned June 30, 1964	Advances [1]	Repayments and other reductions [1]	Amount owned June 30, 1965
Bonds and notes of Government corporations and other agencies held by the Treasury [1]—Continued					
Secretary of the Treasury (Federal Civil Defense Act of 1950, as amended).	Jan. 12, 1951, as amended	$105,000.00		$71,090.78	$33,909.22
Tennessee Valley Authority	Aug. 6, 1959	85,000,000.00	$95,000,000.00	85,000,000.00	95,000,000.00
U.S. Information Agency, informational media guaranties fund	Apr. 3, 1948, as amended, and July 18, 1956.	21,292,940.67	763,200.00		22,056,140.67
Veterans' Administration (veterans' direct loan program)	Apr. 20, 1950, as amended	1,730,077,996.00			1,730,077,996.00
Virgin Islands Corporation	Sept. 2, 1968, as amended	1,225,000.00			1,225,000.00
Defense Production Act of 1950, as amended:					
General Services Administration	Sept. 8, 1950, as amended	1,920,700,000.00	70,000,000.00	46,000,000.00	1,944,700,000.00
Secretary of Agriculture	do	66,337,947.82	12,114,621.82		78,452,569.64
Secretary of the Interior (Defense Minerals Exploration Administration).	do	32,130,000.00	805,000.00		32,935,000.00
D.C. Commissioners:					
Stadium sinking fund, Armory Board, D.C	Sept. 7, 1957, as amended	655,800.00	831,600.00	655,800.00	831,600.00
Total bonds and notes		29,256,102,071.56	7,449,973,835.18	8,351,656,842.12	28,354,419,064.62
Securities of Government agencies held by Government corporations and other agencies:					
Guaranteed securities:					
Federal Housing Administration debentures held by:					
Housing and Home Finance Agency:					
Federal Housing Administration	June 27, 1934, as amended	123,867,650.00	88,967,050.00	87,273,250.00	125,561,450.00
Federal National Mortgage Association:					
Management and liquidating functions	Aug. 2, 1954, as amended	23,558,050.00	17,672,250.00	39,378,050.00	1,862,250.00
Secondary market operations	do	4,996,460.00	64,548,900.00	63,542,650.00	5,992,650.00
Special assistance functions	do	6,928,100.00	24,177,500.00	25,138,600.00	5,967,000.00
Total guaranteed securities		159,340,200.00	195,365,700.00	215,332,550.00	139,373,350.00
Nonguaranteed securities:					
Banks for cooperatives debentures held by:					
Housing and Home Finance Agency:					
Federal National Mortgage Association:					
Government mortgage liquidation fund	Sept. 2, 1964		7,340,000.00	3,480,000.00	3,860,000.00
Secondary market operations	Aug. 2, 1954, as amended		20,000,000.00	20,000,000.00	

Housing and Home Finance Agency: held by:				
Federal ...				
Secondary ...	...do...		7,000,000.00	7,000,000.00
Veterans' ...		25,000,000.00		25,000,000.00
U.S. ... life ... fund...	June 7, 1924, as amended...			
Federal ... the loan bank ... as held by:				
Housing and Home Finance ...				
Federal ...	Aug. 2, 1954, as amended...		27,500,000.00	27,500,000.00
... Salary ... the credit bank ... held by:		27,500,000.00		
Housing and Home Finance ...				
Federal ...	Sept. 2, 1964...	18,005,000.00	2,750,000.00	15,255,000.00
... mortgage ... fund	Aug. 2, 1954, as amended...	14,000,000.00	14,000,000.00	
Secondary				
Total nonguaranteed securities...		25,000,000.00	93,845,000.00	74,730,000.00	44,115,000.00

1 Excludes refundings.
2 Represents purchase of preferred stock by the Association subject to subsequent repurchase by the Secretary of the Treasury as may be required.
3 See also table 110.

4 Includes $15,000,000 advanced to the urban renewal fund as of June 30, 1964, after publication of the daily Treasury statement.
NOTE.—See table 112 for data on other securities held by agencies representing loans made.

TABLE 109.—*Borrowing authority and outstanding issues of Government corporations and other business-type activities whose securities are issued to the Secretary of the Treasury, June 30, 1965*

[In millions of dollars. On basis of daily Treasury statements]

Corporation or activity [1]	Borrowing authority	Outstanding securities held by Treasury	Unused borrowing authority
Agency for International Development:			
Mutual defense program—economic assistance	662	662	
Foreign investment guaranty fund	199		199
India emergency food aid	23	23	
Loan to Spain	27	27	
Commodity Credit Corporation	14, 500	13, 111	1, 389
Export-Import Bank of Washington	6, 000	513	5, 487
Federal Deposit Insurance Corporation	3, 000		3, 000
Federal home loan banks	1, 000		1, 000
Federal National Mortgage Association:			
Management and liquidating functions	902	881	20
Secondary market operations	2, 250		[2] 2, 250
Special assistance functions	3, 368	1, 018	2, 350
Federal Savings and Loan Insurance Corporation	750		750
Housing and Home Finance Administrator:			
College housing loans	2, 875	1, 983	892
Flood insurance	500		500
Public facility loans	600	195	405
Urban mass transportation fund	50		50
Urban renewal fund	1, 000	575	425
Panama Canal Company	10		10
Public Housing Administration	1, 500		1, 500
Rural Electrification Administration	5, 137	4, 075	1, 062
Saint Lawrence Seaway Development Corporation	140	124	16
Secretary of Agriculture, Farmers Home Administration:			
Rural housing loan program	663	551	113
Direct loan account	598	598	
Agricultural credit insurance fund	[3] 106	86	20
Secretary of Commerce:			
Area Redevelopment Administration, area redevelopment fund	300		300
Maritime Admin., Federal ship mortgage insurance fund	[4] 5	5	
Secretary of the Interior, Bureau of Mines:			
Development and operation of helium properties	36	22	14
Secretary of the Treasury (Federal Civil Defense Act of 1950, as amended)	[5] (*)	(*)	
Smithsonian Institution:			
John F. Kennedy Center parking facilities	15		15
Tennessee Valley Authority	[6] 150	95	55
U.S. Information Agency, informational media guaranties fund	28	22	6
Veterans' Administration (veterans' direct loan program)	1, 996	1, 730	266
Virgin Islands Corporation	1	1	(*)
Defense Production Act of 1950, as amended:			
General Services Administration	1, 959	1, 945	14
Secretary of Agriculture	86	78	8
Secretary of the Interior, Defense Minerals Exploration Admin.	36	33	3
Unallocated	19		19
D.C. Commissioners, stadium sinking fund, Armory Board, D.C.	[7] 1	1	
Total	50, 493	28, 354	22, 139

*Less than $500,000.

[1] Excludes authorizations to borrow from the public; also excludes authorizations to expend from public debt receipts for subscriptions to capital stock of the following agencies: International Bank for Reconstruction and Development, $6,350 million; International Monetary Fund, $2,325 million; International Finance Corporation, $35 million; and certain Government corporations, $1,207 million. In addition, the authorized credit to the United Kingdom, of which $3,149 million is outstanding, has been excluded.

[2] The balance shown represents unused portion of authorization to expend from public debt receipts available for loans to the secondary market operations fund without further action by Congress. Because of the borrowing and capital structure of the fund, the maximum it could borrow from the Treasury without adjusting its other borrowing or its capital structure as of June 30, 1965, would be as follows:

Borrowing authorized (10 times capital plus surplus) _____ $3, 751, 596, 436
Securities outstanding _____ −1, 797, 494, 000

Unused balance of borrowing authorized _____ 1, 954, 102, 436

[3] Includes amount due Treasury and restored borrowing authority previously withdrawn. Authority to borrow from the Treasury is indefinite in amount. Funds may be borrowed as needed to carry out provisions of an act approved Aug. 8, 1961 (7 U.S.C. 1929(c)).

[4] Authority to borrow from the Treasury is indefinite in amount. Funds may be borrowed as needed to purchase insured defaulted mortgages as provided by an act approved July 15, 1958 (46 U.S.C. 1275(b)).

[5] Borrowing authority of $249.9 million was administratively cancelled during the fiscal year 1965. Remaining authority as of June 30, 1965, amounting to $33,909.22 is equal to the outstanding securities.

[6] Represents amount of interim securities outstanding which may be issued to the Secretary of the Treasury under specified conditions as provided by an act approved Aug. 6, 1959 (16 U.S.C. 831n–4(c)).

[7] Funds may be borrowed from the Secretary of the Treasury under certain conditions as provided by an act approved July 28, 1958 (2 D.C. Code 1727).

TABLE 110.—*Description of securities of Government corporations and other business-type activities held by the Treasury, June 30, 1965*

[On basis of daily Treasury statements, see "Bases of Tables"]

Title and authorizing act	Date of issue	Date payable [1]	Rate of interest	Principal amount
Agency for International Development:				
Act of Apr. 3, 1948, as amended:			*Percent*	
Note of Administrator (ECA)	May 26, 1951	June 30, 1977	1⅞	$27,082,218.00
Notes of Administrator (ECA)	Various dates	June 30, 1984	1⅞	662,111,352.97
Act of June 15, 1951:				
Notes of Director (MSA)	Feb. 6, 1952	Dec. 31, 1986	2	22,995,512.59
Total				712,189,083.56
Commodity Credit Corporation, act of Mar. 8, 1938, as amended:				
Notes, Series Seventeen-1965	Various dates	July 31, 1965	3¾	1,220,000,000.00
Notes, Series Seventeen-1965	do	do	3⅞	11,275,000,000.00
Notes, Series Seventeen-1965	do	do	4	616,000,000.00
Total				13,111,000,000.00
Export-Import Bank of Washington, act of July 31, 1945, as amended:				
Notes, Series 1965	Various dates	Dec. 31, 1965	2⅝	99,300,000.00
Note, Series 1972	Jan. 4, 1965	June 30, 1972	3	215,100,000.00
Note, Series 1977	June 30, 1959	June 30, 1977	2⅜	198,700,000.00
Total				513,100,000 00
Federal National Mortgage Association, act of Aug. 2, 1954, as amended:				
Management and liquidating functions:				
Note, Series C	June 1, 1961	July 1, 1965	3⅜	9,020,000.00
Notes, Series C	Various dates	Various dates	3½	594,960,000.00
Note, Series C	July 1, 1962	July 1, 1967	3⅝	270,180,000.00
Note, Series C	Apr. 2, 1965	July 1, 1969	4⅛	7,000,000.00
Subtotal				881,160,000.00
Special assistance functions:				
Notes, Series D, subseries BMR	Various dates	Various dates	3⅛	131,822,000.00
Notes, Series D and subseries BMR	do	do	3⅜	14,460,000.00
Notes, Series D	do	do	3½	113,020,000.00
Notes, Series D	do	do	3⅝	233,060,000.00
Notes, Series D	do	do	3¾	525,570,000.00
Subtotal				1,017,932,000.00
Total Federal National Mortgage Association				1,899,092,000.00
Housing and Home Finance Administrator:				
College housing loans, act of Apr. 20, 1950, as amended:				
Note, Series CH	Jan. 22, 1963	July 1, 1976	2½	299,375,000.00
Note, Series CH	do	July 1, 1977	2¾	181,143,000.00
Note, Series CH	do	July 1, 1978	2⅝	283,071,000.00
Note, Series CH	do	July 1, 1980	2⅞	258,026,000.00
Note, Series CH	do	July 1, 1981	3⅛	301,010,000.00
Note, Series CH	June 30, 1963	July 1, 1983	3¼	550,143,000.00
Note, Series CH	June 30, 1964	July 1, 1984	3⅜	95,000,000.00
Note, Series CH	Jan. 28, 1965	do	3½	15,000,000.00
Subtotal				1,982,768,000.00
Public facility loans, act of Aug. 11, 1955:				
Note, Series PF	Nov. 30, 1961	July 31, 1973	3⁶⁄₁₀	47,710,400.00
Note, Series PF	Sept. 18, 1964	July 1, 1976	3⅛	70,000,000.00
Note, Series PF	June 30, 1963	July 1, 1977	3¼	50,858,000.00
Note, Series PF	June 30, 1964	June 30, 1978	3⅜	25,000,000.00
Note, Series PF	Dec. 3, 1964	July 1, 1979	3½	1,000,000.00
Subtotal				194,568,400.00

Footnotes at end of table.

TABLE 110.—*Description of securities of Government corporations and other business-type activities held by the Treasury, June 30, 1965*—Continued

Title and authorizing act	Date of issue	Date payable [1]	Rate of interest	Principal amount
Housing and Home Finance Administrator—Con.				
Urban renewal fund, act of July 15, 1949, as amended:			*Percent*	
Notes	Various dates	Various dates	3⅝	$55,000,000.00
Notes	do	do	3¾	85,000,000.00
Notes	do	do	4	215,000,000.00
Note	June 30, 1960	Dec. 31, 1965	4⅜	25,000,000.00
Note	June 30, 1961	Dec. 31, 1966	3⅜	55,000,000.00
Note	Dec. 31, 1962	June 30, 1968	3½	40,000,000.00
Note	Dec. 31, 1958	Dec. 31, 1968	3	60,000,000.00
Note	June 30, 1965	Dec. 31, 1970	4⅛	40,000,000.00
Definitive note	May 25, 1964	May 1, 1998	5	240,000.00
Subtotal				575,240,000.00
Total Housing and Home Finance Administrator				2,752,576,400.00
Rural Electrification Administration, act of May 20, 1936, as amended:				
Notes of Administrator	Various dates	Various dates	2	4,075,000,735.12
St. Lawrence Seaway Development Corp., act of May 13, 1954, as amended:				
Revenue bonds	Various dates	Dec. 31, 1965	2⅝	500,000.00
Revenue bonds	do	Dec. 31, 1966	2¾	900,000.00
Revenue bonds	do	Various dates	2⅞	5,100,000.00
Revenue bonds	do	do	3	7,800,000.00
Revenue bonds	do	do	3⅛	8,200,000.00
Revenue bonds	do	do	3¼	24,600,000.00
Revenue bonds	do	do	3⅜	15,900,000.00
Revenue bonds	do	do	3½	9,900,000.00
Revenue bonds	do	do	3⅝	31,100,000.00
Revenue bonds	do	do	3¾	4,600,000.00
Revenue bonds	do	do	3⅞	2,500,000.00
Revenue bonds	do	do	4	6,600,000.00
Revenue bonds	do	do	4⅛	5,276,050.53
Revenue bonds	do	do	4¼	700,000.00
Total				123,676,050.53
Secretary of Agriculture, Farmers Home Administration:				
Rural housing loan program, act of Aug. 7, 1956, as amended:				
Notes	Various dates	Various dates	3¾	15,000,000.00
Notes	do	do	3⅞	120,717,972.54
Notes	do	do	4	220,000,000.00
Notes	do	do	4⅛	130,000,000.00
Notes	do	do	4¼	65,000,000.00
Subtotal				550,717,972.54
Direct loan account, acts of July 8, 1959, June 29, 1960, and June 30, 1961:				
Notes	Various dates	Various dates	3	280,500,000.00
Note	Feb. 21, 1962	June 30, 1966	3⅞	37,500,000.00
Note	May 28, 1962	do	3⅝	8,000,000.00
Note	June 30, 1964	June 30, 1969	4	4,963,355.49
Note	June 30, 1965	June 30, 1970	4⅛	266,996,251.85
Subtotal				597,959,607.34
Agricultural credit insurance fund, act of Aug. 14, 1946, as amended:				
Note	June 30, 1961	June 30, 1966	3⅜	1,400,000.00
Notes	do	June 30, 1967	3½	27,135,000.00
Notes	June 30, 1963	June 30, 1968	3⅝	2,060,000.00
Notes	Various dates	do	3¾	775,000.00
Notes	do	do	3⅞	17,075,000.00
Notes	do	June 30, 1969	4	20,375,000.00
Notes	do	do	4⅛	17,670,000.00
Subtotal				86,490,000.00
Total Secretary of Agriculture				1,235,167,579.88

Footnotes at end of table.

TABLE 110.—*Description of securities of Government corporations and other business-type activities held by the Treasury, June 30, 1965*—Continued

Title and authorizing act	Date of issue	Date payable [1]	Rate of interest	Principal amount
Secretary of Commerce, Maritime Administration:				
Federal ship mortgage insurance fund, act of July 15, 1958:			*Percent*	
Note	Mar. 18, 1963	Mar. 18, 1968	3⅝	$4,975,000.00
Note	July 30, 1963	July 30, 1968	3¾	330,000.00
Total				5,305,000.00
Secretary of the Interior, Bureau of Mines:				
Development and operation of helium properties, act of Sept. 13, 1960:				
Notes	Various dates	Sept. 13, 1985	4⅛	17,500,000.00
Notes	do	do	4¼	4,500,000.00
Total				22,000,000.00
Secretary of the Treasury, Federal Civil Defense Act of 1950, as amended:				
Note, Series FCD	July 1, 1964	July 1, 1969	4	33,909.22
Tennessee Valley Authority, act of Aug. 6, 1959:				
Advances	Various dates	Various dates	4	95,000,000.00
U.S. Information Agency:				
Informational media guaranties fund, act of Apr. 3, 1948, as amended:				
Note of Administrator (ECA)	Oct. 27, 1948	June 30, 1986	1⅞	1,410,000.00
Note of Administrator (ECA)	do	do	2	1,305,000.00
Note of Administrator (ECA)	do	do	2⅛	2,272,610.67
Note of Administrator (ECA)	Jan. 24, 1949	do	2½	775,000.00
Note of Administrator (ECA)	do	do	2⅝	75,000.00
Note of Administrator (ECA)	do	do	2¾	302,389.33
Note of Administrator (ECA)	do	do	2⅞	1,865,000.00
Note of Administrator (ECA)	do	do	3	1,100,000.00
Note of Administrator (ECA)	do	do	3⅛	510,000.00
Note of Administrator (ECA)	do	do	3¼	3,431,548.00
Note of Administrator (ECA)	do	do	3⅜	495,000.00
Note of Administrator (ECA)	do	do	3⅝	220,000.00
Note of Administrator (ECA)	do	do	3¾	2,625,960.00
Notes of Administrator (ECA)	Various dates	Various dates	3⅞	3,451,000.00
Notes of Administrator (ECA)	do	do	4	1,234,332.67
Notes of Administrator (ECA)	Aug. 12, 1959	June 30, 1989	4⅛	983,300.00
Total				22,056,140.67
Veterans' Administration (veterans' direct loan program), act of Apr. 20, 1950, as amended:				
Agreements	Various dates	Indefinite	2½	88,342,741.00
Agreements	do	do	2¾	53,032,393.00
Agreements	do	do	2⅞	102,845,334.00
Agreements	do	do	3	118,763,868.00
Agreement	Dec. 31, 1956	do	3⅜	49,736,333.00
Agreements	Mar. 29, 1957	do	3¼	49,768,442.00
Agreement	June 28, 1957	do	3½	49,838,707.00
Agreement	Apr. 7, 1958	do	3⅛	49,571,200.00
Agreements	Various dates	do	3⅝	315,945,113.00
Agreements	do	do	3¾	99,889,310.00
Agreements	do	do	3⅞	392,344,555.00
Agreements	do	do	4¼	109,387,321.00
Agreements	do	do	4½	99,909,137.93
Agreement	Feb. 5, 1960	do	4⅝	20,000,000.00
Agreement	Apr. 1, 1960	do	4⅛	20,703,541.07
Agreements	Various dates	do	4	110,000,000.00
Total				1,730,077,996.00
Virgin Islands Corporation, act of Sept. 2, 1958, as amended:				
Notes	Various dates	Various dates	3¾	450,000.00
Notes	do	do	3⅞	110,000.00
Notes	do	do	4	631,100.00
Note	Sept. 30, 1959	Sept. 30, 1979	4⅛	10,000.00
Note	Oct. 15, 1959	Oct. 15, 1979	4⅜	500.00
Note	Feb. 24, 1960	Feb. 24, 1980	4½	23,400.00
Total				1,225,000.00

Footnotes at end of table.

TABLE 110.—*Description of securities of Government corporations and other business-type activities held by the Treasury, June 30, 1965*—Continued

Title and authorizing act	Date of issue	Date payable [1]	Rate of interest	Principal amount
Defense Production Act of 1950, as amended:				
General Services Administration:			*Percent*	
Notes of Administrator, Series D	Various dates	Various dates	3½	$155,000,000.00
Notes of Administrator, Series D	do	do	3⅝	334,000,000.00
Notes of Administrator, Series D	do	do	3¾	155,000,000.00
Notes of Administrator, Series D	do	do	3⅞	165,000,000.00
Notes of Administrator, Series D	do	do	4	845,700,000.00
Notes of Administrator, Series D	do	do	4⅛	290,000,000.00
Subtotal				1,944,700,000.00
Secretary of Agriculture:				
Notes	Various dates	Various dates	3⅝	13,590,016.49
Note	July 1, 1963	July 1, 1968	3¾	2,540,931.33
Notes	Various dates	Various dates	4	62,321,621.82
Subtotal				78,452,569.64
Secretary of the Interior, Defense Minerals Exploration Administration:				
Notes	Various dates	Various dates	2⅞	6,000,000.00
Note	Aug. 31, 1956	July 1, 1966	3	1,000,000.00
Note	Nov. 19, 1956	do	3¼	1,000,000.00
Note	Jan. 30, 1957	do	3½	1,000,000.00
Note	Apr. 22, 1957	do	3⅜	1,000,000.00
Note	Oct. 11, 1957	July 1, 1967	3¾	1,000,000.00
Note	Jan. 17, 1958	do	3⅛	1,000,000.00
Notes	Various dates	Various dates	3⅞	20,935,000.00
Subtotal				32,935,000.00
Total Defense Production Act of 1950, as amended				2,056,087,569.64
District of Columbia Commissioners:				
Stadium sinking fund, Armory Board, D.C., act of Sept. 7, 1957, as amended:				
Note	Nov. 30, 1964	When funds are available.	3⅞	415,800.00
Note	June 1, 1965	do	4	415,800.00
Total				831,600.00
Total securities [2]				28,354,419,064.62

[1] Securities may be redeemed at any time.
[2] These securities were issued to the Treasury in exchange for advances by the Treasury from public debt receipts under congressional authorization for specified Government corporations and business-type activities to borrow from the Treasury.

TABLE 111.—*Summary statements of financial condition of Government corporations and other business-type activities, June 30, 1965*

[In thousands of dollars. On basis of reports received from activities]

Account	Administrative budget funds			Trust funds	
	Public enterprise revolving funds ·	Intragovernmental revolving funds	General and special funds	Trust revolving funds	Government-sponsored enterprises
ASSETS					
Cash in banks, on hand, and in transit...	175,062	3,558	1,434	6	84,248
Fund balances with the U.S. Treasury ¹	6,191,190	2,918,885	5,955,321	248,001	55,570
Investments:					
Public debt securities (par value).....	2,068,995	----------	3,606	444,545	4,970,568
Securities of Government enterprises.	133,381	----------	----------	5,993	----------
Unamortized premium, or discount (−)................................	−8,896	----------	(*)	−6,331	−28,811
Other securities.....................	293,508	----------	5,724,208	----------	6,000
Advances to contractors and agents:					
Government agencies................	4,848	8,357	5,048	2	----------
Other.....	12,972	67,953	16,290	----------	----------
Accounts and notes receivable:					
Government agencies................	320,789	816,679	121,053	54,798	12
Other (net).......................	794,091	92,360	2,118,485	1,999	1,832
Inventories.........................	5,347,590	6,007,925	6,877,344	482	51
Allowance for losses (−)...........	−972,896	−147	----------	----------	----------
Accrued interest receivable:					
On public debt securities...........	12,578	----------	15	4,315	37,815
On securities of Government enterprises.........................	2,004	----------	738,560	214	----------
Other.....	185,884	----------	522,943	9,710	86,399
Loans receivable:					
Government agencies...............	49,900	----------	----------	----------	3,450
Other: U.S. dollar loans...........	17,671,524	----------	10,074,922	2,091,556	9,205,781
Foreign currency loans.......	1,119,776	----------	3,802,150	----------	----------
Allowance for losses (−)......	−549,569	----------	−14,827	−57,617	−13,022
Acquired security or collateral (net).....	894,341	----------	308	5,200	369
Land, structures, and equipment........	6,021,908	622,448	8,350,092	890	10,179
Accumulated depreciation (−).......	−1,747,832	−265,415	−3,639,229	−244	−1,815
Foreign currencies....................	461	----------	840,198	----------	----------
Other assets (net)....................	2,940,556	164,406	3,085,288	14,891	21,058
Total assets...................	²40,962,164	10,437,009	²44,583,209	2,818,407	14,439,684
LIABILITIES					
Accounts payable:					
Government agencies...............	89,671	336,879	211,748	424	4,950
Other......	550,506	455,937	797,329	55,826	2,250
Accrued liabilities:					
Government agencies...............	760,165	998	12,478	1,307	3
Other......	192,854	147,686	151,550	18,409	123,152
Advances from:					
Government agencies...............	95	1,639,776	39,810	----------	----------
Other......	1,503	7,343	18	----------	----------
Trust and deposit liabilities:					
Government agencies...............	210,586	2,818	34,563	1	180
Other......	169,252	367	15,342	22,400	1,174,976
Bonds, debentures, and notes payable:					
Government agencies...............	142,873	----------	----------	----------	3,450
Other: Guaranteed by the United States............	431,114	----------	----------	----------	----------
Not guaranteed by the United States............	225,011	----------	----------	1,797,494	7,991,225
Other liabilities (including reserves).....	4,933,784	398,370	1,181,994	14,538	238,662
Total liabilities................	7,707,415	2,990,174	2,444,832	1,910,457	9,538,848

Footnotes at end of table.

TABLE 111.—*Summary statements of financial condition of Government corporations and other business-type activities, June 30, 1965*—Continued

[In thousands of dollars]

Account	Administrative budget funds			Trust funds	
	Public enterprise revolving funds	Intragov-ernmental revolving funds	General and special funds	Trust revolving funds	Govern-ment-sponsored enterprises
NET INVESTMENT					
U.S. interest:					
Interest-bearing investment:					
Capital stock	100, 000				
Borrowings from the U.S. Treasury	22, 709, 928		5, 337, 942		
Other	1, 496, 395				
Noninterest-bearing investment:					
Capital stock	1, 041, 000			50, 000	184, 113
Appropriations	15, 620, 918	590, 688	27, 482, 307		
Capitalization of assets (net)	1, 603, 341	406, 972	2, 669, 787		
Other	1, 739, 165	6, 331, 437	12, 587, 604		
Accumulated net income, or deficit (−)	−10, 665, 219	117, 738	−3, 067, 335	44, 818	3, 007, 741
Deposits of general and special fund revenues (−)	−390, 779		−2, 871, 927		
Total U.S. interest	33, 254, 749	7, 446, 835	42, 138, 377	94, 818	3, 191, 854
Trust and private interest:					
Principal of fund				247, 044	
Capital stock				93, 392	1, 434, 062
Accumulated net income, or deficit (−)				472, 695	274, 919
Total trust and private interest				813, 132	1, 708, 982
Total liabilities and investment	40, 962, 164	10, 437, 009	44, 583, 209	2, 818, 407	14, 439, 684

*Less than $500.

1 Consist mainly of unexpended balances of general, special, and revolving fund accounts against which checks may be drawn to pay proper charges under these funds. The funds are considered assets of the agencies, but not of the U.S. Government since funds must be provided out of cash balances of the Treasurer of the United States and future receipts to take care of checks to be issued against the balances.

2 Includes foreign currency assets, representing loans and other receivables recoverable in foreign currencies in U.S. depositaries, aggregating $5,835 million in dollar equivalent. These currencies, acquired primarily without dollar payments, were generated under various Government programs, but principally the Agricultural Trade Development and Assistance Act of 1954, as amended, and the Mutual Security Acts, as amended. Dollar equivalents are computed for reporting purposes to provide a common denominator for the currencies of the many countries involved. Foreign currencies on hand and on deposit and loans under section 104(e) of the Agricultural Trade Development and Assistance Act of 1954, as amended, are stated at the rates as of June 30, 1965, at which the United States could purchase currencies on the market for regular operating purposes. Other loans are stated at the rates at which they are to be repaid or at rates in effect when the loans were extended. Currencies that are dollar denominated or guaranteed as to rate of exchange are stated at rates specified in the agreements.

NOTE.—Business-type activities reporting pursuant to Department Circular No. 966, issued Jan. 30, 1956. Statements of financial condition by type of fund, department, and agency are published quarterly in the monthly *Treasury Bulletin.*

TABLE 112.—*Statement of loans outstanding of Government corporations and other business-type activities, June 30, 1965*

[In thousands of dollars]

Type of loan and lending agency [1]	U.S. dollar loans			Foreign currency loans [2]
	Total	Public enterprise revolving funds	Certain other activities	
TO AID AGRICULTURE				
Loans to cooperative associations:				
Farmers Home Administration:				
Direct loan account	42, 551	42, 551		
Rural Electrification Administration	4, 072, 259		4, 072, 259	
Crop, livestock, and commodity loans:				
Commodity Credit Corporation	[3] 2, 494, 386	[3] 2, 494, 386		
Farmers Home Administration:				
Direct loan account	1, 502	1, 502		
Emergency credit revolving fund	104, 702	104, 702		
Storage facility and equipment loans:				
Commodity Credit Corporation	39, 527	39, 527		
Farm mortgage loans:				
Farmers Home Administration:				
Agricultural credit insurance fund	108, 626	108, 626		
Direct loan account	345, 813	345, 813		
Rural housing and other loans	664, 566		664, 566	
Other loans:				
Economic opportunity loan fund:				
Loans to aid farmers and rural families	17, 018	17, 018		
Farmers Home Administration:				
Direct loan account	719, 674	719, 674		
Rural housing for the elderly revolving fund	1, 108	1, 108		
Rural housing and other loans	16, 904		16, 904	
Total to aid agriculture	8, 628, 635	3, 874, 907	4, 753, 729	
TO AID HOMEOWNERS				
Mortgage loans:				
Federal Housing Administration	145, 656	145, 656		
Federal National Mortgage Association:				
Management and liquidating functions	1, 019, 175	1, 019, 175		
Special assistance functions	1, 116, 638	1, 116, 638		
Federal Savings and Loan Insurance Corporation	224, 404	224, 404		
Housing and Home Finance Administrator:				
Community disposal operations fund	3, 643	3, 643		
Interior Department:				
Bureau of Indian Affairs:				
Liquidation of Hoonah housing project	159	159		
Public Housing Administration	206	206		
Veterans' Administration:				
Direct loans to veterans and reserves	1, 115, 070	1, 115, 070		
Loan guaranty revolving fund	9, 965	9, 965		
Other loans:				
Veterans' Administration:				
Direct loans to veterans and reserves	29, 885	29, 885		
Loan guaranty revolving fund	494, 052	494, 052		
Total to aid homeowners	4, 158, 854	4, 158, 854		
TO AID INDUSTRY				
Loans to railroads:				
Expansion of defense production:				
Treasury Department	8, 539	8, 539		
Other purposes:				
Interstate Commerce Commission	14, 076		14, 076	
Treasury Department:				
Miscellaneous loans and certain other assets	4, 781		4, 781	
Ship mortgage loans:				
Commerce Department:				
Federal ship mortgage insurance fund	20, 373	20, 373		
Maritime Administration	86, 516		86, 516	
Other loans:				
Expansion of defense production:				
Interior Department	8, 055	8, 055		
Treasury Department	8, 206	8, 206		
Defense production guarantees:				
Air Force Department	6, 766	6, 766		
Army Department	2, 128	2, 128		
Navy Department	5, 551	5, 551		

Footnotes at end of table.

TABLE 112.—*Statement of loans outstanding of Government corporations and other business-type activities, June 30, 1965*—Continued

[In thousands of dollars]

Type of loan and lending agency [1]	U.S. dollar loans			Foreign currency loans [2]
	Total	Public enterprise revolving funds	Certain other activities	
To AID INDUSTRY—Continued				
Other loans—Continued				
Other purposes:				
Commerce Department:				
Area Redevelopment Administration:				
Area redevelopment fund	103, 753	103, 753		
Federal ship mortgage insurance fund	379	379		
Housing and Home Finance Administrator:				
Urban mass transportation fund	2, 500	2, 500		
Interior Department:				
Bureau of Commercial Fisheries:				
Fisheries loan fund	5, 981	5, 981		
Office of Minerals Exploration	1, 750		1, 750	
Small Business Administration:				
Revolving fund (lending operations)	851, 950	851, 950		
Treasury Department:				
Miscellaneous loans and certain other assets	679		679	
Total to aid industry	1, 131, 983	1, 024, 182	107, 801	
To AID EDUCATION				
Health, Education, and Welfare Department:				
Office of Education:				
Loans to institutions and nonprofit schools	7, 542		7, 542	
Loans to students in institutions of higher education	534, 262		534, 262	
Public Health Service:				
Loans to institutions and nonprofit schools	13, 242		13, 242	
Housing and Home Finance Administrator:				
College housing loans	1, 926, 461	1, 926, 461		
Total to aid education	2, 481, 507	1, 926, 461	555, 046	
To AID STATES, TERRITORIES, ETC.				
Commerce Department:				
Area Redevelopment Administration:				
Area redevelopment fund	22, 298	22, 298		
General Services Administration:				
Public Works Administration (in liquidation)	58, 012		58, 012	
Health, Education, and Welfare Department:				
Public Health Service	4, 512		4, 512	
Housing and Home Finance Administrator:				
Public facility loans	183, 776	183, 776		
Liquidating programs	6, 532	6, 532		
Urban renewal fund	195, 784	195, 784		
Interior Department:				
Bureau of Reclamation	90, 421		90, 421	
Office of Territories:				
Alaska public works	15, 412		15, 412	
National Capital Planning Commission	566		566	
Public Housing Administration	58, 871	58, 871		
Treasury Department:				
Miscellaneous loans and certain other assets	138, 250		138, 250	
Total to aid States, Territories, etc.	774, 435	467, 262	307, 173	
FOREIGN LOANS				
Military assistance credit sales:				
Defense Department:				
Air Force Department	5, 619		5, 619	
Army Department	44, 045		44, 045	
Navy Department	29, 357		29, 357	
Other purposes:				
Agency for International Development:				
Alliance for Progress, development loans	503, 170	503, 170		
Development loans	1, 633, 148	1, 633, 148		
Development loan fund liquidation account	279, 499	279, 499		1, 119, 776

Footnotes at end of table.

TABLE 112.—*Statement of loans outstanding of Government corporations and other business-type activities, June 30, 1965*—Continued

Type of loan and lending agency [1]	U.S. dollar loans			Foreign currency loans [2]
	Total	Public enterprise revolving funds	Certain other activities	
FOREIGN LOANS—Continued				
Other purposes—Continued				
Agency for International Development—Con.				
Loans to U.S. firms and domestic or foreign firms in foreign countries				137,084
All other loans	1,669,952		1,669,952	3,665,066
Commerce Department:				
Maritime Administration	69		69	
Export-Import Bank of Washington:				
Regular lending activities	[4] 3,511,880	[4] 3,511,880		
Treasury Department:				
Miscellaneous loans and certain other assets	3,154,130		3,154,130	
Total foreign loans	10,830,868	5,927,696	4,903,172	4,921,926
OTHER LOANS				
General Services Administration:				
Surplus property credit sales and liquidation activities	100,251		100,251	
Housing and Home Finance Administrator:				
Housing for the elderly	94,927	94,927		
Liquidating programs	6,894	6,894		
Interior Department:				
Bureau of Indian Affairs:				
Loans for Indian assistance	10		10	
Revolving fund for loans	23,709	23,709		
Public Housing Administration	597	597		
Small Business Administration:				
Revolving fund (lending operations)	156,765	156,765		
State Department:				
Loans to United Nations	107,074		107,074	
Treasury Department:				
Federal Farm Mortgage Corporation liquidation fund	33	33		
Miscellaneous loans and certain other assets	45		45	
Veterans' Administration:				
Insurance appropriations policy loans	964		964	
Service-disabled veterans' insurance fund	4,233	4,233		
Soldiers' and sailors' civil relief	23	23		
Veterans' special term insurance fund	4,889	4,889		
Vocational rehabilitation revolving fund	92	92		
Total other loans	500,507	292,163	208,344	
Total loans [5]	[6] 28,506,789	17,671,524	[7] 10,835,265	4,921,926

[1] Includes purchase money mortgages, mortgages purchased from insured lending institutions to prevent default, and similar long-term paper held by the agencies. Prior to June 30, 1960, these assets had been classified as accounts and notes receivable or other assets. This table excludes interagency loans and those made by deposit and trust revolving funds.
[2] The dollar equivalents of these loans are computed for reporting purposes at varying rates. Where the loan agreements stipulate a dollar denominated figure, the loans outstanding are generally valued at the agreement rates of exchange. Loans executed in units of foreign currency are valued at the market rates (i.e., the rates of exchange at which the Treasury sells such currencies to Government agencies).
[3] Certificates of interest in the amount of $419 million, issued against certain of these loans, were outstanding as of June 30, 1965.
[4] Participation certificates in the amount of $1,022 million, issued against certain of these loans, were outstanding as of June 30, 1965.
[5] Excludes World War I funded and unfunded indebtedness of foreign governments, and World War II indebtedness of foreign governments involving lend-lease articles, surplus property sales agreements, and certain other credits shown in table 105.
[6] Does not include foreign currency loans.
[7] Includes loans in the amount of $760 million excluded from table 111.

NOTE.—The *Treasury Bulletin* for November 1965 contained on pp. 154-5, a table by years beginning with 1955 showing loans outstanding including those by deposit and trust revolving funds. Statistical statements of financial condition by agencies as of June 30, 1965, were published in the same issue. Statements of income and expense, and source and application of funds by agencies as of June 30, 1965, were published in the *Treasury Bulletin* for December 1965.

TABLE 113.—*Dividends, interest, and similar earnings received by the Treasury from Government corporations and other business-type activities, fiscal years 1964 and 1965*

Agency and nature of earnings	Amounts	
	1964	1965
Agency for International Development:		
Development loan fund liquidation account, earnings	$19,780,494.19	$8,491,548.78
Mutual defense program—economic assistance, interest on borrowings	13,112,241.37	12,538,946.83
Civil Service Commission, investigations, earnings	17,655.80	5,203.39
Commerce Department:		
National Bureau of Standards, working capital fund, earnings		63,268.22
Maritime Administration, Federal ship mortgage insurance fund, interest on borrowings	263,067.57	352,907.43
Commodity Credit Corporation:		
Interest on capital stock	3,375,000.00	3,625,000.00
Interest on borrowings	195,793,746.09	455,236,493.75
Export-Import Bank of Washington:		
Regular activities:		
Dividends	50,000,000.00	50,000,000.00
Interest on borrowings	34,381,031.87	15,139,091.63
Farm Credit Administration:		
Banks for cooperatives, franchise tax	2,170,282.79	1,873,609.52
Federal intermediate credit banks, franchise tax	2,731,557.23	3,093,150.30
Farmers Home Administration:		
Rural housing loan program, interest on borrowings	16,860,645.96	19,799,764.16
Direct loan account, interest on borrowings	12,018,972.73	13,805,468.15
Agricultural credit insurance fund, interest on borrowings	2,296,044.33	2,762,728.91
Federal National Mortgage Association:		
Management and liquidating functions:		
Earnings	15,000,000.00	15,000,000.00
Interest on borrowings	42,051,742.74	36,838,176.94
Secondary market operations:		
Dividends	3,887,804.35	2,712,844.52
Interest on borrowings	90,634.53	1,260,656.59
Special assistance functions, interest on borrowings	57,358,122.03	50,033,712.11
Federal Prison Industries, Inc., earnings	4,000,000.00	4,000,000.00
General Services Administration:		
Buildings management fund, earnings	2,958,080.84	898,750.86
Federal telecommunications fund, earnings		1,998,337.46
General supply fund, earnings	6,862,324.26	4,802,170.98
Working capital fund, earnings	114,932.20	66,906.06
Government Printing Office, earnings	6,731,791.17	8,003,282.89
Housing and Home Finance Administrator:		
College housing loans, interest on borrowings	41,393,954.75	48,968,488.66
Public facility loans, interest on borrowings	3,540,311.31	4,902,842.95
Urban renewal fund, interest on borrowings	5,343,592.54	5,894,658.10
Interior Department:		
Bureau of Reclamation:		
Colorado River Dam fund, Boulder Canyon project, interest	2,945,942.87	2,857,153.08
Upper Colorado River storage project, interest		751,635.00
Virgin Islands Corporation:		
Interest on appropriations and paid-in capital	355,305.28	358,154.04
Interest on borrowings	47,868.88	47,868.88
Labor Department:		
Farm labor supply revolving fund, repayment of earnings		399,197.99
Office of Economic Opportunity:		
Economic opportunity loan fund, interest on appropriations		124,230.30
Panama Canal Company, interest on net direct investment of the Government	10,894,217.87	11,335,731.95
Public Housing Administration, low rent public housing program fund, interest on borrowings	2,099,014.02	187,065.17
Rural Electrification Administration, interest on borrowings	74,202,686.96	77,489,648.33
St. Lawrence Seaway Development Corp., interest on borrowings	2,952,363.24	4,000,000.00
Secretary of the Treasury (Federal Civil Defense Act of 1950, as amended), interest on borrowings	7,651.92	4,198.03
Small Business Administration, interest on appropriations	26,521,070.71	30,740,195.05
Tennessee Valley Authority:		
Earnings	40,206,431.91	42,599,978.53
Interest on borrowings	694,644.38	2,395,518.94
Treasury Department:		
Federal Farm Mortgage Corp. liquidation fund, dividends	411,299.98	279,243.60
U.S. Information Agency, informational media guaranties fund, interest on borrowings	621,848.00	656,068.05

TABLE 113.—*Dividends, interest, and similar earnings received by the Treasury from Government corporations and other business-type activities, fiscal years 1964 and 1965*—Continued

Agency and nature of earnings	Amounts	
	1964	1965
Veterans' Administration:		
Canteen service revolving fund, profits	$1,500,000.00	$1,119,679.00
Direct loans to veterans and reserves, interest on borrowings	48,795,130.25	36,324,414.84
Rental, maintenance, and repair of quarters, profits	384.61	243.50
Supply fund, earnings	172,774.67	
Defense Production Act of 1950, as amended:		
General Services Administration, interest on borrowings	153,023,671.29	111,475,844.26
Secretary of Agriculture, interest on borrowings	282,931.33	12,114,621.82
Secretary of the Interior (Defense Minerals Exploration Administration), interest on borrowings		1,357,200.00
Secretary of the Treasury, interest on borrowings	987,139.79	
D.C. Commissioners, stadium sinking fund, Armory Board, D.C., interest on borrowings	27,366.18	6,611.53
Total	908,883,774.79	1,108,792,511.08

Government Losses in Shipment

TABLE 114.—*Government losses in shipment revolving fund, June 30, 1965*

[Established July 8, 1937, under authority of the Government Losses in Shipment Act, as amended (5 U.S.C. 134–134b)]

SECTION I—STATUS OF FUND

Transactions	Cumulative through June 30, 1964	Fiscal year 1965	Cumulative through June 30, 1965
Receipts:			
Appropriations	$1,352,000.00		$1,352,000.00
Transferred from securities trust fund pursuant to 5 U.S.C. 134b	91,803.13		91,803.13
Transferred from the account "Unclaimed partial payments on U.S. savings bonds" pursuant to:			
Public Law 85–354	50,000.00		50,000.00
Public Law 86–561	100,000.00		100,000.00
Public Law 87–575	525,000.00		525,000.00
Recoveries of payments for losses	ʳ 486,274.64	$377.34	486,651.98
Repayments to the fund	3,924.32		3,924.32
Total receipts	2,609,002.09	377.34	2,609,379.43
Expenditures:			
Payment for losses	2,384,941.94	44,210.04	2,429,151.98
Other payments (refunds, etc.)	92.57		92.57
Total expenditures	2,385,034.51	44,210.04	2,429,244.55
Balance in fund	ʳ 223,967.58	−43,832.70	180,134.88

ʳ Revised.

NOTE.—This statement excludes contingent liabilities for pending claims against the fund as of June 30, 1965, totaling $15,237.52.

TABLE 114.—*Government lossesi n shipment revolving'fund, June 30, 1965*—Continued

SECTION II—AGREEMENTS OF INDEMNITY ISSUED BY THE TREASURY
DEPARTMENT

Agreements of indemnity [1]	Number	Amount
Issued through June 30, 1964	1,859	$3,451,996.55
Issued during the fiscal year 1965	13	229,076.03
Total issued	1,872	3,681,072.58
Canceled through June 30, 1965	32	1,056,192.03
In force as of June 30, 1965	1,840	2,624,880.55

[1] The Government has not sustained any actual monetary loss in connection with its liability under these agreements of indemnity.

SECTON III—CLAIMS MADE AND SETTLED

Claims	Number	Amount
Received:		
Through June 30, 1964	7,290	$8,757,018.07
During fiscal year 1965 and processed by:		
Bureau of Accounts	149	84,962.73
Bureau of the Public Debt	111	33,418.90
Total claims received through June 30, 1965	7,550	8,875,399.70
Settled:		
Through June 30, 1964	7,265	8,746,768.76
During fiscal year 1965 and processed by:		
Bureau of Accounts:		
For payment out of the fund	29	14,620.07
For credit in appropriate accounts	105	58,538.83
Without payment or credit	4	3,442.49
Bureau of the Public Debt:		
For payment out of the fund:		
U.S savings bonds redemption cases	112	29,408.09
Armed Forces leave bonds redemption cases	1	181.88
Without payment or credit, U.S. savings bonds redemption cases	7	5,332.49
Total claims settled through June 30, 1965	7,523	8,858,292.61
Unadjusted as of June 30, 1965 [1]	27	17,107.09
Total	7,550	8,875,399.70

[1] Includes claims in process of adjustment by the Bureau of the Public Debt.

Personnel

TABLE 115.—*Number of employees in the departmental and field services of the Treasury Department quarterly from June 30, 1964, to June 30, 1965* [1]

Organizational unit	June 30, 1964	Sept. 30, 1964	Dec. 31, 1964	March 31, 1965	June 30, 1965	Increase or decrease(−) since June 30, 1964
Office of the Secretary [2]	[2] 786	804	·804	795	834	48
Comptroller of the Currency, Office of	1, 540	1, 524	1, 527	1, 581	1, 687	147
Customs, Bureau of	9, 125	9, 224	9, 215	9, 333	9, 567	442
Engraving and Printing, Bureau of	2, 938	2, 898	2, 864	2, 902	2, 996	58
Fiscal Service:						
Accounts, Bureau of	1, 664	1, 616	1, 579	1, 539	1, 518	−146
Public Debt, Bureau of the	2, 107	2, 101	2, 049	2, 027	2, 014	−93
Treasurer of the United States, Office of the	1, 001	965	958	953	994	−7
Internal Revenue Service	59, 357	58, 362	58, 292	[4] 65, 532	60, 360	1, 003
Mint, Bureau of	1, 190	1, 287	1, 353	1, 425	1, 485	295
Narcotics, Bureau of	429	423	422	425	444	15
U.S. Coast Guard	5, 229	5, 150	5, 069	5, 151	5, 322	93
U.S. Savings Bonds Division	543	544	541	534	548	5
U.S. Secret Service	839	849	851	922	992	153
Total civilian employees	86, 748	85, 747	85, 524	93, 119	88, 761	2, 013
Military employees—U.S. Coast Guard	32, 248	32, 241	31, 824	31, 672	31, 776	−472
Grand total	118, 996	117, 988	117, 348	124, 791	120, 537	1, 541

[1] Actual number of employees on the last day of month and any intermittent employees who worked at any time during the month.
[2] Includes Office of the Assistant Secretary for International Affairs.
[3] Includes four employees (Office of Defense Lending) transferred to the Bureau of Accounts on July 1, 1964, by authority of Treasury Order No. 185–2, dated June 24, 1964.
[4] Includes seasonal employees.

INDEX

A

Lightning Source UK Ltd.
Milton Keynes UK
UKHW021108160119
335572UK00008B/291/P